U. Tietze · Ch. Schenk

Electronic Circuits
Design and Applications

With the Assistance of
E. Schmid

With 1168 Figures

Springer-Verlag Berlin Heidelberg NewYork
London Paris Tokyo Hong Kong Barcelona

Dr.-Ing. Ulrich Tietze

Lecturer at the Technical Electronics Institute,
University of Erlangen-Nuremberg
Cauerstraße 9, W-8520 Erlangen, FRG

Dr.-Ing. Christoph Schenk

General Manager, Dr. Schenk GmbH,
Industrial Instrumentation
Einsteinstraße 37, W-8033 Martinsried/Munich, FRG

Dipl.-Ing. Eberhard Schmid

Senior Engineer, Siemens AG
W-8520 Erlangen, FRG

Translation of
Tietze, U.; Schenk, Ch.: Halbleiter-Schaltungstechnik. 9. Aufl. Aktualisierter Nachdruck.
Berlin, Heidelberg, New York, London, Paris, Tokyo, Barcelona: Springer 1990

Also available in
Polish: Naukowo-Techniczne, Warsaw 1976, 1987
Hungarian: Müszaki, Budapest 1974, 1981, 1990
Russian: Mir, Moscow 1982
Spanish: Marcombo, Barcelona 1983
Chinese: 1985

ISBN 3-540-50608-X Springer-Verlag Berlin Heidelberg New York
ISBN 0-387-50608-X Springer-Verlag New York Berlin Heidelberg

Typesetting: Macmillan India Ltd, Bangalore
Offsetprinting: Mercedes-Druck, Berlin; Bookbinding: Lüderitz & Bauer, Berlin
61/3020-543210 – Printed on acid-free paper

Preface

Electronic circuits have become increasingly more important in all areas of science and engineering, their use being no longer limited to communications and data processing. They are indispensable whenever there is anything to be measured, regulated or controlled. Electronic circuit operation and design has therefore ceased to be a subject of the specialist, and its understanding is essential for engineers and scientists in many fields.

The purpose of this book is to help the reader understand ready-made circuits and to enable him to design his own circuitry. It therefore contains both elementary electronics and the advanced circuitry. The enormous success of the German version – it will shortly appear in its 10th edition – and the warm reception of five other translations all indicate that this comprehensive approach is practical and covers the requirements of all those involved in design and applications of electronic circuits.

The chapters of Part I are of an introductory nature. They contain the material of a one-year's undergraduate course on elementary electronics and describe the circuit components by their electrical behavior rather than by their involved semiconductor physics. When analyzing particular circuits, we neglect secondary effects from the outset since we want to keep the reader's mind clear for the inherent and essential principles. The understanding of the underlying concepts and rules is a prerequisite for creative design and is therefore much more important than the development of accurate mathematical models. The precise calculation of circuit parameters is in any case inappropriate in view of the considerable manufacturing tolerances involved. The tool employed nowadays for accurate modelling of electronic circuits is the SPICE simulation program. It is used to advantage for verification of design rather than for determining the circuit scheme, because simulation for a variety of parameters and structures can become very tedious. Modelling aspects are treated in the specialized literature.

The second part of the book is structured according to the particular fields of circuit application. Chapters have been written to stand on their own, with a minimum of cross-reference. This should allow the advanced reader to familiarize himself quickly with the various areas of application. Each chapter offers a critical and detailed overview of various solutions to a given problem. In order to enable the reader to proceed quickly from an idea to a working circuit, we discuss only those solutions we have tested thoroughly on the bench. For many cases, the design approach is illustrated by a real example.

Particular attention is paid to the use of integrated circuits (ICs) since a large variety of special chips is available. The goal of circuit design is therefore no longer to minimize the number of logic gates or operational amplifiers but rather to combine in an ideal manner the most suitable special ICs. For this purpose, application-specific IC tables are given with examples of available chips and the pertinent manufacturers. Obviously, the lists cannot be comprehensive nor fully up-to-date, but they should indicate to the reader which data are relevant and of which manufacturer he should consult the appropriate data books. A directory of manufacturers' addresses is therefore also included.

Development of digital circuitry has ceased to be a task of tieing together different chips of the 7400 family and is concerned nowadays with the application of semi-custom ICs in the form of PLDs (programmable logic devices) which are to be programmed by the user. The availability of development software which can be run on inexpensive personal computers, has provided the basis for their popularity. For the representation of digital circuit elements, we adopt international standard symbols of IEEE. Their recent introduction on the basis of dependency notation provides a powerful tool to describe even the most complex modules. We have paid particular attention to this point in order to facilitate comprehension of the new data sheets for this kind of circuit.

Often, the simplest solution – and also the easiest to understand – is to use a microprocessor, and the development of a circuit configuration is then reduced to programming. Modern microprocessor technology is far advanced and intricate details may be difficult to understand. For this reason, we have based the description on the 6800 family because, although quite old, it provides all the basic functions and, due to its simple structure, makes study of microprocessor operation easy. On this basis, extrapolation to more recent microprocessor families should be no problem for the interested reader, particularly since our overviews contain the most modern types, and single-chip microcomputer applications are also discussed. In order to facilitate transition from conventional digital circuitry to microprocessor arrangements, we have treated hardware and software aspects equally and have devoted two entire chapters to this subject.

There are indications that university syllabuses are tending to neglect analog circuits in favour of digital circuitry, simply because the latter seem to be used more extensively. We hope to have given fair treatment to both as we feel that analog circuits are still important for most routine applications. In any case, our world is basically an analog one and no digital circuit could communicate with it without at least using an analog interface. Many tasks today involve transformation of some physical quantity into an equivalent analog electrical signal which is then smoothed, filtered, rectified, amplified or otherwise treated in some fashion. It may subsequently be converted into a digital signal and processed further. All devices required in this chain, starting from the sensor and ending with the microcomputer or display, are dealt with in this book. We hope that its comprehensive nature will be of help to both the circuit designer and the student.

No book is free of errors, but many readers have helped with their feedback in improving this one. We greatly appreciate their support and we hope that the feedback will continue to be tight and be extended to the English-speaking readership.

We should like to thank Ellis Griffin for doing the bulk of the translation work and Eberhard Schmid for his thorough technical revision and his close collaboration with the authors. We are also grateful for the continued good cooperation with the publishers.

Erlangen and Munich,   U. Tietze Ch. Schenk
December 1990

Table of contents

Part I. Basics

Part I. Basics

1 Definitions and nomenclature

We hope that the following list of definitions will help to avoid confusion and enable a better understanding. Where possible, the definitions are based on IEC recommendations.

Voltage. A voltage between two points x and y is denoted by U_{xy}. It is defined as being positive if point x is positive with respect to point y, and negative, if point x is negative with respect to point y. Therefore, $U_{xy} = - U_{yx}$. The statement

$$U_{BE} = - 5V$$

or

$$- U_{BE} = 5V$$

or

$$U_{EB} = 5V$$

thus indicates that there is a voltage of 5V between E and B where E is positive with respect to B. In a circuit diagram, the double indices are often omitted and the notation U_{xy} is replaced by a voltage arrow U *pointing from node* x *to node* y.

Potential. The potential V is the voltage of a node with relation to a common reference node 0:

$$V_x = U_{x0} \ .$$

In electrical circuits, the reference potential is denoted by a ground symbol. Often U_x is used when actually implying V_x. Specialists then speak, although not quite correctly, of the voltage of a node, e.g. the anode voltage. For the voltage between two nodes, x and y,

$$U_{xy} = V_x - V_y \ .$$

Current. The current is indicated by a current arrow on the connecting line. One defines the current I as being positive if the current in its conventional sense, i.e. the transport of positive charge, flows in the direction of the arrow. I is thus positive if the arrow of the current flowing through a load points from the larger to the smaller potential. The directions of the current and voltage arrows in a circuit diagram are not important as long as the actual values of U and I are given the correct signs.

If current and voltage arrow of a circuit element have the same direction, Ohm's law, with the above definitions, is $R = U/I$. If they have opposite directions, it changes to $R = - U/I$. This fact is illustrated in Fig. 1.1.

$$R = \frac{U}{I}$$

$$R = -\frac{U}{I}$$

Fig. 1.1 Ohm's law

Resistance. If the resistance is voltage- or current-dependent, a static resistance $R = U/I$ and an incremental resistance $r = \partial U/\partial I \approx \Delta U/\Delta I$ can be defined. These formulae are valid if the voltage and current arrows point in the same direction. If the directions are opposed, a negative sign must be inserted, as in Fig. 1.1.

Voltage and current source. A real voltage source can be described by the equation

$$U_\text{o} = U_0 - R_\text{int} I_\text{o} \; , \tag{1.1}$$

where U_0 is the no-load voltage and $R_\text{int} = -\,\mathrm{d}U_\text{o}/\mathrm{d}I_\text{o}$ the internal resistance. This is represented by the equivalent circuit in Fig. 1.2. An ideal voltage source is characterized by the property $R_\text{int} = 0$, i.e. the output voltage is independent of the current.

A different equivalent circuit for a real voltage source can be deduced by rewriting Eq. (1.1):

$$I_\text{o} = \frac{U_0 - U_\text{o}}{R_\text{int}} = I_\text{sc} - \frac{U_\text{o}}{R_\text{int}} \; , \tag{1.2}$$

where $I_\text{sc} = U_0/R_\text{int}$ is the short-circuit current. The appropriate circuit is shown in Fig. 1.3. It is obvious that, the larger R_int, the less the output current depends on the output voltage. For $R_\text{int} \to \infty$, one obtains an ideal current source.

According to Figs. 1.2 and 1.3, a real voltage source can be represented either by an ideal voltage source or by an ideal current source. Which representation is chosen depends on whether the internal resistance R_int is small or large in comparison with the load resistance R_L.

Kirchhoff's current law (KCL). For the calculation of the parameters of many electronic circuits, we use Kirchhoff's current law. It states that the sum of all currents flowing into a node is zero. Currents flowing towards the node are

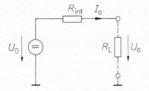

Fig. 1.2 Equivalent circuit of a real
voltage source

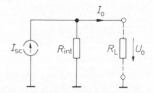

Fig. 1.3 Equivalent circuit of a real
current source

counted as being positive, and currents flowing from the node are negative. Figure 1.4 demonstrates this fact. It can be seen that, for node N,

$$\sum_i I_i = I_1 + I_2 - I_3 = 0 \; .$$

Ohm's law states that:

$$I_1 = \frac{U_1 - U_3}{R_1} \; ,$$

$$I_2 = \frac{U_2 - U_3}{R_2} \; ,$$

$$I_3 = \frac{U_3}{R_3} \; .$$

By substitution we obtain

$$\frac{U_1 - U_3}{R_1} + \frac{U_2 - U_3}{R_2} - \frac{U_3}{R_3} = 0 \; ,$$

giving the result

$$U_3 = \frac{U_1 R_2 R_3 + U_2 R_1 R_3}{R_1 R_2 + R_1 R_3 + R_2 R_3} \; .$$

Kirchhoff's voltage law (KVL). Kirchhoff's voltage law states that the sum of all voltages around any loop in an electrical network is zero. The voltage is entered in the appropriate equation with a positive sign if its arrow points in the direction in which one proceeds around the loop; the voltage is entered with a negative sign if the voltage arrow points against this direction. For the example in Fig. 1.5,

$$\sum_i U_i = U_1 + U_4 - U_2 - U_3 = 0 \; .$$

AC circuits (alternating-current circuits). If the circuit can be described by a DC (direct-current) transfer characteristic $U_o = f(U_i)$, this relationship necessarily also holds for any time-dependent voltage, i.e. $U_o(t) = f[U_i(t)]$, as long as the changes in the input voltage are quasi-stationary, i.e. not too fast. For this

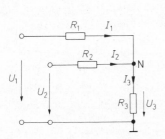

Fig. 1.4 Example to demonstrate Kirchhoff's current law (KCL)

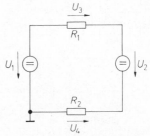

Fig. 1.5 Example to demonstrate Kirchhoff's voltage law (KVL)

reason, we use upper-case letters for DC as well as for time-dependent quantities, e.g. $U = U(t)$.

However, cases exist where a transfer characteristic is only valid for alternating voltages without DC components and it is therefore sensible to have a special symbol to distinguish such alternating voltages. We use the lower-case letter u to denote their instantaneous values.

A particularly important special case is that of sinusoidally alternating voltages, i.e.

$$u = \hat{U}\sin(\omega t + \varphi_u) \ , \tag{1.3}$$

where $\hat{U}$ is the peak value (amplitude). Other values for the characterization of the voltage magnitude are the root-mean-square value $U_{\text{r.m.s.}} = \hat{U}/\sqrt{2}$ or the peak-to-peak value $U_{\text{pp}} = 2\hat{U}$.

The calculus for trigonometric functions is rather involved, but that for exponential functions fairly simple. Euler's theorem

$$e^{j\alpha} = \cos\alpha + j\sin\alpha \tag{1.4}$$

enables a sine function to be expressed by the imaginary part of the complex exponential function:

$$\sin\alpha = \text{Im}\{e^{j\alpha}\} \ .$$

Equation (1.3) can therefore also be written as

$$u = \hat{U}\cdot\text{Im}\{e^{j(\omega t + \varphi_u)}\} = \text{Im}\{\hat{U}\,e^{j\varphi_u}\cdot e^{j\omega t}\} = \text{Im}\{\underline{U}\,e^{j\omega t}\} \ ,$$

where $\underline{U} = \hat{U}e^{j\varphi_u}$ is the complex amplitude. Its magnitude is given by

$$|\underline{U}| = \hat{U}\cdot|e^{j\varphi_u}| = \hat{U}[\cos^2\varphi_u + \sin^2\varphi_u] = \hat{U} \ ;$$

i.e. it is equal to the peak value of the sine wave. Time-dependent currents are treated in an analogous way. The corresponding symbols are then

$$I, \quad I(t), \quad i, \quad \hat{I}, \quad \underline{I} \ .$$

Arrows can also be assigned to alternating voltages and currents. Of course, the direction of the arrow then no longer indicates polarity but denotes the mathematical sign with which the values must be entered in the formulae. The rule illustrated in Fig. 1.1 for DC voltages also applies in this case.

In analogy to the resistance in a DC circuit, a complex resistance is defined as the impedance $\underline{Z}$:

$$\underline{Z} = \frac{\underline{U}}{\underline{I}} = \frac{\hat{U}e^{j\varphi_u}}{\hat{I}e^{j\varphi_i}} = \frac{\hat{U}}{\hat{I}}e^{j(\varphi_u - \varphi_i)} = |\underline{Z}|e^{j\varphi} \ ,$$

where φ is the phase angle between current and voltage. If the voltage is leading with respect to the current, φ is positive. For a purely ohmic resistance, $\underline{Z} = R$; for a capacitance

$$\underline{Z} = \frac{1}{j\omega C} = -\frac{j}{\omega C}$$

and for an inductance $\underline{Z} = j\omega L$. The laws for the DC circuit quantities can be applied to complex quantities as well [1.1, 1.2].

One can also define a complex gain

$$\underline{A} = \frac{\underline{U}_\text{o}}{\underline{U}_\text{i}} = \frac{\hat{U}_\text{o} e^{j\varphi_\text{o}}}{\hat{U}_\text{i} e^{j\varphi_\text{i}}} = \frac{\hat{U}_\text{o}}{\hat{U}_\text{i}} e^{j(\varphi_\text{o} - \varphi_\text{i})} = |\underline{A}| e^{j\varphi} \ ,$$

where φ is the phase angle between input and output voltage. If the output voltage is leading with respect to the input voltage, φ is positive; for a lagging output voltage, it is negative.

Logarithmic voltage ratio. In electrical engineering, a logarithmic value $|\underline{A}|^*$ is often used to express the voltage ratio $|\underline{A}| = \hat{U}_\text{o}/\hat{U}_\text{i}$, i.e. the gain of a circuit. The relationship between $|\underline{A}|^*$ and $|\underline{A}|$ is given by

$$|\underline{A}|^* = 20\,\text{dB}\,\lg\frac{\hat{U}_\text{o}}{\hat{U}_\text{i}} = 20\,\text{dB}\,\lg|\underline{A}| \ .$$

The table in Fig. 1.6 lists some values.

Linear voltage ratio $|A|$	Logarithmic voltage ratio $|A|^*$
0.5	$-6\,\text{dB}$
$1/\sqrt{2} \approx 0.7$	$-3\,\text{dB}$
1	$0\,\text{dB}$
$\sqrt{2} \approx 1.4$	$3\,\text{dB}$
2	$6\,\text{dB}$
10	$20\,\text{dB}$
100	$40\,\text{dB}$
1000	$60\,\text{dB}$

Fig. 1.6 Table for conversion of voltage ratios

Logarithms. The logarithm of a denominate number (e.g. $\lg 1.0\,\text{Hz}$) is not defined. We therefore write, for example, not $\lg f$ but $\lg(f/\text{Hz})$. The difference of logarithms is a different matter: the expression $\Delta \lg f = \lg f_2 - \lg f_1$ is well defined since it can be written in the form $\lg(f_2/f_1)$.

Mathematical symbols. We often use a shortened notation for the time derivatives:

$$\frac{dU}{dt} = \dot{U} \quad \text{and} \quad \frac{d^2U}{dt^2} = \ddot{U} \ .$$

The symbol $\sim$ represents a *proportional* relationship; the symbol $\approx$ stands for *approximately equal to*; the symbol $\cong$ means *corresponding to*. The symbol ‖ means *parallel*. We use it to indicate that resistors are connected in parallel, i.e.

$$R_1 \| R_2 = \frac{R_1 R_2}{R_1 + R_2} .$$

List of the most important symbols

U	any time-dependent voltage, also DC voltages
u	alternating voltage without DC component
$\hat{U}$	amplitude (peak value) of a voltage
$\underline{U}$	complex voltage amplitude
$U_{\text{r.m.s.}}$	root-mean-square value of a voltage
E	computing unit voltage
U_T	thermal voltage kT/e_0 (k = Boltzmann's constant, T = absolute temperature, e_0 = charge of electron)
U_b	supply voltage
V^+	positive supply potential; in circuit diagrams indicated by (+)
V^-	negative supply potential; in circuit diagrams indicated by (−)
I	any time-dependent current, also direct currents
i	alternating current without DC component
$\hat{I}$	amplitude (peak value) of a current
$\underline{I}$	complex current amplitude
$I_{\text{r.m.s.}}$	root-mean-square value of a current
R	ohmic resistance
r	incremental resistance
$\underline{Z}$	complex resistance (impedance)
t	time
τ	time constant
T	period, cycle time
$f = 1/T$	frequency
f_c	3 dB cutoff frequency
f_{cA}	3 dB cutoff frequency of the open-loop gain $\underline{A}_D$ of an operational amplifier
f_T	gain-bandwidth product; unity-gain bandwidth
B	3 dB bandwidth
$\omega = 2\pi f$	angular frequency
$\Omega = \omega/\omega_0$	normalized angular frequency
$s = j\omega + \sigma$	complex angular frequency
$S = p/\omega_0$	normalized complex angular frequency
$A = \partial U_o/\partial U_i$	small-signal voltage gain for low frequencies
$\underline{A}(j\omega) = \underline{U}_o/\underline{U}_i$	complex voltage gain; frequency response
$A(p)$	general transfer function

A_{D}	differential gain, difference mode gain, open-loop gain of an operational amplifier
g	loop gain
G	common-mode rejection ratio, CMRR
k	feedback factor
$\beta = \partial I_2 / \partial I_1$	small-signal current gain
$g_{\mathrm{f}} = \partial I_{\mathrm{C}} / \partial U_{\mathrm{BE}}$	forward transconductance of a bipolar transistor, further index e.g. E for *emitter* connection
$g_{\mathrm{r}} = \partial I_{\mathrm{B}} / \partial U_{\mathrm{CE}}$	reverse transconductance of a bipolar transistor, further index e.g. E for *emitter* connection
$g_{\mathrm{f}} = \partial I_{\mathrm{D}} / \partial U_{\mathrm{GS}}$	forward transconductance of a FET, further index e.g. S for *source* connection
ϑ	temperature on the Celsius scale
T	temperature on the Kelvin scale; absolute temperature
$y = x_1 \cdot x_2$	logic AND operation (conjunction)
$y = x_1 + x_2$	logic OR operation (disjunction)
$y = \bar{x}$	logic NOT operation (negation)
$y = x_1 \oplus x_2$	logic exclusive-OR operation
$\dot{x}$	first derivative of x with respect to time
$\ddot{x}$	second derivative of x with respect to time
$^a\log x$	logarithm to the base a
$\lg x$	logarithm to the base 10
$\ln x$	logarithm to the base e
$\operatorname{ld} x$	logarithm to the base 2
arccos	inverse function of cos
arctan	inverse function of tan
Arsinh	inverse function of sinh
Arcosh	inverse function of cosh

2 Passive *RC* and *LRC* networks

RC networks are of fundamental importance to circuit design. As their effect is the same in all circuits, their operation will be described in some detail.

2.1 The lowpass filter

A lowpass filter is a circuit which passes low-frequency signals unchanged and attenuates at high frequencies, introducing a phase lag. Figure 2.1 shows the simplest type of *RC* lowpass filter circuit.

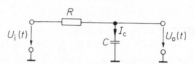

Fig. 2.1 Simple lowpass filter

2.1.1 Frequency-domain analysis

To calculate the frequency response of the circuit, we use the voltage divider formula, written in complex notation as:

$$\underline{A}(j\omega) = \frac{\underline{U}_o}{\underline{U}_i} = \frac{1/j\omega C}{R + 1/j\omega C} = \frac{1}{1 + j\omega RC} \ . \tag{2.1}$$

Factoring according to

$$\underline{A} = |\underline{A}| e^{j\varphi}$$

we obtain the frequency response of the absolute value or magnitude and of the phase shift:

$$|\underline{A}| = \frac{1}{\sqrt{1 + \omega^2 R^2 C^2}} \ , \qquad \varphi = - \arctan \omega RC \ . \tag{2.2}$$

The two curves are shown in Fig. 2.2.

To calculate the 3 dB cutoff frequency f_c, we substitute

$$|\underline{A}| = \frac{1}{\sqrt{2}} = \frac{1}{\sqrt{1 + \omega_c^2 R^2 C^2}}$$

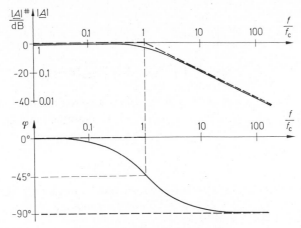

Fig. 2.2 Bode plot of a lowpass filter

into Eq. (2.2), which gives

$$f_c = \frac{1}{2\pi}\omega_c = \frac{1}{2\pi RC} .$$ (2.3)

From Eq. (2.2), the phase shift at this frequency is $\varphi = -45°$.

As we can see from Fig. 2.2, the amplitude-frequency response $|\underline{A}| = \hat{U}_o/\hat{U}_i$ can be easily constructed using the two asymptotes:

1) At low frequencies $f \ll f_c$, $|\underline{A}| = 1 \cong 0$ dB.
2) At high frequencies $f \gg f_c$, from Eq. (2.2) $|\underline{A}| \approx 1/\omega RC$, i.e. the gain is inversely proportional to the frequency. When the frequency is increased by a factor of 10, the gain is reduced by the same factor, i.e. it decreases by 20 dB/decade or 6 dB/octave.
3) At $f = f_c$, $|\underline{A}| = 1/\sqrt{2} \cong -3$ dB.

2.1.2 Time-domain analysis

In order to analyze the circuit in the time domain, we apply a step function of voltage to the input, as shown in Fig. 2.3. To calculate the output voltage, we apply Kirchhoff's current law to the (unloaded) output and obtain in accordance with Fig. 2.1

$$\frac{U_i - U_o}{R} - I_C = 0 .$$

With $I_C = C\dot{U}_o$, we obtain the differential equation

$$RC\dot{U}_o + U_o = U_i = \begin{cases} U_r & \text{for } t > 0 \text{ in Case a ,} \\ 0 & \text{for } t > 0 \text{ in Case b .} \end{cases}$$ (2.4)

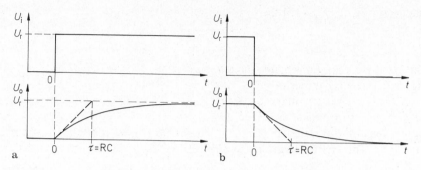

Fig. 2.3 a and b Step-response of a lowpass filter

It has the following solutions:

Case a: Case b:

$$U_\mathrm{o}(t) = U_\mathrm{r}(1 - \mathrm{e}^{-\frac{t}{RC}}) \; ; \qquad U_\mathrm{o}(t) = U_\mathrm{r}\mathrm{e}^{-\frac{t}{RC}} \; . \qquad (2.5)$$

This curve is also plotted in Fig. 2.3. We can see that the steady-state values $U_\mathrm{o} = U_\mathrm{r}$ or $U_\mathrm{o} = 0$ are only attained asymptotically. As a measure of the response time, a *time constant* τ is therefore defined. This indicates how long it takes for the deviation from the steady-state value to equal $1/\mathrm{e}$ times the step

Response accuracy	37%	10%	1%	0.1%
Response time	τ	$2.3\,\tau$	$4.6\,\tau$	$6.9\,\tau$

Fig. 2.4 Response time of a lowpass filter

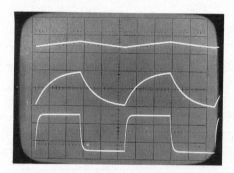

Fig. 2.5 Square-wave response of a lowpass filter for various frequencies

Upper curve:	$f_\mathrm{i} = 10 f_\mathrm{c}$
Middle curve:	$f_\mathrm{i} = f_\mathrm{c}$
Lower curve:	$f_\mathrm{i} = \frac{1}{10} f_\mathrm{c}$

magnitude. From Eq. (2.5) the time constant is

$$\boxed{\tau = RC}\ . \tag{2.6}$$

The response time for smaller deviations can also be derived from Eq. (2.5). Figure 2.4 lists a number of important parameters.

If a square-wave voltage of period T is applied as the input signal, the e-function is truncated after time $T/2$ by the subsequent step. Which final value is obtained at the output depends on the ratio between the time $T/2$ and the time constant τ. This characteristic is clearly illustrated by the oscillogram in Fig. 2.5.

Lowpass filter as an integrating circuit

In the previous section we saw that the alternating output voltage is small compared with the input voltage if a signal frequency $f \gg f_c$ is selected. The lowpass filter operates then as an integrating circuit. This property can be inferred directly from differential Eq. (2.4). Assuming that $|U_o| \ll |U_i|$, it follows that

$$RC\dot{U}_o = U_i\ ,$$

$$U_o = \frac{1}{RC} \int_0^t U_i(\tilde{t})\, d\tilde{t} + U_o(0)\ .$$

Lowpass filter as an averaging circuit

For unsymmetrical alternating voltages, the above condition $f \gg f_c$ is not satisfied. The Fourier expansion in fact contains a constant which is identical to the *arithmetic mean*

$$\boxed{\bar{U}_i = \frac{1}{T} \int_0^T U_i(t)\, dt}$$

where T is the period of the input voltage. If all the higher-order terms of the Fourier series are combined, a voltage $U_i'(t)$ is obtained whose characteristic corresponds to that of the input voltage, but which is displaced from zero such that its arithmetic mean is zero. The input voltage may therefore be expressed in the form

$$U_i(t) = \bar{U}_i + U_i'(t)\ .$$

For voltage $U_i'(t)$, the condition $f \gg f_c$ can be satisfied; it is integrated, whereas the DC component is transferred linearly. The output voltage therefore becomes

$$U_o = \underbrace{\frac{1}{RC} \int_0^t U_i'(\tilde{t})\, d\tilde{t}}_{\text{residual ripple}} + \underbrace{\bar{U}_i}_{\text{mean value}}\ . \tag{2.7}$$

If the time constant $\tau = RC$ is made sufficiently large, the ripple is insignificant compared with the mean value and we get

$$U_o \approx \bar{U}_i \; . \tag{2.8}$$

2.1.3   Rise time and cutoff frequency

Another parameter for characterizing lowpass filters is the rise time t_r. This denotes the time taken for the output voltage to rise from 10 to 90% of the final value when a step is applied to the input. From the e-function in Eq. (2.5) we obtain

$$t_r = t_{90\%} - t_{10\%} = \tau(\ln 0.9 - \ln 0.1) = \tau \ln 9 \approx 2.2\tau \; .$$

Consequently, with $f_c = 1/2\pi\tau$

$$\boxed{t_r \approx \frac{1}{3f_c}} \; . \tag{2.9}$$

In approximation this relation is also true for higher-order lowpass filters.

If a number of lowpass filters with various rise times t_{ri} are connected in series, the resultant rise time is

$$t_r \approx \sqrt{\sum_i t_{ri}^2} \; , \tag{2.10}$$

and the cutoff frequency is

$$f_c \approx \left(\sum_i f_{ci}^{-2}\right)^{-\frac{1}{2}} \; .$$

Hence, for n lowpass filters having the same cutoff frequency

$$\boxed{f_c \approx \frac{f_{ci}}{\sqrt{n}}} \; . \tag{2.11}$$

2.2   The highpass filter

A highpass filter is a circuit which passes high-frequency signals unchanged and attenuates at low frequencies, introducing a phase lead. Figure 2.6 shows the simplest form of *RC* highpass filter circuit. The frequency response of the gain and phase shift is again obtained from the voltage divider formula:

$$\underline{A}(j\omega) = \frac{\underline{U}_o}{\underline{U}_i} = \frac{R}{R + 1/j\omega C} = \frac{1}{1 + 1/j\omega RC} \; . \tag{2.12}$$

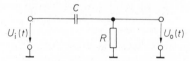

Fig. 2.6 Simple highpass filter

This yields

$$|\underline{A}| = \frac{1}{\sqrt{1 + 1/\omega^2 R^2 C^2}} \quad \text{and} \quad \varphi = \arctan \frac{1}{\omega RC} . \tag{2.13}$$

The two curves are shown in Fig. 2.7. For the cutoff frequency, we obtain as with the lowpass filter:

$$f_c = \frac{1}{2\pi RC} . \tag{2.14}$$

At this frequency the phase shift is $+45°$.

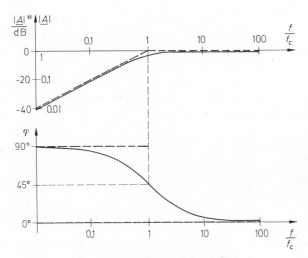

Fig. 2.7 Bode plot of a highpass filter

As in the case of the lowpass filter, the amplitude-frequency response can be easily plotted on a double-logarithmic scale using the asymptotes:

1) At high frequencies $f \gg f_c$, $|\underline{A}| = 1 \triangleq 0 \text{ dB}$.
2) At low frequencies $f \ll f_c$, from Eq. (2.13) $|\underline{A}| \approx \omega RC$, i.e. the gain is proportional to the frequency. The slope of the asymptote is therefore $+20 \text{ dB/decade}$ or $+6 \text{ dB/octave}$.
3) For $f = f_c$, $|\underline{A}| = 1/\sqrt{2} \triangleq -3 \text{ dB}$, as with the lowpass filter.

To calculate the step response, we apply Kirchhoff's current law to the (unloaded) output:

$$C \cdot \frac{d}{dt}(U_i - U_o) - \frac{U_o}{R} = 0 . \tag{2.15}$$

With $\dot{U}_i = 0$, this yields the differential equation

$$RC\dot{U}_o + U_o = 0 \tag{2.16}$$

the solution of which is

$$U_o(t) = U_{oo}e^{-\frac{t}{RC}} . \tag{2.17}$$

The time constant is therefore $\tau = RC$, as in the case of the lowpass filter.

In order to determine the initial value $U_{oo} = U_o(t = 0)$, we have to consider that at the instant when the input voltage changes abruptly, the capacitor charge remains unchanged. The capacitor therefore acts as a voltage source of value $U = Q/C$. The output voltage accordingly shows the same step ΔU as the input voltage. If U_i goes from zero to U_r, the output voltage likewise jumps from zero to U_r (see Fig. 2.8a) then decays exponentially to zero again in accordance with Eq. (2.17).

If the input voltage now goes abruptly from U_r to zero, U_o jumps from zero to $-U_r$ (see Fig. 2.8b). Note that the output voltage assumes negative values even though the input voltage is always positive. This distinctive characteristic is frequently used in circuit design.

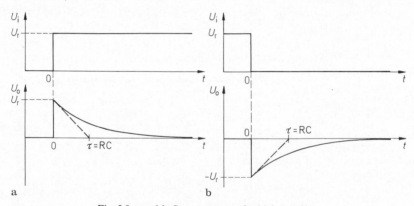

Fig. 2.8 a and b Step response of a highpass filter

Use as an RC coupling network

If a square-wave voltage periodic in $T \ll \tau$ is applied to the input, the capacitor charge barely changes during one half-cycle; the output voltage is identical to the input voltage apart from an additive constant. As no direct current can flow via the capacitor, the arithmetic mean of the output voltage is zero. No DC component of the input voltage is therefore transferred. It is this property which enables a highpass filter to be used as an *RC* coupling network.

Use as a differentiating circuit

If input voltages with frequencies $f \ll f_c$ are applied, $|\underline{U}_o| \ll |\underline{U}_i|$. Consequently, from differential Eq. (2.15)

$$U_o = RC\frac{dU_i}{dt} .$$

Low-frequency input voltages are therefore differentiated.

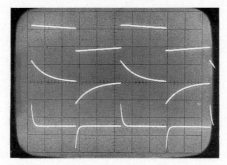

Fig. 2.9 Square-wave response of a highpass filter for various frequencies

Upper curve: $f_i = 10 f_c$
Middle curve: $f_i = f_c$
Lower curve: $f_i = \frac{1}{10} f_c$

The oscillograms in Fig. 2.9 summarize the transient response of a highpass filter.

Series connection of several highpass filters

If a number of highpass filters are connected in series, the resultant cutoff frequency is

$$f_c \approx \sqrt{\sum_i f_{ci}^2} \ . \tag{2.18}$$

Consequently, for n highpass filters having identical cutoff frequencies

$$\boxed{f_c \approx f_{ci} \cdot \sqrt{n}} \ . \tag{2.19}$$

2.3   Compensated voltage divider

It is frequently the case that a resistive voltage divider is capacitively loaded, making it a lowpass filter. The lower the resistance selected for the voltage divider, the higher the cutoff frequency of the filter. However, limits are imposed in that the input resistance of the divider should not be reduced below a specified value.

Another possible way of raising the cutoff frequency is to use a highpass filter to compensate for the effect of the lowpass filter. This is the purpose of capacitor C_k in Fig. 2.10. It is dimensioned such that the resultant parallel-connected capacitive voltage divider has the same division ratio as the resistive voltage divider. Consequently, the same voltage division is produced at high and low frequencies. This means that

$$\frac{C_k}{C_L} = \frac{R_2}{R_1} \ .$$

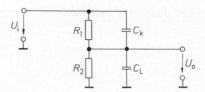

Fig. 2.10 Compensated voltage divider

For optimum adjustment of C_k, it is useful to test with the step function. For the correct value C_k, the step response becomes ideal.

2.4 Passive *RC* bandpass filter

By connecting a highpass and a lowpass filter in series, we obtain a bandpass filter whose output voltage is zero for high and low frequencies. One widely used combination is shown in Fig. 2.11. We shall now calculate the output voltage at medium frequencies and the phase shifts introduced. In complex notation, the formula for the unloaded voltage divider yields:

$$\underline{U}_o = \frac{\dfrac{1}{\dfrac{1}{R} + j\omega C}}{\dfrac{1}{\dfrac{1}{R} + j\omega C} + R + \dfrac{1}{j\omega C}}\underline{U}_i \ ,$$

$$\underline{U}_o = \frac{j\omega RC}{(j\omega RC + 1)^2 + j\omega RC}\underline{U}_i \ .$$

Simplifying with $\omega RC = \Omega$, we obtain for the gain

$$\underline{A}(j\Omega) = \frac{\underline{U}_o}{\underline{U}_i} = \frac{j\Omega}{1 + 3j\Omega - \Omega^2} \ . \tag{2.20}$$

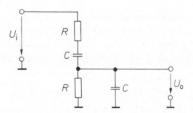

Fig. 2.11 Passive *RC* bandpass filter

Hence the magnitude and phase shift are given by

$$|\underline{A}| = \frac{1}{\sqrt{\left(\dfrac{1}{\Omega} - \Omega\right)^2 + 9}} \quad , \qquad \varphi = \arctan\frac{1 - \Omega^2}{3\Omega} \quad . \tag{2.21}$$

The output voltage is maximum for $\Omega = 1$. The resonant frequency is therefore

$$f_r = \frac{1}{2\pi RC} \quad . \tag{2.22}$$

The quantity Ω initially introduced for simplification expresses the normalized frequency

$$\Omega = \frac{\omega}{\omega_r} = \frac{f}{f_r} \quad .$$

The phase shift at resonance is zero and the gain $A_r = 1/3$. The frequency response of $|\underline{A}|$ and φ is shown in Fig. 2.12.

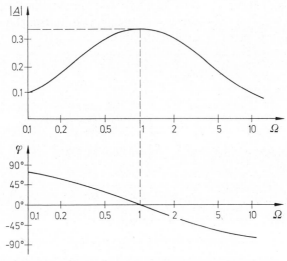

Fig. 2.12 Bode plot of the passive *RC* bandpass filter

2.5 Wien-Robinson bridge

If the bandpass filter shown in Fig. 2.11 is modified by inserting resistors R_1 and $2R_1$, as shown in Fig. 2.13, a Wien-Robinson bridge is obtained. The resistive voltage divider furnishes the voltage $\frac{1}{3}U_i$ irrespective of frequency. At the resonant frequency, the output voltage is therefore zero. Unlike the bandpass filter response, the frequency response of the Wien-Robinson bridge is then minimum. The circuit is therefore useful for suppressing a given frequency band.

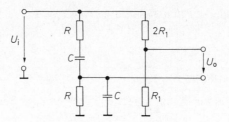

Fig. 2.13 Wien-Robinson bridge

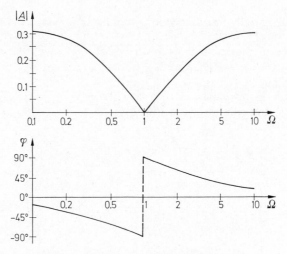

Fig. 2.14 Bode plot of the Wien-Robinson bridge

The output voltage can be calculated from Eq. (2.20):

$$\underline{U}_o = \frac{1}{3}\underline{U}_i - \frac{j\Omega}{1 + 3j\Omega - \Omega^2}\underline{U}_i \; .$$

Hence

$$\underline{A}(j\Omega) = \frac{1}{3}\cdot\frac{1 - \Omega^2}{1 + 3j\Omega - \Omega^2} \; . \tag{2.23}$$

The magnitude of the gain and the phase shift are

$$|\underline{A}| = \frac{|1 - \Omega^2|}{3\sqrt{(1 - \Omega^2)^2 + 9\Omega^2}} \; , \qquad \varphi = \arctan\frac{3\Omega}{\Omega^2 - 1} \quad \text{for } \Omega \neq 1 \; .$$

The frequency response $|\underline{A}|$ and φ is plotted in Fig. 2.14.

2.6   Parallel-T filter

The parallel-T filter in Fig. 2.15 has a very similar frequency response to that of the Wien–Robinson bridge and is therefore also suitable for suppressing

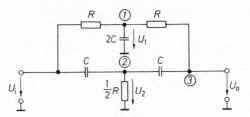

Fig. 2.15 Parallel-T filter

a given range of frequencies. However, it differs from the Wien-Robinson bridge in that the output voltage can be measured with respect to ground. For high and low frequencies, $\underline{U}_o = \underline{U}_i$. High frequencies are transferred without attenuation via the two capacitors C and low frequencies via the two resistors R.

To calculate the frequency response we apply Kirchhoff's current law to points 1, 2 and 3 in Fig. 2.15 and obtain, for an unloaded output:

Node *1*: $\dfrac{\underline{U}_i - \underline{U}_1}{R} + \dfrac{\underline{U}_o - \underline{U}_1}{R} - \underline{U}_1 \cdot 2j\omega C = 0$,

Node *2*: $(\underline{U}_i - \underline{U}_2)\,j\omega C + (\underline{U}_o - \underline{U}_2)\,j\omega C - \dfrac{2\underline{U}_2}{R} = 0$,

Node *3*: $(\underline{U}_2 - \underline{U}_o)\,j\omega C + \dfrac{\underline{U}_1 - \underline{U}_o}{R} = 0$.

Thus, by eliminating $\underline{U}_1$ and $\underline{U}_2$ and with the normalization $\Omega = \omega RC$, we obtain for the gain:

$$\underline{A}(j\Omega) = \frac{1 - \Omega^2}{1 + 4j\Omega - \Omega^2} \; . \tag{2.24}$$

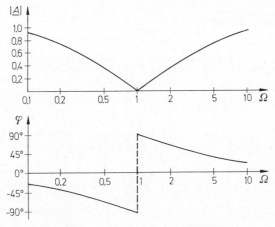

Fig. 2.16 Bode plot of the parallel-T filter

Hence the magnitude and phase shift are given by:

$$|\underline{A}| = \frac{|1 - \Omega^2|}{\sqrt{(1 - \Omega^2)^2 + 16\Omega^2}} \quad, \qquad \varphi = \arctan\frac{4\Omega}{\Omega^2 - 1} \quad.$$

The two curves have been plotted in Fig. 2.16.

2.7   Resonant circuit

In this section we shall list the most important formulae for the lossy parallel resonant circuit shown in Fig. 2.17. No detailed description will be given, as the resonant circuit is well documented in the literature. With $R_P \gg R_L$, its impedance is given by

$$\underline{Z} = \frac{j\omega L + R_L}{1 + j\omega\left[R_L C + \dfrac{L}{R_P}\right] - \omega^2 LC} \quad . \tag{2.25}$$

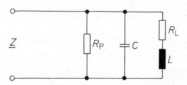

Fig. 2.17 Lossy parallel resonant circuit

This yields the following data:

Resonant frequency, undamped: $\quad \omega_0 = \dfrac{1}{\sqrt{LC}}$

Resonant frequency, damped: $\quad \omega_D = \omega_0\sqrt{1 - R_L^2\dfrac{C}{L}}$

Circuit attenuation: $\quad d = R_L\sqrt{\dfrac{C}{L}} + \dfrac{1}{R_P}\sqrt{\dfrac{L}{C}}$

Circuit Q-factor: $\quad Q = \dfrac{1}{d}$

Bandwidth: $\quad B = f_0 d = f_0/Q$

Resonant resistance: $\quad R_0 = \dfrac{L}{R_L C + \dfrac{L}{R_P}}$

3 Diodes

Diodes are semiconductor devices which favor current flow in one direction. They have two terminals: an anode A and a cathode C. Their circuit symbol is shown in Fig. 3.1. If a positive voltage $U_{AC} > 0$ is applied, the diode becomes biased in the forward direction. With a negative voltage $U_{AC} < 0$, the diode is reverse biased. The reverse current is generally some orders of magnitude smaller than the maximum permissible forward current.

Fig. 3.1 Diode symbol

3.1 Characteristics and relevant data

The behavior of a diode is described by its $I = I(U_{AC})$ characteristic (Fig. 3.2). The forward current rises steeply when small positive voltages U_{AC} are applied. A defined maximum value I_{max} must not be exceeded, as thermal effects would otherwise destroy the diode. A rough idea of the shape of the characteristic can be obtained from the specified forward voltage U_D at currents of the order of 0.1 I_{max}. This so-called threshold voltage is between 0.2 and 0.4 V for germanium and between 0.5 and 0.8 V for silicon.

Figure 3.2 shows that the reverse current rises to values approaching those of the forward current when high voltages $|U_{AC}| > U_{rev\,max}$ are applied. Normal diodes must not be operated in this region, as local heating could destroy them even if the losses are well below the maximum permissible dissipation. The maximum reverse voltage may be between 10 V and 10 kV depending on the type of diode.

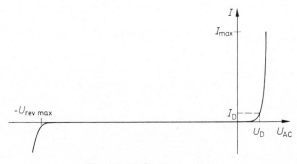

Fig. 3.2 Diode characteristic

The diode characteristic can be described mathematically by means of an e-function [3.1]:

$$I = I_S(T)(e^{\frac{U_{AC}}{mU_T}} - 1)\ ,$$ (3.1)

where I_S is the theoretical reverse current or reverse saturation current and $U_T = kT/e_0$ the thermal voltage. At room temperature the latter is given by

$$U_T = \frac{kT}{e_0} = \frac{1.38 \cdot 10^{-23}\,\text{J/K} \cdot 296\,\text{K}}{1.60 \cdot 10^{-19}\,\text{C}} = 25.5\,\text{mV}\ .$$ (3.2)

The correction factor m allows for the deviation from the simple Shockley diode theory. It lies between 1 and 2.

Equation (3.1) only accurately expresses the actual diode characteristic in the forward direction, and even then only for currents which are not excessively high. The actual reverse current is substantially larger than I_S and increases with the reverse voltage due to surface effects.

Figure 3.3 shows the characteristic, calculated from Eq. (3.1), for a silicon and a germanium diode with the following typical data:

Germanium diode: $I_S = 100\,\text{nA}$, $mU_T = 30\,\text{mV}$, $I_{max} = 100\,\text{mA}$

Silicon diode: $I_S = 10\ \ \text{pA}$, $mU_T = 30\,\text{mV}$, $I_{max} = 100\,\text{mA}$

For the forward voltage at $\frac{1}{10} I_{max}$, we obtain theoretical values of 0.35 V and 0.62 V which correspond well with those measured in practice.

U_D is often defined as the forward voltage of a diode at the knee of the forward characteristic and is called threshold voltage. In reality, however, the forward characteristic has no knee, as the comparison with the semi-logarithmic graph in Fig. 3.4 shows. It is merely the linear representation of the e-function that makes a knee appear to be present. Its position therefore depends entirely on the scales selected.

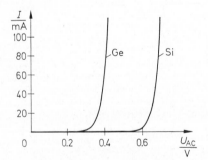

Fig. 3.3 Diode characteristics in
linear representation

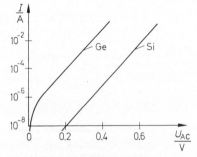

Fig. 3.4 Diode characteristics in
semi-logarithmic representation

Using Eq. (3.1) it is easy to calculate that the forward voltage increases by

$$mU_\mathrm{T}\ln 10 = (1 \ldots 2)\cdot 26\,\mathrm{mV}\cdot\ln 10 = 60 \ldots 120\,\mathrm{mV}$$

when the forward current increases by a factor of 10.

As both U_T and I_s are a function of the temperature, the forward voltage is also temperature-dependent for a given current. As an approximation

$$\left.\frac{\partial U_\mathrm{AC}}{\partial T}\right|_{I=\mathrm{const}} \approx -\frac{2\,\mathrm{mV}}{\mathrm{K}}. \tag{3.3}$$

The linear decrease in the forward voltage for constant current indicates that the current increases exponentially with temperature if a constant voltage is applied.

This behavior is also exhibited by the reverse current, which doubles if the temperature increases by 10 K. For a 100 K temperature rise, it therefore increases by a factor of 1000.

Dynamic response

The transition from forward to reverse bias operation is not instantaneous, as the charge stored in the pn junction must be recovered. This effect can be demonstrated by the simple rectifier circuit in Fig. 3.5. We shall use the square wave shown in Fig. 3.6 as the input voltage. When U_i is positive, the diode conducts and the output voltage becomes equal to the forward voltage. When U_i becomes negative, the diode assumes the blocking state and U_o must become equal to U_i. As can be seen from Fig. 3.6, this transition does not occur until the *recovery time* t_R has elapsed. The latter is longer, the higher the forward current prior to the transition. Typical values for small-signal diodes are 10 to 100 ns. For power diodes, the recovery time is in the µs range.

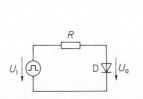

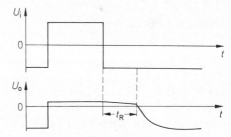

Fig. 3.5 Test circuit for determining the
recovery time

Fig. 3.6 Effect of recovery time

We can see from Fig. 3.6 that the period of the input voltage must be large compared with the recovery time, otherwise the rectifying effect would be lost.

Very short switching times can be achieved using *Schottky diodes*. Instead of a pn junction, these have a metal-semiconductor junction which likewise produces a rectifying effect. With this type of diode, however, the stored charge is extremely small. Consequently, the switching time is minimal—in the order of 100 ps. Another feature of this device is its threshold voltage of about 0.3 V, which is smaller than that of silicon junction diodes.

The symbol for a Schottky diode is shown in Fig. 3.7.

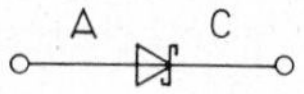

Fig. 3.7 Schottky diode

3.2   Zener diodes

With all diodes, the reverse current rises sharply when the maximum reverse blocking voltage is exceeded. In the case of *Zener diodes*, the breakdown voltage at which this steep rise occurs is precisely specified. It is known as the Zener voltage U_Z. Diodes of this kind can be used for DC voltage stabilization. Figure 3.8 shows the circuit symbol for a Zener diode and Fig. 3.9 its characteristic.

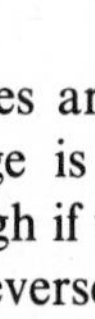

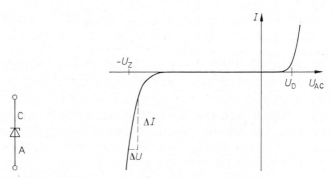

Fig. 3.8 Zener diode symbol   Fig. 3.9 Zener diode characteristic

Zener diodes are available with breakdown voltages of 3 to 200 V; their forward voltage is approximately 0.6 V. As shown in Fig. 3.9, the reverse resistance is high if the reverse voltages $|U_{AC}| < U_Z$. When the Zener voltage is reached, the reverse current rises steeply. The stabilizing effect of the device depends on the fact that a large current change ΔI only produces a small voltage change ΔU. The steeper the curve and therefore the smaller the incremental internal resistance $r_Z = \Delta U/\Delta I$, the better the stabilization. In the case of Zener diodes with $U_Z \approx 8$ V, the incremental internal resistance is at its lowest; below this level, r_Z increases markedly as the Zener voltage decreases, with the result that the stabilizing effect is very poor for low Zener voltages.

In the case of Zener voltages of less than 5.7 V, the Zener effect with negative temperature coefficient predominates; above this figure, the avalanche effect with positive temperature coefficient predominates. The temperature coefficient is in the range $\pm\,0.1\%$ per degree (see Section 18.4.1).

3.3 Varactor diodes

The junction capacitance of a diode decreases as the reverse voltage increases. Diodes in which this effect is exceptionally pronounced are known as varactor diodes. Figure 3.10 shows the circuit symbol, Fig. 3.11 some typical characteristics. The maximum capacitance is between 5 and 300 pF depending on the type of diode. The ratio of maximum to minimum capacitance can be as much as $1:5$.

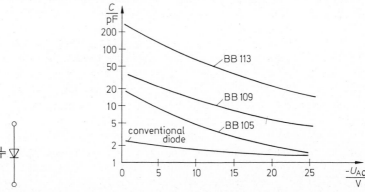

Fig. 3.10 Varactor diode symbol   Fig. 3.11 Junction capacitance as a function
                                                                       of voltage

Owing to their high Q-factor into the UHF range, varactor diodes are suitable for the design of resonant circuits having a voltage-controlled resonance frequency.

4 Bipolar transistors

The transistor is a three-electrode semiconductor device used for amplifying or switching a signal. There are silicon and germanium transistors, both of which exist in pnp and npn types. The circuit symbols are shown in Figs. 4.1 and 4.2.

Fig. 4.1 npn transistor with diode equivalent   Fig. 4.2 pnp transistor with diode equivalent

A transistor consists of two diodes connected back-to-back with a common n-layer or p-layer whose associated electrode is called the base B. The other two electrodes are known as the emitter E and the collector C. This arrangement is illustrated by the diode equivalent circuit next to the graphical symbols. Although this does not fully represent how a transistor actually operates, it provides a general idea of the reverse and forward voltages involved. Normally the emitter-base junction is biased in the forward direction and the collector-base junction is reverse biased, in which case the voltage sources must have the polarities indicated in Figs. 4.3 and 4.4.

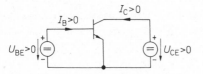

Fig. 4.3 Polarity of an npn transistor

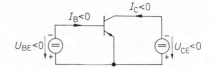

Fig. 4.4 Polarity of a pnp transistor

The main feature of a transistor is that a collector current I_C flows which is a defined multiple of the base current I_B. The ratio $B = I_C/I_B$ is termed the *current gain*. The behavior of a transistor is more precisely described by reference to its various characteristic curves. The following considerations apply to npn transistors. For pnp transistors, all the voltages and currents are of opposite sign.

4.1   Characteristics and small-signal parameters

In order to analyze the transistor characteristics, an input voltage U_{BE} is applied and the output current I_C is measured as a function of the output voltage U_{CE}. By increasing the input voltage in a number of steps, we obtain the family of output characteristics shown in Fig. 4.6.

A noticeable feature is that, above a particular voltage, the collector current is only slightly dependent on U_{CE}. This behavior is similar to that of a pentode. The voltage at which a knee occurs in the characteristic curves is termed the saturation voltage $U_{CE\,sat}$.

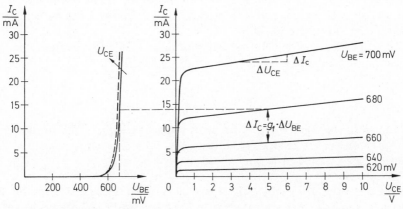

Fig. 4.5 Transfer characteristic   Fig. 4.6 Output characteristics

Another distinctive feature is that even a small input voltage change is sufficient to produce a relatively large variation in the collector current. The variation, i.e. the distance between the curves, increases markedly as the collector current rises. This property can be seen even more clearly from the transfer characteristic in Fig. 4.5, where I_C is plotted as a function of U_{BE}, whereas U_{CE} is varied as a parameter. The figure shows that the transfer characteristic, like the diode characteristic, is exponential in form. However, unlike in Eq. (3.1), the correction factor m is now virtually unity [4.1]. Therefore

$$\boxed{I_C = I_{CS}(T, U_{CE})e^{U_{BE}/U_T}}\,, \tag{4.1}$$

as long as I_C is large compared with the reverse saturation current I_{CS}.

It is often required that a transistor be operated as a linear amplifier. This is achieved in approximation by specifying a particular operating point having the quiescent values I_{CQ}, U_{CEQ} and applying a small amount of drive at this point. For the design of such circuits, we replace the curves in the vicinity of the operating point by their tangents. The gradients of the tangents are known as the differential or small-signal parameters.

The change in the collector current I_C in response to a change in U_{BE} is characterized by the *transconductance* g_f

$$g_f = \frac{\partial I_C}{\partial U_{BE}}\bigg|_{U_{CE} = \text{const}} .$$

It can be calculated by differentiating Eq. (4.1):

$$g_f = \frac{I_{CS}}{U_T} e^{U_{BE}/U_T} = \frac{I_C}{U_T} . \qquad (4.2)$$

It is proportional to the collector current and independent of the individual characteristics of the particular transistor. Consequently, it can be calculated without reference to a data sheet.

The dependence of the collector current on the collector-emitter voltage is characterized by the *incremental output resistance*

$$r_{CE} = \frac{\partial U_{CE}}{\partial I_C}\bigg|_{U_{BE} = \text{const}} .$$

We can see from Fig. 4.6 that it becomes smaller at higher collector currents, since the slope of the characteristic increases. To a good approximation, it is inversely proportional to I_C, i.e.

$$r_{CE} = \frac{U_Y}{I_C} . \qquad (4.3)$$

The proportionality constant U_Y is known as the Early voltage [4.2]. This can be determined by measuring r_{CE}, from which it is then possible to calculate the output resistance for any collector currents. Typical values for U_Y are between 80 and 200 V for npn transistors and between 40 and 150 V for pnp transistors.

Unlike electron tubes, bipolar transistors cannot be driven without current. This can be seen from the input characteristic in Fig. 4.7 which, like the transfer characteristic Eq. (4.1), is an exponential function. However, the correction

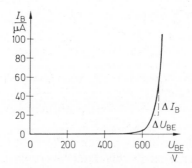

Fig. 4.7 Input characteristic

factor m is not unity and therefore is not negligible in this case. Consequently

$$I_B = I_{BS}e^{U_{BE}/mU_T} \ .$$

To characterize the load due to the input current, the *incremental input resistance*

$$r_{BE} = \frac{\partial U_{BE}}{\partial I_B}\bigg|_{U_{CE}=\text{const}}$$

is defined. Its magnitude is obtained by differentiating the input characteristic:

$$r_{BE} = \frac{mU_T}{I_B} \ .$$

However, it cannot be calculated precisely, as the correction factor m is not known for each particular case.

The collector current is, to a first approximation, proportional to the base current, as can be seen from Fig. 4.8. The ratio of I_C to I_B is known as the *static current gain*:

$$B = \frac{I_C}{I_B} \ . \tag{4.4}$$

As the input characteristic, unlike the transfer characteristic, incorporates the correction factor $m = 1$, the current gain is not a constant but dependent on the collector current. The typical response is shown in Fig. 4.9.

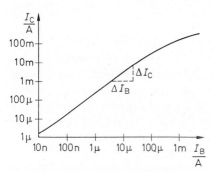

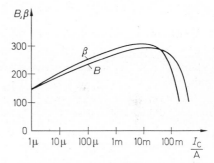

Fig. 4.8 Typical plot of collector current versus base current for a small-signal transistor

Fig. 4.9. Typical plot of the static and incremental current gain for a small-signal transistor

In order to calculate *current changes* around the operating point, the *incremental (small-signal) current gain*

$$\beta = \frac{\partial I_C}{\partial I_B}\bigg|_{U_{CE}=\text{const}}$$

is defined. Its dependence on the collector current is also shown in Fig. 4.9. In the case of power transistors, the maximum of the current gain is in the ampere range; its absolute value is, however, much lower than for small-signal transistors.

Knowing β, the input resistance r_{BE} can be calculated from the transconductance:

$$\boxed{r_{BE} = \frac{\partial U_{BE}}{\partial I_B} = \frac{\partial U_{BE}}{\partial I_C/\beta} = \frac{\beta}{g_f} = \frac{\beta U_T}{I_C}}\ . \tag{4.5}$$

The input characteristic in Fig. 4.7 should strictly speaking be represented by a family of curves with U_{CE} as the parameter. However, the dependence on U_{CE} is so slight that the curves virtually coincide. For small-signal analysis, this dependence is characterized by the *reverse voltage feedback ratio A_r* or the *reverse transconductance g_r*:

$$A_r = \frac{\partial U_{BE}}{\partial U_{CE}}\bigg|_{I_B = \text{const}} \quad , \qquad g_r = \frac{\partial I_B}{\partial U_{CE}}\bigg|_{U_{BE} = \text{const}} = -\frac{A_r}{r_{BE}}\ .$$

For small collector currents, the reverse voltage feedback is *positive,* for large collector currents it is *negative.* The absolute values are less than 10^{-4} so that the feedback effect is negligible in practice. Feedback does, however, increase at higher frequencies. This can be allowed for by taking the collector-base capacitance into account. We shall return to this aspect in Chapter 16 (broadband amplifiers).

Using these parameters, each change in base or collector current can be calculated on a general basis. For this purpose we write

$$I_B = I_B(U_{BE}, U_{CE})\ ,$$

$$I_C = I_C(U_{BE}, U_{CE})\ .$$

The total differentials are

$$dI_B = \frac{\partial I_B}{\partial U_{BE}}\bigg|_{U_{CE}} \cdot dU_{BE} + \frac{\partial I_B}{\partial U_{CE}}\bigg|_{U_{BE}} \cdot dU_{CE}\ ,$$

$$dI_C = \frac{\partial I_C}{\partial U_{BE}}\bigg|_{U_{CE}} \cdot dU_{BE} + \frac{\partial I_C}{\partial U_{CE}}\bigg|_{U_{BE}} \cdot dU_{CE}\ .$$

Using the differential quotients introduced and disregarding the feedback $(g_r = \partial I_B/\partial U_{CE} \approx 0)$, we obtain the basic equations

$$\boxed{\begin{aligned} dI_B &= \frac{1}{r_{BE}} \cdot dU_{BE} \\[2mm] dI_C &= g_f \cdot dU_{BE} + \frac{1}{r_{CE}} \cdot dU_{CE} \end{aligned}}$$

$$\tag{4.6}$$
$$\tag{4.7}$$

The set of equations can be expressed in matrix notation as:

$$\begin{pmatrix} dI_B \\ dI_C \end{pmatrix} = \begin{pmatrix} 1/r_{BE} & 0 \\ g_f & 1/r_{CE} \end{pmatrix} \begin{pmatrix} dU_{BE} \\ dU_{CE} \end{pmatrix} = Y_e \begin{pmatrix} dU_{BE} \\ dU_{CE} \end{pmatrix}\ .$$

In network theory, this matrix of coefficients is termed the Y-matrix. Also used is the H-matrix:

$$\begin{pmatrix} \mathrm{d}U_{BE} \\ \mathrm{d}I_C \end{pmatrix} = \begin{pmatrix} h_{11e} & h_{12e} \\ h_{21e} & h_{22e} \end{pmatrix} \begin{pmatrix} \mathrm{d}I_B \\ \mathrm{d}U_{CE} \end{pmatrix} = H_e \begin{pmatrix} \mathrm{d}I_B \\ \mathrm{d}U_{CE} \end{pmatrix} .$$

The relationship between the matrix elements is

$$1/r_{BE} = y_{11e} = 1/h_{11e} ,$$

$$g_r = y_{12e} = -h_{12e}/h_{11e} \approx 0 ,$$

$$g_f = y_{21e} = h_{21e}/h_{11e} = \beta/r_{BE} ,$$

$$1/r_{CE} = y_{22e} = \frac{1}{h_{11e}}(h_{11e}h_{22e} - h_{21e}h_{12e}) \approx h_{22e} .$$

The subscript "e" associated with the network parameters indicates that the transistor is operated in the common-emitter mode. This means that the emitter terminal is used jointly for the input and output ports. The various operating modes of a transistor are dealt with in more detail in the following sections.

4.2 Transistor ratings

There are various ratings for a transistor which are specified and must not be exceeded. The lowest of the permissible reverse bias voltages is usually the *emitter-base breakdown voltage* U_{EBO}. With silicon transistors, considerable emitter-base leakage currents are generally permissible. The conditions are then similar to those obtaining in a Zener diode.

The highest of the permissible reverse bias voltages is the *collector-base breakdown voltage* U_{CBO}. The maximum permissible *collector-emitter voltage* is generally lower, often only half of U_{CBO}. It is increased if, instead of leaving the base open-circuited, a resistor R is connected between emitter and base. The collector-base leakage current will then flow through R. Without R, it would be amplified in the same way as an external base current. The resultant breakdown voltage is designated as U_{CER}. Figure 4.10 shows the output characteristics for high collector-emitter voltages, indicating the various breakdown voltages [4.3].

It can be seen that the smaller the resistance R, the larger the value of U_{CER}. For $R = 0$, the maximum value U_{CES} (shorted base) is obtained. The reverse-bias

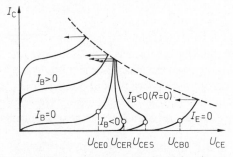

Fig. 4.10 Output characteristics for high voltages

collector-base characteristic $(I_E = 0)$ is given for comparison. Note the relationship

$$U_{CEO} < U_{CER} < U_{CES} < U_{CBO} .$$

The dashed curve in Fig. 4.10 indicates the onset of secondary breakdown [4.4].

One of the most important parameters for power transistors is the *maximum power dissipation*. The power converted into heat in the transistor is

$$P_T = U_{CE} \cdot I_C + U_{BE} \cdot I_B \approx U_{CE} \cdot I_C .$$

As the junction temperature must not exceed a defined value ϑ_j, the maximum permissible power dissipation is dependent on the cooling system. Data sheets usually quote the maximum power dissipation $P_{T\,max}$ for a case temperature of 25°C. Above this temperature the power dissipation must remain below the specified maximum value (derating), because ϑ_j would otherwise be exceeded. Typical values for ϑ_j are 90°C for germanium and 175°C for silicon transistors.

If power dissipation P_T occurs in a transistor, the junction heats up by $\Delta\vartheta_C = R_{\theta C} \cdot P_T$ with respect to the case, where $R_{\theta C}$ is the thermal resistance between semiconductor and case. The case heats up by $\Delta\vartheta_A = R_{\theta A} \cdot P_T$ with respect to the ambient. The junction therefore heats up by $\Delta\vartheta_{tot} = (R_{\theta C} + R_{\theta A})P_T$ with respect to the ambient. $R_{\theta A}$ is the case-to-ambient thermal resistance and depends greatly on the cooling of the case. If a transistor is operated without heat sink and in still air, $R_{\theta A}$ depends solely on the shape of the case and $R_{\theta\,tot} = R_{\theta C} + R_{\theta A}$ is specified to describe the transistor thermal behavior. The power at which ϑ_j is exceeded can therefore be calculated using the formula:

$$P_{\vartheta_j} = \frac{\vartheta_j - \vartheta_A}{R_{\theta\,tot}}$$

where ϑ_A is the temperature of the ambient air. As $R_{\theta C}$ is smaller than $R_{\theta A}$, P_{ϑ_j} is almost totally dependent on the type of the case. The most commonly used types are shown in Fig. 4.11. The maximum power dissipations produced in typical silicon transistors are listed in Fig. 4.12.

The right-hand column contains the typical maximum power dissipation values which can be obtained if the transistor case is maintained at 25°C. However, in practice it is very difficult to achieve this extreme condition. In order to achieve power dissipations which are higher than those for free mounting in still air, it is necessary to use heat sinks which considerably reduce the case-to-ambient thermal resistance. $R_{\theta A}$ is then made up of the ambient-to-sink thermal resistance and the sink-to-case thermal resistance. As the collectors of power transistors are generally connected to the case, a mica plate or a silicone plastic film are required for insulation. However, the insulator produces an additional thermal resistance. P_{ϑ_j} is generally calculated as follows:

$$P_{\vartheta_j} = \frac{\vartheta_j - \vartheta_A}{\sum R_\theta} \qquad (4.8)$$

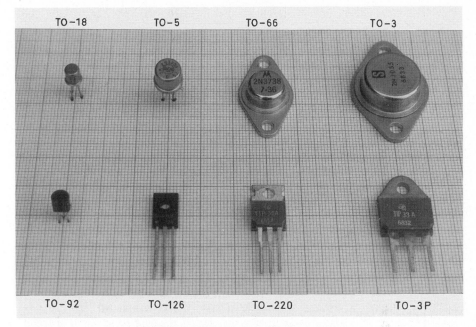

Fig. 4.11 Commonly used transistor cases.
Back row: metal cases TO-18, TO-5, TO-66, TO-3
Front row: plastic cases TO-92, TO-126, TO-220, TO-3 P

Type of case		$P_{\mathrm{T\,max}}$ with free mounting in still	Examples of $P_{\mathrm{T\,max}}$ at 25°C case temperature
Metal	Plastic	air at 25°C	
TO-18	TO-92	300 mW	600 mW
TO-5	TO-126	1 W	5 W
TO-66	TO-220	2 W	25 W
TO-3	TO-3 P	3 W	100 W

Fig. 4.12 Maximum power dissipation of silicon transistors

where $\sum R_\theta$ is the sum of all the thermal resistances between junction and ambient, the latter remaining at constant temperature. We give a worked example in Section 17.7.

Figure 4.13 shows the permissible operating range of a transistor with respect to the output characteristics. The limits are formed by the maximum collector current $I_{\mathrm{C\,max}}$, the maximum power dissipation P_{ϑ_j}, the secondary breakdown and the maximum collector-emitter voltage U_{CE0}. The resultant permissible operating range is known as the safe operating area (SOA).

The above information for each transistor is provided by the manufacturer in the form of a *data sheet*. Data for a small-signal transistor and a power

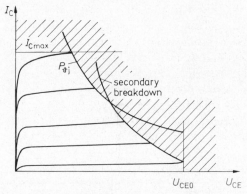

Fig. 4.13 Safe operating area of a transistor

Type		BC237B	BD249A
Manufacturer		Texas Instr.	Texas Instr.
		Motorola	Motorola
		Siemens	
Polarity		npn	npn
Complementary type		BC307B	BD250A
Maximum ratings:			
Collector-emitter voltage	U_{CE0}	45 V	60 V
Collector current	$I_{C\,max}$	100 mA	25 A
Emitter-base voltage	U_{EB0}	6 V	5 V
Base current	$I_{B\,max}$	50 mA	5 A
Power dissipation	$P_{T\,max}$	300 mW	125 W
Characteristics			
Collector-emitter leakage current	I_{CE0}	0.2 nA	0.5 mA
Collector-base capacitance	C_{CB}	3 pF	500 pF
Emitter-base capacitance	C_{EB}	8 pF	
Characteristics for	I_C	**10 µA**	**0.1 A**
Base-emitter voltage	U_{BE}	0.5 V	0.7 V
Saturation voltage	$U_{CE\,sat}$	100 mV	70 mV
Current gain	β	approx. 150	approx. 100
Characteristics for	I_C	**1 mA**	**1 A**
Base-emitter voltage	U_{BE}	0.6 V	0.8 V
Saturation voltage	$U_{CE\,sat}$	60 mV	200 mV
Current gain	β	240 . . . 500	40 . . . 180
Gain bandwidth product	f_T	100 MHz	3 MHz
Characteristics for:	I_C	**100 mA**	**10 A**
Base-emitter voltage	U_{BE}	0.8 V	1.3 V
Saturation voltage	$U_{CE\,sat}$	200 mV	700 mV
Current gain	β	approx. 200	approx. 40

Fig. 4.14 Typical data for a small-signal and a power transistor

transistor are listed in Fig. 4.14 as examples. The current and power dissipation ratings are markedly different.

The data show a pronounced variation in current gain. Circuits must therefore be selected and dimensioned such that the actual size of the current gain has no appreciable effect on operation.

At high current levels, power transistors exhibit certain peculiarities. Base-emitter voltages and collector-emitter saturation voltages are unusually high due to parasitic internal resistances. The current gain falls sharply at high currents, having a value of only about 10 at the maximum collector current of 25 A.

4.3 Common-emitter connection

There are three basis connections for a transistor operated as an amplifier. Depending on whether the emitter, collector or base is at constant potential, we distinguish between the common-emitter, common-collector or common-base modes and shall now examine these configurations in some detail, as they form the basis of all transistor circuits. For reasons of simplicity we shall describe them in terms of npn transistors, only using pnp transistors when there is a particular reason to do so. It is possible to replace npn transistors by pnp types and vice versa in all the circuits if at the same time the polarity of the operating voltages (and of electrolytic capacitors) is reversed. Specific data given are based on silicon transistors which can be assumed to possess an emitter-base voltage of $U_{\text{BEQ}} \approx 0.6$ V at the operating point.

4.3.1 Principle

In order to analyze the common-emitter circuit in Fig. 4.15, we apply an input voltage U_i of about 0.6 V and thereby produce a collector current in the

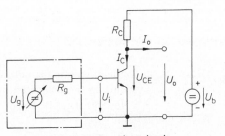

Fig. 4.15 Complete circuit   Fig. 4.16 Simplified representation

Voltage gain $A = \dfrac{\Delta U_o}{\Delta U_i} = -g_{\text{fE}}(R_c \| r_{\text{CE}})$

Input resistance: $r_i = r_{\text{BE}}$

Output resistance: $r_o = R_C \| r_{\text{CE}}$

mA range. If we now increase the input voltage by a small amount ΔU_i, the collector current I_C increases in accordance with Figs. 4.5 or 4.6. As the output characteristics are virtually horizontal, we shall initially make the approximating assumption that I_C is only dependent on U_{BE} and not on U_{CE}. The increase is therefore

$$\Delta I_C \approx g_{fE} \cdot \Delta U_{BE} = g_{fE} \cdot \Delta U_i .$$

As the collector current flows from the operating voltage source into the transistor via the load resistor R_C, the voltage drop across the latter becomes larger due to this increase, i.e. the output voltage U_o increases by

$$\Delta U_o = - \Delta I_C \cdot R_C \approx - g_{fE} R_C \cdot \Delta U_i$$

$$A = \frac{\Delta U_o}{\Delta U_i} \approx - g_{fE} R_C . \tag{4.9}$$

To calculate the current gain precisely, we use basic equation (4.7), substituting the relations derived from Fig. 4.16 for $I_o = 0$.

$$U_{BE} = U_i , \qquad U_{CE} = U_o , \qquad dU_o = - dI_C R_C .$$

This gives

$$- \frac{dU_o}{R_C} = g_{fE} dU_i + \frac{dU_o}{r_{CE}} .$$

Solving with respect to dU_o, we obtain the voltage gain

$$A = \frac{dU_o}{dU_i} = - g_{fE} \frac{R_C r_{CE}}{R_C + r_{CE}} = - g_{fE}(R_C \| r_{CE}) . \tag{4.10}$$

Thus, for the limiting case $R_C \ll r_{CE}$

$$A = - g_{fE} R_C ,$$

in accordance with Eq. (4.9). By substituting Eq. (4.2) we then obtain

$$A = - \frac{I_C R_C}{U_T} . \tag{4.11}$$

The voltage gain is therefore proportional to the voltage drop across the collector resistor R_C.

A numerical example will serve as an illustration. Let us calculate the voltage gain at $I_C = 1$ mA and $R_C = 5$ kΩ. From Eq. (4.2) we obtain the transconductance $g_{fE} = 1$ mA/26 mV $= 38.5$ mA/V. A typical value for r_{CE} at 1 mA is 100 kΩ. We therefore obtain from Eq. (4.10) the voltage gain

$$A = - 38.5 \text{ mA/V} \cdot (5 \text{ k}\Omega \| 100 \text{ k}\Omega) = - 183 .$$

As $R_C \ll r_{CE}$, we can also use Eq. (4.11), obtaining

$$A \approx - \frac{5 \text{ V}}{26 \text{ mV}} = - 192 .$$

We shall now examine the other limiting case, $R_C \gg r_{CE}$. It is difficult to implement this condition using just an ohmic collector resistor R_C as, according to Eq. (4.3), the voltage drop across R_C would have to be large compared with $U_Y \approx 100$ V. One possibility is to use a constant current source as the collector resistor. As we shall see in Section 4.6, high incremental resistances can be achieved in this way, even at low voltage levels. With $R_C \gg r_{CE}$, Eq. (4.10) yields the maximum gain

$$\mu = \lim_{R_c \to \infty} |A| = \lim_{R_c \to \infty} g_{fE}(R_C \| r_{CE}) = g_{fE}r_{CE} .$$

This is *independent* of the collector current, as g_{fE} is directly proportional and r_{CE} inversely proportional to I_C. Using Eqs. (4.2) and (4.3) we obtain

$$\boxed{\mu = g_{fE}r_{CE} = \frac{I_C}{U_T} \cdot \frac{U_Y}{I_C} = \frac{U_Y}{U_T}} . \tag{4.12}$$

Typical values are between 3000 and 7500 for npn transistors and 1500 to 5500 for pnp transistors.

Input and output resistance

In calculating the voltage gain, we have so far disregarded the effect of the signal-source resistances R_g and of the load resistance R_L. In order to calculate their effects, it is necessary to know two additional parameters of the amplifier circuit: the input resistance r_i and the output resistance r_o as shown in Fig. 4.17.

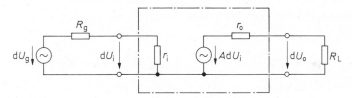

Fig. 4.17 Equivalent circuit for the effect of the input and output resistance of an amplifier circuit

The input resistance is defined as

$$r_i = \left. \frac{\partial U_i}{\partial I_i} \right|_{I_o = 0} .$$

It must therefore be determined for an open-circuited output. In accordance with Fig. 4.17, the reduced signal voltage

$$dU_i = \frac{r_i}{r_i + R_g} \cdot dU_g$$

appears at the input of the (unloaded) amplifier. Multiplying this voltage by the voltage gain A, we obtain the output voltage of the circuit under no-load conditions.

In order to calculate r_i, we use the basic equation (4.6) and, with $\mathrm{d}U_{BE} = \mathrm{d}U_i$ and $\mathrm{d}I_B = \mathrm{d}I_i$, directly obtain the result $r_i = r_{BE}$. Using Eq. (4.5), we therefore have

$$r_i = r_{BE} = \frac{\beta}{g_{fE}} = \frac{\beta U_T}{I_C} \ . \tag{4.13}$$

The smaller the collector current and the larger the current gain β, the larger the value of r_i. At a fixed operating point, the voltage gain is independent of I_C per Eq. (4.11). The collector current should therefore be selected such that the input resistance is substantially greater than R_g.

In order to calculate the voltage gain under load, it is necessary to know the output resistance r_o of the circuit. This indicates how much the output voltage falls if the output is loaded with current $\mathrm{d}I_o$ and the signal voltage U_g is kept constant. In the same way as for the internal resistance of a voltage source, we define

$$r_o = -\left. \frac{\partial U_o}{\partial I_o} \right|_{U_g = \text{const}}$$

Under load with resistance R_L, r_o and R_L form a voltage divider, i.e. the voltage gain is reduced by a factor of $R_L/(r_o + R_L)$. This smaller value is known as the *operating gain* A_b:

$$A_b = \left. \frac{\partial U_o}{\partial U_i} \right|_{R_L} = A \cdot \frac{R_L}{r_o + R_L} \ .$$

For the ratio of the output voltage under load to the no-load voltage of the signal source, we therefore obtain the relation

$$\left. \frac{\partial U_o}{\partial U_g} \right|_{R_L, R_g} = \frac{r_i}{r_i + R_g} \cdot A_b = \frac{r_i}{r_i + R_g} \cdot A \cdot \frac{R_L}{r_o + R_L} \ .$$

In order to calculate r_o, we apply Kirchhoff's current law to the output of the common-emitter circuit in Fig. 4.16 and obtain

$$-\mathrm{d}I_C - \mathrm{d}I_o - \frac{\mathrm{d}U_o}{R_C} = 0 \ .$$

Substitution into the basic equation (4.7) gives

$$-\mathrm{d}I_o - \frac{\mathrm{d}U_o}{R_C} = g_{fE}\mathrm{d}U_{BE} + \frac{1}{r_{CE}}\mathrm{d}U_o \ .$$

Because feedback is negligible, $\mathrm{d}U_{BE} = 0$ follows directly from $\mathrm{d}U_g = 0$, yielding the result

$$r_o = -\frac{\mathrm{d}U_o}{\mathrm{d}I_o} = \frac{R_C r_{CE}}{R_C + r_{CE}} = R_C \| r_{CE} \ . \tag{4.14}$$

Therefore, we can now also calculate the operating gain A_b. Using Eqs. (4.10) and (4.14) we get

$$A_b = \frac{AR_L}{R_L + r_o} = -g_{fE}\frac{R_C r_{CE} R_L}{R_C r_{CE} + R_L R_C + R_L r_{CE}}$$

$$= -g_{fE}(R_C \| r_{CE} \| R_L) \ . \qquad (4.15)$$

The small-signal behavior is therefore defined by the parallel connection of the resistances R_C, r_{CE} and R_L. This conclusion also can be readily deduced from the small-signal equivalent circuit in Fig. 4.18. The section of the circuit within the broken line represents, as may easily be verified, the basic equations (4.6) and (4.7) for the particular operating point selected. As only small variations around the operating point are of interest, the voltage sources are imagined as comprising a DC voltage source U_A and an AC voltage source u connected in series, the amplitude of the latter being small enough for it to be regarded as approximating to the differential change dU. Thus

$$U_g = U_{gA} + u_g \quad \text{with} \quad dU_g = u_g \ .$$

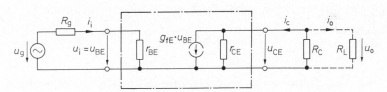

Fig. 4.18 Representation of the common-emitter connection using the small-signal equivalent circuit of a transistor

In the same way, the currents involved are broken down into a DC component and a small AC component. Only the alternating voltages and currents are marked on the small-signal equivalent circuit. It is therefore possible to regard the differential resistances as ohmic and apply the rules of calculation for linear networks. The supply voltage source is thus regarded as a short circuit, as its AC component is zero. As comparison with Fig. 4.15 shows, the collector resistance R_C therefore appears connected between collector and ground. It is therefore in parallel with r_{CE} and R_L.

According to Fig. 4.18, current $g_{fE} u_{BE}$ flows through this parallel circuit. The derived relations for A_b, A, r_o and r_i can therefore be obtained directly.

4.3.2 Nonlinear distortions

Owing to the pronounced nonlinearity of the transfer characteristic, distortions occur unless the amplitude of the input signal u_i is infinitely small. The distortions are measured in terms of the distortion factor

$$D = \frac{\text{total harmonic r.m.s. voltage}}{\text{total r.m.s. voltage}} = \frac{\sqrt{\sum_{n=2}^{\infty} U_n^2}}{\sqrt{\sum_{n=1}^{\infty} U_n^2}} = \frac{\sqrt{\sum_{n=2}^{\infty} \hat{U}_n^2}}{\sqrt{\sum_{n=1}^{\infty} \hat{U}_n^2}} \approx \frac{\sqrt{\sum_{n=2}^{\infty} \hat{U}_n^2}}{\hat{U}_1} .$$

This gives the r.m.s. voltage ratio of the harmonics to the fundamental at the output if the input is driven sinusoidally about the operating point, i.e.

$$U_i(t) = U_{iQ} + \hat{U}_i \sin \omega t .$$

Using the large-signal transfer equation (4.1), we obtain the collector current

$$I_C(t) = I_{CS} e^{\frac{U_{iQ}}{U_T}} e^{\frac{\hat{U}_i}{U_T} \sin \omega t}$$

Thus, by power series expansion

$$I_C(t) = I_{CS} e^{\frac{U_{iQ}}{U_T}} \left[1 + \frac{\hat{U}_i}{U_T} \sin \omega t + \frac{\hat{U}_i^2}{4U_T^2}(1 - \cos 2\omega t) + \ldots \right] .$$

Whence we can derive the amplitude of the fundamental and second harmonic, obtaining

$$D \approx \frac{\hat{I}_{C2}}{\hat{I}_{C1}} = \frac{\hat{U}_i}{4U_T} .$$

The distortion factor is therefore proportional to the input amplitude and independent of the position of the operating point. We can now calculate the maximum input amplitude for a distortion factor not exceeding 1%:

$$U_{i\,max} = \frac{4U_T}{100} \approx 1 \text{ mV} .$$

For a voltage gain $A \approx 200$, this gives a maximum output amplitude of about 200 mV.

4.3.3 Common-emitter connection with current feedback

The negative feedback principle can be used to reduce nonlinear distortion. For this purpose, a portion of the output signal is fed back to the input in such a way as to oppose the input signal. Although this reduces the gain, it enables it to be essentially determined by an ohmic resistance ratio rather than by the nonlinear transfer characteristic of the transistor.

In the circuit in Fig. 4.19, feedback is provided by resistor R_E inserted in the emitter lead. If U_i is increased, the collector current increases. As $I_E \approx I_C$, the voltage drop $U_E = I_E R_E$ increases in the same proportion. The change in $U_{BE} = U_i - U_E$ is therefore only a fraction of ΔU_i. The emitter voltage change occurring thus counteracts the amplification of ΔU_i. Negative feedback is

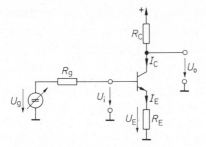

Fig. 4.19 Common-emitter connection with current feedback

Voltage gain: $\displaystyle A = \frac{dU_o}{dU_i} = - \frac{R_C}{R_E + \dfrac{1}{g_{fE}} + \dfrac{R_C}{\mu}} \approx - \frac{g_{fE}R_C}{1 + g_{fE}R_E} \approx - \frac{R_C}{R_E}$

Input resistance: $r_i \approx r_{BE} + \beta R_E$

Output resistance: $r_o \approx R_C$

therefore present. As it is produced by the flow of emitter current, a more precise term would be current feedback or series feedback.

Disregarding the change in U_{BE}, we obtain as a first approximation

$$\Delta U_E \approx \Delta U_i \ .$$

As virtually the same current flows through R_C as through R_E, the change in the voltage drop across R_C exceeds ΔU_E by a factor R_C/R_E. The voltage gain of the circuit with feedback is therefore approximately

$$A = \frac{\Delta U_o}{\Delta U_i} \approx - \frac{R_C}{R_E} \ ;$$

i.e. no other current-dependent transistor parameters are involved.

To calculate the voltage gain more precisely, we take the relations

$$dU_{BE} = dU_i - dU_E \ ; \qquad dU_o = - R_C dI_C \ ;$$

$$dU_{CE} = dU_o - dU_E \ ; \qquad dU_E \approx R_E dI_C$$

from Fig. 4.19 and substitute them in basic equation (4.7). With $g_{fE}r_{CE} = \mu \gg 1$, this gives:

$$A = \frac{dU_o}{dU_i} = - \frac{g_{fE}R_C}{1 + g_{fE}R_E + \dfrac{R_C}{r_{CE}}} = - \frac{R_C}{R_E + \dfrac{1}{g_{fE}} + \dfrac{R_C}{\mu}} \ . \tag{4.16}$$

In order to examine the limiting cases we consider the reciprocal

$$- \frac{1}{A} = \frac{1}{g_{fE}(R_C \| r_{CE})} + \frac{R_E}{R_C} \ . \tag{4.17}$$

For $R_E \to 0$, A tends to $-g_{fE}(R_C \| r_{CE})$, i.e. to the value without feedback, as expected. In the case of strong feedback, i.e. $R_C/R_E \ll g_{fE}(R_C \| r_{CE})$, we obtain

$$\boxed{A = -R_C/R_E} \, , \tag{4.18}$$

in accordance with the initial qualitative analysis.

For $R_C \ll r_{CE}$, Eq. (4.16) yields the approximation

$$A \approx -\frac{g_{fE}R_C}{1 + g_{fE}R_E} = -\frac{R_C}{R_E + 1/g_{fE}} \, .$$

The resultant expression

$$\boxed{g_{fE\,red} = \frac{g_{fE}}{1 + g_{fE}R_E} = \frac{1}{R_E + 1/g_{fE}}} \tag{4.19}$$

is known as the reduced transconductance. It represents the transconductance of a transistor with current feedback provided by R_E. This gives a simple relation for the current gain:

$$A = -g_{fE\,red} \cdot R_C \, .$$

Calculating the input resistance

As we have seen, the change in U_{BE} and thus the voltage gain is reduced by the current feedback. As the input current dI_B is also reduced as a result, the input resistance is increased by the same factor as the voltage gain is reduced. Using the approximation $r_{CE} \gg R_C$, we obtain

$$r_i = r_{BE}(1 + g_{fE}R_E) = r_{BE} + \beta R_E = \beta\left(\frac{1}{g_{fE}} + R_E\right) \, . \tag{4.20}$$

The output resistance is slightly increased by the current feedback and tends towards R_C in the limiting case of heavy feedback.

4.3.4 Voltage feedback

Another possible use of feedback is to add part of the output voltage to the input voltage via a resistor R_N, as shown in Fig. 4.20. As the common-emitter circuit is an inverting amplifier, this reduces the input voltage (parallel feedback).

In order to obtain a clear understanding of how this circuit operates, we study an increase of the input voltage by ΔU_i. This causes U_{BE} to increase and the output voltage is reduced by $|\Delta U_o| \gg \Delta U_{BE}$. If we now assume that the resistance R_N is not much greater than r_{BE}, the current change is $\Delta I_B \ll \Delta I_N$. Hence

$$\Delta I_N \approx \Delta I_i \, .$$

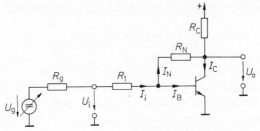

Fig. 4.20 Common-emitter connection with voltage feedback

Voltage gain: $\qquad A \approx -\dfrac{R_N}{R_1}$

Input resistance: $\qquad r_i \approx R_1$

Output resistance: $\qquad r_o \approx \dfrac{1}{g_{fE}}\left(1 + \dfrac{R_N}{R_1}\right)$

If the resistance R_1 is selected so large that $\Delta U_i \gg \Delta U_{BE}$, then

$$\Delta I_i \approx \frac{\Delta U_i}{R_1} \ .$$

We thus obtain the output voltage change

$$\Delta U_o = \Delta U_{BE} - \Delta I_N R_N \approx -\Delta I_N R_N \approx -\frac{R_N}{R_1}\Delta U_i \ .$$

In order to calculate the voltage gain more precisely, we apply Kirchhoff's current law to the base and collector terminals and obtain

$$dI_i - dI_B - dI_N = 0 \ ,$$

$$dI_N - dI_C - dU_o/R_C = 0 \ .$$

With

$$dI_i = \frac{dU_i - dU_{BE}}{R_1} \quad \text{and} \quad dI_N = \frac{dU_{BE} - dU_o}{R_N} \ ,$$

and using basic equations (4.6) and (4.7), we obtain the voltage gain

$$\frac{1}{A} = \frac{dU_i}{dU_o} = -\frac{1 + R_1/(r_{BE}\,\|\,R_N)}{\left(g_{fE} - \dfrac{1}{R_N}\right)(R_C\,\|\,r_{CE}\,\|\,R_N)} - \frac{R_1}{R_N} \ .$$

Using the approximation $R_N \gg 1/g_{fE}$, this gives

$$\frac{1}{A} = -\frac{1 + R_1/(r_{BE}\,\|\,R_N)}{g_{fE}(R_C\,\|\,r_{CE}\,\|\,R_N)} - \frac{R_1}{R_N} \ . \qquad (4.21)$$

For $R_1 \to 0$, we get, as expected, the gain without feedback

$$A = - g_{fE}(R_C \| r_{CE} \| R_N) \ .$$

This shows that R_N should not be too small compared with R_C, as otherwise the loading of the output by R_N would excessively reduce the voltage gain. However, as we have seen earlier from the qualitative analysis, R_N must not be very much higher than r_{BE}, as feedback would be ineffective. A practical compromise is to select $R_N \approx R_C \approx r_{BE}$. In the case of heavy feedback, i.e. R_1 of the order of R_N, we therefore obtain the voltage gain

$$A = - R_N/R_1 \ , \tag{4.22}$$

in accordance with the previous analysis.

The input resistance can be easily calculated by considering the following: a voltage change ΔU_{BE} brings about an output voltage change $\Delta U_o = - g_{fE}(R_C \| r_{CE} \| R_N)\Delta U_{BE}$. The current change due to R_N is therefore

$$\Delta I_N = \frac{\Delta U_{BE} - \Delta U_o}{R_N} \approx \frac{\Delta U_{BE}}{R_N} \cdot g_{fE}(R_C \| r_{CE} \| R_N) \ .$$

The feedback resistor R_N therefore acts with respect to the input resistance like a resistance $R_N/g_{fE}(R_C \| r_{CE} \| R_N)$ between base and ground. We therefore obtain

$$r_i = R_1 + \left[r_{BE} \middle\| \frac{R_N}{g_{fE}(R_C \| r_{CE} \| R_N)} \right] \approx R_1 \ . \tag{4.23}$$

The output resistance is likewise reduced by the voltage feedback because, owing to resistor R_N, the base current increases with the collector potential. Consequently, an increased collector current change is produced when an output voltage change is applied. Under the assumptions made, we obtain

$$r_o = - \left. \frac{\partial U_o}{\partial I_o} \right|_{U_g = \text{const}} \approx \frac{1}{g_{fE}} \left(1 + \frac{R_N}{R_1} \right) \ . \tag{4.24}$$

4.3.5 Biasing

The above considerations apply to small-signal operation of a transistor at a given operating point Q with I_{CQ}, U_{CEQ}. The operating point can be adjusted as shown in Fig. 4.21 by connecting a DC voltage source set to the value U_{BEQ} in series with a small-signal voltage source. However, this solution is expensive because a floating voltage source is required. The base voltage U_{BEQ} is therefore produced as shown in Fig. 4.22 from the operating voltage V^+ and the alternating signal voltage u_i is injected (coupled) via a capacitor. The DC voltage U_{CEQ} superimposed at the output is removed (decoupled) by a second capacitor. The circuit therefore contains two highpass filters whose lower cutoff frequency must be selected such that the lowest signal frequency is still fully transmitted.

The steep slope of the transfer characteristic in Fig. 4.5 shows that the U_{BEQ} setting is extremely critical. Small variations produce large changes in the

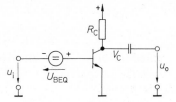

Fig. 4.21 Principle of biasing

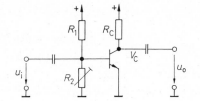

Fig. 4.22 Biasing using a base voltage divider

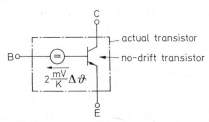

Fig. 4.23 Equivalent circuit showing the effect of base-emitter voltage drift

collector current. Owing to the unavoidable manufacturing variances, it is necessary to adjust U_{BEQ} individually for each transitor using trimmer R_2.

The circuit is also particularly unsatisfactory in terms of its temperature drift. The base-emitter voltage associated with a given collector current increases by about 2 mV per degree rise in temperature. This is illustrated in Fig. 4.23 in which the base lead contains an imaginary voltage source whose output is zero at room temperature and increases by 2 mV per degree. In the circuit in Fig. 4.22, this voltage source is in series with the signal voltage and is amplified in the same way. Consequently, for a gain of $A = -150$, the drift of the quiescent collector potential is

$$\frac{\partial V_{CQ}}{\partial \vartheta} = A \cdot \frac{2\,\mathrm{mV}}{\mathrm{K}} \approx -300\,\frac{\mathrm{mV}}{\mathrm{K}}\ .$$

For a 20 K temperature rise, the quiescent collector potential decreases by about 6 V. Such a large deviation from the desired operating point is generally intolerable.

Biasing the base current

The effect of U_{BE} on the quiescent collector potential can be overcome by setting the operating point using a constant base current. For this purpose the base is connected to the supply voltage via a high-value resistor, as shown in Fig. 4.24. The base current required is obtained from the desired quiescent collector current:

$$I_B = I_C/B\ .$$

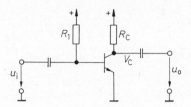

Fig. 4.24 Biasing by constant base current

This current must flow through R_1. Thus, for R_1:

$$R_1 = \frac{V^+ - U_{\mathrm{BEQ}}}{I_{\mathrm{B}}} \approx \frac{V^+}{I_{\mathrm{B}}} .$$

As V^+ is generally large compared to U_{BEQ}, the latter has virtually no effect on the base current, thus eliminating the major source of drift. There still remains the temperature dependence of the current gain B. As an approximation it may be assumed that B increases by 1% per degree temperature rise. The problem is that the relatively large manufacturing variances of B have a significant effect on the quiescent collector current and hence on the quiescent collector potential. The circuit is therefore just as unsatisfactory as the previous one.

Biasing by means of DC feedback

The best method of selecting a stable operating point is to provide a feedback path for low frequencies using an RC network (R_{E}, C_{E} in Fig. 4.25). In this way, the base-emitter voltage drift is only amplified by a factor of $R_{\mathrm{C}}/R_{\mathrm{E}}$. If both a negative and a positive supply voltage are available, the version shown in Fig. 4.26 can be used. In this case the quiescent base potential can be set to zero, thereby obviating the need for a voltage divider at the input if the signal voltage source has a DC path for the quiescent base current.

If no feedback is required for alternating voltages, capacitor C_{E} must short-circuit the alternating voltage in the frequency range of interest. To select its value, we consider the gain-frequency response produced by C_{E}. For this

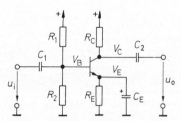

Fig. 4.25 Stabilizing the operating point by DC feedback

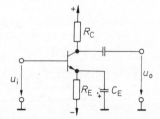

Fig. 4.26 Simplified operating point stabilization using additional negative supply voltage

purpose, we replace R_E in Eq. (4.16) by

$$\underline{Z}_E = R_E \left\| \frac{1}{j\omega C_E} = \frac{R_E}{1 + j\omega R_E C_E} \right. . \tag{4.25}$$

Above frequency $f_1 = 1/2\pi R_E C_E$, the absolute value of this impedance is reduced, i.e. the gain increases in proportion to the frequency until it attains the value $g_{fE} R_C$, as shown in Fig. 4.27. This yields

$$f_2 = \frac{g_{fE} R_C}{R_C/R_E} f_1 = g_{fE} R_E f_1 = \frac{1}{2\pi C_E/g_{fE}} . \tag{4.26}$$

If alternating voltage feedback is also required, which must, however, be weaker than for DC, it is possible to connect a resistor $R'_E < R_E$ in series with capacitor C_E.

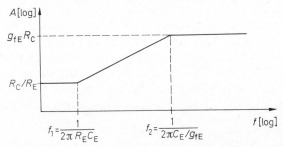

Fig. 4.27 Effect of capacitor C_E on the gain-frequency response

The process of dimensioning the circuit in Fig. 4.25 will now be illustrated by a worked example. Let there be a source with an internal resistance $R_g = 10\,\text{k}\Omega$. Let the current gain of the transistor be $B \approx \beta \approx 250$, the supply voltage $V^+ = 15\,\text{V}$. In order to avoid overloading the signal voltage source, we select the collector current sufficiently large to provide an input resistance of at least $20\,\text{k}\Omega$ for alternating voltages. This resistance is made up of R_1, R_2 and r_{BE} connected in parallel, as we can regard capacitor C_E as a short circuit in the frequency range of interest. Selecting $I_C = 200\,\mu\text{A}$, we obtain from Eq. (4.13)

$$r_{BE} = \frac{\beta U_T}{I_C} = \frac{250 \cdot 26\,\text{mV}}{200\,\mu\text{A}} = 32.5\,\text{k}\Omega . $$

Provided voltage divider R_1, R_2 is not given an excessively low resistance value, the requirement placed on the resulting input resistance can therefore be met.

We now have to specify the quiescent potential. The stability of the operating point is better the higher the voltage drop across R_E, as the change in U_{BE} then remains small compared to V_E and therefore has little effect on the collector current. If we select $V_E = 2\,\text{V}$, the collector current only changes by

$$\frac{\partial I_C/\partial \vartheta}{I_C} \approx \frac{\partial V_E/\partial \vartheta}{V_E} = \frac{2\,\text{mV/K}}{2\,\text{V}} = \frac{0.1\%}{\text{K}} . $$

In specifying the quiescent collector potential, care must be taken to ensure that, during operation, the collector-emitter voltage of the transistor does not fall to the saturation voltage $U_{\text{CE sat}} \approx 0.3$ V, as this would cause the parameters β, g_{fE} and r_{CE} to increase sharply as in Fig. 4.6. This saturated state is undesirable in the linear amplifier mode, because it produces severe distortion. On the other hand, the quiescent collector potential selected must not be excessively high, as this would cause the voltage drop across R_{C} and thus the voltage gain to be small. We shall assume that the maximum drive at the output must be $\Delta V_{\text{C max}} = \pm 2$ V about the quiescent potential. We then have

$$V_{\text{CQ}} > V_{\text{E}} + U_{\text{CE min}} + |\Delta V_{\text{C max}}| = 2 \text{ V} + 1 \text{ V} + 2 \text{ V} = 5 \text{ V} .$$

In order to avoid falling below this value, also allowing for the tolerances on U_{BEQ}, V^+ and the resistances, we select $V_{\text{CQ}} = 7$ V.

We can therefore now calculate the values of R_{C} and R_{E}:

$$R_{\text{E}} = \frac{V_{\text{E}}}{I_{\text{C}}} = \frac{2 \text{ V}}{200 \text{ µA}} = 10 \text{ k}\Omega ,$$

$$R_{\text{C}} = \frac{V^+ - V_{\text{CQ}}}{I_{\text{C}}} = \frac{15 \text{ V} - 7 \text{ V}}{200 \text{ µA}} = 40 \text{ k}\Omega .$$

The drift of the quiescent collector potential is therefore

$$\frac{\partial V_{\text{CQ}}}{\partial \vartheta} = -2 \frac{\text{mV}}{\text{K}} \cdot \frac{R_{\text{C}}}{R_{\text{E}}} = -8 \text{ mV/K} .$$

It is now necessary to adjust the quiescent base potential in such a way that the required 2 V is actually dropped across R_{E}. In the case of small collector currents, U_{BE} is about 0.6 V in accordance with Fig. 4.5. Hence

$$V_{\text{B}} = V_{\text{E}} + U_{\text{BEQ}} \approx 2.6 \text{ V} .$$

The base current is

$$I_{\text{B}} = \frac{I_{\text{C}}}{B} = \frac{200 \text{ µA}}{250} = 0.8 \text{ µA} .$$

It must not significantly affect the base potential. Consequently, we allow a voltage divider transverse current of about $10 I_{\text{B}}$ to flow through R_1 and R_2. This gives

$$R_1 = \frac{15 \text{ V} - 2.6 \text{ V}}{8 \text{ µA} + 0.8 \text{ µA}} = 1.4 \text{ M}\Omega , \qquad R_2 = \frac{2.6 \text{ V}}{8 \text{ µA}} = 330 \text{ k}\Omega .$$

The resistance values calculated are shown in Fig. 4.28. The AC input resistance is

$$r_{\text{i}} = \frac{u_{\text{i}}}{i_{\text{i}}} = r_{\text{BE}} \| R_1 \| R_2 = 29 \text{ k}\Omega .$$

Let $r_{\text{CE}} = 500$ kΩ for a collector current of 200 µA. Using Eq. (4.10) we then

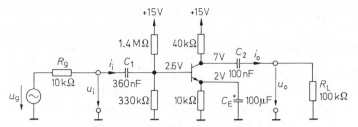

Fig. 4.28 Typical design values for a low-frequency amplifier stage

obtain under no-load conditions a voltage gain of

$$A = \frac{u_o}{u_i} = -\frac{I_C}{U_T}(R_C \| r_{CE}) = -285 \ .$$

The resultant output resistance is

$$r_o = -\frac{u_o}{i_o}\bigg|_{u_g=0} = R_C \| r_{CE} = 40 \text{ k}\Omega \| 500 \text{ k}\Omega = 37 \text{ k}\Omega \ .$$

With a load $R_L = 100 \text{ k}\Omega$, the open-circuit voltage of the signal generator is accordingly amplified by a factor of

$$\frac{u_o}{u_g}\bigg|_{R_L=100 \text{ k}\Omega} = \frac{r_i}{R_g + r_i} \cdot A \cdot \frac{R_L}{R_L + r_o} = -139 \ .$$

We require this value to be maintained constant down to a frequency of $f_{min} = 20$ Hz. As the circuit contains three highpass filters, the cutoff frequencies f_c of the individual high-pass networks must be selected lower than f_{min}. If they are all made equal, from Eq. (2.19):

$$f_c \approx \frac{f_{min}}{\sqrt{n}} = \frac{20 \text{ Hz}}{\sqrt{3}} = 11.5 \text{ Hz} \ .$$

We therefore obtain

$$C_1 = \frac{1}{2\pi f_c(R_g + r_i)} = 0.36 \ \mu\text{F} \ ,$$

$$C_E = \frac{g_{fE}}{2\pi f_c} = \frac{I_C}{2\pi f_c U_T} \approx 100 \ \mu\text{F} \ ,$$

$$C_2 = \frac{1}{2\pi f_c(r_o + R_L)} \approx 100 \ \text{nF} \ .$$

4.4   Common-base connection

Comparing the common-base connection in Fig. 4.29 to the common-emitter configuration in Fig. 4.16, we can see that the signal voltage source is

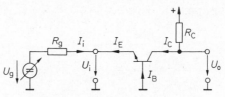

Fig. 4.29 Common-base connection

Voltage gain: $A = g_{fE}(R_C \| r_{CE})$

Input resistance: $r_i \approx 1/g_{fE}$

Output resistance: $r_o \approx R_C$

located between the same terminals. Consequently, the same voltage gain is produced, but this time with positive polarity, as the relation $dU_{BE} = -\,dU_i$ now applies instead of $dU_{BE} = dU_i$. The basic difference between the two circuits is that in the common-base configuration the signal voltage source is grounded together with the base terminal. As is immediately apparent from Fig. 4.29, it is now loaded with the emitter current instead of the base current. The input resistance is therefore smaller by a factor β than in the common-emitter connection.

For a more precise calculation we extract from Fig. 4.29 the relations

$$dI_i = -\,dI_E = -\,dI_B - dI_C\,, \qquad dU_{BE} = -\,dU_i\,,$$

$$dU_{CE} = dU_o - dU_i \approx dU_o = -\,dI_C R_C\,.$$

Hence, using basic equations (4.6) and (4.7):

$$r_i = \frac{r_{BE}(R_C + r_{CE})}{g_{fE}r_{BE}r_{CE} + R_C + r_{CE}} = \left(\frac{1}{g_{fE}} + \frac{R_C}{g_{fE}r_{CE}}\right)\Big\| r_{BE}\,.$$

Using the approximation $R_C \ll r_{CE}$, we therefore obtain

$$\boxed{r_i \approx \frac{1}{g_{fE}} = \frac{r_{BE}}{\beta}}\,, \qquad\qquad (4.27)$$

in accordance with the qualitative approach.

The resulting output resistance is

$$r_o = R_C \Big\| r_{CE}\left(1 + \beta\frac{R_g}{r_{BE} + R_g}\right)\,.$$

For $R_g \to 0$, it follows that $r_o = R_C \| r_{CE}$, as with the common-emitter connection. The increase in the output resistance due to R_g is therefore due to the fact that R_g is now providing current feedback.

Owing to its low input resistance, the common-base connection is little used for low-frequency applications. However, in the high-frequency range it offers advantages over the common-emitter configuration. This range of applications is described in greater detail in Chapter 16 (wideband amplifiers).

4.5   Common-collector connection, emitter follower

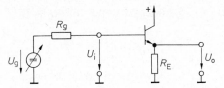

Fig. 4.30 Emitter follower

Voltage gain: $A = \dfrac{g_{fE} R_E}{1 + g_{fE} R_E} \approx 1$

Input resistance: $r_i \approx \beta R_E$

Output resistance: $r_o \approx R_E \left\| \left(\dfrac{1}{g_{fE}} + \dfrac{R_g}{\beta} \right) \right.$

The common-collector connection operates as follows: if an input voltage U_i greater than 0.6 V is applied, a collector current flows which produces a voltage drop across R_E. The output voltage increases until a base-emitter voltage of about 0.6 V is established. We therefore have

$$U_o = U_i - U_{BEQ} \approx U_i - 0.6 \text{ V} .$$

If U_i is made larger, the collector current and hence the voltage drop across R_E increases. Due to the steepness of the input characteristic, U_{BEQ} increases only slightly as the collector current rises. The output voltage therefore increases virtually in the same way as the input voltage, giving a voltage gain of

$$A = \frac{\Delta U_o}{\Delta U_i} \approx 1 .$$

As the emitter potential follows the base potential, the common-collector connection is generally known as an *emitter follower*.

To calculate the voltage gain more precisely, we use the basic equation (4.7) and obtain with

$$dU_{CE} = - dU_o , \qquad dU_{BE} = dU_i - dU_o , \qquad dI_C = \frac{dU_o}{R_E}$$

the result

$$A = \frac{dU_o}{dU_i} = \frac{1}{1 + \dfrac{1}{g_{fE}(R_E \| r_{CE})}} \approx \frac{g_{fE} R_E}{1 + g_{fE} R_E} = g_{f\,red} \cdot R_E . \qquad (4.28)$$

Given that $R_E \gg 1/g_{fE}$, it follows that

$$\boxed{A \approx 1} ,$$

in accordance with the qualitative assessment.

As far as the input resistance is concerned, there is no difference between the emitter follower and the common-emitter connection with current feedback. Accordingly, from Eq. (4.20) under the condition $R_E \gg 1/g_{fE}$ we obtain the result

$$\boxed{r_i = r_{BE} + \beta R_E \approx \beta R_E} \ . \tag{4.29}$$

The output resistance can be easily found for $R_g = 0$: for $\Delta U_g = 0$, the output of the emitter follower has the same behavior as the input of the common-base connection. In this case, therefore,

$$r_o(R_g = 0) = \frac{1}{g_{fE}} \bigg\| R_E \approx \frac{1}{g_{fE}} \ .$$

In order to allow for R_g, we return to basic equations (4.6) and (4.7) and obtain

$$\boxed{r_o = \left(\frac{1}{g_{fE}} + \frac{R_g}{\beta} \right) \bigg\| R_E} \ . \tag{4.30}$$

A worked example will demonstrate how low the output resistance can become: with $I_C = 2$ mA, $\beta = 300$, $R_E = 3$ kΩ and $R_g = 40$ kΩ we obtain

$$r_o = \left(\frac{26 \text{ mV}}{2 \text{ mA}} + \frac{40 \text{ k}\Omega}{300} \right) \bigg\| 3 \text{ k}\Omega = (13 \ \Omega + 133 \ \Omega) \| 3 \text{ k}\Omega = 140 \ \Omega \ .$$

With these values the input resistance is

$$r_i = 300(13 \ \Omega + 3 \text{ k}\Omega) = 904 \text{ k}\Omega \ .$$

It is therefore 6000 times greater than r_o. Consequently, the emitter follower is also known as an impedance converter: it delivers virtually the no-load voltage of the signal source, but has a substantially lower internal resistance than the signal source. By interposing an emitter follower it is possible to couple a high-impedance stage to a low-impedance stage.

The operating point is set in the same way as for the common-emitter connection with current feedback. However, a greater degree of freedom is available for selecting the quiescent emitter potential, as the collector potential is equal to V^+ irrespective of the drive. Higher values may therefore be chosen for V_{EQ} than in the case of the common-emitter connection with current feedback. It is therefore possible simply to connect the emitter follower directly to the output of the preceding stage, as shown in Fig. 4.31. For a collector current of 2 mA to flow under the given condition for the potentials, it is necessary to select

$$R_E = (7 \text{ V} - 0.6 \text{ V})/2 \text{ mA} = 3.2 \text{ k}\Omega \ .$$

The emitter follower is peculiar in that only when it is driven with very low alternating voltages can it have a resistive load as low as might be expected from the low output resistance. This is because, for AC conditions, the load resistor R_L is connected in parallel with the feedback resistor R_E. If R_L is made low with respect to R_E, some small voltage drive ΔV_E will easily produce

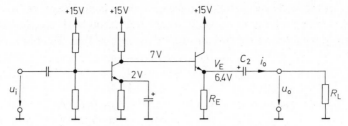

Fig. 4.31 Example of a directly coupled emitter follower

a current drive as large as the quiescent current, and distortion will occur. In order to keep it small, it is necessary that

$$\Delta I_C = \frac{\Delta V_E}{R_E \| R_L} < I_{CQ} = \frac{V_{EQ}}{R_E} \; .$$

Hence the condition

$$\Delta V_E < \frac{R_E \| R_L}{R_E} V_{EQ} \; . \tag{4.31}$$

For our worked example, e.g. with $R_L = r_o = 140\,\Omega$, the maximum permissible amplitude is therefore

$$\Delta V_E < \frac{3.2\,\mathrm{k}\Omega \| 140\,\Omega}{3.2\,\mathrm{k}\Omega} \cdot 6.4\,\mathrm{V} = 268\,\mathrm{mV} \; .$$

We can see from Eq. (4.31) that for an output of $U_o = \frac{1}{2} V_{EQ}$ it is necessary to select the load resistor such that

$$\boxed{R_L > R_E} \; .$$

4.6   Transistor as a constant current source

An ideal current source impresses upon a load R_L a current independent of the voltage drop across R_L. In accordance with the equivalence illustrated in Figs. 1.2 and 1.3, one way of implementing a circuit of this kind is to connect a very large ohmic resistance R_i in series with a voltage source U_0.

In order to avoid the short-circuit current I_0 being unreasonably small, it is necessary to select very high voltages for U_0. For example, if $I_0 = 1\,\mathrm{mA}$ and $R_{int} = 10\,\mathrm{M}\Omega$, U_0 would have to be $10\,\mathrm{kV}$. This requirement can be easily obviated if one is prepared to accept that the output resistance is large only for a given range of output voltages. In this range, therefore, only the *incremental* output resistance

$$r_o = -\frac{\mathrm{d}U_o}{\mathrm{d}I_o}$$

has to be high, whereas the static internal resistance can be low. The output characteristic of a transistor has this property. While U_{CE}/I_C can be of the order of a few kΩ, dU_{CE}/dI_C can, above $U_{CE\,sat}$, be a few 100 kΩ. This incremental output resistance value can be increased by several orders of magnitude by means of feedback. We shall now examine some simple circuits incorporating a single transistor; precision current sources with operational amplifiers are dealt with in Chapter 13.

4.6.1 Basic circuit

The current source in Fig. 4.32 is based on the common-emitter connection with current feedback. The basic difference is that here the load is connected in series with the transistor. The output current remains constant as long as the transistor is not overdriven, i.e. as long as $U_{CE} > U_{CE\,sat}$. In order to calculate the output resistance we derive the following relations:

$$dI_o = dI_C , \qquad dU_{CE} \approx -dU_o , \qquad dI_E = dI_C + dI_B ,$$

$$dU_{BE} = -dI_B(R_1 \| R_2) - dI_E R_E .$$

Hence, using basic equations (4.6) and (4.7)

$$r_o = -\frac{dU_o}{dI_o} = r_{CE}\left[1 + \frac{\beta R_E}{(R_1 \| R_2) + r_{BE} + R_E}\right] . \qquad (4.32)$$

This result indicates three special cases when $R_1 \| R_2 \ll r_{BE}$:

1) For $R_E = 0$, it follows that $r_o = r_{CE}$, i.e. the output resistance of the transistor determines the output resistance of the circuit.

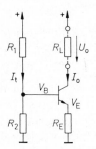

Fig. 4.32 Constant current source with voltage divider

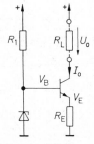

Fig. 4.33 Constant current source with Zener diode

Output current: $\qquad\qquad I_o = \dfrac{V_E}{R_E} = \dfrac{V_B - U_{BEQ}}{R_E}$

Output resistance: $\qquad r_o = -\dfrac{dU_o}{dI_o} = r_{CE}\left[1 + \dfrac{\beta R_E}{(R_1 \| R_2) + r_{BE} + R_E}\right]$

2) For $R_E \ll r_{BE}$ it follows that

$$r_o = r_{CE}\left(1 + \frac{\beta}{r_{BE}} R_E\right) = r_{CE}(1 + g_{fE}R_E) = r_{CE} + \mu R_E \ .$$

In this range the output resistance therefore increases linearly with R_E.
3) For $R_E \gg r_{BE}$ it follows that

$$r_o = r_{CE}(1 + \beta) \approx \beta r_{CE} \ .$$

In this range the output resistance does not increase any further if the emitter resistance is increased. Consequently, this is the largest output resistance that can be achieved using a bipolar transistor.

When designing a constant current source it is first necessary to specify the voltage drop across R_E. The larger the value selected, the higher the output resistance for a given output current and the smaller the maximum voltage drop across the load R_L for a fixed supply voltage. We typically select $V_E = 5$ V at $V^+ = 15$ V. Thus, for a desired output current of 1 mA, the emitter resistance is $R_E = 5$ kΩ. The resistance of the base voltage divider must be selected sufficiently low so that it does not appreciably impair the output resistance of the circuit. For a current gain $\beta = 300$, we therefore select

$$R_1 \| R_2 \approx r_{BE} = \frac{\beta}{g_{fE}} = \beta \frac{U_T}{I_C} = 300 \cdot 26 \ \Omega = 7.8 \ \text{k}\Omega \ .$$

At this value a relatively large transverse current $I_t \approx I_o$ flows through the voltage divider. For the output resistance of the circuit we obtain, with $r_{CE} = 100$ kΩ,

$$r_o = 100 \ \text{k}\Omega\left[1 + \frac{300 \cdot 5 \ \text{k}\Omega}{7.8 \ \text{k}\Omega + 7.8 \ \text{k}\Omega + 5 \ \text{k}\Omega}\right] = 7.4 \ \text{M}\Omega \ .$$

The internal resistance of the base voltage divider can also be kept small by replacing R_2 by a Zener diode. This possibility is shown in Fig. 4.33. This additionally makes the base potential largely independent of operating voltage fluctuations.

4.6.2   Bipolar current source

A current source is sometimes required which can provide a positive or negative output current I_o proportional to the input voltage U_i applied. For this purpose it is possible to combine two complementary current sources, as in Fig. 4.34. When $U_i = 0$, the two currents I_1 and I_2 are of equal magnitude; the output current I_o is zero. If a positive input voltage is applied, I_2 increases and I_1 decreases. Consequently, a negative output current flows. The reverse is true with negative input voltages.

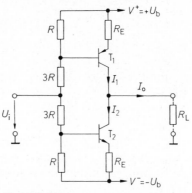

Fig. 4.34 Bipolar constant current source

Output current: $I_o = -U_i/2R_E$

In order to calculate the output current, we first calculate currents I_1 and I_2. In accordance with Fig. 4.34:

$$I_1 = \frac{\frac{1}{4}(U_b - U_i) - U_{\text{BEQ}}}{R_E} \ ,$$

$$I_2 = \frac{\frac{1}{4}(U_b + U_i) - U_{\text{BEQ}}}{R_E} \ .$$

From which we obtain

$$I_o = I_1 - I_2 = -\frac{U_i}{2R_E} \ ,$$

as stated above.

The circuit only operates properly if the current sources are not overdriven. To achieve this, the value of the input voltage must be less than $U_b - 4U_{\text{BE}}$, as one of the two transistors would otherwise be turned off. On the other hand, the load resistor must have a value low enough to ensure that the output voltage does not exceed $\frac{1}{2}U_b$, as this would cause one transistor to be driven into saturation.

4.6.3   Current mirror

In the basic circuit of a current source in Fig. 4.32 the emitter potential increases by 2 mV per degree. This temperature effect can be compensated for by ensuring that the base potential V_B decreases by 2 mV per degree. For this purpose a diode can be connected in series with R_2 as in Fig. 4.35. We then have

$$I_o \approx I_E = \frac{V_B - U_{\text{BEQ}}}{R_E} = \frac{I_i R_2 + U_D - U_{\text{BEQ}}}{R_E} \approx \frac{R_2}{R_E} I_i \ .$$

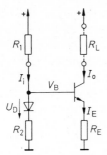

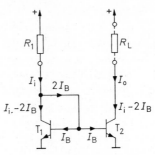

Fig. 4.35 Simple current mirror

Fig. 4.36 Current mirror with transistor diode

Output current: $I_\mathrm{o} \approx \dfrac{R_2}{R_\mathrm{E}} I_\mathrm{i}$

Output current: $I_\mathrm{o} \approx I_\mathrm{i}$

Because I_o is proportional to I_i, this arrangement is known as a current mirror. In order to better satisfy the condition $U_\mathrm{D} \approx U_\mathrm{BEQ}$, a transistor is frequently used instead of a diode, with the collector and base connected as in Fig. 4.36. In this mode $U_\mathrm{CE} = U_\mathrm{BE} > U_\mathrm{CE\,sat}$. Transistor T_1 therefore operates outside saturation. The collector current of T_1 is $I_\mathrm{i} - 2I_\mathrm{B}$. If the two transistors are identical, current $I_\mathrm{o} = I_\mathrm{i} - 2I_\mathrm{B}$ also flows through T_2. Hence, with current gain $B = I_\mathrm{o}/I_\mathrm{B}$:

$$I_\mathrm{o} = \frac{B}{B + 2} I_\mathrm{i} \approx I_\mathrm{i} \; .$$

The circuit basically functions without emitter resistors. However, in order to increase the output resistance and to compensate for matching errors, they are generally not omitted completely.

A current mirror which presents a high output resistance even without emitter resistors is the Wilson circuit shown in Fig. 4.37. Here we have a closed control loop which makes the voltage drop across transistor diode T_2 increase

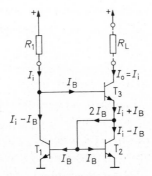

Fig. 4.37 Wilson current mirror

Output current: $I_\mathrm{o} = I_\mathrm{i}$

until a collector current $I_i - I_B$ flows through T_1. The steady-state condition is then achieved and the currents flowing are as indicated in Fig. 4.37.

Using the current mirror it is also possible to generate integral multiples or fractions of the input current by connecting the appropriate number of transistors in parallel with T_2 or T_1, respectively.

Correct operation of the circuit requires is a tight matching tolerance on the transistors. This cannot be achieved using discrete transistors. Transistor arrays or special integrated current mirrors such as series TL011 to TL021 from Texas Instruments are therefore employed [4.5].

4.7   Darlington circuit

In many cases, particularly in an emitter follower configuration, the current gain of one transistor is insufficient. In this case it is possible to connect an emitter follower before a transistor, as in Fig. 4.38. The resultant Darlington circuit may be regarded as a transistor with terminals E', B' and C'. We shall now calculate its characteristics.

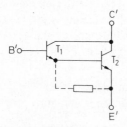

Fig. 4.38 Darlington circuit

Fig. 4.39 Circuit symbol

Equivalent characteristics:

Current gain:	$\beta' = \beta_1 \cdot \beta_2$
Input resistance:	$r_{B'E'} = 2r_{BE1} = 2\beta'\dfrac{U_T}{I_{C'}}$
Transconductance:	$g'_{fE} = I_{C'}/2U_T$
Output resistance:	$r_{C'E'} = \frac{2}{3}r_{CE2}$

As the emitter current of T_1 is equal to the base current of T_2, we obtain the current gain

$$\beta' = \frac{\mathrm{d}I_{C'}}{\mathrm{d}I_{B'}} = \beta_1 \beta_2 \ . \tag{4.33}$$

For the input resistance of this circuit we obtain using Eq. (4.20)

$$r_{B'E'} = r_{BE1} + \beta_1 r_{BE2} \ .$$

Hence, with $I_{C2} \approx \beta_2 I_{C1}$, from Eq. (4.4)

$$r_{BE2} = \frac{1}{\beta_1} r_{BE1} \tag{4.34}$$

and therefore

$$r_{B'E'} = 2r_{BE1} = 2\beta' \frac{U_T}{I_{C'}} . \tag{4.35}$$

In order to calculate the output resistance

$$r_{C'E'} = \left. \frac{\partial U_{C'E'}}{\partial I_{C'}} \right|_{U_{B'E'} = \text{const}}$$

we apply basic equations (4.6) and (4.7) to transistors T_1 and T_2 and obtain, with

$$dU_{B'E'} = dU_{BE1} + dU_{BE2} = 0 , \qquad dI_{B2} = dI_{C1}$$

the result

$$r_{C'E'} = r_{CE2} \left\| \frac{r_{CE1}(1 + g_{fE1}r_{BE2})}{\beta_2} = r_{CE2} \right\| \frac{2r_{CE1}}{\beta_2} . \tag{4.36}$$

Because of Eq. (4.3), $r_{CE1} = \beta_2 r_{CE2}$. This yields

$$r_{C'E'} = r_{CE2} \| 2r_{CE2} = \tfrac{2}{3} r_{CE2} . \tag{4.37}$$

In order to be able to turn off transistor T_2 more quickly, a resistor is frequently connected in parallel with its base-emitter junction.

Complementary Darlington circuit

It is also possible to interconnect two complementary transistors to form a Darlington circuit, as in Fig. 4.40. In this case transistor T_1 basically determines circuit operation, whereas T_2 merely provides current gain. If a pnp

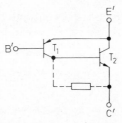

Fig. 4.40 Complementary Darlington circuit

Equivalent characteristics:

Current gain: $\qquad\qquad \beta' = \beta_1 \cdot \beta_2$

Input resistance: $\qquad\quad r_{B'E'} = r_{BE1} = \beta' \dfrac{U_T}{I_{C'}}$

Transconductance: $\qquad\; g'_{fE} = I_{C'}/U_T$

Output resistance: $\qquad r_{C'E'} = \tfrac{1}{2} r_{CE2} = \tfrac{1}{2} U_Y/I_{C'}$

transistor is used for T_1 as in Fig. 4.40, the entire arrangement operates like a pnp transistor possessing quite similar equivalent characteristics to those of the normal Darlington connection.

In order to ensure that a collector current flows through transistor T_1, it is necessary to apply an input voltage $U_{B'E'} = U_{BE1} \approx -0.6$ V. The input resistance of the circuit is

$$r_{B'E'} = \frac{dU_{B'E'}}{dI_{B'}} = \frac{dU_{BE1}}{dI_{B1}} = r_{BE1} \ .$$

As the collector current of T_1 is equal to the base current of T_2, the collector current

$$dI_{C2} = \beta_2 dI_{C1} = \beta_1 \beta_2 dI_{B1} \ ,$$

flows through T_2. The current gain is therefore

$$\beta' = \frac{dI_{C'}}{dI_{B'}} = \beta_1 \beta_2 \ , \tag{4.38}$$

as in the previous circuit. For the output resistance we obtain

$$r_{C'E'} = \frac{dU_{C'E'}}{dI_{C'}} = \frac{dU_{C'E'}}{dI_{C1} + dI_{C2}} = r_{CE2} \left\| \frac{r_{CE1}}{\beta_2} = \tfrac{1}{2} r_{CE2} \ . \tag{4.39}$$

4.8 Differential amplifier

4.8.1 Basic circuit

A differential amplifier is a symmetrical DC voltage amplifier with two inputs and two outputs. The basic circuit is shown in Fig. 4.41. It is characterized by a constant current source in the common emitter lead. This ensures that the sum of the emitter currents $I_{E1} + I_{E2} = I_k$ remains constant. In the quiescent state, $U_{i1} = U_{i2} = 0$. In this case the constant current I_k is equally divided between the two transistors T_1 and T_2 for reasons of symmetry. Therefore

$$I_{E1} = I_{E2} = \tfrac{1}{2} I_k \ .$$

Hence, disregarding the base current

$$I_{C1} = I_{C2} \approx \tfrac{1}{2} I_k \ .$$

This situation is unaltered if the two input voltages are varied by the same amount (common-mode drive). As the collector currents remain constant in this mode of operation, the output voltages also remain constant, i.e. the common-mode gain is zero.

However, if we make $U_{i1} > U_{i2}$, the current distribution in the differential amplifier then changes: I_{C1} increases and I_{C2} decreases. However, the sum remains constantly equal to I_k. Consequently

$$\Delta I_{C1} = - \Delta I_{C2} \ .$$

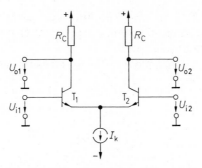

Fig. 4.41 Basic differential amplifier circuit

Differential-mode gain:
$$A_D = \frac{dU_{o1}}{dU_D} = -\frac{dU_{o2}}{dU_D} = -\tfrac{1}{2} g_{fE}(R_C \| r_{CE}) \text{ with } U_D = U_{i1} - U_{i2}$$

Common-mode gain:
$$A_{CM} = \frac{dU_{o1}}{dU_{CM}} = \frac{dU_{o2}}{dU_{CM}} = -\frac{1}{2} \cdot \frac{R_C}{r_k} \text{ with } U_{CM} = \tfrac{1}{2}(U_{i1} + U_{i2})$$

Common-mode rejection ratio (CMRR):
$$G = \frac{A_D}{A_{CM}} \approx g_{fE} r_k \ (r_k = \text{output resistance of current source})$$

Differential input resistance:
$$r_D = \frac{dU_D}{dI_{i1}} = -\frac{dU_D}{dI_{i2}} = 2r_{BE}$$

Common-mode input resistance:
$$r_{CM} = \frac{dU_{CM}}{dI_{i1}} = \frac{dU_{CM}}{dI_{i2}} = 2\beta r_k$$

Output resistance:
$$r_o = R_C \| r_{CE}$$

Quiescent input current:
$$I_B = \tfrac{1}{2}(I_{i1} + I_{i2}) = \frac{1}{2} \cdot \frac{I_k}{B}$$

An input voltage difference therefore produces a change in the output voltages, unlike a common-mode drive.

A temperature-induced change in the base-emitter voltage has the same effect as a common-mode drive signal: It does not affect the output. Consequently, the differential amplifier is suitable as a DC voltage amplifier. Because of its small temperature drift, the differential amplifier is also used if the intention is to amplify a single input voltage rather than a voltage difference. In this case one of the two inputs is connected to zero potential. We then have $U_D = U_i$ or $U_D = -U_i$ depending on which input is used.

In order to calculate the voltage gain more precisely, the input voltages are broken down into two components, namely the common-mode voltage U_{CM} and the differential voltage U_D:

$$U_{i1} = U_{CM} + \tfrac{1}{2} U_D \quad \text{and} \quad U_{i2} = U_{CM} - \tfrac{1}{2} U_D \ .$$

Hence

$$U_{CM} = \tfrac{1}{2}(U_{i1} + U_{i2}) \quad \text{and} \quad U_D = U_{i1} - U_{i2} \ .$$

We first consider the case of purely *differential drive*, i.e. we select

$$dU_{i1} = - dU_{i2} = \tfrac{1}{2} dU_D .$$

For reasons of symmetry the emitter potential remains constant and we obtain

$$dU_{BE1} = - dU_{BE2} = \tfrac{1}{2} dU_D .$$

The two transistors therefore operate as if in common-emitter mode and produce a voltage gain of

$$\frac{dU_{o1}}{dU_D} = \frac{dU_{o1}}{2 dU_{BE1}} = - \tfrac{1}{2} g_{fE}(R_C \| r_{CE}) = A_D$$

or   (4.40)

$$\frac{dU_{o2}}{dU_D} = \frac{dU_{o2}}{- 2 dU_{BE2}} = + \tfrac{1}{2} g_{fE}(R_C \| r_{CE}) = - A_D .$$

The collector voltage changes are of equal magnitude but of opposite polarity and are only half as large as in the common-emitter connection, because the input voltage is now equally divided between two transistors.

In order to calculate the common-mode gain, we must assume a real current source in the emitter lead. We shall denote its output resistance by r_k. If the same voltage U_{CM} is applied to the two inputs, the current is equally divided between the two transistors. In this case they operate like two parallel-connected emitter followers with common emitter resistor r_k. The emitter potential therefore varies by the value dU_{CM} and we obtain the current change

$$dI_k = \frac{dU_{CM}}{r_k} .$$

The collector currents only change by half this amount, producing an output voltage change

$$dU_{o1} = dU_{o2} = - \frac{R_C}{2r_k} dU_{CM}$$

in phase at both collectors. Hence, the common-mode gain is

$$A_{CM} = \frac{dU_{o1}}{dU_{CM}} = \frac{dU_{o2}}{dU_{CM}} = - \frac{R_C}{2r_k} .$$ (4.41)

Typical values are 10^{-3}, whereas the differential gain may be 100 or more.

With simultaneous differential and common-mode drive, the output voltage changes are obtained by linear superposition:

$$dU_{o1} = - \tfrac{1}{2} g_{fE}(R_C \| r_{CE})U_D - \frac{R_C}{2r_k} U_{CM} ,$$

$$dU_{o2} = + \tfrac{1}{2} g_{fE}(R_C \| r_{CE})U_D - \frac{R_C}{2r_k} U_{CM} .$$

A criterion for the quality of the differential amplifier is the ratio of differential to common-mode gain. This is known as the *common-mode rejection ratio*

(CMRR). From Eqs. (4.40) and (4.41) we obtain

$$G = \frac{A_{\mathrm{D}}}{A_{\mathrm{CM}}} \approx g_{\mathrm{fE}} r_{\mathrm{k}} \ . \tag{4.42}$$

In the worked example in Section 4.6.1, we obtained an output resistance of 7.4 MΩ for a 1 mA current source. The transistor transconductance at $I_{\mathrm{C}} = \frac{1}{2}I_{\mathrm{k}} = 0.5$ mA is

$$g_{\mathrm{fE}} = 0.5 \ \mathrm{mA}/26 \ \mathrm{mV} = 19 \ \mathrm{mA/V} \ .$$

This gives a common-mode rejection ratio of $G \approx 140\,000 \triangleq 103$ dB. In practice, however, values are generally lower and it is also found that the output voltages do not vary in an in-phase manner, in contrast to the result in Eq. (4.41). This is because the transistor data do not precisely tally, as assumed in the calculation. The upper limit of the common-mode rejection ratio is therefore determined by the matching tolerance of the transistors. With well-matched transistors, values of between 80 and 100 dB are achieved.

Owing to the parasitic collector-base capacitances, the magnitude of the common-mode gain increases with frequency and the common-mode rejection ratio therefore decreases. The cutoff frequency of the common-mode rejection ratio is much lower than that of the differential gain, as the high output resistance of the current source determines the frequency response of $\underline{G}$. For the frequency response of the differential gain $\underline{A}_{\mathrm{D}}$ only the comparatively low-value collector resistance R_{C} is the determining factor. The typical frequency response is shown in Fig. 4.42 for a collector current of approximately 1 mA. At lower currents, the cutoff frequencies are correspondingly lower.

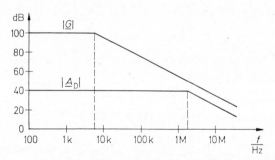

Fig. 4.42 Frequency response of the differential gain $\underline{A}_{\mathrm{D}}$ and common-mode rejection ratio $\underline{G}$

Input resistance

The input data of a differential amplifier can be accurately described by the equivalent circuit in Fig. 4.43. The input currents are composed of three components: the quiescent input current I_{B}, which also flows when $U_{\mathrm{i}1} = U_{\mathrm{i}2} = 0$ V; a contribution which flows through r_{D} and therefore only occurs in the case of differential drive and a component which is caused by resistances r_{CM}.

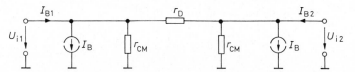

Fig. 4.43 Equivalent circuit for the input of a differential amplifier

The quiescent input current is derived from the current gain of the transistors:

$$I_B = I_C/B \approx I_E/B = I_k/2B \ .$$

The common-mode input resistance r_{CM} is the input resistance measured with pure common-mode drive. It results from the finite internal resistance r_k of the constant current source:

$$r_{CM} = \frac{\Delta U_{CM}}{\Delta I_B} = \frac{\Delta U_{CM}}{\Delta I_E} \beta = \frac{\Delta U_{CM}}{\Delta I_k} \cdot 2\beta = 2\beta r_k \ .$$

The common-mode input resistance is in the GΩ range, as the already large source resistance r_k is multiplied by a further 2β.

In the case of pure differential drive, the emitter potential remains constant and the differential voltage applied is divided equally between the two emitter-base voltages. This results in a differential input resistance of

$$r_D = \frac{\Delta U_D}{\Delta I_B} = 2\frac{\Delta U_{BE}}{\Delta I_B} = 2r_{BE} \ .$$

It is therefore twice as large as in the common-emitter connection.

4.8.2   Large-signal characteristics

So far we have examined the transfer characteristic of the differential amplifier in the linear dynamic range. We shall now calculate the large-signal behavior. Using the transfer characteristic Eq. (4.1) we obtain

$$I_{C1} = I_{CS}e^{U_{BE1}/U_T} \ ,$$

$$I_{C2} = I_{CS}e^{U_{BE2}/U_T} \ .$$

From the circuit we take the additional equations

$$I_k = I_{C1} + I_{C2}$$

and

$$U_D = U_{BE1} - U_{BE2} \ .$$

Consequently

$$\boxed{\frac{I_{C1}}{I_{C2}} = e^{\frac{U_D}{U_T}}} \qquad\qquad (4.43)$$

and

$$I_{C1} = \frac{I_k e^{\frac{U_D}{U_T}}}{1 + e^{\frac{U_D}{U_T}}} = \frac{I_k}{2}\left(1 + \tanh\frac{U_D}{2U_T}\right). \tag{4.44}$$

This transfer characteristic is plotted in Fig. 4.44. We can see that for $U_D = 0$ identical collector currents $\frac{1}{2}I_k$ flow through the two transistors. Around $U_D = 0$, a relatively large linear operating range of $U_D/U_T \approx \pm 1$, i.e. $U_D \approx U_T \approx \pm 25\,\text{mV}$ is found. With differential voltages of $\pm 4U_T \approx \pm 100\,\text{mV}$, 98% of I_k flows through one and only 2% through the other transistor.

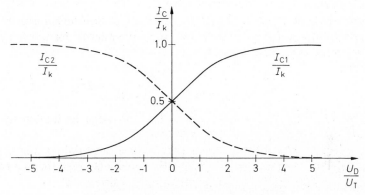

Fig. 4.44 Large-signal transfer characteristic

From the transfer characteristic we can easily calculate the distortion factor. For this purpose we expand tanh in a series up to the third power and obtain:

$$I_{C1} = \frac{I_k}{2}\left(1 + \frac{U_D}{2U_T} - \frac{U_D^3}{24U_T^3} + \cdots\right).$$

Hence, with $U_D = \hat{U}_D \sin\omega t$

$$I_{C1} \approx \frac{I_k}{2}\left[1 + \frac{\hat{U}_D}{2U_T}\sin\omega t - \frac{\hat{U}_D^3}{96U_T^3}(3\sin\omega t - \sin 3\omega t)\right].$$

From the ratio of the harmonic amplitude to the fundamental amplitude we obtain the distortion factor

$$D = \frac{\dfrac{\hat{U}_D^3}{96U_T^3}}{\dfrac{\hat{U}_D}{2U_T} - \dfrac{3\hat{U}_D^3}{96U_T^3}} \approx \frac{1}{48}\left(\frac{\hat{U}_D}{U_T}\right)^2. \tag{4.45}$$

It therefore increases as the square of U_D, but is much smaller than in the common-emitter configuration. For the purposes of comparison, we shall calculate the amplitude $\hat{U}_{D\,\text{max}}$ for which the distortion factor attains the value 1%. It is given by

$$\hat{U}_{D\,max} = 0.7\,U_T = 18\ \text{mV} .$$

Assuming a differential gain of 80, this corresponds to an output amplitude of 1.4 V as against 0.2 V in the common-emitter mode.

4.8.3 Differential amplifier with current feedback

Current feedback can be employed not only for the common-emitter connection, but also for the differential amplifier. The purpose is to arrive at a differential gain which is virtually independent of transistor parameters. Therefore, each transistor is assigned an emitter resistor, as shown in Fig. 4.45. If the voltage difference $U_D = U_{i1} - U_{i2}$ is changed by ΔU_D, the voltage across the two resistors also changes by approximately ΔU_D. This produces a collector current change of

$$\Delta I_{C1} = -\,\Delta I_{C2} \approx \frac{\Delta U_D}{2R_E} .$$

This yields the voltage gain

$$A_D \approx -\frac{R_C}{2R_E} .$$

The common-mode gain is unaffected by resistors R_E.

If two constant current sources are used, as in Fig. 4.46, it is possible to produce the current feedback using a single feedback resistor. In contrast to the resistors R_E in the circuit in Fig. 4.45, no current flows through it in the quiescent state. Consequently, it can be used to vary the gain without changing the quiescent potentials.

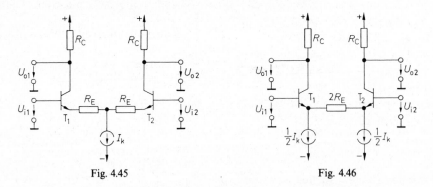

Fig. 4.45   Fig. 4.46

Figs. 4.45 and 4.46 Differential amplifier with current feedback

Differential gain: $A_D = -\dfrac{1}{2}\cdot\dfrac{g_{fE}R_C}{1 + g_{fE}R_E} = -\dfrac{1}{2}g_{fE\,red}R_C \approx -\dfrac{R_C}{2R_E}$ for $R_E \gg \dfrac{1}{g_{fE}}$

Differential input resistance: $r_D = 2(r_{BE} + \beta R_E)$

4.8.4 Offset voltage

For the same current I_C, two transistors will always differ in their base-emitter voltage U_{BE}, even if only slightly. Thus, the input voltage difference is never precisely zero if we make $U_D = 0$. An *offset voltage* U_O is now defined as the input voltage difference which must be applied so that $U_{o1} = U_{o2}$. If monolithic double transistors with well-matched collector resistors are used, typical values for the offset voltage are a few mV.

For many applications these values are too high. There are various ways of adjusting the offset voltage of a differential amplifier to zero. These are indicated in Fig. 4.47.

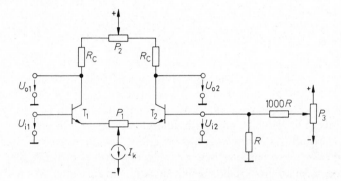

Fig. 4.47 Differential amplifier with zeroing devices

If only one input is required, it is possible to apply a DC voltage to the other input to compensate for the offset voltage. Potentiometer P_3 is used for this purpose. In order to provide a convenient means of adjusting the small voltages required, it is advisable to insert a voltage divider.

If both inputs are required, the two base-emitter voltages can be equalized using emitter resistors. Potentiometer P_1 is used for this purpose. However, it also produces current feedback, like R_E in Fig. 4.45. If this is undesirable, the potentiometer resistance must be selected smaller than $1/g_{fE}$.

The third possibility for equalizing the base-emitter voltages consists of varying the magnitude of the collector currents. For this purpose potentiometer P_2 is used. If it is set e.g. to the left-hand stop, the collector resistance of T_2 is larger than that of T_1. The two output voltages are equal if the collector current of T_2 is correspondingly smaller than that of T_1. U_{BE2} is therefore reduced with respect to U_{BE1}. In this way the offset voltage can be made zero. In order to equalize an original offset voltage of e.g. 3 mV, the current ratio in the quiescent state must, in accordance with Eq. (4.43), assume the value

$$\frac{I_{C1}}{I_{C2}} = e^{U_O/U_T} = 1.12 \ .$$

Using P_2 as a zeroing device instead of P_1 is preferable in that its tap is at constant potential, whereas the full common-mode input voltage appears across P_1. The terminals of P_2 can therefore be brought out more easily.

Offset voltage drift

The base-emitter voltage of transistors decreases by 2 mV per degree temperature rise at constant collector current. In the case of a differential amplifier, this has the same effect as applying a common-mode voltage of 2 mV per degree to transistors having a zero temperature coefficient. This appears at the output, with A amplified, as the output voltage drift. The better the common-mode rejection ratio, the smaller the output voltage drift. The temperature drift of U_{BE} is therefore amplified substantially less than the input voltage difference. This is the reason why the differential amplifier has gained importance as a DC voltage amplifier.

However, two transistors of the same type never have precisely the same temperature coefficients for the same collector currents. Consequently, in addition to the common-mode voltage of 2 mV per degree, a differential voltage is produced which can be several orders of magnitude smaller. However, it is amplified like the wanted signal with differential gain A_D. In order to minimize the differential drift, it is necessary to bring the transistors to the same temperature and to use two samples which are as identical as possible. This requirement can best be fulfilled using monolithic double transistors. Whereas an offset voltage drift of 100 μV/K must be taken into account for single transistors, double transistors achieve 0.1 to 5 μV/K (e.g. LM 394 from National).

The temperature coefficient of the base-emitter voltage is slightly dependent on the collector current. It reduces by 200 μV/K when the current is increased by a factor of 10, i.e. U_{BE} increases by 60 mV. The offset voltage drift of a differential amplifier consequently changes by 3.3 μV/K if the difference between the base-emitter voltages is varied by 1 mV.

Consequently, the offset voltage drift of a differential amplifier can be reduced by selecting slightly different collector currents. On the other hand, this means that a deliberate offset voltage cannot be set by varying the collector currents, as this increases the drift.

4.9   Measuring some transistor parameters

In principle, the small-signal parameters of a transistor can be inferred from the characteristics of the data sheet. However, for many purposes this method is too inaccurate or too laborious. We shall therefore discuss a few circuits with which it is possible to measure the most important transistor data directly using alternating voltages. Figure 4.48 shows a circuit for measuring the small-signal current gain β and the input resistance r_{BE} as well as the transconductance g_f.

The quiescent collector current is set to the desired value I_{CQ} by means of direct current feedback as described in Section 4.3.5 with the aid of resistor R_E,

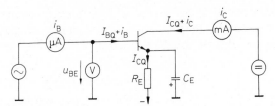

Fig. 4.48 Circuit for measuring the current gain, transconductance and input resistance

whereas the emitter is grounded for AC voltages via capacitor C_E. Consequently $\Delta U_{BE} = u_{BE}$. By measuring the AC components i_B and i_C, we directly obtain

$$\beta = \frac{i_C}{i_B}\bigg|_{U_{CEQ}} \quad , \qquad g_f = \frac{i_C}{u_{BE}}\bigg|_{U_{CEQ}} \quad , \qquad r_{BE} = \frac{u_{BE}}{i_B}\bigg|_{U_{CEQ}} \quad .$$

In order to measure r_{CE} it is possible to use the same method for setting the operating point, and with $u_{BE} = 0$ we obtain the parameter

$$r_{CE} = \frac{u_{CE}}{i_C}\bigg|_{U_{BEQ}} \quad .$$

For variation of the collector-emitter voltage, an alternating voltage source and a direct voltage source can be connected in series. However, a simpler method (Fig. 4.49) is to use a source of alternating voltage onto which a direct voltage can be superimposed internally.

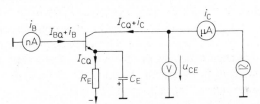

Fig. 4.49 Circuit for measuring the output resistance and the reverse transconductance

By measuring the AC base current component i_B it is possible to calculate the reverse transconductance

$$g_r = \frac{i_B}{u_{CE}}\bigg|_{U_{BEQ}} \quad .$$

However, care must be taken to ensure that the nA-meter in the base lead is of sufficiently low resistance, so that the measuring condition $U_{BE} = $ const, i.e. $u_{BE} = 0$, is fulfilled.

The breakdown voltages of a transistor can be easily measured by impressing a small current and measuring the voltage drop across the transistor. Figure 4.50 shows a circuit for measuring U_{EBO}. A current source is connected to the emitter-base diode which allows a defined reverse current to flow. The voltage

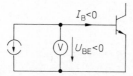 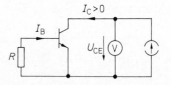

Fig. 4.50 Circuit for measuring the emitter-base breakdown voltage U_{EBO} Fig. 4.51 Circuit for measuring the maximum collector-emitter voltage U_{CER}

U_{EBO} can then be read on the voltmeter. As a current source, it is possible to use e.g. a voltage source whose voltage is large compared to U_{EBO}, with a high-value resistor connected in series.

In order to measure the maximum collector-emitter voltage, a current source is connected between collector and emitter (Fig. 4.51). As Fig. 4.10 shows, the constant current must be selected larger than the collector-base leakage current, but small enough to prevent secondary breakdown occurring. Depending on the size of R, the following voltages can then be measured:

$$R = 0 \quad \rightarrow \quad U_{CES} ,$$

$$R > 0 \quad \rightarrow \quad U_{CER} ,$$

$$R = \infty \quad \rightarrow \quad U_{CEO} .$$

4.10   Transistor noise

Due to the thermal agitation of the electrons, each resistor produces a noise voltage, whose frequency band extends from the lowest to the highest frequencies. Noise is described as "white" if the spectral noise power density dP_n/df is independent of frequency. This condition is fulfilled to a first approximation in the case of resistor noise. The noise power density produced in a resistor is given by:

$$\frac{\Delta P_n}{\Delta f} = \frac{P_n}{B} = 4kT ,$$

where k is the Boltzmann constant, T the absolute temperature and B the noise bandwidth. At room temperature:

$$4kT = 1.6 \cdot 10^{-20} \text{ Ws} .$$

In the case of white noise, the spectral noise power density is independent of frequency and therefore the noise power P_n is proportional to the bandwidth considered:

$$P_n = 4kTB .$$

For an amplifier with power matching, a quarter of this power will be supplied to a load. From the noise power it is possible to calculate the no-load noise voltage for a given resistance R:

$$U_{\text{n r.m.s.}} = \sqrt{P_{\text{n}}R} = \sqrt{4kTBR} \ . \tag{4.46}$$

Transistors are also noisy. The transistor noise magnitude is always expressed in terms of the internal resistance R_{g} of the signal voltage source. The noise of the transistor is conceived of as being produced concomitantly in R_{g}; consequently the noise power in R_{g} must be greater than the pure resistance noise. The transistor itself is then assumed to be noise-free. The *noise factor* F is the factor by which the noise power of resistor R_{g} must be multiplied in order to obtain the noise power actually present at the output of the supposedly noise-free transistor. The power in R_{g} is therefore assumed to be

$$\frac{U_{\text{n r.m.s.}}'^{2}}{R_{\text{g}}} = 4kTBF \ .$$

The no-load noise voltage in R_{g} is therefore given by

$$U_{\text{n r.m.s.}}' = \sqrt{4kTBFR_{\text{g}}} \ . \tag{4.47}$$

For the input circuit of the transistor we obtain the equivalent circuit in Fig. 4.52. R_{g} is the internal resistance, now assumed to be noise-free, of the signal voltage source u_{g}. The voltage appearing at the transistor input is given by

$$U_{\text{BE r.m.s.}} = \sqrt{U_{\text{g r.m.s.}}^{2} + U_{\text{n r.m.s.}}'^{2}} \ \frac{r_{\text{BE}}}{R_{\text{g}} + r_{\text{BE}}} \ . \tag{4.48}$$

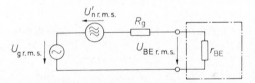

Fig. 4.52 Equivalent circuit for transistor noise

Instead of the noise factor F, the noise figure $F^{*} = 10 \text{ dB lg } F$ is also frequently specified. In order to evaluate a circuit, the quantity of interest is the factor by which $U_{\text{g r.m.s.}}$ is greater than $U_{\text{n r.m.s.}}'$. The quotient $S_{\text{N}} = U_{\text{g r.m.s.}}/U_{\text{n r.m.s.}}'$ is known as the signal-to-noise ratio. The corresponding logarithmic quantity, measured in dB, is $S_{\text{N}}^{\#} = 20 \text{ dB lg } S_{\text{N}}$.

If small voltages are to be dealt with, it is pointless to increase the gain by any amount unless one simultaneously reduces the amplifier noise; otherwise the amplifier noise referred to the input may outweigh the input signal. The limit of voice intelligibility is reached at a signal-to-noise ratio of 0 dB; 40 dB ensures good reproduction and at 60 dB the noise is virtually no longer discernible against the signal. We shall now give an example of how to calculate the required noise factor of an amplifier: a microphone with an internal resistance

$R_g = 200\,\Omega$ produces a no-load voltage $U_{g\,r.m.s.} = 300\,\mu V$. For a bandwidth of 15 kHz, a signal-to-noise ratio of 60 dB is required at the amplifier output.
Hence the no-load noise voltage is given by

$$S_N^{\#} = 60\,dB = 20\,dB\,\lg\frac{300\,\mu V}{U'_{n\,r.m.s.}} \ .$$

Hence:

$$U'_{n\,r.m.s.} = 0.3\,\mu V \ .$$

From Eq. (4.47) we obtain:

$$F = 1.88\ \text{bzw.}\quad F^{*} = 2.74\,dB \ .$$

The amplifier must therefore exhibit a noise factor of no more than about 3 dB.

The noise factor of a transistor is largely dependent on its operating characteristics, particularly the frequency range, the collector current and the internal resistance R_g of the signal source. In Fig. 4.53 the noise factor has been plotted as a function of frequency [4.6]. In the region below about 1 kHz, it is inversely proportional to the frequency. This effect is known as $1/f$ noise.

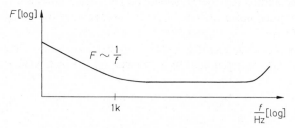

Fig. 4.53 Frequency response of the noise factor

The noise factor is largely dependent on the collector current and the internal source resistance R_g. At a particular collector current it exhibits a minimum which is displaced towards smaller collector currents as R_g increases. This is shown in Fig. 4.54.

The effect of R_g on the noise voltage is immediately apparent from Fig. 4.54, as, in accordance with Eq. (4.47), the product $F \cdot R_g$ determines the noise voltage. As $R_g \to 0$, F tends to infinity, so that the product $F \cdot R_g$ has a finite limit value. The dependence of the noise voltage on R_g is shown in Fig. 4.55 for various collector currents. We can see that for high generator resistances R_g small collector currents are desirable, whereas larger collector currents are desirable for small generator resistances.

As we have seen, the noise factor depends on both, on the source resistance R_g and on the collector current. It cannot be determined for very small and very large values of R_g. It is therefore better to define the equivalent noise voltage $U'_{n\,r.m.s.}$ directly instead of the noise factor F, as has been done in Fig. 4.55. Theory shows, however, that it is possible to express the relationship between

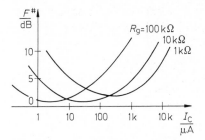

Fig. 4.54 Typical dependence of the noise factor on the collector current

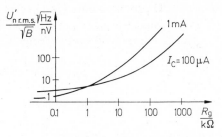

Fig. 4.55 Typical plot of the noise voltage as a function of the source resistance, at 1 Hz bandwidth

$U'_{n\,r.m.s.}$ and R_g explicitly using the following equation [4.7]:

$$U'^2_{n\,r.m.s.} = U^2_{n0\,r.m.s.} + I^2_{n0\,r.m.s.} \cdot R^2_g \;. \tag{4.49}$$

The two quantities $U_{n0\,r.m.s.}$ and $I_{n0\,r.m.s.}$ depend only on the collector current. If they are known, $U'_{n\,r.m.s.}$ can be calculated for all values of R_g. This simplifies the problem significantly and some semiconductor manufacturers have recently begun to specify the noise current $I_{n0\,r.m.s.}$ and the noise voltage $U_{n0\,r.m.s.}$ instead of the noise factor F.

The size of the voltage at the input of the supposedly noise-free transistor in Fig. 4.52 can now be calculated in a generalized manner. Using Eq. (4.48) we obtain

$$U_{BE\,r.m.s.} = \frac{r_{BE}}{R_g + r_{BE}} \sqrt{U^2_{g\,r.m.s.} + U^2_{n0\,r.m.s.} + I^2_{n0\,r.m.s.} \cdot R^2_g} \;. \tag{4.50}$$

An equivalent circuit satisfying Eq. (4.50) is shown in Fig. 4.56.

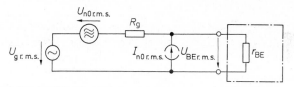

Fig. 4.56 Equivalent circuit for the input noise voltage $U_{BE\,r.m.s.}$ composed of the noise voltage $U_{n0\,r.m.s.}$ and the noise current $I_{n0\,r.m.s.}$

As the dependence of R_g is now explicitly known, the two limiting cases $R_g \to 0$ and $R_g \to \infty$ can also be stated directly. For $R_g \to 0$ we obtain

$$U_{BE\,r.m.s.} = \sqrt{U^2_{g\,r.m.s.} + U^2_{n0\,r.m.s.}} \;. \tag{4.51}$$

Hence for $R_g \to \infty$

$$U_{BE\,r.m.s.} = r_{BE} \sqrt{I^2_{g\,r.m.s.} + I^2_{n0\,r.m.s.}} \;. \tag{4.52}$$

The limiting case $R_g = \infty$ occurs when $R_g \gg r_{BE}$.

4 Bipolar transistors

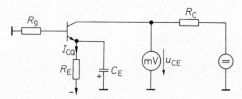

Fig. 4.57 Circuit for measuring the noise voltage and noise current

Equations (4.51) and (4.52) directly provide a test method for the noise current and the noise voltage: in the circuit in Fig. 4.57 it is sufficient to measure the noise voltage at the transistor output for the two limiting cases $R_g \ll r_{BE}$ and $R_g \gg r_{BE}$ and to divide by the voltage gain. This gives two values for $U_{BE\,r.m.s.}$. From Eqs. (4.51) and (4.52) one can then determine the two wanted values using $U_{g\,r.m.s.} = 0$ and $I_{g\,r.m.s.} = 0$:

$$U_{n0\,r.m.s.} = U_{BE\,r.m.s.} \qquad \text{for} \quad R_g \ll r_{BE} \; ,$$

$$I_{n0\,r.m.s.} = U_{BE\,r.m.s.}/r_{BE} \quad \text{for} \quad R_g \gg r_{BE} \; .$$

5 Field effect transistors

Field effect transistors are semiconductor devices which, unlike bipolar transistors, are controlled by an electric field, i.e. they are voltage-controlled.

5.1 Classification

There are six different types of field effect transistor (FET). Their circuit symbols are shown in Fig. 5.1. The *gate* G is the control electrode enabling the resistance between the *drain* D and the *source* S to be controlled. The control voltage is U_{GS}. Many FETs are symmetrical, i.e. their characteristics remain the same when S and D are interchanged. In the case of *junction FETs* (JFETs), the gate is separated from the DS *channel* by a pn or an np junction. When U_{GS} is of correct polarity, this diode blocks current, insulating the gate; with the opposite polarity, it becomes conducting. In the case of *MOSFETs*, a thin SiO_2 layer insulates the gate from the DS channel. Consequently, a gate current can never flow, irrespective of the gate polarity. With JFETs, the gate currents flowing under operating conditions are between 1 pA and 1 nA; with small-signal MOSFETs they can be even smaller. The associated input resistances are 10^{10} to $10^{13}\,\Omega$.

Just as there are pnp and npn bipolar transistors, so there are p- and n-channel FETs. With the n-channel type, the channel current becomes smaller as the gate potential is reduced. The reverse is true of p-channel FETs, as can also be seen from the characteristic curves in Fig. 5.1. For simplicity's sake we shall discuss circuits employing n-channel FETs, referring to the p-channel type only if there is a particular reason for doing so. N-channel FETs can be replaced by p-channel FETs if the polarity of the supply voltages is reversed. Of course, any diodes and electrolytic capacitors present must then also be reversed in polarity.

With JFETs, the highest drain current flows when voltage $U_{GS} = 0$. These devices are therefore 'normally-on' and are designated as *depletion* FETs. The same characteristic is exhibited by depletion MOSFETs. *Enhancement* MOSFETs, on the other hand, are nonconducting when $U_{GS} = 0$. They are therefore 'normally-off' types. With n-channel enhancement MOSFETs, a drain current only flows when U_{GS} exceeds a certain positive value. This can also be seen from the characteristics shown in Fig. 5.1. Intermediate types between enhancement and depletion MOSFETs are available, e.g. in which a medium drain current flows when $U_{GS} = 0$.

In MOSFETs, a fourth terminal, the *substrate* (bulk or body B) is frequently brought out. This electrode has a similar controlling function to that of the gate, but it is insulated from the channel by a junction only. Its controlling effect is

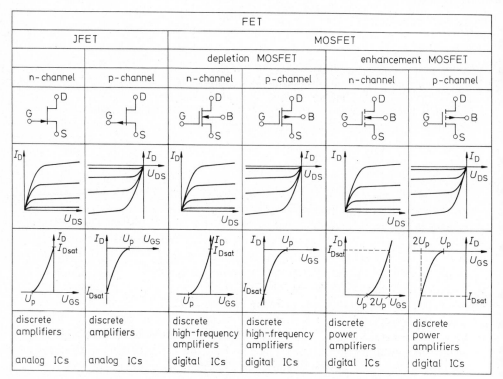

FET					
JFET		MOSFET			
		depletion MOSFET		enhancement MOSFET	
n-channel	p-channel	n-channel	p-channel	n-channel	p-channel
discrete amplifiers	discrete amplifiers	discrete high-frequency amplifiers	discrete high-frequency amplifiers	discrete power amplifiers	discrete power amplifiers
analog ICs	analog ICs	digital ICs	digital ICs	digital ICs	digital ICs

Fig. 5.1 Classification, symbols, characteristics and applications of FETs

normally not utilized, the electrode then being connected to the source electrode. If two control electrodes are required, MOSFETs tetrodes are used which possess two equivalent gates.

In the case of n-channel FETs, the source electrode potential must be more negative than that of the drain electrode. If the polarity is reversed, the drain electrode assumes the function of the source electrode so that, with n-channel FETs, the channel electrode with the lower potential acts as the source.

5.2 Characteristics and small-signal parameters

Figure 5.2 shows a circuit for measurement of the characteristics. The characteristic curves of a typical small-signal JFET are plotted in Figs. 5.3 and 5.4. Qualitatively, they look quite similar to those of a bipolar transistor, the drain electrode corresponding to the collector, the source electrode to the emitter and the gate electrode to the base. Unlike that of the npn transistor, however, the operating range of the gate-source voltage has negative values. The gate voltage at which I_D (apart from a small leakage current) has fallen to zero is known as the *pinch-off voltage* U_p.

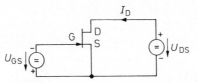

Fig. 5.2 Operation of an n-channel JFET

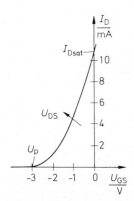

Fig. 5.3 Transfer characteristic of an n-channel JFET

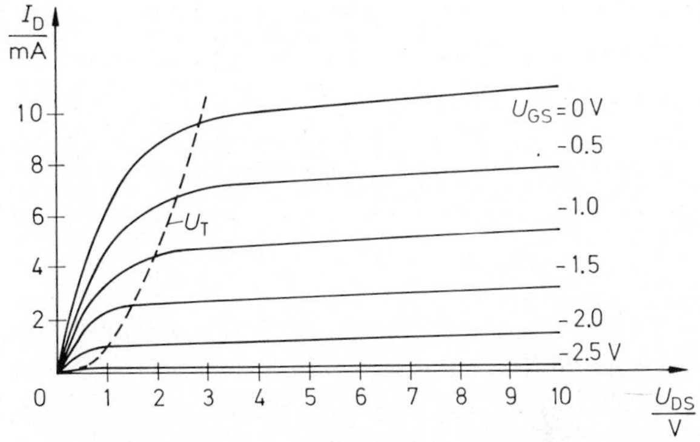

Fig. 5.4 Output characteristics of an n-channel JFET

Above $U_{GS} = U_p$, the transfer characteristics in Fig. 5.3 can be described [5.1] by the relation

$$I_D = I_{Dsat}\left(1 - \frac{U_{GS}}{U_p}\right)^2 , \qquad (5.1)$$

where I_{Dsat} is the saturation drain current at $U_{GS} = 0$. This represents the maximum drain current achievable for JFETs in practice, as positive gate-source voltages are avoided in order not to lose the advantage of the low gate current.

It appears from Eq. (5.1) that the drain current at $U_{GS} = U_p$ is zero. However, this is only an approximation. The pinch-off voltage is therefore normally defined as the value of U_{GS} for a drain current in the μA region. However, the value thus obtained is not always suitable for the calculation using Eq. (5.1). It is therefore preferable to plot $\sqrt{I_D}$ as a function of U_{GS} and to extrapolate the resultant straight line onto the current $I_D = 0$.

Equation (5.1) can also be applied to MOSFETs [5.2], both the depletion and enhancement types, if U_{GS} and U_p are inserted with the correct sign. For the current I_{Dsat} of the enhancement types, it is necessary to use the current at $U_{GS} = 2U_p$. This can be shown by comparing the transfer characteristics in Fig. 5.1. With MOSFETs, the gate-source voltage can be increased to the breakdown voltage of the gate oxide, which may be as much as 50 V. With these devices, considerably higher currents than $I_{D\,sat}$ can therefore be allowed to flow.

The transfer characteristic yields the forward transconductance:

$$g_f = \left.\frac{\partial I_D}{\partial U_{GS}}\right|_{U_{DS}=const}$$

By differentiating Eq. (5.1) we obtain

$$g_f = \frac{2I_{D\,sat}}{U_p^2}(U_{GS} - U_p) = \frac{2}{|U_p|}\sqrt{I_{D\,sat}\,I_D} \ . \tag{5.2}$$

Of particular interest is the transconductance at $I_D = I_{D\,sat}$ which we shall denote by $g_{f\,sat}$. This is the maximum transconductance achievable with junction FETs. From Eq. (5.2) we obtain

$$g_{f\,sat} = \frac{2I_{D\,sat}}{|U_p|} \ . \tag{5.3}$$

This formula provides a simple means of determining the pinch-off voltage from the parameters $g_{f\,sat}$ and $I_{D\,sat}$. They can be easily measured.

The family of output curves in Fig. 5.4 indicates the relationship between I_D and U_{DS} for fixed values of U_{GS}. The characteristics have essentially the same shape for depletion and enhancement type FETs. At low values of U_{DS}, I_D increases approximately proportionally to U_{DS}. In this region, the FET behaves like an ohmic resistance whose magnitude can be controlled by U_{GS}. Below the *threshold voltage*

$$\boxed{U_T = U_{GS} - U_p} \tag{5.4}$$

the output characteristics can be described [5.2, 5.3] by the relation

$$I_D = \frac{I_{D\,sat}}{U_p^2}[2(U_{GS} - U_p)U_{DS} - U_{DS}^2] \ . \tag{5.5}$$

This portion of the characteristics is known as the *linear region*.

The portion of the characteristics beyond the threshold voltage is known as the *saturation region*. Here the drain current is only slightly dependent on U_{DS} and is almost entirely determined by U_{GS} in accordance with Eq. (5.1). The remaining dependence on U_{DS} is characterized by the *differential output resistance*

$$r_{DS} = \left.\frac{\partial U_{DS}}{\partial I_D}\right|_{U_{GS}=const}$$

As in bipolar transistors, the output resistance decreases as the drain current increases, though not in inverse proportion to I_D. It decreases only in approximately inverse proportion to $\sqrt{I_D}$.

The maximum gain

$$\mu = g_f \cdot r_{DS} \tag{5.6}$$

Type code		BF245B	IRF530
Manufacturer		Texas Instr.	Intern. Rectif.
		Siemens	Siliconix
Technology		Junction	MOS
Type		n-channel	n-channel
		depletion	enhancement
Maximum ratings:			
Drain-source voltage	$U_{DS\,max}$	30 V	100 V
Drain current	I_{Dmax}	25 mA	10 A
Gate-source voltage	$U_{GS\,max}$	-30 V	± 20 V
Dissipation	P_{max}	300 mW	75 W
Characteristics:			
Pinch-off voltage	U_p	$-1.5 \ldots -4.5$ V	$1.5 \ldots 3.5$ V
Drain current (saturation)	$I_{D\,sat}$	$6 \ldots 15$ mA	5 A
Maximum transconductance	$g_{f\,sat}$	5 mA/V	5 A/V
Minimum resistance	$R_{DS\,on}$	200 Ω	0.14 Ω
Max. gate leakage current	$I_{G\,max}$	5 nA	0.5 mA
Max. drain leakage current	$I_{D\,max}$	10 nA	1 mA
Input capacitance	$C_{i\,SOURCE}$	4 pF	750 pF
Output capacitance	$C_{o\,SOURCE}$	1.6 pF	300 pF
Reverse capacitance	$C_{r\,SOURCE}$	1.1 pF	50 pF
Transconductance cutoff frequency	f_g	700 MHz	
Turn-on delay	t_{on}		30 ns
Turn-off delay	t_{off}		50 ns

Fig. 5.5 Data for small-signal JFET BF245B and power MOSFET IRF530

is, to a first approximation, independent of current, as the transconductance of FETs is proportional to $\sqrt{I_D}$. However, it is much lower than that of bipolar transistors, being in the range

$$\mu = 50 \ldots 300 \; .$$

This is because FETs have a much lower transconductance than bipolar transistors at the same current.

If μ is known, the current dependence of r_{DS} can be given by

$$r_{DS} = \frac{\mu}{g_f} = \frac{\mu |U_p|}{2\sqrt{I_{D\,sat}}} \cdot \frac{1}{\sqrt{I_D}} \; . \tag{5.7}$$

The data for two commonly used FETs are given in Fig. 5.5. Note the relatively large tolerance of the pinch-off voltage. This is due to fabrication techniques, and the user must take this into account when designing circuits.

Due to their high transconductance cutoff frequency and low capacitances, small-signal FETs are ideally suited for high-frequency amplifiers. The switching times of power MOSFETs are a factor of 10 less than those of equivalent bipolar transistors. They are therefore particularly suitable for use as high-speed switches. However, their high capacitances must be taken into account for the drive arrangement.

Field effect transistors are available from a large number of manufacturers. A particularly wide selection of JFETs is offered by Siliconix, Intersil, Teledyne-Crystalonics, Motorola and Texas Instruments. Small-signal MOSFETs are made by General Instrument. A particularly large range of power MOSFETs is available from International Rectifier, Siliconix, Hitachi, Siemens, Intersil and Motorola.

5.3 Ratings

Field effect transistor ratings are quite similar to those of bipolar transistors. However, as there is no secondary breakdown, power FETs offer advantages over power transistors [5.4].

MOSFETs are subject to a special limitation: the maximum permissible gate voltages must not be exceeded, otherwise the gate oxide breaks down and the transistor is damaged. Such voltages can very easily occur due to the high input resistance. Particularly harmful are static charges, which can destroy the FET even by touch alone. When handling MOSFETs, it is therefore necessary for the workbench, the apparatus, the soldering iron and oneself to be properly grounded. In order to protect MOSFETs, Zener diodes are often inserted between gate and substrate.

5.4 Basic circuits

Similarly to bipolar transistor circuits, a distinction is drawn between source, drain and gate connections depending on which electrode is at constant potential.

5.4.1 Source connection

The source connection in Fig. 5.6 corresponds to the emitter connection of bipolar transistors. The difference is that the gate-channel diode is reverse

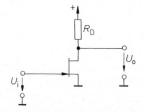

Fig. 5.6 Source connection

Voltage gain: $\qquad A = - g_{\mathrm{f}}(R_{\mathrm{D}} \| r_{\mathrm{DS}})$

Input resistance: $\qquad r_{\mathrm{i}} = r_{\mathrm{GS}} \approx \infty$

Output resistance: $\qquad r_{\mathrm{o}} = R_{\mathrm{D}} \| r_{\mathrm{DS}}$

biased. Consequently, virtually no input current flows and the input resistance is very high.

In order to analyze the circuit, we can use the results obtained in the previous chapter for bipolar transistors. Comparing the characteristics and small-signal parameters, we obtain the following correspondences:

$$
\begin{aligned}
I_C &\to I_D & g_f &\to g_f \\
I_E &\to I_S & g_r &\to g_r \approx 0 \\
I_B &\to I_G \approx 0 & r_{BE} &\to r_{GS} \approx \infty \\
U_{CE} &\to U_{DS} & r_{CE} &\to r_{DS} \\
U_{BE} &\to U_{GS} & \beta &\to g_f r_{GS} \approx \infty
\end{aligned}
\tag{5.8}
$$

Thus, from Eqs. (4.6) and (4.7) we directly obtain the basic FET equations:

$$
dI_G \approx 0 \tag{5.9}
$$

$$
dI_D = g_{fs} \cdot dU_{GS} + \frac{1}{r_{DS}} \cdot dU_{DS} \ , \tag{5.10}
$$

where g_{fs} is the forward transconductance for the source connection.
From Eq. (4.10), using the correspondences Eq. (5.8), the voltage gain of the source connection is given by

$$
A = - g_{fs}(R_D \| r_{DS}) \ . \tag{5.11}
$$

Consequently, for $R_D \gg r_{DS}$, the maximum gain is given by

$$
A = - g_{fs} r_{DS} = - \mu \ .
$$

In the range

$$
0.1 I_{Dsat} < I_D < I_{Dsat}
$$

it is only slightly dependent on the drain current, being between 100 and 300 in the case of n-channel FETs. With p-channel FETs it is only half that figure. The maximum gain of FETs is therefore only about one tenth of the maximum gain of bipolar transistors.

It is instructive to compare the distortion factor of the source connection with that of the emitter connection. For this purpose we again calculate the large-signal transfer characteristic. With a sinusoidal input voltage swing about the operating point Q such that

$$
U_i(t) = U_{iQ} + \hat{U}_i \sin \omega t
$$

we obtain from Eq. (5.1) the drain current

$$
I_D(t) = I_{Dsat}\left(1 - \frac{U_{iQ} + \hat{U}_i \sin \omega t}{U_p}\right)^2 \ ,
$$

$$I_D(t) = I_{Dsat}\left[\left(1 - \frac{U_{iQ}}{U_p}\right)^2 + \frac{\hat{U}_i^2}{2U_p^2} - \frac{2\hat{U}_i}{U_p}\left(1 - \frac{U_{iQ}}{U_p}\right)\sin \omega t - \frac{\hat{U}_i^2}{2U_p^2}\cos 2\omega t\right].$$

Thus, the distortion factor is

$$D \approx \frac{\hat{I}_{D2}}{\hat{I}_{D1}} = \frac{\hat{U}_i}{4(U_{iQ} - U_p)} = \frac{\hat{U}_i}{4|U_p|}\sqrt{\frac{I_{Dsat}}{I_{DQ}}}.$$

It is therefore proportional to the input amplitude, as with the bipolar transistor, but dependent on the operating point. It decreases in inverse proportion to $\sqrt{I_{DQ}}$. If a drain current $I_{DQ} = 3$ mA is selected for a FET with $U_p = -3$ V and $I_{Dsat} = 10$ mA, the distortion factor is

$$D = \hat{U}_i/6.6\,\text{V}\ .$$

In order to ensure that it does not exceed 1%, the input amplitude $\hat{U}_i$ must remain below 66 mV. For a voltage gain of 20, this corresponds to a maximum output amplitude of 1.3 V. This is considerably more than can be achieved using bipolar transistors in the equivalent connection.

In terms of noise, there is a significant difference between field effect and bipolar transistors in that with FETs the noise current is much smaller, whereas with junction FETs the noise voltage is of the same order. As shown by the equivalent circuit in Fig. 4.56, this means that much less noise is produced when using high-resistance signal sources, whereas it is approximately the same for low-resistance sources.

With MOSFETs, $1/f$ noise occurs even at frequencies of 100 kHz, i.e. these devices are much noisier in the low-frequency range than junction FETs. MOSFETs are therefore suitable for low-noise circuits in high-frequency applications only.

Biasing

In the case of bipolar transistors, DC feedback has been found to be the best method of biasing. This method can also be used to good effect with FETs. With the depletion types, it is even possible to make the quiescent gate potential zero, as in Fig. 5.7.

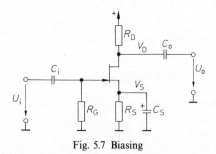

Fig. 5.7 Biasing

To design the circuit, we specify the drain current. From the transfer characteristic in Fig. 5.3 we obtain the associated value of U_{GS}. This can be between zero and U_p depending on the drain current selected. We cannot therefore assume a virtually constant value as with a bipolar transistor. To calculate U_{GS} we use Eq. (5.1) and obtain

$$U_{GS} = U_p \left(1 - \sqrt{\frac{I_D}{I_{Dsat}}} \right) . \tag{5.12}$$

This yields the source resistance

$$R_s = \frac{|U_{GS}|}{I_D} = \frac{|U_p|}{I_D} \left(1 - \sqrt{\frac{I_D}{I_{Dsat}}} \right) . \tag{5.13}$$

As a worked example, let us take a FET with $I_{Dsat} = 10$ mA and $U_p = -3$ V and select $I_D = 3$ mA. Thus

$$U_{GS} = -3 \, V \left(1 - \sqrt{\frac{3\,mA}{10\,mA}} \right) = -1.36 \, V$$

and therefore $R_s = 1.36\,V/3\,mA = 452\,\Omega$.

The quiescent drain potential V_{DQ} must be selected high enough to ensure that U_{DS} does not fall below the value U_T even at maximum drive ΔV_{Dmax}. This prevents distortions which would be produced by a transition to the ohmic region. Consequently, the condition for the quiescent drain potential is

$$V_{DQ} > V_S + U_T + |\Delta V_{Dmax}| .$$

Using $V_S = -U_{GS}$ and Eq. (5.4) we obtain

$$V_{DQ} > |U_p| + |\Delta V_{Dmax}| .$$

For an output swing of ± 2 V and a tolerance allowance of 2 V, we obtain $V_{DQ} = 7$ V. At a supply voltage of $V^+ = 15$ V the drain resistance is

$$R_D = \frac{15\,V - 7\,V}{3\,mA} = 2.7\,k\Omega .$$

In accordance with Eq. (5.2), the transconductance at the operating point is

$$g_{fs} = \frac{2}{3\,V} \sqrt{10\,mA \cdot 3\,mA} = 3.7\,mA/V .$$

Thus, above the lower cutoff frequency we obtain a voltage gain of

$$A \approx -g_{fs} R_D \approx -10 .$$

If, as in the worked example in Section 4.3.5, we require a lower cutoff frequency of 20 Hz and for this purpose give each of the three high-pass filters a cutoff frequency of $f_c = 11.5$ Hz, using Eq. (4.26) it follows that

$$C_S = \frac{g_{fs}}{2\pi f_c} = \frac{3.7\,mA/V}{2\pi \cdot 11.5\,Hz} = 51\,\mu F .$$

We have considerable latitude in selecting R_G. The upper limit is determined by the fact that the voltage drop due to the gate leakage current must be small compared to $|U_{GS}|$. This result in values in the MΩ range.

5.4.2   Gate connection

The gate connection is little used with FETs because the high gate-channel resistance is not utilized to advantage.

5.4.3   Drain connection, source follower

The drain connection possesses a higher input resistance than the source connection. However, this is generally of little interest as it is already very high in the source connection. A possible advantage is that the input capacitance is reduced. Unlike the output resistance of the emitter follower, that of the source follower is independent of the internal resistance R_g of the signal generator.

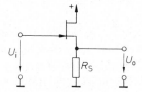

Fig. 5.8 Source follower

Voltage gain:
$$A = \frac{1}{1 + \dfrac{1}{g_{fs}(R_s \| r_{DS})}} \approx \frac{g_{fs}}{1 + g_{fs}R_s}$$

Input resistance:
$$r_i \approx \infty$$

Output resistance:
$$r_o = R_s \left\| \frac{1}{g_{fs}} \right.$$

We shall again calculate typical values for the voltage gain and the output resistance of the source follower in a worked example. With a transconductance $g_{fs} = 5 \text{ mA/V}$ and a source resistance $R_s = 1 \text{ k}\Omega$, we obtain

$$A \approx \frac{5\dfrac{\text{mA}}{\text{V}} \cdot 1 \text{ k}\Omega}{1 + 5\dfrac{\text{mA}}{\text{V}} \cdot 1 \text{ k}\Omega} = 0.83$$

and

$$r_o = \frac{1}{5\dfrac{\text{mA}}{\text{V}}} \left\| 1 \text{ k}\Omega = 200 \, \Omega \| 1 \text{ k}\Omega = 167 \, \Omega \right. .$$

Clearly, with a source follower, it is impossible to achieve such a low output resistance as with an emitter follower. This is because FETs have a lower transconductance than bipolar transistors.

5.5   FETs as constant current sources

The circuit in Fig. 5.9 operates similarly to the bipolar transistor current source in Fig. 4.32. In order to calculate the feedback resistance R_S, we determine U_{GS} for the required current I from the transfer characteristic and obtain the result, using Eq. (5.12)

$$R_S = \frac{U_H + |U_{GS}|}{I_D} = \frac{U_H + |U_p|(1 - \sqrt{I_D/I_{Dsat}})}{I_D} \ .$$

In order to calculate the output resistance, we use Eq. (4.32) for the bipolar transistor. For values β, $r_{BE} \to \infty$ and using Eq. (5.8) this yields

$$r_o = r_{DS}(1 + g_{fs}R_S) = r_{DS} + \mu R_S \ . \tag{5.14}$$

With depletion FETs, a current also flows if the auxiliary voltage U_H is made zero. This mode is of particular interest as it is then possible to use the circuit as a pure two-terminal network as in Fig. 5.10. It can then be substituted for any ohmic resistance. Consequently, it is also known as a field effect diode. Field effect diodes are available in the standard E12 range for currents between 0.1 mA and 5 mA; examples include the series CR 022 to CR 470 from Siliconix or TCR 5278 to TCR 5315 from Teledyne.

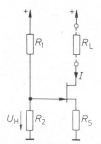

Fig. 5.9 FET constant current source

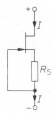

Fig. 5.10 FET constant current source without auxiliary voltage

Output resistance: $r_o = r_{DS}(1 + g_{fs}R_S)$

A worked example will serve to clarify the design of a FET constant current source. A current of 1 mA is to be provided using a FET ($U_p = -3$ V, $I_{Dsat} = 10$ mA, $\mu = 200$). The source resistance is given by

$$R_S = \frac{|U_p|}{I_D}\left(1 - \sqrt{\frac{I_D}{I_{Dsat}}}\right) = \frac{3\,\text{V}}{1\,\text{mA}}\left(1 - \sqrt{\frac{1\,\text{mA}}{10\,\text{mA}}}\right) = 2.05\,\text{k}\Omega \ .$$

In order to calculate the output resistance of the circuit, we must first calculate the output resistance r_{DS} of the FET at a current of $I_D = 1$ mA. Using Eq. (5.7):

$$r_{DS} = \frac{\mu}{g_{fs}} = \frac{\mu |U_p|}{2\sqrt{I_{D\,sat} \cdot I_D}} = \frac{200 \cdot 3 \text{ V}}{2\sqrt{10 \text{ mA} \cdot 1 \text{ mA}}} = 95 \text{ k}\Omega \ .$$

From this and using Eq. (5.14), we obtain the output resistance of the circuit

$$r_o = r_{DS} + \mu R_S = 95 \text{ k}\Omega + 200 \cdot 2.05 \text{ k}\Omega = 505 \text{ k}\Omega \ .$$

This value is much lower than that for comparable current sources incorporating bipolar transistors.

Comparison of Eqs. (5.14) and (4.32) reveals a fundamental difference between a FET and a bipolar transistor current source: if resistance R_E or R_S is made very large, the output resistance of the FET current source tends to infinity, whereas with the bipolar transistor it is limited to a maximum value of βr_{CE}. A typical plot of r_o against R_E or R_S is shown in Fig. 5.11. We can see that better results can be achieved using the FET current source at high feedback-resistance values.

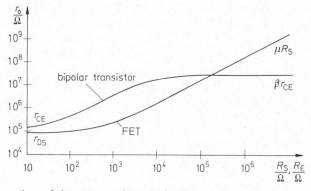

Fig. 5.11 Comparison of the output resistance of FET and bipolar transistor current sources, showing typical values for a constant current of 1 mA

In order to attain this order of magnitude, it is necessary to design the feedback resistance itself as a current source. If a bipolar transistor current source is used for this purpose, as in Fig. 5.12, we obtain, in accordance with the worked example in Section 4.6.1, a differential feedback resistance of $r_S \approx 7$ MΩ at a current of 1 mA. Using the FET data given above, this results in a current source output resistance of 1.1 GΩ.

A current mirror is shown in Fig. 5.13. It corresponds to the circuit incorporating bipolar transistors in Fig. 4.36. If the two MOSFETs are identical, they both carry the same current, as they are operated with an identical gate-source voltage. However, this is precisely the case only if the drain-source voltages match. Otherwise, output current I_o differs from input current I_i, depending on the output resistance r_{DS} of T_2.

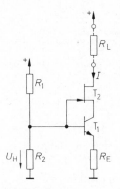

Fig. 5.12 Cascading of current sources

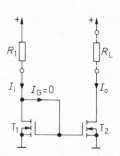

Fig. 5.13 Current mirror

Output current: $I = (U_H - U_{BEQ})/R_E$

Output resistance: $r_o = g_{f2} r_{DS} r_{CE}(1 + g_{f1} R_E) \approx \mu_1 \mu_2 R_E$

$I_o = I_i$

$r_o = r_{DS}$

A current mirror as shown in Fig. 5.13 can be implemented only with depletion type FETs, since $U_{DS} = U_{GS}$ at the operating point. The voltage drop is larger than with bipolar transistors, amounting to between U_p and $2U_p$.

5.6   FET differential amplifier

Many applications require differential amplifiers with a high input resistance. For this purpose it would be possible, in principle, to replace the bipolar transistors in Fig. 4.41 by Darlington circuits. However, considerably better results in terms of input current, bandwidth and noise can be achieved using FETs.

The basic circuit for a FET differential amplifier is shown in Fig. 5.14. In order to calculate the small-signal performance we can usefully employ the relations given in Section 4.8.1. When designing the circuit, care must be taken to ensure that a constant current $I_k \leq I_{DS}$ is selected so that the gate-channel diodes remain blocking even at higher drive levels.

Unlike that of the bipolar transistor, the large-signal transfer characteristic is dependent on I_k. In order to calculate it, we use Eq. (5.1) for the two FETs. With

$$U_D = U_{GS1} - U_{GS2} \quad \text{and} \quad I_{D1} + I_{D2} = I_k$$

we obtain the relation

$$\frac{U_D}{|U_p|} = \sqrt{\frac{I_k}{I_{Dsat}}} \left(\sqrt{\frac{I_{D1}}{I_k}} - \sqrt{1 - \frac{I_{D1}}{I_k}} \right) . \qquad (5.15)$$

It is plotted in Fig. 5.15 for various values of I_k/I_{Dsat}. We can see that if $I_k = I_{Dsat}$, a differential voltage of $U_D = \pm |U_p|$ is required in order to drive the

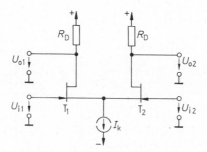

Fig. 5.14 Basic circuit for a FET differential amplifier

Differential-mode gain: $$A_D = \frac{dU_{o1}}{dU_D} = -\frac{dU_{o2}}{dU_D} = -\frac{1}{2}g_{fs}(R_D \| r_{DS}) \text{ with } U_D = U_{i1} - U_{i2}$$

Common-mode gain: $$A_{CM} = \frac{dU_{o1}}{dU_{CM}} = \frac{dU_{o2}}{dU_{CM}} = -\frac{1}{2}\frac{R_D}{r_k} \text{ with } U_{CM} = \tfrac{1}{2}(U_{i1} + U_{i2})$$

Common-mode rejection ratio: $$G = \frac{A_D}{A_{CM}} \approx g_{fs}r_k \, (r_k = \text{current source output resistance})$$

Differential input resistance: $r_D \approx \infty$

Common-mode input resistance: $r_{CM} \approx \infty$

Output resistance: $r_o = R_D \| r_{DS}$

Input bias current: $I_G \approx 0$

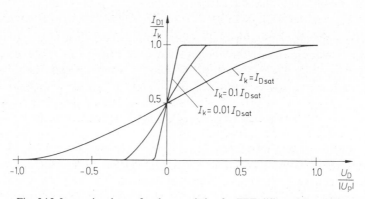

Fig. 5.15 Large-signal transfer characteristic of a FET differential amplifier

differential amplifier to full output, whereas lower voltages are sufficient with smaller values of I_k.

Offset voltage drift

In Section 4.8.4 we saw that the temperature coefficient of the base-emitter junction of a bipolar transistor is in the region of $-2\,\text{mV/K}$, its magnitude decreasing slightly as the current increases. The temperature coefficient of the

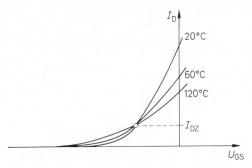

Fig. 5.16 Temperature dependence of the transfer characteristic of a FET

gate-source voltage is of the same order, but it is considerably more current-dependent. As Fig. 5.16 shows, it is negative at low currents and positive at high currents. At current I_{DZ} it is zero. It will be preferable to drive the differential amplifier at this current, as the offset voltage drift is no longer so heavily dependent on the FET matching tolerance.

As described in [5.5], current I_{DZ} can be calculated from the relation

$$I_{DZ} \approx 0.4\,V^2 \cdot \frac{I_{D\,sat}}{U_p^2} = 100 \ldots 600\,\mu A \ . \tag{5.16}$$

At this operating point it is possible to achieve an offset voltage drift of 1 to 50 μV/K using monolithic dual FETs.

The transconductance of an FET at I_{DZ} can be given directly. By substituting Eq. (5.16) in Eq. (5.2) we obtain the result

$$g_{fZ} = \frac{I_{DZ}}{0.32\,V} \ . \tag{5.17}$$

5.7 FET as a controllable resistor

As may be clearly seen from the output characteristics in Fig. 5.4, at low drain-source voltages FETs behave approximately like ohmic resistances whose magnitude can be varied over a wide range using the gate-source voltage. In order to illustrate this effect more clearly, in Fig. 5.17 we have represented the family of curves around the origin in enlarged form.

In order to calculate the resistance we use Eq. (5.5) for the linear region and obtain with $U_{DS} \ll U_k$

$$R_{DS} = \frac{U_{DS}}{I_D} = \frac{U_p^2}{2I_{D\,sat}(U_{GS} - U_p)} \ . \tag{5.18}$$

Using Eq. (5.2) it follows that

$$R_{DS} = \frac{1}{g_f} \ . \tag{5.19}$$

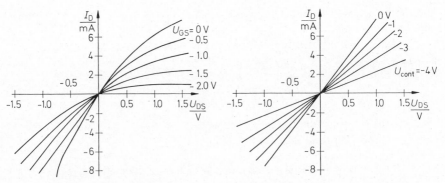

Fig. 5.17 Output characteristics at low
drain-source voltages

Fig. 5.18 Linearized output characteristics

The smallest value is obtained for $U_{GS} = 0$ and is given by

$$R_{DS\,on} = \frac{|U_p|}{2I_{D\,sat}} = \frac{1}{g_{f\,sat}} \ . \tag{5.20}$$

In the case of small-signal FETs, it is of the order of 50 to 500 Ω. Types with $R_{DS\,on}$ values of less than 10 Ω are available specifically for use as variable resistors or switches.

Figure 5.19 shows a FET in a controllable voltage divider. The divider ratio is

$$\frac{U_o}{U_i} = \frac{R_{DS}}{R_1 + R_{DS}} \ .$$

$R_1 \gg R_{DS\,on}$ is selected such that, by using control voltage U_{GS}, the division ratio can be varied over a wide range. As we can see from Fig. 5.17, R_{DS} is nonlinear at high output voltages. Indeed, the FET characteristics are curved such that the drain current at higher drain-source voltages is lower than that of a corresponding ohmic resistance. The characteristics can therefore be linearized by adding a portion of the drain-source voltage to the gate voltage, as shown in Fig. 5.20. As the drain-source voltage increases, so the gate-source voltage also becomes greater and the increase in R_{DS} is compensated. If U_{DS} becomes negative,

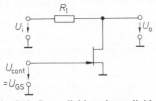

Fig. 5.19 Controllable voltage divider

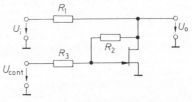

Fig. 5.20 Controllable voltage divider for
larger output amplitudes

U_{GS} decreases due to the compensation circuit. Consequently, the voltage-dependent decrease in R_{DS} is likewise compensated for in the third quadrant.

Figure 5.18 shows the linearized family of curves at optimum adjustment of resistors R_2, R_3. The nonlinearities are then less than 1% up to $|U_{DS}| \approx 1$ V. The optimum linearization is obtained for $R_2 \approx R_3 \gg R_{DS}$. We then have

$$U_{GS} = \tfrac{1}{2}(U_{cont} + U_{DS}) \ .$$

If this value is substituted in Eq. (5.5), the square term U_{DS}^2 cancels out and we obtain without approximation

$$R_{DS} = \frac{U_p^2}{2I_{Dsat}(\tfrac{1}{2}U_{cont} - U_p)} \ . \tag{5.21}$$

6 Optoelectronic components

6.1 Basic photometric terms

The human eye perceives electromagnetic waves in the range 400 to 700 nm as light. The wavelength produces the sensation of color, the intensity that of brightness. In order to quantify brightness, it is necessary to define a number of photometric quantities. The *luminous flux* Φ is a measure of the number of quanta of light (photons) passing through a cross-sectional area of observation A per unit time. It is expressed in lumen (lm). The luminous flux Φ is unsuitable for characterizing the brightness of a light source, as it is generally a function of the cross-sectional area A and the distance r from the light source. In the case of a spherically symmetrical point source, the luminous flux is proportional to the solid angle Ω. This is defined as the spherical surface area intercepted on a sphere of radius r to the square of the radius and is actually dimensionless. However, it is generally assigned the unit *steradian* (sr). The solid angle that encloses the entire surrounding sphere is given by

$$\Omega_0 = \frac{4\pi r^2}{r^2} \text{ sr} = 4\pi \text{ sr} .$$

A circular cone of aperture angle $\pm \varphi$ encloses the solid angle

$$\Omega = 2\pi(1 - \cos \varphi) \text{ sr} . \tag{6.1}$$

At $\pm 33°$, Ω is approximately unity. For small solid angles, we can, as an approximation, replace the spherical surface by a flat surface, obtaining

$$\Omega = \frac{A_n}{r^2} \text{ sr} , \tag{6.2}$$

where r is the distance of the surface from the center.

As the luminous flux of a point source of light is proportional to the solid angle Ω, the brightness of the light source can be characterized by the quantity $I = d\Phi/d\Omega$, the *luminous intensity*. The unit of luminous intensity is the candela (cd). The relationship between the above units is given by 1 cd = 1 lm/sr. A light source therefore possesses a luminous intensity of 1 cd if it emits a luminous flux of 1 lm into a solid angle of 1 sr. In the case of spherical symmetry, the total emitted luminous flux is therefore $\Phi_{tot} = I\Omega_0 = 1 \text{ cd } 4\pi \text{ sr} = 4\pi \text{ lm}$. 1 cd is defined as the luminous intensity of a black body with a surface area of 1.6667 mm^2 at the temperature of solidifying platinum (1769°C). A large candle flame has a luminous intensity of approximately 1 cd. For incandescent lamps, the relation $I = 1 \frac{\text{cd}}{\text{W}} P$ can be used as an approximation, where P is the rated power of the incandescent lamp.

In the case of extended light sources, the *luminance* $L = \mathrm{d}I/\mathrm{d}A_n$ is generally specified, A_n being the projection of the light source area onto the plane perpendicular to the direction of observation. If the angle between the surface normal and the specified direction is ε, then $\mathrm{d}A_n = \mathrm{d}A \cdot \cos \varepsilon$. The unit of luminance is the stilb (sb): $1\ \mathrm{sb} = 1\ \mathrm{cd/cm^2}$.

A measure of how bright an illuminated area A appears to the observer is the *illuminance* $E = \mathrm{d}\Phi/\mathrm{d}A_n$. The unit is the lux (lx): $1\ \mathrm{lx} = 1\ \mathrm{lm/m^2}$. A full moon gives an illuminance of 0.1 to 0.2 lx. A newspaper is just readable at an illuminance of 0.5 to 2 lx. At a writing desk there should be an illuminance of 500 to 1000 lx. Daylight can produce illuminances of up to 50 000 lx.

We shall now calculate the illuminance produced by a point source of light having a given luminance at a specified distance r (Fig. 6.1).

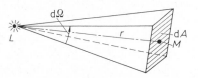

Fig. 6.1 Relationship between luminous intensity and illuminance

In order to calculate the illuminance, we assume that the area term $\mathrm{d}A$ is small compared to r^2 and is perpendicular to the connecting line LM. From Eq. (6.2), the solid angle $\mathrm{d}\Omega$ subtended by $\mathrm{d}A$ at point L is therefore given by:

$$\mathrm{d}\Omega = \frac{\mathrm{d}A}{r^2}\ \mathrm{sr}\ .$$

As defined, the luminous flux emitted by the lamp L is:

$$\mathrm{d}\Phi = I\,\mathrm{d}\Omega = I\frac{\mathrm{d}A}{r^2}\ \mathrm{sr}\ .$$

For the illuminance we obtain:

$$E = \frac{\mathrm{d}\Phi}{\mathrm{d}A} = \frac{I}{r^2}\ \mathrm{sr}\ . \tag{6.3}$$

The illuminance is therefore inversely proportional to the square of the distance.

As each quantum of light possesses the energy hf, a relationship can be established between the light power P_L and the luminous flux Φ for a specific frequency. At a wavelength of 555 nm,

$$P_\mathrm{L} = \frac{1.47\ \mathrm{mW}}{\mathrm{lm}}\ \Phi\ .$$

Thus the illuminance is given by

$$1\ \mathrm{lx} = 1\frac{\mathrm{lm}}{\mathrm{m^2}} \,\hat{=}\, \frac{1.47\ \mathrm{mW}}{\mathrm{m^2}}\ .$$

When giving approximate values for various luminous intensities, we stated that an incandescent lamp of rated power $P = 10$ W possesses a luminous intensity of about 10 cd. It therefore radiates a luminous flux $\Phi_{tot} = 4$ sr $\cdot$ 10 cd $= 126$ lm into the full solid angle; at a wavelength $\lambda = 555$ nm, this corresponds to a light power $P_L = 0.185$ W. An incandescent lamp consequently has an efficiency $\eta = P_L/P \approx 2\%$. In addition to the photometric units given above, other units are often used particularly in the American literature. They are listed in Fig. 6.2.

Physical quantities	Relationship	Units
Luminous flux	Φ	1 lm = 1 cd sr $\hateq$ 1.47 mW ($\lambda = 555$ nm)
Luminous intensity	$I = \dfrac{d\Phi}{d\Omega}$	1 cd = 1 $\dfrac{lm}{sr}$ $\hateq$ 1.47 $\dfrac{mW}{sr}$
Luminance	$L = \dfrac{dI}{dA_n}$	1 sb = 1 $\dfrac{cd}{cm^2}$ = π lambert = $\pi \cdot 10^4$ apostilb = 2919 foot-lambert
Illuminance	$E = \dfrac{d\Phi}{dA_n}$	1 lx = 1 $\dfrac{lm}{m^2}$ = 0.0929 foot-candle $\hateq$ 0.147 $\dfrac{\mu W}{cm^2}$

Fig. 6.2   Table of photometric quantities

6.2   Photoconductive cell

Photoconductive cells are junctionless semiconductor devices whose resistance is a function of the illuminance. Figure 6.3 shows the circuit symbol, Fig. 6.4 the characteristic.

A photoconductive cell behaves like an ohmic resistor, i.e. its resistance is neither a function of the voltage applied nor of its sign. With moderate illuminance the relationship $R \sim E^{-\gamma}$ applies, where γ is a constant between 0.5 and 1. With higher illuminance the resistance tends to a minimum value. At low

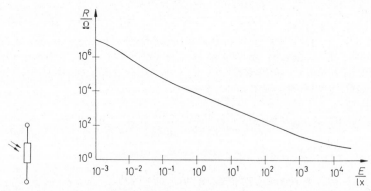

Fig. 6.3   Circuit symbol   Fig. 6.4   Characteristic of a photoconductive cell

illuminance the value of γ increases, and at very low illuminance the resistance tends to the dark resistance. The dark-to-light resistance ratio may exceed 10^6.

The resistance is markedly temperature-dependent at low illuminance. This is shown by Fig. 6.5.

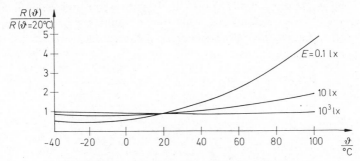

Fig. 6.5 Temperature dependence of photoconductive cell

When the cell is illuminated, a steady-state resistance value is not established immediately. The photoconductive cell requires a certain settling time. This is in the millisecond range at illuminances of a few thousands lux, but may exceed several seconds at values below 1 lx. The steady-state value at which the resistance settles, depends not only on the illuminance but also on the preceding optical history. After comparatively long exposure to high illuminance, higher resistance values are obtained than if the photoconductive cell had been kept in the dark.

Photoconductive cells are generally made of cadmium sulfide, for which the figures quoted above apply. Photoconductive cells made of cadmium selenide are characterized by shorter settling times and a higher dark-to-light resistance ratio. However, they possess higher temperature coefficients and exhibit greater dependence on the past optical history. Cadmium-based photoconductive cells are sensitive in the spectral range from 400 to 800 nm. Some types can be used over the entire frequency range, while others possess a quite specific color sensitivity. Photoconductive cells with high infrared sensitivity are fabricated from lead sulfide or indium antimonide. They are suitable for wavelengths up to some 3 or 7 μm, but are considerably less sensitive than cadmium-based cells.

Photoconductive cells have a sensitivity comparable to that of photomultipliers. They are therefore suitable for measuring low levels of illumination. They can also be employed as controllable resistors. As the load may be several watts, components such as relays can be directly connected without additional amplification.

Clairex offer a particularly wide range of types.

6.3 Photodiode

The reverse current of a diode increases on exposure to light. This effect can be used to measure light. For this purpose, photodiodes are provided with a glass window in the package. Figure 6.6 shows the circuit symbol, Fig. 6.7 the equivalent circuit diagram and Fig. 6.8 the characteristics. Essentially, a short-circuit current flows which is proportional to the illuminance. Thus, in contrast to photoconductive cells, no external voltage source is required. Typical sensitivity values are of the order of 0.1 µA/lx. When a reverse bias is applied, the photo-electric current remains virtually unchanged. This operating mode is useful if short response times are required, as the junction capacitance decreases if the reverse bias is increased.

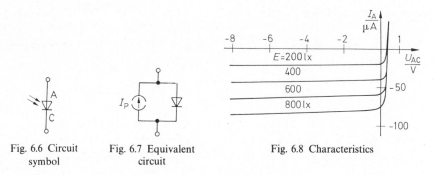

Fig. 6.6 Circuit   Fig. 6.7 Equivalent   Fig. 6.8 Characteristics
    symbol   circuit

As the illuminance increases, the no-load voltage rises to approximately 0.5 V in the case of silicon photodiodes. As Fig. 6.8 shows, the diode voltage decreases only slightly on load as long as the current is smaller than the short-circuit current I_P determined by the illuminance. Photodiodes are therefore suitable not only for measurement of light, but also for generation of electrical energy. For this purpose particularly large-area photodiodes are manufactured which are known as solar cells.

The spectral sensitivity range of silicon photodiodes is between 0.6 and 1 µm, that of germanium photodiodes is between 0.5 and 1.7 µm. The relative spectral response is shown in Fig. 6.9.

Photodiodes have considerably shorter response times than photoconductive cells. Their cutoff frequency is typically 10 MHz, although cutoff frequencies

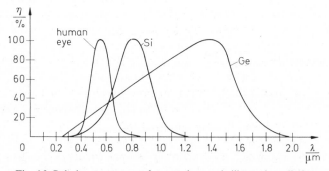

Fig. 6.9 Relative response η of germanium and silicon photodiodes

of up to 1 GHz can be obtained using pin photodiodes. Manufacturers include AEG-Telefunken and Hewlett-Packard.

Due to their low photo-electric current, photodiodes generally require an amplifier. In order to obtain maximum bandwidth, the voltage across the photodiodes is held constant, as the charge of their junction capacitance need not then be reversed. The corresponding operational amplifier circuits are shown in Figs. 6.10/6.11. These are current-voltage converters which will be described in greater detail in Section 13.2. In the circuit in Fig. 6.10, no voltage is dropped across the photodiode—apart from the small offset voltage of the operational amplifier. Consequently, with this circuit the dark current is particularly small. In the circuit in Fig. 6.11, the photodiode is driven with negative bias. It therefore has low junction capacitance and higher bandwidths can be achieved.

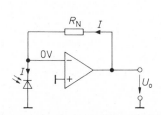

Fig. 6.10 Current-voltage converter for particularly low dark current

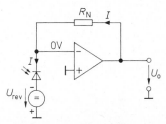

Fig. 6.11 Current-voltage converter for particularly large bandwidth

Figs. 6.10 and 6.11 Output voltage: $U_o = R_N \cdot I$

The input bias current of the operational amplifiers must always be small compared to the photocurrent. The feedback resistance R_N must be low in capacitance, otherwise it limits the circuit bandwidth. A resistance $R_N = 1\ \text{G}\Omega$ in parallel with a capacitance $C_N = 1\ \text{pF}$ results in a cutoff frequency of as low as

$$f_c = 1/2\pi R_N C_N = 160\ \text{Hz}\ .$$

In such cases, it is advisable to use special resistors with internal shielding, whose parallel capacitance is a factor of 100 lower.

6.4   Phototransistor

In a phototransistor, the collector-base junction is designed as a photodiode. Figure 6.12 shows its circuit symbol, Fig. 6.13 its equivalent circuit.

The way a phototransistor operates can be easily explained by reference to the equivalent circuit in Fig. 6.13: the current through the photodiode causes a base current and thus an amplified collector current to flow. Whether it is preferable to connect the base or leave it open depends on the particular circuit. Phototransistors in which the base lead is not brought out are known as photo-duodiodes.

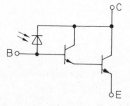

Fig. 6.12 Phototransistor symbol

Fig. 6.13 Equivalent circuit of a phototransistor

Fig. 6.14 Equivalent circuit of a photo-Darlington connection

In order to achieve a particularly high current gain, a Darlington-connected phototransistor can be used. Its equivalent circuit is shown in Fig. 6.14.

The equivalent circuits show that phototransistors have a similar performance to that of comparable photodiodes in terms of their spectral range. However, their cutoff frequency is considerably lower. For phototransistors it is of the order of 300 kHz and for photo-Darlington connections some 30 kHz.

Figure 6.15 shows a phototransistor used as a photodetector. Denoting the photocurrent through the collector-base diode by I_P, we obtain an output voltage

$$U_o = V^+ - BR_1 I_P \; .$$

Correspondingly, for the circuit in Fig. 6.16

$$U_o = BR_1 I_P \; .$$

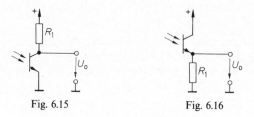

Fig. 6.15   Fig. 6.16

Figs. 6.15 and 6.16 Simple photodetectors

A wide range of phototransistors is available from AEG-Telefunken and Optek.

6.5   Light-emitting diodes

Light-emitting diodes (LEDs) are not made from silicon or germanium, but from gallium arsenide phosphide (III-V compound). These diodes emit light when a forward current flows. The spectral range of the luminous flux emitted is quite sharply delimited, its frequencies depending on the basic material used. Figure 6.17 shows the circuit symbol, Fig. 6.18 provides an overview of the most important characteristics.

A ⚡ C

Fig. 6.17 LED symbol

Color	Wavelength at max. intensity [nm]	Basic material	Forward voltage at 10 mA [V]	Luminous intensity at 10 mA and ± 45° aperture angle [m cd]	Light power at 10 mA [μW]
infrared	900	gallium arsenide	1.3 . . . 1.5		50 . . . 200
red	655	gallium arsenide phosphide	1.6 . . . 1.8	1 . . . 5	2 . . . 10
bright red	635	gallium arsenide phosphide	2.0 . . . 2.2	5 . . . 25	12 . . . 60
yellow	583	gallium arsenide phosphide	2.0 . . . 2.2	5 . . . 25	13 . . . 65
green	565	gallium phosphide	2.2 . . . 2.4	5 . . . 25	14 . . . 70
blue	490	gallium nitrite	3 . . . 5	1 . . . 4	3 . . . 12

Fig. 6.18 Summary of the principal characteristics of light-emitting diodes

The efficiency of infrared LEDs is 1 to 5%, that of the other types less than 0.05%. The luminance is proportional to the forward current over a wide range. Currents of a few mA are sufficient to provide a clearly visible display. LEDs are therefore particularly suitable as display elements in semiconductor circuits. They are also available as seven-segment or matrix units.

LEDs are supplied by most semiconductor manufacturers. A particularly wide selection is offered by Hewlett-Packard, AEG-Telefunken and Siemens.

6.6 Optocouplers

If a LED is combined with a photodetector, e.g. a phototransistor, it is possible to convert an input current into a floating output current at any potential. Optocoupler devices of this kind are available in standard IC packages. In order to achieve a high level of efficiency, they are generally operated in the infrared region. The most important feature of an optocoupler is the transformation ratio $\alpha = I_o/I_i$. This is essentially determined by the detector characteristics. Typical values are listed in Fig. 6.19. We can see that the highest current gain is obtained using photo-Darlingtons, although they exhibit the lowest cutoff frequency.

Optocouplers are suitable for transmitting both digital and analog signals. The relevant circuits are described in Sections 21.5.7 and 25.1.3.

For sensor applications, optocouplers are also designed as slotted optical switches or reflective optical switches.

Detector	Transformation ratio $\alpha = I_o / I_i$	Cutoff frequency
Photodiode	approx. 0.1%	10 MHz
Phototransistor	10 . . . 300%	300 kHz
Photo-Darlington circuit	100 . . . 1000%	30 kHz

Fig. 6.19 Comparison of optocouplers

The main manufacturers of optocouplers are AEG-Telefunken, Clairex, Hewlett-Packard, Motorola, Siemens and Optek.

6.7   Visual display

Digital information can be displayed in many ways, e.g. using incandescent lamps, glow lamps, LEDs or liquid crystals. LED and liquid crystal displays (LCDs) have assumed paramount importance as they can be operated with low voltages and low currents. The application is simplified by the large number of integrated drivers available.

LCDs are not semiconductor components. Unlike LEDs, they themselves generate no light, relying instead on external illumination. An optical effect is produced because a liquid crystal element is transparent when no voltage is applied and therefore appears bright, whereas it is opaque when a voltage is applied and therefore appears dark [6.4]. The liquid crystal element comprises two electrodes with an organic substance sandwiched between them. This substance contains crystals whose orientation can be varied by an electric field. The state of the element therefore depends on the electric field strength; it behaves, in effect, like a capacitor.

The device is driven by AC voltages at a frequency high enough to ensure that no flicker occurs. On the other hand, the frequency selected is low enough to ensure that the alternating current flowing through the capacitor remains small. In practice the values selected are between 30 and 100 Hz. The driving AC

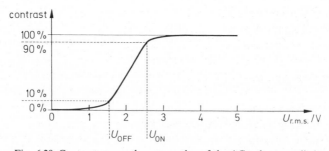

Fig. 6.20 Contrast versus the r.m.s. value of the AC voltage applied

voltage must not contain any DC component, as even at 50 mV electrolytic processes are induced which reduce service life.

In Fig. 6.20 the contrast is plotted as a function of the r.m.s. value of the alternating voltage amplitude applied. For AC voltages of less than $U_{\text{OFF r.m.s.}} \approx 1.5 \text{ V}$, the display is virtually invisible; voltages of more than $U_{\text{ON r.m.s.}} \approx 2.5 \text{ V}$ produce maximum contrast.

As the capacitance of a liquid crystal element is only about 1 nF/cm^2, the currents required for driving the device are well below 1 μA. This extremely low current requirement represents a significant advantage over LEDs.

6.7.1 Binary display

LEDs require a forward current of 5 to 20 mA for good visibility in daylight. These currents can be provided most conveniently using gates as in Figs. 6.21/6.22. In Fig. 6.21, the LED lights when an H-level appears at the gate output by applying an L-level at the input. In Fig. 6.22 the reverse is true. Current limiting is provided in each case via the resistors incorporated in the gates. It is only with TTL circuits that an external current-limiting resistor is required in Fig. 6.22. Due to the relatively high load due to the LEDs, the gate outputs have no specified voltage level and must not therefore be used for logic operations. This is indicated on the circuit diagram by a cross at the gate output.

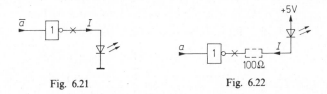

Fig. 6.21   Fig. 6.22

Figs. 6.21 and 6.22 LED drive logic

$$I \approx \begin{cases} 20 \text{ mA} & \text{with} & 74 \text{ LS} & \text{gates} \\ 4 \text{ mA} & \text{with} & 74 \text{ C} & \text{gates} \\ 25 \text{ mA} & \text{with} & 74 \text{ HC} & \text{gates} \end{cases}$$

In order to control the light output, it is possible to use gates with a second input at which a square-wave AC voltage is applied. Its duty cycle then enables the average diode current to be reduced to zero. The frequency must be at least 100 Hz to ensure that no flicker is visible.

Drive signal generation for liquid crystal displays is somewhat more complicated, assuming that standard gates with a 5 V operating voltage are used. An alternating voltage must be generated whose r.m.s. value is sufficiently high and whose mean value is zero. The easiest way to achieve this is to connect the display between two switches (Fig. 6.23) which are switched back and forth between ground and operating voltage V^+ either in phase or in antiphase. For

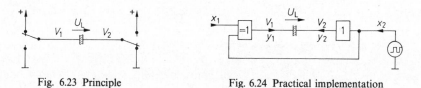

Fig. 6.23 Principle   Fig. 6.24 Practical implementation

Figs. 6.23 and 6.24 Drive of a liquid crystal display from a single supply voltage, without DC offset

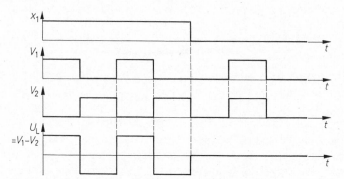

Fig. 6.25 Voltage waveform for liquid crystal display switched on and off

in-phase operation, $U_L = 0$, for antiphase operation $U_{L\,r.m.s.} = V^+$. This is illustrated by the waveform diagram in Fig. 6.25.

The practical implementation of this principle is shown in Fig. 6.24. When $x_1 = 0$, $y_1 = y_2 = x_2$; the two terminals of the display therefore switch in phase with square-wave signal x_2. For $x_1 = 1$, $y_1 = \bar{x}_2$, and the display receives antiphased signals. CMOS gates are most suitable for this purpose, as their output levels with purely capacitive loading only differ by a few millivolts from V^+ or zero potential. In addition, only the use of CMOS gates fully exploits the low power requirement of liquid crystal displays.

6.7.2   Analog display

A quasi-analog display can be obtained using a row of indicating elements. This provides a dot-position display if only the element belonging to a particular indication value is turned on. A bargraph display is obtained if all the lower elements are turned on as well. Figure 6.26 compares these two alternatives.

A dot-position display can be driven by binary signals using a 1-out-of-n encoder (see Section 9.6.1). In this case, only the LED connected to the output selected is turned on. The bargraph display in Fig. 6.28 is obtained when all the LEDs below the selected output are also turned on via the additional output gates.

In order to drive a display row using analog signals, it is advisable to employ an analog-digital converter in a parallel arrangement, as the signals required for

Fig. 6.26 Dot-position (above) and bargraph display (below)

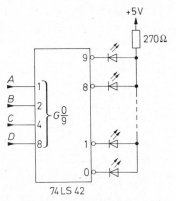

Fig. 6.27 Binary dot-position display drive

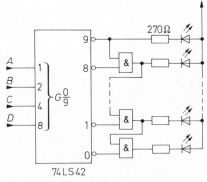

Fig. 6.28 Binary bargraph display drive

driving a bargraph display are then produced directly. As shown in Fig. 6.29, the input voltage is compared with a reference voltage by means of a comparator chain. As a result, all the comparators whose reference voltages are smaller than the input voltage are activated. With this method, additional gates are required in order to implement a dot-position display, as shown in Fig. 6.30.

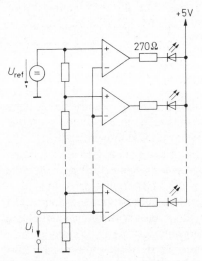

Fig. 6.29 Analog dot-position display drive

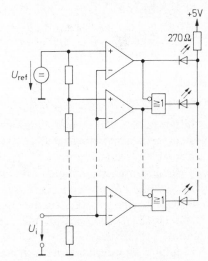

Fig. 6.30 Analog bargraph display drive

Analog dot-position/bargraph display drivers are available as integrated circuits. Some types are listed in Fig. 6.31. Bargraph displays are available as modules from a number of LED manufacturers such as Hewlett-Packard or AEG-Telefunken. Modules may contain between 5 and 100 indicating elements (dots).

Type	Manufacturer	Elements	Dot-position	Bargraph	Internal current limiting
U 237	Telefunken	5		×	×
TL 490	Texas Instr.	10		×	
LM 3914	National	10	×	×	×
UAA 180	Siemens	12		×	×
U 1096 B	Telefunken	30	×		×
HEF 4754 V	Valvo	18	×	×	LCD
TSC 827	Teledyne	101		×	LCD
ICL 7182	Intersil	101		×	LCD

Fig. 6.31 Dot-position/bargraph display drivers with analog input

6.7.3 Numerical display

The simplest means of representing the numerals 0 to 9 is to arrange seven indicating elements to form a 7-segment display (Fig. 6.32). Depending on which combination of segments *a* to *g* is turned on, all digits can be represented with adequate readability.

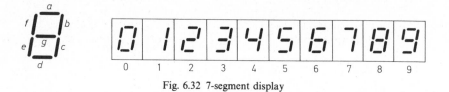

Fig. 6.32 7-segment display

In order to drive a 7-segment display, it is necessary to assign each digit, which is normally present in binary coded form (BCD), the associated combination of segments. A circuit of this type is known as a BCD 7-segment decoder. Its truth table is shown in Fig. 6.33. The principles for connecting LED and liquid crystal displays are those of Figs. 6.22 and 6.24 respectively. The respective circuits are given in Figs. 6.34 and 6.35.

BCD 7-segment decoders are available as integrated circuits; examples are listed in Fig. 6.36. Some of the LED-driving types possess current source outputs, in which case the external current-limiting resistors are not required. In addition to the decoders for driving common-anode displays, types are also available for common cathode. In the case of the liquid-crystal driving decoders,

Digit	BCD-input				7-segment output						
Z	2^3	2^2	2^1	2^0	a	b	c	d	e	f	g
0	0	0	0	0	1	1	1	1	1	1	0
1	0	0	0	1	0	1	1	0	0	0	0
2	0	0	1	0	1	1	0	1	1	0	1
3	0	0	1	1	1	1	1	1	0	0	1
4	0	1	0	0	0	1	1	0	0	1	1
5	0	1	0	1	1	0	1	1	0	1	1
6	0	1	1	0	1	0	1	1	1	1	1
7	0	1	1	1	1	1	1	0	0	0	0
8	1	0	0	0	1	1	1	1	1	1	1
9	1	0	0	1	1	1	1	1	0	1	1

Fig. 6.33 Truth table for a BCD 7-segment decoder

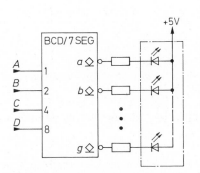

Fig. 6.34 Connection of a LED display to
a 7-segment decoder

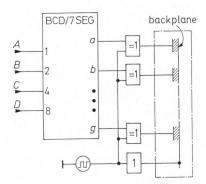

Fig. 6.35 Connection of a liquid crystal
display to a 7-segment decoder

the exclusive-OR gates are already incorporated. The only external device required is therefore the square-wave generator.

Some 7-segment decoders allow the numbers 10 to 15 to be represented by upper-case letters A to F. However, 11 and 13 are represented as lower case b and d respectively, because they would otherwise be indistinguishable from 8 and 0. Decoders of this type are known as hexadecimal decoders. Decoders for multi-digit displays will be dealt with in Section 21.11.

6.7.4 Alphanumeric display

7-segment displays only allow a few letters to be represented. In order to display the entire alphabet, a higher resolution is required. This can be achieved by using 16-segment displays or 35-dot matrices.

Type	Manufacturer	Technology	Internal memory	Hexa-decimal	Common anode/ cathode	Maximum output current	Internal current limiting
For LED displays							
74 LS 47	Texas Instr.	TTL	no	no	anode	24 mA	no
74 LS 247	Texas Instr.	TTL	no	no	anode	24 mA	no
9368	Fairchild	TTL	yes	yes	cathode	20 mA	yes
9370	Fairchild	TTL	yes	yes	anode	40 mA	no
9374	Fairchild	TTL	yes	no	anode	15 mA	yes
NE 587	Signetics	TTL	yes	no	anode	5 ... 50 mA	yes
NE 589	Signetics	TTL	yes	yes	cathode	5 ... 50 mA	yes
CA 3161	RCA	TTL	yes	no	anode	25 mA	yes
4511	numerous	CMOS	yes	no	cathode	25 mA	no
For liquid-crystal displays (LCD)							
4055	numerous	CMOS	no	no			
4056	numerous	CMOS	yes	no			
4543	numerous	CMOS	yes	no			
4544	numerous	CMOS	yes	no			

Fig. 6.36 7-segment decoder

16-segment displays

The arrangement of the segments in a 16-segment display is shown in Fig. 6.37. In comparison with the 7-segment display in Fig. 6.32, segments a, d and g are divided into two sections and segments h to m are added. This enables generation of the character set shown in Fig. 6.38. It is usually limited to 64 characters which include the upper-case letters, the numerals and the most important special characters.

16-segment displays are available in LED and LCD form. LED types are manufactured by Hewlett-Packard, Monsanto and Siemens. The Siemens displays incorporate decoders. A suitable decoder for the other types is, for example, the AC 5947 from Texas Instruments. It is connected to the display in exactly the same way as the 7-segment decoder in Fig. 6.34. Decoders for multi-digit displays are described in Section 21.11.

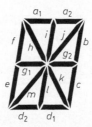

Fig. 6.37 16-segment display. The two additional dots are not shown here

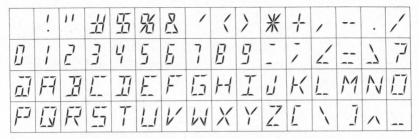

Fig. 6.38 Usual character set of a 16-segment display

35-dot matrix displays

A better resolution than that of a 16-segment display is obtained by using a 5×7 dot matrix as shown in Fig. 6.39. This allows an approximate representation of virtually all conceivable characters. Figure 6.41 shows how all the 96 ASCII characters and 32 additional special characters can be represented using commercially available character generators.

Due to the large numbers of leads involved in matrix displays, a terminal is not brought out from each dot element. Instead the elements are also connected as a matrix. This is shown in Fig. 6.40 using LEDs as an example. There are only 12 external connections. However, as the matrix makes it impossible to turn on all the required elements simultaneously, the display is driven on a time-division multiplex basis by selecting row by row and activating the desired combination of display elements each time. If the progression is sufficiently fast, the observer has the impression that all the dots addressed are activated simultaneously. If

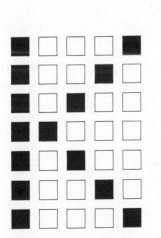

Fig. 6.39 Arrangement of dots in a 35-dot
matrix in 7 rows and 5 columns

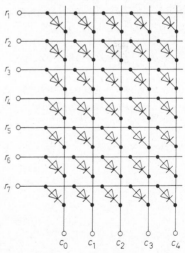

Fig. 6.40 Matrix arrangement of display
elements using LEDs as an example

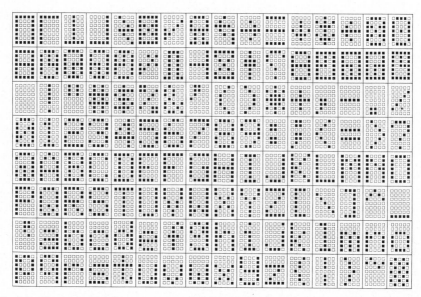

Fig. 6.41 Character set of character generators MM 6061 from MMI or MCM 6674 from Motorola

the cycle frequency is more than 100 Hz, the display appears virtually flicker-free to the human eye.

Figure 6.42 shows schematically a drive circuit for LED matrices. Rows are selected one by one using the straight binary counter and the 1-out-of-8 decoder. The row number together with the ASCII code for the desired character is fed to the character generator. The latter determines, in accordance with Fig. 6.40, which dots of the particular row are to be turned on. Character generators are available as mask-programmed ROMs providing the symbols shown in Fig. 6.41. If other character sets are required, it is advisable to program an

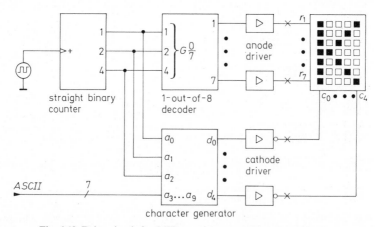

Fig. 6.42 Drive circuit for LED matrices comprising 5 × 7 elements

Row number	ROM address										ROM contents				
	ASCII "K"							i			Column code				
i	a_9	a_8	a_7	a_6	a_5	a_4	a_3	a_2	a_1	a_0	c_0	c_1	c_2	c_3	c_4
1	1	0	0	1	0	1	1	0	0	1	1	0	0	0	1
2	1	0	0	1	0	1	1	0	1	0	1	0	0	1	0
3	1	0	0	1	0	1	1	0	1	1	1	0	1	0	0
4	1	0	0	1	0	1	1	1	0	0	1	1	0	0	0
5	1	0	0	1	0	1	1	1	0	1	1	0	1	0	0
6	1	0	0	1	0	1	1	1	1	0	1	0	0	1	0
7	1	0	0	1	0	1	1	1	1	1	1	0	0	0	1

Fig. 6.43 Character generator contents for representing the character "K"

EPROM accordingly. Figure 6.43 gives the character generator contents required for the character "K". A typical matrix display with integrated drive electronics is the DLR 7136 from Siemens.

The multiplex drive arrangement of liquid crystal displays is somewhat more complicated, as it is impossible to prevent an AC voltage from being applied to the non-selected dots. For this reason, a 3-level signal is used to drive the display, its amplitude at the non-selected elements remaining below the turn-on threshold (see Fig. 6.20). Triplex decoders of this type are likewise available as integrated circuits [6.5]; some of the types available are listed in Section 21.11.

7 Operational amplifiers

There is basically no difference between a normal amplifier and an operational amplifier (op amp). Both are used to provide voltage or power gain. However, whereas the characteristics of a normal amplifier are governed by its internal design, an operational amplifier is so constructed that its mode of operation can be determined primarily by external feedback circuitry. In order to make this possible, operational amplifiers are designed as direct-coupled amplifiers with zero quiescent input and output potential. They exhibit high voltage gain, high input resistance and low output resistance. High-quality amplifiers of this kind were at one time used exclusively in analog computers for performing mathematical operations such as addition and integration, hence the term "operational".

Nowadays they are available as monolithic integrated circuits in a wide variety of types and differ little from individual transistors in terms of size and price. As their characteristics are virtually ideal in many respects, they are much easier to use than individual transistors. Consequently, the operational amplifier has replaced the latter in many areas of linear circuit design.

Knowledge of a few characteristic data is generally adequate for assessing which type of operational amplifier is suitable for a particular application. However, many special classes of application call for in-depth knowledge of the internal design, a point which we shall examine in greater detail in Section 7.5.

After discussing the characteristics used to describe real operational amplifiers, we shall examine the basic principles of the external circuitry design. We shall also examine the limitations of the usual approximations based on the assumption of an "ideal" device. The results of this analysis can be applied as a general principle to the operational amplifier applications described in later chapters.

7.1 Characteristics of an operational amplifier

Figure 7.1 shows the circuit symbol of an operational amplifier. As the input stage is designed as a differential amplifier, the operational amplifier has two inputs. At low frequencies, the output voltage U_o is in phase with the input voltage difference

$$U_D = U_P - U_N \ .$$

Consequently, the P-input is termed the non-inverting input and is indicated by a plus sign on the circuit symbol. The N-input is known as the inverting input and is denoted by a minus sign.

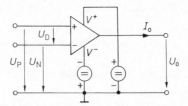

Fig. 7.1 Circuit symbol of an operational amplifier

In order to be able to drive the inputs and the output positively and negatively, the operational amplifier requires a positive and a negative supply potential. This must be provided by two voltage sources connected to the two supply voltage terminals as shown in Fig. 7.1. For a standard IC operational amplifier, operating potentials of ± 15 V are generally employed. For the sake of clarity, only the input and output terminals are indicated on basic circuit diagrams.

In practice there is no such thing as an ideal operational amplifier. In order to assess how near an operational amplifier comes to the ideal, various parameters must be specified.

The *differential gain*

$$A_D = \frac{\Delta U_o}{\Delta U_D} = \frac{\Delta U_o}{\Delta(U_P - U_N)} = \begin{cases} \Delta U_o/\Delta U_P & \text{for } U_N = \text{const} \\ -\Delta U_o/\Delta U_N & \text{for } U_P = \text{const} \end{cases} \quad (7.1)$$

possesses a finite value of the order of 10^4 to 10^5. It is also known as *open-loop gain*, i.e. gain without external feedback.

Figure 7.2 shows a typical plot of the output voltage versus U_D. In the range $U_{o\,min} < U_o < U_{o\,max}$, the output voltage is approximately a linear function of U_D. This range is known as the *maximum output voltage swing*. When this limit is reached, U_o ceases to increase if U_D is increased still further, i.e. the amplifier is overdriven. The limits $U_{o\,max}$ and $U_{o\,min}$ are approximately 3 V below the positive or negative supply voltages. Thus, for a supply voltage of ± 15 V, the output swing is typically ± 12 V.

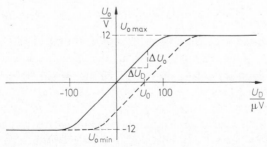

Fig. 7.2 Output voltage as a function of the input voltage difference. Dashed curve: without offset compensation

With an ideal operational amplifier, the transfer characteristic passes through the origin. However, with a real amplifier, it is slightly displaced, as indicated by the dashed curve in Fig. 7.2. This means that a small voltage difference must be applied to the inputs in order to make the output voltage zero. This difference is known as the *input offset voltage* U_O. It is of the order of a few mV and may be disregarded in many applications. In critical cases it can be compensated for (nulled), as described in connection with the differential amplifier in Section 4.8.4. For this purpose, suitable access points are brought out on most IC operational amplifiers.

When the input offset voltage has been adjusted, its only noticeable variation is as a function of temperature, time and supply voltage:

$$dU_O(\vartheta, t, U_b) = \frac{\partial U_O}{\partial \vartheta}\, d\vartheta + \frac{\partial U_O}{\partial t}\, dt + \frac{\partial U_O}{\partial U_b}\, dU_b \ ,$$

where $\partial U_O/\partial \vartheta$ is the *temperature drift*. Typical values are 3 to 10 µV/K. The *long-term drift* $\partial U_O/\partial t$ is of the order of a few µV per month. The *power supply rejection ratio* $\partial U_O/\partial U_b$ characterizes the effect of supply voltage changes on the offset voltage. It can range from 10 to 100 µV/V. Therefore, if small offset voltage changes are an important consideration, the supply voltage changes must not exceed a few mV.

Let us assume that the offset voltage has been nulled. From Eq. (7.1) it therefore follows that

$$U_o = A_D U_D = A_D(U_P - U_N) \ . \tag{7.2}$$

The output voltage is therefore proportional to the input voltage difference within the limits of the swing.

If the same voltage U_{CM} is applied to the P- and N-input, U_D remains equal to zero. Equation (7.2) states that U_o should remain equal to zero for a common mode input of this kind. However, as we have already seen in Section 4.8.1, with real differential amplifiers this is not precisely the case, i.e. the *common mode gain*

$$A_{CM} = \frac{\Delta U_o}{\Delta U_{CM}}$$

is not exactly zero. As we can see from Fig. 7.3, it increases sharply at higher common mode input voltages. The usable range is known as the *common mode input voltage range*. This is generally some 2 V lower than the positive or negative supply voltage. The deviation from the ideal response when a common mode signal is applied is more accurately characterized by the *common mode rejection ratio* (CMRR) $G = A_D/A_{CM}$. Typical values are 10^4 to 10^5. The differential gain is by definition always positive, which is not the case with the common mode gain. Consequently, G may assume positive or negative values. Although the data sheets only give a figure for G, it must be inserted in the formulae with the correct sign. If one is merely interested in the absolute value of the deviation produced by a finite CMRR, the sign is naturally irrelevant.

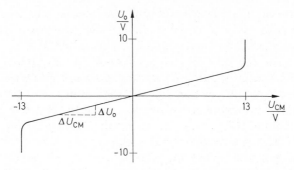

Fig. 7.3 Output voltage as a function of the common mode input voltage

The existence of common mode gain makes it necessary to define the differential gain more precisely; A_D is more strictly defined as the partial differential quotient:

$$A_D = \frac{\partial U_o}{\partial U_D}\bigg|_{U_{CM}=\text{const}} .$$

The general relation for the output voltage is therefore

$$\Delta U_o = \frac{\partial U_o}{\partial U_D}\bigg|_{U_{CM}} \cdot \Delta U_D + \frac{\partial U_o}{\partial U_{CM}}\bigg|_{U_D} \cdot \Delta U_{CM} ,$$

$$\Delta U_o = A_D \cdot \Delta U_D + A_{CM} \cdot \Delta U_{CM} . \tag{7.3}$$

This relation yields a second useful definition for the common mode rejection ratio: for $\Delta U_o = 0$, we have

$$G = \frac{A_D}{A_{CM}} = -\frac{\Delta U_{CM}}{\Delta U_D}\bigg|_{U_o=\text{const}} .$$

Consequently, the common mode rejection ratio also indicates which differential voltage must be applied in order to compensate for the effect of a common mode signal on the output.

As the transfer characteristics in Figs. 7.2 and 7.3 are approximately linear within the limits of the output swing, instead of Eq. (7.3) we can also write, taking the offset voltage U_O into account:

$$U_o = A_D(U_D - U_O) + A_{CM}U_{CM} , \tag{7.4}$$

$$\boxed{U_o = A_D\left[(U_D - U_O) + \frac{1}{G}U_{CM}\right]} .$$

For U_O and $U_{CM} \rightarrow 0$, this relation transposes to Eq. (7.1). Solving for U_D, we obtain

$$U_D = U_O + \frac{U_o}{A_D} - \frac{U_{CM}}{G} . \tag{7.5}$$

With an ideal operational amplifier, $U_O = 0$, $A_D = \infty$ and $G = \infty$. This means that infinitely small values of U_D are theoretically sufficient to produce any finite output voltage U_o.

As we shall see in Section 7.5, for a general-purpose operational amplifier the differential gain frequency response must, for reasons of stability, be like that of a first-order lowpass filter at least up to the frequency at which $|\underline{A}_D| = 1$. In order to satisfy this requirement, the amplifier must contain a lowpass filter with a very low cutoff frequency. Figure 7.4 shows the typical frequency response of the differential gain of a "compensated" amplifier of this kind. The differential gain is written in complex notation as

$$\underline{A}_D = \frac{A_D}{1 + j\dfrac{f}{f_{cA}}} . \tag{7.6}$$

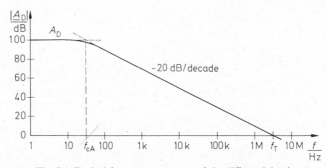

Fig. 7.4 Typical frequency response of the differential gain

In this equation A_D is the low-frequency limit value of $\underline{A}_D$. Above the 3 dB cutoff frequency f_{cA}, the value of $\underline{A}_D$ decreases in inverse proportion to the frequency. In this range therefore

$$\boxed{|\underline{A}_D| \cdot f = A_D f_{cA} = f_T} . \tag{7.7}$$

At the *transit frequency* f_T, $|\underline{A}_D| = 1$. Because of Eq. (7.7) this is also known as the *gain bandwidth product*.

Input resistance

Real operational amplifiers have a finite input resistance. A distinction is drawn between the differential and the common mode input resistance. Their effect is illustrated by the equivalent schematic of the input stage in Fig. 7.5 (see also the differential amplifier in Fig. 4.43). In the case of operational amplifiers with bipolar input transistors, the differential input resistance r_D is in the MΩ range and the common mode input resistance r_{CM} is in the GΩ range. The currents flowing through these resistances are just a few nA.

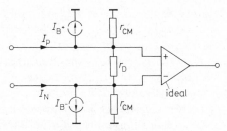

Fig. 7.5 Equivalent circuit for the effect of the differential input resistance, common mode input resistance and input bias current

The constant currents superimposed at the inputs are, however, much higher. The input bias current is defined as

$$I_B = \tfrac{1}{2}(I_{B^+} + I_{B^-})$$

and the input offset current as

$$I_O = |I_{B^+} - I_{B^-}| \; .$$

For standard bipolar operational amplifiers, the input bias current is between 20 and 200 mA. For FET-input amplifiers, it is no more than a few pA.

The principal data for real operational amplifiers are listed in Fig. 7.6. The μA741 type (Texas Instruments, National, Silicon General, etc.) represents the

Parameter	Symbol	Standard amplifier		Special amplifier	
		μA741 (bipolar)	TL081 (FET)	OP77 (bipolar)	OPA 128 (FET)
Differential gain	A_D	10^5	$2 \cdot 10^5$	10^7	$3 \cdot 10^6$
Common mode rejection ratio	G	$3 \cdot 10^4$	$2 \cdot 10^4$	10^7	10^6
3-dB bandwidth	f_{cA}	10 Hz	30 Hz	0.06 Hz	0.3 Hz
Gain-bandwidth product	f_T^-	1 MHz	3 MHz	0.6 MHz	1 MHz
Differential input resistance	r_D	1 MΩ	$10^{12}\,\Omega$	45 MΩ	$10^{13}\,\Omega$
Common mode input resistance	r_{CM}	1 GΩ	$10^{14}\,\Omega$	200 GΩ	$10^{15}\,\Omega$
Input bias current	I_B	80 nA	30 pA	1 nA	**0.04 pA**
Input offset voltage	U_O	1 mV	5 mV	**25 μV**	0.14 mV
Offset voltage drift	$\Delta U_O/\Delta \vartheta$	6 μV/K	10 μV/K	**0.1 μV/K**	5 μV/K
Supply voltage rejection ratio	$\Delta U_O/\Delta U_b$	15 μV/V	50 μV/V	0.7 μV/V	1 μV/V
Input voltage range	$U_{CM\,max}$	± 13 V	+ 14.5 V, − 12 V	± 14 V	± 12 V
Output voltage swing	$U_{o\,max}$	± 13 V	± 13 V	± 14 V	± 13 V
Maximum output current	$I_{o\,max}$	± 20 mA	± 20 mA	± 20 mA	± 20 mA
Output resistance	r_o	1 kΩ	100 Ω	60 Ω	100 Ω
Supply current drain	I_b	1.7 mA	1.4 mA	2 mA	1 mA

Fig. 7.6 Typical data for IC operational amplifiers without external circuitry, operated from a ± 15 V supply

generation of simple amplifiers realized in bipolar technology. Type TL081 (Texas Instruments) is a commonly used FET-input operational amplifier. Ion implantation has now made it possible to combine high-quality p-channel junction FETs with bipolar transistors on a single chip (BIFET technology).

Special operational amplifiers are available for specific applications, e.g. types with particularly low offset voltage drift or with particularly low input bias current. However, these are considerably more expensive than standard amplifiers. We have given the specifications for type OP77 (PMI) and type OPA128 (Burr Brown) as examples.

The normal pin configuration for all commonly used operational amplifiers is shown in Fig. 7.7. There are differences for the connection of a nulling circuit.

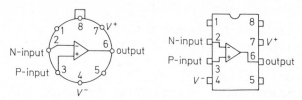

Fig. 7.7 Pin connections of operational amplifiers in TO can and 8-pin dual-in-line package (top view)

7.2   Principle of negative feedback

The basic feedback arrangement for an operational amplifier is shown in Fig. 7.8. A portion of the output voltage is returned to the input via a feedback network. If the fed-back voltage is subtracted from the input voltage, as in Fig. 7.8, this is known as negative feedback; if it is added, it is termed positive feedback. We shall now consider the case of negative feedback.

In order to analyze the circuit in Fig. 7.8 qualitatively, we let the input voltage jump from zero to a positive value U_i. Initially the output voltage U_o (and therefore the fed-back voltage kU_o) remains zero, causing voltage $U_D = U_i$ to appear at the amplifier input. As this voltage is amplified with the high positive value A_D, U_o rapidly increases to positive values and with it kU_o, thereby reducing the amplifier input voltage U_D. The fact that the output voltage change counteracts the input voltage change is typical of negative feedback. It follows that a stable final state will be established. This is achieved

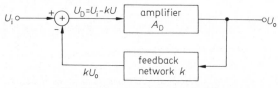

Fig. 7.8 Negative feedback principle

when the output voltage has just become high enough to satisfy the condition

$$U_o = A_D U_D = A_D(U_i - kU_o) \; .$$

Solving for U_o, we obtain

$$\boxed{A = \frac{U_o}{U_i} = \frac{A_D}{1 + kA_D}} \; . \tag{7.8}$$

For values $kA_D \gg 1$, the resultant gain of the feedback arrangement is given by

$$\boxed{A \approx \frac{1}{k}} \; . \tag{7.9}$$

This being so, the gain is then determined by the external feedback network alone and not by the amplifier. In its simplest form, the feedback network consists of a voltage divider. The circuit then operates as a linear amplifier whose gain is determined solely by the divider ratio. If an RC network is used as the feedback circuit, an active filter is produced. Finally, it is also possible to use non-linear components, e.g. diodes or transistors, and perform non-linear mathematical operations in this manner. Such applications will be dealt with in detail in later chapters. Here we shall confine ourselves to the case of resistive feedback.

As we can see from Eq. (7.8), the deviation from the ideal behavior can be described by how much larger the factor

$$g = kA_D \approx A_D/A \tag{7.10}$$

is compared to unity. This factor is known as the *loop gain*, a term derived from control engineering. As we shall see again in Chapter 27, Fig. 7.8 is merely the block diagram of a simple control circuit: the amplifier adjusts its output voltage such that $kU_o \approx U_i$. The adjustment accuracy is determined by the loop gain g.

The loop gain can be interpreted as follows. We make $U_i = 0$ and open the control loop, e.g. at the input of the feedback network. We now apply a test signal U_S to the feedback network and measure the magnitude of the signal arriving at the other end of the break. In the example selected, this is the output voltage U_o of the amplifier. Figure 7.8 directly yields the relation

$$U_o = -kA_D U_S = -gU_S \; .$$

The test signal is therefore amplified with loop gain g as it passes through the opened loop.

The loop gain can also be measured in the closed loop. For this purpose, a voltage U_i is applied to the input and the ratio of the feedback network output voltage kU_o to the amplifier input voltage U_D is measured. This gives

$$\frac{kU_o}{U_D} = \frac{kU_o}{U_o/A_D} = kA_D = g \; .$$

We shall now calculate the amount by which the gain A of the feedback configuration deviates from the ideal value $A_{id} = 1/k$. For the relative deviation we obtain from Eq. (7.8)

$$\frac{A_{id} - A}{A_{id}} = \frac{\dfrac{1}{k} - \dfrac{A_D}{1 + kA_D}}{1/k} = \frac{1}{1 + g} \approx \frac{1}{g} \; . \tag{7.11}$$

The fact that, for $g \gg 1$, the gain A as formulated in Eq. (7.8) is largely independent of A_D also has a favorable effect on the bandwidth of the feedback configuration. In the event of a frequency-dependent decrease in $|\underline{A}_D|$, the gain remains at $|\underline{A}| \approx 1/k$ as long as $|\underline{A}_D| \gg 1/k$. If $|\underline{A}_D|$ becomes smaller than the value set by $1/k$, from Eq. (7.8) $\underline{A} \approx \underline{A}_D$, giving the characteristic plotted for $|\underline{A}|$ in Fig. 7.9. In order to calculate the resultant cutoff frequency, we substitute $\underline{A}_D$ in Eq. (7.8) in complex notation and obtain using Eq. (7.6)

$$\underline{A} = \frac{\underline{A}_D}{1 + k\underline{A}_D} \approx \frac{1/k}{1 + \mathrm{j} \dfrac{f}{kA_D f_{cA}}} \; . \tag{7.12}$$

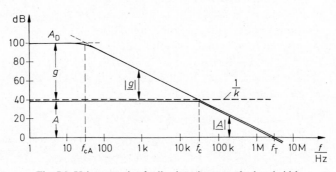

Fig. 7.9 Using negative feedback to increase the bandwidth

The resultant cutoff frequency is therefore given by

$$f_c = kA_D \cdot f_{cA} = g \cdot f_{cA} \; , \tag{7.13}$$

where g is the low-frequency limit value of the loop gain $\underline{g}$. Using Eq. (7.10) we obtain

$$f_c = \frac{A_D}{A} \cdot f_{cA} \; , \qquad \text{i.e.} \qquad \boxed{f_c \cdot A = f_{cA} \cdot A_D = f_T} \; . \tag{7.14}$$

The gain bandwidth product of the entire circuit is therefore equal to the gain bandwidth product of the amplifier.

7.3 Non-inverting amplifier

If a simple voltage divider is used as the feedback network and the subtraction is performed using the differential inputs of an operational amplifier, we obtain the basic circuit of a negative-feedback non-inverting amplifier, as shown in Fig. 7.10. The feedback factor is $k = R_1/(R_1 + R_N)$. Assuming ideal characteristics, the gain is given by

$$\boxed{A = \frac{U_o}{U_i} = \frac{1}{k} = 1 + \frac{R_N}{R_1}} \;. \tag{7.15}$$

The value of A for a finite differential gain A_D has already been calculated in Eq. (7.8). However, for a real operational amplifier we must additionally take into account that the subtraction is not ideal, i.e. the common mode rejection ratio G only possesses a finite value. In order to calculate the resultant gain more precisely, we therefore return to Eq. (7.4) and make the offset voltage U_O equal to zero. With $U_{CM} = U_i$ and $U_D = U_i - kU_o$ it follows that

$$A = \frac{A_D}{1 + kA_D}\left(1 + \frac{1}{G}\right) \;. \tag{7.16}$$

For $G \gg 1$ and $g = kA_D \gg 1$ we obtain the result stated above.

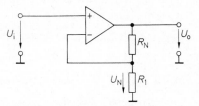

Fig. 7.10 Non-inverting amplifier

$$A = \frac{U_o}{U_i} = 1 + \frac{R_N}{R_1}$$

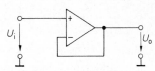

Fig. 7.11 Voltage follower

$$A = \frac{U_o}{U_i} = 1$$

An important special case occurs for $k = 1$, i.e. for $R_N = 0$ and $R_1 = \infty$. This is illustrated in Fig. 7.11. From Eq. (7.15) we obtain a gain $A = 1$ for the configuration shown. An operational amplifier operated in this way is therefore known as a *voltage follower* (follower-with-unit-gain). Like the emitter follower, it is used as an impedance converter. Its main advantage is that the offset between the input and output voltage is only a few mV.

The effect of the offset voltage may be easily examined by reference to the equivalent circuit in Fig. 7.12. We can see that for the circuits shown in Figs. 7.10 and 7.11 the input offset voltage is in series with the input voltage. It is therefore also amplified by the factor A.

Input resistance

In order to calculate the resulting input resistance, we insert the equivalent circuit of Fig. 7.5 into the feedback arrangement and obtain the circuit shown in

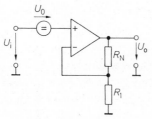

Fig. 7.12 Equivalent circuit for the effect
of the offset voltage

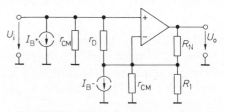

Fig. 7.13 Equivalent circuit for the effect of
the input resistances

Fig. 7.13. Due to the negative feedback, only a very small voltage

$$U_D = \frac{U_o}{A_D} = \frac{U_i}{g}$$

is developed across resistor r_D. The current flowing through the resistor is
therefore only U_i/gr_D. The differential input resistance is therefore boosted by
the feedback by a factor g. This type of feedback is known as *electrometer
feedback*. From Fig. 7.13, the resulting input resistance is given by

$$\boxed{r_i = \frac{\Delta U_i}{\Delta I_i} = gr_D \| r_{CM} \approx r_{CM}} \; . \qquad (7.17)$$

Even in the case of operational amplifiers having bipolar transistor inputs it is
higher than $10^9 \, \Omega$. However, we must not overlook the fact that this is only
a *differential* quantity; that is to say, the current *changes* ΔI_i are small, whereas
a possibly high input bias current I_B may be superimposed.

We shall illustrate the quantities involved by a worked example. Let there be
a signal voltage source with an internal resistance of $R_g = 1 \, M\Omega$. The gain error
due to the input resistance must not exceed 0.1%. This requires that

$$r_i \approx r_{CM} \geqq 1 \, G\Omega \; .$$

Reference to Fig. 7.6 shows that this requirement can already be met using
a type 741 operational amplifier. However, its input bias current $I_B = 80 \, nA$
would produce a voltage drop of 80 mV across the internal resistance of the
signal source. In principle, this can be compensated for by making the internal
resistance of the feedback voltage divider identical to R_g, in which case only
the input current difference has an effect. However, this method seldom
produces the desired result, as the source resistance is rarely well defined.
For high-resistance sources in excess of 50 kΩ, it is advisable to use FET-
input operational amplifiers. This is also advantageous in terms of noise, as
FET operational amplifiers are ideal for such sources due to their low input
noise current.

Output resistance

As the table in Fig. 7.6 shows, real operational amplifiers fall somewhat short of the ideal as far as their output resistance is concerned. However, the output resistance is substantially reduced by negative feedback. A reduction in the output voltage due to loading is in fact transmitted to the N-input via voltage divider R_N, R_1. The resultant increase in U_D counteracts the assumed decrease in output voltage.

The output resistance of an operational amplifier without feedback is defined as

$$r_o = - \left. \frac{\partial U_o}{\partial I_o} \right|_{U_D = \text{const}},$$

but the output resistance of the feedback circuit in Fig. 7.10 is given by

$$r'_o = - \left. \frac{\partial U_o}{\partial I_o} \right|_{U_i = \text{const}}.$$

During negative feedback operation, U_D is not constant under loaded conditions, but varies by

$$dU_D = - dU_N = - k dU_o . \tag{7.18}$$

By linear superposition, the resultant output voltage change is given by

$$dU_o = A_D dU_D - r_o dI_o , \tag{7.19}$$

disregarding the current through the feedback voltage divider. By substituting Eq. (7.18), we obtain

$$\boxed{r'_o = \frac{r_o}{1 + k A_D} \approx \frac{r_o}{g}} . \tag{7.20}$$

If the gain is set at $A = 10$ and the differential gain at $A_D = 10^5$, the output resistance is reduced by negative feedback from 1 kΩ to 0.1 Ω. However, this only applies up to the 3 dB cutoff frequency f_{cA} of the operational amplifier. At higher frequencies, the output resistance increases because $|g|$ decreases at 20 dB per decade. It therefore exhibits an inductive response.

7.4   Inverting amplifier

Another important feedback method consists of connecting the P-input of the operational amplifier in Fig. 7.10 to ground and injecting the input signal at the low end of resistor R_1. This produces the circuit depicted in Fig. 7.14. For purposes of qualitative analysis, we produce an input voltage step from zero to a positive value U_i. U_N then jumps to the value

$$U_N = \frac{R_N}{R_N + R_1} U_i ,$$

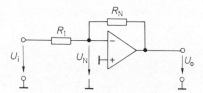

Fig. 7.14 Inverting amplifier

$$A = \frac{U_o}{U_i} = -\frac{R_N}{R_1}$$

as U_o is initially still equal to zero. Voltage $U_D = U_P - U_N$ is therefore negative. Due to the high gain A_D, the output voltage rapidly falls to negative values, thus reducing U_N. The output voltage changes until the voltage U_N has become virtually zero.

In order to calculate the output voltage at which $U_N \approx 0$, we apply Kirchhoff's current law to the N-input, bearing in mind that no input current flows in an ideal operational amplifier:

$$\frac{U_i}{R_1} + \frac{U_o}{R_N} \approx 0 \ .$$

This yields the result:

$$\boxed{U_o \approx -\frac{R_N}{R_1} U_i} \ . \tag{7.21}$$

The feedback effect may be summarized as follows: within its linear operating range, an operational amplifier ensures that an output voltage U_o is established such that $U_N \approx 0$. The N-input therefore behaves like a ground terminal, although there is no passive low-resistance connection to ground. In this circuit it is therefore referred to as *virtual ground* or summing junction. In contrast to non-inverting amplifiers, there is no common mode signal, and the output voltage is in antiphase to the input voltage.

In order to calculate the voltage gain of the feedback arrangement more precisely, we cannot neglect the very small voltage

$$U_N = - U_o/A_D$$

and obtain

$$A = - (1 - k) \frac{A_D}{1 + kA_D} \ , \tag{7.22}$$

with $k = R_1/(R_1 + R_N)$. Assuming that

$$g = kA_D \gg 1$$

it follows that

$$A = - \frac{1 - k}{k} = - \frac{R_N}{R_1} \ , \tag{7.23}$$

in accordance with Eq. (7.21). The deviation from the ideal behavior is determined by the loop gain $g = kA_D$, as in the case of the non-inverting amplifier.

The input resistance of the circuit is here considerably lower than the input resistance of the amplifier itself. It can be obtained directly from Fig. 7.14, taking into account that $U_N \approx 0$. Consequently

$$\boxed{r_i = R_1} \, . \qquad (7.24)$$

For $U_i = \text{const}$, the two circuits in Figs. 7.14 and 7.10 are identical as far as small signals are concerned, so that for the output resistance the same considerations apply as in the case of the non-inverting amplifier.

7.5 Internal design of operational amplifiers

In the previous sections we have postulated the following requirements for an operational amplifier:

1) DC coupling,
2) Zero quiescent input and output potential,
3) Good zero stability,
4) High input resistance and low output resistance,
5) High voltage gain,
6) Defined frequency response.

In order to achieve the desired high voltage gain, several amplifier stages are required. If npn transistors are used, the quiescent potential is increased from stage to stage, due to the DC coupling. In order to ensure that the quiescent output potential is zero, it is therefore necessary to decrease the potential at least once somewhere in the amplifier. There are basically four different ways of achieving this. They are listed in Fig. 7.15:

a) *Voltage dividers* can adapt the potential, but they invariably attenuate the wanted signal.

b) *Zener diodes* cause minimal attenuation of the wanted signal due to their low incremental internal resistance. However, a sufficient current must

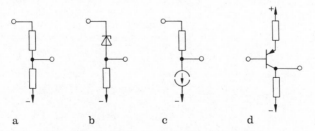

a   b   c   d

Fig. 7.15a–d Methods of adapting the potential

flow through the Zener diode to ensure that its noise does not become troublesome. Consequently, these devices should only be used after emitter followers.

c) *Constant current coupling*: a constant current produces a constant voltage drop across a resistor. If the lower resistor in a) is replaced by a constant current source, the wanted signal is not attenuated.

d) *Complementary transistors* represent the simplest and most elegant method of coupling different potentials.

We shall now examine how the offsets of the individual stages affect the circuit as a whole. For this purpose, let us consider a two-stage amplifier. Designating the offset voltages of the two stages by U_{o1} and U_{o2}, we obtain for $U_i = 0$ an output voltage of

$$U_{oO} = A_2(U_{o2} + A_1 U_{o1}) \ .$$

Consequently, the offset voltage of the first stage has, by its DC voltage gain, a greater effect on the output than that of the second stage. In order to minimize it, the input stage is always a differential amplifier. Normally, output voltages symmetrical about ground are not required. The circuit, whose input is symmetrical, can therefore be allowed at some point to operate unsymmetrically. The gain up to that point should be high enough for the amplified offset of the input stages to be large compared to the offset of the subsequent unsymmetrical stage. The latter then does not appreciably contribute to the offset of the entire circuit.

Simplest design

Due to the abovementioned requirements placed on an operational amplifier, a differential amplifier is required at the input and an emitter follower at the output. This represents the simplest possible op-amp design, as shown in Fig. 7.16.

In order to ensure that transistor T_2 is not driven into saturation in response to small positive common mode signals, its quiescent collector potential must

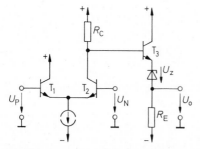 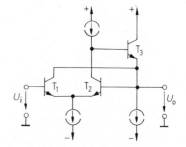

Fig. 7.16 Simple operational amplifier   Fig. 7.17 Voltage follower

not have too low a positive value, e.g. $\frac{1}{2} V^+$. The quiescent output potential must, however, be zero. The Zener diode is used to provide DC coupling of the signal across this potential difference. In the example given, the Zener voltage must have the value $\frac{1}{2} V^+ - 0.6$ V. If the common mode voltage at the input is zero, the collector potential of T_2 can be driven between zero and V^+ if above quiescent potentials are selected. The output voltage swing is therefore $\pm \frac{1}{2} V^+$. For a positive common mode voltage at the input, the negative output voltage swing is reduced correspondingly.

In practice, an operational amplifier with single-stage voltage gain is suitable only as a voltage follower as in Fig. 7.11, because $A = 1$ still obtains a good loop gain. For this specific application, some further improvements can be made, as shown in Fig. 7.17. In order to increase the loop gain and the output voltage swing, the two resistors R_C and R_E have been replaced by constant current sources.

The emitter potential of the differential amplifier is $U_i - 0.6$ V. As negative feedback ensures that $U_o = U_i$, the base potential of T_3 is $U_i + 0.6$ V. The collector-emitter voltage of T_1 is therefore 0.6 V and that of T_2 is 1.2 V, irrespective of the input voltage applied. The circuit operates perfectly with this potential distribution, thereby obviating the need for a Zener diode to drop the output potential as in Fig. 7.16. As all the potentials of T_1 follow the input potential, the circuit exhibits a very high input resistance and a very low input capacitance. Voltage followers operating on this principle are available as monolithic ICs (e.g. LM310 from National).

7.6   Standard IC operational amplifiers

General-purpose operational amplifiers require a higher differential gain than can be obtained with a single stage. A circuit design frequently employed with, for example, type 741 devices is shown in Fig. 7.18.

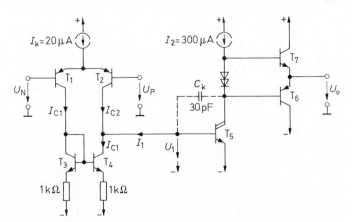

Fig. 7.18 Basic circuit diagram of IC operational amplifier type μA741

The input differential amplifier comprises pnp transistors T_1, T_2. Current source T_4 is used as the load resistor for T_2. Its current is not constant, however, as it and T_3 together form a *current mirror* for the collector current of T_1. The output current of the input stage is therefore given by

$$I_1 = I_{C1} - I_{C2} .$$

This subtraction suppresses in-phase collector current changes, thereby improving the common mode rejection ratio. On the other hand, antiphase changes are added, doubling the available current I_1. Consequently, a current mirror is the most suitable circuit to interpose between the balanced input circuit and the unbalanced output of an operational amplifier.

The emitter terminals of transistors T_3 and T_4 are brought out for *nulling* purposes. Connection of an external potentiometer allows the quiescent collector currents of T_1 and T_2 to be varied in opposite directions.

Darlington transistor T_5 forms the second amplifier stage. It is operated in common-emitter mode using a constant current source as the load resistance. Capacitor C_k is used for frequency compensation. The capacitance value required will be discussed in greater detail in the next section.

Transistors T_6, T_7 form the output stage and operate as complementary emitter followers with low quiescent current (push-pull AB mode). This operating mode will be described in greater detail in connection with power amplifiers in Chapter 17.

We shall now estimate the differential gain of the circuit. In order to achieve low input currents, the input transistors are operated with a collector current of only 10 µA. Their transconductance g_{fE} is 0.4 mA/V at this current. As we saw in Section 4.8.1, the transconductance of a differential amplifier is half this value. Since the input transistors actually consist of pairs of transistors, the transconductance is halved yet again. However, this reduction is cancelled by current mirror T_3, T_4. The resulting transconductance for the input stage is therefore given by

$$g_D = \frac{\partial I_1}{\partial U_D}\bigg|_{U_1 = \text{const}} = \frac{I_C}{2U_T} = \frac{I_k}{4U_T} = 0.2 \, \frac{\text{mA}}{\text{V}} . \tag{7.25}$$

In order to calculate the operating gain of the input stage, we must take the resulting load resistance into account, in the same way as in Fig. 4.18. For the given quiescent currents, it has a value $r_{tot} = 2 \, \text{M}\Omega$ in accordance with the small-signal equivalent circuit in Fig. 7.19. We therefore obtain an operating gain of 400 for the input stage.

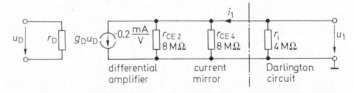

Fig. 7.19 Small-signal low-frequency equivalent circuit of the input stage

The transconductance g' of the Darlington stage is approximately 6 mA/V at $I'_C = 300\,\mu\text{A}$, in accordance with Section 4.7. For an output load of $R_L = 2\,\text{k}\Omega$, the small-signal equivalent circuit in Fig. 7.20 indicates an operating gain of 450 for the output stage.

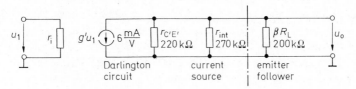

Fig. 7.20 Small-signal low-frequency equivalent circuit of the output stage

The total gain of the operational amplifier is therefore

$$A_D = 400 \cdot 450 = 1.8 \cdot 10^5 \ .$$

However, in practice lower values are obtained. The difference is due to the thermal feedback from the output stage to the input stage which cannot be neglected [7.1].

As we can see from Fig. 7.20, the output emitter follower is driven with a comparatively high signal source resistance, since the output resistance of the second amplifier stage appears as the signal source resistance. As shown in Fig. 7.20, it has a value of 120 kΩ. If the current gain of the output transistors is assumed to be 100, the output resistance of the amplifier is 1.2 kΩ.

FET operational amplifiers

The use of field effect transistors in the input differential amplifier of operational amplifiers has various advantages; the input bias current is reduced to the low gate leakage current. The drain current must be selected ten times larger than for bipolar transistors to obtain the same transconductance. As we shall see in the next section, this also increases the slew rate and large-signal bandwidth by a factor of 10. In addition, the input FETs have a higher cutoff frequency than the pnp transistors, which, in monolithic bipolar circuits, possess very poor characteristics. Consequently, the small-signal bandwidth is considerably greater.

There are three types of FET operational amplifiers:

1) Those with JFETs at the input (BIFET technology). These include the TL054.
2) Those with MOSFETs at the input (BIMOS technology). A typical example is the CA3160 from RCA.
3) Operational amplifiers consisting exclusively of MOSFETs (CMOS technology). One such range is the TLC series from Texas Instruments.

The most commonly used CMOS operational amplifier circuit is shown in Fig. 7.21. Transistors T_1 and T_2 form the input differential amplifier. The signal is fed via the current mirror T_3, T_4 to the second amplifier stage T_5 and to the source follower T_7. In this respect the circuit is identical to the bipolar amplifier in Fig. 7.18. The only difference is that here the negative output currents are generated by transistor T_6 operating in source configuration.

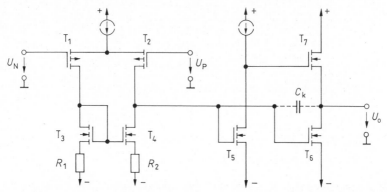

Fig. 7.21 CMOS operational amplifier of the TLC series. The substrates of the n-channel FETs are connected to the negative supply voltage, those of the p-channel FETs to the positive supply voltage

The magnitude of the quiescent currents determines the bandwidth and power dissipation of the circuit. They are all proportional to one another in the range 10 µA to 1 mA. Some types have a fixed quiescent current, while on others it can be changed via an additional terminal [7.2].

The problem with CMOS amplifiers lies in implementing an input differential amplifier having a low offset voltage and offset voltage drift. Good results have been obtained by the introduction of silicon gate technology [7.3].

7.7   Frequency compensation

7.7.1   Basic principles

Due to the parasitic capacitances and multistage construction, an operational amplifier behaves like a higher-order lowpass filter. If there is no compensating capacitance C_k, the typical frequency response of the differential gain $\underline{A}_D$ is as shown in Fig. 7.22. Above frequency f_1, the RC network with the lowest cutoff frequency determines the frequency response. The rolloff is 20 dB/decade and the phase shift between $\underline{U}_D$ and $\underline{U}_o$ is $\varphi = -90°$. The output voltage therefore lags the input voltage difference by 90°. Above f_2, a second lowpass filter also takes effect: the rolloff is now 40 dB/decade and the phase shift between $\underline{U}_D$ and $\underline{U}_o$ is $\varphi = -180°$. However, this means that the roles of the P and the N input are reversed, i.e. the negative feedback which always acts from the output on the inverting input becomes positive in this frequency range.

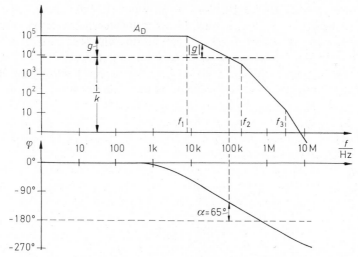

Fig. 7.22 Typical Bode diagram for the differential gain of an operational amplifier

Consequently, negative feedback amplifiers are prone to oscillate. In Section 15.1.1 we shall show that self-sustained oscillations will occur if there is a frequency at which the phase shift in the loop becomes zero (phase condition) and, simultaneously, the absolute value of the loop gain is $|g| = |\underline{k} \cdot \underline{A}_D| \geqq 1$ (amplitude condition), where k is the attenuation of the feedback circuit. For inverting and non-inverting amplifiers it is given by

$$k = \frac{R_1}{R_1 + R_N} ,$$

as is shown by the comparison of the two circuits in Figs. 7.23 and 7.24 for $U_i = 0$. From Eqs. (7.15) and (7.23) the relationship between k and A is given by

$$\frac{1}{k} \approx \begin{cases} A & \text{for the non-inverting amplifier} \\ 1 - A & \text{for the inverting amplifier ,} \end{cases}$$

A being the low-frequency limit value of the resultant gain in the case of negative feedback.

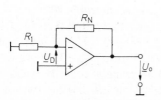

Fig. 7.23 Feedback factor for an inverting amplifier

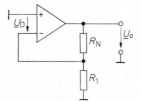

Fig. 7.24 Feedback factor for a non-inverting amplifier

In order to calculate component values for frequency compensation, the stability condition must be examined rather more closely. Complying with this condition simply avoids self-sustained oscillation. In practice, however, precise information about the transient response is also significant.

For this purpose, a critical frequency f_{crit} is defined as the frequency at which $|g|$ becomes unity, and we consider the phase shift of the loop gain at that frequency. If it is $-180°$, we have an undamped oscillation. If it is less than $180°$, a damped oscillation is obtained, because in this case the phase condition required for a self-sustained oscillation is only achieved at a frequency above f_{crit}. In this frequency range, however, $|g| < 1$ by definition for a lowpass system, i.e. only a damped oscillation occurs. An approximate measure of the damping can be given in the form of the *phase margin* α. This is the amount by which the phase shift is less than $-180°$ at the critical frequency:

$$\boxed{\alpha = 180° - |\varphi(f_{crit})|} \; . \tag{7.26}$$

The transient response for an input step function has been plotted in Fig. 7.25 for various values of α. For $\alpha = 90°$, an aperiodically damped transient response is obtained, whereas $\alpha = 65°$ produces an overshoot of 4%. At this value, a maximally flat frequency response of $|\underline{A}|$ is obtained (Butterworth characteristic). It is therefore frequently employed in practice. At smaller values of α, the step response is less damped, and the frequency response of $|\underline{A}|$ exhibits an increasing peak in the region of f_{crit}. At $\alpha = 0$, an undamped continuous oscillation occurs.

This allows us to obtain the damping characteristic of a negative feedback amplifier, for a given feedback factor k, directly from the Bode diagram of the open-looped amplifier. As an example, we have drawn the case $1/k = 8000$ in Fig. 7.22. Here $f_{crit} = 100 \, \text{kHz}$ and $\alpha = 65°$. Adequate damping is obtained for

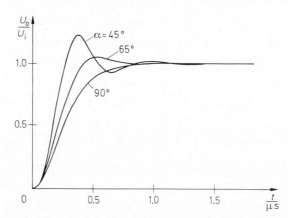

Fig. 7.25 Step response of an operational amplifier having negative feedback, for various phase margins (time scale for type LM301 as example)

this negative feedback. With tighter negative feedback, α rapidly decreases and reaches zero for $1/k = 300$.

7.7.2 General frequency compensation

If an amplifier is to be used as a general-purpose device, its phase shift must be less than $120°$ over the entire range in which $|\underline{A}_D| > 1$. This gives a phase margin of over $60°$ for any resistive feedback $0 \leq k \leq 1$. This condition can be satisfied, for example, by correcting the differential gain frequency response in such a way that its characteristic is the same as that of a first-order lowpass filter, in the range $|\underline{A}_D| > 1$. However, it is impossible to eliminate the unwanted parasitic lowpass filters having the cutoff frequencies f_2 and f_3 shown in Fig. 7.22. Consequently, the only remedy is to reduce the cutoff frequency f_1 of the first lowpass filter by means of an additional compensating capacitor C_k until the absolute value of $\underline{A}_D$ is less than 1, before the second lowpass filter takes effect.

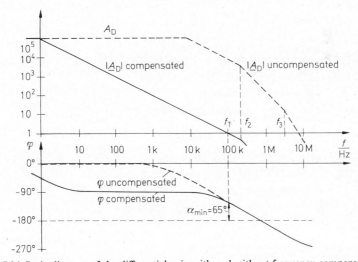

Fig. 7.26 Bode diagram of the differential gain with and without frequency compensation

This is shown in Fig. 7.26. We can see that in this case a phase margin of $\alpha = 65°$ is maintained even in the worst-case condition of full negative feedback ($k = 1$), whereas $90°$ is invariably obtained for weaker feedback. We can also see that the open-loop bandwidth is drastically reduced by the frequency compensation required.

By these measures of correction, the phase shift is increased to $90°$ at low frequencies, but is unaffected at high frequencies. There is therefore no compensation of the phase shift. For this reason, the frequently used term "phase compensation" is inappropriate for frequency compensation.

Implementation

We shall now examine how frequency compensation can be implemented and shall use the μA741 in Fig. 7.18 as an example. The circuit has two high-impedance points, namely the output of the differential amplifier and the output of the Darlington stage. We can assume that these points each possess a parasitic capacitance of about 10 pF to ground. In accordance with the equivalent circuit in Fig. 7.19, the differential amplifier output consequently forms a lowpass filter with a cutoff frequency of

$$f_1 = \frac{1}{2\pi[8\ \text{M}\Omega \| 8\ \text{M}\Omega \| 4\ \text{M}\Omega] \cdot 10\ \text{pF}} = 8\ \text{kHz} \ .$$

For the output-side lowpass filter of the Darlington stage we obtain, using the equivalent circuit in Fig. 7.20, a cutoff frequency of

$$f_2 = \frac{1}{2\pi[220\ \text{k}\Omega \| 270\ \text{k}\Omega \| 200\ \text{k}\Omega] \cdot 10\ \text{pF}} = 210\ \text{kHz} \ .$$

Due to the low gain-bandwidth product of the integrated pnp transistors, a third cutoff frequency is obtained:

$$f_3 \approx 3\ \text{MHz} \ .$$

Above this frequency, a number of other lowpass filters take effect. However, these can be disregarded in the following analysis.

In order to retain a phase margin of 65° at full negative feedback ($k = 1$), it is necessary to select a gain-bandwidth product (transit frequency) of

$$f_T \approx \tfrac{1}{2} f_2 \ .$$

This value has already been indicated in Fig. 7.26. In order to achieve the desired value for the transit frequency, it is necessary to lower the first cutoff frequency f_1 from 8 kHz to the value

$$f_{cA} = \frac{f_T}{A_D} = \frac{100\ \text{kHz}}{10^5} = 1\ \text{Hz} \ .$$

To achieve this, it would be necessary to insert a capacitor with $C_k = 80$ nF to ground at the output of the differential amplifier.

However, capacitances of this size cannot be integrated in monolithic circuits. A substantial reduction can be achieved by connecting the capacitor to the collector of the following amplifier stage instead of to ground, as shown in Fig. 7.18. This produces frequency-dependent voltage feedback in this stage (Miller integrator). In order to explain its effect, let us consider the equivalent circuit in Fig. 7.27. Due to the inverting negative feedback, the input of the Darlington stage becomes virtual ground at higher frequencies, and we obtain the output voltage

$$\underline{U}_o = \frac{g_D \underline{U}_D}{j\omega C_k} \ .$$

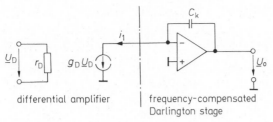

differential amplifier   frequency-compensated
                                      Darlington stage

Fig. 7.27 Small-signal equivalent circuit for frequency compensation by internal voltage feedback

Consequently

$$\underline{A}_D = \frac{U_o}{U_D} = \frac{g_D}{j\omega C_k} \ .$$ (7.27)

At the transit frequency f_T, $|\underline{A}_D|$ becomes unity as per definition. C_k is therefore given by

$$\boxed{C_k = \frac{g_D}{2\pi f_T}} \ .$$ (7.28)

where g_D is the transconductance of the input stage. Using the value $g_D = 0.2\,\mathrm{mA/V}$ and $f_T = 100\,\mathrm{Hz}$ given in the previous section, we obtain $C_k = 320\,\mathrm{pF}$ which is 250 times smaller than the value calculated above.

The voltage feedback of the second stage has yet another important advantage: the output resistance of this stage is reduced. This increases the cutoff frequency f_2 of its output-side lowpass filter from 200 kHz to over 10 MHz. The compensating capacitance C_k therefore decreases f_1 as well as increasing f_2. This separation of the cutoff frequencies is known as *pole splitting*.

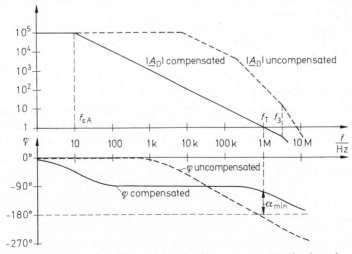

Fig. 7.28 Bode diagram of the differential gain for frequency compensation by pole splitting

Due to the raising of f_2 to values above f_3, the gain-bandwidth product can be increased to around f_3. With $f_T = 1$ MHz, the frequency response illustrated in Fig. 7.28 is obtained. The open-loop bandwidth increases to 10 Hz. To calculate C_k, we use Eq. (7.28) and obtain

$$C_k = \frac{0.2 \text{ mA/V}}{2\pi \cdot 1 \text{ MHz}} \approx 30 \text{ pF} \; .$$

This compensating capacitance is monolithically integrated in such devices as the μA 741.

7.7.3   Adapted frequency compensation

The general frequency compensation method described in the previous section ensures an adequate phase margin for any amount of resistive feedback. Its drawback, however, is that the bandwidth of the feedback circuit decreases in inverse proportion to the selected gain A in accordance with Eq. (7.14). This fact is also readily apparent from Fig. 7.29. For weaker feedback, however, only a correspondingly small reduction in the gain would be required for stabiliz-ation, as in this case the point $|\underline{g}| = 1$ is reached when $|\underline{A}_D| = 1/k > 1$. As we can see from Fig. 7.30, it is possible, for instance, to increase the open-loop bandwidth from 10 Hz to 100 Hz for $1/k = 10$, obtaining a bandwidth of 1 MHz as against 100 kHz for a feedback circuit with internal compensation. For this purpose, the compensating capacitance must be reduced from 30 pF to 3 pF.

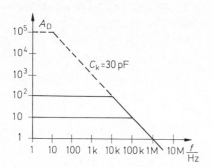

Fig. 7.29 Bandwidth as a function of the chosen gain with general frequency compensation

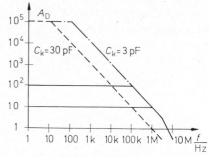

Fig. 7.30 Bandwidth as a function of the chosen gain with adapted frequency compensation

In order to provide adjustable frequency compensation of this kind, IC operational amplifiers are also available which contain no compensating capacitance, the appropriate terminals being brought out instead (e.g. μA748, TL080). Other versions are internally compensated, though with a reduced capacitance. For these amplifiers the minimum permissible gain $A_{\min}$ ensuring stability is always specified.

If gains of more than 10 are selected, the gain-bandwidth product cannot be increased by further reducing C_k, as the phase margin would be reduced due to the absence of pole splitting.

7.7.4 Slew rate

In addition to reducing the bandwidth, frequency compensation has yet another disadvantage: the rate of change of the output voltage (*slew rate*) is limited to a relatively low maximum value. It can be easily calculated from the equivalent circuit in Fig. 7.27. As we saw in Fig. 7.18, with the µA 741 the output current of the differential amplifier input stage is limited to a value of

$$I_{1\,max} = I_k = 20\,\mu A \ .$$

The slew rate is therefore given by

$$\left. \frac{dU_o}{dt} \right|_{max} = \frac{I_{1\,max}}{C_k} = \frac{I_k}{C_k} \ . \tag{7.29}$$

With $I_k = 20\,\mu A$ and $C_k = 30\,pF$, we get

$$\left. \frac{dU_o}{dt} \right|_{max} = 0.6\,V/\mu s \ .$$

Due to the limited slew rate, distortion is caused by rapid voltage changes which cannot be eliminated by negative feedback. This is known as transient inter-modulation (TIM).

We shall now calculate how high the frequency of a sinewave may be in order to just avoid transient intermodulation when the amplifier is driven to full output $\hat{U}_o = 10\,V$. The rate of change is maximum at the zero crossing and is given by

$$\left. \frac{dU_o}{dt} \right|_{max} = 2\pi f \hat{U}_o \ . \tag{7.30}$$

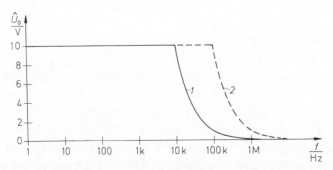

Fig. 7.31 Available output voltage swing versus frequency

Curve *1*: Slew rate: 0.6 V/µs (µA741, µA748 with $C_k = 30\,pF$)
Curve *2*: Slew rate: 6 V/µs (µA748 with $C_k = 3\,pF$, i.e. stability limit $A_{min} = 10$)

For a slew rate of 0.6 V/μs, this gives $f_{max} = 10\,kHz$, i.e. a value substantially lower than the small-signal bandwidth for heavy feedback. Equation (7.30) also indicates the permissible magnitude of the output voltage amplitude at frequencies above f_{max}. The curve is shown in Fig. 7.31 for $C_k = 30\,pF$ and $C_k = 3\,pF$. We can see that it is also advantageous in terms of slew rate to adjust the frequency compensation for gains higher than unity.

Improving the slew rate

In order to examine possible ways of improving the slew rate, it is first necessary to ascertain the amplifier characteristics which ultimately determine it. For this purpose we substitute Eq. (7.29) in Eq. (7.28) for the compensating capacitance and obtain

$$\left.\frac{dU_o}{dt}\right|_{max} = 2\pi f_T \frac{I_k}{g_D} \ . \tag{7.31}$$

For a given gain-bandwidth product f_T, the slew rate is greater the higher the current I_k for a given transconductance. However, with bipolar transistors the ratio I_k/g_D is constant, as the transconductance is also proportional to I_k. The ratio is given by Eq. (7.25) as

$$\frac{I_k}{g_D} = \frac{I_k}{I_k/4U_T} = 4\,U_T \approx 100\,mV \ .$$

It is possible to increase this ratio using current feedback, and this method is sometimes employed with wideband operational amplifiers. Its disadvantage, however, is that the offset voltage drift is greatly increased, as the feedback resistors cannot be matched with the required degree of accuracy.

In the case of operational amplifiers with FET input, the conditions are much more favorable. The lower transconductance of the FETs is now an advantage and produces a faster slew rate. FETs require an appreciably higher current to achieve the same transconductance as bipolar transistors. Thus, the differential amplifier in the TL081 has a transconductance $g_D = 0.3\,mA/V$ for

		Bipolar op amp		FET op amp	
		μA741	μA748 with $C_k = 3\,pF$	TL081	TL080 with $C_k = 3\,pF$
Stability limit	A_{min}	1	10	1	5
Gain-bandwidth product	f_T	1 MHz	10 MHz	3 MHz	12 MHz
Large-signal bandwidth		10 kHz	100 kHz	200 kHz	800 kHz
Slew rate		0.6 V/μs	6 V/μs	13 V/μs	50 V/μs

Fig. 7.32 Dynamic operational amplifier (op amp) data

a constant current of $I_k = 200\,\mu\text{A}$. Consequently, $I_k/g_D = 670\,\text{mV}$, i.e. more than six times larger than for bipolar transistors.

The p-channel FETs at the input of FET amplifiers offer yet another advantage: their gain-bandwidth product is considerably higher than that of lateral pnp transistors. The TL081 therefore has a gain-bandwidth product of $f_T = 3\,\text{MHz}$. Using Eq. (7.28), this gives a compensating capacitance of $C_k = 15\,\text{pF}$ and, from Eq. (7.29), a slew rate 13 V/μs. Thus, from Eq. (7.30) the large-signal bandwidth is 200 kHz as against 10 kHz for a standard type μA741 bipolar amplifier. A comparison of the dynamic characteristics of these operational amplifiers is given in Fig. 7.32.

7.7.5 Practical applications of operational amplifiers

Even internally compensated operational amplifiers may oscillate under certain operating conditions. This is usually due to positive feedback from the output stage to the input stage via the supply voltage sources. Even when regulated power supplies with low internal resistance are used, it is usually necessary to short-circuit high-frequency voltages directly at the amplifier as, in the MHz range, the supply leads may possess considerable inductive impedance. For this purpose ceramic capacitors between 10 nF and 220 nF are used.

Capacitive loading

If the output of an operational amplifier is capacitively loaded, the load combines with the output resistance to form a lowpass filter which introduces an additional phase lag. This reduces the phase margin, and the circuit will oscillate even with low load capacitances. This can be remedied (Fig. 7.33) by connecting a capacitor C_C in parallel with the feedback resistor. It produces a phase lead in the fed-back voltage at higher frequencies, allowing the phase lag caused by load capacitance C_L to be compensated in the region of the critical frequency. This method is known as *lead compensation*.

The effect of capacitor C_C can be increased by inserting a decoupling resistor R_C of 10 to 100 Ω, as shown in Fig. 7.33. Voltage $\underline{U}_1$, which leads output voltage $\underline{U}_o$, is therefore fed back via capacitor C_C.

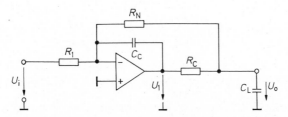

Fig. 7.33 Lead compensation for capacitive loading

Using partially compensated amplifiers

The slew rate and large-signal bandwidth of an operational amplifier can be considerably increased by using partially compensated amplifiers or amplifiers with corresponding external frequency compensation, such as the TL080. However, this is only possible in applications where gain values above the stability limit A_{min} are needed. If lower gains are required, an additional frequency compensation circuit must be inserted. This can be connected at the input of the operational amplifier as shown in Fig. 7.34. The advantage of this arrangement is that the slew rate and large-signal bandwidth of the partially compensated operational amplifier are retained.

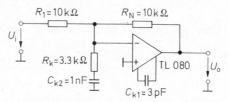

Fig. 7.34 Using a partially compensated amplifier for a gain less than A_{min}

In the circuit in Fig. 7.34, resistors R_k and R_1 combine to attenuate the fed-back signal by a factor of five. The condition $A_{min} = 5$ is thus achieved by attenuation in the feedback loop. Capacitor C_{k2} renders this attenuation ineffective for low frequencies to avoid an unnecessary reduction of the loop gain and zero stability.

Operation with a single supply voltage

Operational amplifiers are primarily designed to operate from a positive and a negative supply voltage source, this being the only way of achieving a bipolar common mode input voltage range and a bipolar output voltage swing. Often however, only a positive supply voltage is available, especially in battery-operated equipment or in digital circuits.

In such cases it is also possible to employ op amps if the operation is limited to a unipolar range. Figure 7.35 shows a voltage follower for positive voltages. The negative supply voltage terminal is at zero potential.

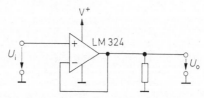

Fig. 7.35 Example of operating an operational amplifier from a single supply voltage source

$$U_o = U_i \quad \text{for} \quad 0 \leq U_i \leq V^+ - 1.5\,\text{V}$$

The absence of a negative amplitude range is acceptable in many cases, although it is essential that the exclusively positive amplitude range of this operating mode includes zero potential. However, with a standard amplifier, the common mode input voltage range and the maximum output voltage swing are only a few volts below the supply voltages. This means for the unipolar operating mode in Fig. 7.35 that the input and output signals must be at least some 2 V above zero potential, because the negative supply voltage is zero.

This limitation does not exist if we use an operational amplifier whose common-mode input voltage range extends to the value of the negative supply voltage. The table in Fig. 7.40 gives a number of examples.

The LM324 offers the added advantage that also the output voltage swing extends to the negative supply voltage if the load resistor (Fig. 7.35) is inserted to pull down the output. When using this type of op amp, the voltage follower in Fig. 7.35 operates in the range

$$0 \leqq U_i \leqq V^+ - 1.5 \text{ V} .$$

Operational amplifier input protection

The input voltages of an operational amplifier must not exceed the supply voltages. Otherwise, an internal diode is turned on and melts unless the current is limited to low values of approx. 10 mA. In the case of CMOS operational amplifiers, this limit is considerably lower (approx. 1 mA), as at this level a parasitic thyristor may be fired, short-circuiting the supply voltages. During normal operation, the risk of a signal exceeding the supply voltage is small, as there is generally no voltage higher than the supply voltage. However, the damage may occur when the supply voltage is switched off, if a capacitor is connected at the input of an amplifier as in Fig. 7.36. The worst-case condition therefore occurs when the capacitor is charged to around the supply voltage and the latter is then disconnected. The capacitor is then discharged via a diode in the operational amplifier. The resultant currents are higher the faster the supply voltage falls and the larger the capacitance. For capacitors of over 10 nF, it is therefore advisable to insert a protective resistor R_S between capacitance and

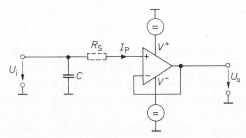

Fig. 7.36 Protecting an operation amplifier input with R_S when a capacitor is connected

input, as in Fig. 7.36. This resistor limits the current to innocuous values:

$$R_S = \frac{V^+}{I_{max}} = \frac{15\,V}{10\,mA} = 1.5\,k\Omega \; .$$

7.8 Measuring operational amplifier data

When determining the small-signal parameters of an operational amplifier, care must be taken not to overdrive the amplifier. Due to the very high voltage gain, this can only be achieved by providing negative feedback. The data of interest must therefore be obtained indirectly in the feedback mode [7.4].

Measurement of the differential gain

By way of example, Fig. 7.37 illustrates the basic arrangement for measuring the differential gain $\underline{A}_D$. The input amplitude is selected such that the output is not overdriven and that no transient intermodulation occurs at higher frequencies. The ratio

$$\underline{A}_D = -\frac{U_o}{U_N}$$

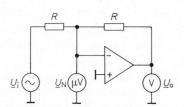

Fig. 7.37 Principle of differential gain
measurement

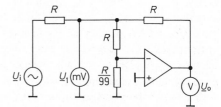

Fig. 7.38 Practical circuit for measuring the
differential gain

is measured. Due to the high gain, the amplitude $\hat{U}_N$ assumes very low values. In order to avoid the resultant measuring problems, the test setup can be modified as shown in Fig. 7.38. Due to the voltage divider at the N-input, voltage $\underline{U}_1$ assumes the value

$$\underline{U}_1 = 100\,\underline{U}_N$$

and is therefore considerably easier to measure. By varying the frequency, we can determine the frequency response of $\underline{A}_D$. For this purpose it is advisable to use an oscilloscope in order to ensure, at each frequency, that the amplifier is not overdriven. The phase shift can be measured at the same time using a high-resolution phase meter.

From the frequency response of the phase shift it is possible to obtain the phase margin for any gain. The phase margin can also be calculated for a specific value of A by oscillographing the step response of the corresponding feedback circuit and comparing it to Fig. 7.25.

Measuring the input bias current

In principle, the input bias current can be measured directly using an ammeter. However, particularly in the case of FET amplifiers, extremely sensitive special equipment would be required and it would also be necessary to shield the entire test setup from external interference.

This complexity can be obviated by using the sample amplifier itself as an impedance converter, as in Fig. 7.39. At the start of the measurement, switch S is open. The capacitor is then charged by the input bias current, and we obtain a linear voltage rise with time:

$$\frac{\Delta U_o}{\Delta t} = - \frac{I_{B^+}}{C} \; .$$

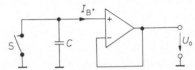

Fig. 7.39 Circuit for measuring the input bias current

This voltage change with time can be measured at the low-impedance amplifier output. Stray noise is averaged out by the capacitor whose value must be selected such that a voltage change of a few hundred mV is produced in a conveniently measurable time interval. For an input bias current of e.g. 30 pA, with $C = 1.5$ nF a voltage rise of 200 mV occurs in 10 s.

In order to minimize measuring errors due to leakage currents, the voltage across the capacitor must not be allowed to attain high values. In addition, capacitors with high insulation resistance must be used. Suitable types include high-performance styroflex capacitors or glass capacitors. If the dielectric is inadequate, the voltage rise over time is nonlinear, tending towards a finite limit value.

7.9   Survey of types available

The number of commercially available operational amplifiers is vast. In Fig. 7.40 we have attempted to select representative examples for every application. Many applications require not just a single operational amplifier but two, four or even more. In these cases, multiple op amps are particularly suitable because they lead to cheaper and more compact solutions. For this reason, we have given preference to dual and quad op amps in the types listed; single and dual types with the same characteristics are also available in many cases.

The general-purpose types are the least expensive and their data are adequate for many applications. The LM324 was one of the first quad op amps. Most subsequent types, many of which represent a marked improvement, have adopted its pin configuration, allowing direct interchangeability of most quad operational amplifiers.

Whereas the differential gain of the general-purpose types is around $A_D \approx 10^5$, that of the precision devices is considerably greater, as may be seen from Fig. 7.40. Consequently, they provide considerably higher loop gains $g = A_D/A$ and therefore smaller deviations from the ideal characteristic. In addition, the precision types have a much lower input offset voltage, thereby frequently obviating the need for nulling even in critical applications.

Operational amplifiers with low offset voltage drift are suitable for amplifying very small signals, such as those from thermocouples. They not only exhibit very small offset voltage drift, but also very low offset voltages. For this reason, it is possible to dispense with nulling, even for amplifying very small voltages. However, care must be taken to ensure that the wiring and soldered joints do not produce thermoelectric voltages which cancel out the excellent amplifier performance.

Types MAX400 to TSC916 are chopper-stabilized operational amplifiers using an additional op amp to perform automatic nulling of the main amplifier. The mode of operation is based on the principle illustrated in Fig. 16.17. In order to minimize the drift of the auxiliary amplifier, it alternately nulls itself and the main amplifier under the control of an internal oscillator, the offset voltages being stored in capacitors. With certain types, such as the MAX430 and TSC914, these capacitors are actually incorporated in the device.

The low-noise operational amplifiers are particularly suitable for amplifying very small signals. When using the types listed to design an amplifier with a bandwidth of 10 kHz, the calculations can be based on an input noise voltage of only 0.1 to 0.3 μV. The OPA2111 with FET input is particularly useful for high-impedance signal sources. Its input noise current is lower by a factor of about 1000 than that of bipolar types.

Some FET-input operational amplifiers employ FETs with exceptionally low gate leakage currents. These are particularly suitable for amplifying very high-impedance signals, such as are generated by pH-meter electrodes in chemical solutions. Once again, of course, the input currents double for every 10 degree temperature rise. Therefore, care must be taken to ensure that the op amps remain as cold as possible during operation and are not subject to additional heating due to high output currents.

For battery-operated equipment, operational amplifiers with particularly low current drain are available. However, this is achieved at the expense of a correspondingly low slew rate. On some types, the current drain can be adjusted externally, with the slew rate varying proportionally.

The low supply voltage types are likewise designed for battery operation. Their circuitry is so designed that the input voltage range (common-mode) and output voltage swing closely approach the positive and negative supply voltages respectively. This is necessary in order to enable these types to be usefully employed at low supply voltages. In the case of the NE5230, the input voltage range exceeds the supply voltage limits by as much as 250 mV. This is made possible by two complementary input differential amplifiers (similar to Fig. 16.9), one of which is operative when the other is in the OFF state [7.3]. A special feature of the LM10 is an additional 0.2 V reference voltage source.

The op amps for high voltages fall into two categories: the simple, inexpensive monolithics and the high-performance hybrid types. Using hybrid technology, it is possible to overcome the limitations of monolithic circuits without requiring appreciably more space. However, hybrid circuits are 5 to 10 times more expensive.

The high output current op amps incorporate a power output stage and, like power transistors, require effective cooling.

Some high bandwidth op amps have no internal frequency compensation for $A_{min} = 1$ in order not to sacrifice bandwidth at higher gain. They can also be operated below the specified value of A_{min}, but in this case external components are required to provide additional frequency compensation. In this respect, current-feedback types (see Section 16.7) are particularly useful, as their bandwidth is independent of the gain setting over a wide range. Types operating on this principle include the Elantec and Comlinear devices.

With wideband circuits, frequent use is made of signal lines having a defined surge impedance of 50 Ω to 100 Ω, the line ends being terminated with the surge impedance. In this case, the usual output loading capacity of 10 to 20 mA is generally insufficient to provide the required amplitude. Consequently, higher output current types are preferably employed.

Transimpedance amplifiers will be dealt with in more detail in Chapter 16 (wideband amplifiers).

Type	Manufacturer	Offset voltage	Input bias current	Slew rate	Op amps per package	Specialities
General-purpose types						
μA741	various	2 mV	100 nA	0.6 V/μs	1	obsolete
LF356	various	3 mV	3 pA	12 V/μs	1	up to 10 nF at output
LT1097	Lin. Techn.	10 μV	40 pA	0.2 V/μs	1	cheap, precision
LM324	various	2 mV	50 nA	0.6 V/μs	4	cheap
TL054	Texas Instr.	0.5 mV	5 pA	18 V/μs	4	FET-input
TLC274	Texas Instr.	3 mV	1 pA	5 V/μs	4	MOS-input
LF444	National	3 mV	5 pA	1 V/μs	4	FET-input
LF347	National	5 mV	25 pA	13 V/μs	4	FET-input
LMC660	National	1 mV	20 pA	1 V/μs	4	MOS-input
OP421	PMI	2 mV	5 nA	0.5 V/μs	4	Bipol-input
MC33179	Motorola	0.15 mV	100 nA	2 V/μs	4	Bipol-input
MC34084	Motorola	1 mV	60 pA	25 V/μs	4	FET-input
LT1079	Lin. Techn.	30 μV	50 pA	0.1 V/μs	4	Bipol-input
Precision types						
HA5147	Harris	10 μV	10 nA	35 V/μs	1	$A_D = 2 \cdot 10^6$
LM627	National	15 μV	3 nA	5 V/μs	1	$A_D = 5 \cdot 10^6$
OP177	PMI	10 μV	0.3 nA	0.3 V/μs	1	$A_D = 12 \cdot 10^6$
LT1028	Lin. Techn.	10 μV	25 nA	15 V/μs	1	$A_D = 30 \cdot 10^6$
OPA2111	Burr Brown	100 μV	2 pA	2 V/μs	2	$A_D = 2 \cdot 10^6$
OP227	PMI	40 μV	7 nA	3 V/μs	2	$A_D = 2 \cdot 10^6$
OP471	PMI	250 μV	7 nA	8 V/μs	4	$A_D = 1 \cdot 10^6$
OP470	PMI	100 μV	6 nA	2 V/μs	4	$A_D = 2 \cdot 10^6$
HA5134	Harris	25 μV		1 V/μs	4	$A_D = 2 \cdot 10^6$
OP400	PMI	40 μV	0.1 nA	0.15 V/μs	4	$A_D = 5 \cdot 10^6$
LT1014	Lin. Techn.	40 μV	0.15 nA	0.4 V/μs	4	$A_D = 8 \cdot 10^6$
Low noise						
AD9610*	Analog Dev.	300 μV	5 μA	3000 V/μs	1	$U_n = 0.7\,nV$, $I_n = 23$ pA[1]
LT1115	Lin. Techn.	50 μV	50 nA	15 V/μs	1	$U_n = 0.9\,nV$, $I_n = 1.2$ pA
HA5147	Harris	10 μV	10 nA	35 V/μs	1	$U_n = 3$ nV, $I_n = 0.4$ pA
HFA0002	Harris	500 μV	200 nA	250 V/μs	1	$U_n = 3$ nV, $I_n = 5$ pA
OP47	Raytheon	20 μV	10 nA	30 V/μs	1	$U_n = 3$ nV, $I_n = 0.4$ pA
OP227	PMI	40 μV	10 nA	3 V/μs	2	$U_n = 3$ nV, $I_n = 0.4$ pA
OP470	PMI	100 μV	6 nA	2 V/μs	4	$U_n = 3$ nV, $I_n = 0.4$ pA
LM837	National	300 μV	500 nA	10 V/μs	4	$U_n = 5$ nV, $I_n = 0.7$ pA
OPA627	Burr Brown	40 μV	8 pA	55 V/μs	1	$U_n = 5$ nV, $I_n = 1.6$ fA
OPA2111	Burr Brown	100 μV	2 pA	2 V/μs	2	$U_n = 6$ nV, $I_n = 0.8$ fA

* in hybrid technology   [1] noise voltage and noise current per $\sqrt{Hz}$ at 1 kHz

Fig. 7.40 Typical op amp data

Type	Manufacturer	Offset voltage	Input bias current	Slew rate	Op amps per package	Specialities

Low offset voltage

Type	Manufacturer	Offset voltage	Input bias current	Slew rate	Op amps per package	Specialities
LT1028	Lin. Techn	10 μV	25 nA	15 V/μs	1	$dU_O/d\vartheta = 0.1$ μV/K
HA5147	Harris	10 μV	10 nA	35 V/μs	1	$dU_O/d\vartheta = 0.2$ μV/K
HA5177	Harris	10 μV	2 nA	1 V/μs	1	$dU_O/d\vartheta = 0.1$ μV/K
OP177	PMI	10 μV	1.2 nA	0.3 V/μs	1	$dU_O/d\vartheta = 0.1$ μV/K
MAX400	Maxim	10 μV	0.7 nA	0.3 V/μs	2	$dU_O/d\vartheta = 0.2$ μV/K
AD708	Analog Dev.	10 μV	0.5 nA	0.3 V/μs	2	$dU_O/d\vartheta = 0.1$ μV/K
OP227	PMI	40 μV	10 nA	3 V/μs	2	$dU_O/d\vartheta = 0.3$ μV/K
OP400	PMI	40 μV	0.75 nA	0.15 V/μs	4	$dU_O/d\vartheta = 0.3$ μV/K
LT1014	Lin. Techn.	40 μV	15 nA	0.4 V/μs	4	$dU_O/d\vartheta = 0.3$ μV/K
LTC1050[2]	Lin. Techn.	0.5 μV	20 pA	4 V/μs	1	$dU_O/d\vartheta = 0.01$ μV/K
TLC2652[1]	Texas Instr.	0.5 μV	4 pA	3 V/μs	1	$dU_O/d\vartheta = 0.01$ μV/K
TSC915[1]	Teledyne	3 μV	30 pA	0.5 V/μs	1	$dU_O/d\vartheta = 0.01$ μV/K
MAX426[2]	Maxim	1 μV	0.2 pA	10 V/μs	1	$dU_O/d\vartheta = 0.01$ μV/K
MAX420[1]	Maxim	1 μV	15 pA	0.5 V/μs	1	$dU_O/d\vartheta = 0.02$ μV/K
ICL7650[1]	Intersil	2 μV	2 pA	2.5 V/μs	1	$dU_O/d\vartheta = 0.1$ μV/K
LTC1052[2]	Lin. Techn.	0.5 μV	20 pA	4 V/μs	2	$dU_O/d\vartheta = 0.01$ μV/K
LTC1054[2]	Lin. Techn.	0.5 μV	20 pA	4 V/μs	4	$dU_O/d\vartheta = 0.01$ μV/K
TSC914[2]	Teledyne	5 μV	30 pA	2.5 V/μs	4	$dU_O/d\vartheta = 0.05$ μV/K

Low input current

Type	Manufacturer	Offset voltage	Input bias current	Slew rate	Op amps per package	Specialities
AD549	Analog Dev.	0.3 mV	40 fA	3 V/μs	1	$U_n = 35$ nV, $I_n = 0.1$ fA
OPA128	Burr Brown	0.2 mV	75 fA	3 V/μs	1	$U_n = 27$ nV, $I_n = 0.1$ fA
OP80	PMI	0.4 mV	200 fA	0.4 V/μs	1	$U_n = 70$ nV

Low supply current

Type	Manufacturer	Offset voltage	Input bias current	Slew rate	Op amps per package	Specialities
TCL25L4	Texas Instr.	1 mV	1 pA	10 V/ms	4	$I_b = 10$ μA/amp
LT1179	Lin. Techn.	0.1 mV	200 pA	40 V/ms	4	$I_b = 15$ μA/amp
OP490	PMI	0.2 mV	4 nA	12 V/ms	4	$I_b = 20$ μA/amp
LP324	National	1 mV	1 nA	50 V/ms	4	$I_b = 25$ μA/amp
LPC660	National	1 mV	40 fA		4	$I_b = 40$ μA/amp
HA5144	Harris	0.5 mV	45 nA	1000 V/ms	4	$I_b = 50$ μA/amp
TL034	Texas Instr.	0.6 mV	3 pA	3500 V/ms	4	$I_b = 200$ μA/amp
MC34184	Motorola	1 mV	60 pA	10000 V/ms	4	$I_b = 250$ μA/amp

Low supply voltage

Type	Manufacturer	Offset voltage	Input bias current	Slew rate	Op amps per package	Specialities
LM10	National	0.3 mV	10 nA	100 V/ms	1	$U_b \geq 1.1$ V
TLC254	Texas Instr.	1 mV	1 pA	10 V/ms	4	$U_b \geq \pm 0.5$ V
OP490	PMI	0.2 mV	4 nA	12 V/ms	4	$U_b \geq \pm 0.8$ V
NE5234	Valvo	0.2 mV	90 nA	800 V/ms	4	$U_b \geq \pm 0.9$ V
LT1179	Lin. Techn.	0.1 mV	200 pA	40 V/ms	4	$U_b \geq \pm 0.9$ V
LT1012	Lin. Techn.	10 μV	30 pA	200 V/ms	1	$U_b \geq \pm 1.2$ V

[1] Chopper-stabilized amplifier, capacitors external

[2] Chopper-stabilized amplifier, capacitors on chip

Fig. 7.40 Typical op amp data (*continued*)

Type	Manufacturer	Offset voltage	Input bias current	Slew rate	Op amps per package	Specialities
High output voltage						
LM343	National	2 mV	8 nA	2.5 V/μs	1	$I_o = $ 15 mA, $U_o = \pm 30$ V
HA2645	Harris	2 mV	12 nA	2.5 V/μs	1	$I_o = $ 15 mA, $U_o = \pm 35$ V
OPA445	Burr Brown	0.5 mV	20 pA	10 V/μs	1	$I_o = $ 15 mA, $U_o = \pm 35$ V
1480*	Philbrick	1 mV	50 pA	100 V/μs	1	$I_o = 100$ mA, $U_o = \pm 140$ V
PA85*	Apex	0.5 mV	5 pA	1000 V/μs	1	$I_o = 200$ mA, $U_o = \pm 225$ V
PA89*	Apex	0.5 mV	5 pA	30 V/μs	1	$I_o = $ 75 mA, $U_o = \pm 500$ V
High output current						
TCA365	Siemens	1 mV	100 nA	5 V/μs	1	$I_o = $ 2.5 A, $U_o = \pm 13$ V
L465	SGS	2 mV	300 nA	14 V/μs	1	$I_o = $ 2.5 A, $U_o = \pm 16$ V
ULN3753	Sprague	1 mV	80 nA	10 V/μs	2	$I_o = $ 2.5 A, $U_o = \pm 16$ V
LM675	National	1 mV	200 nA	8 V/μs	1	$I_o = $ 3 A, $U_o = \pm 20$ V
OPA541	Burr Brown	2 mV	4 pA	10 V/μs	1	$I_o = $ 5 A, $U_o = \pm 35$ V
OPA2541	Burr Brown	2 mV	4 pA	10 V/μs	2	$I_o = $ 5 A, $U_o = \pm 35$ V
OPA512*	Burr Brown	2 mV	12 nA	4 V/μs	1	$I_o = 10$ A, $U_o = \pm 40$ V
LM12	National	2 mV	150 nA	9 V/μs	1	$I_o = 10$ A, $U_o = \pm 35$ V
PA04*	Apex	5 mV	10 pA	50 V/μs	1	$I_o = 20$ A, $U_o = \pm 90$ V
PA03*	Apex	1 mV	10 pA	10 V/μs	1	$I_o = 30$ A, $U_o = \pm 65$ V

*in hybrid technology

Fig. 7.40 Typical op amp data (*continued*)

Type	Manufacturer	Offset voltage	Input bias current	Slew rate	Op amps per package	Specialities

Large bandwidth

Type	Manufacturer	Offset voltage	Input bias current	Slew rate	Op amps per package	Specialities
LM6313	National	5 mV	2 μA	250 V/μs	1	$I_o = 300$ mA, $f_P =$ 4 MHₓ
LM6365	National	1 mV	2.5 μA	300 V/μs	1	$I_o = 20$ mA, $f_P =$ 5 MHₓ
HA2541	Harris	1 mV	6 μA	300 V/μs	1	$I_o = 20$ mA, $f_P =$ 4 MHₓ
HA2542	Harris	3 mV	25 μA	350 V/μs	1	$I_o = 100$ mA, $f_P =$ 5 MHₓ
EL2423	Elantec	1 mV	1 μA	350 V/μs	4	$I_o = 50$ mA $f_P =$ 5 MHₓ
AD840	Analog Dev.	1 mV	5 μA	400 V/μs	1	$I_o = 50$ mA, $f_P =$ 6 MHₓ
OPA621	Burr Brown	0.2 mV	18 μA	500 V/μs	1	$I_o = 150$ mA, $f_P =$ 8 MHₓ
OP260[1]	PMI	1 mV	1 μA	550 V/μs	2	$I_o = 50$ mA, $f_P =$ 9 MHₓ
HFA0005	Harris	6 mV	15 μA	600 V/μs	1	$I_o = 50$ mA, $f_P =$ 25 MHₓ
EL2020[1]	Elantec	3 mV	5 μA	600 V/μs	1	$I_o = 33$ mA, $f_P =$ 8 MHₐ
EL2232[1]	Elantec	3 mV	5 μA	600 V/μs	2	$I_o = 33$ mA, $f_P =$ 8 MHₐ
EL2029	Elantec	0.2 mV	0.3 nA	900 V/μs	1	$I_o = 50$ mA $f_P =$ 10 MHₓ
PA19*	Apex	0.5 mV	10 pA	900 V/μs	1	$I_o = 2$ A, $f_P =$ 3 MHₐ
OPA603[1]	Burr Brown	3 mV	3 μA	1000 V/μs	1	$I_o = 150$ mA, $f_P =$ 8 MHₐ
EL2038	Elantec	0.5 mV	5 μA	1000 V/μs	1	$I_o = 50$ mA, $f_P =$ 16 MHₓ
HFA0001	Harris	1 mV	15 μA	1000 V/μs	1	$I_o = 50$ mA, $f_P =$ 43 MHz
CLC400[1]	Comlinear	2 mV	10 μA	1600 V/μs	1	$I_o = 50$ mA, $f_P =$ 30 MHz
AD844[1]	Analog Dev.	0.1 mV	0.2 μA	2000 V/μs	1	$I_o = 50$ mA, $f_P =$ 32 MHz
EL2030[1]	Elantec	1 mV	5 μA	2000 V/μs	1	$I_o = 100$ mA, $f_P =$ 30 MHz
CLC404[1]	Comlinear	2 mV	15 μA	2500 V/μs	1	$I_o = 100$ mA, $f_P =$ 150 MHz
AD9610*[1]	Analog Dev.	0.3 mV	5 μA	3000 V/μs	1	$I_o = 50$ mA, $f_P =$ 50 MHz
CLC206*[1]	Comlinear	4 mV	4 μA	3400 V/μs	1	$I_o = 100$ mA, $f_P =$ 60 MHz
WA01*[1]	Apex	5 mV	10 μA	4000 V/μs	1	$I_o = 400$ mA, $f_P =$ 40 MHz
CLC203*[1]	Comlinear	0.5 mV	5 μA	6000 V/μs	1	$I_o = 200$ mA, $f_P =$ 60 MHz

* in hybrid technology   [1] transimpedance amplifier

[2] $f_P = (dU/dt)/(\pi U_{oSS}) =$ bandwidth at full output swing (= power bandwidth)

Fig. 7.40 Typical op amp data (*continued*)

8   Latching circuits

8.1   The transistor as a digital component

In the case of the linear circuits, we set the collector quiescent potential between V^+ and $U_{CE\,sat}$, thus enabling them to be driven about this operating point. The characteristic feature of the linear circuits is that the swing is kept so small that the output voltage is a linear function of the input voltage. Consequently, the output voltage must not attain the positive or negative limits of the swing, as this would result in distortion. With *digital* circuits, on the other hand, only two operating states are employed. We are only interested in whether a voltage is greater than a specified value U_H or less than a specified value $U_L < U_H$. If the voltage exceeds U_H, it is referred to as being in the H (high) state, and if it is below U_L, it is said to be in the L (low) state.

The absolute values of levels U_H and U_L depend entirely on the circuit design. For an unambiguous interpretation, steady state levels between U_H and U_L must not occur. The circuit design implications of this will now be discussed with reference to the level inverter in Fig. 8.1. The circuit must exhibit the following characteristics:

$$\text{For } U_i \leqq U_L \rightarrow U_o \geqq U_H$$

and

$$\text{for } U_i \geqq U_H \rightarrow U_o \leqq U_L \ .$$

This relationship must hold good even under worst case conditions; i.e. for $U_i = U_L$, U_o must not be lower than U_H, and for $U_i = U_H$, U_o must not be higher than U_L. This condition can only be satisfied by selecting suitable values for U_H, U_L and R_C and R_B. The following worked example should serve to indicate a possible approach:

When the transistor in Fig. 8.1 is turned off, the output voltage under no-load conditions is equal to V^+. Let us assume that the lowest output load resistance is $R_V = R_C$; in this case U_o is consequently equal to $\frac{1}{2}V^+$. This is therefore the lowest output voltage in the H state. To be on the safe side, we specify $U_H < \frac{1}{2}V^+$ for a supply voltage of $V^+ = 5$ V, e.g. $U_H = 1.5$ V. In accordance with the abovementioned requirement, the input voltage must be in state L for $U_o \geqq U_H$. U_L is therefore defined as the highest input voltage for which the transistor is just sure to remain in the blocking state. For a silicon transistor, we can therefore take a value of 0.4 V if the device is at ambient temperature. Consequently, we select $U_L = 0.4$ V. Having determined the two levels U_H and U_L in this way, we must now select component values for the circuit in such a way that an output voltage $U_o \leqq U_L$ is obtained for $U_i = U_H$. Even under worst case conditions we require a certain safety margin, namely that the output

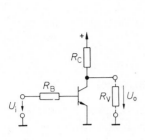

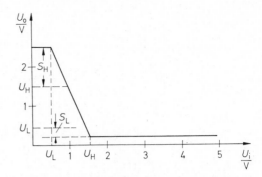

Fig. 8.1 Transistor as inverter

Fig. 8.2 Transfer characteristic for $R_V = R_C$.

S_L: L noise margin. S_H: H noise margin

voltage shall remain below $U_L = 0.4$ V for $U_i = U_H = 1.5$ V. The collector resistance R_C is chosen low enough to ensure that the switching times are sufficiently short, but without making the current drain unnecessarily high. We typically select $R_C = 5$ kΩ. We must now select a value for R_B which ensures that the output voltage falls below the value $U_L = 0.4$ V for an input voltage of $U_i = 1.5$ V. For this to occur, a collector current of $I_C \approx V^+/R_C = 1$ mA has to flow. Transistors for this kind of application normally have a current gain of $B = 100$. The base current required is therefore $I_{B\,min} = I_C/B = 10$ μA. In order to ensure that the transistor is driven into saturation, we select $I_B = 100$ μA, i.e. it is 10 times overdriven. We thus obtain

$$R_B = \frac{1.5\,\text{V} - 0.6\,\text{V}}{100\,\mu\text{A}} = 9\,\text{k}\Omega \ .$$

Figure 8.2 shows the transfer characteristic for these parameters.

For $U_i = U_L = 0.4$ V, the output voltage $U_o = 2.5$ V at full load ($R_V = R_C$) and is therefore 1 V above the minimum value $U_H = 1.5$ V required. We now specify an H noise margin $S_H = U_o - U_H$ for $U_i = U_L$. In our example it is 1 V. Similarly, we can define an L noise margin $S_L = U_L - U_o$ for $U_i = U_H$. In Fig. 8.1 it is identical to the voltage difference between U_L and the collector-emitter saturation voltage $U_{CE\,sat} \approx 0.2$ V and has a value of $S_L = 0.4$ V $- 0.2$ V $= 0.2$ V. The noise margins are a measure of circuit performance reliability. Their general definition is:

$$\left.\begin{array}{l} S_H = U_o - U_H \\ S_L = U_L - U_o \end{array}\right\} \quad \text{for worst-case condition at input} \ .$$

If we wish to improve the L noise margin, it is necessary to increase U_L, as voltage $U_o(U_i = U_H) \approx U_{CE\,sat}$ cannot be reduced much further. For this purpose, we can insert one or more diodes in front of the base, as in Fig. 8.3a. Resistor R_2 serves as a drain for the collector-base reverse current, thereby ensuring that the transistor turns off reliably. Another possibility is to simply insert a preceding voltage divider, as shown in Figs. 8.3b or 8.3c.

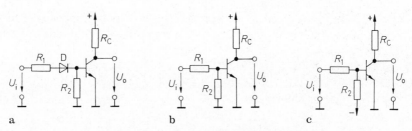

a   b   c

Fig. 8.3a–c Methods of improving the L noise margin

The output loading capability (fan-out) of the inverter in Fig. 8.1 is low. No more than two identical inputs can be connected to one output, otherwise the output voltage would fall below 2.5 V in the H state.

Dynamic characteristics

When using a transistor as a switch, the main parameter of interest is the switching time. Within the square-wave response we differentiate between various periods, as shown in Fig. 8.4.

We can see that the storage time t_S is considerably greater than the other switching times. It is incurred when a previously saturated transistor ($U_{CE} = U_{CEsat}$) is turned off. If, for the conducting transistor, U_{CE} is greater than U_{CEsat}, the storage time is considerably reduced. We exploit this fact in high-speed switches and prevent U_{CEsat} from being reached. Digital circuits operating on this principle are known as *unsaturated logic*. Their design will be discussed for the relevant circuits in Section 9.4.5.

The time behavior of digital circuits is generally characterized by the propagation delay time t_{pd}:

$$t_{pd} = \tfrac{1}{2}(t_{pdL} + t_{pdH})$$

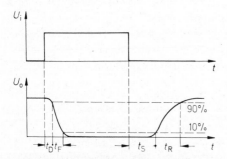

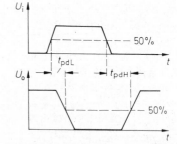

Fig. 8.4 Square-wave response of inverter

    t_S: Storage time
    t_R: Rise time
    t_D: Delay time
    t_F: Fall time

Fig. 8.5 Defining the propagation delay time

where $t_{pd\,L}$ is the time difference between the 50% value of the input edge and the 50% value of the falling output edge. $t_{pd\,H}$ is the corresponding time difference for the rising output edge. This is illustrated in Fig. 8.5.

In the circuit in Fig. 8.1 we saw that the H level was well below the supply voltage and was a function of the load. In order to avoid this, an emitter follower can be connected as shown in Fig. 8.6.

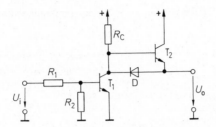

Fig. 8.6 Push-pull output stage for digital circuits

If T_1 is off, the output current flows via emitter follower T_2, thus keeping the current in collector resistor R_C low. If T_1 becomes conducting, its collector potential falls to low levels. With a resistive output load, the output voltage likewise falls. With capacitive loading, the circuit must pick up the capacitor discharge current. As transistor T_2 is blocking in this case, diode D is inserted to allow the discharge current to flow via conducting transistor T_1. However, this increases the output voltage to about 0.8 V in the L state.

8.2   Latching circuits using saturated transistors

Latching circuits are positive-feedback digital circuits. They differ from positive-feedback linear circuits (oscillators) in that their output voltage does not vary continuously but only jumps back and forth between two fixed values. This *switching process* can be initiated in various ways: in the case of *bistable* circuits, the output state only changes when switching is initiated by an input signal. With a *flip-flop* (latch), a short pulse suffices, whereas a *Schmitt trigger* requires a sustained input signal.

A *monostable* circuit has a *single* stable state. Its other state is only stable for a fixed length of time determined by the circuit component values. When this time has elapsed, the circuit automatically returns to the stable state. It is therefore also known as a time switch, monostable multivibrator or one-shot.

An *astable* circuit has no stable state, but constantly oscillates between states without external triggering. It is therefore known also as a multivibrator.

The three types of circuit can be implemented using the basic configuration shown in Fig. 8.7. The only difference is in the nature of the two coupling devices C, as listed in Fig. 8.8.

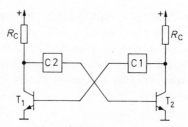

Fig. 8.7 Basic latching configuration using saturated transistors

Type	Name	Coupling device 1	Coupling device 2
Bistable	Flip-flop, Schmitt trigger	R	R
Monostable	One-shot	R	C
Astable	Multivibrator	C	C

Fig. 8.8 Coupling networks required for the various types of latching circuit

8.2.1   Bistable circuits

Flip-flop

As shown in Fig. 8.9, a bistable circuit can be implemented by connecting two inverters in series and providing positive feedback. We can see that the two inverters have equal status, and so the symmetrical circuit diagram given in Fig. 8.10 is generally preferred.

The mode of operation is as follows: a positive voltage at the set input S renders T_1 conducting. This causes its collector potential to fall, thereby reducing the base current of T_2 whose collector potential increases. This increase causes the base current of T_1 to rise via resistor R_1. The steady-state condition is therefore reached when the collector potential of T_1 has fallen to the saturation voltage. T_2 then turns off and T_1 is maintained ON via resistor R_1. Consequently, the voltage at the S-input can be made zero again at the end of

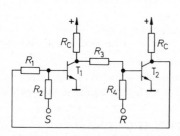

Fig. 8.9 Positive-feedback circuit comprising two inverters

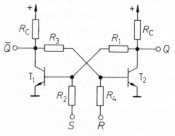

Fig. 8.10 *RS* flip-flop

the switching process without inducing any further changes. The flip-flop can be returned to its original state by applying a positive voltage pulse to the reset input R. When the two input voltages are zero, the flip-flop retains the last state assumed. This characteristic allows it to be used as a data *memory*.

If the two input voltages are simultaneously changed to the H state, both transistors become conducting during this time. However, in this case the base currents are supplied only by the control voltage sources and not by the adjacent transistor, as the two collector potentials are low. Consequently, this state is not stable. If the two control voltages are again made zero, this causes the two collector potentials to rise simultaneously. However, as there is never complete symmetry, one collector potential rises somewhat faster than the other. Due to the positive feedback, this difference is amplified so that a stable state is eventually reached in which one transistor is OFF and the other is ON. However, as it is impossible to predict definitively which of the two stable states the flip-flop will assume, the input state $R = S = $ H is logically impermissible. If it is avoided, the output states are always complementary. This process is summarized by the truth table in Fig. 8.11.

R	S	Q	$\bar{Q}$
H	H	(L)	(L)
H	L	L	H
L	H	H	L
L	L	as before	

Fig. 8.11 Truth table for RS flip-flop

Schmitt trigger

The RS flip-flop described above is caused to change state by applying a positive voltage pulse to the base of the currently nonconducting transistor in order to turn it on. Another possibility consists of only using one input voltage and initiating the process by making the input voltage alternately positive and negative. A flip-flop operated in this way is known as a *Schmitt trigger*. Its simplest circuit is shown in Fig. 8.12.

When the input voltage exceeds the upper trigger threshold $U_{i\,ON}$, the output voltage jumps to the positive saturation limit $U_{o\,max}$. It only returns to zero when the input voltage falls below the lower trigger threshold $U_{i\,OFF}$. This characteristic allows the Schmitt trigger to be used as a square-wave generator. By way of example, Fig. 8.14 shows how a sine wave is converted into a square wave. Due to positive feedback, the change from one state to the other is instantaneous, even though the input voltage changes only slowly.

The transfer characteristic is illustrated in Fig. 8.13. The voltage difference between the turn-on and turn-off levels is termed the *hysteresis*. This is smaller

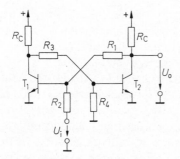

Fig. 8.12 Schmitt trigger

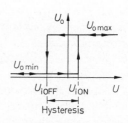

Fig. 8.13 Transfer characteristic of Schmitt trigger

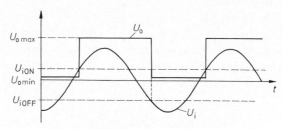

Fig. 8.14 Schmitt trigger as square-wave generator

the more the difference between $U_{o\,max}$ and $U_{o\,min}$ is reduced, or the greater the attenuation in voltage divider R_1, R_2. Any attempt to reduce the hysteresis will adversely affect the positive feedback in the Schmitt trigger and could result in it ceasing to be bistable. For $R_1 \to \infty$, the circuit becomes a conventional two-stage amplifier.

8.2.2   Monostable circuits

A one-shot is basically an RS flip-flop in which one of the two feedback resistors is replaced by a capacitor, as shown in Fig. 8.15. As the capacitor blocks DC, transistor T_2 is ON and transistor T_1 is OFF under steady-state conditions.

A positive input pulse turns on transistor T_1, causing its collector potential to jump from its steady-state value V^+ to zero. This jump is transmitted by high-pass filter network RC to the base of T_2, causing its base potential to go from 0.6 V to $-V^+ + 0.6$ V $\approx -V^+$, and T_2 turns off. T_1 is maintained ON via feedback resistor R_1, even if the input voltage has already returned to zero.

Capacitor C is charged via resistor R connected to V^+. As described in Chapter 2, the base potential of T_2 increases in accordance with the relation

$$V_{B2}(t) \approx V^+(1 - 2e^{-t/RC}) . \tag{8.1}$$

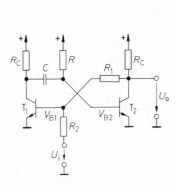

Fig. 8.15 One-shot

Turn-on time: $t_{ON} = RC \ln 2$

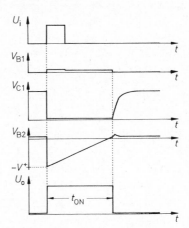

Fig. 8.16 Voltage waveforms

Transistor T_2 remains in the blocking state until V_{B2} has risen to approximately $+0.6$ V. We can obtain the time t_{ON} required for this by substituting $V_{B2} \approx 0$ in Eq. (8.1), giving

$$t_{ON} \approx RC \ln 2 \approx 0.7\, RC \ . \tag{8.2}$$

When this time has elapsed, transistor T_2 begins to conduct once more, i.e. the circuit flips back to its stable state. Figure 8.16 shows the relevant voltage waveforms.

The output returns to its initial state within the defined turn-on time even if the input pulse is longer than the turn-on time. In this case transistor T_1 remains ON until the input pulse disappears, and the positive feedback has no effect. T_2 does not therefore begin to conduct instantaneously, but only in accordance with the rate of rise of V_{B2}.

When the switching cycle is complete, capacitor C must be charged via R_C. If the capacitor is not fully charged until the next turn-on pulse occurs, the subsequent turn-on time is reduced. If this is to affect the turn-on time by less than 1%, T_1 must remain OFF for a recovery time of at least $5R_C \cdot C$.

The supply voltage of the circuit should not rise above 5 V, as this could cause the emitter-base breakdown voltage of T_2 to be exceeded when T_1 becomes conducting. This effect would reduce the turn-on time as a function of the supply voltage.

8.2.3 Astable circuit (multivibrator)

If the second feedback resistor of a one-shot is also replaced by a capacitor, as in Fig. 8.17, the two states are each stable only for a limited period of time. The circuit therefore continuously oscillates between the two states once it is triggered (multivibrator). From Eq. (8.2), the switching times are given by

$$t_1 = R_1 C_1 \ln 2$$

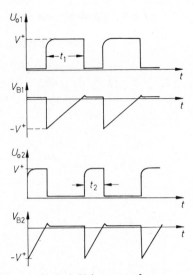

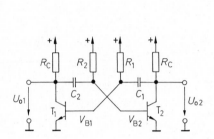

Fig. 8.17 Multivibrator

Fig. 8.18 Voltage waveforms

Switching times: $t_1 = R_1 C_1 \ln 2$
$$t_2 = R_2 C_2 \ln 2$$

and

$$t_2 = R_2 C_2 \ln 2 \ .$$

The voltage waveforms are shown in Fig. 8.18. As we can see, t_1 is the OFF-time of T_1 and t_2 the OFF-time of T_2. The circuit therefore always changes state when the hitherto nonconducting transistor is turned on.

The circuit designer has little latitude in selecting the values of resistors R_1 and R_2. On the one hand, they must be small compared to βR_C so that sufficient current flows through them to drive the conducting transistor into saturation. On the other hand, they must be large compared to R_C so that the capacitors can be charged up to the supply voltage. This condition can be expressed as

$$R_C \ll R_1 \ , \quad R_2 \ll \beta R_C \ .$$

As with the one-shot in Fig. 8.15, the supply voltage must not be selected larger than 5 V in order not to exceed the emitter-base breakdown voltage.

It is possible that the multivibrator in Fig. 8.17 will not start oscillating. For example, if one output is short-circuited, both transistors go into saturation, and this condition continues to obtain even when the short circuit is removed.

At frequencies below 100 Hz, the capacitors are unwieldy and large, and at frequencies above 10 kHz, the switching times of the transistors become a noticeable problem. Consequently, the circuit in Fig. 8.17 is of little practical use. The precision circuits with comparators (Section 8.5.3) are preferable for low-frequency applications, whereas the emitter-coupled multivibrators in Section 8.3.2 tend to be used for high-frequency applications.

8.3   Latching circuits with emitter-coupled transistors

8.3.1   Emitter-coupled Schmitt trigger

A non-inverting amplifier can also be implemented by using a differential amplifier. By applying positive feedback through a resistive voltage divider, we obtain the emitter-coupled Schmitt trigger shown in Fig. 8.19. Both of its trigger thresholds are positive.

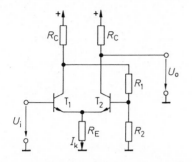
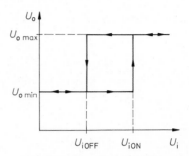

Fig. 8.19 Emitter-coupled Schmitt trigger   Fig. 8.20 Transfer characteristic

By selecting suitable component values for the circuit, we can cause current I_k to switch from one transistor to the other when the circuit changes state, without the transistors becoming saturated. This eliminates the storage time t_S during switchover, and very high switching frequencies can be achieved. This principle is known as "unsaturated logic".

8.3.2   Emitter-coupled multivibrator

Due to the elimination of the storage times, considerably higher frequencies can be achieved with emitter-coupled multivibrators than using saturated transistors. A suitable circuit is shown in Fig. 8.21.

To explain how the circuit operates, let us assume that the amplitude of the AC voltages present is small at all points in the circuit, say $U_{pp} \approx 0.5$ V. When T_1 is OFF, its collector potential is virtually equal to the supply voltage, resulting in an emitter potential of $V^+ - 1.2$ V at T_2. Its emitter current is $I_1 + I_2$. In order to produce the required amplitude of oscillation at R_1, the value $R_1 = 0.5 \text{ V}/(I_1 + I_2)$ must therefore be selected. This gives us an emitter potential of $V^+ - 1.1$ V at T_4 under this operating condition. As long as T_1 is OFF, the current from the left current source flows via capacitor C, causing the emitter potential of T_1 to fall at a rate of

$$\frac{\Delta V_{E1}}{\Delta t} = -\frac{I_1}{C} .$$

T_1 begins to conduct when its emitter potential has fallen to $V^+ - 1.7$ V. The

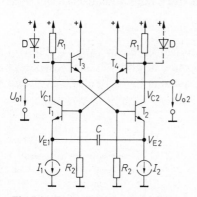

Fig. 8.21 Emitter-coupled multivibrator

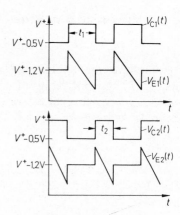

Fig. 8.22 Voltage waveforms

base potential of T_2 then falls by 0.5 V, turning the device off, and its collector potential rises to V^+. The base potential of T_1 rises with it via emitter follower T_4, causing the emitter potential of T_1 to jump to $V^+ - 1.2$ V. This step is transferred via capacitor C to the emitter of T_2, producing a potential increase from $V^+ - 1.2$ V to $V^+ - 0.7$ V across this device.

During the OFF-time of T_2, current I_2 flows via capacitor C and causes the emitter potential of T_2 to fall at a rate of

$$\frac{\Delta V_{E2}}{\Delta t} = -\frac{I_2}{C} .$$

Transistor T_2 remains OFF until its emitter potential has fallen from $V^+ - 0.7$ V to $V^+ - 1.7$ V, giving a switching time of

$$t_2 = \frac{1\,\text{V} \cdot C}{I_2} \quad \text{or, more generally,} \quad t_2 = 2\left(1 + \frac{I_1}{I_2}\right) R_1 C . \tag{8.3}$$

Similarly, we obtain

$$t_1 = \frac{1\,\text{V} \cdot C}{I_1} \quad \text{or, more generally,} \quad t_1 = 2\left(1 + \frac{I_2}{I_1}\right) R_1 C . \tag{8.4}$$

The voltage waveforms for the circuit are shown in Fig. 8.22. We can see that by selecting $U_{pp} = 0.5$ V, none of the transistors is driven into saturation. This circuit allows frequencies of more than 100 MHz to be achieved with no great cost or complexity.

The circuit is particularly suitable for frequency modulation. For this purpose we select the currents $I_1 = I_2 = I$ and control them with a common modulation voltage. In order to ensure that the oscillation amplitude at R_1 remains constant, a diode can be connected in parallel with it in each case, as shown by the dashed lines in Fig. 18.21. The oscillation frequency then becomes

$$f = \frac{1}{t_1 + t_2} = \frac{I}{4U_D C} \, ,$$

where U_D is forward voltage of the diodes.

Emitter-coupled multivibrators are available as monolithic integrated circuits, usually incorporating a TTL- or ECL-compatible output stage.

IC types:

TTL	XR 2209;	$f_{max} =$	1 MHz (Exar)
TTL	SN 74 LS 624...629;	$f_{max} =$	20 MHz (Texas Inst.)
ECL	MC 1658;	$f_{max} =$	150 MHz (Motorola)

8.4 Latching circuits using gates

Latching circuits can be implemented not only using transistors, but also using integrated logic devices (gates), as described in Chapter 9. Readers who are unfamiliar with basic logic functions should therefore read that chapter first.

8.4.1 Flip-flop

Let us return to the flip-flop in Fig. 8.10. Transistor T_1 is ON when a positive voltage is dropped across resistor R_1 or resistor R_2. If we also take into account the level inversion produced by the transistor, we can see that components R_1, R_2, T_1 and R_C form a NOR gate. The same applies to the other half of the circuit. Inserting the appropriate circuit symbols, we obtain the circuit diagram shown in Fig. 8.23 with the associated truth table (Fig. 8.24).

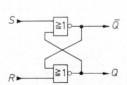

Fig. 8.23 Flip-flop comprising NOR gates

R	S	Q	$\bar{Q}$
0	0	as before	
0	1	1	0
1	0	0	1
1	1	(0)	(0)

Fig. 8.24 Truth table

8.4.2 One-shot

The circuit in Fig. 8.25 provides a simple means of generating short pulses with a duration of just a few gate propagation delay times. As long as the input variable $x = 0$, a logic 0 will be produced at the output of the AND gate. If $x = 1$, the AND element produces a logic 1 until the signal has passed through the inverter chain. When the input signal returns to zero, the AND condition is not satisfied.

The timing diagram is shown in Fig. 8.26. The duration of the output pulse is equal to the delay in the inverter chain. This can be specified by an appropriate number of gates, taking care to ensure that there is an odd number of gates. As we can see from Fig. 8.26, for this one-shot the trigger signal must be present at least for the duration of the output pulse.

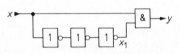   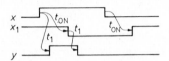

Fig. 8.25 One-shot for short switching times   Fig. 8.26 Waveform pattern
Turn-on time: t_{ON} = sum of inverter propagation delay times
              t_1 = propagation delay time of AND gate

To obtain longer switching times, the delay chain becomes unmanageably long. In this case it is preferable to employ integrated one-shots (monostable multivibrators) whose switching times are determined by an external RC network.

IC types:

CMOS   CD4098(RCA); 74HC123   (Motorola)
TTL   74LS121...123, 422, 423   (Texas Instr.)
ECL   MC10198   (Motorola)

If the AND gate in Fig. 8.25 is replaced by an exclusive-NOR gate, we obtain a one-shot which produces an output pulse on each edge of the input signal. Figure 8.27 shows the relevant circuit, Fig. 8.28 the associated waveform pattern. Under steady-state conditions, the inputs of the exclusive-NOR gate are complementary and the output signal is zero. If the input variable x changes its state, temporarily identical input signals appear at the exclusive-NOR gate due to the delay through the inverters. During this time the output signal y becomes logic 1.

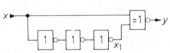   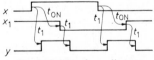

Fig. 8.27 Two-edge-triggered one-shot   Fig. 8.28 Waveform diagram

Turn-on time: $t_{ON} = 3t_{pd}$, t_1 = propagation delay time of exclusive NOR gate

8.4.3   Multivibrator

A simple multivibrator comprising two inverters is shown in Fig. 8.29. In order to explain how it works, let us assume that signal x is in the H state and

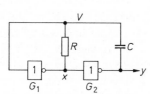

Fig. 8.29 Multivibrator comprising two
inverters

Cycle time: $T = 2 \ldots 3RC$

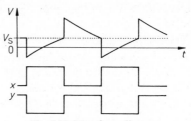

Fig. 8.30 Waveform diagram

Switching level: V_S

y is therefore in the L state. This causes capacitor C to charge up via resistor R until potential V exceeds the switching level V_S of gate G_1. x then changes to the L state and y to the H state, causing potential V to go positive by the amplitude of the output signal. The capacitor then discharges via resistor R until the voltage falls below the switching level.

The voltage waveform is shown in Fig. 8.30. Assuming that the switching level lies half-way between the output levels, the cycle time is given by

$$T = 2RC \ln 3 \approx 2.2RC \ .$$

In general, this assumption is only approximately satisfied in practical circuits. Additional deviations are caused by the fact that the input of gate G_1 loads the RC network. In the case of low-power Schottky TTL circuits, there is but little choice for resistor R: 1 kΩ ... 3.9 kΩ.

When using CMOS gates, a high value can be selected for resistor R, thereby achieving relatively large cycle times. However, in this case a series resistor is required at the input of gate G_1 in order to minimize the load on the RC network. This load would be caused by the protection circuit at the input of G_1 becoming conducting as long as V exceeds the supply voltage or falls below ground potential.

A circuit in which this problem does not arise is shown in Fig. 8.31. In this circuit, capacitor C is charged via resistor R to the switch-off level of the Schmitt trigger and then discharged to the switch-on level. We can see from Fig. 8.32 that the voltage across the capacitor oscillates between the two trigger levels. When using low-power Schottky TTL circuits, R must be selected sufficiently low to

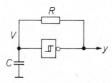

Fig. 8.31 Multivibrator using Schmitt trigger

Cycle time: (TTL) $T = 1.4 \ldots 1.8RC$
(5 V-CMOS) $T = 0.5 \ldots 1RC$

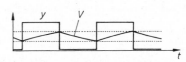

Fig. 8.32 Waveform diagram

ensure that it can pull the input below the switch-on level for the input current flowing. Recommended values are between 220 Ω and 680 Ω. These limitations do not apply to CMOS Schmitt triggers.

Particularly high frequencies above 50 MHz can be achieved by employing ECL gates. If positive feedback is applied to a line receiver (e.g. MC10116), we get a Schmitt trigger which can be configured as a multivibrator, similar to Fig. 8.31. The external circuitry and internal design are shown in Figs. 8.33 and 8.34.

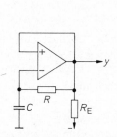

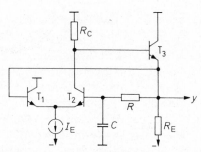

Fig. 8.33 Multivibrator with ECL line
receiver

Fig. 8.34 Internal design of line-receiver
multivibrator

Cycle time: $T \approx 3RC$

8.5   Latching circuits using comparators

8.5.1   Comparators

An operational amplifier without feedback, as in Fig. 8.35, represents the basic circuit of a comparator. Its output voltage is given by

$$U_o = \begin{cases} U_{o\,max} & \text{for } U_1 > U_2 \\ U_{o\,max} & \text{for } U_1 < U_2 \ . \end{cases}$$

The corresponding transfer characteristic is shown in Fig. 7.21. Owing to the high gain, the circuit responds to very small voltage differences $U_1 - U_2$. It is thus suitable for the comparison of two voltages, and operates with high accuracy.

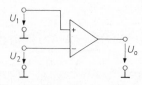

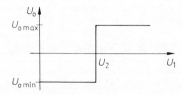

Fig. 8.35 Operational amplifier as
comparator

Fig. 8.36 Transfer characteristic

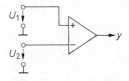

Fig. 8.37 Comparator with logic output

$y = 1$ for $U_1 > U_2$

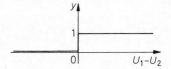

Fig. 8.38 Transfer characteristic

At zero crossing of the input voltage difference, the output voltage does not immediately reach the saturation level because the transition is limited by the slew rate. For frequency-compensated standard operational amplifiers it is about 1 V/μs. A rise from -12 V to $+12$ V therefore takes 24 μs. An additional delay is incurred due to the recovery time needed after the amplifier has been saturated.

As the amplifier possesses no negative feedback, it also does not require any frequency compensation. Its omission can improve the slew rate and recovery time by a factor of about 20.

Considerably shorter response times can be attained when using special comparator amplifiers which are designed for use without feedback and have especially small recovery times. However, the gain and hence the accuracy of the threshold are somewhat lower than those of operational amplifiers. Usually, the amplifier output is directly connected to a level-shift circuit which permits compatible operation with logic circuits. Its application and characteristics are shown in Figs. 8.37 and 8.38. A number of commonly used comparators are listed in Fig. 8.39.

Type	Manufacturer	Comparators per package	Output	Consumption per unit		Switching time	
TLC 3704	Texas Instr.	4	CMOS	0.05	mW	2500	ns
TLC 374	Texas Instr.	4	Open Drain	0.5	mW	1000	ns
LP 365	National	4	Open Coll.	8	mW	1000	ns
LM 339	National	4	Open Coll.	8	mW	600	ns
LM 311	various	1	Open Coll.	140	mW	200	ns
NE 5105	Signetics	1	TTL	100	mW	50	ns
LT 1016	Linear Techn.	1	TTL	140	mW	10	ns
NE 521	Signetics	2	TTL	100	mW	8	ns
AM 686	AMD	1	TTL	300	mW	8	ns
MAX 900	Maxim	4	TTL	18	mW	8	ns
AD 9698	Analog Dev.	2	TTL			4.5	ns
AD 9687	Analog Dev.	2	ECL	215	mW	2.7	ns
SP 93808	Plessey	8	ECL	60	mW	1	ns
10 GO 12	GBL	2	ECL	140	mW	0.2	ns

Fig. 8.39 Examples of comparators

Window comparator

A window comparator can determine whether or not the value of the input voltage lies between two reference voltage levels. Figure 8.40 shows that two comparators are used to decide whether the input voltage is above a lower *and* below an upper reference voltage. When this condition arises, both comparator amplifiers produce Boolean "one", the AND gate providing the defined logic evaluation. The characteristics in Fig. 8.41 illustrate the operation.

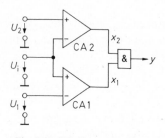

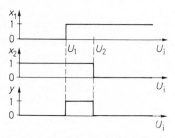

Fig. 8.40 Window comparator

$$y = 1 \quad \text{for} \quad U_1 < U_i < U_2$$

Fig. 8.41 Variables as a function of the input voltage

8.5.2   Schmitt trigger

The Schmitt trigger is a comparator, for which the positive and negative transitions of the output occur at different levels of the input voltage. Their difference is characterized by the hysteresis ΔU_i. As described in earlier sections, Schmitt triggers can be realized by transistors, but in the following section some designs involving comparators are discussed.

Inverting Schmitt trigger

In the Schmitt trigger of Fig. 8.42 the hysteresis is produced by a positive feedback of the comparator, via the voltage divider R_1, R_2. If a large negative voltage U_i is applied, $U_o = U_{o\,max}$. At the P-input, the potential is then given as

$$V_{P\,max} = \frac{R_1}{R_1 + R_2} U_{o\,max} \; .$$

If the input voltage is changed towards positive values, U_o does not change at first; only when U_i reaches the value $V_{P\,max}$, does the output voltage reduce and therefore also V_P. The difference $U_D = V_P - V_N$ becomes negative. Due to the positive feedback, U_o falls very quickly to the value $U_{o\,min}$. The potential V_P assumes the value

$$V_{P\,min} = \frac{R_1}{R_1 + R_2} U_{o\,min} \; .$$

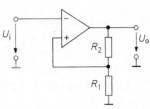

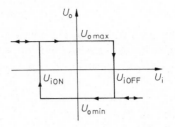

Fig. 8.42 Inverting Schmitt trigger.   Fig. 8.43 Transfer characteristic

Switch-on level: $U_{iON} = \dfrac{R_1}{R_1 + R_2} U_{omin}$

Switch-off level: $U_{iOFF} = \dfrac{R_1}{R_1 + R_2} U_{omax}$

Hysteresis: $\Delta U_i = \dfrac{R_1}{R_1 + R_2}(U_{omax} - U_{omin})$

U_D is negative and large, this resulting in a stable state. The output voltage changes to U_{omax} only when the input voltage has reached V_{Pmin}. The corresponding transfer characteristic is shown in Fig. 8.43.

The circuit has two stable states only if the loop gain

$$g = \frac{A_D R_1}{R_1 + R_2} > 1 \; .$$

Figure 8.44 shows the output of the Schmitt trigger for a sinusoidal input voltage.

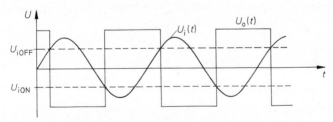

Fig. 8.44 Voltage waveshapes of the inverting Schmitt trigger

Non-inverting Schmitt trigger

The input signal for the Schmitt trigger in Fig. 8.42 can also be applied to the low end of the feedback voltage divider when at the same time the input is grounded. The new configuration is the non-inverting Schmitt trigger in Fig. 8.45.

If a large positive input voltage U_i is applied, $U_o = U_{omax}$. When reducing U_i, U_o does not change until V_P crosses zero. This is the case for the input

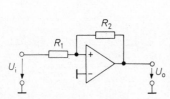

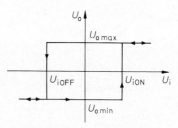

Fig. 8.45 Non-inverting Schmitt trigger   Fig. 8.46 Transfer characteristic

Switch-on level: $U_{iON} = -\dfrac{R_1}{R_2} U_{omin}$

Switch-off level: $U_{iOFF} = -\dfrac{R_1}{R_2} U_{omax}$

Hysteresis: $\Delta U_i = \dfrac{R_1}{R_2}(U_{omax} - U_{omin})$

voltage

$$U_{iOFF} = -\frac{R_1}{R_2} U_{omax} \;.$$

The output voltage jumps to U_{omin} as soon as U_i reaches or falls below this value. The transition is initiated by U_i but is then determined only by the positive feedback via R_2. The new state is stable until U_i returns to the level

$$U_{iON} = -\frac{R_1}{R_2} U_{omin} \;.$$

Figure 8.47 depicts the time function of the output voltage for a sinusoidal input. Since, at the instant of transition, $V_P = 0$, the formulae for the trigger level have the same form as those for the inverting amplifier.

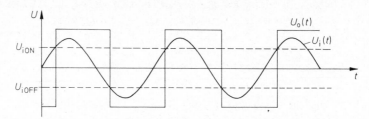

Fig. 8.47 Voltage waveshapes of the non-inverting Schmitt trigger

Precision Schmitt trigger

In the Schmitt triggers described, the switching levels are not as precise as one would expect from operational amplifier circuits. This is because the trigger levels are influenced by the imprecisely defined output voltages U_{omax} or U_{omin}. This drawback can be overcome, as in Fig. 8.48, by using two comparators which compare the input signal with the required switching levels. They then set

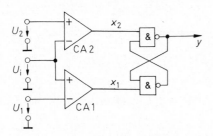

Fig. 8.48 Precision Schmitt trigger

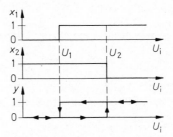

Fig. 8.49 Variables as a function of
input voltage

Switch-on level: $U_{\text{iON}} = U_2$ $\Big\}$ for $U_2 > U_1$
Switch-off level: $U_{\text{iOFF}} = U_1$

an *RS* flip-flop if the upper trigger level is exceeded and reset it if the lower trigger level is undershot. The mode of operation is illustrated in Fig. 8.49.

The precision Schmitt trigger in Fig. 8.48 can be implemented particularly simply using the dual comparator NE 521, as the latter already incorporates the two NAND gates required. For low frequencies there is yet another single-chip solution using an NE 555 timer which will be described in greater detail in the next section.

8.5.3 Multivibrators

If an inverting Schmitt trigger is configured such that the output signal is fed to the input with a delay, we obtain a multivibrator of the type shown in Fig. 8.50.

When the potential at the N-input exceeds the trigger level, the circuit changes state, and the output voltage jumps to the opposite output limit. The potential at the N-input attempts to follow the transition in the output voltage but the capacitor prevents it from changing rapidly. The potential therefore rises or falls gradually until the other trigger level is reached. The circuit then flips back to its initial state. The voltage waveshapes are shown in Fig. 8.51. From

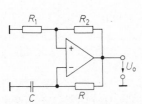

Fig. 8.50 Multivibrator using an operational
amplifier

Cycle time: $T = 2RC \ln(1 + 2R_1/R_2)$

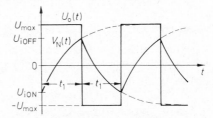

Fig. 8.51 Voltage waveshapes of the
multivibrator

Fig. 8.42, the trigger levels for $U_{o\,max} = -U_{o\,min} = U_{max}$ are given by

$$U_{i\,ON} = -\alpha U_{max}$$

and

$$U_{i\,OFF} = \alpha U_{max} ,$$

where $\alpha = R_1/(R_1 + R_2)$.

The differential equation for V_N can be taken directly from the circuit diagram as

$$\frac{dV_N}{dt} = \frac{\pm U_{max} - V_N}{RC} .$$

With the initial condition $V_N(t = 0) = U_{i\,ON} = -\alpha U_{max}$, we obtain the solution

$$V_N(t) = U_{max}[1 - (1 + \alpha)e^{-t/RC}] .$$

The switching level $U_{i\,OFF} = \alpha U_{max}$ is reached after a time

$$t_1 = RC \ln \frac{1 + \alpha}{1 - \alpha} = RC \ln\left(1 + \frac{2R_1}{R_2}\right) .$$

The period is therefore

$$T = 2t_1 = 2RC \ln\left(1 + \frac{2R_1}{R_2}\right) . \tag{8.5}$$

For $R_1 = R_2$,

$$T = 2RC \ln 3 \approx 2.2\,RC .$$

Multivibrator using a precision Schmitt trigger

The frequency stability of the multivibrator in Fig. 8.50 can be improved by incorporating the precision Schmitt trigger of Fig. 8.48. The resultant circuit is shown in Fig. 8.52. The enclosed section represents integrated timer NE 555 which offers the simplest solution for low frequency applications. Depending on the external circuitry, it can be operated as an astable (Fig. 8.52), a one-shot (Fig. 8.54) or a precision Schmitt trigger (Fig. 8.48).

The internal voltage divider R defines the trigger levels as $\frac{1}{3}V^+$ and $\frac{2}{3}V^+$, but these can be adjusted within certain limits using terminal 5. When the capacitor potential exceeds the upper threshold, $\bar{R} = L$ (low). The output voltage of the flip-flop assumes the L-state and transistor T is turned on. Capacitor C is then discharged by the resistor R_2 until the lower threshold $\frac{1}{3}V^+$ is reached, this process requiring the time

$$t_2 = R_2 C \ln 2 \approx 0.693 R_2 C .$$

On reaching the threshold, $\bar{S} = L$ and the flip-flop resumes its former state. The output voltage assumes the H (high)-state and transistor T is turned off. Charging of the capacitor takes place via the series connection of R_1 and R_2.

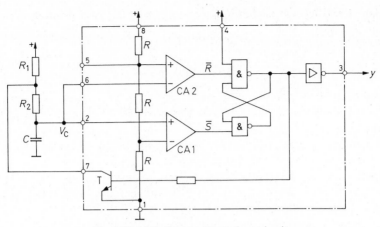

Fig. 8.52 Mulivibrator using a timer circuit.

Period: $T = (R_1 + 2R_2)C \ln 2 \approx 0.7(R_1 + 2R_2)C$

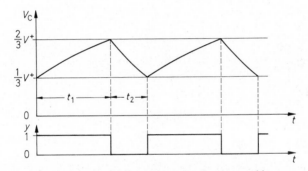

Fig. 8.53 Voltage waveshapes for timer as astable

The time interval needed to reach the upper trigger level is

$$t_1 = (R_1 + R_2)C \ln 2 \approx 0.693(R_1 + R_2)C .$$

Hence the frequency

$$f = \frac{1}{t_1 + t_2} \approx \frac{1.44}{(R_1 + 2R_2)C} .$$

The waveshapes of the signals y and V_C are shown in Fig. 8.53. The reset input 4 allows interruption of the oscillation.

When supplying a voltage to pin 5, the trigger thresholds can be shifted. In this way, the charging time t_1 and therefore the frequency of the multivibrator can be varied. A change in the potential $V_5 = \frac{2}{3}V^+$ by ΔV_5 results in a relative frequency shift of

$$\frac{\Delta f}{f} \approx -3.3 \cdot \frac{R_1 + R_2}{R_1 + 2R_2} \cdot \frac{\Delta V_5}{V^+} .$$

As long as the voltage deviation is not too large, the frequency modulation is reasonably linear.

8.5.4   One-shots

The timer 555 is also useful for generating single pulses (one-shot), and pulse times of a few µs to several minutes can be achieved. The required external wiring is shown in Fig. 8.54.

When the capacitor potential exceeds the upper trigger threshold, the flip-flop is reset, i.e. the output voltage resumes the L-state. Transistor T becomes conducting and discharges the capacitor. As the lower comparator is no longer connected to the capacitor, this state remains unchanged until the flip-flop is set by an L-pulse at trigger input 2. The ON-time t_1 is equal to the time required by the capacitor potential to rise from zero to the upper threshold $\frac{2}{3}V^+$. It is

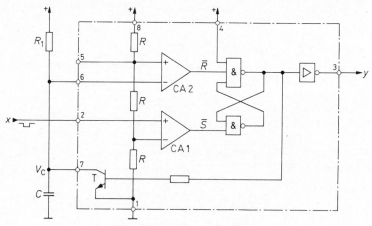

Fig. 8.54 One-shot with timer

ON-*time*: $t_1 = R_1 C \ln 3 \approx 1.1\, R_1 C$

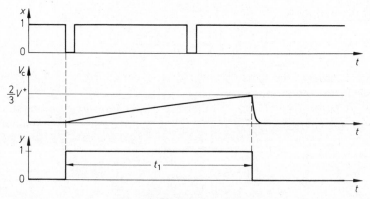

Fig. 8.55 Signals for one-shot

given by

$$t_1 = R_1 C \ln 3 \approx 1.1 R_1 C \ .$$

If a new trigger pulse occurs during this time interval, the flip-flop remains set and the pulse is ignored. Figure 8.55 shows the signals involved.

Discharging of capacitor C at the end of t_1 is not as fast as could be wished, as the collector current of the transistor is limited. The discharge time is known as *recovery time*. If a trigger pulse occurs during this interval, the ON-time is curtailed and is therefore no longer precisely defined.

Retriggerable timer

There are cases where the ON-time is not to be counted from the first pulse of a pulse train, as in the previous circuit, but from the last pulse of the train.

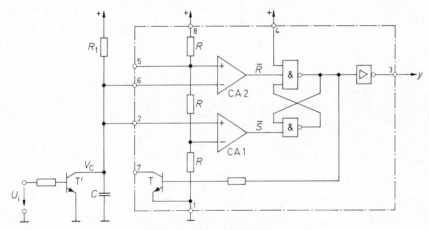

Fig. 8.56 Retriggerable timer

ON-*time*: $t_1 = R_1 C \ln 3 \approx 1.1 R_1 C$

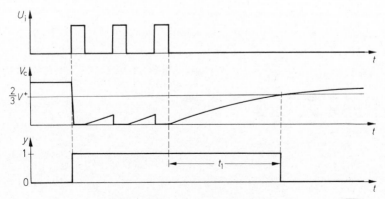

Fig. 8.57 Signals of the retriggerable timer

Circuits having this characteristic are termed retriggerable timers. The appropriate connection of the timer 555 is shown in Fig. 8.56, where use is made only of its function as a precision Schmitt trigger.

When the capacitor potential exceeds the upper trigger threshold, the output voltage of the flip-flop assumes the L-state. The capacitor will not discharge as transistor T is not connected. The capacitor potential therefore rises to V^+, this being the stable state. The capacitor must be discharged by a sufficiently long positive trigger pulse applied to the base of the external transistor T′. The flip-flop is set by the lower comparator and the output voltage assumes the H-state. If a new trigger pulse occurs before the end of the ON-time, the capacitor is discharged again and the output voltage remains in the H-state. It flips back only if no new trigger pulse occurs for at least a time interval of

$$t_1 = R_1 C \ln 3 .$$

The circuit is therefore also called the "missing pulse detector". The signals within the circuit are shown in Fig. 8.57 for several consecutive trigger pulses.

9 Basic logic circuits

Although digital equipment appears at first sight to be relatively complicated, its design is based on the simple concept of the repeated use of a small number of basic logic circuits. We can work out how these basic logic elements have to be linked by applying purely formal methods to the problem. This approach is based on Boolean algebra which, when applied specifically to digital circuit design, is known as switching algebra. In the next few paragraphs we shall summarize the basics of switching algebra.

9.1 The basic logic functions

Unlike a variable in conventional algebra, a logic variable can only assume two discrete values (binary variable), generally referred to as logic or Boolean one and logic or Boolean zero, for which the symbols "0" and "1" or H and L or simply 0 and 1 are used. The latter designation will be used in the following. There is no risk of confusion with the numbers 0 and 1, as it is always clear from the context whether a number or a logic value is meant.

There are three basic relations linking logic variables: conjunction, disjunction and negation. Using the mathematical signs of numerical algebra:

$$\text{Conjunction:} \quad y = x_1 \wedge x_2 = x_1 \cdot x_2 = x_1 x_2$$

$$\text{Disjunction:} \quad y = x_1 \vee x_2 = x_1 + x_2$$

$$\text{Negation:} \quad y = \bar{x}$$

A number of theorems relating these operations are listed below [9.1]:

Commutative law:

$$x_1 x_2 = x_2 x_1 \tag{9.1a}$$

$$x_1 + x_2 = x_2 + x_1 \tag{9.1b}$$

Associative law:

$$x_1(x_2 x_3) = (x_1 x_2) x_3 \tag{9.2a}$$

$$x_1 + (x_2 + x_3) = (x_1 + x_2) + x_3 \tag{9.2b}$$

Distributive law:

$$x_1(x_2 + x_3) = x_1 x_2 + x_1 x_3 \tag{9.3a}$$

$$x_1 + x_2 x_3 = (x_1 + x_2)(x_1 + x_3) \tag{9.3b}$$

Absorption law:

$$x_1(x_1 + x_2) = x_1 \tag{9.4a}$$

$$x_1 + x_1 x_2 = x_1 \tag{9.4b}$$

Tautology:

$$xx = x \qquad (9.5a)$$ | $$x + x = x \qquad (9.5b)$$

Law of negation:

$$x\bar{x} = 0 \qquad (9.6a)$$ | $$x + \bar{x} = 1 \qquad (9.6b)$$

Double negation:

$$\overline{(\bar{x})} = x \qquad (9.7)$$

De Morgan's law:

$$\overline{x_1 x_2} = \bar{x}_1 + \bar{x}_2 \qquad (9.8a)$$ | $$\overline{x_1 + x_2} = \bar{x}_1 \bar{x}_2 \qquad (9.8b)$$

Operations with 0 and 1:

$$x \cdot 1 = x \qquad (9.9a)$$ | $$x + 0 = x \qquad (9.9b)$$

$$x \cdot 0 = 0 \qquad (9.10a)$$ | $$x + 1 = 1 \qquad (9.10b)$$

$$\bar{0} = 1 \qquad (9.11a)$$ | $$\bar{1} = 0 \qquad (9.11b)$$

Many of these laws are already familiar from ordinary algebra. However, Eqs. (9.3b), (9.4a, b), (9.5a, b) and (9.10b) do not apply to algebraic numbers, and the term "negation" is not used at all in connection with numbers. Expressions such as $2x$ and x^2 do not occur in switching algebra due to the tautology.

If one compares the equations on the left with those on the right, the important principle of duality becomes apparent: if conjunction and disjunction and 0 and 1 are interchanged in any identity, an identity is again obtained.

Using Eqs. (9.9) to (9.11), it is possible to work out the conjunction and disjunction for all the possible values of variables x_1 and x_2. Figure 9.1 shows the function or truth table for conjunction and Fig. 9.2 the truth table for disjunction.

We can see from Fig. 9.1 that y is only 1 if x_1 *and* x_2 are 1. Consequently, conjunction is also known as the AND operation. In the case of disjunction, y is always 1 if x_1 *or* x_2 is 1. This operation is therefore also known as the OR operation. Both of these logic operations can be extended to apply to any number of variables.

x_1	x_2	y
0	0	0
0	1	0
1	0	0
1	1	1

x_1	x_2	y
0	0	0
0	1	1
1	0	1
1	1	1

Fig. 9.1 Truth table for conjunction (AND)   Fig. 9.2 Truth table for disjunction (OR)
$$y = x_1 x_2 \qquad\qquad\qquad\qquad y = x_1 + x_2$$

The question now is how to implement these logic operations by electrical circuits. As logic variables can only assume two discrete values, the only candidates are circuits possessing two clearly distinguishable operating states. The simplest means of representing a logic variable is a switch, as shown in Fig. 9.3. An open switch can now be defined as representing a logic "zero" and a closed switch a logic "one". Switch S therefore represents variable x if it is closed for $x = 1$. It represents variable $\bar{x}$ if it is open for $x = 1$.

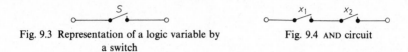

Fig. 9.3 Representation of a logic variable by a switch

Fig. 9.4 AND circuit

Let us first determine which logic function is obtained when two switches x_1 and x_2 are connected in series, as in Fig. 9.4. The value of dependent variable y is characterized by whether the resulting switch arrangement between the terminals is open or closed. As we can see, current can only flow if x_1 and x_2 are closed, i.e. both 1. The series connection therefore represents an AND operation. Similarly, an OR operation is obtained by connecting switches in parallel.

Using this switching logic, we can now verify the theorems stated above. We shall illustrate this by taking the tautology as an example. In Fig. 9.5, both sides of Eq. (9.5a) have been realized by switch arrangements. We can see that the given identity is satisfied, because two switches connected in series and simultaneously opened and closed have the same effect as a single switch.

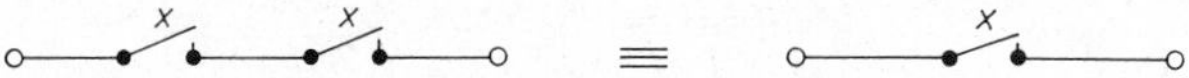

Fig. 9.5 Illustration of the tautology $xx = x$

As we saw in Section 8.1, another way of representing logic variables is by electrical voltages. To the two distinct levels H and L we can now assign the logic states 1 and 0. By making H = 1 and L = 0 we obtain what is known as positive logic. Conversely we can also make H = 0 and L = 1, this being termed negative logic.

The basic logic functions can be implemented by appropriate electronic circuits with one or more inputs and a single output. These are generally known as "gates". The voltage levels at the inputs and the types of logic operation determine the output level. As a logic function can be implemented electronically in a variety of ways, to simplify matters circuit symbols have been introduced which only show the logic function and give no indication of the internal design. These symbols are given in Figs. 9.6 to 9.8. The complete standard can, for instance, be found in IEC 617-12 and IEEE Std 91-1984. For an explanation, see e.g. [9.2, 9.3, 9.4]. To facilitate understanding of old-style circuit diagrams, the symbols formerly used are shown in Figs. 9.9 to 9.11.

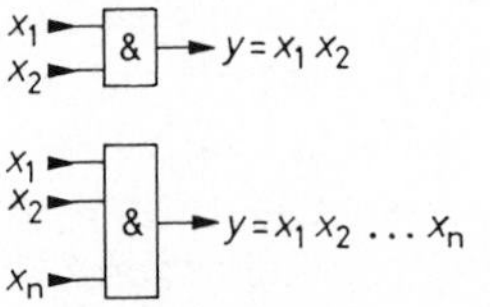

Fig. 9.6 AND circuit 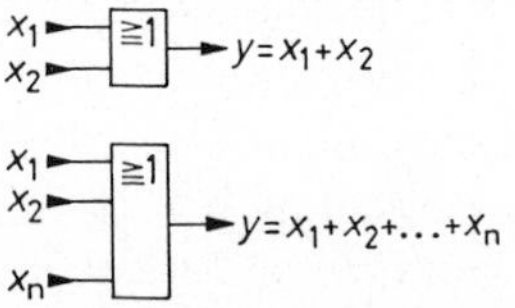   Fig. 9.7 OR circuit 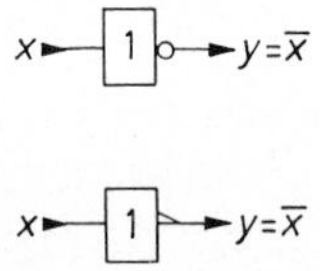   Fig. 9.8 NOT circuit

Figs. 9.6 to 9.8 Circuit symbols to IEC 617-12 and IEEE Std 91-1984

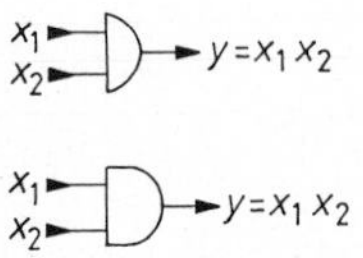

Fig. 9.9 AND circuit 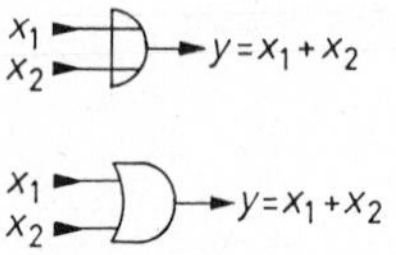   Fig. 9.10 OR circuit 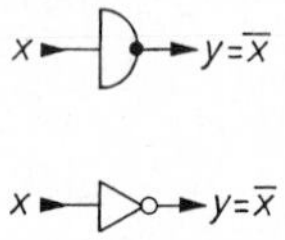   Fig. 9.11 NOT circuit

Figs. 9.9 to 9.11 Old-style circuit symbols

In digital circuits, we are not concerned with the voltage as a physical quantity, but merely with the logic state it represents. Instead of denoting the input and output signals by U_1, U_2, etc., they are therefore expressed directly using the logic variables shown.

9.2   Tabulation of logic functions

In digital circuit design the task is generally presented in the form of a function table, also known as a truth table. The objective is then to find a logic function which satisfies this truth table. The next step is to reduce this function to its simplest form, so that it can be implemented by a suitable combination of basic logic circuits. The logic function is generally given in the *disjunctive normal form* (sum-of-products, standard product terms, canonical products). The procedure is as follows:

1) We find all the rows in the truth table in which the output variable y is 1.
2) From each of these rows we form the logical product (conjunction) of all the input variables, substituting x_i if the relevant variable is 1 and using $\bar{x}_i$ if the variable is 0. We thus obtain as many product terms as there are rows with $y = 1$.
3) We obtain the required function by forming the logical sum (disjunction) of all the product terms found.

By way of example, let us consider the truth table in Fig. 9.12. In rows 3, 5 and 7, we have $y = 1$. We must therefore form the logical products of these rows.

Row	x_1	x_2	x_3	y
1	0	0	0	0
2	0	0	1	0
3	0	1	0	1
4	0	1	1	0
5	1	0	0	1
6	1	0	1	0
7	1	1	0	1
8	1	1	1	0

Fig. 9.12 Example of a truth table

$$\text{Row 3:}\quad K_3 = \bar{x}_1 x_2 \bar{x}_3 \; ,$$
$$\text{Row 5:}\quad K_5 = x_1 \bar{x}_2 \bar{x}_3 \; ,$$
$$\text{Row 7:}\quad K_7 = x_1 x_2 \bar{x}_3 \; .$$

The required function is now obtained as the sum of the products (disjunction of the conjunctions):

$$y = \quad K_3 \quad + \quad K_5 \quad + \quad K_7 \; ,$$
$$y = \bar{x}_1 x_2 \bar{x}_3 + x_1 \bar{x}_2 \bar{x}_3 + x_1 x_2 \bar{x}_3 \; .$$

This is the disjunctive normal form of the required logic function. To simplify, we now apply Eq. (9.3a) and obtain

$$y = [\bar{x}_1 x_2 + x_1(\bar{x}_2 + x_2)]\bar{x}_3 \; .$$

Equations (9.6b) and (9.9a) yield a further simplification

$$y = (\bar{x}_1 x_2 + x_1)\bar{x}_3 \; .$$

From Eq. (9.3b)

$$y = (x_1 + x_2)(x_1 + \bar{x}_1)\bar{x}_3 \; .$$

By again applying Eqs. (9.6b) and (9.9a), we finally obtain the simple result

$$y = (x_1 + x_2)\bar{x}_3 \; .$$

If the output variable y has more "ones" than "zeros", a large number of product terms is obtained. Simplification can now be performed from the outset by considering the complemented (negated, barred) output variable $\bar{y}$ instead of y. There are sure to be fewer "ones" than "zeros" for this negated variable. Consequently, by expressing the logic function for the complemented variable $\bar{y}$, we obtain from the start a smaller number of product terms, i.e. a simpler function. It only needs to be negated at the end to obtain the required function for y. To do this, we merely interchange the operations $(+)$ and $(\cdot)$ and complement all the variables and constants individually.

9.2.1   The Karnaugh map

The Karnaugh map provides an important means of obtaining a logic function in its simplest form. It is basically another version of the truth table. However, the values of the input variables are not simply written one below the other but arranged at the horizontal and vertical sides of an area divided into squares like a chess board. If the number of input variables is even, half are written horizontally and half vertically. If the number of input variables is odd, one side will have one variable more than the other.

The various combinations of input function values must be arranged in such a way that only *one* variable changes from one square to the next. In the squares themselves are entered the values of the output variables y associated with the input variable values written at the sides. Figure 9.13 shows once again the truth table of the AND function for two input variables, Fig. 9.14 the corresponding Karnaugh map.

x_1	x_2	y
0	0	0
0	1	0
1	0	0
1	1	1

x_2 \ x_1	0	1
0	0	0
1	0	1

Fig. 9.13 Truth table for the AND function   Fig. 9.14 Karnaugh map for the AND function

As the Karnaugh map is merely a simplified version of the truth table, it can be used for obtaining the disjunctive normal form of the associated logic function in the manner described above. Its advantage is that it makes it easier to spot possible simplifications. We shall illustrate this by the example in Fig. 9.15.

To write the disjunctive normal form, we must first, as described above, form the logical product of all the input variables for each cell containing a 1. For the cell in the top left-hand corner we obtain

$$K_1 = \bar{x}_1\bar{x}_2\bar{x}_3\bar{x}_4 \ .$$

For the cell on the immediate right

$$K_2 = \bar{x}_1 x_2 \bar{x}_3 \bar{x}_4 \ .$$

If we finally form the sum of all the products, one possible expression is

$$K_1 + K_2 = \bar{x}_1\bar{x}_2\bar{x}_3\bar{x}_4 + \bar{x}_1 x_2 \bar{x}_3 \bar{x}_4 \ .$$

This can be simplified to

$$K_1 + K_2 = \bar{x}_1\bar{x}_3\bar{x}_4(\bar{x}_2 + x_2) = \bar{x}_1\bar{x}_3\bar{x}_4 \ .$$

This illustrates the general simplification rule for the Karnaugh map.

x_1	x_2	x_3	x_4	y
0	0	0	0	1
0	0	0	1	1
0	0	1	0	1
0	0	1	1	1
0	1	0	0	1
0	1	0	1	0
0	1	1	0	0
0	1	1	1	0
1	0	0	0	1
1	0	0	1	0
1	0	1	0	1
1	0	1	1	1
1	1	0	0	0
1	1	0	1	0
1	1	1	0	1
1	1	1	1	1

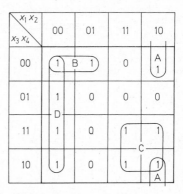

Fig. 9.15 Truth table with corresponding Karnaugh map

If a rectangle or square with 2, 4, 8, 16, etc. cells contains all "ones", the logical product of the entire block can be obtained directly *by only taking into account the input variables possessing a constant value in all the cells of the block*.

Therefore, in our example we obtain for pair **B** the logical product

$$K_B = \bar{x}_1 \bar{x}_3 \bar{x}_4$$

corresponding to the function given above. It is also possible to block together those cells located at the left and right extremities of a row or at the top and bottom of a column.

For the block of four, D, in Fig. 9.15 we obtain

$$K_D = \bar{x}_1 \bar{x}_2 \ .$$

Similarly, for the block of four, C, the logical product is given by

$$K_C = x_1 x_3 \ .$$

That still leaves the 1 in the top right-hand corner. As shown, it can be combined with the 1 at the bottom of that column to form a pair K_A. Another possibility would be to combine it with the 1 at the other end of the same row. However, the simplest solution is to note that there is a 1 at each corner of the Karnaugh map. These can be combined to form a block of four and we obtain

$$K'_A = \bar{x}_2 \bar{x}_4 \ .$$

For the disjunctive normal form we now obtain the already considerably simplified result:

$$y = K'_A + K_B + K_C + K_D \ ,$$

$$y = \bar{x}_2 \bar{x}_4 + \bar{x}_1 \bar{x}_3 \bar{x}_4 + x_1 x_3 + \bar{x}_1 \bar{x}_2 \ .$$

9.3   Derived basic functions

In the preceding discussion we have shown that every logic function can be represented by a suitable combination of the basic functions OR, AND and NOT. We shall now consider a number of derived functions which occur so frequently in circuit design that they have been given names of their own. Their truth tables and circuit diagrams are shown in Fig. 9.16.

input variables x_1 x_2	$y = x_1 + x_2$ $= x_1$ OR x_2	$y = x_1 \cdot x_2$ $= x_1$ AND x_2	$y = \overline{x_1 + x_2}$ $= x_1$ NOR x_2	$y = \overline{x_1 \cdot x_2}$ $= x_1$ NAND x_2	$y = x_1 \oplus x_2$ $= x_1$ EXOR x_2 $= x_1$ ANTIV x_2	$y = \overline{x_1 \oplus x_2}$ $= x_1$ EXNOR x_2 $= x_1$ EQUIV x_2
0 0	0	0	1	1	0	1
0 1	1	0	0	1	1	0
1 0	1	0	0	1	1	0
1 1	1	1	0	0	0	1

Fig. 9.16 Basic functions derived from the AND or OR functions

The NOR and NAND functions are the complements of the OR and AND functions respectively: NOR = not or; NAND = not and. Thus:

$$x_1 \text{ NOR } x_2 = \overline{x_1 + x_2} = \bar{x}_1 \bar{x}_2 , \tag{9.12}$$

$$x_1 \text{ NAND } x_2 = \overline{x_1 x_2} = \bar{x}_1 + \bar{x}_2 . \tag{9.13}$$

In the case of the *equivalence function*, $y = 1$ if the two input variables are the same. By writing the disjunctive normal form, we obtain from the truth table

$$y = x_1 \text{ EQUIV } x_2 = \bar{x}_1 \bar{x}_2 + x_1 x_2 .$$

The *antivalence (non-equivalence) function* is a complemented equivalence function for which y is 1 if the input variables are different. Written in the disjunctive normal form:

$$y = x_1 \text{ ANTIV } x_2 = \bar{x}_1 x_2 + x_1 \bar{x}_2 .$$

The truth table reveals another meaning of the antivalence function: it coincides with the OR function in all values except in the case where all the input variables are 1. It is therefore also known as the exclusive-OR (EXOR) function. Similarly, the equivalence function may also be termed the exclusive-NOR function (EXNOR).

When using integrated circuits, it is sometimes preferable to implement functions using only NAND or NOR gates. For this purpose the functions are modified such that only the desired logic operations occur. A simple method of doing this is to replace the basic functions by NAND and NOR operations. For the

AND function

$$x_1 x_2 = \overline{\overline{x_1 x_2}} = \overline{x_1 \text{ NAND } x_2} \ ,$$

$$x_1 x_2 = \overline{\overline{x}_1 \overline{x}_2} = \overline{\overline{x}_1 + \overline{x}_2} = \overline{x}_1 \text{ NOR } \overline{x}_2 \ .$$

For the OR operation we similarly obtain

$$x_1 + x_2 = \overline{\overline{x}}_1 + \overline{\overline{x}}_2 = \overline{\overline{x}_1 \overline{x}_2} = \overline{x}_1 \text{ NAND } \overline{x}_2 \ ,$$

$$x_1 + x_2 = \overline{\overline{x_1 + x_2}} = \overline{x_1 \text{ NOR } x_2} \ .$$

This yields the possible implementations shown in Fig. 9.17.

Operation	Gate	
	NAND	NOR
NOT	$x \rightarrow$ & $\rightarrow y = \overline{x}$	$x \rightarrow \geq 1 \rightarrow y = \overline{x}$
AND	x_1 x_2 & & $\rightarrow y = x_1 \cdot x_2$	x_1 ≥ 1 x_2 ≥ 1 ≥ 1 $\rightarrow y = x_1 \cdot x_2$
OR	x_1 & x_2 & & $\rightarrow y = x_1 + x_2$	x_1 ≥ 1 x_2 ≥ 1 $\rightarrow y = x_1 + x_2$

Fig. 9.17 Implementation of basic functions using NOR and NAND gates

9.4 Circuit implementation of the basic functions

In the preceding paragraphs we have manipulated logic circuits without concerning ourselves with their internal design. This approach is justified because nowadays digital circuitry is based virtually exclusively on integrated circuits which, apart from their power supply connections, possess only the inputs and outputs mentioned.

For implementation of the individual basic operations a wide variety of circuit technologies exists, with differing characteristics in terms of power consumption, supply voltage, H and L level, gate propagation delay and fanout. In order to make an appropriate choice, it is necessary to have at least a broad understanding of the internal design of these circuits. We have therefore summarized the principal families of circuits below.

When interconnecting ICs, a large number of gate inputs are often connected to one output. The number of inputs of the same family of circuits which can be connected without falling below the guaranteed noise margin is characterized by the *fanout*. A fanout of 10 therefore means that 10 gate inputs can be connected. If the fanout is inadequate, a *buffer* is used instead of a standard gate.

It is the characteristic of a gate that a specific output state is associated with each input state. As described in Chapter 8, these states can be designated by H and L depending on whether the voltage is greater than U_H or less than U_L. The operation of a gate can be described by a level table as in Fig. 9.18. However, this does not determine which logic function the gate will implement, as we have not yet defined the assignment of levels to logic states. Although this assignment is arbitrary, it is advisable to adopt a uniform system within the equipment. The level/state assignment

$$H \triangleq 1 \, , \qquad L \triangleq 0$$

is termed positive logic and produces, in our example, the truth table in Fig. 9.19 which may be identified as that of the NAND operation. The assignment

$$H \triangleq 0 \, , \qquad L \triangleq 1$$

is known as negative logic. In our example, it results in the truth table in Fig. 9.20, i.e. the NOR operation.

One and the same circuit can therefore represent either a NOR or a NAND circuit depending on the type of logic selected. The logic functions of digital circuits are normally described in positive logic. In negative logic, the operations are reversed as follows:

$$NOR \iff NAND \, ,$$

$$OR \iff AND \, ,$$

$$NOT \iff NOT \, .$$

U_1	U_2	U_o
L	L	H
L	H	H
H	L	H
H	H	L

Fig. 9.18 Example of a level table (function table)

x_1	x_2	y
0	0	1
0	1	1
1	0	1
1	1	0

Fig. 9.19 Truth table for positive logic: NAND function

x_1	x_2	y
1	1	0
1	0	0
0	1	0
0	0	1

Fig. 9.20 Truth table for negative logic: NOR function

9.4.1   Resistor-transistor logic (RTL)

RTL circuits are the IC implementation of the latching circuits involving saturated transistors, as in Fig. 8.10 for example. If one input voltage of the RTL gate in Fig. 9.21 is in the H state, the relevant transistor is turned on and the output goes low (L). We therefore obtain a NOR operation in positive logic. The

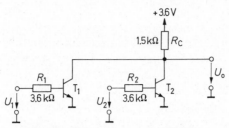

Fig. 9.21 RTL NOR gate, type MC717

Power dissipation: 5 mW

Gate propagation delay: $t_{pd} = 25$ ns

relatively low-value base resistors ensure that the transistors are turned fully on even for low current gains. However, the fanout is consequently low. The following circuits are considerably better in this respect and nowadays, RTL circuits are no longer used.

9.4.2   Diode-transistor logic (DTL)

In the DTL circuit in Fig. 9.22, the base current for the output transistor is injected via resistor R_1 if input diodes D_1 and D_2 are blocking, i.e. when all the input voltages are in the H state. In this case, transistor T_1 is turned on and the output voltage goes low. We thus obtain a NAND operation in positive logic. If the same NAND gates are reconnected to the output, the output voltage in the H state is not loaded by the inputs. It therefore assumes, in the H state, the value V^+. DTL circuits are no longer used due to the large gate propagation delay caused by the saturation of the transistors.

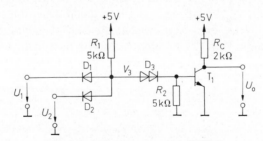

Fig. 9.22 DTL NAND gate, type MC849

Power dissipation: 15 mW;   *Gate propagation delay:* $t_{pd} = 25$ ns

9.4.3   High-level logic (HLL)

Modified DTL circuits are available for use in equipment in which high noise levels are unavoidable. In these circuits the double diode D_3 is replaced by a Zener diode as in Fig. 9.23. This increases the switching level at the input to

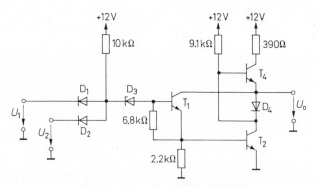

Fig. 9.23 HLL NAND gate, type FZH101A

Power dissipation: 180 mW;   *Gate propagation delay:* $t_{pd} = 175$ ns

approximately 6 V and a noise margin of 5 V is obtained for a 12 V supply voltage. In order to increase the fanout, the HLL circuits have a push-pull stage as shown in Fig. 8.6. The switching time is artificially increased by using low-speed transistors and it can be increased still further by means of an external capacitor. As a result, short spikes have no effect even if their amplitude is greater than the noise margin. HLL circuits are also known as low-speed logic circuits (LSL).

9.4.4   Transistor-transistor logic (TTL)

TTL gates basically operate in exactly the same way as DTL gates. The only difference is in the design of the diode gate and amplifier. With the standard TTL gate in Fig. 9.24, the diode gate is replaced by transistor T_1 incorporating several emitters. If all the input levels are in the H state, the current from R_1 flows via the forward-biased base-collector diode of the input transistor to the base of T_2, turning it on. If one input is at low potential, the relevant base-

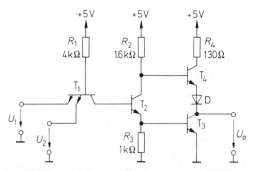

Fig. 9.24 Standard TTL NAND gate, type 7400

Power dissipation: 10 mW;   *Gate propagation delay:* $t_{pd} = 10$ ns

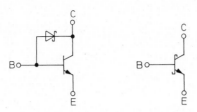

Fig. 9.25 Transistor with Schottky anti-saturation diode and corresponding circuit symbol

emitter diode becomes conducting and takes over the base current of T_2. This turns T_2 off and the output potential goes high.

In TTL circuits, the amplifier consists of drive transistor T_2 and a push-pull output stage (totem-pole circuit).

When T_2 is conducting, T_3 is also ON and T_4 is OFF. The output is at L and transistor T_3 can accept high currents originating e.g. from the connected gate inputs. (In the L state, a current flows from the inputs!)

When T_2 is OFF, T_3 is also OFF. In this case T_4 is turned on and delivers an H signal to the output. The transistor operated as an emitter follower can then supply high output currents and thus rapidly charge up load capacitances. Standard TTL circuits as shown in Fig. 9.24 are no longer used due to the gate propagation delay caused by the saturation of the transistors.

One method of preventing saturation consists of connecting a Schottky diode in parallel with the collector-base junction (Fig. 9.25). When the transistor is conducting, it provides voltage feedback to prevent the collector-emitter voltage falling below about 0.3 V. A TTL gate employing "Schottky transistors" of this type is shown in Fig. 9.26 which is actually a simplified representation of a low-power Schottky TTL gate. Comparison with the standard TTL gate in Fig. 9.24 shows that the values of the circuit resistors are a factor of 5 higher. The power consumption is lower by a factor of 5, being only 2 mW. Nevertheless, the gate propagation delay is no greater, being only 10 ns. The input diode gate, as

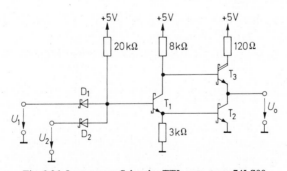

Fig. 9.26 Low-power Schottky TTL gate, type 74LS00

Power dissipation: 2 mW;   *Gate propagation delay:* $t_{pd} = 10$ ns in DTL circuits, consists of separate diodes. The diode D required in the output stage for level shifting (Fig. 9.24) is here replaced by Darlington pair T_3.

The transfer characteristic of the low-power Schottky TTL inverter (NOT operation) is shown in Fig. 9.27. We can see that the switching level is around 1.1 V at the input. The specified tolerance limits are well exceeded: at the maximum permissible L level at the input of 0.8 V, an H level of at least 2.4 V must be present at the output. For the minimum H level at the input of 2.0 V, the L level at the output must be no more than 0.4 V.

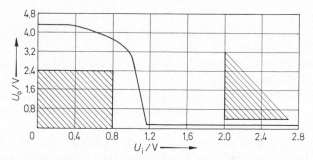

Fig. 9.27 Transfer characteristic of a low-power Schottky TTL inverter.

Hatched areas: Tolerance limits

Open-collector outputs

The problem sometimes arises that a large number of gate outputs must be logically linked. For 20 outputs, for instance, a gate with 20 inputs would be required with 20 individual lines leading to them. This complexity can be avoided by using gates with an *open-collector output*. As shown in Fig. 9.28, their output stage consists merely of an npn transistor whose emitter is connected to ground. Outputs of this kind can simply be paralleled, unlike the push-pull output stages otherwise used, and provided with a common collector resistor as in Fig. 9.28.

The output potential therefore only goes high if *all* the outputs are high. Consequently, in positive logic an AND operation is produced. On the other hand we can see that the output voltage then goes low if one or more of the outputs assumes the L state. We therefore have an OR operation in negative logic. As the

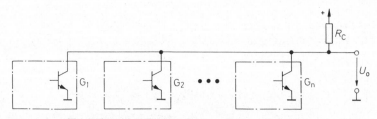

Fig. 9.28 Logical linking of open-collector gate outputs

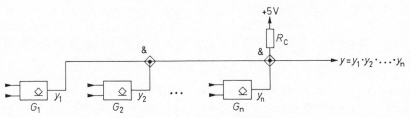

Fig. 9.29 Representation of a wired-AND operation with logic symbols. The $\Diamond$-symbol in the gates means open-collector ,output

operation is realized by the external wiring, it is referred to as a wired-AND or wired-OR circuit. As the gates are at low impedance in the L state only, they are also known as active-low outputs. The wired-AND operation is represented using logic symbols as shown in Fig. 9.29.

An OR operation can also be implemented using open-collector outputs by applying the wired-AND operation to the complemented variables. De Morgan's law states that:

$$y_1 + y_2 + \ldots + y_n = \overline{\bar{y}_1 \cdot \bar{y}_2 \cdot \ldots \cdot \bar{y}_n} \; .$$

The corresponding circuit is shown in Fig. 9.30.

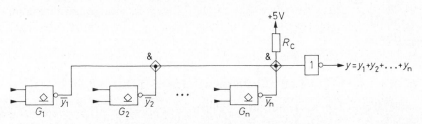

Fig. 9.30 Wired-OR circuit with open-collector outputs

A disadvantage of using open-collector outputs is that the output voltage rises more slowly than with push-pull outputs, because the circuit capacitances can only charge up via resistor R_C. In this respect, open-collector TTL gates have the same disadvantages as the RTL circuits in Fig. 9.21. There, the logical linking can likewise be interpreted as a wired-AND operation.

Tristate outputs

There is another important application in which circuit simplification can be achieved by paralleling gate outputs, namely when any one of several gates connected to a signaling line is to determine the logic state. This is then referred to as a *bus system*.

This end can also be attained using open-collector gates, as shown in Fig. 9.29, by placing all the outputs, apart from one, in the high-impedance H state. However, the main disadvantage of the low rate of rise can be avoided in this particular application by using gates with *tristate* output instead of gates with open-collector output. The tristate output is a genuine push-pull output with the additional property that it can be placed in a high-impedance state using a special control signal. This state is known as the Z state.

The basic circuit implementation is shown in Fig. 9.31. When the *enable* signal $EN = 1$, the circuit operates as a normal inverter: for $x = 0$, $z_1 = 0$ and $z_2 = 1$, i.e. T_1 is OFF and T_2 is ON. For $x = 1$, T_1 is turned on and T_2 is turned off. However, if the control variable $EN = 0$, we also have $z_1 = z_2 = 0$, and both output transistors are OFF. This is the high-impedance Z state.

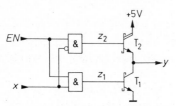

Fig. 9.31 Inverter with tristate output   Fig. 9.32 Circuit symbol of an inverter with
                                                tristate output

Due to their favorable electrical characteristics, the variety of types available and their low price, low-power Schottky TTL circuits are the most commonly used family of logic circuits. The various Schottky TTL families are listed in Fig. 9.46.

9.4.5   Emitter-coupled logic (ECL)

We saw in Fig. 4.44 that, in a differential amplifier with an input voltage difference of about $\pm 100\,\text{mV}$, current I_k can be completely switched from one transistor to the other. The amplifier therefore possesses two defined switching states, namely $I_C = I_k$ or $I_C = 0$. It is therefore also known as a current switch. If, for this switch mode, suitably low-resistance components are selected to ensure that the change in voltage across the collector resistors remains sufficiently low, the conducting transistor can be prevented from being driven into saturation.

Figure 9.33 shows a typical ECL gate. Transistors T_2 and T_3 form a differential amplifier. A constant potential V_{ref} is applied to the base of T_3 via the voltage divider. If all the input voltages are in the L state, transistors T_1 and T_2 are turned off. The emitter current in this case flows via transistor T_3, producing a voltage drop across R_2. Output voltage U_{o1} is therefore in the L state, U_{o2} in the H state. When at least one input level goes high, the output states are reversed. Positive logic gives an OR operation for U_{o1} and an NOR operation for U_{o2}.

We shall now examine the potentials within the circuit. When transistor T_3 is OFF, only a small voltage of about 0.2 V is dropped across R_2, due to the base current of T_5. Consequently the emitter potential of T_5 is in this case -0.9 V.

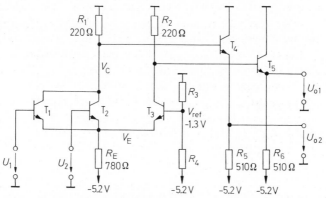

Fig. 9.33 ECL NOR-OR gate, type MC10102. Emitter resistors R_5 and R_6 are not incorporated in the IC and must be connected externally if required

Power dissipation per gate:	25 mW
Power dissipation R_5, R_6, each:	30 mW
Gate propagation delay:	$t_{pd} = 2$ ns

This is the output H level. If this level is applied e.g. to the base of T_2, the emitter potential is

$$V_E = -0.9 \text{ V} - 0.7 \text{ V} = -1.6 \text{ V} .$$

In order to ensure that T_2 is not driven into saturation, its collector-emitter voltage must not fall below 0.6 V. Consequently, the minimum collector potential is

$$V_C = -1.6 \text{ V} + 0.6 \text{ V} = -1.0 \text{ V} .$$

This produces an L level at the output of -1.7 V. V_{ref} must now be selected such that the input transistors are sure to be ON at an input voltage of $U_H = -0.9$ V and OFF at an input voltage of $U_L = -1.7$ V. This condition can best be satisfied by setting V_{ref} half-way between U_H and U_L, i.e. at about -1.3 V. The complete transfer characteristic is shown in Fig. 9.34. We can see that the switching level is -1.3 V. At the maximum permissible input L level of -1.5 V, an H level of at least -1.0 V must be produced at the NOR output. At the lowest input H level of -1.1 V, the L level at the output must not exceed -1.65 V.

In contrast to other logic circuit families, the input voltage of ECL in the H state is tightly constrained at the upper limit. If it exceeds -0.8 V, the relevant input transistor will be driven into saturation. This can be seen from the bend in the transfer characteristic for the NOR output, at -0.4 V input voltage. As the voltage increases further, the collector potential V_C increases with the emitter potential due to the saturation of transistor T_2, and therefore output voltage U_{o2} also increases.

We can see from Fig. 9.34 that the logic levels are much closer to zero potential than to the negative supply voltage (-5.2 V). Moreover, the

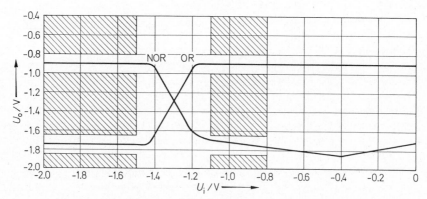

Fig. 9.34 Transfer characteristic of an ECL gate of the MC10000 series.

Hatched areas: Tolerance limits

magnitude of the supply voltage does not affect the H level, as this is determined only by the base-emitter voltage of the emitter followers. If the negative terminal of the supply voltage had been made zero potential, i.e. the level reference, + 5.2 V would be superimposed on all the levels. In view of the low switching levels, reliable operation would be impossible.

Of all the logic families, ECL circuits have the smallest gate propagation delays. Indeed, they are even faster than Schottky TTL circuits which can also be operated unsaturated. The difference is that the collector-emitter voltage across the conducting transistors is higher – never less than 0.6 V. This provides not only a greater margin to the saturation voltage, but also results in a lower collector-base junction capacitance.

Another reason for the high speed of ECL circuits lies in the small signal amplitudes of only 0.8 V involved in switching. The unavoidable switching capacitances can therefore be reverse-charged rapidly. The low output resistance of the emitter followers also promotes fast switching times. From Eq. (4.30) this is given by

$$r_o \approx 1/g_f = U_T/I_C = 26 \text{ mV}/7.7 \text{ mA} = 3.4 \, \Omega \ .$$

The high speed of ECL circuits is obtained at the expense of high power dissipation. For a gate of the MC10.000 series this can be as much as 25 mW. To this must be added the power dissipation in the emitter resistors. For an average output voltage of − 1.3 V, there is a power dissipation of 30 mW in a 510 Ω emitter resistor, i.e. more than in the entire gate. For this reason emitter resistors will only be connected to the outputs used. The dissipation in the emitter resistors can be reduced to 10 mW if, instead of connecting 510 Ω resistors to the − 5.2 V supply, 50 Ω resistors are used on an additional supply voltage of $V_{TT} = - 2$ V. However, the associated cost and complexity is only justifiable for extensive ECL circuitry. Additional care must be taken to ensure that the − 2 V supply voltage is generated with high efficiency in the power supply. Otherwise the problem of power dissipation is merely shifted from the circuit to the power supply. For this reason it is impractical to produce the -2 V from the -5.2 V using a series regulator.

Wired-OR operation

By connecting ECL outputs in parallel, it is possible – as with open-collector outputs – to implement a logic operation. This possibility is illustrated in Fig. 9.35. As the H level is predominant when the emitter followers are connected in parallel (active high), we obtain an OR operation in positive logic. The advantage of a wired-OR operation using ECL circuits is that the speed is not reduced. We not only save one gate but also one gate propagation delay.

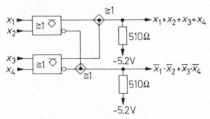

Fig. 9.35 Wired-OR operation for ECL circuits. The $\lozenge$ symbol in the gates means open-emitter output

To summarize, let us enumerate once more the main considerations for using ECL gates in high-speed logic circuits:

1) They exhibit the shortest gate propagation delays.
2) Their power consumption is independent of the switching state. No voltage spikes occur during switching. Consequently high-frequency noise injected into the power supply remains low.
3) The balanced outputs allow noise-immune signal transmission over comparatively large distances (see Section 9.5).

A list of the various ECL families is given in Fig. 9.46.

9.4.6 Complementary MOS logic (CMOS)

CMOS logic circuits constitute a family characterized by extremely low power consumption. Figure 9.36 shows an inverter circuit. It is noticeable that the circuit consists exclusively of enhancement-type MOSFETs. The source electrode of the n-channel FET is connected to ground and that of the p-channel FET to the supply voltage V_{DD}. The two FETs therefore operate in source connection and amplify the input voltage on an inverting basis, with one transistor constituting the pull-up resistance for the other.

The pinch-off voltage of the two MOSFETs is about 1.5 V. For a supply voltage of 5 V, at least one of the two MOSFETs is therefore ON. If we make

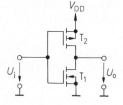

$(V_{DD} = 5\,V)$	Standard	High speed
Type	74C04	74HC04
Power dissipation	$0.3\,\mu W/kHz$	$0.5\,\mu W/kHz$
Gate propagation delay	90 ns	10 ns

Fig. 9.36 CMOS inverter

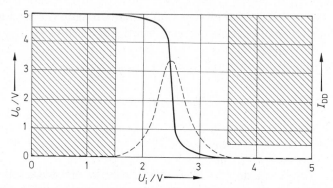

Fig. 9.37 Transfer characteristic and cross-over current of a CMOS gate for a 5 V supply voltage.

Hatched areas:	Tolerance limits
Broken line:	Current drain I_{DD}

$U_i = 0$, the p-channel FET T_2 is ON and the n-channel FET T_1 is OFF. The output voltage is equal to V_{DD}. For $U_i = V_{DD}$, T_2 is OFF and T_1 is ON. The output voltage becomes zero. We can see that under steady-state conditions no current flows through the circuit. It is only during switching that a small cross-over current flows as long as the input voltage is in the range $|U_p| < U_i < V_{DD} - |U_p|$. The cross-over current I_{DD} and transfer characteristic are plotted in Fig. 9.37.

The logic levels depend on the supply voltage selected. The permissible supply voltage range for CMOS circuits is very large. In the case of silicon gate circuits it is between 3 V and 6 V, for metal gate circuits it is even 3 to 15 V. For reasons of symmetry, the switching level is always at half the supply voltage. Consequently, for a supply voltage of 5 V the H level must be above 3.5 V, as we can see from Fig. 9.37. In order to drive a CMOS gate input with a TTL gate output, an additional pull-up resistor is therefore required. On the other hand, HCT (high-speed CMOS TTL) circuits are fully TTL-compatible because they have input transistors with an adapted pinch-off voltage.

The current drawn by a CMOS gate consists of three components: if the input voltage is constantly equal to zero or V_{DD}, only a small reverse current of a few microamps flows. If the input signal changes state, a cross-over current temporarily flows through the two transistors. In addition, the circuit capacitances must be charged when the output goes high. The transferred charge due to the two effects in an L-H-L cycle can be described using an imaginary "power dissipation capacitance" C_P in the form: $Q = C_P \cdot V_{DD}$. For a switching frequency f, the mean current $I = Q \cdot f$ flows. The power dissipation is therefore given by

$$P = V_{DD} \cdot I = V_{DD} \cdot Q \cdot f = C_P \cdot V_{DD}^2 \cdot f \ .$$

Consequently, the power dissipation – apart from the small reverse current losses – is proportional to the frequency at which the circuit is operated.

The potential of open CMOS inputs is *undefined*. The open inputs must therefore be connected to ground or V_{DD}. This is necessary even for unused gates, because otherwise an input potential is created at which an undefined but high cross-over current flows through the two transistors, resulting in an unexpectedly high power dissipation.

Precautions when employing CMOS circuits

The gate electrodes of MOSFETs are highly sensitive to static charges. The inputs of MOS integrated circuits are therefore protected by diodes, as shown in Fig. 9.38. Nevertheless, careful handling is required.

These protective diodes, however, introduce a further constraint affecting the use of CMOS circuits [9.5]. Due to the junction insulation of the two MOSFETs T_1 and T_2, a parasitic thyristor is produced between the supply voltage terminals, as shown in Fig. 9.39. This thyristor normally has no effect, as transistors T_3 and T_4 are in the OFF state. Their reverse currents are drained off via resistors R_2 and R_3. However, if one of the protective diodes acting as an additional emitter is biased in the forward direction, thyristor T_3, T_4 may fire. This will cause the two transistors to turn on, short-circuiting the supply voltage, and the high currents produced will destroy the IC. In order to prevent this "latch-up" effect, the input voltage must not fall below the ground potential or exceed the supply voltage. If this cannot be avoided, the current flowing via the protective diodes should at least be limited to values of 1 to 100 mA

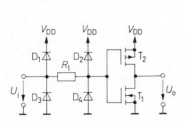

Fig. 9.38 Input protection circuit of CMOS gates

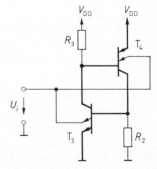

Fig. 9.39 Parasitic thyristor caused by the junction insulation of the MOSFET

depending on the technology. A simple series resistor is generally adequate for this purpose. The parasitic thyristor will also be fired if a voltage is applied to the output which exceeds the supply voltage range.

CMOS gates

Figure 9.40 shows a CMOS NOR gate operating on the same principle as the inverter described above. In order to ensure that the pull-up resistance is high when one of the input voltages assumes the H state, a suitable number of p-channel FETs must be connected in series. By replacing the parallel circuit with a series arrangement, the NOR gate becomes the NAND gate shown in Fig. 9.41.

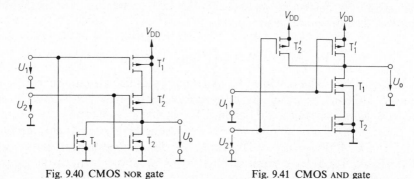

Fig. 9.40 CMOS NOR gate   Fig. 9.41 CMOS AND gate

Transmission gate

In Section 9.1 we saw that logic operations can also be implemented using switches. This possibility is also utilized in MOS technology, as it frequently results in circuit simplification. The resultant component is known as a transmission gate and is used in addition to the conventional gates. Its circuit symbol and equivalent circuit are shown in Fig. 9.42. The way it operates is that input and output are either connected via a very low ON resistance or isolated. As the two terminals are interchangeable in effect, the signal can be transmitted in both directions with minimal delay.

Whereas the logic level in conventional gates is always regenerated, no level regeneration occurs here. The noise margin therefore deteriorates as the number of interconnected transmission gates is increased. Consequently, they are only used in conjunction with conventional gates.

Circuit implementation in CMOS technology is shown in Fig. 9.43. The actual switch is formed by the two complementary MOSFETs T_1 and T_2. The drive arrangement consists of the inverter producing complementary gate potentials. When $U_{contr.} = 0$, $V_{GN} = 0$ and $V_{GP} = V_{DD}$. This causes the two MOSFETs to be turned off provided the signal voltages U_1 and U_2 lie within the range zero to V_{DD}. If, on the other hand, we make $U_{contr.} = V_{DD}$, then

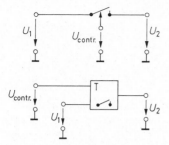

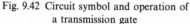

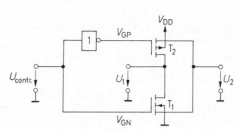

Fig. 9.42 Circuit symbol and operation of   Fig. 9.43 Internal design of a transmission
a transmission gate   gate

$V_{GN} = V_{DD}$ and $V_{GP} = 0$. In this case there is always at least one MOSFET conducting as long as U_1 and U_2 are within the permissible signal voltage range.

As we shall see in Chapter 22, this configuration can also be used as an analog switch. It differs from the transmission gate in that the gate electrodes of T_1 and T_2 are not controlled with logically complementary signals, but driven with signals of opposite polarity. This makes it possible to switch positive and negative signal voltages.

Due to their low power requirement and wide supply voltage range, CMOS circuits are particularly suitable for battery-operated equipment. The various CMOS families are listed in Fig. 9.46.

9.4.7 NMOS logic

The feature of NMOS ICs is that they consist exclusively of n-channel MOSFETs. They are therefore particularly easy to manufacture and, for this reason, are mainly used in large-scale integrated (LSI) circuits.

The NMOS NOR gate in Fig. 9.44 is a close relative of the RTL NOR gate in Fig. 9.21. For technological reasons, a MOSFET is used instead of the ohmic pull-up resistor. As with the input FETs, an enhancement type is employed. To make it conduct, a high gate potential V_{GG} must be applied. If the output voltage in the H state is to rise to the drain potential V_{DD}, the auxiliary potential V_{GG} must be selected higher than V_{DD} by at least the pinch-off voltage. In addition, a negative substrate bias V_{BB} is often required in order to turn off the input FETs reliably and to reduce the junction capacitances.

As we can see from Fig. 9.44, T_3 operates as a source follower for V_{GG}. The internal resistance r_o therefore has the value $1/g_{fs}$. In order to achieve the high resistance values required, it is given a considerably lower transconductance than the input FETs.

The positive auxiliary voltage V_{GG} can be dispensed with by using a depletion-type MOSFET for T_3. This possibility is illustrated in Fig. 9.45, in which T_3 is operated as a constant current source as in Fig. 5.10. However, the

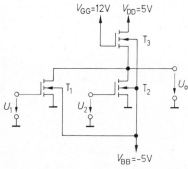

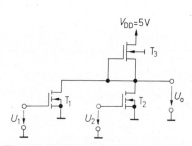

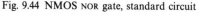

Fig. 9.44 NMOS NOR gate, standard circuit   Fig. 9.45 NMOS NOR gate with depletion
                                                                                load

input FETs must always be of the enhancement type, as the control voltage
would otherwise have to be negative, whereas the output voltage is always
positive. Direct coupling of such gates would therefore be impossible.

Using ion implantation, it is possible to integrate depletion and enhancement type MOSFETs on the same chip. The negative auxiliary voltage can be
eliminated by selecting suitable pinch-off voltages or can be generated from the
positive supply voltage using a voltage converter incorporated in the device.

Only LSI circuits are available in NMOS technology, i.e. no single circuits
such as gates.

9.4.8   Summary

Figure 9.46 provides a list of the most commonly used logic families. In each
case, the data refer to a single gate. We can see that each technology is available
in various versions which differ in terms of power dissipation and gate propagation delay. An attribute of the quality of a circuit family is the delay-power
product. This indicates whether a gate has a small propagation delay despite low
power dissipation. Clearly, the newer families such as the 74AS, 74ALS, 74F,
10H100 and 100.100 possess a noticeably low delay-power product. The reason
for this is that they are dielectrically insulated and therefore have smaller
switching capacitances than the older junction-insulated types.

An equally important technological advance is represented by the silicon
gate CMOS circuits [9.6]. These are faster by a factor of 10 than the metal gate
types with otherwise identical characteristics.

Most circuit families are offered by various manufacturers, which are indicated by the prefix. Manufacturers are listed in Fig. 9.47.

The power consumptions of the logic circuit families vary greatly. We can see
from Fig. 9.48 that the CMOS circuits perform well at low frequencies. However, above 1 MHz there is little difference in power dissipation between low-
power Schottky and CMOS circuits. It is noticeable that in this frequency range
the power consumption of TTL circuits also rises. The reason for this is that

Family	Type	Prefix	Supply voltage	Power dissipation P	Gate propagation delay t_{pd}	Delay-power product $P \cdot t_{pd}$
TTL						
standard	7400	SN, MC, DM, ⊔	5 V	10 mW	10 ns	100 pJ
LP Schottky	74 LS 00	SN, MC, DM, ⊔	5 V	2 mW	10 ns	20 pJ
Schottky	74 S 00	SN, DM, ⊔	5 V	19 mW	3 ns	57 pJ
LP advanced	74 ALS 00	SN, MC, DM	5 V	1 mW	4 ns	4 pJ
fast	74 F 00	F, MC, ⊔, SN	5 V	4 mW	3 ns	12 pJ
advanced	74 AS 00	SN	5 V	10 mW	1.5 ns	15 pJ
ECL						
standard	10.100	MC, F, ⊔	− 5.2 V	35 mW[1]	2 ns	70 pJ
	10.200	MC	− 5.2 V	35 mW[1]	1.5 ns	53 pJ
high speed	1.600	MC	− 5.2 V	70 mW[1]	1 ns	70 pJ
	10 H 100	MC	− 5.2 V	35 mW[1]	1 ns	35 pJ
	100.100	F, ⊔	− 4.5 V	50 mW[1]	0.75 ns	38 pJ
	100 E 100	M	− 4.5 V	30 mW[1]	0.6 ns	18 pJ
CMOS						
standard	4.000 / 14.000	CD, TC / MC	5 V	$0.3 \frac{\mu W}{kHz}$	90 ns	$0.03 \frac{pJ}{kHz}$
	74 C 00	MM	15 V	$3 \frac{\mu W}{kHz}$	30 ns	$0.09 \frac{pJ}{kHz}$
high speed	74 HC 00 / 74 HCT 00	MC, MM, SP / SN, TC, PC, CD	5 V	$0.5 \frac{\mu W}{kHz}$	10 ns	$0.005 \frac{pJ}{kHz}$
advanced	74 AC 00 / 74 ACT 00	SN, PC, F / SN, F	5 V	$0.8 \frac{\mu W}{kHz}$	3 ns	$0.002 \frac{pJ}{kHz}$
TTL output	74 BCT 00	SN	5 V	1 mW	3 ns	3 pJ

[1] inclusive of a 50 Ω emitter resistor connected to $V_{TT} = - 2$ V, producing on average 10 mW

Fig. 9.46 The most commonly used logic circuit families in TTL, ECL and CMOS technology. LP means low power.

Am	AMD	DM, MM	National
F	Fairchild	CD	RCA
HD	Hitachi	⊔	Signetics
MC	Motorola	SN	Texas Instr.
PC	Valvo	SP	SPI
M	SGS-Thom.	TC	Toshiba

Fig. 9.47 Prefixes of the various manufacturers (⊔ = blank)

a cross-over current flows through the totem-pole output stage at each switching cycle which increases significantly the power consumption at high frequencies. ECL circuits do not have this drawback. Consequently, apart from being more expensive, ECL circuits offer nothing but advantages at frequencies above 30 MHz.

Digital ICs will only function properly with a well-designed power supply arrangement. All the logic circuit families generate high-frequency current pulses on the supply lines during switching. As all the signals are referred to ground potential, low-resistance and low-inductance grounding of all ICs is required. This requirement is best satisfied on a printed circuit board by means of a reticular arrangement of the ground conductor. At frequencies above 50 MHz it is advisable to metallize one side of the board completely as a ground conductor plane and only cut out the terminals (see next section). In order to prevent the current pulses from contaminating the supply voltage during switching, the latter must be fed to the ICs with very low resistance and inductance. If the ground connection is well made, interference can be prevented by smoothing the supply voltage with capacitors. For this purpose, 10 to 100 nF ceramic capacitors are used. Electrolytic capacitors are unsuitable due to their poor high-frequency performance. Depending on requirements, one capacitor is assigned to 2 to 5 ICs.

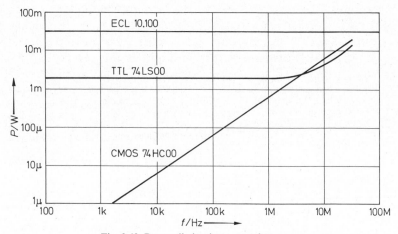

Fig. 9.48 Power dissipation versus frequency

9.5 Connecting lines

So far we have assumed that the digital signals are transmitted undistorted from one IC to another. However, with steep-edged signals the effect of the connecting lines is not negligible. As a rule of thumb, a simple connecting wire is no longer adequate if the delay on that wire attains the order of magnitude of the rise time of the circuit. Consequently, the maximum length for such connections is approximately

10 cm per nanosecond rise time .

If this length is exceeded, severe pulse deformations, reflections and more or less damped oscillations occur. This problem can be overcome by using lines of defined characteristic impedance (coaxial cable, microstrip lines), which are terminated in their characteristic (surge) impedance. This is generally between 50 and 300 Ω.

Microstrip lines can be produced by fabricating all the connecting tracks on the underside of a circuit board and fully metallizing the component side while providing small clearances for the insulation of the component terminals. In this way, all the connecting tracks on the underside become microstrip lines. If the circuit board used has a relative permittivity $\varepsilon_r = 5$ and a thickness $d = 1.2$ mm, we obtain a surge impedance of 75 Ω for a conductor track width of $w = 1$ mm [9.2].

For connections from one board to another, coaxial cables can be used. However, they have the major disadvantage that they are difficult to run via multi-pin connectors. It is much simpler to run the signal via a simple insulated twisted wire pair which can be connected to two adjacent pins of normal multi-pin connectors. If these twisted-pair lines have approximately 100 turns per meter, a characteristic impedance of about 110 Ω is obtained [9.2].

The simplest method of transmitting signals on a twisted-pair line is shown in Fig. 9.49. Due to the low-impedance termination required, the sending-end gate must be able to deliver a correspondingly high output current. Such gates are available in IC form as "line drivers" (buffers). It is advisable to use a Schmitt trigger gate as receiver to re-shape the signal edges. Signal transmission unsymmetrical-about-ground as illustrated in Fig. 9.49 is relatively sensitive to external disturbances, such as voltage spikes on the ground wire. In larger systems, *symmetrical* signal transmission (differential line driver, complementary driver) as shown in Fig. 9.50 is therefore preferable. Here complementary signals are

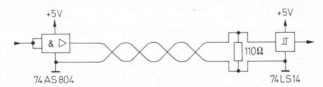

Fig. 9.49 Data transmission via an unsymmetrically driven twisted-pair line

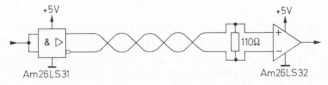

Fig. 9.50 Data transmission via a symmetrically driven twisted-pair line

transmitted on the two wires of the twisted-pair line and a comparator is used as receiver. In this mode of operation, the information is contained in the polarity of the difference voltage rather than in its absolute value. A noise voltage therefore only causes a common-mode input which remains ineffective due to subtraction in the comparator.

When forming the complementary signals, it must be ensured that there is no time delay between the two signals. Consequently, a special circuit with complementary outputs (e.g. Am26LS31 from Advanced Micro Devices) must be used with TTL circuits instead of a simple inverter.

Complementary outputs of this type are inherent in ECL gates. They are therefore particularly well suited to symmetrical data transmission. In order to exploit their high speed capability, a simple differential amplifier with ECL-compatible output is used as comparator. It is known as a *line receiver*. The relevant circuit arrangement is shown in Fig. 9.51.

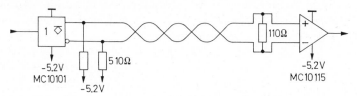

Fig. 9.51 Data transmission in ECL systems via a symmetrically driven twisted-pair line

9.6   Combinatorial logic circuitry

The term "combinatorial logic system" is used to describe an arrangement of digital circuits which contains no means of storing logic variables. The output variables are defined by the input variables alone. It is this property that differentiates them from *sequential logic systems* in which the variables are additionally dependent on the state of the system at any time and hence on its previous history.

The correlation between the output and input variables is described by truth tables or Boolean functions. For circuit implementation, read-only memories (ROMs) can be employed in which the truth table is stored. The input variables are then used as ROM address variables. The second possibility is to use gates or programmable gate arrays (PLD, programmable logic devices) to synthesize the Boolean function. A few simple arrays are described below. Combinatorial logic systems used for performing digital calculations are described in Chapter 19.

Combinatorial logic circuits are frequently used for calculating and recording numbers. If these numbers are to be represented by logic variables, they must be converted into a series of *binary* digits. One binary digit is known as a *bit*. A special binary notation is the straight (natural) binary notation in which the bits are assigned weightings in ascending powers of 2. The symbol 1 identifies logic "one", the symbol 0 logic "zero". Logic variables characterize the individual bits, and we shall identify them by lower-case letters; the entire number will be symbolized by a capital letter. Therefore, an N-bit number in straight binary code is represented as follows:

$$X_N = x_{N-1} \cdot 2^{N-1} + x_{N-2} \cdot 2^{N-2} + \ldots + x_1 \cdot 2^1 + x_0 \cdot 2^0 \ .$$

Obviously, one must always differentiate clearly between an arithmetic operation involving numbers and a Boolean operation of logic variables. An example should clarify the difference. The expression $1 + 1$ is to be calculated. If we interpret the operational sign $(+)$ as an instruction to add in the decimal system, we get

$$1 + 1 = 2 \ .$$

Addition in the straight binary system gives

$$1 + 1 = 10_2 \quad (\text{read: one-zero}) \ .$$

On the other hand, if we interpret the sign $(+)$ as the Boolean sum of logic variables, we obtain

$$1 + 1 = 1 \ .$$

9.6.1 1-out-of-n decoder

A 1-out-of-n decoder is a circuit with n outputs and ld n inputs. Outputs y_J are numbered from 0 to $(n - 1)$. An output therefore goes to "one" precisely when the input binary number A is identical to the number J of the relevant output. Figure 9.52 shows the truth table for a 1-out-of-4 decoder. The variables a_0 and a_1 represent the straight binary code of the number A. The sum of the products (disjunctive normal form) of the recoding functions can be taken directly from the truth table. Figure 9.53 shows the corresponding implementation.

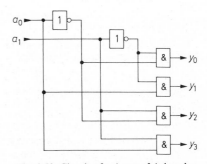

A	a_1	a_0	y_3	y_2	y_1	y_0
0	0	0	0	0	0	1
1	0	1	0	0	1	0
2	1	0	0	1	0	0
3	1	1	1	0	0	0

Fig. 9.52 Truth table of a 1-out-of-4 decoder

$y_0 = \bar{a}_0 \bar{a}_1, y_1 = a_0 \bar{a}_1, y_2 = \bar{a}_0 a_1, y_3 = a_0 a_1$

Fig. 9.53 Circuit of a 1-out-of-4 decoder

When using monolithic integrated circuits, NAND functions are often chosen rather than AND functions, so that most of the output variables are complemented (barred).

Types of IC:	TTL	CMOS
10 outputs	74LS42	4028

For further IC types, see the following section on demultiplexers.

9.6.2 Demultiplexer

A demultiplexer can be used to distribute input information d to various outputs. It represents an extension of the 1-out-of-n decoder. The addressed output does not go to "one", but assumes the value of input variable d. Figure 9.54 illustrates the principle by means of switches, Fig. 9.55 shows its implementation using gates. If we make $d = \text{const} = 1$, the multiplexer operates as a 1-out-of-n decoder. Commonly used demultiplexers are listed in Fig. 9.56.

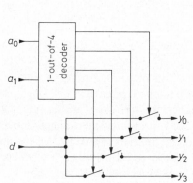

Fig. 9.54 Basic mode of operation

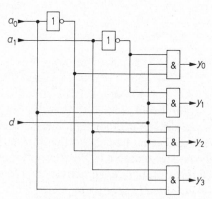

Fig. 9.55 Demultiplexer circuit

$$y_0 = \bar{a}_0\bar{a}_1 d, \; y_1 = a_0\bar{a}_1 d, \; y_2 = \bar{a}_0 a_1 d,$$
$$y_3 = a_0 a_1 d$$

Outputs	TTL	ECL	CMOS
16	74 LS 154		4514
8	74 LS 138	10162	74 HC 138
8	74 ALS 538[1]		40 H 138
2 × 4	74 LS 139	10172	74 HC 139
2 × 4	74 ALS 539[1]		4555

[1] Output polarity reversible

Fig. 9.56 Integrated demultiplexers

9.6.3 Multiplexer

The opposite of a demultiplexer is a multiplexer. Starting from the circuit in Fig. 9.54, it can be implemented by swapping the outputs and input to give the basic circuit in Fig. 9.57. This provides a particularly simple illustration of the mode of operation: a 1-out-of-n decoder selects from n inputs the one whose number coincides with the number entered and switches it to the output. The corresponding gate implementation is shown in Fig. 9.58.

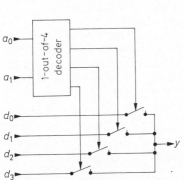

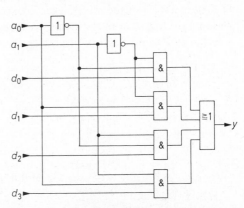

Fig. 9.57 Basic multiplexer operation

Fig. 9.58 Multiplexer circuit

$$y = \bar{a}_0 \bar{a}_1 d_0 + a_0 \bar{a}_1 d_1 + \bar{a}_0 a_1 d_2 + a_0 a_1 d_3$$

In CMOS technology, a multiplexer can be implemented using both gates and analog switches (transmission gates). When analog switches are employed, signal transmission is bidirectional. In this case, therefore, the multiplexer is identical to the demultiplexer, as comparison of Figs. 9.54 and 9.57 will show. The circuit is then known as an analog multiplexer/demultiplexer.

The OR operation required in multiplexers can also be implemented using a wired-OR connection. This possibility is shown for open-collector outputs in

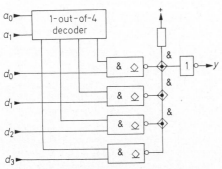

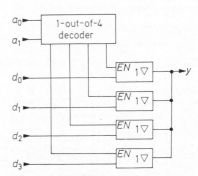

Fig. 9.59 Multiplexer with open-collector gates

Fig. 9.60 Multiplexer with tristate gates

Fig. 9.59. In positive logic, this connection results in an AND operation, it is necessary to resort to the complemented signals – as in Fig. 9.30.

In order to overcome the disadvantage associated with open-collector outputs, namely the higher switching time, tristate outputs can be connected in parallel, with only one being activated at a time. This alternative is shown in Fig. 9.60.

Although the possible implementations of the OR operation shown in Figs. 9.59 and 9.60 are not employed in integrated multiplexers, they are useful if the signal sources of the multiplexer are spatially distributed. Arrangements of this kind are found in bus systems, as we shall describe in Chapter 21.

Some commonly used multiplexers are listed in Fig. 9.61.

Inputs	TTL	ECL	CMOS digital	CMOS analog
16	74 LS 150		4515	4067
2 × 8	74 LS 451[1]			4097
8	74 LS 151	10164	4512	4051
4 × 4	74 LS 453[1]			
2 × 4	74 LS 153	10174	4539	4052
8 × 2	74 LS 604			
4 × 2	74 LS 157	10159	4519	4066

[1] Manufacturer: MMI

Fig. 9.61 Integrated multiplexers. "CMOS analog" means multiplexer/demultiplexer with transmission gate

9.6.4 Priority decoder

The 1-out-of-n code can be converted to straight binary code by using a *priority decoder*. At its outputs a straight binary number appears which corresponds to the highest input number which is logic 1. The value of the

J	x_9	x_8	x_7	x_6	x_5	x_4	x_3	x_2	x_1	y_3	y_2	y_1	y_0
0	0	0	0	0	0	0	0	0	0	0	0	0	0
1	0	0	0	0	0	0	0	0	1	0	0	0	1
2	0	0	0	0	0	0	0	1	×	0	0	1	0
3	0	0	0	0	0	0	1	×	×	0	0	1	1
4	0	0	0	0	0	1	×	×	×	0	1	0	0
5	0	0	0	0	1	×	×	×	×	0	1	0	1
6	0	0	0	1	×	×	×	×	×	0	1	1	0
7	0	0	1	×	×	×	×	×	×	0	1	1	1
8	0	1	×	×	×	×	×	×	×	1	0	0	0
9	1	×	×	×	×	×	×	×	×	1	0	0	1

Fig. 9.62 Truth table of a priority decoder. × ≙ any.

lower-index input variables is irrelevant, hence the name *priority decoder*. This property enables the circuit to convert not only the 1-out-of-*n* code but also a sum code in which not just one variable is 1, but also all the less significant bits. The truth table of the priority decoder is shown in Fig. 9.62.

IC types:

1-out-of-10 code:	SN74147 (TTL)
1-out-of-8 code, extendable:	SN 74148 (TTL); MC 10165 (ECL);
	MC 14532 (CMOS)

9.7 Dependency notation

The new standard for digital circuit symbols (IEC 617-12 and IEEE Std 91-1984) does not merely involve replacing the earlier round symbols by square ones. It also constitutes a significant advance by introducing the so-called dependency notation which allows complex circuits to be represented in a readily comprehensible manner [9.3, 9.4, 9.5].

The underlying concept is the use of precisely defined labeling rules extending beyond the gate symbol itself to indicate how specific variables affect other variables. Controlling terminals are differentiated from controlled terminals. A controlled terminal can in turn also act as a controlling terminal for other terminals.

Various types of dependency have been standardized. These are denoted by specific letters as shown in Fig. 9.63. The relevant letter is written inside the circuit symbol next to the controlling terminal. The letter is followed by an identification number which is also entered at all the terminals affected by the relevant operation.

Symbol	Meaning
G	AND
V	OR
N	Exclusive-OR (controllable negation)
Z	Unaltered transmission
C	Clock, Timing
S	Set
R	Reset
EN	Enable
M	Mode
L	Load
T	Toggle
A	Address
CT	Content (e.g. of a counter)
+	Increment counter
−	Decrement counter

Fig. 9.63 Dependency notation symbols

By way of example, Fig. 9.64 shows the extension of a driver gate to form an
AND gate using the dependency notation. Similarly, Figs. 9.65 and 9.66 show the
extension to OR or EXOR gates.

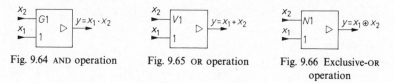

Fig. 9.64 AND operation   Fig. 9.65 OR operation   Fig. 9.66 Exclusive-OR
                                                                         operation

Figs. 9.64–9.66 Dependency notation demonstrated by the example of a driver

A terminal can be controlled simultaneously by several other terminals. In
this case the various identification numbers are separated by commas, as in
Fig. 9.67. The relevant operations must be carried out successively from left
to right.

As an example, Fig. 9.68 shows how a control terminal acts on several other
terminals. A bar over the identification number indicates that the variable in
question must be linked with the negated control variable.

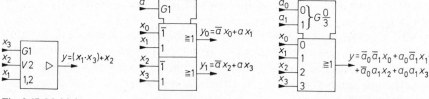

Fig. 9.67 Multiple control   Fig. 9.68 Control of several   Fig. 9.69 Control block
      of an input   inputs, using two 2-to-1   with several control
                                   multiplexers as an example   variables, using a 4-to-1
                                                                      multiplexer as an example

As shown in Fig. 9.69, several terminals can be combined to form one control
variable. In this case the identification number is a straight binary number
resulting from the weighting written inside the brace. The number range in
question is entered after the function symbol. The notation $\frac{0}{3}$ means 0 to 3. In the
example, input x_0 is only effective if control inputs a_0 and a_1 represent the
straight binary number 0.

From the examples given so far, it is clear that controlled inputs are
designated only by identification numbers. However, there are cases in which
a mnemonic designation of a terminal is desirable for other reasons, e.g. D for
data. In such cases the identification numbers are placed before the designation
letter.

Figure 9.70 gives an example of the use of various modes (M) and the effect
and control action of a content (CT). The example shown is of an up-down

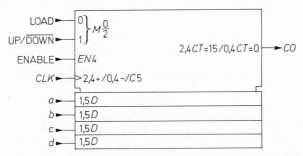

Fig. 9.70 Description of several operating modes using the example of an up-down counter with synchronous parallel loading inputs

counter with parallel loading inputs. Depending on mode, the clock CLK has various effects.

The notation $2,4+$ at the clock input means that the count is incremented $(+)$ when mode 2 is present $(LOAD = 0, UP = 1)$ and $ENABLE = 1$. Similarly, in mode 0 the count is decremented. The condition for this is $0,4-$. The various modes of a terminal are simply written alongside one another, separated by obliques.

In the third mode, the clock initiates parallel data transfer at the D inputs (loading). The notation $1,5\,D$ means that the parallel loading process in mode 1 is taking place in synchrony with the clock. Similarly the notation $1\,D$ would mean a clock-independent (i.e. asynchronous) data transfer.

The carry output CO is controlled by the counter content. It is "1" if the content is 15 when counting up $(2,4\,CT = 15)$ or if the content is "0" when counting down $(0,4\,CT = 0)$.

10 Sequential logic systems

A sequential logic system is an arrangement of digital circuits which can carry out logic operations and, in addition, store the states of individual variables. It differs from a combinatorial logic system in that the output variables y_j are not only dependent on the input variable x_i, but also on the previous history which is represented by the state of flip-flops.

In the following we shall first discuss the design and operation of integrated flip-flops.

10.1 Integrated flip-flops

In Section 8.2.1 we described simple transistor flip-flops. We shall now demonstrate the operation of flip-flops with reference to gates. This approach defines their basic operation irrespective of the particular technology employed.

10.1.1 Transparent flip-flops

By connecting two NOR gates in a feedback arrangement as in Fig. 10.1, we obtain a flip-flop which has complementary outputs Q and $\bar{Q}$ and two inputs S (Set) and R (Reset).

If the complementary input state $S = 1$ and $R = 0$ is applied, we have

$$\bar{Q} = \overline{S + Q} = \overline{1 + Q} = 0$$

and

$$Q = \overline{R + \bar{Q}} = \overline{0 + 0} = 1 \ .$$

The two outputs, therefore, assume complementary states. Similarly, for $R = 1$ and $S = 0$, the opposite output state is obtained. If we make $R = S = 0$, the old output state is retained. This explains why RS flip-flops are used as memories. When $R = S = 1$, the two outputs become simultaneously 0; however, the output state is no longer defined when R and S then become simultaneously 0. Consequently, the input state $R = S = 1$ is generally disallowed. The switching states are summarized in the truth table in Fig. 10.2, with which we are already familiar from the transistor circuit in Fig. 8.10.

In Section 9.2 we showed that a logic equation does not change if all the variables are negated and the arithmetic operations $(+)$ and $(\cdot)$ are interchanged. Applying this rule here, we arrive at the RS flip-flop comprising NAND gates shown in Fig. 10.3, which has the same truth table as that shown in Fig. 10.2. However, note that the input variables are now $\bar{R}$ and $\bar{S}$. As we shall be

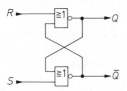

Fig. 10.1 *RS* flip-flop comprising NOR gates

S	R	Q	$\bar{Q}$
0	0	Q_{-1}	$\bar{Q}_{-1}$
0	1	0	1
1	0	1	0
1	1	(0)	(0)

Fig. 10.2 Truth table for an *RS* flip-flop

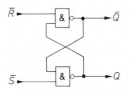

Fig. 10.3 *RS* flip-flop comprising NAND
gates

$\bar{S}$	$\bar{R}$	Q	$\bar{Q}$
0	0	(1)	(1)
0	1	1	0
1	0	0	1
1	1	Q_{-1}	$\bar{Q}_{-1}$

Fig. 10.4 Truth table for an *RS* flip-flop
comprising NAND gates

frequently using the *RS* flip-flop comprising NAND gates, we have given its truth table for input variables $\bar{R}$ and $\bar{S}$ in Fig. 10.4.

Clocked RS flip-flop

We frequently require an *RS* flip-flop which only reacts to the input state at a specific point in time. This time is determined by an additional clock variable C. Figure 10.5 shows a statically clocked *RS* flip-flop of this kind. If $C = 0$, then $\bar{R} = \bar{S} = 1$. In this case the flip-flop stores the old state. For $C = 1$, we get

$$R = R' \quad \text{and} \quad S = S' \; .$$

The flip-flop then behaves like a normal *RS* flip-flop.

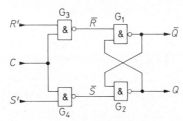

Fig. 10.5 Statically clocked *RS* flip-flop

Clocked D flip-flop

We shall now examine how the value of a logic variable D can be stored using the flip-flop in Fig. 10.5. We have seen that $Q = S$ if complementary input states are applied and $C = 1$. In order to store the value of a variable D, we therefore need only make $S = D$ and $R = \bar{D}$. The inverter G_5 in Fig. 10.6 is used for this purpose. In the resulting data latch, $Q = D$ as long as clock $C = 1$. This may also be seen from the truth table in Fig. 10.7. Due to this property, the clocked data latch is also known as a transparent D flip-flop. If we make $C = 0$, the existing output state is stored.

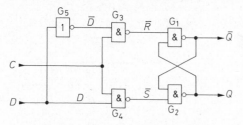

Fig. 10.6 Transparent D flip-flop (D latch)

C	D	Q
0	0	Q_{-1}
0	1	Q_{-1}
1	0	0
1	1	1

Fig. 10.7 Truth table for the transparent D-flip-flop

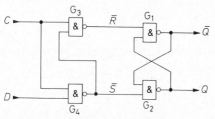

Fig. 10.8 Practical implementation of a transparent D flip-flop

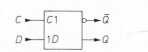

Fig. 10.9 Circuit symbol for a transparent D flip-flop

We can see that NAND gate G_4 in Fig. 10.6 acts as an inverter for D when $C = 1$. Inverter G_5 can therefore be omitted, producing the practical implementation of a D latch shown in Fig. 10.8. The circuit symbol is given in Fig. 10.9.

IC types:

74 LS 75 (TTL);   10133 (ECL);   4042 (CMOS)

10.1.2   Flip-flops with intermediate storage

For many applications, such as counters and shift registers, transparent flip-flops are unsuitable. In these cases flip-flops are required which temporarily store the input state and only transfer it to the output when the inputs are inhibited once more. They therefore comprise two flip-flops: the master flip-flop at the input and the slave flip-flop at the output.

Two-edge-triggered flip-flops

Figure 10.10 shows a master-slave flip-flop of this kind. It consists of two statically clocked RS flip-flops of the type shown in Fig. 10.5. The two flip-flops

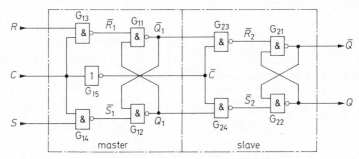

Fig. 10.10 *RS* master-slave flip-flop

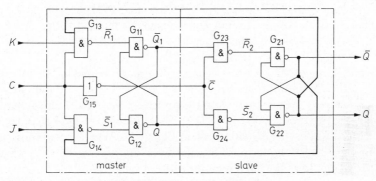

Fig. 10.11 *JK* master-slave flip-flop

are mutually inhibited by complementary clock signals. Gate G_{15} is used for clock inversion. As long as clock $C = 1$, the input information is read into the master. The output state remains unchanged, because the slave is disabled.

When the clock goes to 0, the master is disabled, thereby freezing the state present immediately prior to the negative-going edge of the clock signal. The slave is simultaneously triggered, thus transferring the state of the master to the output. Data transmission therefore occurs on the negative-going edge; however, there is no clock state in which the input data have a direct effect on the output, as is the case with transparent flip-flops.

The input combination $R = S = 1$ necessarily results in an undefined behavior, because inputs $\bar{S}_1$, $\bar{R}_1$ in the master simultaneously go from 00 to 11 when clock C goes to 0. In order to be able to make use of this input combination, the complementary output data are additionally applied to the input gates. The feedback circuit shown in heavy type in Fig. 10.11 is used for this purpose. The external inputs are then designated J and K respectively. We can see from the truth table in Fig. 10.12 that the output state for $J = K = 1$ is inverted at each clock pulse. This is the same as dividing the frequency by two, as Fig. 10.13 shows. Consequently, JK master-slave flip-flops provide a particularly simple means of constructing counters.

J	K	Q
0	0	Q_{-1} (unchanged)
0	1	$\left.\begin{matrix} 0 \\ 1 \end{matrix}\right\}$ $(Q = J)$
1	0	
1	1	$\bar{Q}_{-1}$ (inverted)

Fig. 10.12 Output state of a JK master-slave flip-flop after a (010) clock cycle

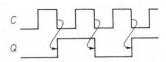

Fig. 10.13 JK master-slave flip-flop as frequency divider $(J = K = 1)$

However, because of the feedback, operation of the JK flip-flop is subject to an important *limitation*: the truth table in Fig. 10.12 only applies if the state at the JK inputs remains unchanged as long as clock C is 1. This is because, unlike the RS master-slave flip-flop in Fig. 10.10, the master-slave flip-flop here can only change state once and cannot change back, as one of the two input NAND gates is always disabled by the feedback. Failure to observe this limitation is a frequent source of errors in digital circuits.

Special types of JK master-slave flip-flops are available which are not subject to this limitation. They are provided with data lockout: the input state read in is precisely the one present on the positive-going edge. Immediately after this edge, the two input gates are disabled and no longer react to changes in the input states [10.1]. This is made clear in Fig. 10.14. Whereas with normal JK flip-flops the J and K inputs must not change as long as clock $C = 1$, with a data lockout JK flip-flop they must remain constant only during the positive-going edge of the clock signal. The common feature of both flip-flops is that the information read in on the positive-going edge of the clock signal does not appear at the output until the negative-going edge. Due to this delay, the circuit symbol in Fig. 10.15 additionally has a delay sign at the outputs.

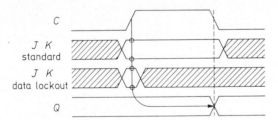

Fig. 10.14 Timing diagram of the input and output signals of JK master-slave flip flops

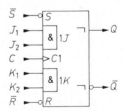

Fig. 10.15 Circuit symbol of a JK master-slave flip-flop

JK flip-flops frequently have several J and K inputs leading to an internal AND gate. The internal J and K variables are then only 1 when all the respective J and K inputs are 1.

In addition to the JK inputs, the JK flip-flops additionally possess Set and Reset inputs which operate independently of the Clock—i.e. asynchronously. This enables master and slave flip-flops to be set or cleared. The RS inputs have priority over the JK inputs. In order to allow clock-controlled operation, either $R = S = 0$ or $\bar{R} = \bar{S} = 1$.

Typical IC types:

	TTL	ECL	CMOS
Standard	7476	10135	4027
Data lockout	74 LS 111		

Single-edge-triggered flip-flops

Flip-flops with intermediate storage can also be implemented by connecting two transparent D flip-flops (Fig. 10.8) in series and clocking them with complementary signals. This produces the circuit shown in Fig. 10.16. As long as clock $C = 0$, the master follows the input signal and we have $Q_1 = D$. The slave meanwhile stores the old state. When the clock goes to 1, the data D present at that instant is frozen in the master and transferred to the slave and thus to the Q output. The information present at the D input on the positive-going edge of the clock signal is therefore instantaneously transmitted to the Q output. The state of the D input has no effect for the rest of the time. This can also be seen from Fig. 10.17. Instead of waiting for the negative-going edge, as in the JK flip-flop with data lockout, the input value appears at the output immediately. For this reason, the circuit symbol in Fig. 10.18 also has no delay symbols. This

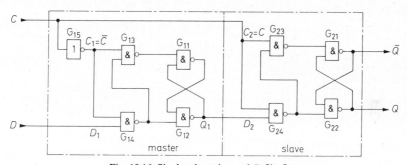

Fig. 10.16 Single-edge-triggered D flip-flop

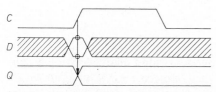

Fig. 10.17 Timing diagram for the input and output signals in the single-edge-triggered D flip-flop

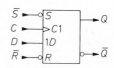

Fig. 10.18 Circuit symbol for the single-edge-triggered D flip-flop

constitutes a significant advantage, in that the entire clock cycle is now available for forming the new D signal. If JK flip-flops are used, this process must take place while the clock is zero, i.e. with symmetrical clock pulses in half the time.

Examples of IC types:

74 LS 74 (TTL);   10131 (ECL);   4013 (CMOS)

Single-edge-triggered D flip-flops can also be operated as toggle flip-flops. For this purpose we make $D = \bar{Q}$ as in Fig. 10.19. The output state therefore inverts at each positive-going edge of the clock signal. This is illustrated in Fig. 10.20. If transparent D flip-flops were used, an oscillation would be obtained while clock $C = 1$, instead of a frequency division. It is caused by the transparent propagation of the signal through the circuit, resulting in a signal inversion after every propagation delay time.

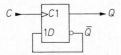

Fig. 10.19 Single-edge-triggered D flip-flop as a frequency divider

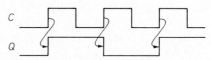

Fig. 10.20 Timing pattern in the frequency divider

It is also possible to make the inversion dependent on a control variable by providing feedback from either $\bar{Q}$ or Q to the D input via a multiplexer. The latter is controlled by the toggle input T in Fig. 10.21. The same mode of operation is possible using the JK flip-flop in Fig. 10.22 with interconnected JK inputs.

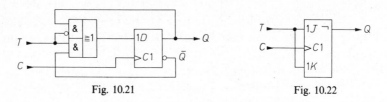

Fig. 10.21   Fig. 10.22

Fig. 10.21/22 Controllable toggle flip-flops

$$Q = \begin{cases} Q_{-1} \\ \bar{Q}_{-1} \end{cases} \text{for} \quad \begin{matrix} T = 0 \\ T = 1 \end{matrix}$$

Multi-purpose flip-flops can be obtained by additionally providing synchronous data input. The multiplexer can then be given another input preceding the D input. This additional input is selected via Load input L as shown in Fig. 10.23. If $L = 1$, then $y = D$ and therefore, after the next clock signal, $Q = D$. When $L = 0$, the circuit operates in exactly the same way as that in Fig. 10.21.

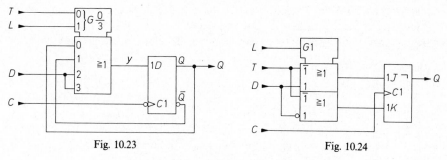

Fig. 10.23   Fig. 10.24

Figs. 10.23/24 Multifunction flip-flops

T = Toggle, L = Load, D = Data, C = Clock

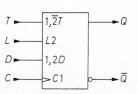

L	T	Q
0	0	Q_{-1}
0	1	Q_{-1}
1	0	D
1	1	D

Fig. 10.25a Circuit symbol of a multifunction   Fig. 10.25b Function table of a multifunction
flip-flop   flip-flop

The mode of operation of this multifunction flip-flop is summarized in Fig. 10.25.

The same behavior can also be obtained using a JK flip-flop as shown in Fig. 10.24. When $L = 1$, $J = D$ or $K = \bar{D}$. Therefore, after the next clock signal, $Q = D$. When $L = 0$, we have $J = K = T$; the circuit then operates as in Fig. 10.22. In the case of JK flip-flops, it must be remembered that the data have to be present before the positive-going edge of the clock signal, but only appear after the output on the negative-going edge. With normal JK flip-flops (as in Fig. 10.11), it must also be ensured that the J and K inputs do not change as long as $C = 1$. During this time the L, T and D inputs must therefore also remain unchanged.

Due to their versatility, the multifunction flip-flops in Figs. 10.23/24 constitute the basic building blocks of counters.

10.2   Straight binary counters

Counters are an important group of sequential logic systems. A counter may be any circuit which, within certain limits, has a defined relationship between the number of input pulses and the state of the output variables. As each output variable can have only two values, for n outputs, there are 2^n possible output combinations, although often only some of these are used. It is

Z	z_3	z_2	z_1	z_0
	2^3	2^2	2^1	2^0
0	0	0	0	0
1	0	0	0	1
2	0	0	1	0
3	0	0	1	1
4	0	1	0	0
5	0	1	0	1
6	0	1	1	0
7	0	1	1	1
8	1	0	0	0
9	1	0	0	1
10	1	0	1	0
11	1	0	1	1
12	1	1	0	0
13	1	1	0	1
14	1	1	1	0
15	1	1	1	1
16	0	0	0	0

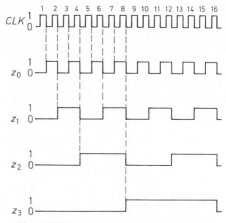

Fig. 10.26 State table of a straight binary
counter

Fig. 10.27 Output states of a straight binary
up-counter, as a function of time

unimportant which number is assigned to which combination, but it is useful to choose a representation which can subsequently be easily processed. The simplest circuits are obtained for the straight binary notation.

Figure 10.26 shows the relationship between the number, Z, of input pulses and the values of output variables z_i, for a 4-bit straight binary counter. If this table is read from top to bottom, two patterns emerge:

1) an output variable z_i always changes state when the next lower value z_{i-1} changes from 1 to 0.
2) an output variable z_i always changes state when all lower variables $z_{i-1}, \ldots, z_0$ have the value 1 and a new pulse arrives.

These patterns can also be seen in the timing diagram in Fig. 10.27. Pattern (1) is the basis of an asynchronous counter (ripple counter), whereas pattern (2) yields the synchronous counter.

Occasionally, counters are required, whose output state is reduced by 1 for each count pulse. The operational principle of such a *down-counter* can also be inferred from the table in Fig. 10.26 by reading it from the bottom up. It follows that

1a) an output variable z_i of a down-counter changes state whenever the next lower variable z_{i-1} changes from 0 to 1.
2a) an output variable z_i of a down-counter always changes state when all lower variables $z_{i-1}, \ldots, z_0$ have the value 0 and a new clock pulse arrives.

10.2.1   Asynchronous straight binary counter

A straight binary asynchronous (ripple) counter can be implemented by arranging flip-flops in a chain, as in Fig. 10.28, and by connecting each clock input C to the output Q of the previous flip-flop. If the circuit is to be an up-counter, the flip-flops must change their output states when their clock inputs C change from 1 to 0. Edge-triggered flip-flops are therefore required, e.g. JK master-slave flip-flops where $J = K = 1$. The counter may be extended to any size. Using this principle, one can count up to 1023 with only 10 flip-flops.

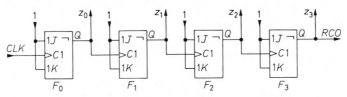

Fig. 10.28 Asynchronous straight binary counter

CLK = Clock RCO = Ripple Carry Output

Flip-flops triggered by the positive-going edge of the clock pulse can also be employed, e.g. single-edge triggered D flip-flops. If they are connected in the same way as in Fig. 10.28, down-counter operation is obtained. For up-counter operation, their clock pulse must be inverted. This is achieved by connecting each clock input to the $\bar{Q}$-output of the previous flip-flop.

Every counter is also a frequency divider. The frequency at the output of flip-flop F_0 is half the counter frequency. A quarter of the input frequency appears at the output of F_1, an eighth at the output of F_2, etc. This property of frequency division can be seen clearly in Fig. 10.27.

IC-types:

Length	TTL	ECL	CMOS
4 bit	74 LS 93	10178	
7 bit			4024
8 bit	74 LS 393		
24 bit			4521
30 bit	74 LS 292		

10.2.2   Synchronous straight binary counters

It is characteristic of an *asynchronous* counter that the clock pulse is applied only to the input of the first flip-flop, while the remaining flip-flops are indirectly controlled. This means that the input signal of the last flip-flop does not arrive until all the preceding stages have changed state. Each change of the output states z_0 to z_n is therefore delayed by the set-up time of a flip-flop. For long chains and high counter frequencies, this may result in z_n changing with a delay of one or more clock cycles. After the last clock pulse, it is therefore necessary to wait for the delay time of the entire counter chain before the result can be evaluated. If evaluation of the counter state is required during counting, the period of the clock pulse must not be smaller than the delay time of the counter chain.

Synchronous counters do not have these drawbacks, as the clock pulses are applied *simultaneously* to all clock inputs C. In order that the flip-flops do not all change state at every clock pulse, controllable toggle flip-flops as shown in Figs. 10.21 or 10.22 are used which only change state when the control variable $T = 1$. In accordance with Fig. 10.26, a flip-flop of a straight binary counter may only change state when all the lower-order flip-flops are 1. To bring this about, we make $T_0 = 1$, $T_1 = z_0$, $T_2 = z_0 \cdot z_1$ and $T_3 = z_0 \cdot z_1 \cdot z_2$. The AND gates required for this purpose are shown in Fig. 10.29.

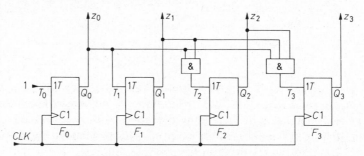

Fig. 10.29 Synchronous straight binary counter

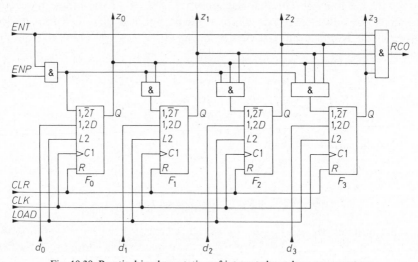

Fig. 10.30 Practical implementation of integrated synchronous counters.

ENT = Enable T ENP = Enable P
CLR = Clear CLK = Clock
RCO = Ripple Carry Output

Integrated synchronous counters have yet more inputs and outputs whose function and application will be described in further detail with reference to Fig. 10.30. The entire counter can be initialized using the Clear input CLR ($Z = 0$). It can be set to any number $Z = D$ via the Load input. Whereas the Clear input always operates asynchronously like any Reset input, both synchronous and asynchronous types are available for the load process.

Very large (multiple-bit) counters can be implemented by cascading several 4-bit counter stages. The stages are connected via the ripple carry output RCO and the enable input ENT, which can be used to inhibit the entire counter stage and the carry output. The latter must therefore go to 1 when a count of 1111 is reached and all the lower-order stages likewise produce a carry. For this to occur, the logic operation

$$RCO = ENT \cdot z_0 \cdot z_1 \cdot z_2 \cdot z_3$$

must be performed in each counter stage. The corresponding output gate is shown in Fig. 10.30.

To cascade the counter stages, it is merely necessary to connect the ENT input of a stage to the RCO output of the next lower-order stage. However, as the delays are cumulative due to the cascaded AND operations, multiple-bit counters are subject to a reduction in the maximum possible counting frequency. In this case it is preferable to perform the required AND operations in parallel in each counter stage. To do this, the lowest-order stage is omitted from the serial RCO-ENT operation and the enabling of the higher-order stages is controlled in parallel via the ENP inputs. In this way the parallel AND operation can be implemented without external gates, as shown in Fig. 10.31.

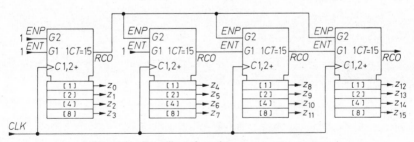

Fig. 10.31 Cascading of synchronous counter stages.

CT = Content

Typical IC types:

Length	Reset	TTL	ECL	CMOS
4 bit	asynchronous	74 LS 161A		4161
4 bit	synchronous	74 LS 163A	10136	4163
8 bit	synchronous	74 LS 590		

10.2.3   Up-down counters

A distinction is drawn between up-down counters with one clock input and a second input which determines the mode of counting, and those with two clock inputs, one for incrementing the count, the other for decrementing it.

Counters with up-down control

As may be seen from Fig. 10.26, the switching condition for counting down is that a flip-flop must change state if all the lower-order bits are zero. In order to decode this, the up-counter logic used in Fig. 10.30 can be connected to the $\bar{Q}$ outputs. In the case of the counter with up-down control in Fig. 10.32, either the top part of the up-counter logic or the bottom part of the down-counter logic is enabled via up-down changeover input $U/\bar{D}$.

A carry into the next higher counter stage can occur in two cases, namely when the count is 1111 during "up" operation ($U/\bar{D} = 1$), or when the count is 0000 during "down" operation. The carry variable is therefore given by

$$RCO = [z_0 z_1 z_2 z_3 \, U/\bar{D} + \bar{z}_0 \bar{z}_1 \bar{z}_2 \bar{z}_3 \, \overline{U/\bar{D}}]ENT \ .$$

This variable is applied to the enable input of the next counter stage, as in Fig. 10.31. The carry is always interpreted with correct sign if the counting direction is changed over simultaneously for all the counters.

Typical IC types:

Length	TTL	ECL	CMOS
4 bit	74 LS 191	10136	4516
8 bit	74 AS 867		
10 bit	74 LS 491 (MMI)		

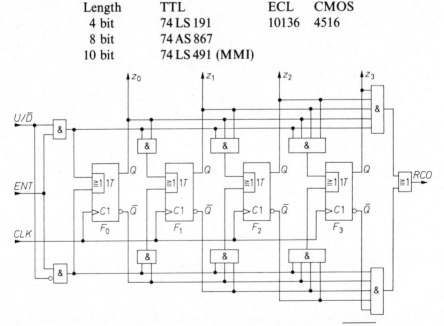

Fig. 10.32 Binary counter with up/down control. $U/\bar{D} = UP/\overline{DOWN}$

Counters with separate up and down inputs

Figure 10.33 shows a counter with two clock inputs for counting up and down respectively. In the previous circuits, the clock signal was fed to all the flip-flops. Those flip-flops not intended to change state were disabled via control input T. In the case of the counter in Fig. 10.33, the clock pulses are prevented from reaching particular flip-flops. An "up" clock signal CUP is only applied to the clock inputs of those flip-flops whose predecessors are at 1. Similarly, a "down" clock signal CDN is only fed to those flip-flops for which all preceding outputs are at 0.

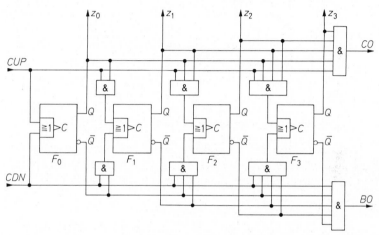

Fig. 10.33 Straight binary counter with clock-up and clock-down inputs. F_0 to F_3 are toggle flip-flops.

$$CUP = \text{Clock Up} \qquad CDN = \text{Clock Down}$$
$$CO = \text{Carry Output} \qquad BO = \text{Borrow Output}$$

As the flip-flops which are to change state receive their clock pulses virtually at the same time, the flip-flops for the more significant bits change state simultaneously with those for the less significant. The circuit therefore operates as a synchronous counter. The AND gates at the output determine the carry for up-counter operation and that for down-counter operation. It is possible to connect another identical counter which is in itself synchronous but delayed with respect to the first, i.e. operating asynchronously. This mode of operation is termed semisynchronous.

IC type:

4 bit   74 LS 193 (TTL)

Coincidence cancellation

The interval between two count pulses and their duration must not be smaller than the set-up time t_{su} of the counter, or the second pulse would be incorrectly processed. Counters with only one clock input can therefore count at a maximum possible frequency of $f_{max} = 1/2t_{su}$. For the counter in Fig. 10.33, the situation is more complicated. Even if the counter frequencies at the up-clock and at the down-clock input are considerably lower than f_{max}, the interval between an up- and a down-clock pulse may, in asynchronous systems, be smaller than t_{su}. Such close or even coinciding pulses result in a spurious counter state. This can be avoided only by preventing these pulses reaching the counter inputs. The state of the counter then remains unchanged as would also be the case after one up- and one down-clock pulse.

Such a coincidence cancellation circuit can, for example, be designed as in Fig. 10.34, where one-shots are used [10.2]. The one-shots (monostable multi-vibrators) M_1 and M_2 convert the counter pulses CUP and CDN into the signals x_{UP} and x_{DN}, each having a defined length t_1. Their trailing edges are used to trigger the two one-shots M_4 and M_5 which in turn generate the output pulses. Gate G_1 decides whether the normalized input pulses x_{UP} and x_{DN} overlap. If this is the case, a positive-going edge appears at its output which triggers one-shot M_3. Both output gates G_2 and G_3 are then disabled for a time t_2, and no pulses can appear at the output. In order that pulses are safely suppressed, the following relationship must hold:

$$t_2 > t_1 + t_3 .$$

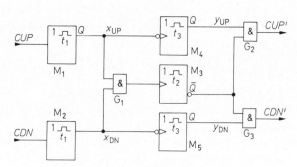

Fig. 10.34 Coincidence cancellation circuit

Time t_3 defines the duration of the output pulses. The interval between them is shortest just before coincidence is detected, i.e. $\Delta t = t_1 - t_3$. For correct operation of the counter, the additional conditions

$$t_3 > t_{su} \quad \text{and} \quad t_1 - t_3 > t_{su}$$

must therefore be fulfilled. The shortest permissible on-times of the one-shots are thus $t_3 = t_{su}, t_1 = 2t_{su}$ and $t_2 = 3t_{su}$. The maximum counter frequency at the two inputs of the coincidence detector is then

$$f_{max} = 1/t_2 = 1/3t_{su} .$$

The coincidence cancellation circuit therefore reduces f_{max} by a factor of 1.5.

The "anti-race clock generator" in the 40110 counter (CMOS) operates on this principle.

Subtraction method

A considerably more elegant method consists of counting off the up and down pulses in separate counters and then subtracting the results, as in Fig. 10.35. Coinciding counter pulses then produce no unwanted effects. A further advantage is that the simpler logic circuitry of an up-counter inherently permits a higher clock frequency.

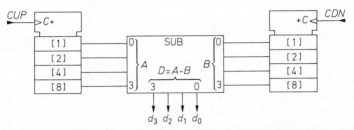

Fig. 10.35 Straight binary up/down counter insensitive to coinciding clock pulses

The carry bit of the subtractor cannot be used to indicate the mathematical sign, as a positive difference would be misinterpreted as being negative should one of the two counters overflow. However, the result is obtained with correct sign if the difference is interpreted – in our example – as a four-digit 2's-complement number. Bit d_3 therefore exhibits the correct sign, provided the difference does not exceed the permissible range -8 to $+7$.

10.3   BCD counters in 8421 code

10.3.1   Asynchronous BCD counter

The table in Fig. 10.26 shows that a 3-bit counter can count up to 7 and a 4-bit counter up to 15. In a counter for straight BCD numbers, a 4-bit straight binary counter used as a decade counter is required for each decimal digit. This decade counter differs from the normal straight binary counter in that it is reset to zero after every tenth count pulse and produces a carry. This carry bit controls the decade counter for the next higher decimal digit.

With BCD counters, a decimal display of the count is achieved much more easily than for the straight binary counter, as each decade can be separately decoded and displayed as a decimal digit.

In straight BCD code, each decimal digit is represented by a 4-bit straight binary number, the bit weightings of which are 2^3, 2^2, 2^1 and 2^0. It is therefore also known as the 8421 code. The state table of a decade counter employing 8421 code is shown in Fig. 10.36. By definition, it must be identical with that in

Z	z_3	z_2	z_1	z_0
	2^3	2^2	2^1	2^0
0	0	0	0	0
1	0	0	0	1
2	0	0	1	0
3	0	0	1	1
4	0	1	0	0
5	0	1	0	1
6	0	1	1	0
7	0	1	1	1
8	1	0	0	0
9	1	0	0	1
10	0	0	0	0

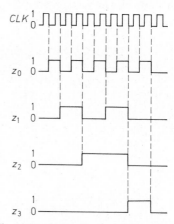

Fig. 10.36 State table for 8421 code

Fig. 10.37 Timing diagram of the output states of an 8421-code counter

Fig. 10.26 up to the number 9, but the number ten $= 10_{\text{dec.}}$ is represented again by 0000. The associated timing diagram for the output variables is shown in Fig. 10.37.

Obviously, additional logic circuitry is required to reset the counter at every tenth input pulse. However, gates may be saved by using JK flip-flops with several J and K inputs, as in Fig. 10.38. In contrast to the normal straight binary counter in Fig. 10.28, the circuit operates as follows: flip-flop F_1 may not change state at the tenth counting pulse, even though z_0 changes from 1 to 0. From Fig. 10.28, we deduce a simple criterion for this case: z_1 must be kept at 0 if z_3 is 1 prior to the clock signal. To achieve this, the J input of F_1 is connected to $\bar{z}_3$. The condition that z_2 must remain 0 at the tenth pulse is therefore automatically satisfied.

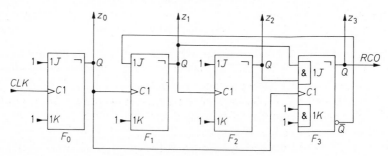

Fig. 10.38 Asynchronous BCD counter

The second difference with respect to a straight binary counter is that z_3 changes from 1 to 0 at the tenth pulse. However, if the clock input of F_3 were connected to z_2 as in a normal straight binary counter, z_3 would be unable to change after the eighth counting pulse, since flip-flop F_1 is disabled by the feedback signal. The clock input of F_3 must therefore be connected to the output of the flip-flop which is not disabled by the feedback signal, in this case z_0.

On the other hand, the J inputs must be controlled so that they prevent flip-flop F_3 from changing state prematurely. Figure 10.36 indicates that z_3 must not go to 1 unless both z_1 and z_2 are 1 prior to the clock signal. This may be achieved by connecting the two J inputs of F_3 to z_1 and z_2 respectively. Then, at the eighth counting pulse $z_3 = 1$. Since z_1 and z_2 become zero simultaneously, z_3 resumes the state $z_3 = 0$ as soon as possible, i.e. at the tenth counting pulse when z_0 has its next transition from 1 to 0. Figure 10.36 indicates that this is precisely the right instant.

IC types:

| 4 bit | 74 LS 90 (TTL) | 10138 (ECL) |
| 2 × 4 bit | 74 LS 390 (TTL) | |

10.3.2 Synchronous BCD counter

The synchronous decade counter in Fig. 10.39 has largely similar circuitry to the synchronous straight binary counter in Fig. 10.30. As with the asynchronous decade counter, two additional features are again required to ensure that, at the transition from $9 = 1001_2$ to $0_{dec.} = 0000$, flip-flop F_3 changes state and not flip-flop F_1. The disabling of F_1 is achieved in Fig. 10.39 via the feedback path of $\bar{Q}_3$, the change of state of F_3 by additionally decoding the 9 at the toggle control input.

Examples of synchronous BCD counters:
74 LS160 (TTL);   4160 (CMOS);

with up-down control:
74 LS190 (TTL);   10137 (ECL);   4510 (CMOS);

with up/down clock input:
74 LS192 (TTL)

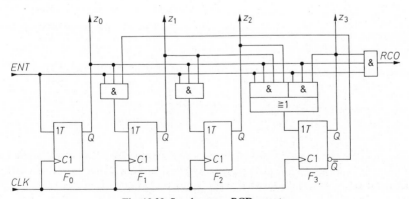

Fig. 10.39 Synchronous BCD counter

10.4 Presettable counters

Presettable counters are circuits which produce an output signal when the number of input pulses equals a predetermined number M. The output signal can be used to trigger any desired process and is employed to stop the counter or reset it to its initial state. If the counter is allowed to continue counting after reset, it operates as a modulo-M counter, the counting cycle of which is determined by the preselected number M.

The most obvious method of implementing a presettable counter consists of comparing the count Z with the preselected number M, as in Fig. 10.40. For this purpose we can use an identity comparator as described in Section 19.4. If $Z = M$ after M clock pulses, y becomes 1 and the counter is cleared ($Z = 0$). The equality signal y is present for the duration of the clearing process. With an asynchronous CLR input, this time only amounts to a few gate propagation delays. For this reason a synchronous clear input is preferable; then the equality signal is present for precisely one clock period. The counter in Fig. 10.40 therefore returns to zero after $M + 1$ clock pulses. It thus represents a modulo-$(M + 1)$ counter.

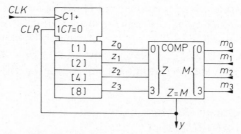

Fig. 10.40 Modulo-$(M + 1)$ counter with comparator

The comparator in Fig. 10.40 can be dispensed with by using the LOAD inputs generally provided in synchronous counters (Fig. 10.30). The circuits in Figs. 10.41/42 make use of this possibility. The counter in Fig. 10.41 is loaded with the number $P = Z_{max} - M$. After M clock pulses, the maximum count Z_{max} is therefore reached which is internally decoded and produces a carry

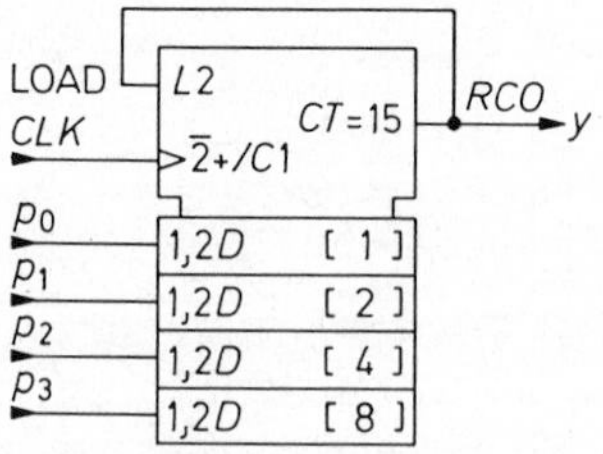

Fig. 10.41 Modulo-$(M + 1)$ counter with parallel input of $P = Z_{max} - M$ for $Z = 15$

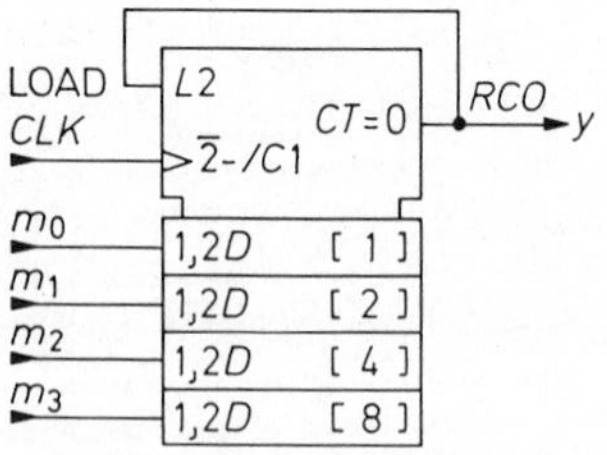

Fig. 10.42 Modulo-$(M + 1)$ counter with parallel input of M for $Z = 0$ using a down counter

$RCO = 1$. If this output is connected to the LOAD input as in Fig. 10.41, the preset number P is reloaded with clock pulse $M + 1$. Once again we have a modulo-$(M + 1)$ counter. For straight binary counters, the number P is particularly easy to determine: it is equal to the 1's-complement of M (see Section 19.1.3).

The counter in Fig. 10.42 is loaded with the preset number M itself. It then counts down to zero. At zero, a carry RCO is generated (see Fig. 10.32) which can be used to reload the counter.

10.5   Shift registers

Shift registers are chains of flip-flops which allow data applied to the input to be advanced by one flip-flop with each clock pulse. After passing through the chain, the data are available at the output with a delay but otherwise unchanged.

10.5.1   Basic circuit

The shift-register principle is illustrated in Fig. 10.43. On the first clock pulse, the information D_1 present at the input is read into flip-flop F_1. On the second clock pulse, it is passed on to flip-flop F_2; simultaneously, new information is read into flip-flop F_1. As an example, Fig. 10.44 illustrates the mode of operation for a 4-bit shift register. We can see that the shift register is filled serially

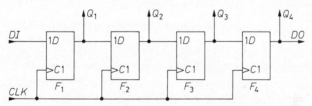

Fig. 10.43 Simplest version of a 4-bit shift register.

DI = Data Input DO = Data Output
CLK = Clock

CLK	Q_1	Q_2	Q_3	Q_4
1	D_1	–	–	–
2	D_2	D_1	–	–
3	D_3	D_2	D_1	–
4	D_4	D_3	D_2	D_1
5	D_5	D_4	D_3	D_2
6	D_6	D_5	D_4	D_3
7	D_7	D_6	D_5	D_4

Fig. 10.44 Function table of a 4-bit shift register

with input data after four clock pulses. These are then available in parallel at the four flip-flop outputs Q_1 to Q_4, or they can be extracted serially once more at output Q_4 on subsequent clock pulses. All flip-flops with intermediate storage can be used. Transparent flip-flops are unsuitable because the information applied to the input would immediately pass through to the last flip-flop when the clock goes to 1.

10.5.2   Shift register with parallel input

If, as in Fig. 10.45, a multiplexer is connected in front of each D input, it is possible to switch over to parallel data input via the Load input. On the next clock pulse, data d_1 to d_4 are loaded in parallel and appear at Q_1 to Q_4. This allows not only *serial-to-parallel conversion* but also *parallel-to-serial conversion*.

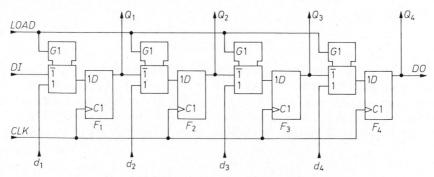

Fig. 10.45 Shift register with parallel LOAD inputs

A shift register with parallel load inputs can also be operated as a bidirectional shift register. For this purpose the parallel load inputs are connected to the output of the next flip-flop on the right. If $LOAD = 1$, the data are shifted from right to left.

Typical IC types

Length	TTL	ECL	CMOS
4 bit	74 LS 194 A	10141	40194
8 bit	74 LS 164, 299		4014
16 bit	74 LS 673		4006
2 × 64 bit	TDC 1005 J (TRW)		4517
8 × 1 ... 16 bit	Am 29525		

10.6   Processing of asynchronous signals

Sequential logic circuits can be realized either in asynchronous or synchronous, i.e. clocked, mode. Asynchronous operation normally requires simpler circuits but creates a number of problems: it must be ensured that the spurious transitions (hazards) which may temporarily appear because of the difference in propagation delay times, are not decoded as valid states. For a synchronous system, the conditions are far more simple. Any transition within the system can only take place at the edge of a clock pulse. The clock pulse therefore indicates when the system is in the steady-state condition. It is advisable to construct the system so that all changes consistently occur on one edge of the clock pulse. If, for instance, all the circuits are triggered by the trailing edge, the system is certain to be in the steady-state condition whenever the clock pulse is 1.

As a rule, external data fed to the system are not synchronized with its clock. In order that they may be processed synchronously, they must be conditioned by special circuits, some examples of which are described below.

10.6.1 Debouncing of mechanical contacts

If a mechanical switch is opened or closed, vibrations usually generate a pulse train. A counter then registers an undefined number of pulses instead of the single pulse intended. One way of avoiding this is to use mercury-wetted contacts, although this is rather expensive. A simple method of electronic debouncing by means of an RS flip-flop is illustrated in Fig. 10.46. When the switch U is in its lower position (break contact) $\bar{R} = 0$ and $\bar{S} = 1$, i.e. $x = 0$. When the switch is operated, a pulse train initially occurs at the $\bar{R}$ input because the break contact is opened. Since $\bar{R} = \bar{S} = 1$, this being the storing condition, the output remains unchanged. After the complete opening of the break contact a pulse train is generated by the opposite make contact. With the very first pulse, $\bar{R} = 1$ and $\bar{S} = 0$, which makes the flip-flop change state so that $x = 1$. This state is stored during the bouncing that follows. The flip-flop changes to its former state only when the lower break contact is touched again. The timing diagram in Fig. 10.47 illustrates this behavior.

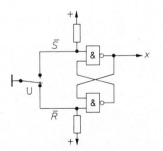

Fig. 10.46 Switch debouncing

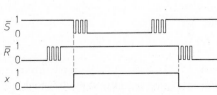

Fig. 10.47 Timing diagram

10.6.2   Edge-triggered *RS* flip-flop

A flip-flop with *RS* inputs is set as long as $S = 1$ and reset as long as $R = 1$. Both inputs must not be 1 simultaneously. To achieve this, we can generate short R or S pulses. A simpler possibility is shown in Fig. 10.48. Here the input signals are fed to the inputs of positive-edge-triggered *D* flip-flops. This ensures that only the instant of the positive-going edge is important and the rest of the clock pulse is immaterial. When a positive-going Set edge occurs, $Q_1 = Q_2$. This results in the exclusive-or operation

$$y = \bar{Q}_1 \oplus Q_2 = \bar{Q}_2 \oplus Q_2 = 1 \; .$$

When a positive-going Reset edge occurs, $Q_2 = \bar{Q}_1$. In this case $y = 0$. Output y therefore behaves like the Q output of an *RS* flip-flop.

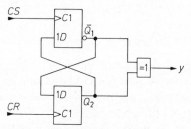

Fig. 10.48 Edge-triggered *RS* flip-flop.

CS = Clock Set CR = Clock Reset

However, the time characteristics of the input signals are once again subject to a limitation: the positive-going input edges must not occur simultaneously. They must be separated in time by at least the propagation delay time plus the data setup time. In TTL circuits of the 74LS series, this amounts to approximately 50 ns. If the input pulse edges occur simultaneously, the output signal is inverted.

10.6.3   Pulse synchronization

The simplest method of synchronizing pulses employs *D*-type flip-flops. As shown in Fig. 10.49, the external unsynchronized signal x is applied to the *D*-input, and the system clock Φ to the *C*-input. In this manner, the state of the input variable x is monitored and transferred to the output on the positive-going edge of the clock pulse. As the input signal can also change during the positive-going edge of the clock pulse, metastable states may occur in flip-flop F_1. Additional flip-flop F_2 has therefore been provided to prevent errors occurring in output signal y.

Figure 10.50 shows a typical timing diagram. Any pulse too short to be registered by the leading edge of a clock pulse is ignored. This case is also shown in Fig. 10.50. If such short pulses are not to be lost, they must be read into

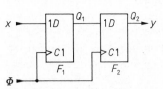

Fig. 10.49 Synchronization circuit

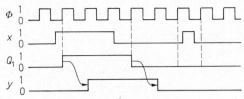

Fig. 10.50 Timing diagram

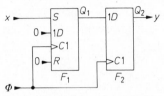

Fig. 10.51 Detection of short pulses

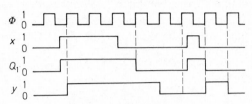

Fig. 10.52 Timing diagram

an intermediate store before being transferred to the D flip-flop. The D flip-flop F_1 in Fig. 10.51 serves this purpose. It is set asynchronously via the S-input when x becomes 1. With the next positive-going edge, $y = 1$. If, at this moment, x has already returned to zero, flip-flop F_1 is reset by the same edge. A short pulse x is thus prolonged until the next clock edge occurs and cannot therefore be lost. This property may also be seen in the example in Fig. 10.52.

10.6.4   Synchronous one-shot

It is possible, using the circuit in Fig. 10.53, to generate a pulse which is in synchronism with the clock. The pulse length equals one clock period and is independent of the length of the trigger signal x.

If x changes from 0 to 1, $Q_1 = 1$ at the positive-going edge of the next clock pulse, i.e. $y = 1$. On the subsequent leading edge, $\bar{Q}_2$ becomes 0 and y becomes 0 again. This state remains unchanged until x has been zero for at least one clock period and has returned to 1. Short trigger pulses which are not registered by the leading edge of a clock pulse are lost, as with the synchronizing circuit in

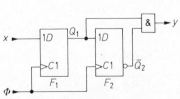

Fig. 10.53 Generation of a single, but clock-synchronous pulse

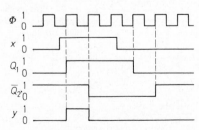

Fig. 10.54 Timing diagram

Fig. 10.49. If they too are to be considered, an additional flip-flop as in Fig. 10.51 must store the pulses until they are transferred to the main flip-flop. The timing diagram in Fig. 10.54 shows an example of operation.

A synchronous one-shot for ON-times longer than one clock period can be realized quite simply by using a synchronous counter, as is shown in Fig. 10.55. If the trigger variable x is at 1, the counter is loaded in the parallel-in mode on the next clock pulse. The following clock pulses are used to count to the maximum output state Z_{max}. At this number, the carry output $RCO = 1$. The counter is then inhibited via count-enable input ENP; the output variable y is 0. The ordinary enable input ENT cannot be employed for this purpose as it not only affects the flip-flops but also RCO directly, and this would result in an unwanted oscillation.

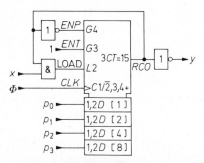

Fig. 10.55 Synchronous one-shot

A new cycle is started by parallel read-in. Immediately after loading, RCO becomes zero and y is then 1. The feedback from RCO to the AND gate at the x-input prevents a new loading process unless the counter has reached the state Z_{max}. By this time, x should have returned to 0; if not, the counter is loaded again, i.e. is operating as a modulo-$(M + 1)$ counter as in Fig. 10.41.

The timing diagram is shown in Fig. 10.56 for an ON-time of 7 clock pulses. If a 4-bit straight binary counter is employed, it must, for this particular ON-time, be loaded with $P = 8$. The first clock pulse is needed for the loading process and the remaining 6 pulses for counting up to 15.

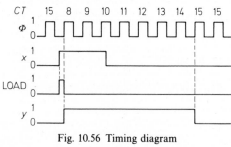

Fig. 10.56 Timing diagram
CT = Content

10.6.5   Synchronous edge detector

A synchronous edge detector gives an output signal in synchronism with the clock pulse whenever the input variable x has changed. For the implementation of such an arrangement, we consider the one-shot circuit in Fig. 10.53. It produces an output pulse whenever x changes from 0 to 1. In order that a pulse is also obtained at the transition from 1 to 0, the AND gate must be replaced by an exclusive-OR gate, producing the circuit in Fig. 10.57. Its characteristics are illustrated by the timing diagram in Fig. 10.58.

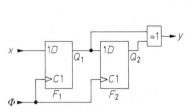

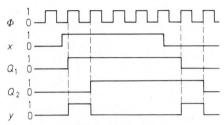

Fig. 10.57 Synchronous edge detector   Fig. 10.58 Timing diagram

10.6.6   Synchronous clock switch

The problem often arises of how to switch the clock on and off without interrupting the clock pulse generator. In principle, an AND gate could be used for this purpose, but this would result in the first and the last pulse being of undefined length if the switching signal is not clock-synchronized. This effect can be avoided by employing a single-edge triggered D-type flip-flop for the synchronization, as is shown in Fig. 10.59. If $EN = 1$, at the next leading pulse edge $Q = 1$ and therefore $\Phi' = 1$. The first pulse of the switched clock Φ' always has the full length because of the edge-triggering property.

The leading pulse edge cannot be used to switch off since, directly after the transition, $Q = 0$, which would result in a very short output pulse. The flip-flop is therefore cleared asynchronously via the reset input when EN and Φ are 0, achieved by the NOR gate at the R-input. As is obvious from Fig. 10.60, only full-length clock pulses can reach the output of the AND gate.

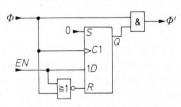

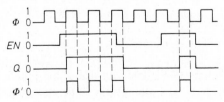

Fig. 10.59 Synchronous clock switch   Fig. 10.60 Timing diagram

10.7   Systematic design of sequential circuits

10.7.1   State diagram

To enable the systematic design of sequential circuits, it is necessary to obtain a clear description of the problem in hand. The starting point is the block diagram in Fig. 10.61.

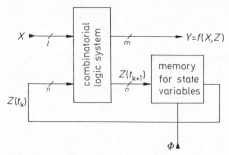

Fig. 10.61 Basic arrangement of a sequential logic system.

Input vector:	X	State vector: Z
Output vector:	Y	Clock: Φ

In contrast to a combinatorial logic system, the output variables y_j depend not only on the input variables x_i but also on the previous history of the system. All the system logic variables affecting the transition to the next state, apart from the input variables, are called state variables z_n. To ensure that they can become effective on the next clock signal, they are stored in the state variable memory for one clock pulse.

The number of input variables x_i is called the input vector:

$$X = \{x_1, x_2 \ldots x_l\} \ .$$

The number of output variables y_j is called the output vector:

$$Y = \{y_1, y_2 \ldots y_m\} \ .$$

The number of state variables z_n is called the state vector:

$$Z = \{z_1, z_2 \ldots z_n\} \ .$$

We shall denote by S_z the various states through which the sequential logic system passes. To simplify the notation, the state vector is preferably read as a straight binary number and the corresponding decimal number is simply written as a subscript.

The new state $S(t_{k+1})$ is determined both by the old state $S(t_k)$ and by the input variables (qualifiers) x_i. The sequence in which the states occur can therefore be influenced using the qualifiers X. The appropriate assignment is made by a combinatorial logic system: if the old state vector $Z(t_k)$ is applied to its inputs, the new state vector $Z(t_{k+1})$ appears at its output. The corresponding system state must obtain until the next clock pulse. Consequently, the state vector $Z(t_{k+1})$ must not be transmitted to the outputs of the flip-flops until the next clock pulse. For this reason, edge-triggered flip-flops must be used.

There are a few important special types of sequential logic circuit. For example, a special case arises when the state variables can be used directly as outputs. A second simplification occurs when the sequence of states is always the same, in which case no input variables are required. We have made use of these simplifications for the counters.

A general description of the state sequence is provided by a state diagram, as shown in Fig. 10.62. Each state S_Z of the system is illustrated by a circle. The transition from one state to another is shown by an arrow. The symbol on the arrow indicates under which condition a transition is to occur. For the example in Fig. 10.62, state $S(t_k) = S_1$ is followed by state $S(t_{k+1}) = S_2$ if $x_1 = 1$. For $x_1 = 0$, however, $S(t_{k+1}) = S_0$. An unmarked arrow stands for an unconditional transition.

For a *synchronous* sequential circuit there is an additional condition that a transition will only occur at the next clock pulse edge and not immediately the transition condition is fulfilled. As this restriction applies to all transitions in the system, it is usually not entered in the state diagram, but indicated in the description. We deal below only with synchronous sequential circuits, as their design is less problematic.

If the system is in the state S_Z and no transition condition is fulfilled which might lead out of this state, the system remains in the state S_Z. This obvious fact can sometimes be emphasized by entering an arrow which starts and ends at S_Z (wait state). Such a case is illustrated at state S_2 in Fig. 10.62.

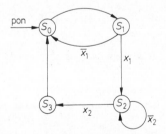

Fig. 10.62 Example of a state diagram.

State 0: Initial state
State 1: Branching state
State 2: Wait state
State 3: Temporary state

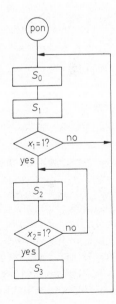

Fig. 10.63 Equivalent flow diagram

When the power supply is switched on, a sequential circuit must be set to a defined initial state. This is the "pon" condition ("power on"). Its signal is produced by a special logic circuit and is 1 for a short time after switch-on of the supply and is otherwise zero. This signal is generally used to clear the state variable memory by applying it to the RESET inputs of the flip-flops.

The operation of a sequential circuit can also be represented by a flow chart, as shown for the same example in Fig. 10.63. This representation suggests the implementation of a sequential circuit by a microcomputer, as discussed in Chapter 20.

10.7.2   Design example for a programmable counter

We shall demonstrate the design process for a counter, the counting cycle of which is either 0, 1, 2, 3 or 0, 1, 2 depending on whether the control variable x is 1 or 0. The appropriate state diagram is given in Fig. 10.64. As the system can assume 4 stable states, we require two flip-flops for storage of the state vector Z which consists of two variables, z_0 and z_1. Since these variables immediately indicate the state of the counter, they are simultaneously used as output variables. In addition, a carry y should be produced when the counter state is 3 for $x = 1$, or 2 for $x = 0$.

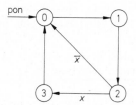

Fig. 10.64 State diagram of a counter with programmable counting cycle.

$$Counting\ cycle = \begin{cases} 3 & \text{if } x = 0 \\ 4 & \text{if } x = 1 \end{cases}$$

We thus obtain the circuit in Fig. 10.65 with, the truth table given in Fig. 10.66. The left-hand side of the table shows all the possible bit combinations of the input and state variables. The state diagram in Fig. 10.64 shows which is the next system state for each combination. This is shown at the right-hand side of the table. The respective values of the carry bit y are also entered.

If a ROM (read-only memory) is used to realize the combinatorial system, the truth table of Fig. 10.66 can be directly employed to program the memory, the state and input variables being used as address variables. The new value Z' of the state vector Z, and the output variable y are stored at the appropriate addresses. Hence, to implement our example, we require a ROM for 8 words of 3 bits. The smallest PROM can store 32 words of 8 bits (see Chapter 11) so that only one tenth of its memory capacity is used.

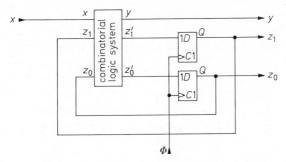

Fig. 10.65 Sequential circuit for implementing the programmable counter

	$Z(t_k)$			$Z(t_{k+1})$	
x	z_1	z_0	z_1'	z_0'	y
0	0	0	0	1	0
0	0	1	1	0	0
0	1	0	0	0	1
0	1	1	0	0	0
1	0	0	0	1	0
1	0	1	1	0	0
1	1	0	1	1	0
1	1	1	0	0	1

ROM address   ROM contents

Fig. 10.66 Truth table for the state diagram in Fig. 10.64

The truth table in Fig. 10.66 supplies the following Boolean functions:

$$z_1' = z_0\bar{z}_1 + x\bar{z}_0z_1 \; ,$$

$$z_0' = \bar{z}_0\bar{z}_1 + x\bar{z}_0 \; ,$$

$$y = \bar{x}\bar{z}_0z_1 + xz_0z_1 \; .$$

Figure 10.67 shows the realization of this combinatorial system by means of gates. It can be seen that the number of integrated circuits involved is many times greater than when using a ROM. The application of a ROM also has another decisive advantage, namely flexibility: the ROM need only be reprogrammed to provide a circuit with different properties without further changes.

The use of gates for a sequential circuit is thus recommended only in certain simple cases, for instance in the standard counters described in the previous sections.

When constructing complex sequential systems, a limit is soon reached even for the ROM solution, where the required memory capacity rises excessively. The following section therefore describes some strategies by which this problem can, to a large extent, be overcome.

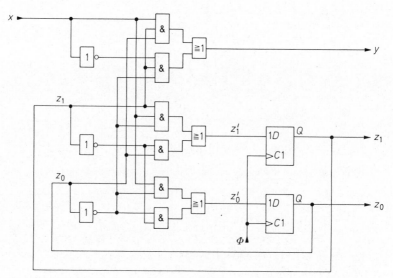

Fig. 10.67 Programmable counter using a combinatorial system consisting of gates

10.7.3   Reduction of memory requirement

As can be seen from the basic circuit in Fig. 10.61, the combinatorial circuit contained in the sequential logic system has $n + l$ inputs and $n + m$ outputs, where n is the number of state variables, l the number of input variables x (qualifiers) and m the number of output variables y. When implementing it using a ROM, a memory of

$$2^{(n+l)} \text{ words at } (n + m) \text{ bits} = (n + m)2^{(n+l)} \text{ bits}$$

is needed. It is possible to assign an output vector Y to each combination of state and input variables. In practice, however, the values of most of the output variables are already fully defined by the state variables, and only a few are dependent on only some of the qualifiers.

This fact allows the ROM to be split into two ROMs as in Fig. 10.68. One is the program ROM containing the system states only and no output states. The output states are formed by an output ROM from the state variables and a small number of the input variables. Therefore l_2 is usually small compared to l. There may also be cases for which an input variable affects only the decoding at the output but not the sequence of the states. For the two-ROM solution in Fig. 10.68, such qualifiers may then be connected directly to the output ROM and omitted for the program ROM. Therefore, $l_1 < l$ is also possible.

As only those qualifiers required for sequential and output control are connected to the two ROMs, a considerably smaller memory is needed. The worst-case condition is where all the l qualifiers are used for both ROMs. The required memory capacity of both ROMs together is then just as large as that of the single ROM in Fig. 10.61.

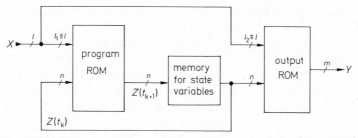

Fig. 10.68 Reduction of the required total memory capacity by replacing a large ROM by two small ones

Although there is no saving in memory capacity, the solution employing two ROMs (Fig. 10.68) is advantageous even in this case, since the system can be more easily adapted to different operating conditions. There are many cases for which the state sequence is identical and which differ only in the output instructions. For an adaptation, only the output ROM need be replaced while the program ROM remains unchanged.

Input multiplexer

A second property of practical sequential logic circuits can also be used to reduce the required memory space. The number l of qualifiers is often so large that the number of address variables of a ROM is greatly exceeded. On the other hand, only relatively few of the 2^l possible combinations are decoded. It is therefore reasonable not to use the qualifiers directly as address variables but to employ a multiplexer to read the variables relevant for each state of the system. This results in the block diagram of Fig. 10.69.

Apart from the state variables, only the output x of the multiplexer is connected to the address inputs of the ROM. The multiplexer is controlled by the straight binary number Q taken from some additional outputs of the ROM. The qualifier selected by this number is denoted by x_Q.

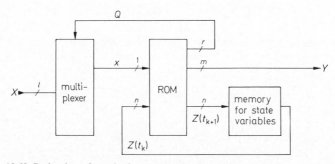

Fig. 10.69 Reduction of required memory capacity using a multiplexer at the input

If, at a single transition, several qualifiers are to be identified, the determination must be carried out serially, as only one variable can be selected at a time. For this purpose, the appropriate state is divided into several sub-states for which only one qualifier need be determined. There is therefore a larger total number of system states, and they can be represented with the help of a few additional state variables. This extension is small, however, compared to the saving in memory locations by using the multiplex qualifier identification.

This fact is demonstrated by the following typical example. A sequential logic circuit having the state diagram in Fig. 10.70 is to be constructed. It has four states and six qualifiers. The realization based on the principle in Fig. 10.61 would require a ROM with 8 inputs and a memory capacity of $2^8 = 256$ words. Assuming that two output variables are to be generated, and taking the two state variables into account, a word length of 4 bits, i.e. a total memory of 1024 bits is needed.

For the implementation using an input multiplexer, the states A and C must be each divided into three sub-states for which only one of the qualifiers shown

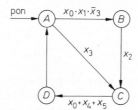

Fig. 10.70 State diagram for the example

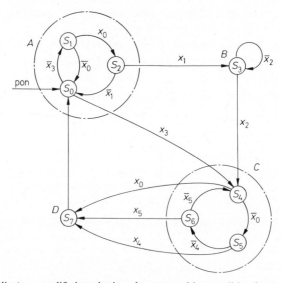

Fig. 10.71 State diagram, modified to obtain only one transition condition for each change of state

in Fig. 10.70 is determined at a time. In this manner, the modified state diagram in Fig. 10.71 is obtained. There is now a total of eight states, denoted by S_0 to S_7. A transition from macrostate A to macrostate B occurs only when $x_3 = 0$ *and* $x_0 = x_1 = 1$, in accordance with the original state diagram in Fig. 10.70. The appropriate combination for an OR operation is seen at macrostate C.

The representation of the eight states requires three state variables. The ROM in Fig. 10.69 must also possess three outputs for the control of the 8-input multiplexer, as well as two y-outputs. This amounts to a word length of 8 bits. Apart from the three state variables, only the output of the multiplexer serves as an address variable so that a memory capacity of 2^4 words of 8 bits each $= 128$ bits is needed. This is only about one tenth of that required by the standard solution.

$Z(t_k)$	x	$Z(t_{k+1})$	Q
0	0	1	3
0	1	4	3
1	0	0	0
1	1	2	0
2	0	0	1
2	1	3	1
3	0	3	2
3	1	4	2
4	0	5	0
4	1	7	0
5	0	6	4
5	1	7	4
6	0	4	5
6	1	7	5
7	0	0	×
7	1	0	×

Fig. 10.72 State table (× = don't-care condition)

Address				Contents					
z_2	z_1	z_0	x	z'_2	z'_1	z'_0	a_2	a_1	a_0
0	0	0	0	0	0	1	0	1	1
0	0	0	1	1	0	0	0	1	1
0	0	1	0	0	0	0	0	0	0
0	0	1	1	0	1	0	0	0	0
0	1	0	0	0	0	0	0	0	1
0	1	0	1	0	1	1	0	0	1
0	1	1	0	0	1	1	0	1	0
0	1	1	1	1	0	0	0	1	0
1	0	0	0	1	0	1	0	0	0
1	0	0	1	1	1	1	0	0	0
1	0	1	0	1	1	0	1	0	0
1	0	1	1	1	1	1	1	0	0
1	1	0	0	1	0	0	1	0	1
1	1	0	1	1	1	1	1	0	1
1	1	1	0	0	0	0	0	0	0
1	1	1	1	0	0	0	0	0	0

Fig. 10.73 PROM programming table

The compilation of the truth table is not difficult. The state table in Fig. 10.72 can be directly deduced from the state diagram in Fig. 10.71. It indicates which state $Z(t_{k+1})$ follows the state $Z(t_k)$, depending on whether x equals 1 or 0. The binary number Q identifies the qualifier x_Q selected at the state $S_{Z(t_k)}$. The numbers $Z(t_k)$, $Z(t_{k+1})$ and Q need now only be written as straight binary numbers to obtain the programming table in Fig. 10.73. In the "contents" column we have entered only the 6 bits required for the sequential control. Extra bits for the output can be added as required.

11 Semiconductor memories

Semiconductor memories fall into two main categories, as shown in Fig. 11.1: *table memories* and *function memories*. With table memories, an address A is defined in the range

$$0 \leq A \leq n = 2^N - 1 .$$

The word width of the address is between $N = 5 \ldots 22$, depending on the size of memory. Data can be stored at each of the 2^N addresses. The data word width is $m = 1 \ldots 16$ bits. Figure 11.2 shows an example for $N = 3$ address bits and $m = 2$ data bits.

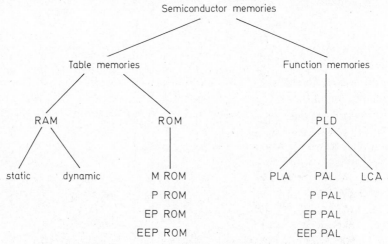

Fig. 11.1 Categories of commonly used semiconductor memories

RAM = Random Access Memory	PLD = Programmable Logic Device
ROM = Read Only Memory	PLA = Programmable Logic Array
M = Mask programmed	PAL = Programmable Array Logic
P = Programmable	LCA = Logic Cell Array
EP = Erasable and Programmable	EEP = Electrically Erasable and Programmable

The memory capacity $K = m \cdot n$ is specified in bits, and also in bytes $(K/8)$ for data word widths of 8 or 16 bits. When using several memory chips, both the address space and the word width can be increased by any amount. This will allow any tables such as truth tables, computer programs or results of measurements (numbers) to be stored.

Function memories store logic functions instead of tables. Each variable of a truth table can be expressed as a logic function. Written in standard product

	A			D		
	a_2	a_1	a_0	d_1	d_0	
0	0	0	0	d_{01}	d_{00}	D_0
1	0	0	1	d_{11}	d_{10}	D_1
2	0	1	0	d_{21}	d_{20}	D_2
3	0	1	1	d_{31}	d_{30}	D_3
4	1	0	0	d_{41}	d_{40}	D_4
5	1	0	1	d_{51}	d_{50}	D_5
6	1	1	0	d_{61}	d_{60}	D_6
7	1	1	1	d_{71}	d_{70}	D_7

Fig. 11.2 Layout of a table

Address word width $N = 3$ bits
Data word width $m = 2$ bits

terms, the logic function of variable d_0 in Fig. 11.2 becomes

$$d_0 = \bar{a}_2\bar{a}_1\bar{a}_0 d_{00} + \bar{a}_2\bar{a}_1 a_0 d_{10} + \ldots + a_2 a_1 a_0 d_{70} \ .$$

If d_0 contains no regularity, and the zeros and ones are therefore statistically distributed, we get $n/2$ — in this case four — non-vanishing product terms. This situation occurs, for instance, when programs are being stored. In this case the implementation of the logic function is more complex than its storage in a table.

However, if a truth table is used as the starting point, extensive simplification is possible for the logic function due to the underlying regularity. One such case is when there are only very few "ones". For example, if in the function d_0 only $d_{70} = 1$, we only require a single conjunction $d_0 = a_2 a_1 a_0$. Another case is when the logic functions can be simplified using Boolean algebra. For example, if $d_0 = a_1$ in Fig. 11.2, an extremely simple function is obtained, even though it contains four "ones". In such cases, the use of function memories generally produces much better solutions than storage in a table.

Table memories are subdivided into two distinct categories, namely RAMs and ROMs. RAM is a general designation for read-write memories. The contents of the memory can be both read and written during normal operation. The abbreviation actually stands for Random Access Memory. "Random access" means that any data word within the memory can be accessed at any time, in contrast to shift register memories in which data can only be read from the memory in the same sequence in which they were written into it. As shift register memories are no longer very important, the term RAM has become a generic term for memories with read-write capabilities. This is somewhat misleading, in that ROMs also allow random access to any data word.

ROM is an abbreviation for Read-Only Memory. This designation identifies memory ICs which retain their contents when there is no supply voltage, even without backup batteries. In normal operation, data are only read from such memories but not written into them. Special equipment is normally required for writing the data, the storage procedure being referred to as programming. The sub-categories listed in Fig. 11.1 differ in the type of programming employed, which is described in greater detail below.

11.1 Random Access Memories (RAMs)

11.1.1 Static RAMs

A RAM is a memory device in which data can be stored under a specified address and subsequently read out from that address (random access). For technological reasons the individual memory cells are not arranged linearly but in a square matrix. To select a particular memory cell, address A is decoded, as shown in Fig. 11.3, by a row and column decoder.

In addition to its address inputs, a RAM has an extra data input D_{in}, a data output D_{out}, a read/$\overline{write}$ pin $R/\overline{W}$ and a chip select CS or chip enable CE pin. The latter is used for multiplexing more than one memory operated via a common data line (bus system). When $CS = 0$, the data output D_{out} assumes high

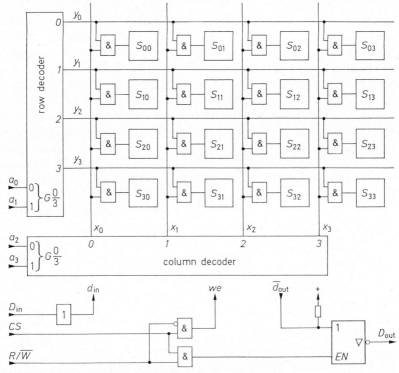

Fig. 11.3 Internal structure of a RAM. Example showing 16-bit memory capacity.

D_{in} = Data input D_{out} = Data output

CS = Chip Select $R/\overline{W}$ = Read/$\overline{Write}$

we = write enable

impedance and thus has no effect on the data line. To allow this change of state, the data output is always implemented as an open-collector gate or tristate gate.

During the write process ($R/\bar{W} = 0$), the output gate is likewise switched to high impedance by an additional logic operation. This allows D_{in} to be connected to D_{out}, enabling data to be transmitted in both directions via the same line (bidirectional bus system).

Another logic operation prevents a switchover to the write state ($we = 1$), if $CS = 0$. This prevents data being written accidentally until the relevant memory has been selected.

Figure 11.3 shows the logic operations mentioned above. Lines d_{in}, d_{out} and we (write enable) are connected to each memory cell internally, as illustrated schematically in Fig. 11.4. Data should only be read into the memory cell when address condition $x_i = y_i = 1$ is satisfied and also $we = 1$. This logic operation is performed by gate G_1. The contents of the memory cell must only reach the output if the address condition is satisfied. This operation is performed by gate G_2, which has an open-collector output. When the cell is not addressed, the output transistor is off. The outputs of all the cells are internally wire-ANDed together and connected to the memory output D_{out} via the tristate gate shown in Fig. 11.3.

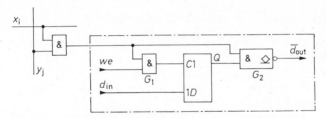

Fig. 11.4 Equivalent logic circuit for the structure of a memory cell

Unless the supply voltage is switched off, the memory contents are retained until they are modified by a write command. Such memories are referred to as static to distinguish them from dynamic memories in which the contents have to be refreshed at regular intervals to prevent them from being lost.

The circuit symbol for a RAM is shown in Fig. 11.5. As we can see, there are N address inputs. These are decoded by the address decoder in such a way that precisely that memory cell is selected (out of 2^N) which corresponds to the address applied. The read-write changeover $R/\bar{W}$ is only activated when chip enable $CE = 1$ or $\overline{CE} = 0$. The tristate output is therefore activated for $R/\bar{W} = 1$; for $R/\bar{W} = 0$ it is high impedance. For this reason, the data input and output can be internally interconnected in the memory IC. This produces a bidirectional data port whose direction of operation is determined by the $R/\bar{W}$ signal.

Frequently, not just a single bit, but an m-digit word is stored at an address. The storage of entire words may be seen as a spatial extension of the block diagram in Fig. 11.3. The additional bits are then stacked in further memory

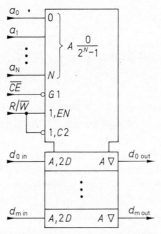

Fig. 11.5 RAM circuit symbol

layers; their control lines x, y and we are connected in parallel, and their data lines form the input or output word.

Timing considerations

For a satisfactory operation of the memory, a number of timing conditions must be observed. Figure 11.6 shows the sequence of a write operation. To prevent the data being written into the wrong cell, the write command must not be applied until a certain time has elapsed after definition of the address. This time is called the address setup time t_{AS}. The duration of the write pulse must not be less than the minimum value t_{WP} (write pulse width) The data are read in at the end of the write pulse. They must be valid, i.e. stable, for a minimum

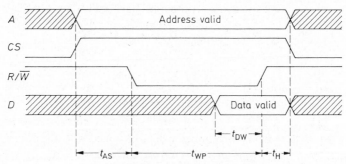

Fig. 11.6 Timing of a write operation

t_{AS} = Address Setup Time
t_{WP} = Write Pulse Width
t_{DW} = Data Valid to End of Write Time
t_H = Hold Time

Capacity	Organization	Type	Manufacturer	Operating power, typical	Access time, max.	Pins
CMOS: ($V_{DD} = 5$ V, $f = f_{max}$)						
16 kbit	**2 k × 8**	**6116**	**Hi, Ne, To**	**160 mW**	**100 ns**	**24**
	2 k × 8	DS 1220[1]	Da	250 mW	150 ns	24
	4 k × 4	6168	Id, Mh, Cy, Is	225 mW	15 ns	20
	16 k × 1	6167		200 mW	12 ns	20
64 kbit	**8 k × 8**	**6264**	**Hi, Ne, To**	**200 mW**	**100 ns**	**28**
	8 k × 8	DS 1225[1]	Da	200 mW	150 ns	28
	8 k × 8	7164	Id, Mh, Cy, Is	250 mW	20 ns	28
	4 k × 16	71586	Id, To	900 mW	25 ns	40
	16 k × 4	7188	Id, Mh, Cy, I	300 mW	15 ns	22
	64 k × 1	7187	Id, Mh, Cy, Is	250 mW	15 ns	22
256 kbit	**32 k × 8**	**62256**	**Hi, Ne, To, Fu**	**300 mW**	**100 ns**	**28**
	32 k × 8	DS 1230[1]	Da	300 mW	150 ns	28
	32 k × 8	71256	Id, Hi, Ne, Cy, Mh	250 mW	35 ns	28
	64 k × 4	71258	Id, Hi, Ne, Cy, Mh	350 mW	25 ns	28
	256 k × 1	71257	Id, Hi, Ne, Cy, Is	350 mW	25 ns	24
1 Mbit	**128 k × 8**	**628128**	**Hi, Ne, To, Fu**	**250 mW**	**70 ns**	**32**
	128 k × 8	DS 1245[1]	Da	250 mW	70 ns	32
	128 k × 8	71024	Id, Hi, Ne	500 mW	35 ns	32
	256 k × 4	71028	Id, Hi, Ne	500 mW	35 ns	28
	1024 k × 1	71027	Id, Ne	500 mW	35 ns	28
4 Mbit	**512 k × 8**		**To**	**350 mW**	**30 ns**	**32**
	512 k × 8	CYM 1464[2]	Cy, Id	1200 mW	45 ns	32
	256 k × 16	CYM 1641[2]	Cy, Id	6000 mW	25 ns	48
8 Mbit	1024 k × 8	MS 81000[2]	Hm	300 mW	85 ns	35
	256 k × 32	CYM 1841[2]	Cy	4000 mW	35 ns	64
ECL: ($V_{EE} = -5.2$ V)						
1 kbit	256 k × 4	10422	Cy, Ne	1000 mW	3 ns	24
4 kbit	1 k × 4	10474	Cy, Ne	1200 mW	3 ns	24
	4 k × 1	10470	Fu, Ne	900 mW	7 ns	18
16 kbit	4 k × 4	10484	Fu, Hi	1300 mW	8 ns	28
	16 k × 1	10480	Fu, Hi, Ne	1100 mW	8 ns	20
64 kbit	16 k × 4	10494	Id, Cy, Fu, Ne, Na	600 mW	8 ns	28
	64 k × 1	10490	Id, Cy, Fu, Ne	420 mW	8 ns	22
256 kbit	64 k × 4	10504	Fu, Na, Hi, Id	1000 mW	15 ns	32
	256 k × 1	10500	Fu, Na, Hi, Ne	800 mW	15 ns	24

[1] Containing lithium battery; data retention: 10 years   [2] Hybrid circuit (module)

Manufacturers: Cy = Cypress, Da = Dallas, Fu = Fujitsu, Hi = Hitachi, Hm = Hybrid Memory, Id = IDT, Is = Inmos, Mh = Matra Harris, Na = National, Ne = NEC, St = SGS-Thomson, To = Toshiba, Vt = VTI

Fig. 11.8 Examples of static RAMs

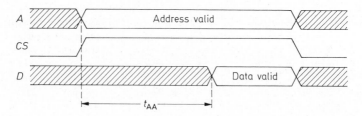

Fig. 11.7 Timing of a read operation

t_{AA} = Address Access Time

period prior to this. This time is called t_{DW} (Data Valid to End of Write). In a number of memories the data and addresses must also be present for a further time t_H after the end of the write pulse (Hold Time). As can be seen from Fig. 11.6, the time required to execute a write operation is expressed as

$$t_W = t_{AS} + t_{WP} + t_H$$

This is referred to as the Write Cycle Time.

The read operation is shown in Fig. 11.7. After the address is applied, it is necessary to wait for time t_{AA} until the data at the output are valid. This time is referred to as the Address Access Time or simply Access Time.

A list of some of the most widely-used static RAMs in bipolar and MOS technology is given in Fig. 11.8.

11.1.2 Dynamic RAMs

As we wish to maximize the number of cells in a memory, every effort must be made to implement them as simply as possible. They normally consist of just a few transistors [11.1]; in the case of static CMOS RAMs, a 6-transistor cell is normally used. In the simplest case, even the flip-flop is omitted and replaced by a MOSFET whose gate-source capacitance is used to store 1 bit as a charge.

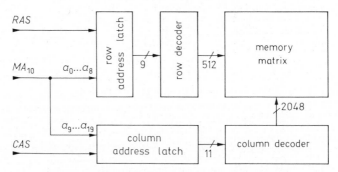

Fig. 11.9 Address decoding in a dynamic 1 Mbit memory.

RAS: Row Address Strobe (simultaneously Chip Enable)
CAS: Column Address Strobe

This makes a single-transistor cell possible. However, as the charge is only retained for a short time, the capacitor must be recharged at regular intervals (every 2 to 8 ms approx.). This operation is known as *refresh*, the memories are called *dynamic RAMs*.

This disadvantage is offset by several advantages. Dynamic memories can provide about four times more storage capacity on the same printed-circuit board area, with the same current drain and at the same cost.

To save on pins, with dynamic memories the address is entered in two stages and buffered in the IC.

The block diagram of a 1 Mbit RAM is shown in Fig. 11.9. In the first step, address bits a_0 to a_8 are stored in the row-address latch with the RAS signal, and simultaneously bit a_9 in the column-address latch. In the second step, address bits a_{10} to a_{19} are loaded into the column-address latch with the CAS signal. This makes it possible to accommodate a 1 Mbit memory in an 18-pin package. Figure 11.10 lists commonly used IC types.

Capacity	Organization	Type	Manufacturer[1]	Operating power, typical	Access time, max.	Pins
CMOS: ($V_{DD} = 5$ V, $f = f_{max}$)						
256 kbit	256 k × 1	51256	Hitachi	200 mW	100 ns	16
	64 k × 4	51464	Hitachi	250 mW	100 ns	18
1 Mbit	**1 M × 1**	**511000**	**Toshiba**	**300 mW**	**80 ns**	**18**
	256 k × 4	514256	Toshiba	300 mW	80 ns	20
	128 k × 8	658128[2]	Hitachi	200 mW	80 ns	32
4 Mbit	**4 M × 1**	**514100**	**Toshiba**	**400 mW**	**80 ns**	**20**
	1 M × 4	514400	Toshiba	400 mW	80 ns	20
	512 k × 8	514800	Hitachi	400 mW	80 ns	28
	512 k × 8	658512[2]	Hitachi	350 mW	80 ns	32
9 Mbit	**1 M × 9**	**THM91000[3]**	**Toshiba**	**2500 mW**	**80 ns**	**30**
36 Mbit	4 M × 9	THM94000[3]	Toshiba	3500 mW	80 ns	30
	1 M × 36	HB56D136B[3]	Hitachi	3500 mW	80 ns	72
72 Mbit	2 M × 36	HB56D236B[3]	Hitachi	4000 mW	80 ns	72

[1] Other manufacturers: Fujitsu, Hitachi, NEC, Oki, Texas Instr.
[2] Pseudo-static since it has an integrated refresh controller
[3] Hybrid circuit (module)

Fig. 11.10 Examples of dynamic RAMs

Dynamic RAM controllers

To operate dynamic RAMs, additional circuitry is required. For a normal memory access, the address has to be loaded into the RAM in two consecutive steps. To avoid loss of data it is necessary to call up all the *row* addresses at least once within (usually) 8 ms. If the contents of memory are not read out cyclically, extra circuitry is required to effect cyclic addressing between normal memory

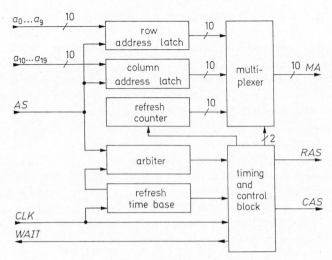

Fig. 11.11 Design of a dynamic RAM controller for 1 Mbit RAMs.

AC = Address Strobe RAS Row Address Strobe
MA = Memory Address CAS Column Address Strobe

accesses. These circuits are referred to as "dynamic RAM controllers". Figure 11.11 shows the block diagram for a circuit of this type [11.2, 11.3].

For a normal memory access, the externally-applied address is stored in the row and column address latch when address strobe AS becomes 1, indicating that the address is valid. An access cycle is simultaneously initiated in the timing and control block, and first, row address $a_0 \ldots a_9$ is forwarded to the memory via the multiplexer. Then, the row address strobe becomes 1, causing the address to be transferred to memory. Subsequently the column address $a_{10} \ldots a_{19}$ is produced and also read into memory with the column address strobe. This sequence is illustrated in Fig. 11.12. Following address input, the address strobe has to remain at logic 1 until data transmission is completed. The next memory access may not occur immediately, but only after a "precharge time" which is of the same order of magnitude as the address access time.

In order to perform the refresh, the lowest 512 addresses must be applied once every 8 ms. For a refresh cycle time of 300 ns, a total of some 150 µs is required for this purpose. Memory availability is thereby reduced by less than 2%. Three different methods can be used to organize the refresh time:

1) *Burst refresh.* In this mode, normal operation is interrupted after 8 ms and a refresh is performed for all memory cells. In many cases, however, it is undesirable for the memory to be inaccessible for 150 µs.

2) *Cycle stealing.* To avoid disabling the memory for a continuous 150 µs period, the refresh process can be subdivided and spread out over 8 ms: if the status of the refresh counter is incremented by one every 15 µs, then after

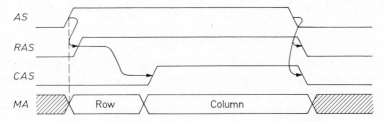

Fig. 11.12 Address input timing sequence for a dynamic RAM

$512 \cdot 15\,\mu s \approx 8\,ms$ all the row addresses will have been applied once, as required. With *cycle stealing* the processor is stopped every 15 μs for one cycle and a refresh step is performed. For this purpose, the refresh time base shown in the block diagram in Fig. 11.11 reduces the frequency of the clock signal *CLK* so that the timing and control block receives a refresh command every 15 μs.

When a refresh cycle is initiated, the status of the refresh counter is transferred via the multiplexer to the memory and the *RAS* signal is temporarily set to 1. The counter is then incremented by 1. During the refresh cycle, the memory user is inhibited by a wait signal. This means that the on-going process is stopped every 15 μs for 0.3 μs, i.e. likewise slowed down by 2%.

3) *Transparent or hidden refresh*. With this method, a refresh step is also performed every 15 μs, but the refresh controller is synchronized in such a way that, instead of inhibiting the memory user, the refresh is performed at the precise instant when the user is not accessing the memory. This means that no time is lost. If any overlapping of an external access with the refresh cycle cannot be totally eliminated, an additional priority decoder (arbiter) can be employed, as shown in Fig. 11.11. It acknowledges an external request with a wait signal until the current refresh cycle is complete and then executes the request.

Refresh controllers:

for 256k-RAMs:	THCT 4502	CMOS	Texas Instr., VTI
	DP8420A	CMOS	National
	74F764	TTL	Signetics
for 1 M-RAMs:	SN74ACT4503	CMOS	Texas Instr.
	DP8421A	CMOS	National
	74F1764	TTL	Signetics
	673104	TTL	AMD
for 4M-RAMs:	DP8422A	CMOS	National
	Am 29 C 688	CMOS	AMD

11.2   RAM expansions

11.2.1   Two-port memories

Two-port memories are special RAMs which allow two independent processes to access common data. This enables data to be exchanged between the two processes [11.4, 11.5]. To be able to do this, the 2-port memory must have two separate sets of address, data and control lines, as shown in Fig. 11.13. Implementation of this principle is subject to limitations, since it is basically impossible to write into the same memory cell simultaneously from both ports.

Fig. 11.13 External connections of a 2-port memory

The "Read-While-Write" memories overcome this problem by only reading from one of the two ports and only writing at the other. Figure 11.14 shows that memories of this type have two separate address decoders which allow *simultaneous* writing to one address while reading from another.

If reading and writing are to take place at both ports of a two-port memory, an access conflict can generally only be avoided by preventing simultaneous memory access. To do this, the address, data and control lines can be made available via multiplexers to the port accessed, as shown in Fig. 11.15. In many

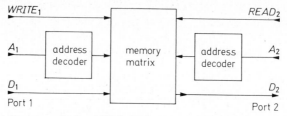

Fig. 11.14 Structure of a Read-While-Write memory with separate address inputs

cases, the two processes accessing the memory are synchronized to prevent simultaneous access. If this is not possible, a priority decoder (arbiter) can be used which, in the event of access overlap, temporarily stops one of the two processes by a wait signal. Some integrated 2-port memories are listed in Fig. 11.16. Their capacities, however, are limited. In order to implement large two-port memories, it is advisable to use normal RAMs in conjunction with a dual-port RAM controller. In this case the Valvo 74LS764 offers particular advantages, since it supports the operation of dynamic RAMs as two-port memories.

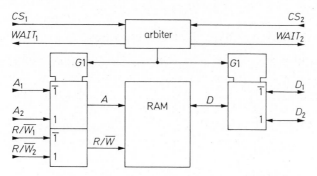

Fig. 11.15 Two-port memory with standard RAMs

Capacity	Organization	Type	Manufacturer	Operating power, typical	Access time, max.	Pins
8 kbit	1 k × 8	IDT 7130	Id, Cy, Am	325 mW	35 ns	48
16 kbit	2 k × 8	IDT 7132	Id, Cy, Vt	325 mW	35 ns	48
32 kbit	4 k × 8	IDT 7134	Id	500 mW	35 ns	48
32 kbit	2 k × 16	IDT 7133	Id	375 mW	45 ns	68
64 kbit	8 k × 8	IDT 7005	Id	750 mW	35 ns	68
64 kbit	4 k × 16	IDT 7024	Id	750 mW	30 ns	84
128 kbit	16 k × 8	IDT 7006	Id	750 mW	35 ns	68
128 kbit	8 k × 16	IDT 7025	Id	750 mW	30 ns	84

Manufacturers: Am = AMD, Cy = Cypress, Id = IDT, Vt = VTI

Fig. 11.16 Examples of two-port memories (CMOS)

11.2.2 RAMs as shift registers

RAMs can be operated as shift registers if the addresses are applied cyclically. The counter shown in Fig. 11.17 is used for this purpose. For each address, the stored data are first read out and new data are then read in. The timing diagram is shown in Fig. 11.18. The positive-going edge of the signal increments the counter. If the CLK signal is simultaneously used as the $R/\overline{W}$ signal, the memory contents are then read out and stored in the output flip-flop on the negative-going edge. While $CLK = 0$, the new data D_{in} are written into the memory cell which has just been read out. In this case the minimum clock cycle is shorter than the sum of the read and write cycle times, since the address remains constant. It is equal to what is known as the "Read-Modify-Write Cycle Time".

The difference between this type of shift register and the normal type (see Section 10.5) is that only the address, which acts as a pointer to the fixed data, is shifted, not the data themselves. The advantage of this method is that normal

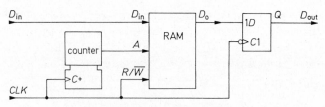

Fig. 11.17 RAM operated as a shift register

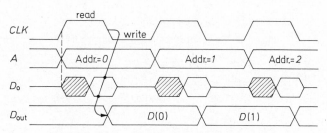

Fig. 11.18 Timing diagram for a RAM shift register

RAMs can be employed, and these are obtainable with memory capacities far greater than those of normal shift registers. If the clock frequency is higher than 64 kHz, dynamic 1 Mbit-RAMs can even be used without refresh logic, since this frequency ensures that the lowest 512 addresses are processed in 8 ms.

Even at high shift frequencies, low-cost RAMs can still be used if several data bits are processed in parallel and a serial-parallel converter is provided at the input and a parallel-serial converter at the output, in order to obtain the required shift frequency.

11.2.3 First-In-First-Out Memories (FIFOs)

A FIFO is a special type of shift register. The common feature is that the data appear at the output in the same order as they were read in: the first word read in is also the first one read out. With a FIFO, as opposed to a shift register, this process can take place completely asynchronously, i.e. the read-out clock is independent of the read-in clock. FIFOs are therefore used for linking asynchronous systems [11.6].

Operation is very similar to that of a waiting line: the data do not move at a fixed rate from input to output, but only remain in the register long enough for all the previous data to be read out. This is shown schematically in Fig. 11.19. With first-generation FIFOs, the data were actually shifted through a register chain, as illustrated in Fig. 11.19. On entry, the data were passed on to the lowest free memory location and shifted onwards from there to the output by the read clock. One disadvantage of this principle was the long fall-through time. This is particularly noticeable when the FIFO is empty, as the input data then have to pass through all the registers before being available at the output. This means that even the smallest FIFOs exhibit fall-through times of several microseconds. Other disadvantages include the complex shift logic and the large number of shift operations, thereby precluding a current-saving implementation in CMOS technology.

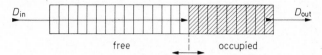

Fig. 11.19 Schematic diagram of FIFO operation

To overcome these drawbacks, in the second-generation FIFOs it is no longer the data that are shifted, but merely two pointers which specify the input and output address in a RAM. This is illustrated in Fig. 11.20. The input counter points to the first free address A_{in}, the output counter to the last occupied address A_{out}. Both pointers therefore rotate during on-going data input and output.

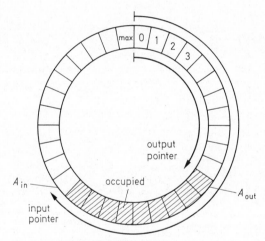

Fig. 11.20 FIFO as ring memory

The distance between the two pointers indicates how full the FIFO is. When $A_{in} - A_{out} = A_{max}$, the FIFO is full. No more data must then be entered, as this would mean overwriting data which have not yet been read out. When $A_{in} = A_{out}$, the FIFO is empty. No data must now be read out, as this would mean receiving old data a second time. An overflow or empty condition can only be avoided if the average data rates for input and output are identical. To achieve this, it is necessary to monitor the occupancy of the FIFO and to attempt to control the source or sink in such a way that the FIFO is on average half full. The FIFO can then accommodate short-term fluctuations, assuming it has a sufficient storage capacity.

The design of a FIFO is shown in Fig. 11.21. It is similar to the RAM shift register in Fig. 11.17. Read-while-write memories with separate address inputs (see Fig. 11.14) are particularly suitable here, as reading and writing can occur asynchronously. The more recent FIFOs, examples of which are listed in Fig. 11.22, operate on this principle.

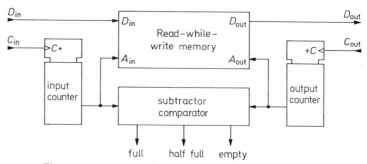

Fig. 11.21 FIFO implementation with read-while-write memory

Capacity	Organization	Type	Manufacturer	Operating power, typical	Clock frequency max.	Pins
Standard FIFOs, (MOS: ($V_{DD} = 5$ V, $f = f_{max}$)						
320 bit	**64 × 5**	**IDT 72404**	**Id, Am, Cy**	**175 mW**	**45 MHz**	**18**
576 bit	64 × 9	CY 7C 409 A	Cy	350 mW	35 MHz	28
2 kbit	256 × 9	IDT 7200	Id, Am	300 mW	40 MHz	28
5 kbit	512 × 9	IDT 7201	Id, Am, Cy, Da, St	300 mW	40 MHz	28
9 kbit	**1 k × 9**	**IDT 7202**	**Id, Am, Cy, Da, St**	**300 mW**	**40 MHz**	**28**
18 kbit	2 k × 9	IDT 7203	Id, Am, Cy, Da, St	375 mW	30 MHz	28
36 kbit	**4 k × 9**	**IDT 7204**	**Id, Da**	**375 mW**	**30 MHz**	**28**
36 kbit	4 k × 9	IDT 72 B04	Id		65 MHz	28
72 kbit	8 k × 9	IDT 7205	Id		20 MHz	28
72 kbit	4 k × 18	IDT 72045	Id		20 MHz	48
144 kbit	**16 k × 9**	**IDT 7206**	**Id**		**20 MHz**	**28**
144 kbit	**8 k × 9**	**IDT 72055**	**Id**		**20 MHz**	**48**
256 kbit	32 k × 8	μPD42532[1,2]	Ne	300 mW	10 MHz	40
1 Mbit	256 k × 4	TMS4C 1050[1]	Ti	250 mW	20 MHz	16
Bidirectional FIFOs, CMOS: ($V_{DD} = 5$ V, $f = f_{max}$)						
9 kbit	512 × 9	67C4701	Am	350 mW	16 MHz	28
18 kbit	512 × 18	IDT 72511	Id	450 mW	30 MHz	68
36 kbit	1 k × 18	IDT 72521	Id	350 mW	30 MHz	68

[1] Contains dynamic RAM   [2] Refresh controller integrated

Manufacturers: Am = AMD, Cy = Cypress, Da = Dallas, Id = IDT, Ne = NEC,
St = SGS-Thomson, Ti = Texas Instr.

Fig. 11.22 Examples of FIFOs

FIFO implementation using standard RAMs

For implementation of large FIFOs it is advisable to use standard RAMs, thereby providing the maximum degree of integration. This involves replacing the read-while-write memory in Fig. 11.21 by a two-port memory implemented using standard RAMs as shown in Fig. 11.15. The resultant configuration is shown in Fig. 11.23.

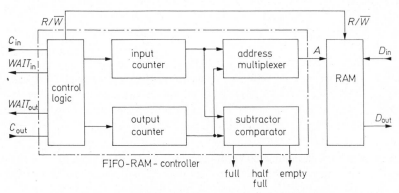

Fig. 11.23 FIFO implementation with standard RAMs

Since it is not possible to read and write simultaneously with a normal RAM, these operations must be performed sequentially. Coordination is provided by an "arbiter" in the control logic. If data are to be entered while a read-out is in progress, the read cycle is first completed and the input delayed via a "wait" signal, and vice versa if an output is to take place while an input is in progress. The cycle that was first requested is executed first in each case. If the read and write clock pulses coincide, the arbiter makes a random decision. Owing to the possible "wait" delay, the access time can double under worst-case conditions. The control logic required to operate a RAM as a FIFO can be obtained in the form of an integrated circuit known as a FIFO RAM controller:

512 ... 64 k words, 10 MHz,   TTL: 674219, MMI
512 ... 64 k words, 15 MHz,   CMOS: ISP 9119, Intersil
256 ... 16 k words, 60 MHz,   ECL: HXA 241-141, Valvo (RTC)

11.2.4 Error detection and correction

When data are stored in RAMs, two different types of error can occur: permanent and transient errors. The permanent errors (hard errors) are caused by faults in the ICs themselves or in the associated controller circuits. The transient errors (soft errors) only occur randomly and are not therefore reproducible. They are mainly caused by α-radiation of the package. It may not only discharge memory capacitors in dynamic RAMs but also cause flip-flops in static RAMs to change state. Transient errors can also result from noise pulses generated inside or outside the circuit [11.7].

The occurrence of memory errors can have far-reaching consequences. Thus a single error in a computer memory might not only produce an incorrect result, but even cause the program to crash completely. Methods have therefore been developed to indicate the occurrence of errors. In order to do this, one or more check bits must be processed in addition to the actual data bits. The more check bits used, the more errors can be detected or even corrected.

Parity bit

The simplest method of error detection consists of transmitting a parity bit p. Even or odd parity can be defined. For even parity check, the parity bit added to the data word is set to zero if the number of ones in the data word is even. It is set to one if this number is odd. This means that the total number of ones transmitted in a data word including parity bits is always even, or, for odd parity, always odd.

The even parity bit can also be interpreted as the sum (modulo-2) of the data bits. This checksum can be calculated as the exclusive-OR of the data bits.

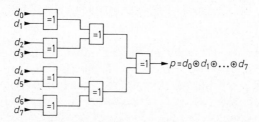

Fig. 11.24 Parity generator for even parity with 8 inputs.
IC types: 8-bit: SN 74180 (TTL);   9-bit: SN 74 S280 (TTL);
12-bit: MC 10160 (ECL);   MC 14531 (CMOS)

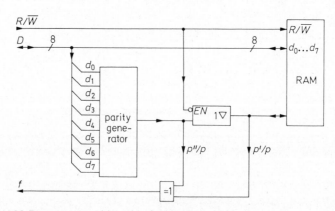

Fig. 11.25 Data memory with parity checking (using 8-bit data words as an example)

The implementation of a parity generator is shown in Fig. 11.24. The exclusive-OR gates can be in any sequence. It is chosen such that the sum of the delay times involved remains as small as possible.

For error detection purposes, the parity bit is stored together with the data bits. When the data are read out, the parity can then be regenerated as shown in Fig. 11.25 and compared with the stored parity bit by an exclusive-OR operation. If they differ, an error has occurred and the error output becomes $f = 1$. This allows each single-bit error to be detected. However, no correction is possible, since the bit containing the error cannot be located. If *several* bits contain errors, an odd number of errors can be detected, whereas an even number cannot.

Hamming code

The Hamming code principle consists of using several check bits in order to refine error detection to the point where it is possible not just to detect single-bit errors but also to pinpoint their location. Once the error bit in a binary code is located, it can be corrected by complementing it.

The question of how many check bits are required for this purpose is easily answered: with k check bits, 2^k different bit locations can be identified. With m data bits, the resultant total word length is $m + k$. An additional check bit combination is required to indicate whether the data word received is correct. This yields the condition

$$2^k \geq m + k + 1 \ .$$

The most important practical solutions are listed in Fig. 11.26. It can be seen that the relative proportion of check bits is smaller the greater the word length.

We shall now examine the procedure for determining the check bits, using a 16-bit word as an example. Figure 11.26 shows that to safeguard 16 bits we need 5 check bits, i.e. a total word length of 21 bits. In accordance with Hamming, the individual check bits are evaluated as parity bits for different parts of the data word. In our example we therefore require 5 parity generators. Their inputs are allocated to data bits in such a way that each data bit is connected to at least 2 of the 5 generators. If a data bit is now read incorrectly, there is a difference only between those parity bits affected by that particular data bit. Using this method we therefore obtain a 5-bit error word, the syndrome word, instead of a parity error signal f. It can assume 32 different values which allow us to pinpoint the error bit. It can be seen that the identification of a single-bit error is unique only if a different parity bit combination is selected for each data bit location. If a difference in just *one* parity bit is detected, only the

Number of data bits	m	1 ... 4	5 ... 11	12 ... 26	27 ... 57	58 ... 120	121 ... 247
Number of check bits	k	3	4	5	6	7	8

Fig. 11.26 Minimum number of check bits required to detect and correct a single-bit error, relative to the length of the data word

parity bit *itself* can be in error since the parity bit combination chosen means that, for an incorrect data bit, at least two parity bits have to differ. If all the data bits and parity bits are read without error, the calculated parity bits match those stored and the syndrome word becomes $F = 0$.

An example of the assignment of the five parity bits to the individual data bits is given in Fig. 11.27. This shows that data bit d_0 affects parity bits p_0 and p_1, data bit d_1 affects parity bits p_0 and p_2, etc. As required, each data bit affects a different combination of parity bits. To simplify the circuitry, the combinations have been distributed in such a way that each parity generator has 8 inputs.

Parity bits	Data bits d_i															
	0	1	2	3	4	5	6	7	8	9	10	11	12	13	14	15
p_0	×	×	×	×							×	×	×		×	
p_1	×				×	×	×				×	×	×	×		
p_2			×		×			×	×		×			×	×	×
p_3				×		×		×		×		×		×	×	×
p_4			×	×	×		×		×	×			×			×

Fig. 11.27 Example of parity bit generation using Hamming code for a 16-bit word

During reading ($R/\overline{W} = 1$) the syndrome generator in Fig. 11.28 compares the stored parity word P' with parity word P'' calculated from data D'. If errors occur, the syndrome word becomes $F = P' \oplus P'' \neq 0$. The syndrome decoder then defines which data bit must be corrected and causes the bit in question to be inverted in the data corrector.

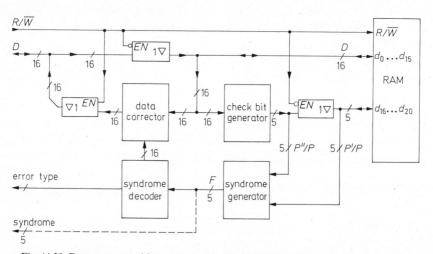

Fig. 11.28 Data memory with error correction (using 16-bit data words as an example)

The operation of the syndrome generator will be explained more precisely with reference to Fig. 11.29. Depending on the syndrome word $f_0 \ldots f_4$, three types of error can be identified: Data errors $d_0 \ldots d_{15}$, check bit errors $p_0 \ldots p_4$ and multiple errors. The latter type, however, are not completely detected when a Hamming matrix of minimum size is used, and cannot be corrected [11.8, 11.9].

Syn-drome word	No error	Data error				Check bit error					Multiple error			
		d_0	d_1	$d_2 \ldots d_{14}$	d_{15}	p_0	p_1	p_2	p_3	p_4				
f_0	0	1	1	1 ... 1	0	1	0	0	0	0	0	1 ... 0	1
f_1	0	1	0	0 0	0	0	1	0	0	0	1	0 1	1
f_2	0	0	1	0 1	1	0	0	1	0	0	1	0 1	1
f_3	0	0	0	1 1	1	0	0	0	1	0	0	1 1	1
f_4	0	0	0	1 0	1	0	0	0	0	1	0	0 1	1

Fig. 11.29 Table of the syndrome words and their significance

The particular advantage of memories with error correction facilities is that the occurrence of memory errors can be registered, while remaining ineffective as a result of the correction procedure. However, in order to derive maximum benefit from this, a number of factors have to be taken into consideration: the probability of non-correctable multiple errors must be minimized. For this reason a separate memory IC should be used for each data bit $d_0 \ldots d_{15}$ and each check bit $p_0 \ldots p_4$. Otherwise several data bits would be simultaneously falsified in the event of total failure of a memory chip. In addition, it is necessary for each error detected to be rectified as quickly as possible. Consequently, a program is interrupted when an error is detected in the computer memory and an error service program is executed. This must first establish whether this error is a transient error which can be rectified by writing the corrected data word back into memory and then reading it out again. If the error persists, it is a permanent error. In this case the syndrome word is read out, as this allows the memory IC involved to be located and the IC number together with the

Word length	Type	Manufacturer	Check bits	Correction time	Power dissipation	Pins
8 bit	74LS636	Texas Instr.	5	45 ns	450 mW	20
16 bit	74LS630	Texas Instr.	6	50 ns	600 mW	28
16 bit	IDT39C60	IDT	7	30 ns	300 mW	48
16 bit	Am29C60	AMD	7	50 ns	250 mW	48
32 bit	74ALS632	Texas Instr.	7	60 ns	780 mW	52
32 bit	IDT49C460	IDT	8	35 ns	350 mW	68
32 bit	Am29C660	AMD	8	50 ns	300 mW	68

Fig. 11.30 Error correction ICs

frequency of failure are listed in a table. This table can then be scanned at regular intervals so that defective chips can be replaced. This enables the reliability of a memory with EDC (Error Detection and Correction) to be continually increased.

Figure 11.30 lists some of the integrated EDC controllers available. All types use an additional check bit which enables *all* double errors to be detected; however, only the single errors can be corrected [11.10].

11.3   Read-only memories (ROMs)

The term ROM refers to table memories which are normally only read. They are therefore suitable for storing tables and programs. Their advantage is that the memory content is retained when the supply voltage is disconnected. Their disadvantage is that putting data into the table is much more intricate than with RAMs. The categories shown in Fig. 11.1 (MROM, PROM, EPROM, EEPROM) differ with respect to the input procedure.

11.3.1   Mask-programmed ROMs (MROMs)

With these devices, the memory content is entered during the final manufacturing stage using a specific metallization mask. This process is only cost-effective for large production quantities (from 10,000 approx.) and generally requires several months for implementation.

11.3.2   Programmable ROMs (PROMs)

A PROM is a read-only memory whose content is programmed-in by the user. The programmable components are usually fuses which are implemented in the ICs by means of exceptionally thin metallization links. Diodes are also used, which can be shorted by overloading them in the reverse-bias direction. The latest programmable elements for PROMs are special MOSFETs with an additional "floating gate". This is charged up during programming, causing it to change the pinch-off voltage of the MOSFET. As the floating gate has all-round SiO_2 insulation, it can be guaranteed to retain its charge for 10 years.

We shall now describe the internal design of a PROM using the example of the fuse-type PROM in Fig. 11.31. For technological reasons, the individual memory cells are not arranged linearly but as a square matrix. A particular memory cell is addressed by applying a logical 1 to the appropriate column or row connection. For this purpose the address vector $A = (a_0 \ldots a_n)$ must be decoded accordingly. The column and row decoders used operate as 1-out-of-n decoders.

The memory cell selected is activated by the AND gate at the intersection of the selected row or column line. The ORing of all the memory cell outputs

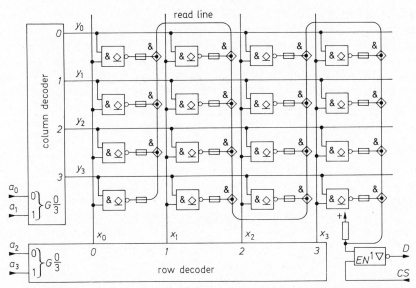

Fig. 11.31 Internal structure of a PROM. Example showing 16-bit memory capacity

produces output signal D. In order to obviate the need for a gate with 2^n outputs, wired-OR logic is used. In the case of open-collector outputs, this can be implemented by wired-ANDing the negated signals. This method has already been described in Fig. 9.30.

In its basic state, each memory cell addressed generates output signal $D = 1$. To program a zero, the fusible link at the output of the desired cell is blown as follows. One selects the address of the corresponding cell, turning on the output transistor of the NAND gate. A powerful current pulse is then injected into the read line which is just large enough to blow the fusible link at the NAND gate output. A timing sequence precisely defined by the manufacturer must be adhered to. Special programming devices are therefore used, which can be tailored to the particular type of memory.

In the case of PROMs, not just 1 bit but an entire 4-bit or 8-bit word is usually stored at an address. These devices therefore possess a corresponding number of data outputs. Specifying a memory capacity as, say, $1 \text{k} \times 8$ bits means that the memory contains 1024 8-bit words. The contents are specified in the form of a programming table. By way of example, Fig. 11.32 shows its organization for a 32×8-bit PROM.

The circuit symbol of a PROM is like that of the RAM in Fig. 11.5. The write-read switch here becomes the programming input and the data inputs are omitted.

Figure 11.33 lists some of the more common PROM types realized in various technologies.

Inputs					Outputs							
x_4	x_3	x_2	x_1	x_0	d_7	d_6	d_5	d_4	d_3	d_2	d_1	d_0
0	0	0	0	0								
0	0	0	0	1								
0	0	0	1	0								
0	0	0	1	1								
$\approx$	$\approx$	$\approx$	$\approx$	$\approx$	$\approx$	$\approx$	$\approx$	$\approx$	$\approx$	$\approx$	$\approx$	$\approx$
1	1	1	1	0								
1	1	1	1	1								

Fig. 11.32 Example of a programming table for a PROM containing 32 8-bit words

Capacity	Organization	Type	Manufacturer	Memory cell	Operating power, typical	Access time, max.	Pins
TTL: ($V_{CC} = 5$ V)							
256 bit	32×8	TBP38S30	Ti, Am, Si	FL	400 mW	15 ns	16
2 kbit	256×8	TBP38S22	Ti, Si	FL	400 mW	25 ns	20
8 kbit	$1 k \times 8$	Am 27S281	Am, Ti, Si	FL	500 mW	30 ns	24
16 kbit	$2 k \times 8$	Am 27S291	Am, Ti, Si	FL	600 mW	35 ns	24
64 kbit	$8 k \times 8$	Am 27S49	Am	FL	800 mW	40 ns	24
CMOS; ($V_{DD} = 5$ V, $f = f_{max}$)							
16 kbit	$2 k \times 8$	CY7C245A	Cy	FG	600 mW	15 ns	24
16 kbit	**2 k $\times$ 8**	**CY7C291**	**Cy, Ws, At, Am**	**FG**	**300 mW**	**30 ns**	**24**
64 kbit	**8 k $\times$ 8**	**CY7C264**	**Cy, Ws, At, Am**	**FG**	**400 mW**	**30 ns**	**24**
128 kbit	$16 k \times 8$	CY7C251	Cy, Ws, Am	FG	450 mW	35 ns	28
256 kbit	**32 k $\times$ 8**	**CY7C271**	**Cy, Ws**	**FG**	**500 mW**	**40 ns**	**28**
256 kbit	$32 k \times 8$	27C256P	To, Hi, Ne, Ti	FG	150 mW	150 ns	28
512 kbit	$64 k \times 8$	CY7C285	Cy	FG	600 mW	30 ns	28
1 Mbit	$128 k \times 8$	27C1001P	To, Hi, Ne, Am	FG	150 mW	200 ns	32

Manufacturers: Am = AMD, At = Atmel, Cy = Cypress, Hi = Hitachi, Ne = NEC, Si = Signetics, Ti = Texas Instr.

Memory cell: FL = fusible link, FG = floating gate = MOSFET

Fig. 11.33 Examples of PROMs

11.3.3   UV-erasable PROMs (EPROMs)

An EPROM (erasable PROM) is a PROM which can not only be user-programmed, but also erased with ultraviolet light. MOSFETs incorporating an additional floating gate are used exclusively as the memory element. This is charged up during programming (as with many PROMs), thereby changing the pinch-off voltage of the transistor. With EPROMs, however, this charge can be erased again in about 20 minutes by irradiation with UV light. For this purpose, the package is provided with a quartz glass window. Due to the additional package complexity involved, EPROMs are more expensive than non-window PROMs, even though they are realized in the same technology. Consequently, EPROMs are useful at the development stage of equipment, but for equipment mass production, the equivalent PROMs are to be preferred.

EPROMs are programmed on a word-by-word basis, i.e. for the usual 8-bit organization one byte at a time. In the case of older EPROMs (e.g. 2716; $2 \text{ k} \times 8$ bit) the programming procedure is still simple. One applies a programming voltage of $V_{PP} = 25$ V, together with the required address and the bit pattern to be programmed. Then a programming command lasting 50 ms is applied to store the data. Programming can then be terminated or the process can be repeated for another address using the associated bit pattern. In the case of a 2-kbyte EPROM, programming the entire device takes about two minutes. However, programming a 128 kbyte memory would take almost 2 hours. As this is clearly not tolerable, it was necessary to modify the technology and programming algorithms for larger EPROMs. All fast programming algorithms are based on the fact that most of the bytes of an EPROM can be programmed in considerably less than 50 ms. However, as "slower" bytes occur from time to time, it is impossible to generally reduce the programming time. Instead, a variable programming pulse length is employed.

The "fast" or "intelligent" programming algorithm generally used nowadays is shown in Fig. 11.34. The programming voltage $V_{PP} = 12.5$ V is applied and the supply voltage is raised to $V_{CC} = 6$ V. The higher supply voltage speeds up the programming process, as the transistors assume lower impedance, and also constitutes the worst-case condition for verification purposes. The address then becomes $A = 0$ and the associated data are applied. Now follows the procedure for programming this byte. For this purpose, an auxiliary counter is set to $n = 0$. A 1 ms programming command is then issued. After the auxiliary counter has been incremented, the memory content is read out to check whether progamming has already been successful. If not, up to another 24 programming commands are issued. If the byte has still not been programmed, the chip is deemed to be defective. Only a few programming pulses are normally required. However, it is still not certain that the floating gate has sufficient charge to last for 10 years. In order to make sure, the charge is trebled. This is done by overprogramming for $3n \cdot 1$ ms.

The first byte is thus programmed and the process can be repeated for the next address using new data. At the end of programming, we switch back to the

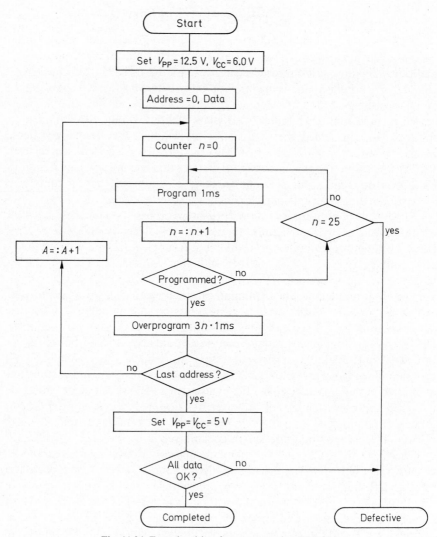

Fig. 11.34 Fast algorithm for programming EPROMs

read mode and check once more that the entire memory content is in order. The fast programming algorithm reduces the programming time for a 1 Mbit EPROM from around 2 h to less than 10 min. By reducing the programming pulse duration to 100 μs, times of less than 1 min can be achieved with some EPROMs.

Commonly used EPROMs are listed in Fig. 11.35.

Capacity	Organization	Type	Manufacturer	Operating power, typical	Access time, max.	Pins
CMOS: ($V_{DD} = 5$ V, $f = f_{max}$)						
16 kbit	2 k × 8	Cy7C291	Cy, Ws	250 mW	35 ns	24
64 kbit	**8 k × 8**	**27C64**	**Ti, Fu, Na, Am**	**100 mW**	**150 ns**	**28**
	8 k × 8	27HC64	At, Cy, Ws	300 mW	45 ns	28
	4 k × 16	WS57C65	Ws	300 mW	55 ns	40
128 kbit	16 k × 8	27C128	Ti, Fu, Am	150 mW	150 ns	28
	16 k × 8	Cy7C251	Cy, Ws	400 mW	45 ns	28
256 kbit	**32 k × 8**	**27C256**	**Ti, At, Fu, Hi, Mi, Ne, Na**	**150 mW**	**150 ns**	**28**
	32 k × 8	27HC256	At, Cy, Ws	350 mW	55 ns	28
	16 k × 16	27C202	In, Ws	500 mW	55 ns	40
512 kbit	64 k × 8	27C512	Ti, At, Fu, Mi, Ne, Na	150 mW	150 ns	28
	64 k × 8	27C285	Cy	700 mW	30 ns	28
1 Mbit	**128 k × 8**	**27C010**	**Am, To, Fu, Hi, Mi, Na, In**	**150 mW**	**200 ns**	**32**
	64 k × 16	**27C1024**	**Am, To, Fu, Ti, Mi, At, Na**	**250 mW**	**200 ns**	**40**
	64 k × 16	27HC1024	At, In	500 mW	55 ns	40
2 Mbit	256 k × 8	27C2001	Ne, In, Am	200 mW	200 ns	32
	128 k × 16	27C220	In, Am	250 mW	200 ns	40
4 Mbit	512 k × 8	27C4001	Ne, Ws, To	150 mW	150 ns	32
	256 k × 16	27C240	In, Hi, Am	250 mW	200 ns	40

Manufacturers: Am = AMD, At = Atmel, Cy = Cypress, Fu = Fujitsu, Hi = Hitachi, In = Intel, Mi = Mitsubishi, Na = National, Ne = NEC, Ti = Texas Instr., To = Toshiba, Ws = Wafer Scale

Fig. 11.35 Examples of EPROMs

11.3.4 Electrically erasable PROMs (EEPROMs)

The term EEPROM (electrically erasable PROM) refers to a PROM which, unlike the EPROM, can also be erased *electrically*. With the more recent types, the voltage converter for generating the programming voltage and the timer for determining the programming pulse duration are incorporated in the same chip. In order to program a byte, merely the address and data must be applied. If programming is then initiated by a write command, the EEPROM stores the address and data internally and immediately re-enables the address and data lines. The subsequent process takes place autonomously on the chip. The old byte is first erased and the new byte is then programmed. This process is internally monitored to ensure that the programmed charge is adequate. The process lasts 1 to 10 ms, i.e. the same order of magnitude as with EPROMs. Some EEPROMs are capable of storing not just one byte but an entire "page" containing 16 to 64 bytes in one programming process. To do this, the page is read into an internal RAM before issuing the programming command. This gives effective programming times of 30 μs per byte.

However, despite these simple, fast erase and write procedures, one should not be tempted to use an EEPROM as a RAM. The number of possible write cycles is in fact limited: no byte must be written more than 10^4 to 10^6 times (depending on type). With a programming time of 1 ms, the end of the operating life of a byte or page may be reached in as little as 10 s if continuous programming is performed [11.11, 11.12].

For this reason EEPROMs are sometimes combined with RAMs. The contents of these types of memory are only transferred to the EEPROM if the supply voltage fails. During normal operation, the RAM provides a short write cycle which is not associated with reduction in lifetime [11.13].

Some examples of EEPROMs are listed in Fig. 11.36. With many EEPROMs, as with most memories, the power dissipation is reduced when they are not selected by $CS = 1$. The smallest power dissipation obviously occurs when the supply voltage is disconnected completely. This does not result in the data being lost — as in the case of all ROMs — but the access time after application of the supply voltage is increased due to the transient response of the read amplifiers. For this reason it is inadvisable to switch on the supply voltage only when the memory is accessed.

Capacity	Organization	Type	Manufacturer	Operating power, typical	Access time, max.	Pins
Standard EEPROMs, CMOS: ($V_{DD} = 5$ V, $f = f_{max}$)						
16 kbit	2 k × 8	28C16	At, Se, Xi	100 mW	200 ns	24
16 kbit	2 k × 8	28HC16	At	300 mW	35 ns	24
64 kbit	**8 k × 8**	**28C64**	**At, Se, Xi**	**120 mW**	**200 ns**	**28**
64 kbit	8 k × 8	28HC64	At	280 mW	45 ns	28
256 kbit	**32 k × 8**	**28C256**	**At, Se, Xi**	**150 mW**	**200 ns**	**28**
256 kbit	32 k × 8	28HC256	At	350 mW	70 ns	28
1 Mbit	128 k × 8	28C010	At, Se, Xi	300 mW	200 ns	32
1 Mbit	64 k × 16	28C1024	At	400 mW	150 ns	40
Flash EEPROMs, CMOS: ($V_{DD} = 5$ V, $f = f_{max}$)						
256 kbit	32 k × 8	28F256	In, At, Am	150 mW	150 ns	32
512 kbit	64 k × 8	28F512	In, Se, Am	150 mW	150 ns	32
1 Mbit	**128 k × 8**	**28F010**	**In, Se, Am**	**150 mW**	**150 ns**	**32**
RAMs with subordinate EEPROMs: ($V_{DD} = 5$ V)						
512 bit	128 × 4	X22C13	Xi		120 ns	18
4 kbit	512 × 8	X2004	Xi	400 mW	200 ns	28
16 kbit	2 k × 8	X20C16	Xi		120 ns	24
64 kbit	8 k × 8	PNC11C68	Pl	250 mW	35 ns	24

Manufacturer: Am = AMD, At = Atmel, In = Intel, Pl = Plessy, Se = Seeq, Xi = Xicor

Fig. 11.36 Examples of EEPROMs

Flash EEPROMs are intermediates between EPROMs and EEPROMs. Like EEPROMs they can be erased electrically, not byte by byte, however, as can the EPROMs, but the entire chip is erased at once. This is the reason for their name. They are erased much more simply than EPROMs: a single erase pulse lasting for a few seconds is required. It is not necessary to take the package from the circuit and put it for 20 min into an eraser unit. Flash EEPROM technology is little more complicated than that of EPROMs. Correspondingly large integration densities consistent with low prices can therefore be achieved. In order to arrive at economical solutions, the converter for the programming voltage and the timer for the programming process normally incorporated in EEPROM devices is omitted in flash EEPROMs. Flash EEPROMs are therefore programmable in the same way as EPROMs.

A comparison of the write and read performance of the various ROM types with that of RAMs is shown in Fig. 11.37. We can see that the strength of RAMs is their fast write and read processes which can be repeated any number of times. With all the ROM variants, writing is subject to more or less severe limitations, although all ROMs have the advantage of retaining their contents even in the absence of supply voltage. This characteristic can be achieved for RAMs by adding a buffer battery. As we can see from Fig. 11.8, the current drain of many CMOS-RAMs is generally lower than the self-discharge of a battery. Hence, data retention of 10 years can be ensured by using appropriate batteries.

	RAM	ROM			
		MROM	PROM	EPROM	EEPROM
Write					
No.	any	once	once	... 100 times	$10^4 ... 10^6$ times
Time	10 ... 200 ns	months	minutes	minutes	milliseconds
Read					
No.	any	any	any	any	any
Time	10 ... 200 ns	approx. 100 ns	10 ... 300 ns	30 ... 300 ns	30 ... 300 ns

Fig. 11.37 Comparison of RAMs and ROMs in terms of their write and read performance

11.4   Programmable logic devices (PLDs)

PLDs are used for storing logic functions. The categories in Fig. 11.1 show that there are three variants: PLAs, PALs and LCAs. The differences between them are in respect of programming flexibility. PALs (programmable array logic) are the easiest to program. They are therefore particularly popular and are available in a wide range of designs. PLAs (programmable logic arrays) are basically more flexible, but programming them is more complicated. They have therefore ceased to be of major importance. LCAs (logic cell arrays) are very recent components. They can not only be programmed as various individual PLDs, but also with any data paths between those PLDs. This enables them to replace simple gate arrays. They can therefore also be described as user-programmable gate arrays.

When logic functions are implemented using the standard product terms, it is first necessary to AND together the input variables and then form the sum of the products. In order to be able to show these operations clearly, we use the

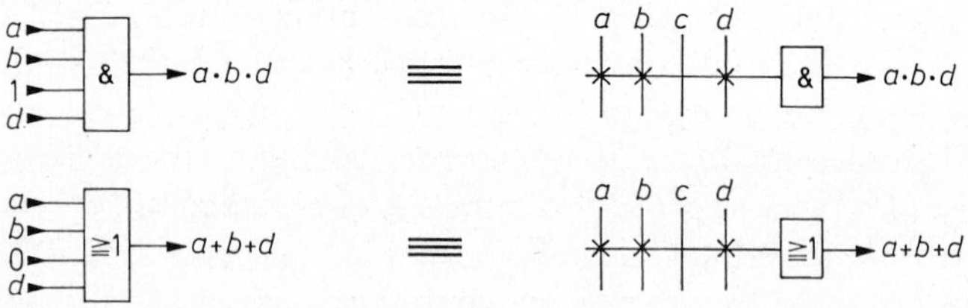

Fig. 11.38 Simplified representation of the AND and OR operations. The crosses indicate which input is connected. An unconnected input has no effect since it is 1 for the AND operation and 0 for the OR operation.

simplified representation in Fig. 11.38. The internal design of PLAs and PALs can then be illustrated very easily, as shown in Fig. 11.39. The input variables or their negation and the intersecting inputs of AND gates form a matrix which enables all the required logical products to be formed. In a corresponding second matrix, the connections between the AND gates and the OR gates can then be established in order to form the required logical sums. This requires only one OR gate per output variable. In the case of a PLA (Fig. 11.39a), both matrices are user-programmable. In the case of a PAL (Fig. 11.39b), the OR matrix is permanently preset (fixed) by the manufacturer, and only the AND matrix can be programmed.

A PROM can also be understood as a function memory if the address decoder, having a truth table as shown in the left half of Fig. 11.40, is interpreted as an AND matrix. Then we can make use of the representation in Fig. 11.39. For every address applied, only a single AND operation is 1, namely that corresponding to the address applied. There are therefore $n = 2^N$ product terms, whereas the PLAs and PALs have substantially fewer. Whether the associated function value is 1 or 0 is determined by the programming of the OR matrix.

PROMs designed for implementing logic functions are also known as PLEs (programmable logic elements). The differences become apparent by considering the example in Fig. 11.40. All the connections not required for these functions have been programmed "open". Figure 11.41 shows that all the required logical products are formed in the AND matrices of the PLA and PAL. In the case of the PLA, it is even possible to use a product, which is required several times, twice in the OR matrix. This freedom is not availabe in the case of the (simple) PALs, as their OR matrix is not programmable.

With a PROM, it is always the particular product corresponding to the input combination that is 1. Consequently, it is necessary in the OR matrix to program connections for all combinations that are 1 in the truth table. We can see from this that a PROM is the image of the truth table, whereas the PLA and PAL represent the logic functions. A PROM can be used to store any kind of truth table, whereas only a limited number of products and sums are available in a PLA or PAL. For this reason, it is not possible to realize any truth table, but only those which can be converted into simple logic functions. This requires utmost simplification of the functions using Boolean algebra and, if necessary,

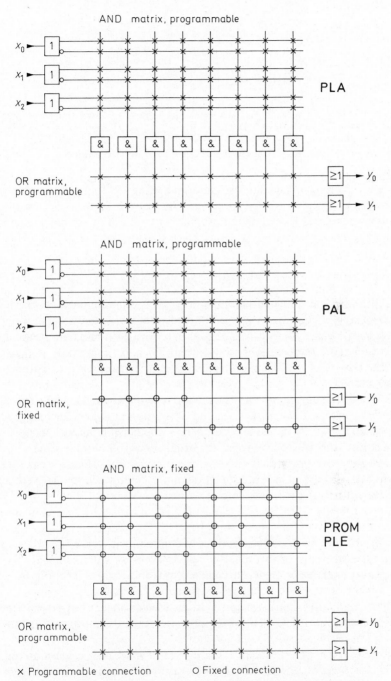

× Programmable connection   O Fixed connection

Fig. 11.39 Comparison of the structures of PLA, PAL and PROM/PLE devices

Z	x_2	x_1	x_0	y_1	y_0
0	0	0	0	1	0
1	0	0	1	0	0
2	0	1	0	1	1
3	0	1	1	0	0
4	1	0	0	0	1
5	1	0	1	1	1
6	1	1	0	1	1
7	1	1	1	0	1

$$y_0 = x_2 + \bar{x}_0 x_1$$
$$y_1 = \bar{x}_0 x_1 + \bar{x}_0 \bar{x}_2 + x_0 \bar{x}_1 x_2$$

Fig. 11.40 Example of a truth table and its logic functions

transformation from AND into OR operations using De Morgan's Law, in order to utilize the PALs as efficiently as possible. Nowadays this is no longer done manually but using special design programs which can be run on any personal computer. Their application is described in greater detail in Section 11.4.2.

11.4.1   Programmable logic array (PAL)

PALs are the principal representatives of programmable logic devices (PLDs) [11.14]. They are available in a wide range of variants, all of which are based on the principle shown in Fig. 11.39b. The differences are in the implementation of the OR operations at the output. The most commonly used variants are listed in Fig. 11.42. Each different type is designated by the relevant letter shown.

The high (H) output represents the basic type shown in Fig. 11.39. In the case of the low (L) type, the output is negated. The C output is complementary. In the programmable (P) type, the user can define whether the output function or its inversion is true. For this purpose the exclusive-OR output gate is used, whose second input can be made 0 or 1 by the programming. The user has then the freedom to form the negated function and thereby utilize the PAL more efficiently if necessary. In the case of the EXOR (X) output, there is likewise an exclusive-OR gate at the output; however, it is controlled by two OR operations. This variant is used for simple implementation of adders.

The sharing (S) output has features in common with the PLAs. Here the OR matrix is also partly programmable: two adjacent OR gates can share the AND operations available to them. This makes it possible to form functions for which the number of OR gates would otherwise be insufficient.

With many PALs, an output can also be used as an input or programmed as a bidirectional port (I/O). This is the purpose of the tristate gate at the output, whose ENABLE is itself a logic function.

An important application of PALs is in sequential logic systems. In order to obviate the need for additional chips, the required registers (R) are incorporated in the PALs. They have a common clock terminal to enable construction of synchronous systems. In addition, the output signals are generally fed back

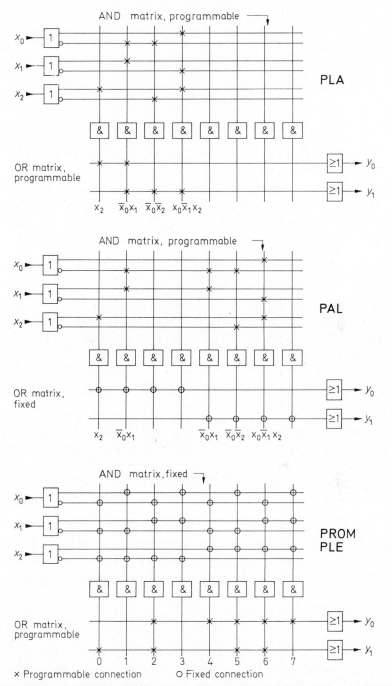

Fig. 11.41 Implementation of the functions of Fig. 11.40 using a PLA, PAL and PROM

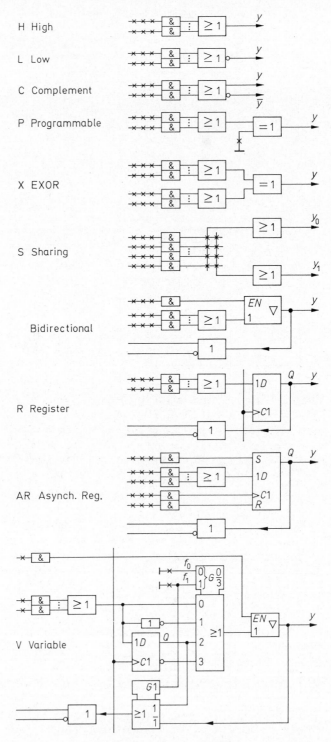

L Low

C Complement

P Programmable

X EXOR

S Sharing

Bidirectional

R Register

AR Asynch. Reg.

V Variable

Fig. 11.42 Output circuits of PALs

internally to the AND matrix, thereby eliminating external feedback circuitry (see Fig. 10.61) and saving on pins.

PALs are also available which are designed for implementing asynchronous sequential logic systems. They allow the clock for each register to be defined by an additional logic function (AR in Fig. 11.42). In addition, these PALs usually have a freely definable set and reset function. Similar to the synchronous type, they may have internal feedback features.

Using the optimum PAL for each application would require a large number of different types — as Fig. 11.42 shows. In order to reduce the variety of types, PALs with a programmable output structure are becoming increasingly common. One such variable "macrocell" (V) is also shown in Fig. 11.42. It is built around a multiplexer which can be used to select any of four different operating modes. These are defined by programming the function bits f_0 and f_1. The different operating modes are listed in Fig. 11.43. Bit f_0 determines whether or not the output is negated. Bit f_1 switches between combinatorial and registered mode. It also determines, via a second multiplexer, whether feedback is taken from the output or from the register. We can see that most PALs can be implemented in this way using a single type.

f_1	f_0	Type	Output	Feedback
0	0	H	Function	Output
0	1	L	Function, negated	Output
1	0	R	Register	Register
1	1	R	Register, negated	Register

Fig. 11.43 Operating modes of the variable macrocell

11.4.2 Computer-aided PLD design

In order to "personalize" a PAL, it is first necessary to specify which connections are to be programmed and then to carry out the programming in a second step. PAL design is no longer a manual process, now that software packages are available which will run on any PC (personal computer). The various design phases are shown in Fig. 11.44. There are usually various input formats, of which only the most commonly used will be presented here. The logic function or truth table is entered using a text editor. When designing sequential logic systems it is also possible to start from a state diagram and specify the transition conditions.

A particularly effective method is to enter the logic diagram. For this a library can be used in which the most common TTL functions are already defined as macros. In addition to gates and flip-flops, the library also provides multiplexers and demultiplexers, adders and comparators as well as counters and shift registers. This is not only useful for converting an old design incorporating TTL devices into a PLD design, but also simplifies the design of new

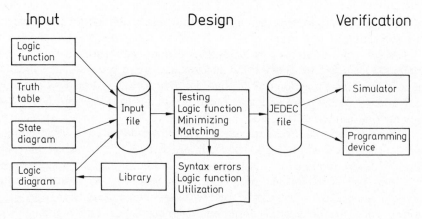

Fig. 11.44 Computer-aided PLD design

circuits in which the TTL devices are used merely as conceptual models. The input method is supported by a graphic character editor.

After input by whatever method, all the data are converted to logic functions and a syntax check is performed. The logic functions are then minimized in accordance with the rules of Boolean algebra. However, this does not yet guarantee that they fit the relevant PLD in their optimum form. For matching, AND operations, for instance, are converted to OR operations using De Morgan's Law. The programming data (fuse map) are finally stored in a standard format, the *JEDEC* file.

Programming is carried out either by connecting a programming device to the PC via a serial interface or by inserting a programming card in the PC. Although not quite so universally applicable, the latter solution is much more cost-effective.

Before programming, it is advisable to check that the design actually has the desired characteristics. This can be done by a simulation program. A table of input combinations (test vectors) is compiled and the resulting output signals are checked. Signals in the PLD can be observed which are not accessible in the hardware. Timing diagrams can also be generated in the simulation as on an oscilloscope, which also allows the dynamic performance to be tested.

The best-known manufacturer-specific design software is PALASM from AMD. Program packages for the general user are LOGIC from Kontron, ABEL from Data-I/O, DASH from Futurenet and CUPL from Personal-CAD-Systems.

11.4.3 Survey of types available

PALs are available in a wide variety of types, ranging from simple PALs with a complexity of 50 gate equivalents to very complex PALs with up to 2000 gate equivalents. Even though not all the functions of a PAL are usually required, it is clear that a whole conglomeration of TTLs can be replaced by a single chip in this way.

Most manufacturers' type designations give an indication of the internal design of the PAL. Figure 11.45 explains the meanings of the individual characters.

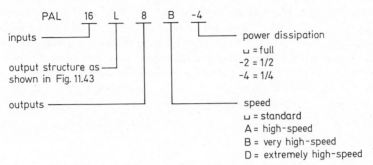

Fig. 11.45 Type designation of PALs ($\sqcup$ = blank)

We can see from Fig. 11.46 that PALs may be divided into two large categories: types with a dedicated output structure and more recent types with a variable macrocell. The advantage of the latter is that a single type can be used in place of an entire group of different dedicated PALs.

In the *architecture* column, we can see that most PALs have a number of bidirectional terminals in addition to the fixed inputs and outputs. This not only enables us to program a bidirectional signal path, but also to increase the number of inputs or outputs, as required.

The number of *inputs* specified in the type designation (first number in the matrix column) basically indicates the inputs of the AND matrix. In most cases, the specified number of inputs is accessible only if all the bidirectional terminals are programmed as inputs. However, an output may then no longer be available. Consequently, the maximum number of matrix inputs can only be utilized if some of the inputs are implemented by internal feedback paths from the output register. However, it is precisely this connection that is required for constructing sequential logic systems and the internal feedback even allows an external connection to be saved.

The second number in the matrix column indicates the total number of AND operations available. One such operation is required for controlling each bidirectional terminal. The remainder can be used to form the logic functions. Dividing them by the number of outputs, we obtain the average possible AND operations for a logic function.

Conventional PALs are manufactured in TTL technology and are fuse-programmed. Nowadays they are available with various power dissipations and speeds, e.g. type 16L8. The same variety is found in types 16R8, 20L8 and 20R8.

Some PALs are now available in ECL technology, although the speed advantage is not so marked. The choice between TTL and ECL technology is automatically determined by the circuit environment. The use of level converters would cancel out all the advantages.

Another innovation are PALs in CMOS technology, which offer a markedly lower power dissipation for identical speed. In addition, they are invariably designed in EPROM or EEPROM technology, and so the programming is erasable and the PALs can be re-used. This is a significant advantage in terms of circuit design and is no disadvantage as far as production is concerned [11.15].

PALs incorporating the versatile macrocell represent the most interesting development. Types 16V8 or EP320 can emulate most 20-pin PALs and the 20V8 most 24-pin PALs. The fourth standard type, the 22V10, provides even more complex functions, as it has virtually twice as many product terms.

Other variable PALs possess an even greater complexity and can sometimes replace several simple PALs.

PLAs and LCAs

PALs have largely ousted PLAs commercially. The only new development in this field is the GAL6001 made by Lattice. Its AND matrix can form 75 products of 39 input variables; its OR matrix forms 36 sums of 64 variables. Constructed in EEPROM CMOS technology, it can emulate complex PALs [11.16].

LCAs are a new family of programmable logic devices. They may be regarded as a matrix of PALs of type 5V2 which can be individually programmed. Their new feature is that connections between the individual PALs can also be programmed, giving them virtually the same degree of flexibility as gate arrays. The XC2000-, XC3000- and XC4000-families employ CMOS-technology and are manufactured by Xilinx and AMD. These LCAs consist of 64 . . . 900 PALs ("configurable logic blocks", CLBs) corresponding to a complexity of 1200 . . . 20000 gates. As the programming stored in an additional RAM in the LCA is lost when the supply voltage is turned off, it must be reloaded each time the device is activated. This is performed automatically by the LCA in a few milliseconds. It is merely necessary to connect an EPROM in which the configuration (10 . . . 65 kbit) is stored [11.17].

Type	Manufacturer	Architecture					Electrical		Pins
		In	In/ Out	Out	Matrix	Prog.	Time max.	Power typical	
TTL-PALs									
16L8	Am, Na, Ti	10	6	2	16 × 64	P	35 ns	600 mW	20
16L8A	Am, Na, Ti	10	6	2	16 × 64	P	25 ns	600 mW	20
16L8A-2	Am, Na, Ti	10	6	2	16 × 64	P	35 ns	300 mW	20
16L8A-4	Am, Na, Ti	10	6	2	16 × 64	P	55 ns	150 mW	20
16L8B	Am, Na, Ti	10	6	2	16 × 64	P	15 ns	600 mW	20
16L8B-2	Am, Na, Ti	10	6	2	16 × 64	P	25 ns	300 mW	20
16L8B-4	Am, Na, Ti	10	6	2	16 × 64	P	35 ns	150 mW	20
16L8D	Am, Na, Ti	10	6	2	16 × 64	P	10 ns	600 mW	20
16R8B	Am, Na, Ti	8	—	8	16 × 64	P	15 ns	600 mW	20
20L8B	Am, Na, Ti	12	6	2	20 × 72	P	15 ns	700 mW	24
20R8B	Am, Na, Ti	12	—	8	20 × 72	P	15 ns	700 mW	24
ECL-PALs									
1016C4	Na, Cy	16	—	4	16 × 32	P	2 ns	900 mW	24
1016P8	Na, Cy, Am	16	—	8	16 × 64	P	3 ns	1000 mW	24
10H20EV8	Am	12	—	8	20 × 90	P	6 ns	1100 mW	24
CMOS–PALs				macro cells					
16V8	**Am, La, Vt**	**10**	**8**	**8**	**16 × 64**	**EEP**	**15 ns**	**350 mW**	**20**
20V8	**Am, La, Vt**	**12**	**8**	**8**	**20 × 64**	**EEP**	**15 ns**	**350 mW**	**24**
22V10	**Am, La, Vt**	**12**	**10**	**10**	**22 × 130**	**EEP**	**15 ns**	**400 mW**	**24**
24V10	**Am**	**14**	**10**	**10**	**24 × 130**	**EEP**	**15 ns**	**420 mW**	**28**
26V12	**Am, La, Se**	**14**	**12**	**12**	**26 × 150**	**EEP**	**15 ns**	**450 mW**	**28**
MACH110	Am	6	32	32	2 × 22 × 64	EEP	15 ns	500 mW	44
MACH210	Am	6	32	64	4 × 22 × 64	EEP	15 ns	600 mW	44
MACH230	Am	6	64	128	8 × 22 × 64	EEP	15 ns		84
EP320	Al, In	10	8	8	18 × 72	EP	25 ns	60 mW	20
EP610	**Al, In, Ti**	**4**	**16**	**16**	**20 × 160**	**EP**	**25 ns**	**120 mW**	**24**
EP910	**Al, In, Ti**	**12**	**24**	**24**	**36 × 240**	**EP**	**30 ns**	**150 mW**	**40**
EP1810	Al, In, Ti	12	48	48	60 × 480	EP	35 ns	400 mW	68
EPM5016	Al	8	8	16	56 × 128	EP	20 ns	300 mW	20
EPM5024	Al	8	12	24	80 × 192	EP	20 ns	450 mW	24
EPM5032	**Al, Cy**	**8**	**16**	**32**	**120 × 256**	**EP**	**20 ns**	**600 mW**	**28**
EPM5064	Al, Cy	8	28	64	4 × 64 × 128	EP	30 ns	700 mW	40
EPM5127	**Al, Cy**	**8**	**28**	**128**	**8 × 64 × 128**	**EP**	**30 ns**	**750 mW**	**40**
EPM5128	Al, Cy	8	52	128	8 × 64 × 128	EP	30 ns	750 mW	68

Manufacturers: Am = AMD, Al = Altera, Cy = Cypress, In = Intel, La = Lattice, Na = National, Se = Seeq, Ti = Texas Instruments, Vt = VTI

Programming technology: P = PROM, EP = EPROM, EEPROM.

Power: The CMOS types of the EP series have a reduced power consumption in the "non-turbo-mode"

Fig. 11.46 Examples of PALs

Part II. Applications

12 Linear and non-linear operational circuitry

Digital computers allow mathematical operations to be performed to a very high standard of accuracy. The quantities involved are often continuous signals, for instance in the form of voltages, which in turn may be the analogs for some other measured quantities. In such cases the digital computer requires two additional units, an analog-to-digital converter and a digital-to-analog converter. Such expenditure is only justified if the accuracy required is too high to be met by analog computer circuitry involving operational amplifiers. An upper limit for the accuracy of this kind of circuit is in the order of 0.1%.

In the following sections the most important families of operational circuits are classified and described. They are circuits for the four fundamental arithmetic operations, for differential and integral operations, and for the synthesis of transcendental or any other chosen functions. In order to illustrate as clearly as possible the operating principles of these circuits, we initially assume ideal characteristics of the operational amplifiers involved. When using real operational amplifiers, restrictions and additional conditions must be observed in the choice of the circuit parameters, and these are treated thoroughly in Chapter 7. We want to discuss in more detail only those effects that play a special role in the performance of the particular circuit.

12.1 Summing amplifier

For the addition of several voltages, an operational amplifier can be used when it is connected as an inverting amplifier. As Fig. 12.1 indicates, the input voltages are connected via series resistors to the N-input of the operational amplifier. Since this node represents virtual ground, Kirchhoff's current law

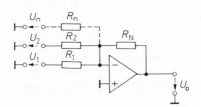

Fig. 12.1 Inverting summing amplifier

Output voltage: $\quad -U_o = \dfrac{R_N}{R_1} U_1 + \dfrac{R_N}{R_2} U_2 + \ldots + \dfrac{R_N}{R_n} U_n$

(KCL) directly yields the relation for the output voltage:

$$\frac{U_1}{R_1} + \frac{U_2}{R_2} + \ldots + \frac{U_n}{R_n} + \frac{U_o}{R_N} = 0 .$$

The inverting summing amplifier can also be used as an amplifier with a wide-range zero adjustment if a DC voltage is added to the signal voltage in the manner described.

12.2 Subtracting circuits

12.2.1 Reduction to an addition

A subtraction can be reduced to the problem of an addition by inverting the signal to be subtracted. This requires the circuit shown in Fig. 12.2. The operational amplifier OA 1 inverts the input voltage U_2; the output voltage is then

$$U_o = A_P U_2 - A_N U_1 . \tag{12.1}$$

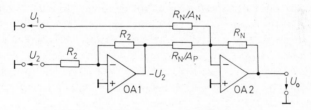

Fig. 12.2 Subtracting circuit using summing amplifier

Output voltage: $\qquad\qquad U_o = A_D(U_2 - U_1)$

Condition for coefficients: $\qquad A_N = A_P = A_D$

An evaluation of the actual difference based on the equation $U_o = A_D(U_2 - U_1)$ can be carried out if both gains, A_P and A_N, are made equal to the desired differential gain A_D. The deviation of this voltage from the result of an ideal subtraction is determined by the common-mode rejection ratio (CMRR) which is defined as $G = A_D/A_{CM}$. The deviation can be calculated by allowing

$$U_2 = U_{CM} + \tfrac{1}{2}U_D$$

and $\qquad\qquad\qquad\qquad\qquad\qquad\qquad\qquad\qquad\qquad\qquad$ (12.2)

$$U_1 = U_{CM} - \tfrac{1}{2}U_D .$$

Equation (12.1) will then give

$$U_o = \underbrace{(A_P - A_N)}_{A_{CM}}U_{CM} + \underbrace{\tfrac{1}{2}(A_P + A_N)}_{A_D}U_D , \tag{12.3}$$

where U_{CM} is the common-mode voltage and U_D is the difference signal voltage.

From Eq. (12.3) the common-mode rejection ratio can be determined as

$$G = \frac{A_D}{A_{CM}} = \frac{1}{2} \cdot \frac{A_P + A_N}{A_P - A_N} .$$ (12.4)

We can now write:

$$A_N = A - \tfrac{1}{2}\Delta A ,$$

$$A_P = A + \tfrac{1}{2}\Delta A ,$$

where A is the arithmetic mean of A_N and A_P. Introducing these expressions into Eq. (12.4) yields the result

$$G = \frac{A}{\Delta A} .$$ (12.5)

The common mode rejection ratio thus equals the reciprocal of the relative matching of the individual gains.

12.2.2 Subtraction using a single operational amplifier

To calculate the output voltage of the subtracting amplifier in Fig. 12.3, we may use the principle of superposition. We therefore write

$$U_o = k_1 U_1 + k_2 U_2 .$$

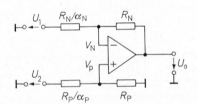

Fig. 12.3 Subtracting circuit using a single amplifier (subtracting amplifier)

Output voltage: $\qquad\qquad\qquad U_o = \alpha(U_2 - U_1)$

Condition for coefficients: $\qquad \alpha_N = \alpha_P = \alpha$

For $U_2 = 0$, the circuit is an inverting amplifier where $U_o = -\alpha_N U_1$. It follows that $k_1 = -\alpha_N$. For $U_1 = 0$, the circuit represents a non-inverting amplifier having a voltage divider connected at its input. The potential

$$V_P = \frac{R_P}{R_P + R_P/\alpha_P} U_2$$

is thus amplified by the factor $(1 + \alpha_N)$, this resulting in the output voltage

$$U_o = \frac{\alpha_P}{1 + \alpha_P}(1 + \alpha_N)U_2 .$$

If both resistor ratios are the same, i.e if $\alpha_N = \alpha_P = \alpha$, it follows that

$$U_o = \alpha U_2$$

and that $k_2 = \alpha$. We now obtain the output voltage for the general case as

$$U_o = \alpha(U_2 - U_1) \ .$$

Should the ratios of the resistors at the P and N inputs not be precisely equal to α, the circuit does not evaluate the precise difference of the input voltages. In this case

$$U_o = \frac{1 + \alpha_N}{1 + \alpha_P} \alpha_P U_2 - \alpha_N U_1 \ .$$

To calculate the common-mode rejection ratio we use the formulation of Eq. (12.2) again and obtain

$$G = \frac{A_D}{A_{CM}} = \frac{1}{2} \cdot \frac{(1 + \alpha_N)\alpha_P + (1 + \alpha_P)\alpha_N}{(1 + \alpha_N)\alpha_P - (1 + \alpha_P)\alpha_N} \ .$$

With $\alpha_N = \alpha - \frac{1}{2}\Delta\alpha$ and $\alpha_P = \alpha + \frac{1}{2}\Delta\alpha$, the expression may be rewritten and expanded into a series. Neglecting higher-order terms one obtains

$$G \approx (1 + \alpha)\frac{\alpha}{\Delta\alpha} \ . \tag{12.6}$$

For constant α, the common-mode rejection ratio is inversely proportional to the tolerance of the resistor ratios. If the resistor ratios are identical, $G = \infty$, although this applies to ideal operational amplifiers only. In order to obtain a particularly high common-mode rejection ratio under real conditions, R_P may be varied slightly. In this way, $\Delta\alpha$ can be adjusted and the finite common-mode rejection ratio of the operational amplifier can be compensated for.

Equation (12.6) also shows that the common-mode rejection ratio for a given resistor matching tolerance $\Delta\alpha/\alpha$ is approximately proportional to the chosen differential gain $A_D = \alpha$. This is a great improvement over the previous circuit.

An example may best illustrate this: two voltages of about 10 V are to be subtracted one from the other. Their difference is no more than 100 mV. This value is to be amplified and to appear at the output of the subtraction amplifier as a voltage of 5 V, with an accuracy of 1%. The differential gain must therefore be $A_D = 50$. The absolute error at the output must be smaller than $5 \, V \cdot 1\% = 50 \, mV$. If we assume the favorable case of the common-mode gain representing the only source of error, we then find it necessary to limit the common-mode gain to

$$A_{CM} \leqq \frac{50 \, mV}{10 \, V} = 5 \cdot 10^{-3} \ ,$$

i.e.

$$G \geqq \frac{50}{5 \cdot 10^{-3}} = 10^4 \triangleq 80 \, dB \ .$$

For the subtracting amplifier in Fig. 12.3, this requirement can be met by a relative resistor matching tolerance of $\Delta\alpha/\alpha = 0.5\%$, as follows from Eq. (12.6). For the subtraction circuit of Fig. 12.2, however, Eq. (12.5) yields a maximum tolerable mismatch of 0.01%.

Figure 12.4 shows an expansion of the subtracting amplifier for any number of additional summing and/or subtracting inputs. The determining factor for the proper functioning of the circuit is that the specified coefficient condition is satisfied. If this is not achieved with the coefficients α_i and α_i' specified, the voltage 0 can be added or subtracted using the missing coefficient required to satisfy the equation.

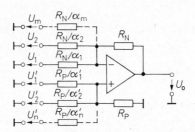

Fig. 12.4 Multiple-input subtracting amplifier

Output voltage: $$U_o = \sum_{i=1}^{n} \alpha_i' U_i' - \sum_{i=1}^{m} \alpha_i U_i$$

Condition for coefficients: $$\sum_{i=1}^{n} \alpha_i' = \sum_{i=1}^{m} \alpha_i$$

In order to deduce the relationships given below Fig. 12.4, we apply Kirchhoff's current law to the N-input:

$$\sum_{i=1}^{m} \frac{U_i - V_N}{\left(\dfrac{R_N}{\alpha_i}\right)} + \frac{U_o - V_N}{R_N} = 0 \ .$$

Hence

$$\sum_{i=1}^{m} \alpha_i U_i - V_N\left[\sum_{i=1}^{m} \alpha_i + 1 \right] + U_o = 0 \ .$$

Similarly, we obtain for the P-input:

$$\sum_{i=1}^{n} \alpha_i' U_i' - V_P\left[\sum_{i=1}^{n} \alpha_i' + 1 \right] = 0 \ .$$

With $V_N = V_P$ and the coefficient condition

$$\sum_{i=1}^{m} \alpha_i = \sum_{i=1}^{n} \alpha_i' \ , \tag{12.7}$$

the subtraction of the two equations results in

$$U_o = \sum_{i=1}^{n} \alpha_i' U_i' - \sum_{i=1}^{m} \alpha_i U_i .$$

For $n = m = 1$, the multiple-input subtracting amplifier becomes the basic circuit of Fig. 12.3.

The inputs of computing circuits represent loads to the signal voltage sources. The output resistances of the latter have to be sufficiently low to minimize the computing errors. If the sources themselves are feedback amplifiers, this condition is generally well satisfied. When using other signal sources it may become necessary to employ impedance converters connected to the inputs. These converters often take the form of non-inverting amplifiers, and the resulting subtracting circuits are then called instrumentation amplifiers. They are commonly used in the field of measurement, and are dealt with extensively in Chapter 25.

12.3 Bipolar-coefficient circuit

The circuit in Fig. 12.5 allows the multiplication of the input voltage by a constant factor, the value of which can be set between the limits $+ n$ and $- n$ by the potentiometer R_2. If the slider of the potentiometer is positioned as far to the right as possible, then $q = 0$ and the circuit operates as an inverting amplifier with gain $A = - n$. In this case, the resistor $R_1/(n - 1)$ is ineffective since there is no voltage across it.

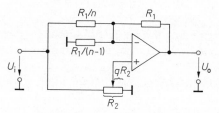

Fig. 12.5 Bipolar-coefficient circuit

Output voltage: $U_o = n(2q - 1)U_i$

For $q = 1$, the full input voltage U_i is at the P-input. The voltage across R_1/n is therefore zero, and the circuit operates as a non-inverting amplifier having the gain

$$A = 1 + \frac{R_1}{R_1/(n - 1)} = + n .$$

For intermediate positions the gain is

$$A = n(2q - 1) .$$

It is thus linearly dependent on q and can be easily adjusted, for instance by means of a calibrated helical potentiometer. The factor n determines the range of the coefficient. The smallest value is $n = 1$; the resistor $R_1/(n-1)$ may in this case be omitted.

12.4   Integrators

One of the most important operational amplifier applications in analog computing circuits is as an integrator. Its output voltage can be expressed by the general form

$$U_o(t) = K \int_0^t U_i(\tilde{t}) d\tilde{t} + U_o(t = 0) \ .$$

12.4.1   Inverting integrator

The inverting integrator in Fig. 12.6 differs from the inverting amplifier in that the feedback resistor R_N is replaced by the capacitor C. The output voltage is then expressed by

$$U_o = \frac{Q}{C} = \frac{1}{C}\left[\int_0^t I_C(\tilde{t}) d\tilde{t} + Q_0 \right] ,$$

where Q_0 is the charge on the capacitor at the beginning of the integration ($t = 0$). As $I_C = - U_i/R$, it follows that

$$U_o = - \frac{1}{RC} \int_0^t U_i(\tilde{t}) d\tilde{t} + U_{oo} \ .$$

The constant U_{oo} represents the initial condition: $U_{oo} = U_o(t = 0) = Q_0/C$. It has to be set to a defined value by the additional measures described in the next section.

Let us now look at two special cases. If the input voltage U_i is constant, the output voltage is

$$U_o = - \frac{U_i}{RC} t + U_{oo} ,$$

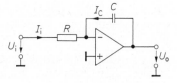

Fig. 12.6 Inverting integrator

Output voltage: $U_o = - \dfrac{1}{RC} \int_0^t U_i(\tilde{t}) d\tilde{t} + U_{oo}$

which increases linearly with time. The circuit is thus very well suited to the generation of triangular and sawtooth voltages.

If U_i is a cosinusoidal alternating voltage $u_i = \hat{U}_i \cos \omega t$, the output voltage becomes

$$U_o(t) = -\frac{1}{RC} \int_0^t \hat{U}_i \cos \omega \tilde{t} \, d\tilde{t} + U_{o0} = -\frac{\hat{U}_i}{\omega RC} \sin \omega t + U_{o0} \, .$$

The amplitude of the alternating output voltage is therefore inversely proportional to the angular frequency ω. When the amplitude-frequency response is plotted in log-log coordinates, the result is a straight line having the slope -6 dB/octave. This characteristic is a simple criterion for determining whether a circuit behaves like an integrator.

The behavior in the frequency domain can also be determined directly with the help of complex calculus:

$$\underline{A} = \frac{\underline{U}_o}{\underline{U}_i} = -\frac{\underline{Z}_C}{R} = -\frac{1}{j\omega RC} \, . \tag{12.8}$$

Hence, it follows that for the ratio of the amplitudes

$$\frac{\hat{U}_o}{\hat{U}_i} = |\underline{A}| = \frac{1}{\omega RC} \, ,$$

as shown before.

As regards the frequency compensation, it must be noted that, unlike all the circuits previously discussed, the feedback network causes a phase shift. This means that the feedback factor becomes complex:

$$\underline{k} = \frac{V_N}{\underline{U}_o}\bigg|_{U_i = 0} = \frac{j\omega RC}{1 + j\omega RC} \, . \tag{12.9}$$

For high frequencies, $\underline{k}$ approaches $\underline{k} = 1$ and the phase shift becomes zero. Therefore, in this range of frequency the same conditions obtain as for a unity-gain inverting amplifier (see Chapter 7). The frequency compensation necessary for the latter case must therefore also be used for the integrator circuit. Internally compensated amplifiers are normally designed for this application, and are therefore suitable for use as integrators.

The frequency range usable for integration can be seen in Fig. 12.7, to give a typical example. The integration time constant chosen is $\tau = RC = 100$ μs. It is apparent that by doing so, a maximum loop gain of $|g| = \underline{k}\underline{A}_D| \approx 600$ is attained, this corresponding to an output accuracy of about $1/|g| \approx 0.2\%$. In contrast to that of the inverting amplifier, the output accuracy falls not only at high, but also at low frequencies.

For the real operational amplifier, the input bias current I_B and the offset voltage U_O may be very troublesome, as their effects accumulate with time. If the input voltage U_i is reduced to zero, the capacitor carries the error current

$$\frac{U_O}{R} + I_B \, .$$

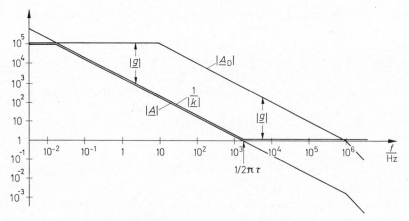

Fig. 12.7 Amplitude-frequency response of the loop gain g

This results in a change in output voltage

$$\frac{dU_o}{dt} = \frac{1}{C}\left(\frac{U_O}{R} + I_B\right) . \tag{12.10}$$

An error current of $I_B = 1\,\mu A$ causes the output voltage to rise at a rate of 1 V/s if $C = 1\,\mu F$. Equation (12.10) indicates that for a given time constant, the contribution of the input bias current is smaller, the larger the value of C chosen. The contribution of the offset voltage remains constant. Because there is a limit to the size of C, one should at least make certain that the effect of I_B does not exceed that of U_O. This is the case if

$$I_B < \frac{U_O}{R} = \frac{U_O C}{\tau} .$$

If a time constant of $\tau = 1$ s has to be achieved with a capacitance of $C = 1\,\mu F$, an operational amplifier having an offset voltage of $U_O = 1$ mV should possess an input bias current smaller than

$$I_B = \frac{1\,\mu F \cdot 1\,mV}{1\,s} = 1\,nA .$$

Operational amplifiers with bipolar input transistors rarely have such low input bias currents. Their undesirable effects can be reduced by not connecting the P-input directly to ground, but via a resistor which also has the value R. The voltage $I_B R$ is then dropped across both resistors and the error current through capacitor C is therefore zero. The remaining error source is now only the difference between the input bias currents, i.e. the offset current, which, however, is generally small in comparison.

In the case of FET op amps, the input bias current is usually negligible. They are therefore preferred if the integration time constants are large, even though

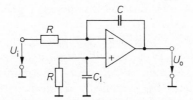

Fig. 12.8 Integrator having input bias current compensation. Capacitor C_1 shorts noise voltages at
the P-input

their offset voltages are often much larger than for op amps with bipolar input
transistors.

A further source of error may be leakage currents through the capacitor. As
electrolytic capacitors have leakage currents in the order of µA, they cannot be
used as integration capacitors. One is therefore obliged to use foil capacitors
which make capacitances of over 10 µF very unwieldy.

12.4.2 Initial condition

An integrator can often be used only if its output voltage $U_o(t = 0)$ can be set
independently of the input voltage. With the circuit in Fig. 12.9 it is possible to
stop integration and set the initial condition.

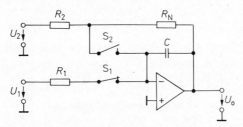

Fig. 12.9 Integrator having three modes of operation: integrate, hold, set initial condition

$$\text{Initial condition:} \quad U_o(t = 0) = -\frac{R_N}{R_2} U_2$$

If the switch S_1 is closed and S_2 open, the circuit operates like that in
Fig. 12.6; the voltage U_1 is integrated. If switch S_1 is now opened, the charging
current becomes zero in the case of an ideal integrator, and the output voltage
remains at the value it had at the time of switching. This may be of use if one
wants to interrupt computation, e.g. in order to read the output voltage at
leisure. To set the initial condition, S_1 is left open and S_2 is closed. The
integrator becomes an inverting amplifier with an output voltage of

$$U_o = -\frac{R_N}{R_2} U_2 \; .$$

However, the output assumes this voltage only after a certain delay determined by the time constant $R_N C$.

Figure 12.10 shows one possibility of replacing the switches by electronic components. The two FETs T_1 and T_2 replace the switches S_1 and S_2 of Fig. 12.9. They are conducting (ON) if the corresponding mode control signal voltage is greater than zero. For sufficiently negative control voltages they are in the OFF-state. The precise operation of the FET switches and of the diodes D_1 to D_6 is described in more detail in Chapter 22.

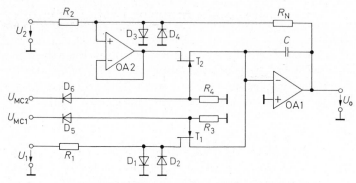

Fig. 12.10 Integrator with electronic mode control

$$\text{Initial condition:} \quad U_o(t = 0) = -\frac{R_N}{R_2} U_2$$

The voltage follower OA 2 reduces the delay time constant for setting the initial condition, from the value $R_N C$ to the small value of $R_{DS\,ON} \cdot C$.

12.4.3   Summing integrator

Just as the inverting amplifier can be extended to become a summing amplifier, so an integrator can be developed into a summing integrator. The relationship given for the output voltage can be directly derived by applying KCL to the summing point.

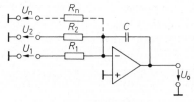

Fig. 12.11 Summing integrator

$$\text{Output voltage:} \quad U_o = -\frac{1}{RC} \int_0^t \left(\frac{U_1}{R_1} + \frac{U_2}{R_2} + \ldots + \frac{U_n}{R_n} \right) d\tilde{t} + U_{o\,0}$$

12.4.4 Non-inverting integrator

For integration without polarity reversal, an inverting amplifier can be added to the integrator. Another solution is shown in Fig. 12.12. The circuit basically consists of a lowpass filter as the integrating element. A NIC, having internal resistance $-R$, is connected in parallel with the filter and simultaneously acts as an impedance converter (see Chapter 13). To calculate the output voltage, we appply KCL to the P-input and obtain

$$\frac{U_o - V_P}{R} + \frac{U_i - V_P}{R} - C\frac{dV_P}{dt} = 0 \ .$$

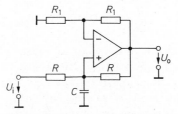

Fig. 12.12 Non-inverting integrator

Output voltage: $U_o = \dfrac{2}{RC}\int\limits_0^t U_i(\tilde{t})\,d\tilde{t} + U_{oo}$

Hence, with $V_P = V_N = \frac{1}{2}U_o$, we arrive at the result

$$U_o = \frac{2}{RC}\int\limits_0^t U_i(\tilde{t})\,d\tilde{t} \ .$$

It must be noted that the input voltage source must have a very low impedance, otherwise the stability condition for the NIC is not fulfilled. The operational amplifier evaluates differences between large quantities, and therefore this integrator does not have the same precision as the basic circuit in Fig. 12.6.

12.5 Differentiators

12.5.1 Basic circuit

If the resistor and capacitor of the integrator in Fig. 12.6 are interchanged, we obtain the differentiator in Fig. 12.13. The application of KCL to the summing point yields the relationship

$$C\frac{dU_i}{dt} + \frac{U_o}{R} = 0 \ , \qquad U_o = -RC\frac{dU_i}{dt} \ . \tag{12.11}$$

Thus, for sinusoidal alternating voltages $u_i = \hat{U}_i \sin \omega t$ we obtain the output voltage

$$u_o = -\omega RC\hat{U}_i \cos \omega t \ .$$

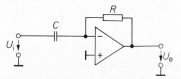

Fig. 12.13 Differentiator

$$\text{Output voltage:} \quad U_o = -RC\frac{dU_i}{dt}$$

For the ratio of amplitudes, it follows that

$$\frac{\hat{U}_o}{\hat{U}_i} = |\underline{A}| = \omega RC \ . \tag{12.12}$$

When the frequency response of the gain is plotted in log-log coordinates, the result is a straight line with the slope + 6 dB/octave. In general, a circuit is said to behave as a differentiator in a particular frequency range if, in that range, the amplitude-frequency response rises at a rate of 6 dB/octave.

The behavior in the frequency domain can also be determined directly with the help of complex calculus:

$$\underline{A} = \frac{\underline{U}_o}{\underline{U}_i} = -\frac{R}{\underline{Z}_C} = -j\omega RC \ . \tag{12.13}$$

Hence,

$$|\underline{A}| = \omega RC \ ,$$

in accordance with Eq. (12.12).

12.5.2   Practical implementation

The practical implementation of the differentiator circuit in Fig. 12.13 presents certain problems since the circuit is prone to oscillations. These are caused by the feedback network which, at higher frequencies, gives rise to a phase lag of 90°, as the feedback factor is:

$$\underline{k} = \frac{1}{1 + j\omega RC} \ . \tag{12.14}$$

This lag is added to the phase lag of the operational amplifier which in the most favorable case is already 90°. The remaining phase margin being zero, the circuit is therefore unstable. The instability can be overcome if one reduces the phase shift of the feedback network at high frequencies by connecting a resistor R_1 in series with the differentiating capacitor, as in Fig. 12.14. This measure need not necessarily reduce the usable frequency range, since the reduction in loop gain limits the satisfactory operation of the differentiator at higher frequencies.

For the cutoff frequency f_1 of the lowpass element R_1C, it is advisable to choose the value for which the loop gain becomes unity. To find this value, one

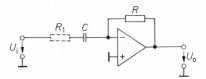

Fig. 12.14   Practical design of a differentiator

Output voltage: $U_o = -RC \dfrac{dU_i}{dt}$ for $f \ll \dfrac{1}{2\pi R_1 C}$

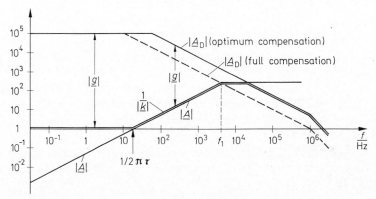

Fig. 12.15 Example for the frequency response of the loop gain $f_1 = \sqrt{f_T/2\pi\tau}$ where $\tau = RC$ and f_T is the unity gain bandwidth

considers a fully compensated amplifier, the amplitude-frequency response of which is shown in the example of Fig. 12.15 as a dashed line. The phase margin at frequency f_1 is then approximately 45°. Since, in the vicinity of frequency f_1, the amplifier has a feedback factor of less than unity, one can obtain an increase in the phase margin by reducing the frequency compensation, and hence approach a transient behavior of near critical damping.

To optimize the compensation capacitor C_k, a triangular voltage is applied to the input of the differentiator and C_k is reduced so that the rectangular output voltage is optimally damped.

12.5.3   Differentiator with high input impedance

The input impedance of the differentiator described exhibits capacitive behavior and this can lead to difficulties in some cases; for example, an operational amplifier circuit used as an input voltage source can easily become unstable. The differentiator in Fig. 12.16 is better in this respect. Its input impedance does not fall below the value of R, even at high frequencies.

The operation of the circuit is best illustrated as follows. Alternating voltages of low frequency are differentiated by the RC network at the input. In this

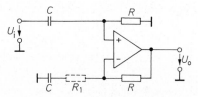

Fig. 12.16 Differentiator with high input impedance

Output voltage: $U_o = RC \dfrac{dU_i}{dt}$

Input impedance: $|Z_i| \geqq R$

frequency range, the operational amplifier corresponds to a non-inverting amplifier, having the gain $A = 1$.

Alternating voltages of high frequency pass the input RC element unchanged and are differentiated by the feedback amplifier. If both time constants are equal, the effects of differentiation at low frequencies and at high frequencies overlap and make a smooth changeover.

As regards stabilization against likely oscillations, the same principles apply as for the previous circuit. The damping resistor R_1 is shown by the dashed line in Fig. 12.16.

12.6   Solving differential equations

There are many problems which can be described most easily in the form of differential equations. One obtains the solution by using the analog computing circuits described above to model the differential equation and by measuring the resulting output voltage. In order to avoid stability problems, the differential equation is transformed in such a way that only integrators are required rather than differentiators.

We shall illustrate this method using the example of a linear second-order differential equation

$$y'' + k_1 y' + k_0 y = f(x) \ . \tag{12.15}$$

In the first step, the independent variable x is replaced by the time variable t:

$$x = \frac{t}{\tau} \ .$$

Since

$$y' = \frac{dy}{dt} \cdot \frac{dt}{dx} = \tau \dot{y} \quad \text{and} \quad y'' = \tau^2 \ddot{y} \ ,$$

the differential equation (12.15) becomes

$$\tau^2 \ddot{y} + k_1 \tau \dot{y} + k_0 y = f(t/\tau) \ . \tag{12.16}$$

In the second step, the equation is solved for the undifferentiated quantities:

$$k_0 y - f(t/\tau) = -\tau^2 \ddot{y} - k_1 \tau \dot{y} \ .$$

Thirdly, the equation is multiplied throughout by the factor $-1/\tau$ and integrated:

$$-\frac{1}{\tau} \int [k_0 y - f(t/\tau)] \, dt = \tau \dot{y} + k_1 y \ . \tag{12.17}$$

In this way, an expression is formed on the left-hand side of Eq. (12.17), which can be computed by a simple summing integrator. Its output voltage is termed the state variable, z_n, where n is the order of the differential equation; here $n = 2$. Therefore

$$z_2 = -\frac{1}{\tau} \int [k_0 y - f(t/\tau)] \, dt \ . \tag{12.18}$$

In this equation, the output variable y is initially taken as known.

By inserting Eq. (12.18) in Eq. (12.17), we arrive at

$$z_2 = \tau \dot{y} + k_1 y \ . \tag{12.19}$$

This differential equation is now treated in the same way as Eq. (12.16) and we obtain therefore

$$z_2 - k_1 y = \tau \dot{y} \ ,$$
$$-\frac{1}{\tau} \int [z_2 - k_1 y] \, dt = -y \ . \tag{12.20}$$

The left-hand side represents the state variable z_1:

$$z_1 = -\frac{1}{\tau} \int [z_2 - k_1 y] \, dt \ . \tag{12.21}$$

This expression is formed by a second summing integrator. Substitution in Eq. (12.20) gives the equation for the output

$$y = -z_1 \ . \tag{12.22}$$

Since there are no longer any derivatives, the procedure is terminated. The last

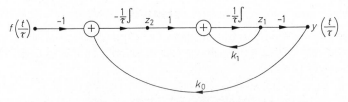

Fig. 12.17 Signal flow graph for solving the differential equation

$$\tau^2 \ddot{y} + k_1 \tau \dot{y} + k_0 y = f\left(\frac{t}{\tau}\right)$$

equation, (12.22), provides the missing relation for the output variable y which had initially been taken as known.

The operations necessary for solving the differential equation (Eqs. (12.18), (12.21) and (12.22)) can be represented clearly with the aid of a signal flow graph as in Fig. 12.17. The appropriate analog computing circuit is shown in Fig. 12.18. In order to save an additional inverting amplifier for the computation of the expression $-k_1 y$ in Eq. (12.21), we make use of the fact that, from Eq. (12.22), $z_1 = -y$.

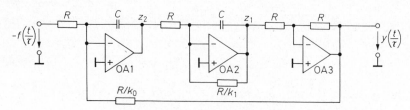

Fig. 12.18 Practical analog computing circuit

12.7 Function networks

The problem often arises that two voltages U_1 and $U_2 = f(U_1)$ have to be assigned one to the other, where f is a given function, so that for example

$$U_2 = U_A \log \frac{U_1}{U_B} \; ,$$

or

$$U_2 = U_A \sin \frac{U_1}{U_B} \; .$$

The correlation can also be given in the form of a diagram or table.

There are three possibilities for realizing such relationships. One can either make use of a physical effect that complies with the correlation required, or one can approximate the function by a series of straight lines or a power series. Below, we give some examples for these methods.

12.7.1 Logarithm

A logarithmic amplifier must produce an output voltage that is proportional to the logarithm of the input voltage. It is therefore possible to make use of the diode characteristic

$$I_A = I_S (e^{\frac{U_{AC}}{mU_T}} - 1) \; . \tag{12.23}$$

In this equation, I_S is the saturation leakage current, U_T is the thermal voltage kT/e_0 and m is a correction factor between 1 and 2. For the forward-biased diode, when $I_A \gg I_S$, Eq. (12.23) can be approximated with good accuracy to

$$I_A = I_S e^{\frac{U_{AC}}{mU_T}} . \tag{12.24}$$

Hence, the forward voltage

$$U_{AC} = mU_T \ln \frac{I_A}{I_S} , \tag{12.25}$$

which is the required logarithmic function. The simplest way of using this relationship for computation of the logarithm is shown in Fig. 12.19, where a diode is incorporated in the feedback loop of an operational amplifier. This amplifier converts the input voltage U_i to a proportional current $I_A = U_i/R_1$. At the same time, the voltage $U_o = - U_{AC}$ appears at its low-impedance output. Therefore

$$U_o = - mU_T \ln \frac{U_i}{I_S R_1} = - mU_T \ln 10 \lg \frac{U_i}{I_S R_1} , \tag{12.26}$$

or, at room temperature,

$$U_o = - (1 \ldots 2) \cdot 60 \, \text{mV} \lg \frac{U_i}{I_S R_1} .$$

The usable range is limited by two effects. The diode possesses a parasitic series resistance, across which a considerable voltage is present at high currents, leading to errors in the computation of the logarithm. In addition, the correction factor m is current-dependent. A satisfactory accuracy can therefore only be achieved over an input voltage range of one or two decades.

The unfavorable effect of the varying correction factor m can be eliminated by replacing the diode D by a transistor T, as shown in Fig. 12.20. For the collector current we write in accordance with Eq. (4.1) if $I_C \gg I_{CS}$:

$$I_C \approx I_{CS} e^{U_{BE}/U_T} \tag{12.27}$$

hence

$$U_{BE} = U_T \ln \frac{I_C}{I_{CS}} . \tag{12.28}$$

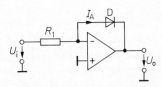

Fig. 12.19 Diode logarithmic amplifier

Output voltage: $U_o = - mU_T \ln \dfrac{U_i}{I_S R_1}$

for $U_i > 0$

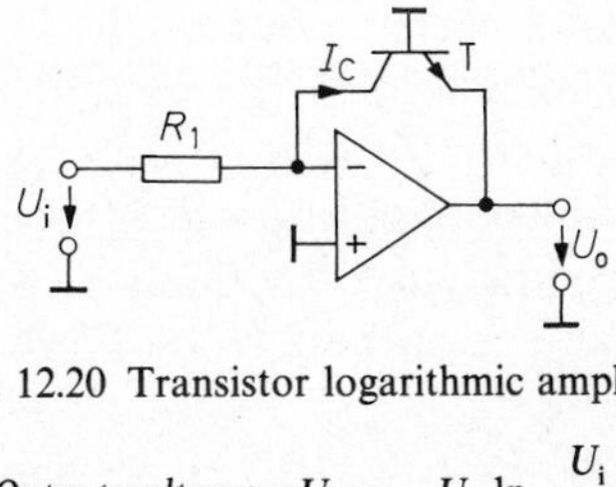

Fig. 12.20 Transistor logarithmic amplifier

Output voltage: $U_o = - U_T \ln \dfrac{U_i}{I_{CS} R_1}$

for $U_i > 0$

It follows that the output voltage of the transistor logarithmic amplifier in Fig. 12.20 is

$$U_\text{o} = - U_\text{BE} = - U_\text{T} \ln \frac{U_\text{i}}{I_\text{CS} R_1} \ .$$

As well as eliminating the correction factor m, the circuit in Fig. 12.20 has two further advantages: no distortion due to the collector-base leakage current occurs, as $U_\text{CB} = 0$. In addition, the magnitude of the current gain does not affect the result, as the base current flows away to ground. When suitable transistors are employed, the collector current can be varied from the pA to the mA region, i.e. over nine decades. However, operational amplifiers with very low input currents are needed to exploit this range to the full.

Since the transistor T increases the loop gain by its own voltage gain, the circuit is prone to oscillations. The voltage gain of the transistor stage can be reduced quite simply by connecting a resistor R_E between emitter and amplifier output, as in Fig. 12.21. This limits the voltage gain of the transistor by means of current feedback to the value R_1/R_E. The resistance R_E must not, of course, give rise to voltage saturation of the operational amplifier at the largest possible output current. The capacitor C can further improve stability of the circuit by derivative action in the feedback. It must be noted, however, that the upper cutoff frequency decreases proportionally to the current because of the non-linear transistor characteristic.

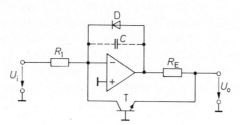

Fig. 12.21 Practical implementation of a logarithmic amplifier

Enhanced performance is achieved if the transistor is operated from a high-impedance current source. The loop gain is then $g_\text{f} \cdot R_1$, where g_f is the transconductance of the drive circuit. As it is independent of the collector current, frequency compensation can be optimized over the entire current range. Operational amplifiers which have a current output are available as integrated "transconductance amplifiers", e.g. types CA 3060 and CA 3080 from RCA. The disadvantage of these types, however, is that they have a relatively large input bias current.

Diode D in Fig. 12.21 prevents the op amp from being overdriven in the event of negative input voltages. This ensures that transistor T is not damaged by excessively high emitter-base reverse voltage and shortens the recovery time.

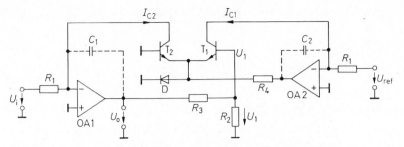

Fig. 12.22 Temperature-compensated logarithmic amplifier

Output voltage: $U_\text{o} = - U_\text{T} \cdot \dfrac{R_3 + R_2}{R_2} \ln \dfrac{U_\text{i}}{U_\text{ref}}$ for $U_\text{i}, U_\text{ref} > 0$

One disadvantage of the logarithmic amplifier described is its strong temperature dependence. The reason for this is that U_T and I_CS vary markedly with temperature. For a temperature rise from 20 °C to 50 °C, U_T increases by 10% while the reverse current multiplies tenfold. The influence of the reverse current can be eliminated by computing the difference between two logarithms. We employ this principle in Fig. 12.22, where the differential amplifier stage T_1, T_2 is used to find the logarithm. In order to examine the operation of the circuit, we determine the current sharing in the differential amplifier stage. From Kirchhoff's voltage law (KVL) it follows that

$$U_1 + U_\text{BE 2} - U_\text{BE1} = 0 \ .$$

The transfer characteristics of the transistors may be written as

$$I_\text{C1} = I_\text{CS} e^{\dfrac{U_\text{BE1}}{U_\text{T}}} \ ,$$

$$I_\text{C2} = I_\text{CS} e^{\dfrac{U_\text{BE 2}}{U_\text{T}}} \ ;$$

and therefore

$$\frac{I_\text{C1}}{I_\text{C2}} = e^{\dfrac{U_1}{U_\text{T}}} \ . \tag{12.29}$$

From Fig. 12.22, we infer the additional equations

$$I_\text{C2} = \frac{U_\text{i}}{R_1} \ , \qquad I_\text{C1} = \frac{U_\text{ref}}{R_1} \ , \qquad U_1 = \frac{R_2}{R_3 + R_2} U_\text{o} \ ,$$

if R_2 is not chosen to be too large. By substitution, we get the output voltage

$$U_\text{o} = - U_\text{T} \frac{R_3 + R_2}{R_2} \ln \frac{U_\text{i}}{U_\text{ref}} \ . \tag{12.30}$$

The value of R_4 does not appear in the result. Its resistance is chosen so that the voltage across it is smaller than the maximum possible output voltage swing of amplifier OA 2.

Logarithmic amplifiers providing an output voltage of 1 V/decade are frequently required. To determine the size of R_2 and R_3 for this special case we rewrite Eq. (12.30) in the form

$$U_o = - U_T \frac{R_3 + R_2}{R_2} \cdot \frac{1}{\lg e} \cdot \lg \frac{U_i}{U_{ref}} = - 1\,V \lg \frac{U_i}{U_{ref}} \,.$$

With $U_T = 26\,mV$, the resulting condition is

$$\frac{R_3 + R_2}{R_2} = \frac{1\,V \cdot \lg e}{U_T} \approx 16.7 \,.$$

If we select $R_2 = 1\,k\Omega$, then $R_3 = 15.7\,k\Omega$.

As regards the frequency compensation of both amplifiers, the same argument holds as for the previous circuit. C_1 and C_2 are the additional compensation capacitors. The temperature effect of U_T can be offset by letting resistor R_2 have a positive or R_3 a negative temperature coefficient of 0.3%/K. This possibility is utilized in the ICL 8084 from Intersil. Another solution is to maintain the differential amplifier at constant temperature using a transistor array with two additional transistors. One of these is then used as a temperature sensor and the other as a heater. A suitable transistor array is e.g. the MAT 04 from PMI [12.1].

12.7.2   Exponential function

Figure 12.23 shows an exponential function amplifier whose design is analogous to that of the logarithmic amplifier in Fig. 12.20. When a negative voltage is applied to the input, the current flowing through the transistor is given by Eq. (12.27):

$$I_C = I_{CS}\,e^{\frac{U_{BE}}{U_T}} = I_{CS}e^{-\frac{U_i}{U_T}} \,,$$

and the output voltage is therefore

$$U_o = I_C R_1 = I_{CS}R_1 e^{-\frac{U_i}{U_T}} \,.$$

As with the logarithmic amplifier in Fig. 12.22, the temperature stability can be improved by using a differential amplifier. The appropriate circuit is represented

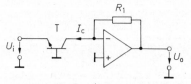

Fig. 12.23 Simple exponential amplifier
$$U_o = I_{CS}R_1 e^{-\frac{U_i}{U_T}} \quad \text{for } U_i < 0$$

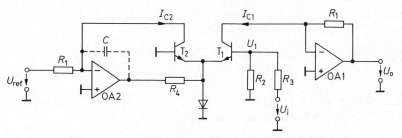

Fig. 12.24 Temperature-compensated exponential amplifier

$$U_o = U_{ref}\, e^{\frac{R_2}{R_3 + R_2} \cdot \frac{U_i}{U_T}} \quad \text{for } U_{ref} > 0$$

in Fig. 12.24. Again, from Eq. (12.29)

$$\frac{I_{C1}}{I_{C2}} = e^{\frac{U_1}{U_T}}\ .$$

From Fig. 12.24 we deduce the following equations

$$I_{C1} = \frac{U_o}{R_1}\ , \qquad I_{C2} = \frac{U_{ref}}{R_1}\ , \qquad U_1 = \frac{R_2}{R_3 + R_2}\, U_i\ .$$

By substitution we obtain the output voltage

$$U_o = U_{ref}\, e^{\frac{R_2}{R_3 + R_2} \frac{U_i}{U_T}}\ . \tag{12.31}$$

It can be seen that I_{CS} no longer appears in the result if the transistors are well matched. The resistor R_4 limits the current through the transistors T_1 and T_2, and its resistance does not affect the result as long as operational amplifier OA 2 is not saturated.

A particularly important design is obtained if the output voltage increases by a factor of 10 for an increase in input voltage of 1 V. The required condition may be derived from Eq. (12.31):

$$U_o = U_{ref} \cdot 10^{\frac{R_2}{R_3 + R_2} \cdot \frac{U_i}{U_T} \cdot \lg e} = U_{ref} \cdot 10^{\frac{U_i}{1\,V}}\ .$$

Consequently, with $U_T = 26\,\text{mV}$

$$\frac{R_3 + R_2}{R_2} = \frac{1\,V \cdot \lg e}{U_T} \approx 16.7$$

i.e. the same component values as for the logarithmic amplifier in Fig. 12.22.

A typical integrated exponential function amplifier with internal temperature compensation is the ICL 8049 from Intersil.

The exponential amplifiers described enable the computation of expressions of the form

$$y = e^{ax}\ .$$

Since

$$b^{ax} = (e^{\ln b})^{ax} = e^{ax \ln b} \; ,$$

exponential functions to any base b can be computed according to

$$y = b^{ax}$$

by amplifying the input signal x by the factor $\ln b$, and by applying the result to the input of an exponential function amplifier.

12.7.3   Computation of power functions using logarithms

The computation of power expressions of the form

$$y = x^a$$

can be performed for $x > 0$ by means of logarithmic and exponential function amplifiers because

$$x^a = (e^{\ln x})^a = e^{a \ln x} \; .$$

The basic arrangement for such a circuit is shown in Fig. 12.25. The equations mentioned apply to the logarithmic-function amplifier of Fig. 12.22 and the exponential-function amplifier of Fig. 12.24, where $R_2 = \infty$, $R_3 = 0$. We therefore obtain the output voltage

$$U_o = U_{ref} e^{\dfrac{aU_T \ln \dfrac{U_i}{U_{ref}}}{U_T}} = U_{ref} \left(\dfrac{U_i}{U_{ref}} \right)^a \; .$$

The logarithm and the exponential function can be obtained using a single integrated circuit if so-called multifunction converters are used, such as the LH 0094 from National or the AD 538 from Analog Devices.

Fig. 12.25 General power-function network

$$U_o = U_{ref} \left(\dfrac{U_i}{U_{ref}} \right)^a \quad \text{for } U_i > 0$$

Involution (raising to the power) by means of logarithms is in principle defined for positive input voltages only. However, from a mathematical point of view, bipolar input signals are also permitted for whole-number exponents a. This case can be realized by using the multipliers described in Section 12.8.

12.7.4 Sine and cosine functions

The output of a sine-function network should approximate the expression

$$U_o = \hat{U}_o \sin\left(\frac{\pi}{2} \cdot \frac{U_i}{\hat{U}_i}\right) \tag{12.32}$$

within the range $-\hat{U}_i \leqq U_i \leqq +\hat{U}_i$. For small input voltages,

$$U_o = \hat{U}_o \cdot \frac{\pi}{2} \cdot \frac{U_i}{\hat{U}_i} \ .$$

It is advisable to choose a value for $\hat{U}_o$ so that near the origin, $U_o = U_i$. This is the case for

$$\hat{U}_o = \frac{2}{\pi} \cdot \hat{U}_i \ . \tag{12.33}$$

For small input voltages, the sine-function network must accordingly have unity gain, whereas at higher voltages the gain must decrease. Figure 12.26 represents a circuit fulfilling these conditions, based on the principle of *piecewise approximation*.

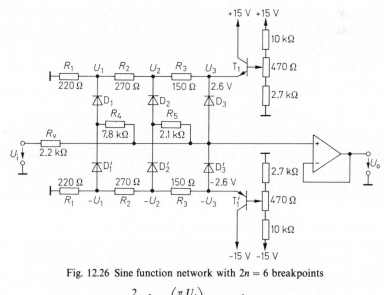

Fig. 12.26 Sine function network with $2n = 6$ breakpoints

$$U_o \approx \frac{2}{\pi} \cdot \hat{U}_i \sin\left(\frac{\pi}{2} \frac{U_i}{\hat{U}_i}\right) \quad \text{for} \quad \hat{U}_i = 5.0 \text{ V}$$

For small input voltages, all the diodes are reverse biased, and $U_o = U_i$, as required. If U_o rises above U_1, diode D_1 becomes forward biased. U_o then increases more slowly than U_i because of the voltage divider formed by R_v and R_4. If U_o becomes larger than U_2, the output of the network is additionally loaded with R_5, so that the rise in voltage is slowed down even more. Diode D_3

finally produces the horizontal tangent at the top of the sine curve. The diodes D_1' to D_3' have the corresponding effects for the negative part of the sine function. Considering that diodes do not become conducting suddenly, but have an exponential characteristic, one can obtain low distortion factors of U_o with only a small number of diodes.

In order to determine the parameters of the network, one begins by choosing the breakpoints of the approximation curve. It can be shown that the first n odd harmonics disappear if $2n$ breakpoints are assigned to the following values of the input voltage [12.2]:

$$U_{ik} = \pm \frac{2k}{2n+1} \hat{U}_i , \quad \text{for } 0 < k \leq n . \tag{12.34}$$

According to Eqs. (12.32) and (12.33), the corresponding output voltages are

$$U_{ok} = \pm \frac{2}{\pi} \hat{U}_i \sin \frac{\pi k}{2n+1} , \quad \text{for } 0 < k \leq n . \tag{12.35}$$

Therefore, the slope of the line segment above the kth breakpoint is given as

$$m_k = \frac{U_{o(k+1)} - U_{ok}}{U_{i(k+1)} - U_{ik}} = \frac{2n+1}{\pi} \left[\sin \frac{\pi(k+1)}{2n+1} - \sin \frac{\pi k}{2n+1} \right] . \tag{12.36}$$

For the highest breakpoint, when $k = n$, the slope becomes zero, as was stipulated earlier in the qualitative description. The slope m_0 must be chosen equal to unity.

For reasons of symmetry, no even harmonics appear. With the r.m.s. values of the odd harmonics present in the waveform, we obtain a theoretical distortion factor of 1.8% if $2n = 6$ breakpoints are chosen, this being reduced to 0.8% for $2n = 12$. However, as real diode characteristics do not have sharp breakpoints, the actual distortion is considerably lower. This is illustrated by the following example.

A voltage of triangular waveshape with a peak value of $\hat{U}_i = 5$ V is to be converted into a sinusoidal voltage. According to Eq. (12.33), the amplitude of the latter must be 3.18 V, so that the slope of the line segment around the origin is unity. For the approximation, we want to use $2n = 6$ breakpoints. Following Eq. (12.35), they must appear at the output voltages ± 1.4 V, ± 2.5 V and ± 3.1 V. For real diodes we assume that a sizeable current flows only for forward voltages of more than 0.5 V. The diode bias voltages must then be reduced by this amount. We thus obtain the voltages $U_1 = 0.9$ V, $U_2 = 2.0$ V and $U_3 = 2.6$ V which define the values for the voltage divider chain R_1, R_2, R_3 shown in Fig. 12.26. The emitter-followers T_1 and T_1' serve as low-impedance sources for U_3 and simultaneously as temperature compensation for the forward voltages of the diodes.

From Eq. (12.36), we obtain for the slopes of the three segments: $m_1 = 0.78$, $m_2 = 0.43$ and $m_3 = 0$. We choose $R_v = 2.2 \text{ k}\Omega$. From

$$m_1 = \frac{R_4}{R_v + R_4} ,$$

disregarding the internal resistance of the divider chain, we obtain $R_4 = 7.8\ \text{k}\Omega$. The slope of the second segment is

$$m_2 = \frac{(R_5 \| R_4)}{R_v + (R_5 \| R_4)}\ ,$$

thus $R_5 = 2.1\ \text{k}\Omega$.

For fine adjustment of the network, it is advisable to use a notch filter for the fundamental (see Chapter 14.9) and to display of the remaining error voltage on the screen of an oscilloscope. The optimum is attained when the peaks of the deviation curve have the same height, as can be seen in the oscillogram in Fig. 12.27. The distortion factor measured for this case was 0.42% and therefore clearly below the theoretical value for ideal diodes.

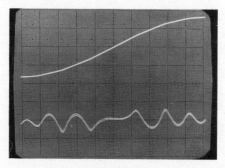

Fig. 12.27 Output voltage and error voltage (amplified 50 times) as a function of the input voltage. Vertical: 2 V/div; Horizontal: 1 V/div

Power series expansion

Another method for the approximation of a sine function is to use a power series, since

$$\sin x = x - \frac{x^3}{3!} + \frac{x^5}{5!} - + \cdots\ .$$

To keep the number of components low, the series is truncated after the second term and this results in an error. If the range of values of the argument is now limited to $-\dfrac{\pi}{2} \leq x \leq \dfrac{\pi}{2}$, the error can be minimized by slightly changing the coefficients [12.3]. If one selects

$$\sin x \approx y = 0.9825x - 0.1402x^3\ , \tag{12.37}$$

the error becomes zero for $x = 0,\ \pm 0.96$ and $\pm \pi/2$. Between these values, the absolute error is less than 0.57% of the amplitude. The distortion factor is 0.6%. It can be reduced to 0.25% by a slight variation of the coefficients, and is therefore somewhat smaller than for the piecewise approximation method using

2×3 breakpoints. The lack of breakpoints is particularly advantageous when the signal is to be differentiated.

For a practical circuit, we define

$$x = \frac{\pi}{2} \cdot \frac{U_i}{\hat{U}_i} \quad \text{and} \quad y = \frac{U_o}{\hat{U}_o} .$$

Furthermore, we select $\hat{U}_i = \hat{U}_o$ and thus obtain from Eq. (12.37)

$$U_o = 1.543\, U_i - 0.543 \frac{U_i^3}{\hat{U}_i^2} \approx \hat{U}_i \sin\left(\frac{\pi}{2} \frac{U_i}{\hat{U}_i}\right) .$$

The block diagram for this operation is represented in Fig. 12.28 where the input voltage amplitude $\hat{U}_i$ is equal to the computing unit E for the multipliers. We shall discuss the analog multipliers required in the next section.

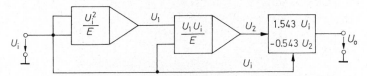

Fig. 12.28 Approximation of the sine function by a power series

$$U_o \approx \hat{U}_i \sin\left(\frac{\pi}{2} \cdot \frac{U_i}{\hat{U}_i}\right) \quad \text{for } \hat{U}_i = E$$

Differential amplifier stage

Another way of approximating a sine wave is based on the fact that the function $\tanh x$ has a similar shape for small x. This function can be easily generated using a differential amplifier stage, as in Fig. 12.29. It was shown in

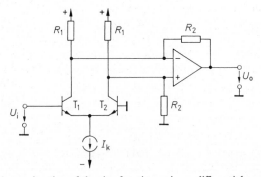

Fig. 12.29 Approximation of the sine function, using a differential amplifier stage

$$U_o \approx I_k R_2 \cdot \sin\left(\frac{\pi}{2} \frac{U_i}{\hat{U}_i}\right) \quad \text{for } \hat{U}_i = 2.8\, U_T \approx 73 \text{ mV}$$

Section 12.7.1, that for a differential amplifier, using Eq. (12.29)

$$\frac{I_{C1}}{I_{C2}} = e^{\frac{U_i}{U_T}} \quad \text{and} \quad I_{C1} + I_{C2} \approx I_k .$$

Therefore

$$I_{C1} - I_{C2} = \frac{e^{\frac{U_i}{U_T}} - 1}{e^{\frac{U_i}{U_T}} + 1} I_k = I_k \tanh \frac{U_i}{2U_T} . \tag{12.38}$$

The operational amplifier forms the difference between the two collector currents such that

$$U_o = R_2 (I_{C1} - I_{C2}) .$$

It follows that

$$U_o = I_k R_2 \tanh \frac{U_i}{2U_T} . \tag{12.39}$$

This function can be interpreted as approximating the sine function

$$U_o = \hat{U}_o \sin \left(\frac{\pi}{2} \cdot \frac{U_i}{\hat{U}_i} \right) \quad \text{for} \quad -\frac{\pi}{2} \leq x \leq \frac{\pi}{2} .$$

The quality of the sine approximation is dependent on the peak value $\hat{U}_i$ chosen. For $\hat{U}_i = 2.8 U_T \approx 73 \text{ mV}$, the error becomes minimal and $\hat{U}_o$ is $0.86 I_k R_2$. However, the error is still 3%. It can be reduced to 0.02% by providing the differential amplifier with 2 additional appropriately biased transistors. This is the operating principle of the AD 639 from Analog Devices which can be used to produce all the other trigonometric functions as well as the sine function [12.3, 4].

Cosine function

The cosine function can be generated for values $0 \leq x \leq \pi$ by means of the sine function networks previously described. The input voltage U_i, which should be between zero and $U_{i\,max}$, is first converted to an auxiliary voltage

$$U_1 = U_{i\,max} - 2U_i . \tag{12.40}$$

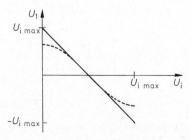

Fig. 12.30 Shape of the auxiliary voltage for generating the cosine function (dashed line)

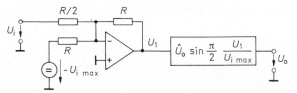

Fig. 12.31 Generation of a cosine function by means of a sine function network

$$U_o = \hat{U}_o \cos\left(\pi\frac{U_i}{U_{i\,max}}\right) \quad \text{for } 0 \leq U_i \leq U_{i\,max}$$

As can be seen in Fig. 12.30, this equation is already a linear approximation of the cosine function. For the necessary rounding-off of the curve near the maximum and minimum, one applies U_1 to the input of a sine function network. As is obvious from Fig. 12.31, the addition of a summing amplifier is all that is needed to convert a sine function network to a cosine function network.

Simultaneous generation of the sine and cosine function for arguments $-\pi \leq x \leq \pi$

With the networks described so far, sine and cosine functions can be generated over a half-period. In cases where the range of argument has to be a full period or more, one initially generates triangular functions as a linear approximation, and uses sine networks to round off the peaks. The shape of the required triangular voltages is represented in Fig. 12.32.

Voltage U_1 approximates the cosine function. For $U_i > 0$, it is identical to the voltage U_1 in Fig. 12.30. For $U_i < 0$, it is symmetrical about the y-axis. We can therefore use Eq. (12.40) by replacing U_i by $|U_i|$, and obtain

$$U_1 = U_{i\,max} - 2|U_i| \ . \tag{12.41}$$

The relationships for the sine function are somewhat more complicated, since we

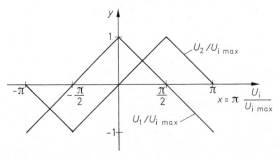

Fig. 12.32 Shape of the auxiliary voltages for generating the sine and cosine function for $-\pi \leq x \leq \pi$

must differentiate between three cases:

$$U_2 = \begin{cases} -2(U_i + U_{i\,max}) & \text{for} \quad -U_{i\,max} \le U_i \le -\tfrac{1}{2}U_{i\,max}\,, & (12.42a) \\ 2U_i & \text{for} \quad -\tfrac{1}{2}U_{i\,max} \le U_i \le \tfrac{1}{2}U_{i\,max}\,, & (12.42b) \\ -2(U_i - U_{i\,max}) & \text{for} \quad \tfrac{1}{2}U_{i\,max} \le U_i \le U_{i\,max}\,. & (12.42c) \end{cases}$$

Such functions are best implemented using the general precision function network which is described below.

12.7.5 Variable function network

In Fig. 12.26 a diode network was used for the piecewise linear approximation of functions. Calculation of the circuit parameters is only possible to an approximation because the forward voltage of the diodes and the loading of the voltage divider chains must be taken into account. Furthermore, the sign of the slope of each linear segment is defined already by the structure of the network. Therefore, such a circuit can be optimized for one particular function only, and its parameters cannot be changed easily.

Figure 12.33, on the other hand, represents a circuit that allows the breakpoint and slope of each individual segment to be set precisely with a separate potentiometer. The part of the circuit formed by operational amplifiers OA 1 and OA 2 permits a segment for positive input voltages to be formed, while operational amplifiers OA 5 and OA 6 are effective for negative input voltages. Amplifier OA 4 determines the slope about the origin. The circuit can be

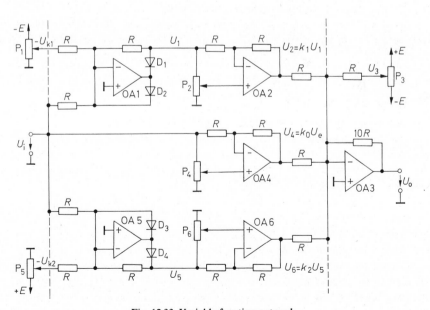

Fig. 12.33 Variable function network

extended for any number of segments by adding further sections identical to those mentioned.

Amplifiers OA 2, OA 4 and OA 6 are connected as bipolar-coefficient circuits, as in Fig. 12.5 for $n = 1$. Their gain can be adjusted to values between $-1 \leq k \leq +1$ by the associated potentiometers; and their output voltages are added by the summing amplifier OA 3. An additional DC voltage can be added by means of potentiometer P_3.

Near zero input voltage, only amplifier OA 4 contributes to the output voltage:

$$U_4 = k_0 U_i \; .$$

Both voltages U_1 and U_5 are zero in this case because diodes D_1 and D_4 are reverse biased, and amplifiers OA 1 and OA 5 have a feedback path via conducting diodes D_2 and D_3.

When the input voltage becomes greater than U_{k1}, diode D_1 is forward biased, and we obtain

$$U_1 = -(U_i - U_{k1}) \quad \text{for} \quad U_i \geq U_{k1} \geq 0 \; .$$

Amplifier OA 1 therefore operates as a half-wave rectifier, with a positive bias voltage U_{k1}. Operational amplifier OA 5 behaves correspondingly for negative input voltages:

$$U_5 = -(U_i - U_{k2}) \quad \text{for} \quad U_i \leq U_{k2} \leq 0 \; .$$

Hence, we obtain the general relationship for the slope of the output voltage U_o as

$$m = \frac{\Delta U_o}{\Delta U_i} = 10 \cdot \begin{cases} -k_0 + k_1 + \cdots + k_m & \text{for} \quad U_i > U_{km} > 0 \\ -k_0 + k_1 & \text{for} \quad U_i > U_{k1} > 0 \\ -k_0 & \text{for} \quad U_{k2} < U_i < U_{k1} \quad (12.43) \\ -k_0 + k_2 & \text{for} \quad U_i < U_{k2} < 0 \\ -k_0 + k_2 + \cdots + k_n & \text{for} \quad U_i < U_{kn} < 0 \; . \end{cases}$$

As an example, we shall demonstrate the implementation of the voltage waveshape $U_2 / U_{i\,max}$ in Fig. 12.32. A positive breakpoint at $U_{k1} = \frac{1}{2} U_{i\,max}$ and a negative breakpoint at $U_{k2} = -\frac{1}{2} U_{i\,max}$ are required. According to Eq. (12.42b) the slope of the segment through the origin must have the value $m = +2$, therefore $k_0 = -0.2$. Above the positive breakpoint, the slope must be -2. For this region, we take from Eq. (12.43)

$$m = 10(-k_0 + k_1)$$

and therefore obtain $k_1 = -0.4$, and correspondingly $k_2 = -0.4$. The shapes of the output voltage functions resulting from this process are shown in Fig. 12.34.

Even if no calibrated potentiometers are available, the network output can be given the desired shape in a simple way, using the following procedure. Initially, all the breakpoint voltages and slopes are set to their maximum value and the input voltage is made zero. This ensures that $|U_i| < |U_{ki}|$. Only the

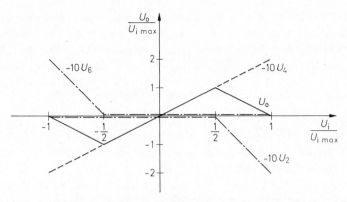

Fig. 12.34 Voltage components for generating voltage U_2 in Fig. 12.32

zeroing potentiometer P_3 affects the output; it is used to adjust the output voltage $U_o(U_i = 0)$ to the desired value. In the next step, U_i is made equal to U_{k1} and P_4 is set so that $U_o(U_i = U_{k1})$ assumes the level required. The factor k_0 is now defined. P_1 is then adjusted to a point where the output voltage just begins to change; this occurs when the setting of P_1 corresponds to U_{k1}. Now U_i is set to the value of the next higher breakpoint (or to the end of the range if there is no higher breakpoint), and P_2 is adjusted so that U_o attains the desired value. In this way, k_1 is defined. The remaining breakpoints and slopes are dealt with in the same manner.

In cases where no calibrated potentiometers are needed for the adjustment of the segment slopes, the circuit may be simplified. One can replace the bipolar

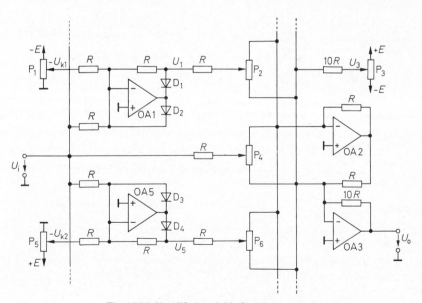

Fig. 12.35 Simplified variable function network

coefficient circuits by simple potentiometers that are connected to a multiple-input subtracting amplifier, as in Fig. 12.35. The subtracting amplifier consists of operational amplifiers OA 2 and OA 3 and is based on the principle of Fig. 12.2.

12.8   Analog multipliers

So far, we have described circuits for addition, subtraction, differentiation and integration. Multiplication could be carried out only if a constant factor was involved. Below, we deal with the most important principles for the multiplication and division of two variable voltages.

12.8.1   Multipliers with logarithmic amplifiers

Multiplication and division can be reduced to an addition and subtraction of logarithms:

$$\frac{xy}{z} = \exp\left[\ln x + \ln y - \ln z\right] \ .$$

The function can be implemented by using three logarithmic amplifiers, one exponential function amplifier and one adder/subtractor circuit. The latter can be eliminated by using the inputs of the differential amplifier for the exponential function amplifier in Fig. 12.24 to perform the subtraction and by considering the fact that the terminal for the reference voltage can be used as an additional signal input.

The logarithmic amplifiers in Fig. 12.36 produce the expressions

$$V_1 = -U_T \ln \frac{U_y}{I_{CS}R_1} \quad \text{and} \quad V_2 = -U_T \ln \frac{U_z}{I_{CS}R_1} \ .$$

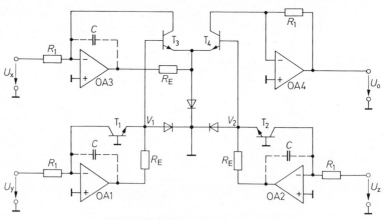

Fig. 12.36 Multiplication by means of logarithms

$$U_o = \frac{U_x U_y}{U_z} \quad \text{for } U_x, U_y, U_z > 0$$

The exponential function generator therefore provides an output voltage of the form

$$U_o = U_x e^{\frac{V_2 - V_1}{U_T}} = \frac{U_x U_y}{U_z} \ .$$

We can see that, in this case, not only the reverse saturation currents I_{CS} but also voltage U_T are eliminated, thereby obviating the need for temperature compensation. However, it is essential that the four transistors have the same characteristics and are at the same temperature. They must therefore be integrated on one chip.

An inherent disadvantage of this method is that all input voltages must be positive and may not even be zero. Such multipliers are called one-quadrant multipliers.

Multipliers such as those in Fig. 12.36 can be implemented using multifunction converters such as the LH 0094 (National) or the AD 538 (Analog Dev.). They are also available as complete ICs, such as the RC 4200 from Raytheon [12.5].

12.8.2   Transconductance multipliers

As shown in Chapter 4, the transconductance of a transistor is defined as

$$g_f = \frac{dI_C}{dU_{BE}} = \frac{I_C}{U_T} \ ,$$

and is therefore proportional to the collector current.

The variation of the collector current is then proportional to the product of the input voltage variation and the quiescent collector current. This property is made use of for multiplication, in the differential amplifier shown in Fig. 12.37.

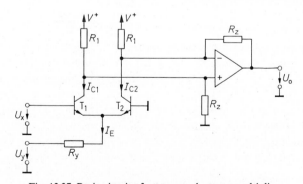

Fig. 12.37 Basic circuit of a transconductance multiplier

$$U_o \approx \frac{R_z}{R_y} \frac{U_x U_y}{2U_T} \quad \text{for } U_y < 0$$

The operational amplifier evaluates the difference between the collector currents:

$$U_o = R_z(I_{C2} - I_{C1}) \ . \tag{12.44}$$

Applying a negative voltage U_y and setting U_x to zero, the currents through both transistors are equal, and the output voltage remains zero. If U_x is made positive, the collector current through T_1 rises and that of T_2 falls; the output voltage is negative. Correspondingly, U_o becomes positive when U_x is negative. The resulting difference in collector currents is greater, the larger the emitter current, i.e. the higher the value $|U_y|$. It can therefore be assumed that U_o is at least approximately proportional to $U_x \cdot U_y$. For a more precise calculation we determine the current sharing within the differential amplifier stage. As was shown in Section 12.7.4, Eq. (12.38) states that

$$I_{C1} - I_{C2} = I_E \tanh \frac{U_x}{2U_T} \ . \tag{12.45}$$

A power series expansion up to the fourth order gives

$$I_{C1} - I_{C2} = I_E \left(\frac{U_x}{2U_T} - \frac{U_x^3}{24U_T^3} \right) \ . \tag{12.46}$$

Hence,

$$I_{C1} - I_{C2} \approx I_E \cdot \frac{U_x}{2U_T} \quad \text{for} \quad |U_x| \ll U_T \ . \tag{12.47}$$

If $|U_y| \gg U_{BE}$, then

$$I_E \approx -\frac{U_y}{R_y} \ .$$

Substitution in Eq. (12.47) gives, in conjunction with Eq. (12.44), the result

$$U_o \approx \frac{R_z}{R_y} \cdot \frac{U_x U_y}{2U_T} \ . \tag{12.48}$$

The voltage U_x must be $|U_x| < 0.35 U_T \approx 9$ mV, if the error in Eq. (12.48) is not to exceed 1%. Because of the small value of U_x, transistors T_1 and T_2 must be closely matched to prevent the offset voltage drift affecting the result.

For the correct operation of the circuit, it is necessary that U_y is always negative while the voltage U_x may have either polarity. Such a multiplier is called a two-quadrant multiplier.

There are several properties of the transconductance multiplier in Fig. 12.37 which can be improved. In deducing the output equation (12.48), we had to use the approximation that $|U_y| \gg U_{BE} \approx 0.6$ V. This condition can be dropped if resistor R_y is replaced by a controlled current source for which I_E is proportional to U_y.

A further disadvantage of the circuit in Fig. 12.37 is that $|U_x|$ must be limited to small values in order to minimize the error. This can be avoided by not applying U_x directly, but rather its logarithm.

An expansion to a four-quadrant multiplier, i.e. a multiplier for input voltages of either polarity, it is possible if a second differential amplifier stage is connected in parallel, the emitter current of which is controlled by U_y in opposition to that of the first transistor pair.

All these aspects are considered in the four-quadrant transconductance multiplier in Fig. 12.38. The differential amplifier stage T_1, T_2 is the same as that of Fig. 12.37. It is supplemented symmetrically by differential amplifier T'_1, T'_2. Transistors T_5, T_6 form a differential amplifier with current feedback. The collectors represent the outputs of two current sources which are controlled by U_y simultaneously but in opposition, as required:

$$I_5 = I_8 + \frac{U_y}{R_y} , \qquad I_6 = I_8 - \frac{U_y}{R_y} . \qquad (12.49)$$

For the difference in the collector currents in the two differential amplifier stages T_1, T_2 and T'_1, T'_2, we obtain, in analogy to the previous circuit,

$$I_1 - I_2 = I_5 \tanh \frac{U_1}{2U_T} = \left(I_8 + \frac{U_y}{R_y} \right) \tanh \frac{U_1}{2U_T} , \qquad (12.50)$$

$$I'_1 - I'_2 = I_6 \tanh \frac{U_1}{2U_T} = \left(I_8 - \frac{U_y}{R_y} \right) \tanh \frac{U_1}{2U_T} . \qquad (12.51)$$

As before, the operational amplifier evaluates the difference of the collector currents according to

$$\Delta I = (I_2 + I'_1) - (I'_2 + I_1) = (I'_1 - I'_2) - (I_1 - I_2) . \qquad (12.52)$$

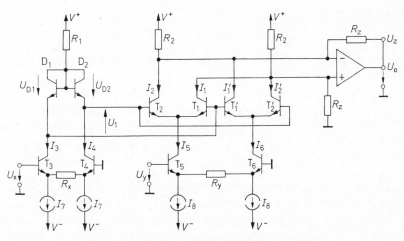

Fig. 12.38 Four-quadrant transconductance multiplier

$$U_o = \frac{2R_z}{R_x R_y} \cdot \frac{U_x U_y}{I_7} \quad \text{for } I_7 > 0$$

By subtracting Eq. (12.50) from Eq. (12.51), it follows that

$$\Delta I = - \frac{2U_y}{R_y} \tanh \frac{U_1}{2U_T} , \tag{12.53}$$

where U_y may now have either polarity. By expanding this expression into a series, one can see that the same approximation to multiplication is involved as for the previous circuit.

We shall now examine the relationship between U_1 and U_x. Two transistors are connected as diodes (transdiodes), D_1 and D_2, and these are used to form the logarithm of the input signals:

$$U_1 = U_{D2} - U_{D1} = U_T \ln \frac{I_4}{I_{CS}} - U_T \ln \frac{I_3}{I_{CS}} .$$

Hence,

$$U_1 = U_T \ln \frac{I_4}{I_3} = U_T \ln \frac{I_7 - \dfrac{U_x}{R_x}}{I_7 + \dfrac{U_x}{R_x}} . \tag{12.54}$$

Substitution in Eq. (12.53) gives the current difference

$$\Delta I = \frac{2U_x U_y}{R_x R_y I_7} . \tag{12.55}$$

From this, the operational amplifier configured as a current subtractor forms the output voltage

$$U_o = \Delta I R_z = \frac{2R_z}{R_x R_y I_7} \cdot U_x U_y = \frac{U_x U_y}{E} , \tag{12.56}$$

where $E = R_x R_y I_7 / 2R_z$ is the computing unit. This is usually chosen to be 10 V. Good temperature compensation is attained, since U_T cancels out. Equation (12.55) or (12.56) is obtained without recourse to power expansion, and therefore a considerably larger range of input voltages U_x is permissible. The limits of the input range are reached when one of the transistors in the controlled current source is turned off. Therefore,

$$|U_x| < R_x I_7 \quad \text{and} \quad |U_y| < R_y I_8 .$$

If the currents I_7 are controlled by a further input voltage U_7, simultaneous division and multiplication is possible. However, the usable range for I_7 is limited because I_7 influences all the quiescent potentials within the multiplier and also the permissible range for U_x.

A simpler way of achieving division is to open the connection between U_o and U_z and to link the voltages U_y and U_o instead. Because of the resulting feedback, the output voltage assumes a value such that $\Delta I = U_z/R_z$. Therefore, from Eq. (12.55),

$$\Delta I = \frac{2U_x U_y}{R_x R_y I_7} = \frac{U_z}{R_z} .$$

Thus the new output voltage is

$$U_o = U_y = \frac{R_x R_y I_7}{2R_z} \cdot \frac{U_z}{U_x} = E \frac{U_z}{U_x} . \tag{12.57}$$

However, stability is only guaranteed if U_x is negative, otherwise the negative feedback becomes positive. The signal U_z, on the other hand, can have either polarity, and therefore the circuit is a two-quadrant divider. The limitation on the sign of the denominator is not peculiar to this arrangement, but is common to all divider circuits.

Transconductance multipliers operating on the principle shown in Fig. 12.38, are available as monolithic integrated circuits. The achievable accuracy is 0.25% referred to computing unit E, i.e. 25 mV for a computing unit of 10 V. As we shall see in Section 12.8.5, the simple types require four trimmers in order to achieve this degree of accuracy. The better types are already internally adjusted by the manufacturer [12.5], and external adjustment is generally unnecessary.

The 3 dB-bandwidth is in the order of 1 MHz, at which frequency the computing error is already 30%. As a deviation of this magnitude is unacceptable in the majority of applications, a better reference point is the frequency at which the output voltage is reduced by 1%.

IC Type	Manufacturer	Accuracy		Bandwidth	
		without adjustment	with adjustment	1%	3 dB
MPY 100	Burr Brown	0.5%	0.35%	70 kHz	0.5 MHz
MPY 634	Burr Brown		0.5%	100 kHz	10 MHz
MPY 600	Burr Brown	1%			75 MHz
AD 533	Analog Dev.		0.5%	75 kHz	1 MHz
AD 534	Analog Dev.	0.25%	0.1%	50 kHz	1 MHz
AD 539	Analog Dev.		0.5%		60 MHz
AD 834	Analog Dev.	2%			500 MHz

Transconductance divider with improved accuracy

We have mentioned two methods of division, one using the logarithmic multiplier (Fig. 12.36) and the other using the transconductance multiplier described above. For a division, a basic problem arises in the region of zero input, as the output voltage is then chiefly determined by the input offset error. This error is particularly large for the transconductance multiplier, since in the input log-amplifier a positive constant (i.e. I_7 in Eq. (12.54)) is added to the input signal to avoid a change of polarity in the argument. The conditions are considerably more favorable if the circuit in Fig. 12.36 is used for the division. However, only one quadrant is available.

The advantages of the two methods, i.e. two-quadrant division and good accuracy near zero input, can be combined. This is achieved not by adding a constant to the argument of the logarithm (to avoid the change in sign) but by adding to the numerator a quantity proportional to the denominator [12.7].

The divider output should conform to the expression

$$U_o = E \frac{U_x}{U_z} \;.$$

Assuming that $U_z > 0$ and $|U_x| < U_z$, two auxiliary voltages

$$U_1 = U_z - \tfrac{1}{2} U_x \;, \qquad U_2 = U_z + \tfrac{1}{2} U_x \;, \tag{12.58}$$

can be generated which are always positive. The logarithms of these two voltages are computed according to the block diagram of Fig. 12.39, each by means of the simple logarithmic amplifier in Fig. 12.20. Using a differential amplifier stage, as in Fig. 12.37, the hyperbolic tangent of the difference of the output voltages U_3 and U_4 is calculated so that

$$U_o = R_z I_E \tanh \frac{U_T \ln(U_2/U_1)}{2 U_T} \;.$$

Therefore, with Eq. (12.58),

$$U_o = \frac{R_z I_E}{2} \cdot \frac{U_x}{U_z} \;.$$

With this method, an accuracy of 0.1% of the computing unit E can be obtained over a dynamic range of 1:1000 (e.g. with model 436 from Analog Devices).

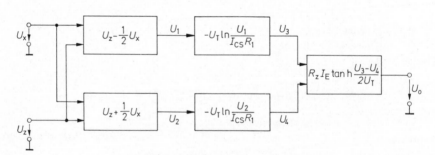

Fig. 12.39 Two-quadrant transconductance divider

$$U_o = \frac{R_z I_E}{2} \cdot \frac{U_x}{U_z} \quad \text{for } U_z > 0 \text{ and } |U_x| \le U_z$$

12.8.3 Multiplier using electrically isolated couplers

A voltage can be multiplied by a constant, using a simple voltage divider. Analog multiplication is possible if, by employing closed-loop control, one ensures that the constant is proportional to a second input voltage.

The principle of such a circuit is illustrated in Fig. 12.40. The arrangement contains two identical coefficient elements K_x and K_z, the output voltages of which are proportional to their input voltages. Their constant of proportionality k can be controlled by voltage U_1. Due to the feedback via K_z, the output voltage U_1 of the operational amplifier assumes a level such that $kU_z = U_y$, this resulting in $k = U_y/U_z$. If the voltage U_x is applied to the second coefficient element K_x, its output voltage becomes

$$U_o = kU_x = \frac{U_x U_y}{U_z} \; .$$

Voltage U_z must be larger than zero so that the negative feedback does not become positive. Whether voltage U_y is allowed to go both positive *and* negative, depends on the design of the coefficient elements. If the latter permits bipolar coefficients, U_y may also be bipolar.

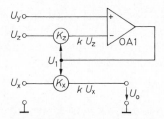

Fig. 12.40 Principle of the circuit

$$U_o = \frac{U_x U_y}{U_z} \quad \text{for } U_z > 0$$

Voltage U_x can be bipolar in any case. It has the additional advantage that it is not transferred through balancing amplifier OA 1. Consequently very high bandwidths can be achieved for U_x.

FETs can be employed as electrically controlled resistors, as in the circuit in Fig. 12.41. Amplifier OA 1 operates as a controller for adjusting the coefficients. Its output voltage causes the resistance R_{DS} to vary so that

$$\frac{\alpha U_z}{R_{DS}} + \frac{U_y}{R_4} = 0 \; .$$

Hence,

$$R_{DS} = - \alpha R_4 \frac{U_z}{U_y} \; .$$

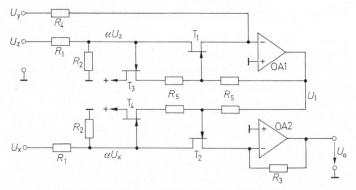

Fig. 12.41 Multiplier with FETs as controlled resistors

$$U_o = \frac{R_3}{R_4} \frac{U_x U_y}{U_z} \quad \text{for } U_z > 0, \, U_y < 0$$

The output voltage of operational amplifier OA 2 is

$$U_o = -\alpha \frac{R_3}{R_{DS}} U_x = \frac{R_3}{R_4} \cdot \frac{U_x U_y}{U_z} \, .$$

In order that FETs may be operated as resistors, the voltage across them must be kept below approx. 0.5 V. Voltage dividers R_1, R_2 provide the necessary attenuation. The resistors R_5 make the voltage-current characteristic of the FET more linear, as is described in Section 5.7. In order to prevent any reactive effect of control voltage U_1 on input signals U_z and U_x, the circuit incorporates the two additional source followers T_3 and T_4 respectively. The magnitude of their gate-source voltage is irrelevant, as it is controlled by operational amplifier OA 1. It is merely essential for them to be well matched. Double FETs should therefore be used.

To ensure negative feedback in the control circuit, U_z must be positive. As only positive coefficients can be realized using the simple coefficient elements shown in Fig. 12.41, U_y must always be negative to allow balancing [12.8]. However, U_x can have either polarity.

In order to achieve a high degree of accuracy, FETs T_1 and T_2 should be well matched over a wide range of resistances. This requirement can only be met using monolithic double FETs, such as type VCR 11N from Intersil.

12.8.4   Adjustment of multipliers

A multiplier should conform to the expression

$$U_o = \frac{U_x U_y}{E} \, ,$$

where E is the computing unit, e.g. 10 V. In practice, there is a small offset voltage superposed on any terminal voltage. Therefore, in general

$$U_{o} + U_{oO} = \frac{1}{E}(U_{x} + U_{xO})(U_{y} + U_{yO}) \; .$$

Thus

$$U_{o} = \frac{U_{x}U_{y}}{E} + \frac{U_{y}U_{xO} + U_{x}U_{yO} + U_{xO}U_{yO}}{E} - U_{oO} \; . \qquad (12.59)$$

The product $U_{x}U_{y}$ must be zero whenever U_{x} or U_{y} is zero. This is only possible if the parameters U_{xO}, U_{yO} and U_{oO} become zero independently. Therefore, three trimmers are essential for compensating the offset voltages. A suitable trimming procedure is as follows. Firstly, U_{x} is made zero. Then, according to Eq. (12.59)

$$U_{o} = \frac{U_{y}U_{xO} + U_{xO}U_{yO}}{E} - U_{oO} \; .$$

When voltage U_{y} is now varied, the output voltage also changes because of the term $U_{y}U_{xO}$. The nulling circuit for U_{x} is adjusted in such a way that, despite variation of U_{y}, a constant output voltage is obtained; U_{xO} is then zero.

In a second step, U_{y} is nulled and U_{x} is varied. In the same way as above, the offset of U_{y} can now be compensated. Thirdly, U_{x} and U_{y} are made zero and the third trimmer is adjusted such that the output offset U_{oO} becomes zero.

A fourth trim potentiometer may often be necessary for adjusting the constant of proportionality, E, to the desired value.

12.8.5 Expansion of one- and two-quadrant multipliers to four-quadrant multipliers

There are cases where one- and two-quadrant multipliers have to be operated with input voltages of a polarity for which they are not designed. The most obvious remedy would then be to invert the polarity of the input and output of the multiplier whenever the impermissible polarity combination occurs. However, this method involves a large number of components and is not particularly fast. It is more convenient to add constant voltages U_{xk} and U_{yk} to the input voltages U_{x} and U_{y}, so that the resulting input voltages remain within the permissible limits under all conditions. Then, for the output voltage,

$$U_{o} = \frac{(U_{x} + U_{xk})(U_{y} + U_{yk})}{E} \; .$$

Hence,

$$\frac{U_{x}U_{y}}{E} = U_{o} - \frac{U_{xk}}{E}U_{y} - \frac{U_{yk}}{E}U_{x} - \frac{U_{xk}U_{yk}}{E} \; .$$

It follows that a constant voltage, and also two voltages each proportional to an input voltage, must be subtracted from the output voltage of the multiplier. The circuits required for these operations are described in the first sections of this chapter.

The block diagram of the resulting arrangement is shown in Fig. 12.42. The constant voltages and coefficients are selected such that the range of control is fully exploited. If the input voltage U_x is within $-E \leq U_x \leq +E$, the range for the voltage $U_1 = 0.5\,U_x + 0.5\,E$ is $0 \leq U_1 \leq E$. Therefore, the output voltage obtained is

$$U_o = 4\,\frac{\frac{1}{2}(U_x + E)\cdot\frac{1}{2}(U_y + E)}{E} - U_x - U_y - E = \frac{U_x U_y}{E}\,.$$

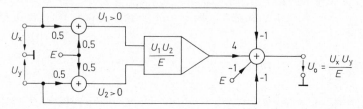

Fig. 12.42 Expansion of a one-quadrant multiplier to a four-quadrant multiplier

12.8.6   Multiplier as a divider or square-rooter

Figure 12.43 illustrates a method by which a multiplier without division input can be used as a divider. Because of negative feedback, the output voltage of the operational amplifier finds a level such that

$$\frac{U_o U_z}{E} = U_x\,.$$

Thus, the circuit evaluates the quotient $U_o = E U_x / U_z$, but only as long as $U_z > 0$. For negative denominators, the feedback is positive.

A multiplier can be employed as a square-rooter by operating it as a squarer and inserting it in the feedback loop of an operational amplifier, as shown in

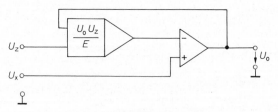

Fig. 12.43 Multiplier used as divider

$$U_o = E\,\frac{U_x}{U_z} \quad \text{for } U_z > 0$$

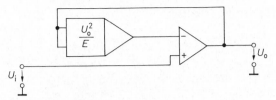

Fig. 12.44 Multiplier used as square-rooter

$$U_o = \sqrt{EU_i} \quad \text{for } U_i > 0$$

Fig. 12.44. The output voltage finds a level such that

$$\frac{U_o^2}{E} = U_i \ , \quad \text{hence } U_o = \sqrt{EU_i} \ .$$

Correct operation is ensured only for positive input and output voltages. Difficulties may arise if the output becomes momentarily negative, e.g. at switch-on. In such a case, the squarer causes a phase inversion in the feedback loop so that positive feedback occurs, and the output voltage becomes more negative until it reaches the negative level of output saturation. The circuit is then said to be in "latch-up" and is inoperable. Therefore, additional circuitry must be used to ensure that the output voltage cannot become negative.

12.9   Transformation of coordinates

Cartesian as well as polar coordinates play an important role in many technical applications. We therefore discuss in this section some circuits which allow transformation from one coordinate system to the other.

12.9.1   Transformation from polar to Cartesian coordinates

In order to implement the transformation equations

$$x = r \cos \varphi \ ,$$
$$y = r \sin \varphi \tag{12.60}$$

by means of an analog computing circuit, the coordinates must be expressed as voltages. We let

$$\varphi = \pi \frac{U_\varphi}{E} \quad \text{for } -E \leqq U_\varphi \leqq +E \ .$$

The range of argument is therefore defined between $\pm \pi$. We define the remaining coordinates as

$$x = \frac{U_x}{E} \ ; \quad y = \frac{U_y}{E} \ ; \quad r = \frac{U_r}{E} \ .$$

Thus, Eq. (12.60) can be rewritten

$$U_x = U_r \cos\left(\pi \frac{U_\varphi}{E}\right), \qquad U_y = U_r \sin\left(\pi \frac{U_\varphi}{E}\right). \tag{12.61}$$

To generate the sine and cosine functions for the range of argument $\pm\,\pi$, we employ the network described in Section 12.7.4 and, in addition, two multipliers. The complete circuit is represented in the block diagram of Fig 12.45.

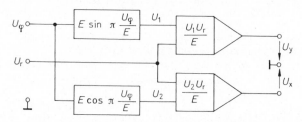

Fig. 12.45 Transformation from polar to Cartesian coordinates

$$U_x = U_r \cos\left(\pi \frac{U_\varphi}{E}\right); \qquad U_y = U_r \sin\left(\pi \frac{U_\varphi}{E}\right)$$

12.9.2   Transformation from Cartesian to polar coordinates

Inversion of the transformation equation (12.60) yields

$$r = \sqrt{x^2 + y^2} \quad \text{or} \quad U_r = \sqrt{U_x^2 + U_y^2}\,, \tag{12.62}$$

$$\varphi = \arctan\frac{y}{x} \quad \text{or} \quad U_\varphi = \frac{E}{\cdot\,\pi}\arctan\frac{U_y}{U_x} \tag{12.63}$$

respectively. The magnitude, U_r, of the vector can be computed according to the block diagram in Fig. 12.46, using two squarers and one square-rooter. A more simple circuit which also has a larger range of input voltage can be deduced by applying a few more mathematical operations. From Eq. (12.62)

$$U_r^2 - U_y^2 = U_x^2\,,$$

$$(U_r - U_y)(U_r + U_y) = U_x^2\,.$$

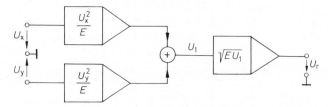

Fig. 12.46 Computation of the magnitude of a vector (vector voltmeter)

$$U_r = \sqrt{U_x^2 + U_y^2}$$

Hence,

$$U_r = \frac{U_x^2}{U_r + U_y} + U_y \; .$$

The implicit equation for U_r can be implemented by means of a multiplier with division input, as in Fig. 12.47. The summing amplifier S_1 evaluates the expression

$$U_1 = U_r + U_y \; ,$$

and therefore

$$U_2 = \frac{U_x^2}{U_r + U_y} \; .$$

In order to obtain U_r, this voltage U_2 is added to the input voltage U_y using the summing amplifier S_2.

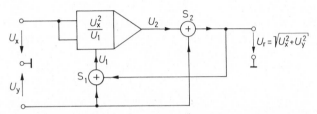

Fig. 12.47 Simplified circuit for computing the vector magnitude

The fact that voltage U_y must always be positive may be easily explained by reference to the special case $U_x = 0$. We thus have $U_2 = 0$ and $U_r = U_y$. This is the correct solution only for positive values of U_y. In addition, as practical dividers cannot handle a sign change in the denominator, it is necessary to form the absolute value for bipolar values of U_y, e.g. using the circuit shown in Fig. 25.20. This does not limit the vector calculation, as the intermediate variable U_y^2 is positive in each case.

The simplest implementation of a vector meter is one in which multiplication and division are performed via logarithms, because both operations can be performed using a single circuit, as shown in Fig. 12.36. However, in this case it is necessary to form also the absolute value of U_x.

This is not required when using transconductance multipliers, as these generally allow four-quadrant operation. However, in this case separate circuits are required for multiplication and division. It is advisable, as shown in Fig. 12.48, to perform division before multiplication, as the dynamic range would otherwise be reduced due to the presence of the variable U_x^2.

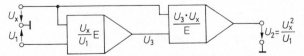

Fig. 12.48 Use of transconductance multipliers to compute the vector magnitude according to the method in Fig. 12.47

13 Controlled sources and impedance converters

In linear network synthesis, not only passive components are used, but also idealized active elements such as controlled current and voltage sources. In addition, idealized converter circuitry such as the negative impedance converter (NIC), the gyrator and the circulator is often employed. In the following sections we describe the most important ways of implementing these circuits.

13.1 Voltage-controlled voltage sources

A voltage-controlled voltage source is characterized by having an output voltage U_2 proportional to the input voltage U_1. It is therefore nothing more than a voltage amplifier. Ideally, the output voltage should be independent of the output current and the input current should be zero. Hence, the transfer characteristics are

$$I_1 = 0 \cdot U_1 + 0 \cdot I_2 = 0 \; ,$$
$$U_2 = A_v U_1 + 0 \cdot I_2 = A_v U_1 \; .$$

In practice, the ideal source can only be approximated. Considering that the reaction of the output on the input is usually negligibly small, the equivalent circuit of a real source is as shown in Fig. 13.1, the transfer characteristics of which are

$$I_1 = \frac{1}{r_i} U_1 + 0 \cdot I_2 \; ,$$
$$U_2 = A_v U_1 - r_o I_2 \; . \tag{13.1}$$

The internal voltage source shown must be assumed to be ideal. The input resistance is r_i, and the output resistance is r_o.

Voltage-controlled voltage sources of low output resistance and of defined, but adjustable gain have already been described in Chapter 7 in the form of inverting amplifiers and non-inverting (electrometer) amplifiers. They are shown for the sake of completeness in Figs. 13.2 and 13.3. It is easy to obtain output resistances of far less than $1 \, \Omega$ and therefore to approach the ideal behavior

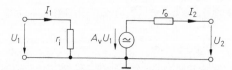

Fig. 13.1 Low-frequency equivalent circuit of a voltage-controlled voltage source

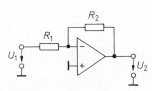

Fig. 13.2 Inverting amplifier as voltage-controlled voltage source

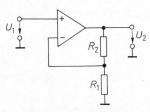

Fig. 13.3 Electrometer amplifier as voltage-controlled voltage source

Ideal transfer
characteristic: $\quad U_2 = -\dfrac{R_2}{R_1} U_1$

Input impedance: $\quad \underline{Z}_i = R_1$

Output impedance: $\quad \underline{Z}_o = \dfrac{r_o}{\underline{g}}$

Ideal transfer
characteristic: $\quad U_2 = \left(1 + \dfrac{R_2}{R_1}\right) U_1$

Input impedance: $\quad \underline{Z}_i = r_{CM} \left\|\dfrac{1}{j\omega C}\right.$

Output impedance: $\quad \underline{Z}_o = \dfrac{r_o}{\underline{g}}$

fairly closely. It should be noted, however, that the output impedance is somewhat inductive, i.e. it rises with increasing frequency (see Chapter 7).

The input resistance of a electrometer amplifier is very high. At low frequencies, one easily attains values in the GΩ-range and hence very nearly ideal conditions. The high (incremental) input resistance must not lead us to overlook the additional errors that may arise due to the constant input bias current I_B, particularly when the output resistance of the signal source is high. In critical cases an amplifier with FET input should be employed.

For low-resistance signal sources, the inverting amplifier circuit in Fig. 13.2 can be used, as its low input resistance R_1 then causes no error. The advantage is that no inaccuracies due to common-mode signals can arise.

13.2 Current-controlled voltage sources

The equivalent circuit of a current-controlled voltage source, shown in Fig. 13.4, is identical to that of the voltage-controlled voltage source in Fig. 13.1. The only difference between the two sources is that the input current is now the controlling signal. It should be influenced by the circuit as little as possible, a condition fulfilled in the ideal case when $r_i = 0$. The transfer characteristics,

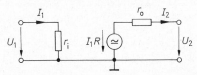

Fig. 13.4 Low-frequency equivalent circuit of a current-controlled voltage source

disregarding the effect of the output on the input, are

$$U_1 = r_i I_1 + 0 \cdot I_2 \qquad U_1 = 0$$
$$U_2 = R I_1 - r_o I_2 \qquad \Rightarrow \qquad U_2 = R I_1 \qquad (13.2)$$
$$\text{(real)} \qquad\qquad \text{(ideal, } r_i = r_o = 0).$$

When implementing this circuit as in Fig. 13.5, we use the fact that the summing point of an inverting amplifier represents virtual ground. Because of this, the input resistance is low, as required. The output voltage becomes $U_2 = - R I_1$ if the input bias current of the amplifier is negligible compared with I_1. If very small currents I_1 are to be used as control signals, an amplifier with FET input must be employed. Additional errors may occur due to the offset voltage and these will increase if the output resistance R_g of the signal source is reduced, since the offset voltage is amplified by a factor of $(1 + R/R_g)$.

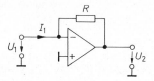

Fig. 13.5 Current-controlled voltage source

Ideal transfer characteristic: $U_2 = - R I_1$

Input impedance: $\qquad\qquad \underline{Z}_i = \dfrac{R}{\underline{A}_D}$

Output impedance: $\qquad\qquad \underline{Z}_o = \dfrac{r_o}{\underline{g}}$

For the output impedance of the circuit, the same conditions hold as for the previous circuit where the loop gain $\underline{g}$ is dependent on the output resistance R_g of the signal source and is given by

$$\underline{g} = \underline{k} \underline{A}_D = \frac{R_g}{R + R_g} \underline{A}_D .$$

A current-controlled voltage source with a floating input is discussed in Section 25.2.1.

13.3   Voltage-controlled current sources

The purpose of voltage-controlled current sources is to impress on a load a current I_2 which is independent of the output voltage U_2 and is determined only by the control voltage U_1. Therefore

$$I_1 = 0 \cdot U_1 + 0 \cdot U_2 ,$$
$$I_2 = g_f U_1 + 0 \cdot U_2 . \qquad (13.3)$$

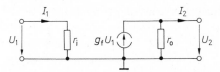

Fig. 13.6 Low-frequency equivalent circuit of a voltage-controlled current source

In practice, these conditions can be fulfilled only approximately. Taking into account that the effect of the output on the input is normally very small indeed, the equivalent circuit of a real current source becomes that shown in Fig. 13.6. The transfer characteristics are then

$$I_1 = \frac{1}{r_i} U_1 + 0 \cdot U_2 \ ,$$

$$I_2 = g_f U_1 - \frac{1}{r_o} U_2 \ .$$

(13.4)

For $r_i \to \infty$ and $r_o \to \infty$, one obtains the ideal current source. Tha parameter g_f is the forward transconductance or transfer conductance.

13.3.1 Current sources for floating loads

In inverting and electrometer amplifiers, the current through the feedback resistor is $I_2 = U_1/R_1$ and is therefore independent of the voltage across the feedback resistor. Both circuits can thus be used as current sources if the load R_L is inserted in place of the feedback resistor, as shown in Figs. 13.7 and 13.8.

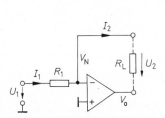

Fig. 13.7 Inverting amplifier as voltage-controlled current source

Ideal transfer
  characteristic: $I_2 = U_1/R_1$

Input impedance: $\underline{Z}_i = R_1$

Output impedance: $\underline{Z}_o = A_D R_1 \left\| \dfrac{A_D R_1 \omega_{cA}}{j\omega} \right.$

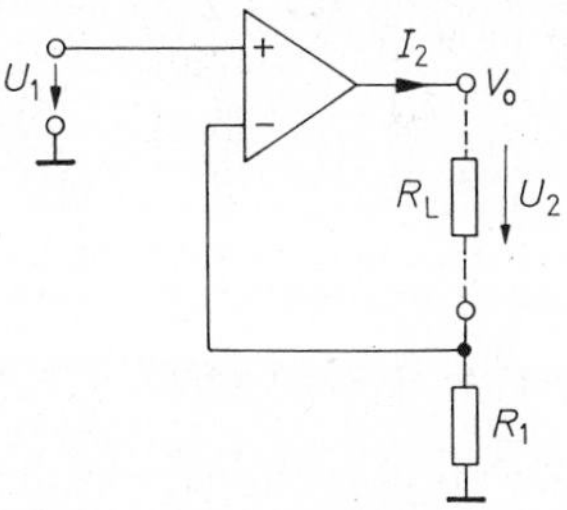

Fig. 13.8 Electrometer amplifier as voltage-controlled current source

Ideal transfer
  characteristic: $I_2 = U_1/R_1$

Input impedance: $\underline{Z}_i = r_{CM} \left\| \dfrac{1}{j\omega C_{CM}} \right.$

Output impedance: $\underline{Z}_o = A_D R_1 \left\| \dfrac{A_D R_1 \omega_{cA}}{j\omega} \right.$

For the input impedance the same conditions obtain as for the corresponding voltage-controlled voltage sources in Figs. 13.2 and 13.3.

For a finite open-loop gain A_D of the operational amplifier, the output resistance assumes finite values only, as the potential difference $U_D = V_P - V_N$ does not remain precisely zero. To determine the output resistance, we take the following relationships from Fig. 13.7

$$I_1 = I_2 = \frac{U_1 - V_N}{R_1} \,, \qquad V_N = -\frac{V_o}{A_D} \,, \qquad U_2 = V_N - V_o$$

and obtain

$$I_2 = \frac{U_1}{R_1} - \frac{U_2}{R_1(1 + A_D)} \approx \frac{U_1}{R_1} - \frac{U_2}{A_D R_1} \,,$$

and therefore for the output resistance

$$r_o = -\frac{\partial U_2}{\partial I_2} = A_D R_1 \tag{13.5}$$

which is thus proportional to the differential gain of the operational amplifier.

Since the open-loop gain A_D of a frequency-compensated operational amplifier has a fairly low cutoff frequency (e.g. $f_{cA} \approx 10$ Hz for the 741 type), one must take into account that A_D is complex even at low frequencies. Equation (13.5) must then be rewritten in its complex form

$$\underline{Z}_o = \underline{A}_D R_1 = \frac{A_D}{1 + j\dfrac{\omega}{\omega_{cA}}} R_1 \,. \tag{13.6}$$

This output impedance may be represented by a parallel connection of a resistor R_o and a capacitor C_o, as the following rearrangement of Eq. (13.6) shows:

$$\underline{Z}_o = \frac{1}{\dfrac{1}{A_D R_1} + \dfrac{j\omega}{A_D R_1 \omega_{cA}}} = R_o \left\| \frac{1}{j\omega C_o} \right. \,, \tag{13.7}$$

where $R_o = A_D R_1$ and $C_o = \dfrac{1}{A_D R_1 \omega_{cA}}$.

With an operational amplifier having $A_D = 10^5$ and $f_{cA} = 10$ Hz, one obtains for $R_1 = 1\,\text{k}\Omega$

$$R_o = 100\,\text{M}\Omega \quad \text{and} \quad C_o = 159\,\text{pF} \,.$$

For a frequency of 10 kHz, the value of the output impedance is reduced to 100 kΩ.

The same considerations apply to the output impedance of the circuit in Fig. 13.8. As far as their electrical data are concerned, the two current sources in Figs. 13.7 and 13.8 are well suited for many applications. However, they have a serious technical disadvantage: The load R_L must be floating, i.e. it must not be connected to a fixed potential, otherwise the amplifier output or the N-input is short-circuited. The following circuits overcome this restriction.

13.3.2   Current sources for grounded loads

The principle of the current source in Fig. 13.9 is based on the fact that the output current is measured as the voltage drop across R_1. The output voltage of the operational amplifier finds a value such that this voltage is equal to a given input voltage. In order to determine the output current, we apply KCL to the N-input, the P-input and to the output. Thus

$$\frac{V_o - V_N}{R_2} - \frac{V_N}{R_3} = 0 \ , \qquad \frac{U_1 - V_P}{R_1 + R_2} + \frac{U_2 - V_P}{R_3} = 0 \ ,$$

$$\frac{V_o - U_2}{R_1} + \frac{V_P - U_2}{R_3} - I_2 = 0 \ .$$

Since $V_N = V_P$, we obtain the output current as

$$I_2 = \frac{U_1}{R_1} + \frac{R_2^2 - R_3^2}{R_1 R_3 (R_2 + R_3)} U_2 \ .$$

We can see that the output current for $R_2 = R_3$ is independent of the output voltage. The output resistance then becomes $r_o = \infty$ and the output current is $I_2 = U_1/R_1$. In practice, resistance R_1 is made low so that the voltage across it remains in the order of a few volts. Resistance R_2 is selected large in comparison with R_1, so that the operational amplifier and the voltage source U_1 are not unnecessarily loaded. The output resistance of the current source can, at low frequencies, be adjusted to infinity even for a real operational amplifier, by slightly varying R_3. The internal resistance R_g of the controlling voltage source is connected in series with R_1 and R_2. In order to avoid an incorrect result, it must be negligibly small.

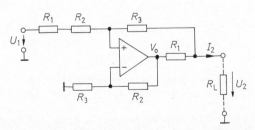

Fig. 13.9 Voltage-controlled current source for grounded loads

Output current: $I_2 = \dfrac{U_1}{R_1}$ for $R_3 = R_2$

The circuit can also be designed as a current source with *negative output resistance*. For this purpose we select $R_3 < R_2$ and obtain

$$r_o = \frac{\Delta U_2}{\Delta I_2} = \frac{R_1 R_3 (R_2 + R_3)}{R_3^2 - R_2^2} < 0 .$$

An alternative for the same application is shown in Fig. 13.10, where both op amps are operated as inverting amplifiers having no common-mode signal. In addition, the loading of the controlling source is independent of U_2 and hence of the load resistance R_L.

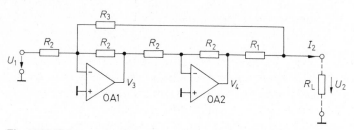

Fig. 13.10 Voltage-controlled current source without common-mode voltage

Output current: $\quad I_2 = \dfrac{U_1}{R_1} \quad$ for $R_3 = R_2 - R_1$

To determine the output current, we use KVL for the circuit and obtain

$$V_4 = - V_3 = U_1 + \frac{R_2}{R_3} U_2 .$$

Applying KCL to the output gives

$$\frac{V_4 - U_2}{R_1} - \frac{U_2}{R_3} - I_2 = 0 .$$

Eliminating V_4, we obtain

$$I_2 = \frac{U_1}{R_1} + \frac{R_2 - R_3 - R_1}{R_1 R_3} U_2 .$$

The output current becomes independent of the output voltage when the condition

$$R_3 = R_2 - R_1$$

is fulfilled.

13.3.3 Precision current sources using transistors

Simple single-ended current sources employ a bipolar transistor or a field-effect transistor to supply loads having one terminal connected to a constant potential. Such circuits have been described in introductory Chapters 4 and 5.

Their disadvantage is that the output current is affected by U_{BE} or U_{GS} and therefore cannot be precisely defined. An operational amplifier can be used to eliminate this effect. Figure 13.11 shows the relevant circuits for a bipolar transistor and for a FET. The output voltage of the operational amplifier finds a value such that the voltage across the resistance R_1 equals U_1. Obviously, this holds for positive voltages only, as otherwise the transistors are OFF. Since the current through R_1 is U_1/R_1, the load current is

for the bipolar transistor: $\qquad I_2 = \dfrac{U_1}{R_1}\left(1 - \dfrac{1}{B}\right)$,

and for the FET: $\qquad\qquad\qquad I_2 = \dfrac{U_1}{R_1}$.

The difference between these currents is due to the fact that, in the bipolar transistor, part of the emitter current flows through the base. As the current transfer ratio B is dependent on U_{CE}, the current I_B also changes with the output voltage U_2. As shown in Section 4.6, this effect limits the output resistance to the value βr_{CE}, even if the operational amplifier is assumed to be ideal.

The effect of the finite current transfer ratio can be reduced if the bipolar transistor is replaced by a Darlington circuit. It can be virtually eliminated by using a FET because the gate current is extremely small. The output resistance of the circuit in Fig. 13.11b is limited only by the finite gain of the operational amplifier. It can be determined by the following relationships obtained directly from the circuit for $U_1 = \text{const}$:

$$dU_{DS} \approx -\,dU_2 \ ,$$

$$dU_{GS} = dU_G - dU_S = -\,A_D R_1 dI_2 - R_1 dI_2 \approx -\,A_D R_1 dI_2 \ .$$

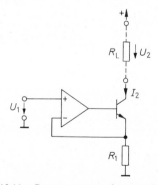

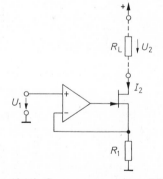

Fig. 13.11a Current source using a transistor

Output current: $\qquad I_2 = \dfrac{U_1}{R_1}\left(1 - \dfrac{1}{B}\right)$

$\qquad\qquad\qquad$ for $U_1 > 0$

Output resistance: $r_o = \beta r_{CE}$

Fig. 13.11b Current source using a FET

Output current: $\qquad I_2 = \dfrac{U_1}{R_1}$

$\qquad\qquad\qquad$ for $U_1 > 0$

Output resistance: $r_o = \mu A_D R_1$

Using the basic equation (5.10),

$$dI_2 = g_f dU_{GS} + \frac{1}{r_{DS}} dU_{DS} \ ,$$

we obtain for the output resistance

$$r_o = -\frac{dU_2}{dI_2} = r_{DS}(1 + A_D g_f R_1) \approx \mu A_D R_1 \ . \tag{13.8}$$

It is thus greater by a factor $\mu = g_f \cdot r_{DS} \approx 150$ than that of the corresponding current source in Fig. 13.8 which uses an operational amplifier without field-effect transistor. Using the same values as in the example given for the circuit in Fig. 13.8, we obtain the very high output resistance of approximately 15 GΩ. Because of the frequency dependence of the open-loop gain A_D, this value holds only for frequencies below the cutoff frequency f_{cA} of the operational amplifier. For higher frequencies, we must take into account that the differential gain is complex and obtain, instead of Eq. (13.8), the output impedance

$$\underline{Z}_o = \underline{A}_D \mu R_1 = \frac{A_D}{1 + j\dfrac{\omega}{\omega_{cA}}} \mu R_1 \ . \tag{13.9}$$

A comparison with Eqs. (13.6) and (13.7) shows that this impedance is equivalent to connecting a resistance $R_o = \mu A_D R_1$ in parallel with a capacitance $C_o = 1/\mu A_D R_1 \omega_{cA}$. For the practical example mentioned, we obtain $C_o = 1$ pF. The capacitance of the FET of the order of a few pF will appear in parallel.

When larger output currents are required, a power FET may be used, as shown in Fig. 13.12. This does not change the properties of the circuit since, as before, no current flows into the gate.

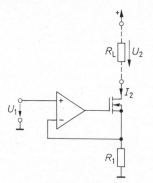

Fig. 13.12 Current source for large output currents

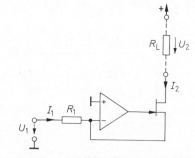

Fig. 13.13 Inverting FET current source

Output current: $\quad I_2 = \dfrac{U_1}{R_1}$ for $U_1 > 0$

Output resistance: $\quad r_o = \mu A_D R_1$

Output current: $\quad I_2 = -\dfrac{U_1}{R_1}$ for $U_1 < 0$

Output resistance: $\quad r_o = \mu A_D R_1$

The circuit in Fig. 13.11b can be modified by connecting the input voltage directly to R_1 and by grounding the P-input terminal. Figure 13.13 shows the resulting circuit. U_1 must always be negative to ensure that the FET is not turned off. In contrast to the circuit in Fig. 13.11b, the control voltage source is loaded by the current $I_1 = -I_2$.

When a current source is required, the output current of which flows in the opposite direction to that in the circuit of Fig. 13.11b, the n-channel FET is simply replaced by a p-channel FET, as shown in the circuit in Fig. 13.14. If no p-channel FET is available, the arrangement in Fig. 13.15 can also be used. In contrast to the previous circuits, the source terminal here serves as the output. However, this does not affect the output current since it is controlled, as before, by the voltage across R_1. Negative feedback is established in the following manner. If the output current falls, V_P rises, resulting in an amplified increase of the gate potential, and U_{GS} is therefore reduced. This counteracts the reduction in current. The output resistance is considerably smaller than that of the previous circuits.

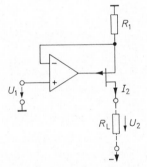

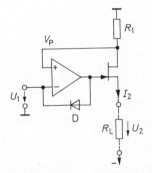

Fig. 13.14 Current source using a
p-channel FET

Fig. 13.15 Current source with a quasi-p-
channel FET

Output current: $I_2 = -\dfrac{U_1}{R_1}$ for $U_1 < 0$ Output current: $I_2 = -\dfrac{U_1}{R_1}$ for $U_1 < 0$

Output resistance: $r_o = \mu A_D R_1$ Output resistance: $r_o = A_D R_1$

If, due to an excessively large input signal, the gate-channel diode becomes forward biased, the output voltage of the operational amplifier reacts directly on the P-input. Positive feedback then occurs, and the output reaches positive saturation. To avoid this latch-up, a diode D is inserted as in Fig. 13.15.

Transistor current sources for bipolar output currents

One disadvantage of all the current sources previously described is that they can supply only unidirectional output currents. By combining the circuits in Figs. 13.11 and 13.14, we obtain the current source in Fig. 13.16 which can supply currents of either polarity. For zero control voltage, $V_{P1} = \frac{3}{4}V^+$ and

$V_{P2} = \frac{3}{4}V^-$. In this case,

$$I_2 = I_{D1} - I_{D2} = \frac{V^+}{4R_1} + \frac{V^-}{4R_1} = 0 \quad \text{for} \quad V^+ = -V^- \; .$$

For positive input voltages U_1, current I_{D2} increases by $U_1/4R_1$, whereas I_{D1} decreases by the same amount. Therefore, one obtains a negative output current

$$I_2 = -\frac{U_1}{2R_1} \; .$$

For negative input voltages, I_{D2} decreases while I_{D1} becomes larger, this resulting in a positive output current. The limit for the control voltage is reached when one of the FETs is turned off. This is the case for $U_1 = \pm V^+$. In order to turn off the FETs, the absolute value of the gate potential must be higher than the supply voltage V^+. Therefore, operational amplifiers OA 1 and OA 2 require higher supply voltages, and these are designated in Fig. 13.16 as V^{++} and V^{--} respectively.

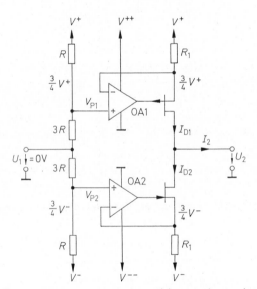

Fig. 13.16 Bipolar FET current source (potentials entered are quiescent values)

$$\text{Output current:} \quad I_2 = -\frac{U_1}{2R_1}$$

The circuit has a rather poor zero stability. This is because the output current is itself the difference between the two relatively large currents, I_{D1} and I_{D2}, which are additionally affected by changes in the supply voltages.

The circuit in Fig. 13.17 is considerably better in this respect. It differs from the former circuit in that it uses a different kind of control [13.1]. The two output stages are controlled by the currents I_3 and I_4, flowing in the supply

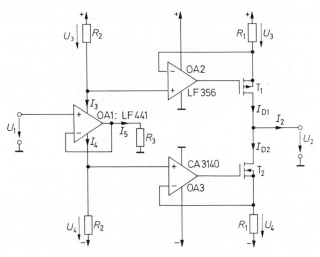

Fig. 13.17 Bipolar FET current source for large output currents

$$\text{Output current:}\quad I_2 = \frac{R_2}{R_1 R_3} U_1$$

terminals of the amplifier OA 1. For the drain currents

$$I_{D1} = \frac{U_3}{R_1} = \frac{R_2}{R_1} I_3 \;,\qquad I_{D2} = \frac{U_4}{R_1} = \frac{R_2}{R_1} I_4 \;. \tag{13.10}$$

The output stages therefore operate as current mirrors. Hence, the output current

$$I_2 = I_{D1} - I_{D2} = \frac{R_2}{R_1}(I_3 - I_4) \;. \tag{13.11}$$

Amplifier OA 1 operates as a voltage follower. Therefore, the voltage across resistor R_3 is equivalent to the input voltage U_1. Thus, its current is

$$I_5 = \frac{U_1}{R_3} \;. \tag{13.12}$$

For further processing of this signal, use is made of the fact that the operational amplifier can be regarded as a current node for which, by applying KCL, the sum of the currents must equal zero. As the input currents are negligible and as there is usually no ground connection, the following relationship holds with very good accuracy:

$$I_5 = I_3 - I_4 \;. \tag{13.13}$$

Substitution in Eqs. (13.12) and (13.11) yields the output current

$$I_2 = \frac{R_2}{R_1 R_3} U_1 = \frac{U_1}{R_1} \quad \text{for} \quad R_2 = R_3 \;.$$

For zero input, $I_5 = 0$ and $I_3 = I_4 = I_Q$, where I_Q is the quiescent current flowing in the supply leads of the amplifier OA 1. It is small in comparison with the maximum possible output current, I_5, of the amplifier. For a positive differential input voltage, $I_3 \approx I_5 \gg I_4$. The output current I_2 is then supplied virtually only from the upper output stage whereas the lower stage is disabled. The inverse is true for a negative input voltage difference. The circuit is therefore of the class-AB push-pull type. Since the quiescent current in the output stage is

$$I_{D1Q} = I_{D2Q} = \frac{R_2}{R_1} I_Q \qquad (13.14)$$

and is small relative to the maximum output current, the output current at zero input signal is now determined by the difference of small quantities. This results in a very good zero-current stability. A further advantage is that of high efficiency, this being of special interest if the circuit is to be designed for high output currents. For this reason, the device selected for OA 1 is an operational amplifier with low quiescent current drain I_Q, such as the LF 441.

In the case of the circuit in Fig. 13.17, it is particularly advisable to use power MOSFETs. As they are of the enhancement type, their gate potentials are within the supply voltage range, thereby obviating the need for positive and negative auxiliary voltages for operational amplifiers OA 2 and OA 3 respectively. However, amplifiers must be used whose common-mode input voltage range extends to the positive or negative supply voltage. The types specified satisfy this condition.

If resistor R_3 in Fig. 13.17 is not grounded but connected to the output of a second voltage follower, the input voltage difference will determine the output current [13.2].

13.3.4   Floating current sources

In the previous sections we discuss two types of current sources. Neither load terminal in the circuits of Figs. 13.7 and 13.8 may be connected to a fixed potential. Such a load is called off-ground or floating and is illustrated in Fig. 13.18a. For this kind of operation, the load may in practice consist only of

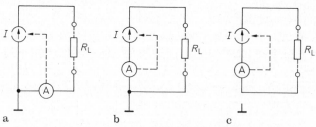

Fig. 13.18 (a) Current source for floating loads. (b) Current source for grounded loads (single-ended current source). (c) Floating current source for any load

passive elements, since for active loads there is normally a connection to ground via the supply.

Grounded loads can be supplied by a current source based on the arrangement in Fig. 13.18b. Its practical design is shown in Figs. 13.9 to 13.17.

If one or other load terminal is to be connected to any desired potential without the current being affected, a floating current source is required. It can be constructed using two grounded current sources which supply equal but opposite currents, as shown in Fig. 13.19.

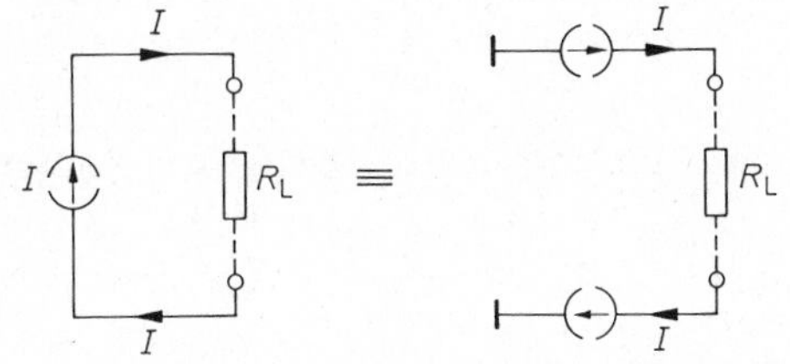

Fig. 13.19 Implementation of a floating current source by two single-ended current sources

13.4   Current-controlled current sources

The equivalent circuit of the current-controlled current source is identical to that of the voltage-controlled current source in Fig. 13.6. The only difference is that the input current is now the controlling signal and should be affected as little as possible by the circuit. This is so for the ideal condition where $r_i = 0$. When the effect of the output on the input is neglected, the transfer characteristics are

$$U_1 = r_i I_1 + 0 \cdot U_2 \qquad U_1 = 0$$
$$I_2 = A_1 I_1 - \frac{1}{r_o} \cdot U_2 \implies \qquad I_2 = A_1 I_1 \qquad (13.15)$$

(real) $\qquad$ (ideal, $r_i = 0$, $r_o = \infty$) .

In Figs 13.7 and 13.13, we show two voltage-controlled current sources of finite input resistance. They can be operated as current-controlled current sources having virtually ideal characteristics if the resistor R_1 is made zero; then $I_2 = I_1$.

Current-controlled current sources allowing polarity reversal of the output currents are of particular interest. They are called current mirrors, and one example is shown in Fig. 13.20. It is based on the voltage-controlled current source in Fig. 13.11b, and the current-to-voltage conversion is effected by the additional resistor R. However, this results in non-ideal conditions for the input resistance.

The maximum freedom in specifying the circuit parameters is obtained if a circuit from Section 13.2 is used for the current-to-voltage conversion and one

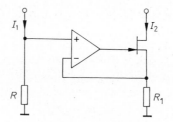

Fig. 13.20 Current mirror

Output current: $\quad I_2 = \dfrac{R}{R_1} I_1$

of the voltage-controlled current sources described in Section 13.3 is connected in series.

13.5   NIC (negative impedance converter)

There are cases when negative resistances or voltage sources having negative internal resistances are required. By definition, the resistance $R = + U/I$, if the arrows for current and voltage have the same direction. If the voltage U across and the current I through a two-terminal network then have opposite signs, the quotient U/I becomes negative. Such a network is said to have a negative resistance. Negative resistances can, in principle, be implemented only by the active circuits known as NICs. There are two types: the UNIC which reverses the polarity of the voltage without affecting the direction of the current, and the INIC which reverses the current without changing the polarity of the voltage. The implementation of the INIC is particularly simple. Its ideal transfer characteristics are

$$U_1 = U_2 + 0 \cdot I_2 \, , \qquad I_1 = 0 \cdot U_2 - I_2 \, . \tag{13.16}$$

These equations can be implemented as shown in Fig. 13.21, by a voltage-controlled voltage source and a current-controlled current source. However, both functions can also be performed by a single operational amplifier, as shown in Fig. 13.22.

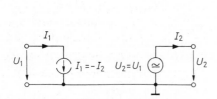

Fig. 13.21 Circuit of an INIC using controlled sources

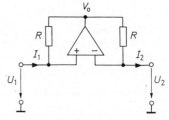

Fig. 13.22 INIC using a single amplifier

For the ideal operational amplifier, $V_P = V_N$, and therefore $U_1 = U_2$, as required. The output potential of the amplifier has the value

$$V_o = U_2 + I_2 R \ .$$

Hence, the current at port 1 is, as required,

$$I_1 = \frac{U_2 - V_o}{R} = -I_2 \ .$$

For this deduction we have tacitly assumed stability of the circuit. However, since it simultaneously employs positive and negative feedback, the validity of this assumption must be examined separately in each case. To do so, we determine what proportion of the output voltage affects the P-input and N-input respectively. Figure 13.23 shows the INIC in a general application, where R_1 and R_2 are the internal resistances of the circuits connected to it. The feedback of the voltage

$$V_P = V_o \frac{R_1}{R_1 + R} \quad \text{is positive ,}$$

and that of

$$V_N = V_o \frac{R_2}{R_2 + R} \quad \text{is negative .}$$

The circuit is stable if the positive-feedback voltage V_P is smaller than V_N, i.e. if

$$R_1 < R_2 \ .$$

The circuit in Fig. 13.24 illustrates the use of the INIC for producing negative resistances. When a positive voltage is applied to port 1, $U_2 = U_1$ becomes positive according to Eq. (13.16), and hence I_2 is also positive. From Eq. (13.16)

$$I_1 = -I_2 = -\frac{U_1}{R_2} \ .$$

A negative current thus flows into port 1 even though a positive voltage has been

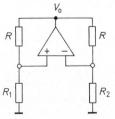

Fig. 13.23 INIC in a general application

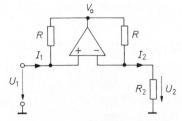

Fig. 13.24 Implementation of negative resistances

Negative resistance: $\dfrac{U_1}{I_1} = -R_2$

applied. Port 1 therefore behaves as if it were a negative resistance with the value

$$\frac{U_1}{I_1} = - R_2 \ . \tag{13.17}$$

This arrangement is stable as long as the internal resistance R_1 of the circuit connected to port 1 is smaller than R_2. For this reason, the arrangement is stable even under short-circuit conditions. It is also possible to have a negative resistance which is stable at open-circuit, by reversing the INIC, i.e. by connecting the resistance R_2 to port 1.

Since Eq. (13.16) also holds for alternating currents, one can replace the resistance R_2 by a complex impedance $\underline{Z}_2$ and in this way obtain any desired negative impedance.

The INIC can also be operated as a voltage source of negative output resistance. A voltage source having no-load voltage U_0 and source resistance r_o, yields, at load I, an output voltage $U = U_0 - Ir_o$. For normal voltage sources, r_o is positive, this resulting in a reduction of U under load. For a voltage source with negative output resistance, however, U increases with load. The circuit in Fig. 13.25 exhibits this behavior. It follows from the circuit that

$$U_2 = V_1 = U_0 - I_1 R_1 \ .$$

Since $I_1 = - I_2$, then

$$U_2 = U_0 + I_2 R_1 \ .$$

Here, the INIC is connected in such a way that the voltage source is stable under no-load conditions.

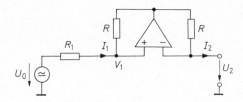

Fig. 13.25 Voltage source with negative output resistance

Output voltage: $U_2 = U_0 + I_2 R_1$

Output resistance: $r_o = - \dfrac{dU_2}{dI_2} = - R_1$

Negative resistances can be connected in series and in parallel just like conventional resistors, and the same laws apply. For example, a voltage source with negative output resistance can be used to compensate for the resistance of a long line so that, at the end of the line, the voltage U_0 is obtained with zero source resistance.

13.6   Gyrator

The gyrator is a converter circuit by which any impedance can be converted into its dual-transformed counterpart, e.g. a capacitance can be changed into an

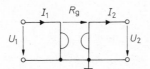

Fig. 13.26 Symbol of the gyrator

inductance. The graphic symbol of a gyrator is represented in Fig. 13.26. The ideal transfer characteristics are

$$I_1 = 0 \cdot U_1 + \frac{1}{R_g} U_2 \; , \qquad I_2 = \frac{1}{R_g} U_1 + 0 \cdot U_2 \; , \qquad (13.18)$$

where R_g is the gyration resistance. Hence, the current at one port is proportional to the voltage at the other port. For this reason, the gyrator can be constructed from two voltage-controlled current sources having high input and output resistances, as shown schematically in Fig. 13.27.

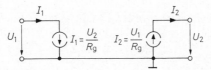

Fig. 13.27 Implementation of a gyrator by two voltage-controlled current sources

Another method of implementing a gyrator is based on the combination of two INICs [13.2] and is illustrated in Fig. 13.28. To determine the transfer characteristics, we apply KCL to the P-inputs and N-inputs of OA 1 and OA 2 and obtain for

$$\text{node } P_1: \qquad \frac{V_3 - U_1}{R_g} - \frac{U_1}{R_g} + I_1 = 0 \; ,$$

$$\text{node } N_1: \qquad \frac{V_3 - U_1}{R_g} + \frac{U_2 - U_1}{R_g} = 0 \; ,$$

$$\text{node } P_2: \qquad \frac{V_4 - U_2}{R_g} + \frac{U_1 - U_2}{R_g} - I_2 = 0 \; ,$$

$$\text{node } N_2: \qquad \frac{V_4 - U_2}{R_g} - \frac{U_2}{R_g} = 0 \; .$$

By eliminating V_3 and V_4, the transfer characteristics become

$$I_1 = \frac{U_2}{R_g} \quad \text{and} \quad I_2 = \frac{U_2}{R_g} \; ,$$

which are the desired relationships as given in Eq. (13.18).

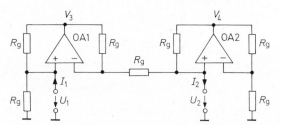

Fig. 13.28 Gyrator using two INICs

Some applications of the gyrator are described below. In the first example, a resistor R_2 is connected to the right-hand port. Since the arrows of I_2 and U_2 have the same direction, $I_2 = U_2/R_2$, following Ohm's law. Insertion of this relationship in the transfer characteristics gives

$$U_1 = I_2 R_g = \frac{U_2 R_g}{R_2} \quad \text{and} \quad I_1 = \frac{U_2}{R_g} \; .$$

Port 1 therefore behaves like a resistance having the value

$$R_1 = \frac{U_1}{I_1} = \frac{R_g^2}{R_2} \; , \tag{13.19}$$

and is thus proportional to the reciprocal of the load resistance connected to port 2.

The conversion of resistances is also valid for impedances and, according to Eq. (13.19), gives

$$\underline{Z}_1 = \frac{R_g^2}{\underline{Z}_2} \; . \tag{13.20}$$

This relationship indicates an interesting application of the gyrator: if a capacitor of the value C_2 is connected to one side, the impedance measured on the other side is

$$\underline{Z} = R_g^2 \cdot j\omega C_2 \; ,$$

which is the inductance

$$L_1 = R_g^2 C_2 \; . \tag{13.21}$$

The importance of the gyrator is due to the fact that it can be used to emulate large low-loss inductances. The appropriate circuit is depicted in Fig. 13.29. The two free terminals of the gyrator behave, according to Eq. (13.21), as if an inductance $L_1 = R_g^2 C_2$ were connected between them. With $C_2 = 1\,\mu\text{F}$ and $R_g = 10\,\text{k}\Omega$, one obtains $L_1 = 100\,\text{H}$.

If a capacitor C_1 is connected in parallel with the inductance L_1, the result is a parallel resonant circuit which can be used to construct high-Q "L"C-filters.

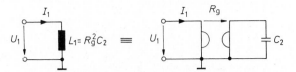

Fig. 13.29 Emulation of an inductance

The Q-factor of the parallel resonant circuit, for $C_1 = C_2$, is well suited to describe the deviation of a real gyrator from the ideal behavior, and is also called the Q-factor of the gyrator. The losses of a real gyrator can be represented by two equivalent resistances R_1 connected in parallel to the two ports. For the circuit involving current sources shown in Fig. 13.27, these resistances are given by the parallel connection of the input resistance of one source with the output resistance of the other. For the circuit involving INICs shown in Fig. 13.28, the equivalent resistances are defined by the matching tolerance of the resistors. The equivalent circuit of a parallel-resonant circuit incorporating a real gyrator with losses, is shown in Fig. 13.30a. When the conversion equation (13.20) is applied to the right-hand side, the transformed equivalent circuit in Fig. 13.30b is obtained. From this, according to Section 2.7, the gyrator Q-factor can be determined as $Q = R_1/2R_g$.

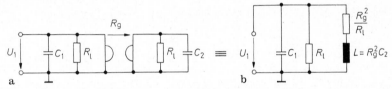

Fig. 13.30 (a) Emulation of a resonant circuit using a lossy gyrator. (b) Equivalent circuit of a lossy resonant circuit

This relationship, however, is only valid for low frequencies, as the Q-factor is very sensitive to phase displacements between current and voltage of the transfer characteristics (Eqs. (13.18)). According to [13.4], a first order approximation is

$$Q(\varphi) = \cfrac{1}{\cfrac{1}{Q_0} + \varphi_1 + \varphi_2} \, ,$$

where Q_0 is the low-frequency limit value of the Q-factor. The terms φ_1 and φ_2 are the phase displacements between current $\underline{I}_1$ and voltage $\underline{U}_2$, and current $\underline{I}_2$ and voltage $\underline{U}_1$ respectively, at resonant frequency of the circuit. For lagging phase angles, the Q-factor rises with increasing resonant frequency. For $|\varphi_1 + \varphi_2| \geq 1/Q_0$, the circuit becomes unstable, and an oscillation at the resonant frequency of the circuit occurs. For leading phase angles the Q-factor decreases with increasing resonant frequency.

Not only two-terminal, but also four-terminal networks can be converted using gyrators. For this purpose the four-terminal network to be converted

Fig. 13.31 Dual transformation of four-terminal networks

is connected between two gyrators with identical gyration resistances, as in Fig. 13.31. The dual-transformed counterpart of the middle two-port then appears between the two outer ports. To deduce the transfer characteristics, the product of the chain matrices is calculated. The four-terminal network to be transformed has the chain matrix

$$(A) = \begin{pmatrix} A_{11} & A_{12} \\ A_{21} & A_{22} \end{pmatrix} .$$

From Eq. (13.18), we obtain the following relationship for the gyrator

$$\begin{pmatrix} U_1 \\ I_1 \end{pmatrix} = \underbrace{\begin{pmatrix} 0 & R_g \\ 1/R_g & 0 \end{pmatrix}}_{(A_g)} \begin{pmatrix} U_2 \\ I_2 \end{pmatrix} . \tag{13.22}$$

The chain matrix $(\bar{A})$ of the resulting four-terminal network is then

$$(\bar{A}) = (A_g)(A)(A_g) = \begin{pmatrix} A_{22} & A_{21} \cdot R_g^2 \\ A_{12}/R_g^2 & A_{11} \end{pmatrix} \tag{13.23}$$

which is the matrix of the dual-transformed middle two-port.

As an example, Fig. 13.32 shows how a circuit of three inductors can be replaced by the dual circuit containing three capacitors.

If a capacitor is externally connected in parallel with each of the inductances L_1 and L_2, one obtains an inductance-coupled bandpass filter consisting exclusively of capacitors. If C_a and C_b are short-circuited, a floating inductance L_3 is obtained.

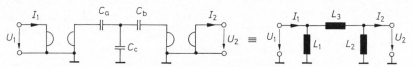

Fig. 13.32 Example of dual transformation

Transformation equations: $L_1 = R_g^2 C_a$
$L_2 = R_g^2 C_b$
$L_3 = R_g^2 C_c$

13.7 Circulator

A circulator is a circuit with three or more terminals, the graphic symbol for which is shown in Fig. 13.33. It has the characteristic that a signal applied to one

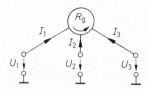

Fig. 13.33 Symbol for a circulator

of the terminals is transferred in the direction of the arrow. If a terminal is open, the signal passes unchanged, whereas at a short-circuited terminal the polarity of the signal voltage is inverted. If a resistor $R = R_g$ is connected between one terminal and ground, the signal voltage appears across this resistor and will, in this case, not be passed on to the next terminal.

A circuit having these properties is shown in Fig. 13.34 [13.5]. It can be seen that it consists of three identical stages, one of which is shown again in Fig. 13.35. The operation of the individual stage is examined below; several cases can be distinguished:

If terminal 1 is left open, $I_1 = 0$ and $V_P = U_i = V_N$. Hence, no current flows through the feedback resistor, and $U_o = U_i$.

If terminal 1 is short-circuited, $U_1 = 0$, and the circuit acts as an inverting amplifier with unity gain. In this case, we obtain the output voltage $U_o = - U_i$.

If a resistor $R_1 = R_g$ is connected to terminal 1, the circuit operates as a subtracting amplifier for two equal input voltages U_i, and the voltage U_o is therefore zero.

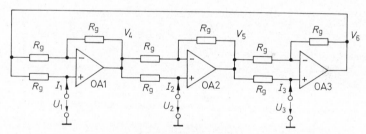

Fig. 13.34 A possible implementation of a circulator

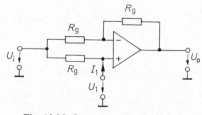

Fig. 13.35 One stage of a circulator

If U_i is made zero and a voltage U_1 applied to terminal 1, the circuit behaves like a non-inverting amplifier having the gain 2, and we obtain the output voltage $U_o = 2U_1$.

From these characteristics, the operation of the circuit in Fig. 13.34 can be easily understood. Let us assume that voltage U_1 is applied to terminal 1, that a resistor R_g is connected between terminal 2 and ground, and that terminal 3 is left open. We already know that the output voltage of OA 2 becomes zero. OA 3 has unity gain because of the open terminal 3 and its output voltage is therefore also zero. OA 1 consequently operates as a non-inverting amplifier with gain 2, so that its output voltage is $2U_1$. Half this voltage (U_1) appears at terminal 2 since this is terminated in R_g. Other special cases can be analyzed in an identical manner.

If a more general case is to be considered, the transfer characteristics of the circulator are used to determine the properties of the circuit. For this purpose we apply KCL to the P-inputs and N-inputs:

<table>
<tr><td align="center">P-inputs</td><td align="center">N-inputs</td></tr>
<tr><td align="center">$$\frac{V_6 - U_1}{R_g} + I_1 = 0$$</td><td align="center">$$\frac{V_6 - U_1}{R_g} + \frac{V_4 - U_1}{R_g} = 0$$</td></tr>
<tr><td align="center">$$\frac{V_4 - U_2}{R_g} + I_2 = 0$$</td><td align="center">$$\frac{V_4 - U_2}{R_g} + \frac{V_5 - U_2}{R_g} = 0$$</td></tr>
<tr><td align="center">$$\frac{V_5 - U_3}{R_g} + I_3 = 0$$</td><td align="center">$$\frac{V_5 - U_3}{R_g} + \frac{V_6 - U_3}{R_g} = 0.$$</td></tr>
</table>

Eliminating V_4 to V_6, the transfer characteristics become

$$I_1 = \frac{1}{R_g}(U_2 - U_3) \, ,$$

$$I_2 = \frac{1}{R_g}(-U_1 + U_3) \, , \tag{13.24}$$

$$I_3 = \frac{1}{R_g}(U_1 - U_2) \, .$$

It is obvious from Eq. (13.24) that a circulator can also be implemented by three voltage-controlled current sources with differential input, as shown in Fig. 13.36. A current source suitable for this purpose is shown in Fig. 13.17.

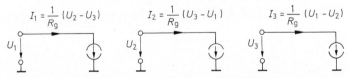

$$I_1 = \frac{1}{R_g}(U_2 - U_3) \qquad I_2 = \frac{1}{R_g}(U_3 - U_1) \qquad I_3 = \frac{1}{R_g}(U_1 - U_2)$$

Fig. 13.36 Circulator composed of voltage-controlled current sources

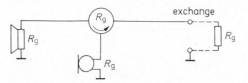

Fig. 13.37 Circulator used as a telephone hybrid set

Figure 13.37 shows a circulator employed as an active hybrid set for telephone circuits. It consists of a circulator having three ports all of which are terminated in the transfer resistance R_g. The signal from the microphone is relayed to the exchange and does not reach the receiver. The signal from the exchange is transferred to the receiver but not to the microphone. The cross-talk attenuation is largely determined by the degree to which the terminating resistances are matched.

14 Active filters

14.1 Basic theory of lowpass filters

Simple lowpass and highpass filters were discussed in Sections 2.1 and 2.2, the circuit of the simplest lowpass filter being shown again in Fig. 14.1. The ratio of output voltage to input voltage can be expressed from Eq. (2.1) as

$$\underline{A}(j\omega) = \frac{\underline{U}_o}{\underline{U}_i} = \frac{1}{1 + j\omega RC} \; ,$$

and is called the frequency response of the circuit. Replacing $j\omega$ by $j\omega + \sigma = s$ gives the transfer function

$$A(s) = \frac{L\{U_o(t)\}}{L\{U_i(t)\}} = \frac{1}{1 + sRC} \; .$$

This is the ratio of the Laplace transformed output and input voltages for signals of any time dependence. On the other hand, the transition from the transfer function $A(s)$ to the frequency response $\underline{A}(j\omega)$ for sinusoidal input signals is made by setting σ to zero.

In order to present the problem in a more general form, it is useful to normalize the complex frequency variable s by defining

$$S = \frac{s}{\omega_c} \; .$$

Hence, for $\sigma = 0$,

$$S = \frac{j\omega}{\omega_c} = j\frac{f}{f_c} = j\Omega \; .$$

The circuit in Fig. 14.1 has the cutoff frequency $f_c = 1/2\pi RC$. Therefore, $S = sRC$ and

$$A(S) = \frac{1}{1 + S} \; . \tag{14.1}$$

For the absolute value of the transfer function, i.e. for the amplitude ratio with sinusoidal input signals, we obtain

$$|\underline{A}(j\Omega)|^2 = \frac{1}{1 + \Omega^2} \; .$$

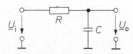

Fig. 14.1 Simplest passive lowpass filter

If $\Omega \gg 1$, i.e. $f \gg f_c$, then $|\underline{A}| = 1/\Omega$; this corresponds to a reduction in gain of 20 dB per frequency decade.

If a steeper decrease in gain is required, n lowpass filters can be connected in series. The transfer function is then expressed in the form

$$A(S) = \frac{1}{(1 + \alpha_1 S)(1 + \alpha_2 S) \ldots (1 + \alpha_n S)} \, , \qquad (14.2)$$

where the coefficients $\alpha_1, \alpha_2, \alpha_3 \ldots$ are real and positive. For $\Omega \gg 1$, $|\underline{A}|$ is proportional to $1/\Omega^n$; the gain therefore falls off at $n \cdot 20$ dB per decade. It can be seen that the transfer function possesses n real negative poles. This is characteristic of n-th order passive RC lowpass filters. If decoupled lowpass filters of identical cutoff frequencies are cascaded, then

$$\alpha_1 = \alpha_2 = \alpha_3 = \cdots = \alpha = \sqrt{\sqrt[n]{2} - 1} \, ,$$

this being the condition for which critical damping occurs. Each individual lowpass filter then has a cutoff frequency a factor $1/\alpha$ higher than that of the filter as a whole.

The transfer function of a lowpass filter has the general form

$$A(S) = \frac{A_0}{1 + c_1 S + c_2 S^2 + \cdots + c_n S^n} \, , \qquad (14.3)$$

where $c_1, c_2 \ldots c_n$ are positive and real. The order of the filter is equal to the highest power of S. It is advantageous for filter design if the denominator polynomial is written in factored form. If complex poles are also permitted, a separation into linear factors as in Eq. (14.2) is no longer possible, and a product of quadratic expressions is obtained:

$$A(S) = \frac{A_0}{(1 + a_1 S + b_1 S^2)(1 + a_2 S + b_2 S^2) \ldots} \, , \qquad (14.4)$$

where a_i and b_i are positive and real. For odd orders n, the coefficient b_1 is zero.

There are several different theoretical aspects with respect to which the frequency response can be optimized. Any such aspect leads to a different set of coefficients a_i and b_i. As will be seen, conjugate complex poles arise. They cannot be realized by passive RC elements, as comparison with Eq. (14.2) shows. One way of implementing conjugate complex poles is to use LRC networks. For high frequencies, the design of the necessary inductances usually presents no difficulties, but in the low frequency range, large inductances are often required. These are unwieldy and have poor electrical properties. However, the use of inductances at low frequencies can be avoided by the addition of active elements (e.g. operational amplifiers) to the RC network. Such circuits are called active filters.

Let us first compare the most important optimized frequency responses, the technical realizations of which are discussed in the following sections.

Butterworth lowpass filters have an amplitude-frequency response which is flat for as long as possible and falls off sharply just before the cutoff frequency.

Their step response shows a considerable overshoot which increases for higher-order filters.

Chebyshev lowpass filters have an even steeper roll-off above the cutoff frequency. In the passband, however, the gain varies and has a ripple of constant amplitude. For a given order, the decrease above the cutoff frequency is steeper the larger the permitted ripple. The overshoot in the step response is even greater than for the Butterworth filters.

Bessel lowpass filters have the optimum square-wave response. The prerequisite for this is that the group delay is constant over the largest possible frequency range, i.e. that the phase shift in this frequency range is proportional to the frequency. The amplitude-frequency response of Bessel filters does not fall off as sharply as that of Butterworth or Chebyshev filters.

Figure 14.2 shows the amplitude-frequency responses of the four described filter types for the orders 4 and 10. It can be seen that the Chebyshev lowpass filter has the most abrupt transition from the passband to the stopband. This is advantageous but has the side effect of a ripple in the amplitude-frequency response in the passband. As this ripple is gradually reduced, the behavior of the

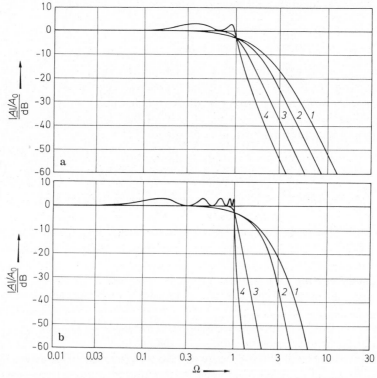

Fig. 14.2a and b Comparison of the amplitude-frequency response for different filter types. (a) Fourth order. (b) Tenth order.
Curve *1*: Lowpass filter with critical damping. Curve *2*: Bessel lowpass filter. Curve *3*: Butterworth lowpass filter. Curve *4*: Chebyshev lowpass filter with 3 dB ripple

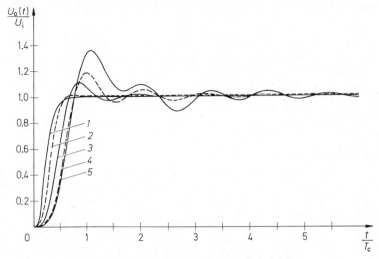

Fig. 14.3 Step response of fourth-order lowpass filters.
Curve *1*: Lowpass filter with critical damping. Curve *2*: Bessel lowpass filter. Curve *3*: Butterworth lowpass filter. Curve *4*: Chebyshev lowpass filter with 0.5 dB ripple. Curve *5*: Chebyshev lowpass filter with 3 dB ripple. $T_c = 1/f_c$

Chebyshev filter approaches that of a Butterworth filter [14.1]. Both kinds of filter show a considerable overshoot in the step response, as is seen in Fig. 14.3. Bessel filters, on the other hand, have only negligible overshoot. Despite their unfavorable amplitude-frequency response they will always be used where a good step response is important. A passive *RC* lowpass filter exhibits no overshoot; however, the relatively small improvement over the Bessel filter involves a considerable deterioration in the amplitude-frequency response. In addition, the corners in the step response are much rounder than for the Bessel filter. The table in Fig. 14.4 compares the rise times, delay times and the overshoots. The rise time is the time in which the output signal rises from 10% to 90% of its final-state value. The delay time is that in which the output signal increases from 0 to 50% of the final-state value.

It can be seen that the rise time does not depend to any great extent on the order nor the type of the filter. Its value is approximately $1/3f_c$, as shown in Section 2.1.3. On the other hand, the delay time and overshoot increase, the higher the order. The Bessel filters are an exception in that the overshoot decreases for orders higher than 4.

It will be seen later that a single circuit is sufficient to implement any of these filter types for a particular order; the values of resistances and capacitances determine the type of filter. In order that the circuit parameters can be defined, the frequency response of the individual filter types must be known for each order. We shall therefore discuss these in more detail in the following sections.

	Order				
	2	4	6	8	10
Critical damping					
Normalized rise time t_r/T_c	0.344	0.342	0.341	0.341	0.340
Normalized delay time t_d/T_c	0.172	0.254	0.316	0.367	0.412
Overshoot %	0	0	0	0	0
Bessel					
Normalized rise time t_r/T_c	0.344	0.352	0.350	0.347	0.345
Normalized delay time t_d/T_c	0.195	0.329	0.428	0.505	0.574
Overshoot %	0.43	0.84	0.64	0.34	0.06
Butterworth					
Formalized rise time t_r/T_c	0.342	0.387	0.427	0.460	0.485
Normalized delay time t_d/T_c	0.228	0.449	0.663	0.874	1.084
Overshoot %	4.3	10.8	14.3	16.3	17.8
Chebyshev, 0.5 dB ripple					
Normalized rise time t_r/T_c	0.338	0.421	0.487	0.540	0.584
Normalized delay time t_d/T_c	0.251	0.556	0.875	1.196	1.518
Overshoot %	10.7	18.1	21.2	22.9	24.1
Chebyshev, 1 dB ripple					
Normalized rise time t_r/T_c	0.334	0.421	0.486	0.537	0.582
Normalized delay time t_d/T_c	0.260	0.572	0.893	1.215	1.540
Overshoot %	14.6	21.6	24.9	26.6	27.8
Chebyshev, 2 dB ripple					
Normalized rise time t_r/T_c	0.326	0.414	0.491	0.529	0.570
Normalized delay time t_d/T_c	0.267	0.584	0.912	1.231	1.555
Overshoot %	21.2	28.9	32.0	33.5	34.7
Chebyshev, 3 dB ripple					
Normalized rise time t_r/T_c	0.318	0.407	0.470	0.519	0.692
Normalized delay time t_d/T_c	0.271	0.590	0.912	1.235	1.557
Overshoot %	27.2	35.7	38.7	40.6	41.6

Fig. 14.4 Comparison of lowpass filters. Rise time and delay time are normalized to the reciprocal cutoff frequency $T_c = 1/f_c$

14.1.1   Butterworth lowpass filters

From Eq. (14.3), the absolute value of the gain of an n-th order lowpass filter has the general form

$$|\underline{A}|^2 = \frac{A_0^2}{1 + k_2\Omega^2 + k_4\Omega^4 + \cdots + k_{2n}\Omega^{2n}} .$$ (14.5)

Odd powers of Ω do not occur since the square of $|\underline{A}|$ must be an even function.

Below the cutoff frequency of the Butterworth lowpass filter, the function $|\underline{A}|^2$ must be maximally flat. Since for this range $\Omega < 1$, this condition is best fulfilled if $|\underline{A}|^2$ is dependent only on the highest power of Ω. The reason for this is that for $\Omega < 1$, the lower powers of Ω contribute most to the denominator and therefore to the fall-off in gain. Hence,

$$|\underline{A}|^2 = \frac{A_0^2}{1 + k_{2n}\Omega^{2n}} .$$

The coefficient k_{2n} is defined by the "normalizing condition", namely, that the gain at $\Omega = 1$ is reduced by 3 dB. Thus

$$\frac{A_0^2}{2} = \frac{A_0^2}{1 + k_{2n}} ,$$

$$k_{2n} = 1 .$$

Therefore, the square of the gain of n-th order Butterworth lowpass filters is given by

$$|\underline{A}|^2 = \frac{A_0^2}{1 + \Omega^{2n}} . \tag{14.6}$$

To implement a Butterworth lowpass filter, a circuit must be designed in which the square of the gain has the form given above. However, the circuit analysis initially gives the complex gain $\underline{A}$, and not the gain squared, $|\underline{A}|^2$. It is therefore necessary to know the complex gain involved in Eq. (14.6). This is found by calculating the absolute value of Eq. (14.3) and by comparing the coefficients with those of Eq. (14.6). In this way, the desired coefficients $c_1 \ldots c_n$ can be defined. The denominators of Eq. (14.3) are then the Butterworth polynomials, the first four orders of which are shown in Fig. 14.5.

n	
1	$1 + S$
2	$1 + \sqrt{2}S + S^2$
3	$1 + 2S + 2S^2 + S^3 = (1 + S)(1 + S + S^2)$
4	$1 + 2.613S + 3.414S^2 + 2.613S^3 + S^4 = (1 + 1.848S + S^2)(1 + 0.765S + S^2)$

Fig. 14.5 Butterworth polynomials

According to reference [14.2], it is possible to determine analytically the poles of the transfer function. By combining the conjugate complex poles, we immediately obtain the coefficients, a_i and b_i of the quadratic expressions in Eq. (14.4):

even order n:

$$a_i = 2\cos\frac{(2i - 1)\pi}{2n} \quad \text{for } i = 1 \ldots \frac{n}{2} ,$$

$$b_i = 1 ,$$

odd order n:

$$a_1 = 1 \; ,$$

$$b_1 = 0$$

and

$$a_i = 2\cos\frac{(i-1)\pi}{n} \quad \text{for } i = 2 \ldots \frac{n+1}{2} \; ,$$

$$b_i = 1 \; .$$

The coefficients of the Butterworth polynomials up to the order 10 are shown in Fig. 14.4.

It can be seen that the first-order Butterworth lowpass filter is a passive lowpass filter having the transfer function of Eq. (14.1). The higher Butterworth polynomials possess conjugate complex zeros. Comparison with Eq. (14.2) shows that such denominator polynomials cannot be implemented by passive RC networks, because in the case of the latter, all the zeros are real. In such cases, the only choice is to use LRC circuits with all their disadvantages, or active RC filters. The frequency response of the gain is shown in Fig. 14.6.

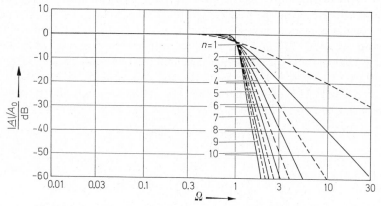

Fig. 14.6 Amplitude-frequency response of Butterworth lowpass filters

14.1.2   Chebyshev lowpass filters

At low frequencies, the gain of a Chebyshev lowpass filter has the value A_0, but varies below the cutoff frequency, having a predetermined ripple. Polynomials which have a constant ripple within a defined range (equal ripple) are the Chebyshev polynomials

$$T_n(x) = \begin{cases} \cos(n\arccos x) & \text{for} \quad 0 \leq x \leq 1 \\ \cosh(n\,\mathrm{Arcosh}\,x) & \text{for} \quad x > 1 \; , \end{cases}$$

the first four of which are shown in Fig. 14.7. For $0 \leq x \leq 1$, $|T(x)|$ oscillates

n	
1	$T_1(x) = x$
2	$T_2(x) = 2x^2 - 1$
3	$T_3(x) = 4x^3 - 3x$
4	$T_4(x) = 8x^4 - 8x^2 + 1$

Fig. 14.7 Chebyshev polynomials

between 0 and 1; for $x > 1$, $T(x)$ rises steadily. In order to obtain the equation of a lowpass filter from the Chebyshev polynomials, one defines

$$|\underline{A}|^2 = \frac{kA_0^2}{1 + \varepsilon^2 T_n^2(x)} \ . \tag{14.7}$$

The constant k is chosen such that for $x = 0$ the square of the gain $|\underline{A}|^2$ becomes A_0^2, i.e. $k = 1$ for odd n and $k = 1 + \varepsilon^2$ for even n. The factor ε is a measure of the ripple and is given by

$$\frac{A_{max}}{A_{min}} = \sqrt{1 + \varepsilon^2}$$

and

$$\left.\begin{array}{l} A_{max} = A_0\sqrt{1 + \varepsilon^2} \\ A_{min} = A_0 \end{array}\right\} \quad \text{for even orders}$$

and

$$\left.\begin{array}{l} A_{max} = A_0 \\ A_{min} = A_0/\sqrt{1 + \varepsilon^2} \end{array}\right\} \quad \text{for odd orders .}$$

In Fig. 14.8, the appropriate values are listed for different ripples. In principle, the complex gain can be calculated from $|\underline{A}|^2$ and hence the coefficients of the factored form can be determined. However, as shown in [14.3], it is possible to derive the poles of the transfer function directly from those of the Butterworth filters. By combining the conjugate complex poles, the coefficients a_i and b_i in

	Ripple			
	0.5 dB	1 dB	2 dB	3 dB
A_{max}/A_{min}	1.059	1.122	1.259	1.413
k	1.122	1.259	1.585	1.995
ε	0.349	0.509	0.765	0.998

Fig. 14.8 Comparison of some Chebyshev parameters

Eq. (14.4) are determined as follows:

even order n:

$$b_i' = \cfrac{1}{\cosh^2\gamma - \cos^2\dfrac{(2i - 1)\pi}{2n}}$$

$$a_i' = 2b_i' \cdot \sinh\gamma \cdot \cos\frac{(2i - 1)\pi}{2n} \quad \Bigg\} \quad \text{for } i = 1 \ldots \frac{n}{2} \,,$$

odd order n:

$$b_1' = 0 \,,$$

$$a_1' = 1/\sinh\gamma \,,$$

$$b_i' = \cfrac{1}{\cosh^2\gamma - \cos^2\dfrac{(i - 1)\pi}{n}}$$

$$a_i' = 2b_i' \cdot \sinh\gamma \cdot \cos\frac{(i - 1)\pi}{n} \quad \Bigg\} \quad \text{for } i = 2 \ldots \frac{n + 1}{2} \,,$$

where $\gamma = \dfrac{1}{n} \operatorname{Arsinh} \dfrac{1}{\varepsilon}$.

If the coefficients a_i' and b_i' found in this way replace a_i and b_i in Eq. (14.4), Chebyshev filters are obtained. However, S is then not normalized with respect to the 3 dB cutoff frequency ω_c, but rather to the frequency $\omega_{c\,min}$ at which the gain assumes the value A_{min} for the last time.

For an easy comparison of the different filter types, it is useful to normalize S to the 3 dB cutoff frequency. The variable S is replaced by αS and the normalizing constant α is determined such that the gain, for $S = j$, has the value $1/\sqrt{2}$. The quadratic expressions in the denominator of the complex gain are then

$$(1 + a_i'\alpha S + b_i'\alpha^2 S^2) \,.$$

Hence, by comparing the coefficients with those of Eq. (14.4):

$$a_i = \alpha a_i' \quad \text{and} \quad b_i = \alpha^2 b_i' \,.$$

The coefficients a_i and b_i are shown in the table of Fig. 14.14 up to the tenth order, and for ripple values of 0.5, 1, 2 and 3 dB. The frequency response of the gain is shown in Fig. 14.9 for ripple values of 0.5 and 3 dB. Figure 14.10 makes possible a direct comparison of fourth-order Chebyshev filters having different amounts of ripple. It can be seen that the differences in the frequency response in the stopband are very small, and that they become even smaller for higher orders. It is also obvious that even the Chebyshev filter response having the small ripple of 0.5 dB emerges from the passband much more steeply than that of the Butterworth filter.

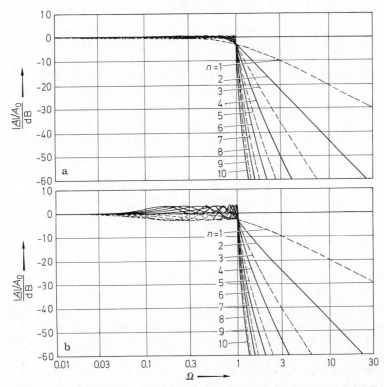

Fig. 14.9a and b Amplitude-frequency response of Chebyshev lowpass filters. (a) 0.5 dB ripple. (b) 3 dB ripple

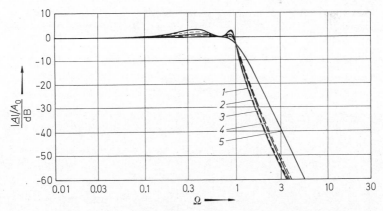

Fig. 14.10 Comparison of fourth-order Chebyshev lowpass filters. Ripple: Curve *1*: 3 dB. Curve *2*: 2 dB. Curve *3*: 1 dB. Curve *4*: 0.5 dB. Curve *5*: Fourth-order Butterworth lowpass filter for comparison

The transition from the passband to the stopband can be made even steeper. To accomplish this, zeros are introduced into the amplitude-frequency response above the cutoff frequency. One way of optimizing the design is to give the amplitude-frequency response a constant ripple in the stopband also. Such filters are called *Cauer filters*. The transfer function differs from the ordinary lowpass filter equation in that the numerator is a polynomial, instead of the constant A_0. For this reason, the "steepened" lowpass filters cannot be designed with the simple circuits of Section 14.4. However, in Section 14.11 we discuss a universal filter with which any numerator polynomial can be implemented. The coefficients of the Cauer polynomials can be found in the tables of reference [14.4].

14.1.3   Bessel lowpass filters

As previously shown, Butterworth and Chebyshev lowpass filters have a considerable overshoot in their step response. An ideal square-wave response is achieved by filters having frequency-independent group delay, i.e. having a phase shift proportional to frequency. This behavior is best approximated by Bessel filters, sometimes also called Thomson filters. The approximation consists of selecting the coefficients such that the group delay below the cutoff frequency $\Omega = 1$ is dependent as little as possible on Ω. This procedure is equivalent to a Butterworth approximation of the group delay, i.e. the optimization of a maximally flat group delay.

From Eq. (14.4), with $S = j\Omega$, the gain of a second-order lowpass filter is given by

$$\underline{A} = \frac{A_0}{1 + a_1 S + b_1 S^2} = \frac{A_0}{1 + ja_1 \Omega - b_1 \Omega^2} \, .$$

Therefore the phase shift is

$$\varphi = - \arctan \frac{a_1 \Omega}{1 - b_1 \Omega^2} \, . \tag{14.8}$$

The group delay is defined as

$$t_{\text{gr}} = - \frac{\mathrm{d}\varphi}{\mathrm{d}\omega} \, .$$

To simplify further calculations, we introduce the normalized group delay

$$T_{\text{gr}} = \frac{t_{\text{gr}}}{T_{\text{c}}} = t_{\text{gr}} \cdot f_{\text{c}} = \frac{1}{2\pi} t_{\text{gr}} \cdot \omega_{\text{c}} \, , \tag{14.9a}$$

where T_{c} is the reciprocal of the cutoff frequency. We thus obtain

$$T_{\text{gr}} = - \frac{\omega_{\text{c}}}{2\pi} \cdot \frac{\mathrm{d}\varphi}{\mathrm{d}\omega} = - \frac{1}{2\pi} \cdot \frac{\mathrm{d}\varphi}{\mathrm{d}\omega} \tag{14.9b}$$

and with Eq. (14.8)

$$T_{gr} = \frac{1}{2\pi} \cdot \frac{a_1(1 + b_1\Omega^2)}{1 + (a_1^2 - 2b_1)\Omega^2 + b_1^2\Omega^4} \cdot \qquad (14.9c)$$

In order to find the Butterworth approximation of the group delay, we use the fact that, for $\Omega \ll 1$,

$$T_{gr} = \frac{a_1}{2\pi} \cdot \frac{1 + b_1\Omega^2}{1 + (a_1^2 - 2b_1)\Omega^2} \quad \text{for } \Omega \ll 1 \; .$$

This expression becomes independent of Ω if the coefficients of Ω^2 in the numerator and denominator are identical. The condition for this is that

$$b_1 = a_1^2 - 2b_1$$

or   (14.10)

$$b_1 = \tfrac{1}{3}a_1^2 \; .$$

A second relationship is derived from the normalizing condition, $|\underline{A}|^2 = \tfrac{1}{2}$ for $\Omega = 1$:

$$\frac{1}{2} = \frac{1}{(1 - b_1)^2 + a_1^2} \; .$$

Hence, with Eq. (14.10)

$$a_1 = 1.3617 \; ,$$

$$b_1 = 0.6180 \; .$$

For higher filter orders, a corresponding calculation becomes very involved since a system of non-linear equations arises. Using a different concept [14.5], however, it is possible to define the coefficients c_i in Eq. (14.3) by a recursion formula

$$c_1' = 1 \; ,$$

$$c_i' = \frac{2(n - i + 1)}{i(2n - i + 1)} c_{i-1}' \; .$$

The denominators of Eq. (14.3) obtained in such a way are the Bessel polynomials, and are shown in Fig. 14.11 up to the fourth order. However, it should be noted that, in this representation, the frequency S is not normalized with

n	
1	$1 + S$
2	$1 + S + \tfrac{1}{3}S^2$
3	$1 + S + \tfrac{2}{5}S^2 + \tfrac{1}{15}S^3$
4	$1 + S + \tfrac{3}{7}S^2 + \tfrac{2}{21}S^3 + \tfrac{1}{105}S^4$

Fig. 14.11 Bessel polynomials

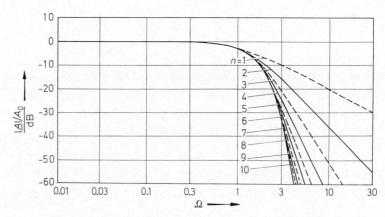

Fig. 14.12 Amplitude-frequency response of Bessel lowpass filters

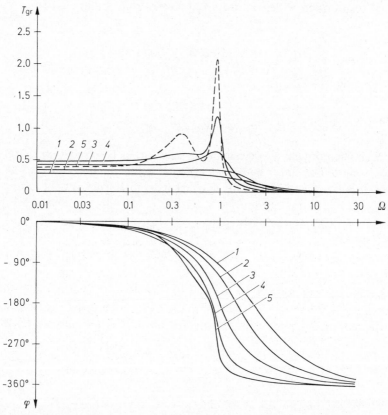

Fig. 14.13 Comparison of the frequency response of the group delay and phase shift of fourth-order filters.
Curve *1*: Lowpass filter with critical damping. Curve *2*: Bessel lowpass filter. Curve *3*: Butterworth lowpass filter. Curve *4*: Chebyshev lowpass filter with 0.5 dB ripple. Curve *5*: Chebyshev lowpass filter with 3 dB ripple

respect to the 3 dB cutoff frequency, but to the reciprocal of the group delay for $\Omega = 0$. However, this is of little use for the design of lowpass filters. We have therefore recalculated the coefficients c_i for the 3 dB cutoff frequency, as in the previous section, and in addition have broken down the denominator into quadratic expressions. The coefficients a_i and b_i of Eq. (14.4) thus obtained are listed in Fig. 14.14 for up to the tenth order. The frequency response of the gain is plotted in Fig. 14.12.

In order to demonstrate the amount of phase distortion of other filters in comparison with the Bessel filters, we have illustrated in Fig. 14.13 the frequency response of the phase shift and of the group delay for fourth-order filters. These curves can best be calculated from the factored transfer function in Eq. (14.4) by adding together the phase shifts of each individual second-order filter stage and by adding the individual group delays. For a filter of a given order, the following relations are derived from Eqs. (14.8) and (14.9c):

$$\varphi = - \sum_i \arctan \frac{a_i \Omega}{1 - b_i \Omega^2}$$

and

$$T_{gr} = \frac{1}{2\pi} \sum_i \frac{a_i(1 + b_i \Omega^2)}{1 + (a_i^2 - 2b_i)\Omega^2 + b_i^2 \Omega^4} \ .$$

14.1.4   Summary of theory

We have seen that the transfer functions of all lowpass filters have the form

$$A(S) = \frac{A_0}{\prod_i (1 + a_i S + b_i S^2)} \ . \tag{14.11}$$

The order n of the filter is determined by the highest power of S in Eq. (14.11) when the denominator is multiplied out. It defines the slope of the asymptote of the amplitude-frequency response as having the value $- n \cdot 20$ dB/decade. The rest of the amplitude-frequency response curve for a particular order is determined by the type of filter. Of special interest are the Butterworth, Chebyshev and Bessel filters which all have different values for the coefficients a_i and b_i in Eq. (14.11). The values of the coefficients are summarized in Fig. 14.14 for up to the tenth order. In addition, the 3 dB cutoff frequency of each individual filter stage is indicated by the ratio f_{ci}/f_c. Although this value is not needed for the design, it is useful for checking the correct operation of the individual filter stages.

Also listed are the pole-pair quality factors Q_i of the individual filter stages. In analogy to the Q-factors of the bandpass filters in Section 14.6.1, they are defined as

$$Q_i = \frac{\sqrt{b_i}}{a_i} \ .$$

n	i	a_i	b_i	f_{ci}/f_c	Q_i
Critically damped filters					
1	1	1.0000	0.0000	1.000	–
2	1	1.2872	0.4142	1.000	0.50
3	1	0.5098	0.0000	1.961	–
	2	1.0197	0.2599	1.262	0.50
4	1	0.8700	0.1892	1.480	0.50
	2	0.8700	0.1892	1.480	0.50
5	1	0.3856	0.0000	2.593	–
	2	0.7712	0.1487	1.669	0.50
	3	0.7712	0.1487	1.669	0.50
6	1	0.6999	0.1225	1.839	0.50
	2	0.6999	0.1225	1.839	0.50
	3	0.6999	0.1225	1.839	0.50
7	1	0.3226	0.0000	3.100	–
	2	0.6453	0.1041	1.995	0.50
	3	0.6453	0.1041	1.995	0.50
	4	0.6453	0.1041	1.995	0.50
8	1	0.6017	0.0905	2.139	0.50
	2	0.6017	0.0905	2.139	0.50
	3	0.6017	0.0905	2.139	0.50
	4	0.6017	0.0905	2.139	0.50
9	1	0.2829	0.0000	3.534	–
	2	0.5659	0.0801	2.275	0.50
	3	0.5659	0.0801	2.275	0.50
	4	0.5659	0.0801	2.275	0.50
	5	0.5659	0.0801	2.275	0.50
10	1	0.5358	0.0718	2.402	0.50
	2	0.5358	0.0718	2.402	0.50
	3	0.5358	0.0718	2.402	0.50
	4	0.5358	0.0718	2.402	0.50
	5	0.5358	0.0718	2.402	0.50
Bessel filters					
1	1	1.0000	0.0000	1.000	–
2	1	1.3617	0.6180	1.000	0.58
3	1	0.7560	0.0000	1.323	–
	2	0.9996	0.4772	1.414	0.69
4	1	1.3397	0.4889	0.978	0.52
	2	0.7743	0.3890	1.797	0.81
5	1	0.6656	0.0000	1.502	–
	2	1.1402	0.4128	1.184	0.56
	3	0.6216	0.3245	2.138	0.92

Fig. 14.14 Coefficients of the individual filter types

n	i	a_i	b_i	f_{ci}/f_c	Q_i
6	1	1.2217	0.3887	1.063	0.51
	2	0.9686	0.3505	1.431	0.61
	3	0.5131	0.2756	2.447	1.02
7	1	0.5937	0.0000	1.684	–
	2	1.0944	0.3395	1.207	0.53
	3	0.8304	0.3011	1.695	0.66
	4	0.4332	0.2381	2.731	1.13
8	1	1.1112	0.3162	1.164	0.51
	2	0.9754	0.2979	1.381	0.56
	3	0.7202	0.2621	1.963	0.71
	4	0.3728	0.2087	2.992	1.23
9	1	0.5386	0.0000	1.857	–
	2	1.0244	0.2834	1.277	0.52
	3	0.8710	0.2636	1.574	0.59
	4	0.6320	0.2311	2.226	0.76
	5	0.3257	0.1854	3.237	1.32
10	1	1.0215	0.2650	1.264	0.50
	2	0.9393	0.2549	1.412	0.54
	3	0.7815	0.2351	1.780	0.62
	4	0.5604	0.2059	2.479	0.81
	5	0.2883	0.1665	3.446	1.42

Butterworth filters

n	i	a_i	b_i	f_{ci}/f_c	Q_i
1	1	1.0000	0.0000	1.000	–
2	1	1.4142	1.0000	1.000	0.71
3	1	1.0000	0.0000	1.000	–
	2	1.0000	1.0000	1.272	1.00
4	1	1.8478	1.0000	0.719	0.54
	2	0.7654	1.0000	1.390	1.31
5	1	1.0000	0.0000	1.000	–
	2	1.6180	1.0000	0.859	0.62
	3	0.6180	1.0000	1.448	1.62
6	1	1.9319	1.0000	0.676	0.52
	2	1.4142	1.0000	1.000	0.71
	3	0.5176	1.0000	1.479	1.93
7	1	1.0000	0.0000	1.000	–
	2	1.8019	1.0000	0.745	0.55
	3	1.2470	1.0000	1.117	0.80
	4	0.4450	1.0000	1.499	2.25
8	1	1.9616	1.0000	0.661	0.51
	2	1.6629	1.0000	0.829	0.60
	3	1.1111	1.0000	1.206	0.90
	4	0.3902	1.0000	1.512	2.56

Fig. 14.14 (*continued*)

n	i	a_i	b_i	f_{ci}/f_c	Q_i
9	1	1.0000	0.0000	1.000	–
	2	1.8794	1.0000	0.703	0.53
	3	1.5321	1.0000	0.917	0.65
	4	1.0000	1.0000	1.272	1.00
	5	0.3473	1.0000	1.521	2.88
10	1	1.9754	1.0000	0.655	0.51
	2	1.7820	1.0000	0.756	0.56
	3	1.4142	1.0000	1.000	0.71
	4	0.9080	1.0000	1.322	1.10
	5	0.3129	1.0000	1.527	3.20

Chebyshev filters, 0.5 dB ripple

n	i	a_i	b_i	f_{ci}/f_c	Q_i
1	1	1.0000	0.0000	1.000	–
2	1	1.3614	1.3827	1.000	0.86
3	1	1.8636	0.0000	0.537	–
	2	0.6402	1.1931	1.335	1.71
4	1	2.6282	3.4341	0.538	0.71
	2	0.3648	1.1509	1.419	2.94
5	1	2.9235	0.0000	0.342	–
	2	1.3025	2.3534	0.881	1.18
	3	0.2290	1.0833	1.480	4.54
6	1	3.8645	6.9797	0.366	0.68
	2	0.7528	1.8573	1.078	1.81
	3	0.1589	1.0711	1.495	6.51
7	1	4.0211	0.0000	0.249	–
	2	1.8729	4.1795	0.645	1.09
	3	0.4861	1.5676	1.208	2.58
	4	0.1156	1.0443	1.517	8.84
8	1	5.1117	11.9607	0.276	0.68
	2	1.0639	2.9365	0.844	1.61
	3	0.3439	1.4206	1.284	3.47
	4	0.0885	1.0407	1.521	11.53
9	1	5.1318	0.0000	0.195	–
	2	2.4283	6.6307	0.506	1.06
	3	0.6839	2.2908	0.989	2.21
	4	0.2559	1.3133	1.344	4.48
	5	0.0695	1.0272	1.532	14.58
10	1	6.3648	18.3695	0.222	0.67
	2	1.3582	4.3453	0.689	1.53
	3	0.4822	1.9440	1.091	2.89
	4	0.1994	1.2520	1.381	5.61
	5	0.0563	1.0263	1.533	17.99

Fig. 14.14 (*continued*)

n	i	a_i	b_i	f_{ci}/f_c	Q_i
Chebyshev filters, 1 dB ripple					
1	1	1.0000	0.0000	1.000	–
2	1	1.3022	1.5515	1.000	0.96
3	1	2.2156	0.0000	0.451	–
	2	0.5442	1.2057	1.353	2.02
4	1	2.5904	4.1301	0.540	0.78
	2	0.3039	1.1697	1.417	3.56
5	1	3.5711	0.0000	0.280	–
	2	1.1280	2.4896	0.894	1.40
	3	0.1872	1.0814	1.486	5.56
6	1	3.8437	8.5529	0.366	0.76
	2	0.6292	1.9124	1.082	2.20
	3	0.1296	1.0766	1.493	8.00
7	1	4.9520	0.0000	0.202	–
	2	1.6338	4.4899	0.655	1.30
	3	0.3987	1.5834	1.213	3.16
	4	0.0937	1.0423	1.520	10.90
8	1	5.1019	14.7608	0.276	0.75
	2	0.8916	3.0426	0.849	1.96
	3	0.2806	1.4334	1.285	4.27
	4	0.0717	1.0432	1.520	14.24
9	1	6.3415	0.0000	0.158	–
	2	2.1252	7.1711	0.514	1.26
	3	0.5624	2.3278	0.994	2.71
	4	0.2076	1.3166	1.346	5.53
	5	0.0562	1.0258	1.533	18.03
10	1	6.3634	22.7468	0.221	0.75
	2	1.1399	4.5167	0.694	1.86
	3	0.3939	1.9665	1.093	3.56
	4	0.1616	1.2569	1.381	6.94
	5	0.0455	1.0277	1.532	22.26
Chebyshev filters, 2 dB ripple					
1	1	1.0000	0.0000	1.000	–
2	1	1.1813	1.7775	1.000	1.13
3	1	2.7994	0.0000	0.357	–
	2	0.4300	1.2036	1.378	2.55
4	1	2.4025	4.9862	0.550	0.93
	2	0.2374	1.1896	1.413	4.59
5	1	4.6345	0.0000	0.216	–
	2	0.9090	2.6036	0.908	1.78
	3	0.1434	1.0750	1.493	7.23

Fig. 14.14 (continued)

n	i	a_i	b_i	f_{ci}/f_c	Q_i
6	1	3.5880	10.4648	0.373	0.90
	2	0.4925	1.9622	1.085	2.84
	3	0.0995	1.0826	1.491	10.46
7	1	6.4760	0.0000	0.154	–
	2	1.3258	4.7649	0.665	1.65
	3	0.3067	1.5927	1.218	4.12
	4	0.0714	1.0384	1.523	14.28
8	1	4.7743	18.1510	0.282	0.89
	2	0.6991	3.1353	0.853	2.53
	3	0.2153	1.4449	1.285	5.58
	4	0.0547	1.0461	1.518	18.69
9	1	8.3198	0.0000	0.120	–
	2	1.7299	7.6580	0.522	1.60
	3	0.4337	2.3549	0.998	3.54
	4	0.1583	1.3174	1.349	7.25
	5	0.0427	1.0232	1.536	23.68
10	1	5.9618	28.0376	0.226	0.89
	2	0.8947	4.6644	0.697	2.41
	3	0.3023	1.9858	1.094	4.66
	4	0.1233	1.2614	1.380	9.11
	5	0.0347	1.0294	1.531	29.27

Chebyshev filters, 3 dB ripple

n	i	a_i	b_i	f_{ci}/f_c	Q_i
1	1	1.0000	0.0000	1.000	–
2	1	1.0650	1.9305	1.000	1.30
3	1	3.3496	0.0000	0.299	–
	2	0.3559	1.1923	1.396	3.07
4	1	2.1853	5.5339	0.557	1.08
	2	0.1964	1.2009	1.410	5.58
5	1	5.6334	0.0000	0.178	–
	2	0.7620	2.6530	0.917	2.14
	3	0.1172	1.0686	1.500	8.82
6	1	3.2721	11.6773	0.379	1.04
	2	0.4077	1.9873	1.086	3.46
	3	0.0815	1.0861	1.489	12.78
7	1	7.9064	0.0000	0.126	–
	2	1.1159	4.8963	0.670	1.98
	3	0.2515	1.5944	1.222	5.02
	4	0.0582	1.0348	1.527	17.46
8	1	4.3583	20.2948	0.286	1.03
	2	0.5791	3.1808	0.855	3.08
	3	0.1765	1.4507	1.285	6.83
	4	0.0448	1.0478	1.517	22.87

Fig. 14.14 (*continued*)

n	i	a_i	b_i	f_{ci}/f_c	Q_i
9	1	10.1759	0.0000	0.098	–
	2	1.4585	7.8971	0.526	1.93
	3	0.3561	2.3651	1.001	4.32
	4	0.1294	1.3165	1.351	8.87
	5	0.0348	1.0210	1.537	29.00
10	1	5.4449	31.3788	0.230	1.03
	2	0.7414	4.7363	0.699	2.94
	3	0.2479	1.9952	1.094	5.70
	4	0.1008	1.2638	1.380	11.15
	5	0.0283	1.0304	1.530	35.85

Fig. 14.14 (*continued*)

The larger the pole-pair Q-factor, the more likely the filter is to be unstable. Filters with real poles have pole-pair Q-factors of $Q \leq 0.5$.

The frequency response of the gain, phase shift and group delay can be calculated using the coefficients a_i and b_i of the factored transfer function:

$$|\underline{A}|^2 = \frac{A_0^2}{\prod_i [1 + (a_i^2 - 2b_i)\Omega^2 + b_i^2\Omega^4]} \, , \tag{14.12}$$

$$\varphi = -\sum_i \arctan \frac{a_i\Omega}{1 - b_i\Omega^2} \, , \tag{14.13}$$

$$T_{gr} = \frac{1}{2\pi} \sum_i \frac{a_i(1 + b_i\Omega^2)}{1 + (a_i^2 - 2b_i)\Omega^2 + b_i^2\Omega^4} \, . \tag{14.14}$$

14.2   Lowpass/highpass transformation

In the logarithmic representation, the amplitude-frequency response of a lowpass filter is transformed into the analogous highpass filter response by plotting its mirror image about the cutoff frequency, i.e. by replacing Ω by $1/\Omega$ and S by $1/S$. The cutoff frequency remains the same, and A_0 changes to A_∞. Equation (14.11) then becomes

$$A(S) = \frac{A_\infty}{\prod_i \left(1 + \dfrac{a_i}{S} + \dfrac{b_i}{S^2}\right)} \, . \tag{14.15}$$

In the time domain, the performance cannot be transformed, as the step response shows a basically different behavior. This can be seen in Fig. 14.15, where an oscillation about the final-state value occurs even in highpass filters having critical damping. The analogy to the corresponding lowpass filters

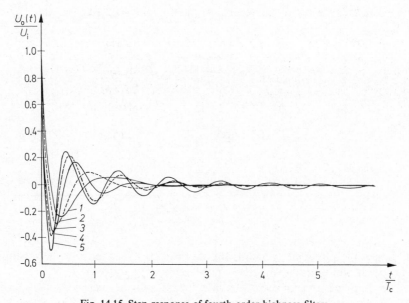

Fig. 14.15 Step response of fourth order highpass filters.
Curve *1*: Highpass filter having critical damping. Curve *2*: Bessel highpass filter. Curve *3*: Butterworth highpass filter. Curve *4*: Chebyshev highpass filter with 0.5 dB ripple. Curve *5*: Chebyshev
highpass filter with 3 dB ripple

still applies in as much as the transient oscillation decays more slowly, the higher
the pole-pair Q-factors.

14.3   Realization of first-order lowpass and highpass filters

According to Eq. (14.11), the transfer function of a first-order lowpass filter
has the general form

$$A(S) = \frac{A_0}{1 + a_1 S} . \tag{14.16}$$

It can be implemented by the simple RC network in Fig. 14.1. From Section 14.1
it follows that for this circuit

$$A(S) = \frac{1}{1 + sRC} = \frac{1}{1 + \omega_c RCS} .$$

The low-frequency gain is defined by the value $A_0 = 1$, but the parameter a_1 can
be chosen freely. Its value is found by comparing the coefficients

$$RC = \frac{a_1}{2\pi f_c} .$$

As can be seen from the table in Fig. 14.14, all filter types of the first order are identical and have the coefficient $a_1 = 1$. When higher-order filters are implemented by cascading filter stages of lower orders, first-order filter stages may be required for which $a_1 \neq 1$. The reason for this is that individual filter stages have, as a rule, a cutoff frequency different from that of the filter as a whole, namely $f_{c1} = f_c/a_1$.

The simple RC network in Fig. 14.1 has the disadvantage that its properties change when it is loaded. Therefore an impedance converter (buffer) is usually connected in series. If it is given voltage gain A_0, the low-frequency gain can then be chosen freely. An appropriate circuit is presented in Fig. 14.16.

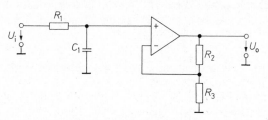

Fig. 14.16 First-order lowpass filter with impedance converter

$$A(S) = \frac{(R_2 + R_3)/R_3}{1 + \omega_c R_1 C_1 S}$$

In order to arrive at the corresponding highpass filter, the variable S in Eq. (14.16) must be replaced by $1/S$. In the circuit itself, the conversion is achieved by simply exchanging R_1 and C_1.

Somewhat simpler circuits for first-order lowpass and highpass filters are obtained if the filtering network is included in the feedback loop of the operational amplifier. The corresponding lowpass filter is shown in Fig. 14.17. For the actual design, one defines the cutoff frequency, the low frequency gain A_0 which in this case is negative, and the capacitance C_1. Comparing the coefficients to those of Eq. (14.16), it follows that

$$R_2 = \frac{a_1}{2\pi f_c C_1} \quad \text{and} \quad R_1 = -\frac{R_2}{A_0}.$$

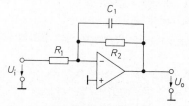

Fig. 14.17 First-order lowpass filter with inverting amplifier

$$A(S) = -\frac{R_2/R_1}{1 + \omega_c R_2 C_1 S}$$

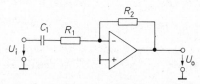

Fig. 14.18 First-order highpass filter with inverting amplifier

$$A(S) = -\frac{R_2/R_1}{1 + \dfrac{1}{\omega_c R_1 C_1} \cdot \dfrac{1}{S}}$$

Figure 14.18 shows the corresponding highpass filter. By comparing coefficients with Eq. (14.15) it follows that

$$R_1 = \frac{1}{2\pi f_c a_1 C_1} \quad \text{and} \quad R_2 = -R_1 A_\infty \; .$$

The transfer functions given for the previous circuits apply only to the range of frequency for which the open-loop gain of the operational amplifier is large with respect to the absolute value of $\underline{A}$. This condition is difficult to fulfill for high frequencies, as the magnitude of the open-loop gain falls at a rate of 6 dB/octave because of the necessary frequency compensation. For a standard operational amplifier at 10 kHz, $|\underline{A}_D|$ is only about 100.

14.4   Realization of second-order lowpass and highpass filters

According to Eq. (14.11), the transfer function of a second-order lowpass filter has the general form

$$A(S) = \frac{A_0}{1 + a_1 S + b_1 S^2} \; . \tag{14.17}$$

As can be seen from the table in Fig. 14.14, the optimized transfer functions of second and higher orders have conjugate complex poles. Such transfer functions cannot be implemented by passive RC networks, as discussed in Section 14.1. One possibility of realizing these circuits is to use inductances and this is demonstrated in the following example.

14.4.1   *LRC* filters

The conventional implementation of second-order filters involves using LRC networks as shown in Fig. 14.19. Comparison of the coefficients with those of Eq. (14.17) yields

$$R = \frac{a_1}{2\pi f_c C} \quad \text{and} \quad L = \frac{b_1}{4\pi^2 f_c^2 C} \; .$$

From Fig. 14.14, the coefficients of a second-order Butterworth lowpass filter are $a_1 = 1.414$ and $b_1 = 1.000$. For a given cutoff frequency of $f_c = 10$ Hz and

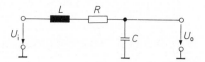

Fig. 14.19 Passive second-order lowpass filter

$$A(S) = \frac{1}{1 + \omega_c RCS + \omega_c^2 LCS^2}$$

a capacitance of $C = 10\ \mu\text{F}$, the remaining design parameters are $R = 2.25\ \text{k}\Omega$ and $L = 25.3\ \text{H}$. Obviously, such a filter is extremely difficult to implement because of the size of the inductance. However, this can be avoided by emulating the inductance with an active RC circuit. The gyrator in Fig. 13.32 is useful for this purpose, although its implementation involves a considerable number of components.

The desired transfer functions can be put into practice much more simply without inductance emulation by connecting suitable RC networks around operational amplifiers.

14.4.2   Filter with multiple negative feedback

An active second-order RC lowpass filter is shown in Fig. 14.20. By comparing the coefficients with those of Eq. (14.17), we obtain the relations

$$A_0 = -R_2/R_1 \ ,$$

$$a_1 = \omega_c C_1 \left(R_2 + R_3 + \frac{R_2 R_3}{R_1} \right) ,$$

$$b_1 = \omega_c^2 C_1 C_2 R_2 R_3 \ .$$

For the actual specification, the values of the resistors R_1 and R_3, for example, can be predetermined; the parameters R_2, C_1 and C_2 can then be calculated from the above equations. Such a determination is possible for all positive values of a_1 and b_1, so that any desired filter type can be realized. The gain at zero frequency, A_0, is negative. At low frequencies, therefore, the filter inverts the signal.

In order to achieve the desired frequency response, the circuit elements must not have too large a tolerance. This requirement is easy to fulfill for resistors, as they can be obtained off-the-shelf with one percent tolerance, in the E 96 standard series. The situation is different with capacitors, which, as a rule, are available off-the-shelf only in the E 6 series. It is therefore advantageous in filter

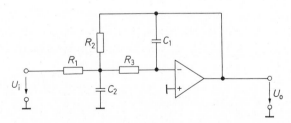

Fig. 14.20 Active second-order lowpass filter with multiple negative feedback

$$A(S) = - \cfrac{R_2/R_1}{1 + \omega_c C_1 \left(R_2 + R_3 + \dfrac{R_2 R_3}{R_1} \right) S + \omega_c^2 C_1 C_2 R_2 R_3 S^2}$$

design to predetermine the capacitors and calculate the values for the resistors. We therefore solve the design equations for the resistances and obtain

$$R_2 = \frac{a_1 C_2 - \sqrt{a_1^2 C_2^2 - 4 C_1 C_2 b_1 (1 - A_0)}}{4\pi f_c C_1 C_2},$$

$$R_1 = \frac{R_2}{-A_0},$$

$$R_3 = \frac{b_1}{4\pi^2 f_c^2 C_1 C_2 R_2}.$$

In order that the value for R_2 be real, the condition

$$\frac{C_2}{C_1} \gtreqqless \frac{4 b_1 (1 - A_0)}{a_1^2}$$

must be fulfilled. The most favorable design is obtained if the ratio C_2/C_1 is chosen not much larger than is prescribed by this condition. The filter parameters are relatively insensitive to the tolerances of the components, and therefore the circuit is particularly suited to the realization of filters having high Q-factors.

14.4.3   Filter with single positive feedback

Active filters can also be designed using amplifiers with positive feedback. However, the gain must be fixed at a precise value by an internal negative feedback ("controlled source"). The voltage divider $R_3, (\alpha - 1)R_3$ in Fig. 14.21 provides this negative feedback and determines the internal gain as having the value α. The positive feedback is provided by capacitor C_2.

The design can be considerably simplified if it is restricted to certain special cases. One possible case is to define the internal gain as $\alpha = 1$. Then $(\alpha - 1)R_3 = 0$, and both resistors R_3 can be omitted. Such operational amplifiers with unity feedback factor are available as integrated voltage followers (e.g.

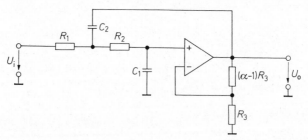

Fig. 14.21 Active second order lowpass filter with single positive feedback

$$A(S) = \frac{\alpha}{1 + \omega_c [C_1(R_1 + R_2) + (1 - \alpha)R_1 C_2]S + \omega_c^2 R_1 R_2 C_1 C_2 S^2}$$

type BUF-03 from PMI or LT1010 from Linear Technology). A simple impedance converter or buffer, for instance an emitter or source follower, is often sufficient. In this way, filters in the MHz range can also be realized. For the special case when $\alpha = 1$, the transfer function is given by

$$A(S) = \frac{1}{1 + \omega_c C_1 (R_1 + R_2)S + \omega_c^2 R_1 R_2 C_1 C_2 S^2} .$$

Defining C_1 and C_2 and comparing the coefficients with those of Eq. (14.17) gives

$$A_0 = 1 ,$$

$$R_{1/2} = \frac{a_1 C_2 \mp \sqrt{a_1^2 C_2^2 - 4b_1 C_1 C_2}}{4\pi f_c C_1 C_2} .$$

In order to arrive at values that are real, the condition

$$\frac{C_2}{C_1} \geq \frac{4b_1}{a_1^2}$$

must be fulfilled. As for the filter with multiple negative feedback, the most favorable design is obtained if the ratio C_2/C_1 is chosen not much larger than is prescribed by this condition.

A further interesting special case occurs when identical resistors and capacitors are employed in the circuit, i.e. when $R_1 = R_2 = R$ and $C_1 = C_2 = C$. To enable implementation of the different filter types, the internal gain must, in this case, be variable. The transfer function then becomes

$$A(S) = \frac{\alpha}{1 + \omega_c RC(3 - \alpha)S + (\omega_c RC)^2 S^2} .$$

By comparing the coefficients with those in Eq. (14.17) we obtain the relations

$$RC = \frac{\sqrt{b_1}}{2\pi f_c} ,$$

$$\alpha = A_0 = 3 - \frac{a_1}{\sqrt{b_1}} = 3 - \frac{1}{Q_1} .$$

As can be seen, the internal gain α is dependent only on the pole-pair Q-factor and not on the cutoff frequency f_c. The value of α therefore determines the type of filter. Insertion of the coefficients given in Fig. 14.14 for a second-order filter results in the values for α given in Fig. 14.22. For $\alpha = 3$, the circuit produces

	Critical	Bessel	Butterworth	3 dB-Chebyshev	Undamped
α	1.000	1.268	1.586	2.234	3.000

Fig. 14.22 Internal gain for single positive feedback (second order)

a self-contained oscillation at the frequency $f = 1/2\pi RC$. It can be seen that the adjustment of the internal gain becomes more difficult as one approaches the value $\alpha = 3$. For the Chebyshev filter in particular, a very precise adjustment is therefore necessary. This is a slight disadvantage compared with the previous filters. A considerable advantage, however, is due to the fact that the type of filter is solely determined by α and is not dependent on R and C. Hence, the cutoff frequency of this filter circuit can be changed particularly easily, for example using a dual-gang potentiometer for the two identical resistors R_1 and R_2 in Fig. 14.21.

If the resistors and capacitors are interchanged, one arrives at the *highpass filter* in Fig. 14.23. To simplify the design process, we choose the special case where $\alpha = 1$ and $C_1 = C_2 = C$. Comparing the coefficients with those of Eq. (14.15) gives

$$A_\infty = 1 \ ,$$

$$R_1 = \frac{1}{\pi f_c C a_1} \ ,$$

$$R_2 = \frac{a_1}{4\pi f_c C b_1} \ .$$

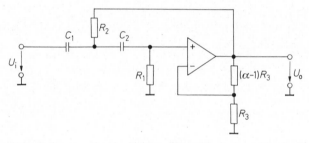

Fig. 14.23 Active second-order highpass filter with single positive feedback

$$A(S) = \frac{\alpha}{1 + \dfrac{R_2(C_1 + C_2) + R_1 C_2(1 - \alpha)}{R_1 R_2 C_1 C_2 \omega_c} \cdot \dfrac{1}{S} + \dfrac{1}{R_1 R_2 C_1 C_2 \omega_c^2} \cdot \dfrac{1}{S^2}}$$

14.5   Realization of higher-order lowpass and highpass filters

In cases where the filter characteristic is not steep enough, filters of higher orders must be employed. For this purpose, first- and second-order filters are cascaded, thereby multiplying the frequency responses of the individual filters. It would, however, be wrong to cascade two second-order Butterworth filters, for example, to obtain a fourth-order Butterworth filter. The resulting filter would have a different cutoff frequency and also a different filter characteristic. The coefficients of the individual filters must therefore be chosen such that the product of the frequency responses gives the desired optimized filter type.

To simplify the determination of the circuit parameters of the individual filters, we have factored the polynomials of the different filter types. The coefficients a_i and b_i of the individual filter stages are given in Fig. 14.14. Each factor with $b_i \neq 0$ can be implemented by one of the second-order filters described previously. It is merely necessary to replace the coefficients a_1 and b_1 by a_i and b_i. To calculate the circuit parameters from the given formulae, the desired cutoff frequency of the *resulting total filter* must be inserted. As a rule, the individual filter stages possess cutoff frequencies different from that of the filter as a whole, as can be seen in Fig. 14.14. Odd-order filters contain a factor in which $b_i = 0$. The corresponding filter stage can be implemented by one of the first-order filters described if a_1 is replaced by a_i. In this case also, the cutoff frequency f_c of the total filter must be inserted. Because of the defined value of a_i, this filter stage automatically has the cutoff frequency f_{ci} given in Fig. 14.14.

The sequence in which the individual filter stages are cascaded is, in principle, not significant, as the resulting frequency response remains the same. In practice, however, there are several design considerations governing the best sequence of the filter stages. One such aspect is the permissible voltage swing, for which it is useful to arrange the filter stages according to their cutoff frequencies, with the one having the lowest cutoff frequency at the input; otherwise it may be saturated while the output of the second stage is still below the maximum permissible voltage swing. The reason for this is that the filter stages having the higher cutoff frequencies also invariably have the higher pole-pair Q, and therefore show a rise in gain in the vicinity of their cutoff frequency. This can be seen in Fig. 14.24 where the amplitude-frequency responses of a tenth-order 0.5 dB Chebyshev lowpass filter and of its five individual stages are shown. It is

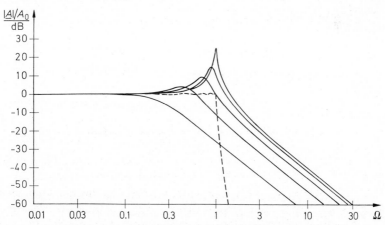

Fig. 14.24 Amplitude-frequency responses of a tenth-order Chebyshev filter with 0.5 dB ripple and of its five individual filter stages

obvious that the permissible voltage swing is highest if the filter stages having low cutoff frequencies are at the input of the filter cascade.

Another aspect which may have to be considered for a suitable arrangement of the filter stages is noise. In this case, just the reverse sequence is most favorable, as then the filters with the lower cutoff frequencies at the end of the filter chain reduce the noise introduced by the input stages.

The design process is demonstrated for a third-order Bessel lowpass filter. It is to be constructed from the first-order lowpass filter in Fig. 14.16 and the second-order lowpass filter in Fig. 14.21, for which the special case of $\alpha = 1$ (described in Section 14.4.3) is chosen. The low-frequency gain is defined as unity. To achieve this, the impedance converter in the first-order filter stage must have the gain $\alpha = 1$. The resulting circuit is represented in Fig. 14.25.

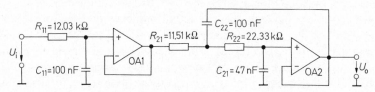

Fig. 14.25 Third-order Bessel lowpass filter having a cutoff frequency $f_c = 100$ Hz

The desired cutoff frequency is $f_c = 100$ Hz. For the calculation of the first filter stage, we predetermine $C_{11} = 100$ nF and obtain, according to Section 14.3, with the coefficients from Fig. 14.14:

$$R_{11} = \frac{a_1}{2\pi f_c C_{11}} = \frac{0.7560}{2\pi \cdot 100 \text{ Hz} \cdot 100 \text{ nF}} = 12.03 \text{ k}\Omega \ .$$

For the second filter stage, we set $C_{22} = 100$ nF and obtain, in accordance with Section 14.4.3, the condition for C_{21}:

$$C_{21} \leqq C_{22} \frac{a_2^2}{4b_2} = 100 \text{ nF} \cdot \frac{(0.9996)^2}{4 \cdot 0.4772} \ ,$$

$$C_{21} \leqq 52.3 \text{ nF} \ .$$

We choose the nearest standard value $C_{21} = 47$ nF and arrive at

$$R_{21/22} = \frac{a_2 C_{22} \mp \sqrt{a_2^2 C_{22}^2 - 4b_2 C_{21} C_{22}}}{4\pi f_c C_{21} C_{22}} \ ,$$

$$R_{21} = 11.51 \text{ k}\Omega \ , \qquad R_{22} = 22.33 \text{ k}\Omega \ .$$

For third-order filters, it is possible to omit the first operational amplifier. The simple lowpass filter of Fig. 14.1 is then connected in front of the second-order filter. Due to the mutual loading of the filters, a different method of calculation must be employed which is considerably more difficult than in the

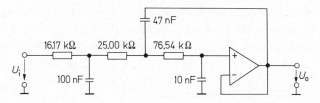

Fig. 14.26 Simplified third-order Bessel lowpass filter having a cutoff frequency $f_c = 100$ Hz

decoupled case. Figure 14.26 shows such a circuit having the same character-istics as that in Fig. 14.25.

14.6   Lowpass/bandpass transformation

In Section 14.2 it is shown how, by transforming the frequency variable, a given lowpass frequency response can be converted to the corresponding highpass frequency response. With a very similar transformation, the frequency response of a bandpass filter can be created, i.e. by replacing the frequency variable S in the lowpass transfer function by the expression

$$\frac{1}{\Delta\Omega}\left(S + \frac{1}{S}\right) .$$
(14.18)

By means of this transformation, the amplitude response of the lowpass filter in the range $0 \leq \Omega \leq 1$ is converted into the pass range of a bandpass filter between the center frequency $\Omega = 1$ and the upper cutoff frequency Ω_{max}. On a logarith-mic frequency scale, it also appears as a mirror image below the center fre-quency. The lower cutoff frequency is then $\Omega_{min} = 1/\Omega_{max}$ [14.7]. Figure 14.27 illustrates this process.

The normalized bandwidth $\Delta\Omega = \Omega_{max} - \Omega_{min}$ can be chosen freely. The described transformation results in the bandpass filter having the same gain at Ω_{min} and Ω_{max} as the corresponding lowpass filter at $\Omega = 1$. If the lowpass filter,

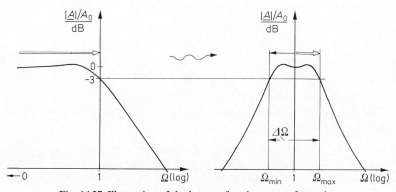

Fig. 14.27 Illustration of the lowpass/bandpass transformation

as in the table Fig. 14.14, is normalized with respect to the 3 dB cutoff frequency, $\Delta\Omega$ represents the normalized 3 dB bandwidth of the bandpass filter. Since $\Delta\Omega = \Omega_{max} - \Omega_{min}$ and $\Omega_{max} \cdot \Omega_{min} = 1$, we obtain for the normalized 3 dB cutoff frequencies

$$\Omega_{max/min} = \tfrac{1}{2}\sqrt{(\Delta\Omega)^2 + 4} \pm \tfrac{1}{2}\Delta\Omega \ .$$

14.6.1 Second-order bandpass filters

The simplest bandpass filter is obtained by applying the transformation equation (14.18) to a first-order lowpass filter where

$$A(S) = \frac{A_0}{1 + S} \ .$$

Therefore the transfer function of the second-order bandpass filter is

$$A(S) = \frac{A_0}{1 + \dfrac{1}{\Delta\Omega}\left(S + \dfrac{1}{S}\right)} = \frac{A_0 \Delta\Omega S}{1 + \Delta\Omega S + S^2} \ . \tag{14.19}$$

The interesting parameters of bandpass filters are the gain A_r at the resonant frequency f_r, and the quality factor Q. It follows directly from the given transformation characteristic that $A_r = A_0$. This can be easily verified by making $\Omega = 1$, i.e. $S = j$ in Eq. (14.19). Since A_r is real, the phase shift at resonant frequency is zero.

As for a resonant circuit, the Q-factor is defined as the ratio of the resonant frequency f_r to the bandwidth B. Therefore,

$$Q = \frac{f_r}{B} = \frac{f_r}{f_{max} - f_{min}} = \frac{1}{\Omega_{max} - \Omega_{min}} = \frac{1}{\Delta\Omega} \ . \tag{14.20}$$

Inserting this in Eq. (14.19) gives

$$A(S) = \frac{(A_r/Q)S}{1 + \dfrac{1}{Q}S + S^2} \ . \tag{14.21}$$

This equation is the transfer function of a second-order bandpass filter and allows direct identification of all parameters of interest.

With $S = j\Omega$, we obtain from Eq. (14.21) the frequency response of the amplitude and the phase

$$|\underline{A}| = \frac{(A_r/Q)\Omega}{\sqrt{1 + \Omega^2\left(\dfrac{1}{Q^2} - 2\right) + \Omega^4}} \ , \tag{14.22}$$

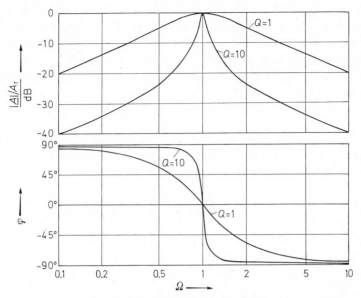

Fig. 14.28 Frequency response of amplitude and phase of second-order bandpass filters with $Q = 1$ and $Q = 10$

$$\varphi = \arctan \frac{Q(1 - \Omega^2)}{\Omega} \ . \qquad (14.23)$$

These two functions are shown in Fig. 14.28 for the Q-factors 1 and 10.

14.6.2   Fourth-order bandpass filters

The amplitude-frequency response of second-order bandpass filters becomes more peaked the larger the Q-factor selected. However, there are many applications where the curve must be as flat as possible in the region of the resonant frequency but must also have a steep transition to the stopband. This optimization problem may be solved by applying the lowpass/bandpass transformation to higher-order lowpass filters. It is then possible to choose freely not only the bandwidth $\Delta\Omega$, but also the most suitable filter type.

The application of the lowpass/bandpass transformation to lowpass filters of the second order is particularly important. It results in a mathematical description of fourth-order bandpass filters. Such filters are investigated below. By inserting the transformation equation (14.18) in the second-order lowpass equation (14.17), we obtain the bandpass transfer function

$$A(S) = \frac{S^2 A_0 (\Delta\Omega)^2 / b_1}{1 + \dfrac{a_1}{b_1} \Delta\Omega S + \left[2 + \dfrac{(\Delta\Omega)^2}{b_1} \right] S^2 + \dfrac{a_1}{b_1} \Delta\Omega S^3 + S^4} \ . \qquad (14.24)$$

It can be seen that the asymptotes of the amplitude-frequency response at low and high frequencies have the slope $\pm\,12\,\text{dB/octave}$. At the center frequency $\Omega = 1$, the gain is real and has the value $A_m = A_0$.

In Fig. 14.29 we have plotted the frequency response of the amplitude and phase of a Butterworth bandpass filter, and of a 0.5 dB Chebyshev bandpass filter, both having a normalized bandwidth $\Delta\Omega = 1$. The frequency response of a second-order bandpass filter with the same bandwidth is shown for comparison.

As in the case of the lowpass filters, we shall simplify the design process by splitting the denominator into quadratic factors. For reasons of symmetry we can choose a more simple formulation and write

$$A(S) = \frac{S^2 A_m (\Delta\Omega)^2 / b_1}{\left[1 + \dfrac{\alpha S}{Q_i} + (\alpha S)^2\right]\left[1 + \dfrac{1}{Q_i}\left(\dfrac{S}{\alpha}\right) + \left(\dfrac{S}{\alpha}\right)^2\right]}\,. \qquad (14.25)$$

By multiplying out and comparing the coefficients with those in Eq. (14.24), we

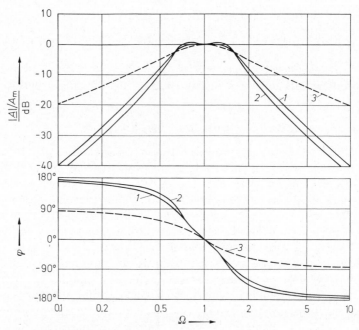

Fig. 14.29 Frequency response of amplitude and phase for bandpass filters with a bandwidth $\Delta\Omega = 1$.

Curve *1*: Fourth order Butterworth bandpass filter. Curve *2*: Fourth order Chebyshev bandpass filter with 0.5 dB ripple. Curve *3*: Second order bandpass for comparison

arrive at the equation for α:

$$\alpha^2 + \left[\frac{\alpha\Delta\Omega a_1}{b_1(1+\alpha^2)}\right]^2 + \frac{1}{\alpha^2} - 2 - \frac{(\Delta\Omega)^2}{b_1} = 0 \ . \tag{14.26}$$

For any particular application it can be easily solved numerically with the aid of a pocket calculator. Having determined α, the pole-pair quality factor Q_i of an individual filter stage is

$$Q_i = \frac{(1+\alpha^2)b_1}{\alpha\Delta\Omega a_1} \ . \tag{14.27}$$

There are two possible ways of implementing the filter, depending on how the numerator is factored. Splitting-up into a constant factor and a factor containing S^2 yields the cascade connection of a highpass and a lowpass filter. This design is useful for realizing large bandwidths $\Delta\Omega$.

For smaller bandwidths, $\Delta\Omega \lesssim 1$, it is preferable to use a cascade connection of two second-order bandpass filters which are not tuned to precisely the same center frequency. This method is called "staggered tuning". For the design of the individual bandpass filter stages, we split the numerator of Eq. (14.25) into two factors containing S and obtain

$$A(S) = \frac{(A_r/Q_i)(\alpha S)}{1 + \dfrac{\alpha S}{Q_i} + (\alpha S)^2} \cdot \frac{(A_r/Q_i)(S/\alpha)}{1 + \dfrac{1}{Q_i}\left(\dfrac{S}{\alpha}\right) + \left(\dfrac{S}{\alpha}\right)^2} \ . \tag{14.28}$$

Comparing the coefficients with those of Eq. (14.25) and Eq. (14.23), we obtain the parameters of the two individual bandpass filters:

	f_r	Q	A_r	
1st filter stage	f_m/α	Q_i	$Q_i\Delta\Omega\sqrt{A_m/b_1}$	(14.29)
2nd filter stage	$f_m \cdot \alpha$	Q_i	$Q_i\Delta\Omega\sqrt{A_m/b_1}$	

where f_m is the center frequency of the resulting bandpass filter and A_m is the gain at this frequency. The factors α and Q_i are given by Eqs. (14.26) and (14.27).

The determination of the parameters of the individual filter stages will be demonstrated by an example. A Butterworth bandpass is required with a center frequency of 1 kHz and a bandwidth of 100 Hz. The gain at the center frequency is required to be $A_m = 1$. To begin with, we take the coefficients of a second-order Butterworth lowpass filter from the table in Fig. 14.14: $a_1 = 1.4142$ and $b_1 = 1.000$. As $\Delta\Omega = 0.1$, Eq. (14.26) gives $\alpha = 1.0360$. Equation (14.27) yields $Q_i = 14.15$, and from Eq. (14.29) $A_r = 1.415$, $f_{r1} = 965$ Hz and $f_{r2} = 1.036$ kHz.

14.7   Realization of second-order bandpass filters

The cascade connection of a highpass and a lowpass filter of first order, as in Fig. 14.30, gives a bandpass filter with the transfer function

$$A(s) = \cfrac{1}{1 + \cfrac{1}{\alpha s RC}} \cdot \cfrac{1}{1 + \cfrac{sRC}{\alpha}} = \cfrac{\alpha s RC}{1 + \cfrac{1 + \alpha^2}{\alpha} sRC + (sRC)^2} .$$

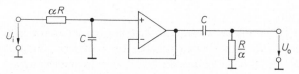

Fig. 14.30 Bandpass filter consisting of a first-order highpass and lowpass filter

$$A(S) = \cfrac{\alpha S}{1 + \cfrac{1 + \alpha^2}{\alpha} S + S^2}$$

With the resonant frequency $\omega_r = 1/RC$, we obtain the normalized form. Comparison of the coefficients with those of Eq. (14.21) gives the Q-factor

$$Q = \frac{\alpha}{1 + \alpha^2} .$$

For $\alpha = 1$, $Q_{max} = \frac{1}{2}$, which is the highest Q-factor that can be achieved by cascading first-order filters. For higher Q-factors, the denominator of Eq. (14.21) must have complex zeros, but such a transfer function can only be implemented by LRC circuits or by special active RC circuits which are discussed below.

14.7.1   LRC bandpass filter

A common method of designing selective filters having high quality factors is the use of resonant circuits. Figure 14.31 shows such a circuit, the transfer function of which is

$$A(s) = \frac{sRC}{1 + sRC + s^2 LC} .$$

With the resonant frequency $\omega_r = 1/\sqrt{LC}$, we obtain the normalized expression as given in Fig. 14.31. Comparison of the coefficients with those of Eq. (14.21) gives

$$Q = \frac{1}{R}\sqrt{\frac{L}{C}} \quad \text{and} \quad A_r = 1 .$$

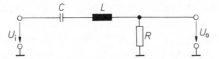

Fig. 14.31 *LRC* bandpass filter

$$A(S) = \frac{R\sqrt{\dfrac{C}{L}}\,S}{1 + R\sqrt{\dfrac{C}{L}}\,S + S^2}$$

For high frequencies, the inductances required can be easily implemented and have very little loss. For the low-frequency range, the inductances become unwieldy and have a poor electrical performance. If, for example, a filter having the resonant frequency $f_r = 10$ Hz is to be implemented using the circuit in Fig. 14.31, the inductance $L = 25.3$ H is required if a capacitance of $10\,\mu$F is selected. As has been already shown in Section 14.4.1 for the lowpass and highpass filters, such inductances can be emulated, e.g. using gyrators. In most cases, the desired transfer function of Eq. (14.21) can be put into practice much more easily by inserting suitable RC networks in the feedback loop of an operational amplifier.

14.7.2 Bandpass filter with multiple negative feedback

The principle of multiple negative feedback can also be applied to bandpass filters. The appropriate circuit is shown in Fig. 14.32. As can be seen by comparison with Eq. (14.21), the coefficient of S^2 must be unity. Therefore, the resonant frequency is given by

$$f_r = \frac{1}{2\pi C}\sqrt{\frac{R_1 + R_3}{R_1 R_2 R_3}}\,. \tag{14.30}$$

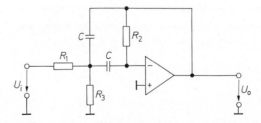

Fig. 14.32 Bandpass filter with multiple negative feedbaok

$$A(S) = \frac{-\dfrac{R_2 R_3}{R_1 + R_3}\,C\omega_r S}{1 + \dfrac{2R_1 R_3}{R_1 + R_3}\,C\omega_r S + \dfrac{R_1 R_2 R_3}{R_1 + R_3}\,C^2\omega_r^2 S^2}$$

Inserting this relation in the transfer function and comparing the remaining coefficients with those of Eq. (14.21) gives the other parameters

$$- A_r = \frac{R_2}{2R_1} , \tag{14.31}$$

$$Q = \frac{1}{2} \sqrt{\frac{R_2(R_1 + R_3)}{R_1 R_3}} = \pi R_2 C f_r . \tag{14.32}$$

It can be seen that the gain, the Q-factor and the resonant frequency can be freely chosen.

From Eq. (14.32), we obtain the bandwidth of the filter

$$B = \frac{f_r}{Q} = \frac{1}{\pi R_2 C} ,$$

which is independent of R_1 and R_3. On the other hand, it can be seen from Eq. (14.31) that A_r is not dependent on R_3. It is therefore possible to vary the resonant frequency by R_3 without affecting the bandwidth B and the gain A_r.

If resistor R_3 is omitted, the filter remains functional, but the Q-factor becomes dependent on A_r. This is because, with $R_3 \to \infty$, Eq. (14.32) becomes

$$- A_r = 2Q^2 .$$

In order that the loop gain of the circuit be very much larger than unity, the open-loop gain of the operational amplifier must be large compared to $2Q^2$. Using resistor R_3, high Q-factors can be attained even for a low gain A_r. As can be seen in Fig. 14.32, the low gain is due only to the fact that the input signal is attenuated by the voltage divider R_1, R_3. Therefore, the open-loop gain of the operational amplifier must in this case also be large compared to $2Q^2$. This requirement is particularly exacting as it must be met around the resonant frequency; it determines the choice of the operational amplifier, especially for applications at higher frequencies.

The determination of the circuit parameters is shown by the following example. A selective filter is required, having a resonant frequency $f_r = 10$ Hz and a quality factor $Q = 100$. Therefore, the cutoff frequencies lie at approximately 9.95 Hz and 10.05 Hz. The gain at resonant frequency is required to be $- A_r = 10$. One of the parameters can be freely chosen, e.g. $C = 1$ μF, and the remainder must be calculated. To begin with, from Eq. (14.32)

$$R_2 = \frac{Q}{\pi f_r C} = 3.18 \text{ M}\Omega .$$

Hence, from Eq. (14.31)

$$R_1 = \frac{R_2}{- 2A_r} = 159 \text{ k}\Omega .$$

The resistance R_3 is given by Eq. (14.30) as

$$R_3 = \frac{- A_r R_1}{2Q^2 + A_r} = 79.5 \ \Omega .$$

The open-loop gain of the operational amplifier must, at resonant frequency, still be large compared to $2Q^2 = 20 \cdot 10^3$.

One advantage of the circuit is that it has no tendency to oscillate at resonant frequency, even if the circuit elements do not quite match their theoretical values. Obviously, this is true only if the operational amplifier is correctly frequency compensated; otherwise high-frequency oscillations occur.

14.7.3 Bandpass filter with single positive feedback

The application of single positive feedback results in the bandpass circuit in Fig. 14.33. The negative feedback via the resistors R_1 and $(k-1)R_1$ fixes the internal gain at value k. Comparison of the coefficients with those of Eq. (14.21) yields the equations given for determining the circuit parameters.

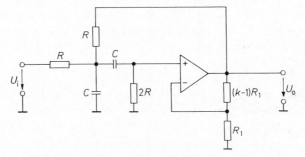

Fig. 14.33 Bandpass filter with single positive feedback

$$A(S) = \frac{kRC\omega_r S}{1 + RC\omega_r(3-k)S + R^2C^2\omega_r^2 S^2}$$

Resonant frequency: $f_r = \dfrac{1}{2\pi RC}$ *Gain at f_r:* $A_r = \dfrac{k}{3-k}$ *Q-factor:* $Q = \dfrac{1}{3-k}$

A disadvantage is that Q and A_r cannot be chosen independently of one another. The advantage, however, is that the Q-factor may be altered by varying k without at the same time changing the resonant frequency.

For $k = 3$, the gain is infinite, and an undamped oscillation occurs. The adjustment of the internal gain therefore becomes more critical the closer it approaches the value 3.

14.8 Lowpass/band-stop filter transformation

Selective rejection of a particular frequency requires a filter whose gain is zero at the resonant frequency and rises to a constant value at higher and lower frequencies. Such filters are called *rejection filters, band-stop filters* or *notch filters*. To characterize the selectivity, the rejection quality factor is defined as

$Q = f_r/B$, where B is the 3 dB bandwidth. The larger the Q-factor of the filter, the more steeply the gain falls off in the vicinity of the resonant frequency f_r.

As in the case of the bandpass filter, the amplitude-frequency response of the band-rejection filter can be derived from the frequency response of a lowpass filter by using a suitable frequency transformation. To accomplish this, the variable S is replaced by the expression

$$\frac{\Delta\Omega}{S + \dfrac{1}{S}} \, , \tag{14.33}$$

where $\Delta\Omega = 1/Q$ is the normalized 3 dB bandwidth. By means of this transformation, the amplitude of the lowpass filter in the range $0 \leq \Omega \leq 1$ is converted to the pass band of the band-rejection filter between $0 \leq \Omega \leq \Omega_{c1}$. In addition, it appears as a mirror image about the resonant frequency, when plotted on a logarithmic scale. At the resonant frequency $\Omega = 1$, the transfer function is zero. As with the bandpass filter, the order of the filter is doubled by the transformation. It is of particular interest to apply the transformation to a first-order lowpass filter. This results in a notch filter of the second order, having a transfer function

$$A(S) = \frac{A_0(1 + S^2)}{1 + \Delta\Omega S + S^2} = \frac{A_0(1 + S^2)}{1 + \dfrac{1}{Q}S + S^2} \, . \tag{14.34}$$

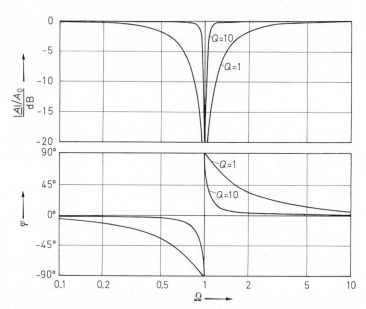

Fig. 14.34 Frequency response of amplitude and phase for second-order band-stop filters with $Q = 1$ and $Q = 10$

From this, we obtain the relations for the amplitude-frequency response and the phase-frequency response

$$|\underline{A}| = \frac{A_0|(1 - \Omega^2)|}{\sqrt{1 + \Omega^2\left(\dfrac{1}{Q^2} - 2\right) + \Omega^4}} \quad, \qquad \varphi = \arctan \frac{\Omega}{Q(\Omega^2 - 1)} \;.$$

The corresponding curves are shown in Fig. 14.34 for the rejection quality factors 1 and 10.

The denominator of Eq. (14.34) is identical to that of Eq. (14.21) for band-pass filters. It follows from Eq. (14.21) that a maximum Q-factor of only $Q = \frac{1}{2}$ can be attained with passive RC circuits; for higher Q-factors, LRC networks or special active RC circuits must be employed.

14.9   Realization of second-order band-stop filters

14.9.1   *LRC* band-stop filter

A well known method of implementing rejection filters involves using series-tuned oscillating circuits as in Fig. 14.35. At resonant frequency, the arrangement represents a short-circuit and the output voltage is zero. The transfer function of the circuit is

$$A(s) = \frac{1 + s^2 LC}{1 + sRC + s^2 LC} \;.$$

Hence, the resonant frequency $\omega_r = 1/\sqrt{LC}$, and we obtain the normalized form as given in Fig. 14.35. The rejection quality factor is found by comparing the coefficients with those of Eq. (14.21),

$$Q = \frac{1}{R}\sqrt{\frac{L}{C}} \;.$$

This holds for lossless inductors only, because only for such inductors can the output voltage fall to zero. In addition, the same considerations for the use of inductances apply here as for the bandpass filters.

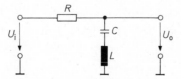

Fig. 14.35 *LRC* band-stop filter

$$A(S) = \frac{1 + S^2}{1 + R\sqrt{\dfrac{C}{L}}\, S + S^2}$$

14.9.2   Active parallel-T RC band-stop filter

As shown in Section 2.6, the parallel-T filter represents a passive RC rejection filter. From Eq. (2.24), its rejection Q-factor is $Q = 0.25$, which can be raised by incorporating the parallel-T filter in the feedback loop of an amplifier. One possible implementation is shown in Fig. 14.36.

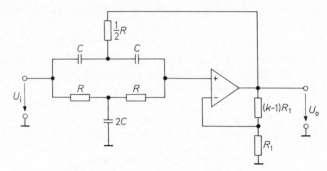

Fig. 14.36 Active parallel-T band-stop filter

$$A(S) = \frac{k(1 + S^2)}{1 + 2(2 - k)S + S^2}$$

Resonant frequency: $f_r = \dfrac{1}{2\pi RC}$

Gain: $A_0 = k$

Rejection Q-factor: $Q = \dfrac{1}{2(2 - k)}$

For high and low frequencies, the parallel-T filter transfers the input signal unchanged. The output voltage of the impedance converter is then kU_i. At the resonant frequency, the output voltage is zero. In this case, the parallel-T filter behaves as if resistor $R/2$ were connected to ground. Therefore, the resonant frequency $f_r = 1/2\pi RC$, remains unchanged. From the transfer function, the filter data given below Fig. 14.36 can be directly deduced. If the voltage follower has unity gain, $Q = 0.5$. For an increase in gain, Q rises towards infinity as k approaches 2.

A precondition for the correct operation of the circuit is the precise adjustment of the resonant frequency and gain of the parallel-T filter. This is difficult to achieve for higher Q-factors since varying one resistance always affects both parameters simultaneously. The active Wien-Robinson band-stop filter is more favorable in this respect.

14.9.3   Active Wien-Robinson band-stop filter

As is shown in Section 2.5, the Wien-Robinson bridge also behaves like a notch filter. However, its Q-factor is not much higher than that of the parallel-T filter, but it can also be raised to any desired value by incorporating

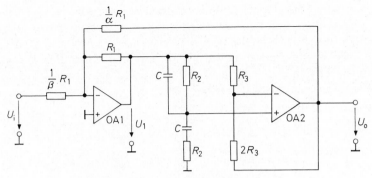

Fig. 14.37 Active Wien-Robinson band-stop filter

$$A(S) = -\frac{\dfrac{\beta}{1+\alpha}(1+S^2)}{1+\dfrac{3}{1+\alpha}S+S^2}$$

Resonant frequency: $f_r = \dfrac{1}{2\pi R_2 C}$

Gain: $A_0 = \dfrac{\beta}{1+\alpha}$

Rejection Q-factor: $Q = \dfrac{1+\alpha}{3}$

the filter in the feedback loop of an operational amplifier. The corresponding circuit is shown in Fig. 14.37, and its transfer function is obtained from the relation for the Wien-Robinson bridge:

$$\underline{U}_o = \frac{1-\Omega^2}{1+3j\Omega-\Omega^2}\underline{U}_1$$

which directly yields the filter data given below Fig. 14.37. For the actual design of the circuit, the parameters f_r, A_0, Q and C are defined and the remaining parameters are then

$$R_2 = \frac{1}{2\pi f_r C}, \qquad \alpha = 3Q-1 \quad \text{and} \quad \beta = 3A_0 Q .$$

In order to tune the filter to the resonant frequency, the capacitors C are changed in steps and the two resistors R_2 can be varied continuously using potentiometers. If the resonant frequency is not fully suppressed due to a slight mismatch of the bridge components, the final adjustment can be made by slightly varying resistor $2R_3$.

14.10   Allpass filters

14.10.1   Basic principles

The filters discussed so far are circuits for which the gain and phase shift are frequency dependent. In this section, we examine circuits for which the gain remains constant but the phase shift is dependent on the frequency. These are called allpass filters, and they are used for phase correction and signal delay.

Initially, we show how the frequency response of an allpass filter can be derived from the frequency response of a lowpass filter. To do this, the constant factor A_0 in the numerator of Eq. (14.11) is replaced by the conjugate complex denominator and, in this way, constant unity gain and phase shift doubling is obtained:

$$A(S) = \frac{\prod_i (1 - a_i S + b_i S^2)}{\prod_i (1 + a_i S + b_i S^2)} = \frac{\prod_i \sqrt{(1 - b_i \Omega^2)^2 + a_i^2 \Omega^2}\, e^{-j\alpha}}{\prod_i \sqrt{(1 - b_i \Omega^2)^2 + a_i^2 \Omega^2}\, e^{+j\alpha}} \qquad (14.35)$$

$$= 1 \cdot e^{-2j\alpha} = e^{j\varphi} ,$$

where

$$\varphi = -2\alpha = -2\sum_i \arctan \frac{a_i \Omega}{1 - b_i \Omega^2} . \qquad (14.36)$$

The use of allpass filters for signal delay is of particular interest. Constant gain is one prerequisite for undistorted signal transfer, a condition always fulfilled by allpass filters. The second prerequisite is that the group delay of the circuit is constant for all frequencies considered. The filters which best fulfill this condition are Bessel lowpass filters for which the group delay is Butterworth-approximated. Therefore, in order to obtain a "Butterworth allpass filter", the Bessel coefficients must be inserted in Eq. (14.35).

It is advisable, however, to re-normalize the frequency responses thus obtained, as the 3 dB cutoff frequency of the lowpass filters is in this case meaningless. For this reason, we recalculate the coefficients a_i and b_i so that the group delay at $\Omega = 1$ is reduced to $1/\sqrt{2}$ of its low-frequency value. The coefficients obtained in this way are shown in Fig. 14.38 for filters of up to the tenth order.

The group delay is the time interval by which the signal is delayed in the allpass filter. According to the definition, Eq. (14.9b), it can be determined from Eq. (14.36):

$$T_{gr} = \frac{t_{gr}}{T_c} = t_{gr} \cdot f_c = -\frac{1}{2\pi} \cdot \frac{d\varphi}{d\Omega}$$

$$= \frac{1}{\pi} \sum_i \frac{a_i(1 + b_i \Omega^2)}{1 + (a_i^2 - 2b_i)\Omega^2 + b_i^2 \Omega^4} , \qquad (14.37)$$

and therefore at low frequencies has the value

$$T_{gr0} = \frac{1}{\pi} \sum_i a_i ,$$

which is given for each order in Fig. 14.38. In addition, the pole-pair quality factor $Q_i = \sqrt{b_i}/a_i$ is given. As it is unaffected by the renormalization, it has the same values as for the Bessel filters.

n	i	a_i	b_i	f_i/f_c	Q_i	T_{gr0}
1	1	0.6436	0.0000	1.554	–	0.2049
2	1	1.6278	0.8832	1.064	0.58	0.5181
3	1	1.1415	0.0000	0.876	–	0.8437
	2	1.5092	1.0877	0.959	0.69	
4	1	2.3370	1.4878	0.820	0.52	1.1738
	2	1.3506	1.1837	0.919	0.81	
5	1	1.2974	0.0000	0.771	–	1.5060
	2	2.2224	1.5685	0.798	0.56	
	3	1.2116	1.2330	0.901	0.92	
6	1	2.6117	1.7763	0.750	0.51	1.8395
	2	2.0706	1.6015	0.790	0.61	
	3	1.0967	1.2596	0.891	1.02	
7	1	1.3735	0.0000	0.728	–	2.1737
	2	2.5320	1.8169	0.742	0.53	
	3	1.9211	1.6116	0.788	0.66	
	4	1.0023	1.2743	0.886	1.13	
8	1	2.7541	1.9420	0.718	0.51	2.5084
	2	2.4174	1.8300	0.739	0.56	
	3	1.7850	1.6101	0.788	0.71	
	4	0.9239	1.2822	0.883	1.23	
9	1	1.4186	0.0000	0.705	–	2.8434
	2	2.6979	1.9659	0.713	0.52	
	3	2.2940	1.8282	0.740	0.59	
	4	1.6644	1.6027	0.790	0.76	
	5	0.8579	1.2862	0.882	1.32	
10	1	2.8406	2.0490	0.699	0.50	3.1786
	2	2.6120	1.9714	0.712	0.54	
	3	2.1733	1.8184	0.742	0.62	
	4	1.5583	1.5923	0.792	0.81	
	5	0.8018	1.2877	0.881	1.42	

Fig. 14.38 Allpass filter coefficients for a maximally flat group delay

To enable the correct operation of the individual filter stages to be checked, we have also shown the ratio f_i/f_c in Fig. 14.38. Here, f_i is the frequency at which the phase of the particular filter stage approaches the value $-180°$ for a second-order, or $-90°$ for a first-order filter stage. This frequency is considerably easier to measure than the cutoff frequency of the group delay.

The frequency response of the group delay is shown in Fig. 14.39 for allpass filters of the first to the tenth order.

The following example shows the steps in the design of an allpass filter. A signal having a frequency spectrum of 0 to 1 kHz is to be delayed by

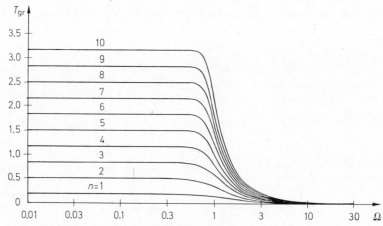

Fig. 14.39 Frequency response of the group delay for orders 1 to 10

$t_{\mathrm{gr}0} = 2$ ms. In order that the phase distortion is not too large, the cutoff frequency of the allpass filter must be $f_c \geqq 1$ kHz. From Eq. (14.9a), it is therefore necessary that

$$T_{\mathrm{gr}0} \geqq 2 \text{ ms} \cdot 1 \text{ kHz} = 2.00 \; .$$

From Fig. 14.38, it can be seen that a filter of at least seventh order is needed for which $T_{\mathrm{gr}0} = 2.1737$. To make the group delay exactly 2 ms, the cutoff frequency must be selected, in accordance with Eq. (14.9a), as

$$f_c = \frac{T_{\mathrm{gr}0}}{t_{\mathrm{gr}0}} = \frac{2.1737}{2 \text{ ms}} = 1.087 \text{ kHz} \; .$$

14.10.2   Realization of first-order allpass filters

The circuit in Fig. 14.40 exhibits gain $+1$ at low frequencies and gain -1 at high frequencies, i.e. the phase shift changes from zero to $-180°$. The circuit is an allpass filter if the magnitude of the gain is also unity for the middle frequency range. To examine this, we consider the transfer function in Fig. 14.40. The

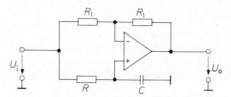

Fig. 14.40 First-order allpass filter

$$A(S) = \frac{1 - sRC}{1 + sRC} = \frac{1 - RC\omega_c S}{1 + RC\omega_c S}$$

absolute value of the gain is indeed constant and unity. Comparing the coefficients with those of Eq. (14.35) gives

$$RC = \frac{a_1}{2\pi f_c} .$$

With Eq. (14.37), the low-frequency value of the group delay is therefore

$$t_{gr0} = 2\,RC .$$

The first-order allpass filter in Fig. 14.40 is very well suited for use as a phase shifter over a wide range of phase delays. By varying the value of resistor R, the phase delay can be adjusted to values between 0 and $-180°$ without affecting the amplitude. The phase shift is

$$\varphi = -2\arctan(\omega RC) .$$

14.10.3 Realization of second-order allpass filters

The second-order allpass filter transfer function can be implemented, for example, by subtracting the output voltage of a bandpass filter from its input voltage. The transfer function of this circuit is then

$$A(S') = 1 - \frac{\dfrac{A_r}{Q}S'}{1 + \dfrac{1}{Q}S' + S'^2} = \frac{1 + \dfrac{1 - A_r}{Q}S' + S'^2}{1 + \dfrac{1}{Q}S' + S'^2} .$$

It can be seen that for $A_r = 2$, the transfer function of an allpass filter is obtained. It is normalized not to the cutoff frequency of the allpass, but to the resonant frequency of the bandpass filter. For a correct normalization, we take

$$\omega_c = \beta\omega_r$$

and obtain

$$S' = \frac{s}{\omega_r} = \frac{\beta s}{\omega_c} = \beta S .$$

Hence, the transfer function

$$A(S) = \frac{1 - \dfrac{\beta}{Q}S + \beta^2 S^2}{1 + \dfrac{\beta}{Q}S + \beta^2 S^2} .$$

Comparing the coefficients with those of Eq. (14.35) yields

$$a_1 = \frac{\beta}{Q} \quad\text{and}\quad b_1 = \beta^2 .$$

The data of the required bandpass filter are therefore

$$A_r = 2 \ ,$$

$$f_r = f_c/\sqrt{b_1} \ ,$$

$$Q = \sqrt{b_1}/a_1 = Q_1 \ .$$

As an example, let us consider the implementation using the bandpass in Fig. 14.32. As the Q-factors are relatively small, resistor R_3 may be omitted and the gain adjusted by resistor R/α in Fig. 14.41 instead. The component values are obtained by comparing the coefficients of the transfer function with those of Eq. (14.35):

$$R_1 = \frac{a_1}{4\pi f_c C} \ , \qquad R_2 = \frac{b_1}{\pi f_c C a_1} \quad \text{and} \quad \alpha = \frac{a_1^2}{b_1} = \frac{1}{Q_1^2} \ .$$

From the transfer function, a further application of the circuit in Fig. 14.41 can be deduced. If

$$2R_1 - \alpha R_2 = 0 \ ,$$

a band-stop filter circuit is obtained.

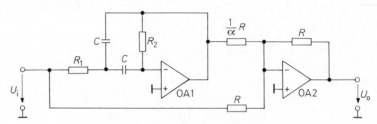

Fig. 14.41 Second-order allpass filter

$$A(S) = -\frac{1 + (2R_1 - \alpha R_2)C\omega_c S + R_1 R_2 C^2 \omega_c^2 S^2}{1 + 2R_1 C\omega_c S + R_1 R_2 C^2 \omega_c^2 S^2} \ .$$

14.11   Adjustable universal filter

As shown previously, the transfer function of a second-order filter element has the general form

$$A(S) = \frac{d_0 + d_1 S + d_2 S^2}{c_0 + c_1 S + c_2 S^2} \ . \tag{14.38}$$

The filter families described so far can be deduced from Eq. (14.38) by assigning special values to the coefficients of the numerator:

lowpass filter: $d_1 = d_2 = 0$;
highpass filter: $d_0 = d_1 = 0$;
bandpass filter: $d_0 = d_2 = 0$;
band-stop filter: $d_1 = 0$, $d_0 = d_2$;
allpass filter: $d_0 = c_0$, $d_1 = -c_1$, $d_2 = c_2$.

The numerator coefficients may have either sign, whereas the coefficients of the denominator must always be positive for reasons of stability. The pole-pair Q-factor is defined by the denominator coefficients

$$Q_i = \frac{\sqrt{c_0 c_2}}{c_1} \; . \tag{14.39}$$

Filter with variable coefficients

In the previous sections we have shown specific and, if possible, simple circuits for each filter type. Sometimes, however, a single circuit is required to realize all the described kinds of filters, as well as the more general types in Eq. (14.38) with any numerator coefficients. This problem can be solved by using the circuit in Fig. 14.42. This circuit has the added advantage that the individual coefficients can be set independently of one another, as each coefficient is determined by only one circuit component. In the transfer function given below Fig. 14.42, ω_0 is the normalizing frequency and $\tau = RC$ is the time constant of the two integrators. The coefficients k_i and l_i are resistance ratios and therefore always positive. If the sign of a numerator coefficient is to be changed, the input voltage of the filter must be inverted by an additional amplifier to which the corresponding resistor is connected.

To realize a higher-order filter, the number of integrators can be raised accordingly. However, it is usually easier to split the filter into second-order stages and cascade them.

The design process for the circuit is illustrated by the following example: a second-order allpass filter is required, the group delay curve of which is maximally flat and has, at low frequencies, the value 1 ms. From the table in Fig. 14.38 we take the values $a_1 = 1.6278$, $b_1 = 0.8832$ and $T_{\mathrm{gr}0} = 0.5181$. Equation (14.9a) gives the cutoff frequency

$$f_c = \frac{T_{\mathrm{gr}0}}{t_{\mathrm{gr}0}} = \frac{0.5181}{1 \text{ ms}} = 518.1 \text{ Hz} \; .$$

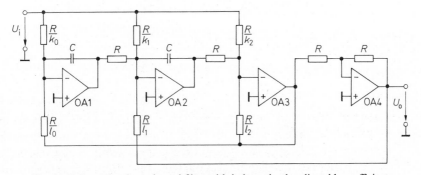

Fig. 14.42 Second-order universal filter with independently adjustable coefficients

$$A(S) = \frac{k_0 - k_1 \omega_0 \tau S + k_2 \omega_0^2 \tau^2 S^2}{l_0 + l_1 \omega_0 \tau S + l_2 \omega_0^2 \tau^2 S^2} \; .$$

We select $\tau = 1$ ms and, by comparing the coefficients of Eqs. (14.40) and (14.35), and using $\omega_0 = 2\pi f_c = 3.26$ kHz, obtain the values

$$l_0 = k_0 = 1 \ , \qquad l_1 = k_1 = \frac{a_1}{\omega_0\tau} = 0.500 \ , \qquad l_2 = k_2 = \frac{b_1}{(\omega_0\tau)^2} = 0.0833 \ .$$

Such a low value of l_2 is difficult to obtain in practice. However, it increases more rapidly than the other coefficients when τ is reduced. We therefore choose $\tau = 0.3$ ms and obtain

$$l_0 = k_0 = 1 \ , \qquad l_1 = k_1 = 1.67 \quad \text{and} \quad l_2 = k_2 = 0.926 \ .$$

Filter with adjustable parameters

For some applications of a bandpass filter, it is desirable that the resonant frequency, the Q-factor and the gain at resonant frequency can be set independently. As a comparison of Eq. (14.40) and Eq. (14.21) shows, the two coefficients l_1 and k_1 should be simultaneously adjustable to enable the Q-factor to be set without affecting the gain. Figure 14.43 shows a circuit in which such a dependence is eliminated.

The circuit is interesting in that it acts simultaneously as a bandpass filter, as a band-stop filter, as a lowpass and as a highpass filter, depending on which output is used. To calculate the filter parameters, we obtain from the circuit the following relationships if we use $\tau = RC$ for the integration time constant:

$$U_{\text{BS}} = -U_{\text{BP}} - \frac{R_1}{R_2}U_i \ , \qquad U_{\text{HP}} = -\frac{R_3}{R_1}U_{\text{LP}} - \frac{R_3}{R_4}U_{\text{BS}}$$

$$U_{\text{BP}} = -U_{\text{HP}}/s\tau \ ; \qquad U_{\text{LP}} = -U_{\text{BP}}/s\tau \ .$$

By eliminating three of the four output voltages, we obtain the stated transfer functions. The circuit parameters are obtained by comparing the coefficients with those in Eqs. (14.11), (14.15), (14.21) and (14.34). This is particularly simple if we put $\tau \cdot \omega_c = 1$, i.e. select $RC = 1/2\pi f_c$:

Lowpass filter	Highpass filter	Bandpass, band-stop filter
given: R_1	given: R_1	given: R_1
$R_3 = R_1/b_i$	$R_3 = R_1 b_i$	$R_3 = R_1$
$R_4 = R_1/a_i$	$R_4 = R_1 b_i/a_i$	$R_4 = R_1 Q$
$R_2 = R_1 a_i/A_0$	$R_2 = R_1 a_i/A_\infty$	$R_2 = -R_1/A_r$.

We can see from these equations that R_3 and R_4 determine the filter type for highpass and lowpass filters, and R_2 the gain. For any given type of filter, the cutoff frequency and the gain can be adjusted independently of one another.

Even for bandpass and band-rejection filter operation, the resonant frequency, gain and Q-factor can be varied without one affecting the other. This is because the resonant frequency is determined solely by the product $\tau = RC$. As

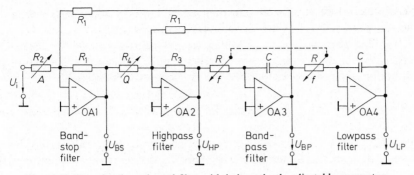

Fig. 14.43 Second-order universal filter with independently adjustable parameters
Integration time constant $\tau = RC$

$$\frac{\underline{U}_{LP}}{\underline{U}_i} = \frac{\dfrac{R_1^2}{R_2 R_4}}{1 + \dfrac{R_1}{R_4}\tau\omega_c S + \dfrac{R_1}{R_3}\tau^2\omega_c^2 S^2} \qquad \text{(Lowpass filter)}$$

$$\frac{\underline{U}_{HP}}{\underline{U}_i} = \frac{\dfrac{R_1 R_3}{R_2 R_4}}{1 + \dfrac{R_3}{R_4\tau\omega_c}\cdot\dfrac{1}{S} + \dfrac{R_3}{R_1\tau^2\omega_c^2}\cdot\dfrac{1}{S^2}} \qquad \text{(Highpass filter)}$$

$$\frac{\underline{U}_{BP}}{\underline{U}_i} = \frac{-\dfrac{R_1^2}{R_2 R_4}\tau\omega_r S}{1 + \dfrac{R_1}{R_4}\tau\omega_r S + \dfrac{R_1}{R_3}\tau^2\omega_c^2 S^2} \qquad \text{(Bandpass filter)}$$

$$\frac{\underline{U}_{BS}}{\underline{U}_i} = \frac{-\dfrac{R_1}{R_2}\left(1 + \dfrac{R_1}{R_3}\tau^2\omega_c^2 S^2\right)}{1 + \dfrac{R_1}{R_4}\tau\omega_r S + \dfrac{R_1}{R_3}\tau^2\omega_c^2 S^2} \qquad \text{(Band-stop filter)}$$

these variables do not occur in the equations for A and Q, the frequency can be varied without affecting A and Q. These two parameters can be set independently using resistors R_2 and R_4.

Universal filters are available as integrated circuits. The only external circuitry required is a pair of resistors for determining the filter type and the cutoff frequency. However, they have now been largely superseded by integrated switched-capacitor filters (SC filters) which are described in Section 14.12. The continuously tunable filters described here are nowadays only used if the 70 to 90 dB signal-to-noise ratio of the SC filters is insufficient.

Electronic control of filter parameters

As the resistors R have large values for low filter frequencies, it may in this case be advantageous to replace them by fixed resistors connected to voltage

dividers. The voltage divider can then be realized by low resistance potentiometers. This method may also be used for the resistors R_1 and R_2.

If a filter parameter is to be voltage controlled, the voltage divider can be
replaced by an analog multiplier, where the control voltage is connected to the
second input, as shown in Fig. 14.44. The effective resistance is then

$$R_x = R_0 \cdot \frac{E}{U_{control}} \, ,$$

where $U_{control}$ is the controlling voltage. If two such circuits are inserted instead
of the two frequency-determining resistors R, the resonant frequency of the
bandpass filter becomes

$$f_r = \frac{1}{2\pi R_0 C} \cdot \frac{U_{control}}{E} \, ,$$

and is proportional to the control voltage.

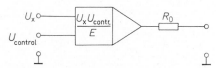

Fig. 14.44   Multiplier as a controlled resistor

For numerical control of filter parameters, e.g. via a computer, digital-
to-analog (D/A) converters can be used instead of analog multipliers. These
provide an output voltage proportional to the product of the applied number
and reference voltage:

$$U_o = U_{ref} \frac{Z}{Z_{max} + 1} \, .$$

The types preferred for use in filters are those whose reference voltage can
assume any positive or negative value. Consequently, the multiplying D/A
converters with CMOS switches described in Section 23.2 are particularly
suitable for this purpose, but as they possess considerable resistor tolerances,
they cannot simply be inserted as series resistors in Fig. 14.43. However, the
effect of the absolute resistance value can be eliminated by providing a following
operational amplifier with a feedback path via a resistor incorporated in the
D/A converter. The resulting circuit for digital frequency adjustment is shown in
Fig. 14.45. The two integrators are preceded by a D/A converter. The resulting
integration time constant is

$$\tau = RC(Z_{max} + 1)/Z \, . \tag{14.40}$$

If the number Z equals the maximum value Z_{max}, i.e. all the bits are one,
virtually the same resonant frequency is obtained as in the circuit shown in
Fig. 14.43.

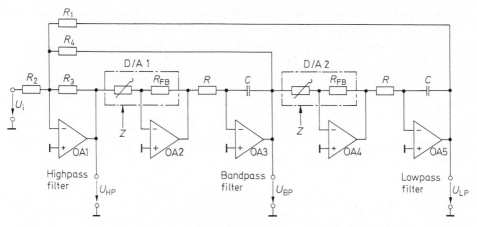

Fig. 14.45 Universal filter with digitally adjustable frequency. Integration time constant:

$$\tau = RC(Z_{max} + 1)/Z$$

$$\frac{U_{LP}}{U_i} = \frac{-R_1/R_2}{1 + \dfrac{R_1}{R_4}\tau\omega_c S + \dfrac{R_1}{R_3}\tau^2\omega_c^2 S^2} \qquad \text{(Lowpass filter)}$$

$$\frac{U_{HP}}{U_i} = \frac{-R_1/R_2}{1 + \dfrac{R_3}{R_4\tau\omega_c}\cdot\dfrac{1}{S} + \dfrac{R_3}{R_1\tau^2\omega_c^2}\cdot\dfrac{1}{S^2}} \qquad \text{(Highpass filter)}$$

$$\frac{U_{BP}}{U_i} = \frac{-\dfrac{R_1}{R_2}\tau\omega_r S}{1 + \dfrac{R_1}{R_4}\tau\omega_r S + \dfrac{R_1}{R_3}\tau^2\omega_c^2 S^2} \qquad \text{(Bandpass filter)}$$

In comparison with Fig. 14.43, the arrangement of the feedback loops is modified somewhat, because the D/A converters in conjunction with the associated operational amplifiers and following integrators form a *non-inverting integrator*. However, the resulting transfer functions are quite similar. Selecting component values is particularly simple if one selects $\tau\omega_c = 1$, i.e. $f_c = 1/2\pi\tau$:

Lowpass filter	Highpass filter	Bandpass filter
given: R_1	given: R_1	given: R_1
$R_3 = R_1/b_i$	$R_3 = R_1 b_i$	$R_3 = R_1$
$R_4 = R_1/a_i$	$R_4 = R_3/a_i$	$R_4 = R_1 Q$
$R_2 = -R_1/A_0$	$R_2 = -R_3/A_\infty$	$R_2 = -R_1 Q/A_r$.

Substituting the integration time constant in Eq. (14.40), we can see that the cutoff and resonant frequencies become proportional to the number Z:

$$f_c = \frac{1}{2\pi\tau} = \frac{1}{2\pi RC}\cdot\frac{Z}{Z_{max} + 1} \; .$$

The outputs of the D/A converters must have a large dynamic range in order to be able to adjust the frequency over a wide band. To prevent any DC errors in the circuit, it is necessary to use operational amplifiers with low offset voltage. One suitable type, which also features a high slew rate, is the OP 227 from PMI. Suitable devices for D/A conversion include the AD 7528 (8 bit) or the AD 7537 (12 bit) from Analog Devices, as these incorporate two D/A converters with a common computer interface.

A considerably simpler way of implementing an adjustable filter is to use SC filters of the type described in Section 14.12. These are also available in a variety of IC versions.

14.12   Switched capacitor filters

14.12.1   Basic principle

The active filters described above require an active component in the form of an operational amplifier as well as passive elements in the form of capacitors and resistors. Normally, filters with variable cutoff frequency are only realized by varying the capacitors or resistors (see Fig. 14.45). However, it is also possible to simulate a resistor by means of a switched capacitor. Figure 14.46 shows the principle involved.

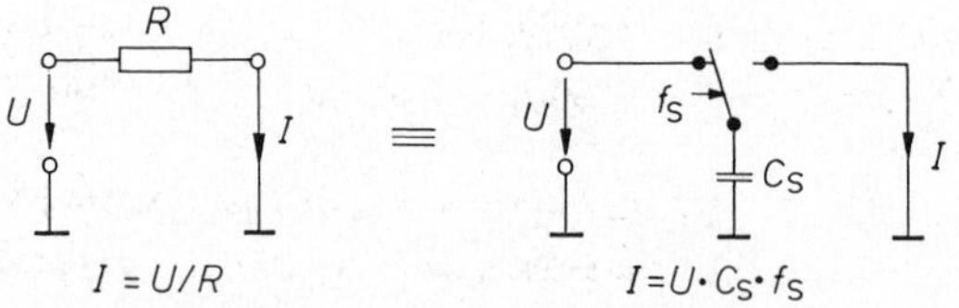

Fig. 14.46 Equivalence of switched capacitor and ohmic resistor

If the switch in the arrangement shown connects the switched capacitor to the input voltage, capacitor C receives the charge $Q = C_S \cdot U$. In the other switch position, the capacitor delivers the same charge again. In each switching period it therefore transfers the charge $Q = C_S \cdot U$ from the input to the output of the circuit. This produces an average current flow of $I = C_S \cdot U/T_S = C_S \cdot Uf_S$. Comparing this relation with Ohm's Law, the basic equivalence between the switched capacitor and an ohmic resistor can be expressed in the form

$$I = U/R_{equiv} = U \cdot C_S \cdot f_S \quad \text{with} \quad R_{equiv} = 1/C_S \cdot f_S \ .$$

Note the proportional relationship between the switching frequency and the equivalent conductance. It is this property that is utilized in switched capacitor (SC) filters.

14.12.2   The SC integrator

The switched capacitor can replace the ohmic resistor in the conventional integrator shown in Fig. 14.47. The result is the SC integrator of Fig. 14.48. In an

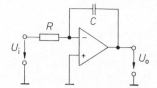

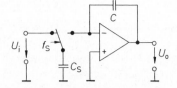

Fig. 14.47 Inverting integrator in RC technology   Fig. 14.48 Inverting integrator in SC technology

$$\tau = RC \qquad \frac{U_o'}{U_i} = -\frac{1}{\tau p} \qquad\qquad \tau = \frac{1}{f_s}\cdot\frac{C}{C_s} \qquad \frac{U_o}{U_i} = -\frac{1}{\tau p}$$

arrangement of this kind, the integration time constant

$$\tau = CR_{\text{equiv}} = \frac{C}{C_s f_s} = \frac{\eta}{2\pi f_s} \tag{14.41}$$

can be set by the switching frequency f_s. The capacitance ratio $C/C_s = \eta/2\pi$ is permanently preset by the manufacturer; the parameter η can be obtained from the data sheet. It is generally between 50 and 200 [14.9].

However, using switched capacitors has yet more advantages: the implementation of a non-inverting integrator in conventional technology requires an inverting integrator with a preceding or following voltage inverter. With the SC integrator, the polarity of the input voltage can be changed simply by connecting the capacitor, which has been charged up to the input voltage to be sampled, with *reversed* terminals to the operational amplifier input during the following charge transfer phase. Reversal of the terminals can be effected as shown Fig. 14.49 using an additional changeover switch S_2 which switches simultaneously with S_1.

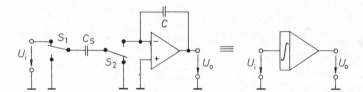

Fig. 14.49 The non-inverting integrator in SC technology and its circuit symbol

$$U_o = +f_s\frac{C_s}{C}\int U_i\,dt = \frac{1}{\tau}\int U_i\,dt \qquad \frac{U_o}{U_i} = \frac{f_s}{s}\cdot\frac{C_s}{C} = \frac{1}{\tau\cdot s}$$

The charging and discharging of the capacitor C_s does not occur instantaneously, but exponentially due to the unavoidable resistances in the switches. Instantaneous charging and discharging would also be completely undesirable, because neither the input voltage source nor the operational amplifier could supply the required currents. On the other hand, these parasitic resistances also determine the maximum switching frequency, as a complete charge-discharge cycle is impossible at too high a switching frequency.

14.12.3   First-order SC filter

The two basic SC integrators circuits can be extended by a feedback resistor to produce a first-order lowpass filter similar to that in Fig. 14.17. However, a different basic structure is generally selected for the monolithic version. This consists of an SC-type integrator preceded by an additional summing amplifier with three supplementary resistors then connected as shown in Fig. 14.50. This arrangement simultaneously provides a highpass and a lowpass filter.

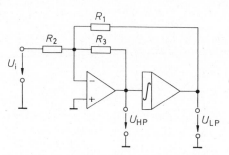

Fig. 14.50 First-order highpass and lowpass filter

$$\text{Integration time constant:}\quad \tau = \frac{C}{C_s f_s} = \frac{\eta}{2\pi f_s}$$

$$\frac{U_{LP}}{U_i} = \frac{-R_1/R_2}{1 + \dfrac{\tau\omega_c R_1}{R_3}\cdot S} \qquad\qquad \frac{U_{HP}}{U_i} = \frac{-R_3/R_2}{1 + \dfrac{R_3}{\tau\omega_c R_1}\cdot\dfrac{1}{S}}$$

To determine the component values, we simply select $f_s/f_c = \eta$. The transfer functions then yield

Lowpass filter	Highpass filter
given: R_1	given: R_1
$R_3 = R_1/a_1$	$R_3 = R_1 a_1$
$R_2 = -R_1/A_0$	$R_2 = -R_3/A_\infty$

In the case of first-order filters, for which $a_1 = 1$ in accordance with Fig. 14.14, we therefore have $R_3 = R_1$. The gains of lowpass and highpass filter are therefore equal, the circuit thus representing complementary highpass and lowpass filters.

14.12.4   Design of second-order SC filters

Second-order SC filters are mainly designed as "biquad" structures as in Fig. 14.45. As non-inverting integrators are once again employed, we obtain the same structure and identical transfer functions (monolithic IC universal filters always contain this biquad structure). Unlike in the RC-filter case, the integration time constant τ as formulated in Eq. (14.41) is determined by the switching frequency f_s selected.

To determine the transfer function, we derive the following relations from the circuit in Fig. 14.51:

$$U_{HP} = -\frac{R_3}{R_1}U_i - \frac{R_3}{R_4}U_{BP} - \frac{R_3}{R_2}U_{LP} \, ,$$

$$U_{BP} = \frac{1}{\tau s}U_{HP} \, ; \qquad U_{LP} = \frac{1}{\tau s}U_{BP} \, .$$

From these, we can calculate the specified transfer function for the individual filters. If the switching frequency is again made equal to the η-th multiple of the cutoff frequency (or resonant frequency), we get $\tau\omega_c = 1$, and obtain the following design equations:

Lowpass filter	Highpass filter	Bandpass filter
given: R_1	given: R_1	given: R_1
$R_3 = R_1/b_1$	$R_3 = R_1 b_1$	$R_3 = R_1$
$R_4 = R_1/a_1$	$R_4 = R_3/a_1$	$R_4 = R_1 Q$
$R_2 = -R_1/A_0$	$R_2 = -R_3/A_\infty$	$R_2 = -R_1 Q/A_r \, .$

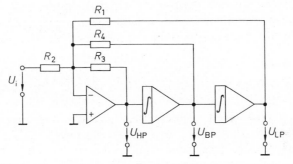

Fig. 14.51 SC biquad to synthesize second-order highpass, lowpass and bandpass filters

Integration time constant: $\quad \tau = \dfrac{C}{C_s f_s} = \dfrac{\eta}{2\pi f_s}$

$$\frac{U_{LP}}{U_i} = \frac{-R_1/R_2}{1 + \dfrac{R_1\tau\omega_c}{R_4}S + \dfrac{R_1\tau^2\omega_c^2}{R_3}S^2} \qquad \text{(Lowpass)}$$

$$\frac{U_{HP}}{U_i} = \frac{-R_3/R_2}{1 + \dfrac{R_3}{R_4\tau\omega_c}\dfrac{1}{S} + \dfrac{R_3}{R_1\tau^2\omega_c^2}\dfrac{1}{S}} \qquad \text{(Highpass)}$$

$$\frac{U_{BP}}{U_i} = \frac{-S\tau\omega_r R_1/R_2}{1 + \dfrac{R_1\tau\omega_r}{R_4}S + \dfrac{R_1\tau^2\omega_r^2}{R_3}S^2} \qquad \text{(Bandpass)}$$

When the component values of one filter type have been defined, the other two do not, of course, necessarily have the same filter parameters. For the cutoff frequencies (or the resonant frequency) the following relation applies:

$$f_{cLP}/\sqrt{b_1} = f_{rBP} = f_{cHP}\sqrt{b_1} \ .$$

As $b_1 = 1$ for second-order filters, the three frequencies coincide. In this case the gains are given by

$$A_0 = A_r/Q = A_\infty \ .$$

As a design example, we shall calculate the component values of a second-order lowpass filter with a cutoff frequency $f_c = 1$ kHz, a gain in the pass band of $A_0 = -1$ and Butterworth characteristic. From Fig. 14.14, $a_1 = 1.4142$ and $b_1 = 1$. We select $R_2 = 10$ kΩ and thus obtain $R_1 = R_3 = 10$ kΩ and $R_4 = 7.15$ kΩ. For $\eta = 100$, the switching frequency must be $f_s = 100$ kHz. For these values we additionally obtain a highpass filter with $A_\infty = -1$ and Butterworth characteristic, as well as a bandpass filter with $A_r = -0.707$ and $Q = 0.707$.

Higher-order SC filters can be produced by cascading. The coefficients of the filter sections must then be selected from Fig. 14.14.

14.12.5   Implementation of SC filters as ICs

SC filters are of course implemented not with discrete components but using integrated circuits containing capacitors and operational amplifiers in addition to the switches. This not only is simpler for the user but also offers significant advantages, as will be shown below.

SC filter ICs employ the 2-switch arrangement illustrated in Fig. 14.49, because this arrangement compensates for the effect of stray capacitances. The changeover switches are realized in the form of a transmission gate and are driven by an internal clock generator which provides non-overlapping timing signals. This ensures that no charge is lost during switching.

As we can see, the capacitance ratio C/C_S together with the switching frequency f_s determine the integration time constant. The basic advantage of an IC implementation is that capacitance ratios with 0.1% tolerance can be produced. The use of monolithic SC filters therefore provides well-reproducible accuracies. In addition, the time constant is temperature-invariant, as the two capacitors exhibit identical temperature dependence if both are integrated on the same chip. Reproducible time constants, which are otherwise difficult and costly to achieve in IC technology, can be easily provided using SC devices. To achieve this, the ratio of the two capacitances must be appropriately selected.

14.12.6   General considerations for using SC filters

Despite the clearly superior characteristics of modern SC circuit design, the use of these components is subject to certain limitations, as these are actually sampling systems. Every time Shannon's sampling theorem is violated, one has to contend with unwanted mixing products in the base frequency band (aliasing). Consequently, the input system must not contain any frequency components above half the switching frequency f_S. In order to ensure this, analog filtering is generally required at the input which must introduce sufficient attenuation (some 70–90 dB) at $\frac{1}{2}f_S$. As the typical sampling frequency of SC filter ICs is approximately 50 to 100 times the cutoff frequency, a second-order analog filter acting as an anti-aliasing filter is normally adequate for this purpose.

The output signal of an SC filter always has a staircase waveform, as the output voltage only changes at the switching instant. It therefore contains spectral components associated with the switching frequency. Consequently, an analog smoothing filter must also be provided at the output to suit the particular application.

14.12.7 Survey of available types

The SC filters available nowadays mainly contain complete functional blocks comprising SC integrators, summing circuits and the associated (controllable) oscillators for clock generation. Their arrangement on the chip is either permanently fixed by masks (filters with fixed characteristics) or the components can be combined by the user as required (universal filters with variable characteristics). As the universal filters require external circuitry, the IC package involved must have more pins. The number of pins thus limits the complexity of the filter and, therefore, universal filter ICs are for low orders only. However, twin types in a single package are generally available, which can then be simply cascaded, thus allowing fourth-order filters to be realized on a single chip [14.10].

Switching by means of the clock frequency produces background noise in the filters which limits the signal-to-noise ratio to about 70–90 dB (Fig. 14.52). This constitutes a disadvantage compared with "continuous" RC filters [14.11].

Several manufacturers additionally offer freely configurable operational amplifiers on the same chip. These can be used as smoothing or anti-aliasing filters. Figure 14.52 shows a number of representative SC filters. In addition to these standard types, all manufacturers offer special semi-custom circuits.

Type	Manufacturer	Filter type	Filter order	Clock frequency			Dynamic range	Speciality
Universal filters								
CS 7008	Crystal	4 biquads	8	. . .	1	MHz	72 dB	μP-interface
LTC 1059	Lin. Tech.	2 biquads	2	. . .	2	MHz	90 dB	Op amp
LTC 1060	Lin. Tech.	2 biquads	2 × 2	. . .	1.5	MHz	90 dB	2 × LTC 1059
LTC 1061	Lin. Tech.	3 biquads	3 × 2	. . .	1.5	MHz	90 dB	3 × LTC 1059
LTC 1064	Lin. Tech.	4 biquads	4 × 2	. . .	1.5	MHz	90 dB	4 × LTC 1059
MAX 262	Maxim	2 biquads	2 × 2	40 Hz . . .	4	MHz		μP-interface
MAX 266	Maxim	2 biquads	2 × 2	40 Hz . . .	4	MHz		dig. prog.
LMF 100	National	2 biquads	2 × 2	. . .	10	MHz		
RF 5620	Reticon	1 biquad	2	500 kHz . . .	2	MHz	90 dB	dig. prog.
RF 5621	Reticon	2 biquads	2 × 2	25 Hz . . .	750	kHz	95 dB	
RF 5622	Reticon	4 biquads	4 × 2	25 Hz . . .	750	kHz	95 dB	
SC 22324	Sierra	4 biquads	4 × 2					dig. prog.
Lowpass filters								
XR 1001	EXAR	Butterworth	4	100 Hz . . .	1	MHz	72 dB	
XR 1003	EXAR	Bessel	4	100 Hz . . .	1	MHz	72 dB	
XR 1005	EXAR	Chebyshev	4	100 Hz . . .	1	MHz	72 dB	ripple 0.1 dB
LMF 40	National	Butterworth	4	5 Hz . . .	2	MHz	88 dB	
LMF 60	National	Butterworth	6	5 Hz . . .	2	MHz	88 dB	2 op amps
RF 5609	Reticon	Cauer	7	1 kHz . . .	2.5	MHz	75 dB	2 op amps
RF 5613	Reticon	Bessel	7	1 kHz . . .	2.5	MHz	75 dB	2 op amps
TSG 8512	Thomson	Cauer	7	1 kHz . . .	2	MHz	85 dB	2 op amps
TSG 8513	Thomson	Chebyshev	8	1 kHz . . .	1.5	MHz	85 dB	2 op amps
TSG 8514	Thomson	Butterworth	8	1 kHz . . .	1	MHz	87 dB	2 op amps
LTC 1064-2	Lin. Tech.	Butterworth	8	100 Hz . . .	7	MHz	90 dB	
LTC 1064-3	Lin. Tech.	Bessel	8	100 Hz . . .	7	MHz	90 dB	
LTC 1064-4	Lin. Tech.	Cauer	8	100 Hz . . .	7	MHz	90 dB	
Highpass filters								
RF 5611	Reticon	Chebyshev	5	5 kHz . . .	2.5	MHz	80 dB	
TSG 8531	Thomson	Cauer	6	4 kHz . . .	1.8	MHz	80 dB	2 op amps
TSG 8532	Thomson	Chebyshev	6	5 kHz . . .	1.8	MHz	85 dB	2 op amps
Bandpass filters								
MAX 268	Maxim		2 × 2	40 Hz . . .	4	MHz		
MF 8	National	Cheb. Butt.	2 × 2	100 Hz . . .	2	MHz		Q prog.
RM 5614	Reticon	Chebyshev	6	55 Hz . . .	1	MHz	76 dB	various Q
RF 5633	Reticon		6	1 kHz . . .	1.5	MHz	75 dB	filter bank
TSG 8550	Thomson	Cauer	6	1 kHz . . .	1.2	MHz	78 dB	2 op amps
TSG 8551	Thomson	Güte 35	8	4 kHz . . .	3.8	MHz	90 dB	2 op amps
Notch filters								
LMF 90	National	Cauer	4	10 Hz . . .	3	MHz	50 dB	cryst. osc.
RF 5612	Reticon		4	5 kHz . . .	2.5	MHz	65 dB	

Fig. 14.52 Examples of monolithic SC filters

15 Signal generators

In this Chapter we shall describe circuits which generate sinusoidal signals. In the case of LC oscillators, the frequency is determined by a tuned circuit, in the case of crystal-controlled oscillators a piezoelectric crystal is used, and with the Wien and differential-equation oscillators, RC networks are the frequency-determining components. The function generators primarily produce a triangular signal, which can be converted into sinusoidal form using a suitable function network.

15.1 *LC* oscillators

The simplest method of generating a sinewave is to use an amplifier to eliminate the damping of an LC resonant circuit. In the following section, we deal with some of the basic aspects of this method.

15.1.1 Condition for oscillation

Figure 15.1 shows the principle of an oscillator circuit. The amplifier multiplies the input voltage by the gain $\underline{A}$, and thereby causes a parasitic phase shift α between $\underline{U}_2$ and $\underline{U}_1$. The load resistance R_L and a frequency-dependent feedback network, for example a resonant circuit, are connected to the amplifier output. The voltage feedback is therefore $\underline{U}_3 = \underline{k}\underline{U}_2$, and the phase shift between $\underline{U}_3$ and $\underline{U}_2$ is denoted by β.

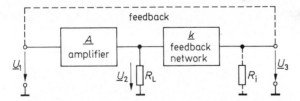

Fig. 15.1 Basic arrangement of an oscillator

To establish whether the circuit can produce oscillations, the feedback loop is opened. An additional resistor R_i is introduced at the output of the feedback network, representing the input resistance of the amplifier. An alternating voltage $\underline{U}_1$ is applied to the amplifier and $\underline{U}_3$ is measured. The circuit is capable of producing oscillations if the output voltage is the same as the input voltage. Hence, the necessary condition for oscillation

$$\underline{U}_1 = \underline{U}_3 = \underline{k}\underline{A}\underline{U}_1 \;.$$

The loop gain must therefore be

$$g = \underline{k}\underline{A} = 1 \; , \tag{15.1}$$

from which two conditions can be deduced, i.e.

$$|\underline{g}| = |\underline{k}| \cdot |\underline{A}| = 1 \tag{15.2}$$

and

$$\alpha + \beta = 0, 2\pi, \ldots \; . \tag{15.3}$$

Equation (15.2) is the *amplitude condition* which states that a circuit can oscillate only if the amplifier eliminates the attenuation due to the feedback network. The *phase condition* of Eq. (15.3) states that an oscillation can arise only if the output voltage is in phase with the input voltage. Details of the oscillation, e.g. frequency and waveform, can only be obtained with additional information on the feedback network. To this end, let us consider the *LC* oscillator in Fig. 15.2 as an example.

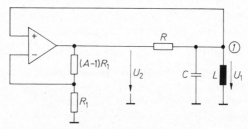

Fig. 15.2 Principle of an *LC* oscillator

The non-inverting amplifier multiplies the voltage $U_1(t)$ by the gain A. As the output resistance of the amplifier is low, the resonant circuit is damped by the parallel resistor R. To calculate the feedback voltage, we apply KCL to node 1 and obtain

$$\frac{U_2 - U_1}{R} - C\dot{U}_1 - \frac{1}{L}\int U_1 \, dt = 0 \; .$$

As $U_2 = AU_1$, it follows that

$$\ddot{U}_1 + \frac{1 - A}{RC}\dot{U}_1 + \frac{1}{LC}U_1 = 0 \; . \tag{15.4}$$

This is the differential equation of a damped oscillation. To abbreviate,

$$\gamma = \frac{1 - A}{2RC} \quad \text{and} \quad \omega_0^2 = \frac{1}{LC} \; ,$$

and therefore

$$\ddot{U}_1 + 2\gamma\dot{U}_1 + \omega_0^2 U_1 = 0 \; ,$$

the solution of which is given by

$$U_1(t) = U_0 \cdot e^{-\gamma t} \sin(\sqrt{\omega_0^2 - \gamma^2}\,t) \ . \tag{15.5}$$

One must differentiate between three cases:

1) $\gamma > 0$, i.e. $A < 1$.
   The amplitude of the AC output voltage decreases exponentially; the oscillation is damped.
2) $\gamma = 0$, i.e. $A = 1$.
   The result is a sinusoidal oscillation with the frequency $\omega_0 = \dfrac{1}{\sqrt{LC}}$ and with constant amplitude.
3) $\gamma < 0$, i.e. $A > 1$.
   The amplitude of the AC output voltage rises exponentially.

With Eq. (15.2) we have the necessary condition for an oscillation. This can now be described in more detail: For $A = 1$, a sinusoidal output voltage of constant amplitude and the frequency

$$\omega = \omega_0 = \frac{1}{\sqrt{LC}}$$

is obtained. With reduced feedback, the amplitude falls exponentially and with increased feedback, the amplitude rises exponentially. To ensure that the oscillation builds up after the supply has been switched on, the gain A must initially be larger than unity. The amplitude then rises exponentially until the amplifier begins to saturate. Because of the saturation, A decreases until it reaches the value 1; the output, however, is then no longer sinusoidal. If a sinusoidal output is required, an additional gain control circuit must ensure that $A = 1$ before the amplifier saturates. For the high-frequency range, resonant circuits with high Q-factors are usually simple to implement. The voltage of the resonant circuit is still sinusoidal, even if the amplifier saturates. For this frequency range, additional amplitude control is usually not required, and the voltage across the resonant circuit is then taken as the output voltage.

15.1.2 Meissner oscillator

The feature of a Meissner circuit that the feedback is provided by a transformer. A capacitor C, together with the transformer primary winding, forms the frequency-determining resonant circuit. Figures 15.3 to 15.5 show three Meissner oscillators, each in common-emitter connection. At the resonant frequency

$$\omega_0 = \frac{1}{\sqrt{LC}} \ ,$$

the amplified input voltage appears at the collector with maximum amplitude and with a phase shift of 180°. Part of this alternating voltage is fed back via the secondary winding. To fulfill the phase condition, the transformer must effect a further phase displacement of 180°. This is achieved by AC-grounding the secondary winding at the end having the same voltage polarity as the collector end of the primary winding. The dots on the two windings indicate which winding ends have the same polarity. The turns ratio is selected such that the magnitude of the loop gain $\underline{k}\underline{A}$ at resonant frequency is always larger than unity. Oscillation then begins when the supply is switched on, its amplitude rising exponentially until the transistor saturates. Saturation reduces the mean value of the gain until $|\underline{k}\underline{A}| = 1$ and the amplitude of the oscillation remains constant. Two saturation effects can be distinguished, that at the input and that at the output. The output saturation arises when the collector-base junction is forward biased. This is the case for the circuits in Figs. 15.3 and 15.5 when the collector potential goes negative. The maximum amplitude of the oscillation is therefore $\hat{U}_C = V^+$. The maxima of the collector potential are then $\hat{U}_{CE\,max} = 2V^+$. This affects the choice of the transistor. For the circuit in Fig. 15.4, the maximum amplitude is smaller than V^+, the reduction being due to the Zener voltage.

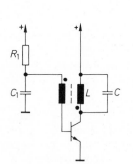

Fig. 15.3 Biasing by a constant base current

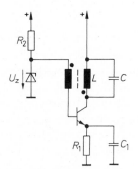

Fig. 15.4 Biasing by series feedback

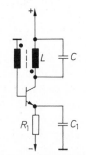

Fig. 15.5 Series feedback for a negative supply voltage

With heavy feedback, input saturation can also occur. Large input amplitudes arise which are rectified at the emitter-base junction. The capacitor C_1 is therefore charged, and the transistor conducts only during the positive peaks of the AC input voltage.

In the circuit of Fig. 15.3, a few oscillations may be sufficient to charge the capacitor C_1 to such a high negative voltage that the oscillation stops altogether. It restarts only after the base potential has risen to $+0.6$ V with the relatively large time constant $R_1 C_1$. In this case, a sawtooth voltage appears across C_1. This arrangement was therefore often used as a sawtooth generator, such a circuit being known as a *blocking oscillator*.

To prevent the circuit from operating in the blocking oscillator mode, the input saturation must be reduced by choosing a correspondingly smaller turns ratio. In addition, the resistance of the base biasing circuit should be kept as low as possible [15.1]. This is difficult to achieve for the circuit in Fig. 15.3 as the base current would then be excessively high. Biasing by series feedback, as in Figs. 15.4 and 15.5, is therefore preferable.

15.1.3   Hartley oscillator

The Hartley oscillator resembles a Meissner oscillator. The only difference is that the transformer is replaced by a tapped winding (auto-transformer). The inductance of this winding, together with the parallel-connected capacitor, determines the resonant frequency.

Figure 15.6 shows a Hartley oscillator in common-emitter connection. An alternating voltage is applied to the base via capacitor C_2; it is in phase opposition to the collector voltage, so that positive feedback occurs. The amplitude of the feedback voltage can be adjusted to the required value by appropriate positioning of the tap. As with the Meissner oscillator in Fig. 15.5, the collector quiescent current is determined by the series feedback resistor R_1.

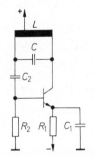

Fig. 15.6 Hartley oscillator in
common-emitter connection

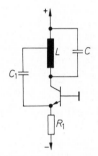

Fig. 15.7 Hartley oscillator in
common-base connection

For the Hartley oscillator in Fig. 15.7, the transistor is operated in common-base connection. Therefore, a voltage must be taken from the inductor L by means of capacitor C_1, in phase with the collector voltage.

15.1.4   Colpitts oscillator

A characteristic of the Colpitts circuit is the capacitive voltage divider determining the fraction of the output voltage that is fed back. The series connection of the capacitors acts as the oscillator capacitance, i.e.

$$C = \frac{C_a C_b}{C_a + C_b} \cdot$$

The common-emitter circuit of Fig. 15.8 corresponds to the circuit in Fig. 15.6, but requires an additional collector resistor R_3 for applying the positive supply voltage.

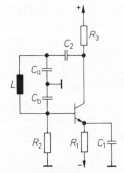

Fig. 15.8 Colpitts oscillator in
common-emitter connection

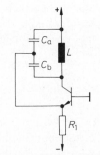

Fig. 15.9 Colpitts oscillator in
common-base connection

The common-base connection is again much simpler, as can be seen in
Fig. 15.9. It corresponds to the Hartley oscillator of Fig. 15.7.

15.1.5   Emitter-coupled *LC* oscillator

A simple way of realizing an oscillator is to use a differential amplifier, as in
Fig. 15.10. As the base potential of T_1 is in phase with the collector potential of
T_2, positive feedback can be attained by directly connecting the two terminals.
The loop gain is proportional to the transconductance of the transistors. It can
be adjusted over a wide range by varying the emitter current. As the transistors
are operated at $U_{CB} = 0$, the amplitude of the output voltage is limited to about
0.5 V.

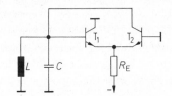

Fig. 15.10 Emitter-coupled oscillator

The amplifier of the emitter-coupled oscillator, together with an output stage
and amplitude control, is available as an IC (MC 1648 from Motorola). It is
suitable for frequencies of up to about 200 MHz.

15.1.6   Push-pull oscillators

Push-pull circuits are used in power amplifiers in order to achieve higher
output powers and better efficiency. For the same reason these circuits can also
be employed for the design of oscillators. One such design is shown in Fig. 15.11,

consisting basically of two Meissner oscillators in which the transistors T_1 and T_2 are alternately conducting.

As the base potential of one transistor is in phase with the collector potential of the other, the secondary winding normally required for phase inversion can be omitted. This version is shown in Fig. 15.12. The positive feedback is provided by the capacitive voltage dividers C_1, C_2. The parallel resistive voltage dividers provide the bias.

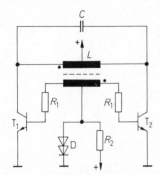

Fig. 15.11 Push-pull oscillator with
inductive feedback

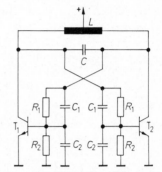

Fig. 15.12 Push-pull oscillator with
capacitive feedback

Both circuits, in addition to providing larger output power, also generate fewer harmonics than the single-ended oscillators.

Another simple way of designing a push-pull oscillator is to use a bipolar current source, as in Fig. 4.34, to feed the resonant circuit (see Fig. 15.13). The voltage of the resonant circuit is fed back to the current source via the emitter follower T_3. As the damping of the resonant circuit is only very slight, alternating voltages with low distortion can be generated. Resistor R_6 ensures a smooth cut-in of voltage limiting, thereby keeping distortion low, even at saturation of the current sources.

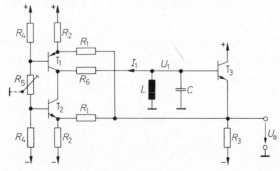

Fig. 15.13 Push-pull oscillator with controlled current sources

The voltage divider R_4, R_5 determines the limit of this saturation and thereby the amplitude of the alternating voltage. R_5 can be used for balancing. The resistances R_2 define the quiescent current of the current source. If a low distortion factor is important, R_2 should be chosen such that the transistors T_1 and T_2 are in class-A operation. The resistances R_1 determine the amount of feedback.

The circuit can be interpreted as a negative resistance which cancels out the damping of the resonant circuit. To determine its value, we assume a positive change in voltage, ΔU_1, which causes a fall of $\Delta U_1/R_1$ in the collector current of T_2 and an equally large rise in the collector current of T_1. Current I_1 is therefore reduced by $2\Delta U_1/R_1$. This corresponds to a resistor connected in parallel to the resonant circuit, having a value

$$R = \frac{\Delta U_1}{\Delta I_1} = -\tfrac{1}{2}R_1 \ .$$

To ensure that the condition for oscillation is fulfilled, $\tfrac{1}{2}R_1$ must be somewhat smaller than the resistance of the LC circuit at resonance.

15.2   Crystal oscillators

The frequency of the LC oscillators described is not sufficiently constant for many applications, as it depends on the temperature coefficients of capacitance and inductance of the resonant circuit. Considerably more stable frequencies can be achieved using quartz crystals. Such a crystal can be excited by electric fields to vibrate mechanically and, when provided with electrodes, behaves electrically like a resonant circuit having a high Q-factor. The temperature coefficient of the resonant frequency is very small. The frequency stability that can be attained by a crystal oscillator is in the order of

$$\frac{\Delta f}{f} = 10^{-6} \ldots 10^{-10} \ .$$

15.2.1   Electrical characteristics of a quartz crystal

The electrical behavior of a quartz crystal can be described by the equivalent circuit in Fig. 15.14. The two parameters C and L are well defined by the mechanical properties of the crystal. The resistance R is small and characterizes

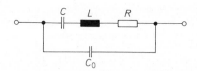

Fig. 15.14 Equivalent circuit of a quartz crystal

the damping. C_0 represents the value of the capacitance formed by the electrodes and leads. Typical values for a 4 MHz crystal are

$$L = 100 \, \text{mH} \, , \qquad\qquad R = 100 \, \Omega \, ,$$
$$C = 0.015 \, \text{pF} \, , \qquad C_0 = 5 \, \text{pF} \, ,$$

giving a Q-factor of

$$Q = \frac{1}{R}\sqrt{\frac{L}{C}} = 26000 \, .$$

To calculate the resonant frequency we initially determine the impedance of the quartz crystal. From Fig. 15.14, and neglecting R

$$\underline{Z}_q = \frac{j}{\omega} \cdot \frac{\omega^2 LC - 1}{C_0 + C - \omega^2 LCC_0} \, . \tag{15.6}$$

It can be seen that there is a frequency for which $\underline{Z}_q = 0$ and another for which $\underline{Z}_q = \infty$. The quartz crystal therefore has a series and a parallel resonance. To calculate the series resonant frequency f_s, the numerator of Eq. (15.6) is set to zero, and thus

$$f_s = \frac{1}{2\pi\sqrt{LC}} \, . \tag{15.7}$$

The parallel resonant frequency is calculated by setting the denominator to zero:

$$f_P = \frac{1}{2\pi\sqrt{LC}} \sqrt{1 + \frac{C}{C_0}} \, . \tag{15.8}$$

As can be seen, the series resonant frequency is dependent only on the well-defined product LC, whereas the parallel resonant frequency is influenced by the electrode capacitance C_0 which is far more susceptible to variations.

The frequency of a quartz oscillator must often be adjustable within a small range. This can be achieved by simply connecting a capacitor C_S in series with the quartz crystal, as in Fig. 15.15; C_S must be large compared to C.

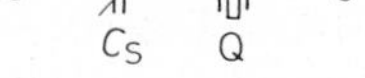

Fig. 15.15 Tuning the series resonant frequency

To calculate the shift in the resonant frequency, we determine the impedance of the series connection. With Eq. (15.6) we obtain

$$\underline{Z}'_q = \frac{1}{j\omega C_S} \cdot \frac{C + C_0 + C_S - \omega^2 LC(C_0 + C_S)}{C_0 + C - \omega^2 LCC_0} \, . \tag{15.9}$$

Setting the numerator to zero gives the new series resonant frequency

$$f'_s = \frac{1}{2\pi\sqrt{LC}}\sqrt{1 + \frac{C}{C_0 + C_s}} = f_s\sqrt{1 + \frac{C}{C_0 + C_s}}\ . \qquad (15.10)$$

By expanding this into a power series, we arrive at the approximation

$$f'_s = f_s\left[1 + \frac{C}{2(C_0 + C_s)}\right]$$

if $C \ll C_0 + C_s$. The relative shift in frequency is therefore

$$\frac{\Delta f}{f} = \frac{C}{2(C_0 + C_s)}\ .$$

The parallel resonant frequency is not changed by C_s as the poles of Eq. (15.9) are independent of C_s. A comparison of Eqs. (15.10) and (15.8) shows that for $C_s \rightarrow 0$, the series resonant frequency cannot be raised to a value higher than that of the parallel resonant frequency.

15.2.2 Fundamental frequency oscillators

In the Pierce oscillator in Fig. 15.16, the crystal in conjunction with capacitors C_s and C_1 forms a series resonant circuit with a series capacitance of

$$\frac{1}{C_{Stot}} = \frac{1}{C_s} + \frac{1}{C_1}\ .$$

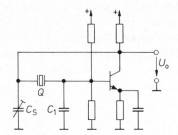

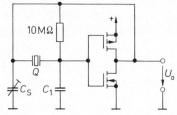

Fig. 15.16 Pierce oscillator with amplifier in common-emitter connection

Fig. 15.17 Pierce oscillator with CMOS inverter as amplifier

The resonant circuit is excited via the collector. Assuming that the current in the oscillatory circuit is large compared to the excitation current, antiphase signals will be produced at C_1 and C_s, resulting in positive feedback.

Nowadays, the amplifiers are usually CMOS inverters. The resulting circuit is shown in Fig. 15.17. It requires not only fewer components, but also imposes little damping on the crystal as its input resistance is high. The resistor fixes the operating point at $U_i = U_o \approx \frac{1}{2}U_b$. Its resistance may be very high, as virtually no input current flows.

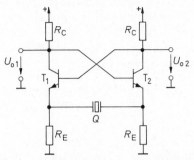

Fig. 15.18 Emitter-coupled crystal multivibrator

The crystal-controlled oscillator in Fig. 15.18 operates in the same way as the emitter-coupled multivibrator in Fig. 8.21[15.2]. The amount of positive feedback can be adjusted via the transconductance of the transistors using the emitter resistors. It is selected such that the circuit reliably begins to oscillate but is not excessively overdriven. The output voltage difference and hence the current flowing through the crystal is then virtually sinusoidal. An automatic gain control device of this kind is incorporated, for example, in type MC 12061.

A precision crystal oscillator allowing grounded crystals to be employed is shown in Fig. 15.19. In order not to impair the Q-factor of the crystal, the circuit must be driven at the lowest possible impedance (series resonance). Emitter follower T_1 is used for this purpose. The current ΔI flowing through the crystal is translated into a voltage $\Delta V_{C2} = \Delta I R_2$ in transistor T_2 configured as a current-voltage converter. Positive feedback is provided via the emitter follower T_4 and the base of T_1. The reduced transconductance of T_1 and hence the loop gain of the circuit is at its maximum at the series resonant frequency of the

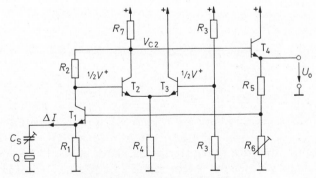

Fig. 15.19 Precision crystal oscillator

crystal. Attenuator R_5, R_6 is adjusted such that the AC voltage across the
crystal is only a few 10 mV. The power dissipation in the crystal is then so small
that the frequency stability is unimpaired. It is preferable to use an electrically
controllable attenuator, e.g. a transconductance multiplier, which is set to the
correct value using an amplitude control circuit. This also ensures reliable
start-up of the oscillator, and the output voltage has a good sinusoidal waveform. This principle is employed by the SL 680 C from Plessey. A number of
integrated circuits are listed in Fig. 15.20.

Type	Manufacturer	Output	Max. frequency
74 LS 320	Texas Instr.	TTL	20 MHz
74 LS 624	Texas Instr.	TTL	20 MHz
ICM 7209	Intersil	CMOS	10 MHz
MC 12061	Motorola	TTL, ECL	20 MHz
SL 680 C	Plessey	Analog	100 MHz

Fig. 15.20 IC crystal oscillators for external quartz crystals

15.2.3 Harmonic oscillators

Crystals for frequencies above 30 MHz are difficult to manufacture. To
obtain high frequencies of this kind with crystal accuracy, one can either
stabilize an LC oscillator via a PLL (Sect. 26.4.5) using a low-frequency crystal,
or excite a crystal at a harmonic of its characteristic frequency.

If we examine the frequency response of the crystal impedance shown in
Fig. 15.21, we can see that it also possesses resonance points at odd-numbered
harmonics. However, the circuits considered so far are unsuitable for operating
a crystal at a harmonic. For such a circuit, we require an amplifier which
provides maximum gain close to the desired frequency. This can be achieved by
using an additional LC resonant circuit.

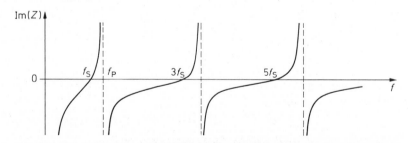

Fig. 15.21 Typical impedance-frequency response of a quartz crystal (imaginary part)

If the positive feedback of the Hartley oscillator in Fig. 15.7 is obtained via
a crystal, we obtain the circuit shown in Fig. 15.22. The LC resonant circuit is
tuned to the required harmonic. The gain is then maximum for this frequency,

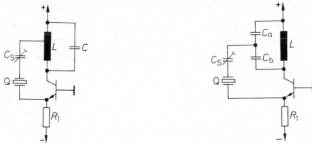

Fig. 15.22 Hartley oscillator with crystal   Fig. 15.23 Colpitts oscillator with crystal

and the crystal will tend to be excited at the corresponding harmonic. The suitably modified Colpitts oscillator of Fig. 15.9 is shown in Fig. 15.23.

A harmonic oscillator can also be implemented using the emitter-coupled oscillator in Fig. 15.10. For this purpose, a crystal is inserted in the positive feedback loop, as shown in Fig. 15.24. This arrangement provides positive feedback with the required crystal harmonic at the resonant frequency of the LC resonant circuit. The simplest way of implementing the high-frequency amplifier required is to use an ECL gate. In this case a line receiver provides a particularly effective solution, as the reference potential V_{BB} is accessible. If the resonant circuit is connected as in Fig. 15.24, the amplifier will be optimally biased. Capacitor C_1 serves merely to short-circuit V_{BB} at high frequencies. The resultant output voltage is very nearly sinusoidal. If a squarewave ECL signal is required, it is merely necessary to connect another line receiver at the output [15.3].

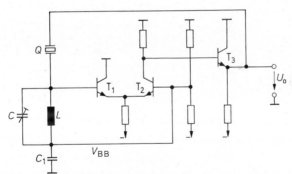

Fig. 15.24 Emitter-coupled crystal-controlled oscillator. Frequencies of up to 100 MHz or more can be achieved using ECL line receiver 10.116

15.3 Wien–Robinson oscillator

In the low-frequency range, LC oscillators are less satisfactory because the inductances and capacitances required become unmanageably large. Consequently, oscillators are preferred in which RC networks are used to determine the frequency.

In principle an *RC* oscillator can be realized by replacing the resonant circuit in Fig. 15.2 by a passive *RC* bandpass filter. However, the maximum attainable Q-factor would then be limited to $\frac{1}{2}$, as is shown in Section 14.1. Consequently, the frequency stability of the resulting sinewave would be poor, as can be seen from the frequency response of the phase shift shown in Fig. 15.25. The phase shift of a passive lowpass filter with $Q = \frac{1}{3}$ is 27° at half the resonant frequency. In the case of the amplifier causing a phase shift of $-27°$, the circuit would oscillate at half the resonant frequency, as the total phase shift is then zero. For good frequency stability, a feedback network is thus required for which the gradient of the phase-frequency response at zero phase is as steep as possible. High-Q resonant circuits and the Wien-Robinson bridge have this characteristic. However, the output voltage of the Wien-Robinson bridge is zero at resonant frequency and the bridge is therefore suitable as a feedback network only under certain conditions. When employed in oscillators, it must be slightly detuned, as in Fig. 15.26, where ε is positive and small compared to unity.

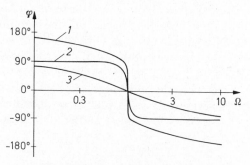

Fig. 15.25 Frequency response of the phase shift.
Curve *1*: Wien-Robinson bridge for $\varepsilon = 0.01$. Curve *2*: Resonant circuit for $Q = 10$. Curve *3*: Passive bandpass filter for $Q = \frac{1}{3}$

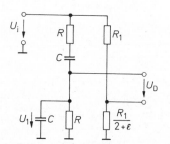

Fig. 15.26 Detuned Wien-Robinson bridge

The frequency dependence of the phase shift of a detuned Wien-Robinson bridge can be determined qualitatively: At high and low frequencies, $\underline{U}_1 = 0$, and thus $\underline{U}_D \approx -\frac{1}{3}\underline{U}_i$ and the phase shift is $\pm 180°$. At resonant frequency, $\underline{U}_1 = +\frac{1}{3}\underline{U}_i$ and

$$\underline{U}_D = \left(\frac{1}{3} - \frac{1}{3+\varepsilon}\right)\underline{U}_i \approx \frac{\varepsilon}{9}\underline{U}_i \;,$$

i.e. $\underline{U}_D$ is in phase with $\underline{U}_i$. To determine quantitatively the shape of curve 1 in Fig. 15.25, we first calculate the transfer function

$$\frac{\underline{U}_D}{\underline{U}_i} = -\frac{1}{3+\varepsilon} \cdot \frac{(1+S^2) - \varepsilon S}{1 + \dfrac{9+\varepsilon}{3+\varepsilon}S + S^2} \;.$$

Hence, neglecting higher powers of ε, the frequency response of the phase is

$$\varphi = \arctan \frac{3\Omega(\Omega^2 - 1)(3 + 2\varepsilon)}{(\Omega^2 - 1)^2(3 + \varepsilon) - 9\varepsilon\Omega^2} \;,$$

which is shown in Fig. 15.25 for $\varepsilon = 0.01$. It can be seen that the phase shift of the detuned Wien-Robinson bridge increases to $\pm 90°$ within a very narrow frequency range. It is narrower the smaller the value of ε. As far as this aspect is concerned, the Wien-Robinson bridge is comparable to high-quality resonant circuits, and an additional advantage is that the phase shift is not limited to $\pm 90°$ but to $\pm 180°$. Harmonics are thereby strongly damped. One disadvantage of the Wien-Robinson bridge is that the attenuation at resonant frequency becomes higher the smaller the value of ε. In general, the attenuation at resonant frequency is

$$\frac{\hat{U}_D}{\hat{U}_i} = k \approx \frac{\varepsilon}{9} \;,$$

and, in our example, $k \approx \frac{1}{900}$. To fulfill the amplitude condition of an oscillator, the amplifier must compensate for the attenuation. Such an oscillator circuit is represented in Fig. 15.27.

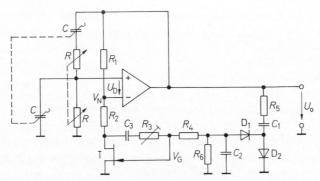

Fig. 15.27 Simple Wien-Robinson oscillator

Resonant frequency: $f_0 = 1/2\pi RC$

If the amplifier has open-loop gain A_D, the detuning factor ε must have the value

$$\varepsilon = 9k = \frac{9}{A_D}$$

to fulfill the amplitude condition $kA_D = 1$. If ε is slightly larger, the oscillation amplitude increases until the amplifier begins to saturate. If ε is too small or negative, there will be no oscillation. However, it is impossible to adjust the resistors R_1 and $R_1/(2 + \varepsilon)$ with the required precision. Therefore, one of the two resistances must be controlled automatically depending on the output amplitude. This is the purpose of the field-effect transistor T in Fig. 15.27. As shown in Sect. 5.7, the channel resistance R_{DS} is dependent only on the voltage U_{GS} if U_{DS} remains sufficiently small. To ensure that U_{DS} does not become too large, only part of V_N is applied to the FET and the rest appears at R_2. The sum of R_2 and R_{DS} must have the value $R_1/(2 + \varepsilon)$. The smallest possible value of R_{DS} is R_{DSON}, and hence R_2 must be smaller than

$$\tfrac{1}{2}R_1 - R_{DSON} \ .$$

When the supply voltage is switched on, V_G is initially zero and therefore $R_{DS} = R_{DSON}$. If the above design condition is fulfilled, the sum of R_2 and R_{DS} is then smaller than $\tfrac{1}{2}R_1$. At resonant frequency of the Wien–Robinson bridge, there is therefore a relatively large voltage difference U_D. As a consequence, oscillation begins and the amplitude increases. The output voltage is rectified by the voltage doubler D_1, D_2. The gate potential thereby becomes negative and R_{DS} increases. The amplitude of the output voltage rises until

$$R_{DS} + R_2 = \frac{R_1}{2 + \varepsilon} = \frac{R_1}{2 + \dfrac{9}{A_D}} \ .$$

The distortion factor of the output voltage is dependent mainly on the linearity of the FET output characteristic which can be greatly improved if part of the drain-source voltage is added to the gate potential, as in Fig. 5.20. This is the purpose of the two resistors R_3 and R_4. The capacitor C_3 ensures that no direct current will flow into the N-input of the operational amplifier, as this would cause an output offset. In practice, $R_3 \approx R_4$ but, by fine adjustment of R_3, the distortion factor can be reduced to a minimum and values below 0.1% can be achieved.

If R is made adjustable, the frequency can be continuously controlled. Good matching of the two resistors is important since the greater their mismatch, the more efficient the amplitude control must be. The maximum value of R should be low enough to ensure that there is no noticeable voltage arising from the input bias current of the operational amplifier. On the other hand, R must not be too low, or the output will be overloaded. To adjust the frequency within a range of 1:10, fixed resistors with the value $R/10$ are connected in series with the potentiometers R. If, in addition, switches are used to select different values for the capacitances C, a range of output frequencies from 10 Hz to 1 MHz can be covered by this circuit. To ensure that the amplitude control does not cause distortion even at the lowest frequency, the charge and discharge time constants, $R_5 C_2$ and $R_6 C_2$ respectively, must be larger than the longest oscillation period by a factor of at least 10.

The data of the field-effect transistor T determine the output amplitude. The stability of the output voltage amplitude is not particularly good, since some deviation in amplitude is required to effect a noticeable change in the resistance of the FET. It can be improved by amplifying the gate voltage, and such a circuit is shown in Fig. 15.28.

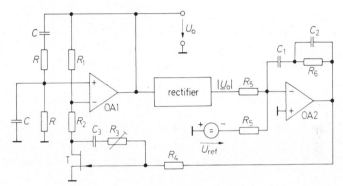

Fig. 15.28 Wien-Robinson oscillator with precise amplitude control

$$Amplitude: \qquad \hat{U}_o = \frac{\pi}{2} U_{ref}$$

The rectified AC output voltage is applied to OA 2, configured as a modified PI-controller (Fig. 27.7). This adjusts the gate potential of the FET in such a way that the mean value of $|U_o|$ equals U_{ref}. The controller time constant must be large compared to the oscillation period, or the gain will change even within a single cycle, resulting in considerable distortion. A pure PI-controller cannot therefore be used; it is better to have a modified type in which a capacitor is connected in parallel with R_6. The alternating voltage at R_6 is thereby short-circuited even at the lowest oscillator frequency. The proportional controller action comes into effect only below this frequency.

15.4 Differential equation oscillators

Low-frequency oscillations can be generated by programming operational amplifiers to solve the differential equation of a sinewave. From Section 15.1.1

$$\ddot{U}_o + 2\gamma \dot{U}_o + \omega_0^2 U_o = 0 , \qquad (15.11)$$

the solution of which is

$$U_o(t) = \hat{U}_o e^{-\gamma t} \sin(\sqrt{\omega_0^2 - \gamma^2} t) \ . \tag{15.12}$$

Since operational amplifiers are better suitable for integration than for differentiation, the differential equation is rearranged by integrating it twice:

$$U_o + 2\gamma \int U_o \, dt + \omega_0^2 \iint U_o \, dt^2 = 0 \ .$$

This equation can be simulated using two integrators and an inverting amplifier, and several methods of programming are available. One of these, particularly suitable for an oscillator, is shown in Fig. 15.29. For this circuit, the damping is given by $\gamma = -\alpha/20\,RC$ and the resonant frequency $f_0 = 1/2\pi RC$. Hence, from Eq. (15.12), the output voltage

$$U_o(t) = \hat{U}_o \, e^{\frac{\alpha}{20\,RC} t} \sin\left(\sqrt{1 - \frac{\alpha^2}{400} \frac{t}{RC}} \right) \ . \tag{15.13}$$

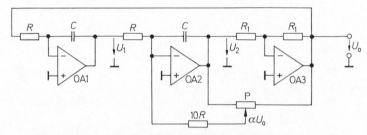

Fig. 15.29 Second-order differential equation for sinewave generation

Resonant frequency: $f_0 = 1/2\pi RC$

It is evident that the damping of the oscillation is adjusted by α. At the right-hand stop of potentiometer P, $\alpha = 1$. At the left-hand stop, $\alpha = -1$; in the middle, $\alpha = 0$. The damping can thus be varied between positive and negative values. For $\alpha = 1$, the oscillation amplitude is increased, within 20 cycles, by the factor e, for $\alpha = -1$ it is decreased by the factor $1/e$. For $\alpha = 0$, the oscillation is undamped although this is so only for ideal conditions. In practice, for $\alpha = 0$, a slightly damped oscillation will occur, and to achieve constant amplitude, α must be given a small positive value. The adjustment is so critical that the amplitude can never be kept constant over a longer period and one must therefore introduce automatic amplitude control. As for the Wien–Robinson oscillator in Fig. 15.28, the amplitude at the output can be measured by a rectifier and α controlled, depending on the difference between this amplitude and a reference voltage. As shown previously, the controller time constant must be large compared to the period of oscillation to ensure that amplitude control causes no distortion. This requirement is increasingly difficult to fulfill for frequencies below 10 Hz.

The difficulties arise from the fact that a whole cycle of the oscillation must be allowed to occur before the correct amplitude is known. Such problems can be eliminated if the amplitude is measured at every instant of the oscillation period. This is possible for the circuit in Fig. 15.29 where, in the case of an undamped oscillation,

$$U_o = \hat{U}_o \sin \omega_0 t$$

and

$$U_1 = -\frac{1}{\tau}\int U_o \, dt = \hat{U}_o \cos \omega_0 t \; .$$

The amplitude can now be determined at any instant by solving the following expression:

$$U_o^2 + U_1^2 = \hat{U}_o^2(\sin^2 \omega_0 t + \cos^2 \omega_0 t) = \hat{U}_o^2 \; . \tag{15.14}$$

It is obvious that the expression $U_o^2 + U_1^2$ is dependent only on the amplitude of the output signal and not on its phase. A pure DC voltage is therefore obtained which requires no filtering and which can be directly compared with the reference voltage.

A differential-equation oscillator whose amplitude is controlled in this way is shown in Fig. 15.30. Analog multipliers M_1 and M_2 form the square of U_1 and U_o respectively. To these two portions, the reference voltage at the summation point of automatic gain control (AGC) amplifier OA 4 is now added, giving an output voltage U_3 such that

$$\frac{U_1^2}{ER_2} + \frac{U_o^2}{ER_2} - \frac{U_{ref}}{R_2} = 0 \; .$$

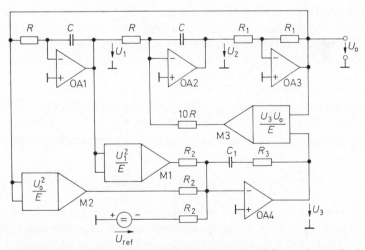

Fig. 15.30 Differential-equation oscillator and supplementary circuit for precise amplitude control

Frequency: $f_0 = 1/2\pi RC$,   Amplitude: $\hat{U}_o^2 = EU_{ref}$

Applying Eq. (15.14), this is the case for an amplitude of $\hat{U}_o^2 = EU_{ref}$. The amplifier time constant is determined by RC network $R_3 C_1$. The circuit design is described in Chapter 27.

Voltage $U_o U_3 / E$ is present at the output of multiplier M_3. This voltage is applied to resistor $10R$ instead of potentiometer P in Fig. 15.29, making $\alpha = U_3 / E$. If the amplitude increases, $\hat{U}_o^2 > EU_{ref}$ and both U_3 and α become negative, i.e. the oscillation is damped. If the amplitude decreases, U_3 becomes positive and the oscillation is undamped.

Apart from providing a good method of controlling the amplitude, sinewave generation by solving a second-order differential equation offers a further advantage in that it allows virtually ideal frequency modulation. If this is to be accomplished for LC oscillators, the value of L or C must be varied. However, this will alter the energy of the oscillator and hence the oscillation amplitude, and parametric effects arise. For the differential equation method, however, the resonant frequency can be changed by varying the two resistors R without affecting the oscillator energy.

As each of the two resistors is connected to virtual ground, multipliers connected in front of them can be used to modulate the frequency. The multipliers then produce the output voltages

$$U'_o = \frac{U_c}{E} U_o \quad \text{and} \quad U'_1 = \frac{U_c}{E} U_1 \ .$$

This is equivalent to an increase in the resistance R by the factor E/U_c, so that the resonant frequency is given by

$$f_0 = \frac{1}{2\pi RC} \cdot \frac{U_c}{E} \ ,$$

i.e. it is proportional to the control voltage U_c.

The frequency can also be controlled digitally by connecting D/A converters instead of analog multipliers in front of the integrators. This produces the same arrangement as for the digitally tunable filter in Fig. 14.45. In this way, frequency bands of $1 : 100$ can be covered with a high degree of accuracy. In order to keep the damping of the oscillator as constant as possible over such a large frequency range, it is advisable to connect a small capacitance in parallel with input resistor R_1 at OA 3. This will compensate for the increased attenuation due to the phase lag of the operational amplifier at higher frequencies.

15.5 Function generators

As we have seen, the amplitude control involved in the generation of low-frequency sinewaves is rather cumbersome. It is much easier to use a Schmitt trigger and an integrator to generate a triangular alternating voltage. A sinewave can then be produced if the sine function network of Section 12.7.4 is employed. Since with this method, a triangular wave, a square wave and a sinusoidal wave are obtained simultaneously, circuits based on this principle are called function generators. The block diagram of such a circuit is shown in Fig. 15.31.

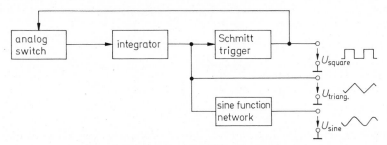

Fig. 15.31 Block diagram of a function generator

The principle consists in applying a constant voltage to an integrator. This voltage is either positive or negative depending on the direction in which the integrator output voltage is to be changed. If the integrator output voltage reaches the switch-on or switch-off level of the following Schmitt trigger, the sign at the integrator input is inverted. This produces at the output a triangular voltage which oscillates between the trigger levels.

15.5.1 Basic arrangement

Two approaches are possible, which differ in the way in which integration is implemented. In the case of the circuit in Fig. 15.32, $+ U_i$ or $- U_i$ is applied to an integrator depending on the position of the analog switch. With the circuit in Fig. 15.33, current $+ I_i$ or $- I_i$ is impressed on capacitor C via an analog switch. This also results in a linear voltage rise or fall. In order not to falsify the triangular voltage across the capacitor due to loading, an impedance converter is generally required. The advantage of the method in Fig. 15.33, however, is that it facilitates implementation of the impedance converter and current switch for higher frequencies [15.4].

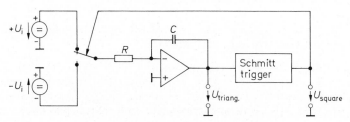

Fig. 15.32 Function generator with integrator

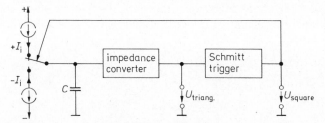

Fig. 15.33 Function generator with constant current sources

15.5.2 Practical implementation

The simplest method of implementation is to start from the principle illustrated in Fig. 15.32 and to use the output voltage of the Schmitt trigger itself as the input voltage for the integrator. The resulting circuit is shown in Fig. 15.34. The Schmitt trigger supplies a constant output voltage which is integrated by the integrator. If the integrator output voltage reaches the trigger level of the Schmitt trigger, the voltage U_{square} to be integrated instantaneously changes sign, causing the integrator output to reverse direction until the other trigger level is reached. In order to ensure that the absolute values of the positive and negative slopes are the same, the comparator must have a symmetrical output voltage $\pm U_{square\,max}$. In accordance with Section 8.5.2, the amplitude of the triangular voltage is given by

$$\hat{U}_{triang.} = \frac{R_1}{R_2} U_{square\,max} \,.$$

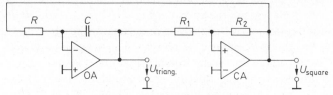

Fig. 15.34 Simple function generator

$$Frequency: \quad f = \frac{R_2}{4R_1} \cdot \frac{1}{RC}, \quad Amplitude: \quad \hat{U}_{triang.} = \frac{R_1}{R_2} U_{square\,max}$$

The oscillation period is equal to four times the time required by the integrator to change from zero to $\hat{U}_{triang}$. It is therefore

$$T = 4\frac{R_1}{R_2} RC \,.$$

An example of a practical implementation of the circuit principle of Fig. 15.33 is shown in Fig. 15.35. The controlled current switch consists of

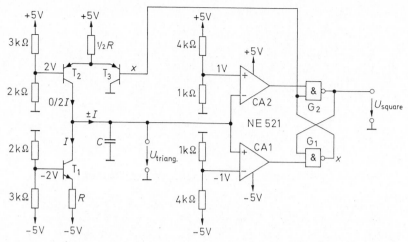

Fig. 15.35 High-speed function generator with current switch and precision comparator

$$\text{Frequency:} \quad f = \frac{I}{4\hat{U}_{\text{triang.}} \cdot C} = \frac{0.6}{RC}, \qquad \text{Amplitude:} \quad \hat{U}_{\text{triang.}} = 1 \text{ V}$$

transistors T_1 to T_3. As long as control signal $x = L$, the capacitor is discharged via T_1 with current I. If the triangular voltage falls below -1 V, the precision Schmitt trigger realized in accordance with Fig. 8.48 changes state, and $x = H$. This turns T_3 off and current source T_2 is turned on. The latter supplies twice as much current as T_1, namely $2I$. This means that capacitor C is charged with current I and T_1 need not be turned off.

If the triangular voltage exceeds the upper trigger level of $+1$ V, the Schmitt trigger reverts to the state $x = L$, and capacitor C is discharged again.

Dual comparator NE 521 from Signetics is particularly suitable for implementing the precision Schmitt trigger, as it already contains the two gates required. This comparator additionally features particularly short switching times of only some 8 ns, enabling frequencies of up to several MHz to be generated. The impedance converter shown in Fig. 15.33 is only required if the triangular voltage is to be loaded at low impedance. The subsequent comparators place virtually no load on the triangular voltage.

15.5.3 Function generators with controllable frequency

Using the principle illustrated in Fig. 15.32, the frequency can be controlled quite easily by varying voltages $+U_i$ and $-U_i$. An example of a function generator of this type is shown in Fig. 15.36. Voltages $+U_i$ or $-U_i$ are available at low impedance at the outputs of OA1 and OA2. These voltages are applied to the integrator input via transistor T_1 or T_2, depending on the switching state of the Schmitt trigger. If the output voltages of the comparator

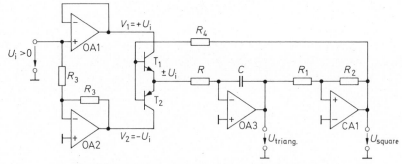

Fig. 15.36 Function generator with controllable frequency

$$Frequency: \quad f = \frac{R_2}{4R_1} \cdot \frac{1}{RC} \cdot \frac{U_i}{U_{square\,max}}, \qquad Amplitude: \quad \hat{U}_{triang.} = \frac{R_1}{R_2} U_{square\,max}$$

are greater than $\pm U_i$, the two transistors operate as saturated emitter followers and therefore only have a voltage drop of a few millivolts, as described in Section 22.2.3.

The Schmitt trigger once again determines the amplitude of the triangular signal, given by

$$\hat{U}_{triang.} = \frac{R_1}{R_2} U_{square\,max} \ .$$

The rate of change of the triangular voltage is

$$\frac{\Delta U_{triang.}}{\Delta t} = \pm \frac{U_i}{RC} \ .$$

The period is equal to four times the time required by the integrator to go from zero to $\hat{U}_{triang.}$. The frequency is therefore

$$f = \frac{U_i}{4RC\hat{U}_{triang.}} = \frac{R_2}{4R_1} \cdot \frac{1}{RC} \cdot \frac{U_i}{U_{square\,max}}$$

i.e. it is proportional to the input voltage U_i, and so the circuit is suitable for use as a voltage-frequency converter. If we select

$$U_i = U_{i0} + \Delta U_i \ ,$$

we obtain a linear frequency modulation.

If accuracy and stability of amplitude and frequency are essential, care must be taken to ensure that they are not dependent on $U_{square\,max}$. This is easily achieved by using a precision Schmitt trigger, as in Fig. 15.35. However, one then requires an additional amplifier to generate the bipolar signals necessary for driving T_1 and T_2. In this case it is simpler to replace the transistors by CMOS analog switches, such as the DG 301 from Siliconix (see Chapter 22).

Variable duty ratio

In order to generate a squarewave voltage with variable duty ratio, we can use a comparator to compare a symmetrical triangular voltage with a DC voltage. The relationships are somewhat more difficult if, as in Fig. 15.37, not only the squarewave but also the triangular voltage is to be asymmetrical in form.

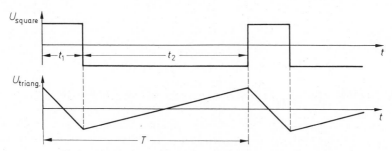

Fig. 15.37 Voltage waveform for a duty factor of $t_1/T = 20\%$

One solution is to use the circuit shown in Fig. 15.36, applying two different absolute values for the potentials V_1 and V_2. The rise and fall times of the triangular voltages between $\pm \hat{U}_{triang.}$ are therefore

$$t_1 = \frac{2RC\hat{U}_{triang.}}{V_1} , \qquad t_2 = \frac{2RC\hat{U}_{triang.}}{|V_2|} .$$

If we now want to change the symmetry without changing the frequency, we have to increase the absolute value of one potential and reduce that of the other, so that

$$T = t_1 + t_2 = 2RC\hat{U}_{triang.}\left(\frac{1}{V_1} + \frac{1}{|V_2|}\right) \qquad (15.15)$$

remains constant. This condition can also be easily satisfied by using the drive circuit in Fig. 15.38 [15.5]. Its output potentials are given by

$$\frac{1}{V_1} + \frac{1}{|V_2|} = \frac{1}{U_i R_3}[R_3 + (1-\alpha)R_4 + R_3 + \alpha R_4] = \frac{1}{U_i R_3}[2R_3 + R_4] .$$

As required, this expression holds irrespective of the symmetry factor α selected. By substitution in Eq. (15.15), we obtain the frequency in the form

$$f = \frac{R_3}{2RC[2R_3 + R_4]} \cdot \frac{U_i}{\hat{U}_{triang.}} .$$

The duty factor t_1/T or t_2/T can be set between

$$\frac{R_3}{2R_3 + R_4} \quad \text{and} \quad \frac{R_3 + R_4}{2R_3 + R_4} ,$$

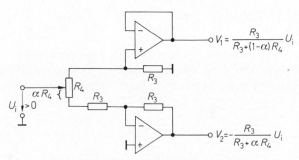

Fig. 15.38 Extension for variable duty ratio

using potentiometer R_4. With $R_4 = 3R_3$, we obtain values between 20% and 80%.

Function generators which not only produce triangular and squarewave voltages, but also contain a sinewave function network, are available in IC form:

Type	Manufacturer	Max. frequency
ICL 8038	Intersil	300 kHz
XR-205	Exar	4 MHz
XR-2206	Exar	1 MHz

Use of these circuits constitutes the simplest method of implementing function generators. However, signal quality and the usable frequency range are limited.

15.5.4 Function generators for simultaneously producing sine and cosine signals

The easy amplitude stabilization of function generators can also be utilized for the simultaneous generation of sine and cosine signals. Taking the triangular signal of a function generator, its changes in sign can be determined by means of a comparator. They are phase-shifted by 90° with respect to the squarewave. Using a second integrator, the resulting squarewave signal can be converted to a triangular signal which is also phase-shifted by 90° with respect to the original triangular signal.

A simple version of this principle is illustrated in Fig. 15.39. Operational amplifier OA 1 and comparator CA 1 constitute a function generator of the type shown in Fig. 15.34. Comparator CA 2 produces the phase-shifted squarewave signal and integrator OA 2 the associated triangular signal.

However, the circuit would not operate without a feedback path via R_3: integrator OA 2 would invariably be overdriven due to the unavoidable symmetry and offset errors. This can be avoided by inserting an additional resistor

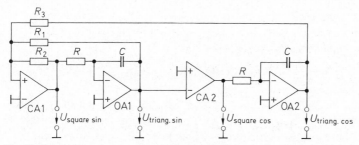

Fig. 15.39 Function generator for producing triangular and squarewave signals phase-shifted by 90°

$$\text{Frequency}: \quad f = \frac{R_2}{4R_1} \cdot \frac{1}{RC}, \quad \text{Amplitude}: \quad \hat{U}_{\text{triang.}} = \frac{R_1}{R_2} U_{\text{square max}}$$

R_3. Voltage $U_{\text{triang. sin}}$ can be shifted via this resistor towards positive or negative values, thereby also allowing the duty factor of $U_{\text{square cos}}$ to be varied. The feedback via R_3 virtually cancels out the DC voltage superimposed at output $U_{\text{triang. cos}}$.

It is not immediately apparent why the triangular voltage present at output $U_{\text{triang. cos}}$ and fed back via R_3, does not impair the operation of function generator CA 1, OA 1. The reason may be seen from Fig. 15.40, which shows that triangular voltage $U_{\text{triang. cos}}$ is zero at the peak values of $U_{\text{triang. sin}}$ and does not therefore alter the switching instant of Schmitt trigger CA1. This can only happen due to a superimposed DC voltage.

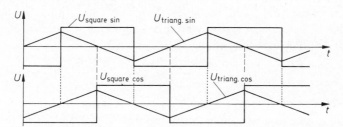

Fig. 15.40 Time diagram of triangular and squarewave voltages shifted by 90°

The circuit in Fig. 15.39 can be extended to obtain signals with a controllable phase shift of between 0° and 180° [15.6, 15.7].

16   Wideband amplifiers

When designing amplifier circuits with an upper cutoff frequency higher than 100 kHz, certain special aspects must be considered. These are discussed below. There are two main effects which influence the value of the upper cutoff frequency:

1) the frequency dependence of the current gain which is governed by the internal structure of the transistor;
2) stray capacitances which, together with the external resistances, form lowpass filters.

16.1   Frequency dependence of the current gain

The frequency response of the current gain $\underline{\beta} = \underline{I}_C/\underline{I}_B$ of a bipolar transistor can be described with good accuracy by a first-order lowpass filter characteristic, i.e.

$$\underline{\beta} = \frac{\beta}{1 + j\dfrac{f}{f_\beta}} \, , \tag{16.1}$$

where β is the current gain at low frequencies and f_β is the 3 dB cutoff frequency.

Instead of the 3 dB cutoff frequency, the gain-bandwidth product f_T is often given. This is the frequency at which the magnitude of $\underline{\beta}$ becomes unity. From Eq. (16.1) with $\beta \gg 1$, it follows that

$$\boxed{f_T = \beta f_\beta} \, . \tag{16.2}$$

The gain-bandwidth product is also known as the transit frequency.

The best way to study the effect of the frequency response of the current gain on the frequency response of the voltage gain of a circuit is to use the Johnson–Giacoletto model depicted in Fig. 16.1. The frequency dependence of the current gain is represented by the "diffusion capacitance", C_D, of the forward-biased base-emitter diode. The additional depletion layer capacitance $C_{CB'}$ is ignored for the moment. The relationship between C_D and f_T is, according to [16.1]

$$C_D = \frac{I_C}{2\pi f_T U_T} = \frac{g_i}{2\pi f_T} = \frac{\beta}{2\pi f_T r_{BE}} \, . \tag{16.3}$$

To the first approximation, the gain-bandwidth product f_T is independent of the mean value of the emitter current. The capacitance C_D must therefore be proportional to I_C, in accordance with Eq. (16.3).

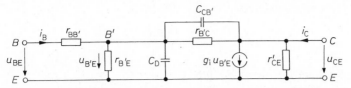

Fig. 16.1 Giacoletto equivalent circuit for the common-emitter connection. Relation of the equivalent parameters to the low-frequency values of the y-parameters:

Internal base-emitter resistance:	$r_{B'E} \approx r_{BE}$
Base spreading resistance:	$r_{BB'} \approx \frac{1}{10} r_{BE}$
Internal transconductance:	$g_i \approx g$
Internal collector-base resistance:	$r_{B'C} \approx 1/g_r$
Internal collector-emitter resistance:	$r'_{CE} \approx r_{CE}$

If a transistor in common-emitter connection is operated from a high-impedance signal voltage source, i.e. with an impressed base current I_B, the cutoff frequency is determined by the lowpass filter consisting of $r_{B'E}$ and C_D as follows:

$$\underline{I}_C = g_i \underline{U}_{B'E} = g_i \frac{r_{B'E}}{1 + j\omega r_{B'E} C_D} \underline{I}_B = \frac{\beta}{1 + j \dfrac{f}{f_T/\beta}} \underline{I}_B \ . \tag{16.4}$$

The cutoff frequency is therefore f_T/β and thus equal to f_β, as required by the definition.

If the common-emitter circuit is controlled by a low-impedance voltage source, the cutoff frequency of the circuit is determined by the time constant

$$\tau = (r_{BB'} \| r_{B'E}) C_D \approx r_{BB'} C_D \ .$$

Therefore the frequency response of the transconductance

$$\underline{g}_f = \frac{\underline{I}_C}{\underline{U}_{BE}} = \frac{g_f}{1 + j\omega r_{BB'} C_D} = \frac{g_f}{1 + j \dfrac{f}{f_g}} \ , \tag{16.5}$$

where g_f is the low-frequency value of the transconductance and $f_g = 1/2\pi r_{BB'} C_D$, the cutoff frequency of the transconductance. The latter is larger than the β-cutoff frequency, f_β, by a factor of $r_{B'E}/r_{BB'} \approx 10$.

If the transistor is operated as a common-base amplifier with voltage control, the same result is obtained, as the control voltage is applied across the same two terminals.

The conditions change if the emitter current is impressed. Since the collector current is practically the same as the emitter current for $|\beta| \gg 1$, the gain begins to decrease only in the region of the transit frequency f_T. The relationship between collector and emitter current with $i_E = i_C + i_B$ and $i_B = i_C/\beta$ is given by

$$\alpha = \frac{i_C}{i_E} = \frac{\beta}{1+\beta} \; .$$

In complex notation, using Eq. (16.1),

$$\underline{\alpha} = \frac{\underline{\beta}}{1+\underline{\beta}} = \frac{\alpha}{1+j\dfrac{\alpha f}{\beta f_\beta}} \; .$$

Hence, we obtain the α-cutoff frequency

$$\boxed{f_\alpha = \frac{\beta f_\beta}{\alpha} \approx f_T} \; .$$

When operating the transistor as an emitter follower, a cutoff frequency of the voltage gain is obtained which lies between the values f_g and f_T, depending on the load resistance.

To summarize,

$$\boxed{f_\beta \ll f_g \ll f_\alpha \approx f_T} \; .$$

16.2   Effect of transistor and stray capacitances

In every circuit, there are a number of unavoidable transistor and stray capacitances which, together with the circuit's resistances, form lowpass filters, as shown in Fig. 16.2. It can be seen that the circuit contains two lowpass filters. The capacitances C_3 and C_4, together with the parallel resistance R_C, produce

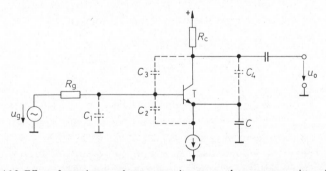

Fig. 16.2 Effect of transistor and stray capacitances on the common-emitter circuit

C_1: stray capacitance, in particular that of the input lead
C_2: emitter-base capacitance
C_3: collector-base capacitance
C_4: collector-emitter capacitance

a lowpass filter at the output. They reduce the dynamic collector impedance at high frequencies and thereby reduce the voltage gain. At the input, the capacitances C_1, C_2 and C_3 form a lowpass filter together with R_g. The effective input capacitance of the circuit is

$$C_i = C_1 + C_2 + |A|C_3 \; ,$$

where A is the voltage gain of the circuit. The increase of the collector-base capacitance is known as the *Miller effect* and is caused by the fact that a voltage appears across the capacitance C_3 which is $(|A| + 1)$ times that at the input. If $|A| \gg 1$, the term $|A|C_3$ outweighs the remaining transistor capacitances, and we obtain approximately

$$C_i \approx |A|C_3 \; .$$

For this reason, the input lowpass filter has a large effect and the bandwidth of a common-emitter circuit is therefore relatively small.

The conditions are more favorable for the common-base amplifier. As can be seen from Fig. 16.3, the effective input capacitance in this application is

$$C_i = C_1 + C_2 - AC_4 \quad \text{with} \quad A > 0 \; .$$

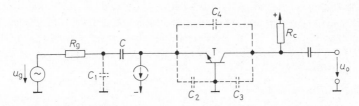

Fig. 16.3 Effect of transistor and stray capacitances on the common-base circuit

Here, the input capacitance is reduced instead of increased. The low input resistance, however, is a disadvantage.

16.3   Cascode amplifier

The disadvantage of the low input resistance of the common-base circuit can be overcome by connecting two transistors in series in the form of a "cascode circuit", as shown in Fig. 16.4. Here, the input transistor T_1 operates in common-emitter connection, and the output transistor T_2 is operated in common-base connection with current control. Since T_2 has at its emitter terminal the low input resistance $1/g_f$, the voltage gain of the input stage is

$$A_1 = - g_f \cdot \frac{1}{g_f} = - 1 \; .$$

In this way, the Miller effect is eliminated. As practically the same collector

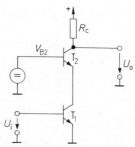

Fig. 16.4 Cascode amplifier

Voltage gain:	$\underline{A} = - g_f R_C$
Input resistance:	$r_i = r_{BE1}$
Output resistance:	$r_o = R_C$

current flows through the two transistors, the voltage gain of the circuit as a whole becomes

$$\underline{A} = - g_f \cdot R_C ,$$

as for the normal common-emitter circuit. The transconductance cutoff frequency of the circuit is not adversely affected by transistor T_2. This is because T_2 is in common-base connection and is current controlled, and therefore the high frequency $f_\alpha \approx f_T \gg f_g$ is the determining cutoff frequency of this stage.

The base potential V_{B2} of T_2 determines the collector potential of T_1. It is selected high enough to ensure that the collector-emitter voltages of T_1 and T_2 do not fall below a few volts; this is to minimize the voltage-dependent collector-base capacitances.

16.4   Differential amplifier as a wideband amplifier

Another way of increasing the low input resistance of the common-base circuit is to connect an emitter follower to its input. This results in the asymmetric differential amplifier shown in Fig. 16.5. Since transistor T_1 is operated with a constant collector potential, the Miller effect does not occur. Transistor T_2 is operating in common-base connection with voltage control; the cutoff frequency of this stage is therefore the transconductance cutoff frequency f_g. As the cutoff frequency of the emitter follower lies above this frequency, f_g is also the transconductance cutoff frequency of the entire arrangement and is the same as for the cascode amplifier. However, the absolute value of the total transconductance is not the same as that of the cascode amplifier. For its calculation we use the fact that an emitter follower with low-impedance control has the output resistance $r_{o1} = 1/g_{f1}$, and that the common-base circuit has the input resistance $r_{i2} = 1/g_{f2}$. Both transistors are operated with the same collector quiescent current and therefore have the same transconductance g_f. Therefore,

$$r_{o1} = r_{i2} .$$

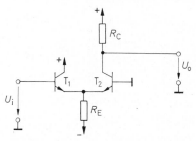

Fig. 16.5 Asymmetric differential amplifier

Voltage gain: $\qquad A = \frac{1}{2} g_f R_C$

Input resistance: $\qquad r_i = 2 r_{BE}$

Output resistance: $\qquad r_o \approx R_C$

Thus, exactly half of the input alternating voltage appears at the emitter of T_2, and we obtain the total transconductance as

$$g_{f\,tot} = \frac{I_{C2}}{U_i} = \frac{I_{C2}}{-2 U_{BE\,2}} = -\frac{1}{2} g_f$$

and the voltage gain as

$$A = \frac{1}{2} g_f R_C \;.$$

The voltage gain is therefore half that of the cascode amplifier.

The advantage of the differential amplifier over the cascode circuit is that the base-emitter voltages of the two transistors compensate one another.

The good high-frequency properties of the differential amplifier are only attained if, as in Fig. 16.5, the collector of the input transistor and the base of the output transistor have constant potential. In order to obtain a symmetrical wideband differential amplifier, some extensions are required, and these are discussed in the following section.

16.5 Symmetrical wideband amplifiers

16.5.1 Differential amplifier using cascode circuits

In Fig. 16.6, a wideband differential amplifier is shown having a symmetrical input and output. In order to avoid the Miller effect, the two transistors of the basic differential amplifier circuit are each replaced by a cascode amplifier.

In wideband amplifiers, negative feedback across several stages is usually associated with considerable stability problems. To achieve a defined gain, however, each stage can be given its own feedback. This is the purpose of the two

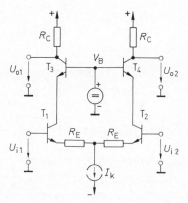

Fig. 16.6 Differential amplifier using cascode circuits

Differential gain: $A_D = -\frac{1}{2}g_f' R_C$

Reduced transconductance: $g_f' = \dfrac{g_f'}{1 + g_f' R_E}$

resistors R_E, each providing current feedback. They reduce the transconductance $\underline{g}_f$ of the input transistors to the value

$$\underline{g}_f' = \frac{1}{R_E + 1/\underline{g}_f} \quad . \tag{16.6}$$

It can be seen that the larger the value of R_E compared to $|1/\underline{g}_f|$, the more the transconductance is determined by the feedback resistance. In addition, the cutoff frequency of the transconductance is increased: by inserting Eq. (16.5) in (16.6), we obtain the frequency response of the reduced transconductance as

$$\underline{g}_f' = \frac{g_f'}{1 + j\dfrac{f}{f_g(g_f/g_f')}} \quad . \tag{16.7}$$

The transconductance cutoff frequency is therefore increased to

$$f_g' = f_g(1 + g_f R_E) = f_g \frac{g_f}{g_f'} \quad . \tag{16.8}$$

The design process may be illustrated by an example: a bandwidth of $B = 100\ \text{MHz}$ is required. It is advisable to select the cutoff frequency f_c of the lowpass filter at the output and the transconductance cutoff frequency f_g', as being roughly the same. For a cascade connection of n lowpass filters all having the same cutoff frequency f_c, the approximation holds that

$$f_{cn} \approx \frac{1}{\sqrt{n}} \cdot f_c \quad . \tag{16.9}$$

Hence, for this example, it is necessary that

$$f'_g \approx f_c \approx 100 \text{ MHz} \cdot \sqrt{2} \approx 150 \text{ MHz} .$$

The transistor and stray capacitances are assumed to have a total value of 6 pF. Thus, for the collector resistance

$$R_C = \frac{1}{2\pi f_c C_S} \approx 180 \, \Omega .$$

In view of this low resistance value, a large transconductance, i.e. a large collector current, is required in order to obtain sufficient voltage gain. The upper limit is given by the permissible power dissipation of the transistor and by the reduction of the gain-bandwidth product at higher collector currents. We select $I_C = 10 \text{ mA}$ and obtain $1/g_f = U_T/I_C \approx 3 \, \Omega$. In order to achieve effective feedback, we make $R_E \gg 1/g_f$. With $R_E = 15 \, \Omega$,

$$g'_f = \frac{1}{3 \, \Omega + 15 \, \Omega} = \frac{1}{18 \, \Omega} = 56 \frac{\text{mA}}{\text{V}} ,$$

and therefore a low-frequency voltage gain

$$A_D = \frac{u_{o1}}{u_{i1} - u_{i2}} = -\tfrac{1}{2} g'_f R_C = -5 .$$

It is now clear that using a wideband amplifier stage with feedback, only a relatively low voltage gain can be achieved. It is also obvious that FETs cannot be used to provide sufficient voltage gain, as their transconductance is too small. If a high input resistance is required, FET source followers may be connected to the input transistors.

From Eq. (16.8), we can determine the necessary transconductance cutoff frequency of the input transistors:

$$f_g = \frac{g'_f}{g_f} f'_g = \frac{3 \, \Omega}{18 \, \Omega} \cdot 150 \text{ MHz} = 25 \text{ MHz} .$$

The gain-bandwidth product must therefore be over 250 MHz. Such values could be attained even with audio transistors but these are unsuitable because of their large capacitances.

There are several ways of increasing the bandwidth by incorporating preemphasis in the circuit. For instance, the current feedback can be made ineffective at high frequencies by connecting a capacitor between the emitter terminals of T_1 and T_2. For a lower cutoff frequency of 100 MHz, we obtain, in our example, a value of 53 pF. A further possibility is to increase the impedance of the collector resistors in the vicinity of the cutoff frequency by series-connecting an inductance. In our example, it would have the approximate value of 0.3 μH. This method is known as 'peaking'.

16.5.2 Differential amplifier using inverting amplifiers

A wideband differential amplifier operating in a similar way to that described above, is represented in Fig. 16.7. The input stage is identical. To obtain a large bandwidth, the collector potentials of the input transistors must again remain constant. For this reason, the transistors T_3 and T_4 of the following differential amplifier have individual feedback via resistors R_C. Their base terminals therefore represent summing points for which the changes in voltage remain small [16.2]. Hence, the alternating voltage at the output is

$$\underline{U}_{o1} = R_C \underline{I}_{C1} = \tfrac{1}{2} g_f' R_C (\underline{U}_{i1} - \underline{U}_{i2}) \ .$$

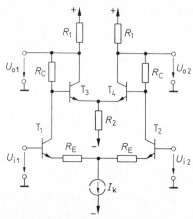

Fig. 16.7 Differential amplifier using inverting amplifiers

Differential gain: $A_D = \tfrac{1}{2} g_f' R_C$

For this circuit, the feedback resistors R_C determine the voltage gain. The resistors R_1 are used to adjust the collector quiescent potentials. They are selected in the order of magnitude of R_C, giving

$$U_{o1} = V^+ - (I_{C1} + I_{C3}) R_1 \ .$$

These two circuits are particularly suited for application as DC amplifiers in wideband oscilloscopes. When transistors having a gain-bandwidth product of several GHz are used in suitably low-impedance circuits, bandwidths of over 500 MHz can be achieved [16.3].

16.5.3 Differential amplifier using complementary cascode circuits

With a single wideband amplifier stage, a voltage gain of not much more than 10 is possible and it is therefore necessary to cascade a number of amplifiers. When DC coupling is involved, a problem arises in that the quiescent output potentials of the circuits described are higher than the quiescent input potentials. Therefore, the quiescent potentials increase from stage to stage, i.e. the number of stages is limited.

This disadvantage can be avoided if pnp transistors are used in the output stage of the cascode differential amplifier of Fig. 16.6, as shown in Fig. 16.8. It is then possible to make the input and output quiescent potentials zero.

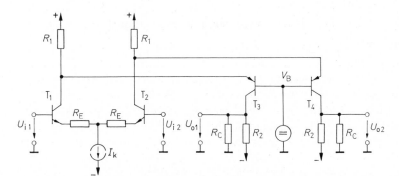

Fig. 16.8 Differential amplifier using complementary cascode circuits

Differential gain: $A_D = -\tfrac{1}{2} g_f' (R_C \| R_2)$

Section 16.5.1 showed that the cutoff frequency of the circuit is determined by the transconductance cutoff frequency f_g' of the input transistors providing feedback, as the output stage has a very much higher cutoff frequency $f_\alpha \approx f_T$. Therefore, the fact that the gain-bandwidth product for pnp transistors is usually lower than that for npn transistors, is of no significance for the circuit in Fig. 16.8.

The base potential V_B determines the collector potential of the input differential amplifier, since $V_{C1} = V_B + 0.7$ V. Hence, the current through the resistors R_1 is constant and has the magnitude

$$I = I_{C1} + I_{C3} = \frac{V^+ - V_{C1}}{R_1} = \frac{V^+ - V_B - 0.7 \text{ V}}{R_1} .$$

If the collector current I_{C1} increases, I_{C3} decreases by the same amount. For the AC collector currents therefore

$$\underline{I}_{C3} = -\underline{I}_{C1} .$$

Apart from the polarity, this is the same relationship as for the normal cascode amplifier.

The resistors R_2 are given values such that the output quiescent potential is zero for the collector current selected. The resistances obtained in this way are usually larger than can be tolerated for a given bandwidth. Therefore, the resistors R_C are inserted, the values of which can be chosen freely, as no DC voltage appears across them. Hence, for the voltage gain

$$\underline{A} = \frac{\underline{U}_{o1}}{\underline{U}_{i1} - \underline{U}_{i2}} = -\tfrac{1}{2} g'_f (R_C \| R_2) \ .$$

16.5.4 Push-pull differential amplifier

During large-signal operation, the wideband amplifiers described have different responses for the leading and the trailing edge of a pulse. This is due to the fact that the transistor current can usually be increased faster than it can be decreased. To obtain equal slew rates for both edges, the principle of push-pull operation is applied. An amplifier of this kind consists of transistors which are controlled in opposition so that, on leading as well as on trailing edges, an increase in current occurs in one half of the circuit, with a simultaneous decrease in the other half.

To achieve this, the circuit in Fig. 16.8 can be extended symmetrically by complementary transistors, as shown in Fig. 16.9.

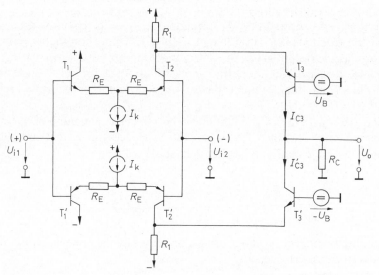

Fig. 16.9 Push-pull differential amplifier

Differential gain: $A_D = g'_f R_C$

For zero input, the current through transistors T_3 and T'_3 is the same, and the output quiescent potential is nil. If a positive input voltage difference $U_D = U_{i1} - U_{i2}$ is applied, the collector current of T_3 increases by $U_D \cdot g'_f$ whereas I'_{C3} decreases by the same amount. The difference between the two currents flows through resistor R_C, and the voltage gain becomes

$$\underline{A}_D = \frac{\underline{U}_o}{\underline{U}_D} = g_f' R_C \ .$$

As in the previous circuit, no DC voltage appears across the resistor R_C. The value of the latter can therefore be freely selected for the bandwidth required.

If an output voltage opposite in polarity to that of U_o is required, a second output stage may be connected to transistors T_1 and T_1'.

16.6 Wideband voltage follower

An emitter follower as in Fig. 16.10 is, in principle, well suited for use as a wideband voltage follower, since its cutoff frequency is higher than the transconductance cutoff frequency. A disadvantage of the circuit, however, is that the output voltage is offset by 0.6 V with respect to the input voltage. Moreover, this offset voltage is appreciably temperature-dependent ($-2\,\text{mV/K}$). This disadvantage can be overcome by using depletion-type FETs, as in Fig. 16.11, where FET current source T_2 is used as the source resistance. If the two transistors are identical, $U_{GS} = -U_R$ for both, as the same current flows through them (for zero load at the output); consequently $U_o = U_i$. Dual FETs are required in order to achieve tight matching tolerances. The resistors R determine the quiescent current flowing. For $R = 0$, the maximum drain current I_{DS} flows. However, in this case the load current must be kept small, as otherwise the gate-channel diode of T_1 may become forward-biased, and the input voltage source may be loaded.

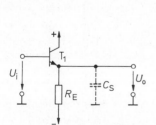

Fig. 16.10 Emitter follower

$U_o \approx U_i - 0.6\,\text{V}$

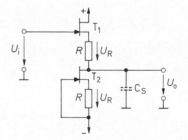

Fig. 16.11 Source follower

$U_o \approx U_i$

The bandwidth of the two circuits is larger, the higher the quiescent current is made. However, for large signals, an extremely unsymmetrical transient behavior is incurred. This is because the stray capacitance C_S can be charged relatively quickly, since the conducting transistor in Fig. 16.10 has an output resistance of only $1/g_f$, whereas the discharge can take place only via resistor R_E, the transistor being reverse-biased for trailing edges. This difficulty can again be overcome by the use of push-pull circuits.

16.6.1   Push-pull voltage follower

Push-pull circuits can be particularly easily realized using junction FETs, as no auxiliary voltages are required to define the operating point. In the circuit in Fig. 16.12, the desired quiescent current is adjusted by means of series feedback resistors R_1 and R_2. In the first step of the design, the quiescent current I_{DQ} is defined. In order that the output quiescent potential is zero, resistor R_1 must have a voltage $|U_{GS1}(I_{DQ})|$ across it. Because of the parabolic transfer characteristic of Eq. (5.1),

$$U_{GS} = U_p(1 - \sqrt{I_D/I_{Dsat}}) \ .$$

Hence

$$R_1 = \frac{|U_{p1}|}{I_{DQ}}\left(1 - \sqrt{\frac{I_{DQ}}{I_{Dsat1}}}\right) \quad \text{and} \quad R_2 = \frac{U_{p2}}{I_{DQ}}\left(1 - \sqrt{\frac{I_{DQ}}{I_{Dsat2}}}\right) \ .$$

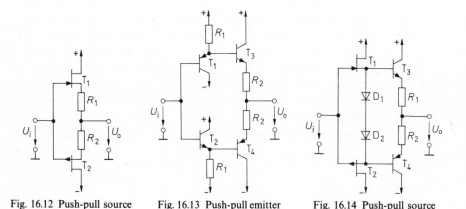

Fig. 16.12 Push-pull source
follower

Fig. 16.13 Push-pull emitter
follower

Fig. 16.14 Push-pull source
follower as driver for a push-
pull emitter follower

If output currents of more than about 10 mA are required, bipolar transistors must be used. A suitable circuit is shown in Fig. 16.13. In order to ensure that a quiescent current flows through the two output transistors T_3 and T_4, the voltage between the two base terminals must be about 1.4 V. This voltage is generated by means of the two emitter followers T_1 and T_2, which also act as impedance converters. The quiescent current is stabilized by the series feedback effect of resistors R_2. Values between 3 Ω and 30 Ω are usually chosen.

Resistors R_1 provide the emitter currents for the drive circuit and the base currents for the output stage. They must be of such a low resistance that, even for the maximum input signal, their current is larger than the base current required by the appropriate output transistor. At large-signal operation it is better to replace them by constant current sources.

Emitter followers are prone to parasitic high-frequency oscillations. These can be damped by inserting a series resistor at each base. They are chosen as small as possible so as not to affect the output resistance and cutoff frequency. Practicable values lie between 20 Ω and 200 Ω.

The complementary source follower in Fig. 16.12 can also be used as bias generator for a complementary emitter follower. In this case diodes D_1 and D_2 in Fig. 16.14 limit the base voltage difference to 1.4 V. For nulling purposes, source followers T_1 and T_2 are additionally loaded with a constant current source having adjustable current. The majority of wideband voltage follower ICs operate on this principle. They are listed in Fig. 16.15.

Type	Manufacturer	Technology	Slew rate	Power bandwidth	Input current	Output current
EL 2002	Elantec	monol.	1000 V/μs	15 MHz	3 μA	100 mA
HA 5002	Harris	monol.	1300 V/μs	11 MHz	2 μA	200 mA
MAX 460	Maxim	hybrid	1500 V/μs	15 MHz	2 pA	100 mA
OPA 633	Burr Brown	hybrid	2500 V/μs	40 MHz	15 μA	100 mA
LH 4010	National	hybrid	2500 V/μs	30 MHz	500 pA	100 mA
EL 2009	Elantec	monol.	3000 V/μs	50 MHz	5 μA	1000 mA
LH 4011	National	hybrid	5000 V/μs	80 MHz	10 pA	200 mA
EL 2031	Elantec	hybrid	7000 V/μs	100 MHz	10 nA	70 mA
LH 4009	National	hybrid	10000 V/μs	150 MHz	5 nA	200 mA
LH 4012	National	hybrid	11 500 V/μs	200 MHz	200 μA	200 mA
WB05	Apex	hybrid	15000 V/μs	70 MHz	150 μA	1000 mA

Fig. 16.15 Some wideband voltage follower ICs

16.7   Wideband operational amplifiers

Wideband operational amplifiers are implemented by taking a wideband differential amplifier, providing it with constant current sources as pull-up resistances and connecting a wideband voltage follower to its output. This produces sufficient differential gain and at the same time a low output resistance.

Using the complementary cascode circuit in Fig. 16.8, we obtain the op amp shown in Fig. 16.16. Current mirror T_5, T_6 provides the high-value collector resistance required for T_4, while simultaneously utilizing the output signal from T_3. The push-pull emitter follower in Fig. 16.13 has been provided as impedance converter. Examples of circuits employing this principle are the LM 6365 from National and the HA 2541/42 from Harris.

If the circuit is based on the push-pull differential amplifier in Fig. 16.9, it is merely necessary to omit the ohmic load resistor R_C and replace it by a following

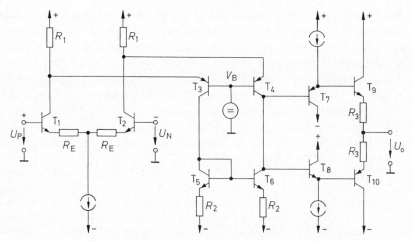

Fig. 16.16 Wideband op amp with cascode differential amplifier

impedance converter. Figure 16.17 shows the resulting circuit. However, in order to realize it as a monolithic device, high-quality pnp transistors have to be manufactured, which is only possible at the expense of a fabrication process providing dielectric insulation. The high-speed op amps from Harris, e.g. types HA 2539 and HA 5160, are realized in this technology.

In order to be able to provide the operation amplifier with external feedback circuitry, it is necessary to ensure an adequate phase margin, i.e. the absolute

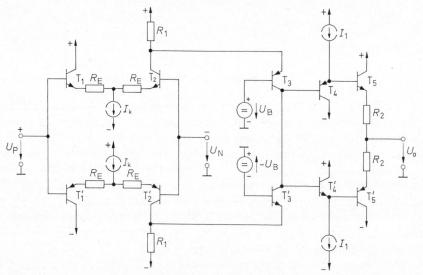

Fig. 16.17 Wideband operational amplifier

value of the loop gain must be less than unity before the phase shift reaches $-180°$. For this purpose it is theoretically possible to connect an RC network to the collectors of T_3 and T_3. However, this greatly impairs the slew rate of the output voltage. A much better solution is to adjust the desired transient response by varying the current feedback resistors R_E.

16.8 Transimpedance amplifiers

A disadvantage of the wideband operational amplifier described is that, in order to retain optimum bandwidth, it is necessary to match the emitter resistors to the required gain. However, this is not possible in an IC; nor can the resistors be looped in externally, because this would require too many connections, and the signals involved are too sensitive.

In order to avoid this problem, the input differential amplifier from Fig. 16.17 can be modified in such a way that the inverting input is formed by the emitters of transistors T_2, T_2'. The resulting circuit (Fig. 16.18) allows the current feedback of amplifier stage T_2, T_2' and hence the differential gain of the entire circuit to be determined by a single resistor connected at the inverting input.

The inputs are here quite different: the input resistance of the non-inverting input is high, since it is preceded by transistors T_1, T_1' as emitter follower; the input resistance of the inverting input is very low, as transistors T_2, T_2' are

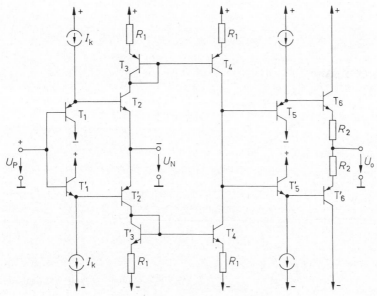

Fig. 16.18 Transimpedance amplifier

Operational amplifiers

Amplifier equivalent circuit

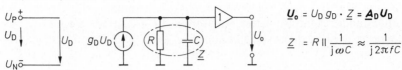

$$\underline{U}_o = U_D\, g_D \cdot \underline{Z} = \underline{A}_D U_D$$

$$\underline{Z} = R \parallel \frac{1}{j\omega C} \approx \frac{1}{j\,2\pi f C}$$

Open-loop frequency response

$$\underline{A}_D = \frac{\underline{U}_o}{\underline{U}_D} = g_D \underline{Z} = \frac{A_{D0}}{1 + j\,\dfrac{f}{f_{cA}}} \approx \frac{f_T}{jf} \quad \text{with} \quad
\begin{aligned}
A_{D0} &= g_D R \\
f_{cA} &= 1/2\,\pi\,RC \\
f_T &= A_{D0}\cdot f_{cA}
\end{aligned}$$

Amplifier with external circuitry

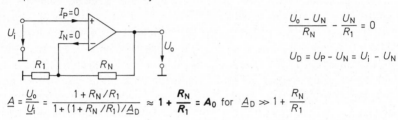

$$\frac{U_o - U_N}{R_N} - \frac{U_N}{R_1} = 0$$

$$U_D = U_P - U_N = U_i - U_N$$

$$\underline{A} = \frac{\underline{U}_o}{\underline{U}_i} = \frac{1 + R_N/R_1}{1 + (1 + R_N/R_1)/\underline{A}_D} \approx 1 + \frac{R_N}{R_1} = A_0 \quad \text{for} \quad \underline{A}_D \gg 1 + \frac{R_N}{R_1}$$

Closed-loop frequency response

$$\underline{A} = \frac{A_0}{1 + j\,\dfrac{A_0}{f_T}\,f} \quad \text{therefore} \quad f_c = \frac{f_T}{A_0} \quad \text{dependent on } R_N \text{ and } R_1$$

Loop gain

$$g_0 = \frac{R_1}{R_1 + R_N}\, A_{D0} = \frac{A_{D0}}{A_0} \quad \text{dependent on } R_N \text{ and } R_1$$

Frequency response

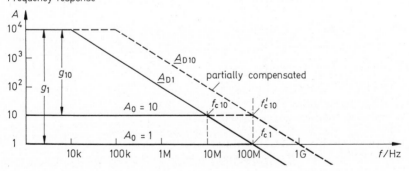

Fig. 16.21 Comparison of operational amplifiers

Transimpedance amplifier

Amplifier equivalent circuit

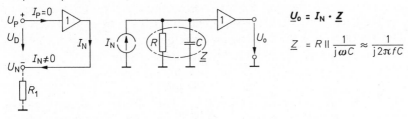

$$\underline{U}_o = I_N \cdot \underline{Z}$$

$$\underline{Z} = R \parallel \frac{1}{j\omega C} \approx \frac{1}{j 2\pi f C}$$

Open-loop frequency response

$$\underline{A}_D = \frac{\underline{U}_o}{\underline{U}_D} = \frac{\underline{Z}}{R_1} = \frac{A_{D0}}{1 + j\dfrac{f}{f_{cA}}} \quad \text{with} \quad \begin{array}{l} A_{D0} = R/R_1 \\ f_{cA} = 1/2\pi RC \end{array}$$

Amplifier with external circuitry

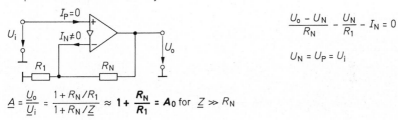

$$\frac{U_o - U_N}{R_N} - \frac{U_N}{R_1} - I_N = 0$$

$$U_N = U_P = U_i$$

$$\underline{A} = \frac{\underline{U}_o}{\underline{U}_i} = \frac{1 + R_N/R_1}{1 + R_N/\underline{Z}} \approx 1 + \frac{R_N}{R_1} = A_0 \text{ for } \underline{Z} \gg R_N$$

Closed-loop frequency response

$$\underline{A} = \frac{A_0}{1 + R_N \cdot j 2\pi f C} \quad \text{therefore} \quad f_c = 1/2\pi R_N C \text{ independent of } R_1$$

Loop gain

$$A_{D0} = \frac{R}{R_N \parallel R_1} = \frac{R}{R_N} A_0 = g_0 A_0 \quad \text{therefore} \quad g_0 = \frac{R}{R_N} \quad \text{independent of } R_1$$

Frequency response

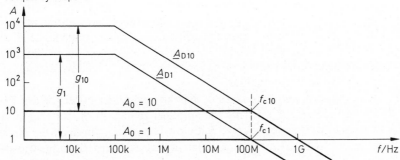

and transimpedance amplifiers

operated in common-base connection. However, as with any operational amplifier, only the voltage difference between the two inputs is amplified.

In order to ensure that the low-resistance input becomes the inverting input of the circuit, we replace the cascode circuit in Fig. 16.17 by current mirrors T_3, T_4 and T'_3, T'_4. Currents I_k determine the quiescent currents in the circuit because transistors T_1, T_2 and T'_1, T'_2 form current mirrors for I_k. Hence

$$I_{C1} = I_{C1'} = I_{C2} = I_{C2'} = I_{C3} = I_{C3'} = I_{C4} = I_{C4'} \ .$$

The operation of a transimpedance amplifier can best be described with reference to its equivalent circuit in Fig. 16.19. The input stage operates, ideally, as a voltage follower. The inputs of the circuit are formed by the high-resistance non-inverting input and the low-resistance output of the voltage follower. As with any op amp, the input voltage difference is therefore zero.

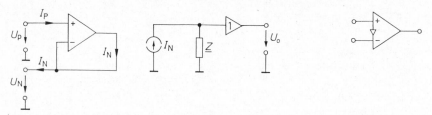

Fig. 16.19 Equivalent circuit of a transimpedance amplifier   Fig. 16.20 Circuit symbol

The current flowing in the non-inverting input produces, via a current-controlled current source (in Fig. 16.18, transistors T_3, T'_3, T_4, T'_4), a voltage drop $I_N \cdot \underline{Z}$ across *impedance* $\underline{Z}$. This voltage drop furnishes the output voltage via an impedance converter (T_5, T'_5, T_6, T'_6). The voltage gain of the circuit can only be specified after having connected a resistor (e.g. R_1 in Fig. 16.21) at the inverting input. Current $I_N = U_P/R_1$ then flows, giving an output voltage of

$$U_o = I_N \cdot \underline{Z} = \frac{\underline{Z}}{R_1} U_P \ .$$

The voltage gain $\underline{Z}/R_1$ can therefore be adjusted externally, as required. In order to achieve high gains, transimpedance amplifiers have a high impedance $\underline{Z}$, the real part of which is between $100 \, k\Omega$ and $1 \, M\Omega$. Resistances $R_1 = 200 \, \Omega \ldots$ $2 \, k\Omega$ thus produce loop gains in the order of 1000, which is a common compromise for wideband amplifiers.

The high value of the impedance $\underline{Z}$ has an important consequence. The currents I_N required for fully driving the amplifier remain in the μA region. As the external circuitry must be selected with low impedance, these currents may be disregarded. Since the input voltage difference is again zero, the same transfer equations are obtained as for conventional op amps.

The great advantage of transimpedance amplifiers is that their differential gain is proportional to the external gain if the former is adjusted by R_1 and if R_N

is kept constant. Their loop gain is then constant, as is the bandwidth and the transient response of the circuit in feedback mode. With conventional op amps, this can only be achieved by matching the frequency compensation to the particular gain. Figure 16.21 shows the similarities and differences [16.4, 16.5, 16.6]. Examples of commercially available transimpedance amplifiers are given in Fig. 7.40. The types listed with the best slew rate are all of transimpedance design.

16.9 Wideband composite amplifiers

The DC characteristics of broadband operational amplifiers are considerably worse than one might otherwise expect from operational amplifiers. The series-feedback resistors R_E necessary for stable operation cause a low DC voltage gain and a high offset voltage. As the input transistors must carry a relatively high collector current because of the required bandwidth, the input bias currents are correspondingly high.

These disadvantages may be overcome if a wideband amplifier OA 2 is combined with a DC amplifier OA 1, as in Fig. 16.22. The wideband amplifier then determines the high-frequency characteristics and the DC amplifier the low-frequency characteristics of the circuit. The only disadvantage is that a non-inverting input is no longer available. *For DC voltages*, the circuit provides the gain

$$|\underline{A}| = A_{D1} A_{D2} \ .$$

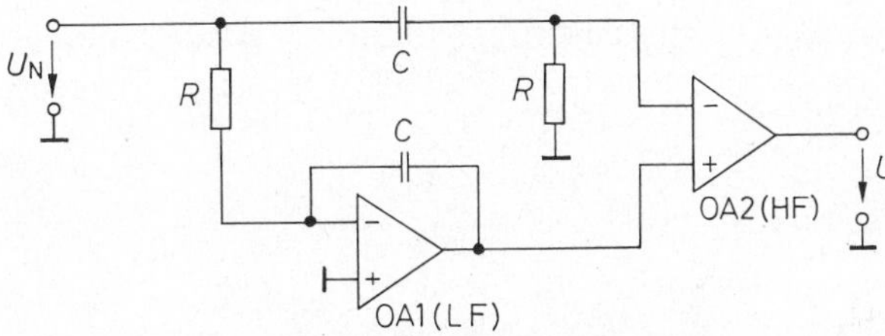

Fig. 16.22 DC-stabilized wideband amplifier
(HF = high freq., LF = low freq.)

Since the voltage appearing at the input of OA 2 is already amplified by the very large factor A_{D1}, the offset voltage of OA 2 is no longer of any importance. The input bias current of wideband amplifier OA 2 flows through resistor R and so bypasses the input. The circuit has therefore the low input bias current and the low offset voltage of OA 1.

At low frequencies, OA 1 operates as an integrator. Its gain therefore falls off at -20 dB per decade, whereas that of wideband amplifier OA 2 remains constant. In this frequency range the circuit therefore provides a gain of

$$|A| = |A_1| A_{D2} = \frac{1}{2\pi f RC} A_{D2} \ .$$

This characteristic is shown in Fig. 16.23.

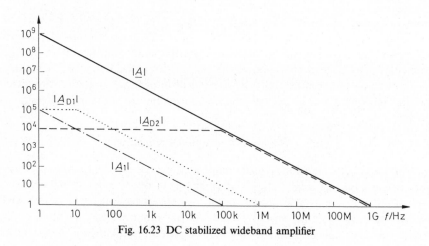

Fig. 16.23 DC stabilized wideband amplifier

At high frequencies, wideband amplifier OA 2 provides the gain by itself. To achieve this, the time constant RC is selected such that, at the cutoff frequency f_{c2} of OA 2, the highpass filter also has its cutoff frequency, and the gain of the integrator has fallen to unity.

Consequently

$$RC = 1/2\pi f_{c2} \ .$$

If we select $R = 10\,\text{k}\Omega$, the example in Fig. 16.23 gives, with $f_{c2} = 100\,\text{kHz}$, a value of $C = 160\,\text{pF}$. This ensures an unbroken continuation of the frequency response $|\underline{A}|$, as may be seen from Fig. 16.23. For high frequencies, the circuit gain is $|\underline{A}| = |\underline{A}_{D2}|$.

17   Power amplifiers

Power amplifiers are designed to provide large output powers with the voltage gain playing only a minor role. Normally, the voltage gain of a power output stage is near unity and the power gain is thus mainly due to the current gain of the circuit. Output voltage and current must be able to assume positive and negative values. Power amplifiers with unidirectional output current are known as power supplies. They are discussed in Chapter 18.

17.1   Emitter follower as a power amplifier

The operation of the emitter follower has already been described in Section 4.4. Here, we define some of the parameters which are of particular interest for its application as a power amplifier. Firstly, we calculate the load resistance for which the circuit delivers maximum power without distortion. If the output is negative, R_L carries some of the current flowing through R_E. The limit for control of the output voltage is reached when the current through the transistor becomes zero. This is the case for the output voltage

$$U_{o\,min} = -\frac{R_L}{R_E + R_L} \cdot V_b \ .$$

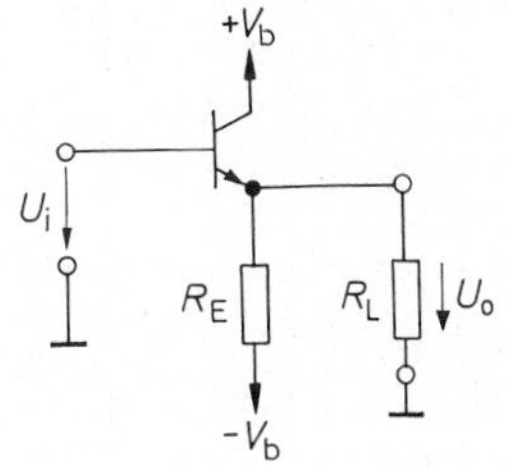

Fig. 17.1 Emitter follower as a power amplifier

Voltage gain:	$A \approx 1$
Current gain if load is matched to internal resistance:	$A_i = \frac{1}{2}\beta$
Load resistance if matched:	$R_L = R_E$
Output power for matched load and full sinusoidal output swing:	$P_{L\,max} = \dfrac{V_b^2}{8R_E}$
Maximum efficiency:	$\eta_{max} = \dfrac{P_{L\,max}}{P_{tot}} = 6.25\%$
Max. dissipation of the transistor:	$P_T = \dfrac{V_b^2}{R_E} = 8P_{L\,max}$

If the output voltage is to be controlled sinusoidally around 0 V, its amplitude must not exceed the value

$$\hat{U}_{o\,max} = \frac{R_L}{R_E + R_L} \cdot V_b \;.$$

The power delivered to R_L is then

$$P_L = \frac{1}{2}\frac{\hat{U}_{o\,max}^2}{R_L} = \frac{V_b^2 R_L}{2(R_E + R_L)^2} \;.$$

With $\dfrac{dP_L}{dR_L} = 0$, it follows that for $R_L = R_E$ the maximum output power

$$P_{L\,max} = \frac{V_b^2}{8R_E}$$

is attained. This result is surprising in that one would normally expect maximum power output when the load resistance equals the output resistance r_o of the voltage source. However, this is so only for constant open-circuit voltage. Here, the open-circuit voltage is not constant as it must be reduced when R_L is small.

In the next step we determine the power consumption within the circuit for any output voltage amplitude and any load resistance. For a sinusoidal voltage, the power

$$P_L = \frac{1}{2}\frac{\hat{U}_o^2}{R_L}$$

is supplied to the load resistance R_L. The power dissipation of the transistor is

$$P_T = \frac{1}{T}\int_0^T (V_b - U_o(t))\left(\frac{U_o(t)}{R_L} + \frac{U_o(t) + V_b}{R_E}\right) dt \;.$$

For $U_o(t) = \hat{U}_o \sin \omega t$ it follows that

$$P_T = \frac{V_b^2}{R_E} - \frac{1}{2}\hat{U}_o^2\left(\frac{1}{R_L} + \frac{1}{R_E}\right) \;.$$

The power dissipation of the transistor is largest for zero input signal. Similarly, the power in R_E is given by

$$P_E = \frac{V_b^2}{R_E} + \frac{1}{2}\frac{\hat{U}_o^2}{R_E} \;.$$

The circuit therefore draws from the power supplies a total power of

$$P_{tot} = P_L + P_T + P_E = 2\frac{V_b^2}{R_E} \;.$$

This is a surprising result since it shows that the total power of the circuit is independent of the drive voltage and of the load, and that it remains constant as long as the circuit is not overdriven. The efficiency η_{max} is defined as the ratio of the maximum obtainable output power to the power consumption at full voltage swing. The results for $P_{L\,max}$ and P_{tot} give $\eta_{max} = 1/16 = 6.25\%$. The following characteristics are typical for this circuit:

1) The current through the transistor is never zero.
2) The total power consumption is independent of the input drive voltage and the load.

These are the characteristics of *class-A operation*.

17.2   Complementary emitter followers

The output power of the emitter follower in Fig. 17.1 is limited in that the resistor R_E restricts the maximum output current. A considerably higher output power and a better efficiency can be attained if R_E is replaced by a second emitter follower, as in Fig. 17.2.

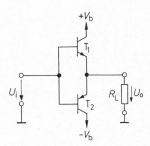

Fig. 17.2 Complementary emitter follower

Voltage gain:	$A \approx 1$
Current gain:	$A_i = \beta$
Output power at full sinusoidal output swing:	$P_L = \dfrac{V_b^2}{2R_L}$
Efficiency at full sinusoidal output swing:	$\eta_{max} = \dfrac{P_L}{P_{tot}} = 78.5\%$
Max. dissipation of one transistor:	$P_{T1} = P_{T2} = \dfrac{V_b^2}{\pi^2 R_L} = 0.2\,P_L$

17.2.1   Complementary class-B emitter follower

For positive input voltages, T_1 operates as an emitter follower and T_2 is reverse biased; vice versa for negative drive. The transistors thus carry the current alternately, each for half a period. Such a mode of operation is known as *push-pull class-B operation*. For $U_i = 0$, both transistors are turned off and therefore no quiescent current flows in the circuit. The current taken from the positive or negative power supply is thus the same as the output current. The circuit therefore has a considerably better efficiency than the normal emitter follower. A further advantage is that, at any load, the output can be driven between $\pm V_b$ as the transistors do not limit the output current. The difference between the input and output voltage is determined by the base-emitter voltage of the current-carrying transistor. As it changes only very slightly with load, $U_o \approx U_i$, irrespective of the load current. The output power is inversely proportional to the resistance R_L and has no extremum, and therefore no matching is required between the load resistance and any internal circuit resistance. The maximum power output is determined instead by the permissible peak currents and the maximum power dissipation of the transistors, which, for full sinusoidal drive, is given by

$$P_L = \frac{\hat{U}_o^2}{2R_L} \; .$$

We now determine the power dissipation P_{T1} of transistor T_1. As the circuit is symmetrical, it is identical to that of T_2.

$$P_{T1} = \frac{1}{T} \int_0^{T/2} (V_b - U_o(t)) \frac{U_o(t)}{R_L} \, dt \; .$$

For $U_o(t) = \hat{U}_o \sin \omega t$, this is

$$P_{T1} = \frac{1}{R_L} \left(\frac{\hat{U}_o V_b}{\pi} - \frac{\hat{U}_o^2}{4} \right) \; .$$

Hence, the efficiency of the circuit

$$\eta = \frac{P_L}{P_{tot}} = \frac{P_L}{2P_{T1} + P_L} = \frac{\pi}{4} \cdot \frac{\hat{U}_o}{V_b} \approx 0.785 \frac{\hat{U}_o}{V_b} \; .$$

It is therefore proportional to the output amplitude and, for full output swing ($\hat{U}_o = V_b$), attains a value of $\eta_{max} = 78.5\%$.

The power dissipation of the transistors reaches its maximum not at full output voltage swing, but at

$$\hat{U}_o = \frac{2}{\pi} V_b \approx 0.64 V_b \; .$$

This follows from the extremum condition

$$\frac{dP_{T1}}{d\hat{U}_o} = 0 \; .$$

In this case the power dissipation for each transistor is

$$P_{T\,max} = \frac{1}{\pi^2} \frac{V_b^2}{R_L} \approx 0.1 \frac{V_b^2}{R_L} \; .$$

The curves of output power, power dissipation and total power as functions of the relative output voltage swing $\hat{U}_o/V_b$ are given in Fig. 17.3.

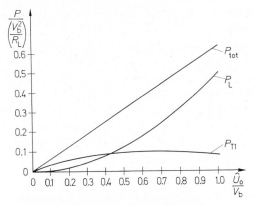

Fig. 17.3 Power and loss curves for the complementary emitter follower as a function of the output amplitude

We can see that the power consumption

$$P_{tot} = 2P_{T1} + P_L = \frac{2V_b}{\pi R_L} \hat{U}_o \approx 0.64 \frac{V_b}{R_L} \hat{U}_o$$

is proportional to the output amplitude. This is characteristic of *class-B operation*.

As described above, only one transistor carries current at any given time. However, this only applies to input frequencies which are small compared to the gain-bandwidth product of the transistors. Some time is needed for the transistor to change from the ON to the OFF state. If the period of the input voltage is smaller than this time, both transistors may conduct simultaneously. Very high crossover currents then flow through both transistors from $+V_b$ to $-V_b$ and will destroy them instantaneously. Oscillations at this critical frequency can occur in amplifiers with feedback or if the emitter followers supply leading loads. For the protection of the transistors, a current limiter should therefore be incorporated.

17.2.2 Complementary class-AB emitter followers

Figure 17.4 represents the transfer characteristic $U_o = U_o(U_i)$ for push-pull class-B operation, as described for the previous circuit. Near zero voltage, the current in the forward-biased transistor becomes very small and the transistor impedance increases. The output voltage at load therefore no longer changes linearly with the input voltage, as indicated by a bend in the characteristic, near the origin. This gives rise to distortion of the output voltage, known as *crossover distortion*. If a small quiescent current flows through the transistors, their impedance near the origin is reduced and the transfer characteristic in Fig. 17.5 is obtained. The transfer characteristic of each individual emitter follower is

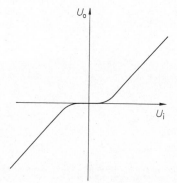
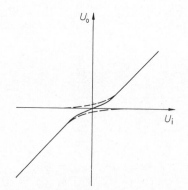

Fig. 17.4 Crossover for push-pull class-B   Fig. 17.5 Crossover for push-pull class-AB
operation   operation

shown by a dashed line. It can be seen that the crossover distortion is considerably reduced. If the quiescent current is made as large as the maximum output
current, the resulting mode of operation would be called push-pull class-A, in
analogy to Section 17.1. However, the crossover distortion is already greatly
reduced if only a fraction of the maximum output current is permitted to flow as
quiescent current. This mode is called push-pull class-AB operation and its
crossover distortion is so small that it can be easily reduced to tolerable values
by means of feedback.

Additional distortion may arise if positive and negative voltages are amplified at different gains. This is the case if the complementary emitter followers are
driven from a high-impedance source and the transistors have different current
transfer ratios. If strong feedback is undesirable, the transistors must be selected
for identical current transfer ratios.

Figure 17.6 shows the basic circuit for the realization of class-AB operation.
To obtain a small quiescent current, a DC voltage of about 1.4 V is applied
between the base terminals of T_1 and T_2. If the two voltages U_1 and U_2 are the
same, the quiescent potential of the output approximately equals that of the
input. The bias voltage can also be supplied by a single voltage source,
$U_3 = U_1 + U_2$, as represented in Fig. 17.7. In this case, the potential difference
between output and input is about 0.7 V.

The main problem of class-AB operation is keeping the required quiescent
current constant over a wide temperature range. As the transistors get warmer,
the quiescent current increases, which may itself further increase the temperature and finally lead to destruction of the transistors. This effect is known as
positive thermal feedback. The increase of the quiescent current can be avoided
if the voltages U_1 and U_2 are each reduced by 2 mV for every degree of
temperature rise. For this purpose, diodes or thermistors can be mounted on the
heat sinks of the power transistors.

However, temperature compensation is never quite perfect, as the temperature difference between junction and case is usually considerable. Therefore,

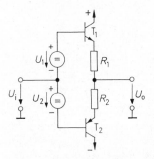

Fig. 17.6 Realization of class-AB operation using two auxiliary voltages

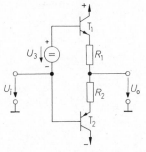

Fig. 17.7 Realization of class-AB operation using a single auxiliary voltage

additional stabilization is required in the form of resistors R_1 and R_2 which provide series feedback. This is more effective the larger the resistances chosen. As the resistors are connected in series with the load, they reduce the available output power and must therefore be selected small compared to the load resistance. This dilemma can be avoided by using Darlington circuits, as will be shown in Section 17.4.

17.2.3 Generation of the bias voltage

One way of providing a bias voltage is shown in Fig. 17.8. The voltage of $U_1 = U_2 \approx 0.7\,\text{V}$ across each of the diodes D_1 and D_2 just allows a small quiescent current to flow through the transistors T_1 and T_2. To attain a higher input resistance, the diodes can be replaced by emitter followers, this resulting in the circuit of Fig. 17.9.

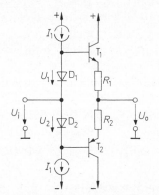

Fig. 17.8 Bias voltage generation by diodes

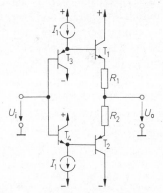

Fig. 17.9 Bias voltage generation by transistors

Figure 17.10 represents a driver arrangement which allows adjustment of the bias voltage and its temperature coefficient over a wide range. Feedback is applied to transistor T_3 by means of voltage divider R_5, R_6. For negligible base

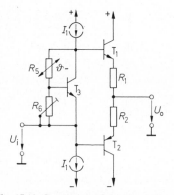

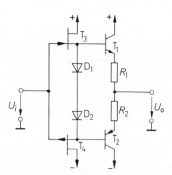

Fig. 17.10 Generation of the bias voltage
having an adjustable temperature coefficient

Fig. 17.11 Bias voltage generation by FETs

current, its collector-emitter voltage has the value

$$U_{CE} = U_{BE}\left(1 + \frac{R_5}{R_6}\right).$$

To obtain the desired temperature coefficient, R_5 is, in practice, a resistor network containing an NTC resistor mounted on the heat sink of the output transistors. In this way, the quiescent current can to a large extent be made temperature-independent even though the temperature of the case is lower than that of the output transistor junctions.

In circuits using diodes for bias voltage generation, no current can flow from the input into the base of the output transistors. The base current for the output transistors must therefore be supplied from the constant-current sources. The constant current I_1 must be larger than the maximum base current of T_1 and T_2 so that diodes D_1 and D_2 (or transistors T_3 and T_4) will not be turned off before maximum permissible output voltage swing is reached. It would for this reason be inadvisable to replace the constant-current sources by resistors, as this would cause the current to decrease with rising output voltage.

The most favorable driver circuit would be one supplying a larger base current for increasing output voltage, and such a circuit is represented in Fig. 17.11. The FETs T_3 and T_4 operate as source followers. The difference in their source voltages settles, due to series feedback, to a value of about 1.4 V. FETs having a large saturation drain current $I_{D\,sat}$ are suitable for this purpose.

17.3 Complementary Darlington circuits

With the circuits described so far, output currents of up to a few hundred milli-amperes can be obtained. For higher output currents, transistors having higher current transfer ratios must be used. They can be made up of two or more individual transistors if they are operated in a Darlington, or even in a complementary Darlington connection. Such circuits and their parameters have already been discussed in Section 4.6. The basic circuit of a Darlington power amplifier is shown in Fig. 17.12, where the transistor pairs T_1, T_1' and T_2, T_2' are Darlington connected.

For the implementation of push-pull class-AB, the adjustment of the quiescent current presents problems, as four temperature-dependent base-emitter voltages must now be compensated. These difficulties can be avoided by allowing the quiescent current to flow only through the driver transistors T_1 and T_2. The output transistors then become conducting only for larger output currents. To achieve this, the bias voltage U_1 is selected such that a voltage of approx. 0.4 V appears across each of resistors R_1 and R_2; thus $U_1 \approx 2(0.4 \text{ V} + 0.7 \text{ V}) = 2.2 \text{ V}$. Then, for zero input, the output transistors carry virtually no current, even at higher junction temperatures.

At higher output currents, the base-emitter voltages of the output transistors rise to about 0.8 V. This limits the current through R_1 and R_2 to double the quiescent value, and therefore most of the emitter current of the driver transistors is available as base current for the output transistors.

Resistors R_1 and R_2 also discharge the base of the output transistors. The lower their resistance, the faster the output transistors can be turned off. This is particularly important when the input voltage changes polarity, as one transistor can become conducting before the other is turned off. In this way, a large crossover current can flow through both output transistors, and the resulting *secondary breakdown* will destroy them immediately. This effect determines the attainable large-signal bandwidth.

Sometimes it is preferable to use output power transistors of the same type. In such cases the Darlington circuit T_2, T_2' in Fig. 17.12 is replaced by the complementary Darlington connection, as described in Section 4.6. The resulting circuit, shown in Fig. 17.13, is known as a *quasi-complementary* power amplifier. To arrive at the same quiescent current conditions as for the previous circuit, a voltage of about 0.4 V is impressed across resistor R_1. Voltage U_1 must then be 0.4 V + 2·0.7 V = 1.8 V. The quiescent current flows via T_2 and R_2 to the negative supply. If $R_1 = R_2$, a bias voltage of 0.4 V is also obtained for T_2'. The purpose of resistors R_1 and R_2 is the same as for the previous circuit, that is to discharge the base of the output current transistors.

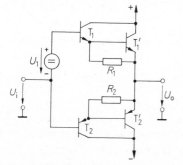

Fig. 17.12 Complementary Darlington pairs

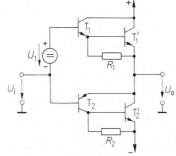

Fig. 17.13 Quasi-complementary Darlington pairs

The entire arrangement is available as a monolithic integrated circuit. Type TDA 1420 from SGS can supply a maximum output current of 3 A. The permissible power dissipation is 30 W for a case temperature of 60 °C. Type L 149 from SGS has additional protection circuits which ensure that the safe operating area (SOA) cannot be exceeded.

17.4 Complementary source followers

The major advantage of power MOSFETs over bipolar power transistors is that they can be turned on and off considerably faster. Whereas bipolar power transistors have switching times of between 100 ns and 1 µs, the corresponding range for MOSFETs is 10 ns to 100 ns. It is therefore preferable to employ power MOSFETs in output stages for frequencies above 100 kHz up to 1 MHz.

As power MOSFETs possess large drain-gate and gate-source capacitances, possibly a few hundred pF, it is advantageous to operate them as source followers. This prevents the drain-gate capacitance from being dynamically increased due to the Miller effect, and the gate-source capacitance is even considerably reduced by bootstrapping.

Figure 17.14 shows the basic circuit diagram for a complementary source follower. The two auxiliary voltages U_1 are used, as in the case of the bipolar transistor in Fig. 17.6, to set the required quiescent current. For $U_1 = U_p$, no quiescent current flows at all: class-B operation is established. However, in order to minimize the transfer distortion, a quiescent current is usually caused to flow by selecting $U_1 > U_p$. The magnitude of the quiescent current is stabilized by current feedback via resistors R_1, R_2. The magnitude of U_1 results from the

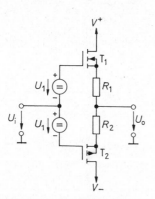

Fig. 17.14 Principle of a complementary source follower

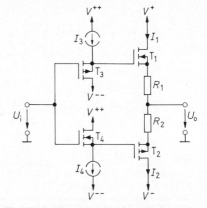

Fig. 17.15 Bias generation for complementary source followers. Examples of transistor types from International Rectifier:

| T_3: IRFD 112 | T_1: IRF 531 |
| T_4: IRFD 9112 | T_2: IRF 9531 |

transfer characteristic of the MOSFETs, i.e.

$$U_1 = I_D R_1 + U_p \left(1 + \sqrt{\frac{I_D}{I_{D\,sat}}} \right) .$$

The resulting voltages are markedly higher than for bipolar transistors, as the pinch-off voltage U_p of power MOSFETs is between 1 V and 4 V. A simple means of producing the required bias is to replace emitter followers T_3, T_4 in Fig. 17.9 by source followers. The resultant circuit is shown in Fig. 17.15. Here, T_3 produces as bias voltage of

$$U_1 = U_{p3} \left(1 + \sqrt{\frac{I_3}{I_{D\,sat3}}} \right) .$$

If low-power MOSFETs T_3 and T_4 are fabricated in the same process as the power MOSFETs T_1, T_2, and therefore have the same pinch-off voltages, the maximum quiescent current produced for $R_1 = R_2 = 0$ is

$$I_1 = \frac{I_{D\,sat1}}{I_{D\,sat3}} I_3 .$$

This can be reduced using R_1, R_2. Currents I_3, I_4 are selected sufficiently large to charge the input capacitor of source followers T_1, T_2 at the highest frequency occurring.

Operation of the drive circuit generally requires a supply voltage 10 V higher than for the output stage. Otherwise, the maximum achievable output voltage may be as much as 10 V below the supply voltage, resulting in unacceptably poor efficiency.

17.5 Electronic current limiting

Due to their low output resistance, power amplifiers can be easily overloaded and therefore easily destroyed. Consequently, it is advisable to limit the output current to a defined maximum value by means of an additional control circuit. The various possibilities are exemplified by the simple complementary emitter follower in Fig. 17.8. A particularly simple circuit is shown in Fig. 17.16. Limiting takes effect when multiple diode D_3 or D_4 begins to conduct, because this prevents any further increase in the voltage dropped across R_1 or R_2. The maximum output current is therefore

$$I_{o\,max}^+ = \frac{U_{D3} - U_{BE1}}{R_1} = \frac{0.7\,V}{R_1} (n_3 - 1) ,$$

$$I_{o\,max}^- = -\frac{U_{D4} - |U_{BE2}|}{R_2} = -\frac{0.7\,V}{R_2} (n_4 - 1) .$$

where n_3 and n_4 are the number of diodes used for D_3 and D_4 respectively.

Another method of current limiting is shown in Fig. 17.17. If the voltage drop across R_1 or R_2 exceeds a value of about 0.7 V, transistor T_3 or T_4 begins to conduct, thereby preventing any further rise in the base current of T_1 or T_2. This control arrangement limits the output current to a maximum value of

$$I_{o\,max}^+ \approx \frac{0.7\ V}{R_1} \qquad \text{or} \qquad I_{o\,max}^- \approx \frac{0.7\ V}{R_2}\ .$$

The advantage here is that the circuit is no longer subject to the widely varying base-emitter voltage of the power transistors, but only to the base-emitter voltage of the limiting transistors. Resistors R_3 and R_4 are used to protect these transistors from excessively large base-current peaks.

In the event of a short circuit, current $I_{o\,max}$ flows through T_1 and T_2 for half a period in each case, while the output voltage is zero. The power dissipation in the output-stage transistors is therefore

$$P_{T1} = P_{T2} \approx \tfrac{1}{2} V_b I_{o\,max}\ .$$

As comparison with Section 17.2 shows, this is five times the dissipation during normal operation. Consequently, the ratings of the power transistors and heat sinks must be such that the circuits in Figs. 17.16 and 17.17 are short-circuit proof.

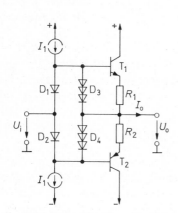

Fig. 17.16 Current limiting with diodes

$$I_{o\,max} = \pm\ 1.4\ V/R_{1,\,2}$$

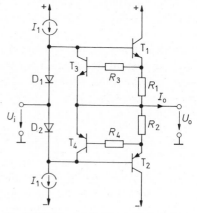

Fig. 17.17 Current limiting with transistors

$$I_{o\,max} = \pm\ 0.7\ V/R_{1,\,2}$$

Amplitude-dependent current limiting

The need for additional short-circuit protection at the output stage can be obviated by only allowing resistive loads of a defined value R_L to be connected. It can then be assumed that, for small output voltages, only small output currents will flow. The current limiting does not therefore have to be defined by the maximum current $I_{o\,max} = U_{o\,max}/R_L$, but the output current can be limited to $I_o = U_o/R_L$, i.e. as a function of the output voltage. The maximum current under short-circuit conditions ($U_o = 0$) can therefore be selected correspondingly low.

In order to make the current limit dependent on the output voltage, the bias voltage applied to transistors T_3 and T_4 in Fig. 17.18 is increased as the output

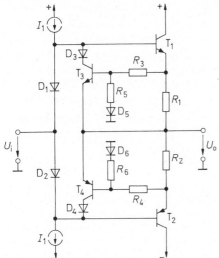

Fig. 17.18 Voltage-dependent current limiting

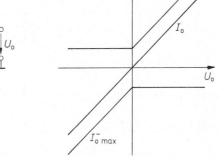

Fig. 17.19 Current limit and output current characteristics for resistive load

$$|I_{o\,max}| = \frac{0.7\,\text{V}}{R_{1,2}} + \frac{R_{3,4}}{R_{5,6}} \cdot \frac{U_o}{R_{1,2}}$$

voltage rises. Resistors R_5 and R_6, which have high values compared to R_3 and R_4, are used for this purpose. For low output voltages, we therefore obtain the same current limit as in Fig. 17.17. For higher positive output voltages, an additional voltage drop of $U_o R_3/R_5$ appears across R_3, thereby raising the current limit to

$$I_{o\,max}^+ \approx \frac{0.7\,\text{V}}{R_1} + \frac{R_3}{R_5} \frac{U_o}{R_1}.$$

Diode D_5 prevents transistor T_3 from receiving a positive bias when the output voltages are negative, which could result in it being turned on unintentionally. Diode D_3 prevents the collector-base diode of T_3 from conducting when a larger voltage is dropped across R_2 in the event of negative output voltages. Otherwise the drive circuit would be subject to additional loading. Similar considerations apply to the negative current limiting by T_4.

These characteristics are graphically illustrated in Fig. 17.19. Using this form of voltage-dependent current limiting, it is therefore possible to utilize fully the safe operating area (SOA) of the power transistors. Consequently, it is also known as SOA current limiting. Driver ICs providing current limiting in this way include types ICL 8063 (Intersil) and LM 391 (National).

17.6 Four-quadrant operation

A power output stage is subject to the most severe operating conditions when a constant current limit $I_{o\,max}^+$ and $I_{o\,max}^-$ is required for any given positive and negative output voltage. Such requirements invariably arise if no resistive

load is present, but a load which can feed energy back to the output stage. Loads
of this kind include capacitors, inductors and electric motors. In this case, it is
necessary to fall back on the current limiting arrangements in Figs. 17.16 or
17.17. The critical operating condition for the negative output-stage transistor
T_2 occurs when the load feeds the current-limit value $I_{o\,max}^-$ into the circuit while
the output voltage is $U_o = U_{o\,max} \approx V^+$. Current $I_{o\,max}^-$ then flows through T_2 at
a voltage of $U_{CE\,2} \approx 2V^+$, resulting in a power dissipation of $P_{T2} = 2V^+ \cdot I_{o\,max}^-$.
However, for a voltage of $2V^+$, secondary breakdown limits the majority of
bipolar transistors to be loaded only to a fraction of their thermal rating.
Therefore, it is generally necessary to connect several power transistors in
parallel or, preferably, to employ power MOSFETs, which are not subject to
secondary breakdown.

One method of halving the voltage across the output-stage transistors is
shown in Fig. 17.20. The basic idea is to control the collector potentials of T_1
and T_2 together with the input voltage. For positive input voltages, we obtain

$$V_1 = U_i + 0.7\ \text{V} + 3\ \text{V} - 0.7\ \text{V} - 0.7\ \text{V} = U_i + 2.3\ \text{V}\ .$$

Transistor T_1 is therefore being operated well outside saturation. For negative
input voltages, diode D_3 takes over the current, and we have $V_1 = -0.7\ \text{V}$. If
the input voltage falls to $U_i = U_{i\,min} \approx V^-$, a voltage of only $U_{CE\,1\,max} \approx V^-$ is
dropped across T_1. The maximum voltage across T_3 is likewise no larger. It
occurs when $U_i = 0$ and is given by $U_{CE\,3\,max} \approx V^+$. The maximum power
dissipated in T_1 and T_3 is therefore $P_{max} = V^+ \cdot I_{o\,max}^+$. Consequently, not only is
the maximum collector-emitter voltage halved, but also the power dissipation.
For the negative side, T_2, T_4 produce corresponding results due to the symmetry
of the circuit. To make this clear, the characteristics of V_1 and V_2 are plotted in
Fig. 17.21.

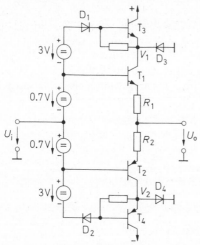

Fig. 17.20 Push-pull stage for four-quadrant
operation

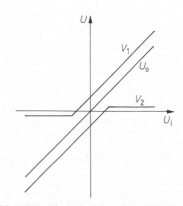

Fig. 17.21 Characteristics of output voltage
and auxiliary potentials V_1 and V_2

17.7 Rating a power output stage

To illustrate the design process for a power output stage in more detail, we use the circuit of Fig. 17.22 and determine the rating of its components for an output power of 50 W. The circuit is based on the power amplifier of Fig. 17.12.

The amplifier is required to supply a load, $R_L = 5\,\Omega$, with a power of 50 W at sinusoidal output. The amplitude of the output voltage is then $\hat{U}_o = 22.4$ V, and that of the current $\hat{I}_o = 4.48$ A. To determine the supply voltage, we calculate the minimum voltage across T_1', T_1, T_3 and R_3. For the base-emitter voltages of T_1 and T_1' at I_{max}, we must allow about 2 V in all. A diode forward voltage is dropped across R_3 i.e. 0.7 V. The collector-emitter voltage of T_3 should not fall below 0.9 V at full input drive. The output stage is intended for operation from an unregulated supply, the voltage of which may fall by about 3 V at full load. We therefore obtain the no-load supply voltage

$$V_b = 22.4 \text{ V} + 2 \text{ V} + 0.7 \text{ V} + 0.9 \text{ V} + 3 \text{ V} = 29 \text{ V} \ .$$

For reasons of symmetry, the negative supply voltage must have the same value. The maximum ratings of transistors T_1' and T_2' can now be determined. The maximum collector current is 4.48 A. To be on the safe side, we choose $I_{C\,max} = 10$ A. The maximum collector-emitter voltage occurs at full output swing and is $V_b + \hat{U}_o = 51.4$ V. We choose the reverse collector-emitter voltage as $U_{CER} = 60$ V. Using the relation

$$P_T = 0.1 \frac{V_b^2}{R_L}$$

from Section 17.2.1, we obtain $P_{T1'} = P_{T2'} = 17$ W. It can be shown that the

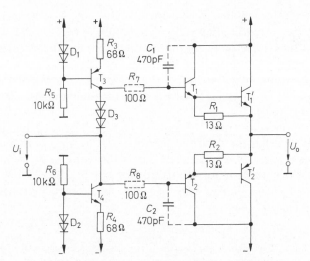

Fig. 17.22 Power output stage for 50 W sinusoidal output

relation between the power dissipation and the thermal resistance is

$$P_{\vartheta_j} = \frac{\vartheta_j - \vartheta_A}{R_{\theta A} + R_{\theta C}} .$$

The maximum junction temperature ϑ_j is normally 175°C for silicon transistors. The ambient temperature ϑ_A within the housing of the amplifier should not exceed 55°C. The thermal resistance between heat sink and air is assumed to be $R_{\theta A} = 4$ K/W. Hence, the value of the thermal resistance between junction and the transistor case must not be larger than

$$17 \text{ W} = \frac{175°\text{C} - 55°\text{C}}{\dfrac{4 \text{ K}}{\text{W}} + R_{\theta C}} .$$

i.e.

$$R_{\theta C} = \frac{3.1 \text{ K}}{\text{W}} .$$

Instead of the thermal resistance $R_{\theta C}$, the maximum power dissipation P_{25} at 25°C case temperature is often given in the specifications. It can be calculated from

$$P_{25} = \frac{\vartheta_j - 25°\text{C}}{R_{\theta C}} = \frac{150 \text{ K}}{\dfrac{3.1 \text{ K}}{\text{W}}} = 48 \text{ W} .$$

The transistors selected in this way are assumed to have a current transfer ratio of 30 at maximum output current. We can therefore determine the data of the driver transistors T_1 and T_2. Their maximum collector current is

$$\frac{4.48 \text{ A}}{30} = 149 \text{ mA} ,$$

although this value applies to low frequencies only. For frequencies above $f_c \approx 20$ kHz, the current transfer ratio of audio power transistors falls markedly. When the current rises steeply, the driver transistor must therefore momentarily supply the largest proportion of the output current. To obtain the largest possible bandwidth we choose $I_{C \max} = 1$ A. Transistors within this range of collector currents, having gain-bandwidth products in the region of 50 MHz, are still reasonably priced.

We have shown in Section 17.3 that it is useful to allow the quiescent current to flow only through the driver transistors, and to have a voltage of about 400 mV across resistors R_1 and R_2. This is the purpose of the three silicon diodes D_3 which have a total forward voltage of about 2.1 V. We select a quiescent current of approx. 30 mA to keep the crossover distortion reasonably small. Thus

$$R_1 = R_2 = \frac{400 \text{ mV}}{30 \text{ mA}} = 13 \, \Omega .$$

The power dissipation of the driver transistors is, at zero input voltage, 30 mA · 29 V ≈ 0.9 W, and at maximum input is still 0.75 W. A small power transistor in a TO-5 case with cooling fins is obviously sufficient. A value of 100 is usual for the current transfer ratio of such a transistor. The maximum base current is then

$$I_{B\,max} = \frac{1}{100}\left(\frac{4.48\ A}{30} + \frac{0.8\ V}{13\ \Omega}\right) \approx 2\ mA\ .$$

The current through the constant current sources T_3 and T_4 must be large compared to this value, and we select approx. 10 mA.

Emitter followers are prone to unwanted oscillations in the region of the transit frequency of the output transistors [17.1]. These oscillations can be damped by additionally loading the output by a series RC element (approx. 1 Ω; 0.22 μF). However, this also reduces the efficiency at higher frequencies. Another way of damping which may also be used in addition to that above, is to provide series resistors in the base lead of the driver transistors in conjunction with an increased collector-base capacitance. If $R_7 = R_8 = 100\ \Omega$, as shown in Fig. 17.22, the voltage across these resistors remains below 0.2 V. The achievable output voltage swing is therefore not significantly reduced.

17.8 Driver circuits with voltage gain

The power amplifiers described have a certain amount of crossover distortion in the region of zero output voltage, but this can be largely eliminated by feedback. The output stage is connected to a pre-amplifier stage, and negative feedback is applied across both stages. Figure 17.23 shows a simple possibility. The output stage drive is supplied via current source T_3 which, in conjunction with T_7, forms a current mirror for I_{C6}. Differential amplifier T_5, T_6 provides the required voltage gain. Its total collector resistance is relatively high, being produced by the paralleled current-source internal resistances T_3, T_4 and the input resistances of emitter followers T_1, T_2.

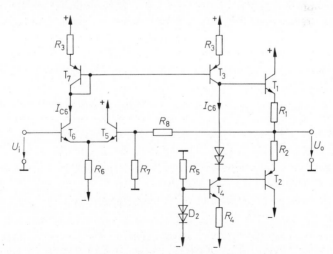

Fig. 17.23 Simple driver circuit with voltage gain

The whole arrangement has feedback via resistors R_7 and R_8, and therefore has a voltage gain $A = 1 + R_8/R_7$. In order to produce sufficient loop gain, A must not be selected too large, practicable values being between 5 and 30.

If we only wish to amplify AC voltages, the zero stability of the circuit can be improved by connecting a coupling capacitor in series with R_7, thereby reducing the DC voltage gain to unity.

Most power amplifier ICs, such as the TDA 2002 from SGS, operate on this principle.

Wideband drive circuit

A larger drive circuit bandwidth can be obtained by driving the two current sources T_3, T_4 in opposite directions and operating them in common-base mode. This produces the circuit in Fig. 17.24, which has similarities with the wideband op amp in Fig. 16.16. However, as a power amplifier requires no differential input, half of the push-pull differential stage has been omitted and replaced by the push-pull stage of the op amp. The latter stabilizes the quiescent potential in accordance with the principle described in Fig. 16.22. The overall circuit behaves like an inverting op amp with a feedback path via R_{15} and R_{16}. Its gain is therefore $A = - R_{16}/R_{15}$.

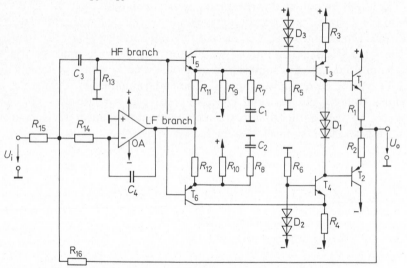

Fig. 17.24 Broadband power amplifier (HF = high freq., LF = low freq.)

To begin the dimensioning of the circuit, the collector currents of the transistors T_3 to T_6 are defined. We choose 10 mA. A current of 20 mA must then flow through resistors R_3 and R_4. A voltage of 1.4 V is dropped across R_3 and R_4. Hence

$$R_3 = R_4 = \frac{1.4 \text{ V}}{20 \text{ mA}} = 70 \, \Omega \ .$$

The output quiescent potential of the operational amplifier is determined by the offset voltage of the power output stage and is close to zero. Hence, with no input drive, the current through resistors R_{11} and R_{12} is virtually zero. The collector currents of T_5 and T_6 must therefore flow through resistors R_9 and R_{10}. With supply potentials of ± 15 V, it follows that

$$R_9 = R_{10} \approx \frac{15\ \text{V}}{10\ \text{mA}} = 1.5\ \text{k}\Omega\ .$$

To attain full swing of the current sources T_3 and T_4, the collector currents of T_5 and T_6 must be controlled between zero and 20 mA. These values should be reached for full output swing of the operational amplifier. Thus, for resistors R_{11} and R_{12},

$$R_{11} = R_{12} \approx \frac{10\ \text{V}}{10\ \text{mA}} = 1\ \text{k}\Omega\ .$$

The op amp OA is configured as an integrator. Its gain is defined by the external circuitry and is selected such that it is markedly below the open-loop gain of the operational amplifier. If we select $R_{14} = 10\ \text{k}\Omega$ and $C_4 = 160\ \text{pF}$, for instance, the gain is unity at a frequency of 100 kHz. The lower cutoff frequency of the highpass filter C_3, R_{13} in the high-frequency path must have a lower value, e.g. 1 kHz.

The total gain of the circuit can be set by resistors R_{15} and R_{16} to values between 1 and 10. A higher gain is inadvisable, as the loop gain in the high-frequency path then becomes too low. The open-loop gain of the high-frequency path can be varied by means of resistors R_7 and R_8. They are adjusted so as to obtain the desired transient response for the whole circuit. For the operational amplifier, the internal standard frequency compensation is sufficient. To avoid oscillations in the VHF range, it may be necessary to insert resistors in the base leads of some of the transistors [17.1].

17.9 Boosting the output current of integrated operational amplifiers

The output current of integrated operational amplifiers is normally limited, the maximum being about 20 mA. There are many applications for which about ten times this current is required but where the number of additional components must be kept to a minimum. In such cases the power output stages described above may be employed. For low signal frequencies, the number of components can be reduced by the use of push-pull class-B emitter followers. However, owing to the finite slew rate of the operational amplifier, noticeable crossover distortion occurs even with feedback. It can be reduced considerably by inserting a resistance R_1 as in Fig. 17.25, which by-passes the emitter followers in the region of zero voltage. In this case, the slew rate required of the amplifier is reduced from infinity to a value which is $1 + R_1/R_L$ times that of the rate of change of the output voltage.

The arrangement in Fig. 17.26 has the same characteristics as the previous circuit. Here, however, the output transistors are controlled by the supply

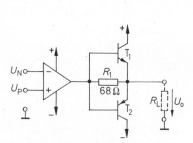

Fig. 17.25 Current booster with
complementary emitter followers

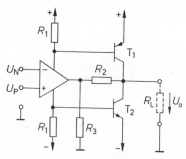

Fig. 17.26 Current booster with
complementary common-emitter circuits

terminals of the operational amplifier. This, together with the output transistors
of the operational amplifier, results in two complementary Darlington connections if we make $R_2 = 0$.

At small output currents, the two output transistors T_1 and T_2 are turned off.
The operational amplifier then supplies the whole output current. At larger
output currents, transistors T_1 and T_2 become alternately conducting and
supply the largest proportion of the output current. The contribution of the
operational amplifier remains limited to approximately $0.7 \text{ V}/R_1$.

The circuit has an advantage over the previous one in that the quiescent
current of the operational amplifier causes biasing of the base-emitter junctions
of the power output transistors. The values of the resistors R_1 are such that the
bias is about 400 mV. This considerably reduces the range of crossover without
the need for a quiescent current in the output transistors, the stabilization of
which would require additional measures.

Using voltage divider R_2, R_3 the output stage can provide an additional
voltage gain $1 + R_2/R_3$. This enables the output voltage swing of the amplifier
to be increased to a value only falling short of the supply voltage by the
saturation voltage of T_1 or T_2. The likelihood of oscillation within the complementary Darlington circuits is also reduced.

18   Power supplies

Every electronic circuit requires a power supply providing one or more DC voltages. For larger power requirements, batteries are not economical. The DC voltage is therefore obtained from the AC line supply by transformation and subsequent rectification. The DC voltage thus obtained usually has considerable ripple, and changes in response to variations in the line voltage and the load. Therefore, a voltage regulator is often connected to the rectifier to keep the DC output voltage constant and counteract these variations. The following two sections describe ways of providing the unregulated DC voltage; regulator circuits will be dealt with later.

18.1   Properties of power transformers

The internal resistance R_i of the power transformer plays an important part in the design of rectifier circuits. It can be calculated from the rating of the secondary winding $U_{\sec n}$, $I_{\sec n}$, and from the loss factor f_1 which is defined as the ratio of the no-load voltage $U_{\sec 0}$ to the nominal voltage $U_{\sec n}$

$$f_1 = \frac{U_{\sec 0}}{U_{\sec n}} \; . \tag{18.1}$$

Hence, the relation for the internal ohmic resistance

$$R_i = \frac{U_{\sec 0} - U_{\sec n}}{I_{\sec n}} = \frac{U_{\sec n}(f_1 - 1)}{I_{\sec n}} \; . \tag{18.2}$$

We define a rated load $R_n = U_{\sec n}/I_{\sec n}$ and obtain from Eq. (18.2)

$$R_i = R_n(f_1 - 1) \; . \tag{18.3}$$

The data of M-core transformers normally used are listed in the table of Fig. 18.1; the corresponding data for toroidal transformers are given in Fig. 18.2.

As toroidal transformers are more difficult to wind, they are significantly more expensive, particularly for low powers. However, this is offset by the advantage of minimal magnetic flux leakage, higher magnetizing reactance and therefore lower magnetizing current and small no-load losses. For further details, see e.g. [18.1, 18.2].

The values in Figs. 18.1 and 18.2 are based on a line voltage $U_{p\,r.m.s.} = 220$ V at 50 Hz and a maximum flux density of $\hat{B} = 1.2$ T. Should the line voltage slightly deviate from this value, w_1 must be recalculated proportionally with $U_{p\,r.m.s.}$ and d_1 with $1/\sqrt{U_{p\,r.m.s.}}$. If the line frequency is 60 Hz, $\hat{B}$ is reduced to 1 T and the parameters w_1, d_1 in Figs. 18.1 and 18.2 include a safety margin.

Core type (lateral length)	Rated power	Loss factor	Number of primary turns	Primary wire gauge	Normalized number of secondary turns	Normalized secondary wire gauge
	P_n	f_1	w_1	d_1	w_2/U_2	$d_2/\sqrt{I_2}$
[mm]	[W]			[mm]	[1/V]	$[\text{mm}/\sqrt{\text{A}}]$
M 42	4	1.31	4716	0.09	28.00	0.61
M 55	15	1.20	2671	0.18	14.62	0.62
M 65	33	1.14	1677	0.26	8.68	0.64
M 74	55	1.11	1235	0.34	6.24	0.65
M 85a	80	1.09	978	0.42	4.83	0.66
M 85b	105	1.06	655	0.48	3.17	0.67
M 102a	135	1.07	763	0.56	3.72	0.69
M 102b	195	1.05	513	0.69	2.45	0.71

Fig. 18.1 Typical data of M-core supply transformers for a primary voltage of $U_{\text{pr.m.s.}} = 220\,\text{V}$ at 50 Hz

External diameter approx.	Rated power	Loss factor	Number of primary turns	Primary wire gauge	Normalized number of secondary turns	Normalized secondary wire gauge
D	P_n	f_1	w_1	d_1	w_2/U_2	$d_2/\sqrt{I_2}$
[mm]	[W]			[mm]	[1/V]	$[\text{mm}/\sqrt{\text{A}}]$
60	10	1.18	3500	0.15	19.83	0.49
61	20	1.18	2720	0.18	14.83	0.54
70	30	1.16	2300	0.22	12.33	0.55
80	50	1.15	2140	0.30	11.25	0.56
94	75	1.12	1765	0.36	9.08	0.58
95	100	1.11	1410	0.40	7.08	0.60
100	150	1.09	1100	0.56	5.42	0.61
115	200	1.08	820	0.60	4.00	0.62
120	300	1.07	715	0.71	3.42	0.63

Fig. 18.2 Typical data of toroidal core supply transformers for a primary voltage of $U_{\text{pr.m.s.}} = 220\,\text{V}$ at 50 Hz

18.2   Power rectifiers

18.2.1   Single-phase half-wave rectifier

The easiest way to rectify an AC voltage is to charge a capacitor via a diode, as in Fig. 18.3. If the output is not loaded, the capacitor C is charged during the positive half cycle to the peak value $U_{o0} = \sqrt{2}\,U_{\text{sec 0 r.m.s.}} - U_D$, where U_D is the forward voltage of the diode. The peak reverse voltage of the diode occurs when

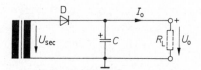

Fig. 18.3 Single-phase half-wave rectifier

No-load output voltage: $\qquad U_{o0} = \sqrt{2}\,U_{\text{sec}\,0\,\text{r.m.s.}} - U_D$

On-load output voltage (C infinitely large): $\qquad U_{o\infty} = U_{o0}\left(1 - \sqrt{\dfrac{R_i}{R_L}}\right)$

Peak reverse voltage: $\qquad U_{pr} = 2\sqrt{2}\,U_{\text{sec}\,0\,\text{r.m.s.}}$

Mean diode current: $\qquad \hat{I}_D = I_o$

Repetitive peak current: $\qquad I_{Dp} = \dfrac{U_{o0}}{\sqrt{R_i R_L}}$

Ripple voltage (peak-to-peak): $\qquad U_{rpp} = \dfrac{I_o}{Cf_s}\left(1 - \sqrt[4]{\dfrac{R_i}{R_L}}\right)$

Lowest value of output voltage: $\qquad U_{o\,\text{min}} \approx U_{o\infty} - \tfrac{2}{3}U_{rpp}$

the transformer voltage is at its negative maximum, and therefore has the value of $2\sqrt{2}\,U_{\text{sec}\,0\,\text{r.m.s.}}$.

When a load resistance R_L is connected to the DC output, it discharges the capacitor C for as long as the diode is reverse-biased. Only when the no-load voltage of the transformer exceeds that of the output by the amount U_D, is the capacitor recharged. The voltage reached by recharging depends on the internal resistance R_i of the transformer. Figure 18.4 shows the shape of the output voltage at steady state. Owing to the unfavorable ratio of recharge/discharge

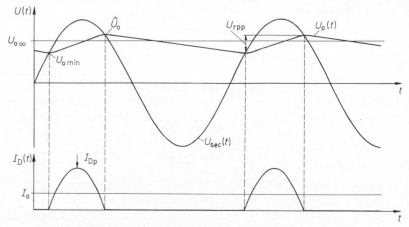

Fig. 18.4 Voltage and current waveforms for a single-phase half-wave rectifier

time, the output voltage is considerably reduced even for a small load, and for this reason the circuit is unsuitable for use in power supplies.

18.2.2   Bridge rectifier

The ratio of recharge/discharge time can be greatly improved by charging the capacitor C during the positive *and* the negative half-cycle. This is achieved by the bridge rectifier in Fig. 18.5.

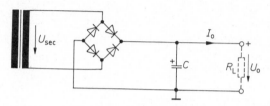

Fig. 18.5 Bridge rectifier

No-load output voltage:	$U_{o0} = \sqrt{2}U_{\text{sec 0 r.m.s.}} - 2U_D$
On-load output voltage (C infinitely large):	$U_{o\infty} = U_{o0}\left(1 - \sqrt{\dfrac{R_i}{2R_L}}\right)$
Peak reverse voltage:	$U_{pr} = 2\sqrt{2}U_{\text{sec 0 r.m.s.}}$
Mean diode current:	$\bar{I}_D = \frac{1}{2}I_o$
Repetitive peak current:	$I_{Dp} = \dfrac{U_{o0}}{\sqrt{2R_iR_L}}$
Ripple voltage (peak-to-peak):	$U_{rpp} = \dfrac{I_o}{2Cf_s}\left(1 - \sqrt[4]{\dfrac{R_i}{2R_L}}\right)$
Lowest value of output voltage:	$U_{o\min} \approx U_{o\infty} - \frac{2}{3}U_{rpp}$
Rated power of transformer:	$P_n = (1.2 \ldots 2)U_{o\infty} \cdot I_o$

During the recharge period, the diodes connect whichever terminal of the transformer is negative to ground, and the positive terminal to the output. The repetitive peak reverse voltage is identical to the no-load output voltage:

$$U_{o0} = \sqrt{2}U_{\text{sec 0 r.m.s.}} - 2U_D = \sqrt{2}U_n f_1 - 2U_D \;, \tag{18.4}$$

and is only half that of the half-wave rectifier.

To calculate the voltage reduction at load, we initially assume an infinitely large reservoir capacitor C. The output voltage is then a pure DC voltage which we define as $U_{o\infty}$. The more the output voltage decreases due to the load, the longer the recharge time. Steady state is reached when the incoming charge of the capacitor equals the outgoing charge, i.e. that supplied to the load. Hence,

$$U_{o\infty} = U_{o0}\left(1 - \sqrt{\frac{R_i}{2R_L}}\right), \tag{18.5}$$

where $R_L = U_{o\infty}/I_o$ is the load resistance. The deduction of this equation is based on calculations involving the approximation of sine waves by parabolas and is omitted here because of its complexity. As comparison with the half-wave circuit in Fig. 18.3 shows, in this bridge rectifier only half the internal resistance of the transformer is responsible for the voltage drop at load.

To dimension the rectifier correctly, the currents must be known. As no DC current flows through the capacitor, the mean forward current of each bridge arm is half the output current. As the forward voltage is only slightly dependent on the current, the power dissipation of a single diode is given by

$$P_D = \tfrac{1}{2}U_D I_o .$$

During every recharge period a peak current I_{Dp} flows, the value of which may be many times that of the output current:

$$I_{Dp} = \frac{\hat{U}_{sec0} - 2U_D - U_{o\infty}}{R_i} = \frac{U_{o0} - U_{o\infty}}{R_i} .$$

With Eq. (18.5), it follows that

$$I_{Dp} = \frac{U_{o0}}{\sqrt{2R_i R_L}} .$$

It can be seen that the internal resistance R_i of the AC voltage source significantly influences the peak current. If R_i is very small, it may be necessary to series-connect a resistance or inductance so as not to exceed the maximum peak current of the rectifier. This must be taken into account particularly for direct rectification of the line voltage i.e. without transformer. Full-wave rectification is also better in this respect, as the peak current is reduced by a factor of $\sqrt{2}$.

The r.m.s. value of the pulsating charging current is larger than its mean value. Therefore the DC power must always be kept smaller than the rated power of the transformer for resistive load, so as not to exceed the thermal transformer rating. The DC power is determined by the power supplied to the load ($I_o U_{o\infty}$) and the losses in the rectifier (approx. $2U_D I_o$). The rated power of the transformer must therefore be selected as

$$P_n = \alpha I_o(U_{o\infty} + 2U_D) \approx \alpha I_o U_{o\infty} \tag{18.6}$$

where α is the form factor allowing for the increased r.m.s. value of the current. For full-wave rectification, $\alpha \approx 1.2$. However, it is advisable not to operate at the thermal limit as in Eq. (18.6) but to overrate the transformer by using a higher value for α, thereby producing a greater efficiency. The disadvantage of an increased space requirement can be minimized by employing toroidal transformers. Even if they are considerably overrated, the no-load losses remain low.

For a finite capacitance C, a superposed ripple voltage appears at the output. It can be calculated from the charge supplied by the capacitor during the discharge time t_d,

$$U_{rpp} = \frac{I_o t_d}{C} .$$

With Eq. (18.5),

$$t_d \approx \tfrac{1}{2}\left(1 - \sqrt[4]{\frac{R_i}{2R_L}}\right)T_s ,$$

where $T_s = 1/f_s$ is the reciprocal of the AC supply frequency. Hence

$$U_{rpp} = \frac{I_o}{2Cf_s}\left(1 - \sqrt[4]{\frac{R_i}{2R_L}}\right) . \tag{18.7}$$

The lowest instantaneous value of the output voltage is of special interest. It is approximately

$$U_{o\,min} \approx U_{o\,\infty} - \tfrac{2}{3}U_{rpp} . \tag{18.8}$$

The dimensioning of a power rectifier is best illustrated by an example. A DC supply is required having a minimum output voltage of $U_{o\,min} = 30$ V for an output current of $I_o = 1$ A, and a ripple of $U_{rpp} = 3$ V.

To begin with, we obtain from Eq. (18.8)

$$U_{o\,\infty} = U_{o\,min} + \tfrac{2}{3}U_{rpp} = 32 \text{ V} ,$$

and from Eq. (18.6) and $\alpha = 1.5$ the rated power of the transformer

$$P_n = \alpha I_o(U_{o\,\infty} + 2U_D) = 1.5\,\text{A}(32\,\text{V} + 2\,\text{V}) = 51\,\text{W} .$$

It can be seen from the table in Fig. 18.2 that a toroidal type with $D = 80$ mm having a loss factor of $f_i = 1.15$ must be used. We now need to know the internal resistance of the transformer; however, it is dependent on the rated voltage, the value of which is not yet known. For its determination, the system of non-linear equations (18.3) to (18.5) must be solved. This is best done by iteration: We set the initial value of $U_{sec\,n\,r.m.s.}$ to $U_{sec\,n\,r.m.s.} \approx U_{o\,min} = 30$ V. With Eq. (18.3), it follows that

$$R_i = R_n(f_i - 1) = \frac{U^2_{sec\,n\,r.m.s.}}{P_n}(f_i - 1) = \frac{(30\text{ V})^2}{51\text{ W}}\cdot(1.15 - 1) = 2.65\,\Omega .$$

Hence, with Eqs. (18.4) and (18.5)

$$U_{o\,\infty} = (\sqrt{2}U_{sec\,n\,r.m.s.}f_i - 2U_D)\left(1 - \sqrt{\frac{R_i}{2R_L}}\right)$$

$$= (\sqrt{2}\cdot 30\text{ V}\cdot 1.15 - 2\text{ V})\left(1 - \sqrt{\frac{2.65\,\Omega}{2\cdot 32\text{ V}/1\text{ A}}}\right) \approx 37.3\text{ V} .$$

The voltage is about 5 V higher than that initially required. For the first iteration, we decrease the rated transformer voltage by this amount and obtain correspondingly

$$R_i = 1.84\ \Omega \quad \text{and} \quad U_{o\,\infty} = 32.1\ \text{V} \ ,$$

which is already the desired value for the output voltage. The design parameters for the transformer are therefore

$$U_{\text{sec n r.m.s.}} \approx 25\ \text{V} \ ; \qquad I_{\text{sec n r.m.s.}} = \frac{P_n}{U_n} \approx 2\ \text{A} \ .$$

Figure 18.2 gives the winding data for a primary voltage of 220 V/50 Hz:

$$w_1 = 2140 \ , \qquad\qquad d_1 = 0.30\ \text{mm} \ ,$$

$$w_2 = 11.25 \frac{1}{\text{V}} \cdot 25\ \text{V} = 281 \ , \qquad d_2 = 0.56 \frac{\text{mm}}{\sqrt{\text{A}}} \sqrt{2\text{A}} = 0.79\ \text{mm} \ .$$

The capacitance of the reservoir capacitor is given by Eq. (18.7) as

$$C = \frac{I_o}{2U_{\text{rpp}}f_s}\left(1 - \sqrt[4]{\frac{R_i}{2R_L}}\right) = \frac{1\ \text{A}}{2\cdot 3\ \text{V}\cdot 50\ \text{Hz}}\left(1 - \sqrt[4]{\frac{1.84\ \Omega}{2\cdot 32\ \Omega}}\right) \approx 2000\ \mu\text{F} \ .$$

The no-load output voltage is 39 V. The capacitor must be rated for at least this voltage.

The calculation for transformers having several secondary windings is the same as that above. For P_n, the rated power of the corresponding secondary winding must be inserted. The total power is the sum of the individual powers of the secondary windings. This determines the choice of the core and therefore the loss factor f_i.

18.2.3   Center-tap circuit

Full-wave rectification can also be achieved by rectifying two antiphase AC voltages on a half-wave basis. This principle is illustrated by the center-tap circuit in Fig. 18.6. As we can see from the data given, the advantages of the bridge circuit are retained.

An additional advantage is that the current need only flow through one diode at a time and not through two as in the case of the bridge circuit. As

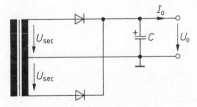

Fig. 18.6 Center-tap circuit

a result, the voltage drop caused by the forward voltages of the diodes is halved. On the other hand, the internal resistance of the transformer is doubled, as each part-winding must be rated for half the output power, thereby further increasing the voltage drop. The ratio of the output voltage to the forward voltage of the diode will dictate which effect predominates. The center-tap circuit is better for low output voltages, the bridge rectifier circuit for high output voltages.

Double center-tap circuit

The negative half-cycles, which remain unutilized in the circuit in Fig. 18.6, can be rectified in a second center-tap circuit using diodes of opposite polarity, thereby simultaneously producing a negative DC voltage. This method of generating voltages that are balanced to ground is shown in Fig. 18.7. An IC bridge rectifier can be used to provide the four diodes required. The nominal transformer rating must again be 1.2 to 2 times the DC output.

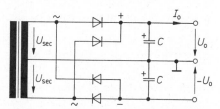

Fig. 18.7 Center-tap circuit for balanced-to-ground output voltages

No-load output voltage:

$$U_{o0} = \sqrt{2}U_{\text{sec 0 r.m.s.}} - U_{\text{D}}$$

On-load output voltage: (C infinitely large)

$$U_{o\infty} = U_{o0}\left(1 - \sqrt{\frac{R_i}{2R_L}}\right)$$

Peak reverse voltage:

$$U_{\text{pr}} = 2\sqrt{2}U_{\text{sec 0 r.m.s.}}$$

Mean forward current:

$$I_{\text{D}} = \tfrac{1}{2}I_o$$

Repetitive peak current:

$$I_{\text{D}_p} = \frac{U_{o0}}{\sqrt{2R_i R_L}}$$

Ripple voltage:

$$U_{\text{rpp}} = \frac{I_o}{2Cf_s}\left(1 - \sqrt[4]{\frac{R_i}{2R_L}}\right)$$

Minimum output voltage:

$$U_{o\text{min}} \approx U_{o\infty} - \tfrac{2}{3}U_{\text{rpp}}$$

18.3   Linear voltage regulators

Electronic circuits generally require a DC voltage accurate to within 5 to 10% of a specified value. This tolerance must be maintained over the entire range of line voltage, load current and temperature variations. The ripple voltage must not exceed the millivolt range. For these reasons, the output voltage of the rectifier circuits described is not directly usable as a supply voltage for electronic circuits, but requires stabilization and smoothing by a following voltage regulator.

The principal characteristics of a voltage regulator are:

1) The output voltage and its tolerance.
2) The maximum output current and the short-circuit current.
3) The minimum voltage drop required by the voltage regulator to maintain the output voltage. This is termed "dropout voltage" in data sheets.
4) Suppression of input voltage variations, i.e. line regulation.
5) Counteraction to load current variations, i.e. load rejection.

18.3.1 Basic circuit

Output voltage variations due to supply voltage and load current fluctuations can be reduced by inserting a controlled series resistance, this method being known as series loss regulation.

The simplest series regulator is an emitter follower with its base connected to a reference voltage source. The reference voltage can, for instance, be obtained from the unstabilized input voltage U_i using a Zener diode as in Fig. 18.8. Other possibilities will be discussed in Section 18.4. Due to current feedback, the output voltage is

$$U_o = U_{ref} - U_{BE} \; .$$

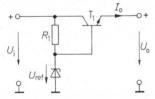

Fig. 18.8 Voltage stabilization using emitter follower

Output voltage: $U_o = U_{ref} - U_{BE}$

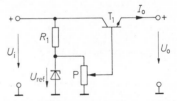

Fig. 18.9 Additional circuitry for output voltage adjustment

$0 \leq U_o \leq U_{ref} - U_{BE}$

The extent to which the voltage varies with load is related to the output resistance

$$r_0 = -\frac{\partial U_o}{\partial I_o} = \frac{1}{g} = \frac{U_T}{I_o} \; .$$

With $U_T \approx 26\,\text{mV}$, we obtain approximately $0.3\,\Omega$ for $I_o = 100\,\text{mA}$.

Input voltage variations are compensated by the low differential resistance r_Z of the Zener diode. The output voltage variation is given by

$$\Delta U_o = \Delta U_{ref} = \frac{r_Z}{R_1 + r_Z} \Delta U_i \approx \frac{r_Z}{R_1} \Delta U_i \ .$$

This represents 1 to 10% of the input voltage variation depending on the component values selected.

If an adjustable output voltage is required, a portion of the reference voltage can be tapped off at a potentiometer, as shown in Fig. 18.9. The potentiometer resistance selected must be small compared to r_{BE}, so that the circuit output resistance is not appreciably increased.

18.3.2   Voltage regulators with fixed output voltage

The simple circuits in Figs. 18.8/9 are largely inadequate or fail to meet the requirements that voltage regulators must satisfy. Consequently, IC voltage regulators contain a gain-controlled amplifier and a reference voltage source, as well as several additional modules to protect the power transistor [18.4]. These are shown in the block diagram in Fig. 18.10.

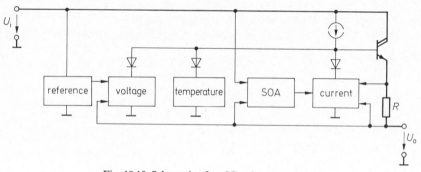

Fig. 18.10 Schematic of an IC voltage regulator

The current-limiting circuit monitors the voltage drop across current-sensing resistor R. The safe operating area (SOA) of the power transistor is monitored in an additional block. If the voltage drop across the power transistor increases, the current limit is reduced accordingly.

A thermal protection device monitors the crystal temperature and reduces the output voltage if hazardous overheating is likely to occur. The diodes ensure that the output voltage is determined by the lowest of the four correcting variables. The amplifier holds the output voltage at the nominal value only as long as no limit value is exceeded.

The practical implementation of a 7800-series IC voltage regulator is shown in Fig. 18.11. The requirements placed on the amplifier are not particularly stringent, as an emitter follower alone already constitutes an effective voltage regulator. Consequently, it is sufficient to have a simple differential amplifier T_3, T_4 operating in conjunction with Darlington circuit T_1 as a power op amp. It acts as a non-inverting amplifier via voltage divider R_1, R_2 in the feedback path and produces at the output an amplified reference voltage of

$$U_o = (1 + R_2/R_1)U_{ref} .$$

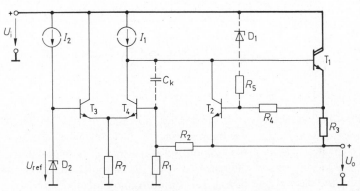

Fig. 18.11 7800-series IC voltage regulator

$$U_o = \left(1 + \frac{R_2}{R_1}\right)U_{ref} \qquad I_{o\,max} = \frac{0.6\ \text{V}}{R_3}$$

Transistor T_2 has a current-limiting function. If the voltage drop across R_3 reaches 0.6 V, T_2 is turned on, thereby reducing the output voltage. Due to the feedback path produced, the output voltage is adjusted so that the voltage drop across R_3 is stabilized to the value 0.6 V. This is equivalent to a constant output current

$$I_{o\,max} = 0.6\ \text{V}/R_3 .$$

Under these conditions the output voltage is determined by load resistor R_L in accordance with $U_o = I_{o\,max}R_L$.

When the maximum current is reached, the power dissipation in output transistor T_1 is given by

$$P = I_{o\,max}(U_i - U_o) .$$

In the event of a short circuit at the output, it is much higher than during normal operation, since the output voltage then falls below the nominal value to zero. In order to prevent this increased power dissipation, the current limit can be reduced as the output voltage decreases. This produces the foldback characteristic shown in Fig. 18.12.

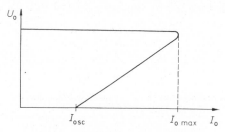

Fig. 18.12 Foldback current limiting

A marked increase in power dissipation may also occur if the input voltage U_i is increased, as in this case the difference $U_i - U_o$ likewise increases. Consequently, the best way of protecting output transistor T_1 is to match the current limit $I_{o\,max}$ to the voltage difference $U_i - U_o$. Resistor R_5 and Zener diode D_1 shown by the dashed line in Fig. 18.11 are used for this purpose.

If the potential difference $U_i - U_o$ is less than the Zener voltage U_Z of diode D_1, no current flows through resistor R_5. Consequently, the current limit in this case remains $0.6 \text{ V}/R_3$. If the potential difference exceeds the value U_Z, voltage divider R_5, R_4 causes a positive base-emitter bias to be applied to transistor T_2. As a result, the latter will be turned on in response to a correspondingly smaller voltage drop across R_3.

Capacitor C_k provides the frequency compensation required for stability. To provide additional stabilization, it is generally necessary to connect capacitors with approximately 100 nF to ground at the input and output.

18.3.3   Voltage regulators with adjustable output voltage

In addition to the fixed voltage regulators described above, adjustable types are also available (series 78 G). In the latter, voltage divider R_1, R_2 is omitted and the amplifier input is brought out as shown in Fig. 18.13. These regulators therefore have four terminals. By connecting voltage divider R_1, R_2 externally, any output voltage between $U_{ref} \approx 5 \text{ V} \leq U_o < U_i - 3 \text{ V}$ can be selected.

Adjustable voltage regulators with only three terminals can be realized by dispensing with the ground connection and diverting the supply current of the amplifier to the output. In order to make this difference clear, Fig. 18.13 shows a 78 G-series adjustable voltage regulator with four terminals alongside a 317-series adjustable voltage regulator with three terminals (Fig. 18.14). Here the

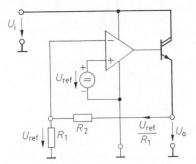

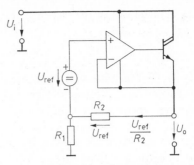

Fig. 18.13 Adjustable voltage regulator with four terminals (78 G-series)

Fig. 18.14 Adjustable voltage regulator with three terminals (317-series)

$$U_o = \left(1 + \frac{R_2}{R_1}\right) U_{ref} \; ; \quad U_{ref} = 5\,\text{V}$$

$$U_o = \left(1 + \frac{R_1}{R_2}\right) U_{ref} \; ; \quad U_{ref} = 1.25\,\text{V}$$

reference voltage source is not connected to ground but to the midpoint of the feedback voltage divider. The output voltage therefore increases until voltage U_{ref} is dropped across R_2. The input voltage difference of the op amp is then zero.

The output of the voltage regulator in Fig. 18.14 must not be in open-circuit, as this would prevent the amplifier supply current loop from being closed. It is therefore advisable to select low values for voltage divider R_1, R_2, typically $R_2 = 240\,\Omega$; a transverse current of 5 mA therefore flows for a reference voltage of $U_{ref} = 1.25\,\text{V}$. Consequently, the current of approximately 100 μA flowing out of the reference voltage source cannot appreciably alter the voltage drop across R_1.

18.3.4   Voltage regulator with reduced dropout voltage

As we can see from Fig. 18.11, the minimum voltage drop between the input and output of the voltage regulator is made up of the voltage drop of 0.6 V across current-sensing resistor R_3, the Darlington circuit's base-emitter voltage of 1.6 V and the minimum voltage drop of about 0.3 V across current source I_1. The minimum voltage drop (dropout voltage) is therefore 2.5 V. This is particularly troublesome for regulating low output voltages: in the case of a 5 V regulator, at least 50% of the output power is dissipated. As an additional voltage drop is required to compensate for line and load changes, an even higher power dissipation results, generally just as large as the output power.

Removal of the heat generated frequently poses problems. Although IC voltage regulators are provided with thermal protection, this means that the maximum output current is reduced accordingly if cooling is inadequate. It is therefore important to keep the minimum voltage drop as small as possible. This can be achieved in the circuit in Fig. 18.11 by operating the current source I_1 from an auxiliary voltage a few volts above the input voltage. This method is used in type LM 396-5.

A simpler method is to use a pnp transistor as the power transistor, as in Fig. 18.15. The minimum voltage drop across the voltage regulator is here equal to the saturation voltage of power transistor T_1. It can be held below 0.5 V if an appropriately high base current is applied. However, in order to provide the required base currents for T_1, a Darlington pair should not be used, as the minimum voltage drop would be increased by an emitter-base voltage. Transistor T_2 is therefore operated in a common-emitter connection. Current feedback via R_3 limits the maximum output current and simultaneously improves the stability of the regulation circuit. However, ICs employing this principle are only available for relatively low output currents, (e.g. LM 2940), as pnp power transistors are difficult to manufacture as monolithic circuits.

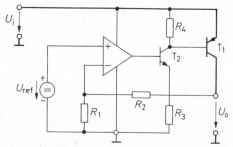

Fig. 18.15 Voltage regulator with low dropout voltage; $U_o = \left(1 + \dfrac{R_2}{R_1}\right) U_{\text{ref}}$

For high currents, it is necessary to use discrete pnp power transistors. The drive circuit can be constructed from commercially available op amps. A particularly simple solution is to use the UC 3834 voltage regulator from Unitrode which has been specially developed for this application. Its internal design and external circuitry are shown in Fig. 18.16. It comprises voltage regulator OA 1, current regulator OA 2, a reference voltage source and supervisory logic (not shown).

The voltage regulating circuit corresponds to that in Fig. 18.15. OA 1 provides an output voltage such that the output voltage of the divider R_1, R_2 is equal to the reference voltage. In this example an output voltage of 5 V is obtained.

For current monitoring purposes, the voltage drop across R_8 is measured. If it is equal to the value determined by voltage source U_2, OA 2 assumes the regulating function and limits the output current to a value of $I_o = U_2/R_8$. If $U_2 = \text{const}$, a square output characteristic is produced. This will be the case, for instance, if the control input (pin 4) for the voltage-controlled voltage source is left open. We then have $U_2 = 150$ mV. However, a foldback current limiting

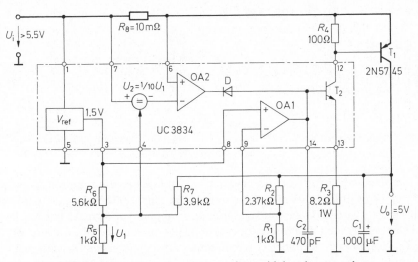

Fig. 18.16 Implementation of a voltage regulator with low dropout voltage

Output voltage: $U_o = 5$ V   *Minimum input voltage:* $U_{i\,min} = 5.5$ V

Maximum output current: $I_{o\,max} = 10$ A   *Minimum voltage drop:* $\Delta U_{min} = 0.5$ V

Short-circuit current: $I_{osc} = 2$ A

characteristic as shown in Fig. 18.12 can be obtained by reducing the control voltage U_1 as the output voltage decreases. Resistors R_5 to R_7 are used for this purpose. For a nominal output voltage of 5 V, we obtain $U_1 = 1$ V. Consequently, the maximum output current is

$$I_{omax} = U_2/R_8 = \tfrac{1}{10} U_1/R_8 = 100\,\text{mV}/10\,\text{m}\Omega = 10\,\text{A} \ .$$

In the event of a short circuit ($U_o = 0$ V), U_1 is reduced to 200 mV; the short-circuit current is therefore $I_{osc} = 2$ A.

Capacitors C_1 and C_2 are used for frequency compensation of the current and voltage regulating circuits. C_1 simultaneously compensates for the increase in the output impedance which, at higher frequencies, is produced by the reduction in loop gain in the voltage regulating circuit.

18.3.5 Voltage regulator for negative voltages

The voltage regulators described above can also be used for stabilizing negative output potentials if a floating input source is available. The relevant circuit is shown in Fig. 18.17. We can see that it will cease to operate if the unstabilized voltage source is grounded at either of the terminals, because the voltage regulator or the output voltage would then be shorted. This problem arises, for instance, if we use the simplified circuit (Fig. 18.7) for simultaneously generating a positive and a negative supply voltage. As the center tap is grounded, the negative supply potential cannot be stabilized as in Fig. 18.17. In

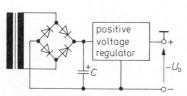

Fig. 18.17 Stabilizing a negative voltage

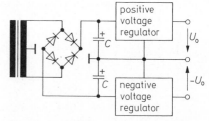

Fig. 18.18 Stabilizing two voltages balanced
to ground

this case voltage regulators for negative output voltages are required, as shown in Fig. 18.18. If IC types complementary to the 7800 or 317 series are used, the power transistor is operated in common-emitter configuration, as this results in an easily fabricated npn transistor. The mode of operation of the circuits shown in Figs. 18.19 and 18.20 thus corresponds to the voltage regulator with reduced dropout voltage in Fig. 18.15. For this reason, the negative voltage regulator ICs have a significantly lower dropout voltage than the corresponding positive voltage regulators.

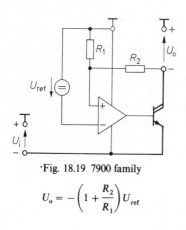

·Fig. 18.19 7900 family

$$U_o = -\left(1 + \frac{R_2}{R_1}\right)U_{ref}$$

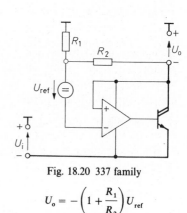

Fig. 18.20 337 family

$$U_o = -\left(1 + \frac{R_1}{R_2}\right)U_{ref}$$

18.3.6   Symmetrical division of a floating voltage

The problem often arises, especially in battery operated equipment, of obtaining two regulated balanced-to-ground voltages from a floating un-stabilized voltage source. To solve this problem, the sum of the two voltages can be stabilized to the desired value using one of the circuits previously described. A second circuit is then required to ensure that the voltage is split in the correct ratio. In principle, we could use a voltage divider with its tap grounded. The division of the voltage is kept constant if the internal resistance of the voltage divider is low, but the loss in the voltage divider is then considerably increased. It is therefore better to replace the divider by two transistors. Only the transistor

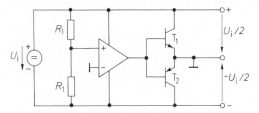

Fig. 18.21 Balancing a floating voltage

connected to the DC bus carrying the smaller load current is turned on at any one time. The relevant circuit is shown in Fig. 18.21.

The voltage divider formed by the two resistors R_1 halves the voltage U_i. It may have a high internal resistance, as its only load is the input bias current of the operational amplifier. If the tap of the voltage divider is at zero potential, the voltage U_i is split into a positive and a negative voltage in the ratio $1:1$, as required. The operational amplifier therefore compares the tap potential with the ground potential and adjusts its output voltage so that their difference becomes zero. Negative feedback is provided as follows: if, for instance, the positive output is loaded more than the negative, the positive output voltage falls, thereby reducing the potential at the P-input of the operational amplifier. Because of the high gain, the amplifier output potential reduces even further, so that T_1 is turned off and T_2 is turned on. This counteracts the assumed voltage dip at the positive output. Under steady state conditions, the current through T_2 is just large enough to ensure that the two output voltages share the load equally. Transistors T_1 and T_2 therefore operate as shunt regulators, only one of which is conducting at any one time.

If the load is only slightly unbalanced, the output stage of the operational amplifier can be used directly, instead of transistors T_1 and T_2. The amplifier output is then simply connected to ground.

18.3.7   Voltage regulator with sensor terminals

The resistance R_w of the connecting wires between the voltage regulator and the load, including possible contact resistances, may cancel out the low output resistance of the regulator. This effect can be eliminated by incorporating the unwanted resistances in the feedback loop, i.e. by measuring the output voltage as near to the load as possible. This is the purpose of the sensor terminals S^+ and S^- in Fig. 18.22. The resistors in the sensor leads produce no errors, as only small currents flow in them.

The four-wire regulation method described can also be implemented using IC voltage regulators if the ground or voltage sensor terminal is externally accessible. Suitable types include the 78G, 79G, L 200 or LT 1087.

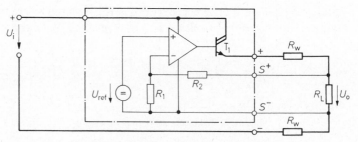

Fig. 18.22 Voltage stabilization at the load

18.3.8   Bench power supplies

The output voltage of the voltage regulators so far described can be adjusted only within a certain range $U_o \geqq U_{ref}$. The current limit serves only to protect the voltage regulator and is therefore fixed at I_{max}.

A bench power supply must have an output voltage and a current limit which are both linearly adjustable between zero and the maximum value. A suitable circuit is shown in Fig. 18.23. Voltage regulation is provided by op amp OA 1 operated as an inverting amplifier. The output voltage

$$U_o = -\frac{R_2}{R_1} U_{ref1}$$

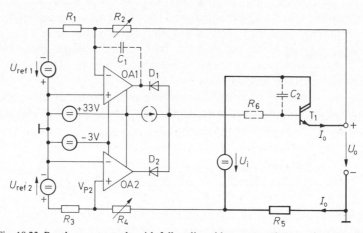

Fig. 18.23 Bench power supply with fully adjustable output voltage and current limit

$$U_o = -\frac{R_2}{R_1} U_{ref1} \; ; \qquad I_{omax} = \frac{R_4}{R_5 R_3} U_{ref2}$$

is proportional to the variable resistance R_2. The voltage can be controlled by varying U_{ref1}. The output current flows from the floating unregulated power voltage source U_i via Darlington transistor T_1 through the load and via current-sensing resistor R_5 back to the source.

The voltage across R_5 is therefore proportional to the output current I_o. It is compared with a second reference voltage $U_{ref\,2}$ by op amp OA 2 operated as an inverting amplifier. As long as

$$\frac{I_o R_5}{R_4} < \frac{U_{ref\,2}}{R_3}$$

V_{P2} remains positive. The output voltage of OA 2 therefore goes to its positive limit, and diode D_2 is reverse biased. In this operating condition, voltage regulation is therefore unaffected. If the output current reaches the limit

$$I_{o\,max} = \frac{R_4}{R_5 R_3} U_{ref\,2}$$

then $V_{P2} = 0$. The output voltage of OA 2 falls, and diode D_2 becomes forward biased. This causes the base potential of the Darlington pair to fall, i.e. current regulation comes into effect. Amplifier OA 1 tries to prevent the fall in output voltage by raising its output potential to the maximum, thereby turning off diode D_1 and current regulation is unimpaired.

In power supplies whose output voltage can be adjusted to zero, exceptionally high power dissipation may occur. In order to be able to achieve $U_{o\,max}$, the unstabilized voltage U_i must be greater than $U_{o\,max}$. Maximum power dissipation in T_1 occurs when the maximum output current $I_{o\,max}$ is allowed to flow at low output voltage levels. It is then approximately $U_i \cdot I_{o\,max}$, i.e. just as high as the maximum available output power. For this reason, it is preferable, when comparatively high powers are involved, to use switched-mode regulators in the output stage. This is because their power dissipation remains small even if the voltage drop is large.

18.3.9   Overview of IC voltage regulators

Apart from a small number of voltage regulators for special applications, these devices can be subdivided into two main families: the 7800 or 317 series (see Fig. 18.24). Both categories also include negative voltage regulators. Whereas types with adjustable output voltage are the exception in the 7800 series, all the 317-series types are adjustable and have only three terminals.

We can see that the dropout voltage for all types is 2 V or more. This is particularly troublesome for 5 V regulators handling large currents, as the power dissipation in the voltage regulator is then in excess of 40% of output power. Consequently, the power supply efficiency is only 25%, which means that three times the power delivered is converted into heat. One solution is to use voltage regulators with reduced dropout voltage. For higher currents, however, these are not available in IC form. Nevertheless, by using suitably rated discrete components as, for example, in Fig. 18.16, even a 5 V power supply can be made to operate at over 50% efficiency.

Another way of minimizing losses is to use switching regulators, as we shall describe in Section 18.5.

Type	Manufacturer	Output voltage U_o		Output current $I_{o\,max}$		Dropout voltage at $I_{o\,max}$	Characteristic features
7800-family							
7800	various	$+ 5$ ... $+ 24$ V		1	A	2 V	3 terminals
7900	various	$- 5$ ... $- 24$ V		1	A	1.1 V	3 terminals
317-family							
317	various	$* + 1.2$ ... $+ 37$ V		1.5	A	2.3 V	3 terminals
317 HV	National	$* + 1.2$ ... $+ 57$ V		1.5	A	2.3 V	3 terminals
350	various	$* + 1.2$ ... $+ 32$ V		3	A	2.3 V	3 terminals
396	National	$* + 1.2$ ... $+ 15$ V		10	A	2.1 V	3 terminals
337	various	$* - 1.2$ ... $- 37$ V		1.5	A	2.3 V	3 terminals
337 HV	National	$* - 1.2$ ... $- 47$ V		1.5	A	2.3 V	3 terminals
333	National	$* - 1.2$ ... $- 32$ V		3	A	2.3 V	3 terminals
Reduced dropout voltage							
L 4920	SGS	$* + 1.2$ ... $+ 20$ V		0.4	A	0.4 V	5 terminals
L 4940	SGS	$+ 5$ ... $+ 12$ V		1.5	A	0.4 V	3 terminals
LM 2940	National	$+ 5$ ... $+ 10$ V		1	A	0.5 V	3 terminals
LM 2941	National	$* + 1.3$ ... $+ 25$ V		1	A	0.5 V	5 terminals
LM 2943	National	$+ 5$ V		3	A		3 terminals
LT 1084	Lin. Techn.	$* + 1.3$ ... $+ 25$ V		5	A	1.3 V	3 terminals
LT 1083	Lin. Techn.	$* + 1.3$ ... $+ 25$ V		7	A	1.3 V	3 terminals
Reduced quiescent current							
LP 2936	National	$+ 5$ V		50	mA	0.2 V	Quies. curr. $15\,\mu A$
LP 2951	National	$* + 1.3$ ... $+ 25$ V		100	mA	0.4 V	Quies. curr. $75\,\mu A$
LT 1020	Lin. Techn.	$*$ 0 ... $+ 30$ V		100	mA	0.5 V	Quies. curr. $40\,\mu A$
MAX 663	Maxim	$* + 1.3$ ... $+ 15$ V		40	mA	0.9 V	Quies. curr. $6\,\mu A$
MAX 664	Maxim	$* - 1.3$ ... $- 15$ V		40	mA	0.5 V	Quies. curr. $6\,\mu A$
Special types							
L 200	SGS	$* + 2.9$ ... $+ 36$ V		$*0$ ... 1.5 A		2 V	$I_{o\,max}$ adjustable
TL 783	Texas Instr.	$* + 1.3$ ... $+ 125$ V		0.5	A	10 V	$U_o =$ high

* The output voltage can be set within the specified range using an external voltage divider.

Fig. 18.24 Typical data for IC voltage regulators

18.4   Reference voltage generation

Every voltage regulator requires a reference voltage with which the output voltage is compared. Output voltage stability is only as good as that of the reference. In this section we shall therefore examine various aspects of reference voltage generation in greater detail.

18.4.1   Reference voltage sources using Zener diodes

The simplest method of generating a reference voltage is to apply the unstabilized input voltage to a Zener diode via a series resistor, as in Fig. 18.25.

The quality of the stabilization is characterized by the suppression of input voltage variations (line regulation) $\Delta U_{\mathrm{i}}/\Delta U_{\mathrm{ref}}$, which is usually given in dB. For the circuit in Fig. 18.25

$$\frac{\Delta U_{\mathrm{i}}}{\Delta U_{\mathrm{ref}}} = 1 + \frac{R}{r_{\mathrm{Z}}} \approx \frac{R}{r_{\mathrm{Z}}} = 10 \ldots 100 \; ,$$

where r_{Z} is the incremental resistance of the Zener diode at the operating point selected. In a first-order approximation, r_{Z} is inversely proportional to the current flowing in the diode. Increasing the series resistance R for a given input voltage will not therefore produce an improvement in stabilization. An important aspect to consider when defining the diode current is the noise in the Zener voltage which increases markedly at low currents. The resistance R is selected such that an adequate diode current will still flow at minimum input voltage and maximum output current.

Considerably improved stabilization can be achieved if the series resistor R is replaced by a current source, as in Fig. 18.26. The simplest method is to use a FET current source, as this has only two terminals (see Fig. 5.10). Stabilization factors of up to 10000 can then be achieved.

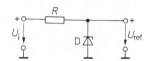

Fig. 18.25 Voltage stabilization using
a Zener diode

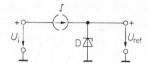

Fig. 18.26 Improving the stabilization using
a constant current source

Another way of operating the Zener diode with a constant current is to connect it to the stabilized output voltage instead of to the unregulated input voltage. As shown in Fig. 18.27, we generate an output voltage

$$U_{\mathrm{ref}} = \left(1 + \frac{R_2}{R_1}\right) U_{\mathrm{Z}}$$

which is higher than Zener voltage U_{Z}. Constant current $I_{\mathrm{Z}} = (U_{\mathrm{ref}} - U_{\mathrm{Z}})/R_3$ then flows through R_3. Line regulation is in this case primarily determined by the supply ripple rejection $D = \Delta U_{\mathrm{b}}/\Delta U_{\mathrm{O}}$ of the operational amplifier, where U_{O} is the op amp offset voltage. Using the relations

$$\Delta U_{\mathrm{O}} = \Delta V_{\mathrm{P}} - \Delta V_{\mathrm{N}} \; , \quad \Delta V_{\mathrm{P}} = \frac{r_{\mathrm{Z}}}{r_{\mathrm{Z}} + R_3} \Delta U_{\mathrm{ref}} \; , \quad \Delta V_{\mathrm{N}} = \frac{R_1}{R_1 + R_2} \Delta U_{\mathrm{ref}}$$

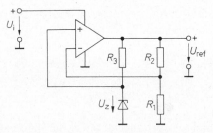

Fig. 18.27 Operating the Zener diode from the regulated voltage

$$U_{ref} = \left(1 + \frac{R_2}{R_1}\right) U_z$$

and $\Delta U_b = \Delta U_i$, we obtain

$$\frac{\Delta U_i}{\Delta U_{ref}} \approx D\left(\frac{r_z}{r_z + R_3} - \frac{R_1}{R_1 + R_2}\right) \approx |D| \frac{R_1}{R_1 + R_2} \approx |D| \ .$$

Values of around 10000 are achieved. If the input voltage variation remains less than 10 V, the output voltage will then vary by less than 1 mV.

Considerably larger variations may occur due to changes in temperature. The temperature coefficient of the Zener voltage is in the order of $\pm 1 \cdot 10^{-3}/K$. For small Zener voltages, it is negative and for larger ones, positive. Its typical characteristic is plotted in Fig. 18.28. We can see that the temperature coefficient is at its smallest for Zener voltages around 6 V. For larger Zener voltages, it can be reduced by connecting forward-biased diodes in series. Although discrete components of this kind are available as *reference diodes*, in most cases IC reference voltage sources containing reference diodes are used, as in Fig. 18.27. Some examples are listed in Fig. 18.31. Temperature coefficients up to $10^{-6}/K \triangleq 1$ ppm are achieved.

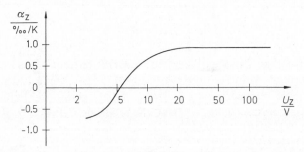

Fig. 18.28 Temperature coefficient $\alpha_z = \dfrac{\Delta U_z}{U_z} \cdot \dfrac{1}{\Delta \vartheta}$ as a function of the Zener voltage

18.4.2 Bandgap reference

In principle, the forward voltage of a diode or the base-emitter voltage of a bipolar transistor can also be used as a voltage reference. However, the temperature coefficient of $-2\,\text{mV/K}$ at 0.6 V is rather high. It can be compensated for by adding a voltage with a temperature coefficient of $+2\,\text{mV/K}$. The characteristic feature of the circuit in Fig. 18.29 is that this voltage is generated by a second transistor. Transistors T_1 and T_2 are driven by different collector currents $I_{C2} > I_{C1}$. From the transfer characteristic, we obtain a voltage drop across R_1 of

$$\Delta U_{BE} = U_{BE2} - U_{BE1} = U_T \ln \frac{I_{C2}}{I_{C1}} \; .$$

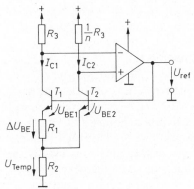

Fig. 18.29 Bandgap reference

$$U_{ref} = U_{BG} \approx 1.205 \text{ V}$$

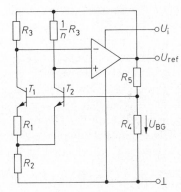

Fig. 18.30 Operating the reference transistor from the regulated voltage

$$U_{ref} = \left(1 + \frac{R_5}{R_4}\right) U_{BG}$$

It is therefore proportional to U_T and, because $U_T = kT/e_0$, it is also proportional to the absolute temperature T. A correspondingly larger voltage is dropped across resistor R_2, as not only current $I_{C1} = \Delta U_{BE}/R_1$ but also current I_{C2} flows through this resistor. The operational amplifier assumes an output voltage such that $I_{C2} = nI_{C1}$. Hence

$$U_{Temp} = R_2(I_{C1} + I_{C2}) = R_2 \frac{\Delta U_{BE}}{R_1}(1 + n) = U_T \frac{R_2}{R_1}(1 + n)\ln n = AU_T \; .$$

We now have the possibility of achieving any gain factor A by selecting suitable values of n and R_2/R_1. Thus, for U_{Temp} we obtain a temperature coefficient of $+2\,\text{mV/K}$ if we select $A \approx 23$, because

$$\frac{dU_{Temp}}{dT} = A \cdot \frac{dU_T}{dT} = A\frac{k}{e_0} = A\frac{U_T}{T} = 23 \cdot \frac{26\,\text{mV}}{300\,\text{K}} = +2\frac{\text{mV}}{\text{K}} \; .$$

According to [18.5] the theoretical value for the temperature coefficient of a bipolar transistor is

$$\frac{dU_{BE}}{dT} = \frac{U_{BE}}{T} - \frac{U_{BG}}{T} \approx -2\frac{mV}{K}$$

where $U_{BG} = E_g/e_0 = 1.205$ V is the bandgap voltage of silicon, E_g being the bandgap. The temperature coefficient of the output voltage $U_{ref} = U_{Temp} + U_{BE2}$ is therefore zero if

$$\boxed{U_{ref} = AU_T + U_{BE} = U_{BG} = 1.205 \text{ V}} \quad .$$

This is a more precise and at the same time simpler adjustment criterion than setting the gain A to some calculated value [18.6].

For the discrete circuit design in Fig. 18.29 we obtain useful component values if $I_{C2} = 10 I_{C1}$. In this case $R_1 \approx R_2$. In order to achieve good matching of T_1 and T_2, a double transistor is necessary, such as an LM 394.

Discrete-component bandgap references are only of interest in special cases, as a wide variety of IC versions is available (see Fig. 18.31). As transistors T_1 and T_2 in Fig. 18.29 are sometimes operated with identical collector currents, different current densities must then be achieved by connecting several transistors in parallel for T_1. The two possibilities are also combined [18.7].

The significant advantage as compared to reference diodes is that bandgap references can be operated with lower voltages, which can be as low as the bandgap voltage $U_{BG} \approx 1.2$ V. Reference diodes, on the other hand, require voltages of 6.4 V and above. Moreover, reference voltages of any magnitude can be produced using bandgap references, when only a portion of the op amp output voltage is fed back to the base terminals, as in Fig. 18.30. In this case the actual reference voltage source T_1, T_2 is operated from the stabilized output voltage. This provides significantly improved line regulation, as in Fig. 18.27.

With many IC bandgap references it is permissible to connect the output to the supply voltage, or the corresponding connection is already established internally. The circuit then has only two terminals brought out and can be used like a Zener diode.

As voltage U_{Temp} is proportional to the absolute temperature, it can be used for temperature measurement (see Chapter 26.1.5). In many circuits, e.g. in REF 43 from PMI or LT 1019 from Linear Technology, $U_{Temp} = 2$ mV/K is brought out to the terminals for this purpose.

18.4.3   Survey of types available

In Fig. 18.31 we have listed a number of commonly used reference voltage sources. Note the tight tolerances and low temperature coefficients. These are achieved by laser adjustment of the relevant resistors during manufacture. The specified values, however, only give a rough indication, as all the circuits are available in various precision categories [18.8].

Those types denoted by * are two-terminal networks. They can only be used like Zener diodes. Consequently, their current must not be zero. Some types have a simple emitter follower at the output. They can therefore only deliver a current, but cannot accept one. Other types have a push-pull emitter follower at the output. They can therefore also accept currents. With these types, operation in Zener diode mode is generally possible if the reference and supply voltage terminals are interconnected.

Type	Manufacturer	Reference voltage	Tolerance	Temperature coefficient	Output current
Bandgap references					
TSC 04	Teledyne	*1.25 V	1 %	50 ppm/K	20 µA–20 mA
LM 385-1.2	National	*1.2 V	1 %	20 ppm/K	10 µA–20 mA
LM 385-2.5	National	*2.5 V	2 %	20 ppm/K	20 µA–20 mA
REF 025	Ferranti	*2.5 V	1 %	25 ppm/K	50 µA–5 mA
TL 431	Texas Instr.	*2.5 V	2 %	30 ppm/K	1 mA–100 mA
MC 1403	Motorola	2.5 V	1 %	10 ppm/K	0–10 mA
REF 43	PMI	2.5 V	0.05%	5 ppm/K	0–10 mA
AD 584	Analog Dev.	2.5 V	0.2 %	10 ppm/K	0–10 mA
LT 1019-2.5	Lin. Techn.	2.5 V	0.05%	3 ppm/K	± 10 mA
REF 050	Ferranti	*5 V	1 %	30 ppm/K	50 µA–5 mA
AD 584	Analog Dev.	5 V	0.2 %	10 ppm/K	0–10 mA
REF 05	PMI	5 V	0.5 %	10 ppm/K	0–10 mA
MAX 673	Maxim	5 V	0.05%	2 ppm/K	0–20 mA
LT 1019-5	Lin. Techn.	5 V	0.05%	3 ppm/K	± 10 mA
REF 10	PMI	10 V	0.5 %	10 ppm/K	0–10 mA
AD 584	Analog Dev.	10 V	0.2 %	10 ppm/K	0–10 mA
MAX 672	Maxim	10 V	0.05%	2 ppm/K	0–20 mA
LT 1019-10	Lin. Techn.	10 V	0.05%	3 ppm/K	± 10 mA
Zener diode references					
AD 586	Analog Dev.	5 V	± 2.5 mV	5 ppm/K	± 10 mA
LT 1021-5	Lin. Techn.	5 V	± 2.5 mV	2 ppm/K	± 10 mA
LT 1021-10	Lin. Techn.	10 V	± 5 mV	2 ppm/K	± 10 mA
REF 102	Burr Brown	10 V	± 2.5 mV	2 ppm/K	± 10 mA
LM 169	National	10 V	± 1 mV	2 ppm/K	± 10 mA
AD 588	Analog Dev.	10 V	± 1 mV	1 ppm/K	± 10 mA
MAX 671	Maxim	10 V	± 1 mV	1 ppm/K	± 10 mA

* Two-terminal network, to be operated like a Zener diode

Fig. 18.31 Typical data for reference voltage sources

18.5   Switched-mode power supplies

The power supplies incorporating linear series regulators described hitherto
are subject to three basic loss factors: the line transformer, the rectifier and the
regulating transistor. The efficiency $\eta = P_{\text{output}}/P_{\text{input}}$ is in most cases only 25%
to 50%. The power dissipation

$$P_{\text{loss}} = P_{\text{input}} - P_{\text{output}} = \left(\frac{1}{\eta} - 1\right) P_{\text{output}}$$

can therefore be up to three times as large as the power output. Consequently
there is not only a large power loss but also an associated cooling problem.

The losses in the series regulator can be substantially reduced by replacing
the continuously controlled transistor by a switch, as in Fig. 18.32. In order to
obtain the required DC output voltage, a lowpass filter is additionally required
to provide time averaging. The magnitude of the output voltage can be determined in this case by the duty cycle with which the switch is closed. If an LC
lowpass filter is used, the regulator no longer possesses an inherently lossy
element. As the switching regulator described is connected on the secondary side
of the power transformer, these circuits are also known as *secondary switched-
mode power supplies*.

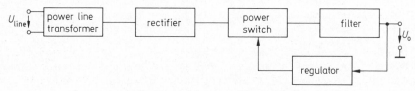

Fig. 18.32 Secondary switching regulator

The losses in the power transformer are of course not reduced by the
switching regulator. However, they can be brought down by transforming
a high-frequency alternating voltage instead of the line voltage. For this purpose, the line voltage is directly rectified as in Fig. 18.33 and an alternating
voltage with a frequency in the range 20 kHz to 200 kHz is generated using
a switching regulator.

As the number of turns required on the power transformer decreases in
inverse proportion to the supply frequency, the copper losses can be greatly

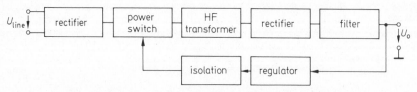

Fig. 18.33 Primary switching regulator (HF = high frequency)

reduced. The secondary voltage is rectified, filtered and then fed directly to the load. The duty cycle of the switches on the primary side is varied to regulate the DC voltage.

Circuits of this kind are known as *primary switched-mode power supplies*. Their efficiency can be 60% to 80%. An additional advantage is their compactness and the low weight of the HF transformer.

If we compare the two basic circuits in Figs. 18.32 and 18.33, we can see that in both cases a switch is used to generate an AC voltage whose duty cycle determines the output voltage. Whereas with the secondary regulator, line isolation is provided by a normal 50 Hz power transformer, with the primary regulator this function is performed by an HF transformer. Consequently the switches in the primary regulator are at line potential. Their withstand voltage must be at least as high as the peak value of the line voltage. The regulator in this case comprises two sections, one which is at line potential and controls the switches, and another which is at output potential and measures the output voltage. Both sections must be suitably insulated from each other.

In spite of these problems and the associated circuit complexity, primary switching power supplies are to be preferred due to their high efficiency. Secondary switching power supplies are mainly used as low-power DC/DC converters.

18.6 Secondary switching regulators

Figures 18.34 to 36 show the three basic types of DC/DC converters. They each consist of three components: a power switch S, a storage choke L and a smoothing capacitor C. However, each of the three circuits delivers a different output voltage. In the case of the circuit in Fig. 18.34, the switch produces an AC voltage whose average value lies between the input voltage and zero depending on the duty cycle.

With the circuit in Fig. 18.35, $U_o = U_i$ if the switch remains permanently in the upper position. If the switch is moved to the lower position, energy is stored in the choke and additionally delivered to the output when the switch is returned to its original position. The output voltage is therefore higher than the input voltage.

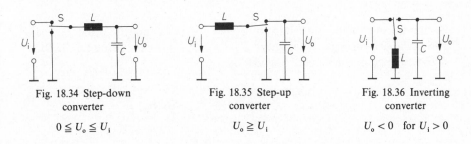

Fig. 18.34 Step-down converter

$0 \leqq U_o \leqq U_i$

Fig. 18.35 Step-up converter

$U_o \geqq U_i$

Fig. 18.36 Inverting converter

$U_o < 0$ for $U_i > 0$

In the circuit in Fig. 18.36, energy is stored in the choke as long as the switch is in the left-hand position. When it switches to the right, the choke current changes direction and charges the capacitor (if the input voltage is positive) to negative values.

In the circuit in Fig. 18.34, current flows continuously into the reservoir capacitor. The circuit is therefore also known as a *forward* converter. This is not true of Figs. 18.35 and 36, because there the capacitor is not recharged as long as the choke is being charged. These circuits are known as *flyback converters*.

18.6.1   Step-down converters

The double-throw switch can be simplified by implementing one arm using a simple one-way switch and the other using a diode. This results in the step-down converter (buck regulator) in Fig. 18.37. As long as the switch is closed, $U_1 = U_i$. When it opens, the choke current retains its direction and U_1 falls until the diode is turned on, i.e. virtually to zero potential. This can be seen from the timing diagram in Fig. 18.38.

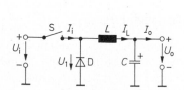

Fig. 18.37 Step-down converter with simple switch

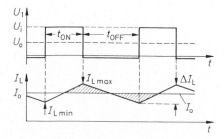

Fig. 18.38 Current and voltage waveforms

$$U_o = \frac{t_{ON}}{T} U_i \quad \text{for } I_o \geq I_{o\min}$$

The time characteristic of the reactor current is deduced from the law of induction

$$U_L = L \cdot \frac{dI_L}{dt} \ . \tag{18.9}$$

During the ON-time t_{ON}, a voltage of $U_L = U_i - U_o$ is applied across the choke; during the OFF-time t_{OFF}, a voltage of $U_L = -U_o$ is present. Using Eq. (18.9), the rate of change of the current is given by

$$\Delta I_L = \frac{1}{L}(U_i - U_o)t_{ON} = \frac{1}{L}U_o t_{OFF} \ . \tag{18.10}$$

From this we can calculate the output voltage:

$$U_o = \frac{t_{ON}}{t_{ON} + t_{OFF}} U_i = \frac{t_{ON}}{T} U_i = p U_i \qquad (18.11)$$

where $T = t_{ON} + t_{OFF} = 1/f$ is the period and $p = t_{ON}/T$ is the duty cycle. We can see that the output voltage is the arithmetic mean of U_1, as we would expect.

The circuit behaves quite differently if the output current I_o becomes smaller than

$$I_{o\,min} = \tfrac{1}{2}\Delta I_L = \frac{T}{2L} U_o \left(1 - \frac{U_o}{U_i} \right). \qquad (18.12)$$

The choke current then falls to zero during the OFF-time of the switch, the diode is turned off and the voltage across the choke becomes zero, as shown in Fig. 18.39 (discontinuous operation). To calculate the output voltage we shall assume that the circuit provides completely lossless operation. The average input power must therefore be equal to the output power:

$$U_i \bar{I}_i = U_o I_o . \qquad (18.13)$$

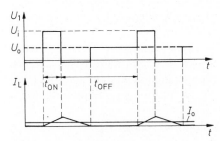

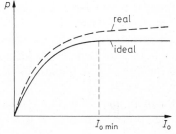

Fig. 18.39 Current and voltage waveforms in the step-down converter for output currents of less than

$$I_{o\,min} = \frac{T}{2L} U_o \left(1 - \frac{U_o}{U_i} \right)$$

Fig. 18.40 Duty cycle $p = t_{ON}/T$ as a function of output current I_o at constant output voltage U_o

The current flowing through the choke rises during t_{ON} from zero to the value $I_L = U_L t_{ON}/L$. The arithmetic mean of the input current is therefore

$$\bar{I}_i = \frac{t_{ON}}{T} \cdot \frac{1}{2} I_L = \frac{t_{ON}^2}{2TL} U_L = \frac{T}{2L} (U_i - U_o) p^2 . \qquad (18.14)$$

Substitution into Eq. (18.13) gives the output voltage and duty cycle respectively

$$U_o = \frac{U_i^2 p^2 T}{2LI_o + U_i p^2 T} , \qquad p = \sqrt{\frac{2L}{T} \frac{U_o}{U_i(U_i - U_o)}} \sqrt{I_o} . \qquad (18.15)$$

In order to prevent the output voltage from rising in the event of low currents $(I_o < I_{o\,min})$, p must be reduced accordingly. This is shown schematically in Fig. 18.40. We can see that very short switching times must be achieved in this region. For currents higher than $I_{o\,min}$, the duty cycle remains constant in accordance with Eq. (18.11). However, this only applies to a lossless circuit. Otherwise p must also be increased – albeit by a much smaller amount – as the output current increases above $I_{o\,min}$, in order to keep the output voltage constant.

Design considerations

If possible the inductance of the storage choke is selected large enough to prevent the current falling below $I_{o\,min}$. From Eq. (18.12) it therefore follows that

$$L = T\left(1 - \frac{U_o}{U_i}\right)\frac{U_o}{2I_{o\,min}} . \qquad (18.16)$$

The maximum current flowing through the storage choke and consequently through the switch and diode is therefore $I_{L\,max} = I_o + I_{o\,min}$. This still leaves the parameter of the period $T = 1/f$. In order to allow a small inductance to be used, the frequency f is selected as high as possible. However, the problem then arises that at high frequencies the switching transistor becomes more costly and the drive circuit more complex. In addition, the dynamic switching losses increase proportionally with the frequency. For these reasons switching frequencies between 20 and 200 kHz are preferred.

Smoothing capacitor C determines the output voltage ripple. The charge current is $I_C = I_L - I_o$. The charge applied and removed during one cycle therefore corresponds to the hatched area in Fig. 18.38. For the ripple we therefore obtain the relation

$$\Delta U_o = \frac{\Delta Q_C}{C} = \frac{1}{C} \cdot \frac{1}{2} \cdot \left(\frac{1}{2}t_{ON} + \frac{1}{2}t_{OFF}\right) \cdot \frac{1}{2}\Delta I_L = \frac{T}{8C}\Delta I_L .$$

Using Eqs. (18.10) and (18.16), the smoothing capacitance is given by

$$C = \left(1 - \frac{U_o}{U_i}\right)\frac{T^2 U_o}{8L\Delta U_o} = \frac{TI_{o\,min}}{4\Delta U_o} . \qquad (18.17)$$

When selecting the smoothing capacitor, care must be taken to ensure that it has the lowest possible series resistance and series inductance. In order to achieve this, it is customary to connect one or more electrolytic and ceramic capacitors in parallel.

18.6.2 Generating the switching signal

The switching signal is generated using two modules: a pulsewidth modulator and a regulator with voltage reference. Figure 18.41 shows the block diagram.

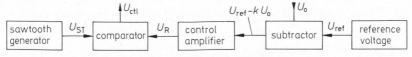

Fig. 18.41 Control unit design

The pulsewidth modulator comprises a sawtooth generator and a comparator. The comparator closes the switch as long as voltage U_R is greater than the triangular voltage. The resultant control voltage U_{ctl} is shown in Fig. 18.42 for U_R ranging from the lower limit to the upper limit. The resulting duty cycle

$$p = \frac{t_{ON}}{T} = \frac{U_R}{\hat{U}_{ST}}$$

is therefore proportional to U_R.

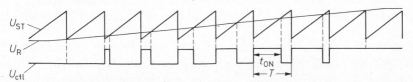

Fig. 18.42 Mode of operation of the pulsewidth modulator

The subtractor takes the difference between the reference voltage and the weighted output voltage $U_{ref} - kU_o$. The PI control amplifier increases U_R until this difference becomes zero. The output then has the value $U_o = U_{ref}/k$.

An example should serve to illustrate the design process for a switching regulator. Let us assume that an output voltage of 5 V at a maximum current of 4 A is required. The minimum output current is to be 0.5 A, the input voltage is approximately 20 V. A suitable switching regulator for this application would be the L 296 from SGS. The resultant circuit is shown in Fig. 18.43. Apart from the LC output filter, only a small number of external resistors and capacitors are required to operate the integrated circuit. The switching regulator is to be operated at a frequency of 50 kHz, giving a period of 20 μs. From Eq. (18.11), we obtain an ON-time of

$$t_{ON} = T\frac{U_o}{U_i} = 20 \,\mu s \, \frac{5 \,V}{20 \,V} = 5 \,\mu s \ .$$

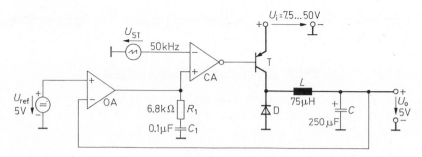

Fig. 18.43 Example of a step-down converter incorporating an L 296 switching regulator

$$U_o = 5 \text{ V} \; ; \quad I_{o\,max} = 4 \text{ A} ; \quad U_i = 7.5 \text{ to } 50 \text{ V}$$

The inductance of the storage choke is obtained from Eq. (18.16):

$$L = T\left(1 - \frac{U_o}{U_i}\right)\frac{U_o}{2I_{o\,min}} = 20 \text{ μs}\left(1 - \frac{5 \text{ V}}{20 \text{ V}}\right)\frac{5 \text{ V}}{2 \cdot 0.5 \text{ A}} = 75 \text{ μH} \ .$$

If the output ripple is to be of the order of 10 mV, the value of the smoothing capacitor is given by Eq. (18.17)

$$C = T\frac{I_{o\,min}}{4\Delta U_o} = 20 \text{ μs}\,\frac{0.5 \text{ A}}{4 \cdot 10 \text{ mV}} = 250 \text{ μF} \ .$$

A voltage divider in the output voltage feedback path is unnecessary, as the internal reference voltage is 5 V. The output voltage remains constant even if the output current is less than the value $I_{o\,min} = 0.5$ A used in the calculation. In this case, the control amplifier reduces the duty cycle via the comparator, as in Fig. 18.40. Problems then arise if the required ON-time is less than the minimum achievable ON-time for transistor T. In this case the output voltage increases so much in response to a turn-on pulse from transistor T that the transistor is then turned off for *several* cycles. This results in very unsmooth operation.

The desired control response is achieved by connecting RC network $R_1 C_1$ at the high-impedance op amp output. It must be remembered that the voltage regulating circuit of switching regulators is prone to instability. This has two causes: firstly, the switching regulator is a sampling system with an average dead time equal to half the period; secondly, the output filter represents a second-order lowpass filter which produces a phase lag of up to 180°. For these reasons it is advisable to ensure that the control amplifier produces no phase lag at high frequencies. Resistor R_1 in Fig. 18.43 is used for this purpose.

The static circuit losses are mainly due to the voltage drops in the power circuit. Although the storage choke can easily be rated high enough to minimize its resistive losses, this still leaves the losses due to the voltage drop across the power switch comprising transistor T and diode D.

During t_{ON}, the output current flows through T, and during t_{OFF} through D. In the case of the L 296, the voltage drop is in each case 1.5 V at 4 A, giving a power dissipation of 6 W at maximum output current. The maximum efficiency neglecting dynamic losses is therefore

$$\eta = \frac{P_{\text{output}}}{P_{\text{input}}} = \frac{20\,\text{W}}{20\,\text{W} + 6\,\text{W}} = 77\% \; .$$

18.6.3 Step-up converters

Figure 18.44 shows a practical implementation of the step-up converter (boost regulator) in Fig. 18.35, and Fig. 18.45 gives the voltage and current waveforms. Once again, the relations required for the design parameters of the circuit can be derived from the rise or fall in the choke current I_L during the two states of switch S. These relations are given below the diagrams. The smallest output voltage is $U_o = U_i$. For a lossless circuit, this is obtained when switch S is continuously open.

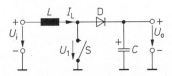

Fig. 18.44 Step-up converter

$$U_o = \frac{T}{t_{\text{OFF}}} U_i \quad \text{for } I_o > I_{o\min}$$

$$I_{o\min} = U_i \left(1 - \frac{U_i}{U_o}\right) \cdot \frac{I}{2L}$$

$$L = U_i \left(1 - \frac{U_i}{U_o}\right) \cdot \frac{T}{2I_{o\min}}$$

$$C \approx \frac{T I_{o\max}}{\Delta U_o}$$

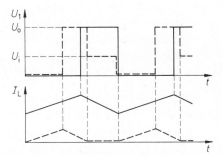

Fig. 18.45 Voltage and current waveforms in the step-up converter

Dashed lines: for $I_o < I_{o\min}$

Here, too, the specified output voltage is only achieved if the choke current does not become zero. If the output value falls below the minimum $I_{o\min}$, the ON-time must be reduced, as in Fig. 18.40, in order to prevent a rise in the output voltage. This case is shown by the dashed lines in Fig. 18.45. The switching signal is generated in precisely the same way as for the step-down converter.

18.6.4 Inverting converter

The inverting converter (inverting regulator) and associated waveforms are shown in Figs. 18.46 and 18.47.

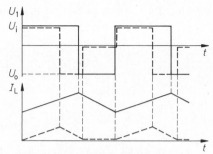

Fig. 18.46   Inverting converter

$$U_o = \frac{t_{ON}}{t_{OFF}} U_i \quad \text{for } I_o > I_{o\min}$$

$$I_{o\min} = \frac{U_i U_o}{U_i + U_o} \cdot \frac{T}{2L}$$

$$L = \frac{U_i U_o}{U_i + U_o} \cdot \frac{T}{2L}$$

$$C \approx \frac{T I_{o\max}}{\Delta U_o}$$

Fig. 18.47   Voltage and current waveforms in
the inverting converter.

Dashed lines: for $I_o < I_{o\min}$

As we can see, the capacitor is charged to a negative voltage via the diode during the OFF-phase. The relations given are again deduced from the reactor current changes being equal during the ON- and OFF-times.

If the output current falls below the value $I_{o\min}$ the reactor current becomes occasionally zero. In order to keep the output voltage constant in this case, the ON-time must again be reduced, as in Fig. 18.40. This is represented by the dashed lines in Fig. 18.47.

18.6.5   Voltage converter with charge pump

If the current requirement is low, there is a simple method of inverting a voltage. For this purpose, the input voltage is converted to an AC voltage using switch S_1, as shown in Fig.18.48. This alternating voltage is made "floating" by capacitor C_1 and then rectified again, this time by switch S_2. In the switch position shown, C_1 is charged up to the input voltage: $U_1 = U_i$. The two switches then change over, causing voltage $-U_1$ to be applied to C_2, and the latter is charged up to the voltage $U_o = -U_1 = -U_i$ after several switching cycles.

Rectification of the output voltage does not necessarily require a controlled switch, but can also be performed by two diodes, as in Fig. 18.49. Depending on which potential is applied to the rectifier and on the polarity of the diodes, voltage U_i can be added to or subtracted from that potential. However, the disadvantage of rectification using diodes is that the output voltage is reduced by the two forward voltages. Consequently, IC voltage inverters such as the ICL 7660 from Intersil employ CMOS switches for rectification. For load currents up to 20 mA, the sum of the voltage drops across the four switches (2×2 switches per cycle) therefore remains below 1 V [18.9].

Additional losses are incurred due to the continual reversal of the capacitor charge. However, these depend only on the size of the voltage difference

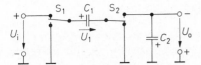

Fig. 18.48 Voltage inverter employing the
charge pump principle

$$U_o = - U_i$$

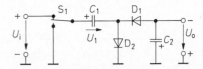

Fig. 18.49 Simplified arrangement for
rectifying the output voltage

$$U_o = - (U_i - 2U_D)$$

produced, which under steady state conditions can easily be minimized by selecting suitably high-value capacitors.

18.6.6   Survey of types available

A number of integrated circuits particularly suitable as voltage converters are listed in Fig. 18.50. The majority of pulsewidth modulators for primary switching regulators can also be used for this purpose. These are given in Fig. 18.74 but require an external power transistor.

Type	Manufacturer	Output current	Output voltage	Voltage reference	Typical frequency
Step-down converters					
MAX 638	Maxim	60 mA	5 V	1.3 V	65 kHz
LM 2575	National	1 A	5 V	yes	52 kHz
L 4960	SGS	2.5 A	5 ... 40 V	5 V	50 kHz
L 296	SGS	4 A	5 ... 40 V	5 V	50 kHz
LT 1074	Lin. Techn.	5 A	2.5 ... 50 V	2.2 V	70 kHz
L 4975	SGS	5 A	5 ... 40 V	5 V	70 kHz
L 4970	SGS	10 A	5 ... 40 V	5 V	70 kHz
Step-up converters					
MAX 644	Maxim	40 mA	5 V	1.3 V	18 kHz
MAX 630	Maxim	60 mA	2.5 ... 25 V	1.3 V	40 kHz
LT 1070	Lin. Techn.	4 A	3 ... 60 V	1.3 V	40 kHz
Inverting converters					
MAX 743	Maxim	100 mA	$\pm$ 12, $\pm$ 15 V	2 V	200 kHz
MAX 634	Maxim	60 mA	$-2.5 ... -20$ V	1.3 V	40 kHz
MAX 680[1]	Maxim	10 mA	$\pm 2U_i$	–	15 kHz
ICL 7660[1]	Various	20 mA	$- U_i$	–	10 kHz
ICL 7662[1]	Intersil	20 mA	$- U_i$	–	10 kHz
Si 7661[1]	Siliconix	80 mA	$- U_i$	–	10 kHz
TSC 962[1]	Teledyne	80 mA	$- U_i$	6.4 V	10 kHz
LT 1054[1]	Lin. Techn.	100 mA	$- U_i$	2.5 V	25 kHz

[1] Voltage inverter employing charge pump principle

Fig. 18.50 Integrated circuits including power transistors for secondary switching regulators

18.7   Primary switching regulators

Primary switching regulators fall into two categories, namely single-ended and push-pull converters. As single-ended types generally require only one power switch, the number of components involved is low. However, their use is limited to low-power applications. For powers in excess of 100 W, push-pull converters are preferred, even though they require two power switches.

18.7.1   Single-ended converters

The single-ended converter in Fig. 18.51 represents the simplest practical primary switching regulator. It is similar to the flyback converter in Fig. 18.46, except that the storage choke has been replaced by a transformer. As long as power switch S is closed, energy is stored in the transformer. This energy is transferred to smoothing capacitor C when the switch opens. The resulting relation for the output voltage is the same as for the circuit in Fig. 18.46. The only difference is that the output voltage is now reduced by the winding ratio W of the transformer, where $W = w_1/w_2$ (see Sect. 18.7.3).

The waveform of the voltage across the switch is plotted in Fig. 18.52. When the switch opens, the voltage rises until diode D is turned on, i.e. to $U_{S\max} = U_i + WU_o$. In order to prevent it from becoming too high, we make the ON-time $t_{ON} \leq 0.5\,T$, which means that $U_{S\max} \leq 2U_i$. As a DC voltage of

$$U_i = 220 \text{ V} \cdot \sqrt{2} = 310 \text{ V}$$

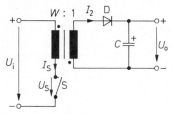

Fig. 18.51 Single-ended flyback converter

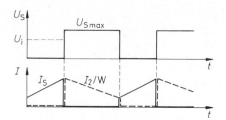

Fig. 18.52 Voltage and current waveforms for $I_o > I_{o\min}$

$$U_o = \frac{t_{ON}}{t_{OFF}} \cdot \frac{U_i}{W} \quad \text{for } I_o > I_{o\min}$$

$$U_{S\max} = U_i\left(1 + \frac{t_{ON}}{t_{OFF}}\right)$$

$$W = w_1/w_2$$

is produced when rectifying the 220 V AC supply, a voltage of $U_{S\max} = 620$ V is present at the power switch. The voltages actually present are even higher due to the unavoidable leakage inductance.

The current characteristic is also shown in Fig. 18.52. As long as the switch is closed, the rate of rise of the current is $\Delta I = U_i t_{ON}/L$. When the switch opens, the diode is turned on and the fall in the current transferred to the primary side obeys the relation $\Delta I = WU_o t_{\text{OFF}}/L$, producing the output voltage indicated. However, the transformer inductance must be large enough to ensure that the current does not fall to zero during the OFF-time.

One disadvantage of the circuit is that the transformer has to provide not only AC line isolation and the required stepping-down of the voltage, but must simultaneously act as a storage choke. Due to the DC biasing which occurs, it has to be considerably overrated. A better solution is to keep the transformer free of any DC component and to use a separate storage choke. All the following circuits operate on this principle.

In the case of the single-ended converter in Fig. 18.53, the primary and secondary windings have the same polarity. Consequently, energy is transferred to the output via diode D_2, as long as the power switch is closed. The circuit is therefore a forward converter. The voltage characteristics are shown in Fig. 18.54. As long as the power switch is closed, the input voltage U_i is present at the primary winding and therefore voltage $U_2 = U_i/W$ is present at the secondary winding. When switch S opens, D_2 is turned off and the current through storage choke L is carried by diode D_3. The conditions on the secondary side are therefore precisely the same as for the forward converter in Fig. 18.37. Consequently, apart from the factor W, we obtain the same relations for the output voltage and the same considerations apply to the design procedure for the storage chokes and the smoothing capacitor.

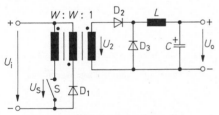

Fig. 18.53 Single-ended forward converter

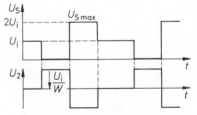

Fig. 18.54 Voltage waveforms

$$U_o = \frac{t_{\text{ON}}}{T} \cdot \frac{U_i}{W} \quad \text{for } I_o > I_{o\min}$$

$$U_{S\max} = 2U_i$$

At the instant the power switch is turned off, diode D_2 also becomes reverse biased. Without further action, the energy stored in the transformer would then generate an extremely high-amplitude voltage spike. In order to prevent this, the transformer is provided with a third winding with the same number of turns as the primary winding, but with a smaller cross section. For the given polarity, diode D_1 then becomes conducting when the induced voltage equals the input voltage. In this way the voltage across the power switch is limited to $U_{S\max} = 2U_i$. In addition, the same energy is fed back to the input voltage source during the OFF-time as was stored in the transformer during the ON-time. In this way the transformer is operated without DC magnetization.

18.7.2   Push-pull converter

With circuits of this type, the DC input voltage is converted to AC form by an inverter comprising at least two power switches. This AC voltage is stepped down in an HF transformer and subsequently rectified.

In the circuit in Fig. 18.55, the period T is subdivided into four time periods. Initially switch S_1 is closed, which means that diode D_1 is ON and voltage $U_3 = U_i/W$ is present at storage choke L. Switch S_1 then re-opens and all the voltages at the transformer fall to zero. Diodes D_1 and D_2 then each carry half the choke current.

In the next time period, switch S_1 remains open, whereas switch S_2 closes. This turns on D_2 which likewise transfers voltage $U_3 = U_i/W$. When S_2 re-opens, all the voltages at the transformer become zero once more, as during the second time period. The relevant voltage waveforms are shown in Fig. 18.56.

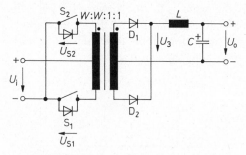

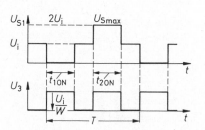

Fig. 18.55 Parallel-fed push-pull converter   Fig. 18.56 Voltage waveforms

$$U_o = 2\frac{t_{ON}}{T} \cdot \frac{U_i}{W} \quad \text{with} \quad \frac{t_{ON}}{T} < 0.5$$

$$U_{S\,max} = 2U_i$$

The secondary side of the circuit therefore operates in basically the same way as the forward converter in Fig. 18.37. However, energy is now transferred to the storage choke twice during period T due to full-wave rectification. Consequently, $\frac{1}{2}T$ instead of T must be substituted in the forward converter equations.

Due to the balanced mode of operation, the transformer operates without direct current. However, this only applies if the ON-times of the power switches are precisely equal, i.e. $t_{1\,ON} = t_{2\,ON} = t_{ON}$. This condition must be fulfilled when drive is applied to the switches, otherwise the transformer will be driven into saturation, the currents will become high and the switches will be destroyed. For the same reason, it is necessary to prevent one switch from not closing at all during a cycle. However, these conditions are taken into account in the majority of IC drive circuits for push-pull switching regulators. The drive arrangement for the power switches is here simplified by the fact that their two negative terminals are at the same potential.

In the case of the push-pull converter in Fig. 18.57, an AC voltage is produced by connecting one end of the primary winding alternately to the positive or negative terminal of the input voltage, while the other is at $\frac{1}{2}U_i$. The power switches are again driven alternately. The voltage waveforms in Fig. 18.58 are the same as for the previous circuit. The only difference is that the amplitude is halved, a feature which is particularly advantageous for switch selection.

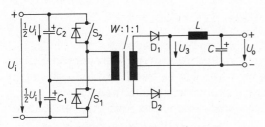

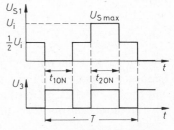

Fig. 18.57 Push-pull converter in a half-bridge configuration

Fig. 18.58 Voltage waveforms

$$U_o = \frac{t_{ON}}{T} \cdot \frac{U_i}{W} \quad \text{with} \quad \frac{t_{ON}}{T} < 0.5$$

$$U_{Smax} = U_i$$

A further advantage of the circuit is that the transformer is always DC-free due to capacitive coupling, even if the ON-times of the two switches are unequal. In this case, only the DC voltage across capacitors C_1 and C_2 is slightly displaced. However, a disadvantage is that the negative terminals of the power switches are at quite different potentials, making the drive arrangement more complex.

18.7.3 High-frequency transformers

Storage chokes are commercially available in a wide variety of types. Various manufacturers offer types rated from 10 µH to 10 mH and from 0.1 A to 60 A. There is therefore little necessity for the user to wind them himself. However, this is not the case with high-frequency transformers. Here one would be lucky to find a ready-made transformer with the appropriate turns ratio. Consequently, the user generally has to calculate the transformer data and also wind the transformers himself if only small quantities are required.

According to the law of electromagnetic induction, the voltage induced in a transformer is given by:

$$U = w\dot{\Phi} = w \cdot A_c \cdot \dot{B} \ , \qquad (18.18)$$

where Φ is the magnetic flux, B the magnetic induction and A_c the cross-sectional area of the core between the two coils. If the number of turns on the primary side is w_1, it follows from Eq. (18.18) that

$$w_1 = \frac{U_1}{A_c \cdot B} = \frac{U_1}{A_c} \cdot \frac{\Delta t}{\Delta B} \; .$$

With $\Delta B = \hat{B}$, the minimum number of turns results from the permissible peak value of the magnetic induction, $\hat{B}$, and from the maximum value of

$$\Delta t = t_{\text{ON max}} = p_{\text{max}} \cdot T = p_{\text{max}}/f = 1/2f \; .$$

Hence

$$w_1 = \frac{U_1}{2A_c \cdot \hat{B} \cdot f} \; . \tag{18.19}$$

We can see that the required number of turns is inversely proportional to the frequency. Consequently, the power which can be transferred for a given core and thus for a given winding area, is proportional to the frequency.

The number of turns on the secondary side results from the voltage ratio:

$$w_2 = w_1 \frac{U_2}{U_1} = \frac{w_1}{W} \; . \tag{18.20}$$

The magnetizing and copper losses can generally be kept negligibly low.

The wire gauge depends on the currents to be handled. Current densities of up to $S = 5$ to $7 \, \text{A/mm}^2$ are permissible in terms of thermal requirements. However, if the copper losses are to be minimized, lower values should be adopted. The wire diameter is given by

$$D = 2\sqrt{\frac{I}{\pi \cdot S}} \; . \tag{18.21}$$

However, due to the *skin effect*, at higher frequencies the current no longer flows uniformly through the entire cross section, but only at the wire surface. For the skin depth (drop to $1/e$) of the current, [18.10] gives us

$$\delta = 2.2 \, \text{mm}/\sqrt{f/\text{kHz}} \; . \tag{18.22}$$

We can see from Fig. 18.59 how the skin depth reduces with increasing frequency. For this reason, it is inadvisable to select the wire diameter greater than twice the skin depth. In order that the required cross sections can still be achieved, litz wire composed of fine, separately insulated strands can be used. It is also preferable to employ ribbon cable or correspondingly thin copper foils.

The principal characteristics of a number of ferroxcube EC cores are listed in Fig. 18.60. The maximum rating is only a rough guideline. If the wire diameter is substantially oversized in order to minimize the losses, it is possible that the next larger size of core will be required in order to provide sufficient winding space.

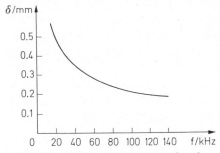

Fig. 18.59 Skin effect: skin depth as a function
of frequency

Core type (lateral length) [mm]	Maximum rating at 20 kHz [W]	Magnetic cross section A_c [mm^2]	Inductance factor A_L [μH]
EC 35	50	71	2.1
EC 41	80	106	2.7
EC 52	130	141	3.4
EC 70	350	211	3.9

Fig. 18.60 Ferroxcube cores for high-
frequency transformers

Recommended max. induction: $\hat{B} = 200\,\text{mT} = 2\,\text{kG}$

Inductance: $L = A_L \cdot w^2$

18.7.4   Power switches

The aspects discussed in this section apply to the power switches of all switching regulators. The components we shall consider here are bipolar transistors and power MOSFETs. The use of thyristors is only of interest when high powers in the kilowatt range are involved; consequently, these devices will not be discussed here. If we look at the safe operating area (SOA) of power transistors, we can see that there are virtually no power transistors that can handle 100 W at high voltage levels. However, when these devices are used as high-speed switches, there are a number of exceptions, as shown in Fig. 18.61.

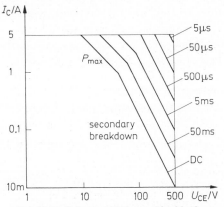

Fig. 18.61 Safe operating area of a bipolar
transistor used as a switch

DC power up to $U_{CE} = 50\,\text{V}$:   50 W

DC power up to $U_{CE} = 500\,\text{V}$:   5 W

Pulse power for 5 μs at $U_{CE} = 500\,\text{V}$:   2500 W

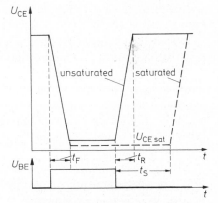

Fig. 18.62 Switching times of a bipolar
transistor with and without saturation

t_F: Fall time
t_R: Rise time
t_S: Storage time

We can see that the power dissipation and secondary breakdown can be exceeded, albeit briefly, and in extreme cases (for a few microseconds) it is even permissible for $U_{CE\,max}$ and $I_{C\,max}$ to be applied simultaneously. It is therefore possible to use a transistor to switch several kilowatts, a characteristic which is utilized in switched-mode power supplies.

However, there is a second reason for switching the transistors on and off quickly: a switch only operates losslessly if the transition from the OFF-state to the ON-state and vice versa is instantaneous. Otherwise so-called switching losses occur. These are greater the longer the switching process lasts. As they occur each time the transistor switches, they are proportional to the switching frequency.

In addition, with most switching regulators it is also preferable to provide short ON-times t_{ON} in order to ensure orderly operation even at low load currents $I_o < I_{o\,min}$. For this purpose it is essential to switch the transistor off rapidly. Consequently, we have to obviate the problem of the storage time of bipolar transistors by preventing them from going into saturation during the conducting phase ($U_{CE} > U_{CE\,sat}$). These two cases are compared in Fig. 18.62. We can see that a slight increase in the voltage drop across the conducting transistor must be tolerated in order to eliminate the storage time.

The basic arrangement for a bipolar transistor operated as a power switch is shown in Fig. 18.63. In order to turn on the transistor, switch S is moved to the upper position, allowing a large base current to flow via resistor R_1. This causes the collector current to rise rapidly, and a short fall time is produced. When the collector potential falls below the base potential, the Schottky diode is turned on, preventing the transistor from being driven into saturation. The major portion of the current through R_1 is now diverted via the diode to the collector, and the remaining base current immediately assumes the value required by the transistor at this operating point. In order to turn off the transistor, it is not enough merely to cut off the base current. Its direction must be reversed in order to remove the charge of the base junction. If this is to be effected rapidly, a large negative base current is required, its magnitude being determined by resistor R_2.

One possible arrangement is shown in Fig. 18.64. Complementary emitter follower T_2, T_3 provides the required base currents. Resistor R_B limits the base current. Antisaturation diode D_1 ensures that the collector potential remains higher than the base potential. Driver ICs operating on this principle include types UAA 4002 and 4006 from Thomson, which can deliver base currents up to ± 1.5 A.

If the power switches have to be used to switch high currents, the required base currents become unmanageably large. In this case, a Darlington circuit can be used, as in Fig. 18.65. However, this increases the saturation voltage of T_1' by U_{BE}. An important requirement to ensure fast turn-off is that the Darlington circuit contains the speed-up diode D_1 for removal of the base charge, since transistor T_1 cannot otherwise be actively turned off.

Power MOSFETs used as power switches offer considerable advantages: they have no secondary breakdown, no storage time and can be turned on and

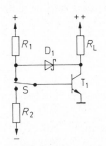

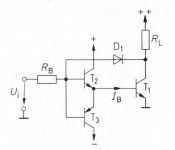

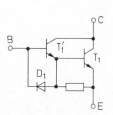

Fig. 18.63 Base drive for short switching times

Fig. 18.64 Practical base drive arrangement

Fig. 18.65 Darlington pair with speed-up diode

off at least a factor of 10 more quickly than comparable bipolar transistors. Although costly, they are to be preferred for frequencies above 50 to 100 kHz. However, the use of MOSFETs should not lead to the erroneous assumption that they can be controlled without power. This may best be explained by reference to Fig. 18.66, in which capacitors C_1 and C_2 represent the parasitic capacitances of the power MOSFET. If we now increase the gate voltage from 0 V to 10 V, the MOSFET is turned on and its drain potential falls from 310 V to about zero. The associated charge variation in the two capacitors is

$$\Delta Q = 500\,\text{pF} \cdot 10\,\text{V} + 50\,\text{pF} \cdot 310\,\text{V} = 5\,\text{nC} + 16\,\text{nC} = 21\,\text{nC}\ .$$

For the gate potential to rise in 100 ns, a current of $I = 21\,\text{nC}/100\,\text{ns} = 210\,\text{mA}$ is required. The gate current is therefore of the same order of magnitude as the base current of bipolar transistors. The only difference is that the gate current only flows at the switching instant. In order to switch power MOSFETs on and off rapidly, low-impedance drivers are therefore required. Figure 18.66 shows a complementary emitter follower and Fig. 18.67 a totem pole output stage of the type commonly used in TTL gates. Being easier to implement in monolithic technology, it is therefore preferred in driver ICs, e.g. the SG 3525 . . . 27 from Silicon General. In terms of their drive circuitry, power MOSFETs have the

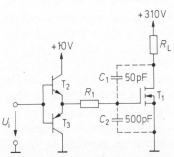

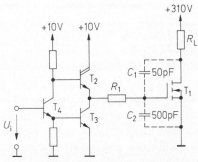

Fig. 18.66 Drive circuit for a power MOSFET with complementary emitter follower

Fig. 18.67 Drive circuit for a power MOSFET with totem pole circuit

advantage of not requiring negative voltage sources as is the case with bipolar transistors.

18.7.5   Generating the switching signals

The switching signals for single-ended converters can be generated using a pulsewidth modulator, as described earlier in Section 18.6.2. However, push-pull converter operation requires two alternately activated pulsewidth modulated outputs. To generate these signals, the pulsewidth modulator in Fig. 18.41 is provided with a toggle flip-flop, giving the circuit in Fig. 18.68. It changes state on each negative-going edge of the sawtooth signal, thereby enabling one or the other of the AND gates. Figure 18.69 shows the waveform diagram. We can see that two signals from the sawtooth generator are required to produce a complete pulse cycle at the output. Its frequency must therefore be twice as high as that at which the HF transformer is to be operated. As the maximum ON-time at its output cannot exceed 50%, this circuit ensures that the two power switches can never be simultaneously ON.

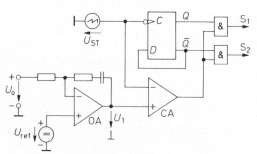

Fig. 18.68 Pulsewidth modulator for
push-pull converters

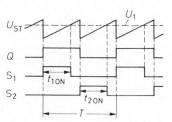

Fig. 18.69 Signal waveforms

An additional problem for controlling primary switching regulators is AC line isolation in the drive circuit, as can be seen in Fig. 18.33. This circuit has the function of monitoring the output voltage as well as providing the switching signals for the power switches which are at line potential. It therefore requires isolation, which should be provided either in respect of the output signal of the regulator in Fig. 18.68 or in respect of switching signals S_1, S_2. An opto-coupler can be used to isolate the control voltage, as in Fig. 18.70. The regulator then additionally compensates for the nonlinearity of the opto-coupler [18.11].

Electrical isolation of the switching signals is an obvious solution, especially when the two power switches are at different potentials, e.g. as in Fig. 18.57, and direct connection to the pulsewidth modulator is therefore impossible. As well as opto-couplers, pulse transformers can also be used to provide isolation. Opto-couplers have the disadvantage of being unable to transfer the necessary drive

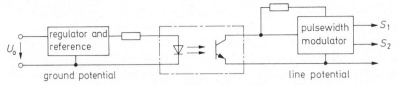

Fig. 18.70 Line isolation using an opto-coupler for the analog regulator signal

power for the power switches. An auxiliary power supply at the potential of the power switches is therefore required [18.12]. Pulse transformers, on the other hand, allow the drive power to be transferred directly. The relevant circuit is particularly simple if power MOSFETs are used. The pulse transformer can simply be switched between driver and MOSFET, as in Fig. 18.71 [18.13]. The coupling capacitor keeps the transformer free of any DC component. However, it should be noted that the gate signal amplitude is a function of the ON-time, as the arithmetic mean of U_2 is zero. This effect is illustrated in Fig. 18.72. For this reason, ON-times of over 50% cannot be achieved without further measures; however, they are rarely required.

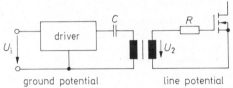

Fig. 18.71 Line isolation using a pulse transformer

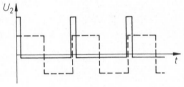

Fig. 18.72 Pulse amplitude as a function of the ON-time

When bipolar power switches are driven via a pulse transformer, it is necessary to have part of the driver at transistor potential. The driver must control the switch-on current and the switch-off current as well as preventing saturation. The simplest solution is to use a floating switch driver such as the SG 3629 from Silicon General.

18.7.6 Loss analysis

There are three types of loss which determine the efficiency of a switching regulator. The *static losses* are due to the current consumption of the pulsewidth modulator and the drivers, and are compounded by the ON-state power losses of the power switches and the output rectifier. These losses are independent of the switching frequency. The *dynamic losses* occur as switching losses in the power switches and as magnetic losses in the HF transformer and in the choke. They are approximately proportional to the switching frequency. The *copper losses* in the HF transformer and in the choke result from the voltage drop across the ohmic resistance of the windings. As fewer windings are required at higher frequencies, as stated in Eq. (18.19), these losses are inversely proportional to the frequency as long as the skin effect can be neglected. Figure 18.73 shows the three loss sources as a function of frequency. An advisable operating range is between 20 and 200 kHz. Although for high-frequency operation the magnetic components are lighter and smaller, the dynamic losses are so predominant in this range that the overall losses increase.

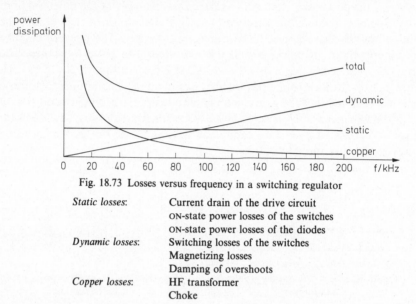

Fig. 18.73 Losses versus frequency in a switching regulator

Static losses:	Current drain of the drive circuit
	ON-state power losses of the switches
	ON-state power losses of the diodes
Dynamic losses:	Switching losses of the switches
	Magnetizing losses
	Damping of overshoots
Copper losses:	HF transformer
	Choke

An additional problem are the overshoots which occur when the power switches are turned off. They are due to the voltages across the leakage inductance of the HF transformer and other circuit inductances. In order to minimize them, all the leads in the power circuit must be kept as short as possible. Nevertheless, during rapid switching, high overshoots may occur even if the leakage inductances are small. To give a numerical example:

$$U = L_{\text{leakage}} \frac{\Delta I}{\Delta t} = 100 \, \text{nH} \, \frac{1 \, \text{A}}{100 \, \text{ns}} = 100 \, \text{V} \ .$$

In order to prevent damage to the power switches, an additional snubber network is required, although this also causes additional dynamic losses [18.14, 18.15].

18.7.7   IC drive circuits

A number of commonly used switching regulators are listed in Fig. 18.74. The control devices for push-pull converters have two outputs which switch

Type	Manufacturer	Control principle	Current limiting	Output current	Characteristic features
Control devices for single-ended converters					
497	Texas Instr.	voltage	dynamic	0.5 A	
3528	Silicon Gen.	voltage/current	dynamic	$\pm$ 0.2 A	1 MHz max.
3842	various	current	dynamic	$\pm$ 1 A	for primary switch reg.
4919	Siemens	voltage/current	dynamic	$\pm$ 0.5 A	with ripple compensation by feed-forward control
Control devices for single-ended and push-pull converters					
493	various	voltage	static	0.2 A	new: 593 ... 595
3624 A	various	voltage	dynamic	0.2 A	
3525	various	voltage	–	$\pm$ 0.4 A	inv. output: 3527
3526	various	voltage	dynamic	$\pm$ 0.2 A	
3825	Unitrode	voltage/current	dynamic	$\pm$ 1.5 A	1 MHz max.
3846	various	current	dynamic	$\pm$ 0.2 A	inv. output: 3847
4918	Siemens	voltage/current	dynamic	$\pm$ 0.5 A	with ripple compensation by feed-forward control

Manufacturers: Unitrode, Silicon General, Texas Instr., SGS

Fig. 18.74 Control devices for switched-mode power supplies

alternately. However, these can also be used in single-ended converters if one output is left uncommitted. If limiting the ON-time to 50% causes problems, it is also possible to OR the two outputs together.

The types with a $\pm$ preceding the output current rating have a push-pull output and are therefore capable of driving power MOSFETs directly. The other types have a single transistor at the output, whose emitter or collector signal can be used. If the obtainable output currents are inadequate, an additional power driver from Fig. 18.75 must be provided at the output.

In the case of *current-controlled* switching regulators, the sawtooth voltage required for pulsewidth regulation is derived from the current flowing through the power switch. This provides a faster reaction to load changes and automatic balance correction in the push-pull circuits. It additionally provides instantaneous ("dynamic") shutdown in the event of an overload.

All pulsewidth modulators have a *soft-start* circuit which makes the ON-time increase gradually to the steady-state value after the supply voltage has been applied. This prevents the power switches from being overloaded.

All the types have a current monitoring facility. Some have a current regulator which is designed to sense the DC output current of the switching regulator. It operates in parallel with the voltage regulator and reduces the output voltage by means of the ON-time if the maximum current is exceeded ("static current limiting"). Other types have "dynamic current limiting", which is designed to supervise the instantaneous value of the current through the power switch and to terminate the prevailing ON-condition if the limit is exceeded.

Type	Manufacturer	No. of drivers	Output current cont./peak	Maximum output voltage	Switching time	Technology
Si 9910[1]	Siliconix	1	0.2/1 A	18 V	100 ns	bipolar
TPQ 6002[2]	Sprague	2	± 0.25/0.5 A	30 V	30 ns	bipolar
D 469	Siliconix	4	± 0.25/0.5 A	14 V	30 ns	MOS
TSC 1428	Teledyne	2	± 0.25/1.5 A	18 V	30 ns	MOS
MAX 628	Maxim	2	± 0.25/1.5 A	18 V	30 ns	MOS
MC 34153	Motorola	2	± 0.4/1.5 A	18 V	15 ns	bipolar
UC 3707	Unitrode	2	± 0.5/1.5 A	38 V	40 ns	bipolar
SG 3626	Silicon Gen.	2	± 0.5/3 A	20 V	25 ns	bipolar
TSC 4429	Teledyne	1	± 0.5/6 A	18 V	35 ns	MOS
L 6203	SGS	2	± 3/5 A	50 V	200 ns	MOS

[1] Contains dU/dt-, dI/dt- and I_{max}-monitoring for MOSFETs
[2] Transistor array comprising 2 npn trans. 2N2219 and 2 pnp trans. 2N2905

Unwanted pulse suppression, which is incorporated in most types, inhibits multiple activation of the power switch during a pulse cycle. This might otherwise occur if the relatively high spikes occurring at the turn-off instant of the power switch are detected by the pulsewidth comparator.

The double-pulse inhibitor ensures that two turn-on pulses are never applied consecutively to one and the same power transistor of a push-pull converter.

19 Digital arithmetic circuitry

There are basically three different methods of digitally performing arithmetic operations:

1) using a microcomputer program,
2) using an arithmetic processor,
3) in parallel using hardware devices.

The first method is the cheapest but also the slowest, as the program has to process the data digit by digit.

With the second method, the microcomputer is augmented by a special arithmetic unit known as a "number cruncher". Although this also operates sequentially, it is specifically optimized for performing arithmetic operations. It therefore operates about 100 times faster.

The third method is the fastest. Here the arithmetic operations are performed in combinatorial logic. Its disadvantage is that the circuitry involved increases markedly with the word length to be processed.

19.1 Number representation

As digital circuits can only process binary, i.e. two-valued, variables, the number representation must be converted from the conventional decimal system to a binary system. The various methods of doing this are summarized in the following sections.

19.1.1 Positive integers in straight binary code

The simplest form of representation is the straight binary code. The digit positions are arranged in ascending powers of 2. For the straight binary representation of an N-digit number, we therefore have:

$$Z_N = z_{N-1} \cdot 2^{N-1} + z_{N-2} \cdot 2^{N-2} + \ldots + z_1 \cdot 2^1 + z_0 \cdot 2^0 = \sum_{i=0}^{N-1} z_i 2^i \; .$$

As in the decimal system, we simply write the digit sequence $\{z_{N-1} \ldots z_0\}$ and think in terms of multiplying the digits by the relevant power of two and adding.

Example:
$$15253_{dec} = \frac{1\;1\;1\;0\;1\;1\;1\;0\;0\;1\;0\;1\;0\;1}{2^{13} \ldots \ldots \ldots \ldots \ldots \ldots 2^0} \quad \begin{array}{l} \text{Straight binary} \\ \text{Weight} \end{array}$$

Octal code

As we can see, the straight binary representation is difficult to read. We therefore use an abbreviated notation by condensing binary numbers into groups of three and writing them as decimal digits. As the resulting digits are arranged in powers of $2^3 = 8$, this is known as octal code.

Example:	3	5	6	2	5	Octal
$15253_{dec} =$	0 1 1	1 0 1	1 1 0	0 1 0	1 0 1	Straight binary
	2^{12} 8^4	2^9 8^3	2^6 8^2	2^3 8^1	2^0 8^0	Weight

Hexadecimal code

Another commonly used abbreviated notation is obtained by combining binary digits into groups of four. As the resulting digits are arranged in powers of $2^4 = 16$, this is known as hexadecimal or simply hex code. Each digit can assume values between 0 and 15. Since we only have 10 decimal digits, the numbers "ten" to "fifteen" are represented by the letters A to F.

Example:	3	B	9	5	Hex
$15253_{dec} =$	0 0 1 1	1 0 1 1	1 0 0 1	0 1 0 1	Straight binary
	2^{12} 16^3	2^8 16^2	2^4 16^1	2^0 16^0	Weight

19.1.2   Positive integers in BCD code

Straight binary numbers are unsuitable for numeric input and output, as we are accustomed to calculating in the decimal system. Binary-coded decimal (BCD) notation has therefore been introduced, in which each individual decimal digit is represented by a binary number, e.g. by the corresponding straight binary number. In this case we have, for example

	1	5	2	5	3	Dec
$15253_{dec} =$	0 0 0 1	0 1 0 1	0 0 1 0	0 1 0 1	0 0 1 1	BCD
	10^4	10^3	10^2	10^1	10^0	Weight

A decimal number encoded in this way could more precisely be termed a BCD number in 8421 code or a natural BCD number. The individual decimal digits can also be represented by other binary combinations of four or more digits. As the 8421 BCD code is the most commonly used, it is often known simply as BCD code. We shall adopt this convention and draw the reader's attention to any deviations from natural BCD code.

Numbers between 0 and 15_{dec} can be represented using a four-digit straight binary number (tetrad). As only ten combinations are used in BCD code, this form of representation requires more bits than straight binary.

19.1.3 Binary integers of either sign

Signed-magnitude representation

A negative number can be characterized quite simply by placing a sign bit s in front of the highest-order digit. Zero means "positive", one means "negative". An unambiguous interpretation is only possible if a fixed word length has been agreed upon.

Example for an 8-bit word length:

$$+ 118_{dec} = \boxed{0} \quad 1 \ 1 \ 1 \ 0 \ 1 \ 1 \ 0_2$$
$$- 118_{dec} = \boxed{1} \quad 1 \ 1 \ 1 \ 0 \ 1 \ 1 \ 0_2$$
$$(-1)^s \quad 2^6 \ 2^5 \ 2^4 \ 2^3 \ 2^2 \ 2^1 \ 2^0$$

Two's-complement representation

The disadvantage of signed-magnitude representation is that positive and negative numbers cannot be added simply. An adder must be switched over to subtraction mode when a minus sign occurs. With two's-complement representation, this is unnecessary.

With 2's-complement representation, the most significant bit is given a negative weight. The rest of the number is represented in normal binary form. Once again a fixed word length must be agreed upon, so that the most significant bit is unambiguously defined. For a positive number, the most significant bit is 0. For a negative number, the most significant bit must be 1, because only this position has a negative weight.

Example for an 8-bit word length:

$$+ 118_{dec} = \boxed{0} \quad \underbrace{1 \ 1 \ 1 \ 0 \ 1 \ 1 \ 0}_{B_N}$$
$$- 118_{dec} = \boxed{1} \quad \underbrace{0 \ 0 \ 0 \ 1 \ 0 \ 1 \ 0}_{X}$$
$$-2^7 \ 2^6 \ 2^5 \ 2^4 \ 2^3 \ 2^2 \ 2^1 \ 2^0$$

The transition from a positive to a negative number of equal magnitude is of course somewhat more difficult than with signed-magnitude representation. Let us assume that the binary number B_N has word length N without the sign bit. The sign digit position therefore has the weight -2^N. The number $-B_N$ is therefore obtained in the form

$$- B_N = - 2^N + X \ .$$

The positive remainder X is therefore

$$X = 2^N - B_N \ .$$

This expression is known as the *two's-complement* $B_N^{(2)}$ to B_N. It can be easily calculated from B_N. For this purpose, we consider the largest number that can be represented in binary form using N digit positions. It has the value

$$1111 \ldots \triangleq 2^N - 1 \ .$$

If we subtract any binary number B_N from this number, we obviously obtain a binary number which is produced by negation of all the digits. This number is known as the *one's-complement* $B_N^{(1)}$ to B_N. We get

$$B_N^{(1)} = 2^N - 1 - B_N = \underbrace{2^N - B_N}_{B_N^{(2)}} - 1$$

and

$$\boxed{B_N^{(2)} = B_N^{(1)} + 1} \ . \tag{19.1}$$

The 2's-complement of a binary number is therefore the result of negation of all the digits and the addition of 1.

It can easily be demonstrated that it is not necessary to deal with the sign digit separately, but that, to change the sign, it is possible merely to form the 2's-complement of the entire number including the sign digit. For binary numbers in 2's-complement representation the following relationship therefore holds

$$\boxed{- B_N = B_N^{(2)}} \ . \tag{19.2}$$

This relation applies to the case in which we likewise consider only N digits in the result and disregard the overflow digit.

Example of an 8-digit binary number in 2's-complement representation:

$118_{dec} =$	01110110
1's complement	10001001
	$+ \qquad 1$
2's-complement	$\overline{10001010} = - 118_{dec}$

Reconversion:

1's-complement	01110101
	$+ \qquad 1$
2's-complement	$\overline{01110110} = + 118_{dec}$.

Sign extension

If we wish to expand a positive number to a larger word length, we simply add to the leading zeros. In 2's-complement, a different rule applies: we have to extend the sign bit.

Example: 8 bit   16 bit
$118_{dec} = 01110110 = 0000000001110110$
$-118_{dec} = 10001010 = 1111111110001010$

sign extension

The proof is simple. For an N-digit negative number, the sign bit has the value -2^{N-1}. If we extend the word length by one bit, we have to insert an additional leading "one". The added sign digit has the value -2^N. The old sign digit changes its value from -2^{N-1} to $+2^{N-1}$. The two together therefore have the value

$$-2^N + 2^{N-1} = -2\cdot 2^{N-1} + 2^{N-1} = -2^{N-1}$$

i.e., it remains unchanged.

Offset binary

Some circuits can only process positive numbers. They therefore always interpret the most significant digit as positive. In such cases we define the midpoint of the number range as being represented as zero (offset binary representation).

Using an 8-digit positive binary number, the range 0 to 255_{dec} can be represented, using an 8-digit 2's-complement number the range -128_{dec} to $+127_{dec}$. To change to offset binary representation, we shift the number range by adding 128 to 0 ... 255. Numbers above 128 are therefore to be treated as positive, numbers under 128 as negative. Range midpoint 128 means zero in this case. The addition of 128 can simply be performed by negating the sign bit in the 2's-complement notation. Some numeric values are listed in Fig. 19.1.

Decimal	2's-complement								Offset binary							
	b_7	b_6	b_5	b_4	b_3	b_2	b_1	b_0	b_7	b_6	b_5	b_4	b_3	b_2	b_1	b_0
127	0	1	1	1	1	1	1	1	1	1	1	1	1	1	1	1
1	0	0	0	0	0	0	0	1	1	0	0	0	0	0	0	1
0	0	0	0	0	0	0	0	0	1	0	0	0	0	0	0	0
-1	1	1	1	1	1	1	1	1	0	1	1	1	1	1	1	1
-127	1	0	0	0	0	0	0	1	0	0	0	0	0	0	0	1
-128	1	0	0	0	0	0	0	0	0	0	0	0	0	0	0	0

Fig. 19.1 Relationship between 2's-complement and offset binary representation

19.1.4   Fixed-point binary numbers

Like a decimal fraction, a binary fraction is defined such that the weights to the right of the point are interpreted as negative powers of 2.

Example:

$$225.8125_{dec} = \frac{1}{2^7} \; \frac{1}{2^6} \; \frac{1}{2^5} \; \frac{0}{2^4} \; \frac{0}{2^3} \; \frac{0}{2^2} \; \frac{0}{2^1} \; \frac{1}{2^0} \; . \; \frac{1}{2^{-1}} \; \frac{1}{2^{-2}} \; \frac{0}{2^{-3}} \; \frac{1}{2^{-4}}$$

In general, a fixed number of digits after the point is stipulated, hence the term fixed-point binary digit. Negative fixed-point numbers are given in signed-magnitude form.

When specifying a defined number of digits, it is possible, by multiplying with the reciprocal of the lowest power of two, to produce integers which can be processed in the notations described. For the numeric output, the multiplication is reversed again.

19.1.5   Floating-point binary numbers

In analogy to floating-point decimal numbers

$$Z_{10} = M \cdot 10^E \; ,$$

a floating-point binary number is defined as

$$Z_2 = M \cdot 2^E \; ,$$

where M is the mantissa and E the exponent.

Example:

225.8125	decimal, fixed point
$= 2.258125E2$	decimal, floating point
$= 11100001.1101$	straight binary, fixed point
$= 1.11000011101E0111$	straight binary, floating point

For computation with floating-point numbers, the notation specified in *IEEE Standard P754* is nowadays universally employed. This notation is used not only in mainframe computers, but also in PCs and even in some signal processors, and is in many cases supported by the corresponding arithmetic processors available. The user can choose between two precision formats: 32-bit single precision and double precision with 64 bit. Internally, computation is performed with 80-bit precision. These three formats are shown in Figs. 19.2 and 19.3. There are three distinct parts in each format: the sign bit S, the exponent E and the mantissa M. The word lengths of the exponent and mantissa are a function of the precision selected. In the IEEE Standard, the mantissa M is specified by the digits $m_0, m_1, m_2 \ldots$ Usually, the mantissa is normalized to $m_0 = 1$:

$$M = 1 + m_1 \cdot 2^{-1} + m_2 \cdot 2^{-2} + \ldots = 1 + \sum_{i=1}^{k} m_i 2^{-i} \; .$$

IEEE format	Word length	Sign S	Exponent length E	range	Mantissa length M	precision
Single	32 bit	1 bit	8 bit	$2^{\pm 127} \approx 10^{\pm 38}$	23 bit $\triangleq$	7 digits$_{dec}$
Double	64 bit	1 bit	11 bit	$2^{\pm 1023} \approx 10^{\pm 308}$	52 bit $\triangleq$	16 digits$_{dec}$
Internal	80 bit	1 bit	15 bit	$2^{\pm 16383} \approx 10^{\pm 4932}$	64 bit $\triangleq$	19 digits$_{dec}$

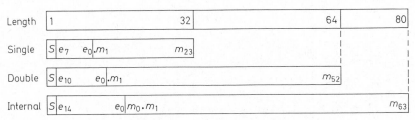

Fig. 19.3 Comparision of floating-point formats

Its absolute value is therefore $1 \le M < 2$. The digit $m_0 = 1$ is only specified for the internal notation, otherwise it is hidden and must be restored for the calculation.

The exponent E is specified in IEEE format as an offset binary number, so that positive and negative values can be defined. For the calculation, an offset amounting to half the range must be subtracted, namely

$$2^7 - 1 = \quad 127 \quad \text{for single precision,}$$
$$2^{10} - 1 = \quad 1023 \quad \text{for double precision,}$$
$$2^{14} - 1 = 16383 \quad \text{for internal precision.}$$

The sign of the integer is determined by the sign bit S, thus producing a signed-magnitude representation. The value of an IEEE number can therefore be calculated in the following manner:

$$Z = (-1)^S \cdot M \cdot 2^{E - \text{offset}} .$$

Taking the example of IEEE 32-bit single precision, we shall now examine this in somewhat greater detail. The segments of a word are shown in Fig. 19.4. The most significant bit is the sign bit S, followed by 8 bits for the exponent and 23 bits for the mantissa. The MSB (most significant bit) of the mantissa $m_0 = 1$ is hidden; the point is to the left of m_1. The weight of m_1 is therefore $\frac{1}{2}$.

The integer can be split up into two words of 16 bits, 4 bytes or 8 nibbles each. It can therefore be expressed by 8 hex characters. A number of examples are given in Fig. 19.5. The normalized number NOR$_1$ has an exponent of 127; after subtracting the offset from 127, we obtain a multiplier of $2^0 = 1$. The noted value of the mantissa is 0.75. This together with the hidden 1 produces the

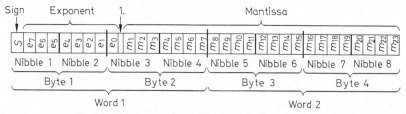

Fig. 19.4 Segmentation of a 32-bit floating-point number

$$\text{NOR}_1 \quad = 3\,F\,E\,0\,0\,0\,0\,0_{\text{hex}} \; = 0 \quad \underbrace{0\,1\,1\,1\,1\,1\,1\,1}_{127}.\underbrace{1\,1\,0\,0\dots0}_{0.75}= +1.75$$
$$+$$

$$\text{NOR}_2 \quad = B\,F\,B\,0\,0\,0\,0\,0_{\text{hex}} \; = 1 \quad \underbrace{0\,1\,1\,1\,1\,1\,1\,1}_{127}.\underbrace{0\,1\,1\,0\dots0}_{0.375}= -1.375$$
$$-$$

$$\text{NOR}_3 \quad = 4\,1\,2\,0\,0\,0\,0\,0_{\text{hex}} \; = 0 \quad \underbrace{1\,0\,0\,0\,0\,0\,1\,0}_{130}.\underbrace{0\,1\,0\,0\dots0}_{0.25}= +10$$
$$+$$

$$\text{NOR}_{\text{max}} = 7F7FFFF_{\text{hex}} \; = 0 \quad \underbrace{1\,1\,1\,1\,1\,1\,1\,0}_{254}.\underbrace{1\,1\,1\,1\dots1}_{1-2^{-23}}= +2^{127}(2-2^{-23})$$
$$+$$

$$\text{INF} \quad = 7\,F\,8\,0\,0\,0\,0_{\text{hex}} \; = 0 \quad \underbrace{1\,1\,1\,1\,1\,1\,1\,1}_{255}.\underbrace{0\,0\,0\,0\dots0}_{0}= +\infty$$
$$-$$

$$\text{ZERO} = 0\,0\,0\,0\,0\,0\,0\,0_{\text{hex}} \; = \times \quad \underbrace{0\,0\,0\,0\,0\,0\,0\,0}_{0}.\underbrace{0\,0\,0\,0\dots0}_{0}= \quad 0$$

Fig. 19.5 Examples of normalized numbers and exceptions in 32-bit floating-point format

specified value $+1.75$. In the second example NOR_2, a negative number has been selected; in this case $S=1$. The number 10 in the third example is represented in normalized form as $10 = 2^3 \cdot 1.25$. We arrive at the given hex representation in the usual way by organizing the bit string into groups of four and using the associated hex symbols. Unfortunately the hex representation of IEEE numbers is very involved, because the first symbol contains the sign and part of the exponent, and the third symbol a mixture of exponent and mantissa.

A couple of special cases are also listed in Fig. 19.5. The largest number that can be represented in 32-bit IEEE format is

$$\text{NOR}_{\text{max}} = 2^{254-127}(1 + 1 - 2^{-23}) = 2^{127}(2 - 2^{-23}) \approx 2^{128} \approx 3.4 \cdot 10^{38} \; .$$

The exponents 0 and 255 are reserved for exceptions. The exponent 255 is interpreted in conjunction with the mantissa as $\pm \infty$, depending on sign. If exponent and mantissa are both 0, the number is defined as $Z = 0$. In this case the sign is immaterial.

19.2   Code converters

19.2.1   Conversion of straight binary integers to BCD numbers

A simple method of binary-to-BCD conversion consists of having a straight binary counter and a decimal counter operating in parallel. If the two counters are started at zero and then stopped when the binary number to be converted is reached, the corresponding BCD number will be available at the output of the decimal counter. The disadvantage of this method is that up to 2^N counting steps have to be executed in order to convert an N-digit binary number. The method described below, on the other hand, requires only N computing steps.

For arithmetic operations in BCD code, results may arise containing the decimal "digits" 10_{dec} to 15_{dec}. Such unintended digits are called *pseudo-tetrads* (pseudo combinations). To correct for them, they must be reduced by $10_{dec} = 1010_2$ and the next higher tetrad increased by 1. This correction can also be achieved by adding $6 = 0110_2$ to the pseudo-tetrad, as shown by the following example:

	tens	:	units		tens	:	units
pseudo 13:	0000	:	1101		0000	:	1101
$- 10_{dec}$:	0000	:	1010	$+ 6$:	0000	:	0110
$+ 10_{dec}$:	0001	:	0000			:	
correct 13:	0001	:	0011		0001	:	0011

The above example illustrates the rule for converting a 4-bit straight binary number to a BCD number.

Numbers up to and including 9 remain unchanged.
Numbers over 9 must undergo the pseudo-tetrad correction.

Binary numbers of more than 4 bits are treated accordingly: beginning with the most significant bit (MSB), the straight binary number is shifted from right to left into a BCD "frame", as shown in Fig. 19.6. If a 1 crosses the boundary between the units- and the tens-column, an error is incurred. This is because, for the straight binary number, the weighting changes due to the shift from 8 to 16, whereas for the BCD number it changes only from 8 to 10. After such a shift, the BCD number has become too small by 6. To allow for this, a 6 must be added whenever a 1 crosses the boundary. Similarly, a 6 must be added in the tens-column when a 1 is transferred to the hundreds-column. The resulting BCD number then has the correct value but may still contain pseudo-tetrads. To avoid this, any pseudo-tetrads that do occur are immediately corrected after every shift by adding 6 to the decade in question and carrying 1 to the next decade. Both corrections require the same arithmetic operation, that is the addition of 6.

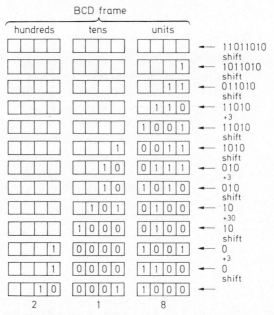

Fig. 19.6 Straight binary-to-BCD conversion; 218_{dec} as an example

Instead of adding 6 after the shift, one can equally well add 3 beforehand, since it can be ascertained before the shift whether or not a correction will be necessary: if the value of a tetrad is smaller than or equal to $4 = 0100_2$, the subsequent shift will result neither in a 1 crossing the column boundary nor in a pseudo-tetrad. The tetrad can therefore be shifted to the left unchanged. If the value of the tetrad before the shift is 5, 6 or 7, there again is no boundary crossing, as the most significant bit is zero. However, the pseudo-tetrads ten, twelve, fourteen, or eleven, thirteen, fifteen may arise depending on whether the next bit entering the frame is 0 or 1. In these cases a pseudo-tetrad correction is necessary, i.e. 3 must be added before the shift.

If the value of the tetrad before the shift is 8 or 9, the boundary crossing of the 1 must be corrected, giving the correct tetrads six or seven, or eight or nine, after the shift. Because of the immediate pseudo-tetrad correction, values higher than nine cannot arise. All possibilities are now taken care of, and we obtain the correction table in Fig. 19.7.

The conversion of a straight binary to the corresponding BCD number can be implemented by left shifting the straight binary into a shift register divided into 4-bit blocks (decades). A correction circuit is connected to each decade, which alters the contents of the register according to the truth table in Fig. 19.7 before the next shift is carried out.

Instead of a solution involving sequential logic circuits, combinatorial logic circuitry can be employed if the shift operation is performed by appropriate wiring. This possibility is shown in Fig. 19.8. Rather than shifting the number

Decimal	Input				Output				Function
I	x_3	x_2	x_1	x_0	y_3	y_2	y_1	y_0	Y
0	0	0	0	0	0	0	0	0	X
1	0	0	0	1	0	0	0	1	X
2	0	0	1	0	0	0	1	0	X
3	0	0	1	1	0	0	1	1	X
4	0	1	0	0	0	1	0	0	X
5	0	1	0	1	1	0	0	0	$X + 3$
6	0	1	1	0	1	0	0	1	$X + 3$
7	0	1	1	1	1	0	1	0	$X + 3$
8	1	0	0	0	1	0	1	1	$X + 3$
9	1	0	0	1	1	1	0	0	$X + 3$

Fig. 19.7 Correction system for the straight binary-to-BCD conversion

from right to left, the BCD frame may be shifted from left to right and each tetrad corrected according to the table in Fig. 19.7. In order to be able to hard-wire the frame shift, an individual correction network is necessary for each decade and each shifting "step". The total circuit may be simplified by omitting a correction network whenever fewer than 3 bits are applied at the input, as in this case a correction is definitely not required. Figure 19.8 shows the combinatorial logic circuit for the conversion of an 8-bit binary number, where the omitted elements are drawn with dashed lines. The circuit can be extended to

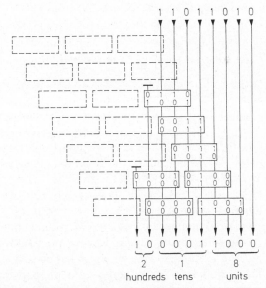

Fig. 19.8 Straight binary-to-BCD conversion using correction networks. The values shown refer to the example of 218_{dec}

deal with larger numbers by expanding its characteristic pattern. The numbers in the diagram apply to the example of Fig. 19.6 and illustrate the conversion procedure.

The correction network is available as a manufacturer-programmed, 256-byte ROM (SN 74 S 485). Five networks are combined to form a block, as in Fig. 19.9. As comparison with Fig. 19.8 shows, an 8-digit binary number can be converted using two ICs. A 16-digit binary number requires eight ICs.

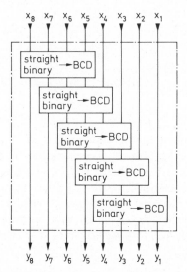

Fig. 19.9 Functional diagram of binary-to-BCD converter SN 74 S 485

19.2.2   Conversion of BCD to straight binary code

In many cases the BCD code can be generated directly in a simple way, e.g. using BCD counters. As will be discussed later, many arithmetic operations can also be performed in BCD code, but sometimes conversion to straight binary numbers is necessary. This can be achieved by a repeated division by 2. To begin with, the binary coded decimal number is divided by 2, and if it is an odd number, a remainder of 1 is obtained, i.e. the 2^0-bit has the value 1. The quotient is again divided by 2. If the remainder is 0, the 2^1-bit is 0, and if the remainder is 1, the 2^1-bit has the value 1. The more significant bits of the straight binary number are obtained accordingly.

The division of a BCD number by 2 can be carried out simply by shifting it one place to the right, since the individual decades are already straight-binary coded. In each case, the remainder is the bit which has been "pushed out" of the BCD frame. If, during shifting, a 1 crosses the boundary between two columns, an error is incurred: when crossing from the tens to the units, the bit weighting of the shifted 1 must be halved from 10 to 5. However, for a straight binary number, the assigned weighting would be 8 so that, for a correction, 3 must be subtracted. Therefore the following correction rule applies: If the MSB of a column (decade) after shifting is 1, a subtraction of 3 is required in this particular decade. The truth table of the correction network in Fig. 19.10 can

Decimal	Input				Output				Function
I	x_3	x_2	x_1	x_0	y_3	y_2	y_1	y_0	Y
0	0	0	0	0	0	0	0	0	X
1	0	0	0	1	0	0	0	1	X
2	0	0	1	0	0	0	1	0	X
3	0	0	1	1	0	0	1	1	X
4	0	1	0	0	0	1	0	0	X
5	0	1	0	1	0	1	0	1	X
6	0	1	1	0	0	1	1	0	X
7	0	1	1	1	0	1	1	1	X
8	1	0	0	0	0	1	0	1	$X - 3$
9	1	0	0	1	0	1	1	0	$X - 3$
10	1	0	1	0	0	1	1	1	$X - 3$
11	1	0	1	1	1	0	0	0	$X - 3$
12	1	1	0	0	1	0	0	1	$X - 3$
13	1	1	0	1	1	0	1	0	$X - 3$
14	1	1	1	0	1	0	1	1	$X - 3$
15	1	1	1	1	1	1	0	0	$X - 3$

$x_3 \ x_2 \ x_1 \ x_0$

BCD → straight binary

$y_3 \ y_2 \ y_1 \ y_0$

Fig. 19.10 Correction system for BCD-to-straight binary conversion

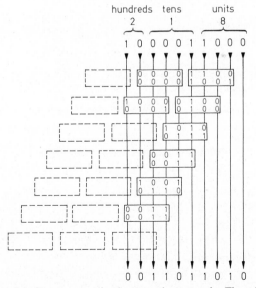

Fig. 19.11 BCD-to-straight binary conversion by correction networks. The values entered refer to the example of 218_{dec}

thus be directly determined. The conversion is complete when the BCD number has been entirely "pushed out" of the frame.

Figure 19.11 shows a combinatorial logic system for the conversion of a $2\frac{1}{2}$-digit BCD number. In analogy to Fig. 19.8, shifting of the BCD frame is achieved by hard-wiring identical correction networks. To illustrate the basic structure, all three correction networks required for each shift are shown. If the MSB is not used, no correction is necessary as can be seen in Fig. 19.10, and the corresponding correction networks can be omitted. In Fig. 19.11, they are shown by dashed lines.

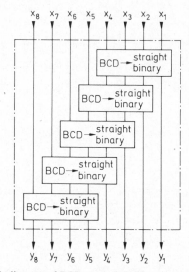

Fig. 19.12 Block diagram of BCD-to-straight binary converter SN 74 S 484

The correction networks are available as blocks of five in the form of manufacturer-programmed 256-byte ROM (SN 74 S 484). To convert two BCD decades, one IC is required. Four BCD decades require five ICs.

19.3 Combinatorial shift register (barrel shifter)

For many arithmetic operations, a bit pattern must be shifted by one or more binary digits. This operation is usually carried out by a shift register, as described in Section 10.5. A single clock pulse results in a shift by one bit. There is a disadvantage, however, in that a sequential controller is necessary to organize loading of the bit pattern into the shift register and the subsequent shifting by a given number of binary digits.

The same operation may be carried out without recourse to clocked sequential control by employing instead a combinatorial network involving multiplexers, as illustrated in Fig. 19.13. For this reason, the unclocked shift registers involved are termed combinatorial or asynchronous shift registers. If, in Fig. 19.13, the address $A = 0$ is applied, then $y_3 = x_3$, $y_2 = x_2$ etc., but if $A = 1$, then $y_3 = x_2$, $y_2 = x_1$, $y_1 = x_0$ and $y_0 = x_{-1}$, due to the wiring arrangement of the multiplexers. The bit pattern X therefore appears at the output left-shifted by one digit. As with a normal shift register, the MSB is lost. If multiplexers with N inputs are used, a shift of $0, 1, 2 \ldots (N - 1)$ bits can be executed. For the example in Fig. 19.13, $N = 4$; the corresponding function table is shown in Fig. 19.14.

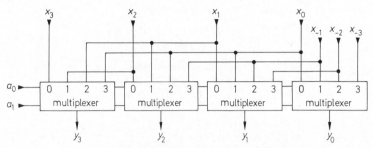

Fig. 19.13 Barrel shifter made up of multiplexers

a_1	a_0	y_3	y_2	y_1	y_0
0	0	x_3	x_2	x_1	x_0
0	1	x_2	x_1	x_0	x_{-1}
1	0	x_1	x_0	x_{-1}	x_{-2}
1	1	x_0	x_{-1}	x_{-2}	x_{-3}

Fig. 19.14 Function table of the barrel shifter

If the loss of MSBs is to be avoided, the shift register may be extended by adding identical elements, as illustrated in Fig. 19.15. For the chosen example, where $N = 4$, a 5-bit number X can be shifted in this way by a maximum of 3 bits without loss of information. The shifted number then appears at outputs y_3 to y_7.

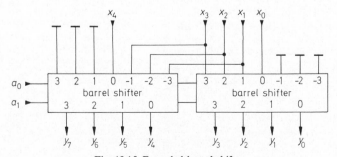

Fig. 19.15 Extended barrel shifter

The circuit in Fig. 19.13 can also be operated as a ring shifter if the extension inputs x_{-1} to x_{-3} are connected to inputs x_1 to x_3, as in Fig. 19.16.

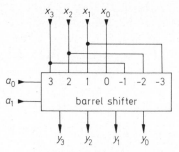

Fig. 19.16 Ring shifter

IC types:

4 bit (TTL):	Am 25 S 10	from AMD
16 bit (TTL):	SN 74 AS 897	from Texas Instruments
32 bit (CMOS):	LSH 32	from Logic Devices.

19.4   Digital comparators

Comparators check two numbers, A and B, against one another, the relations of interest being $A = B$, $A > B$ and $A < B$. We shall first consider comparators which determine whether two binary numbers are equal (identity comparators). The criterion for this is that all corresponding bits of the two numbers are identical. The comparator will produce at its output a logic 1 if the numbers are equal, otherwise a logic 0. In the simplest case, the two numbers consist of only one bit each; to compare them, the EQUIV operation (exclusive-NOR gate) may be used. Two N-bit numbers are compared bit by bit using an EQUIV circuit for each binary digit and the outputs are combined by an AND gate, as shown in Fig. 19.17.

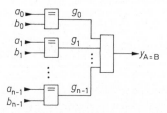

Fig. 19.17 Identity comparator for two N-bit numbers

IC-types:

2 × 8 inputs: SN 74 LS 688 (TTL) from Texas-Instr.
2 × 9 inputs: Am 29809 (TTL) from AMD.
2 × 10 inputs: SN 74 LS 460 from MMI.

Comparators have a wider range of application if, in addition to indicating equality, they can also determine which of two numbers is the larger. Such circuits are known as magnitude comparators. To enable a comparison of the magnitude of two numbers, their code must be known, and for the following, we assume that both numbers are straight binary coded, i.e. that

$$A = a_N \cdot 2^N + a_{N-1} \cdot 2^{N-1} + \cdots + a_1 \cdot 2^1 + a_0 \cdot 2^0 \ .$$

The simplest case is again that of comparing two single-bit numbers. The formulation of the logic functions is based on the truth table of Fig. 19.18. From these, we can directly obtain the circuit in Fig. 19.19.

a	b	$y_{a>b}$	$y_{a=b}$	$y_{a<b}$
0	0	0	1	0
0	1	0	0	1
1	0	1	0	0
1	1	0	1	0

Fig. 19.18 Truth table of a 1-bit magnitude comparator

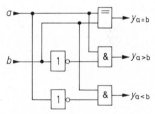

Fig. 19.19 1-bit magnitude comparator

The following algorithm is used for comparing numbers consisting of more than one bit: To begin with, the most significant bit (MSB) of A is compared with the MSB of B. If they are different, these bits are sufficient to determine the result. If they are equal, the next lower significant bit must compared, etc. If the identity variable of digit i is denoted by g_i, as in Fig. 19.17, the magnitude comparison of an N-digit number is given by the general relation

$$y_{A>B} = a_{N-1} \cdot \bar{b}_{N-1} + g_{N-1} \cdot a_{N-2} \cdot \bar{b}_{N-2} + \ldots + g_{N-1} \cdot g_{N-2} \cdot \ldots \cdot g_1 \cdot a_0 \cdot \bar{b}_0 \ .$$

IC types:

for 5-digit comparison: MC 10166 (ECL)
for 8-digit comparison: SN 74 LS 682 . . . 689 (TTL).

The circuits can be cascaded serially or in parallel, Fig. 19.20 showing the serial method. When the 3 most significant bits are the same, the outputs of comparator C_1 determine the result, as they are connected to the LSB inputs of comparator C_2 (LSB = least significant bit).

When comparing many-bit numbers it is better to employ parallel cascading, as in Fig. 19.21, since the propagation delay time is shorter.

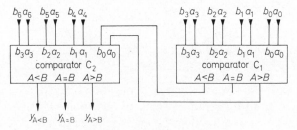

Fig. 19.20 Serial magnitude comparator

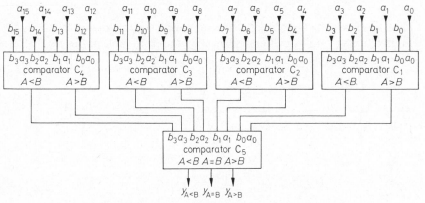

Fig. 19.21 Parallel magnitude comparator

19.5 Adders

19.5.1 Half-adder

Adders are circuits which give the sum of two binary numbers. We shall first describe adders for straight binary numbers. The simplest case is the addition of two single-bit numbers. To devise the logic circuit, all possible cases must first be investigated so that a logic function table can be compiled. The following cases can occur if two single-bit numbers A and B are to be added:

$$0 + 0 = 0 ,$$
$$0 + 1 = 1 ,$$
$$1 + 0 = 1 ,$$
$$1 + 1 = 10 .$$

If both A and B are 1, a carry to the next higher bit is obtained. The adder must therefore have two outputs, one for the sum and one for the carry to the next higher bit. The truth table in Fig. 19.22 can be deduced by expressing the numbers A and B by the logic variables a_0 and b_0. The carry is represented by the variable c_1, and the sum by the variable s_0.

By setting up the canonical products, the Boolean functions

$$c_1 = a_0 b_0$$

and

$$s_0 = \bar{a}_0 b_0 + a_0 \bar{b}_0 = a_0 \oplus b_0$$

are obtained. The carry thus represents an AND operation, the sum an exclusive-OR operation. A circuit implementing both operations is known as a half-adder and is shown in Fig. 19.23.

a_0	b_0	s_0	c_1
0	0	0	0
0	1	1	0
1	0	1	0
1	1	0	1

Fig. 19.22 Truth table of the half-adder

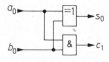

Fig. 19.23 Circuit of the half-adder

19.5.2 Full-adder

If two straight binary numbers of more than one digit are to be added, the half-adder can only be used for the LSB. For all other binary digits, not two but three bits must be added, as the carry from the next lower binary digit must be included. In general, each bit requires a logic circuit with three inputs, a_i, b_i and c_i, and two outputs, s_i and c_{i+1}. Such circuits are called full-adders and can be implemented as in Fig. 19.24, using two half-adders. Their truth table is given in Fig. 19.25.

For each bit, a full-adder is required, but for the LSB a half-adder is sufficient. Figure 19.26 shows a circuit suitable for adding two 4-bit numbers, A and B. Such circuits are available as ICs, but usually a full-adder is used for

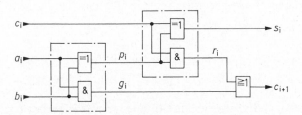

Fig. 19.24 Full-adder. $s_i = a_i \oplus b_i \oplus c_i$; $c_{i+1} = a_i b_i + a_i c_i + b_i c_i$

Input			Internal			Output		Decimal
a_i	b_i	c_i	p_i	g_i	r_i	s_i	c_{i+1}	Σ
0	0	0	0	0	0	0	0	0
0	1	0	1	0	0	1	0	1
1	0	0	1	0	0	1	0	1
1	1	0	0	1	0	0	1	2
0	0	1	0	0	0	1	0	1
0	1	1	1	0	1	0	1	2
1	0	1	1	0	1	0	1	2
1	1	1	0	1	0	1	1	3

Fig. 19.25 Truth table of the full-adder

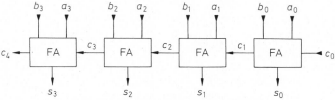

Fig. 19.26 4-bit addition with ripple carry

the LSB also, in order to enable the circuit to be extended as required (SN 74 LS 83).

19.5.3   Look-ahead carry logic

The computing time of the adder in Fig. 19.26 is considerably longer than that of the individual stages, because the carry c_4 can assume its correct value only after c_3 has been determined. The same applies to all the previous carries (ripple carry). To shorten the computing time for the addition of many-bit straight binary numbers, a look-ahead carry generator (parallel or simultaneous carry logic) can be used. In this method, all carries are determined directly from the input variables. From the truth table in Fig. 19.25, the general relation for the carry of stage i can be deduced:

$$c_{i+1} = \underbrace{a_i b_i}_{g_i} + \underbrace{(a_i \oplus b_i)c_i}_{p_i} . \tag{19.3}$$

The quantities g_i and p_i are introduced for brevity and appear as intermediate variables in the full-adder of Fig. 19.24. Their calculation therefore requires no additional complexity. These variables can be interpreted as follows: the quantity g_i indicates whether or not the input combination a_i, b_i results in a carry in stage i, and is therefore called the generate variable. The quantity p_i indicates whether the input combination causes a carry from the next lower-order stage to be absorbed or passed on. It is therefore called the propagate variable.

From Eq. (19.3), we obtain successively the individual carries

$$
\begin{aligned}
c_1 &= g_0 + p_0 c_0 \ , \\
c_2 &= g_1 + p_1 c_1 = g_1 + p_1 g_0 + p_1 p_0 c_0 \ , \\
c_3 &= g_2 + p_2 c_2 = g_2 + p_2 g_1 + p_2 p_1 g_0 + p_2 p_1 p_0 c_0 \ , \\
c_4 &= g_3 + p_3 c_3 = g_3 + p_3 g_2 + p_3 p_2 g_1 + p_3 p_2 p_1 g_0 + p_3 p_2 p_1 p_0 c_0 \\
&\ \ \vdots \qquad\quad \vdots
\end{aligned}
\tag{19.4}
$$

It can be seen that the expressions become ever more complicated, but that they can be computed from the auxiliary variables within the propagation delay time of two gates.

Figure 19.27 shows the block diagram of a 4-bit adder with look-ahead carry logic. The Eqs. (19.4) are implemented in the carry generator. The complete circuit is available on a single chip.

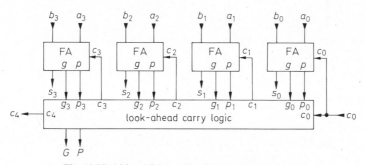

Fig. 19.27 4-bit addition with look-ahead carry logic

IC types:

TTL: SN 74 LS 181; SN 74 S 281; SN 74 LS 381; SN 74 LS 382; SN 74 LS 681
CMOS (4 × 4 bit = 16 bit): L 4 C 381 from Logic Dev.; IDT 7381

Adder networks for more than 4 bits can be realized by cascading several 4-bit blocks. The carry c_4 would then be applied as c_0 to the next block up. This method however, is somewhat inconsistent because the carry is parallel-processed within the blocks but serially between the blocks.

To obtain short computation times, the carries from block to block must therefore also be parallel-processed. The relationship for c_4 in Eq. (19.4) is thus reconsidered:

$$
c_4 = \underbrace{g_3 + p_3 g_2 + p_3 p_2 g_1 + p_3 p_2 p_1 g_0}_{G} + \underbrace{p_3 p_2 p_1 p_0}_{P} c_0 \ .
\tag{19.5}
$$

To abbreviate, the block-generate variable G and the block-propagate variable P are introduced, and

$$c_4 = G + Pc_0$$

is obtained. The form of this equation is the same as that of Eq. (19.3). Within the individual 4-bit adder blocks, only the additional auxiliary variables G and P need be computed; when these are known, the algorithm given in Eq. (19.4) and used for the bit-to-bit carries, can also be used for the carries from block to block. The result is the block diagram given in Fig. 19.28 for a 16-bit adder with look-ahead carry logic. The carry logic is identical to that of the 4-bit adder in Fig. 19.27. It can be obtained as a separate IC. When performing a 16-bit addition with TTL circuits, the computation time is 36 ns; for Schottky-TTL circuits it is reduced to 19 ns.

IC carry blocks:
For 4 digits: SN 74182 (TTL), MC 10179 (ECL), MC 14582 (CMOS)
For 8 digits: SN 74 LS 882 (TTL), 67 S 583 . . . 585 (TTL) from MMI

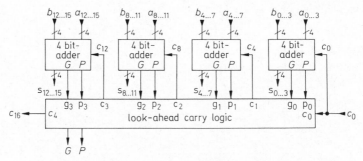

Fig. 19.28 16-bit addition with look-ahead carry logic on two levels

19.5.4   Addition of BCD numbers

For the addition of two BCD numbers, a 4-bit straight binary adder can be used for each decade. After the addition, a correction is necessary, as has already been discussed for straight binary-to-BCD conversion: if a carry arises in a decade, 6 must be added to allow for the difference in the bit weighting. The result obtained is a BCD number already having the correct value, although it may still contain pseudo-tetrads. It is therefore necessary to check whether a number larger than 9 has occurred in any decade. If this is the case, 6 must again be added to eliminate the pseudo-tetrad. The carry thus obtained is transferred to the next higher decade in the same way as the ordinary carry. The described operations are effected most simply by using a second adder for each decade, as shown in Fig. 19.29. The entire arrangement is available as a monolithic integrated circuit.

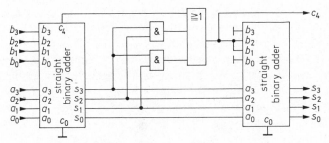

Fig. 19.29 BCD addition with straight-binary adders

IC types (TTL):
N 82 S 82, N 82 S 83 (Signetics), 74 F 582, 74 F 583 (Fairchild)

19.5.5 Subtraction

The subtraction of two numbers can be reduced to an addition, since

$$D = A - B = A + (-B) .$$

(19.6)

If the numbers are represented in 2's-complement, for a specified word length N, we can derive from Eq. (19.2) the simple relation

$$-B_N = B_N^{(2)} .$$

The difference is therefore

$$D_N = A_N + B_N^{(2)} .$$

To calculate the difference, we therefore have to form the 2's-complement of B_N and add it to A_N. For this purpose we must negate all the digits of B_N (1's-complement) and add 1, as stated in Eq. (19.1). The addition of A_N and 1 can be performed by one and the same adder by utilizing the carry input. This results in the 4-bit circuit shown in Fig. 19.30.

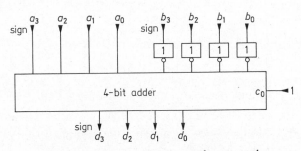

Fig. 19.30 Subtraction of two's complement numbers

$$D = A - B$$

In order to ensure that the difference D_N appears in the correct 2's-complement notation, A_N and B_N must likewise be entered in this format, i.e. for positive numbers the MSB must be 0.

The 181-series integrated adders described in Section 19.5.3 have control inputs enabling the input numbers to be complemented. They are therefore also suitable as subtractors. As further control inputs can be used to select logic operations for the input variables, these devices are generally known as arithmetic logic units. (ALUs).

19.5.6   Two's-complement overflow

When two positive N-digit binary numbers are added together, the result can be an $(N + 1)$-digit number. This overflow is recognizable from the fact that, from the most significant digit, a carry is produced.

In 2's-complement notation, the leftmost digit position is reserved for the sign. When two negative numbers are added, a carry into the overflow position will systematically occur, as the sign digit of the two numbers is 1. When processing 2's-complement numbers of either sign, the occurrence of a carry into the overflow position does not therefore necessarily mean that an overflow has taken place.

An overflow can be detected as follows: when two positive numbers are added, the result must also be positive. If the sum is out of range, a carry into the overflow position occurs, i.e. the result becomes "negative". This indicates a positive overflow. Similarly, a negative overflow is present if a "positive" result is obtained when two negative numbers are added. When a positive and a negative number are added, no overflow can occur, as the magnitude of the difference is then smaller than the numbers entered.

The occurrence of a 2's-complement overflow can be easily detected by comparing the carry c_{N-1} into the sign position with the carry c_N out of the sign position (Fig. 19.31). An overflow has taken place precisely when these two carries are different. This case is decoded by the exclusive-or gate. This output is available on the 4-bit arithmetic unit SN 74 LS 382.

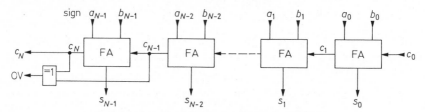

Fig. 19.31 Forming the 2's-complement overflow OV

19.5.7   Addition and subtraction of floating-point numbers

When processing floating-point numbers, the mantissa and exponent must be handled separately. For addition, it is first necessary to adjust the exponents so that they are the same. To do this, we take the difference of the exponents and shift the mantissa associated with the smaller exponent the corresponding number of bits to the right. Then both numbers have the same, namely the larger, exponent. It is passed on via the multiplexer in Fig. 19.32 to the output. The two mantissas can now be added or subtracted, generally producing a non-normalized result, i.e. the leading 1 in the mantissa is not in the correct position. To normalize the result, the leftmost 1 in the mantissa is located using a priority decoder (see Section 9.6.4). The mantissa is then shifted to the left by the corresponding number of bits and the exponent is reduced accordingly [19.1]. Some examples of IC floating-point adders are given in Fig. 19.36.

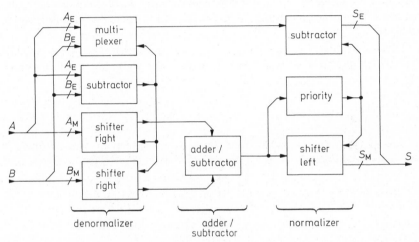

Fig. 19.32 Arrangement for adding/subtracting floating-point numbers A and B (indices: E = exponent, M = mantissa)

19.6 Multiplier

19.6.1 Multiplication of fixed-point numbers

Multiplication of two straight binary numbers is best illustrated by an example. The product $13 \cdot 11 = 143$ is to be calculated:

$$1101 \cdot 1011$$

$$
\begin{array}{r}
1101 \\
+ \quad 1101 \\
+ \quad 0000 \\
+ \quad 1101 \\
\hline
10001111
\end{array}
$$

The calculation is particularly easy because only multiplications by either 1 or 0 occur. The product is obtained by consecutive shifting of the multiplicand to the left by 1 bit at a time, and by adding or not adding, depending on whether the corresponding multiplier bit is 1 or 0. The individual bits are processed consecutively, and this method is therefore known as serial multiplication.

Multiplication can be implemented by combining a shift register and an adder, although such a circuit would require a sequential controller. As is described for the straight binary-to-BCD conversion, the shifting process can also be carried out by a combinatorial network if N adders are suitably staggered and interconnected. This method requires a large number of adders, but the shift register and the sequential controller are no longer needed. The main advantage, however, is the considerably reduced computation time since, instead of the time-consuming clock control, only gate propagation delays are incurred.

Figure 19.33 shows a suitable circuit for a combinatorial 4 × 4-bit multiplier. For the additions, we can usefully employ the SN 74 LS 381 chip, whereby

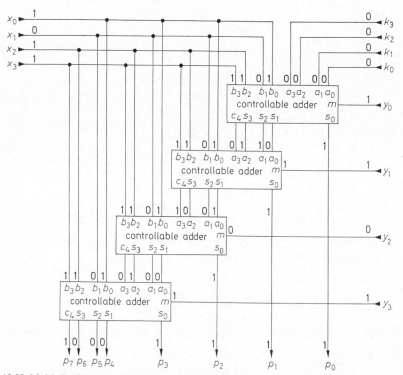

Fig. 19.33 Multiplier for two 4-bit numbers. The values entered refer to the example $13 \cdot 11 = 143$.

Result: $P = X \cdot Y + K$

addition can be activated and deactivated via control inputs, giving

$$S = \begin{cases} A + 0 & \text{for} \quad m = 0 \\ A + B & \text{for} \quad m = 1 \end{cases}.$$

The multiplier is applied bit by bit to the control inputs m. The multiplicand is fed in parallel to the four addition inputs b_0 to b_3.

To begin with, we assume that the number $K = 0$. We then obtain the expression

$$S_0 = X \cdot y_0$$

at the output of the first element, corresponding to the first partial product in the above multiplication algorithm. The LSB of S_0 represents the LSB of the product P; it is transferred directly to the output. The more significant bits of S_0 are added in the second element to the expression $X \cdot y_1$. The resulting sum is the subtotal of the partial products in the first and second line of the multiplication algorithm. The LSB of this sum gives the second lowest bit of P and is therefore transferred to the output p_1. The subsequent subtotals are treated accordingly. We have entered in Fig. 19.33 the numbers of the above example to demonstrate this process.

The additional inputs k_0 to k_3 can be used to add a 4-bit number K to the total product P, so that the multiplier function becomes

$$P = X \cdot Y + K .$$

The method of expansion for larger numbers can now be understood. For each additional bit of the multiplier Y, a further arithmetic unit is added at the bottom left of the circuit. If the multiplicand X is to be increased, the word length is enlarged by cascading an appropriate number of arithmetic units at each stage.

In the multiplication method described, the new partial product is always added to the previous subtotal. This technique requires the fewest elements and results in straightforward and easily extensible circuitry. The computing time can be shortened if as many summations as possible are carried out simultaneously and if the individual subtotals are added afterwards by a fast adder circuit. Several procedures are available which differ only in the adding sequence (Wallace Tree) [19.2]. Another way of reducing the computing time is to use the Booth algorithm [19.3]. The multiplier bits are combined into pairs, thereby halving the number of adders required, and the computing time is reduced accordingly.

Commercially available multipliers not only contain a multiplier core but also an input and output register. Often the results of several multiplications must be accumulated. Therefore many multipliers also contain an adder on the same chip. The most popular type for such a multiplier-accumulator (MAC) is the 1010 offered by various manufacturers under related names. A simplified schematic is shown in Fig. 19.34. Beside the multiplier array there are edge triggered input registers for the two 16-bit operands X and Y. A third register stores the

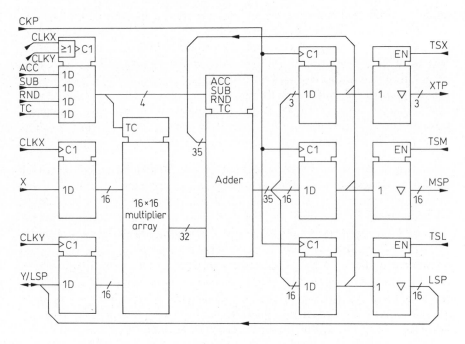

Fig. 19.34 Schematic of a 1010-type multiplier-accumulator (simplified)

control variables Accumulate (ACC), Subtract (SUB), Round (RND) and Two's Complement (TC). The 32 bit output of the multiplier is not directly connected to the output register but an adder is inserted. It can add or subtract the last result stored in the output register or transfer the product unchanged. The accumulate path has 3 additional bits; in this way at least 8 products can be summed without overflow. The result can be rounded to 16 bit by adding a binary 1 to the most significant bit of the LSP with carry. With the TC input the circuit can be switched to two's complement or unsigned magnitude number representation. The new result is transferred to the output register by the CKP clock. It is made available by enabling the tristate buffers at the output. If the LSP output word is needed, it must be multiplexed with the Y input.

Figure 19.36 presents a survey of some popular multipliers. The word length for the operands is between 8 and 32 bits. Multiplication produces a result with double the word length. In order to minimize the pin count, on many types the data are transferred into or out of the multiplier in multiplexed form or via bidirectional lines. Nevertheless, many multipliers have over 100 pins. Arithmetic units nowadays invariably employ CMOS technology. As we can see from Fig. 19.36, they are nevertheless no longer slower than their TTL predecessors.

However, they require only a fraction of the current even at high clock frequencies, thereby completely obviating the need for heat sinks and fans. Systems designed for very high speeds are still being implemented mainly in ECL technology. For these applications, ECL types are the only solution, as the use of level converters would introduce additional delays.

Most types have an input which can be used to specify whether signed-magnitude or 2's-complement calculation is required. Some types additionally have an accumulator, enabling a number to be added to the product. This task arises particularly often in digital signal processing (see Chapter 24).

19.6.2 Multiplication of floating-point numbers

To multiply floating-point numbers, the mantissas of both numbers have to be multiplied and their exponents added, as shown in Fig. 19.35. During this process, an overflow in the mantissa may occur. The result can be renormalized by shifting the mantissa one place to the right and increasing the exponent by 1. Denormalization as used with the floating-point adder in Fig. 19.32 is not required in this case; the complexity lies in the multiplier [19.1].

Some examples of floating-point arithmetic units are listed in Fig. 19.37. The specified computing power means that the operands are loaded at the specified frequency and the results can also be read out at that frequency. However, due to the internal pipeline structure, the results are generally delayed by one or more clock pulses. Consequently, in order to achieve the full computing power, several operations must be begun consecutively before the first result appears at the output.

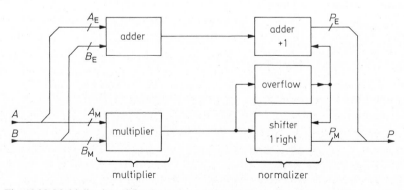

Fig. 19.35 Multiplication of floating-point numbers (indices: E = exponent, M = mantissa)

Type	Manufacturer	Technology	Functions	I/O ports [bit]	Computing power [MOPS]	Power dissipation [mW]
8-bit operands (TDC 1008-, SN 74 S 558-series)						
ADSP 1080 A*	Analog Dev.	CMOS	$\times$	$\to 8 \to 8 \quad 16 \to$	30	275
ADSP 1008 A	Analog Dev.	CMOS	$\times\ \Sigma$	$\to 8 \to 8 \quad 16 \to$	20	100
TMC 2208	TRW	CMOS	$\times\ \Sigma$	$\to 8 \to 8 \quad 16 \to$	25	300
12-bit operands (TDC 1009-series)						
IDT 7212*	IDT	CMOS	$\times$	$\to 12 \to 12 \quad 24 \to$	25	150
IDT 7209*	IDT	CMOS	$\times\ \Sigma$	$\to 12 \to 12 \quad 24 \to$	25	200
MC 10951	Motorola	ECL	$\times$	$\to 12 \to 12 \quad 24 \to$	70	6500
16-bit operands (TDC 1010-, Am 29516-series)						
IDT 7216*	IDT	CMOS	$\times$	$\to 16 \to 16 \to 16 \to$	50	220
IDT 7210*	IDT	CMOS	$\times\ \Sigma$	$\to 16 \to 16 \to 16 \to$	40	220
IDT 738 I	IDT	CMOS	$+\ -$	$\to 16 \to 16 \quad 16 \to$	50	150
IDT 7216	IDT	CMOS	$\times$	$\to 16 \to 16 \to 16 \to$	50	220
IDT 7210	IDT	CMOS	$\times\ \Sigma$	$\to 16 \to 16 \to 16 \to$	40	220
L4 C 381	Logic Dev.	CMOS	$+\ -$	$\to 16 \to 16 \quad 16 \to$	30	60
LMU 18	Logic Dev.	CMOS	$\times$	$\to 16 \to 16 \quad 32 \to$	28	300
PDSP 1601	Plessey	CMOS	$+\ -\ \leftrightarrow$	$\to 16 \to 16 \to 16 \to$	20	300
PDSP 16116	Plessey	CMOS	$\times (a + jb)$	$\to 16^4 \quad 16^2 \to$	10	400
PDSP 16318	Plessey	CMOS	$+\ -\ (a + jb)$	$\to 16^2 \quad 16^2 \to$	20	350
PDSP 16330	Plessey	CMOS	$\sqrt{x^2 + y^2}$	$\to 16^2 \quad 16^2 \to$	20	400
PDSP 16340	Plessey	CMOS	$r, \varphi \to x, y$	$\to 16^2 \quad 16^2 \to$	20	400
ADSP 1110 A	Analog Dev.	CMOS	$\times\ \Sigma$	$\to 16 \to$	12	150
ADSP 1101 A	Analog Dev.	CMOS	$\times\ \Sigma\ +\ -$	$\to 16 \to 16 \to 16 \to$	15	300
ADSP 7018	Analog Dev.	TTL	$\times$	$\to 16 \to 16 \quad 32 \to$	50	3000
ADSP 7011	Analog Dev.	TTL	$\times\ \Sigma$	$\to 16 \to 16 \quad 32 \to$	67	4500
ADSP 8018	Analog Dev.	ECL	$\times$	$\to 16 \to 16 \quad 32 \to$	67	3000
ADSP 8011	Analog Dev.	ECL	$\times\ \Sigma$	$\to 16 \to 16 \quad 32 \to$	80	5500
24-bit operands						
ADSP 1024 A	Analog Dev.	CMOS	$\times$	$\to 24 \to 24 \quad 24 \to$	10	300
32-bit operands						
L 64032	LSI-Logic	CMOS	$\times\ \Sigma$	$\to 32 \to 32 \quad 32 \to$	10	900
Am 29 C 323	AMD	CMOS	$\times\ \Sigma$	$\to 32 \to 32 \quad 32 \to$	10	750
Am 29323	AMD	TTL	$\times\ \Sigma$	$\to 32 \to 32 \quad 32 \to$	14	
Am 29423	AMD	ECL	$\times\ \Sigma$	$\to 32 \to 32 \quad 32 \to$	20	6200
Am 29 C 332	AMD	CMOS	$+\ -\ \leftrightarrow$	$\to 32 \to 32 \quad 32 \to$	10	
74 ACT 8836	Texas Instr.	CMOS	$\times\ \Sigma$	$\to 32 \to 32 \quad 32 \to$	13	
74 AS 8832	Texas Instr.	TTL	$+\ -$	$\to 32 \to 32 \quad 32 \to$	13	
TMC 3211	TRW	CMOS	$\div$	$\to 32 \to 16 \quad 32 \to$	25	350

Function: Σ accumulator; $\leftrightarrow$ barrel shifter; $(a + jb)$ complex numbers; $\sqrt{x^2 + y^2}$ polar $\to$ cartesian; $r, \varphi \to x, y$ cart. $\to$ polar

Input/output: $\to \times \times$ Input, $\to \times \times \to$ bidirectional, $\times \times \to$ output

MOPS: Million Operations Per Second

* Other manufacturers: AMD, Analog Dev., Cypress, IDT, MMI, Logic Dev., LSI-Logic, TRW

16^2: 2×16 I/O bits; 16^4: 4×16 I/O bits

Fig. 19.36 Fixed-point arithmetic units

Type	Manufacturer	Technology	Functions	I/O ports [bit]		Computing power [MFLOPS]	Power dissipation [mW]
32-bit IEEE operands (WTL 1032-, 1033-series)							
WTL 3332	Weitek	CMOS	$+ - \times$	$\rightarrow 32 \rightarrow 32 \rightarrow 32 \rightarrow$		20	700
WTL 3132	Weitek	CMOS	$+ - \times$	$\rightarrow 32 \rightarrow$		20	700
Am 29 C 325	AMD	CMOS	$+ - \times$	$\rightarrow 32 \rightarrow 32$	$32 \rightarrow$	10	900
L 64133	LSI-Logic	CMOS	$+ - \times$	$\rightarrow 32 \rightarrow 32$	$32 \rightarrow$	16	1000
ADSP 3201*	Analog Dev.	CMOS	$\times$	$\rightarrow 32 \rightarrow 32$	$32 \rightarrow$	10	500
ADSP 3202*	Analog Dev.	CMOS	$+ -$	$\rightarrow 32 \rightarrow 32$	$32 \rightarrow$	10	500
TMC 3200	TRW	CMOS	$+ -$	$\rightarrow 16 \rightarrow 16$	$16 \rightarrow$	10	150
TMC 3201	TRW	CMOS	$\times$	$\rightarrow 16 \rightarrow 16$	$16 \rightarrow$	10	150
TMC 3210	TRW	CMOS	$\div$	$\rightarrow 16$	$16 \rightarrow$	2.5	250
64/32-bit IEEE operands (WTL 1064, 1065-series)							
WTL 2264	Weitek	CMOS	$\times$	$\rightarrow 32 \rightarrow 32$	$32 \rightarrow$	10/20	500
WTL 2265	Weitek	CMOS	$+ -$	$\rightarrow 32 \rightarrow 32$	$32 \rightarrow$	20/20	500
WTL 3364	Weitek	CMOS	$+ - \times \div \sqrt{}$	$\rightarrow 32 \rightarrow 32$	$32 \rightarrow$	20	1800
WTL 3164	Weitek	CMOS	$+ - \times \div \sqrt{}$	$\rightarrow 32 \rightarrow$		20	1800
AM 29 C 327*	AMD	CMOS	$+ - \times \div \leftrightarrow$	$\rightarrow 32 \rightarrow 32$	$32 \rightarrow$	10/	1100
IDT 721264	IDT	CMOS	$\times$	$\rightarrow 32 \rightarrow 32$	$32 \rightarrow$	6/12	500
IDT 721265	IDT	CMOS	$+ -$	$\rightarrow 32 \rightarrow 32$	$32 \rightarrow$	12/12	500
74 ACT 8847	Texas Instr.	CMOS	$+ - \times \div \sqrt{}$	$\rightarrow 32 \rightarrow 32$	$32 \rightarrow$	33/33	500
ADSP 3212*	Analog Dev.	CMOS	$\times$	$\rightarrow 32 \rightarrow 32$	$32 \rightarrow$	20/20	1000
ADSP 3222*	Analog Dev.	CMOS	$+ -$	$\rightarrow 32 \rightarrow 32$	$32 \rightarrow$	20/20	1000
ADSP 7110*	Analog Dev.	TTL	$\times \div \sqrt{}$	$\rightarrow 32 \rightarrow 32$	$32 \rightarrow$	20/25	8000
ADSP 7120*	Analog Dev.	TTL	$+ - \leftrightarrow$	$\rightarrow 32 \rightarrow 32$	$32 \rightarrow$	40/40	8000
ADSP 8110*	Analog Dev.	ECL	$+ \leftrightarrow \sqrt{}$	$\rightarrow 32 \rightarrow 32$	$32 \rightarrow$	20/25	8000
ADSP 8120*	Analog Dev.	ECL	$+ - \leftrightarrow$	$\rightarrow 32 \rightarrow 32$	$32 \rightarrow$	40/40	8000
B 3130*	Bipol. Int.	ECL	$+ - \times \div \sqrt{}$	$\rightarrow 64 \rightarrow 64$	$64 \rightarrow$	200	25000

Function: $\leftrightarrow$ barrel shifter
Input/output: $\rightarrow \times \times$ input, $\rightarrow \times \times \rightarrow$ bidirectional, $\times \times \rightarrow$ output
MFLOPS: Million Floating Point Operations Per Second
*can also be used for fixed-point operations with 32-bit or 64-bit word length respectively

Fig. 19.37 Floating-point arithmetic units

19.7   Digital function networks

The function $Y = f(X)$ can be implemented directly in tabular form using ROMs. For a high resolution, many-bit numbers and therefore large memories are required. The latter can be considerably reduced if only part of the table is stored, and if the remaining values of the function are interpolated from it using simple arithmetic operations. Special characteristics of the particular function can then often be used to advantage [19.4].

19.7.1   Sine function

One advantage of the sine function is its periodicity, so that only the function values for $0 \le \theta \le \pi/2$ need be stored. The input is a straight binary fraction, $0 \le X \le 1$, according to

$$X = x_1 \cdot 2^{-1} + x_2 \cdot 2^{-2} + \cdots + x_N \cdot 2^{-N}$$

and

$$\theta = \frac{\pi}{2} X .$$

For an input word length of up to 9 bits (0.2%) and an output word length of up to 8 bits, the mask-programmed ROM MM 5232 (AEI mask) from National can be used. An extension to an output word length of 16 bits is possible with a second ROM MM 5232, programmed with mask AEJ. ROMs Am 29526...29 from AMD have an input word length of 10 bits and an output word length of 16 bits.

For larger input word lengths the required memory capacity quickly rises to unrealistic proportions. For an input and output of 16 bits, it will be already 1 Mbit.

The memory required can be reduced if the input variable X is divided into a part M containing the more significant bits and a part L containing the less significant bits. If

$$X = M + L ,$$

then

$$\sin \theta = \sin \frac{\pi}{2}(M + L) = \sin \frac{\pi}{2}M \cos \frac{\pi}{2}L + \cos \frac{\pi}{2}M \sin \frac{\pi}{2}L . \qquad (19.7)$$

The part L is made small so that, for a given output accuracy,

$$\cos \frac{\pi}{2}L = 1 . \qquad (19.8)$$

Then

$$\sin \frac{\pi}{2}L = \frac{\pi}{2}L , \qquad (19.9)$$

and Eq. (19.7) reduces to

$$\sin \theta = \sin \frac{\pi}{2} M + \underbrace{\frac{\pi}{2} L \cos \frac{\pi}{2} M}_{K} \,. \tag{19.10}$$

The sine and cosine functions for the calculation of this expression require only a short input word length.

We shall now illustrate the method by an example. The sine function is to be calculated with a resolution of 16 bits at the input and the output. To begin with, we determine the word length of L. The error in Eq. (19.8) is largest if L assumes its maximum value. With the condition

$$(\Delta \sin \theta)_{\max} < 0.5 \cdot 2^{-16} = 2^{-17} \,,$$

we obtain from Eq. (19.8)

$$1 - \cos \frac{\pi}{2} L_{\max} < 2^{-17} \,, \quad \text{i.e.} \quad L_{\max} < 2^{-9} \,.$$

In order not to exceed this limit, we can use for L no more than the last 7 bits, i.e. the bit weightings $2^{-10} \ldots 2^{-16}$. Therefore, the 9 MSBs of the straight binary fraction are left for the representation of M, i.e. the bit weightings $2^{-1} \ldots 2^{-9}$. This splitting is illustrated in Fig. 19.38. For the storage of the coarse-increment values, a sine ROM having 2^9 words of 16 bits each is required.

The computation of the interpolation values K in Eq. (19.10) can be performed using a multiplier. However, at its output, the full word length of 16 bits is not required. Eight bits are sufficient (binary weighting $2^{-9} \ldots 2^{-16}$), as the largest possible interpolation value is

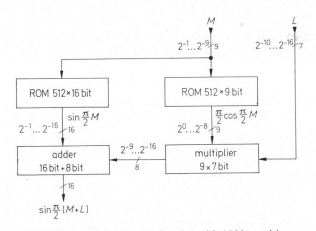

Fig. 19.38 Generating the sine function with 16-bit precision

$$K_{max} = \frac{\pi}{2} L_{max} \cos\left(\frac{\pi}{2}\cdot 0\right) \approx 3.1 \cdot 10^{-3} < 2^{-8} .$$

For the cosine ROM, a resolution of 9 bits is sufficient to keep the error in the product below 2^{-17}. The total capacity of the memories is 13 kbit, i.e. only about 1% of that of a direct ROM implementation.

The 9×7-bit multiplier has the highest component count of the circuit, but if resolution is reduced it can be omitted by incorporating the multiplication in the cosine ROM. For a desired input resolution of 12 bits and an output resolution of 14 bits, a mask-programmed interpolation ROM (MM 5232, mask AEK) is available and can be used in connection with the sine ROMs mentioned, as illustrated in Fig. 19.39. Although the output resolution is still 16 bits, the precision is reduced to 0.7×2^{-14}, as only the 6 MSBs of M are connected to the interpolation ROM.

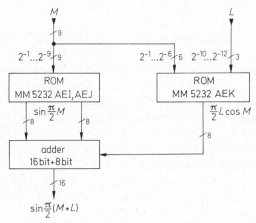

Fig. 19.39 Simplified generation of the sine function, with an input word length of 12 bits and output precision of 14 bits

20 Microcomputer basics

The common feature of microcomputers is that all the basic modules of a computer are concentrated in a single highly integrated circuit or in a small number of such circuits, with capabilities ranging from a simple sequential logic network to a complex data processing system. Powerful microcomputers of this kind are also known as "micro-mainframes".

20.1 Basic structure of a microcomputer

As we can see from the block diagram in Fig. 20.1, a microcomputer basically comprises four functional units:

1) The most important unit is the microprocessor. It constitutes the central control and arithmetic unit and is therefore also known as the central processing unit (CPU).
2) The program memory contains the sequence of commands to be processed, i.e. the program. It generally consists of an EPROM, as the program will then be retained even if the power supply fails. RAMs are used for storage of programs requiring frequent modification. These are generally loaded from an external bulk storage medium (e.g. floppy disk or magnetic tape).
3) The data memory contains the variables. It is therefore always a RAM.
4) The computer communicates with peripherals, such as VDU (visual display unit), keyboard, bulk storage medium, etc., via the input/output (I/O) circuitry.

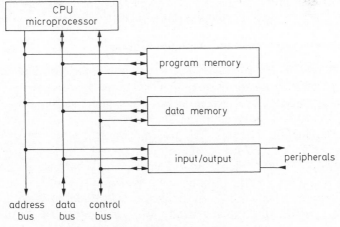

Fig. 20.1 Block diagram of a microcomputer

Communication between the CPU and the other units takes place via three bus systems, as shown in Fig. 20.1. The microprocessor uses the address bus to specify the desired memory address. It uses the control bus to determine whether reading or writing is to take place. Data is exchanged via the data bus, which, unlike the other two, is bidirectional.

The block diagram in Fig. 20.1 gives no indication of the capability of the CPU and the capacity of the main memory. It is simply the block diagram of a computer. Depending on the size of the available memory and on the speed of operation (measured as Million Instructions Per Second, MIPS), a rough distinction can be drawn as follows:

Classification	Storage capability	Word length	Comp. speed
Microcomputer	1 k ... 256 kbyte	4 ... 16 bit	0.1 ... 1 MIPS
Personal Computer	0.5 M ... 8 Mbyte	8 ... 16 bit	0.5 ... 3 MIPS
Workstation	4 M ... 16 Mbyte	16 ... 32 bit	1 ... 10 MIPS
Mainframe Comp.	8 M ... 256 Mbyte	32 ... 64 bit	5 ... 100 MIPS

The microcomputer breakthrough came with the introduction of monolithic microprocessors. Rapidly falling prices have made them attractive not only as simple general-purpose computers but also for use in hardware applications, where, using fixed programs, they can perform relatively complex arithmetic and control tasks. Thus, a standard hardware circuit is adequate for a large number of applications, whereas the development itself is increasingly shifting towards programming (software).

This trend has been further accelerated by the introduction of single-chip microcomputers. Such large-scale integrated circuits contain, in addition to the processor, an I/O unit as well as a small RAM and a ROM. A microcomputer of this kind is therefore fully functional even without external add-ons.

20.2　Operation of a microprocessor

20.2.1　Internal design

In this section we shall examine the mode of operation and instruction format of a microprocessor in somewhat greater detail.

The block diagram of a microprocessor is shown in Fig. 20.2. There are three functional blocks: the execution unit, the sequence controller (sequencer) and the bus interface. The execution unit processes the arithmetic and logic instructions. The operands involved are present either in the data or address registers or are applied via the internal bus. The sequence controller comprises the instruction decoder and the program counter.

The program counter calls up the program instructions in sequence. The instruction decoder then initiates the steps required to execute the instruction. The sequence controller constitutes a sequential logic system (cf. Section 10.7),

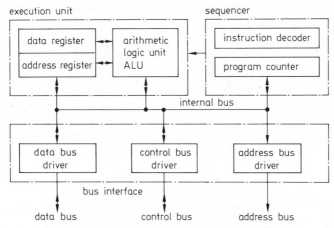

Fig. 20.2 Block diagram of a microprocessor CPU

whose truth table, in more recent microprocessors, is stored in a ROM. The contents of this ROM is known as the microprogram. The external instructions in this case determine the entry addresses into the microprogram.

When a program is started, the program counter is set to the start address. This address is transferred to the memories via the address bus. When a read signal is applied at the address bus, the contents of the relevant memory appear on the data bus and are stored in the instruction decoder. The latter then initiates the operations necessary to execute the instruction. As we shall see, this requires a variable number of machine cycles, depending on the type of instruction. Once the instruction has been executed, the instruction decoder sets the program counter to the address of the next instruction.

In order to allow a description in more practical detail, we shall now consider an actual 8-bit microprocessor. The term "8-bit" refers to the word length of the data bus. As an introduction, the basic 6800-type is particularly

flag register	8 bit
accumulator A	8 bit
accumulator B	8 bit
index register	16 bit
stack pointer	16 bit
program counter	16 bit

Fig. 20.3 List of the registers in the MC 6800 microprocessor which are accessible to the user

instructive, as it is of straightforward design, clearly structured and yet comparatively powerful. Motorola and other manufacturers have since produced a number of further developments which, although more powerful, are more difficult to understand due to their wide range of capabilities. Their characteristics are summarized in Section 20.5.

Figure 20.3 shows the user-accessible registers of the MC 6800 microprocessor. Most arithmetic operations are carried out with the help of the accumulators A and B. The index register stores frequently used addresses, and the stack pointer is used to organize the subroutine techniques. The flag register (condition code register) contains information on the last arithmetic result obtained.

20.2.2   Form of an instruction

The MC 6800 microprocessor operates with an address word length of 16 bits (= 2 bytes) and a data word length of 8 bits (= 1 byte). For the user, bit strings of this length are difficult to read, and for this reason a shortened notation is used. The bits are collected in groups of 4, each represented by a digit which may thus assume 16 different values. The resulting code is therefore called hexadecimal or hex code. For the digits 0 to 9, the normal decimal symbols are used. The digits "ten" to "fifteen" are represented by the capitals A to F, so that the assignment shown in Fig. 20.4 is obtained.

Straight binary	Hex	Decimal	Straight binary	Hex	Decimal
0000	0	0	1000	8	8
0001	1	1	1001	9	9
0010	2	2	1010	A	10
0011	3	3	1011	B	11
0100	4	4	1100	C	12
0101	5	5	1101	D	13
0110	6	6	1110	E	14
0111	7	7	1111	F	15

Fig. 20.4 Comparison of straight binary, hex and decimal notation

Since the base 16 of the hex code is a power of 2, there are two different possibilities for converting a many-digit hex coded number to the corresponding decimal number. The relationship

$$Z_{hex} = z_{N-1} \cdot 16^{N-1} + z_{N-2} \cdot 16^{N-2} + \cdots + z_1 \cdot 16 + z_0$$

indicates one method of conversion. The other way would be to convert each digit separately to a straight binary number and join them together. This method results in the corresponding straight binary number which can then be processed using the methods previously described. The following example illustrates the two methods of conversion:

$$A148_{hex} = 10 \cdot 16^3 + 1 \cdot 16^2 + 4 \cdot 16 + 8 = 41288_{dec} \, ,$$

$$A148_{hex} = \underbrace{1\ 0\ 1\ 0}\ \underbrace{0\ 0\ 0\ 1}\ \underbrace{0\ 1\ 0\ 0}\ \underbrace{1\ 0\ 0\ 0}_2 = 41288_{dec} \; .$$

The 16-bit straight binary address words may thus be represented in the shortened notation by 4-digit hex numbers, and the 8-bit data words by 2-digit hex numbers.

The different instructions which a microprocessor can carry out are represented in machine language (operation code or op code) by 8-bit words, i.e. 2-digit hex numbers. In addition, mnemonics are employed to make programming easier. The instruction "load accumulator A", for example, is shortened to the mnemonic "LDA A". However, this symbol cannot be interpreted by the microprocessor and must therefore be translated into op code. For this purpose, a translating table or a special translating program (assembler) is used.

The instruction LDA A is not yet complete, because the microprocessor must be told *what* the accumulator is to be loaded with, i.e. to which *operand* the instruction is to be applied. There are several methods of indicating this.

1) Extended addressing

The two bytes which follow the instruction in the program contain the complete 16-bit address of the memory location, the contents of which are to be loaded into the accumulator A. The result is the following structure:

instruction		B6		LDA A
higher-order address byte	e.g.	A1	mnem.	A1
lower-order address byte		48		48

The op code of the LDA A (ext) instruction for the MC 6800 is $B6_{hex} = 1011\ 0110_2$. In the above example, we have entered the address

$$A148_{hex} = 1010\ 0001\ 0100\ 1000_2 \; .$$

2) Direct addressing

Only a one-byte address is specified in the program, the microprocessor automatically assuming the higher-order byte to be zero. The corresponding op code for the LDA A (dir.) instruction is 96_{hex}. This addressing mode allows the user to directly address the location 0000 to $00FF_{hex} = 0$ to 255_{dec} (base page), thereby reducing the execution time. It is therefore asvisable to use the base page for the storage of frequently needed variables and constants. The structure of the instruction in the direct addressing mode is as follows:

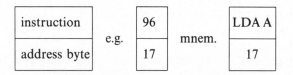

In the example, the contents of the register

$$17_{hex} = 0000\ 0000\ 0001\ 0111_2$$

is read into the accumulator A.

3)   Indexed addressing

With this mode of addressing, the contents of a memory location is read, the address of which is held in the index register. In addition, it is possible to specify an index "offset" by including an 8-bit number in the instruction. The result is a simple method of addressing locations above any desired 16-bit index address, the instruction then reading:

instruction		A6		LDA A, X
offset byte	e.g.	07	mnem.	07

The op code for the LDA A (inx.) instruction is $A6_{hex} = 1010\ 0110_2$. If we assume that the address $A148_{hex}$ is stored in the index register, the contents of the memory location $A148_{hex} + 0007_{hex} = A14F_{hex}$, for our example, are read into accumulator A.

The offset information is read by the microprocessor as a positive 8-bit number. A negative offset is not defined. The largest possible offset is therefore

$$1111\ 1111_2 = FF_{hex} = 255_{dec}\ .$$

It will be seen in Section 20.3.3 (jump and branch instructions) that there is another way of specifying an offset, although this specification is used only to define a program branch and is interpreted as being a 8-bit number in 2's-complement representation.

4)   Immediate addressing

In this mode, the operand is included in the instruction as the second byte:

instruction		86		LDA A #
data byte	e.g.	3F	mnem.	3F

The op code for the LDA A (imm.) instruction is 86_{hex}. In the example, the operand $3F_{hex} = 0011\ 1111_2$ is read into accumulator A. It must be noted that *two* data bytes are needed for the immediate loading of the index register and stack pointer, as their word length is 16 bits.

5)   Inherent addressing

With this form of addressing, the operand need not be specified separately, as it is already defined by the command itself:

> | instruction | e.g. | 4F | mnem. | CLRA |

The example $4F_{hex} = CLRA$ means: clear accumulator A. As we can see, the command can be executed without further information.

Mnemonic code

When writing programs in mnemonic code, certain conventions are employed which are very similar for all the assemblers, whereas the mnemonic abbreviations themselves can vary depending on the processor family.

The following features are specified in the mnemonic notation: the operand is written after the command, with the hex numbers identified by a $-sign. Numbers without identifier are decimals. These are converted to the corresponding hex number during assembling. ASCII characters are indicated by a quotation mark, and are replaced during assembling by the appropriate bit combination in accordance with the table in Fig. 21.25. In some rare cases the operand is written out as a bit combination and is characterized by an &-sign.

Another way of representing an operand is to use a label. This is defined by a value assignment, e.g.

> M1   EQUAL $ A000 .

On the basis of this assignment, the assembler inserts the hex number A000 wherever M1 appears in the program. The EQUAL directive is used by the assembler only during the translation and does not appear in the machine program. Such assignments are known as assembler directives.

Labels are frequently used to mark branch and jump addresses. In this case the value assignment is not made explicitly by the directive EQUAL but implicitly by writing the label at the appropriate address in front of the mnemonic instruction.

The form of addressing of a instruction is not stated explicitly but results indirectly from the operand notation as detailed in Fig. 20.5. It is possible to replace each operand by a label. The first character of a label is generally declared to be a letter and is not preceded by a special character. Consequently, operands without special characters are either decimal numbers or labels. Their distinguishing criterion is whether or not they start with a letter.

When the assembler recognizes a label, it fetches the associated operand from the label table and then determines the type of addressing in accordance with Fig. 20.5.

Type of addressing	Operand	Interpretation
extended	$ ⬚⬚⬚⬚	address hex
direct	$ ⬚⬚	address hex
indexed	$ ⬚⬚ , X	offset hex
	⬚⬚⬚ , X	offset decimal
immediate	# $ ⬚⬚	data hex
	# ⬚⬚	data decimal
	# & ⬚⬚⬚⬚⬚⬚⬚⬚	data binary
	# " ⬚	data ASCII
inherent		data implicit

Fig. 20.5 Types of addressing and their representation in mnemonic notation

Figure 20.6 shows an example of a program in mnemonic notation. On the left-hand side is the translation of the commands into machine code (op code) and the associated address. In the op code also, the operand is often written on the same line, after the instruction. The address of the operand is obtained by counting on. In the example in Fig. 20.6, the operand 3F is consequently at address 1008.

Address	Hex code			Label	Mnem.	Operand	Comment
1000	B6	A1	48		LDA A	$ A148	extended
1003	96	17			LDA A	$ 17	direct
1005	A6	07			LDA A	$ 07, X	indexed
1007	86	3F			LDA A	# $ 3F	immediate
1009	4F				CLR A		inherent
	⌣ assembler				⌣ programmer		

Fig. 20.6 Example of the assembler notation of a program

20.2.3 Execution of an instruction

The execution of an instruction usually requires several machine cycles. Referring to the example LDA A (ext.) $\triangleq$ B6$_{hex}$, we shall explain the manipulation carried out by the microprocessor: if the program counter calls for the address M at which the instruction is stored, the register answers on the data bus with the op-coded instruction, in our example B6$_{hex}$. The microprocessor decodes the instruction and finds that it must fetch the next two bytes from the program memory in order to obtain the address of the operand. To achieve this, it applies the address ($M + 1$) to the address bus and reads the appropriate byte into an auxiliary register. At the next cycle, it issues the address $M + 2$ and reads the appropriate byte into a second auxiliary register. During the fourth cycle, the microprocessor applies the two stored bytes (i.e. the 16-bit address of the operand) in parallel to the address bus and reads the byte which now appears on the data bus into the accumulator A. The execution of the instruction thus requires the four cycles set out in Fig. 20.7. Similar considerations show that the instruction LDA A (dir.) requires three cycles and the instruction LDA A (imm.) two cycles.

Cycle	Address bus	Data bus
1	address M of instruction	op-coded instruction
2	address $M + 1$	higher-order byte of operand address
3	address $M + 2$	lower-order byte of operand address
4	address of operand	operand

Fig. 20.7 Activity on address and data bus when executing the operation LDA A (ext.)

The number of cycles is a direct measure of the execution time of an instruction. For the MC 6800, the cycle time is equal to the clock period. For the maximum clock rate of 1 MHz, a cycle time of 1 µs is therefore attainable so that the operation LDA A (ext.) is executed within 4 µs.

20.3   Instruction set

In this section, a review of the instructions for the MC 6800 is given. This microprocessor can carry out 72 different instructions, most of which may be applied in different addressing modes. Considering the large number of addressing modes, a set of 197 instructions is obtained.

20.3.1   Register operations

In Fig. 20.8, we have listed the operations available for the exchange of data between individual registers. The symbols under the heading "short description of operation" are as follows:

A: contents of accumulator A,
B: contents of accumulator B,
$[M]$:   contents of the memory location having the address M,
X: contents of the index register X,
X_H: higher-order byte of X,
X_L: lower-order byte of X,
C: carry bit in the flag register.

Operation	Mnemonic	Addressing modes					Brief description of operation
		ext.	dir.	inx.	imm.	inher.	
load accumulator	LDA A	B6	96	A6	86		$[M] \rightarrow A$
	LDA B	F6	D6	E6	C6		$[M] \rightarrow B$
store accumulator	STA A	B7	97	A7			$A \rightarrow M$
	STA B	F7	D7	E7			$B \rightarrow M$
transfer accumulator	TAB					16	$A \rightarrow B$
	TBA					17	$B \rightarrow A$
clear	CLR	7F		6F			$00 \rightarrow M$
	CLR A					4F	$00 \rightarrow A$
	CLR B					5F	$00 \rightarrow B$
load index register	LDX	FE	DE	EE	CE		$[M] \rightarrow X_H$ $[M+1] \rightarrow X_L$
store index register	STX	FF	DF	EF			$X_H \rightarrow M,$ $X_L \rightarrow M+1$

Fig. 20.8 Register operations of the microprocessor MC 6800

20.3.2 Arithmetic and Boolean operations

The instructions for arithmetic and Boolean operations are listed in Fig. 20.9. Logic operations are carried out simultaneously for each bit of the data words and each result is transferred to the corresponding bit of the result. The AND operation, for example, produces

$$A: \quad 1001 \ 1101$$
$$B: \quad 0110 \ 1011$$
$$A \cdot B: \quad 0000 \ 1001 \ .$$

The instruction set for arithmetic operations is very limited for most microprocessors. Apart from the conversion to 2's-complement, only addition and subtraction are available. When using the operation DA A (decimal adjust), the addition can also be applied to BCD numbers. In this case, the same corrections are carried out after the addition as are discussed in Section 19.5.4. More complex arithmetic operations in the user program must be composed of the basic operations. Only more recent microprocessors also have operations available for multiplication and division.

To demonstrate the application of the instruction set, we shall write a program for the addition of two 16-bit numbers: the first term of the sum is assumed to be stored in the two registers 0001 and 0002, i.e. the higher-order byte in 0001 and the lower-order byte in 0002. The second term of the sum is stored similarly in registers 0003 and 0004. The result is to be transferred to 0005 and 0006.

In the first step, the two lower-order bytes of the straight binary numbers are added, i.e. the contents of registers 0002 and 0004. As no carry from

Operation	Mnemonic	Addressing modes					Brief description
		ext.	dir.	inx.	imm.	inher.	
add	ADD A	BB	9B	AB	8B		A plus $[M] \to A$
	ADD B	FB	DB	EB	CB		B plus $[M] \to B$
	ABA					1B	A plus $B \quad \to A$
add with carry	ADC A	B9	99	A9	89		A plus $[M]$ plus $C \to A$
	ADC B	F9	D9	E9	C9		B plus $[M]$ plus $C \to B$
decimal adjust A	DAA					19	BCD correction
subtract	SUB A	B0	90	A0	80		A minus $[M] \to A$
	SUB B	F0	D0	E0	C0		B minus $[M] \to B$
	SBA					10	A minus $B \quad \to A$
subtract with carry	SBC A	B2	92	A2	82		A minus $[M]$ minus $C \to A$
	SBC B	F2	D2	E2	C2		B minus $[M]$ minus $C \to B$
2's-complement	NEG	70		60			$[M]^{(2)} \to M$
	NEG A					40	$A^{(2)} \quad \to A$
	NEG B					50	$B^{(2)} \quad \to B$
increment by 1	INC	7C		6C			$[M]$ plus $1 \to M$
	INC A					4C	A plus $1 \quad \to A$
	INC B					5C	B plus $1 \quad \to B$
	INX					08	X plus $1 \quad \to X$
decrement by 1	DEC	7A		6A			$[M]$ minus $1 \to M$
	DEC A					4A	A minus $1 \quad \to A$
	DEC B					5A	B minus $1 \quad \to B$
	DEX					09	X minus $1 \quad \to X$
1's-complement	COM	73		63			$[M]^{(1)} \to M$
	COM A					43	$A^{(1)} \quad \to A$
	COM B					53	$B^{(1)} \quad \to B$

Fig. 20.9 Arithmetic and logic operations of the MC 6800 microprocessor

Operation	Mnemonic	Addressing modes					Brief description
		ext.	dir.	inx.	imm.	inher.	
AND	AND A / AND B	B4 / F4	94 / D4	A4 / E4	84 / C4		$A \cdot [M] \to A$ / $B \cdot [M] \to B$
OR	ORA A / ORA B	BA / FA	9A / DA	AA / EA	8A / CA		$A + [M] \to A$ / $B + [M] \to B$
exclusive-OR	EOR A / EOR B	B8 / F8	98 / D8	A8 / E8	88 / C8		$A \oplus [M] \to A$ / $B \oplus [M] \to B$
rotate left	ROL / ROL A / ROL B	79		69		49 / 59	$[M]$, A, B 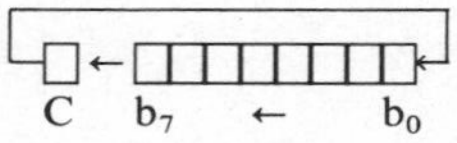
shift left, arithmetic	ASL / ASL A / ASL B	78		68		48 / 58	$[M]$, A, B 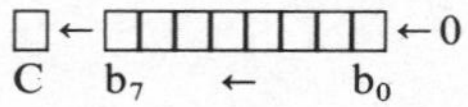
rotate right	ROR / ROR A / ROR B	76		66		46 / 56	$[M]$, A, B 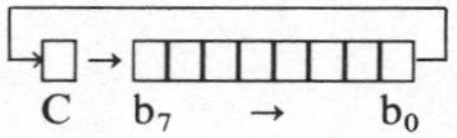
shift right, arithmetic	ASR / ASR A / ASR B	77		67		47 / 57	$[M]$, A, B 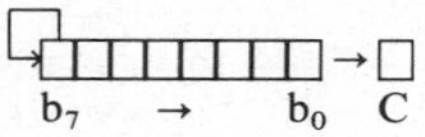
shift right, logic	LSR / LSR A / LSR B	74		64		44 / 54	$[M]$, A, B 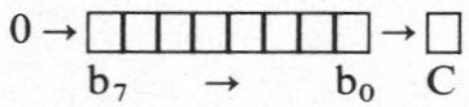
no operation	NOP					01	advances program counter only

Fig. 20.9 Arithmetic and logic operations of the MC 6800 microprocessor (continued)

a previous number is to be taken into account, the operation ADD A is used. The result is stored in register 0006. In the second step, the higher-order bytes are added using the operation ADC A. This ensures that the carry of the previous addition is included, after it has been called by the ALU from the flag register. The result is stored in register 0005. The entire program list is shown in Fig. 20.10.

Address	Hex code	Label	Mnem.	Operand	Comment
1000	96 02	AD 16	LDA A	$ 02	
1002	9B 04		ADD A	$ 04	addition of the two lower-order bytes
1004	01		NOP		
1005	97 06		STA A	$ 06	
1007	96 01		LDA A	$ 01	
1009	99 03		ADC A	$ 03	addition of the two higher-order bytes
100B	01		NOP		
100C	97 05		STA A	$ 05	
100E	39		RTS		

Fig. 20.10 Program for the addition of two 16-bit numbers

With the same program, two 4-digit BCD numbers can be added if the NOP instructions (inserted as dummy operations to reserve space for other operations to be entered later) are replaced by the BCD correction DA A.

20.3.3 Jump and branch instructions

Flag register

One particular strength of the microprocessor is that it can carry out a large number of logic jump and branch instructions. To enable it to do this, various flags are held in the flag register (condition code register) and read when required. The flag register is an 8-bit register in which the two most significant bits are always 1. The individual flags are arranged in the following sequence

1	1	H	I	N	Z	V	C

bit 7   bit 0

where
C: carry flag, carry from bit 7,
V: overflow flag for 2's-complement representation,
Z: zero flag,
N: sign flag (negative flag) for 2's-complement representation,
I: interrupt flag,
H: half carry flag, half carry from bit 3.

The individual flags are set or reset for all register and arithmetic operations. For example, when a number is loaded into the accumulator, bit 7 of which is 1, flag N is set to 1; if the number is represented in 2's-complement, it will then be interpreted as being negative. If, during an addition or subtraction, the condition for overflow in the 2's-complement representation (see Section 19.5.6) is recognized, the overflow flag V is set to 1. The zero flag is set if bits 0 to 7 of an operand are zero.

There is a series of operations the result of which is given only in the form of flag states. If, for instance, it is of interest to know whether the number in the A register is larger than the number in register B, the difference $(A - B)$ may be calculated using the operation SBA and afterwards the sign flag N is tested. If it is set, then $A < B$. The value of the difference is now stored in register A. Should it be of no interest, the operation CBA may be used instead of SBA. Although the difference $(A - B)$ is still computed and the flag register is set, the value of the difference is not stored and, after the operation, the initial operands are still available in the A and B registers.

A series of further instructions for which no results are stored except the flags, is listed in Fig. 20.11.

Operation	Mnemonic	Addressing modes					Brief description
		ext.	dir.	inx.	imm.	inher.	
compare	CMP A	B1	91	A1	81		A minus $[M]$
	CMP B	F1	D1	E1	C1		B minus $[M]$
	CBA						A minus B
	CPX	BC	9C	AC	8C		X_H minus $[M]$, X_L minus $[M + 1]$
bit test	BIT A	B5	95	A5	85		$A \cdot [M]$
	BIT B	F5	D5	E5	C5		$B \cdot [M]$
test, zero or minus	TST	7D		6D			$[M] - 00$
	TST A					4D	$A - 00$
	TST B					5D	$B - 00$
set carry flag	SEC					0D	$1 \to C$
clear carry flag	CLC					0C	$0 \to C$
set overflow flag	SEV					0B	$1 \to V$
clear overflow flag	CLV					0A	$0 \to V$
set interrupt mask	SEI					0F	$1 \to I$
clear interrupt mask	CLI					0E	$0 \to I$

Fig. 20.11 Operations of the MC 6800 microprocessor, manipulating the flag register

Unconditional jumps

An unconditional jump is carried out without reading the flag register. One must differentiate between absolute addressing (jump) and relative addressing (branch). For a *jump*, the address is specified to which the program counter is to be set. Two different methods may be used, extended addressing or indexed addressing. The address is specified either as a hex number or as a label. This results, for example, in the following program sequence:

a) Extended addressing

Address	Hex code	Mnem.	Operand	Comment
⋮	⋮	⋮		
1107	7E 11 8F	JMP	$ 118F	
⋮	⋮ ⋮ ⋮	⋮	⋮	
118F		next instruction to be executed		

b) Indexed addressing

Address	Hex code	Mnem.	Operand	Comment
⋮	⋮	⋮		
1107	6E 1A	JMP	$ 1A, X	
⋮	⋮ ⋮	⋮	⋮	
X + 1A		next instruction to be executed		

For a *branch*, instead of specifying the absolute address of the next instruction to be executed, an offset is given by which the program counter is to be advanced. This has the advantage that the program need not be changed if it is loaded at a different starting address. The offset is specified in the form of a 8-bit number in 2's-complement notation. The range of branching is therefore limited to $-128 \ldots +127$ program steps. The program sequence may, for example, be as follows:

Address	Hex code	Mnem.	Operand	Comment
⋮				
1107	20 0E	BRA	$ 0E	
⋮		⋮		
1109 + 0E = 1117		next instruction to be executed		

The offset is counted from the next instruction following the branch instruction. Offset 00 therefore results in a normal program sequence without branch.

Conditional branch

A conditional branch is carried out only if the appropriate condition of the flag register is true. The branch instructions involved employ relative addressing exclusively. If the condition is not true, the program continues without a jump and executes the instruction following the branch instruction. Figure 20.12 lists the most important jump and branch instructions. For operations referring to 2's-complement arithmetic, the sign bit is correctly interpreted even for an overflow, since the overflow flag is also taken into account. The description column indicates the Boolean operations carried out for each particular branch instruction and also gives information on how to test for particular bit combinations.

The application of conditional branch instructions is best explained by an example: the number sequence 0, 1, 2, 3 . . . is to be stored in the registers 0200 to $M - 1$. The higher-order byte of the address M is assumed to be held in register 0000, the lower-order byte in register 0001.

The program is listed in Fig. 20.13. First, the 16-bit number 0200_{hex} is read into the index register and the accumulator A is cleared. On entry into the loop, the contents of accumulator A is stored in the indexed addressing mode. Subsequently, accumulator A and the index register are incremented. If the resulting address is smaller than M, the program counter jumps back to the loop entry. In this manner, the next value of the number sequence is stored in the next higher register, and so on. When $X = M$, the program counter no longer returns and the program stops at the instruction WAI.

Address	Hex code	Label	Mnem.	Operand	Comment
1000	CE 02 00		LDX	# $ 0200	
1003	4F		CLR A		
1004	A7 00	LOOP	STA A	0, X	entry into loop
1006	4C		INC A		
1007	08		INX		
1008	9C 00		CPX	$ 00	
100A	26 F8		BNE	LOOP	return to LOOP if $X < M$
100C	39		RTS		

Fig. 20.13 Program for loading the memory with 0, 1, 2. . . . , starting at the location 0200

Operation	Mnemonic	Addressing modes				Brief description of the branch condition
		rel.	ext.	inex.	inher.	
jump	JMP		7E	6E		
branch always	BRA	20				
branch if ≠ 0	BNE	26				$Z = 0$
branch if = 0	BEQ	27				$Z = 1$
branch if $\geqq 0$	BCC	24				$C = 0$
branch if $\leqq 0$	BLS	23				$C + Z = 1$
branch if > 0	BHI	22				$C + Z = 0$
branch if < 0	BCS	25				$C = 1$
branch if $V = 0$	BVC	28				$V = 0$
branch if $V = 1$	BVS	29				$V = 1$
branch if $\geqq 0$	BGE	2C				$N \oplus V = 0$
branch if $\leqq 0$	BLE	2F				$Z + (N \oplus V) = 1$
branch if > 0	BGT	2E				$Z + (N \oplus V) = 0$
branch if < 0	BLT	2D				$N \oplus V = 1$
branch if $b_7 = 0$	BPL	2A				$N = 0$
branch if $b_7 = 1$	BMI	2B				$N = 1$
branch to subroutine	BSR	8D				
jump to subroutine	JSR		BD	AD		
return from subroutine	RTS				39	
software interrupt	SWI				3F	
return from interrupt routine	RTI				3B	
wait for interrupt	WAI				3E	

condition when using unsigned arithmetic

condition when using 2's-complement arithmetic

Fig. 20.12 Jump and branch instructions of the MC 6800 microprocessor

Subroutines

The jump or branch to a subroutine (BSR, JSR) is an unconditional jump having the additional feature that the address of the next instruction is stored as a return address in a special register. This enables the user to switch from different parts of the main program to frequently used subroutines. With the instruction RTS (return from subroutine), the program counter is set back to the return address stored at the time.

It is possible to jump from one subroutine to another (nesting). As the return from the first subroutine may only be carried out after the return from the second, the second return address must also be stored. The same applies to all other nested subroutines. The first return jump must be to the address stored last, the second to the one before last and so on. This sequence is organized by a special 16-bit register within the CPU, the so-called *stack pointer*.

For the storage of the return addresses, a range of RAM locations is defined which is not otherwise used. It is known as the *stack*. Its size may be chosen according to the number of nested routines included in the program. After switch-on of the microprocessor, the *highest* address of the stack must be read into the stack pointer of the CPU, using the LDS instruction shown in Fig. 20.14.

If a jump to a subroutine is carried out on the instruction BSR or JSR, the return address (lower-order byte) is automatically stored at the address in-

Operation	Mnemonic	Addressing modes					Brief description
		ext.	dir.	inx.	imm.	inher.	
push accumulator	PSH A					36	$A \to M_{SP}$, SP minus $1 \to$ SP
	PSH B					37	$B \to M_{SP}$, SP minus $1 \to$ SP
pull accumulator	PUL A					32	SP plus $1 \to$ SP, $[M_{SP}] \to$ A
	PUL B					33	SP plus $1 \to$ SP, $[M_{SP}] \to$ B
load stack pointer	LDS	BE	9E	AE	8E		$[M] \to SP_H$, $[M+1] \to SP_L$
store stack pointer	STS	BF	9F	AF			$SP_H \to M$, $SP_L \to M+1$
increment stack pointer	INS					31	SP plus $1 \to$ SP
decrement stack pointer	DES					34	SP minus $1 \to$ SP
stack pntr. $\to$ index reg.	TSX					30	SP plus $1 \to$ X
index reg. $\to$ stack pntr.	TXS					35	X minus $1 \to$ SP

Fig. 20.14 Stack operations of the microprocessor MC 6800

dicated by the stack pointer. The contents of the stack pointer are then decreased by 1 and the higher-order byte of the return address is stored at the address now indicated. The contents of the stack pointer are again decreased by 1, thereby indicating the next free address.

If a jump to another subroutine within that subroutine now occurs, the second return address is stored in the two next lower addresses of the stack in the same way. The stack therefore continues growing downwards as more subroutines are "nested" within the previous one.

With the instruction RTS (return from subroutine), the return address stored last is read from the stack into the program counter and the number in the stack pointer is increased by 2. In this manner, the return addresses are worked through, as required, in the reverse order of their occurrence (Last In First Out: LIFO).

Figure 20.15 shows schematically the program sequence for a subroutine being called up twice by the main program.

Figure 20.16 illustrates the case where one subroutine calls up another. The return addresses to be stored in each case are shown in the stack.

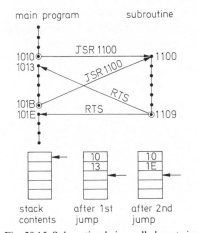

Fig. 20.15 Subroutine being called up twice

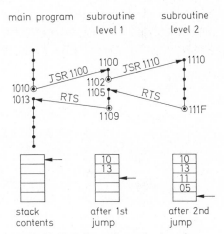

Fig. 20.16 Call-up of nested subroutines

The stack may also be used for economical temporary storage of the accumulator contents by employing the inherent instructions PSHA or PSHB. The contents are then stored in the memory location specified by the stack pointer. The contents of the pointer are subsequently reduced by 1, since the data word, unlike the address word, is only 8 bits long.

The data is retrieved by the instructions PULA or PULB. It is obvious that data stored in this manner must always be retrieved within the *same* subroutine level, as otherwise return addresses and data will be mixed up.

Interrupt

An interrupt routine is a special type of subroutine. It may be distinguished from the ordinary subroutine in that the jump from the current program is not initiated by a jump instruction somewhere within the program, but arbitrarily by an external control signal. This signal must be applied to the interrupt input *IRQ* (interrupt request) of the CPU.

The start address of the interrupt routine is stored in special locations independent of the program. For the MC 6800, the memory locations FFF8 (higher-order byte) and FFF9 (lower-order byte) are reserved for this purpose.

Since the interrupt request may occur at any stage of the program, steps must be taken to ensure that the program can continue without error after the return from the routine. The original data must therefore be available in the temporary registers of the CPU. For this reason, in the event of an interrupt, the contents of the accumulators A and B, of the index register and of the flag register are automatically stored in the stack. On the instruction RTI (return from interrupt) they are re-read into the CPU.

To demonstrate this process, we have listed in Fig. 20.17 the contents of the stack after an interrupt. We assumed that the program before the interrupt was at the second subroutine level and that during the execution of the first (not yet finished) subroutine, the contents of accumulators A and B were stored in the stack.

Address	Stack		
07FF	return address	low	} 1st subroutine
07FE	return address	high	
07FD	accumulator A		PSH A
07FC	accumulator B		PSH B
07FB	return address	low	} 2nd subroutine
07FA	return address	high	
07F9	return address	low	
07F8	return address	high	
07F7	index register	low	
07F6	index register	high	} interrupt
07F5	accumulator A		
07F4	accumulator B		
07F3	flag register		
stack pointer → 07F2			

Fig. 20.17 Example of the stack contents after an interrupt

After termination of the interrupt routine, the interrupted program returns to the second subroutine and from there to the first. At this level, the effect of the two PSH operations must be cancelled by the corresponding PUL instructions before returning to the main program. At the return, the stack pointer indicates again the highest address of the stack (our example: 07FF).

Interrupt mask

The interrupt flag *I* in the flag register enables the user to block the interrupt input *IRQ*. A jump to the interrupt routine is executed only if signal *IRQ* is handed on to the CPU and flag *I* cleared. For this reason, the flag is known as the interrupt mask. It may be set or cleared with the instructions SEI or CLI respectively, which are specified in Fig. 20.11. In the event of a jump to an interrupt routine, the flag is automatically set to prevent this interrupt routine being requested again before it has been completed. Figure 20.18 shows the program sequence following an interrupt request, in the form of a flow diagram.

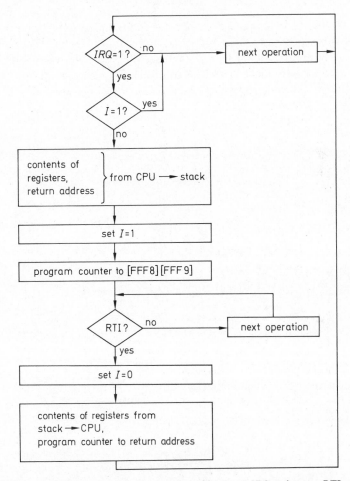

Fig. 20.18 Flow diagram for the execution of interrupt *IRQ* and return RTI

The control input *NMI* (non-maskable interrupt) enables the user to switch to a second interrupt routine, the starting address of which is stored at FFFC (higher-order byte) and FFFD (lower-order byte). In this kind of interrupt, the interrupt mask bit is not tested and both kinds of interrupt routines can therefore be nested.

A third kind of interrupt routine is started by the SWI instruction (software interrupt). Its start address is not stored in the program either, but at locations FFFA and FFFB. It has an advantage over a normal jump instruction in that the contents of the temporary registers are stored in the stack without the need for additional instructions. The return is initiated by the RTI instruction. The interrupt mask bit is not tested.

Restart

The *RESET* input of the CPU offers an additional possibility for interrupting the current program. It is used for starting the computer. When the CPU recognizes the control signal *RESET*, it loads the *restart* address stored permanently in the memory locations FFFE and FFFF (i.e. hardwired or by switches or by a ROM) into the program counter. A list of the different start addresses is shown in Fig. 20.19.

Address	Memory contents		Jump condition	Initiation
FFFF	starting address	low	} reset	*RESET* input
FFFE	starting address	high		
FFFD	starting address	low	} non-maskable interrupt	*NMI* input
FFFC	starting address	high		
FFFB	starting address	low	} software interrupt	SWI instruction
FFFA	starting address	high		
FFF9	starting address	low	} interrupt request	*IRQ* input
FFF8	starting address	high		

Fig. 20.19 Definition of memory locations for the start addresses of the interrupt routines

When the supply voltage is switched on, the stack pointer receives a random value. Consequently, if stack operations are expected during program execution, the LDS instruction must be used at the start of the program to load a defined address into the stack pointer.

20.4 Development aids

As mentioned before, microcomputers are normally employed not as freely programmable computers but as fixed-programmed control and arithmetic units. Their programs are then stored in PROMs.

It has been shown in the previous section that a program may be written directly in hex code by using a programming table. The finished program can be read into a **PROM** by a programming device and the **PROM** inserted in a microcomputer arrangement as shown in Fig. 20.1. However, in most cases it will be found that the program is not functional because it still contains errors. As the arrangement does not allow experimental changes of individual instructions, debugging is very difficult and time consuming. In this section, we shall discuss a number of methods of developing and testing programs before they are read into the PROM.

20.4.1   Programming in hex code

If we wish to make further modifications to a program in the development phase, it must be stored not in a PROM but in a RAM and tested in this condition. In the simplest case, a normal microcomputer (Fig. 20.1) can be used in whose PROM a so-called monitor program has been installed. This is available from several manufacturers in conjunction with single-board microcomputers. The monitor program essentially comprises input and output routines.

Input routine:
Interrogation of a hexadecimal keyboard and loading of the corresponding bit combination into the accumulator.

Output routine:
Reading of the accumulator contents and displaying them in hexadecimal format.

These two subroutines are the basis for the actual operator control routines (PROTO program) which are called up by means of special keys.

Memory input/output: The required register address M is entered in the form of a four-digit hex number and the corresponding contents are obtained in the display in the form of a two-digit hex number, e.g.

The displayed contents can be changed by entering new numbers. The last contents displayed are stored in the register requested. The next-higher address is then called up automatically.

This function of the operator control routine can be used to store the application program in the desired RAM area. Of course, this requires that the program first be manually translated into hex code using a programming table ("do-it-yourself assembler"). This method is therefore only suitable for first attempts.

After the program has been entered, the restart address is switched over from the starting point of the operator control routine to the starting point of the user program and the process is begun with a reset signal. However, the starting address is often permanently set to the start of the monitor program. At the start of the application program we therefore require a special start routine (GO) with which the start address is read in from the keyboard and loaded into the program counter.

Most monitor programs additionally possess a dump or load command with which programs can be stored on tape and reloaded. Another, more convenient way of maintaining comparatively small programs is to program them into an EPROM using a burn command. A large number of small microcomputers offering these facilities are commercially available.

20.4.2   Programming with assembler

For creating larger programs, hex-code programming is out of the question. The program is written in mnemonic code using an editor which allows text corrections. The program steps are not initially assigned an address. Branch addresses are defined by labels only. Comments can be entered together with the program steps.

The resulting text is known as the source listing. It is, of course, considerably more extensive than the associated machine program, the ratio being in the order of 20:1. A bulk storage medium in the form of a hard disk or floppy disk is needed to store it.

The source listing is then translated into hex code using the assembler program. It is advisable to break larger tasks down into several parts and translate them separately. This facilitates debugging, as the various modules can be tested separately. Each module begins with the address 0000.

In the next step, we specify which modules are to be combined in which sequence to form a complete program. If the names of library routines appear in the program, these routines are automatically copied from the library and added to the program. This task is performed by the "linker" program. The result is a coherent program, the steps of which are continuously numbered starting from 0000.

In the third and last step, the start address which the program is to receive in the object computer is specified. Using this information, the loader program numbers all the program steps and stores their hex code in a data field, where it is available for simulation runs or for the EPROM programmer.

Figure 20.20 shows the entire sequence in the form of a flowchart. An equipment which can be used to carry out the steps described is called a development system. The hardware configuration is shown in Fig. 20.21. As the entire translation process is a purely formal text processing activity, the CPU of the development system need not conform to that of the object computer. For example, a wide variety of inexpensive personal computers (PCs) are available as host computers. The cross-software required, comprising the assembler, linker and loader, is available from various software houses and from some microcomputer manufacturers for virtually all types.

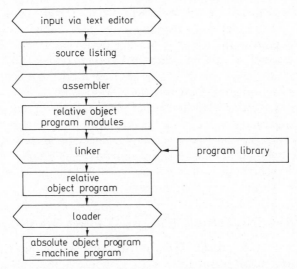

Fig. 20.20 Program creation sequence using a development system

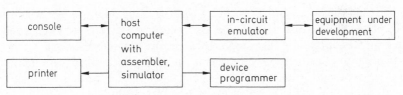

Fig. 20.21 Hardware of a development system

20.4.3   Simulation and emulation

The assembler checks a program for syntax errors during translation, but cannot detect logical errors. Consequently, a program must be tested after development, for which purpose two aids are available: the simulator and the emulator. The simulator is a program which simulates the CPU of the object system on the development system computer (e.g. PC). This makes it possible to observe the register contents, the stack and other memory areas during execution of the program. The better simulators even allow I/O circuits to be incorporated in the simulation and to check the reactions to external signals. The majority of logical program errors can be found in this way. As the hardware of the system to be developed does not have to be available when using the simulator, hardware and software development can proceed in parallel.

The disadvantage of simulators is that they operate orders of magnitude slower than the CPU of the object system and thus cannot be used to examine real-time behavior. For final testing, we therefore require an emulator (in-circuit emulator, ICE). This consists of interface hardware and software which link the development system with the object system. The emulator contains the microprocessor and the program memory of the device to be developed and is connected to the processor socket of the new device via a cable. It allows the program to be tested in real time using the I/O ports of the object system. For checking purposes, "breakpoints" can be inserted in the program, at which the registers and memory areas of interest can be displayed.

Emulators are specific to the particular microprocessor being developed. It must therefore be changed along with the software if programs are to be written for another microprocessor. Simple versions are available for between US $1000 and US $5000. Powerful emulators cost up to US $25,000. Emulators for single-chip microcomputers often contain an EPROM programmer for the EPROM of the particular microcomputer.

20.4.4   Simple development systems without bulk storage

The high cost and complexity of the development systems described is due to the fact that the application program is stored in mnemonic form and has to be processed. This means that a bulk memory with associated operating system is required.

The bulk memory can be dispensed with by using an assembler which will immediately translate each command as it is entered and only store the machine program. Of course, it is then impossible to store comments as well.

In order to obviate the need to operate in hex code for subsequent modifications, we require a program which will convert hex code back into mnemonic format. Such a program is called a disassembler. Contrary to popular belief, labels can also be used with this method. The "line-by-line" assembler merely has to create a label table which is stored along with the program and is available to the disassembler for the re-translation.

An assembler/disassembler of this kind together with a monitor program occupy only about 8 kbytes of memory. It can therefore be accommodated directly in the object computer. This has the advantage of making it possible to test the program directly after input, without using an emulator. The program can be modified without having to go each time through tedious translation procedure detailed in Fig. 20.20.

Consequently, a simple development system of this kind is particularly useful for writing short programs of up to approx. 10 kbytes, as here the primary consideration is to be able to modify quickly, and the disadvantage of not having a commentary is less important.

20.5   Survey of types available

The wide variety of microprocessors available can be subdivided into two product families, one based on the Motorola 6800 and the other on the Intel 8080. Figures 20.22 and 20.23 show the principal representatives of these two families. The 6800 and 8080 are nowadays of merely historical significance, having been superseded by types 6802 and 8085 respectively. However, the latter are largely compatible with the basic types, and more powerful microprocessors have been developed in both families. This improvement is due to a number of factors.

One factor is the increase of the word length in the data registers from 8 to 16 or 32 bits and a corresponding enlargement of the data bus. This means that 2 or 4 bytes can be transmitted and processed in one cycle. In order to make this possible, the data types are defined accordingly.

Similarly, the word length in the address registers has been raised from 16 via 20 and 24 to 32 bits, thereby increasing the address space to up to 4 Gbytes. This also increases the branch range (relative addressing), making it possible with most of the newer microprocessors to also write large relocative programs, i.e. without having to assign definite memory locations.

Performance has been further increased by extending the instruction set. Using new powerful instructions such as a multiply instruction, some operations can be performed much more quickly and without long subroutines. Additional types of addressing are introduced in order to simplify and speed up access to tables.

The increased clock frequency has been achieved by modern integration technology. However, it requires faster RAMs and ROMs. The quality of a microprocessor is evidenced by the fact that it does not request extremely short access times even at high clock frequencies. A microprocessor requiring short access times severely limits the choice of suitable RAMs and ROMs as they are very expensive. The access time can be lengthened by inserting wait states, but this reduces the computing power. The values given in Figs. 20.22/23 refer to operation without wait states. In larger systems, bus drivers are required, and the access time is reduced by their delay times.

Computing speed is expressed on MIPS (Million Instructions per Second). This specifies the average number of instructions that the microprocessor can handle in a second. It must be remembered that a 32-bit processor is more powerful than an 8-bit processor, even if its MIPS figure is identical. It can process a 32-bit operand using a single instruction, whereas the 8-bit processor requires several instructions for this purpose. The computing speed is naturally proportional to the clock frequency, the specified value being referred to the maximum clock frequency.

In addition to the access time of the memories, a limiting factor for the computing speed is the bus bandwidth. Various mechanisms have been developed in order to achieve high computing speed even for moderate requirements (and costs). One frequently used method is "prefetch": even while an instruction is being processed, the next (or in some cases the next but one) instruction is fetched if the bus is free. Problems arise if branches occur in the program, because the next instruction is defined only after the current instruction has been processed. It may happen that the instructions buffered in the prefetch have to be disregarded. During program development, the prefetch is generally a hindrance in the emulation phase, as the instruction just being

Type	Instruction set	Data bus width [bit]	Address space [byte]	Data register [bit]	Address register [bit]	Relative branch range	Multiply instruction
6500-series from Rockwell, WDC, VLSI							
6502	6500	8	64 k	1×8	2×16	± 127	–
65C816	6500 +	8/16	16 M	1×16	$5 \times 16/24$	± 32 k	–
6800-series from Motorola, Hitachi, Thomson, Valvo (68070)							
6800	6800	8	64 k	2×8	3×16	± 127	–
6802	6800	8	64 k	2×8	3×16	± 127	–
6809	6809	8	64 k	2×8	5×16	± 32 k	8×8
68000	68000	16	16 M	8×32	10×32	± 32 k	16×16
68008	68000	8	1 M	8×32	10×32	± 32 k	16×16
68070	68000	16	16 M	8×32	10×32	± 32 k	16×16
68010	68000 +	16	16 M	8×32	11×32	± 32 k	16×16
68020	68000 + +	32	4 G	8×32	11×32	± 2 G	32×32
68030	68000 + + +	32	4 G	8×32	11×32	± 2 G	32×32
68040	68000 + + +	32	4 G	8×32	11×32	± 2 G	32×32

Fig. 20.22 Survey of

Type	Instruction set	Data bus width [bit]	Address space [byte]	Data register [bit]	Address register [bit]	Relative branch range	Multiply instruction
8080-series from Intel, Siemens, AMD, NEC							
8080	8080	8	64 k	8×8	5×16	–	–
8085	8080	8	64 k	8×8	5×16	—	—
8086	8086	16	1 M	4×16	9×16	± 32 k	16×16
8088	8086	8	1 M	4×16	9×16	± 32 k	16×16
80186	8086 +	16	1 M	4×16	9×16	± 32 k	16×16
80188	8086 +	8	1 M	4×16	9×16	± 32 k	16×16
80286	8086 + +	16	16 M	4×16	9×16	± 32 k	16×16
80386	8086 + +	32	4 G	8×32	9×32	± 2 G	32×32
80486	8086 + +	32	4 G	8×32	9×32	± 2 G	32×32
Z80-series from Zilog, NEC, SGS, Sharp							
Z80	8080 +	8	64 k	8×8	4×16	± 127	–
Z180	Z80 +	8	512 k	8×8	4×16	± 127	8×8
Z280	Z8000 +	8/16	16 M	8×8	4×16	± 32 k	16×16
Z320	Z80000	32	4 G	8×32	9×32	± 2 G	32×32

Data types: T = Bit, B = Byte, W = Word (16 bit), L = Long Word (32 bit), Q = Quad Word (64 bit), D = Decimal (BCD), A = ASCII, S = String

Fig. 20.23 Survey of

Clock frequency f std/max [MHz]	Access time std/min [ns]	Computing speed at f_{max} [MIPS]	Data types	Remarks
1/3	650/170	0.3	B, D	
2/8	365/70	0.8	B, D, W	CP
1/2	600/290	0.3	B, D	
1/2	600/230	0.3	B, D	128 byte RAM
1/2	700/330	0.4	B, D, W	
8/16	250/125	1.0	B, D, W, L, T	SY
8/12	250/190	0.7	B, D, W, L, T	SY
10	200	0.8	B, D, W, L, T	SY, VM, MMU, DMA, TIM
8/12	250/190	1.3	B, D, W, L, T	SY, VM
16/25	110/55	5.0	B, D, W, L, T, Q	SY, VM, CA, CP
25/50	70/20	12	B, D, W, L, T, Q	SY, VM, CA, MMU, CP
50	40	17	B, D, W, L, T, Q	SY, VM, CA, MMU, CP, MCP

6800-type microprocessors

Clock frequency f std/max [MHz]	Access time std/min [ns]	Computing speed at f_{max} [MIPS]	Data types	Remarks
1/3	500/200	0.2	B, D	
3/6	300/75	0.4	B, D	
5/10	325/200	1.0	B, D, W	CP
5/8	325/200	0.7	B, D, W	CP
8/12	200/120	1.3	B, D, W, A, S	CP, TIM, DMA, IRC
8/10	200/150	0.9	B, D, W, A, S	CP, TIM, DMA, IRC
6/16	250/100	2.0	B, D, W, A, S	CP, SY, MMU, VM
20/33	60/35	8.0	B, D, W, A, S, Q	CP, SY, MMU, VM
25/33	35/25	18	B, D, W, A, S, Q	CP, SY, MMU, VM, CA, MCP
3/8	360/120	0.6	B, D, T	RC
4/10	250/100	0.7	B, D, T	RC, MMU, DMA, TIM
10/12.5	100/80	1.4	B, D, W, L, S, T	RC, MMU, CA, DMA, TIM, CA
8/10	120/100		B, D, W, L, S, T, Q	SY, MMU, CA

Remarks: CP = Coprocessor-Interface, TIM = Timer, DMA = Direct Memory Access, IRC = Interrupt Controller, MMU = Memory Managment Unit, SY = System or Supervisory mode, VM = Virtual Memory, CA = Cache, MCP = Mathem. Coprocessor, RC = Refresh Controller

8080-type microprocessors

loaded will not be executed next (nor perhaps at all). Consequently, it is usually possible to deactivate the prefetch mechanism.

Another method of speeding up access to programs or even data is to use a cache memory. A cache is a small, fast buffer memory which is frequently integrated in the microprocessor itself. It is used to store the instructions (and data) required most recently. As most programs contain relatively small loops, it is highly probable that the required instructions and operands will still be in the cache, thereby obviating a large number of time-consuming bus accesses. This, of course, reduces program observability.

Programmer and user alike find it very difficult to arrange systematically the large address space provided by the modern microprocessors. Therefore, a memory management unit (MMU) is often inserted between the microprocessor and the memory. It allows a largely flexible allocation between the *logical addresses* of the processor and the *physical memory locations*. This "mapping" is performed by means of a table which is loaded into the MMU. In addition, attributes such as write protection can be defined for each memory segment. One disadvantage of the MMU method is that address translation requires additional time. As a result, it is often necessary to insert an additional wait state. It is thus preferable for the MMU to be integrated on the processor chip, as the delay is then minimized.

More recent microprocessors also support virtual memory (VM) operation. Using this technique, data and programs can be addressed on a hard disk as if they were directly available in a RAM. In the course of executing a program, it may happen that an operand is required which is not in RAM but in external mass storage. In this case, execution of the instruction is interrupted. The operating system loads the data segment containing the operand from mass storage into RAM and then returns to executing the instruction. This allows, for example, the vast 4 Gbyte address space to be utilized.

Microprocessor performance can be considerably increased by connecting a coprocessor in parallel. This device executes complicated operations which would severely tax the microprocessor. The most common types are arithmetic coprocessors which not only carry out the four basic arithmetic operations in fixed-point and IEEE format (see Section 19.1), but can also calculate transcendental functions and convert number notations. There are also graphics, text and DMA coprocessors. To be able to use a coprocessor, the microprocessor must have a coprocessor interface across which data exchange and synchronization can take place. In programming terms, the coprocessor is very transparent: it simply adds a few instructions to the microprocessor's instruction set. During program execution, the processors detect from the instruction code which one of them has to carry out the particular instruction.

With the microprocessors listed in Figs. 20.22 and 20.23, the current drain is not given, as it is virtually negligible compared to the power consumption of the extensive semiconductor memories and mass storage as well as the I/O circuits which are invariably used to operate such processors. Nevertheless, a number of new, particularly complex types have already been realized wholly or partly in CMOS technology. This has not been done to save power, but to be able to cool the chips sufficiently, as they contain more than half a million transistors.

With simple microprocessors, some of which are also used in battery-operated equipment, the current drain is not negligible, and it is desirable to use current-saving CMOS versions. As we can see from Fig. 20.24, the power dissipation for all types is quite small at 1 MHz clock frequency. It increases, however, in proportion to the frequency. If the CMOS types are operated at the maximum permissible frequency, the power dissipation is comparable to that of NMOS types. The CMOS microprocessors, however, all have static memories which enable the clock to be stopped. This characteristic can be used to minimize the average power dissipation even at high clock frequencies by stopping the clock in wait phases. For small, battery-operated equipments, the single-chip microcomputers in Figs. 20.30 and 20.31 frequently offer advantages, as they generally contain all the I/O circuits required.

Basic type	CMOS type	Power dissipation at 1 MHz	Max. clock frequency	Manufacturer
6502	R65C02	20 mW	4 MHz	Rockwell
6809	HD6309	12 mW	3 MHz	Hitachi
68000	HD68HC000	12 mW	12.5 MHz	Hitachi, Motorola
8085	MSM80C85	15 mW	5 MHz	Oki
8086	80C86	50 mW	8 MHz	Harris, Oki, Intel
8086	V30	30 mW	16 MHz	NEC
8088	80C88	50 mW	8 MHz	Harris, Oki, Intel
8088	V20	30 mW	10 MHz	NEC
80186	80C186	50 mW	16 MHz	Intel
80186	V50	35 mW	8 MHz	NEC
80188	80C188	50 mW	16 MHz	Intel
80188	V40	35 mW	8 MHz	NEC
80286	80C286	60 mW	25 MHz	Harris
Z80	TMPZ84C00	20 mW	8 MHz	Toshiba, Zilog
Z180	HD64180	12 mW	8 MHz	Hitachi, Zilog

Fig. 20.24 CMOS microcomputers of the 6800 or 8080 series

20.6   Minimum systems

A microcomputer equipped with a program memory of 2 kbytes, a 128-byte RAM and an I/O circuit already constitutes a very powerful tool, capable of replacing a large number of different hardware sequential logic systems. Therefore, in order to perform specific tasks, one can often dispense with modular expandability, thereby achieving a significant reduction in hardware complexity. We shall now examine this possibility in somewhat greater detail.

20.6.1 Design of a simple microcomputer

If we know from the outset that the microcomputer is to be implemented using only a small number of integrated circuits, we can make an initial simplification by dispensing with all the bus drivers. The second simplification is that it is no longer necessary to decode the addresses completely, as only a small part of the address range is allocated. This possibility of partial decoding will be illustrated with the aid of an example. We shall assume that a 2-kbyte EPROM is used as the program memory and a 128-byte RAM as the data memory. A PIA (see Section 21.4.2) is additionally provided for parallel I/O, i.e. a total of

$$2048 + 128 + 4 = 2180$$

memory locations are used. To differentiate between them, we require 12 address bits which are decoded in accordance with Fig. 20.25: Address bits a_0 to a_{10} denoted by M_3 are applied directly to the EPROM. Bit a_{11} characterizes the program memory area and is applied to the Chip Select input of the EPROM.

Hex address	Type of memory		Straight binary address				

Fig. 20.25 Allocation of memories for minimum system and address decoding. M_1, M_2, M_3 denote address inputs of the appropriate memory. The highest and the lowest address is entered for each memory group

The locations of the input/output registers are designated by the 01 combination at the address lines a_{11} and a_{10}. The internal registers of the PIA are selected by the address bits a_0 and a_1.

The RAM locations are identified by the combination 00 at the address bits a_{11} and a_{10}. The 128 locations are distinguished by the address bit a_0 to a_6 (M_1). By the additional decoding of bits a_7 to a_9, the RAM range can be extended to 1 kbyte without having to change the memory specifier decoder.

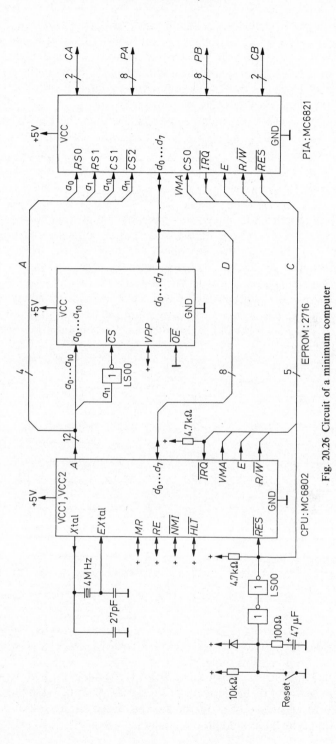

Fig. 20.26 Circuit of a minimum computer

With the partial decoding technique used, address bits a_{12} to a_{15} are not tested, and therefore each location may be called by 16 different 16-bit addresses. The highest digit of the 4-digit hexadecimal number may thus have any value. However, it is advisable to select the addresses in the program as if they were fully decoded. This ensures that the program is operable even in a prototyping computer which decodes the address completely.

Figure 20.26 shows the circuit implemented using the address allocation described. An MC6802, which already contains the 128-byte RAM, has been selected as central processor.

20.6.2   Single-chip microcomputer

Advances in large-scale integration have made it possible to accommodate not only a RAM but also a ROM and several peripheral circuits on the processor chip. This has brought about the development from single-chip microprocessor to single-chip microcomputer. By way of example, Fig. 20.27 shows the block diagram of a type MC68HC11A8. Its CPU has been greatly extended compared with the 6800 microprocessor. It has a second index register, and the two accumulators A and B can be combined to form a 16-bit register. In addition to a large number of new instructions, 8×8 bit multiplication is also provided.

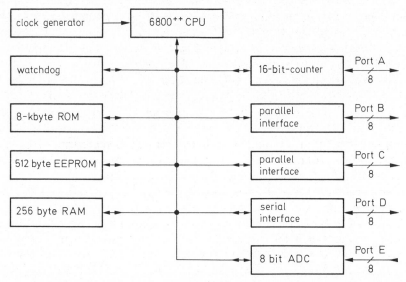

Fig. 20.27 Internal structure of the MC68HC11A8 single-chip microcomputer

The memory consists of an 8-kbyte ROM at the top of the address space and a 256-byte RAM in the "base page" (see Fig. 20.28). The microcomputer also has an EEPROM which can be programmed and erased during operation without having to apply an additional programming voltage. The EEPROM can be used

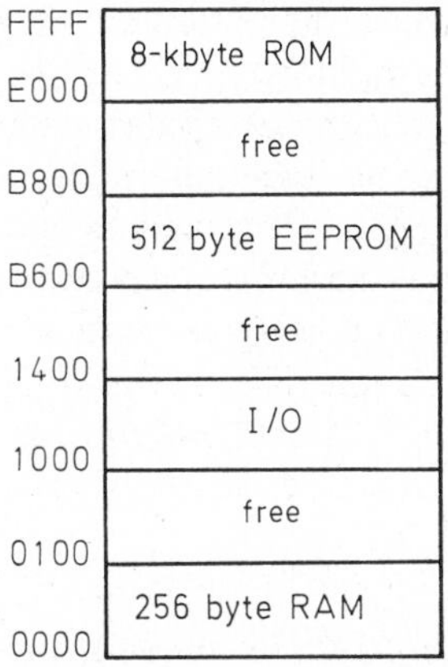

FFFF	8-kbyte ROM
E000	
B800	free
B600	512 byte EEPROM
1400	free
1000	I/O
0100	free
0000	256 byte RAM

Fig. 20.28 Address allocation in the MC68HC11A8

to store data such as calibration values, which although not fixed from the outset, must not be lost in the event of a power failure. The EEPROM can also be used to store programs, e.g. a short main program, which employs a program library stored in a ROM.

The MC68HC11A8 has five I/O interfaces. The address and data bus can be made externally accessible via the two parallel interfaces (ports B and C). This allows external RAMs to be connected as program memories during program development. The serial interface consists of an asynchronous interface for connecting an operator terminal and a synchronous interface for connecting serially driven displays or D/A converters, or for communication with other microcomputers in the same equipment.

The microcomputer has an A/D converter with 8-bit precision for evaluation of analog signals. A preceding multiplexer enables interrogation of 8 different sources. If this level of precision is insufficient, it can be increased to some extent by either taking the average of several measurements or subdividing the measurement range into several parts. If a higher degree of precision is required, it is advisable to connect an external A/D converter to the synchronous serial interface.

The programmable counter can not only count events, but can also be used for frequency and time measurement and as a real-time clock. It is then associated with a watchdog circuit which waits for a regular program action and initiates a restart if it fails to occur. This ensures that the microcomputer automatically resumes the required operation if it jumps out of program sequence due to a program error or an interference pulse. However, single-chip microcomputers are much less prone to interference than multichip solutions, as the line lengths are smaller by some orders of magnitude. This constitutes a significant advantage which must not be lost by using external program memories.

In order to minimize current drain, the 68HC11 is fabricated in CMOS technology. An additional saving can be made by selecting the clock frequency no higher than the processing rate requires. However, an equally effective solution is to let the microcomputer operate at the full clock frequency and to stop it at times when there is nothing to process; this results in shorter reaction times. Such a changeover in the operating mode is supported by virtually all CMOS-based microcomputers. A WAIT command is issued to deactivate the CPU, but the clock generator and the counters continue to run, so that the CPU reactivates itself in response to a pre-programmed timer interrupt. The lowest current drain is achieved in the STOP or SLEEP mode. Here the clock generator is also stopped until an external interrupt is received. The memory contents of the RAM are retained, as the CMOS-RAMs are always static devices.

Virtually all single-chip microcomputers allow external access to be provided to the address and data bus. This makes it possible to connect additional program and data memories as well as I/O circuits. This possibility is illustrated in Fig. 20.29. As we can see, it results in the loss of 18 port connections. In order not to lose yet another 8 lines, the bottom 8 address lines are multiplexed together with the data lines. The address strobe signal AS indicates whether addresses or data are being transmitted. In order to be able to use normal memories and I/O circuits, the 8 lower-order address bits are stored in a latch. The result is that now a regular 16-bit address bus A and 8-bit data bus D is available, as in a normal multichip microcomputer. However, this also cancels out virtually all the advantages of a single-chip device because, in order to recover the lost ports, it is necessary to insert a port replacement unit PRU. The PRU is selected via an address decoder at those addresses which the desired ports had previously occupied in the address space of the microcomputer, and which are now assigned to the external memory (RAM). This level of complexity is only justified in emulators, where it is necessary to emulate the microcomputer exactly. An external program memory is then essential, because is has to be loaded by the development system.

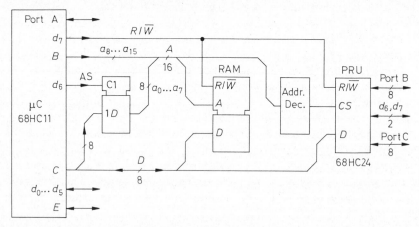

Fig. 20.29 Operation of a single-chip microcomputer in expanded multiplexed mode using a port replacement unit PRU

Figures 20.30 and 20.31 provide an overview of some commonly used microcomputers. As we can see, there are equivalent microcomputers for virtually every microprocessor of the simpler type. Their instruction set is sometimes extended, sometimes reduced, but almost never identical. In addition, instructions for operations using a single bit are often provided. This makes it possible with a single instruction, for instance to set and reset a bit or even branch depending on whether a bit is set or clear.

In the basic version, the microcomputer program memory is always designed as a mask-programmed ROM. However, due to the high mask costs (e.g. US $50,000 or more), this design is only of interest for mass production, but mass-produced microcomputers may sell at well below US $5 per unit. For program development and for production in small lots, four program memory variants are available (depending on type):

1) without program memory
2) with EPROM on the chip
3) with "piggy-back" EPROM
4) with EEPROM.

In the version without program memory, an external RAM or EPROM must be connected, resulting in the loss of 18 ports—as shown in Fig. 20.29. Unfortunately, the remaining ports are normally insufficient, and so it is necessary to adopt the relatively involved approach of replacing them by an additional parallel interface circuit.

A solution to this problem is provided by variants 2) to 4). Here the user can load and modify the program himself without incurring the loss of ports. Therefore, in the lists in Figs. 20.30 and 20.31 preference has been given to microcomputers offering these variants. Where the EPROM is on the chip, the program memory can be programmed and erased like a normal EPROM. There are also versions in plastic packages without window. OTP (One Time Programmable) or ZTAT (Zero Turn-Around Time) versions of this type are considerably cheaper and, for production quantities up to 5000, generally more favorably priced than mask-programmed types. The fact that they cannot be erased presents no disadvantage for large-scale production.

With piggy-back EPROMs, the address and data bus is additionally brought out and connected to a socket for a conventional EPROM which is located on the top of the microcomputer housing. Although this version is a general-purpose type, it is unfortunately very expensive, because the special housing is intricate and the contacting of the many pins is complex. This version is therefore only used during program development and for prototypes.

The more recent successors to EPROMs for program storage are the EEPROMs. These are particularly suitable for microcomputers which already contain a small EEPROM for storing calibration values. These variants are to be found in a number of the latest microcomputers, realized in CMOS technology.

ROM type	EPROM type	Manufacturer	Technology	Instruction set
R 6500/1	R 6500/1 EB[1]	Rockwell	NMOS	6500
M 50753	M 50753 PGYS[1]	Mitsubishi	CMOS	6500
MC 6804 P 2	MC 68704 P 2	Motorola	NMOS	6800 − −
MC 68 HC 04 P 4	MC 68 HC 704 P 4	Motorola	CMOS	6800 − −
MC 68 HC 05 J 2	MC 68 HC 705 J 2	Motorola	CMOS	6800 −
MC 68 HC 05 P 7	MC 68 HC 705 P 9	Motorola	CMOS	6800 −
MC 68 HC 05 C 4	MC 68 HC 705 C 4	Motorola	CMOS	6800 −
MC 68 HC 05 B 6	MC 68 HC 805 B 6[2]	Motorola	CMOS	6800 −
MC 68 HC 05 C 8	MC 68 HC 705 C 8	Motorola	CMOS	6800 −
MC 68 HC 11 D 3	MC 68 HC 711 D 3	Motorola	CMOS	6800 +
MC 68 HC 11 A 8	MC 68 HC 811 A 8[2]	Motorola	CMOS	6800 +
MC 68 HC 11 E 9	MC 68 HC 711 E 9	Motorola	CMOS	6800 +
MC 68 HC 11 K 4	MC 68 HC 711 K 4	Motorola	CMOS	6800 +
PCB 93 C 110		Philips	CMOS	68000

Fig. 20.30 Examples of 6800-series

ROM type	EPROM type	Manufacturer	Technology	Instruction set
Z 8601	Z 8603[1]	Zilog	NMOS	Z 80 −
Z 8820	Z 8822[1]	Zilog	NMOS	Z 80 +
HD 643180 X	HD 647180 X	Hitachi	CMOS	64180
HD 643180 Y	HD 647180 Y	Hitachi	CMOS	64180
8048	8748	Intel, Siemens	NMOS	8080 −
80 C 48		Intel, Siemens	CMOS	8080 −
8051	8751	Intel[3]	NMOS	8080 +
80 C 51	87 C 51	AMD, Oki	CMOS	8080 +
80 C 521	87 HC 521	AMD	CMOS	8080 +
80 C 541	87 C 541	AMD	CMOS	8080 +
8096	8796	Intel	NMOS	8086 −
80 C 196	87 C 196	Intel	CMOS	8086 −

Fig. 20.31 8080-series single-

[1] EPROM attachable (piggy-back)
[2] EEPROM as program memory
[3] Other manufacturers: AMD, Siemens, Valvo

RAM/ROM [byte]	Pins I/O [pins]	Serial I/O	Counter [bit]	AD conv. [channels × bit]	Remarks
64/2 k	32	–	1 × 16	–	
192/6 k	44	Async.	3 × 8	8 × 8	PWM
32/1 k	20	–	1 × 8	–	
156/4 k	20	–	1 × 8	–	$V_{DD} \geqq 2\,V$
64/2 k				–	DOG
128/2 k	21	Async.	1 × 16	4 × 8	DOG
176/4 k	31	As., sync.	1 × 16	–	
176/6 k	32	Async.	1 × 16	8 × 8	DOG, PWM, 256 EE
304/8 k	31	As., sync.	1 × 16	–	DOG
192/4 k	32	As., sync.	1 × 16		DOG
256/8 k	38	As., sync.	1 × 16	8 × 8	DOG, 512 EE
512/12 k	38	As., sync.	1 × 16	8 × 8	DOG, 512 EE
768/24 k	62	As., sync.	1 × 16	8 × 8	DOG, PWM, 640 EE
512/34 k	40	As., sync.	3 × 16	–	DOG, 256 EE

single-chip microcomputers

RAM/ROM [byte]	Pins I/O [bit]	Serial I/O	Counter [bit]	AD conv. [channels × bit]	Remarks
128/2 k	32	Async.	2 × 8	–	
272/8 k	32	Async.	2 × 16	–	
512/16 k	54	As., sync.	2 × 16	–	
1024/32 k	54	As., sync.	2 × 16	6 × 10 bit	
64/1 k	24	–	1 × 8	–	
64/1 k	24	–	1 × 8	–	
128/4 k	32	Async.	2 × 16	–	
128/4 k	32	Async.	2 × 16	–	
256/8 k	32	Async.	2 × 16	–	DOG
256/16 k	32	Async.	2 × 16	–	DOG
232/8 k	40	Async.	2 × 16	8 × 10	DOG, PWM
256/8 k	40	Async.	2 × 16	8 × 10	DOG, PWM

chip microcomputers

Remarks: EE: Bytes of additional EEPROM
        PWM: Pulse Width Modulator
        DOG: Watchdog

21 Modular design of microcomputers

In the previous Chapter the emphasis was on the programming of micro-computers. We shall now discuss the actual circuitry in greater detail. This will entail describing a modular system where each functional unit is accommodated on a separate board. The functional units are interconnected via the microcomputer bus, which connects the corresponding pins of all the boards in parallel.

21.1 Microprocessor board

Figure 21.1 shows the pin configuration of the MC 6802 microprocessor. All the inputs and outputs are TTL-compatible. Most of the pin functions have been described in the previous sections. Their meanings are listed in Fig. 21.2.

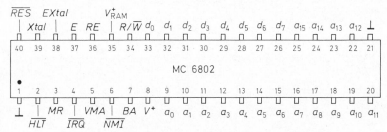

Fig. 21.1 Pin configuration of the MC 6802 microprocessor

As we have already seen in Fig. 20.1, the data pins of the CPU, memories and peripheral circuits are connected in parallel. An arrangement of this type is known as a *bus*. It is obvious that only one user can transfer data on the bus at any one time. This user is selected by the address bus. Additional control signals to determine the direction of the data flow and for synchronization purposes are transmitted via the control bus.

As no more than 10 MOS or 5 low-power-Schottky inputs can be connected to a microprocessor output, larger systems require amplifiers (buffers) at all the outputs. Figure 21.3 shows how they have to be connected to the microprocessor bus. Bidirectional buffers must be used for the bidirectional data bus. These consist of two antiparallel-connected amplifiers with tristate output which are complementarily activated using direction changeover signal $EN1/EN2$. The $R/\overline{W}$ signal of the microprocessor is used to select the direction of data flow. The Enable pin EN of the buffers is linked to the BA output of the microprocessor, causing the data bus to go high impedance when the microprocessor is halted. This mode provides direct memory access (DMA). For the same reason, tristate

Signal	Direction	Function
$a_0 \ldots a_{15}$	Tristate output	Address
$d_0 \ldots d_{15}$	Tri. inp./outp.	Data
$R/\bar{W}$	Tristate output	Read/$\overline{\text{Write}}$ switchover.
VMA	Output	Valid Memory Address. "High" level indicates that a valid address is being output.
BA	Output	Bus Available. Processor in HALT status; all tristate outputs are high impedance.
E	Output	Enable (previously ϕ_2). System clock output.
$EXtal$	Input	External clock input. One quarter of the frequency applied appears as system clock at E.
$Xtal$	Output	Crystal output. Used together with $EXtal$ as crystal connection for the internal clock generator.
$\overline{HLT}$	Input	Halt. "Low" level halts the processor. All tristate outputs go high impedance. $BA = 1$ and $VMA = 0$.
MR	Input	Memory Ready. The processor waits in the status $E = 1$ for as long as $MR = 0$. All outputs remain valid. Maximum duration: 10 µs.
$\overline{IRQ}$	Input	Interrupt Request. Normal interrupt input.
$\overline{NMI}$	Input	Non-Maskable Interrupt.
$\overline{RES}$	Input	Reset input.
RE	Input	RAM Enable. Low level deactivates the installed RAM

Fig. 21.2 Description of input/output signals for the 6802 microprocessor

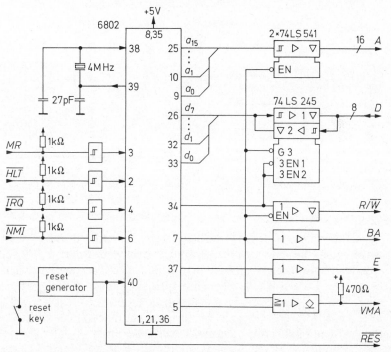

Fig. 21.3 Connecting the 6802 microprocessor via drivers to the address, data and control buses

buffers are also used on the address bus and at the $R/\overline{W}$ output. The following tristate buffers in low-power Schottky TTL technology are well suited to microprocessor applications (many other types are listed in Chapter 28.2):

Unidirectional: Bidirectional:
8 bit:　74 LS 541   8 bit:　74 LS 245

21.1.1　Reset logic

It is essential that when a microcomputer is switched on, it automatically jumps to the program to be executed. For this to happen, the reset input $\overline{RES}$ must be held at low (L) level for a period of time after energization. Although only 8 μs are required for the 6802, this period does not commence until the operating voltage has exceeded the lower tolerance limit of 4.75 V.

A simple circuit for achieving this is shown in Fig. 21.4. After the microprocessor is switched on, the voltage across the capacitor increases much more slowly than the supply voltage. $\overline{RES} = 1$ only when the voltage across the capacitor exceeds the TTL-gate switching level of approx. 1.4 V. The time characteristic of the reset signal is shown in Fig. 21.5. It can be seen that for the values specified the reset status does not disappear until the supply voltage has exceeded 4.75 V.

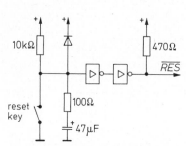

Fig. 21.4 Simple "Power-on/Reset" circuit

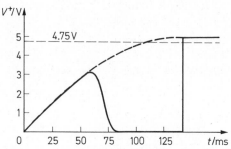

Fig. 21.5 Reset signal $\overline{RES}$ when the supply voltage is switched on

Immediately after switch-on, the Reset signal initially increases with the supply voltage, as the gates are not operating correctly due to the supply voltage being too low. This increase can have detrimental effects, particularly where the system contains CMOS RAMs which are operated as quasi-permanent memories using a standby power supply. As long as the supply voltage is below 4.75 V, neither the microprocessor nor the bus drivers will function correctly. Consequently, unintentional write operations will take place during this period, making the contents of the memory unusable. A Reset signal is therefore required in this case which inhibits the memory all the time the supply voltage is building up.

A Reset signal of this type can only be implemented using the normally-closed contact of a relay, since electronic circuits cannot operate without voltage. An appropriate reset circuit is shown in Fig. 21.6. As long as the relay is not energized, the reset line is connected to ground. $\overline{RES} = 1$ only when the relay is energized. RS flip-flop G_1, G_2 is merely used to debounce the relay contact (see Fig. 10.46).

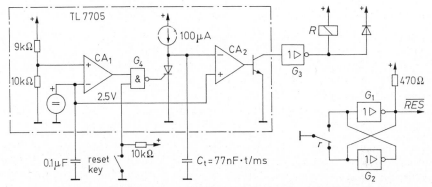

Fig. 21.6 Precision reset generator without switch-on and switch-off disturbances

In this example we have used the TL 7705 Power-on/Reset generator to activate the relay. The suitably reduced supply voltage is compared in this device with a reference voltage of 2.5 V. When the supply voltage exceeds 4.75 V, the comparator output goes to 1, the gate output goes to 0 and the thyristor turns off, because it was operated below its holding current. Capacitor C_t is then charged with a constant current. When the capacitor voltage has increased to 2.5 V, the output of CA_2 goes to zero, the transistor is turned off and the relay is energized via inverter G_3. The delay time can be set to any value by selecting C_t accordingly.

If the supply voltage is less than 4.75 V at switch-off, comparator CA_1 goes to zero, the output of G_4 to 1, and the thyristor fires. This discharges timer capacitor C_t virtually instantaneously, the relay assumes the normal position and the reset signal becomes zero.

The TL 7705 reset generator can also be used without the additional relay. However, the same disturbances then occur during switch-on and switch-off as in the simple circuit in Fig. 21.4/5.

21.1.2 Adjustable restart address

In Fig. 20.19 we saw that the start addresses of the interrupt routines have to be stored in memory area FFF8 to FFFF. If a RAM is providing this address area, the addresses can be loaded into it using, for example, a monitor program. At the start of the monitor program itself, however, its start address must be permanently available at restart point FFFE/FFFF. Figure 21.7 shows one method of removing these two memory locations from the RAM area and replacing them by switches.

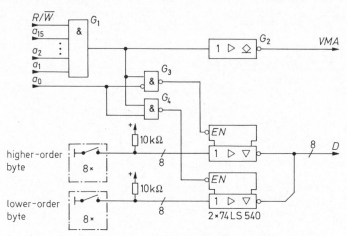

Fig. 21.7 Restart circuit with adjustable start address

If the microprocessor produces addresses FFFE and FFFF and a read signal, the VMA line is pulled down to zero via open collector gate G_2. To make this possible, an open collector gate must also be used as driver for the VMA line on the CPU board, as shown in Fig. 21.3. As $VMA = 0$, no memories are addressed, i.e. not even those installed at addresses FFFE or FFFF. Instead, the switch status is transferred to the data bus via the tristate buffers, with the higher-order byte at address FFFE ($a_0 = 0$) and the lower-order byte at address FFFF ($a_0 = 1$). If binary-coded step switches are used, the restart address can be coded directly in hexadecimal.

21.2   Memory boards

When memory is connected to a microcomputer with modular expansion facilities, a number of points must be taken into consideration which we shall now examine with reference to Fig. 21.8. This shows a memory unit with a 16-kbyte capacity.

To enable the memory ICs to be decoupled from the microcomputer bus, drivers are used on all the bus lines, as on the microprocessor board. Once again, the data drivers must be bidirectional. However, change of direction is now effected in complementary mode: For $R/\overline{W} = 1$ (read), the data drivers must be switched to transfer data to the bus.

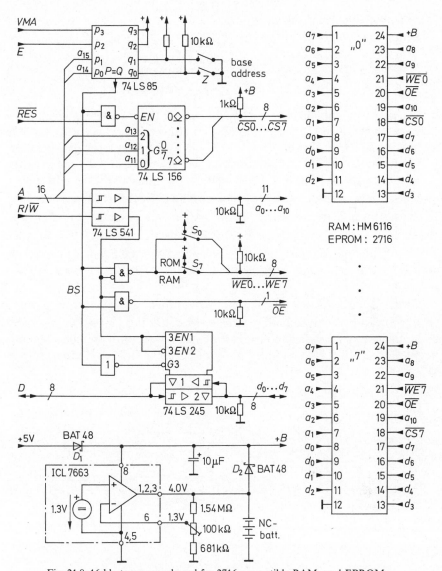

Fig. 21.8 16-kbyte memory board for 2716-compatible RAMs and EPROMs

The circuit in Fig. 21.8 is designed for memory chips with a capacity of 2 kbyte. The addresses within a memory are specified by address bits $a_0 \ldots a_{10}$. The three next higher address bits $a_{11} \ldots a_{13}$ are used, with the aid of a 1-of-8 decoder, to select one of the 8 memory chips. The two highest-order address bits are decoded by a comparator which compares these bits with a manually selectable number Z between 0 and 3 (base address) which can be interpreted directly as the board number. This means that the memory area is divided into four 16-kbyte blocks as shown below:

$$Z = 0: \quad A = 0000 \dots 3\text{FFF}$$
$$Z = 1: \quad A = 4000 \dots 7\text{FFF}$$
$$Z = 2: \quad A = 8000 \dots B\text{FFF}$$
$$Z = 3: \quad A = C000 \dots F\text{FFF}$$

The comparator only delivers the equality signal $BS = 1$ (Board Select) if the address applied is in the area selected. It is also necessary to ensure that the address applied is itself valid, i.e. $VMA \cdot E = 1$. To perform this logic operation, two free comparator bits can be used, as shown in Fig. 21.8, by applying the appropriate adjacent pins to 1. If the board is not selected, the data drivers are switched to high impedance. In addition, no chip is selected ($\overline{CS}_i = 1$) nor is any write attempt undertaken ($\overline{WE}_i = 1$). All outputs are deactivated ($\overline{OE} = 1$). In the event of a read operation, the memory outputs are activated ($\overline{OE} = 0$); when a write operation is initiated, a write command is issued ($\overline{WE} = 0$). However, the read or write command only becomes effective for the memory selected ($\overline{CS}_i = 0$).

Switch S can be used to hold the read/write switchover in the "read" position ($\overline{WE} = 1$) in order to avoid unintentional writes. For this purpose, it is possible either to use a single switch to protect the entire board, or to provide a separate switch for each RAM in order to protect each individual 2-kbyte area ($S_0 \dots S_7$).

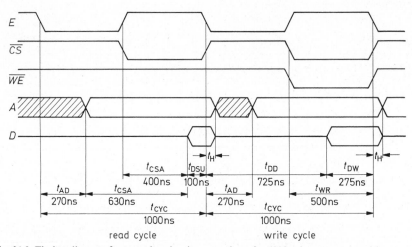

Fig. 21.9 Timing diagram for a read and write operation of a 6802 microprocessor with a system clock frequency of 1 MHz. The times given are for "worst case" conditions

t_{AD}:	Address Delay Time	t_{ADA}:	Address Access Time
t_{DD}:	Data Delay Time	t_{CSA}:	Chip-Select Access Time
t_{DSU}:	Data Setup Time	t_{WR}:	Write Time
t_{H}:	Hold Time	t_{DW}:	Data Valid Time

The timing diagram for a read and a write operation is shown in Fig. 21.9. The timing is controlled by system clock E. A microprocessor cycle begins on the negative-going edge of E. The addresses become valid after Address Delay Time t_{AD}, the data after Data Delay Time t_{DD}. During a read operation the microprocessor reads in the data at the end of a cycle, i.e. at the negative-going edge of E. In order to ensure that it is transferred correctly, it must be valid for at least the "Data Setup Time" prior to this transfer. This fact defines the maximum permissible access time for the memory: the latter must deliver valid data not more than 630 ns after the addresses have been set up and 400 ns after $\overline{CS}$ activation.

In the case of a write cycle, the duration of the write command (Write Time t_{WR}) is 500 ns, but valid data is not available until 275 ns before the end of the cycle (Data Valid Time t_{DW}). The actual access times required are somewhat shorter, as we have ignored the delays of the bus drivers. However, the required times are achieved even by slow memory chips.

21.2.1 Quasi-permanent memory

One of the particular characteristics of CMOS RAMs is that in the quiescent state, i.e. with constant input signals, they only draw a low supply current in the μA range. While in this state, they can therefore be supplied for long periods from a battery, thus providing virtually a permanent (nonvolatile) memory which – unlike EPROMs – can be programmed and erased without any special procedures.

To utilize the benefits of CMOS RAMs, a number of additional circuit features must be incorporated, as already shown in Fig. 21.8. The changeover between external 5 V and internal battery supply is effected using Schottky diodes D_1 and D_2. If the supply voltage falls below 4 V, D_1 is turned off and the battery takes over the supply to the RAMs. The battery voltage can fall to as low as 2 V without the contents of the CMOS RAMs being lost.

The ICL 7663 is used as a voltage regulator for battery charging. As long as the voltage is below 4 V, it supplies a current of 20 mA to allow fast charging. On the other hand, it prevents overcharging of the battery, as the charge current falls rapidly if the specified voltage level is reached. When the supply voltage is disconnected, the voltage regulator loads the battery with only a few microamps.

However, additional measures must be taken to ensure data protection. If, for example, the supply voltage sweeps through the range 0 to about 4.5 V, the bus drivers and the microprocessor operate in an undefined manner and incorrect data may be written into the CMOS RAMs. To prevent this from occurring, we can use the $\overline{RES}$ signal generated on the CPU board (see Fig. 21.6). This signal becomes zero if the supply voltage falls below 4.75 V, i.e. before undefined states occur. It inhibits the 1-of-8 decoder 74 LS 156 shown in Fig. 21.8, and all the output transistors are turned off, regardless of which value between 0 and 4.75 V the supply voltage assumes. This ensures that all the $\overline{CS}$

lines are at $+B$ potential, i.e. no RAM is selected. As a result of the output transistors being in the "off" state, voltage $+B$ is not loaded by the pull-up resistors when the external 5 V supply is switched off.

The resistors on the data and address lines ensure that all the RAM outputs are at a defined potential when the supply voltage is switched off, since it is only then that the CMOS RAMs go into standby mode with low power consumption.

21.2.2   EPROM boards

The circuit in Fig. 21.8 is also suitable for EPROMs, as the HM 6116 CMOS RAMs are pin-compatible with the 2716 EPROMs. The Write Enable input is used there as a programming input V_{PP}. It must be at 5 V during normal operation. This can be achieved by setting write-protect switches $S_0 \ldots S_7$ to ROM.

21.2.3   Expansion to 64 kbyte

On the same principle, the memory capacity of the circuit in Fig. 21.8 can be increased to 64 kbyte by using 8-kbyte RAMs or EPROMs. Pin-compatible types include HM 6264 CMOS RAMs and 2764 EPROMs. In this case address bits a_{11} and a_{12} are additionally applied to the memories and address bits a_{13} to a_{15} are fed to the 1-of-8 decoder. An address comparator is not required in this case, as the entire available addressing area of the 6802 is available on a single memory board. The addresses required for the I/O circuits can be invalidated via the VMA line, as in the restart circuit in Fig. 21.7 [21.1].

21.3   Programming of EPROMs

Programming an EPROM is very similar to writing information into a RAM. The programming voltage ($VPP = 25$ V for the 2716) must first be applied to the selected chip ($\overline{CE/PGM} = 0$). Addresses and data can then be applied. A 50 ms programming pulse is now delivered to the $\overline{CE/PGM}$ input. The next address and the associated data can then be applied and another programming pulse can be sent. The programming voltage need not be switched off in the interim. It is even permissible to read out the memory contents after each programming pulse with the programming voltage applied in order to verify that correct programming has been achieved.

The easiest method of keeping the addresses and data constant during the programming time of 50 ms would be to extend the write cycle of the microprocessor accordingly via the Memory Ready line. However, this is only permissible for 10 µs, as the registers would otherwise lose their contents. The only exceptions are the CMOS types (see Fig. 20.24). Although the HALT line can be used to block all types for any length of time, they will in this case terminate the instruction being executed and then deactivate the address and data drivers. Consequently, the addresses and data have to be buffered on the programming board. This can be achieved with relatively little additional complexity by employing address and bus drivers with built-in memories. These are used in the circuit shown in Fig. 21.10.

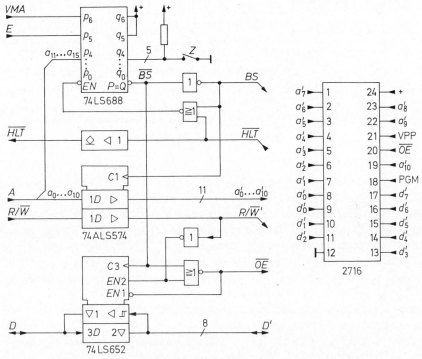

Fig. 21.10 Typical EPROM programmer board for a 2-kbyte EPROM

The timing of the programming operation is shown in Fig. 21.11. On the positive-going edge of the Board Select signal (BS), the address valid at that instant and the $R/\overline{W}$ signal are stored. On the negative-going edge, the associated data is stored.

Controlling the programming sequence requires a time base generator which is triggered by the $R/\overline{W}'$ and BS signals and generates the two signals $\overline{HLT}$ and PGM shown in Fig. 21.11. The $\overline{HLT}$ signal sets the microprocessor to the HALT state. Since this signal can only be generated during the execution phase of the underlying store instruction, the microprocessor cannot be prevented from executing the next instruction. As this might disrupt operation, a NOP instruction should follow.

The $\overline{HLT}$ signal simultaneously disables the address comparator. This ensures that the board cannot be selected during the programming phase.

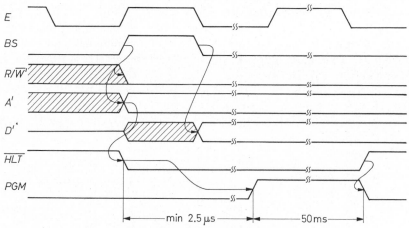

Fig. 21.11 Timing diagram for a programming operation

Before and after the programming command *PGM*, the addresses and data must be present in unchanged form for at least 2 μs. To ensure that this is the case, the programming pulse must start no earlier than 2.5 μs after the *HLT* signal. On the other hand, it is not necessary to extend the *HLT* signal beyond the end of programming, as the addresses and data remain stored on the programming board until the next microprocessor access. The earliest possible access, however, is certain to be more than 2 μs after the *HLT* signal disappears.

There are various possibilities for generating the two timing control signals. The best method is to derive them by appropriate decoding of a counter, which divides down the 1 MHz clock signal *E*.

For a read operation ($R/\bar{W} = 1$) the programming cycle must not be initiated. The circuit in Fig. 21.10 then operates in virtually the same way as a normal memory board. In this case the data must not be stored in the data bus driver, as it would arrive too late at the microprocessor. Consequently, the data bus driver must be wired in such a way that it stores in the direction of the board but not in the direction of the microprocessor.

21.4   Parallel interface

21.4.1   Fixed direction of data

The simplest means of reading data in parallel is to connect tristate buffers to the data bus which are activated using an address decoder, as shown in Fig. 21.12. When the predefined address Q is called, the external data appears on the data bus and is read in by the microprocessor. This operation is precisely the same as calling a memory. The input operation therefore differs from a memory operation only in the selection of the appropriate address. When calling an address, eight external connections can be interrogated in parallel in the case of an 8-bit data bus.

An output register can be implemented in much the same way. In order to ensure that the data remains valid until new values are issued, flip-flops are used for buffering, as shown in Fig. 21.13. If the address defined by the address decoder becomes valid and a write operation is to be performed ($R/\overline{W} = 0$), then $C = 0$. With the falling edge of E, $\overline{BS} = 1$ again and thus $C = 1$ also. Valid data is now present at the flip-flop inputs. It is transferred to the outputs with the rising edge of C and remains there until the next output.

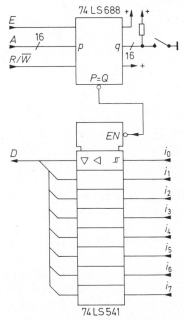

Fig. 21.12 Parallel 8-bit input port

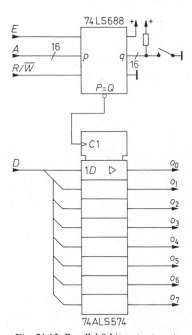

Fig. 21.13 Parallel 8-bit output port

21.4.2 Bidirectional parallel interfaces

The two circuits shown in Fig. 21.12 and 21.13 can be combined to allow either input or output operations. However, for applications of this kind it is easier to use monolithic bidirectional interface ICs, e.g. the PIA (Peripheral Interface Adapter) 6821 whose block diagram is shown in Fig. 21.14. It has two 8-bit input/output channels. The data to be transferred is stored in an output register. A data direction register is assigned to each output register, which is used to specify which line is to be used as an input and which is to operate as an output. A control register is additionally available in each channel, which has further connections for initiating and acknowledging interrupt requests.

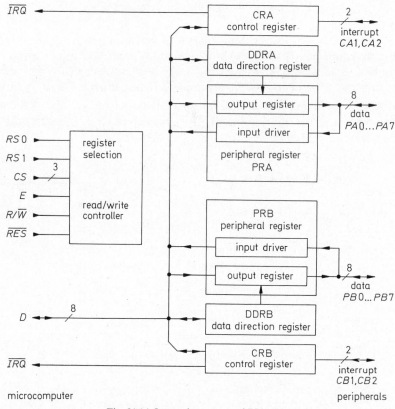

Fig. 21.14 Internal structure of **PIA 6821**

The PIA thus contains a total of six 8-bit registers, but only four registers can be selected by the two available address inputs. Consequently the peripheral registers and the direction registers assigned to them are each given a common address. They are differentiated by means of one bit of the corresponding control register. The address assignment is shown in Fig. 21.15 [21.2].

Address		Switchover bit	Register	
a_1	a_0	u		
0	0	$\begin{cases} u_A = 0 \\ u_A = 1 \end{cases}$	DDRA	data direction register A
			PRA	peripheral register A
0	1	$u_A = $ any	CRA	control register A
1	0	$\begin{cases} u_B = 0 \\ u_B = 1 \end{cases}$	DDRB	data direction register B
			PRB	peripheral register B
1	1	$u_B = $ any	CRB	control register B

Fig. 21.15 Addressing of the six registers in the PIA

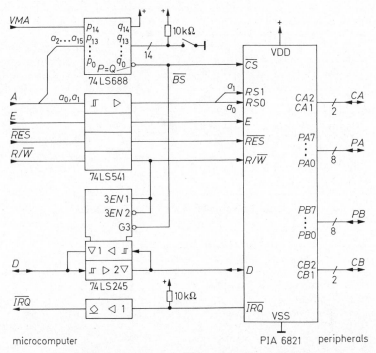

Fig. 21.16 Connection of the PIA to the microcomputer bus

Figure 21.16 shows how the PiA is connected to the microcomputer bus. It is basically operated in the same way as a RAM. One difference, however, is that the Enable signal E is not connected to an address decoder but to a special input of the PIA. This is necessary, since the interrupt inputs are only interrogated at the Enable edge, while, on the other hand, an interrupt request must also be possible when the PIA is not addressed. There is also a Reset input available which can be used to clear all the registers.

Programming of the PIA will now be described with the aid of an example. Bit combination 1101 is to appear on the A-side at pins PA3 ... PA0. The information present at pins PA7 ... PA4 is then to be loaded into accumulator B. The relevant program is listed in Fig. 21.17. We have chosen $F000_{hex}$ as the base address of the PIA. In the control word we only manipulate the switchover bit u assigned to the third-to-last bit position. We set the others to zero, thereby switching off all the interrupt functions. When the program has been run, accumulator B contains the following information:

$B =$	PA7	PA6	PA5	PA4	1	1	0	1

An overview of the main parallel-interface chips of the 6800 family is given in Fig. 21.18. As we can see, there are also types with a third 8-bit port or with

Addr.	Hex code	Mnem.	Operand	Spec. reg.	Comments
1000	CE F0 00	LDX	# $ F000		base address of the PIA
1003	6F 00	CLR	00, X	CRA	$u = 0$ (DDRA access)
1005	86 0F	LDA A	# & 0000 1111		⎫ PA 7 . . . 4 on input
1007	A7 00	STA A	00, X	DDRA	⎰ PA 3 . . . 0 on output
1009	86 04	LDA A	# & 0000 0100		
100B	A7 01	STA A	01, X	CRA	$u = 1$ (PRA access)
100D	86 0D	LDA A	# & 0000 1101		
100F	A7 00	STA A	00, X	PRA	output of 1101 on PA 3 . . . 0
1011	E6 00	LDA B	00, X	PRA	read-in of PA 7 . . . 4
1013	39	RTS			

Fig. 21.17 Example of how the PIA is programmed

Type	Manufacturer	Technology	Port 1	Port 2	Port 3	Timer
6821	Motorola	NMOS	8 + 2	8 + 2		
68 SC 21	Mitel	CMOS	8 + 2	8 + 2		
6522	Rockwell	NMOS	8 + 2	8 + 2	serial	16 bit
65 SC 22	Mitel	CMOS	8 + 2	8 + 2	serial	16 bit
6823	Motorola	NMOS	8	8	8	
146823	Motorola	CMOS	8	8	8	
6525	Commodore	NMOS	8	8	8	
6526	Commodore	NMOS	8	8	serial	2 × 16 bit 24 h-clock

Fig. 21.18 Parallel-interface circuits of the 6800 family with 8-bit data bus

built-in timers. Equivalent CMOS versions are also available for most of the circuits.

21.5   Serial interface

The advantage of serial transmission over parallel transmission is that only a few connecting lines are required. This is of particular significance for data transmission over long distances. However, serial transmission is also often used over short distances, provided it is established at the outset that a slower transmission speed will not cause problems. For this reason, screen-based terminals and printers usually have serial interfaces.

21.5.1   Serial transmission

Data interchange on a bit-serial basis is also possible using parallel input/output circuits, by employing just one port. To do this, the data word to be transmitted must be shifted one bit position via software after each output step. When receiving, the data word can be constructed by step-by-step shifting and addition. It is evident, however, that serial transmission certainly cannot take place very rapidly, since several computations are required for each individual bit.

It is therefore preferable to perform parallel-serial or serial-parallel conversion using a special hardware circuit. At the heart of such a circuit is a shift register with parallel Load inputs as described in Section 10.5.2. In addition, a sequencer is required. This ensures that during transmission the 8 bits are issued sequentially at the desired bit rate.

A central problem in serial data transmission is synchronization between transmitter and receiver. To overcome this, the serial bit sequence is subdivided into individual blocks ("*transmission frames*"). For *synchronous* transmission, a specific bit sequence, which cannot occur elsewhere, is inserted for synchronization purposes (synchronizing code, synchronizing character). This enables the receiver to detect the start of a data block. When no data is present, only synchronizing code is transmitted. Thus the clock generator in the receiver can always lock onto the incoming signal.

With *asynchronous* transmission, the transmit and receive clocks are not synchronized, but only approximately set to the same frequency ($\pm 3\%$). For this reason only short blocks of data can be transmitted between two synchronization characters. ASCII characters containing 7 data bits are normally transmitted, a parity bit is added and the block is framed with a start and a stop bit. Figure 21.19 shows the resulting transmission frame. When there is no data to be transmitted there is a corresponding pause in asynchronous transmission.

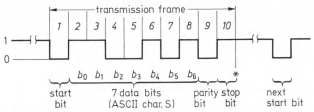

Fig. 21.19 Asynchronous transmission of ASCII character "S".
* = earliest possible occurrence of next start bit

21.5.2   The ACIA

It is evident that considerable circuit complexity is required to control serial data transmission in the way described above. However, a number of monolithic ICs are available for this purpose, e.g. the ACIA MC 6850 (Asynchronous Communications Interface Adapter), the block diagram of which is shown in Fig. 21.20. It contains four registers which are selected as shown below with the

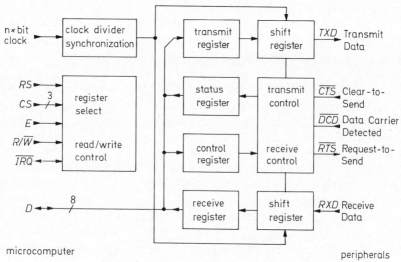

Fig. 21.20 Internal structure of the ACIA 6850

aid of addressing input *RS* and the read/write switchover:

RS	R/$\bar{W}$	
1	0	transmit register for parallel-serial conversion
1	1	receive register for serial-parallel conversion
0	0	control register for specifying the operating mode
0	1	status register for indicating the operating status

It is possible to divide up the registers in this way because the receive and status registers represent two exclusively read registers and the transmit and control registers two exclusively write registers.

The transmission frame and the parity condition can be selected using the 8-bit control register. The condition which will trigger an interrupt can also be defined. In addition, a frequency division for the bit clock can be programmed ($n = 1, 16, 64$). For the $n = 16$ and $n = 64$ settings, automatic synchronization to the start bit occurs during reception.

After the operating voltage is switched on, the ACIA must be readied by applying a "Master Reset". As no hardware RESET connection is available, this operation has to be performed via software by writing a particular bit combination into the control register. An overview of other serial interface circuits is given in Fig. 21.21.

Type	Manufacturer	Technology	Channels	Baud rate internal	Baud rate max
MC 6850	Motorola	NMOS	1	no	19.2 kbaud
HD 6350	Hitachi	CMOS	1	no	19.2 kbaud
COM 8502	SMC	CMOS	1	no	38.4 kbaud
R 65 C 51	Rockwell	CMOS	1	yes	19.2 kbaud
R 65 C 52	Rockwell	CMOS	2	yes	38.4 kbaud
MC 68562	Motorola	NMOS	2	yes	38.4 kbaud
COM 78808	SMC	CMOS	8	yes	19.2 kbaud
SCC 2698	Valvo	CMOS	8	yes	38.4 kbaud

Fig. 21.21 Serial asynchronous interface chips with 8-bit data bus

21.5.3 ACIA board

Figure 21.22 shows how the ACIA is connected to the microcomputer bus. The address decoder and the data bus driver operate in exactly the same way as in the parallel interface shown in Fig. 21.16.

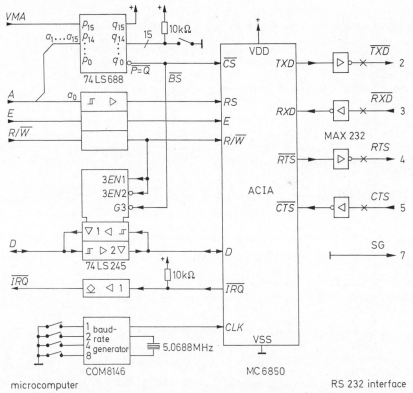

Fig. 21.22 Connecting the ACIA to a microcomputer and to a RS 232 interface for operation as a data terminal equipment (DTE). The numbers on the RS 232 interface give the pin numbers in the 25-pin Cannon connector

The bit clock can be easily generated using baud-rate generator COM 8146 from Standard Microsystems. It is driven by a 5.0688 MHz quartz crystal. This makes it possible to use the four switches to set sixteen times the standard bit rates shown in Fig. 21.23. The drivers illustrated on the peripheral side are used as signal converters for a RS 232 interface. Their functions are discussed in more detail in Section 21.5.6.

50	150	1.8 k	4.8 k
75	**300**	2.0 k	7.2 k
110	600	**2.4 k**	**9.6 k**
135	**1200**	3.6 k	19.2 k

Fig. 21.23 List of standard bit rates. Normal bit rates are shown in bold type.
Unit: 1 bit/s = 1 baud

21.5.4   Programming the ACIA

We shall now discuss ACIA operation with reference to the programming example in Fig. 21.24. Program P0 performs the Master Reset and sets the transmission frame. Control word 09_{hex} has the following meaning:

1 start bit, 7 data bits, even parity bit, 1 stop bit,

with a frequency division of 16 for the bit clock and with disabled interrupt request. We have assumed $F010_{hex}$ to be the base address for the ACIA.

Addr.	Hex code	Label	Mnem.	Operand	Reg. spec.	Comment
1000	CE F0 10	P0	LDX	# $ F010		*Initialization*
3	C6 03		LDA B	# $ 03		
5	E7 00		STA B	00, X	control	master reset
7	C6 09		LDA B	# $ 09		
9	E7 00		STA B	00, X	control	clock, frame
B	39		RTS			
1010	CE F0 10	P1	LDX	# $ F010		*output*
3	E6 00	M1	LDA B	00, X	status	
5	C5 02		BIT B	# $ 02		
7	27 FA		BEQ	M1		transmit reg. empty?
9	A7 01		STA A	01, X	transmit	transmit byte
B	39		RTS			
1020	CE F0 10	P2	LDX	# $ F010		*input*
3	E6 00	M2	LDA B	00, X	status	
5	56		ROR B			
6	24 FB		BCC	M2		receive reg. full?
8	A6 01		LDA A	01, X	receive	read-in byte
A	39		RTS			

Fig. 21.24 Example of programming the ACIA

If a data word is to be transmitted, there must first be an inquiry as to whether the transmit register is empty. The interrogate loop in output program P1 does this by testing bit 1 in the status register. Only when this bit is 1 may the next data word be written into the transmit register.

Input program P2 must first wait until there is a data word in the receive register. Bit 0 in the status register is interrogated for this purpose. A "1" indicates that there is valid data present which can then be loaded into the accumulator.

A bit in the control register can be used to enable the interrupt system in the ACIA. An interrupt is then always generated if there is new data in the receive register. This ensures that the computer performs a read operation only when there is new data present. For the rest of the time, it is available for processing other programs.

Other status bits indicate whether parity conditions are fulfilled or whether a word has been lost because the receive register has been overwritten due to the computer not having called the previous word in time.

21.5.5   ASCII code

For serial data transmission, letters and digits are normally transmitted in ASCII code. This also applies to data transmission on the IEC bus (see Section

hex equiv. (2nd digit)	hex equiv. (1st digit)	0	1	2	3	4		5	6	7	
	$b_6b_5b_4$ / $b_3b_2b_1b_0$	000	001	010	011	100		101	110	111	
0	0 0 0 0	NUL	DLE	SP	0	@	§	P	`	p	
1	0 0 0 1	SOH	DC1	!	1	A		Q	a	q	
2	0 0 1 0	STX	DC2	"	2	B		R	b	r	
3	0 0 1 1	ETX	DC3	#	3	C		S	c	s	
4	0 1 0 0	EOT	DC4	$	4	D		T	d	t	
5	0 1 0 1	ENQ	NAK	%	5	E		U	e	u	
6	0 1 1 0	ACK	SYN	&	6	F		V	f	v	
7	0 1 1 1	BEL	ETB	'	7	G		W	g	w	
8	1 0 0 0	BS	CAN	(	8	H		X	h	x	
9	1 0 0 1	HT	EM	)	9	I		Y	i	y	
A	1 0 1 0	LF	SUB	*	:	J		Z	j	z	
B	1 0 1 1	VT	ESC	+	;	K		[	Ä	k	{	ä
C	1 1 0 0	FF	FS	,	<	L		\	Ö	l			ö
D	1 1 0 1	CR	GS	–	=	M		]	Ü	m	}	ü
E	1 1 1 0	SO	RS	•	>	N		↑	n	~	β
F	1 1 1 1	SI	US	/	?	O		←	o	DEL	

Fig. 21.25 ASCII character set. The right hand side of the columns contains the DIN 66003 character set where this differs from ASCII

21.6) and for displaying data. The ASCII code (American Standard Code for Information Interchange) governs the relationship between the alphanumeric characters and their relevant representation in binary. The code is shown in Fig. 21.25 together with its hexadecimal equivalents [21.3].

There are 96 alphanumeric characters. Digits 0 through 9 are assigned to hexadecimal numbers 30 through 39. The straight binary number for a particular ASCII digit can thus be determined simply by subtracting 30_{hex}.

The first two columns in Fig. 21.25 contain non-displayable special characters whose meanings are listed in Fig. 21.26. The most important, such as carriage return CR and line feed LF, can be generated by special keys on the

Hex. code	ASCII character	Meaning
00	NUL	Null
01	SOH	Start of Heading
02	STX	Start of Text
03	ETX	End of Text
04	EOT	End of Transmission
05	ENQ	Enquiry
06	ACK	Acknowledge
07	**BEL**	**Bell**
08	**BS**	**Backspace**
09	HT	Horizontal Tabulation
0A	**LF**	**Line Feed**
0B	VT	Vertical Tabulation
0C	FF	Form Feed
0D	**CR**	**Carriage Return**
0E	SO	Shift Out
0F	SI	Shift In
10	DLE	Data Link Escape
11	DC 1	Device Control 1
12	DC 2	Device Control 2
13	DC 3	Device Control 3
14	DC 4	Device Control 4
15	NAK	Negative Acknowledge
16	SYN	Synchronous Idle
17	ETB	End of Transmission Block
18	CAN	Cancel
19	EM	End of Medium
1A	SUB	Substitute
1B	**ESC**	**Escape**
1C	FS	File Separator
1D	GS	Group Separator
1E	RS	Record Separator
1F	US	Unit Separator
20	**SP**	**Space**
7F	**DEL**	**Delete**

Fig. 21.26 Meaning of the special characters in ASCII code, also defined in DIN 66033

keyboard. The others are generated using the CTRL key in combination with a character from column 4 or 5. For example, the character BEL $\hat{=}$ 07_{hex} is produced by pressing CTRL and G together. Another important special character is the space SP $\hat{=}$ 20_{hex}.

21.5.6   RS 232 C interface

In the RS 232 standard (DIN 66020, 66022, CCITT V.24) a High level is defined as a voltage of between $+3$ V and $+15$ V and a Low as a voltage between -3 V and -15 V. The data is transmitted in negative logic, the control signals in positive logic. The conventional IC signal converters (level shifters) are types 1488/89. Their disadvantage, however, is that two additional supply voltages of ± 12 V are required, and these are only needed for operation of the RS 232 interface. In this respect, the MAX 232-family from Maxim or the LT 1081 from Linear Techn. offer a considerable simplification. In addition to two level converters for each direction, these also contain the necessary voltage converters in one integrated circuit. They operate on the charge pump principle (see Sect. 18.6.5) and only require four external capacitors.

Figure 21.27 shows the signal lines of a RS 232 transmission link with the corresponding signal converters. The standard baud rates are listed in Fig. 21.23. The line length is restricted to 15 m, since transmission would otherwise be susceptible to interference due to ground loops.

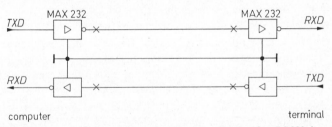

Fig. 21.27 Arrangement of level converters for the data signals of a RS 232 interface. Signal designations apply to two interconnected data terminal equipments

In the RS 232 interface, in addition to the two signal lines, six control lines are defined which can be used to control data interchange. These were originally intended for data transmission using a modem (modulator/demodulator). With this method, the data is encoded by frequency-shift keying (FSK) in the audio-frequency band and transmitted over telephone circuits. Figure 21.28 lists the RS 232 signal designations.

In addition to the two data signals TXD and RXD, there are two control signals RTS and CTS which are used by the computer or the terminal to indicate whether they are ready to receive data. This control option is mainly used by printers, to which data can be transmitted faster than they can print it. They then cancel the RTS signal before their buffers overflow, thereby temporarily

Pin	Abbreviation	Signal name	Meaning
1	FG	Frame Ground	protective ground
2	TXD	Transmit Data	transmit data from DTE
3	RXD	Receive Data	receive data for DTE
4	RTS	Request To Send	DTE can receive data
5	CTS	Clear To Send	DCE can receive data
6	DSR	Data Set Ready	DCE ready to operate
7	SG	Signal Ground	
8	DCD	Data Carrier Detected	DCE has recognized connection
20	DTR	Data Terminal Ready	DTE ready to operate
22	RI	Ring Indicator	DCE has detected call signal

Fig. 21.28 Designation and meaning of signals in a RS 232 interface.

DTE = Data terminal equipment e.g. terminal, printer, computer
DCE = Data communication equipment e.g. modem, computer

inhibiting data output from the computer. Similarly, the computer can inhibit a terminal via the *CTS* signal if it cannot keep up with the rate of data transmission. Control signals *DSR* and *DTR* have a similar effect. They are often used for a handshake, instead of the signals *RTS* and *CTS*. Control signals *DCD* and *RI* are of importance only in conjunction with modems.

When connecting RS 232 interfaces, it must be defined whether data terminal equipment (DTE, e.g. terminals, printers) or data communications equipment (DCE, e.g. modems) is involved. Computers are mostly treated as DTE, as in Fig. 21.22, but sometimes also as DCE. Whether a RS 232 interface is of DTE or DCE type can be seen from the signal "flow" in Fig. 21.29a. For a DTE, the *TXD* signal, for instance, is an output; for a DCE, it is an input. Figure 21.29a also shows that the connection between a DCE and a DTE is established via a 10-core parallel-wired cable.

When connecting two RS 232 interfaces of the same kind, the corresponding signals must be interchanged. Figure 21.29b shows the example of two DTEs. The required swapping of signals can in principle be achieved by a specially wired cable. For more flexibility, however, a standard RS 232 parallel-wired cable is used and swapping is effected by a so-called DCE/DCE (or DTE/DTE) adapter.

If one does not wish to use the control lines, the corresponding inputs on both sides cannot simply be left unassigned, as an open input is usually interpreted as zero and may disable the computer or terminal. To prevent this, a local feedback circuit can be provided by interconnecting pins 4, 5 and 6, 8, 20 in both connectors, as shown in Fig. 21.29c. One of the pins is in each case an output which is at "1" under normal conditions, thereby satisfying the associated inputs. However, if one does not wish to dispense with a handshake, the

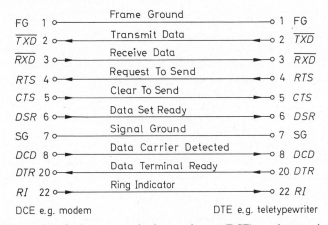

Fig. 21.29a Connection of a data communications equipment (DCE) to a data terminal equipment (DTE) via an RS 232 interface. The numbers define the pin numbers in the 25-pin Cannon connector.

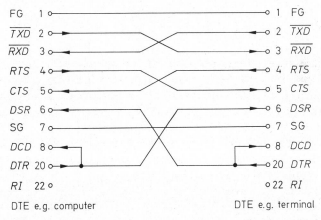

Fig. 21.29b Connection of two data terminal equipments via a DTE-DTE adapter

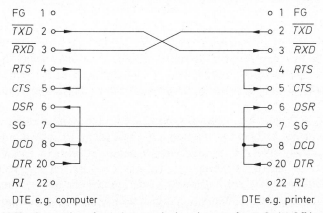

Fig. 21.29c Connection of two data terminal equipments for X-On/X-Off handshake

X-On/X-Off protocoll can be used. In this case the ASCII special character (see Fig. 21.26) DC3 = 13_{hex} = 19_{dec} is transmitted via data lines TXD and RXD to stop the transmitter, or DC1 = 11_{hex} = 19_{dec} is transmitted via these lines to restart it. It is thus possible to connect the RS 232 interface using only a three-conductor connecting cable, as shown in Fig. 21.29c.

21.5.7 Current-loop interface

For data transmission over long distances, electrical isolation is essential in order to suppress unwanted signals which may be produced by currents circulating in the ground wire. The current-loop interface shown in Fig. 21.30 possesses these characteristics.

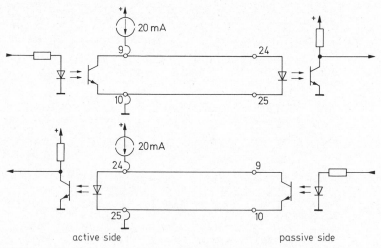

Fig. 21.30 Arrangement of a current-loop interface. The figures at the connections are the pin numbers in the 25-contact Cannon connector as specified in DIN 66021

The current interface, also known as the 20-mA or current-loop or TTY interface, is not a standard interface. It has, however, come to be used worldwide. This interface is described in greater detail in DIN 66258 Part 1 (draft)—"Interfaces and Control Procedures for Data Transmission for the Clinical/Chemical area".

When two devices are linked together, a send loop and a receive loop are formed. A current of 20 mA is injected into these loops, as shown in Fig. 21.30. This is frequently achieved by simply connecting a resistor to a 12 V supply.

The current can be injected at either the send or the receive side. The interface containing the current source is designated the active interface. The source does not need to be floating, since it is sufficient to isolate the potential on one side of the loop, preferably the passive side.

A logic 1 corresponds to a flow of current, logic 0 to no current. The speeds of up to 9.6 kbaud shown in Fig. 21.23 are the permissible transmission rates. The line can be up to 1000 m long.

21.5.8 RS 449 standard

The RS 232 interface standard is already quite old and is designed for low data rates. The new RS 449 standard allows significantly higher data rates over longer distances. With regard to the electrical design, two different versions are available: an unbalanced interface (RS 423 A, CCITT V.10) for up to 300 kbit/s and a balanced interface (RS 422 A, CCITT V.11) for up to 2 Mbit/s [21.4].

Unbalanced interface (RS 423 A)

Figure 21.31 illustrates data transmission over an unbalanced line (single-ended line). The voltage levels are typically specified at ± 3.6 V. The line must be terminated in its characteristic impedance. The maximum data rate is 300 kbit/s for a line length of 30 m, reducing to 15 kbit/s for a line length of 600 m.

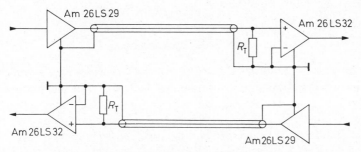

Fig. 21.31 Arrangement of an RS 423 interface

Balanced interface (RS 422 A)

Data rate and line length can be maximized by employing balanced transmission as shown in Fig. 21.32. A maximum of 2 Mbit/s can be transmitted up to a line length of 60 m. For greater lengths, the data rate reduces to 100 kbit/s at 1200 m maximum.

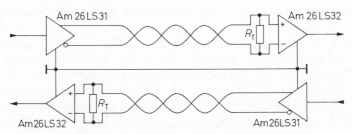

Fig. 21.32 Arrangement of an RS 422 interface

Characteristic	RS 232 C (V.24)	Current interface	RS 423 (V.10)	RS 422 (V.11)
type of transmission	unbalanced	balanced	unbalanced	balanced
type of line	twisted pair	twisted pair	coaxial	twisted pair
max. line length	15 m	300 m	600 m	1200 m
max. data rate	20 k bit/s	10 k bit/s	300 k bit/s	2 M bit/s
max. driver output at no-load	± 25 V	20 mA	± 6 V	± 6 V diff.
max. driver output under load	± 5 ... ± 15 V	20 mA	± 3.6 V	± 2 V diff.
receiver input minimum	± 3 V	10 mA	± 0.2 V	± 0.2 V diff.
sender IC	MAX 232	optocoupler	Am 26 LS 29	Am 26 LS 31
receiver IC	MAX 232	optocoupler	Am 26 LS 32	Am 26 LS 32
manufacturer	Maxim	various	AMD	AMD

Fig. 21.33 Comparison of serial interface characteristics

Figure 21.33 gives an overview of the main electrical characteristics of the four serial interfaces described [21.5].

21.6 IEC bus interface

As we saw in Section 21.1, the bus principle provides a simple method of interconnecting a large number of modules. The same principle can usefully be applied to data interchange between different devices. To enable equipment of different manufacturers to be interconnected in any combination, an internal interface standard has been created in the form of IEEE Standard 488-1978 for the USA and IEC Standard 66.22 for Europe, known as the IEC Bus Standard. Apart from the specification of the connector, both standards are identical.

General Purpose Interface Adapter (GPIA) MC 68488 provides an LSI device which makes connection of the microcomputer bus to the IEC bus very simple. In order to explain its operation, we shall first describe the IEC bus in somewhat greater detail. Its block diagram is shown in Fig. 21.34.

The IEC bus consists of 8 data lines and 8 control lines. Unlike transfer on the microcomputer bus, the addresses of the devices accessed are also transferred via the data lines. They are identified by the control signal "Attention (ATN)". Another difference between this bus and the microcomputer bus is that data is not transmitted synchronously with the clock signal, but asynchronously in the form of an acknowledgement procedure. Control signals "Ready for Data (RFD)", "Data Valid (DAV)" and "Data Accepted (DAC)" are used for this purpose. A "three-wire handshake" of this kind enables data to be transmitted from any one "talker" to any number of "listeners" without having to establish any rules concerning transmission speed. Data validity is maintained until it has been accepted by the slowest listener.

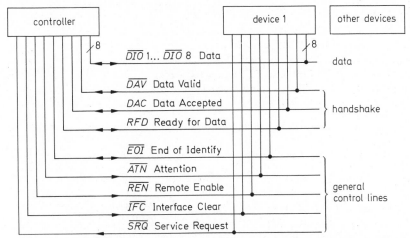

Fig. 21.34 Connection of devices to the IEC bus. For the sake of clarity, the names of the bus lines
have been given in positive logic, not as defined in the Standard

Figure 21.35 shows the sequence of the three-wire handshake. When the
talker has a new byte available, it writes it onto the data bus and tests signal
RFD. It is wired-ANDed using open-collector outputs and consequently only
becomes 1 when all the devices connected to the bus are ready to accept data.
When they are, the talker indicates that the data is valid by setting $DAV = 1$.
The listeners react to this with $RFD = 0$ to indicate that they cannot process any
more data for the time being, and transfer the byte into their input buffer. The
complete acceptance of the data by all the listeners addressed is indicated by
wired-ANDed signal $DAC = 1$. The talker then sets $DAV = 0$. This tells the
listeners that their DAC signal has arrived. They therefore reset it to zero.

Processing of the data will now begin. The end of the processing phase is
indicated by control signal "Ready for Data". When all the devices are ready
again, $RFD = 1$ is set once more. This indicates to the talker that a new byte can
be transmitted. To make this process easier to understand, we have included two
flow charts in Fig. 21.35 together with the timing diagram, showing how the
talker and listeners perform the handshake procedure.

It can be seen that for data transmission from the talker to the listeners it is
not necessary to involve the controller. The latter only comes into action if
new listeners or a new talker is to be addressed. To do this, the control device
sets $ATN = 1$ and transmits the corresponding addresses via the data lines,
initiating the normal handshake procedure. In order to ensure that this function
is performed correctly, the Standard specifies that all the devices will go to the
start of the listener handshake no later than 200 ns after $ATN = 1$ and will do
this regardless of activities being performed at the time.

The addresses of the devices are defined in the Standard in the form of
ASCII characters. The characters in columns 2 and 3 of Fig. 21.25 are permitted

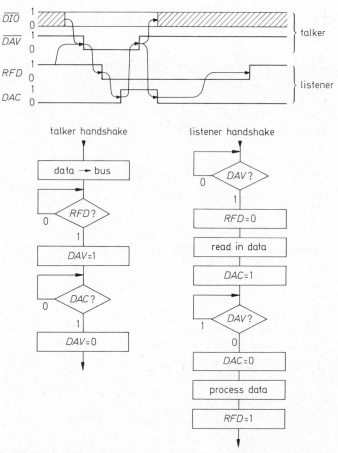

Fig. 21.35 Timing diagram and flow chart for the 3-wire handshake

as listener addresses, those in columns 4 and 5 as talker addresses. Listener and talker addresses for the same device cannot be selected independently but must be identical in their last 5 bits. Listener address "4" is therefore associated with talker address "T". Character "?" is fixed and means "Unlisten". It is used to switch off all the listeners. The corresponding talker address character " ← " means "Untalk" and is used to switch off the current talker. However, it is generally dispensable, as a talker is switched off automatically as soon as another talker address appears on the bus. In all, 31 listener and 31 talker addresses can be freely selected. The remaining ASCII characters are defined as special commands, e.g. DC4 stands for "Device Clear".

Figure 21.36 shows how the GPIA is connected to the microcomputer bus. The three lower-order address bits permit access to 7 write and 8 read registers.

Data input/output is via register 7 of the GPIA. The other registers are used to define the operating mode or for indicating the relevant operating status. The

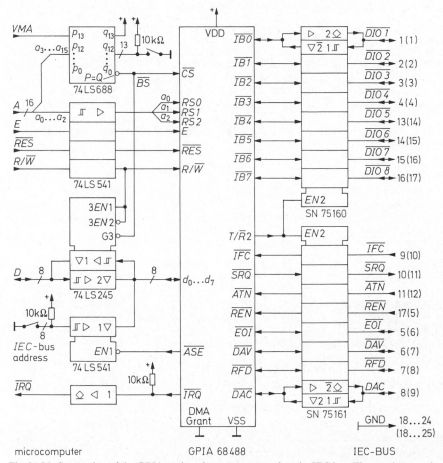

Fig. 21.36 Connection of the GPIA to the microcomputer and to the IEC bus. The numbers on the IEC bus lines indicate the pin numbers on the 24-contact IEEE Amphenol connector. The numbers in brackets are the pin numbers on the 25-contact IEC Cannon connector

device address is stored in register 4, into which it must be loaded by the software. Frequently, however, we may wish to allow this address to be set manually. The address switches are used for this purpose: when register 4 of the GPIA is read, the data outputs remain at high impedance. Instead, the tristate drivers on the switches are activated with signal $\overline{ASE}$. This causes the set address to appear on the data bus, where it can be read by the CPU. The lower-order 5 bits of the ASCII address are set on the switch. The 3 higher-order bits can be used to select the special operating modes "Talk Only" or "Listen Only".

The GPIA is relatively easy to use, as it reacts automatically to the bus commands and automatically handles the handshake procedure. The IEC bus driver also switches its direction of transmission automatically, depending on whether the interface has been addressed as a listener or a talker.

Addr.	Hex. code	Label	Mnem.	Operand	Spec. reg.	Comments
1000	CE F0 20	P0	LDX	#$ F020		*Initialization*
3	E6 04		LDA B	04, X	Address	read address switch
5	E7 04		STA B	04, X	Address	store device address
7	6F 03		CLR	03, X	Command	clear reset bit
9	6F 00		CLR	00, X	Interrupt	switch off interrupt
B	C6 80		LDA B	#$ 80		
D	E7 02		STA B	02, X	Addr. Mode	normal addressing mode
F	39		RTS			
1010	E6 00	P1	LDA B	00, X	Status	*Input*
2	56		ROR B			
3	24 07		BCC	M1		character arrived?
5	A6 07		LDA A	07, X	Input	fetch character
7	BD × × × ×		JSR	V1		process character
A	20 F4		BRA	P1		
C	39	M1	RTS			
1020	E6 00	P2	LDA B	00, X	Status	*Output*
2	C5 40		BIT B	#$ 40		
4	27 06		BEQ	M2		output reg. empty?
6	BD × × × ×		JSR	V2		provide character
9	A7 07		STA A	07, X	Output	transmit character
B	20		BRA	P2		
C	39	M2	RTS			
						Main program
1030	8D CE	P3	BSR	P0		initialization
2	8D DC	M3	BSR	P1		input
4	8D EA		BSR	P2		output
6	20 FA		BSR	M3		reentry

Fig. 21.37 GPIA programming example

The programming example in Fig. 21.37 should illustrate the relationships. We have given the GPIA a base address of F020$_{hex}$ for this example. In the initialization routine we have selected the simplest operating mode, which is adequate for a large number of applications.

The input routine tests whether a character has been read from the IEC bus. If so, the character is loaded into accumulator A. This read procedure automatically sets $RFD = 1$ for the operating mode selected and thereby completes the handshake. Selection of another operating mode, however, allows the RFD signal to be kept at zero and the IEC bus therefore disabled until the character is processed. In this case, RFD must be set to 1 at the required time by a separate command.

After the character has been processed, control returns to the start of the input routine. If no further character has arrived in the interim, an exit from the input routine takes place.

The output routine first checks whether the output register is free. If so, the character to be transmitted is loaded from accumulator A into the output register and from there is transferred automatically via the handshake onto the IEC bus. Completion of the handshake can be detected by the output register being signaled as free again. The next character can then be transferred. If there is no further character to be transmitted, exit from the output routine takes place.

The main program calls up the two routines in turn. This means that the device is available at all times as a listener or talker for the IEC bus.

21.7 Programmable counter

In Section 10.2 we saw that counters with parallel load inputs have a wide variety of applications. When used in conjunction with a microcomputer they could, in principle, be connected to the computer bus via PIAs. However, a large amount of hardware and software can be saved by using a special bus-compatible counter chip, such as "Programmable Timer Module" MC 6840. A block diagram of this module is shown in Fig. 21.38. It contains three independent binary down-counters with a 16-bit word length.

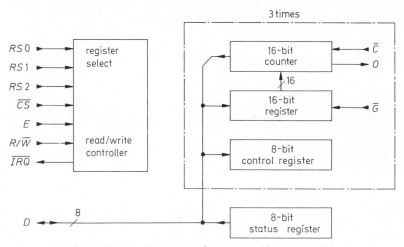

Fig. 21.38 Internal structure of programmable counter 6840

C = external clock
O = counter output
G = gate, inhibit

Each counter is assigned a 16-bit register which is used to store the preselected number and a control register for specifying the operating mode. In "continuous" mode, the counter is automatically loaded with the preselected number as soon as the count reaches zero. Either the external input $\bar{C}$ or the system clock

E can be used to provide the timing signal. Output signal O changes whenever the counter reaches zero. In this way, a symmetrical squarewave signal is obtained whose frequency is lower than the clock frequency by a factor of 2 to 2^{17}, depending on the preselected number.

In "monostable" mode, a single output pulse can be triggered with the G input and its duration set between T and $(2^{16} - 1)T$.

The counter can be operated as an up-down counter if the upward pulses are sent to one counter and the downward pulses to a second counter. The total count is then simply obtained by subtracting the two counter readings, as in the circuit in Fig. 10.35. Here, this process can be performed using software consisting of just a few commands.

The 6840 is also available from Mitel in a CMOS version. Types 6522 and 6526 (see Fig. 21.18) can be used as counters in combination with parallel interfaces. The 146818 from Motorola is a special counter realized in CMOS technology which is programmed as a clock and a calendar. It provides the following data: seconds, minutes, hours, days of the week, days of the month, months and up to 100 years. It takes account of the lengths of the months even in leap years.

21.8 Interrupt Controller

So far we have assumed that the interrupt outputs of all the peripheral devices are connected to the $\overline{IRQ}$ input of the microprocessor by wired-OR circuits. Therefore, if an interrupt occurs, it is first necessary to establish which I/O unit has triggered the interrupt. To do this, a routine at the start of the interrupt program reads in the status words of the I/O units in turn and tests the interrupt bit. This serial interrogation operation is known as "serial polling". Once the routine has established the source of the interrupt, the program jumps to the appropriate service routine.

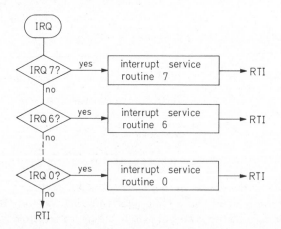

Fig. 21.39 Determining the source of an interrupt by serial polling

If several interrupts occur simultaneously, the decision as to which unit is to be served first is made on the basis of a previously defined priority list. Figure 21.39 demonstrates the process using a flow chart for 8 priority levels. The higher number indicates the higher priority.

It can be seen that the lower the priority, the longer the reaction time This disadvantage can be avoided by using an *interrupt controller*. This allows a direct jump to the appropriate routine without going through the polling procedure.

Interrupt Controller MC 6828 has 8 interrupt inputs $IN0 \ldots IN7$. These are polled on each E-edge. Depending on which interrupt occurs, the microprocessor receives from the interrupt controller a different entry into the interrupt routine when it requests address FFF8/FFF9.

For this purpose, the interrupt controller is combined with an EPROM as shown in Fig. 21.40 and this is installed at the top end of the address space. The start addresses of interrupt routines 0 through 7 are stored at addresses FFE8/9 through FFF6/7. Address bits a_1 to a_4 are not connected directly to the address bus but to the output of the interrupt controller. They are therefore always modified by the controller when the CPU performs a read operation at address FFF8/9. In this way the contents of the EPROM from area FFE8 through FFF7 appear on the data bus, depending on the interrupt.

If no interrupt input is triggered, the addresses are transferred unmodified to the EPROM. In this case, therefore, the contents of register FFF8/9 also appear under address FFF8/9. This allows I/O units which output an interrupt directly onto the IRQ line to be served. The priority of these units is -1 in this case.

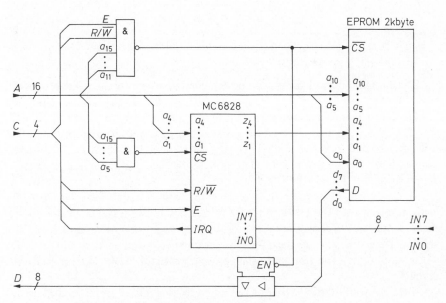

Fig. 21.40 Connection of the interrupt controller to the microcomputer bus

21.9   Direct Memory Access (DMA)

If one wishes to read data files in or out via an interface, several commands have to be executed for each byte. This is illustrated by the program in Fig. 21.41, using as an example a parallel interface whose output register is to be at address F000. The memory area to be transferred has a start address of 1010 and an end address of 1012. To perform the operation, each byte is loaded from the data file into the accumulator and then transferred to the interface. The index register is then incremented and interrogated to determine whether the end has been reached. As long as this is not the case, the program loop continues to be executed and the information is transferred one byte at a time. Figure 21.41 shows that, in order to transfer one byte, 5 commands have to be executed within the loop, requiring a total of 23 clock cycles. If the computer has a cycle time of 1 µs, 23 µs will be required to output a byte, and the program will output a maximum of 43 kbytes per second.

Addr.	Hex. code	Label	Mnem.	Operand	Cycles	Comments
1000	FE 10 00		LDX	#$1010		start address
3	A6 00	LOOP	LDA A	00, X	5	fetch character
5	B7 F0 00		STA A	F000	5	transfer character
8	08		INX		4	next address
9	BC 10 02		CPX	$1012	5	end address
C	26 F5		BNE	LOOP	4	loop
E	39		RTS		23	
1010	00 00		WORD	$0000		start address
2	02 00		WORD	$0200		end address

Fig. 21.41 Program for transferring a memory area via a parallel interface

Much higher output speeds can be achieved if, instead of the microprocessor, a counter is used to generate the addresses. A chip of this type is the 6844 DMA Controller. This contains four identically structured channels, one of which is shown in Fig. 21.42. For initialization, the address register is loaded with the start address and the byte count register with the number of bytes to be transmitted. The control register determines whether counting of addresses is to be up or down and whether data is to be written into memory or read from it.

If the DMA Controller then receives a transfer request $TxRQ$ from the peripherals, it uses the DMA Request to put the microprocessor into a HALT state. When the microprocessor has terminated the current command, it enables the computer bus and notifies the DMA Controller of this fact with the DMA Grant command. The controller then assumes control of the address and $R/\overline{W}$ signals.

The connection of a DMA Controller to the microcomputer and to an output interface is shown in Fig. 21.43. For initialization, the DMA Controller

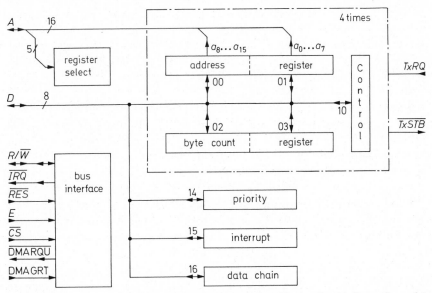

Fig. 21.42 Internal structure of the 6844 DMA Controller. The numbers indicate the register addresses of channel 0

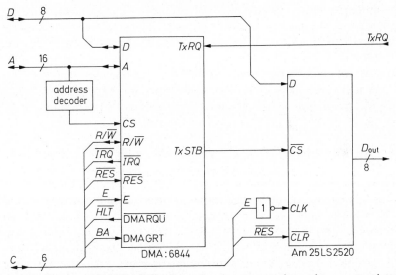

Fig. 21.43 Connection of the DMA Controller to the microcomputer bus and to an output interface

must be connected to the microcomputer bus like any other peripheral circuit. As the DMA Controller generates the address and $R/\overline{W}$ signals during DMA transmission, bidirectional bus drivers are also required for these signals. These devices are set to output in the bus direction with Bus Available signal BA.

To control the output interface, the DMA Controller generates Transfer Strobe signal *TxSTB*. This corresponds to the *VMA* signal of the microprocessor and indicates when the DMA Controller is outputting a valid address, thereby enabling the interface circuit to be selected. If valid data from the memory is then present at the end of the transfer cycle, it is stored in the interface circuit on the negative *E*-pulse edge.

Greater complexity is involved when using interface modules having several registers and requiring initialization, such as the PIA 6821. In this case, in addition to the DMA interface, there must be a normal bus interface through which the microprocessor can have direct access to the registers of the interface circuit. Another register select memory is then required which retains the address of the data register in the I/O circuit during DMA mode.

There are various options for performing DMA transmission. The fastest is block transmission, whereby the microprocessor is halted until the entire data block has been transmitted. In this mode, one byte is transferred with each *E*-clock cycle. Compared to a program-controlled transfer, speed is increased 23-fold. However, as this will only be achieved if the time taken for initializing the DMA Controller is not a major factor, it is not efficient to transmit just a few bytes by DMA.

DMA Controllers are available which also allow DMA transmission between memories. For this purpose, two DMA channels are linked together, one pointing to the source area, the other to the destination area. When data is transmitted, in the first cycle each byte is fetched from the source area and buffered in the DMA Controller. The second cycle then stores it at the destination address. Memory-to-memory transmission therefore requires two cycles, making it only half as fast as memory-to-I/O transmission. However, it does have the advantage that the DMA controller need not be permanently assigned to one I/O circuit, but can also be used if required as DMA board for any data transfers, i.e. to shift data files within memory as well.

21.10   Arithmetic processor

If extensive computations need to be performed with a microcomputer, one would not normally write the programs for this oneself, since ready-made software packages are available for the standard mathematical operations, and these can be used as subroutines (e.g. floating-point ROM MC 68 A 39 for the 6809 processor). The computation times are, however, comparatively long: for the four basic arithmetic operations in 32-bit IEEE floating point format, they are between 2 and 6 ms.

The shortest computation times are achieved with parallel-operating hardware chips of the kind described in Chapter 19. However, the circuit complexity involved is considerable.

An optimum compromise for many applications is to use an arithmetic processor, which is connected to the microcomputer bus in the same way as a peripheral device. The computation time for the four basic arithmetic operations in 32-bit IEEE floating point format is about 100 μs. At present the most widely used, all-purpose types are the Am 9511A and the Am 9512 from AMD. The 9511 can process three types of data: 16-bit and 32-bit fixed point as well as 32-bit floating point. In addition to the four basic arithmetic operations, it can calculate square roots, trigonometric functions, logarithms and exponential functions. The Am 9512 has the advantage of being able to process 32-bit and 64-bit operands in IEEE format. Its disadvantage, however, is that it can only perform the four basic arithmetic functions. Both types have the same pin assignment.

Figure 21.44 shows how an arithmetic processor is connected to the microcomputer bus. The address decoder and the data driver here operate in precisely the same way as on any input/output board. A special feature of the arithmetic processor, however, is that it has separate write or read inputs which may only be activated while the chip is selected ($\overline{CS} = 0$). This type of control is normal in the 8080 family and is described in further detail in Section 21.14. To ensure

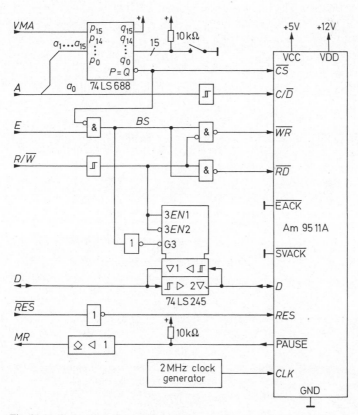

Fig. 21.44 Connection of an arithmetic processor to the microcomputer bus

correct timing, the $\overline{CS}$ input is activated directly after the addresses are set up, but the $\overline{RD}$ or $\overline{WR}$ input only while $E = 1$.

The 9511/12 has an internal stack for data input/output. Before a computation is performed, all the operands are loaded byte by byte into the stack. To initiate a computation, the appropriate command is written into the instruction register. The result is stored in the stack and can be fetched from there. Additional information about the result of the computation (e.g. overflow) can be called from the status register. The registers are selected with the aid of the Command/Data changeover $C/\overline{D}$ using address bit a_0 in the following way:

$C/\overline{D}(a_0)$	$R/\overline{W}$	Register accessed
0	0	data (write)
0	1	data (read)
1	0	command (write)
1	1	status (read)

Synchronization between CPU and arithmetic processor can be provided in a number of ways. The highest-order bit of the status word indicates whether the arithmetic processor is BUSY. If it is zero, reading or writing is possible.

The second option is to apply the $\overline{PAUSE}$ signal to the Memory Ready input MR of the CPU. There is then no need to interrogate the BUSY signal. If the CPU accesses the memory at a time when the arithmetic processor is busy, access is halted until the arithmetic processor is ready again.

Figure 21.45 shows the organization of the stack. Data is entered to the topmost register (Top of Stack, TOS). When the next input takes place, the stack is automatically pushed down by one byte. During output, the opposite occurs.

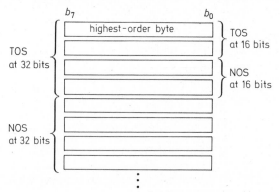

Fig. 21.45 Arrangement of operands in the arithmetic processor stack.
The top 8 bytes out of 16 are shown

TOS = Top of Stack
NOS = Next of Stack

Mnemonic	Hex	Cycles max.*	Description of operation	Result to	Stack operation
16-bit fixed-point operations S					
SADD	6C	18	NOS + TOS	NOS	PULL
SSUB	6D	32	NOS − TOS	NOS	PULL
SMUL	6E	94	NOS * TOS	NOS	PULL
SMUU	76	98	NOS * TOS	NOS	PULL
SDIV	6F	94	NOS : TOS	NOS	PULL
FIXS	1F	214	F → S	TOS	—
CHSS	74	24	$+\circlearrowleft-$	TOS	—
PTOS	77	16	NOS → TOS	—	PUSH
POPS	78	10	Rotate Stack	TOS	PULL
XCHS	79	18	NOS $\circlearrowleft$ TOS	TOS	—
32-bit fixed-point operations D					
DADD	2C	22	NOS + TOS	NOS	PULL
DSUB	2D	40	NOS − TOS	NOS	PULL
DMUL	2E	210	NOS * TOS	NOS	PULL
DMUU	36	218	NOS * TOS	NOS	PULL
DDIV	2F	210	NOS : TOS	NOS	PULL
FIXD	1E	336	F → D	TOS	—
CHSD	34	28	$+\circlearrowleft-$	TOS	—
PTOD	37	20	NOS → TOS	—	PUSH
POPD	38	12	Rotate Stack	TOS	PULL
XCHD	39	26	NOS $\circlearrowleft$ TOS	TOS	—
32-bit floating-point operations F					
FADD	10	368	NOS + TOS	NOS	PULL
FSUB	11	370	NOS − TOS	NOS	PULL
FMUL	12	168	NOS * TOS	NOS	PULL
FDIV	13	184	NOS : TOS	NOS	PULL
SQRT	01	870	SQRT (TOS)	TOS	—
SIN	02	4808	SIN (TOS)	TOS	—
COS	03	4878	COS (TOS)	TOS	—
TAN	04	5886	TAN (TOS)	TOS	—
ASIN	05	7938	ARCSIN (TOS)	TOS	—
ACOS	06	8284	ARCCOS (TOS)	TOS	—
ATAN	07	6536	ARCTAN (TOS)	TOS	—
LOG	08	7132	LOG (TOS)	TOS	—
LN	09	6956	LN (TOS)	TOS	—
EXP	0A	4878	EXP (TOS)	TOS	—
PWR	0B	12032	NOS ↑ TOS	NOS	PULL
FLTS	1D	156	S → F	TOS	—
FLTD	1C	342	D → F	TOS	—
CHSF	15	20	$+\circlearrowleft-$	TOS	—
PTOF	17	20	NOS − TOS	—	PUSH
POPF	18	12	Rotate Stack	TOS	PULL
XCHF	19	26	NOS $\circlearrowleft$ TOS	TOS	—
PUPI	1A	16	π → TOS	TOS	PUSH
NOP	00	4	No Operation	—	—

*Cycle time: 0.5 μs at 2 MHz clock frequency

Fig. 21.46 Instruction list of arithmetic processor Am 9511 A

Figure 21.46 lists the commands for the Am 9511 A. TOS and NOS consist of 2 or 4 bytes depending on the word length specified. Care must be taken to ensure that during input/output all the bytes of an operand are always transmitted, otherwise the internal stack pointer will operate incorrectly.

A simple programming example should serve to illustrate how the arithmetic processor is used. We are assuming here that synchronization is provided by the $PAUSE$ signal, as in the circuit in Fig. 21.44. The program has to calculate the expression $Y = (K - L)/M$ for 16-bit fixed-point numbers. Let the operands be stored in the following registers:

$$
\begin{array}{lll}
0000/0001 & K & \text{(high/low)} \\
0002/0003 & L & \text{(high/low)} \\
0004/0005 & M & \text{(high/low)} \\
0006/0007 & Y & \text{(high/low)}
\end{array}
$$

The arithmetic processor is installed at, say, address F030. The resulting program is listed in Fig. 21.47. Note that the stack can be used to advantage here, as it can in a pocket calculator using reverse Polish notation, to buffer intermediate results.

Addr.	Hex. code	Label	Mnem.	Operand	Comments
1000	CE F0 00	AR 1	LDX	#$ F030	base address of 9511
3	96 01	STO 1	LDA A	$01	
5	A7 00		STA A	0, X	
7	96 00		LDA A	$00	
9	A7 00		STA A	0, X	TOS = K
B	96 03		LDA A	$03	
D	A7 00		STA A	0, X	
F	96 02		LDA A	$02	
11	A7 00		STA A	0, X	TOS = L; NOS = K
3	86 6D	SUB 1	LDA A	#$6D	instruction code for SSUB
5	A7 01		STA A	1, X	TOS := NOS − TOS
7	96 05	STO 2	LDA A	$05	
9	A7 00		STA A	0, X	
B	96 04		LDA A	$04	
D	A7 00		STA A	0, X	TOS = M, NOS = K − L
F	86 6F	DIV 1	LDA A	#$6F	instruction code for SDIV
21	A7 01		STA A	1, X	TOS := NOS : TOS
3	A6 00	REC 1	LDA A	0, X	
5	97 06		STA A	$06	
7	A6 00		LDA A	0, X	
9	97 07		STA A	$07	$Y = \langle 0006 | 0007 \rangle$
102B	39		RTS		

Fig. 21.47 Example of programming the Am 9511 A arithmetic processor to compute the expression $Y = (K - L)/M$ for 16-bit fixed-point numbers

21.11 Output of data to display units

The LED and liquid crystal displays described in Section 6.7 can be used for visual representation of data, the circuits shown in that Section being controlled by the microprocessor via a parallel interface chip. However, in order to minimize the number of drivers and lines required, it is advisable in the case of multi-character displays to connect them together as a matrix and operate them on a time-division multiplex basis. Figure 21.48 shows an arrangement of this kind for an 8-character, 7-segment LED display. The corresponding segments of all the displays are connected in parallel. In order to ensure that the same segments of all the characters do not now light up simultaneously, only one character is activated via the 1-of-8 decoder.

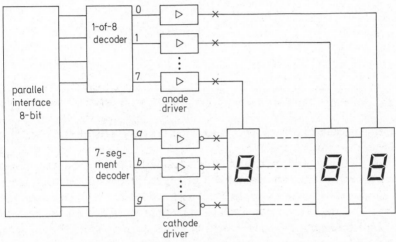

Fig. 21.48 Connection of an 8-character seven-segment display to a parallel output interface (like the one shown in Fig. 21.13)

Therefore, 15 lines are required to operate an 8-character, 7-segment display. A single 8-bit parallel interface is suitable as a microprocessor interface. The 1-of-8 decoder and the 7-segment decoder can even be connected directly to the microcomputer bus, provided they have internal memories. A number of 7-segment decoders are shown in Fig. 6.36. Anode and cathode drivers are listed in Fig. 21.49.

Multiplex operation is performed by the microprocessor program. To do this, the position number is specified with four bits and the character to be represented in BCD code using the other four bits. The output is then repeated for the next character position. In order to ensure that a flicker-free display is produced, the complete display cycle must be executed at least 100 times a second. There are many applications, particularly in simple devices, where the processing time required for driving the display is spare. However, it may be

Type	Manufacturer	Number	Max. current I_{max}	Voltage drop at I_{max}
Anode drivers (current source)				
ULN 2941 B	Sprague	4	1500 mA	1.4 V
ULN 2033	Sprague	7	80 mA	1.3 V
DS 8867	National	8	14 mA	constant current
UDN 2985 A	Sprague	8	300 mA	1.3 V
ULN 2981	Sprague	8	500 mA	2.0 V
Cathode drivers (current sink)				
CA 3262	RCA	4	600 mA	0.6 V
SN 75492	Texas Instr.	6	250 mA	1.3 V
DS 8859	National	6	40 mA	constant current
SN 75497	Texas Instr.	7	125 mA	0.4 V
ULN 2003	Sprague	7	500 mA	2.3 V
NE 590	Signetics	8	250 mA	1.1 V
ULN 2803	Sprague	8	500 mA	2.3 V
L 603	SGS	8	500 mA	2.3 V
UDN 2597 A	Sprague	8	1000 mA	1.0 V
SN 75498	Texas Instr.	9	125 mA	0.4 V

Fig. 21.49 Drivers for LED displays and other applications requiring high output currents

disturbing to have the display flickering when the microprocessor is required for long periods for other tasks.

If the display is to operate without microprocessor support, it must possess a display memory and an internal multiplexing facility in addition to the devices shown in Fig. 21.48. The resulting circuit is shown in Fig. 21.50. The display data is written by the microprocessor into a two-port memory (see Section 11.2) which is connected to the microcomputer bus like a normal RAM. The display

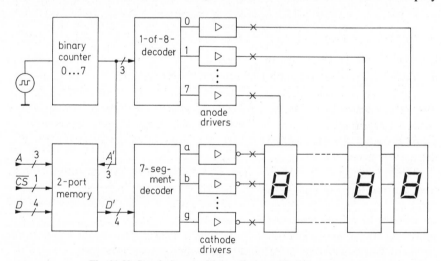

Fig. 21.50 Stand-alone multiplex display with data memory

Type	Manufacturer	Char-acters	Segments per character	Common	Data input
Drivers for LED displays					
ICM 7212	Intersil, Maxim	4	7	anode	4 bit
MM 74C911	National	4	7	cathode	8 bit
MC 14499	Motorola	4	7	cathode	1 bit
MM 74C912	National	6	7	cathode	5 bit
ICM 7218	Intersil, Maxim	8	7	an./cath.	8 bit
ICM 7243	Intersil	8	16	cathode	6 bit
10937	Rockwell	16	16	cathode	1 bit
LED displays with built-in drivers					
PD 1165	Siemens	1	8×8		8 bit
PD 3435	Siemens	4	5×7		8 bit
HDSP 2382	Hewlett-Pack.	4	5×7		1 bit
PD 2816	Siemens	8	16		8 bit
HDSP 2112	Hewlett-Pack.	8	5×7		8 bit
Drivers for LCD displays				stat./mux.	
ICM 7211	Intersil, Maxim	4	7	stat.	4 bit
ICM 7233	Intersil, Maxim	4	16	mux.	6 bit
MSM 58292	Oki	5	7	stat.	1 bit
ICM 7234	Intersil, Maxim	5	7	mux.	1 bit
ICM 7231	Intersil, Maxim	8	7	mux.	6 bit
HD 6103	Hitachi	8	7	stat.	4 bit
ICM 7232	Intersil, Maxim	10	7	mux.	1 bit
HD 6102	Hitachi	25	8	mux.	8 bit
HD 61104	Hitachi	any	80	stat.	4 bit
MSM 5265	Oki	any	80/160	stat./mux.	1 bit

Fig. 21.51 Display interface ICs with data memory (stat. = static, mux. = multiplex)

contents are read from the two-port memory, independently of the bus operation. During this process, the binary counter issues the addresses cyclically and activates the appropriate character positions via the 1-of-8 decoder.

Display drivers operating on this principle are widely available as fully-integrated circuits. Some types are listed in Fig. 21.51. As well as the types with parallel data inputs, there are also versions in which the display data is stored in a shift register. They only require one serial data line and no addresses to control them. Both versions can be expanded. In the case of the RAM types, the required module is selected via a 1-of-n decoder; in the case of the shift register types, the display data can be shifted serially through a number of modules connected in series.

Some LED displays already incorporate the multiplex drivers. "Intelligent displays" of this kind are also listed in Fig. 21.51.

Liquid crystal displays (LCDs) require an AC voltage of a specific amplitude. The push-pull method described in Fig. 6.24 is only used for generating this voltage for a small number of segment drivers. For larger numbers of segments, liquid crystal displays are also linked together to form matrices, in order to minimize the number of connecting lines. However, *three* voltage levels are required (in addition to ground potential) for driving liquid crystal matrices of this kind, in order to ensure that the selected segments receive a sufficiently high and the remainder a suitably low AC voltage. This special type of multiplexing is known as the triplex method [21.6].

21.12   Video output

To display longer texts or graphics, video monitors are preferred because of their higher resolution and lower cost. TV-standard monitors are particularly attractive in terms of cost, since they are largely constructed from the inexpensive components used in television sets. For home computing, normal television receivers are commonly used for video output purposes. However, it is always necessary to convert the screen contents into a standard video signal.

21.12.1   Television standard

Television pictures are generated by writing information to the screen one line at a time and controlling the pixel intensity (and, if required, color also) to produce the desired screen content. This scanning pattern (raster) is shown in Fig. 21.52. In accordance with the PAL television standard, a complete 625-line picture is written in 40 ms, giving a frame repetition rate of 25 Hz. The horizontal (line) frequency is 625 times higher, i.e. $f_H = 15.625$ kHz; this corresponds to a line duration of $t_H = 64$ μs. The US NTSC standard has 525 lines, a frame repetition rate of 30 Hz and, accordingly, a line frequency of 15.75 kHz.

At any instant, only one point on the screen is receiving information. The fact that the impression of a complete picture is gained is due to the persistance of the phosphor and the slow perception of the eye. However, with the scheme depicted in Fig. 21.52, flicker would be clearly visible, as the top half of the picture would already be fading while the bottom half was being written. This problem can be largely overcome by using the interlaced scanning method shown in Fig. 21.53. Here the complete picture is divided into two fields. In the

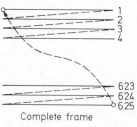

Fig. 21.52 Screen scanning
pattern (raster)

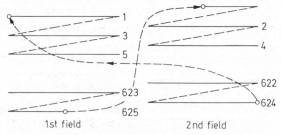

Fig. 21.53 How the two fields are interlaced to form a
complete frame

first field, only the odd-numbered lines are written and in the second only the even-numbered lines. This gives a field period of $t_v = 20\,\text{ms}$ or a vertical deflection frequency of $f_v = 50\,\text{Hz}$.

To produce a picture, the pixel (short for *picture element*) must always be in its correct position on the screen. To ensure that this is the case, a horizontal and vertical synchronizing signal is generated which synchronizes the deflection generators in the monitor. These two signals are combined to form the *composite synchronization* shown in simplified form in Fig. 21.54. As we can see, the line sync signals (shown as vertical marks) occur at 64 µs intervals and the frame sync signals at 20 ms intervals. During frame synchronization, the line sync signals continue at double the frequency to ensure that the horizontal deflection remains in synchronization. Figure 21.54 also shows that the frame sync signals are offset by half a line from field to field [21.7, 21.8].

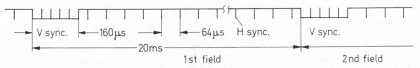

Fig. 21.54 Simplified horizontal/vertical composite synchronization

The composite synchronization signal is added to the frame content. The resulting CVS signal (composite video signal) is shown in Fig. 21.55 for the grey scale. Taking black level as a reference, the synchronization level for normal video signals is 0.3 V lower and the white level 0.7 V higher. Coaxial cable with a characteristic impedance of 75 Ω, signal sources with an output impedance of 75 Ω and loads with 75 Ω input impedance are generally employed for signal transmission. This allows the required bandwidths to be obtained while at the same time avoiding reflections.

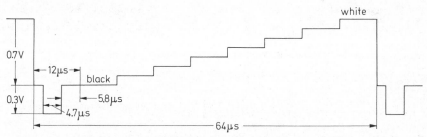

Fig. 21.55 Composite video signal (CVS) of one line, shown for a grey scale. The amplitudes apply to a circuit terminated in 75 Ω

Not all of the line or frame period is available for displaying the picture, as part of the time is required for horizontal or vertical flyback. In order to ensure that the return trace remains invisible, the picture is made dark for this period by the *blanking signal*. The horizontal blanking pulse has a duration of 12 µs, leaving only 52 μs for the display of the line. The vertical blanking pulse lasts for approximately 25 lines, i.e. leaving only 600 displayable lines. In order to ensure that the edge of the picture is not seen, the transmitted picture is somewhat larger than the screen. If, in the case of computer output, one wishes to ensure that the entire output is visible, it is generally possible to use only 512 lines with a duration of about 42 μs. For television receivers, the bandwidth of the picture signal is limited to 5 MHz. This results in a minimum pixel duration of 100 ns, giving a horizontal resolution of 420 pixels. Video monitors normally have a substantially larger bandwidth.

For video output, line interlacing is usually dispensed with and the same field is always written at 50 Hz. Although this halves the usable number of lines to 256, it avoids the problem of annoying flicker of bright lines if they are in one field only and are only being refreshed at 25 Hz.

21.12.2 Alphanumeric video output

For the programmer, the simplest method of writing text on a television screen is to display the contents of a RAM area. The arrangement required for this purpose is shown in Fig. 21.56. The RAM is connected to the microcomputer bus using the normal bus interface and can therefore be written and read by the microprocessor.

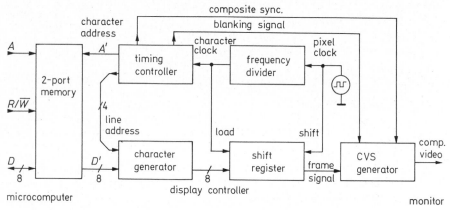

Fig. 21.56 Alphanumeric video interface with two-port memory

On the other hand, the RAM is being continuously read by the video interface. In order to control the timing and generate the synchronization mix, a video timing controller such as the MC 6845 from Motorola or the SY 6545 from Synertek is employed. This device applies to the RAM the address of the particular character to be displayed. All the characters are numbered sequentially on the screen from top left to bottom right and read out from consecutive RAM addresses.

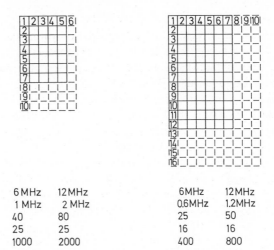

Pixel clock	6 MHz	12 MHz	6 MHz	12 MHz
Character clock	1 MHz	2 MHz	0.6 MHz	1.2 MHz
Characters per row	40	80	25	50
Rows per frame	25	25	16	16
Characters per frame	1000	2000	400	800

Fig. 21.57   Representation of characters in a 5 × 7 or 7 × 12 raster for a usable line duration of 42 µs and 256 lines per frame

Displaying a character requires several lines on the screen. Figure 21.57 shows two examples of how a character is made up. First the top line of all the characters is displayed in one screen line. To do this, the character generator receives from the RAM the ASCII code of the relevant character, and also the topmost line number from the timing controller. When the first line of a row of text is written, the timing controller increments the line number by one and then reads the same row of text from the RAM. This causes the character generator to issue the intensity pattern for the second line of the row of text. The characters belonging to a row of text are read from the RAM as many times as required to display all the associated character lines. Only then is the next row of text written using the same method.

The intensity pattern for a particular line of a character is issued by the character generator in parallel. A shift register is used to perform the parallel-to-series conversion required for serial display on the screen. For this purpose, the shift register is loaded in parallel using the character clock and read out serially using the pixel clock. The ratio between these two timing signals must be equal to the number of pixels in one line of the character, including space.

A mask-programmed read-only memory, such as the MCM 6674 with a 5 × 7 dot matrix, or the MCM 66710 . . . 66790 with a 7 × 12 dot matrix, is normally used as the character generator. Character generators with built-in shift registers are also available. These are known as video display controllers, the most popular being the CRT 8002 from Standard Microsystems Corp. (SMC). It can also process a number of attributes such as inversion, flashing or underscore. These can be stored together with the character code in the RAM. An attribute bit is already available, as the ASCII code only requires 7 bits.

The CVS generator is basically a 2-bit D/A converter. Because of the very low resolution, it can be simply implemented by weighting the two TTL signals via resistors, adding and applying them to an emitter follower acting as an impedance converter. This principle is shown in Fig. 21.58.

If a commercially available television receiver having no video input is to be used, the amplitude-modulated antenna signal must be generated from the composite video signal. The MC 1374 VHF modulator IC made by Motorola is particularly suitable for this purpose.

Microcomputer bus interface

The MC 6845 or R 6545 Video Timing Controller is a microcomputer peripheral circuit which can be connected to the microprocessor bus in precisely the same way as a parallel or serial interface module. It possesses 17 or 19 internal registers in which all the parameters defining the screen format can be entered at initialization [21.9].

The RAM is also connected to the microcomputer bus via a standard bus interface. It is advisable to provide it with separate address switches, so that the RAM addresses can be assigned independently of the timing controller.

A special feature here is that the RAM has to operate as a two-port memory. However, as cost considerations generally dictate the use of standard RAMs, a multiplexer will be required for the addresses, data and the $R/\bar{W}$ line of the RAM. Figure 21.59 shows how these lines are switched between the bus interface and the video interface. Under normal circumstances, the RAM is connected to the video interface. Only when the microprocessor is accessing the RAM does the address decoder become active and connect the RAM to the microcomputer bus.

This causes slight picture disturbance, which is barely noticeable because a line with a length of 1 to 2 characters in one single field only is affected in each case. If disturbance is to be eliminated altogether, care must be taken to ensure

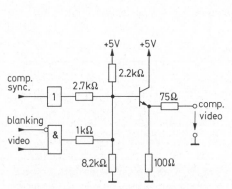

Fig. 21.58 Composite video signal, comprising picture signal, blanking signal and composite synchronization signal for producing an amplitude of 1 V_{PP} at 75 Ω load impedance

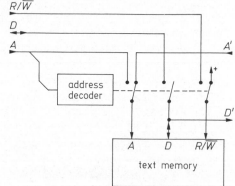

Fig. 21.59 Implementation of the two-port memory

that the microcomputer does not access the RAM during the active picture duration. If 42 μs of the 64 μs line period and 512 of the 625 lines are used, about half the time is available for this purpose. If memory accesses are restricted to the flyback period, only the vertical flyback bit in one of the timing controller registers needs to be interrogated.

Another way of avoiding picture disturbance, without the microprocessor having to wait for access, is to switch the multiplexer back and forth between the video interface and the bus interface in synchronism with the character clock. If microprocessor clock signal E is selected equal to the character clock, the microprocessor can access the RAM as long as $E = 1$ and the video interface as long as $E = 0$, since the microprocessor is certain not to require the RAM during this phase. A typical microprocessor for which clock E can be injected with the basic frequency is the 6800. A slight disadvantage of this approach is that the clock frequency of the microprocessor cannot be freely selected but must be made equal to the character timing. This may call for the faster A or B versions.

21.12.3 Video graphics

The possibilities for displaying graphics via the alphanumeric video interface are limited. Although 160 graphics characters can be stored in the character generator along with the 96 ASCII characters by additionally using the eighth bit, it is not possible to display all types of dot graphics in this way. For full graphics capability, it is necessary to store the intensity of each pixel on the screen. A resolution of 256×256 pixels requires a memory capacity of

$$2^8 \cdot 2^8 \text{ bits} = 2^{16} \text{ bits} = 2^{13} \text{ bytes} = 8 \text{ kbytes} .$$

However, this only allows 1 bit per picture element (pixel) to be stored. If, for example, we wish to store 4 bits per pixel so that 16 shades of grey or colors can be distinguished, this alone requires 32 kbytes of memory capacity. For full resolution of 512×512 pixels, as much as 128 kbytes are needed. Often, however, large memory capacities of this kind are not available at all in the addressing area of a microprocessor.

An additional factor is that one would not normally wish to input graphic elements such as vectors to the display memory dot by dot via software, since this would take up an excessive amount of machine time. Therefore, a Graphic Display Processor (GDP) is normally connected between the microcomputer and the display memory, a typical 6800 module being the EF 9367 from Thomson. Figure 21.60 shows how it is used. It is connected to the microcomputer bus like any other peripheral circuit module via the address, data and control buses, and is used to write information to the display memory. Dynamic RAMs are employed in order to minimize space requirements, power consumption and costs. The necessary refresh is provided here without additional complexity by means of cyclic readout for the video interface. The addresses and CAS or RAS control signals required for this purpose are generated by the GDP

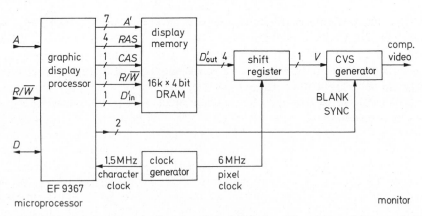

Fig. 21.60 Video interface for alphanumeric and graphic displays. The values apply to a resolution of 256 × 256 pixels

together with the standard television raster; likewise the blanking signal and composite synchronization signal.

In order to enable inexpensive RAMs with long access times to be used, each read operation includes not only the pixel to be displayed, but 4 pixels in parallel, as shown in the example in Fig. 21.60. For high-resolution graphics with 512 pixels per line, as many as 8 pixels are read out. This means that a character clock rate of only 1.5 MHz is required. This is the highest frequency occurring in the GDP and RAM. The serial video signal is again generated using a shift register for parallel-to-series conversion.

The GDP is programmed via its 12 registers. To draw vectors, the start address of the vector is specified in an X and a Y register. The length of the vector, ΔX and ΔY, is specified in two further registers. The vector is then entered into the display memory using a write instruction and the internal vector generator selects the raster elements which most closely approximate the vector [21.10]. After a drawing command has been issued, the X or Y register points out the end of the vector so that drawing can continue directly. Another register is used to specify whether the vector is to be drawn continuously, as dots, as a dashed or dash-dotted line.

In addition to the vector generator, the GDP also has a character generator which can enter alphanumeric characters into the display memory independently. For this reason it is not necessary to program the generation of letters or numbers from a combination of dots or vectors. To display a character, its coordinates are entered in the X and Y registers and the ASCII code is written to the command register. While the GDP writes the corresponding pixels to the display memory, the X register is automatically increased by one character width, so that the next character can be written immediately afterwards.

The EF 9367 can process 256 different commands: 16 general commands, 16 normal vectors, 128 short vectors and 96 ASCII characters. During processing, the contents of the remaining 11 registers are used as parameters [21.11].

Superficially there is a similarity between text output via the alphanumeric interface and via the graphic interface. There is, however, a fundamental difference in the way in which the characters are stored: in the case of the alphanumeric interface, the characters are stored in *ASCII code* and their address determines the position on the screen. With the graphic interface, the *intensity pattern* of the character is stored in the display memory at the position at which it is to appear on the screen.

21.13 Analog input/output

A microcomputer is often used for digital processing of analog signals. This requires two special interface circuits: an analog-to-digital converter module for input and a digital-to-analog converter module for analog signal output. Chapter 23 contains a more detailed description of how the A/D or D/A converters operate. This section will explain the specific aspects which apply to connecting them to a microcomputer.

21.13.1 Analog input

The basic design of an analog input board is shown in Fig. 21.61. To perform a conversion, the analog value is first stored using a sample-and-hold circuit before the start command is issued to the analog-to-digital converter (ADC). The two one-shots which are activated by a read procedure at address base + 2 are used for this purpose. If the input voltage varies only slowly (by less than 1 LSB during conversion) the sample-and-hold circuit and the monostables can even be dispensed with.

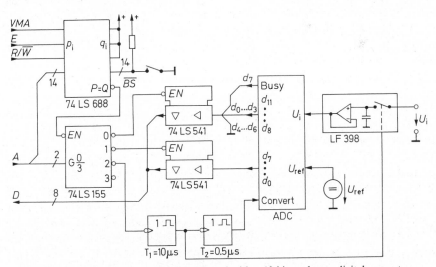

Fig. 21.61 Example of an analog input board with a 12-bit analog-to-digital converter

Reso-lution	Type	Manufacturer	Chan-nels	Conver-sion time	Supply voltages + 5 V and	Internal reference	Output
8 bit	AD 7575	Analog Dev.	1	5 µs	–	–	8 bit
	AD 7769[1]	Analog Dev.	1	2 µs	–	yes	8 bit
	AD 7820*	Analog Dev.	1	1.3 µs	–	–	8 bit
	AD 7824*	Analog Dev.	4	2.5 µs	–	–	8 bit
	AD 7828*	Analog Dev.	8	2.5 µs	–	–	8 bit
	LTC 1099	Lin. Tech.	1	2.5 µs	–	–	8 bit
	ZN 540[1]	Plessey	1	5 µs	–	2.5 V	8 bit
	TLC 540	Texas Instr.	11	12 µs	–	–	1 bit
10 bit	AD 7580	Analog Dev.	1	20 µs	–	–	8 bit
	LTC 1090	Lin. Tech.	8	20 µs	–	–	1 bit
	MAX 151	Maxim	1	3 µs	– 5 V		10 bit
	ADC 1061	National	1	2 µs	–	–	10 bit
	TLC 1540	Texas Instr.	11	21 µs	–	–	1 bit
12 bit	AD 7870	Analog Dev.	1	10 µs	– 5 V	+ 3 V	12 bit
	AD 7874	Analog Dev.	4	10 µs	– 5 V	+ 3 V	12 bit
	AD 1332[2]	Analog Dev.	1	8 µs	± 15 V	– 5 V	12 bit
	AD 1334	Analog Dev.	4	15 µs	± 15 V	– 5 V	12 bit
	AD 1678	Analog Dev.	1	5 µs	± 12 V	+ 5 V	12 bit
	ADS 602	Burr Brown	1	1 µs	± 15 V	yes	12 bit
	ADS 807	Burr Brown	1	10 µs	± 15 V	+ 10 V	12 bit
	ADS 7800	Burr Brown	1	13 µs	– 15 V	yes	8 bit
	SDM 873	Burr Brown	16	17 µs	± 15 V	+ 10 V	12 bit
	CS 5012	Crystal	1	7 µs	– 5 V	–	12 bit
	CS 5412	Crystal	1	1 µs	– 5 V	–	12 bit
	ADC 674 Z	Datel	1	15 µs	+ 12 V	10 V	12 bit
	HY 9674	Harris	1	15 µs	± 15 V	+ 10 V	12 bit
	HY 9712	Harris	16		± 15 V		8 bit
	LTC 1291	Lin. Tech.	1	13 µs	–	–	1 bit
	LTC 1294	Lin. Tech.	8	13 µs	–	–	1 bit
	MAX 163	Maxim	1	8 µs	– 12 V	– 5 V	8/12 bit
	SP 9415	Sipex	8	13 µs	± 15 V	yes	8 bit
13 bit	ADC 1241	National	1	14 µs	– 5 V	–	13 bit
15 bit	MAX 134[3]	Maxim	1	50 ms	– 5 V	–	4 bit
16 bit	AD 1380	Analog Dev.	1	20 µs	± 15 V	yes	16 bit
	DSP 102	Burr Brown	2	5 µs	– 5 V	yes	1 bit
	CS 5126	Crystal	1	10 µs	– 5 V	–	16 bit
	SP 9488	Sipex	16	20 µs	± 15 V	yes	16 bit
	TSC 850[3]	Teledyne	1	25 ms	– 5 V	–	16 bit
20 bit	CS 5503	Crystal	1	50 ms	– 5 V	–	1 bit

[1] additionally contains DACs   [2] contains a lowpass filter   [3] S&H not required
* other manufacturers: Maxim, National

Fig. 21.62 Microcomputer-compatible analog-to-digital converters with integrated sample-and-hold circuit.
Other A/D converters are listed in Fig. 23.42 Supply voltages: + 5 V and additional voltages.
Where a reference voltage is specified, it is externally accessible

During conversion, the Busy bit of the ADC can be tested to establish whether conversion has been completed. To do this, address base $+2$ is read out and a test is performed to establish whether bit 7 is set. When conversion is complete, the measured value can be read out at address base $+0$ and $+1$.

Some A/D converter ICs which are particularly suitable for microprocessor applications are listed in Fig. 21.62. Other types, which can also be connected to the microcomputer bus using appropriate add-ons, are described in Chapter 23. The types in Fig. 21.62 with conversion times in the microsecond range employ the weighing or cascade (extended parallel) method. The slow AD converters in the millisecond range use the counting method. These are particularly suitable for measuring slowly-changing signals and possess good noise suppression characteristics.

The A/D converters with more than one channel have an analog multiplexer at their input which allows one of several input voltage sources to be selected. The multiplexer can be controlled from the microprocessor, thereby allowing a number of input voltage sources to be interrogated in turn.

21.13.2 Analog output

An example of an analog output board with 12-bit resolution is shown in Fig. 21.63. The circuit operates like the parallel output circuit in Fig. 21.13. The 4 higher-order bits are stored at address base $+0$ and, subsequently, the 8 low-order bits are stored at address base $+1$. Only then may the 4 higher-order bits be applied to a digital-to-analog converter (DAC). The higher-order bits must therefore be double buffered. Without the additional memory, the 4 new higher-order bits would be converted—at least temporarily—along with the 8 old lower-order bits into a voltage. The edge-triggered D-flip-flops should not be replaced by D-latches (transparent D-flip-flops), as the data from the

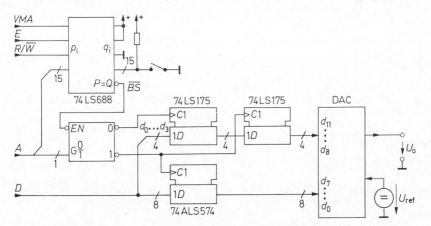

Fig. 21.63 Example of an analog output board with a 12-bit digital-to-analog converter

microprocessor would otherwise continue to be passed on to the DAC all the time that $E = 1$, whereas valid data appears only just before the end of the cycle, as shown in Fig. 21.9. This would cause high-amplitude noise pulses to occur at the analog output.

A number of microprocessor-compatible digital-to-analog converters are listed in Fig. 21.64. They all have an internal data memory; those more than 8 bits wide are normally "double buffered". All types have an internal operational amplifier which provides an output voltage at low impedance [21.12].

Reso-lution	Type	Manufacturer	Chan-nels	Settling time	Supply voltages + 5 V and	Internal reference	Input
8 bit	AD 558	Analog Dev.	1	1 μs	−	yes	8 bit
	AD 7769[1]	Analog Dev.	2	1 μs	−	yes	8 bit
	AD 7226	Analog Dev.	4	5 μs	+ 15 V	−	8 bit
	AD 7228	Analog Dev.	8	5 μs	+ 15 V	−	8 bit
	MAX 500	Maxim	4	3 μs	+ 15 V	−	1 bit
	ZN 540[1]	Plessey	2	1 μs	−	2.5 V	8 bit
	DAC 8800	PMI	8	1 μs	+ 12 V	−	1 bit
12 bit	AD 767	Analog Dev.	1	3 μs	± 12 V	+ 10 V	12 bit
	AD 7248	Analog Dev.	1	5 μs	+ 15 V	+ 5 V	8 bit
	AD 662	Analog Dev.	1	3 μs	−	+ 2.5 V	12 bit
	AD 395	Analog Dev.	2	15 μs	± 12 V	−	12 bit
	AD 664	Analog Dev.	4	10 μs	± 12 V	−	8/12 bit
	DAC 811	Burr Brown	1	4 μs	± 12 V	+ 6.3 V	4/12 bit
	SP 9344	Sipex	4	10 μs	± 15 V	−	12 bit
16 bit	AD 7846	Analog Dev.	1	4 μs	± 15 V	−	16 bit
	AD 1148[2]	Analog Dev.	1	20 μs	± 15 V	yes	16 bit
	PCM 56	Burr Brown	1	1.5 μs	− 5 V	yes	1 bit
	DAC 707	Burr Brown	1	4 μs	± 12 V	yes	16 bit
	DAC 725	Burr Brown	2	4 μs	± 12 V	yes	8 bit
	SP 1148[2]	Sipex	1	20 μs	± 15 V	yes	16 bit
18 bit	AD 1139	Analog Dev.	1	40 μs	± 15 V	− 10 V	18 bit
	AD 1860	Analog Dev.	1	1.5 μs	− 5 V	yes	1 bit
	DSP 202	Burr Brown	2	2 μs	− 5 V	yes	1 bit
	DAC 729	Burr Brown	1	8 μs	± 15 V	+ 10 V	18 bit
	SP 9380	Sipex	1	30 μs	± 15 V	+ 10 V	16/18 bit

[1] additionally contains an ADC　　[2] offset and gain programmable

Fig. 21.64 Microcomputer-compatible digital-to-analog converters with integrated output amplifier.

Other D/A converters without output amplifier are listed in Fig. 23.23.

Where a reference voltage is specified, it is externally accessible

21.14   Special peripheral circuits

The choice of peripheral units can be greatly increased if circuits from other families are also taken into account. However, they often require the kind of control signals normally employed in the 8080 family. Instead of a read/write changeover signal $R/\bar{W}$, they have two control inputs: one for reading ($\overline{RD}$) and one for writing ($\overline{WR}$). A read or write operation is not initiated using the Chip Select signal, as is the case with 6800 devices, but only when the $\overline{WR}$ or $\overline{RD}$ signal is also activated. We have already given an example of the bus interface required, in connection with the arithmetic processor in Fig. 21.44. Figure 21.65 gives a general idea of the principle involved. The timing diagram in Fig. 21.66 shows that the $\overline{CS}$ (8080) signal is generated immediately the set address appears, whereas $\overline{WR}$ or $\overline{RD}$ signals do not become active until $E = 1$.

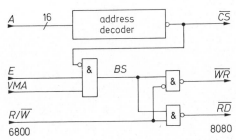

Fig. 21.65 Control signal generation for peripheral circuits of the 8080 family from 6800-bus signals

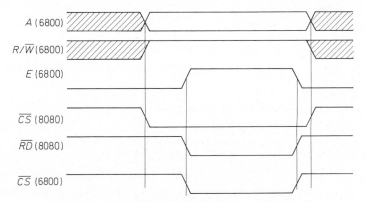

Fig. 21.66 Timing of the control signals for a read operation

In addition to the peripheral circuit applications already described in this section, there are a large number of further applications for which special modules are available. Figure 21.67 lists examples of these types.

Function	Type	Manufacturer
Floppy Disk Controller	WD 1773	Western Digital
	WD 37 C 65 A	Western Digital
	FDC 9267	SMC
	82072	Intel
	µ PD 72067	NEC
Hard Disk Controller	WD 1007 V	Western Digital
	WD 42 C 22 A	Western Digital
	HDC 7261	SMC
	82064	Intel
	HD 63463	Hitachi
	MC 68 HC 99	Motorola
	µ PD 7262	NEC
Hard, -Floppy Disk Controller	HDC 9224	SMC
	µ PD 7260	NEC
Raster Scan Controller	TMS 34020	Texas Instr.
	82786	Intel
	DP 8500	National
	HD 64400	Hitachi
	HD 63484	Hitachi
LCD Graphic Controller	HD 63645	Hitachi
	µ PD 72030	NEC
Keyboard Controller	KR 9600	SMC
Keyboard, -Display Controller	8279	Intel
Speech Synthesizer	TMS 50 C 50	Texas Instr.
	µ PD 7764	NEC
Speech Analyzer	µ PD 7763	NEC
DMA Controller	Am 9517	AMD
Data Encryption Unit	Am 9568	AMD
IEC Bus Controller	µ PD 7210	NEC
	TMS 9914 A	Texas Instr.
Local Area Network Controller	COM 9026	SMC
Ethernet Controller	82586	Intel

Fig. 21.67 Special peripheral circuits

Floppy and hard disk controllers are highly integrated circuits for interfacing with magnetic disks. Many of them are realized as single chip microcontrollers and are specially programmed for this application. They control the spindle and stepper motors of the disk. When writing on the disk, a write clock is generated along with the serial data pulse stream. In order to reduce the "peak shift" advanced hard disk controllers add a write precompensation in form of a pattern dependent delay of the write clock. When reading from the disk, a synchronized read clock is regenerated by a PLL and the data are read, separated and buffered. A CRC (cyclic redundancy check) error detection and correction is usually incorporated.

The raster scan controllers are interface circuits for displays with television-like raster scanning. They contain a timing generator producing the horizontal and vertical video timing signals and coordinating readout and update of the display memory. A drawing processor executes high level commands for graphic elements such as lines, polygons, circles and characters. A display processor is responsible for scrolling, zooming and window generation. Three interfaces are provided: for the microprocessor, the display RAM, and the video display. Unlike other circuits the TMS 34020 contains a user programmable micro-processor optimized for graphic applications. Especially when floating point precision is required it is extremely fast when combined with the TMS 34082 floating point processor. The LCD graphic controllers consist of the same building blocks but contain a display interface for the row and column drivers of LCD displays.

A keyboard controller scans the switch matrix of the keyboard and generates the specific code when an activated key is recognized. Debounce logic is provided. Today's general purpose microcomputers like the 8051 are often programmed for this application.

Speech generation is a question of available memory capacity. For telephone quality, a sampling rate of 8 kHz and a resolution of 12 bit is required resulting in a data rate of 96 kbit/s. When companding to 8 bit per sample and using difference coding the data rate can be reduced to 32 kbit/s. This technique, known as ADPCM is used in the μPD 7755. Data rates of only 1.2 kbit/s are achieved by the linear predictive coding (LPC) in the TMS 50C50. Here only the pitch, the energy and 10 filter coefficients adjusting a digital filter are encoded for a block of samples to reconstruct the human voice. The speech analyzer computes the frequency spectrum and performs a voice pattern matching with representative patterns stored in memory.

A data encryption unit encodes data so that they can be read only by an authorized receiver. The receiver can use the same chip for decryption but the encryption code must be known.

The IEC bus (see Chapter 21.6) is a network for locally restricted automa-tion. Signals are transmitted via a 16 bit parallel cable, its length being limited to 20 m, the maximum data rate being 1 Mbyte/s. The local area networks (LAN) like Ethernet, Cheapernet, Starlan and Arcnet can be extended to larger areas and employ single channel serial transmission; coaxial or twisted pair cables or even optical transmission by glass fibres are used. Data rates up to 10 Mbit/s are usual. The LAN controllers are microprogrammed circuits that contain a CRC generator/checker for error detection and a DMA controller for real time data transfers to and from the host memory.

22 Analog switches and sample-and-hold circuits

An analog switch is designed to switch a continuous input signal on and off. When the switch is in the ON-state, the output voltage must be as close to the input voltage as possible; when the switch is OFF, it must be zero. The principal characteristics of an analog switch are defined by the following parameters:

forward attenuation (ON-state resistance),
reverse attenuation (OFF-state current),
analog voltage range,
switching times.

22.1 Principle

There are several switch arrangements which fulfill the above requirements. They are represented in Fig. 22.1 as mechanical switches.

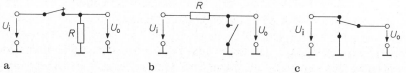

a   b   c

Fig. 22.1 (a) Series switch. (b) Short-circuiting switch. (c) Series/short-circuiting switch

Figure 22.1a shows a single-throw series switch. As long as its contact is closed, $U_o = U_i$. On opening the switch, the output voltage becomes zero, although this only applies to no-load conditions. For capacitive loads, the output voltage will only fall slowly to zero because of the finite output resistance $r_o = R$.

The single-throw short-circuiting switch in Fig. 22.1b overcomes this difficulty. However, in the ON-state, i.e. when the contact is open, the circuit possesses a finite output resistance $r_o = R$.

The double-throw series/short-circuiting switch in Fig. 22.1c combines both advantages, and has a low output resistance in both states. The forward attenuation is low, the reverse attenuation is high. However, the fact that the output is short-circuited in the OFF-state may also cause problems, e.g. if the output voltage is to be stored in a capacitor, as in the sample-and-hold circuits in Section 22.4. In this case, switch S_3 can be inserted, as in Fig. 22.2. When the switch is open, the input signal capacitively coupled via S_1 is short-circuited by S_2; however, the output remains at high impedance due to S_3. This arrangement therefore behaves like the series switch in Fig. 22.1a, but has a much better reverse attenuation for high frequencies.

Extending this principle to several inputs, we obtain the arrangement shown in Fig. 22.3. One or other of the four switches is closed at any one time, which means that the output voltage is equal to the particular input voltage selected. This arrangement is therefore also known as an *analog multiplexer*.

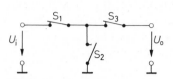

Fig. 22.2 Series switch with improved reverse
attenuation

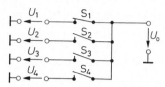

Fig. 22.3 Analog multiplexer-demultiplexer

By inverting the arrangement, an input voltage can be distributed to several outputs, thus providing an *analog demultiplexer* function. The corresponding circuits for digital signals have already been described in Section 9.6.

22.2   Electronic switches

Field effect transistors, diodes or bipolar transistors are used to implement the switches. They possess quite different characteristics and specific advantages and disadvantages. They do, however, have the same basic arrangement, which is shown in Fig. 22.4. In most cases, TTL-compatible control signals are required. These are amplified by a power gate followed by a level converter which generates the voltages required for opening or closing the switch.

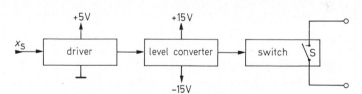

Fig. 22.4 Drive arrangement for a switch

22.2.1   FET switch

As we saw in Section 5.7, a FET behaves like an ohmic resistor whose value can be varied by several orders of magnitude using the gate-source voltage U_{GS} if the drain-source voltages are low. This behavior makes it extremely useful as a series switch (see Fig. 22.5). With positive input voltages, the FET is turned off if we make $U_C \leqq U_p$; with negative input voltages, the control voltage must be less than the input voltage by at least $|U_p|$.

To make the FET conduct, the voltage U_{GS} must be zero. This condition is not so easy to fulfill, as the source potential is not constant. A solution to this problem is shown in Fig. 22.6 where diode D becomes reverse biased if U_C is made larger than the most positive input voltage, and therefore $U_{GS} = 0$, as required.

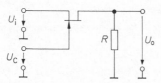

Fig. 22.5 FET series switch

$$U_{C_{ON}} = U_i$$
$$U_{C_{OFF}} \leqq \begin{cases} U_p & \text{for } U_i > 0 \\ U_p + U_{i\,min} & \text{for } U_i < 0 \end{cases}$$

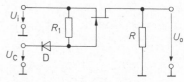

Fig. 22.6 Simplified drive arrangement

$$U_{C_{ON}} = U_{i\,max}$$
$$U_{C_{OFF}} \leqq \begin{cases} U_p & \text{for } U_i > 0 \\ U_p + U_{i\,min} & \text{for } U_i < 0 \end{cases}$$

For sufficiently negative control voltages, diode D is forward biased and the FET is turned off. In this mode, a current flows from the input voltage source via resistor R_1 into the control circuit. This can usually be tolerated, as the output voltage in this case is zero. However, this effect becomes troublesome if the input voltage is connected to the switch via a coupling capacitor, as the latter becomes charged to a negative voltage during the OFF phase.

These problems do not arise if a MOSFET is used for switching. An n-channel MOSFET can be made to conduct by applying a control voltage which is larger than the most positive input voltage. No current flows from gate to channel, so that diode D and resistor R_1 are no longer necessary. To ensure

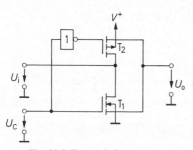

Fig. 22.7 Transmission gate

$$U_{C_{ON}} = V^+$$
$$U_{C_{OFF}} = 0$$

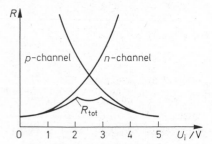

Fig. 22.8 FET resistance versus input voltage for

$$U_C = U_{C_{ON}} = V^+ = 5\,\text{V}$$

Type	Manufac-turer	Switch	ON-state resistance	Analog range	Level converter	Data latches	Latch-up protected
74HC-family							
74HC4016	N, Ti	4 × on	50 Ω	0...12 V	no	no	no
74HC4066	N, Ti	4 × on	30 Ω	0...12 V	no	no	no
74HC4316	N, Ti	4 × on	30 Ω	± 6 V	yes	no	no
200-family							
DG212	A, I, M, S	4 × on	150 Ω	± 15 V	yes	no	yes
DG222	A	4 × on	60 Ω	± 15 V	yes	yes	yes
300-family							
DG302	H, M, S	4 × on	35 Ω	± 15 V	yes	no	yes
DG303	H, M, S	2 × dt	35 Ω	± 15 V	yes	no	yes
MAX343	M	2 × dt	50 Ω	± 50 V	yes	no	yes
MAX345	M	4 × on	50 Ω	± 50 V	yes	no	yes
400-family							
DG412	S	4 × on	25 Ω	± 15 V	yes	no	yes
DG423S	S	2 × dt	25 Ω	± 15 V	yes	yes	yes
TSC447	Ty	4 × on	120 Ω	± 5 V	yes	yes	yes
TSC444	Ty	2 × dt	120 Ω	± 5 V	yes	yes	yes
500-family							
DG541*	S	4 × on	40 Ω	0...12 V	yes	no	yes
DG542*	S	2 × dt	40 Ω	0...12 V	yes	no	yes
5000-family							
IH5043	H, I, M, S	2 × dt	60 Ω	± 15 V	yes	no	yes
IH5053	I	4 × on	50 Ω	± 15 V	yes	no	yes
IH5352*	I, M	4 × on	50 Ω	± 15 V	yes	no	yes

* Switches with high reverse-attenuation at high frequencies, as in Fig. 22.2.
dt = double-throw switch = changeover switch
Manufacturers: A = Analog Devices, H = Harris, I = Intersil, M = Maxim, N = National,
S = Siliconix, Ti = Texas Instr., Ty = Teledyne

Fig. 22.9a Examples of analog switches in CMOS technology

that the bipolar input voltage range is as large as possible, it is better to use, instead of a single MOSFET, a CMOS switch consisting of two complementary MOSFETs connected in parallel as shown in Fig. 22.7.

To turn the switch ON, V^+ is applied to the gate of n-channel MOSFET T_1 and that of p-channel MOSFET T_2 is connected to ground. Around midrange of voltage U_i, both MOSFETs are therefore conducting. If the input voltage increases to higher positive values, U_{GS1} is reduced, making T_1 have higher impedance. However, this has no adverse effect, as the absolute value of U_{GS2} simultaneously increases. This makes T_2 go low impedance, and vice versa for small input voltages. This is illustrated in Fig. 22.8 in which we see that the input voltage can assume any value between 0 and V^+.

Type	Manufacturer	Switch	ON-state resistance	Analog range	Level converter	Data latches	Latch-up protected
74HC-family							
74HC4051	N, Ti	1×8	$30\,\Omega$	± 6 V	yes	no	no
74HC4052	N, Ti	2×4	$30\,\Omega$	± 6 V	yes	no	no
300-family							
MAX369	M	2×4	$150\,\Omega$	± 15 V	yes	yes	yes
MAX368	M	1×8	$150\,\Omega$	± 15 V	yes	yes	yes
500-Standard family							
DG529	H, S	2×4	$400\,\Omega$	± 15 V	yes	yes	yes
DG528	H, S	1×8	$400\,\Omega$	± 15 V	yes	yes	yes
DG527	H, S	2×8	$400\,\Omega$	± 15 V	yes	yes	yes
DG526	H, S	1×16	$400\,\Omega$	± 15 V	yes	yes	yes
500-High-frequency family							
DG538*	S	1×8	$90\,\Omega$	$-5\ldots+10$ V	yes	yes	yes
DG536*	S	1×16	$90\,\Omega$	$0\ldots+10$ V	yes	yes	yes
500-High-voltage family							
DG569	S	2×4	$100\,\Omega$	± 50 V	yes	yes	yes
DG568	S	1×8	$100\,\Omega$	± 50 V	yes	yes	yes
6000-Low-reverse-current family							
IH6208	I, M	2×4	$300\,\Omega$	± 14 V	yes	no	yes
IH6108	I, M	1×8	$300\,\Omega$	± 14 V	yes	no	yes
IH6216	I, M	1×8	$600\,\Omega$	± 11 V	yes	no	yes
IH6116	I, M	1×16	$600\,\Omega$	± 11 V	yes	no	yes

*Switches with high reverse attenuation, as in Fig. 22.2
Manufacturers: H = Harris, I = Intersil, M = Maxim, N = National, S = Siliconix, Ti = Texas Instr.

Fig. 22.9b Examples of analog multiplexers in CMOS technology

With standard CMOS switches, neither the control voltage nor the analog signals must be outside this range, because this could result in the destruction of the switches due to *latch-up*. In this case the channel substrate diode becomes conducting and floods the substrate with charge carriers which could fire the parasitic thyristor shown in Fig. 9.39, short-circuiting the supply voltage. If it cannot be guaranteed that the relevant values will stay within the safe input voltage range, a resistor must be connected at the input to limit the current [22.1].

Because of these problems, most IC CMOS switches are provided with additional protective, i.e. current-limiting, structures or are manufactured with *dielectric insulation* [22.2]. In this case an oxide layer is used as the insulator to the substrate, instead of a p-n junction. Consequently, CMOS components with dielectric insulation are not subject to latch-up effects, but their manufacturing process is considerably more expensive.

Figure 22.9 lists a number of commonly used CMOS switches and multiplexers. The 74HC types are normal, extremely low-cost CMOS gates, but they are prone to latch-up and have only a limited voltage range. The other types are protected against this effect and can therefore be used without any difficulty. The manufacturers listed also offer a wide range of other types, of which just a few examples are given.

The typical reverse currents of the switches are between 0.1 nA and 1 nA at room temperature. These values double for every 10 degrees increase in temperature and can therefore be as much as 100 nA. The switching times are between 100 ns and 300 ns.

22.2.2 Diode switch

Diodes are also suitable for use as switches because of their low forward resistance and high blocking resistance. If a positive control voltage is applied to the circuit in Fig. 22.10, diodes D_5 and D_6 become reverse biased. The impressed current I then flows through branches D_1, D_4 and D_2, D_3 from one current source to the other. The potentials V_1 and V_2 thereby assume the values

$$V_1 = U_i + U_D, \qquad V_2 = U_i - U_D .$$

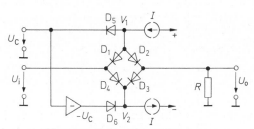

Fig. 22.10 Series switch using diodes

The output voltage then is

$$U_o = V_1 - U_D = V_2 + U_D = U_i ,$$

if the forward voltages U_D are the same. Should this not be the case, an offset voltage occurs.

If the control voltage is made negative, the two diodes D_5, D_6 become forward biased, and the diode bridge is turned off. This means that the output is doubly disconnected from the input and the midpoint is at constant potential. The analog switch therefore has a high reverse attenuation and is of the type shown in Fig. 22.2.

By employing this principle, switching times of less than 1 ns can be achieved if fast-switching diodes are used [22.2]. Suitable types include diode array CA 3019 from RCA or Schottky diode quartet 5082-2813 from Hewlett-Packard.

Rapid switching naturally requires correspondingly fast drive signals. An example of a suitable drive circuit is shown in Fig. 22.11. This consists of a bridge circuit made up of four constant current sources T_1 to T_4. The upper two are switched on alternately by the drive signal. When T_1 is on, a current of magnitude I flows through the diode bridge, causing it to conduct. In order to ensure that, in this case, current sources T_2 and T_3 are not driven into saturation, the reverse voltages are limited by transistors T_5 and T_6. These also ensure that the diode bridge driver is at low impedance during reverse-biased operation. Good reverse attenuation is then achieved due to the reduction of capacitive feedthrough.

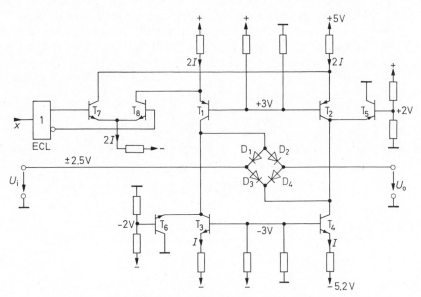

Fig. 22.11 Diode bridge with fast drive circuit

The amplitude of the analog signal must be smaller than the maximum control voltage across the diode bridge. For the values specified, it must be limited to ± 2.7 V by transistors T_5 and T_6. Higher voltages should not be handled by high-speed switches, because components with higher reverse voltages also possess markedly worse high-frequency characteristics in most cases.

22.2.3   Bipolar junction transistor switch

To investigate the suitability of a bipolar junction transistor for use as a switch, we examine its output characteristic curves around the origin, an expanded view of which is given in Fig. 22.12 for small positive and negative collector-emitter voltages.

The first quadrant contains the familiar output characteristics shown in Fig. 4.6. If the voltage U_{CE} is made negative without changing the base current, the output characteristics of the third quadrant are obtained. In this reverse mode polarity, the current gain of the transistor is considerably reduced and is about $\frac{1}{30}\beta$. The maximum permissible collector-emitter voltage in this mode is the breakdown voltage U_{EB0}, since the base-collector junction is forward biased and the base-emitter junction is reverse biased. This type of operation is known as reverse-region operation, and the accompanying current gain is termed the reverse current gain ratio β_r. The collector current is zero for a collector-emitter voltage of about 10 to 50 mV. If the base current exceeds a few mA, this *offset voltage* increases steeply; for small base currents it remains constant over a large range.

The offset voltage can be considerably reduced by ensuring that the transistor is in reverse-region operation when the output current crosses zero. To

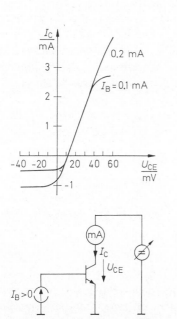

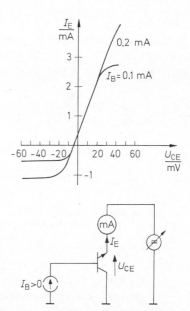

Fig. 22.12 Complete output characteristics of a transistor in common-emitter connection, with associated test circuit

Fig. 22.13 Complete output characteristics for interchanged emitter and collector, with associated test circuit

achieve this, collector and emitter must be interchanged. The resulting output characteristics are shown in Fig. 22.13. At larger output currents, virtually the same curves are obtained as for the normal operation in Fig. 22.12, if U_{CE} is still measured at the correct polarity (collector-to-emitter). The reason for this is that the emitter current, now the output current, is very nearly the same as the collector current.

Near the origin, however, a major difference arises in that the base current can no longer be neglected with respect to the output current. If, for normal operation, the output current is made zero, the emitter current is identical to the base current, i..e. is not zero, and an offset voltage of 10 to 50 mV appears at the output. If collector and emitter are interchanged and the output current is made zero, the collector current is the base current. The collector-base junction is then forward biased (reverse operation). The offset voltage for this mode of operation is usually about $\frac{1}{10}$ that at normal operation, but is also positive since, for the circuit in Fig. 22.13, $U_o = - U_{CE}$. Typical values for the offset voltage are between 1 and 5 mV, and it is therefore desirable to operate transistor switches with interchanged collector and emitter. If the emitter current is kept small, the transistor operates almost exclusively in the reverse mode.

Short-circuiting switch

Figures 22.14 and 22.15 show how a transistor can be used as a short-circuiting switch. In the circuit of Fig. 22.14, the transistor is operating in normal mode whereas in Fig. 22.15, it is in reverse-region mode. To obtain a sufficiently low transistor resistance, the base current must be in the mA-range. The collector current in Fig. 22.14, and the emitter current in Fig. 22.15, should not be much larger in order to ensure that the offset voltage remains small.

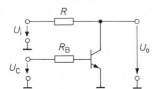

Fig. 22.14 Bipolar transistor as a short-circuiting switch

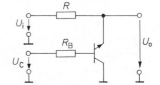

Fig. 22.15 Short-circuiting switch in reverse-region mode

Series switch

Figure 22.16 shows a bipolar transistor used as a series switch. A negative control voltage must be applied to turn off the transistor. It must be more negative than the most negative value of the input voltage, but also has a limit, since the control voltage may not be more negative than $- U_{EBO} \approx - 6$ V.

To render the transistor conducting, a positive control voltage is applied which is larger than the input voltage by a value of $\Delta U = I_B R_B$. The collector-base junction is then forward biased and the transistor operates as a switch in reverse-region mode. The disadvantage is that the base current flows into the input voltage source, and unless the internal resistance of the source is kept very small, large errors may occur.

If this condition can be fulfilled, the circuit is particularly suitable for positive input voltages, as the ON-state emitter current is positive. The offset voltage is therefore reduced and even becomes zero for a particular emitter current, as can be seen in Fig. 22.13. The circuit in this mode of operation is known as a saturated emitter follower, since for control voltages between zero and U_i, it operates as an emitter follower for U_C. This is illustrated in Fig. 22.17 by the transfer characteristics for positive input voltages.

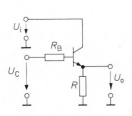

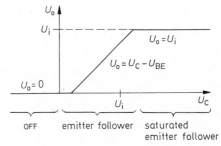

Fig. 22.16 Saturated emitter follower as a series switch

Fig. 22.17 Transfer characteristics for positive input voltages

Series/short-circuiting switch

If the saturated emitter follower in Fig. 22.16 is combined with the short-circuiting switch in Fig. 22.15, a series/short-circuiting switch is obtained having a low offset voltage for both modes of operation. It has the disadvantage that complementary control signals are required. The control arrangement is particularly simple if a complementary emitter follower is used, as in Fig. 22.18. It is

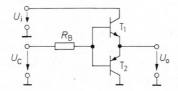

Fig. 22.18 Series/short-circuiting switch

saturated in both the ON and OFF states if $U_{C\max} > U_i$ and $U_{C\min} < 0$. Due to the low output resistance, a fast switchover of the output voltage, between zero and U_i, is possible. A practical implementation of this was shown in the case of the function generator in Fig. 15.36.

22.2.4   Differential amplifier switch

The gain of a differential amplifier is proportional to the transconductance, which is in turn proportional to the collector current. Consequently, the differential gain can be made zero by cutting off the emitter current. Figure 22.19 shows how this principle can be applied to a differential amplifier used as an analog switch.

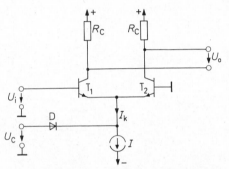

Fig. 22.19 Differential amplifier used as a switch

$$U_o = \begin{cases} 0 & \text{for} \quad U_C = 1\,\text{V} \\ g_f R_C U_i & \text{for} \quad U_C = -1\,\text{V} \end{cases}$$

If the control voltage is made negative, diode D is turned off and the differential amplifier carries emitter current $I_k = I$. If the output voltage is taken from the collectors, we obtain:

$$U_o = g_f R_C U_i = \frac{I_C}{U_T} R_C U_i = \frac{1}{2U_T} I_k R_C U_i \; .$$

If the control voltage is made positive, the diode takes over current I and the transistors are turned off: $I_k = 0$. Although this causes the two output potentials to increase to V^+, the output voltage difference U_o becomes zero.

Figure 22.20 shows how this principle can be employed to design an analog switch for low frequencies. As long as the input voltage $U_D = 0$, the control current I_C is equally divided between the two transistors of the differential amplifier, and current I flows in all the current mirrors. The output current becomes zero. If a positive input voltage is applied, the collector current of T_2

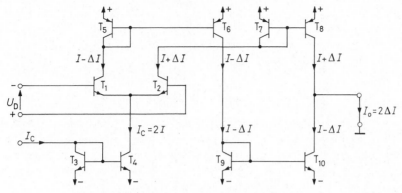

Fig. 22.20 Transconductance amplifier used as a switch

$$I_o = \begin{cases} 0 & \text{for } I_C = 0 \\ I_C U_D / 2U_T & \text{for } I_C > 0 \end{cases}$$

increases by $\Delta I = \frac{1}{2} g_f U_D$ and that of T_1 decreases by the same amount. The output current is therefore

$$I_o = 2\Delta I = g_f U_D = \frac{I_C}{U_T} U_D = \frac{I_C}{2U_T} U_D \;.$$

If the control current I_C is made zero, all the transistors are turned off and the output current also becomes zero.

Amplifiers operating on this principle are known as *transconductance amplifiers*. They are available in IC form: e.g. the CA 3060 or CA 3280 from RCA, or the GAP 01 from PMI. They can also be used as operational amplifiers if the control current remains constant. If the control current is made proportional to a second input voltage, they can also be used as analog multipliers [22.3].

Figure 22.21 shows how the principle illustrated in Fig. 22.19 can be used to design a switch for high frequencies. Here the two operational amplifiers T_1, T_2 and T_3, T_4 employ common collector resistors R_1. However, only one pair is in operation at a time: when the control voltage is positive, the left-hand differential amplifier receives current I; for negative control voltages, current I flows in pair T_3/T_4. This arrangement has an advantage over that in Fig. 22.19 in that the output potentials remain constant during switching.

We therefore have a device which can be used to switch from one input voltage $U_{i1} = U_1 - U_2$ to another $U_{i2} = U_3 - U_4$. If we make $U_3 = U_2$ and $U_4 = U_1$ by connecting the relevant inputs, then $U_{i2} = -U_{i1}$ and we have a polarity changer.

The circuit can be designed as a wideband amplifier, like the complementary cascode differential amplifier shown in Fig. 16.8. Current feedback resistors R_E and cascode circuits T_7, T_8 are used for this purpose. By selecting suitable component values, bandwidths of 100 MHz or more can be achieved. The

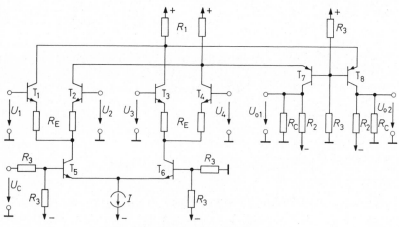

Fig. 22.21 Wideband multiplexer

$$U_{o1} = -U_{o2} = \begin{cases} A(U_1 - U_2) & \text{for} \quad U_C = 1\text{ V} \\ A(U_3 - U_4) & \text{for} \quad U_C = -1\text{ V} \end{cases}$$

$$A = \tfrac{1}{2}g_f'(R_C \| R_2) \qquad\qquad g_f' = g_f/(1 + g_f R_E)$$

circuit can therefore be used, for instance, as a modulator, demodulator or phase detector for telecommunications, and as a channel (beam) chopper in wideband oscilloscopes.

Integrated circuits employing this principle include the OPA 676 from Burr Brown or the AD 539 from Analog Devices for high bandwidth applications, or the AD 630 from Analog Devices for high precision circuits.

22.3   Analog switches with amplifiers

If analog switches are combined with operational amplifiers, a number of special characteristics can be obtained. In the following sections, the switches themselves will only be shown symbolically. The CMOS types listed in Fig. 22.9 are the most suitable for practical implementations.

22.3.1   Analog switches for high voltages

In the circuit in Fig. 22.22, the operational amplifier operates as an inverting amplifier. When the switch is open, the voltage across it is limited by diodes D_1 and D_2 to ± 0.7 V. When the switch is closed, both terminals are at ground potential, as they are connected to the summing point. The circuit operates in this case as an inverting amplifier. The diodes have no effect, as virtually no voltage is dropped across them. The circuit gain can therefore be selected using R_1 and R_2 such that the operational amplifier is not overdriven even at the highest input voltages.

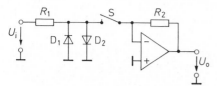

Fig. 22.22 Switching high voltages at low switch voltages

$$U_o = \begin{cases} 0 \\ - U_i R_2/(R_1 + r_{DSON}) \end{cases}$$

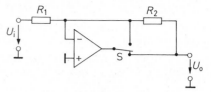

Fig. 22.23 Switching high voltages with high precision

$$U_o = \begin{cases} 0 \\ - U_i R_2/R_1 \end{cases}$$

Another method of switching large voltages is illustrated in Fig. 22.23. In the switch position shown, the op-amp again operates as an inverting amplifier. The advantage in this case is that the switch is inserted in the feedback loop and, as a result, its ON-state resistance has no effect on the gain. However, it is necessary to use switches whose analog voltage range is identical to the maximum output voltage swing of the operational amplifier.

When the switch is changed over, the output is connected via R_2 to the summing point, i.e. to zero potential.

22.3.2   Amplifier with switchable gain

In the circuit in Fig. 22.24, the gain of a non-inverting amplifier can be switched using an analog multiplexer. Depending on which switch of the multiplexer is closed, any gain factor $A \geq 1$ can be realized by selecting suitable component values for the voltage divider chain. The main advantage of this circuit is that the switches of the analog multiplexer can be operated without current. This means that their ON-state resistance does not affect the output voltage. An IC amplifier operating on this principle is the AD 526 from Analog Devices. Its gain can be switched between 1 and 16.

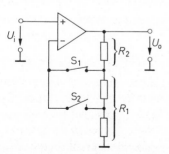

Fig. 22.24 Non-inverting amplifier with switchable gain

$$U_o = (1 + R_2/R_1) U_i$$

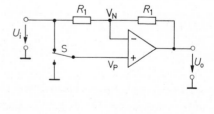

Fig. 22.25 Inverting/non-inverting amplifier

$$U_o = \begin{cases} U_i & \text{for} \quad S = \text{up} \\ - U_i & \text{for} \quad S = \text{down} \end{cases}$$

With the circuit in Fig. 22.25, the sign of the gain can be reversed using switch S. When the switch is in the lower position, the circuit operates as an inverting amplifier providing a gain of $A = -1$.

When the switch is in the upper position, $V_P = U_i$. The output voltage therefore assumes a value such that no voltage is dropped across R_1. This occurs when $U_o = U_i$. The amplifier therefore operates as a non-inverting amplifier. The circuit is very similar to the bipolar coefficient network in Fig. 12.5.

22.4   Sample-and-hold circuits

22.4.1   Basic principles

The output voltage of a sample-and-hold circuit should follow the input voltage when in the ON-state. In this mode, it therefore behaves like an analog switch. In the OFF-state, however, the output voltage must not become zero, but the voltage at the turn-off instant must be stored. This is why sample-and-holds are also known as track-and-hold circuits.

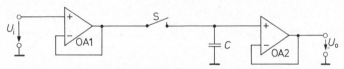

Fig. 22.26 Schematic diagram of a sample-and-hold circuit

The basic arrangement for a sample-and-hold is shown in Fig. 22.26. The central component is the capacitor C which performs the storage function. When switch S is closed, the capacitor is charged up to the input voltage. In order to ensure that the input voltage source is not loaded, an impedance converter is employed. This is implemented by voltage follower OA 1. It must be capable of delivering high output currents in order to be able to charge and discharge the storage capacitor quickly.

When switch S is open, the voltage across capacitor C must be kept constant for as long as possible. Consequently, a voltage follower is connected after it to eliminate loading of the capacitor. In addition, the switch must have a high OFF-state resistance and the capacitor a low leakage current.

The main non-ideal characteristics of a sample-and-hold are given in Fig. 22.27. When the switch is closed by the sample command, the output voltage does not instantaneously increase to the value of the input voltage, but only at a defined maximum *slew rate*. It is primarily determined by the maximum current of the input impedance converter. This is followed by a settling time whose duration is determined by the damping due to the impedance converter and the ON-state resistance of the switch. The *acquisition time* t_{Ac} is defined as the time that elapses after the start of the track command until the output voltage is equal to the input voltage within the specified tolerance. If the

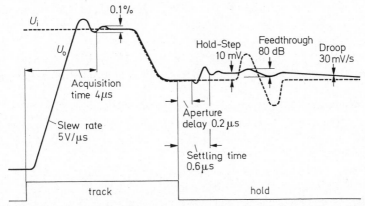

Fig. 22.27 Specifications of a sample-and-hold circuit, showing typical values for an LF 398 with 1 nF capacitor. The duration of the tracking phase must be at least equal to the acquisition time

charging of the storage capacitor is determined solely by the ON-state resistance R_S of the switch, the acquisition time can be calculated from the charging function of an RC network and the required accuracy of acquisition. Thus

$$t_{Ac} = R_S \cdot C \cdot \begin{cases} 4.6 & \text{for} \quad 1\% \\ 6.9 & \text{for} \quad 0.1\% \end{cases}.$$

It is therefore shorter the smaller the value of C selected.

During transition to the hold state, it takes a while for the switch to open. This is known as the *aperture delay* t_{Ap}. It is not usually constant, but tends to vary, often as a function of the particular value of the input voltage. These fluctuations are termed *aperture jitter* Δt_{Ap}.

In general, the output voltage does not now remain at the stored value, but there is a small voltage change ΔU_o (*hold step*) with subsequent settling. This is due to the fact that, when the circuit is switched off, a small charge is coupled by the drive signal via the switch capacitance C_S into storage capacitor C. The resultant hold step is given by

$$\Delta U_o = \frac{C_S}{C} \Delta U_C ;$$

where ΔU_C is the amplitude of the drive signal. This effect is smaller the larger the value selected for C.

Another non-ideal characteristic is the *feedthrough*. This results from the fact that the input voltage has an effect on the output even though the switch is open. This effect is mainly caused by the capacitive voltage divider formed by the capacitance of the open switch with the storage capacitor.

The most important variable in the store condition is the *droop* (hold decay). This is mainly determined by the input current of the impedance converter at the output and the reverse current of the switch. For a discharge current I_L, we have

$$\frac{\Delta U_o}{\Delta t} = \frac{I_L}{C} \ .$$

In order to minimize the discharge current, an FET-input amplifier is used for OA 2.

As we can see, all the characteristics in the hold state are better the larger the value selected for C, whereas during tracking operation small values of C are desirable. Consequently, a compromise has to be found depending on the application.

We have hitherto assumed that the hold capacitor possesses ideal character-istics. It is also possible to find capacitors with virtually no leakage current. Nevertheless, a voltage change can occur in the hold state due to charge storage in the dielectric. This effect may be explained by reference to the equivalent circuit in Fig. 22.28. Capacitor C_1 represents the charge stored in the dielectric. It initially remains unchanged in the event of a hold step and only changes slowly. If the sampling time is short, the charge required for this purpose is taken from capacitor C during the hold phase (dielectric absorption). In the case of a hold step of magnitude U, this produces a subsequent voltage change of

$$\Delta U = \frac{C_1}{C} U \ ,$$

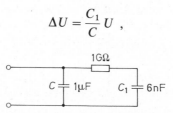

Fig. 22.28 Equivalent circuit of a capacitor. In this example, a 1 μF capacitor with Mylar dielectric is used [22.4]

i.e. 0.6% in the example in Fig. 22.28. The size of this effect depends on the dielectric used. Teflon, polystyrene and polypropylene are good in this respect; polycarbonate, Mylar and most ceramic dielectric materials, on the other hand, are poor [22.4].

22.4.2   Practical implementation

The fastest sample-and-holds can be designed on the principle illustrated in Fig. 22.26 if the diode bridge of Fig. 22.11 is used as a switch and the circuits described in Section 16.6.1 are used as voltage followers. A typical example of this sample-and-hold design is the HTS 0010 from Analog Devices.

A higher degree of accuracy can be achieved using an overall feedback arrangement, as shown in Fig. 22.29. When the switch is closed, the output potential V_1 of amplifier OA 1 assumes a value such that $U_o = U_i$. This elimin-ates offset errors due to OA 2 or the switch. Diodes D_2 and D_3 are nonconduct-

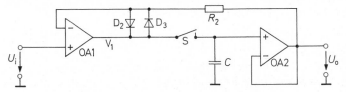

Fig. 22.29 Sample-and-hold with overall feedback

ing in this operating condition, as only a small voltage $V_1 - U_o$ is dropped across them, which is precisely equal to the offset voltage.

If the switch is opened, the output voltage remains constant. Resistor R_2 and diodes D_2, D_3 prevent amplifier OA 1 from being overdriven in this operating condition. This is an important consideration, because any overdriving is followed by a considerable recovery time which is added to the settling time.

This is the principle employed by type LF 398 which, being inexpensive, represents the most commonly used sample-and-hold circuit for general applications.

Sample-and-hold circuit with integrator

Instead of a grounded capacitor with voltage follower, an integrator can also be used as an analog storage device. This possibility is illustrated in Fig. 22.30, in which the series switch is connected to the summing point, this resulting in a simple drive arrangement.

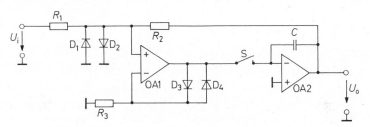

Fig. 22.30 Sample-and-hold with integrator as storage device

When the switch is closed, the output voltage assumes the value $U_o = - U_i R_2 / R_1$ due to the negative feedback. As in the previous circuit, amplifier OA 1 reduces the settling time and eliminates the offset voltage of FET amplifier OA 2.

When the switch is opened, the current flowing through the storage capacitor becomes zero and the output voltage remains constant. In this case overall feedback is ineffective. Instead, diodes D_1 to D_4 come into play and limit the output voltage of OA 1 to ± 1.2 V, thereby preventing it from being overdriven.

With high-speed sample-and-holds, amplifier OA 1 is generally omitted. The circuit is then similar to the integrator in Fig. 12.9. The HTC 0300 from Analog Devices operates on this principle.

Survey of types available

Figure 22.31 lists a selection of sample-and-hold circuits. With the monolithic types, the hold capacitor is connected externally. This makes it possible—within certain limits—to match the data to the particular application. The hybrid circuits should only be considered if speed is vital, as they are several times more expensive.

Type	Manufacturer	Hold capacitor	Settling time	Accuracy	Slew rate	Droop	Technology
LF 398	various	10 nF	20 μs	10 bit	0.5 V/μs	3 mV/s	bipolar
LF 398	various	1 nF	4 μs	10 bit	5 V/μs	30 mV/s	bipolar
HA 2425	Harris	1 nF	6 μs	12 bit	5 V/μs	20 mV/s	bipolar
SMP 10	PMI	5 nF	5 μs	12 bit	10 V/μs	5 V/s	bipolar
AD 585	Analog Dev.	100 pF*	3 μs	12 bit	10 V/μs	0.1 V/s	bipolar
SHC 5320	Burr B.	100 pF*	1.5 μs	12 bit	45 V/μs	0.1 V/s	bipolar
SHM 20	Datel	*	1 μs	12 bit	45 V/μs	0.1 V/s	bipolar
CS 3112	Crystal	*	1 μs	12 bit	4 V/μs	1 mV/s	CMOS
CS 31412[1]	Crystal	*	1 μs	12 bit	4 V/μs	1 mV/s	CMOS
AD 684[1]	Analog Dev.	*	1 μs	12 bit	60 V/μs	10 mV/s	bipolar
HA 5330	Harris	90 pF*	0.5 μs	12 bit	90 V/μs	10 mV/s	bipolar
AM 6420	AMD	50 pF*	0.5 μs	12 bit	50 V/μs	20 V/s	bipolar
AD 681	Analog Dev.	45 pF*	0.5 μs	12 bit	130 V/μs	10 mV/s	bipolar
HS 9716	Sipex	*	10 μs	16 bit	10 V/μs	50 mV/s	hybrid
SHC 76	Burr B.	*	6 μs	14 bit	30 V/μs	0.1 V/s	hybrid
AD 1154	Analog Dev.	*	3 μs	16 bit	10 V/μs	0.02 V/s	hybrid
SHM 91[2]	Datel	*	2 μs	14 bit	45 V/μs	1 V/s	hybrid
SHC 702	Burr B.	*	0.5 μs	16 bit	150 V/μs	0.2 V/s	hybrid
SP 9760	Sipex	*	0.3 μs	16 bit		1 V/s	hybrid
SHC 803	Burr B.	*	0.2 μs	12 bit	160 V/μs	0.5 V/s	hybrid
SHM 45	Datel	*	0.2 μs	12 bit	300 V/μs	0.5 V/s	hybrid
HS 9720	Sipex	*	0.2 μs	12 bit	170 V/μs	0.5 V/s	hybrid
SHM 40	Datel	*	40 ns	8 bit	300 V/μs	20 V/s	hybrid
CLC 942	Comlinear	*	25 ns	12 bit	300 V/μs	20 V/s	hybrid
SHC 601	Burr B.	*	22 ns	12 bit	350 V/μs	20 V/s	hybrid
HTS 0010	Analog Dev.	*	10 ns	8 bit	300 V/μs	50 V/s	hybrid
CLC 940	Comlinear	*	10 ns	8 bit	500 V/μs	20 V/s	hybrid

*Internal hold capacitor   [1] Quad S&H.   [2] Double S&H.

Fig. 22.31 Typical sample-and-hold circuit data

23 D/A and A/D converters

To display or process a voltage digitally, the analog signal must be translated into numerical form. This task is performed by an analog-to-digital converter (A/D converter, ADC). The resultant number Z will generally be proportional to the input voltage U_i:

$$Z = U_i/U_{LSB} \ ,$$

where U_{LSB} is the voltage unit for the least significant bit, i.e. the voltage for $Z = 1$.

To convert a number back into a voltage, a digital-to-analog converter (D/A converter, DAC) is used, whose output voltage is proportional to the numeric input, i.e.

$$U_o = U_{LSB} \cdot Z \ .$$

23.1 Basic principles of D/A conversion

The purpose of a DAC is to convert a digital number into a proportional voltage. There are basically three methods of conversion:

the parallel method,
the weighting method and
the counter method.

These three methods are shown schematically in Fig. 23.1. With the parallel method (Fig. 23.1a), a voltage divider is used to provide all the possible levels of output voltage. The switch to which the required output voltage level is assigned is then closed by the 1-of-n decoder.

With the weighting method in Fig. 23.1b, a switch is assigned to each bit. The output voltage is then added up via appropriately weighted resistors.

The counter method in Fig. 23.1c requires just a single switch which is opened and closed periodically. Its duty cycle is set using a presettable counter in such a way that the arithmetic mean of the output voltage assumes the desired value.

Comparison of the three methods shows that the parallel method requires Z_{max} switches, the weighting method ld Z_{max} switches and the counting method a single switch. Due to its large number of switches, the parallel method is rarely used. Likewise, the counter method is seldom used, its main disadvantage being that the output voltage can only change slowly due to the lowpass filter required. It is mainly employed in frequency meters.

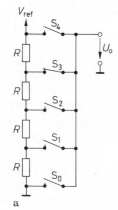

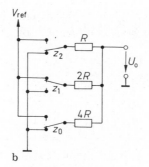

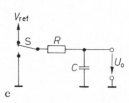

Fig. 23.1a Parallel method   Fig. 23.1b Weighting   Fig. 23.1c Counter method
                                         method

Fig. 23.1 D/A conversion methods

DACs employing the weighting method, on the other hand, are widely used and we shall now describe the various ways in which they can be implemented. Two methods of realizing the switches have become standard: CMOS circuits use the transmission gates shown in Fig. 22.7; in bipolar circuits, constant currents are generated and switched using diodes or differential amplifiers, as in Fig. 22.19.

23.2   D/A converters in CMOS technology

23.2.1   Summation of weighted currents

A simple circuit for converting a straight binary number to a voltage proportional to it is shown in Fig. 23.2. The resistors are selected such that, when the appropriate switch is closed, a current flows through them which is

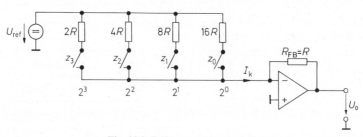

Fig. 23.2 D/A converter principle

$$U_o = - U_{ref} \frac{Z}{16} \; ; \qquad\qquad I_k = \frac{U_{ref}}{R} \cdot \frac{Z}{16} \; .$$

equivalent to the relevant binary weight. The switches must therefore always be closed if a logical "1" appears in the relevant bit position. Due to the op-amp feedback via resistor R_{FB}, the summing point remains at zero potential. The current components are therefore added together without affecting one another.

If the switch controlled by z_0 is closed, the output voltage is

$$U_o = U_{LSB} = -U_{ref} \frac{R_{FB}}{16R} = -\frac{1}{16} U_{ref} \; .$$

In general

$$U_o = \frac{1}{2} U_{ref} z_3 - \frac{1}{4} U_{ref} z_2 - \frac{1}{8} U_{ref} z_1 - \frac{1}{16} U_{ref} z_0 \; ,$$

giving

$$U_o = -\frac{1}{16} U_{ref}(8z_3 + 4z_2 + 2z_1 + z_0) = -U_{ref} \frac{Z}{Z_{max} + 1} \qquad (23.1)$$

23.2.2   D/A converters with double-throw switches

A disadvantage of the above D/A converter is that the voltages across the switches fluctuate considerably. As long as the switches are open, they are at V_{ref} potential; when closed, they are at zero potential. As a result, the charges of the stray capacitances of the switch must be reversed every time the switch operates. This disadvantage can be avoided if double-throw switches are used, as in Fig. 23.3, to connect the resistors either to the summing point or to ground. The current through each resistor therefore remains constant. This has a further advantage over the previous circuit in that the load of the reference voltage source is constant and its internal resistance need not be zero. The input resistance of the network, and thus the load resistance of the reference voltage source, is given by

$$R_i = 2R \| 4R \| 8R \| 16R = \tfrac{16}{15} R \; .$$

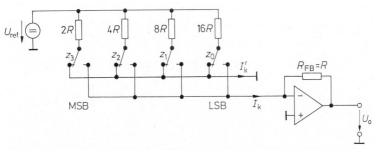

Fig. 23.3 D/A converter with double-throw switches

$$I_k = \frac{U_{ref}}{R} \frac{Z}{Z_{max} + 1} \; ; \qquad I_k' = \frac{U_{ref}}{R} \cdot \frac{Z_{max} - Z}{Z_{max} + 1} \; ; \qquad U_o = -U_{ref} \frac{Z}{Z_{max} + 1}$$

23.2.3   Ladder network

When fabricating integrated D/A converters, the implementation of accurate resistances of widely differing values is extremely difficult. The weighting of the bits is therefore often effected by successive voltage division using a ladder network as in Fig. 23.4. The basic element of such a ladder network is the loaded voltage divider in Fig. 23.5, which is required to have the following character-istics: if it is loaded by a resistor R_p, its input resistance R_i must also assume the value R_p. At this load, the attenuation $\alpha = U_2/U_1$ along the ladder element must have a predetermined value. With these two conditions, we obtain

$$R_d = \frac{(1 - \alpha)^2}{\alpha} R_q \quad \text{and} \quad R_p = \frac{(1 - \alpha)}{\alpha} R_q \; . \tag{23.2}$$

In the case of straight binary code, $\alpha = 0.5$. We define $R_q = 2R$, and obtain

$$R_d = R \quad \text{and} \quad R_p = 2R \; , \tag{23.3}$$

in accordance with Fig. 23.4.

The reference voltage source is loaded by the constant resistance

$$R_i = 2R \| 2R = R \; .$$

The output voltage of the summing amplifier is

$$
\begin{aligned}
U_o &= - R_{FB} I_k \\
&= - U_{ref} \frac{R_{FB}}{16R} (8z_3 + 4z_2 + 2z_1 + z_0) = - U_{ref} \frac{Z}{Z_{max} + 1} \; .
\end{aligned} \tag{23.4}
$$

The D/A converter in Fig. 23.4 only requires resistors of size R if the $2R$ resistors are replaced by two resistors connected in series. This arrangement is therefore ideally suitable for fabrication in monolithic IC form. Although the required

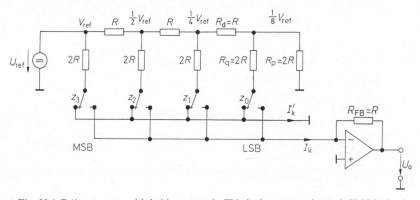

Fig. 23.4 D/A converter with ladder network. This is the commonly used CMOS circuit

$$U_o = - U_{ref} \frac{Z}{Z_{max} + 1}$$

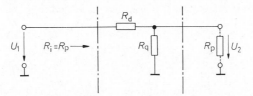

Fig. 23.5 Element of the ladder network

matching tolerances for the resistors can be easily achieved, their absolute values cannot be precisely specified. Consequently, tolerances up to $\pm 50\%$ are common. Of course, currents I_k or I'_k may also deviate by correspondingly large amounts. In order to obtain tight output voltage tolerances despite this deviation, feedback resistor R_{FB} is also integrated. This cancels out the absolute value of R from Eq. (23.4) for the output voltage. For this reason, the internal feedback resistor should always be used for current-voltage conversion, and never an external one.

23.2.4 Inverse operation of a ladder network

Sometimes the ladder network is also operated with transposed input and output (Fig. 23.6), as no summing amplifier is then required. However, one must then accept the drawbacks, mentioned earlier, of a high voltage swing across the switches and a variable loading of the reference voltage source.

To calculate the output voltage we need to know the relationship between the applied voltages U_i and the associated node voltages U'_i. For this purpose we use the superposition principle, i.e. we set all the injected voltages, apart from the voltage U_i in question, equal to zero and add the individual components. If we terminate the network right and left with resistance $R_L = R_p = 2R$, we obtain, as required, a load of $R_p = 2R$ at each node to right and left. This gives

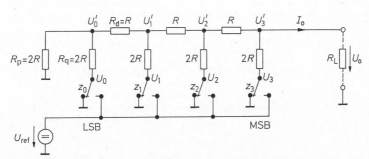

Fig. 23.6 Inversely operated ladder network. This circuit is used in converters with voltage output

$$U_o = U_{ref} \frac{R_L}{R + R_L} \cdot \frac{Z}{Z_{max} + 1} = U_{ref} \frac{R_L}{R + R_L} \cdot \frac{Z}{16}$$

us the voltage components $\Delta U_i' = \frac{1}{3}\Delta U_i$, and by adding the correspondingly weighted components we obtain the output voltage

$$U_o = \tfrac{1}{3}(U_3 + \tfrac{1}{2}U_2 + \tfrac{1}{4}U_1 + \tfrac{1}{8}U_0) = \frac{2U_{ref}}{3}\cdot\frac{Z}{16} \,. \tag{23.5}$$

As the internal resistance of the network, irrespective of the set number Z, has a constant value of

$$R_i = R_p \| R_q = (1 - \alpha)R_q = R \,, \tag{23.6}$$

the weighting is retained even if the load resistance R_L does not possess the initially specified value $R_p = 2R$. From the equivalent circuit diagram in Fig. 23.7, we can calculate the no-load voltage and the short-circuit current directly using Eq. (23.5):

$$U_{o0} = U_{ref}\frac{Z}{16} = U_{ref}\frac{Z}{Z_{max} + 1}\;;\quad I_{o\,s.c.} = \frac{U_{ref}}{R}\cdot\frac{Z}{16} = \frac{U_{ref}}{R}\cdot\frac{Z}{Z_{max} + 1} \,. \tag{23.7}$$

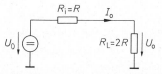

Fig. 23.7 Equivalent circuit for calculating the no-load voltage and short-circuit current

23.2.5   Ladder network for decade weighting

The ladder network in Fig. 23.4 can be extended to any length if longer straight binary numbers are to be converted. For the conversion of BCD numbers the method is somewhat modified, as in Fig. 23.8. Each decimal place (decade) is converted by a 4-bit D/A converter as in Fig. 23.3 or 23.4, and the individual converters are connected to a ladder network. This introduces, from stage to stage, an attenuation of $\alpha = \frac{1}{10}$. In Eq. (23.2), resistance R_q must then be replaced by the input resistance R_i of the D/A converter stages so that the

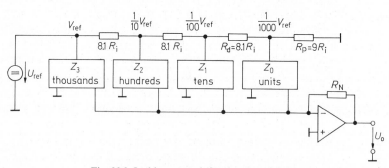

Fig. 23.8 Ladder network for decade weighting

coupling resistors are $R_d = 8.1\,R_i$ and the terminating resistor is $R_p = 9R_i$, as indicated in Fig. 23.8. In this manner, each input voltage for a D/A converter stage is $\frac{1}{10}$ that of the previous stage. For the example of 4 decades, the output voltage

$$U_o = -\frac{U_{ref}}{16}(Z_3 + \tfrac{1}{10}Z_2 + \tfrac{1}{100}Z_1 + \tfrac{1}{1000}Z_0)\ ,$$

is obtained if, for each decade, a ladder network as in Fig. 23.4 is used.

23.3   D/A converters in bipolar technology

With D/A converters employing bipolar technology, it is easy to implement constant-current sources individually contributing to the total output current. The principle is illustrated in Fig. 23.9. The currents are weighted according to the significance of the associated bit position. Depending on whether the relevant binary digit is 1 or 0, the associated current flows to the output or is diverted to ground. The busbar for current I_k need not necessarily be at ground potential, as the current supplied by the current sources is not a function of the voltage. However, this only applies within the output voltage range for constant-current operation (compliance voltage range). Consequently, an ohmic load resistance can be used which need not be connected to virtual ground (as in Fig. 23.4).

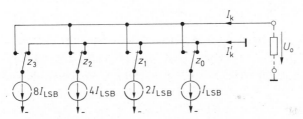

Fig. 23.9 D/A converter with switched current sources

$$U_o = -R_L \cdot I_{LSB} \cdot Z\ ;\quad I_k = I_{LSB} \cdot Z\ ;\quad I_k' I_{LSB}(Z_{max} - Z)$$

Simple transistor current sources of the type shown in Fig. 4.33 are used to generate the constant currents. If all the base potentials are made equal and all the emitter resistors are connected to V^-, the latter must be inversely proportional to the significance of the associated binary digit. This causes tolerancing problems, even in the bipolar process. Consequently, a ladder network is again used for current flow division (Fig. 23.10). Current source bank T_1 to T_6 is at equal base potential which is established via the op-amp in such a way that current $I_{ref} = U_{ref}/R_{ref}$ flows via reference transistor T_1. This is the case when $U_1 = 2R \cdot I_{ref}$. If the emitter-base voltages of the other transistors are identical to that of T_1, we obtain the stated voltage drops across the emitter resistors and therefore the required weighting of the currents.

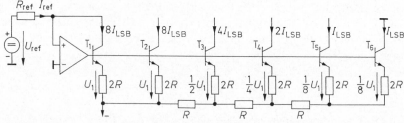

Fig. 23.10 Generation of weighted constant currents. This is the commonly used circuit employing bipolar technology

$$I_{\text{ref}} = \frac{U_{\text{ref}}}{R_{\text{ref}}} = 8I_{\text{LSB}}; \qquad U_1 = I_{\text{ref}} \cdot 2R = \frac{2R}{R_{\text{ref}}} U_{\text{ref}}$$

However, identical emitter-base voltages do not occur even if the transistors are completely identical, as the currents are not the same. From the transfer characteristic in Eq. (4.1) we obtain

$$U_{\text{BE}} = U_{\text{T}} \ln \frac{I_{\text{C}}}{I_{\text{CS}}} .$$

Consequently, the voltage increases by 18 mV if the collector current doubles. To avoid any resultant error, all the transistors are operated using the same collector current density. For this purpose, a sufficient number of transistors are connected in parallel to ensure that only current I_{LSB} flows through each. In integrated circuits, this is taken into account by using correspondingly larger-area transistors for the higher currents.

The $2R$ termination of the ladder network in Fig. 23.10 must not be connected to ground, but a point must be selected which is at emitter potential. This is generated by otherwise unused transistor T_6. For simplicity, its emitter can also be connected in parallel with T_5 and the two emitter resistors combined to form a single resistor of value R.

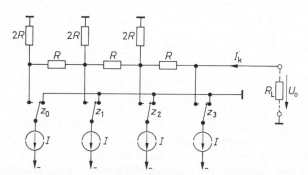

Fig. 23.11 D/A converter with inversely operated ladder network. This circuit is used in video converters

Short-circuit current $(R_L = 0)$: $I_{k\,\text{s.c.}} = \frac{1}{8} I_{\text{MSB}} \cdot Z = I_{\text{LSB}} \cdot Z$

Output voltage: $\qquad\qquad U_{\text{o}} = I_{k\text{o}}(2R \parallel R_L)$

Another method of D/A conversion using switched current sources is shown in Fig. 23.11. Here identical currents are generated which appear at the output after being weighted by a ladder network. The arrangement corresponds to the inversely operated ladder network in Fig. 23.6. The resistors $2R$ providing the attenuation within the chain must be connected to ground, as they would have no effect connected in series with the constant current sources. On the other hand, the attenuation in the chain is unchanged by connecting a current source, as the latter has, theoretically at least, an infinitely high internal resistance.

23.4 D/A converters for special applications

23.4.1 Processing signed numbers

When describing D/A converters, we have hitherto assumed that positive numbers are involved which have to be converted into positive or negative voltages, depending on the circuit. We shall now examine ways of producing bipolar output voltages using the D/A converters described. The conventional representation of binary numbers of either sign is in two's-complement notation (see Section 19.1.3). In this way, the range -128 to $+127$ can be represented with 8 bits, as shown again in Fig. 23.12.

Decimal	Two's complement								Offset binary								Analog	
	v_z	z_6	z_5	z_4	z_3	z_2	z_1	z_0	z_7	z_6	z_5	z_4	z_3	z_2	z_1	z_0	U_1/U_{LSB}	U_o/U_{LSB}
127	0	1	1	1	1	1	1	1	1	1	1	1	1	1	1	1	-255	127
126	0	1	1	1	1	1	1	0	1	1	1	1	1	1	1	0	-254	126
1	0	0	0	0	0	0	0	1	1	0	0	0	0	0	0	1	-129	1
0	0	0	0	0	0	0	0	0	1	0	0	0	0	0	0	0	-128	0
-1	1	1	1	1	1	1	1	1	0	1	1	1	1	1	1	1	-127	-1
-127	1	0	0	0	0	0	0	1	0	0	0	0	0	0	0	1	-1	-127
-128	1	0	0	0	0	0	0	0	0	0	0	0	0	0	0	0	0	-128

Fig. 23.12 Processing negative numbers in D/A converters

$$U_{LSB} = U_{ref}/256$$

To enter data to the D/A converter, the number range is shifted to 0 to 255 by adding 128. Numbers above 128 are deemed to be positive, those below negative. The mid-scale number 128 denotes in this case zero. This characterization of signed numbers by purely positive numbers is known as offset binary representation. The addition of 128 can be performed simply by negation of the sign bit (see Fig. 23.12).

In order to obtain an output voltage of correct sign, the addition of the offset is cancelled out by subtracting $128U_{LSB} = \frac{1}{2}U_{ref}$. Summing op-amp OA 2 in

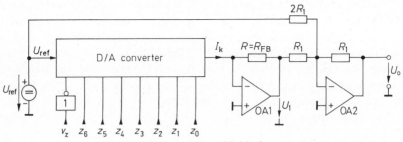

Fig. 23.13 D/A converter with bipolar output

$$U_\text{o} = U_\text{ref} \frac{Z}{256} \quad \text{for} \quad -128 \leqq Z \leqq 127$$

Fig. 23.13 is used for this purpose, providing the output voltage

$$U_\text{o} = -U_1 - \frac{1}{2} U_\text{ref} = U_\text{ref} \frac{Z + 128}{256} - \frac{1}{2} U_\text{ref} = U_\text{ref} \frac{Z}{256}. \qquad (23.8)$$

Its magnitude is listed together with voltage U_1 in Fig. 23.12.

The zero stability of the circuit in Fig. 23.13 can be improved by using the complementary output current I'_k instead of using the reference voltage directly for subtraction of the offset. In the case of two's-complement number 0, which actually corresponds to 128 in offset binary, we have

$$I_k = 128 I_\text{LSB} \quad \text{and} \quad I'_k = 127 I_\text{LSB}.$$

Therefore, if we add an I_LSB to I'_k and subtract the result from I_k, we obtain the correct zero point. This method is illustrated in Fig. 23.14. Operational amplifier OA 1 converts current I_k into the output voltage as before. To eliminate errors, the amplifier is fed back via DAC internal resistor R_FB. Op-amp OA 2 inverts the sum of I_LSB and I'_k and adds this current into the summing point of OA 1.

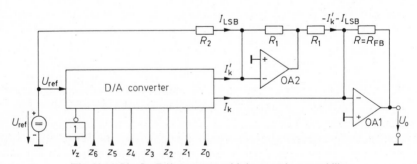

Fig. 23.14 Bipolar D/A converter with improved zero stability

$$U_\text{o} = U_\text{ref} \frac{Z}{128} \quad \text{for} \quad -128 \leqq Z \leqq 127$$

The absolute values of the two resistors R_1 are irrelevant, as long as they are the same. Current I_{LSB} is added via resistor R_2. If $I_{LSB} = U_{ref}/(256R)$, it follows that

$$R_2 = \frac{U_{ref}}{I_{LSB}} = 256\,R \ .$$

To calculate the output voltage we only need to add the currents at the summing point of OA 1 and obtain

$$U_o = R\left[\underbrace{\frac{U_{ref}}{R}\frac{Z+128}{256}}_{I_k} - \underbrace{\frac{U_{ref}}{R}\frac{255-(Z+128)}{256}}_{I'_k} - \underbrace{\frac{U_{ref}}{R}\frac{1}{256}}_{I_{LSB}} \right] = U_{ref}\frac{Z}{128} \ . \quad (23.9)$$

23.4.2   Multiplying D/A converters

As we have seen, D/A converters provide an output voltage proportional to the input number Z and the reference voltage U_{ref}, i.e. they form the product $Z \cdot U_{ref}$. For this reason, types allowing the reference voltage to be varied are also known as *multiplying* D/A converters.

With circuits realized in bipolar technology, the reference voltage can only assume positive values, as the current sources in Fig. 23.10 would otherwise be turned off. With CMOS types, on the other hand, positive and negative reference voltages are permissible. If circuits like those in Figs. 23.13 and 23.14, which allow positive and negative numbers to be converted with their correct signs, are used, this is termed *four-quadrant multiplication*.

23.4.3   Dividing D/A converters

A D/A converter can also be operated in such a way that it *divides* by the input number. To achieve this, it is inserted in the feedback loop of an operational amplifier, as in Fig. 23.15. This means that the reference voltage V_{ref} is set

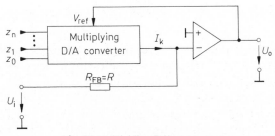

Fig. 23.15 Dividing D/A converter

$$U_o = -U_i \cdot \frac{R}{R_{FB}} \cdot \frac{Z_{max}+1}{Z}$$

such that $I_k = -U_i/R_{FB}$. Using the converter equation

$$I_k = \frac{V_{ref}}{R} \cdot \frac{Z}{Z_{max} + 1}$$

we obtain the output voltage

$$U_o = V_{ref} = I_k R \frac{Z_{max} + 1}{Z} = -U_i \cdot \frac{R}{R_{FB}} \cdot \frac{Z_{max} + 1}{Z}$$

$$= -U_i \cdot \frac{Z_{max} + 1}{Z} . \tag{23.10}$$

This simple means of performing division frequently obviates the need for analog or digital division with its associated cost and complexity, if a higher degree of accuracy is required.

23.4.4   D/A converter as function generator

The output voltage U_o of the usual D/A converter is proportional to the applied number Z: $U_o = a \cdot Z$. If, instead of the proportional function, any other relationship $U_o = f(Z)$ is to be realized, the function $X = f(Z)$ must be generated by a digital function network (see Section 19.7) and this applied to a D/A converter.

If no stringent requirements are imposed on the accuracy, there is a considerably more simple solution: the binary number Z is used to control an analog multiplexer. One applies constant analog input values, each of which is assigned to the appropriate binary number. For each analog value, a separate switch is needed, and the attainable resolution is therefore limited to about 16 steps.

A possible implementation is shown in Fig. 23.16. In contrast to the usual D/A converter, only one of the switches S_0 to S_7 is closed at any time. The values of the output voltage function are thus given by the expression

$$U_o(Z) = \begin{cases} + U_{ref} \dfrac{R_N}{R_Z} & \text{for } Z = 0 \dots 3 \\[2mm] - U_{ref} \dfrac{R_N}{R_Z} & \text{for } Z = 4 \dots 7 \, . \end{cases}$$

An important application of this principle is the digital generation of sine waves (e.g. in modems). A simple and widely used method of generating signals of different frequencies, all synchronized to a common time base, is to employ frequency division. However, a serious drawback for use in analog systems is that the signals obtained are square waves. Sine waves can be produced by filtering the fundamental with a lowpass or bandpass filter, but these filters must always be tuned to the appropriate frequency.

The D/A converter described avoids these problems in that it allows the frequency-independent generation of sine waves. According to Fig. 23.17, we

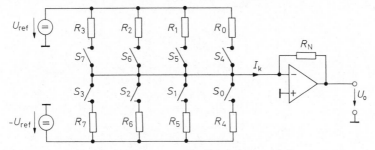

Fig. 23.16 D/A converter for any desired weighting

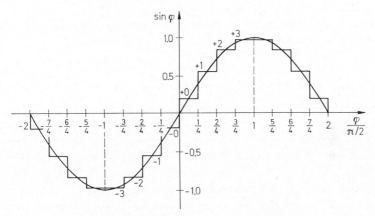

Fig. 23.17 Approximation of a sine wave by 16 steps

require a digital input signal representing a rising and falling sequence of equidistant numbers. This input signal corresponds to the triangular waveshape for sine wave generation by an analog function network, as described in Section 12.7.4.

If the signed-magnitude representation is chosen for the binary numbers, a number sequence having the desired properties can be easily generated by a cyclic straight binary counter [23.1]. The most significant bit represents the sign. The second most significant bit effects a change of counting direction for all lower bits by complementing the corresponding outputs with the aid of exclusive-OR gates. These bits represent the magnitude. When using a four-bit straight binary counter, the circuit in Fig. 23.18 is obtained. The number sequence generated is listed in Fig. 23.19. With a 3-bit number at the input of the analog multiplexer, four positive steps $+0, 1, 2, 3$ of the sine function and correspondingly, four negative steps $-0, -1, -2, -3$ are selected. If the steps are distributed as in Fig. 23.17, the function values in Fig. 23.19 are obtained, and the appropriate resistors can be determined. As the chosen quantization is rather coarse, it is sufficient to select the nearest standard resistance value.

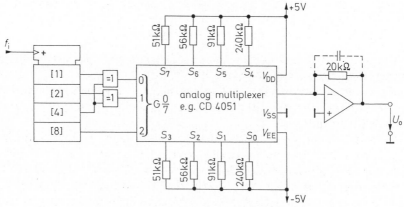

Fig. 23.18 Circuit for generating a continuous sine wave

$$U_o = 2\,\text{V}\sin 2\pi \frac{f_i}{16} t$$

Z	Counter outputs				Multiplexer inputs			Switch closed	Step number	Output voltage
	z_3	z_2	z_1	z_0	C	B	A			$U_o/\hat{U}_o$
0	0	0	0	0	0	0	0	S_0	+ 0	0.20
1	0	0	0	1	0	0	1	S_1	+ 1	0.56
2	0	0	1	0	0	1	0	S_2	+ 2	0.83
3	0	0	1	1	0	1	1	S_3	+ 3	0.98
4	0	1	0	0	0	1	1	S_3	+ 3	0.98
5	0	1	0	1	0	1	0	S_2	+ 2	0.83
6	0	1	1	0	0	0	1	S_1	+ 1	0.56
7	0	1	1	1	0	0	0	S_0	+ 0	0.20
8	1	0	0	0	1	0	0	S_4	− 0	− 0.20
9	1	0	0	1	1	0	1	S_5	− 1	− 0.56
10	1	0	1	0	1	1	0	S_6	− 2	− 0.83
11	1	0	1	1	1	1	1	S_7	− 3	− 0.98
12	1	1	0	0	1	1	1	S_7	− 3	− 0.98
13	1	1	0	1	1	1	0	S_6	− 2	− 0.83
14	1	1	1	0	1	0	1	S_5	− 1	− 0.56
15	1	1	1	1	1	0	0	S_4	− 0	− 0.20

Fig. 23.19 List of the number sequences and resulting voltages

Since in a complete period each step occurs twice, the sine wave is approximated by a total of 16 steps. Correspondingly, the input frequency f_i of the counter must be 16 times that of the sine wave.

23.5   Accuracy of D/A converters

23.5.1   Static characteristics

The *zero error* of a D/A converter is determined by the leakage currents flowing through the open switches.

The *full-scale error* is determined by the on-state resistances of the switches and the accuracy of the feedback resistor R_{FB}. Both errors can be largely eliminated by trimming.

Nonlinearity, on the other hand, cannot be eliminated by adjustment. It is defined as the amount by which a step is larger or smaller than 1 LSB, under worst-case conditions. Figure 23.20 illustrates a nonlinearity of $\pm \frac{1}{2}$ LSB. The critical case occurs at mid-scale: if only the most significant bit is a 1, the current flows via a single switch. If the number is reduced by 1, the total current of all the lower-order switches is reduced by only I_{LSB}.

If the linearity error is greater than 1 LSB, the trend is reversed. The output voltage then falls at the mid-scale point although the number is increased by 1. A serious error of this kind is termed a *monotony error*, an example of which is shown in Fig. 23.21. Most D/A converters are so designed that their non-linearity does not exceed $\pm \frac{1}{2}$ LSB, as the least significant bit would otherwise be meaningless.

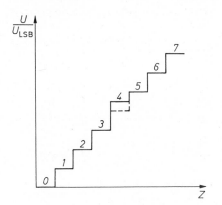

Fig. 23.20 D/A converter with a nonlinearity of $\pm \frac{1}{2}$ LSB

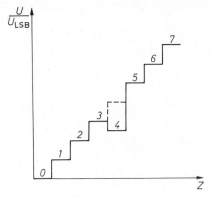

Fig. 23.21 D/A converter with a nonlinearity of $\pm 1\frac{1}{2}$ LSB and associated monotony error

23.5.2   Dynamic characteristics

The *settling time* is defined as the time it takes for the output signal to reach the steady-state value with an accuracy of $\frac{1}{2}$ LSB after the number Z has changed from 0 to Z_{max}. Only then is the analog signal available with the accuracy provided by the resolution of the D/A converter. Defining the settling time with reference to $\frac{1}{2}$ LSB means, of course, that D/A converters with the same time constant but higher resolution settle more slowly to $\frac{1}{2}$ LSB than those with lower resolution.

With many D/A converters, a current is initially formed which can be converted into a voltage, as required, in a following operational amplifier. In this case, the settling time of the op-amp, which is usually much greater than that of the D/A converter, is also added. In order to achieve short settling times for the voltage, methods must be selected which allow a voltage output to be provided even without using an op-amp. For CMOS types, the only option is to use the inversely operated ladder network in Fig. 23.6. Types realized in bipolar technology can all generate a voltage across an ohmic load resistance. In order to achieve bandwidths in the MHz range, it is advisable to use D/A converters whose output currents are so large that they can produce the required amplitudes across load resistors of 50 or 75 Ω.

Unwanted interference pulses (*glitches*) may also occur at the transition from one input number to the other. In most cases, these are due only to a small extent to capacitive feedthrough of the binary drive signals to the output. Large glitches occur if the switches in the D/A converter do not change state simultaneously. The critical point again occurs at mid-scale: if the most significant bit (MSB) is a 1, the current flows via one switch only. If the number is reduced by 1, the switch for the MSB opens and all the others close. If the MSB switch opens before the other switches have closed, the output signal briefly goes to zero. However, if the MSB switch opens slightly late, the output signal momentarily assumes its full-scale value. In this way, unwanted pulses with an amplitude equal to half the range may occur. An example of the switches closing more rapidly than they open is shown in Fig. 23.22.

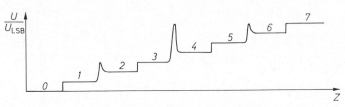

Fig. 23.22 Occurrence of positive glitches if the switches open too slowly

As the glitches are short pulses, they can be reduced using a lowpass filter at the output. As a result of this, however, they become correspondingly longer, the voltage-time area, i.e. the glitch energy, remaining constant.

Glitches can also be eliminated by connecting a sample-and-hold circuit at the output. This can be made to hold during the glitch phase, thereby blanking the glitch. Sample-and-holds specially designed for this purpose are known as *deglitchers*.

A simpler solution, however, is to use low-glitch D/A converters. These generally have an internal edge-triggered data memory for the number Z in order to ensure that the control signals are applied to all the switches simultaneously. The parallel method is also sometimes used for the more significant, critical bits, because this method is intrinsically glitch-free [23.2].

Figure 23.23 gives an overview of the principal D/A converter types.

Reso-lution	Type	Manufacturer	Channels	Latch	Settling time	Output	Input	Technology
8 bit	AD 7524*	Analog Dev.	1	×	200 ns	Summ.	8 bit	CMOS
	AD 7528*	Analog Dev.	2	×	200 ns	Summ.	8 bit	CMOS
	Bt 110	Brooktree	8	×	100 ns	Summ.	8 bit	CMOS
	DAC 830	National	1	×	1 µs	Summ.	8 bit	CMOS
	MP 7628	Micro Power	4	R	200 ns	Summ.	8 bit	CMOS
	Am 6080	AMD	1	×	160 ns	2 mA	8 bit	TTL
	ZN 559	Plessey	1	×	800 ns	2.5 V	8 bit	TTL
	ZN 508	Plessey	2	×	800 ns	2.5 V	8 bit	TTL
	TDC 1018	TRW	1	×	10 ns	30 mA	8 bit	ECL
	AD 9701	Analog Dev.	1	×	8 ns	27 mA	8 bit	ECL
	SDA 8005	Siemens	1	×	7 ns	40 mA	8 bit	ECL
	HDAC 51400	Honeywell	1	×	4 ns	40 mA	8 bit	ECL
	Bt 108	Brooktree	1	×	3 ns	40 mA	8 bit	ECL
	SP 98608	Plessey	1	×	2 ns	40 mA	8 bit	ECL
12 bit	AD 7545*	Analog Dev.	1	×	250 ns	Summ.	12 bit	CMOS
	AD 7547	Analog Dev.	2	×	800 ns	Summ.	12 bit	CMOS
	DAC 7800	Burr Brown	2	×	400 ns	Summ.	1 bit	CMOS
	DAC 7802	Burr Brown	2	×	400 ns	Summ.	12 bit	CMOS
	MAX 543	Maxim	1	×	250 ns	Summ.	1 bit	CMOS
	MP 7622	Micro Power	1	×	1 µs	Summ.	4/12 bit	CMOS
	MP 7680	Micro Power	4	×	1 µs	Summ.	8/12 bit	CMOS
	DAC 1210	National	1	×	1 µs	Summ.	8/12 bit	CMOS
	DAC 8012	PMI	1	R	1 µs	Summ.	12 bit	CMOS
	DAC 8043	PMI	1	×	250 ns	Summ.	1 bit	CMOS
	DAC 8222	PMI	2	×	1 µs	Summ.	12 bit	CMOS
	HS 7584	Sipex	4	×	2 µs	Summ.	8/12 bit	CMOS
	AM 6012*	AMD	1	−	75 ns	4 mA	12 bit	TTL
	AD 565*	Analog Dev.	1	−	250 ns	2 mA	12 bit	TTL
	AD 568	Analog Dev.	1	−	35 ns	10 mA	12 bit	TTL
	Bt 105	Brooktree	1	×	30 ns	40 mA	12 bit	TTL
	TDC 1112	TRW, Comlin.	1	×	30 ns	40 mA	12 bit	TTL
	AD 9713	Analog Dev.	1	×	15 ns	20 mA	12 bit	TTL
	AD 9712	Analog Dev.	1	×	15 ns	20 mA	12 bit	ECL
16 bit	AD 1145	Analog Dev.	1	×	6 µs	5 V	1/16 bit	2 Chips
	DAC 706	Burr Brown	1	×	350 ns	Summ.	16 bit	2 Chips
	MP 7636	Micro Power	1	×	1 µs	Summ.	8/16 bit	CMOS
	SP 9316	Sipex	1	×	3 µs	Summ.	8/16 bit	CMOS
18 bit	PCM 58	Burr Brown	1	×	200 ns	Summ.	1 bit	CMOS
	PCM 64	Burr Brown	1	−	200 ns	Summ.	18 bit	CMOS

* Other manufacturers: Burr Brown, Datel, Maxim, Micro Power Systems, PMI, Sipex.
R = Register with data readback   Summ. = Summing junction

Fig. 23.23 D/A converters without output amplifier (for other types with amplifier, see Fig. 21.64)

23.6   Basic principles of A/D conversion

The purpose of an A/D converter (ADC) is to transform an analog input voltage into a proportional digital number. There are three basically different conversion methods:

the parallel method	(word at a time),
the weighting method	(digit at a time),
the counter method	(level at a time).

The parallel (flash) method compares the input voltage with n reference voltages simultaneously and determines between which two reference levels the value of the input voltage lies. The resulting number is thus obtained in a single operation. However, the circuitry involved is very extensive, as a separate comparator is required for each possible number. For a range of mesurement from 0 to 100 in unit steps, $n = 100$ comparators are needed.

With the weighting (successive approximation) method, the end result is not obtained in a single operation; instead, one bit of the corresponding straight binary number is determined at a time. The input voltage is first checked against the most significant bit, i.e. whether it is larger or smaller than the reference voltage for this bit. If it is larger, the bit is 1 and the reference voltage is subtracted from the input voltage. The remainder is compared with the next lower bit, etc. The number of conversion operations and reference voltages needed is the same as the number of bits in the result.

The simplest method is the counter method. It involves counting how often the reference voltage of the least significant bit must be added to arrive at the input voltage. The number of operations is the required result. If the maximum number to be represented is n, a maximum of n operation steps must be performed to obtain the result.

Approach	Number of steps	Number of reference voltages	Characteristics
Parallel method	1	$n = 2^N$	complex, fast
Weighting method	$N = \mathrm{ld}\, n$	$N = \mathrm{ld}\, n$	
Counter method	$n = 2^N$	1	simple, slow

Fig. 23.24 Comparison of different approaches to A/D conversion

In order to compare the different methods, we have listed their main characteristics in Fig. 23.24. Figure 23.25 shows the accuracy and frequency range in which these methods are implemented.

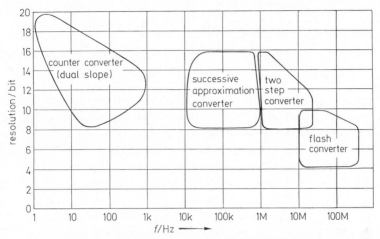

Fig. 23.25 Conversion frequency and resolution of A/D converters

23.7   Accuracy of A/D converters

23.7.1   Static errors

When converting an analog signal to a digital quantity having a finite number of bits, a systematic error is incurred due to the limited resolution, which is known as the quantization error. According to Fig. 23.26, it is $\pm \frac{1}{2} U_{LSB}$, i.e. it corresponds to half the input voltage step required to change the least significant bit.

If the number sequence generated is reconverted by a D/A converter to a voltage, the quantization error gives rise to superimposed noise, the r.m.s. value of which is given by [23.3]

$$U_{n\ r.m.s.} = \frac{U_{LSB}}{\sqrt{12}} \ .$$ (23.11)

For full sinusoidal swing, the r.m.s. output signal voltage for an N-bit converter is determined by

$$U_{s\ r.m.s.} = \frac{1}{\sqrt{2}} \cdot \frac{1}{2} \cdot 2^N \cdot U_{LSB} \ .$$

Hence, the signal-to-noise ratio

$$S = 20\ dB\ lg \frac{U_{s\ r.m.s.}}{U_{n\ r.m.s.}} = N \cdot 6\ dB + 1.8\ dB \approx N \cdot 6\ dB \ .$$ (23.12)

In addition to the systematic quantization error, errors arise from non-ideal circuitry. When the mid-values of the steps are joined, as shown in Fig. 23.26, a straight line is obtained which passes through the origin and has the slope 1. For a real A/D converter, this line misses the origin (offset error) and its slope is different from 1 (gain error). The gain error gives rise to a *relative* deviation of the output quantity from the desired value, which is constant over the whole range of operation. The offset error gives rise to a constant *absolute* deviation. Both errors can usually be eliminated by adjusting the output at zero and full-scale operation. The remaining deviation is then due to drift and non-linearity only.

A linearity error exceeding the quantization error is incurred whenever the steps are of different heights. To determine the linearity error, offset and gain are adjusted and the maximum deviation of the input voltage from the ideal straight line is measured. This value, reduced by the systematic quantization error of $\frac{1}{2}U_{\mathrm{LSB}}$, is the *total nonlinearity*. It is usually quoted as a percentage of the LSB voltage unit. For the example in Fig. 23.27, the total nonlinearity is $\pm\frac{1}{2}U_{\mathrm{LSB}}$.

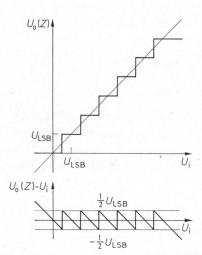

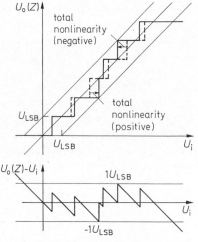

Fig. 23.26 Quantization error of an ideal A/D converter. Voltage $U_\mathrm{o}(Z)$ is obtained by D/A conversion of the number Z at the A/D converter output

Fig. 23.27 Transfer characteristic of an A/D converter having linearity error

A further measure of the linearity error is the *differential non-linearity* which indicates by how much the widths of the individual steps deviate from the desired value U_{LSB}. If this deviation is larger than U_{LSB}, a number is skipped (missing code). For even larger deviations, the number Z may even decrease for an increasing input voltage (monotonicity error).

23.7.2   Dynamic errors

A/D converter applications fall into two categories: those in digital volt-meters and those in signal-processing circuits. Their use in digital voltmeters is based on the assumption that the input voltage remains constant during the conversion process. For signal-processing applications, however, the input voltage changes continually. For digital processing, samples must be taken from the alternating voltage by means of a sample-and-hold circuit. The samples are then A/D converted. It has been shown in Section 24.1 that the resulting number sequence $\{Z\}$ represents the continuous input signal without loss of information only if the *sampling theorem* (*Nyquist theorem*) is satisfied. The sampling frequency f_s must therefore be at least twice the highest signal frequency f_{max}. Consequently, the conversion time of the A/D converter and the settling time of the sample-and-hold circuit must together be less than $1/(2 f_{max})$. In order to meet this requirement without introducing excessive complexity, the signal bandwidth is limited to just the value required. It is therefore customary to insert a preceding low-pass filter.

In order to judge the attainable accuracy, the properties of the A/D converter and of the sample-and-hold circuit must, in this application, be considered together. For example, it is pointless to operate a 12-bit A/D converter in conjunction with a sample-and-hold circuit which does not settle to $1/4096 \approx 0.025\%$ of full scale within the allotted time.

Another dynamic error is incurred due to *aperture jitter*. Due to the aperture time t_{Ap} of the sample-and-hold, the measured value is not extracted until after a delay. If the aperture time is constant, every measured value will be delayed by the same time, and so equidistant sampling will still be ensured. However, if the aperture time varies by the aperture jitter Δt_{Ap}, as in Fig. 23.28, a measuring error is introduced which is equal to the voltage change ΔU over this time. To calculate the maximum error ΔU, the input signal is taken to be a sine wave with the highest frequency f_{max} for which the system is designed. The maximum slope is at the origin

$$\frac{dU}{dt}\bigg|_{t=0} = \hat{U}\,\omega_{max} \ .$$

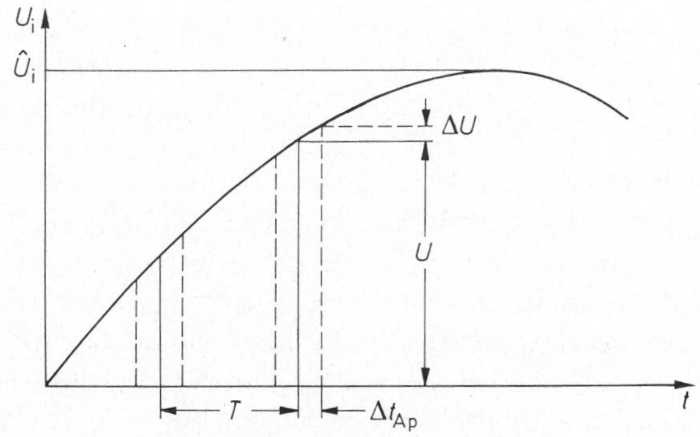

Fig. 23.28   Effect of aperture jitter

Hence, the amplitude error

$$\Delta U = \hat{U}\,\omega_{max}\cdot\Delta t_{Ap}\;.$$

If the error is to be smaller than the smallest conversion voltage U_{LSB} of the A/D converter, the condition for the aperture jitter must be as follows:

$$\Delta t_{Ap} < \frac{U_{LSB}}{\hat{U}\,\omega_{max}} = \frac{U_{LSB}}{\frac{1}{2}U_{max}\omega_{max}}\;. \tag{23.13}$$

It is extremely difficult to fulfill this condition for high signal frequencies, as the following example illustrates. For an 8-bit converter, $U_{LSB}/U_{max} = 1/255$. For a maximum signal frequency of 10 MHz, the aperture jitter must, according to Eq. (23.13), be smaller than 125 ps.

23.8   Design of A/D converters

23.8.1   Parallel method

Figure 23.29 illustrates the application of the parallel method to 3-bit numbers. With three bits, 8 different numbers including zero can be represented, for which 7 comparators are required. The 7 associated equidistant reference voltages can be generated by means of a voltage divider.

For an input voltage having a value between, for instance, $\frac{5}{2}U_{LSB}$ and $\frac{7}{2}U_{LSB}$, the comparators 1 to 3 produce ones, the comparators 4 to 7, zeros. A logic circuit is therefore required to convert these comparator states to the number "3". Figure 23.30 lists the comparator output states and the corresponding straight binary numbers. A comparison with Fig. 9.62 shows that the required conversion can be carried out by the priority decoder described in Section 9.6.4.

However, the priority decoder must not be connected directly to the outputs of the comparators, since totally erroneous straight binary numbers may arise if the input voltage is not constant. The example of a change from 3 to 4, i.e. in straight binary code from 011 to 100, illustrates this. If the most significant bit changes before the two other bits because of a shorter propagation delay, the number 111 (i.e. 7_{dec}) occurs temporarily. This is equivalent to an error of half the range. The result of an A/D conversion is usually transferred to a memory, and there is therefore a certain probability that this erroneous number would be carried over and stored. The use of a sample-and-hold circuit can prevent this effect, as it holds the input voltage constant during the conversion process. However, since the sample-and-hold circuit requires an acquisition time, this measure limits the range of input frequencies. Nevertheless, spurious transitions of the comparators cannot be entirely avoided, since fast sample-and-hold circuits have a considerably drift.

However, these problems can be avoided by storing the digital value after the comparators instead of storing the analog value before them. The edge-triggered D flip-flops at the output of each comparator in Fig. 23.29 are used for this

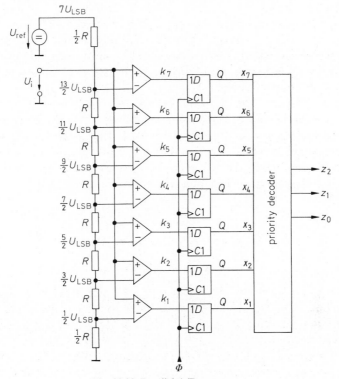

Fig. 23.29 Parallel A/D converter.

$$Z = \frac{U_i}{U_{LSB}} = 7\frac{U_i}{U_{ref}} = Z_{max}\frac{U_i}{U_{ref}}$$

Input voltage	Comparator states							Straight binary number			Decimal equivalent
U_i/U_{LSB}	k_7	k_6	k_5	k_4	k_3	k_2	k_1	z_2	z_1	z_0	Z
0	0	0	0	0	0	0	0	0	0	0	0
1	0	0	0	0	0	0	1	0	0	1	1
2	0	0	0	0	0	1	1	0	1	0	2
3	0	0	0	0	1	1	1	0	1	1	3
4	0	0	0	1	1	1	1	1	0	0	4
5	0	0	1	1	1	1	1	1	0	1	5
6	0	1	1	1	1	1	1	1	1	0	6
7	1	1	1	1	1	1	1	1	1	1	7

Fig. 23.30 States of variables in the parallel A/D converter as a function of the input voltage

purpose, ensuring that the priority decoder receives constant input signals for one complete clock period. Steady-state data is therefore available at the priority decoder output prior to the arrival of the next trigger edge.

A particular advantage of the parallel method is that a *digital sample-and-hold* can be used, making high-speed A/D conversion possible. For frequencies higher than a few MHz, analog sample-and-holds cannot be implemented with the necessary accuracy, even at the cost of considerable complexity.

The sampling instant is essentially determined by the trigger edge of the clock signal, although the actual sampling is performed a little earlier because of the comparator delay. The delay differences therefore determine the aperture jitter. In order to be able to achieve the low values stipulated in the preceding section, the signal delay from the analog input to the storage devices is kept to a minimum. On most types, therefore, the storage element is incorporated in the comparator and inserted directly after the analog input. The resulting input circuit of a comparator of this type is shown in Fig. 23.31 [23.4].

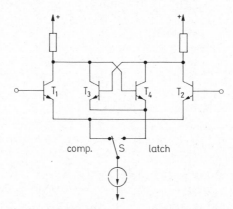

Fig. 23.31 Comparator input with storage flip-flop

If switch S is set to the left, transistors T_1, T_2 operate as a comparator. When the switch is changed over, comparator T_1, T_2 is deactivated and flip-flop T_3, T_4 is activated instead. The latter then stores the state which was present at the comparator output. For this purpose, it is not even necessary for the comparator to have already changed state completely. Since the flip-flop is likewise designed as a differential amplifier, differences of a few millivolts decide whether the flip-flop assumes one state or the other. In this way the aperture jitter can be reduced to 10 ps.

Figure 23.32 lists a number of A/D converters employing the parallel (flash) method. We can see that TRW offers the widest range with types of 4 to 9 bit resolution and sampling frequencies of 20 to 100 MHz. Although CMOS types are of interest due to their low power consumption, they still have a number of disadvantages compared to bipolar types.

The linearity of A/D converters at low signal frequencies is equal to the resolution of $\pm \frac{1}{2}$LSB or even $\pm \frac{1}{4}$LSB in some cases. However, at high signal frequencies, nonlinearity increases, with the result that the least significant or

Resolution	Type	Manufacturer	Sampling frequency max.	Input capacitance	Logic family	Power dissipation
8 bit	AD9048	Analog Dev.	30 MHz	4 pF	TTL	550 mW
	AD9012	Analog Dev.	100 MHz	16 pF	TTL	950 mW
	AD9002	Analog Dev.	150 MHz	20 pF	ECL	750 mW
	AD770	Analog Dev.	200 MHz	19 pF	ECL	2000 mW
	AD9038	Analog Dev.	300 MHz	17 pF	ECL	2200 mW
	ADC304	Datel	20 MHz	30 pF	TTL	360 mW
	ADC303	Datel	100 MHz	35 pF	ECL	1100 mW
	HADC77100	Honeywell	150 MHz	56 pF	ECL	1600 mW
	HADC77300	Honeywell	250 MHz	30 pF	ECL	3200 mW
	IDT75C48	IDT	20 MHz	50 pF	CMOS	500 mW
	MP7684	Micro Power	20 MHz	50 pF	CMOS	300 mW
	MP7688	Micro Power	35 MHz	50 pF	CMOS	350 mW
	SP973T8	Plessey	30 MHz	25 pF	TTL	500 mW
	SP97508	Plessey	110 MHz	35 pF	ECL	1100 mW
	SP97608	Plessey	300 MHz			
	CA3318	RCA	15 MHz	30 pF	CMOS	150 mW
	SDA8010	Siemens	100 MHz	30 pF	ECL	1300 mW
	SP1078	Sipex	50 MHz	3 pF	TTL	560 mW
	CXA1096	Sony	20 MHz	30 pF	TTL	390 mW
	CXA1176	Sony	300 MHz	25 pF	ECL	1500 mW
	TKAD10C	Tektronix	500 MHz	1 pF	ECL	7500 mW
	TDC1038	TRW	20 MHz	75 pF	TTL	500 mW
	TDC1025	TRW	50 MHz	120 pF	ECL	2000 mW
9 bit	TDC1049	TRW	30 MHz	120 pF	ECL	2800 mW
10 bit	AD9020	Analog Dev.	60 MHz	45 pF	TTL	2800 mW
	AD9060	Analog Dev.	75 MHz	45 pF	ECL	2800 mW
	HADC77600	Honeywell	50 MHz	300 pF	ECL	2700 mW
	SP1080	Sipex	25 MHz			
	TDC1020	TRW	25 MHz	260 pF	TTL	6000 mW

Fig. 23.32 Typical data for A/D converters employing the parallel method (flash converters)

even the next-to-least significant bit becomes unusable. The quantizing noise increases correspondingly by 6 or 12 dB in accordance with Eq. (23.12) [23.5].

23.8.2 Extended parallel (half-flash) method

A disadvantage of the parallel conversion (flash) method is that the number of comparators required rises exponentially with the word length. For an 10-bit converter for example, a total of 1023 comparators is needed. This number can be considerably reduced by a small sacrifice in conversion speed. Such a compromise involves combining the parallel method with the weighting method.

A 10-bit converter for the extended parallel conversion method (half-flash converter) is realized in the following manner; initially, the five most significant bits are parallel-converted, as can be seen in the block diagram of Fig. 23.33. The

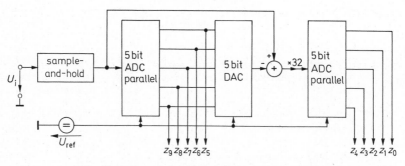

Fig. 23.33 Extended parallel (half-flash) A/D converter

$$Z = Z_{\max}\frac{U_\mathrm{i}}{U_\mathrm{ref}} = 1023\frac{U_\mathrm{i}}{U_\mathrm{ref}}$$

result is the coarsely quantized value of the input voltage. A D/A converter is used to produce the appropriate analog voltage which is then subtracted from the input voltage. The remainder is digitized by a second 5-bit A/D converter.

If the difference between the coarse value and the input voltage is amplified by a factor of 32, two A/D converters with the same input voltage range can be employed. There are, however, different requirements for the accuracy of the two converters: the accuracy of the first 5-bit converter must be as high as that of a 10-bit converter, otherwise the calculated difference is meaningless.

However, parallel A/D converters providing such a high degree of linearity are unobtainable, nor can they be implemented for higher signal frequencies. Consequently, the difference signal exceeds the fine range and overdrives the second A/D converter, resulting in serious errors in the output signal (missing codes).

This problem can be overcome by reducing the gain for the difference signal from 32 to 16, as shown in Fig. 23.34. Bit z_5 is then formed both by the coarse and the fine quantizer. If the fine signal now exceeds the design range due to

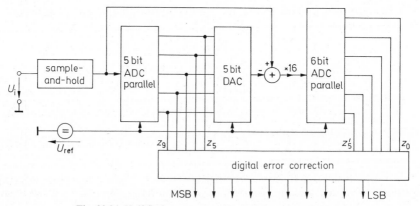

Fig. 23.34 Half-flash converter with digital error correction

linearity errors of the coarse quantizer, the coarse value can be increased or lowered by 1 using z'_5. This allows coarse quantizer linearity errors to be corrected to $\pm \frac{1}{2}$LSB. The coarse quantizer linearity need not be better than the resolution, a requirement which is not as stringent as that for the circuit in Fig. 23.33. It is merely necessary for the D/A converter to have full 10-bit accuracy [23.7].

Coarse and fine values must of course be formed by the same input voltage $U_i(t_j)$ in each case. However, due to the transit through the first stage, a time delay is introduced. Consequently, with this method the input voltage must be kept constant using an analog sample-and-hold until the complete number is formed. This constitutes a serious disadvantage as compared with the purely parallel method. For successful error correction, the coarse and fine quantizer range must overlap by at least one bit. So as not to reduce the resolution of the circuit as a whole, the fine quantizer must therefore have one additional bit.

A number of extended-parallel-type (half-flash) converters are listed in Fig. 23.35.

Reso-lution	Type	Manufacturer	Sampling frequency, max.	S & H incor-porated	Correc-tion	Power dissi-pation		Techno-logy
8 bit	AD 7820	Analog Dev.	0.8 MHz	(yes)	–	35	mW	CMOS
	ADC0820	National	1 MHz	(yes)	–	35	mW	CMOS
	MP7683	Micro Power	3 MHz	(yes)	–	100	mW	CMOS
10 bit	ADC310	Datel	20 MHz	–	–	360	mW	ECL
	CX20220	Sony	20 MHz	–	–	360	mW	ECL
11 bit	MP7685	Micro Power	1 MHz	–	–	100	mW	CMOS
12 bit	CS5412	Crystal	1 MHz	yes	–	700	mW	CMOS
	AD671	Analog Dev.	2 MHz					
	ADC500	Datel	2 MHz	–	2 bit	1.5	W	hybrid
	SP9548	Sypex	2 MHz	–	4 bit	1.7	W	hybrid
	ADC603	Burr Brown	10 MHz	yes	2 bit	6	W	hybrid
	THC1202	TRW, Comlin	10 MHz	yes		2.3	W	hybrid
	AD9005	Analog Dev.	10 MHz	yes		3.1	W	hybrid
	CAV1220	Analog Dev.	20 MHz	yes	1 bit	25	W	module
16 bit	ADC974	Datel	0.4 MHz	–	2 bit	6	W	module
	ADC701	Burr Brown	0.5 MHz	–		2	W	hybrid

Fig. 23.35 Typical data for A/D converters using the extended parallel method (half-flash converters)

23.8.3 Weighting method

The basic design of an A/D converter employing the weighting (or weighing or successive approximation) method is shown in Fig. 23.36. The comparator compares the stored measured value with the output voltage of the D/A converter. When measurement commences, the number Z is set to zero. The most significant bit (MSB) is then set to 1 and a check is performed to ascertain whether the input voltage is greater than $U(Z)$. If so, it remains set. If not, it is canceled again. Thus the MSB is "weighed". The process is then repeated for each additional bit until finally the least significant bit (LSB) is established. In this way a number is produced in the register. This number is converted in the DAC into a voltage corresponding to U_i within the resolution U_{LSB}, giving

$$U(Z) = U_{ref} \frac{Z}{Z_{max} + 1} = U_i$$

i.e.

$$Z = (Z_{max} + 1) \frac{U_i}{U_{ref}} . \tag{23.14}$$

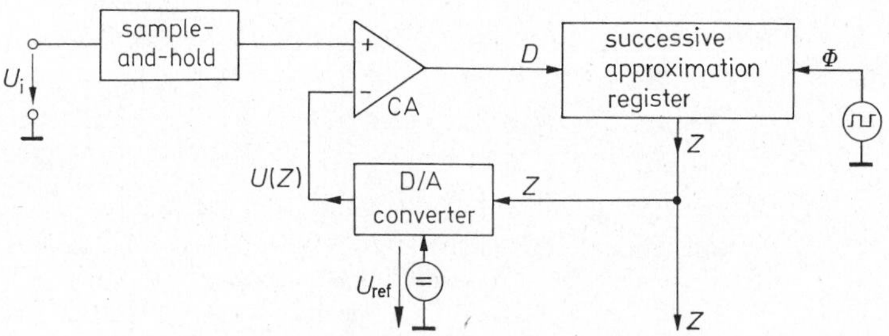

Fig. 23.36 A/D converter based on weighting method

$$Z = (Z_{max} + 1) \frac{U_i}{U_{ref}}$$

If the input voltage changes during the conversion time, a sample-and-hold circuit is required to buffer the sampled values, so that all the digits are formed from the same input voltage value $U_i(t_j)$. If no sample-and-hold is present, an error may occur that is equal to the input voltage variation during the conversion period [23.7].

The flow chart for the first three weighing steps is shown in Fig. 23.37. It can be seen that in each step, a decision is made as to whether the relevant bit is 1 or 0. The previously determined bits remain unchanged.

The timing diagram for the weighing process is shown in Fig. 23.38 for the voltage $U(Z)$ and in Fig. 23.39 for the number Z. Each bit is set on a trial-and-error basis. If, as a result, the input voltage is exceeded, the bit is canceled again. In this example, conversion is therefore complete after 8 weighing steps.

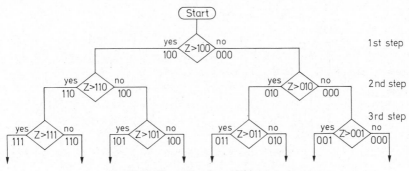

Fig. 23.37 Flow chart for weighing sequence

Conversion is controlled by the successive approximation register (SAR). The basic mode of operation will now be discussed with reference to Fig. 23.40. At the start of conversion, reset signal R is used to clear all the flip-flops. In shift register F'_7 to F'_0, a 1 is shifted one position to the right on each clock pulse, causing bits z_7 to z_0 to be set in turn on a trial-and-error basis. The particular weighing result is stored in latch flip-flops F_7 to F_0 by reading the relevant comparator state D. Only the flip-flop whose associated bit is currently being tested is enabled via the C-input at any one time.

When the least significant bit z_0 has also been established, the last flip-flop F of the shift register is set. This indicates Conversion Complete (CC). Because of the OR gate at the D-input, it retains this state even if further clock pulses are

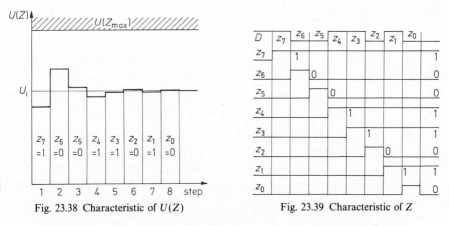

Fig. 23.38 Characteristic of $U(Z)$ Fig. 23.39 Characteristic of Z

Fig. 23.38/39 Timing diagram for A/D conversion based on the weighting method

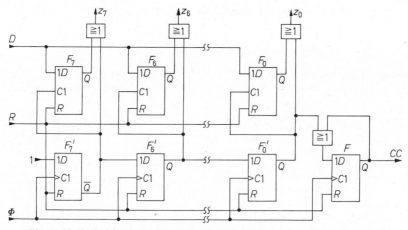

Fig. 23.40 Typical implementation of a successive approximation register (SAR)

applied. It, together with the result, is not cleared until the next conversion begins.

The truth table for the successive approximation register is shown in Fig. 23.41. As we can see, all the outputs are cleared with the reset signal. The only exception is bit z_7 which already exhibits the "1" for the first weighing process. At each step T, the decision D of the comparator is stored in the relevant position and the next less significant bit is weighed. The truth table illustrates the operation of the shift register. After 8 steps, "1" has arrived at the Conversion Complete output (CC), and the conversion is done. The result Z is then available in parallel form. However, it can also be obtained in serial form at the comparator output.

T	R	D	z_7	z_6	z_5	z_4	z_3	z_2	z_1	z_0	CC
0	1	D_7	1	0	0	0	0	0	0	0	0
1	0	D_7	D_7	1	0	0	0	0	0	0	0
2	0	D_6	D_7	D_6	1	0	0	0	0	0	0
3	0	D_5	D_7	D_6	D_5	1	0	0	0	0	0
4	0	D_4	D_7	D_6	D_5	D_4	1	0	0	0	0
5	0	D_3	D_7	D_6	D_5	D_4	D_3	1	0	0	0
6	0	D_2	D_7	D_6	D_5	D_4	D_3	D_2	1	0	0
7	0	D_1	D_7	D_6	D_5	D_4	D_3	D_2	D_1	1	0
8	0	D_0	D_7	D_6	D_5	D_4	D_3	D_2	D_1	D_0	1

Fig. 23.41 Truth table for the successive approximation register

Successive approximation registers are available as integrated circuits:

8 bit: Am 2502, F 74 LS 502 (TTL), SP 74 HCT 502 (CMOS)
12 bit: Am 2504, F 74 LS 504 (TTL), SP 74 HCT 504 (CMOS) .

However, only in exceptional cases is it worth constructing a successive approximation A/D converter from individual chips, as the entire circuit is widely available in IC form. A number of examples are listed in Fig. 23.42.

Resolution	Type	Manufacturer	Conv. time	Int. Ref.	Power dissip.	Output	Technology
8 bit	AD 7574*	Analog Dev.	15 μs	−	30 mW	8 bit	CMOS
	AD 7576	Analog Dev.	10 μs	−	15 mW	8 bit	CMOS
	AD 670	Analog Dev.	10 μs	yes	150 mW	8 bit	bipolar
	Am 6108	AMD	1 μs	+ 2.5 V	600 mW	8 bit	bipolar
	ADC 847	Datel	9 μs	+ 2.5 V	125 mW	8 bit	CMOS
	ZN 448	Plessey	9 μs	+ 2.5 V	125 mW	8 bit	bipolar
	ZN 509	Plessey	5 μs	+ 2.5 V	200 mW	1 bit	bipolar
	ADC 0841	National	40 μs	−	15 mW	8 bit	CMOS
	ADS 908	PMI	6 μs	−	15 mW	8 bit	CMOS
10 bit	AD 575	Analog Dev.	30 μs	yes	200 mW	1 bit	bipolar
	ZN 503	Plessey	15 μs	+ 2.5 V	300 mW	1/10 bit	bipolar
	ADC 1005	National	50 μs	−	15 mW	10 bit	CMOS
	ADC 910	PMI	6 μs	+ 2.5 V	400 mW	10 bit	bipolar
12 bit	AD 7572*	Analog Dev.	5 μs	− 5.2 V	135 mW	8/12 bit	CMOS
	AD 7672*	Analog Dev.	3 μs	−	110 mW	12 bit	CMOS
	AD 574*	Analog Dev.	25 μs	+ 10 V	400 mW	8/12 bit	2 Chips
	AD 674*	Analog Dev.	15 μs	+ 10 V	400 mW	8/12 bit	2 Chips
	AD 7772	Analog Dev.	10 μs	− 5.2 V	135 mW	1 bit	CMOS
	ADC 774	Burr Brown	8 μs	+ 10 V	325 mW	12 bit	2 Chips
	ADC 601	Burr Brown	1 μs	yes	1300 mW	1/12 bit	hybrid
	MAX 170	Maxim	6 μs	− 5.2 V	115 mW	1 bit	CMOS
	MAX 171[1]	Maxim	6 μs	− 5.2 V	265 mW	1 bit	2 Chips
	MAX 172	Maxim	10 μs	− 5.2 V	145 mW	8/12 bit	CMOS
	MAX 162	Maxim	3 μs	− 5.2 V	145 mW	8/12 bit	CMOS
	HI 774*	Harris	9 μs	+ 10 V	400 mW	8/12 bit	hybrid
	Am 6112	AMD	3 μs	+ 2.5 V	500 mW	8 bit	bipolar
	ADC 912	PMI	12 μs	−	85 mW	8/12 bit	CMOS
16 bit	AD 376	Analog Dev.	16 μs	yes	1100 mW	16 bit	hybrid
	AD 1377	Analog Dev.	10 μs	yes	600 mW	16 bit	hybrid
	ADC 700	Burr Brown	17 μs	yes	645 mW	8 bit	2 Chips
	PCM 78	Burr Brown	4 μs	yes	600 mW	1 bit	2 Chips
	ADC 701	Burr Brown	2 μs	+ 10 V	1500 mW	16 bit	hybrid
	HS 9576	Sipex	15 μs	yes	1000 mW	16 bit	hybrid

* Other manufacturers: Burr Brown, Datel, Harris, Maxim, Micro Power Systems, PMI, Sipex.
[1] Optically isolated output

Fig. 23.42 Analog-to-digital converters based on the weighting method (without sample-and-hold).
Other types with sample-and-hold are listed in Fig. 21.62

23.8.4   Counter method

A/D conversion using the counter method requires the least circuit complexity, but the conversion time is considerably longer than with the other methods—generally between 1 ms and 1 s. However, this is adequate for slowly changing signals, such as those involved in temperature measurement, and is also fast enough for digital voltmeters, as there is a limit to how quickly the result can be read off. The counter method can be implemented in various ways. The principal techniques are discussed below, the most important being the dual-slope method, as it allows maximum accuracy to be achieved with minimum circuit complexity.

Compensation method

The compensating A/D converter in Fig. 23.43 is closely related to the successive approximation (SA) type in Fig. 23.36. The basic difference is that an up-down counter is used instead of the SA register.

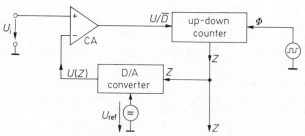

Fig. 23.43 Tracking A/D converter

$$Z = (Z_{max} + 1)U_i/U_{ref}$$

The comparator compares the input voltage U_i with the compensating voltage $U(Z)$. If the difference is positive, it causes the counter to count upwards, and vice versa. This means that the compensating voltage rises or falls until it has reached the level of the input voltage, and then follows the latter as it changes. For this reason, the circuit is also known as a *tracking A/D converter*.

One drawback with the simple circuit in Fig. 23.43 is that, as the clock is never switched off, the counter never stops, but always oscillates by 1 LSB around the input voltage. If this causes problems, the simple comparator can be expanded to form a window comparator. This allows the clock to be inhibited when the compensating voltage $U(Z)$ is within $\pm \frac{1}{2}U_{LSB}$ of the input voltage U_i.

The significant reduction in control logic as compared to the weighting method is achieved at the expense of considerably longer conversion times, as the compensating voltage only changes in U_{LSB}-steps. However, if the input voltage changes only slowly, a short settling time can again be achieved, as approximation is performed continuously because of the tracking characteristic and does not always start at zero as with the weighting method.

Monolithic ICs employing the tracking method include the ADC 856 from Datel and the ZN 433 from Ferranti. These have 10-bit resolution and a conversion time of 1 μs/LSB.

Single-slope method

The sawtooth A/D converter shown in Fig. 23.44 does not require a DAC. The principle here is that the input voltage is initially converted into a proportional time interval using the sawtooth generator in conjunction with window comparator CA_1, CA_2 and G_1.

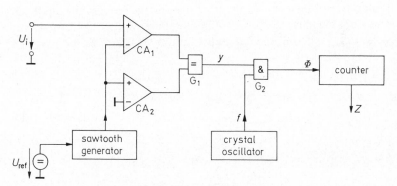

Fig. 23.44 Single-slope A/D converter

$$Z = \tau \cdot f \cdot U_i / U_{ref}$$

The sawtooth voltage can be raised from negative to positive values in accordance with the relation

$$V_s = \frac{U_{ref}}{\tau} t - V_0 \ .$$

Logic 1 is present at EQUIVALENCE gate G_1 only for as long as the sawtooth voltage is between the limits 0 and U_i. The corresponding time interval is $\Delta t = \tau U_i / U_{ref}$. This is measured by counting the oscillations of the crystal-controlled oscillator. If the counter is zeroed at the start of the measurement, the count after the upper comparator threshold has been exceeded, is expressed by

$$Z = \frac{\Delta t}{T} = \tau f \frac{U_i}{U_{ref}} \; . \tag{23.15}$$

If a negative measurement voltage is applied, the sawtooth voltage will first cross the measurement voltage and then through zero. This sequence therefore enables the sign of the measured voltage to be determined. The measuring time is the same; it is purely a function of the magnitude of the measurement voltage. After each conversion the counter must be reset to zero and the sawtooth voltage adjusted to its negative initial value. In order to retain the result, the old count is normally stored until a new one is available.

As Eq. (23.15) indicates, the tolerance of time constant τ directly affects the measuring accuracy. Since it is determined by an RC network, it is subject to the temperature and long-term drift of the capacitor. Consequently, an accuracy of better than 0.1% is difficult to achieve.

Dual-slope method

With this method, not only the reference voltage but also the input voltage is integrated. In the inactive state, switches S_1 and S_2 in Fig. 23.45 are open, switch S_3 is closed. As a result, the integrator output voltage is zero.

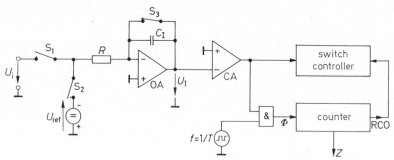

Fig. 23.45 Dual-slope A/D converter

$$Z = (Z_{max} + 1) U_i / U_{ref}$$

At the start of the conversion cycle, the counter is cleared, switch S_3 is opened and S_1 is closed, causing the input voltage U_i to be integrated. If it is positive, the integrator output becomes negative and the comparator enables the clock generator. The end of the cycle is reached when the counter overflows after $Z_{max} + 1$ clock pulses and is thus again at zero. The integrator output voltage is now

$$U_1(t_1) = -\frac{1}{\tau} \int_0^{t_1} U_i dt = -\frac{\bar{U}_i}{\tau} (Z_{max} + 1) T \; . \tag{23.16}$$

The circuit then switches to integration of the reference voltage, which is selected with the opposite sign to that of the input voltage. In this way the magnitude of the integrator voltage is reduced again, as we can see from Fig. 23.46.

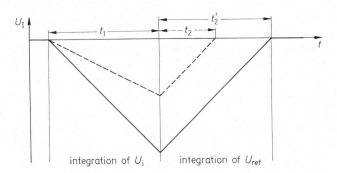

Fig. 23.46 Integrator output voltage versus time for two input voltages

The comparator and the result counter are now used to determine how long it takes to reach the zero crossing once again:

$$t_2 = Z \cdot T = \frac{\tau}{U_{ref}} |U_1(t_1)| \ . \tag{23.17}$$

Using Eq. (23.16), this gives

$$Z = (Z_{max} + 1) \frac{U_i}{U_{ref}} \ . \tag{23.18}$$

This equation reveals the salient feature of the dual-slope method, namely that neither the clock frequency $1/T$ nor the integration time constant $\tau = RC_1$ have any effect on the result. The only requirement is that the clock frequency shall be constant during the time $t_1 + t_2$. This short-term stability can be achieved using simple clock generators. For these reasons, accuracies of $0.01\% = 100$ ppm can be achieved by this method [23.8].

As we have seen, it is not the instantaneous value of the measurement voltage that affects the result, but its average value over measuring time t_1. Consequently, alternating voltages are attenuated more heavily the higher their frequency. Alternating voltages whose frequencies are equal to an integral multiple of $1/t_1$ are rejected completely. It is therefore advisable to adjust the clock generator frequency such that t_1 is equal to the period of the AC supply voltage or a multiple thereof. This will eliminate any hum.

As the dual-slope method allows a high degree of accuracy and noise rejection to be achieved with minimum circuit complexity, it is preferable to use this type of converter in digital voltmeters. In this application, the relatively long conversion time does not present any problem.

The counter in Fig. 23.45 need not be a straight binary counter. The mode of operation is identical if a BCD counter is employed. This possibility is utilized in digital voltmeters, as no binary-to-decimal conversion of the measured value is then required.

Automatic offset adjust

In the description of the dual-slope method, we have seen that the time constant $\tau = RC_1$ and the clock frequency $f = 1/T$ do not affect the result. The accuracy is therefore basically determined by the reference voltage tolerance and the zero errors of the integrator and comparator. These zero errors can be largely eliminated using an automatic zero-balancing arrangement. For this purpose, short-circuit switch S_3 in Fig. 23.45 is replaced, as in Fig. 23.47, by a control circuit which is used to initialize the integrator appropriately.

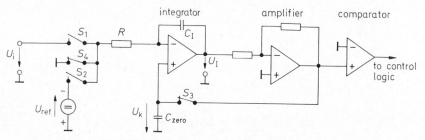

Fig. 23.47 Dual-slope method with offset adjust

In the inactive state, switch S_3 is closed. As a result, the integrator and comparator amplifier together form a voltage follower whose output voltage U_k charges zeroing capacitor C_{zero}. For zero correction, the integrator input is simultaneously applied to zero potential with additional switch S_4, causing U_k to assume the correction value $U_{OI} - I_B R$, where U_{OI} is the integrator offset voltage and I_B its input quiescent current. At steady state, this compensating effect ensures that the current flowing through C_1 is zero, as with an ideal integrator.

To integrate the input voltage, switches S_3 and S_4 are opened and S_1 closed. As voltage U_k remains stored in capacitor C_{zero} during this time, the zero point remains adjusted also during the integration phase. The zero drift is then determined solely by the short-term stability.

The comparator offset error is likewise eliminated to a large extent with this method. In the inactive state, the integrator output voltage U_I does not adopt the value zero as in the previous circuit, but assumes the offset voltage of the comparator amplifier, i.e. the switching threshold of the whole arrangement.

As the compensating circuit consists of two amplifiers connected in series, oscillations can easily occur. Stabilization can be provided by connecting a resistor in series with C_{zero}. It is also advisable to limit the gain of the comparator amplifier to values of less than 100. This makes it easier to achieve the short delay times required for comparator operation during the integration phase.

A/D converters employing the dual-slope principle are widely available as monolithic CMOS integrated circuits. They fall into two main categories: general-purpose types (particularly for connecting to microcomputers) and types specially designed for driving display units. Whereas the former mainly produce binary or BCD code, the latter generally have 7-segment outputs. A number of examples are listed in Fig. 23.48.

Resolution	Type	Manufacturer	Convers. time	Output	Parallel/ multiplex	Supply voltage	Power dissipation
12 bit	ICL7109	I, M, T	40 ms	Dual	Par.	$\pm$ 5 V	7 mW
$3\frac{3}{4}$ digit	MAX134*	M	50 ms	BCD	Mux.	$\pm$ 5 V	1 mW
$4\frac{1}{2}$ digit	ICL7135	I, M, T	200 ms	BCD	Mux.	$\pm$ 5 V	9 mW
16 bit	TSC850	T	25 ms	Dual	Par.	$\pm$ 5 V	20 mW
22 bit	AD1175[1]	Anal. Dev.	50 ms	Dual	Mux.	$\pm$ 15 V[2]	2.5 W
For seven-segment displays							
$3\frac{1}{2}$ digit	ICL7106	I, M, T	200 ms	LCD	Par.	9 V	10 mW
	ICL7107	I, M, T	200 ms	LED	Par.	$\pm$ 5 V	600 mW
	ICL7136	I, M, T	400 ms	LCD	Par.	9 V	1 mW
	ICL7137	I, M, T	400 ms	LED	Par.	$\pm$ 5 V	600 mW
	MAX138	M	200 ms	LCD	Par.	5 V	1 mW
	MAX139	M	200 ms	LED	Par.	5 V	600 mW
	TSC 816*	T	500 ms	LCD	Mux.	9 V	10 mW
$3\frac{3}{4}$ digit	ICL7149*	I	200 ms	LCD	Mux.	9 V	15 mW
$4\frac{1}{2}$ digit	ICL7129	I, M, T	500 ms	LCD	Mux.	9 V	10 mW

* With automatic range switching   [1]module   [2]and $+5$ V

Manufacturers: I = Intersil, M = Maxim, T = Teledyne

Fig. 23.48 Analog-to-digital converters employing the dual-slope method

24 Digital filters

In Chapter 14, several transfer functions are discussed and their realization by active filters is described. The processed signals are voltages which in turn are continuous functions of time. The circuits are made up of resistors, capacitors and amplifiers.

Recently, the trend has been towards signal processing by digital rather than analog circuits. The advantages are high accuracy and consistency in the results and a lower sensitivity to disturbances. The high number of digital components required is a disadvantage, however, but in view of the increase in integration of digital circuitry, is becoming less important.

Sequences of discrete numbers are processed instead of continuous signals, and the circuit elements are memories and arithmetic circuits. The transition from an analog to a digital filter raises three questions:

1) How can a sequence of discrete numerical values be derived from the continuous input voltage without loss of information?
2) How must this numerical sequence be processed in order to obtain the required transfer function?
3) How can the output values be converted back into a continuous voltage?

The embedding of a digital filter in an analog environment is shown schematically in Fig. 24.1. At sampling instants t_μ, the sample-and-hold circuit extracts voltages $U_i(t_\mu)$ from the input signal $U_i(t)$ and holds them constant for one sampling interval. In order to prevent any irreparable errors from occurring during sampling, the input signal must be band-limited to half the sampling rate in accordance with the sampling theorem. Consequently, a lowpass filter is generally required at the input.

The ADC converts the time-discrete voltage sequence $U_i(t_\mu)$ into a numerical sequence $x(t_\mu)$. The x values are usually N-digit binary numbers, the

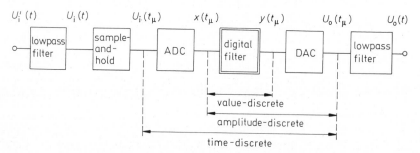

Fig. 24.1 Digital filter in an analog environment

Signal	Sampling frequency	Resolution
Telephone speech	8 kHz	12 bit
CD music	44.1 kHz	16 bit
Digital TV	13.3 MHz	8 bit

Fig. 24.2 Usual sampling frequencies and word lengths for digital signal processing

mantissa N determining the magnitude of the quantizing noise (see Eq. (23.12)). Typical sampling frequencies and resolutions are listed in Fig. 24.2.

The digital filter in Fig. 24.1 produces the filtered number sequence $y(t_\mu)$. In order to convert it back into a voltage, a DAC is used which delivers an amplitude- and time-discrete staircase signal at its output. To convert this to a continuous voltage, a following lowpass smoothing filter is required.

24.1 Sampling theorem

A continuous input signal can be converted to a series of discrete values, by using a sample-and-hold circuit for sampling the signal at equidistant instants $t_\mu = \mu T_s$, where $f_s = 1/T_s$ is the sampling rate. It is obvious from Fig. 24.3 that a staircase function arises, and that the approximation to the continuous input function is better the higher the sampling rate. However, as circuit complexity increases markedly with higher sampling rates, it is essential to keep the latter as low as possible. The question is now: what is the lowest sampling rate at which the original signal can still be reconstructed *error-free*, i.e. without loss of information. This theoretical limit is defined by the sampling theorem (Nyquist criterion) which we shall now discuss in some detail.

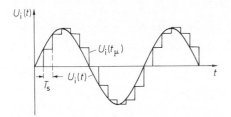

Fig. 24.3 Example of an input signal $U_i(t)$ and sampled values $U_i(t_\mu)$

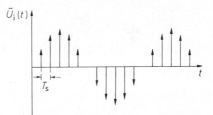

Fig. 24.4 Representation of the input signal by a Dirac impulse sequence

In order to obtain a simpler mathematical description, the staircase function in Fig. 24.3 is replaced by a series of Dirac impulse functions, as illustrated in Fig. 24.4:

$$\tilde{U}_i(t) = \sum_{\mu=0}^{\infty} U_i(t_\mu) T_s \delta(t - t_\mu) \ . \tag{24.1}$$

Their impulse area $U_i(t_\mu) \cdot T_s$ is represented by an arrow. The arrow must not be mistaken for the height of the impulse, as a Dirac function is, by definition, an impulse with infinite height but zero width although its area has a finite value. This area is often misleadingly known as the impulse amplitude. The characteristics of the impulse function are shown by Fig. 24.5, where the Dirac impulse function is approximated by a rectangular pulse r_ε; the limit of the approximation is

$$U_i(t_\mu) T_s \delta(t - t_\mu) = \lim_{\varepsilon \to 0} U_i(t_\mu) r_\varepsilon(t - t_\mu) \ . \tag{24.2}$$

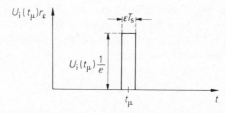

Fig. 24.5 Approximation of a Dirac impulse by a finite voltage pulse

To examine the information contained in the impulse function sequence represented by Eq. (24.1), we consider its spectrum. By applying the Fourier transformation to Eq. (24.1), we obtain

$$\tilde{X}(jf) = T_s \sum_{\mu=0}^{\infty} U_i(\mu T_s) e^{-2\pi j \mu f / f_s} \ . \tag{24.3}$$

It can be seen that this spectrum is a periodic function, the period being identical to the sampling frequency f_s. When Fourier-analyzing this periodic function, it can be shown that the spectrum $|\tilde{X}(jf)|$ is, for $-\frac{1}{2}f_s \leq f \leq \frac{1}{2}f_s$, identical to the spectrum $|X(jf)|$ of the original waveform [24.1]. It thus still contains all the information although only a few values of the function were sampled.

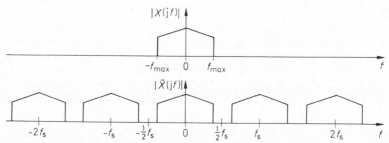

Fig. 24.6 Spectrum of the input voltage before sampling (upper diagram) and after sampling (lower diagram)

There is only one restriction, and this is explained with the help of Fig. 24.6. The original spectrum reappears unchanged only if the sampling rate is chosen such that consecutive bands do not overlap. According to Fig. 24.6, this is the case for

$$\boxed{f_s \geq 2f_{max}} \, , \tag{24.4}$$

this condition being known as the sampling theorem.

Recovery of the analog signal

From Fig. 24.6, the condition for recovery of the analog signal can be directly deduced. The frequencies above $\frac{1}{2}f_s$ in the spectrum must be cut off by a lowpass filter. The lowpass filter must therefore be designed so as to have zero attenuation at f_{max} and infinite attenuation at $\frac{1}{2}f_s$ and above.

To summarize: the original waveform can be recovered from the sampled values of a continuous band-limited function of time as long as the condition $f_s \geq 2f_{max}$ is fulfilled. To ensure this, the sampled values must be transformed into a sequence of Dirac impulse functions which is in turn applied to an ideal lowpass filter with $f_c = f_{max}$.

If the sampling rate is lower than the frequency demanded by the sampling theorem, spectral components arise which have the difference frequency $(f_s - f) < f_{max}$. They are not suppressed by the lowpass filter and are present as a beat in the output signal (aliasing). Figure 24.7 illustrates these conditions. We can see that the spectral components of the input signal above $\frac{1}{2}f_s$ are not simply lost, but are mirrored back into the wanted band. The highest signal frequency $f_{i\,max}$ therefore reappears as the lowest mirror frequency $f_s - f_{i\,max} < \frac{1}{2}f_s$ in the baseband of the output spectrum. Figure 24.8 shows these relationships for an input signal whose spectrum contains just one spectral line at $f_{i\,max} \lessapprox f_s$. We can see from this how a signal with a beat frequency of $f_s - f_{i\,max}$ is produced.

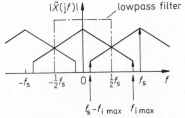

Fig. 24.7 Overlapping of spectra if sampling
frequency too low

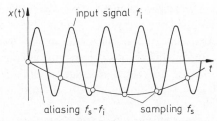

Fig. 24.8 Aliasing due to excessively low
sampling frequency for $f_i \lessapprox f_s$

24.1.1   Practical aspects

For a practical realization, the problem arises that a real system is unable to generate Dirac impulse functions. The impulses must thus be approximated, as in Fig. 24.5, by a finite amplitude and a finite time interval, thereby abandoning the limit concept of Eq. (24.2). By inserting Eq. (24.2) in (24.1), we obtain, for finite ε, the approximated impulse sequence

$$\tilde{U}'_i(t) = \sum_{\mu=0}^{\infty} U_i(t_\mu) r_\varepsilon (t - t_\mu) \ . \tag{24.5}$$

The Fourier transformation yields the spectrum

$$\tilde{X}_1(\mathrm{j}f) = \frac{\sin \pi \varepsilon T_s f}{\pi \varepsilon T_s f} \cdot \tilde{X}_1(\mathrm{j}f) \ , \tag{24.6}$$

which is the same as for the Dirac impulse sequence, except for a superposed weighting function causing an attenuation of the higher frequency components. The case of the staircase function is particularly interesting, as the pulse width εT_s is identical to the sampling interval T_s. The spectrum is then given by

$$\boxed{\tilde{X}'(\mathrm{j}f) = \frac{\sin (\pi f/f_s)}{\pi f/f_s} \cdot \tilde{X}(\mathrm{j}f)} \ . \tag{24.7}$$

The magnitude of the weighting function is represented in Fig. 24.9, along with the symbolic spectrum of the Dirac impulse functions. At half the sampling rate, an attenuation of 0.64 is obtained.

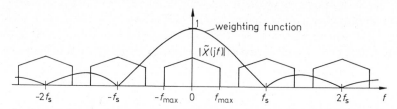

Fig. 24.9 Transition from the spectrum of a Dirac impulse sequence to the spectrum of the staircase function by means of the weighting function $|(\sin \pi f/f_s)/(\pi f/f_s)|$

The example in Fig. 24.10 should serve to illustrate a possible approach for selecting the sampling rate and the input or output filters. Consider an input spectrum for a music signal in the range $0 \leq f \leq f_{max} = 16\,\mathrm{kHz}$ which is to be sampled and reconstructed with the utmost fidelity. In this case it is insignificant whether 16 kHz components actually occur with full amplitude; the linear frequency response should rather indicate that constant gain is required in this range.

Even if it can be ensured that no tones above 16 kHz are present, this does not automatically mean that the spectrum at the sampler input is limited to

16 kHz. A typical source of broadband interference is amplifier noise. For this reason it is always advisable to provide the input lowpass filter shown in Fig. 24.1. This is designed to limit the input spectrum to half the sampling rate in order to prevent aliasing. Its cutoff frequency must be at least f_{max} in order to maintain the true input signal. On the other hand, it is desirable for it to reject completely a frequency that is only slightly higher, in order to allow the lowest possible value to be used for the sampling rate, the point being that the circuit complexity of the A/D or D/A converters and digital filter increases with the

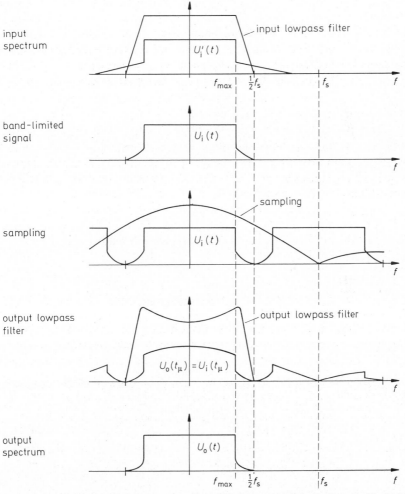

Fig. 24.10 Reconstruction of the input spectrum in a digital system of the type shown in Fig. 24.1 for
$$y(t_\mu) = x(t_\mu)$$

sampling frequency. On the other hand, the complexity of the lowpass filter increases with greater filter cutoff sharpness and stop-band attenuation. It is therefore always necessary to find a compromise between the complexity of the lowpass filter on the one hand and that of the converters and digital filter on the other. In the example with $f_{max} = 16$ kHz, one could select e.g. $\frac{1}{2}f_s = 22$ kHz, i.e. using a sampling rate of $f_s = 44$ kHz.

Sampling causes the band-limited input signal to be continued periodically to f_s, as shown in Fig. 24.10. Consequently, the baseband $0 \leq f \leq \frac{1}{2}f_s$ must be extracted again following D/A conversion. As a staircase function is obtained at the output of the D/A converter, the $(\sin x)/x$ weighting as expressed in Eq. (24.7) must also be taken into account.

The equalization required for this purpose can either be provided in the frequency response of the digital filter or performed in the output lowpass filter. The latter possibility is illustrated in Fig. 24.10. However, the main purpose of the output filter is to extract the baseband $0 \leq f \leq \frac{1}{2}f_s$ from the spectrum: at f_{max} it must still exhibit full passband characteristics, whereas at the sometimes only marginally higher frequency $\frac{1}{2}f_s$ it should attenuate completely. We can see that, in terms of filter steepness, the same problems arise as with the input filter. Consequently, in order to implement the filter, it is again necessary to provide an adequate margin between f_{max} and $\frac{1}{2}f_s$.

The problems of implementing the input or output filter can be mitigated by employing a markedly higher sampling rate, i.e. raising it by a factor of two or four, for example. Although this *oversampling* naturally increases the complexity of the A/D and D/A converters, the sampling rate can be reduced again to the value specified by the sampling theorem by inserting a digital lowpass filter after the A/D converter. This avoids high data rates for transmission or storage. Prior to D/A conversion, intermediate values are recalculated using an interpolator, allowing oversampling again and enabling a simple output lowpass filter to be used [24.2].

24.2   Digital transfer function

As we have seen in Chapter 14, analog filters can be implemented using integrators, adders and coefficient networks. A digital filter is obtained by replacing the integrators by delay elements. The latter can be implemented e.g. by shift registers which are used to shift the input function samples through at the sampling rate f_s. The simplest case is that of delay by one time interval T_s; a delay element of this kind is shown schematically in Fig. 24.11.

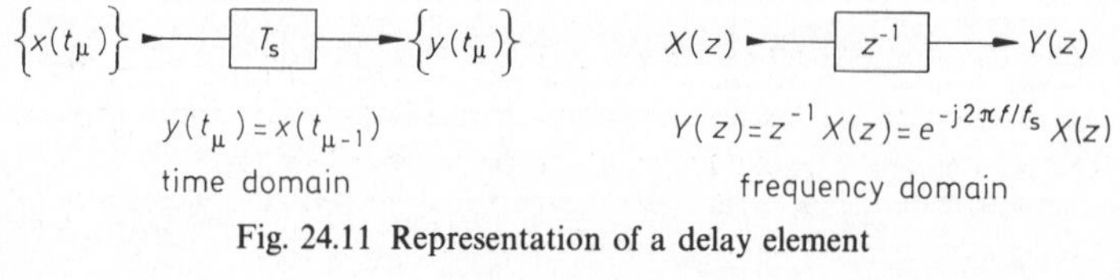

$$\{x(t_\mu)\} \longrightarrow \boxed{T_s} \longrightarrow \{y(t_\mu)\} \qquad\qquad X(z) \longrightarrow \boxed{z^{-1}} \longrightarrow Y(z)$$

$$y(t_\mu) = x(t_{\mu-1}) \qquad\qquad\qquad Y(z) = z^{-1}X(z) = e^{-j2\pi f/f_s}X(z)$$

time domain   frequency domain

Fig. 24.11 Representation of a delay element

24.2.1 Time domain analysis

The number sequence $\{x(t_\mu)\} = \{x_\mu\}$ is given and may be taken as sampling values with a word length of 8, 16 or 32 bits. These are shifted into a register using a corresponding number of parallel-clocked flip-flops. The output sequence $\{y(t_\mu)\} = \{y_\mu\}$ represents the input sequence shifted by one clock period T_s. We therefore have

$$y(t_\mu) = x(t_{\mu-1}) \ . \tag{24.8}$$

24.2.2 Frequency domain analysis

To examine the frequency response, the sinusoidal sequence $x(t_\mu) = x_0 \sin \omega t_\mu$ is applied to the input. If the system is linear, a sinusoidal sequence appears at the output. As for analog filters, the ratio of the amplitudes is equivalent to the magnitude of the transfer function for $s = j\omega$. The linearity of a digital filter is indicated by the linearity of the difference equation. According to Eq. (24.8), the filter in Fig. 24.11 is therefore linear.

The transfer function may be inferred from the circuit with the help of complex calculus, as for analog filters. This requires that the frequency response of a delay element be known. With the harmonic input sequence

$$x(t_\mu) = \hat{x}\, e^{j\omega t_\mu} \ ,$$

the harmonic output sequence

$$y(t_\mu) = \hat{x}\, e^{j\omega(t_\mu - T_s)} = \hat{x}\, e^{j\omega t_\mu} \cdot e^{-j\omega T_s} = x(t_\mu) e^{-j\omega T_s}$$

is obtained, and with $j\omega = s$, the transfer function

$$A(s) = \frac{y(t_\mu)}{x(t_\mu)} = e^{-j\omega T_s} = e^{-sT_s} \ . \tag{24.9}$$

It is a periodic function, the period being $f = f_s = 1/T_s$, where f_s is the sampling, i.e. clock frequency.

To abbreviate,

$$\boxed{z^{-1} = e^{-sT_s} = e^{-j2\pi f/f_s}} \ , \tag{24.10}$$

which results, together with Eq. (24.9), in transfer function

$$\boxed{\tilde{A}(z) = z^{-1}} \ . \tag{24.11}$$

This is the frequency domain description of the delay element shown in Fig. 24.11.

It was mentioned in Chapter 14 that the transfer function $A(s)$ describes the relationship between the output signal and any desired time-dependent input signal if the Laplace transforms according to the equation

$$L\{y(t)\} = A(s) \cdot L\{x(t)\} \tag{24.12}$$

are used. This relationship also holds for a digital system. Using the converted transfer function of Eq. (24.11), the relation for number sequences can be simplified since

$$Z\{y(t_\mu)\} = \tilde{A}(z) \cdot Z\{x(t_\mu)\} \ , \tag{24.13}$$

where

$$Z\{x(t_\mu)\} = X(z) = \sum_{\mu=0}^{\infty} x(t_\mu)z^{-\mu} \tag{24.14}$$

is the Z-transform of the input sequence. The output sequence is obtained by the corresponding reverse transform [24.3/4]. Because of this property, $\tilde{A}(z)$ is called the *digital transfer function*.

From this we can calculate the analog transfer function or the quantities derived from it, such as the magnitude, phase and group delay. For the delay element, it follows from

$$\tilde{A}(z) = \frac{Y(z)}{X(z)} = z^{-1} \quad \text{with} \quad z^{-1} = e^{-j\omega T_s}$$

that

$$\underline{A}(j\omega) = z^{-1} = e^{-j\omega T_s} = \cos \omega T_s - j \sin \omega T_s \ .$$

The magnitude is therefore

$$|\underline{A}(j\omega)| = \sqrt{\cos^2 \omega T_s + \sin^2 \omega T_s} = 1 \ ,$$

the phase

$$\varphi = \arctan \frac{-\sin \omega T_s}{\cos \omega T_s} = \arctan(-\tan \omega T_s) = -\omega T_s = -2\pi \frac{f}{f_s}$$

and the group delay

$$t_{gr} = -\frac{d\varphi}{d\omega} = T_s \ .$$

Example of a lowpass filter

Digital filters may be easily described using the relations for a delay element. The numerical value $x(t_\mu) - \beta_1 y(t_\mu)$ is present at the input of the memory in Fig. 24.12 at instant t_μ. This value appears one clock period later at the memory output. The values of the output sequence are therefore given by the relation

$$y(t_{\mu+1}) = x(t_\mu) - \beta_1 y(t_\mu) \ .$$

This *difference equation* represents the analogon to the differential equation for a continuous system. It can be used as a recursive formula to calculate the output sequence by specifying an initial value $y(t_0)$. As an example, we select $y(t_0) = 0$ and calculate the step response for $\beta_1 = -0.75$. This is plotted in Fig. 24.13. We can see that the circuit exhibits a lowpass characteristic.

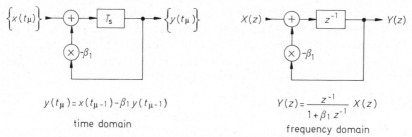

$$y(t_\mu) = x(t_{\mu-1}) - \beta_1 y(t_{\mu-1})$$

time domain

$$Y(z) = \frac{z^{-1}}{1 + \beta_1 z^{-1}} X(z)$$

frequency domain

Fig. 24.12 Example of a recursive first-order digital filter

The frequency response of the lowpass filter used in this example can be calculated in the same way as for the delay element. From the diagram on the right in Fig. 24.12 we take

$$Y(z) = [X(z) - \beta_1 Y(z)]z^{-1} \; .$$

The digital transfer function is therefore

$$\tilde{A}(z) = \frac{Y(z)}{X(z)} = \frac{z^{-1}}{1 + \beta_1 z^{-1}} \; .$$

To calculate the frequency response we put

$$z^{-1} = e^{-j\omega T_s} = \cos \omega T_s - j \sin \omega T_s$$

and obtain

$$\underline{A}(j\omega) = \frac{1}{\beta_1 + e^{j\omega T_s}} = \frac{1}{\beta_1 + \cos \omega T_s + j \sin \omega T_s} \; .$$

With $\omega T_s = 2\pi f/f_s$, the resulting magnitude is

$$|\underline{A}(j\omega)| = \frac{1}{\sqrt{(\beta_1 + \cos 2\pi f/f_s)^2 + (\sin 2\pi f/f_s)^2}} \; .$$

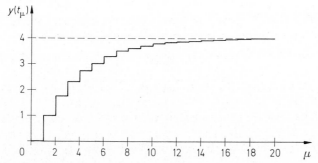

Fig. 24.13 Step response of the digital filter in Fig. 22.12 for $\beta_1 = -0.75$
with an input step from 0 to 1

We can see from Fig. 24.14 that it is periodic with f_s and symmetrical about $\frac{1}{2}f_s$. This characteristic is shared by all digital filters. The frequency range above $\frac{1}{2}f_s$, however, cannot be used, as this would violate the sampling theorem.

An interesting special case arises for $\beta_1 = 1$. The magnitude of the transfer function can now be simplified in accordance with $\cos^2 x + \sin^2 x = 1$:

$$|\underline{A}(j\omega)| = \frac{1}{\sqrt{2 + 2\cos 2\pi f/f_s}} = \frac{1}{\sqrt{4(\sin \pi f/f_s)^2}} = \frac{1}{2\sin \pi f/f_s} \ .$$

Hence, for low frequencies $f \ll f_s$ we obtain, with $\sin x \approx x$

$$|\underline{A}(j\omega)| = \frac{f_s}{2\pi f} \sim \frac{1}{f} \ ,$$

i.e. the frequency response of an integrator. The resulting circuit is the usual arrangement for an adder or accumulator.

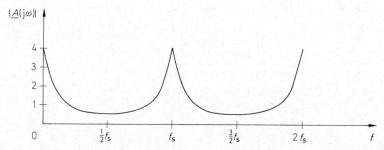

Fig. 24.14 Amplitude-frequency response of the digital filter in Fig. 22.12 for $\beta_1 = -0.75$

24.3 Basic structures

Lattice filters apart, there are three arrangements for implementing digital filters. These are illustrated in Figs. 24.15 to 24.17. All three possess the same transfer functions if the filter coefficients α_k and β_k are used at the locations shown [25.5/6/7].

We can see from Figs. 24.15 to 24.17 that, in addition to the delay elements, the filters require multipliers which multiply the variables by the constant filter

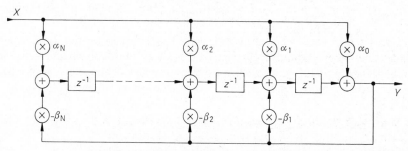

Fig. 24.15 Digital filter with distributed adders

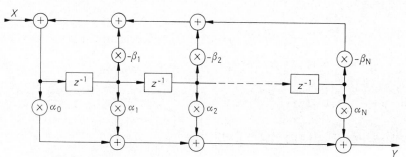

Fig. 24.16 Digital filter with a global adder at the output and input

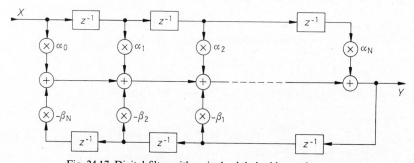

Fig. 24.17 Digital filter with a single global adder at the output

coefficients, and adders which add two or three numbers. The structure shown in Fig. 24.15 is the most commonly used, as in this case each multiplier-accumulator stage (MAC) is separated from the next by a delay element. As a result, a complete clock period is available for these operations. The delay elements here produce a "pipeline" structure. In the other two circuits many variables have to be added in a single clock period. Although this does not require more adders, it does require more computing time.

In the circuit in Fig. 24.16, it can be seen that the input signal for the delay chain is derived from the input signal X and all the weighted intermediate values. Accordingly, the output signal is the weighted sum of all the intermediate values. The adders can therefore be combined to form two global adders: one at the input and one at the output.

The circuit in Fig. 24.17 has a single global adder at the output. It adds both the delayed and weighted input signal as well as the delayed and weighted output signal. For this purpose, an additional delay chain is required which is connected to the output. However, the additional complexity involved is minimal.

The number of filter sections determines the order N of the filter. One delay element (two in Fig. 24.17) and two coefficient multipliers are required for each section, and three addends must be added. Only the first and last section is somewhat simpler.

We shall analyze the circuits taking Fig. 24.15 as an example. The difference equation is of the form

$$y(t_N) = \sum_{k=0}^{N} \alpha_k X_{N-k} - \sum_{k-1}^{N} \beta_k y_{N-k} \ . \tag{24.15}$$

For the transfer function, the circuit yields the relation

$$Y(z) = \sum_{k=0}^{N} \alpha_k z^{-k} X(z) - \sum_{k=1}^{N} \beta_k z^{-k} Y(z) \ .$$

Hence, the transfer function is

$$A(z) = \frac{Y(z)}{X(z)} = \frac{\displaystyle\sum_{k=0}^{N} \alpha_k z^{-k}}{1 + \displaystyle\sum_{k=1}^{N} \beta_k z^{-k}} \ , \tag{24.16}$$

$$A(z) = \frac{\alpha_0 + \alpha_1 z^{-1} + \alpha_2 z^{-2} + \cdots + \alpha_{N-1} z^{-(N-1)} + \alpha_N z^{-N}}{1 + \beta_1 z^{-1} + \beta_2 z^{-2} + \cdots + \beta_{N-1} z^{-(N-1)} + \beta_N z^{-N}} \ .$$

To calculate the complex frequency response, we again put

$$z^{-1} = e^{-j\omega T_s} = \cos \omega T_s - j \sin \omega T_s \ .$$

It is also advisable to normalize all the frequencies to the sampling rate $f_s = 1/T_s$. The normalized frequency variable F is therefore

$$F = \frac{f}{f_s} \quad \text{or} \quad \omega T_s = 2\pi F \quad . \tag{24.17}$$

In order not to contravene the sampling theorem, the following must apply:

$$0 \le f \le \tfrac{1}{2}f_s \quad \text{or} \quad 0 \le F \le \tfrac{1}{2}$$

Thus, for the magnitude of the complex frequency response, it follows from Eq. (24.16) that

$$|\underline{A}(j\omega)| = \sqrt{\frac{\left[\sum\limits_{k=0}^{N} \alpha_k \cos 2\pi kF\right]^2 + \left[\sum\limits_{k=0}^{N} \alpha_k \sin 2\pi kF\right]^2}{\left[\sum\limits_{k=0}^{N} \beta_k \cos 2\pi kF\right]^2 + \left[\sum\limits_{k=0}^{N} \beta_k \sin 2\pi kF\right]^2}} \quad . \tag{24.18}$$

The coefficient β_0 is always 1. The multiplier for β_0 can therefore be omitted in all the filter structures.

Equation (24.18) is extremely useful, as it allows us to calculate the frequency response of any digital filter if the filter coefficients are known. All the frequency responses in this section have been calculated in this way.

An extension of the variants shown in Figs. 24.15/16/17 is the cascade structure, whereby several filter stages are connected in series (Fig. 24.18). The resultant frequency response of the filter as a whole is therefore the product of the individual filter stage frequency responses. To design the filter stages, the transfer function to be implemented is factored. Thus, a Nth-order filter (highest power z^{-N}) is broken down into a number of filter stages which, when recombined, possess the order N. The order of the filter stages selected is basically irrelevant, but it must not be lower than $N_i = 2$ in the case of IIR filters, because it will otherwise not be possible to realize the normally occurring conjugately complex poles of the transfer function. We can see that the order of the filter as a whole is retained in the cascade structure. An obvious advantage of this is that the lower-order filter stages are generally easier to design and verify. These properties are utilized in the analog filters in Chapter 14 and in the recursive filters in Section 24.6.

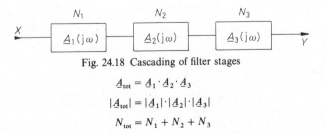

Fig. 24.18 Cascading of filter stages

$$\underline{A}_{\text{tot}} = \underline{A}_1 \cdot \underline{A}_2 \cdot \underline{A}_3$$
$$|\underline{A}_{\text{tot}}| = |\underline{A}_1| \cdot |\underline{A}_2| \cdot |\underline{A}_3|$$
$$N_{\text{tot}} = N_1 + N_2 + N_3$$

24.4   Design analysis of FIR filters

The coefficients β_k in the digital filters (see Figs. 24.15–24.17) determine the amount of feedback. If they are all made zero, there is no feedback and the output signal is merely the weighted sum of the input signal and its delays. Filters of this kind are known as *nonrecursive filters, transversal filters or finite impulse response filters* (FIR). The term FIR means that the impulse response is of finite length ($N + 1$ values). The circuits in Figs. 24.15 to 24.17 then become the simplified circuits in Figs. 24.19/20.

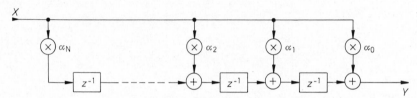

Fig. 24.19 FIR filter with distributed adders

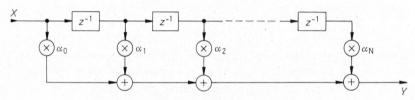

Fig. 24.20 FIR filter with a global adder at the output

24.4.1   Basic equations

The elimination of the coefficients β_k also simplifies the transfer equations. The difference equation is

$$y_N = \alpha_0 x_N + \alpha_1 x_{N-1} + \cdots + \alpha_{N-1} x_1 + \alpha_N x_0 \ , \quad y_N = \sum_{k=0}^{N} \alpha_k x_{N-k} \ . \quad (24.19)$$

For the transfer function we obtain

$$Y(z) = [\alpha_0 + \alpha_1 z^{-1} + \alpha_2 z^{-2} + \cdots + \alpha_{N-1} z^{-(N-1)} + \alpha_N z^{-N}] X(z) \ ,$$

$$\tilde{A}(z) = \frac{Y(z)}{X(z)} = \sum_{k=0}^{N} \alpha_k z^{-k} \ . \quad (24.20)$$

Inserting Euler's relation

$$z^{-1} = e^{-j2\pi F} = \cos 2\pi F - j \sin 2\pi F \ , \quad (24.21)$$

the complex frequency response

$$\underline{A}(j\omega) = \sum_{k=0}^{N} \alpha_k e^{-j2\pi kF} \tag{24.22}$$

is obtained. This relation can be simplified if the coefficients are symmetrical:

$$\alpha_{N-k} = \alpha_k \quad \text{even symmetry} , \tag{24.23}$$

$$\alpha_{N-k} = -\alpha_k \quad \text{odd symmetry} . \tag{24.24}$$

Two terms with coefficients equal in absolute value can then be combined and a common phase factor can be factored out. Equation (24.22) is then simplified as follows:

for even symmetry:

$$\underline{A}(j\omega) = e^{-j\pi NF} \sum_{k=0}^{N} \alpha_k \cos \pi(N - 2k)F , \tag{24.25a}$$

for odd symmetry:

$$\underline{A}(j\omega) = je^{-j\pi NF} \sum_{k=0}^{N} \alpha_k \sin \pi(N - 2k)F . \tag{24.25b}$$

For odd symmetry, the middle coefficient must disappear in even-order filters, i.e. $\alpha_{\frac{1}{2}N} = 0$. We thus obtain an expression in terms of magnitude $B(\omega)$ and phase $e^{j\varphi}$ of the form

$$\underline{A}(j\omega) = \begin{cases} B(\omega)e^{-j\pi NF} & \text{for even symmetry} , \\ B(\omega)je^{-j\pi NF} & \text{for odd symmetry} . \end{cases}$$

In order to calculate the magnitude, we only need to take account of the sum in Eq. (24.25). The phase shift follows from the exponential function

$$\varphi = \begin{cases} -\pi NF & \text{for even symmetry} , \\ -\pi NF + \pi/2 & \text{for odd symmetry} . \end{cases} \tag{24.26}$$

We can see in both cases the *linear phase* behavior which is exactly fulfilled for any symmetrical coefficients.

The group delay is obtained from the definition

$$t_{\text{gr}} = -\frac{d\varphi}{d\omega} = -\frac{d\varphi}{dF} \cdot \frac{dF}{d\omega} = -\frac{T_s}{2\pi} \cdot \frac{d\varphi}{dF} . \tag{24.27}$$

Hence, by differentiating Eq. (24.26)

$$t_{\text{gr}} = \tfrac{1}{2}NT_s . \tag{24.28}$$

Consequently, it is frequency-invariant. Delay distortion cannot therefore occur with symmetrical FIR filters. This is one of their chief advantages and is the reason why FIR filters are only designed with symmetrical coefficients. The design procedures and examples given in this chapter all produce FIR filters with constant group delay.

24.4.2   Simple examples

In order to become familiar with the behavior and design analysis of FIR filters, it is useful to examine a few simple examples.

First-order FIR filter

The circuit shown in Fig. 24.21 is a first-order FIR filter ($N = 1$). As we can see, it is a lowpass filter. Its DC voltage gain is $|A(F = 0)| = 1$. This may also be perceived directly from the circuit: if a unit sequence $x_\mu = 1$ is applied to the input, then $y_\mu = \alpha_0 + \alpha_1 = 0.5 + 0.5 = 1$. This characteristic can be generalized:

> The DC voltage gain of an FIR filter is equal to the sum of all the filter coefficients.

At the highest signal frequency permitted by the sampling theorem, i.e.

$$f = \tfrac{1}{2}f_s \quad \text{or} \quad F = \tfrac{1}{2},$$

a unity input sequence is produced in which the values $+1$ and -1 occur alternately, $\{X_\mu\} = \{ +1, -1, +1, -1 \ldots \}$. Consequently, in Fig. 24.20 the output signal $Y = +0.5 - 0.5 = -0.5 + 0.5 = 0$, i.e. it is constantly zero. This is also apparent from the amplitude-frequency response. This characteristic, too, can be generalized:

> The gain of an FIR filter at half the sampling frequency is equal to the sum of the coefficients alternately weighted with $+1$ and -1.

If all the filter coefficients are multiplied by the same factor, the effect is the same as if the input signal were multiplied by that factor. From this we can derive the general rule:

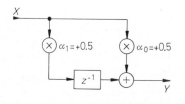
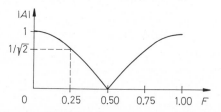

Fig. 24.21   First-order lowpass filter/interpolator

$$\tilde{A}(z) = 0.5(1 + z^{-1}) \qquad\qquad F_c = 0.25$$

$$\underline{A}(j\omega) = 0.5(1 + \cos 2\pi F - j\sin 2\pi F) \qquad \varphi = -\pi F$$

$$|\underline{A}(j\omega)| = |\cos \pi F| \qquad\qquad t_{gr} = 0.5 T_s$$

> If all the coefficients of an FIR filter are multiplied by the same factor, only the basic gain of the filter will be modified, but its filter characteristic will remain unchanged.

To calculate the cutoff frequency we put

$$|\underline{A}(j\omega)| = \cos \pi F_c = 1/\sqrt{2}$$

and obtain $F_c = \frac{1}{4}$ or $f_c = \frac{1}{4}f_s$.

If an input sequence $x(t_\mu)$, which is equal to 1 only on one occasion and is otherwise 0, is applied to an FIR filter, initially the coefficient $y(t_\mu) = \alpha_0$ is obtained at the output, followed by $y(t_{\mu+1}) = \alpha_1$, i.e. the coefficients occur consecutively. Generalizing:

> The unity-impulse response of an FIR filter is the sequence of its coefficients. It is $N + 1$ values long.

A first-order highpass filter is shown in Fig. 24.22. We can see from the coefficients $\alpha_0 = +0.5$ and $\alpha_1 = -0.5$ that their sum is zero. This also results in zero DC voltage gain. With an input sequence of $+1, -1, \ldots$ (highest signal frequency), the same sequence will appear at the output. The gain is therefore unity. The cutoff frequency of the highpass filter, like that of the lowpass filter, is $f_c = \frac{1}{4}f_s$.

The two examples described also reveal the linear phase behavior and the resulting constant group delay. The lowpass filter can also be used for averaging, as may be seen from the coefficients. Similarly, the highpass filter can be used as a differentiator, since for low frequencies

$$|\underline{A}(j\omega)| = \sin \pi F \approx \pi F \;;$$

i.e. the gain is proportional to the frequency.

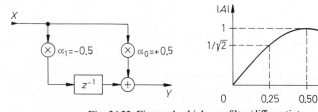

Fig. 24.22 First-order highpass filter/differentiator

$\tilde{A}(z) = 0.5(1 - z^{-1})$	$F_c = 0.25$
$\underline{A}(j\omega) = 0.5(1 - \cos 2\pi F + j \sin 2\pi F)$	$\varphi = \pi(0.5 - F)$
$|\underline{A}(j\omega)| = |\sin \pi F|$	$t_{gr} = 0.5T_s$

Second-order FIR filter

A second-order lowpass filter or interpolator is shown in Fig. 24.23. It may be seen that the argument of the cosine is here twice as large, and consequently, so is the phase shift and the group delay. Its amplitude-frequency response is plotted in log-log form in Fig. 24.24; the first-order lowpass frequency response has also been plotted by way of comparison.

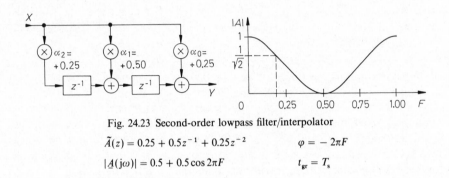

Fig. 24.23 Second-order lowpass filter/interpolator

$$\tilde{A}(z) = 0.25 + 0.5z^{-1} + 0.25z^{-2} \qquad\qquad \varphi = -2\pi F$$

$$|\underline{A}(j\omega)| = 0.5 + 0.5\cos 2\pi F \qquad\qquad t_{gr} = T_s$$

$$F_c = \frac{1}{2\pi}\arccos(\sqrt{2} - 1) = 0.182$$

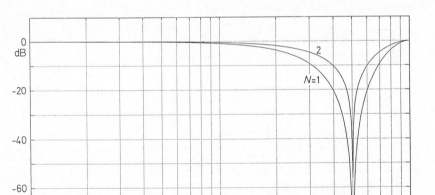

Fig. 24.24 Log-log graph of the frequency responses of the lowpass filters used as examples

$$N = 1:\ \alpha_0 = \alpha_1 = +0.5$$

$$N = 2:\ \alpha_0 = \alpha_2 = +0.25,\quad \alpha_1 = +0.5$$

The corresponding plots for a second-order highpass filter (differentiator) are shown in Figs. 24.25/26. The fact that the sum of the coefficients is zero immediately indicates that we are dealing here with a highpass filter. If we add the coefficients weighted with $+1$ or -1, we can show that the gain at $\frac{1}{2}f_s$ is unity.

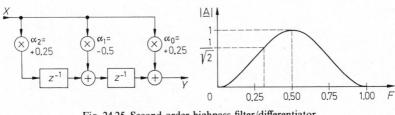

Fig. 24.25 Second-order highpass filter/differentiator

$$\tilde{A}(z) = 0.25 - 0.5z^{-1} + 0.25z^{-2} \qquad \varphi = -2\pi F$$

$$|\underline{A}(j\omega)| = 0.5 - 0.5\cos 2\pi F \qquad t_{gr} = T_s$$

$$F_c = \frac{1}{2\pi}\arccos(1 - \sqrt{2}) = 0.318$$

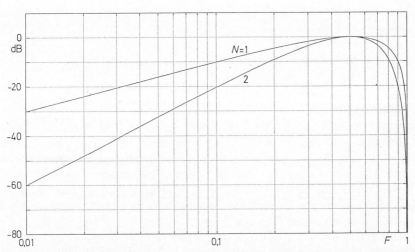

Fig. 24.26 Log-log graph of the frequency responses of the highpass filters used as examples

$$N = 1: \alpha_0 = +0.5, \qquad \alpha_1 = -0.5$$

$$N = 2: \alpha_0 = \alpha_2 = +0.25, \quad \alpha_1 = +0.5$$

For $\alpha_1 = 0$, the band-stop filter (Fig. 24.27) with center frequency $f_r = \frac{1}{4}f_s$ is obtained. We can see here that the values at the output cancel each other out when two consecutive input values are $+1$ and the next two are -1. Accordingly, band-stop filters with low resonant frequency can be realized by likewise making (in a comparatively long delay chain) the first and last coefficient $\alpha_0 = \alpha_N = 0.5$ and setting all the others to zero.

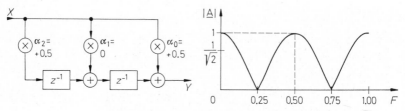

Fig. 24.27 Second-order band-stop filter

$$\tilde{A}(z) = 0.5 + 0.5z^{-2} \qquad\qquad \varphi = -2\pi F$$

$$|\underline{A}(j\omega)| = |\cos 2\pi F| \qquad\qquad t_{gr} = T_s$$

$$F_r = 0.25 \qquad\qquad\qquad Q = F_r/B = 1$$

24.4.3   Calculating the filter coefficients

Two methods are commonly used to calculate the coefficients of FIR filters: the *window method* and the *Remez Exchange Algorithm* [24.8/9/10]. The latter is a numerical method of Chebyshev approximation of a given gain tolerance scheme. It provides a minimal number of coefficients and therefore produces particularly efficient circuits. The advantage of the window method is that it allows a clear understanding of the mode of operation while at the same time being less computationally intensive. We shall now describe how these methods are used to calculate the filter coefficients.

FIR filters possess a particularly distinctive impulse response. If a unity impulse conforming to the sequence

$$\{x(kT_s)\} = \begin{cases} 1 & \text{for } k = 0 \\ 0 & \text{otherwise} \end{cases} \qquad\qquad (24.29)$$

is applied to the input, we obtain in accordance with Figs. 24.19/20 or Eq. (24.19) the unity-impulse response

$$\{y(kT_s)\} = \alpha_0, \alpha_1, \alpha_2 \dots \alpha_N = \{\alpha_k\} \ , \tag{24.30}$$

i.e. the sequence of the filter coefficients.

On the other hand, it can be shown that the impulse response of a system represents the inverse Fourier transform of its frequency response $A_w(j\omega)$ in accordance with

$$y(t) = \int\limits_{-\infty}^{+\infty} A_w(j\omega)e^{j\omega t}d\omega \ . \tag{24.31}$$

With discrete-time systems, the frequency response is periodic with $f_s = 1/T_s$, and the time can be specified as multiples of the sampling period: $t = kT_s$. This simplifies Eq. (24.31) to

$$y(kT_s) = \int\limits_{-1/2f_s}^{+1/2f_s} A_w(jf)e^{j2\pi fkT_s}df \ . \tag{24.32}$$

The required filter coefficients are obtained by equating (24.30) and (24.32) and specifying the desired frequency response $A_w(j\omega)$.

Of particular interest is the case, shown in Fig. 24.28, of the ideal lowpass filter with cutoff frequency $F_c = f_c/f_s$ and a gain of 1 in the passband and 0 in the stop band. If a constant group delay $t_{gr} = \frac{1}{2}NT_s$ is additionally required, $A_w(jf)$ can also be expressed as a delay function

$$\underline{A}_w(jf) = \begin{cases} e^{-j\pi fNT_s} & \text{for } -f_c \leq f \leq f_c \\ 0 & \text{otherwise} \end{cases} \ . \tag{24.33}$$

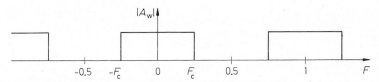

Fig. 24.28 Desired frequency response of an ideal lowpass filter and its periodic continuation

Inserting this ideal frequency response in Eq. (24.32), we obtain

$$\alpha_{kr} = \int\limits_{-f_c}^{f_c} e^{-j\pi fNT_s}e^{j2\pi fkT_s}df = \int\limits_{-F_c}^{F_c} e^{j\pi F(2k-N)}dF \ ,$$

$$\boxed{\alpha_{kr} = 2F_c \frac{\sin(2k-N)\pi F_c}{(2k-N)\pi F_c} \quad \text{for } k = 0,1,2 \dots N} \ . \tag{24.34}$$

These are the filter coefficients sought, but only their raw values, hence the subscript r. They must be modified such that the desired cutoff frequency or gain is achieved precisely. For this reason, we shall simplify by omitting factor $2F_c$ common to all coefficients of Eq. (24.34). This simplification is allowed since factor $2F_c$ will eventually be replaced during the necessary normalization of the gain. To the value $(\sin 0)/0$ occurring for even order, i.e. of odd coefficient numbers, we assign the limit value

$$\lim_{x \to 0} \frac{\sin x}{x} = 1 \ .$$

As in practice only finite orders N can be realized, the sequence α_{kr} must be terminated. This can be interpreted—as in Fig. 24.29—as multiplication by a square window. This of course means that we have an incomplete approximation to the desired frequency response. In Fig. 24.30 we can see a marked deviation from the desired ideal frequency response and a poor stop-band attenuation. This can be greatly improved by using, instead of the square window, a window which gradually reduces the coefficients towards the edge. Commonly used window functions are:

Hamming window,   Hanning window,

Blackman window,   Kaiser window.

We shall use the Hamming window, as it provides good results with minimal computing effort. The Hamming function

$$\boxed{W_k = 0.54 - 0.46 \cos \frac{2\pi k}{N} \quad \text{for} \quad k = 0, 1, 2 \ldots N} \qquad (24.35)$$

is plotted in Fig. 24.29. Its boundary values are

$$W(k = 0) = W(k = N) = 0.08 \ ;$$

in the center it has the value $W(k = \frac{1}{2}N) = 1$. The filter coefficients evaluated using this window function are given below Fig. 24.29, and the resulting frequency response is shown in Fig. 24.30. We can see that the unwanted ripple is largely eliminated and the stop-band attenuation increased.

The low-frequency gain must now be normalized to 1. This is done by dividing each coefficient by the sum of all the coefficients. This step is likewise shown in Figs. 24.29/30.

The resulting filter does not yet possess the desired cutoff frequency. As the value of F_c used in Eq. (24.29) only yields an approximate solution, its value in this equation must therefore be corrected somewhat in order to achieve a gain of $1/\sqrt{2}$ at the desired cutoff frequency. In this case it must be increased to $F_c' = 0.32$. However, to do this it will be necessary to repeat the entire design process using the modified value of F_c. This inevitably entails iteration which

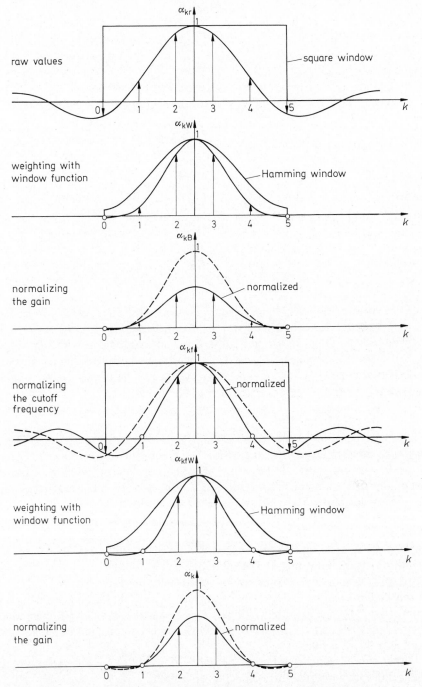

Fig. 24.29 Steps in calculating the filter coefficients based on the example of a fifth-order lowpass filter having a cutoff frequency $F_c = 0.25$

Result: $\alpha_0 = \alpha_5 = -0.00979$, $\alpha_1 = \alpha_4 = +0.00979$, $\alpha_2 = \alpha_3 = 0.5000$

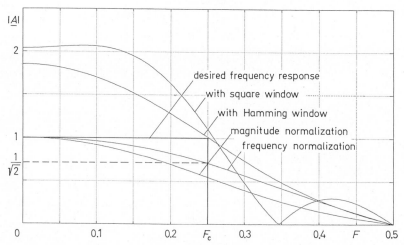

Fig. 24.30 Effect of the individual steps for coefficient calculation on the frequency response of a filter, based on the example of a fifth-order lowpass filter with $F_c = 0.25$

must be performed several times, resulting in a lowpass filter that is normalized in terms of gain and cutoff frequency, as illustrated in Figs. 24.29/30.

The lowpass filters shown in Fig. 24.31 for normalized cutoff frequencies of $F_c = 0.25; 0.1; 0.025$ have been designed using this method. The filter coefficients have been tabulated in Fig. 24.32. The lower the cutoff frequency f_c compared to the sampling rate f_s, i.e. the smaller $F_c = f_c/f_s$, the higher the lowest order N for which a solution exists. If $F_c = 0.025$, then $N = 27$ is the lowest order, whereas for $F_c = 0.01$ it would be $N = 65$.

Here we have limited our considerations to odd-order lowpass filters. These have two advantages: on the one hand, their frequency response has a zero at $F = 0.5$, whereas those of the even-order lowpass filters exhibit a (relative) maximum at that point. This results in a considerably enhanced band-stop characteristic, particularly in the case of lower-order lowpass filters with $F_c = 0.25$. On the other hand, they have an even number of coefficients and therefore integrated FIR filters can generally be better utilized.

In order to arrive at the simplest solution for realizing lowpass filters, we can ask the question: how must the cutoff frequency F_c be chosen to ensure that, in Eq. (24.34), as many filter coefficients as possible become zero? Two special cases of this kind are shown in Fig. 24.33. If we make $F_c = \frac{1}{2}$, all the coefficients apart from the middle one with the value $\alpha(\frac{1}{2}N) = 1$ vanish in even order filters (odd number of coefficients). The resulting filter is an allpass and cannot therefore be used as a lowpass filter.

If the cutoff frequency is halved, *half-band filters* with $F_c = \frac{1}{4}$ are produced. If this condition is inserted in Eq. (24.34), we obtain

$$\alpha_{kr} = \frac{\sin(2k - N)\pi/4}{(2k - N)\pi/4} .$$

(24.36)

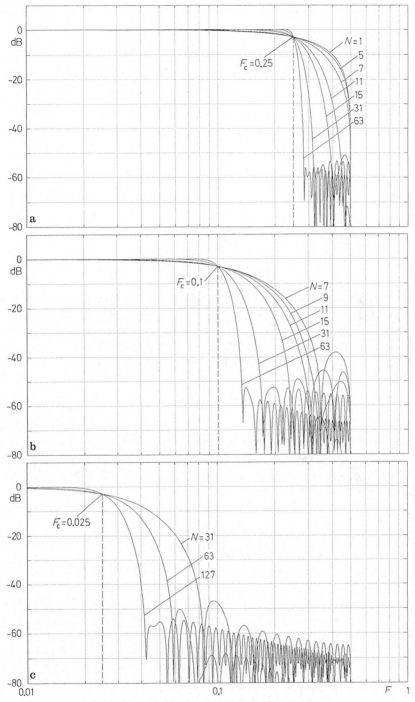

Fig. 24.31 Frequency responses of FIR lowpass filters

Cutoff frequency $F_c = 0.25$

$N = 1$

$\alpha_0 = \alpha_1 = +0.50000$

$N = 5$

$\alpha_0 = \alpha_5 = -0.00979$	$\alpha_1 = \alpha_4 = +0.00979$	$\alpha_2 = \alpha_3 = +0.50000$

$N = 7$

$\alpha_0 = \alpha_7 = +0.00343$	$\alpha_1 = \alpha_6 = -0.03171$	$\alpha_2 = \alpha_5 = +0.03171$
$\alpha_3 = \alpha_4 = +0.49657$		

$N = 11$

$\alpha_0 = \alpha_{11} = -0.00203$	$\alpha_1 = \alpha_{10} = +0.01056$	$\alpha_2 = \alpha_9 = +0.00010$
$\alpha_3 = \alpha_8 = -0.07531$	$\alpha_4 = \alpha_7 = +0.07734$	$\alpha_5 = \alpha_6 = +0.48934$

$N = 15$

$\alpha_0 = \alpha_{15} = +0.00152$	$\alpha_1 = \alpha_{14} = -0.00561$	$\alpha_2 = \alpha_{13} = -0.00175$
$\alpha_3 = \alpha_{12} = +0.02812$	$\alpha_4 = \alpha_{11} = -0.01076$	$\alpha_5 = \alpha_{10} = -0.09143$
$\alpha_6 = \alpha_9 = +0.09879$	$\alpha_7 = \alpha_8 = +0.48112$	

$N = 31$

$\alpha_0 = \alpha_{31} = +0.00074$	$\alpha_1 = \alpha_{30} = -0.00182$	$\alpha_2 = \alpha_{29} = -0.00083$
$\alpha_3 = \alpha_{28} = +0.00404$	$\alpha_4 = \alpha_{27} = +0.00088$	$\alpha_5 = \alpha_{26} = -0.00898$
$\alpha_6 = \alpha_{25} = +0.00024$	$\alpha_7 = \alpha_{24} = +0.01753$	$\alpha_8 = \alpha_{23} = -0.00429$
$\alpha_9 = \alpha_{22} = -0.03102$	$\alpha_{10} = \alpha_{21} = +0.01441$	$\alpha_{11} = \alpha_{20} = +0.05303$
$\alpha_{12} = \alpha_{19} = -0.03900$	$\alpha_{13} = \alpha_{18} = -0.10015$	$\alpha_{14} = \alpha_{17} = +0.12815$
$\alpha_{15} = \alpha_{16} = +0.46707$		

$N = 63$

$\alpha_0 = \alpha_{63} = +0.00036$	$\alpha_1 = \alpha_{62} = -0.00078$	$\alpha_2 = \alpha_{61} = -0.00036$
$\alpha_3 = \alpha_{60} = +0.00105$	$\alpha_4 = \alpha_{59} = +0.00041$	$\alpha_5 = \alpha_{58} = -0.00158$
$\alpha_6 = \alpha_{57} = -0.00045$	$\alpha_7 = \alpha_{56} = +0.00239$	$\alpha_8 = \alpha_{55} = +0.00044$
$\alpha_9 = \alpha_{54} = -0.00356$	$\alpha_{10} = \alpha_{53} = -0.00030$	$\alpha_{11} = \alpha_{52} = +0.00513$
$\alpha_{12} = \alpha_{51} = -0.00006$	$\alpha_{13} = \alpha_{50} = -0.00714$	$\alpha_{14} = \alpha_{49} = +0.00075$
$\alpha_{15} = \alpha_{48} = +0.00968$	$\alpha_{16} = \alpha_{47} = -0.00190$	$\alpha_{17} = \alpha_{46} = -0.01283$
$\alpha_{18} = \alpha_{45} = +0.00372$	$\alpha_{19} = \alpha_{44} = +0.01677$	$\alpha_{20} = \alpha_{43} = -0.00650$
$\alpha_{21} = \alpha_{42} = -0.02179$	$\alpha_{22} = \alpha_{41} = +0.01074$	$\alpha_{23} = \alpha_{40} = +0.02852$
$\alpha_{24} = \alpha_{39} = -0.01743$	$\alpha_{25} = \alpha_{38} = -0.03839$	$\alpha_{26} = \alpha_{37} = +0.02898$
$\alpha_{27} = \alpha_{36} = +0.05549$	$\alpha_{28} = \alpha_{35} = -0.05326$	$\alpha_{29} = \alpha_{34} = -0.09716$
$\alpha_{30} = \alpha_{33} = +0.14016$	$\alpha_{31} = \alpha_{32} = +0.45891$	

Fig. 24.32a Coefficients for FIR filters with cutoff frequency $F_c = 0.25$, i.e. $f_c = 0.25 f_s$. Order $N = 3$ does not exist here, as the two coefficients α_0 and α_3 vanish

Cutoff frequency $F_c = 0.025$

$N = 31$

$\alpha_0 = \alpha_{31} = +0.00077$	$\alpha_1 = \alpha_{30} = +0.00132$	$\alpha_2 = \alpha_{29} = +0.00236$
$\alpha_3 = \alpha_{28} = +0.00417$	$\alpha_4 = \alpha_{27} = +0.00698$	$\alpha_5 = \alpha_{20} = +0.01095$
$\alpha_6 = \alpha_{25} = +0.01613$	$\alpha_7 = \alpha_{24} = +0.02244$	$\alpha_8 = \alpha_{23} = +0.02968$
$\alpha_9 = \alpha_{22} = +0.03754$	$\alpha_{10} = \alpha_{21} = +0.04559$	$\alpha_{11} = \alpha_{20} = +0.05335$
$\alpha_{12} = \alpha_{19} = +0.06033$	$\alpha_{13} = \alpha_{18} = +0.06606$	$\alpha_{14} = \alpha_{17} = +0.07012$
$\alpha_{15} = \alpha_{16} = +0.07222$		

Fig. 24.32c Coefficients for FIR filters with cutoff frequency $F_c = 0.025$, i.e. $f_c = 0.025 f_s$. No solution exists for orders $N < 27$

Cutoff frequency $F_c = 0.1$

$N = 7$

$\alpha_0 = \alpha_7 = +0.00976$ $\alpha_1 = \alpha_6 = +0.04966$ $\alpha_2 = \alpha_5 = +0.16442$
$\alpha_3 = \alpha_4 = +0.27616$

$N = 11$

$\alpha_0 = \alpha_{11} = -0.00470$ $\alpha_1 = \alpha_{10} = -0.00605$ $\alpha_2 = \alpha_9 = +0.00818$
$\alpha_3 = \alpha_8 = +0.07006$ $\alpha_4 = \alpha_7 = +0.17404$ $\alpha_5 = \alpha_6 = +0.25848$

$N = 15$

$\alpha_0 = \alpha_{15} = -0.00101$ $\alpha_1 = \alpha_{14} = -0.00521$ $\alpha_2 = \alpha_{13} = -0.01269$
$\alpha_3 = \alpha_{12} = -0.01214$ $\alpha_4 = \alpha_{11} = +0.01830$ $\alpha_5 = \alpha_{10} = +0.08914$
$\alpha_6 = \alpha_9 = +0.17962$ $\alpha_7 = \alpha_8 = +0.24399$

$N = 31$

$\alpha_0 = \alpha_{31} = -0.00165$ $\alpha_1 = \alpha_{30} = -0.00146$ $\alpha_2 = \alpha_{29} = -0.00037$
$\alpha_3 = \alpha_{28} = +0.00225$ $\alpha_4 = \alpha_{27} = +0.00593$ $\alpha_5 = \alpha_{26} = +0.00823$
$\alpha_6 = \alpha_{25} = +0.00548$ $\alpha_7 = \alpha_{24} = -0.00461$ $\alpha_8 = \alpha_{23} = -0.01979$
$\alpha_9 = \alpha_{22} = -0.03195$ $\alpha_{10} = \alpha_{21} = -0.02944$ $\alpha_{11} = \alpha_{20} = -0.00261$
$\alpha_{12} = \alpha_{19} = +0.04987$ $\alpha_{13} = \alpha_{18} = +0.11780$ $\alpha_{14} = \alpha_{17} = +0.18175$
$\alpha_{15} = \alpha_{16} = +0.22058$

$N = 63$

$\alpha_0 = \alpha_{63} = +0.00065$ $\alpha_1 = \alpha_{62} = +0.00086$ $\alpha_2 = \alpha_{61} = +0.00073$
$\alpha_3 = \alpha_{60} = +0.00022$ $\alpha_4 = \alpha_{59} = -0.00061$ $\alpha_5 = \alpha_{58} = -0.00148$
$\alpha_6 = \alpha_{57} = -0.00194$ $\alpha_7 = \alpha_{56} = -0.00150$ $\alpha_8 = \alpha_{55} = +0.00001$
$\alpha_9 = \alpha_{54} = +0.00223$ $\alpha_{10} = \alpha_{53} = +0.00418$ $\alpha_{11} = \alpha_{52} = +0.00464$
$\alpha_{12} = \alpha_{51} = +0.00272$ $\alpha_{13} = \alpha_{50} = -0.00144$ $\alpha_{14} = \alpha_{49} = -0.00639$
$\alpha_{15} = \alpha_{48} = -0.00973$ $\alpha_{16} = \alpha_{47} = -0.00909$ $\alpha_{17} = \alpha_{46} = -0.00343$
$\alpha_{18} = \alpha_{45} = +0.00593$ $\alpha_{19} = \alpha_{44} = +0.01532$ $\alpha_{20} = \alpha_{43} = +0.01986$
$\alpha_{21} = \alpha_{42} = +0.01560$ $\alpha_{22} = \alpha_{41} = +0.00177$ $\alpha_{23} = \alpha_{40} = -0.01790$
$\alpha_{24} = \alpha_{39} = -0.03551$ $\alpha_{25} = \alpha_{38} = -0.04135$ $\alpha_{26} = \alpha_{37} = -0.02742$
$\alpha_{27} = \alpha_{36} = +0.00903$ $\alpha_{28} = \alpha_{35} = +0.06348$ $\alpha_{29} = \alpha_{34} = +0.12467$
$\alpha_{30} = \alpha_{33} = +0.17761$ $\alpha_{31} = \alpha_{32} = +0.20829$

Fig. 24.32b Coefficients for FIR filters with cutoff frequency $F_c = 0.1$, i.e. $f_c = 0.1 f_s$. No solution exists here for orders $N < 7$

Cutoff frequency $F_c = 0.025$

$N = 63$

$\alpha_0 = \alpha_{63} = -0.00005$ $\alpha_1 = \alpha_{62} = -0.00022$ $\alpha_2 = \alpha_{61} = -0.00042$
$\alpha_3 = \alpha_{60} = -0.00068$ $\alpha_4 = \alpha_{59} = -0.00101$ $\alpha_5 = \alpha_{58} = -0.00141$
$\alpha_6 = \alpha_{57} = -0.00188$ $\alpha_7 = \alpha_{56} = -0.00241$ $\alpha_8 = \alpha_{55} = -0.00295$
$\alpha_9 = \alpha_{54} = -0.00344$ $\alpha_{10} = \alpha_{53} = -0.00383$ $\alpha_{11} = \alpha_{52} = -0.00403$
$\alpha_{12} = \alpha_{51} = -0.00395$ $\alpha_{13} = \alpha_{50} = -0.00350$ $\alpha_{14} = \alpha_{49} = -0.00259$
$\alpha_{15} = \alpha_{48} = -0.00115$ $\alpha_{16} = \alpha_{47} = +0.00089$ $\alpha_{17} = \alpha_{46} = +0.00356$
$\alpha_{18} = \alpha_{45} = +0.00689$ $\alpha_{19} = \alpha_{44} = +0.01084$ $\alpha_{20} = \alpha_{43} = +0.01536$
$\alpha_{21} = \alpha_{42} = +0.02036$ $\alpha_{22} = \alpha_{41} = +0.02573$ $\alpha_{23} = \alpha_{40} = +0.03131$
$\alpha_{24} = \alpha_{39} = +0.03694$ $\alpha_{25} = \alpha_{38} = +0.04243$ $\alpha_{26} = \alpha_{37} = +0.04759$
$\alpha_{27} = \alpha_{36} = +0.05227$ $\alpha_{28} = \alpha_{35} = +0.05618$ $\alpha_{29} = \alpha_{34} = +0.05928$
$\alpha_{30} = \alpha_{33} = +0.06143$ $\alpha_{31} = \alpha_{32} = +0.06252$

Fig. 24.32c Coefficients for FIR filters with cutoff frequency $F_c = 0.025$, i.e. $f_c = 0.025 f_s$.
(continued)

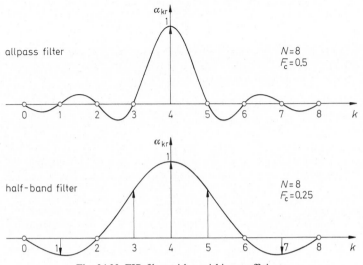

Fig. 24.33 FIR filter with vanishing coefficients

As we can see from Fig. 24.33, an appreciable simplification is again obtained for even order (odd number of coefficients), as every second coefficient becomes zero. In order to arrive at a practicable filter design, the coefficients have still to be evaluated with a window. Using the Hamming window in Eq. (24.35), we obtain with $\alpha_{kw} = \alpha_{kr} \cdot W_k$

$$\alpha_{kw} = \frac{\sin(2k - N)\pi/4}{(2k - N)\pi/4}\left(0.54 - 0.46\cos\frac{2\pi k}{N}\right) \quad \text{for} \quad k = 0, 1, 2 \ldots N \ . \quad (24.37)$$

If filter coefficients for all k have been calculated, it is now merely necessary to normalize them by dividing them by their sum in order to obtain the final coefficients. An iterative process is no longer necessary. Consequently, these filter coefficients may be calculated on a pocket calculator. The resulting cutoff frequencies are of course not precisely $F_c = \frac{1}{4}$, as they have not been normalized; but a normalization is ruled out, as the advantage of every second coefficient vanishing would be lost. The frequency responses of a number of half-band filters are shown in Fig. 24.34 and a coefficient table is given in Fig. 24.35. It may be seen from Fig. 24.34 that the -6 dB cutoff frequencies approach $F_c = 0.25$ more accurately the higher the order, i.e. they approach the "half band". The -3 dB cutoff frequencies normally specified are therefore lower; their precise

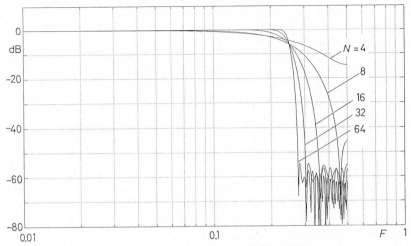

Fig. 24.34 Frequency responses of half-band filters

$N = 4$ 3 coefficients $F_c = 0.205$
$\alpha_0 = \alpha_4 = 0$ $\alpha_1 = \alpha_3 = +0.20371$ $\alpha_2 = +0.59258$

$N = 8$ 5 coefficients $F_c = 0.199$
$\alpha_0 = \alpha_8 = 0$ $\alpha_1 = \alpha_7 = -0.02266$ $\alpha_2 = \alpha_6 = 0$ $\alpha_3 = \alpha_5 = +0.27398$
$\alpha_4 = +0.49737$

$N = 16$ 9 coefficients $F_c = 0.225$
$\alpha_0 = \alpha_{16} = 0$ $\alpha_1 = \alpha_{15} = -0.00524$ $\alpha_2 = \alpha_{14} = 0$ $\alpha_3 = \alpha_{13} = +0.02321$
$\alpha_4 = \alpha_{12} = 0$ $\alpha_5 = \alpha_{11} = -0.07611$ $\alpha_6 = \alpha_{10} = 0$ $\alpha_7 = \alpha_9 = +0.30770$
$\alpha_8 = +0.50087$

$N = 32$ 17 coefficients $F_c = 0.238$
$\alpha_0 = \alpha_{32} = 0$ $\alpha_1 = \alpha_{31} = -0.00189$ $\alpha_2 = \alpha_{30} = 0$ $\alpha_3 = \alpha_{29} = +0.00386$
$\alpha_4 = \alpha_{28} = 0$ $\alpha_5 = \alpha_{27} = -0.00824$ $\alpha_6 = \alpha_{26} = 0$ $\alpha_7 = \alpha_{25} = +0.01595$
$\alpha_8 = \alpha_{24} = 0$ $\alpha_9 = \alpha_{23} = -0.02868$ $\alpha_{10} = \alpha_{22} = 0$ $\alpha_{11} = \alpha_{21} = +0.05072$
$\alpha_{12} = \alpha_{20} = 0$ $\alpha_{13} = \alpha_{19} = -0.09802$ $\alpha_{14} = \alpha_{18} = 0$ $\alpha_{15} = \alpha_{17} = +0.31594$
$\alpha_{16} = +0.50071$

$N = 64$ 33 coefficients $F_c = 0.244$
$\alpha_0 = \alpha_{64} = 0$ $\alpha_1 = \alpha_{63} = -0.00084$ $\alpha_2 = \alpha_{62} = 0$ $\alpha_3 = \alpha_{61} = +0.00110$
$\alpha_4 = \alpha_{60} = 0$ $\alpha_5 = \alpha_{59} = -0.00158$ $\alpha_6 = \alpha_{58} = 0$ $\alpha_7 = \alpha_{57} = +0.00235$
$\alpha_8 = \alpha_{56} = 0$ $\alpha_9 = \alpha_{55} = -0.00344$ $\alpha_{10} = \alpha_{54} = 0$ $\alpha_{11} = \alpha_{53} = +0.00490$
$\alpha_{12} = \alpha_{52} = 0$ $\alpha_{13} = \alpha_{51} = -0.00681$ $\alpha_{14} = \alpha_{50} = 0$ $\alpha_{15} = \alpha_{49} = +0.00927$
$\alpha_{16} = \alpha_{48} = 0$ $\alpha_{17} = \alpha_{47} = -0.01243$ $\alpha_{18} = \alpha_{46} = 0$ $\alpha_{19} = \alpha_{45} = +0.01650$
$\alpha_{20} = \alpha_{44} = 0$ $\alpha_{19} = \alpha_{43} = -0.02192$ $\alpha_{22} = \alpha_{42} = 0$ $\alpha_{23} = \alpha_{41} = +0.02944$
$\alpha_{24} = \alpha_{40} = 0$ $\alpha_{25} = \alpha_{39} = -0.04076$ $\alpha_{26} = \alpha_{38} = 0$ $\alpha_{27} = \alpha_{37} = +0.06025$
$\alpha_{28} = \alpha_{36} = 0$ $\alpha_{29} = \alpha_{35} = -0.10408$ $\alpha_{30} = \alpha_{34} = 0$ $\alpha_{31} = \alpha_{33} = +0.31785$
$\alpha_{32} = +0.50039$

Fig. 24.35 Coefficients for half-band filters

values are additionally given in Fig. 24.35. The inconsistent values for F_c nevertheless allow any cutoff frequencies to be realized by selecting the sampling frequency accordingly:

$$f_s = f_c / F_c \ .$$

We can see in Fig. 24.33 that half the values become zero only for an odd number of coefficients. Consequently, only half-band filters with even order are used. It is also apparent that the boundary coefficients (α_0 and α_8 in the example) vanish for all orders divisible by 4. They are therefore particularly useful, as we can obtain two additional filter orders without an additional multiplication. Even the two delay elements associated with the two vanishing boundary coefficients $\alpha_0 = \alpha_N = 0$ can be dispensed with. However, these advantages can only be exploited if the filter algorithm is programmed on a signal processor. With the hardware filters listed in Fig. 24.43, the advantages of the half-band filters cannot be utilized.

Half-band filters can be used to advantage in cascade arrangements, as shown in Fig. 24.36. Identical filter blocks are used which already possess a high stop-band attenuation at half the sampling frequency. It is therefore possible, without significantly contravening the sampling theorem, to operate the second filter block at half the sampling rate. This reduces the computation by half. In the third and fourth filter block, the sampling frequency is again halved in each case. The cutoff frequency of the entire filter is therefore halved with each additional filter block; this is also shown in Fig. 24.36. In this way, cutoff frequencies can be realized which are well below the sampling frequency and whose implementation would otherwise require considerable complexity [24.16].

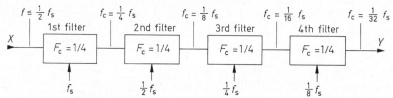

Fig. 24.36 Use of half-band filters in cascade structure with undersampling.
Number of MAC operations to calculate on output value:

$$(N + 1) + \tfrac{1}{2}(N + 1) + \tfrac{1}{4}(N + 1) + \ldots = (N + 1)(1 + \tfrac{1}{2} + \tfrac{1}{4} + \ldots) = 2(N + 1)$$

Highpass filters

Calculating the filter coefficients of highpass filters can be related to the design of lowpass filters. To do this we use the addition theorem of the Fourier transformation, which states that an addition in the frequency domain corresponds to an addition in the time domain. Figure 24.37 shows how this statement can be used to design highpass filters. We can see that a highpass filter is produced in the frequency domain by subtracting a lowpass filter from an allpass filter. The associated filter coefficients are therefore obtained by subtracting the coefficients of the lowpass filter from those of the allpass filter, as is shown on the right-hand side of the figure. Of course, the coefficients must once again be weighted using a window and the magnitude of the gain normalized to 1 at $F = 0.5$ and to $1/\sqrt{2}$ at $F = F_c$.

However, it is apparent that odd-order highpass filters designed using this method have a zero at $F = 0.5$ which makes their performance unsatisfactory. Therefore, only even-order filters, i.e. those with an odd number of coefficients, have been taken into account in the coefficients tables in Fig. 24.38 and the frequency responses in Fig. 24.39.

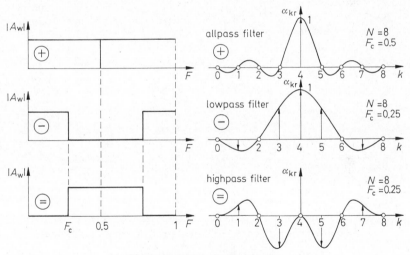

Fig. 24.37 Design of highpass filters

Cutoff frequency $F_c = 0.25$

$N = 1$
$\alpha_0 = -\alpha_1 = +0.5000$

$N = 6$

$\alpha_0 = \alpha_6 = -0.00009$ $\alpha_1 = \alpha_5 = -0.05091$ $\alpha_2 = \alpha_4 = -0.25163$
$\quad\quad\alpha_3 = +0.60528$

$N = 10$

$\alpha_0 = \alpha_{10} = -0.00162$ $\alpha_1 = \alpha_9 = +0.01114$ $\alpha_2 = \alpha_8 = +0.03079$
$\alpha_3 = \alpha_7 = -0.05152$ $\alpha_4 = \alpha_6 = -0.27968$ $\quad\alpha_5 = +0.58179$

$N = 14$

$\alpha_0 = \alpha_{14} = +0.00113$ $\alpha_1 = \alpha_{13} = -0.00587$ $\alpha_2 = \alpha_{12} = -0.01005$
$\alpha_3 = \alpha_{11} = +0.02291$ $\alpha_4 = \alpha_{10} = +0.05852$ $\alpha_5 = \alpha_9 = -0.04623$
$\alpha_6 = \alpha_8 = -0.29895$ $\alpha_7 = +0.55709$

$N = 30$

$\alpha_0 = \alpha_{30} = +0.00053$ $\alpha_1 = \alpha_{29} = -0.00188$ $\alpha_2 = \alpha_{28} = -0.00136$
$\alpha_3 = \alpha_{27} = +0.00375$ $\alpha_4 = \alpha_{26} = +0.00407$ $\alpha_5 = \alpha_{25} = -0.00732$
$\alpha_6 = \alpha_{24} = -0.01026$ $\alpha_7 = \alpha_{23} = +0.01213$ $\alpha_8 = \alpha_{22} = +0.02267$
$\alpha_9 = \alpha_{21} = -0.01739$ $\alpha_{10} = \alpha_{20} = -0.04475$ $\alpha_{11} = \alpha_{19} = +0.02213$
$\alpha_{12} = \alpha_{18} = +0.09366$ $\alpha_{13} = \alpha_{17} = -0.02541$ $\alpha_{14} = \alpha_{16} = -0.31369$
$\quad\alpha_{15} = +0.52709$

$N = 62$

$\alpha_0 = \alpha_{62} = +0.00025$ $\alpha_1 = \alpha_{61} = -0.00082$ $\alpha_2 = \alpha_{60} = -0.00038$
$\alpha_3 = \alpha_{59} = +0.00104$ $\alpha_4 = \alpha_{58} = +0.00064$ $\alpha_5 = \alpha_{57} = -0.00146$
$\alpha_6 = \alpha_{56} = -0.00110$ $\alpha_7 = \alpha_{55} = +0.00209$ $\alpha_8 = \alpha_{54} = +0.00184$
$\alpha_9 = \alpha_{53} = -0.00291$ $\alpha_{10} = \alpha_{52} = -0.00297$ $\alpha_{11} = \alpha_{51} = +0.00389$
$\alpha_{12} = \alpha_{50} = +0.00457$ $\alpha_{13} = \alpha_{49} = -0.00500$ $\alpha_{14} = \alpha_{48} = -0.00680$
$\alpha_{15} = \alpha_{47} = +0.00620$ $\alpha_{16} = \alpha_{46} = +0.00981$ $\alpha_{17} = \alpha_{45} = -0.00744$
$\alpha_{18} = \alpha_{44} = -0.01387$ $\alpha_{19} = \alpha_{43} = +0.00866$ $\alpha_{20} = \alpha_{42} = +0.01938$
$\alpha_{21} = \alpha_{41} = -0.00982$ $\alpha_{22} = \alpha_{40} = -0.02713$ $\alpha_{23} = \alpha_{39} = +0.01085$
$\alpha_{24} = \alpha_{38} = +0.03879$ $\alpha_{25} = \alpha_{37} = -0.01170$ $\alpha_{26} = \alpha_{36} = -0.05873$
$\alpha_{27} = \alpha_{35} = +0.01235$ $\alpha_{28} = \alpha_{34} = +0.10304$ $\alpha_{29} = \alpha_{33} = -0.01275$
$\alpha_{30} = \alpha_{32} = -0.31713$ $\alpha_{31} = +0.51315$

Fig. 24.38a Filter coefficients of FIR highpass filters with cutoff frequency

$F_c = 0.25$,   i.e. $f_c = 0.25 f_s$

Cutoff frequency $F_c = 0.1$

$N = 12$

$\alpha_0 = \alpha_{12} = -0.01015$	$\alpha_1 = \alpha_{11} = -0.01925$	$\alpha_2 = \alpha_{10} = -0.04453$
$\alpha_3 = \alpha_9 = -0.08090$	$\alpha_4 = \alpha_8 = -0.11882$	$\alpha_5 = \alpha_7 = -0.14737$
$\alpha_6 = +0.84203$		

$N = 30$

$\alpha_0 = \alpha_{30} = -0.00160$	$\alpha_1 = \alpha_{29} = -0.00200$	$\alpha_2 = \alpha_{28} = -0.00212$
$\alpha_3 = \alpha_{27} = -0.00117$	$\alpha_4 = \alpha_{26} = +0.00185$	$\alpha_5 = \alpha_{25} = +0.00723$
$\alpha_6 = \alpha_{24} = +0.01375$	$\alpha_7 = \alpha_{23} = +0.01836$	$\alpha_8 = \alpha_{22} = +0.01674$
$\alpha_9 = \alpha_{21} = +0.00479$	$\alpha_{10} = \alpha_{20} = -0.01960$	$\alpha_{11} = \alpha_{19} = -0.05505$
$\alpha_{12} = \alpha_{18} = -0.09628$	$\alpha_{13} = \alpha_{17} = -0.13521$	$\alpha_{14} = \alpha_{16} = -0.16308$
$\alpha_{15} = +0.82679$		

$N = 62$

$\alpha_0 = \alpha_{62} = +0.00048$	$\alpha_1 = \alpha_{61} = +0.00082$	$\alpha_2 = \alpha_{60} = +0.00096$
$\alpha_3 = \alpha_{59} = +0.00079$	$\alpha_4 = \alpha_{58} = +0.00023$	$\alpha_5 = \alpha_{57} = -0.00070$
$\alpha_6 = \alpha_{56} = -0.00176$	$\alpha_7 = \alpha_{55} = -0.00254$	$\alpha_8 = \alpha_{54} = -0.00252$
$\alpha_9 = \alpha_{53} = -0.00134$	$\alpha_{10} = \alpha_{52} = +0.00099$	$\alpha_{11} = \alpha_{51} = +0.00390$
$\alpha_{12} = \alpha_{50} = +0.00629$	$\alpha_{13} = \alpha_{49} = +0.00689$	$\alpha_{14} = \alpha_{48} = +0.00475$
$\alpha_{15} = \alpha_{47} = -0.00020$	$\alpha_{16} = \alpha_{46} = -0.00683$	$\alpha_{17} = \alpha_{45} = -0.01292$
$\alpha_{18} = \alpha_{44} = -0.01572$	$\alpha_{19} = \alpha_{43} = -0.01296$	$\alpha_{20} = \alpha_{42} = -0.00392$
$\alpha_{21} = \alpha_{41} = +0.00984$	$\alpha_{22} = \alpha_{40} = +0.02439$	$\alpha_{23} = \alpha_{39} = +0.03417$
$\alpha_{24} = \alpha_{38} = +0.03350$	$\alpha_{25} = \alpha_{37} = +0.01835$	$\alpha_{26} = \alpha_{36} = -0.01208$
$\alpha_{27} = \alpha_{35} = -0.05455$	$\alpha_{28} = \alpha_{34} = -0.10217$	$\alpha_{29} = \alpha_{33} = -0.14584$
$\alpha_{30} = \alpha_{32} = -0.17650$	$\alpha_{31} = +0.81246$	

Fig. 24.38b Filter coefficients of FIR highpass filters with cutoff frequency

$$F_c = 0.1, \quad \text{i.e.} \quad f_c = 0.1 f_s$$

Cutoff frequency $F_c = 0.025$

$N = 48$

$\alpha_0 = \alpha_{48} = -0.00271$	$\alpha_1 = \alpha_{47} = -0.00288$	$\alpha_2 = \alpha_{46} = -0.00332$
$\alpha_3 = \alpha_{45} = -0.00404$	$\alpha_4 = \alpha_{44} = -0.00503$	$\alpha_5 = \alpha_{43} = -0.00628$
$\alpha_6 = \alpha_{42} = -0.00778$	$\alpha_7 = \alpha_{41} = -0.00951$	$\alpha_8 = \alpha_{40} = -0.01144$
$\alpha_9 = \alpha_{39} = -0.01353$	$\alpha_{10} = \alpha_{38} = -0.01577$	$\alpha_{11} = \alpha_{37} = -0.01811$
$\alpha_{12} = \alpha_{36} = -0.02050$	$\alpha_{13} = \alpha_{35} = -0.02291$	$\alpha_{14} = \alpha_{34} = -0.02530$
$\alpha_{15} = \alpha_{33} = -0.02762$	$\alpha_{16} = \alpha_{32} = -0.02983$	$\alpha_{17} = \alpha_{31} = -0.03189$
$\alpha_{18} = \alpha_{30} = -0.03376$	$\alpha_{19} = \alpha_{29} = -0.03541$	$\alpha_{20} = \alpha_{28} = -0.03680$
$\alpha_{21} = \alpha_{27} = -0.03791$	$\alpha_{22} = \alpha_{26} = -0.03872$	$\alpha_{23} = \alpha_{25} = -0.03921$
$\alpha_{24} = +0.96062$		

Fig. 24.38c Filter coefficients of FIR highpass filters with cutoff frequency

$$F_c = 0.025, \quad \text{i.e.} \quad f_c = 0.025 f_s$$

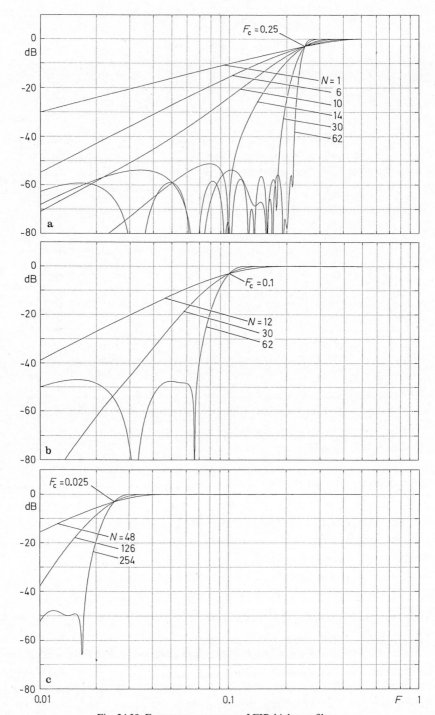

Fig. 24.39 Frequency responses of FIR highpass filters

Bandpass filters and band-stop filters

A bandpass filter can be implemented by subtracting the frequency responses of two lowpass filters from one another, as in Fig. 24.40. In order to obtain a band-stop filter, the frequency response of a bandpass filter can be subtracted from that of an allpass filter. The coefficients of the required filter can therefore be obtained in each case by subtraction of the relevant sets of coefficients.

Another method of obtaining the filter coefficients of bandpass and band-stop filters consists of multiplying together the transfer functions $\tilde{A}(z)$ of a corresponding highpass and lowpass filter. The implementation can then be performed either from the individual filters in a cascade arrangement or, after multiplying out, in a continuous arrangement.

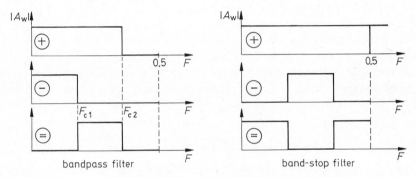

Fig. 24.40 Design of bandpass or bandstop filters

24.5 Realization of FIR filters

To implement FIR filters, Eq. (24.19) must be used to calculate the output values

$$y(t_N) = \sum_{k=0}^{N} \alpha_k x(t_{N-k})$$

as the sum of the N last input values weighted with the coefficients. This operation can be performed either in parallel, i.e. in one step, or serially, i.e. in N steps. In the former case, considerable hardware complexity is involved, in the latter a considerable amount of time, as Fig. 24.41 shows. If we assume e.g. 100 ns for the basic operation, i.e. multiplication and addition (MAC), sampling frequencies of 10 MHz can be achieved with parallel processing, otherwise only the Nth part thereof.

Processing	Multipliers	Adders	Computing time	Memory
Parallel	$N + 1$	N	1 clock period	$2N + 1$
Serial	1	1	$(N + 1)$ clock periods	$2N + 1$

Fig. 24.41 Estimated requirements for Nth-order FIR filters with parallel or serial processing

To calculate Eq. (24.19), all the coefficients and the last N sampling values must of course be available in memory. In both cases this requires a memory for $2N + 1$ values.

The required word length w of the data x is determined by the signal-to-quantizing-noise ratio, which is in the order of $w \cdot 6\,\text{dB}$. The word length available for the coefficients determines the accuracy to which the calculated coefficients can be realized. They are normally selected at least as large as the data word. After multiplication, this produces words of double the word length, i.e. $2w$. When calculating the sum, the word length can increase by one bit in each step, i.e. to $2w + N$. However, the actual increase is smaller, as the majority of the coefficients $\alpha_k \ll 1$. Nevertheless, a rounding down to smaller word length is generally unavoidable if circuit complexity is to be kept within acceptable limits.

24.5.1   Realization of FIR filters by the parallel method

The structure shown in the Fig. 24.19 is particularly suitable for realizing FIR filters by the parallel method, as an entire clock period is available for an MAC operation. Multiplication of the input sequence by the filter coefficients can, in principle, be carried out by parallel multipliers. Their multiplicand is defined by connecting bit by bit to 0 or 1, depending on the value of the coefficients. It would also be possible to work out the multiplication table for each coefficient and store it in an EPROM.

However, both methods are now outdated, as integrated FIR filters are commercially available in numerous versions. These are all based on the principle illustrated in Fig. 24.19. They are highly complex circuits containing

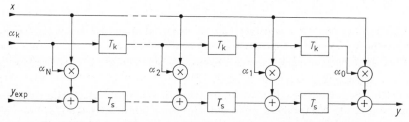

Fig. 24.42 Design of integrated FIR filters employing the parallel method

a large number of parallel multipliers, adders and memories. An additional shift register is often provided for input and storing of the coefficients, as shown in Fig. 24.42. The coefficients are read into the shift register once the supply voltage has been switched on; the filter is then configured. The coefficients may also be exchanged during operation in order to make the filter characteristic adaptive. This facility is used e.g. in echo cancellation. The coefficient input can also be used as a second signal input. In this case the arrangement calculates the cross correlation function of the input signals. The additional input y_{exp} allows similar devices to be cascaded so as to raise the filter order. Data on a number of integrated FIR filters is given in Fig. 24.43.

Type	Manufacturer	No. of coefficients	Word length	Sampling frequency	Power dissipation	Package
TMC 2243	TRW	3	10 bit	20 MHz	0.25 W	68 PGA
TMC 2246	TRW	4	10 bit	30 MHz	0.6 W	120 PGA
TDC 1028	TRW	8	4 bit	10 MHz	2.5 W	48 DIL
ZR 33481	Zoran	4	8 bit	20 MHz	0.6 W	68 LCC
ZR 33881	Zoran	8	8 bit	20 MHz	0.75 W	68 LCC
ZR 33891	Zoran	8	9 bit	20 MHz	0.75 W	84 PGA
IMS A 110	Inmos	21	8 bit	20 MHz	1 W	100 PGA
IMS A 100	Inmos	32	16 bit	2.5 MHz	1 W	84 PGA
L 64243	LSI-Logic	9	8 bit	40 MHz	1 W	68 LCC
L 64240	LSI-Logic	64	8 bit	20 MHz	2.5 W	155 PGA
IM 29 C 128*	Intersil	128	16 bit	78 kHz		64 DIL
DSP 56200*	Motorola	256	16 bit	37 kHz	0.75 W	28 DIL

* Serial

Fig. 24.43 Integrated FIR filters

24.5.2   Realization of FIR filters by the serial method

The serial realization of FIR filters is derived from the basic structure in Fig. 24.20 with a global adder at the output. A shift register is used to store the coefficients, as in Fig. 24.44. It is then possible to replace all the multipliers and adders by a single entity, as shown in Fig. 24.45. To calculate the output value, the multiplier inputs are shifted once through all the stages and the resultant subproducts are added together. The two shift registers are implemented as FIFOs (see Section 11.2.3). It is not necessary to shift the data physically, it is rather only the relevant input and output pointers that are stepped forward. This is illustrated in Fig. 24.46. This method is supported e.g. by filter control chip IM 29 C 128 from Intersil. An EPROM is additionally required in which the coefficients are stored, and a multiplier-accumulator. They are interconnected as

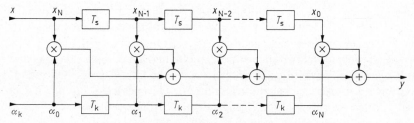

Fig. 24.44 FIR filter with global adder at output

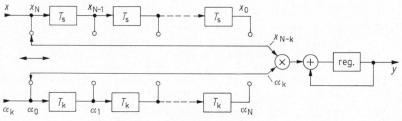

Fig. 24.45 Serial calculation of the subproducts

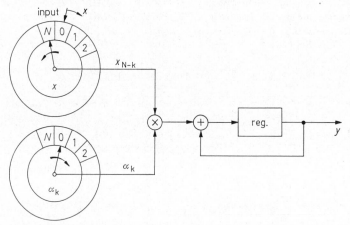

Fig. 24.46 Serial calculation of y. To calculate the output value, the two output pointers are rotated once and all the subproducts are added. Then the next value x is read in

shown in Fig. 24.47. In this way filters with 16-bit word size can be implemented, which additionally allow a sampling frequency of

$$f_s = \frac{1}{128 \cdot \tau_{MAC}} = \frac{1}{12.8 \ \mu s} \approx 78 \ \text{kHz}$$

at the maximum length of 128 coefficients if a computing time of 100 ns is assumed for the MAC [24.13].

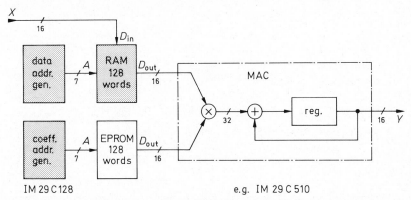

Fig. 24.47 FIR filter employing the serial method, using filter control chip Im29C128 (shaded) from Intersil

FIR processor DSP 56200 from Motorola provides a compact solution. Here the entire arrangement shown in Fig. 24.47 is integrated on a single chip. The maximum filter length is here 256 coefficients. The DSP 56200 is a digital signal processor from the DSP 56000 family which contains an application-specific program for FIR filters. Of course it is also possible to use any other signal processor if one writes the required program oneself. A number of freely programmable signal processors are listed in Fig. 24.60.

24.6 Design analysis of IIR filters

The recursive filters are also known as infinite impulse response (IIR) filters, as their impulse response possesses—at least theoretically—an infinite number of non-zero sampling values. Their basic structure and transfer functions, which have already been discussed in Section 24.3, apply to digital filters in general.

24.6.1 Calculating the filter coefficients

Two methods in particular are commonly used to calculate the filter coeffic-ients, the Yulewalk Algorithm and the bilinear transformation. The Yulewalk Algorithm [24.10/14] approximates a given tolerance scheme in the frequency domain by means of a minimum number of filter coefficients. It thus provides coefficients for a minimized IIR filter and therefore represents the analogon to the Remez Exchange Algorithm for FIR filters. We shall now describe the bilinear transformation in greater detail because it is less computationally intensive and therefore facilitates understanding of the principles involved.

The bilinear transformation is based on the frequency response of an analog filter and attempts to model it as accurately as possible with an IIR filter. However, this is not directly possible, as the transfer function of a digital filter can only be utilized up to half the sampling frequency $\frac{1}{2}f_s$ and must be periodic

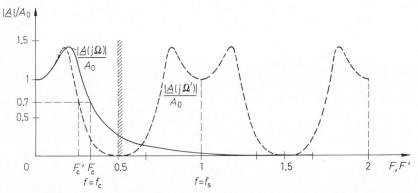

Fig. 24.48 Producing a periodic amplitude-frequency response. Second-order Chebyshev characteristic with 3 dB ripple as example.

Cutoff frequency: $F_c = 0.3$, i.e. $f_c = 0.3 f_s$. Linear plot

beyond that. For this reason, the amplitude frequency response of the analog filter in the range $0 \leq f \leq \infty$ is mapped into the range $0 \leq f' \leq \frac{1}{2} f_s$ of the digital filter and continued periodically. A transformation possessing this characteristic is

$$f = \frac{f_s}{\pi} \tan \frac{\pi f'}{f_s} \ . \tag{24.38}$$

For $f \to \infty$, f' tends to $\frac{1}{2} f_s$, as required. For $f' \ll f_s$, we have $f \approx f'$. The compression of the frequency axis is therefore smaller the higher the clock frequency f_s with respect to the frequency range of interest.

In order to be able to employ normalized frequencies as with the analog filters, we normalize all the frequencies to the sampling frequency:

$$F = f/f_s \quad \text{or} \quad F_c = f_c/f_s \ . \tag{24.39}$$

Equation (24.38) therefore becomes:

$$F = \frac{1}{\pi} \tan \pi F' \ . \tag{24.40}$$

To illustrate the transformation of the frequency axis, we have plotted in Fig. 24.48 the amplitude-frequency response of a second-order Chebyshev low-pass filter. We can see that the typical passband characteristic is retained, although the cutoff frequency is shifted. In order to avoid this effect, we introduce a factor l into Eq. (24.40) for frequency mapping. We select this factor such that the cutoff frequency is retained in the transformation, i.e. $F_c = F_c'$:

$$F = \underbrace{F_c \cot \pi F_c}_{l} \tan \pi F' \ . \tag{24.41}$$

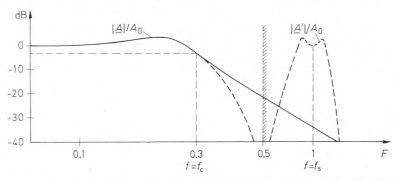

Fig. 24.49 Matching the cutoff frequency. Second-order Chebyshev characteristic with 3 dB ripple as example.

Cutoff frequency: $F_c = 0.3$, i.e. $f_c = 0.3 f_s$. Logarithmic plot

The resultant frequency response curve is shown in Fig. 24.49. We interpret the formally introduced quantity F' as a new frequency variable F and denote the transformed frequency response by $\underline{A}'(j\Omega)$. We can see that this provides a good approximation to the analog filter characteristic.

The transformed frequency response $\underline{A}'(jF)$ now possesses a shape which can be implemented using a digital filter. To calculate the digital transfer function $\tilde{A}(z)$ we now require the transformation equation for the complex frequency variable S. With $S = j\Omega = jF/F_c$, it follows from Eq. (24.41) that

$$S = l \cdot j \tan \pi F .$$

Using the mathematical transformation

$$j \tan x = -\tanh(-jx) = \frac{1 - e^{-2jx}}{1 + e^{-2jx}}$$

and the definition of $z^{-1} = e^{-2\pi jF}$ we therefore obtain

$$\boxed{S = l\frac{1 - e^{-2\pi jF}}{1 + e^{-2\pi jF}} = l\frac{1 - z^{-1}}{1 + z^{-1}} \quad \text{with} \quad l = \cot \pi F_c} . \tag{24.42}$$

This relation is known as the bilinear transformation.

To summarize, an analog filter function can be transformed into a digital function as follows: in the analog transfer function $A(S)$, the normalized frequency variable S is replaced by $l(z - 1)/(z + 1)$ and a transfer function $A(z)$ is obtained which can be implemented by a digital filter. The amplitude-frequency response is therefore very similar in shape to that of the analog filter. The characteristic is compressed on the f axis so that the value $|\underline{A}(j\infty)|$ appears at frequency $\frac{1}{2}f_s$. The resultant deviations are smaller, the larger the value of f_s compared to the frequency range $0 < f < f_{max}$ of interest.

However, the phase-frequency response is changed to a far greater extent. Consequently, the statements relating to analog filters cannot be directly applied to digital filters. It would be of no avail, for example, to approximate the amplitude-frequency response of a Bessel filter, because the linearity of the phase delay is lost. If a filter with linear phase is required, it is preferable to use an FIR filter.

To calculate the filter coefficients of IIR filters, we insert into the frequency response of the linear filter

$$A(S) = \frac{d_0 + d_1 S + d_2 S^2 + \ldots}{c_0 + c_1 S + c_2 S^2 + \ldots} = \frac{\sum\limits_{k=0}^{N} d_k S^k}{\sum\limits_{k=0}^{N} c_k S^k} \qquad (24.43)$$

the bilinear transformation (24.42)

$$S = l \frac{1 - z^{-1}}{1 + z^{-1}} .$$

Coefficient comparison with the general frequency response (24.16) of an IIR filter

$$A(z) = \frac{\alpha_0 + \alpha_1 z^{-1} + \alpha_2 z^{-2} + \ldots}{1 + \beta_1 z^{-1} + \beta_2 z^{-2} + \ldots} = \frac{\sum\limits_{k=0}^{N} \alpha_k z^{-k}}{1 + \sum\limits_{k=1}^{N} \beta_k z^{-k}}$$

then yields the required filter coefficients α_k and β_k.

24.6.2 IIR filters in cascade structure

The simplest method of implementing digital filters, as in the case of analog filters, is to cascade first- and second-order blocks. In this case the values tabulated in Fig. 14.14 for analog filters can also be used to calculate the filter coefficients. The recalculation of the filter coefficients is therefore given below in more detail.

First-order IIR filters

The structure of a first-order IIR filter shown in Fig. 24.50 is derived from Fig. 24.15 for the case $N = 1$. From the first-order *analog* transfer function

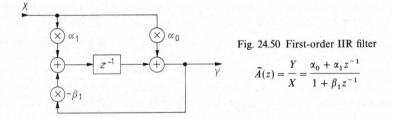

Fig. 24.50 First-order IIR filter

$$\tilde{A}(z) = \frac{Y}{X} = \frac{\alpha_0 + \alpha_1 z^{-1}}{1 + \beta_1 z^{-1}}$$

$$A(S) = \frac{d_0 + d_1 S}{c_0 + c_1 S} \tag{24.44}$$

we obtain, by using the bilinear transformation, the digital transfer function

$$\tilde{A}(z) = \frac{\alpha_0 + \alpha_1 z^{-1}}{1 + \beta_1 z^{-1}} \tag{24.45}$$

with the coefficients

$$\alpha_0 = \frac{d_0 + d_1 l}{c_0 + c_1 l} \; ; \quad \alpha_1 = \frac{d_0 - d_1 l}{c_0 + c_1 l} \; ; \quad \beta_1 = \frac{c_0 - c_1 l}{c_0 + c_1 l} \; . \tag{24.46}$$

Applying these general equations to a lowpass filter:

$$A(S) = \frac{A_0}{1 + a_1 S} \Rightarrow \tilde{A}(z) = \alpha_0 \frac{1 + z^{-1}}{1 + \beta_1 z^{-1}} \; ; \tag{24.47}$$

$$\alpha_0 = \alpha_1 = \frac{A_0}{1 + a_1 l} \; ; \quad \beta_1 = \frac{1 - a_1 l}{1 + a_1 l} \; . \tag{24.48}$$

Similarly, for a highpass filter:

$$A(S) = \frac{A_\infty}{1 + a_1 \dfrac{1}{S}} = \frac{A_\infty S}{a_1 + S} \Rightarrow \tilde{A}(z) = \alpha_0 \frac{1 - z^{-1}}{1 + \beta_1 z^{-1}} \; ;$$

$$\alpha_0 = -\alpha_1 = \frac{A_\infty l}{a_1 + l} \; ; \quad \beta_1 = \frac{a_1 - l}{a_1 + l} \; . \tag{24.49}$$

By way of example, we shall calculate the coefficients for a first-order highpass filter with $a_1 = 1$. Its cutoff frequency shall be $f_c = 100$ Hz, the bandwidth of the input signal 3.4 kHz. We select $f_s = 10$ kHz and obtain the normalized cutoff frequency

$$F_c = f_c/f_s = 100 \text{ Hz}/10 \text{ kHz} = 0.01 \; .$$

This yields the normalization factor

$$l = \cot \pi F_c = \cot \pi \cdot 0.01 = 31.82 \; .$$

Hence, from Eq. (24.49)

$$\alpha_0 = -\alpha_1 = 0.9695 \quad \text{and} \quad \beta_1 = -0.9391 \; .$$

The digital transfer function is therefore

$$\tilde{A}(z) = \frac{\alpha_0 + \alpha_1 z^{-1}}{1 + \beta_1 z^{-1}} = \frac{0.9695 - 0.9695 z^{-1}}{1 - 0.9391 z^{-1}} \; .$$

The ratio of the sampling frequency to the cutoff frequency is determined by the parameters selected and has the value 100. The cutoff frequency is therefore proportional to the sampling frequency. It can therefore be simply controlled using the sampling frequency. This characteristic is peculiar to all digital filters. The only other filters exhibiting this property are the switched-capacitor types described in Section 14.10.

Second-order IIR filters

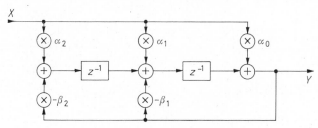

Fig. 24.51 Second-order IIR filter

$$\tilde{A}(z) = \frac{Y}{X} = \frac{\alpha_0 + \alpha_1 z^{-1} + \alpha_2 z^{-2}}{1 + \beta_1 z^{-1} + \beta_2 z^{-2}}$$

A second-order IIR filter obtained by particularizing Fig. 24.15 is shown in Fig. 24.51. Into the linear transfer function

$$A(S) = \frac{d_0 + d_1 S + d_2 S^2}{c_0 + c_1 S + c_2 S^2}$$

we insert the bilinear transformation as defined in Eq. (24.42) and obtain

$$\tilde{A}(z) = \frac{\alpha_0 + \alpha_1 z^{-1} + \alpha_2 z^{-2}}{1 + \beta_1 z^{-1} + \beta_2 z^{-2}} \tag{24.50}$$

with the coefficients

$$\alpha_0 = \frac{d_0 + d_1 l + d_2 l^2}{c_0 + c_1 l + c_2 l^2} \; ; \quad \alpha_1 = \frac{2(d_0 - d_2 l^2)}{c_0 + c_1 l + c_2 l^2} \; ; \quad \alpha_2 = \frac{d_0 - d_1 l + d_2 l^2}{c_0 + c_1 l + c_2 l^2} \; ;$$

$$\beta_1 = \frac{2(c_0 - c_2 l^2)}{c_0 + c_1 l + c_2 l^2} \; ; \quad \beta_2 = \frac{c_0 - c_1 l + c_2 l^2}{c_0 + c_1 l + c_2 l^2} \; .$$

From this, we can calculate the following second-order filters:

Lowpass filter (Eq. (24.51))

$$A(S) = \frac{A_0}{1 + a_1 S + b_1 S^2} \Rightarrow \tilde{A}(z) = \alpha_0 \frac{1 + 2z^{-1} + z^{-2}}{1 + \beta_1 z^{-1} + \beta_2 z^{-2}} \; ;$$

$$\alpha_0 = \frac{A_0}{1 + a_1 l + b_1 l^2} \; ; \quad \beta_1 = \frac{2(1 - b_1 l^2)}{1 + a_1 l + b_1 l^2} \; ; \quad \beta_2 = \frac{1 - a_1 l + b_1 l^2}{1 + a_1 l + b_1 l^2} \; .$$

Highpass filter (Eq. (24.52))

$$A(S) = \frac{A_\infty S^2}{b_1 + a_1 S + S^2} \Rightarrow \tilde{A}(z) = \alpha_0 \frac{1 - 2z^{-1} + z^{-2}}{1 + \beta_1 z^{-1} + \beta_2 z^{-2}} \; ;$$

$$\alpha_0 = \frac{A_\infty l^2}{b_1 + a_1 l + l^2} \; ; \quad \beta_1 = \frac{2(b_1 - l^2)}{b_1 + a_1 l + l^2} \; ; \quad \beta_2 = \frac{b_1 - a_1 l + l^2}{b_1 + a_1 l + l^2} \; .$$

Bandpass filter (Eq. (24.53))

$$A(S) = \frac{A_r S/Q}{1 + S/Q + S^2} \Rightarrow \tilde{A}(z) = \alpha_0 \frac{1 - z^{-2}}{1 + \beta_1 z^{-1} + \beta_2 z^{-2}} \; ;$$

$$\alpha_0 = \frac{l A_r/Q}{1 + l/Q + l^2} \; ; \quad \beta_1 = \frac{2(1 - l^2)}{1 + l/Q + l^2} \; ; \quad \beta_2 = \frac{1 - l/Q + l^2}{1 + l/Q + l^2} \; .$$

Band-stop filter (Eq. (24.54))

$$A(S) = \frac{A_0(1 + S^2)}{1 + S/Q + S^2} \Rightarrow \tilde{A}(z) = \frac{\alpha_0 + A_0 \beta_1 z^{-1} + \alpha_0 z^{-2}}{1 + \beta_1 z^{-1} + \beta_2 z^{-2}} \; ;$$

$$\alpha_0 = \frac{A_0(1 + l^2)}{1 + l/Q + l^2} \; ; \quad \beta_1 = \frac{2(1 - l^2)}{1 + l/Q + l^2} \; ; \quad \beta_2 = \frac{1 - l/Q + l^2}{1 + l/Q + l^2} \; .$$

We shall now discuss the design procedure with the aid of a worked example. We require a second-order Chebyshev lowpass filter with 0.5 dB ripple and a 3 dB cutoff frequency $f_c = 100$ Hz. The analog signal shall have a bandwidth of 3.4 kHz and be sampled at $f_s = 10$ kHz. This gives us a normalized cutoff frequency of $F_c = 0.01$ and a normalizing factor $l = 31.82$. From Table 14.14 we can obtain $a_1 = 1.3614$ and $b_1 = 1.3827$. This produces the continuous transfer function

$$A(S) = \frac{1}{1 + 1.3614 S + 1.3827 S^2} \; .$$

Using Eq. (24.51) we obtain from this the digital transfer function

$$\tilde{A}(z) = 6.923 \cdot 10^{-4} \frac{1 + 2z^{-1} + z^2}{1 - 1.937 z^{-1} + 0.9400 z^{-2}} \; .$$

As a second example, we shall design a bandpass filter. The sampling frequency shall be 10 kHz as before. The resonant frequency shall be $f_r = 1$ kHz. Hence $F_c = 1$ kHz$/10$ kHz $= 0.1$. For $Q = 10$, the continuous transfer function in accordance with Eq. (14.24) for $A_r = 1$ is of the form

$$A(S) = \frac{0.1 S}{1 + 0.1 S + S^2} \; .$$

Using $l = \cot \pi F_c = 3.078$ and Eq. (24.53), we obtain the digital transfer function

$$\tilde{A}(z) = -2.855 \cdot 10^{-2} \frac{1 - z^{-2}}{1 - 1.572 z^{-1} + 0.9429 z^{-2}} \, .$$

Similarly, for $Q = 100$ we obtain

$$\tilde{A}(z) = -2.930 \cdot 10^{-3} \frac{1 - z^{-2}}{1 - 1.613 z^{-1} + 0.9941 z^{-2}} \, .$$

We shall now consider the case $Q = 10$ and $F_r = 0.01$. This gives

$$\tilde{A}(z) = -3.130 \cdot 10^{-3} \frac{1 - z^{-2}}{1 - 1.990 z^{-1} + 0.9937 z^{-2}} \, .$$

We can see that as Q increases or the resonant frequency F_r decreases, the coefficient α_0 becomes continually smaller, whereas $\beta_2 \to 1$ and $\beta_1 \to -2$. The information on the filter characteristic is therefore to be found in the very small deviation with respect to 1 or -2. This means an increasing accuracy requirement on the filter coefficients resulting in a correspondingly large word length in the filter. In order to minimize circuit complexity, the sampling rate must therefore not be selected any larger than necessary.

24.7 Realization of IIR filters

24.7.1 Construction from simple building blocks

We shall now demonstrate the procedure for arriving at the simplest possible circuit, using the first-order highpass filter example from Section 24.6.2. There we have already calculated the digital transfer function for a highpass filter with a cutoff frequency $f_c = 100$ Hz at a sampling rate $f_s = 10\,\text{kHz}$, i.e. $F_c = 0.01$:

$$\tilde{A}(z) = \frac{\alpha_0 + \alpha_1 z^{-1}}{1 + \beta_1 z^{-1}} = \frac{0.9695 - 0.9695 z^{-1}}{1 - 0.9391 z^{-1}} \, .$$

The corresponding circuit is shown in Fig. 24.52. We can see that the three coefficients are close to 1. The numerator coefficients α_0 and α_1 can be rounded to 1 without any appreciable error, as they only determine the gain. This does not apply to coefficient β_1 whose deviation from 1 determines the filter cutoff frequency. However, in this case simplification is possible by the transformation

$$\beta_1 = 1 - \beta_1' = -0.9391 = -(1 - 0.0609) \, ,$$

where $\beta_1' = 1 - \beta_1$ is the deviation from unity. This coefficient possesses substantially fewer significant digits than β_1. The nearest power of two is $2^{-4} = 0.0625$. The binary arithmetic can be greatly reduced by rounding β_1' to this value, as a multiplication by 2^{-4} only represents a shift by 4 digits which can

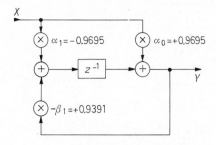

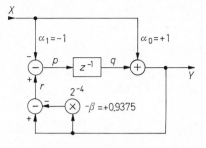

Fig. 24.52 First-order IIR highpass filter

Fig. 24.53 IIR highpass filter with simplified coefficients

$$\tilde{A}(z) = \frac{0.9695 - 0.9695z^{-1}}{1 - 0.9391z^{-1}}$$

$$F_c = f_c/f_s = 0.01$$

$$A(f = 0.5 f_s) = 1$$

$$\tilde{A}(z) = \frac{1 - z^{-1}}{1 - (1 - 2^{-4})z^{-1}}$$

$$F_c = f_c/f_s = 0.0103$$

$$A(f = 0.5 f_s) = 1.032$$

be implemented by appropriate wiring. From Eq. (24.44) the resulting shift in cutoff frequency is given by

$$l = \frac{1 - \beta_1}{\beta_1} = \frac{2 - 2^{-4}}{2^{-4}} = 31 \ , \quad \text{thus} \quad F_c = 0.0103 \ ,$$

i.e. the cutoff frequency increases to $f_c = 103$ Hz.

We simplify further by rounding the numerator coefficients to $\alpha_0 = -\alpha_1 = 1$, and use Eq. (24.44) to obtain, for high frequencies ($f \approx \frac{1}{2}f_s$), the gain

$$A_\infty = \alpha_0 \frac{1 + l}{l} = 1 \frac{1 + 31}{31} = 1.032 \ .$$

This small deviation is also acceptable. The resulting simplified arrangement is shown in Fig. 24.53. We can see that in simple filters it is possible to reduce the circuit considerably by slightly modifying the design objective.

The practical implementation is shown in Fig. 24.54 for an input word length of 4 bit. In order to be able to represent positive and negative numbers, we have selected the two's-complement notation introduced in Section 19.1.3. The highest-order bit is therefore the sign bit. As we can perform the multiplication by shifting, only adding circuits are required. For this purpose we use 4-bit arithmetic circuits of type SN 74 LS 382. These can also be operated as subtractors by controlling appropriate inputs. In this way the computation of the two's-complement of the coefficients $\alpha_1 = -1$ and $-\beta_1 = 1 - 2^{-4}$ can be carried out in the adder.

The two arithmetic circuits IC 8 and IC 9 form the expression

$$r = -\beta_1 y = y - 2^{-4} y \ .$$

Multiplication of y by 2^{-4} is achieved by connecting y, displaced by four digits, to the subtractor. This increases the word length from 4 to 8 bit.

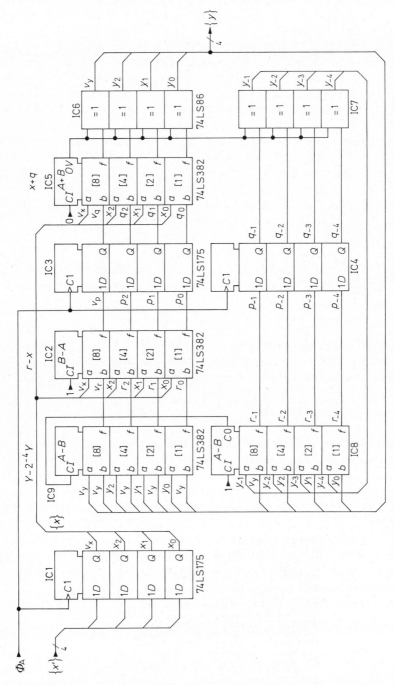

Fig. 24.54 Circuit implementation of a digital IIR highpass filter with a word length of 8 bit internal and 4 bit external

The sign bit v_y must be connected to *all* the vacated digits, so that multiplication of y by 2^{-4} can be carried out correctly for both positive and negative values of y (sign extension).

Arithmetic unit IC 2 performs the subtraction $r - x$ at the input of Fig. 24.53, IC 5 the addition $x + q$ at the output. The delay by one clock period is achieved by ICs 3 and 4, each of which contains four single-edge triggered D flip-flops. The flip-flops in IC 1 are used to synchronize the input signal.

The exclusive-OR gate in IC 6 and 7 provide latch-up protection: as we have already seen in Section 19.1.3, a jump from $+127$ to -128 would occur if the positive number range is exceeded, as the highest-order bit is read as the sign. This unwanted sign change may destabilize the filter in the overdriven state and it may not return to normal operation. This corresponds precisely to the latch-up effect in analog circuitry. One way of preventing it is to set the numbers at the adder output to $+127$ for positive overflow and to -128 for negative overflow. For this purpose the positive and negative overflow would have to be decoded separately.

However, a distinction between these two cases is unnecessary if the outputs are complemented in the event of an overflow. This produces the characteristic shown in Fig. 24.55. To implement it, exclusive-OR gates are connected to the

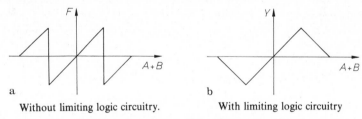

a Without limiting logic circuitry.   b With limiting logic circuitry

Fig. 24.55 Overflow characteristics of the arithmetic units

outputs f_i of those arithmetic units at which an overflow can occur, as in Fig. 24.54. This produces a complementation when $OV = 1$. Arithmetic units 74 LS 382 have an advantage over standard types 74 LS 181 in that the overflow variable OV is directly available and does not have to be generated externally.

The operation of the digital filter is clearly shown by the step response in Fig. 24.56.

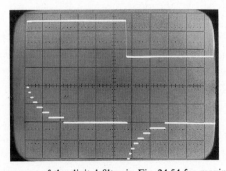

Fig. 24.56 Step response of the digital filter in Fig. 24.54 for maximum input swing

24.7.2 Design using LSI devices

There are three methods of implementing IIR filters using LSI circuitry:

1) using specific IIR filters,
2) using FIR filters,
3) using programmable signal processors.

Few specific IIR filters are available. The MS 2014 from Plessey is a second-order filter block of the type shown in Fig. 24.51 for data with 16 bit and coefficients with 13 bit word length. However, it is relatively slow as its multipliers operate serially. Consequently, sampling rates of no more than 64 kHz are achievable.

An IIR filter can be constructed from two FIR filters, of which numerous versions are available as LSI circuits, as shown in Fig. 24.43. It is possible to start with the basic structure in Fig. 24.16 with global adders at the input and output and to double the delay chain. This results in the circuit shown in Fig. 24.57 in which we can identify the two FIR filters. Whether the FIR filters employ—as shown here—a global adder at the output or distributed adders as in Fig. 24.19, is unimportant. The result is in both cases the same if the coefficients are arranged accordingly. FIR filter IMS A 100 from Inmos represents a particularly efficient implementation of the principle illustrated in Fig. 24.57. Here, two sets of coefficients can be stored and a control variable can be used to specify which set is to be active at any one time. In this way it is possible to calculate first y_1 using the coefficients β_k and then the value y using α_k [24.15]. The additional adder at the input can be implemented by one of the arithmetic units used in Figs. 19.34/36.

The basic structure shown in Fig. 24.17 can also be broken down into two FIR filters if the global adder at the output is split into two sections. In Fig. 24.58 we can see that this produces two FIR filters whose partial effects (i.e. results) can be combined using an additional adder.

Single-chip signal processors are the most suitable devices for serial method implementation of IIR filters, as they possess the required data memories in addition to a parallel multiplier with accumulator. The calculation of the filter output sequence can be programmed at machine level in Assembler, as on a microprocessor. Recently, the programming is being supported in a higher-level language such as "C". For programming, it is best to start from the basic structure with a global adder at the output, as in Fig. 24.58. As Fig. 24.59 shows, the new value of the output sequence can then be calculated in accordance with Eq. (24.15)

$$y_N = \sum_{k=0}^{N} \alpha_k x_{N-k} - \sum_{k=1}^{N} \beta_k y_{N-k} \, ,$$

by weighting all input and feedback signals with the relevant coefficients and subsequently adding. To do this, the tap is shifted along the delay chain and the

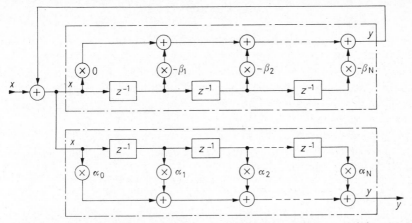

Fig. 24.57 Implementation of an IIR filter with a global adder at the input and the output, from two FIR filters and one additional adder

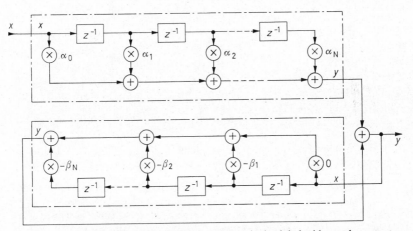

Fig. 24.58 Implementation of an IIR filter using a single global adder at the output, from two FIR filters and one additional adder

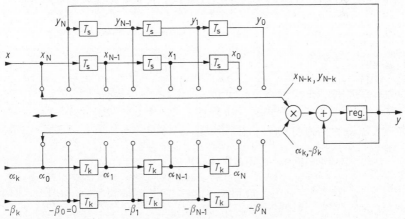

Fig. 24.59 Serial implementation of an IIR filter with a single global adder at the output, preferably using a programmable signal processor

particular coefficient α_k or β_k is selected. When the entire chain has been run through once, the new function value y_N is available. Then the contents of the two shift registers can be shifted forward by one clock, in order to calculate a further function value y in the next pass. The data are, of course, not shifted physically: only the pointers addressing the values x_k, y_k, α_k and β_k are made to rotate.

Using a signal processor it is just as easy to make design calculations for IIR filters in cascade form. For this purpose the order of the filter in Fig. 24.59 is reduced to $N = 2$ and we calculate

$$y_2 = \alpha_0 x_2 + \alpha_1 x_1 + \alpha_2 x_0 - \beta_1 y_1 - \beta_2 y_0$$

using a small subroutine. The entire filter is therefore obtained by repeatedly calling up the program for a second-order filter and exchanging the relevant data or coefficient sets.

Figure 24.60 provides an overview of a number of more recent signal processors. The preferred number notations are 16-bit fixed point numbers for universal applications or 32-bit floating point numbers for high accuracy and dynamic range. The data word length of the accumulator is generally more than twice that size, in order to ensure that the rounding errors have no effect on the result. The majority of signal processors have high-speed data and program memories on the chip. These should be used where possible, because each external memory access results in the insertion of wait states even if the access times are short.

Type	Manufac-turer	Data word length [bit]	Internal memory data/prog. [words]	External memory data/prog. [words]	Cycle time MAC	Power dissi-pation	Package
ADSP 2102	Analog Dev.	16	1 k/2 k	16 k/16 k	80 ns	0.8 W	68 LCC
DSP 16A	AT&T	16	2 k/4 k	64 k/64 k	25 ns	0.5 W	84 LCC
DSP 32C	AT&T	24 E8	1 k/2 k	16 M/16 M	80 ns	1.2 W	133 PGA
MB 86232	Fujitsu	{ 24 24 E8	512/1 k	1 M/64 k	75 ns } 150 ns	1.5 W	208 PGA
DSP 56001	Motorola	24	1 k/512	128 k/64 k	75 ns	0.5 W	88 PGA
DSP 96002	Motorola	24 E8	2 k/1 k	4 G/4 G	75 ns		214 PGA
μPD 77220	NEC	24	1 k/2 k	8 k/4 k	150 ns	1 W	68 PGA
μPD 77230	NEC	24 E8	1 k/2 k	8 k/4 k	150 ns	1.5 W	68 PGA
MSM 699210	Oki	16 E6	512/2 k	64 k/64 k	100 ns	0.4 W	84 LCC
TS 18941	Thomson	{ 16 32	512/0	64 k/64 k	100 ns } 200 ns	0.8 W	144 PGA
TMS 320 C 25	Texas Instr	16	544/4 k	64 k/64 k	80 ns	0.9 W	68 PGA
TMS 320 C 50	Texas Instr.	16	8 k/2 k	128 k/128 k	35 ns		84 LCC
TMS 320 C 30	Texas Instr.	24 E8	2 k/4 k	16 M/16 M	60 ns	1.5 W	180 PGA
ZR 34161	Zoran	16	256/0	64 k/64 k	100 ns	0.5 W	48 DIL
ZR 34325	Zoran	24 E8	128/0	16 M/16 M	80 ns	1 W	84 PGA

Fig. 24.60 More recent signal processors

The time taken to perform a multiplication and accumulation (MAC) operation determines how rapidly a signal processor can process filter algorithms, as these consist virtually exclusively of MAC operations. For an Nth-order FIR filter, $N + 1$ MAC operations are required for each sampled value whereas an IIR filter requires $2N + 1$. In most of the more recent signal processors, a MAC operation is performed in a single machine cycle.

24.8   Comparison of FIR and IIR filters

If we compare the structure of IIR filters in Figs. 24.15–17 with that of FIR filters in Figs. 24.19/20, we can see that IIR filters of the same order require approximately twice as many MAC operations as FIR filters. However, they possess a higher selectivity than FIR filters with the same number of MAC operations. This is illustrated by the example in Fig. 24.61. Generally speaking, the required order for an FIR filter is, for the same performance, more than twice as high as for an IIR filter. In Section 24.6.2 we have shown that a lowpass filter with a low cutoff frequency of $F_c = 0.01$ can be implemented using a first-order IIR filter. For an FIR filter with this cutoff frequency, an order of at least $N = 65$ would have been required since, to a first approximation, a complete cycle at the cutoff frequency F_c is to be weighted with the coefficients, i.e.

$$N \geqq 1/F_c = f_s/f_c \ .$$

However, this characteristic must be set against a number of important advantages of FIR filters. We have seen that FIR filters can easily be used to implement a linear phase behavior, i.e. constant group delay, with precision. All the FIR filters mentioned in this section possess this characteristic, i.e. they produce no phase distortion.

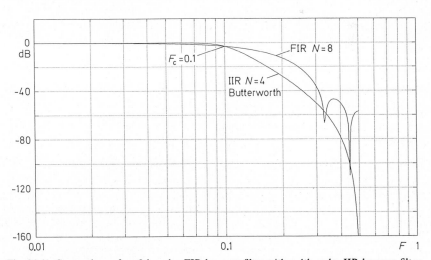

Fig. 24.61 Comparison of an 8th-order FIR lowpass filter with a 4th-order IIR lowpass filter

As FIR filters possess no feedback path, they are also stable for any coefficients. IIR filters, like analog filters, tend to oscillate more the higher their pole Q-factor or the lower their cutoff frequency compared to the sampling frequency (see Section 24.6.2). In order to ensure that no significant deviations from the calculated frequency response are incurred, the coefficients of IIR filters must be realized with considerably more precision than for FIR filters; this requires a larger word length. In addition, with IIR filters the rounding errors due to limited computational accuracy frequently result in *limit cycles*. These are periodic oscillations in the lowest-order bits which are particularly disturbing in the case of small input signals. The various advantages and disadvantages are listed in Fig. 24.62.

Feature	FIR filter	IIR filter
selectivity	low	**high**
order required	high	**low**
no. of MAC operations	many	**few**
memory requirement	high	**low**
linear phase	**easily provided**	rarely possible
constant group delay	**easily provided**	rarely possible
stability	**absolute**	limited
required word length	**reasonable**	high
required coefficient accuracy	**reasonable**	high
limit cycles	**none**	present
adaptive filter	**possible**	rarely possible

Fig. 24.62 Comparison of FIR and IIR filters

25 Measurement circuits

In the previous chapters, a number of methods for processing analog and digital signals are described. Many applications, however, require that even electrical signals must be conditioned before they can be processed in analog computing circuits or A/D converters. In such cases, measurement circuits are needed which have a low-resistance single-ended output, i.e. produce a ground-referenced output voltage.

25.1 Measurement of voltage

25.1.1 Impedance converter

If the signal voltage of a high-impedance source is to be measured without affecting the load conditions, the non-inverting amplifier (follower-with-gain, electrometer amplifier) in Fig. 7.11 can be employed for impedance conversion. It must be noted, however, that the high-impedance input is very sensitive to noise arising from capacitive stray currents in the input lead. Therefore the lead is usually screened, but this results in considerable capacitive loading of the source to ground (30 . . . 100 pF/m). For an internal source resistance of 1 GΩ, for instance, and a lead capacitance of 100 pF, an upper cutoff frequency of only 1.6 Hz is obtained.

The capacitance is not constant but can change, for example when the lead is moved. This gives rise to an additional problem in that this variation produces very large noise voltages. If, for instance, the lead is charged-up to 10 V, a change in capacitance of 1% results in a voltage step of 100 mV.

These disadvantages can be avoided if a non-inverting amplifier is employed to keep the voltage low between the inner conductor and the shield. The shield is then connected not to ground but to the amplifier output, as shown in Fig. 25.1. In this manner, the effect of the lead capacitance is reduced by the open-loop gain of the operational amplifier. Since now only the offset voltage of the amplifier appears across the lead capacitance, the noise also is eliminated to a large extent.

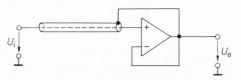

Fig. 25.1 Reduction of shield capacitance and stray current noise by allowing the shield potential to follow the measuring potential

Increasing the output voltage swing

The maximum permissible supply voltage of standard integrated operational amplifiers is usually ± 18 V. The attainable output voltage swing is thereby limited to values of about ± 15 V. This limit can be raised by allowing the operational amplifier supply potentials to follow the input voltage. This is achieved by the bootstrap circuit in Fig. 25.2, using two emitter followers to stabilize the potential differences $V_1 - U_o$ and $U_o - V_2$ to a value $U_Z - 0.7$ V. The maximum output voltage swing is thus no longer determined by the operational amplifier, but by the permissible voltage across the emitter followers and the current sources.

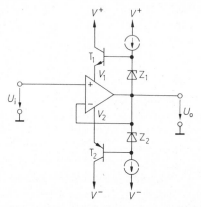

Fig. 25.2 Voltage follower for large input voltages

25.1.2 Potential difference measurement

Measurement of potential differences involves amplifying the voltage difference

$$U_D = V_2 - V_1$$

whilst minimizing the effect of the superimposed common-mode voltage

$$U_{CM} = \tfrac{1}{2}(V_2 + V_1) \ .$$

It is frequently the case that differential voltages in the millivolt range have common-mode voltages of 10 V or more superimposed on them. The quality of a subtractor is therefore characterized by its common-mode rejection

$$G = \frac{A_D}{A_{CM}} = \frac{U_o/U_D}{U_o/U_{CM}} \ .$$

In the example given, G must be greater than $10\,V/1\,mV = 10^4$. Particular problems arise if the superimposed common-mode voltage exhibits very high values or high frequencies.

There are three different methods of amplifying voltage differences:

— operational amplifiers configured as subtractors,
— differential amplifiers with feedback,
— subtraction using switched capacitors.

Subtractor with operational amplifier circuitry

In principle, the subtractor in Fig. 12.3 can be used to measure potential differences. However, the potentials to be measured often cannot be loaded with the input resistance of the subtractor because they possess considerable internal resistance. Using the additional voltage followers in Fig. 25.3 renders the operation of the subtractor independent of the internal resistances of the potentials to be measured.

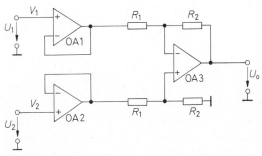

Fig. 25.3 Subtractor with preceding impedance converters

$$U_o = \frac{R_2}{R_1}(V_2 - V_1)$$

A higher common-mode rejection can be achieved by shifting the voltage gain to the impedance converters and giving the subtractor unity gain. This variant is shown in Fig. 25.4. For $R_1 = \infty$, OA 1 and OA 2 operate as voltage followers; in this case, the circuit is virtually identical to the previous one.

The circuit has the further advantage that the differential gain can be adjusted by varying a single resistor. It can be seen in Fig. 25.4 that the potential difference $V_2 - V_1$ appears across resistor R_1. Hence,

$$V_2' - V_1' = \left(1 + \frac{2R_2}{R_1}\right)(V_2 - V_1) \ .$$

This difference is transferred to the single-ended output by the subtracting amplifier OA 3.

For a purely common-mode input drive ($V_1 = V_2 = V_{CM}$), $V_1' = V_2' = V_{CM}$. The common-mode gain of OA 1 and OA 2 is therefore unity, irrespective of the differential gain chosen. With Eq. (12.6), we thus obtain the common-mode

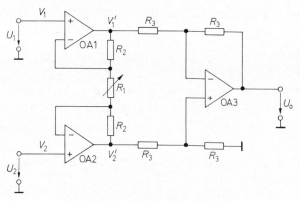

Fig. 25.4 Instrumentation amplifier

$$U_o = \left(1 + \frac{2R_2}{R_1}\right)(V_2 - V_1)$$

rejection ratio as

$$G = \left(1 + \frac{2R_2}{R_1}\right)\frac{2\alpha}{\Delta\alpha} \, ,$$

where $\Delta\alpha/\alpha$ is the relative matching tolerance of the resistors R_3.

With the instrumentation amplifier in Fig. 25.4, one op-amp can be eliminated at the expense of circuit symmetry. Electrometer amplifier OA 2 in Fig. 25.5
has the gain $1 + R_1/R_2$. OA 1 amplifies potential V_2 by $1 + R_2/R_1$ and simultaneously adds voltage V_1' injected at the base point with weighting $- R_2/R_1$.
As a result, the two input potentials are amplified by $1 + R_2/R_1$. If the circuit is
modified as in Fig. 25.6, the gain can again be set by a single resistor.

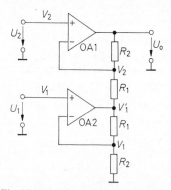

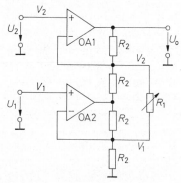

Fig. 25.5 Unbalanced instrumentation
amplifier

$$U_o = \left(1 + \frac{R_2}{R_1}\right)(V_2 - V_1)$$

Fig. 25.6 Subtractor with adjustable gain

$$U_o = 2\left(1 + \frac{R_2}{R_1}\right)(V_2 - V_1)$$

For some applications, it is acceptable to use a subtractor with only one high-impedance input. In this case, only a single operational amplifier is required, as shown in Fig. 25.7. However, the transfer equation reveals the limitation that the gain for U_2 is always less than that for U_1 in absolute-value terms (although this is no disadvantage, for example, in the case of the gain and zero offset of sensor signals). An interesting special case arises for $R_N = R_1 = R$ and $R_2 = \infty$; we then obtain the output voltage $U_o = 2U_2 - U_1$.

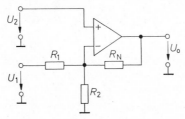

Fig. 25.7 Subtractor with a single high-impedance input

$$U_o = \left(1 + \frac{R_N}{R_1} + \frac{R_N}{R_2}\right) U_2 - \frac{R_N}{R_1} U_1$$

Subtractors for high voltages

To subtract high voltages, we can use the circuit in Fig. 25.3. The three high-voltage operational amplifiers required in this case can often be dispensed with by making $R_1 \gg R_2$; Figure 25.8 shows typical component values. The input resistance now becomes so large that the voltage followers can often be omitted. At the same time, the input voltages present at the subtractor are so low that no high-voltage operational amplifier is required. In the example, input voltages of over 200 V can be applied for a common-mode input voltage range of ± 10 V.

A disadvantage of selecting these circuit parameters is that they result in subtractors with a gain $A = R_2/R_1 \ll 1$. Although it is possible to insert a second amplifier to amplify the voltage difference by the required factor, a simpler solution is to use the circuit shown in Fig. 25.9. Here, the attenuation of high input voltages and the gain can be designed independently. Resistors R_1 and R_2 again determine the gain; the additional resistors R_3 merely reduce the common-mode input voltage. For the component values selected, we obtain unity gain, whereas the common-mode input voltage range is virtually unchanged in comparison with the example in Fig. 25.8. An IC subtractor employing this principle is the Burr Brown INA 117.

However, increasing the common-mode input voltage range with resistors R_3 in Fig. 25.9 also presents problems which must be taken into account when selecting the operational amplifiers. Resistors R_3 actually operate as attenuators for the operational amplifier input signals. They therefore reduce the loop gain

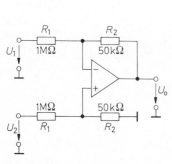

Fig. 25.8 Subtraction of high voltages

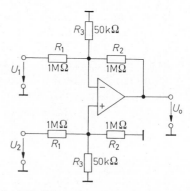

Fig. 25.9 Subtraction of high voltages with freely selectable gain

$$U_o = \frac{R_2}{R_1}(U_2 - U_1) = 0.05(U_2 - U_1)$$

$$U_{CM} = \frac{R_2}{R_1 + R_2}U_2 = 0.048\,U_2$$

$$U_o = \frac{R_2}{R_1}(U_2 - U_1) = U_2 - U_1$$

$$U_{CM} = \frac{R_2\,\|\,R_3}{R_1 + R_2\,\|\,R_3}U_2 = 0.045\,U_2$$

and, consequently, in most cases also the bandwidth. They simultaneously increase, to the same extent, the unwanted amplification of the offset voltage and offset voltage drift. As a result, a high-grade operational amplifier is required. Resistors R_3 must, of course, introduce the same attenuation on both sides, and so it is particularly important to use tightly matched resistors. In order to ensure tight matching tolerances at both operational amplifier inputs, resistors R_2 and R_3 at the non-inverting input should not generally be combined to form a single resistor.

Subtractor with differential amplifiers using negative feedback

The differential gain of a differential amplifier can be reduced to any well defined values by means of current feedback (see Section 4.8.3). On the other hand, we have seen that a differential amplifier can easily be used to obtain a high degree of common-mode rejection by employing a constant current source as the emitter resistance. Figure 25.10 shows a circuit based on this principle. The input differential amplifier T_1, T_2 has a feedback path via resistor R_G. Essentially, the collector current difference produced is converted to the output voltage by the following operational amplifier. However, an equal and opposite current difference

$$\Delta I_C = \frac{V_2 - V_1}{R_G} = -\frac{V_4 - V_3}{R_S}$$

is formed by the second differential amplifier T_3, T_4. This current difference compensates the primary current difference, so that the collector currents of T_1

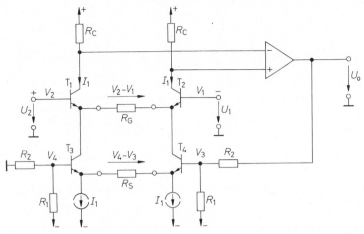

Fig. 25.10 Instrumentation amplifier with negative-feedback differential amplifiers

$$U_o = \left(1 + \frac{R_2}{R_1}\right)\frac{R_S}{R_G}(V_2 - V_1)$$

and T_2 always possess the constant value I_1 of the current sources. This is achieved by feedback via the operational amplifier, whose output voltage assumes a value such that its input voltage difference becomes zero; however, it is precisely then that the collector currents of T_1 and T_2 are of equal magnitude. Allowing for the attenuation of voltage dividers R_1, R_2 in accordance with $V_3 - V_4 = U_o R_1/(R_1 + R_2)$, we obtain under steady-state conditions the output voltage

$$U_o = \left(1 + \frac{R_2}{R_1}\right)\frac{R_S}{R_G}(V_2 - V_1) \ .$$

Resistors R_1 and R_2 are already specified in ICs based on this principle. The user is therefore able to fix the gain at the desired value using R_S and R_G. The advantage of this circuit compared to the operational amplifier subtractor is that the degree of common-mode rejection is not dependent on the matching tolerance of voltage dividers R_1, R_2. For this reason, the circuit in Fig. 25.10 can be manufactured entirely in monolithic IC form, whereas the critical resistors would otherwise have to be implemented separately in thin-film technology.

Subtractors realized in SC technology

Using this method, a capacitor is basically charged up to the voltage difference to be measured and the charge is then transferred to a single-ended capacitor. The resulting circuit is shown in Fig. 25.11. As long as the switch is in the position shown, storage capacitor C_S is charged to the level of the input voltage difference. In the other switch position, the charge is transferred to

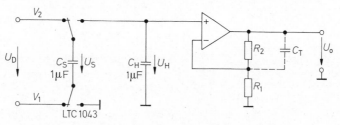

Fig. 25.11 Subtractor in switched-capacitor technology

$$U_o = \left(1 + \frac{R_2}{R_1}\right)(V_2 - V_1)$$

holding capacitor C_H. After a number of switching cycles, voltage U_H will have increased to the steady-state value

$$U_H = U_S = U_D = V_2 - V_1 \ .$$

This voltage can be amplified as required in the following electrometer amplifier, as no further subtraction is required in this case.

The subtraction accuracy is almost entirely determined by stray capacitances of the switches. In order to minimize their effect, we select relatively high values for C_S and C_H, e.g. 1 µF, as proposed in the circuit. If a Linear Technology LTC 1043 is used as the switch, a common-mode rejection ratio of 120 dB = 10^6 can be achieved, and this not only for DC voltages but also up to frequencies of 20 kHz [25.1]. The LTC 1043 is particularly suitable for this purpose, as it contains, in addition to 4 change-over switches, an oscillator which controls the switches.

The circuit contains three lowpass filters which limit the bandwidth. The first lowpass filter is produced when storage capacitor C_S is charged. The on-state resistance of the two switches (2 × 240 Ω for the LTC 1043) and the internal resistance of the source determine the charge time constant. Consequently, for low source resistances it is approximately 0.5 ms.

A second lowpass filter is produced during the charge transfer to holding capacitor C_H. If voltage $U_H = 0$, it increases in the first step to $\frac{1}{2}U_D$, in the second to $\frac{3}{4}U_D$ and in the third to $\frac{7}{8}U_D$, etc. The resulting time constant is therefore approximately 2 switch cycles. In order to minimize parasitic charge transfer during switching, low switching frequencies of around 500 Hz $\hat{=}$ 2 ms are selected. Consequently, the circuit can only process low-frequency difference signals, the upper limit being 10 ... 50 Hz. Superimposed common-mode voltages and ripple voltages of up to 20 kHz have no effect.

A third lowpass filter is provided by capacitor C_T. It is inserted to limit the amplifier bandwidth to the frequency range for which the amplifier is used in order to reduce output noise.

Examples of IC instrumentation amplifiers are listed in Fig. 25.12.

Type	Manufacturer	Gain		Input current		Offset voltage	Circuit Fig.	Remarks
INA 105	Burr Brown	1		20	µA/V	50 µV	25.8	inexpensive
INA 106	Burr Brown	10		50	µA/V	50 µV	25.8	inexpensive
INA 117	Burr Brown	1		2.5	µA/V	120 µV	25.9	$U_i = \pm 200$ V
INA 101	Burr Brown	1	... 1000	5	nA	25 µV	25.4	
INA 102	Burr Brown	1	... 1000	10	nA	100 µV	25.4	$I_b = 0.5$ mA
INA 103	Burr Brown	1	... 100	2.5	µA	50 µV	25.4	$U_n = 1$ nV/$\sqrt{\text{Hz}}$
INA 110	Burr Brown	1	... 500	20	pA	50 µV	25.4	inexpensive
PGA 202	Burr Brown	1	... 1000	10	pA	300 µV	25.4	digit. gain adjust.
LTC 1100	Lin. Techn.	100		25	pA	2 µV	25.5	chopper stab.
LT 1101	Lin. Techn.	10, 100		6	nA	50 µV	25.5	$P = 0.5$ mW
LT 1102	Lin. Techn.	10, 100		10	pA	200 µV	25.5	$\Delta U_o/\Delta t = 25$ V/µs
AMP 01	PMI	0.1	... 10000	1	nA	20 µV	25.10	$I_o = 50$ mA
AMP 02	PMI	1	... 10000	20	pA	20 µV	25.10	
AMP 05	PMI	1	... 1000	20	pA	300 µV	25.10	$\Delta U_o/\Delta t = 5$ V/µs
AD 624	Anal. Dev.	1	... 1000	25	nA	25 µV	25.4	
AD 625	Anal. Dev.	1	... 10000	10	nA	25 µV	25.4	
LM 363	National	10	... 1000	2	nA	30 µV	25.10	inexpensive
LH 0084	National	1	... 100	150	pA	300 µV	25.4	digit. gain adjust

Fig. 25.12 Instrumentation amplifiers

25.1.3   Isolation amplifiers

Using the instrumentation amplifiers described above, voltages from 10 to 200 V can be processed, depending on the circuit principle employed. There are many applications, however, in which the voltage to be measured is superimposed on a considerably higher common-mode voltage of perhaps several kV. To deal with such high potentials, the measuring circuit is split, as in Fig. 25.13, into two electrically isolated units. Electrical isolation may also be required for safety reasons, e.g. in most medical applications. The transmitter unit operates at the measuring potential, the receiver unit at system ground. To enable it to operate in this way, the transmitter must have its own floating supply, the common of which is used as one of the two differential inputs (floating ground). Although this terminal is electrically isolated from system ground, it must not be forgotten that there is still some capacitive coupling due mainly to the capacitance C_s of the supply transformer. This is indicated in Fig. 25.13. To keep the coupling low, it is advisable not to use a mains supply transformer but a high-frequency transformer for about 100 kHz, fed from a separate oscillator. In this way, coupling capacitances C_s of less than 10 pF can be achieved.

If both test points have a high internal resistance, even the reduced stray capacitance current may produce a considerable voltage between test point 2 and floating ground. In such a case, it is advisable to connect the floating ground terminal to a third point and to determine the potential difference between the two measuring points with the instrumentation amplifier of Fig. 25.4. The measuring leads then carry no current; the instrumentation amplifier is connected to the floating supply. The remaining common-mode voltage with respect to floating ground can usually be kept low if the floating ground is connected to a suitable potential within the circuit being tested.

There is still the question of electrically isolated transmission of the measured voltage to the receiver unit. Three methods exist: transformers, opto-couplers or capacitors [25.1, 25.2]. For transmission by transformers or capacitors [25.1, 25.2], the signal must be modulated on a carrier of sufficiently high frequency (amplitude modulation or pulse-width modulation), whereas opto-

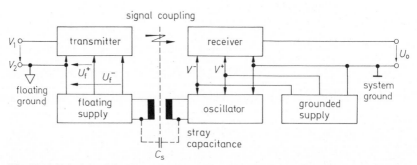

Fig. 25.13 Principle of floating voltage measurement with an electrically isolated amplifier

couplers enable the direct transmission of DC voltages. When high accuracy is required, the analog signal can be digitized at floating-ground potential, and the digital values subsequently transmitted by opto-couplers to the receiver unit. The non-linearity of the opto-coupler is then no longer significant.

A method of optical analog transmission is presented in Fig. 25.14. In order to compensate for the linearity error of the opto-coupler, the operational amplifier OA 1 controls the current though the light-emitting diodes in such a way that the photo-electric current in the reference receiver T_1 equals a desired value. The feedback loop is closed via the reference coupler, so that

$$I_{F1} = \frac{U_f^+}{R_2} + \frac{V_1 - V_2}{R_1} .$$

As the photo-electric current cannot change polarity, a constant current U_f^+/R_2 is superimposed to enable transmission of bipolar input signals. If the two opto-couplers are well matched, we obtain at the receiver side the current $I_{F2} = I_{F1}$, and thus the output voltage

$$U_o = \frac{R_1'}{R_1}(V_1 - V_2) \quad \text{for} \quad \frac{U_f^+}{R_2} = \frac{V^+}{R_2'} .$$

Isolation amplifiers with transformer, opto- or capacitor coupling are available as ready-made modules. A number of such types are listed in Fig. 25.15. Among the most user-friendly are the types which already incorporate the required DC converter. An external voltage converter is only worthwhile if it can be used to drive several isolation amplifiers whose floating ground is at the same potential. In the types with built-in voltage converter, the floating power supply is also available to the user, e.g. for driving a preceding instrumentation amplifier or a sensor. An all-purpose device is the Analog Devices AD 210 in which the receiver circuit also operates from a floating supply. Consequently,

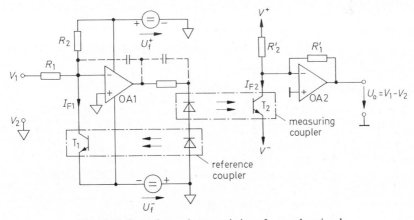

Fig. 25.14 Opto-electronic transmission of an analog signal

the receiver signal ground can in this case be isolated from the power supply ground and, as there are therefore three mutually isolated ground terminals, this arrangement is termed "three-port isolation".

Type	Manufac-turer	Signal transmission	Isolated power supply	Power bandwidth	Isolation voltage	Remarks
ISO 100	Burr Br.	Opto-coupler	external[1]	5 kHz	750 V	obsolete
ISO 122 P	Burr Br.	capacitor	external[1]	3 kHz	1500 V	very inexpensive
ISO 121	Burr Br.	capacitor	external[1]	5 kHz	3500 V	high isolation
ISO 107	Burr Br.	capacitor	for input	10 kHz	2500 V	$\cong$ ISO103
ISO 103	Burr Br.	capacitor	for input	10 kHz	1500 V ⎫	complementary
ISO 113	Burr Br.	capacitor	for output[2]	10 kHz	1500 V ⎬	power supply
ISO 212	Burr Br.	transformer	for input	3 kHz	750 V	inexpensive
AD 202	Anal. Dev.	transformer	for input	2 kHz	1500 V	inexpensive
AD 210	Anal. Dev.	transformer	f. inp. & outp.	20 kHz	2500 V	3-port isolation
1B21	Anal. Dev.	transformer	for output[2]	5 kHz	1500 V	4 . . . 20 mA output

[1] e.g. PWS 725 or HPR 110 from Burr Brown   [2] with output for 20 mA current loops

Fig. 25.15 Examples of isolation amplifiers

25.2 Measurement of current

25.2.1 Floating zero-resistance ammeter

Section 13.2 describes a current-to-voltage converter which is almost ideally suited for the measurement of currents because of its extremely low input resistance. However, as the input represents virtual ground, only currents to ground can be measured.

Floating ammeters can be realized by the instrumentation amplifier in Fig. 25.4 if its two inputs are connected to a measuring shunt. The advantage of

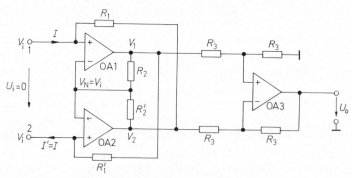

Fig. 25.16 Floating zero-resistance ammeter

$$U_o = 2RI \quad \text{for} \quad R_1 = R_1' = R_2 = R_2' = R$$

the low input resistance is then lost, but if the shunt is incorporated in the feedback loop of the input amplifiers, as illustrated in Fig. 25.16, a floating ammeter is obtained having virtually zero input resistance.

'Due to the feedback via the resistors R_2 and R'_2, the potential V_N assumes a value V_i such that the potential difference across the inputs 1 and 2 becomes zero. If a current I flows into terminal 1, the feedback causes the output potential of OA 2 to have the value

$$V_2 = V_i - IR_1 \ . \tag{25.1}$$

With $V_N = V_i$, we obtain

$$V_1 = V_2 + \left(1 + \frac{R_2}{R'_2}\right)(V_i - V_2) = V_i + \frac{R_1 R_2}{R'_2} I \ . \tag{25.2}$$

Hence, the current leaving terminal 2 is given by

$$I' = \frac{V_1 - V_i}{R'_1} = \frac{R_1 R_2}{R'_1 R'_2} I \ . \tag{25.3}$$

If both inputs are to behave like those of a floating circuit, I' must be the same as I, or the current difference $\Delta I = I' - I$ will flow through the operational amplifier outputs to ground. Hence the condition that

$$\frac{R_1}{R'_1} = \frac{R'_2}{R_2} \ . \tag{25.4}$$

The subtracting amplifier OA 3 computes the difference $V_1 - V_2$. Its output voltage, with Eqs. (25.1) and (25.2), is therefore

$$U_o = R_1 \left(1 + \frac{R_2}{R'_2}\right) I \ , \tag{25.5}$$

i.e. it is proportional to the current I.

25.2.2 Measurement of current at high potentials

The permissible common-mode voltage of the previous circuit is limited to values between the supply voltages. For measurement of currents at higher potentials, the simple circuit of Fig. 13.5 can be employed if it is connected to the floating ground terminal of an isolation amplifier rather than to system ground. Its output voltage is referenced to system ground with the help of the isolation amplifier.

The required circuitry may be reduced quite considerably if a voltage drop of 1 V to 2 V can be tolerated for the measurement of current (e.g. in the anode circuit of high-voltage tubes). In such cases, the current to be measured is made to flow through the light-emitting diode of an opto-coupler, so that a floating supply is no longer needed. For linearization of the transfer characteristic, a reference opto-coupler may be used on the receiver side, as demonstrated in

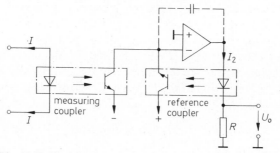

Fig. 25.17 Simple isolation amplifier for current measurement.

$$U_o = R \cdot I$$

Fig. 25.17. Its input current I_2 is controlled by the operational amplifier in such a manner that the photo-electric currents of the reference and the measuring coupler cancel each other out. If the couplers are well matched,

$$I_2 = I \ .$$

This current can be measured as a voltage across the grounded resistor R.

25.3   AC/DC converters

Various quantities are used to characterize alternating voltages: the arithmetic mean absolute value, the root-mean-square (r.m.s.) value and the positive and negative peak value.

25.3.1   Measurement of the mean absolute value

To obtain the absolute values of an alternating voltage, a circuit is required in which the sign of the gain changes with the polarity of the input voltage; i.e. its transfer characteristic must have the shape represented in Fig. 25.18.

A full-wave rectifier of this kind can be realized by a diode bridge. However, the accuracy of such a circuit is limited owing to the forward voltages of the diodes. This effect can be avoided if the bridge rectifier is operated from

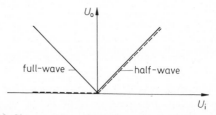

Fig. 25.18 Characteristics of a half-wave and a full-wave rectifier

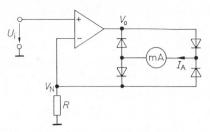

Fig. 25.19 Full-wave rectifier for floating meters.

$$I_A = |U_i|/R$$

a controlled current source; a simple solution is shown in Fig. 25.19. The operational amplifier is employed as a voltage-controlled current source, in accordance with Fig. 13.8. Hence, independently of the diode forward voltage,

$$I_A = \frac{|U_i|}{R} \; .$$

To display the mean value of this current, a moving-coil ammeter can be used, for instance, and this method is therefore often employed in analog multimeters.

For output potentials in the range $-2U_D < V_o < 2U_D$, the amplifier has no feedback, as none of the diodes conduct. While V_o changes from $2U_D$ to $-2U_D$, V_N remains constant, this causing a delay time within the control loop. Because of this, any phase shift can be incurred in the control loop, depending on the frequencies involved, so that stabilization of the operational amplifier is particularly difficult. To reduce the delay time, amplifiers having a fast slew rate must be chosen and the frequency compensation must be stronger than for linear feedback.

Full-wave rectifier with single-ended output

In the previous circuit, the load (i.e. the moving-coil instrument) had to be floating. However, if the signal is to be processed further, e.g. digitized, a ground-referenced output voltage is needed; this can be derived from the current I_A e.g. using a floating current-to-voltage converter. Figure 25.20 shows a simpler method.

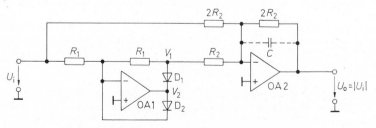

Fig. 25.20 Full-wave rectifier with single-ended output

Let us first consider the operation of OA 1. For positive input voltages, it operates as an inverting amplifier since V_2 is negative, i.e. diode D_1 is forward and D_2 reverse biased. Hence, $V_1 = -U_i$. For negative input voltages, V_2 is positive; D_1 is OFF and D_2 is conducting, thereby applying feedback to the amplifier and preventing OA1 from saturating so that the summing point remains as zero voltage. Since D_1 is reverse biased, V_1 is also zero. Therefore

$$V_1 = \begin{cases} -U_i & \text{for} \quad U_i \geq 0 \;, \\ 0 & \text{for} \quad U_i \leq 0 \;. \end{cases} \qquad (25.6)$$

Amplifier OA1 thus operates as an inverting half-wave rectifier.

The extension to the full-wave rectifier is effected by amplifier OA 2. It computes the expression

$$U_o = -(U_i + 2V_1) \;, \qquad (25.7)$$

which, with Eq. (25.6), becomes

$$U_o = \begin{cases} U_i & \text{for} \quad U_i \geq 0 \;, \\ -U_i & \text{for} \quad U_i \leq 0 \;. \end{cases} \qquad (25.8)$$

This is the desired characteristic of a full-wave rectifier. The operation is illustrated by Fig. 25.21.

Amplifier OA 2 can be extended by the addition of capacitor C to become a first-order lowpass filter. If the filter cutoff frequency is chosen small compared to the lowest signal frequency, a smooth DC voltage is obtained at the output, having the value

$$U_o = \overline{|U_i|} \;.$$

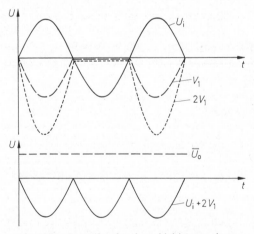

Fig. 25.21 Operation for sinusoidal input voltage

As in the previous circuit, amplifier OA1 must have a fast slew rate to keep the delay time of the change-over from one diode to the other as short as possible.

Rectification by sign reversal

We can see from Eq. (25.8) that with a full-wave rectifier, $A = +1$ for positive voltages and $A = -1$ for negative voltages. This function can also be implemented directly by using an amplifier whose gain can be switched from $+1$ to -1 and controlling the changeover by the sign of the input voltage. This principle is illustrated in Fig. 25.22. If the input voltages are positive, the non-inverting input of the amplifier is used; if they are negative, the comparator changes the switch over to the inverting input.

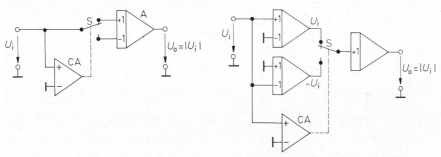

Fig. 25.22 Rectification by sign reversal   Fig. 25.23 Practical implementation of rectification by gain switching

For amplifier A, it would of course be impossible to use an operational amplifier without external circuitry, as its gain $A_D \gg 1$. However, a suitable solution is provided by the circuit in Fig. 22.25, where the gain can be switched between $+1$ and -1 using switch S. For higher frequencies, the wideband multiplexer in Fig. 22.21 is more suitable, and Fig. 25.23 shows how this circuit can be operated as a rectifier. The input amplifier is connected to the input voltage in such a way that signals of opposite polarity are produced. Depending on which input amplifier is selected by the comparator, the output voltage $+U_i$ or $-U_i$ is obtained.

This method of rectification is practicable because there are ICs which operate on this principle, such as the Analog Devices AD 630 which also contains the required comparator. However, at high frequencies the delay due to the comparator introduces appreciable errors, as the delayed changeover then becomes a critical factor.

Wideband full-wave rectifier

A differential amplifier provides an inverting and a non-inverting output and can therefore be used as a fast full-wave rectifier. In this application, two

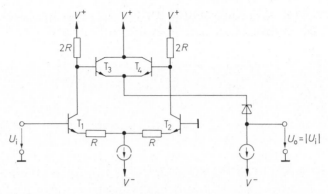

Fig. 25.24 Wideband full-wave rectifier

parallel-connected emitter followers T_3/T_4 are used, as in Fig. 25.24, to connect the more positive collector potential to the output. The Zener diode compensates for the collector quiescent potential to make the output quiescent potential zero.

This method can be used to rectify signal voltages of up to 100 MHz with good linearity. For the detailed design, the same considerations apply as for the wideband differential amplifiers in Section 16.5.

25.3.2   Measurement of the r.m.s. value

Whereas the arithmetic mean absolute value (mean modulus) is defined as

$$\overline{|U|} = \frac{1}{T}\int_0^T |U|\,\mathrm{d}t \ , \tag{25.9}$$

the definition of the root-mean-square value (r.m.s. value) is given as

$$U_{\text{r.m.s.}} = \sqrt{\overline{(U^2)}} = \sqrt{\frac{1}{T}\int_0^T U^2\,\mathrm{d}t} \ , \tag{25.10}$$

where T is the measuring interval which must be large compared to the longest period contained in the signal spectrum. In this manner, a reading is obtained which is independent of T. For strictly periodic functions, averaging over one period is sufficient to get the correct result.

For sinusoidal voltages,

$$U_{\text{r.m.s.}} = \hat{U}/\sqrt{2}$$

so that the r.m.s. value can be determined simply by measuring the peak value. For other waveshapes, this method would produce errors, particularly for highly peaked voltages, i.e. for waveshapes having large *crest factors* $\hat{U}/U_{\text{r.m.s.}}$.

The errors become smaller if the measurement of r.m.s. values is reduced to that of the mean absolute values. For a sinusoidal voltage,

$$\overline{|U|} = \frac{\hat{U}}{T} \int_0^T |\sin \omega t| \, dt = \frac{2}{\pi} \hat{U} \tag{25.11}$$

and, with $U_{\text{r.m.s.}} = \hat{U}/2$,

$$U_{\text{r.m.s.}} = \frac{\pi}{2\sqrt{2}} \overline{|U|} \approx 1.11 \cdot \overline{|U|} \; . \tag{25.12}$$

The relative magnitude of the individual values is demonstrated in Fig. 25.25. The *form factor* of 1.11 is incorporated in the calibration of most available mean-absolute-value meters; for sinusoidal signals, therefore, they show the r.m.s. value although they actually measure the mean-absolute-value. For other waveshapes, this modified reading produces varying deviations from the true r.m.s. value. For a triangular waveshape, $U_{\text{r.m.s.}} = 2\overline{|U|}/\sqrt{3}$; for white noise, $U_{\text{r.m.s.}} = \overline{|U|}\sqrt{\pi/2}$, whereas for a DC voltage, $U_{\text{r.m.s.}} = \overline{|U|}$. The following deviations in the readings are obtained for different waveshapes:

DC, square wave: reading too large by 11%,
triangular wave: reading too small by 4%,
white noise: reading too small by 11%.

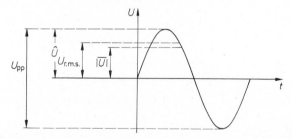

Fig. 25.25 Relative magnitude of peak value, r.m.s. value and mean absolute value, of a sinusoidal signal

True measurement of r.m.s. values

For a true, waveshape-independent measurement of an r.m.s. value, either the definition Eq. (25.10) can be employed, or the power can be measured.

The operation of the circuit in Fig. 25.26 is based on Eq. (25.10). In order to evaluate the mean value of the squared input voltage, a simple first-order lowpass filter is used, the cutoff frequency of which is low compared to the lowest signal frequency.

One drawback of the circuit is that its minimum input signal must be relatively large; if, for instance, a voltage of 10 mV is applied to the input and the computing unit E is 10 V as usual, a voltage of only 10 µV is obtained at the

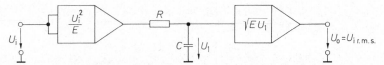

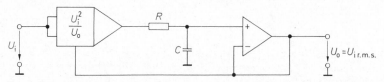

Fig. 25.26 Measurement of r.m.s. values by analog computing circuits

Fig. 25.27 Circuit for r.m.s. measurement, having an improved input voltage range

output of the squarer. This, however, will be drowned by the noise of the square-rooter.

In this respect, the circuit of Fig. 25.27 is preferable, since the square-rooting operation at the output is replaced by a division at the input. The voltage at the output of the lowpass filter is thus

$$U_o = \overline{\left(\frac{U_i^2}{U_o}\right)} . \tag{25.13}$$

At steady state, $U_o = $ const; hence,

$$U_o = \frac{\overline{(U_i^2)}}{U_o} ,$$

i.e.

$$U_o = \sqrt{\overline{(U_i^2)}} = U_{\text{r.m.s.}} .$$

An advantage of this method is that the input voltage U_i is not multiplied by the factor U_i/E which, for low input voltages, is small with respect to unity, but by the factor U_i/U_o which is close to unity. The available input range is therefore considerably larger. However, the precondition for this is that the division U_i/U_o can be carried out sufficiently accurately even for small signals. Divider circuits based on logarithmic operations are best suited for this purpose, as described in Section 12.8.1.

Implicit equation (25.13) can therefore be solved using the principle illustrated in Fig. 25.28 [25.4]. Before taking the logarithm, we must first form the absolute value of the input voltage. Squaring is performed simply by multiplying the logarithm by two. To divide by U_o, the logarithm of the output voltage is subtracted.

The practical implementation of this principle is shown in Fig. 25.29. The full-wave rectified input signal is produced at the summing point of OA 2. The latter forms the logarithm of the input voltage. The voltage doubling required

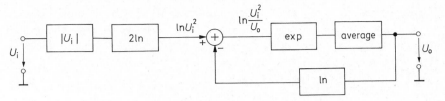

Fig. 25.28 Computation of r.m.s. value via logarithms

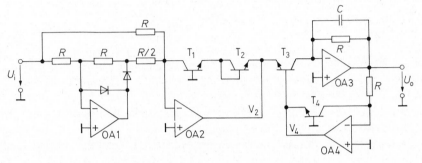

Fig. 25.29 Practical method of r.m.s. calculation

Output voltage: $U_\mathrm{o} = \sqrt{\overline{U_\mathrm{i}^2}} = U_\mathrm{i\,r.m.s.}$

for squaring is effected by the two transistors T_1 and T_2 connected in series:

$$V_2 = -2U_\mathrm{T} \ln \frac{U_\mathrm{i}}{I_\mathrm{CS}R} = -U_\mathrm{T} \ln \left(\frac{U_\mathrm{i}}{I_\mathrm{CS}R} \right)^2 .$$

OA 4 takes the logarithm of the output voltage:

$$V_4 = -U_\mathrm{T} \ln \frac{U_\mathrm{o}}{I_\mathrm{CS}R} .$$

The voltage $V_4 - V_2$ across T_3 implementing the exponential function produces the output voltage

$$U_\mathrm{o} = I_\mathrm{CS}R \exp \frac{V_4 - V_2}{U_\mathrm{T}} = \frac{U_\mathrm{i}^2}{U_\mathrm{o}} . \tag{25.14}$$

Using capacitor C for averaging, the same output voltage is therefore produced as expressed by Eq. (25.13).

Type	Manufacturer	Technology	Accuracy	Bandwidth
AD637	Analog Devices	bipolar	0.1%	80 kHz
AD736	Analog Devices	bipolar	0.3%	30 kHz
AD536	Maxim	bipolar	0.2%	45 kHz
LH0091	National	hybrid	0.2%	80 kHz

Fig. 25.30 True r.m.s. converters

Transistors T_1 to T_4 must be of monolithic IC form to ensure that they possess identical characteristics—as was assumed in the calculation above. It is even possible to integrate the operational amplifiers and resistors on the same chip, as shown in Fig. 25.30.

Thermal conversion

The r.m.s. value of an AC voltage is defined as that DC voltage which will produce the same average power in a resistor, i.e.

$$\overline{U_i^2}/R = U_{\text{r.m.s.}}^2/R \ .$$

The r.m.s. value of an AC voltage U_i can therefore be determined by increasing a DC voltage $U_{\text{r.m.s.}}$ across a resistor R until the latter is exactly as hot as that heated by U_i. This is the principle on which thermal r.m.s. measurement is based. Essentially, any method of temperature measurement can be employed (see Section 26.1). A particularly useful one is to use temperature sensors which can be fabricated together with the heating resistors as an IC. Consequently, diodes are mainly used nowadays as temperature sensors, as illustrated in Fig. 25.31.

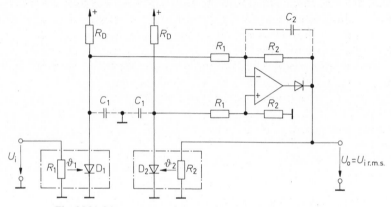

Fig. 25.31 Measurement of r.m.s. values by thermal conversion

Resistor R_1 is heated by the input voltage, resistor R_2 by the output voltage. The latter increases until the difference between the two diode voltages is zero, i.e. both temperatures are the same. In this case the operational amplifier configured as a subtractor with lowpass filter is used as control amplifier. Capacitors C_1 keep high-frequency signals away from the operational amplifier.

The diode at the amplifier output prevents resistor R_2 being heated by a negative voltage, as this would result in latch-up of the circuit due to positive thermal feedback.

Since the thermal power is proportional to the square of U_o, the loop gain is also proportional to U_o^2, giving a nonlinear step response: the switch-off time constant is considerably larger than the switch-on time constant. A considerable improvement is achieved with an additional square-function AC feedback circuit [25.5, 25.6].

As resistors R_1 and R_2 are usually low-value components (50 Ω) in order to achieve a large bandwidth, correspondingly high currents are required to provide drive. Consequently, an emitter follower is generally inserted at the output of the control amplifier. A preamplifier or impedance converter at the input would have to be of considerably more complex design, since it must not only provide high current peaks of several 100 mA but also be capable of handling the bandwidth of the AC input signal. Wideband operational amplifiers or voltage followers are required, as described in Chapter 16.

In order to obtain accurate measurements, the two measuring couples must have good matching characteristics. An IC meeting these requirements is the LT 1088 from Linear Technology, with which accuracies of 1% can be achieved up to 100 MHz.

25.3.3 Measurement of the peak value

The peak value can be measured very simply by charging a capacitor via a diode. To eliminate its forward voltage, the diode is inserted in the feedback loop of a voltage follower, as in Fig. 25.32. For input voltages $U_i < V_C$, the diode is reverse biased. For $U_i > V_C$, the diode conducts and, due to the feedback, $V_C = U_i$. The capacitor therefore charges to the peak input voltage. The voltage follower OA 2 draws only very little current from the capacitor, so that the peak value can be stored over a long period. Push-button switch P discharges the capacitor to prepare it for the next measurement.

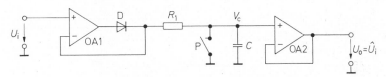

Fig. 25.32 Peak value measurement

The capacitive load of amplifier OA 1 may give rise to oscillations; this effect is eliminated by resistor R_1. However, the charging time is increased as the capacitor voltage now only approaches steady-state conditions asymptotically. A further disadvantage of the circuit is that OA 1 has no feedback if $U_i < V_C$, i.e. is saturated. The resulting recovery time limits the use of this circuit to low-frequency applications.

Both of these drawbacks are avoided with the peak detector in Fig. 25.33. Here, OA 1 is operated in the inverting mode. If U_i exceeds the value of $- V_C$, V_1 becomes negative and diode D_1 conducting. Because of the feedback across the two amplifiers, V_1 assumes such a value that $U_o = - U_i$. In this way the diode forward voltage, as well as the offset voltage of the impedance converter OA 2, is

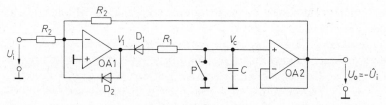

Fig. 25.33 Improved method of peak value measurement

eliminated. If the input voltage falls, V_1 rises, thus reverse biasing diode D_1. The feedback path via R_2 is opened, but V_1 can only rise until diode D_2 becomes conducting and provides feedback for OA 1. In this manner, saturation of OA 1 is avoided.

The inverted positive peak value of U_i remains stored at capacitor C as no leakage current can flow either through D_1 or through the impedance converter OA 2. Before a new reading, capacitor C must be discharged by switch P. For measurement of negative peak voltages, the diodes must be reversed.

Another method of implementing a peak voltmeter consists of using a sample-and-hold circuit and issuing the sample command at the appropriate instant. For this purpose we can simply use a comparator, as shown in Fig. 25.34, to determine when the input voltage is larger than the output voltage, and close switch S of the sample-and-hold at this time. The output signal then

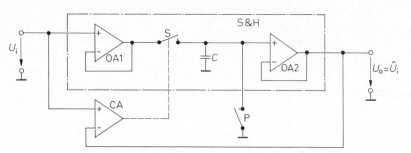

Fig. 25.34 Peak value measurement using sample-and-hold circuit

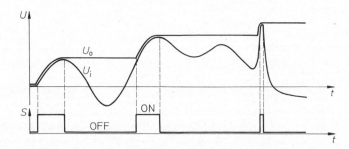

Fig. 25.35 Signal waveforms in the peak voltmeter with sample-and-hold circuit

follows the input signal as long as it rises, and remains stored when it falls again. The output voltage only rises further when the input voltage exceeds the last maximum stored. A typical mode of operation is shown in Fig. 25.35. This circuit can be implemented using the sample-and-holds of Fig. 22.31 and the comparators from Fig. 8.39 [25.7].

An IC containing all the components for a peak voltmeter as well as two electrically controlled switches is the PKD01 from PMI.

Continuous measurement of the peak value

The method described can be adapted for continuous peak voltage measurements if switch P is replaced by a resistor, the value of which is chosen large enough to ensure that the discharge of the capacitor C between two voltage crests is negligible. However, this method has the disadvantage that a decrease in peak amplitude is registered only very slowly.

It is important for many applications, particularly in control circuits, for the peak amplitude to be measured with the shortest possible delay. With the methods described so far, the measuring time is at least one period of the input signal. However, for sinusoidal signals, the peak amplitude can be computed at any instant with the trigonometric equation

$$\hat{U} = \sqrt{\hat{U}^2 \sin^2 \omega t + \hat{U} \cos^2 \omega t} \ . \tag{25.15}$$

We have already used this relationship for the amplitude control of the oscillator in Fig 15.30. There it was particularly practicable since both the sine and the cosine function were available.

For the measurement of an unknown sinusoidal voltage, we must establish the $\cos \omega t$ function from the input signal; a differentiator can be employed for this purpose. We obtain its output voltage as

$$V_1(t) = -RC\frac{dU_i(t)}{dt} = -\hat{U}_i RC\frac{d\sin \omega t}{dt} = -\hat{U}_i \omega RC \cos \omega t \ . \tag{25.16}$$

If the frequency is known, the coefficient ωRC can be adjusted to 1, so that the required term for Eq. (25.15) is obtained. By squaring and adding $U_i(t)$ and $V_i(t)$, a continuous voltage for the amplitude is obtained which requires no filtering.

For variable frequencies, the circuit must be expanded as in Fig. 25.36, by inserting an integrator to enable provision of the $\cos^2 \omega t$ term with frequency-independent amplitude. The output potential of the integrator is

$$V_2(t) = -\frac{1}{RC}\int U_i(t)\,dt = -\frac{1}{RC}\int \hat{U}_i \sin \omega t\,dt = \frac{\hat{U}_i}{\omega RC} \cos \omega t \ , \tag{25.17}$$

where the constant of integration is zero at steady state, because of the resistor R_p. By multiplying V_1 and V_2, the required expression

$$V_3(t) = -\frac{\hat{U}_i^2}{E} \cos^2 \omega t$$

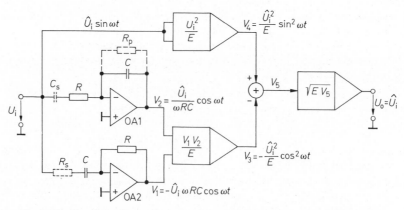

Fig. 25.36 Circuit for the continuous amplitude measurement of sinusoidal signals

is obtained. By subtracting this from V_4 and square-rooting the result, the output voltage

$$U_o = \hat{U}_i$$

is measured which is equal to the amplitude of the input voltage at any instant. For steep changes in the amplitude, a temporary deviation from the correct value is incurred until the integrator output resettles to zero mean voltage. However, the output voltage will instantly change to the correct direction so that a connected controller, for example, obtains accurate information about the trend without delay.

25.3.4   Synchronous demodulator

In a synchronous demodulator (synchronous detector, phase-sensitive rectifier), the sign of the gain is not influenced by the polarity of the input voltage, but rather by an external control voltage $U_{CS}(t)$. For such a circuit, the switches for polarity change described in Sections 22.2.4 and 22.3.2 can be employed.

A synchronous demodulator can be used in the arrangement shown in Fig. 25.37 to separate a sine wave from a noisy signal and to determine its amplitude. The sine wave selected has a frequency equal to that of the control signal, and a phase shift φ which is constant with respect to the control signal. The special case when $f_i = f_{CS}$ and $\varphi = 0$ is illustrated in Fig. 25.38. It can be seen that under these conditions, the synchronous demodulator operates as a full-wave rectifier. If $\varphi \neq 0$ or $f_i \neq f_{CS}$, negative voltage-time areas occur as well as the positive areas and reduce the mean value of the output voltage so that it is always lower than that of the example shown.

The output voltage will now be determined as a function of frequency and phase. The input voltage U_i is multiplied by $+1$ or by -1 in time with the

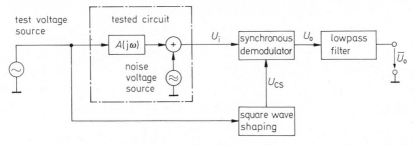

Fig. 25.37 Application of a synchronous demodulator to the measurement of noisy signals

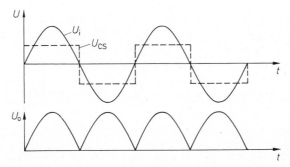

Fig. 25.38 Operation of a synchronous demodulator

control frequency f_{CS}, this effect being represented mathematically as

$$U_o = U_i(t) \cdot S(t) \, , \tag{25.18}$$

where

$$S(t) = \begin{cases} 1 & \text{for } U_{CS} > 0 \\ -1 & \text{for } U_{CS} < 0 \, . \end{cases}$$

By rewriting this in Fourier series form, we obtain

$$S(t) = \frac{4}{\pi} \sum_{n=0}^{\infty} \frac{1}{2n+1} \sin(2n+1)\omega_{CS}t \, . \tag{25.19}$$

Let us now assume the input voltage to be a sinusoidal voltage having the frequency $f_i = m \cdot f_{CS}$ and the phase angle φ_m. With Eqs. (25.18) and (25.19), we then have the output voltage

$$U_o(t) = \hat{U}_i \sin(m\,\omega_{CS}t + \varphi_m) \cdot \frac{4}{\pi} \sum_{n=0}^{\infty} \frac{1}{2n+1} \sin(2n+1)\omega_{CS}t \, . \tag{25.20}$$

The arithmetic mean value of this voltage is evaluated by the subsequent lowpass filter. With the auxiliary equation

$$\frac{1}{T} \int_0^T \sin(m\,\omega_{CS}t + \varphi_m) = 0$$

and the orthogonal property of sinusoidal functions, i.e.

$$\frac{1}{T}\int_0^T \sin(m\,\omega_{CS}t + \varphi_m)\sin l\,\omega_{CS}t\,dt = \begin{cases} 0 & \text{for } m \neq l \\ \frac{1}{2}\cos\varphi_m & \text{for } m = l \end{cases}$$

and with Eq. (25.20), we obtain the final result

$$\bar{U}_o = \begin{cases} \dfrac{2}{\pi m}\,\hat{U}_i\cdot\cos\varphi_m & \text{for } m = 2n+1 \\[2mm] 0 & \text{for } m \neq 2n+1 \ . \end{cases} \qquad (25.21)$$

where $n = 0, 1, 2, 3, \ldots\,$.

If the input voltage is a mixture of frequencies, only those components contribute to the mean value of the output voltage, the frequencies of which are equal to the control frequency or are an odd multiple thereof. This explains why the synchronous demodulator is particularly suitable for selective amplitude measurements. The synchronous demodulator is also known as the *phase-sensitive rectifier* since the mean output voltage is dependent on the phase angle between the appropriate component of the input voltage and the control voltage.

For $\varphi_m = 90°$, $\bar{U}_o$ is zero even if the frequency condition is fulfilled. For our example in Fig. 25.38, we have $\varphi_m = 0$ and $m = 1$. In this case, Eq. (25.21) yields

$$\bar{U}_o = \frac{2}{\pi}\,\hat{U}_i \ ,$$

which is the arithmetic mean of a full-wave rectified sinusoidal voltage; a result which could have been deduced directly from Fig. 25.38.

Equation (25.21) has shown that only those voltages whose frequencies are equal to the control frequency or are odd multiples thereof contribute to the output voltage. However, this holds only if the time constant of the lowpass filter is infinitely large. In practice, this is not possible and is not even desirable, as the upper cutoff frequency would be zero, i.e. the output voltage could not change at all. If $f_c > 0$, the synchronous demodulator no longer picks out

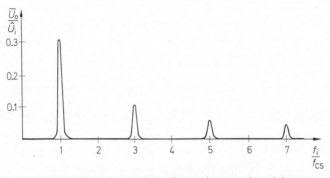

Fig. 25.39 Filter characteristic of a synchronous demodulator

discrete frequencies, but individual frequency bands. The 3 dB bandwidth of these frequency bands is $2f_c$, and Fig. 25.39 shows the resulting filter characteristic.

The mostly unwanted contribution of the odd-order harmonics can be avoided by using an *analog multiplier* for synchronous demodulation instead of the polarity changing switch. The input voltage is then multiplied by a sinusoidal function $U_{CS} = \hat{U}_{CS} \sin \omega t$ rather than by the square wave function $S(t)$. As this sine wave no longer contains harmonics, Eq. (25.21) holds only for $n = 0$. If the amplitude of the control voltage is chosen to be equal to the computing unit voltage E of the multiplier, we obtain, instead of Eq. (25.21), the result

$$\bar{U}_o = \begin{cases} \frac{1}{2}\hat{U}_i \cos \varphi & \text{for } f_i = f_{CS} \\ 0 & \text{for } f_i \neq f_{CS} . \end{cases} \tag{25.22}$$

According to Eq. (25.22), the synchronous demodulator does not produce the amplitude $\hat{U}_i$ directly, but gives the real part $\hat{U}_i \cos \varphi$ of the complex amplitude $\underline{U}_i$. To determine the magnitude $|\underline{U}_i| = \hat{U}_i$, the phase angle of the control voltage can be adjusted by a suitable phase shifting network so that the output voltage of the demodulator is at maximum. The signal $U_i(t)$ and the control voltage $U_{CS}(t)$ are then in phase, and we obtain from Eq. (25.22)

$$\bar{U}_o = \frac{1}{2}\hat{U}_i = \frac{1}{2}|\underline{U}_i|_{f_i = f_{CS}} .$$

If a calibrated phase-shifter is employed, the phase shift φ of the tested circuit can be read directly.

One is often interested only in the amplitude of a spectral input component and not in its phase angle. In such a case, synchronization of the control voltage is no longer necessary if two synchronous demodulators are used as in Fig. 25.40 and operated by two quadrature control voltages:

$$V_1 = E \sin \omega_{CS} t \quad \text{and} \quad V_2 = E \cos \omega_{CS} t$$

where E is the computing unit voltage of the demodulating multipliers. The oscillator in Fig. 15.30 is particularly suitable for generating these two voltages.

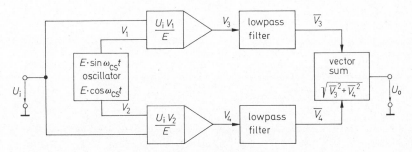

Fig. 25.40 Phase-independent synchronous demodulation.

$$U_o = \frac{1}{2}\hat{U}_i \quad \text{for} \quad f_{CS} = f_i$$

Only the spectral component of the input voltage having the frequency f_{CS} contributes to the output voltages of the two demodulators. If it has the phase angle φ with respect to V_1, it is of the form

$$U_i = \hat{U}_i \sin(\omega_{CS} t + \varphi) \ .$$

According to Eq. (25.22), the upper demodulator produces the output voltage

$$\bar{V}_3 = \tfrac{1}{2} \hat{U}_i \cos \varphi \ , \tag{25.23}$$

whereas the lower demodulator gives

$$\bar{V}_4 = \tfrac{1}{2} \hat{U}_i \sin \varphi \ . \tag{25.24}$$

By squaring and adding, we obtain the output voltage

$$U_o = \tfrac{1}{2} \hat{U}_i \sqrt{\sin^2\varphi + \cos^2\varphi} = \tfrac{1}{2} \hat{U}_i \tag{25.25}$$

which is independent of the phase angle φ. The circuit can therefore be used as a tunable selective voltmeter. Its bandwidth is constant and equal to twice the cutoff frequency of the lowpass filters. The attainable Q-factor is considerably higher than that of conventional active filters: a 1 MHz signal can be filtered with a bandwidth of 1 Hz without any trouble. This corresponds to a Q-factor of 10^6.

If the control frequency is made to sweep through a given range, the circuit operates as a spectrum analyzer.

26 Sensors and measurement systems

This chapter deals with circuits for measuring non-electrical quantities. For this purpose, the latter must first be detected by a *sensor* and then converted into an electrical quantity. The interfacing circuit for the sensor normally converts this quantity into a voltage which, after conditioning, is then displayed or employed for control purposes.

Figure 26.1 shows the individual stages. A concrete example is then given in Fig. 26.2 for a humidity sensor. In this example the sensor has a capacitance which is dependent on the relative humidity. In order to measure it, the sensor must be incorporated in a capacitance measuring circuit, the output of which delivers a voltage proportional to the capacitance but in no way proportional to the humidity. Another circuit is therefore required for linearization and calibration of the sensor. There is a wide variety of sensors for the most diverse measurands and measurement ranges. Figure 26.3 provides an overview of the types available.

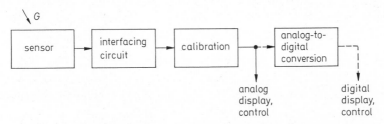

Fig. 26.1 Conversion of a physical quantity G into a calibrated electrical signal

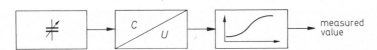

Fig. 26.2 A humidity sensor as an example of how the measured value is obtained

26.1 Temperature measurement

The following paragraphs describe various ways in which temperature can be measured. It is evident from the overview table that the metallic sensors, such as the thermocouple and resistance thermometer, can be employed for a very large range of temperatures. The semiconductor-based temperature sensors

Measurand	Sensor	Measurement range	Principle
Temperature	PTC metal	$-200...+800°$ C	Pos. temperature coefficient of the resistance of metals, e.g. platinum
	PTC thermistor	$-50...+150°$ C	Pos. temperature coefficient of the resistance of semiconductors, e.g. silicon
	NTC thermistor	$-50...+150°$ C	Neg. temperature coefficient of the resistance of metal-oxide ceramic
	Transistor	$-50...+150°$ C	Neg. temperature coefficient of the base-emitter voltage of a transistor
	Thermocouple	$-200...+2800°$ C	Thermo-electric voltage at contact of different metals
	Crystal oscillator	$-50...+300°$ C	Temperature coefficient of the resonant frequency of specially cut quartz crystals
Temperature via heat radiation	Pyrometer	$-100...+3000°$ C	Spectral distribution of the luminance is temperature-dependent
	Pyroelement	$-50...+2200°$ C	Increase in temperature due to radiated heat generates polarization voltage
Light intensity	Photodiode Phototransistor	$10^{-2}...10^{5}$ lx	Current increases with light intensity due to optically-released charge carriers
	Photoresistor	$10^{-2}...10^{5}$ lx	Electrical resistance reduces as illumination increases
	Photomultiplier	$10^{-6}...10^{3}$ lx	Light releases electrons from a photocathode which are multiplied by subsequent dynodes
Sound	Dynamic microphone		Induction of a voltage by movement of a coil within a magnetic field
	Condenser microphone		Voltage of a charged capacitor varies with distance between plates
	Crystal microphone		Piezoelectric effect generates voltage
Magnetic field	Induction coil		Supplies voltage if the magnetic field changes or the coil moves within the field
	Hall-effect device	$10^{-4}...1$ T	Produces a voltage across the semiconductor by deflection of electrons in the magnetic field
	Magnetoresistor	$0.1...1$ T	Resistance increases in semiconductor as a function of field strength

Fig. 26.3 Overview of sensors, part 1

Measurand	Sensor	Measurement range	Principle
Force	Strain gauge	$10^{-2}\ldots 10^7$ N	Force causes elastic elongation of a thin-film resistor, thereby increasing its resistance
Pressure	Strain gauge	$10^{-3}\ldots 10^3$ bar	Bridge circuit of strain gauge on diaphragm is detuned by pressure
Acceleration	Strain gauge	$1\ldots 5000$ g	Strain-gauge bridge is detuned by acceleration force on weighted diaphragm
Linear displacement	Potentiometric displacement transducer	μm$\ldots$m	Potentiometer tap is shifted
	Inductive displacement transducer	μm$\ldots 10^{-1}$ m	Inductive bridge is unbalanced by displacement of a ferrite core
	Incremental displacement transducer, optical	μm$\ldots$m	Reticle pattern is scanned. Number gives displacement
Angle	Incremental angular displacement transducer, optical	$1\ldots 20000$/rev.	Reticle pattern is scanned. Number gives angle of rotation
	Incremental angular displacement transducer, magnetic	$1\ldots 1000$/rev.	Magnetic scanning of a toothed-wheel sensor
	Incremental angular displacement transducer, capacitive	$1\ldots 1000$/rev.	Capacitive scanning of a toothed-wheel sensor
Flow velocity	Windmill-type anemometer		Rotational speed increases with speed of flow
	Heated-wire anemometer		Cooling increases with rate of flow
	Ultrasound transceiver		Doppler shift increases with rate of flow
Gas concentration	Ceramic resistor		Resistance changes with adsorption of test substance
	MOSFET		Change in threshold voltage during adsorption of test substance under the gate
	Absorption spectrum		Absorption lines characteristic for each gas
Humidity	Capacitor	$1\ldots 100\%$	Dielectric constant increases due to water absorption as relative humidity rises
	Resistor	$5\ldots 95\%$	Resistance decreases due to water absorption as relative humidity rises

Fig. 26.3 Overview of sensors, part 2

(PTC and NTC thermistors, transistors) produce a very much larger output signal, therefore allowing lower-cost solutions.

26.1.1 Metals as PTC thermistors

The resistance of metals increases with temperature, i.e. metals possess a positive temperature coefficient. The metals most widely used for temperature measurement are platinum and nickel-iron. To a first approximation, resistance increases linearly by some 0.4% per degree of temperature. Thus, if the temperature increases by 100 K, the resistance increases by a factor of 1.4.

With *platinum temperature detectors*, the resistance R_0 is specified at 0°C. A usual value is 100 Ω (Pt 100), but it can also be 200 Ω (Pt 200), 500 Ω (Pt 500) and 1000 Ω (Pt 1000). In the range $0°C \leq \vartheta \leq 850°C$, the resistance is given by the following equation (DIN 43760 and IEC 571):

$$R_\vartheta = R_0[1 + 3.90802 \cdot 10^{-3}\, \vartheta/°C - 0.580195 \cdot 10^{-6}(\vartheta/°C)^2]$$

and in the range $-200°C \leq \vartheta \leq 0°C$ by

$$R_\vartheta = R_0[1 + 3.90802 \cdot 10^{-3}\, \vartheta/°C - 0.580195 \cdot 10^{-6}(\vartheta/°C)^2 \\ + 0.42735 \cdot 10^{-9}(\vartheta/°C)^3 - 4.2735 \cdot 10^{-12}(\vartheta/°C)^4] \ .$$

The usable temperature range of $-200°C$ to $+850°C$ is very wide. For higher temperatures thermocouples are employed (see Section 26.1.6). The nonlinearity of the equation is relatively small. Within a limited range of temperatures, linearization can therefore often be dispensed with. Examples of interfacing circuits are given in Section 26.1.4.

With *nickel-iron temperature detectors*, the nominal resistance R_0 is specified at 20°C. The temperature curve within the range $-50°C \leq \vartheta \leq 150°C$ is then given by

$$R_\vartheta = R_{20}[1 + 3.83 \cdot 10^{-3}(\vartheta/°C) + 4.64 \cdot 10^{-6}(\vartheta/°C)^2] \ .$$

It can be seen that in addition to the linear term there is a quadratic component which causes a deviation of approximately 25° at 150°C. Linearization is therefore invariably necessary [26.1]. Section 26.4.1 describes the operation and design of the relevant interfacing circuits.

26.1.2 Silicon-based PTC thermistors

The resistance of uniformly doped silicon increases with temperature. The temperature coefficient is approximately twice as large as for metals. The resistance approximately doubles for an increase in temperature of 100 K. The relevant equation takes the form

$$R_\vartheta = R_{25}[1 + 7.95 \cdot 10^{-3}\Delta\vartheta/°C + 1.95 \cdot 10^{-5}(\Delta\vartheta/°C)^2] \ .$$

This only applies precisely to the TS series of sensors from Texas Instruments, and is only approximate for other manufacturers. In the equation, R_{25} is the nominal resistance at 25°C, being mainly between 1 and 2 kΩ. $\Delta\vartheta$ is the difference between the actual temperature and the nominal temperature: $\Delta\vartheta = \vartheta - 25°C$. As with nickel-iron sensors, the usable temperature range is between $-50°C$ and $+150°C$. Section 26.1.4 will show how silicon PTC thermistors are used and how their characteristics are linearized.

26.1.3 NTC thermistors

NTC thermistors are temperature-dependent resistors with a negative temperature coefficient. They are made of metal-oxide ceramic material and their temperature coefficients are very large, being between -3 and -5% per degree. *NTC power thermistors* are used for inrush current limiting. With these devices, heating due to the flow of current is desirable. When hot, they must possess a low resistance and a high current carrying capacity. In contrast, self-heating in *NTC measurement thermistors* is kept to a minimum. What matters here is a resistance curve specified as precisely as possible. The relationship between temperature and resistance can be approximated by the relation [26.2]

$$R_T = R_N \cdot \exp\left[B\left(\frac{1}{T} - \frac{1}{T_N} \right) \right]$$

if the temperature of interest T is close to the nominal temperature T_N. Temperatures must be inserted in Kelvin ($T = \vartheta + 273°$). Depending on the type of thermistor, the constant B is between $B = 1500$ K and 7000 K. To enable the resistance characteristic to be described precisely, even if the temperature differences are large, it is preferable to use the equation

$$\frac{1}{T} = \frac{1}{T_N} + \frac{1}{B}\ln\frac{R}{R_N} + \frac{1}{C}\left(\ln\frac{R}{R_N} \right)^3 \; .$$

This additionally includes the term with the coefficient $1/C$, allowing an accuracy of 0.1 K to be achieved even in a temperature range of 100 K. This naturally requires that the coefficients or the resistance characteristic be specified with sufficient accuracy by the manufacturer. Interfacing circuits for NTC thermistors are dealt with in Section 26.1.4.

26.1.4 Operation of resistive temperature detectors

With the resistive temperature detectors (RTD) described here, resistance is a function of temperature; the relationship is described by the relevant equations $R = f(\vartheta)$. The magnitude of the change in resistance with temperature is given by the temperature coefficient

$$TC = \frac{1}{R} \cdot \frac{dR}{d\vartheta} \; . \tag{26.1}$$

in % per degree. This also allows the resulting temperature tolerance to be calculated from a resistance tolerance:

$$\underbrace{\Delta \vartheta}_{\text{Temperature tolerance}} = \frac{1}{TC} \cdot \underbrace{\frac{\Delta R}{R}}_{\text{Resistance tolerance}} \cdot \qquad (26.2)$$

For a temperature coefficient of 0.3% per degree, a resistance tolerance of $\pm 1\%$ consequently produces a temperature tolerance of ± 3 K. The larger the temperature coefficient, the smaller the temperature tolerance for a given resistance tolerance.

The resistance of resistive temperature detectors can be measured by making a constant current flow through the sensor. This current must be small enough to ensure that no appreciable self-heating occurs, if possible keeping the heat dissipation below 1 mW. A voltage is then obtained at the sensor which is proportional to its resistance. Where there are long leads between the current source and the sensor, it may be useful to employ a four-wire resistance measuring circuit, like the one shown in Fig. 26.4. Here, lead resistances do not falsify the result when measuring U_ϑ with high resistance instruments.

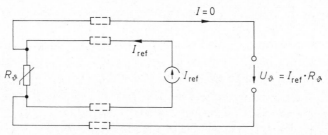

Fig. 26.4 Four-wire resistance measuring circuit providing independence from lead resistances

Although voltage U_ϑ is proportional to the resistance R_ϑ, it is not a linear function of temperature due to the non-linear characteristics. However, if the measured values are digitized, the corresponding temperature can be calculated by solving the relevant characteristic curve equation for ϑ. For analog linearization, a function network of the type described in Section 12.7.5 can be connected at the output.

For most applications, however, adequate linearization is obtained by connecting a suitable fixed resistor R_{lin} in parallel with the sensor, as shown in Fig. 26.5a. Figure 26.6 shows the effect of R_{lin} on a silicon PTC thermistor. As the value of R_ϑ increases, the linearization resistor causes the value of the parallel circuit to increase more slowly. This largely compensates for the quadratic term in the characteristic curve equation. The quality of the linearization is basically dependent on optimizing the linearization resistance for the required measurement range. In the simplest case, this value can be obtained from the data sheet.

The question that remains, however, is how to proceed when no information is available for the required measurement range. The usual requirement is for

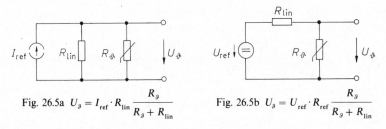

Fig. 26.5a $U_\vartheta = I_{\text{ref}} \cdot R_{\text{lin}} \dfrac{R_\vartheta}{R_\vartheta + R_{\text{lin}}}$

Fig. 26.5b $U_\vartheta = U_{\text{ref}} \cdot R_{\text{ref}} \dfrac{R_\vartheta}{R_\vartheta + R_{\text{lin}}}$

Linearization of an NTC thermistor characteristic using R_{lin}. For $U_{\text{ref}} = I_{\text{ref}} \cdot R_{\text{lin}}$ both circuits produce the same output signal

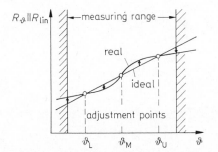

Fig. 26.6 Least-error compensation by three point adjustment

Fig. 26.7 Simplified method of calculating the linearizing resistance

a constant error limit that is as low as possible throughout the range. The linearizing resistance allows the error for three temperatures (ϑ_L, ϑ_M, ϑ_U) to be reduced to zero. These three temperatures are now shifted, selecting an appropriate value of R_{lin}, until the maximum error between them and at either end of the range is of the same magnitude. Figure 26.6 illustrates this process.

A simple approximate value for R_{lin} is obtained by placing temperatures ϑ_L and ϑ_U at the ends of the measurement range and ϑ_M in the middle. This is shown in Fig. 26.7. The linearization condition therefore follows from the requirement that the change in resistance of the parallel circuit ($R_\vartheta \| R_{\text{lin}}$) in the lower half of the measurement range shall be of exactly the same magnitude as in the upper half. For R_{lin} this gives

$$R_{\text{lin}} = \frac{R_{\vartheta M}(R_{\vartheta U} + R_{\vartheta U}) - 2R_{\vartheta L} \cdot R_{\vartheta U}}{R_{\vartheta L} + R_{\vartheta U} - 2R_{\vartheta M}} \tag{26.3}$$

where $R_{\vartheta L}$, $R_{\vartheta M}$ and $R_{\vartheta U}$ are the resistance values of the sensor at the lower (ϑ_L), middle (ϑ_M) and upper (ϑ_U) temperature. We can see that the linearizing resistance tends to infinity, i.e. can be omitted, when $R_{\vartheta M}$ is half way between $R_{\vartheta L}$ and $R_{\vartheta U}$, since then the sensor is itself linear. If $R_{\vartheta M}$ is above the mid-point, R_{lin} becomes negative. This situation occurs when the quadratic term of the sensor characteristic is negative, as, for example, with platinum sensors.

The linearization described is also obtained if the current source in Fig. 26.5a is combined with the linearizing resistance and converted into an equivalent voltage source, as shown in Fig. 26.5b. The linearizing resistance R_{lin} is the same in both cases. Figure 26.8 shows the resulting measurement circuit. Voltage U_ϑ is now the linearized function of the temperature. In order not to influence it by loading, it is applied to the non-inverting input of an instrumentation amplifier. Due to the configuration of R_1, R_2 and R_3, it can simultaneously provide the required gain and zero shift. It can be seen from Fig. 26.8 that the resulting circuit can also be regarded as a measuring bridge.

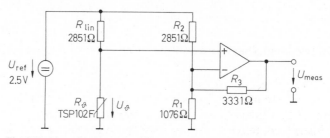

Fig. 26.8 Linearization, zero shift and gain for a silicon PTC thermistor
$U_{meas} = 20 \text{ mV} \vartheta/°C$ for $0° \leq \vartheta \leq 100°C$

Component value selection will now be explained by reference to an example. The circuit is to measure a temperature in the range 0°C to 100°C and produce output voltages between 0 V and 2 V. The reference voltage is to be 2.5 V. The sensor chosen is a silicon PTC thermistor, in this case type TSP 102 F from Texas Instruments. Linearization is to be computed for this range. To do this we take the resistance values at the ends of the range and at mid-range as specified in the data sheet, in accordance with Fig. 26.9. From Eq. (26.3) this gives a linearizing resistance $R_{lin} = 2851 \ \Omega$. The linearization error is greatest half-way between the predetermined accurate values, i.e. at 25°C and 75°C in this case. However, it is only 0.2 K. The values for U_ϑ also given in Fig. 26.9 are then produced at voltage divider R_ϑ, R_{lin}. It can be seen that the differences with respect to mid-range actually become equal in size.

To calculate resistances R_1, R_2 and R_3, one of the values can be prespecified. We select $R_2 = R_{lin} = 2851 \ \Omega$. Resistances R_1 and R_3 determine the gain and the zero point. The gain of the circuit results on the one hand from the output

ϑ	R_ϑ	U_ϑ	U_{meas}
$\vartheta_L = \quad 0°C$	$R_{\vartheta L} = \quad 813 \ \Omega$	$U_{\vartheta L} = 0.555 \text{ V}$	$U_{meas\,L} = 0.00 \text{ V}$
$\vartheta_M = \quad 50°C$	$R_{\vartheta M} = 1211 \ \Omega$	$U_{\vartheta M} = 0.745 \text{ V}$	$U_{meas\,M} = 1.00 \text{ V}$
$\vartheta_U = 100°C$	$R_{\vartheta U} = 1706 \ \Omega$	$U_{\vartheta U} = 0.935 \text{ V}$	$U_{meas\,U} = 2.00 \text{ V}$

Fig. 26.9 Mode of operation of the circuit in Fig. 26.8

voltage required

$$A = \frac{U_{\text{meas U}} - U_{\text{meas L}}}{U_{\vartheta\text{U}} - U_{\vartheta\text{L}}} = \frac{2.00 \text{ V}}{380 \text{ mV}} = 5.263$$

and on the other hand from the formula for the instrumentation amplifier

$$A = 1 + R_3/(R_1 \| R_2) \ .$$

The selection of zero point $U_{\text{meas L}} = 0$ V forces in the circuit of Fig. 26.8 the condition that the voltage drop across the virtual-parallel resistors R_1 and R_3 is precisely U_ϑ,

$$U_{\vartheta\text{L}} = \frac{R_1 \| R_3}{(R_1 \| R_3) + R_2} U_{\text{ref}} \ .$$

From these two conditional equations we obtain

$$R_1 = 1076 \ \Omega \quad \text{and} \quad R_3 = 3331 \ \Omega \ .$$

To implement the circuit, we select the next standard value from the E96 series (see Section 28.2). Circuit balancing is unnecessary in most cases, provided a closely toleranced reference voltage source such as type MC 1403 from Motorola is used.

Where a high degree of accuracy is required, the zero point can be adjusted by varying R_1 and the gain by varying R_3. In order to obviate the need for any iterative adjustment routine here, nulling is initially performed at a temperature at which the voltage at R_3 is zero. Then R_1 can be adjusted, regardless of the value of R_3. In our example

$$U_{\text{meas}} = U_\vartheta = 0.685 \text{ V}$$

for $R_\vartheta = 1076 \ \Omega$ or $\vartheta = 34.3°C$. The gain can then be adjusted for any other temperature (e.g. 0°C or 100°C) at R_3 without affecting the zero point. The general procedure for sensor circuit balancing is given in Section 26.5.

If an operational amplifier is selected whose common-mode voltage range and output voltage swing extend as far as the negative operating voltage, the circuit can be operated from a single 5 V source. In order to achieve nearly zero output, the output should be loaded with an additional 1 kΩ.

To linearize platinum temperature sensors, a negative linearizing resistance is required because of the negative quadratic term in the characteristic. For a Pt 100 sensor operated in the temperature range between 0°C and 400°C, a linearization resistor $R_{\text{lin}} = -2.5$ kΩ is required in accordance with Eq. (26.3). Linearization of the type shown in Fig. 26.8 is therefore impossible. A current source with negative internal resistance must be used in this case. Figure 26.10 shows the equivalent circuit diagram. The current source shown in Fig. 13.9 is particularly suitable for implementing this circuit. If R_3 is given a slightly lower value than would be necessary for a constant current source, a negative resistance is produced

$$r_\text{o} = -\frac{\Delta U_\vartheta}{\Delta I} = \frac{R_1 R_3 (R_2 + R_3)}{R_3^2 - R_2^2} = R_{\text{lin}} \ .$$

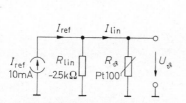

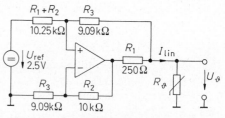

Fig. 26.10 Principle of linearized operation of Pt 100 sensors

Fig. 26.11 Implementation of a current source having a negative output resistance

This is a conditional equation for R_3. If we make $R_1 = 250\,\Omega$, $R_2 = 10\,k\Omega$ and $R_{lin} = -2.5\,k\Omega$, we obtain a value of $9.09\,k\Omega$ for R_3. The circuit thus dimensioned is shown in Fig. 26.11. The circuit for the gain adjustment and zero shift of sensor voltage U_ϑ can be devised in analogy to that of Fig. 26.8.

In a restricted range of temperatures and where the degree of accuracy required is not too great, the resistance characteristic of an NTC thermistor can also be linearized using a parallel resistor. Figure 26.12 shows how this arrangement operates. Optimum linearization can also be obtained here if the inflection point of $R_{lin} \| R_T$ is at the mid-point T_M of the desired temperature range. This gives the following equation for the linearizing resistance [26.2]

$$R_{lin} = \frac{B - T_M}{B + 2T_M} R_{TM} \approx R_{TM} \; ,$$

where B is the B value of the NTC thermistor from the characteristic curve equation. Once again the temperature sensor can be connected in series with the same linearizing resistor R_{lin}, giving a linearized voltage curve. In order to obtain a voltage which increases with temperature, it is advisable to take off the voltage across the linearizing resistor. This is shown in Fig. 26.13. The circuit and its design procedure are otherwise identical to the interfacing circuit for PTC thermistors shown in Fig. 26.8.

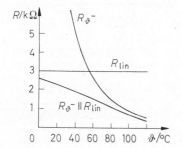

Fig. 26.12 Linearization of an NTC thermistor using a parallel resistor

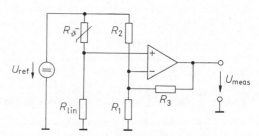

Fig. 26.13 Interfacing circuit providing linearization, zero shift and gain for NTC thermistors

26.1.5   Transistors as temperature sensors

Because of its internal structure, a bipolar transistor is a heavily temperature-dependent component. Its reverse current doubles for an approximately 10 K increase in temperature, and its base-emitter voltage falls by some 2 mV/K (see Section 4.3.5). These otherwise undesirable side-effects can be utilized for temperature measurement. In Fig. 26.14, a transistor configured as a diode is operated with a constant current. This produces the temperature dependence of the base-emitter voltage shown in Fig. 26.15. At room temperature ($T \approx 300$ K), its normal value is about 600 mV. With a temperature increase of 100 K, U_{BE} falls by 200 mV and increases accordingly if the temperature is reduced. The temperature coefficient is therefore

$$\frac{\Delta U}{U \cdot \Delta T} = 0.3\% \ /\text{K} \ .$$

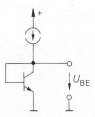

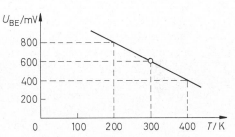

Fig. 26.14 Using the base-emitter voltage for temperature measurement

Fig. 26.15 Temperature versus base-emitter voltage (typical)

Unfortunately the dispersion of the forward voltage and of the temperature coefficient is very large. For this reason, individual transistors are nowadays only used for temperature measurement where the degree of measuring accuracy required is not too great. Improved calibration can be achieved for circuits based on the difference in the base-emitter voltages of two bipolar transistors operated at different current densities. The principle is shown in Fig. 26.16. This is effectively a bandgap reference as described in Section 18.4. The difference between the base-emitter voltages is given by

$$\Delta U_{BE} = U_T \ln \frac{I_{C2}}{I_{CS} A_2} - U_T \ln \frac{I_{C1}}{I_{CS} A_1} = U_T \ln \frac{I_{C2} A_1}{I_{C1} A_2} \ .$$

Since the two collector currents are of the same magnitude and the surface ratio of the transistors is $A_1/A_2 = 10$, it follows that

$$\Delta U_{BE} = \frac{kT}{e} \ln 10 = 200 \frac{\mu V}{K} \cdot T \ .$$

To implement a band-gap reference this voltage is amplified with R_2 so that

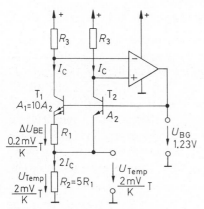

Fig. 26.16 Use of a bandgap reference for
temperature measurement
(e.g. LT1019 from Linear Techn.)

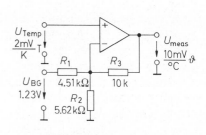

$U_{meas} = 5\,U_{Temp} - 2.22\,U_{BG}$

Fig. 26.17 Supplementary circuit for
implementing a Celsius zero point

a voltage $U_{Temp} \approx (2\,\mathrm{mV/K}) \cdot T$ is produced which compensates for the temperature coefficient of T_2 (see Section 18.4).

Voltage U_{Temp} can be used directly for temperature measurement: it is proportional to absolute temperature T (PTAT). For $\vartheta = 0°\mathrm{C}$

$$U_{Temp} = 2\,\frac{\mathrm{mV}}{\mathrm{K}} \cdot 273\,\mathrm{K} = 546\,\mathrm{mV}\ .$$

To obtain a Celsius zero point, a constant voltage of this magnitude can be subtracted from U_{Temp}. For this purpose, the subtractor in Fig. 26.17 uses the appropriately weighted voltage U_{BG}.

The principle employed in Fig. 26.16 can be modified by connecting the emitters to the same potential. The output voltage of the operational amplifier in Fig. 26.18 again assumes a value such that the two collector currents have the same magnitude. This produces the same value for ΔU_{BE}, but in this case between the base terminals. The voltage across R_1 is therefore proportional to T (PTAT). It can be increased to any value by series connection of additional resistors. In the example shown in Fig. 26.18, it is amplified by a factor of 50:

$$U_{Temp} = 50 \Delta U_{BE} = 10\,\frac{\mathrm{mV}}{\mathrm{K}} \cdot T\ .$$

At room temperature ($T \approx 300\,\mathrm{K}$) this produces a voltage of $U_{Temp} \approx 3\,\mathrm{V}$. The advantage of this variant is that U_{Temp} occurs at the output of the operational amplifier and a load can therefore be applied to it.

Temperature sensors employing the principle shown in Fig. 26.18 are manufactured as ICs by Texas Instr. (STP 35) and National (LM 335). They do not have a separate supply voltage terminal and therefore behave like a Zener diode.

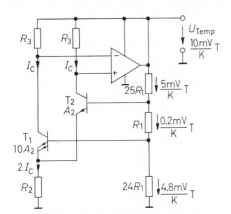

Fig. 26.18 Modified bandgap reference for direct temperature measurement (e.g. STP 35 from Texas Instruments)

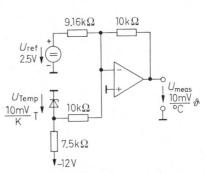

Fig. 26.19 Example of Celsius zero shift for a two-terminal temperature sensor

The operation of this type of temperature sensor with Celsius zero shift will be illustrated by the example in Fig. 26.19. Since the sensor behaves like a Zener diode with a low internal resistance (approx. $0.5\,\Omega$ at 1 mA), the current flowing has virtually no effect on the voltage and the sensor can be operated from an unregulated supply voltage. It is merely necessary to ensure that the minimum operating current (here 0.4 mA) is maintained. On the other hand, an unnecessarily large operating current should not be chosen, so that self-heating is kept to a minimum. If a series resistance of $7.5\,\mathrm{k}\Omega$ is selected in Fig. 26.19, a current of about 1 mA flows through the sensor at 0°C; at 150°C it is still higher than 0.4 mA. To obtain a Celsius zero point, a current of

$$\frac{2.73\,\mathrm{V}}{10\,\mathrm{k}\Omega} = \frac{2.5\,\mathrm{V}}{9.16\,\mathrm{k}\Omega} = 273\,\mu\mathrm{A}$$

must be subtracted. Since the operational amplifier inverts in this case, a positive Celsius scale is obtained at the output, as required.

A sensor incorporating Celsius zero shift is also available. The LM 35 from National, for example, produces a voltage of 10 mV/°C. It represents a significantly simpler solution if only positive temperatures are to be measured.

Voltage ΔU_{BE} which is proportional to temperature can also be used to generate a *current* which is proportional to the absolute temperature. In both Fig. 26.16 and Fig. 26.18, collector current I_{C} is proportional to T. In order to obtain the required current it is therefore sufficient to replace the operational amplifier in Fig. 26.16 with the current balancing circuit in Fig. 26.20. Condition $I_{\mathrm{C1}} = I_{\mathrm{C2}}$ is then still fulfilled. Voltage

$$\Delta U_{\mathrm{BE}} = U_{\mathrm{T}} \ln \frac{A_1}{A_2} = \frac{k}{e} \ln \frac{A_1}{A_2} \cdot T = 86\,\frac{\mu\mathrm{V}}{\mathrm{K}} \ln \frac{A_1}{A_2} \cdot T$$

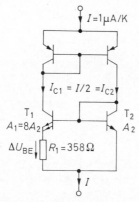

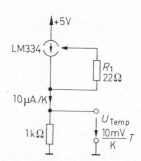

Fig. 26.20 Temperature-controlled current source using the bandgap principle (e.g. AD 592 from Analog Devices)

Fig. 26.21 Temperature-controlled current source with freely-selectable output current (e.g. LM 344 from National)

then results in a current of

$$I = 2I_C = 2\Delta U_{BE}/R_1 \ .$$

A surface ratio of $A_1/A_2 = 8$ and a resistance $R_1 = 358 \, \Omega$ therefore produce a current of

$$I = T \cdot 1 \, \mu A/K \ .$$

An example of a sensor employing this principle is the AD 592 from Analog Devices [26.3].

Sometimes resistor R_1 is not incorporated in the integrated circuit but can be connected externally. This provides the option of selecting any required proportionality constant, i.e. of programming even a relatively large current of $10 \, \mu A/K$. A monolithic sensor which offers this facility is the LM 334 from National. Figure 26.21 shows an example of how it operates. The $22 \, \Omega$ resistor sets the current to $10 \, \mu A/K$. It causes a voltage drop of $10 \, mV/K$ across the load resistance of $1 \, k\Omega$. Since these temperature sensors constitute constant current sources, the supply voltage has no effect on the current, provided that the voltage is not lower than a given minimum (1 V in the case of the LM 334). For this reason, a regulated voltage supply is not required.

26.1.6 The thermocouple

At the contact point of two different metals or alloys the Seebeck effect gives rise to a voltage in the millivolt range known as the thermoelectric voltage. The principle of temperature measurement illustrated in Fig. 26.22 shows that even if one of the two metals is copper we always obtain two thermocouples with opposite polarity. At identical temperatures $\vartheta_M = \vartheta_R$, their thermoelectric voltages therefore compensate one another. Consequently, only the temperature

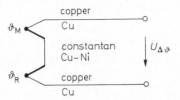

Fig. 26.22 Principle of temperature measurement with thermocouples, using a copper-constantan thermocouple as an example

difference $\Delta\vartheta = \vartheta_M - \vartheta_R$ can be measured. To measure individual temperatures, a *reference junction* with reference temperature ϑ_R is therefore required. The case is particularly simple if $\vartheta_R = 0°C$. This can be achieved by immersing one leg of the thermocouple in ice water. The measured values then indicate by how many degrees ϑ_M exceeds $0°C$.

This method of generating the reference temperature is of course nothing more than a conceptual model which would be very hard to implement. A simpler solution is to construct an oven which can be kept at a constant temperature of e.g. $60°C$ and to use this as a reference temperature. In this case the measured value is therefore referred to $60°C$. To convert it to $0°C$, a constant voltage corresponding to the reference temperature of $60°C$ can simply be added.

However, it is even simpler to leave the temperature of the reference junction as it is [26.4]. It will then be close to the ambient temperature. Nevertheless, if this reference temperature is not taken into account, an error of 20 . . . 50°C can easily occur which would be too large for most applications. But if this temperature is measured (which would be a simple matter using a transistor thermometer IC, for example), the associated voltage can be added into the measuring circuit. This procedure is shown schematically in Fig. 26.23, which also shows the case where neither of the thermocouple metals is copper. In this case an additional unintentional thermocouple occurs at the connection point to a copper wire of the evaluation circuit. In order to ensure that these two thermoelectric voltages compensate for each other, the two additional elements must be at the same temperature.

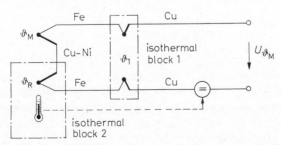

Fig. 26.23 Compensation of reference junction temperature ϑ_R

The arrangement in Fig. 26.23 can be simplified by combining the two isothermal blocks into one with a temperature of ϑ_R and reducing to zero the length of the joining metal lead (iron in this case). This produces the commonly used arrangement shown in Fig. 26.24 which only requires one isothermal block.

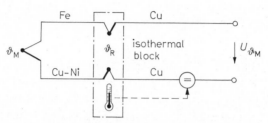

Fig. 26.24 Practical design for a thermocouple system

There are various combinations of metals or alloys for thermocouples and these are standardized under IEC 584 and DIN 43710. They are listed in Fig. 26.25. It is evident that their maximum working temperature varies widely and that the noble metal thermocouples possess markedly lower temperature coefficients. The thermoelectric voltage characteristic is plotted in Fig. 26.26. As we can see, none of the curves is precisely linear. Types T, J, E and K, however, do possess a decent linearity and also deliver relatively high voltages. They are

Type	Metal 1 Pos. terminal	Metal 2 Neg. terminal	Temp. coeff. Average	Usable temperature range
T	Copper	Constantan	42.8 µV/°C	$-200\ldots+400°C$
J	**Iron**	**Constantan**	51.7 µV/°C	$-200\ldots+700°C$
E	Chromel	Constantan	60.9 µV/°C	$-200\ldots+1000°C$
K	**Chromel**	**Alumel**	40.5 µV/°C	$-200\ldots+1300°C$
S	Platinum	Platinum-10% Rhodium	6.4 µV/°C	$0\ldots+1500°C$
R	Platinum	Platinum-13% Rhodium	6.4 µV/°C	$0\ldots+1600°C$
B	Platinum-6% Rhodium	Platinum-30% Rhodium		$0\ldots+1800°C$
G	Tungsten	Tungsten-26% Rhenium		$0\ldots+2800°C$
C	Tungsten-5% Rhenium	Tungsten-26% Rhenium	15 µV/°C	$0\ldots+2800°C$

Fig. 26.25 Overview of thermocouples. The most widely used types, J and K, are shown in bold type. Types B and G are so non-linear that no average temperature coefficient can be specified

Constantan = Copper-nickel, Chromel = Nickel-chromium, Alumel = Aluminum-nickel

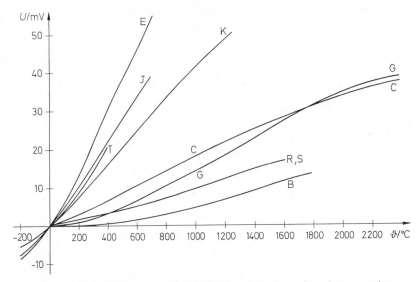

Fig. 26.26 Temperature versus thermoelectric voltage for various thermocouples, at a reference temperature of 0°C

therefore preferred if the temperature range permits their use. For the other types, linearization is required for evaluation if it is not possible to restrict the application to a narrow temperature range.

To evaluate the thermoelectric voltage, a voltage corresponding to reference temperature ϑ_R must be added in accordance with Fig. 26.24 in order to refer the measurement to the "ice point", i.e. 0°C. This correction can either be made at thermocouple level or after amplification. Figure 26.27 gives a schematic representation of the second situation, using an iron-constantan thermocouple as an example. To amplify its voltage to $10\,\mathrm{m\,V/K}$, a gain of

$$A = \frac{10\,\mathrm{m\,V/K}}{51.7\,\mathrm{\mu V/K}} = 193$$

is required. Then the reference temperature must be added with the same sensitivity, i.e. also with $10\,\mathrm{m\,V/K}$. Figure 26.28 shows one way of implementing this principle. Since the thermoelectric voltages are in the µV range, a low-drift

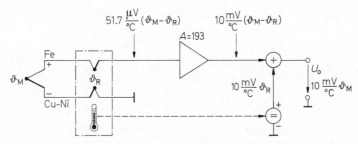

Fig. 26.27 Amplification and reference point compensation for thermocouples,
using an iron-constantan thermocouple as an example

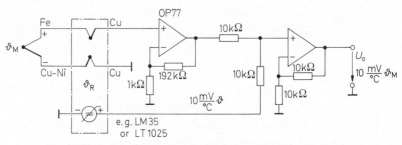

Fig. 26.28 Practical design of the interfacing circuit for thermocouples,
using an iron-constantan type as an example

operational amplifier is necessary. In order to obtain adequate loop gain despite the high voltage gain of 193, the op-amp must possess a high differential gain A_D. Measuring the reference junction temperature can be greatly simplified by using a ready-made temperature sensor with Celsius zero point such as the LM 35 from National or the LT 1025 from Linear Technology. However, any other circuit providing an output signal of 10 mV/K described in this chapter could also be used.

Figure 26.29 shows the alternative principle whereby the ice point correction value is added to the thermocouple voltage before the signal is amplified. For this purpose a voltage of 51.7 µV/K must be added in the case of an iron-constantan thermocouple. The circuit becomes very simple if we make use of the fact that the thermocouple is electrically floating and can therefore simply be connected in series with the correction voltage source, as shown in Fig. 26.30.

The simplest solution is to use specific ICs for operating thermocouples, such as the AD 594 . . . 597 series from Analog Devices. Types AD 594 and 596 of this series are calibrated for the operation of iron-constantan thermocouples (type J) and types AD 595 and AD 597 for Chromel-Alumel (type K). Here the wires of the thermocouple are connected directly to the integrated circuit, as shown in Fig. 26.31. The latter constitutes the isothermal block with reference temperature ϑ_R. It is assumed that the silicon crystal is at the same temperature as the IC pins. The ice point correction is generated for the chip temperature, added to the thermoelectric voltage and amplified. An internal zero point and gain calibration to within 1°C is available. If the inputs are shorted and the thermocouple omitted, only the ice point correction voltage of

$$U_\vartheta = 51.7 \frac{\mu V}{°C} \cdot \vartheta_R \cdot 193 = 10 \frac{mV}{°C} \vartheta_R$$

is produced at the output. The circuit then operates as a transistor temperature sensor with Celsius zero point.

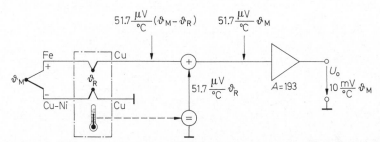

Fig. 26.29 Reference junction compensation prior to amplification of thermocouple signals, using an iron-constantan type as an example

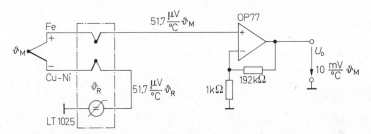

Fig. 26.30 Practical design for reference junction compensation prior to amplification, using iron-constantan thermocouples as an example

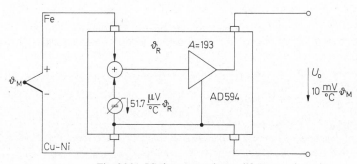

Fig. 26.31 IC thermocouple amplifier

26.1.7 Overview of types

A number of representative manufacturers and products for temperature measurement are listed in Fig. 26.32. There are large variations in price. It is therefore worthwhile comparing different principles and types. Generally it can be said, however, that the more expensive a sensor, the more accurately it has been adjusted (laser trimmed) by the manufacturer.

Type	Manufacturer	Output signal Rated value	Temperature range
Metal PTC thermistor			
Pt 100 . . . 1000	Heraeus	100 . . . 1000 Ω	− 50°C . . . + 500°C
Pt 100 . . . 1000	Murata	100 . . . 1000 Ω	− 50°C . . . + 600°C
Pt 100 . . . 1000	Degussa	100 . . . 1000 Ω	− 250°C . . . + 850°C
Ni 100	Degussa	100 Ω	− 60°C . . . + 180°C
Ni 2000	Honeywell	2 kΩ	− 40°C . . . + 150°C
Silicon PTC thermistor			
TS-Series	Texas Instr.	1 kΩ . . . 2 kΩ	− 50°C . . . + 150°C
KTY-Series	Valvo	1 kΩ . . . 2 kΩ	− 50°C . . . + 300°C
KTY-Series	Siemens	2 kΩ	− 50°C . . . + 150°C
Metal-ceramic NTC thermistor			
M-Series	Siemens	1 kΩ . . . 100 kΩ	− 50°C . . . + 200°C
NTC thermistor	Valvo	1 kΩ . . . 1 MΩ	− 50°C . . . + 200°C
NTC thermistor	Yellow-Springs	100 Ω . . . 1 MΩ	− 80°C . . . + 150°C
Bandgap sensors			
STP 35	Texas Instr.	10 mV/K	− 40°C . . . + 125°C
LM 235 Z	National	10 mV/K	− 40°C . . . + 125°C
LM 35	National	10 mV/°C	0°C . . . + 125°C
LT 1025	Lin. Technology	10 mV/°C*	0°C . . . + 60°C
LM 134 Z	National	0.1 . . . 10 μA/K	− 40°C . . . + 125°C
AD 590	Analog Dev.	1 μA/K	− 55°C . . . + 150°C
Thermocouples			
J, K, S, R, B	Heraeus	see Fig. 26.25	see Fig. 26.25
J, K, S, R, B	Degussa	see Fig. 26.25	see Fig. 26.25
J, K, S	Philips	see Fig. 26.25	see Fig. 26.25
Thermocouple amplifiers			
AD 594	Analog Dev.	10 mV/°C, (type J)	− 55°C . . . + 125°C
AD 595	Analog Dev.	10 mV/°C, (type K)	− 55°C . . . + 125°C

*Additional outputs for reference junction compensation of thermocouple types E, J, K, T, R and S

Fig. 26.32 Examples of temperature sensors

26.2 Pressure measurement

Pressure is defined as force per unit area

$$p = F/A .$$

The unit of pressure is

$$\boxed{1 \text{ Pascal} = \frac{1 \text{ Newton}}{1 \text{ Square meter}} ; \quad 1 \text{ Pa} = \frac{1 \text{ N}}{1 \text{ m}^2}} .$$

The term bar is also widely used. It is related to the above as follows

$$1 \text{ bar} = 100 \text{ kPa} \quad \text{or} \quad 1 \text{ mbar} = 1 \text{ hPa} .$$

Sometimes pressure is defined as the height of a column of water or mercury. The relationships are

$$1 \text{ cm H}_2\text{O} = 98.1 \text{ Pa} = 0.981 \text{ mbar} ,$$

$$1 \text{ mm Hg} = 133 \text{ Pa} = 1.33 \text{ mbar} .$$

In English-language data sheets pressure is usually specified in

$$\text{psi} = \text{pounds per square inch} .$$

This can be converted as follows.

$$1 \text{ psi} = 6.89 \text{ kPa} = 68.9 \text{ mbar} \quad \text{or} \quad 15 \text{ psi} \approx 1 \text{ bar} .$$

Figure 26.33 shows a few examples of the orders of magnitude of pressures occurring in practical applications [26.5].

Pressure sensors can be used in a wide variety of applications. They can even be used to determine flow rates and flow volumes via differences in pressure.

Pressure range	Application
< 40 mbar	Water level of washing machine, dishwasher
100 mbar	Vacuum cleaner, filtration monitoring, flow measurement
200 mbar	Blood pressure measurement
1 bar	Barometer, motor vehicle (correction for ignition and fuel injection)
2 bar	Motor vehicle (tyre pressure)
10 bar	Motor vehicle (oil pressure, compressed air for brakes), cooling compressor
50 bar	Pneumatics, industrial robots
500 bar	Hydraulics, construction machinery

Fig. 26.33 Pressures occurring in practical applications

26.2.1 Pressure sensor design

Pressure sensors record the pressure-induced deflection of a diaphragm. For this purpose a number of strain gauges are mounted on the diaphragm and form a Wheatstone bridge. They vary their resistance as a result of the piezo-resistive effect of deflection, pressure or tensile force. They used to be mainly constructed from vapor-deposited constantan or platinum-iridium layers. Nowadays resistors implanted in silicon are generally used, with the silicon substrate simultaneously acting as the diaphragm. They have the advantage of being cheaper to manufacture and are over ten times more sensitive. Their disadvantage, however, is their higher temperature coefficient.

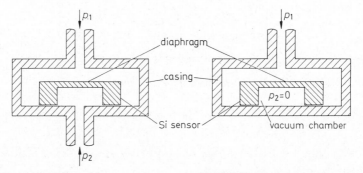

Fig. 26.34a Differential pressure sensor   Fig. 26.34b Absolute pressure sensor

Figure 26.34 gives a schematic representation of a pressure sensor. In the differential pressure sensor shown in Fig. 26.34a, a pressure p_1 is exerted on one side of the diaphragm and a pressure of p_2 on the other. Therefore, only the pressure difference $p_1 - p_2$ governs the deflection of the diaphragm. With the absolute pressure sensor in Fig. 26.34b one side of the diaphragm takes the form of a vacuum chamber [26.6].

Figure 26.35 shows a typical arrangement of the strain gauges on the diaphragm. The left-hand diagram is intended to show that when the diaphragm deflects, zones are produced which are elongated and others which are compressed. It is in these areas—see right-hand diagram—that the four bridge resistors are arranged. They are interconnected in such a way that the resistances in the bridge arms change inversely. This arrangement, as can be seen

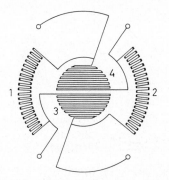

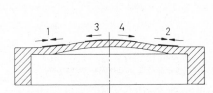

Fig. 26.35a Expansion and compression of   Fig. 26.35b Arrangement of strain gauges on
   the diaphragm of pressure sensors   the diaphragm

from Fig. 26.36, produces a particularly large output signal, while concurring
effects, such as the absolute value of the resistances and their temperature
coefficient, compensate for each other. In spite of this, the output signal is low
because of the very small changes in resistance ΔR. At maximum pressure and at
an operating voltage of $U_{ref} = 5\,V$, it is between 25 and 250 mV depending on
the sensor. The relative change in resistance is therefore between 0.5% and 5%.

   The output signal of a real pressure sensor is made up of a component
proportional to the pressure and an undesirable offset component:

$$U_D = S \cdot p \cdot U_{ref} + O \cdot U_{ref} = U_P + U_O \qquad (26.4)$$

where p is the pressure and

$$S = \frac{\Delta U_D}{\Delta p \, U_{ref}} = \frac{\Delta R}{\Delta p \cdot R}$$

is the sensitivity and O the offset. Both terms provide a contribution which is
proportional to the reference voltage. In order not to obtain too small a signal,
the reference voltage should be as large as possible. However, constraints exist
due to the self-heating of the sensor. Reference voltages between 2 V and 12 V are
therefore used.

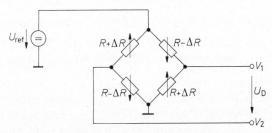

Fig. 26.36 Measuring bridge of a pressure sensor

$$\frac{U_D}{U_{ref}} = \frac{R + \Delta R}{2R} - \frac{R - \Delta R}{2R} = \frac{\Delta R}{R}$$

26.2.2　Operation of temperature-compensated pressure sensors

Silicon-based pressure sensors have such high temperature coefficients that some form of temperature compensation is generally required. The easiest solution is for the user to employ pressure sensors which already have temperature compensation provided by the manufacturer. However, in some cases cost considerations may force users to implement their own temperature compensation. We shall now describe a possible approach.

There are a number of basic considerations relating to the conditioning of pressure sensor signals:

1) Although the four bridge resistors in Fig. 26.36 are well matched beforehand, their absolute value exhibits a large tolerance and is also heavily temperature-dependent. For this reason the output signals must not be loaded, and an instrumentation amplifier is normally used to provide gain.
2) Pressure sensors usually have a zero error which is quite small in absolute terms (e.g. ± 50 mV); however, comparison with the wanted signal shows that it is usually of the order of magnitude of the measurement range. A zero adjuster covering the entire measurement range is therefore required.
3) In general, the sensitivity of a pressure sensor also exhibits significant tolerances (e.g. $\pm 30\%$) so that gain adjustment is additionally required.
4) Zero and gain adjustment must be possible without having to use iteration procedures.
5) Since the wanted signals of a pressure sensor are small, a large amount of amplification is required. This results in appreciable amplifier noise. The pressure sensor itself also produces considerable circuit noise. The bandwidth at the amplifier output must therefore be limited to the frequency range of the pressure variations.
6) The pressure measuring circuit will often be required to operate exclusively from a positive voltage, so that an additional negative supply voltage can be dispensed with.

The circuit normally used for conditioning pressure sensor signals is an instrumentation amplifier [26.7]. In Fig. 26.37, the asymmetrical amplifier from Fig. 25.5 is illustrated as an example. The gain is adjusted by resistor R_1 to suit the sensor. For zeroing purposes, the foot of voltage divider R_2 has not been connected to ground but via impedance converter OA 3 to the zero adjuster. This causes voltage V_Z to be added to the output voltage.

The circuit in Fig. 26.37 can be operated from a single positive supply voltage, since the quiescent potentials are approximately $\frac{1}{2}U_{ref}$. A serious disadvantage, however, is that it is not possible to adjust zero and gain noniteratively. If, for example, the output voltage of the pressure sensor is broken down in accordance with Eq. (26.4) into a pressure-dependent component U_P and the offset voltage U_O, it can be seen that both are amplified by the factor $A = 2(1 + R_2/R_1)$:

$$U_o = A(V_1 - V_2) + V_Z = AU_P + AU_O + V_Z \,,$$

whereas the voltage for zero correction is not amplified. The zero adjustment

$$V_Z = -AU_O$$

is therefore dependent on the gain A. This means that for iteration-free adjustment, the voltage for zero correction must also be amplified by A. Consequently zeroing must *precede* the point in the signal flow at which gain adjustment takes place. Then the zero balance point can be selected such that the resistor for adjusting the gain has no voltage, its value then having no effect on the output voltage.

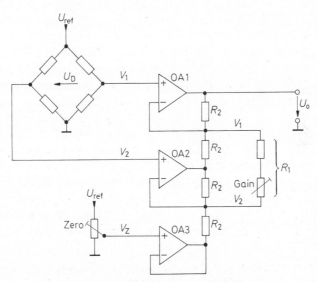

Fig. 26.37 Interfacing circuit for pressure sensors

$$U_o = 2\left(1 + \frac{R_2}{R_1}\right) \cdot (V_1 - V_2) + V_Z$$

$$U_o = \qquad A \quad \cdot \quad U_D \quad - U_O$$

To allow zeroing to be performed before the subtractor containing the gain adjuster, operational amplifiers OA 3 and OA 4 have been added in Fig. 26.38. For potential V_3 this gives:

$$V_3 = V_2 + \frac{R_3}{R_3 + R_4} (\tfrac{1}{2} V_{ref} - V_z) \;.$$

Thus a voltage of up to $\pm \tfrac{1}{2} V_{ref} R_3/(R_3 + R_4)$ can be added to potential V_2, depending on the size of V_z. The amplifier zero has not been fixed at 0 V but at U_{ref} by connecting the foot of voltage divider chain R_2 to U_{ref} instead of to ground. This shifts the zero balance point from zero pressure and zero output voltage to the pressure corresponding to $U_o = U_{ref}$ (see Section 26.5.1). In any case, it is not possible to achieve an output voltage of exactly 0 V in the circuit, as it is operated from a positive supply voltage only.

An example will serve to illustrate component value selection for the circuit. An air pressure meter is to deliver an output voltage of 5 mV/hPa. The KP 100 A 1 from Valvo is to be used as the pressure gauge. At a supply voltage of $U_{ref} = 5$ V, it delivers a signal of 20 . . . 80 µV/hPa; its zero error can be as much as ± 50 mV. To calculate the zero adjustment we specify $R_3 = 1$ kΩ. At a reference voltage of $U_{ref} = 5$ V, this then produces the required adjustment range with $R_4 = 49$ kΩ. The gain must be adjustable between 62.5 and 250, depending on the sensitivity of the sensor. If $R_2 = 10$ kΩ is specified, a minimum value of 80 Ω (fixed resistor) and a maximum value of 330 Ω is obtained for R_1. The variable resistor must therefore have a value of 250 Ω.

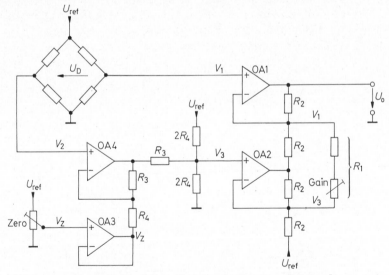

Fig. 26.38 Interfacing circuit for non-iterative calibration

$$U_o = 2\left(1 + \frac{R_2}{R_1}\right)\left[(V_1 - V_2) + \frac{R_3}{R_3 + R_4}(V_z - \tfrac{1}{2} U_{ref})\right] + U_{ref}$$

$$U_o = \underbrace{\qquad A \qquad}_{} \qquad [U_D - U_o] \qquad + U_{ref}$$

To calibrate the circuit, it is first necessary to adjust the zero point. To avoid an iterative process, the pressure at which no voltage is present at the gain adjuster is selected, i.e. $V_1 - V_3 = 0$. This is the case, when $U_o = U_{ref} = 5$ V and corresponds to a pressure of 1000 hPa. The zero adjuster is therefore set so that U_o is actually 5 V at 1000 hPa. Since no voltage is dropped across R_1 after the adjustment, its value has no effect on the adjustment. To calibrate the gain, we select the pressure which is as far away as possible from the zero point at 1000 hPa, i.e. the upper or lower end of the desired measurement range, for example, and adjust the output voltage to the nominal value with R_1. A more detailed description of sensor calibration is given in Section 26.5.

Since the sensor signals are in the microvolt range, it is advisable to use operational amplifiers with low offset voltages and offset voltage drifts. However, as the bandwidth requirements are small, operational amplifiers with low power consumption can be used. A good example is the quad operational amplifier OP 490 from PMI. A ready-made instrumentation amplifier can, of course, be used for the subtractor, although the advantage is not significant: only the four resistors R_2 are saved.

The circuit for conditioning the sensor signals can be greatly simplified if a negative voltage is additionally available or can be generated with a voltage converter. In the circuit shown in Fig. 26.39, one bridge arm of the pressure sensor is in the negative feedback path of amplifier OA 1. If we imagine $V_n = 0$, the output voltage of OA 1 will assume a value such that $V_2 = 0$. The entire bridge signal U_D will therefore be transferred to the right-hand bridge output and subtraction will no longer be required. Therefore the simple non-inverting amplifier OA 2 is all that is required here to provide gain. For nulling purposes, voltage V_n is applied to OA 1. Then $V_2 = V_n$ and

$$V_1 = U_D + V_n = U_P + U_O + V_n \ .$$

The zero point is therefore adjusted for $V_n = - U_O$.

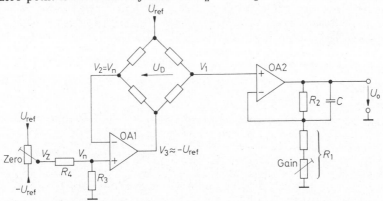

Fig. 26.39 Transfer of the wanted signal to the right-hand bridge arm

$$U_o = \left(1 + \frac{R_2}{R_1}\right)(U_D + V_n) = A(U_D - U_O)$$

A lowpass filter can easily be implemented using capacitor C to limit the noise bandwidth of the circuit. A second-order lowpass filter can also be implemented by connecting a second capacitor to ground directly at the bridge output.

26.2.3 Temperature compensation for pressure sensors

By their nature, the doped silicon resistors of a pressure sensor are temperature-dependent. They are even used for temperature measurement themselves (see Section 26.1). The typical resistance curve is shown in Fig. 26.40. At room temperature the resistor's temperature coefficient is as follows

$$TC_R = \frac{\Delta R}{R \cdot \Delta \vartheta} \approx 1350 \frac{\text{ppm}}{\text{K}} = 0.135 \frac{\%}{\text{K}} \ .$$

In a bridge arrangement of the type employed in pressure sensors, the temperature-induced resistance variation has no adverse effect, provided it is the same in all the resistors and no load is placed on the output signal. However, a problem arises due to the fact that the pressure sensitivity of the sensor is also temperature-dependent; its temperature coefficient is

$$TC_S = \frac{\Delta S}{S \cdot \Delta \vartheta} \approx -2350 \frac{\text{ppm}}{\text{K}} = -0.235 \frac{\%}{\text{K}} \ .$$

Thus, for a temperature increase of 40°C, it has already dropped by 10%, as can be seen from Fig. 26.40. To prevent this from invalidating the measurement, the gain must be increased accordingly with temperature. Naturally, this must not be based on the temperature of the amplifier, but on that of the pressure sensor. The temperature detector must therefore be incorporated into the pressure sensor. Hence, the obvious solution would be to perform the temper-

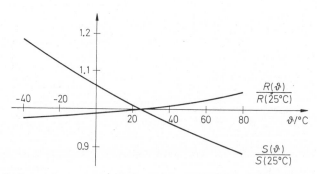

Fig. 26.40 Resistance and sensitivity of silicon pressure sensors as a function of temperature

$$TC_R = \frac{\Delta R}{R \Delta \vartheta} \approx 1350 \frac{\text{ppm}}{\text{°C}} \ , \qquad TC_S = \frac{\Delta S}{S \Delta \vartheta} \approx -2350 \frac{\text{ppm}}{\text{°C}}$$

ature compensation in the sensor itself. This can be done by increasing reference voltage U_{ref} with temperature in such a way that the reduction in sensitivity is just compensated:

$$U_D = S \cdot p \cdot U_{ref} + O \cdot U_{ref} = U_P + U_O .$$

It is usually accepted that the zero point $U_O = O \cdot U_{ref}$ will shift slightly.

Temperature-compensated pressure sensors differ only in the method of temperature compensation employed. Three widely-used methods are illustrated in Fig. 26.41. In Fig. 26.41a an NTC thermistor is used to increase the bridge voltage with temperature. In Fig. 26.41b the negative temperature coefficient of a diode of $-2\,mV/K$ is used. The arrangement of the transistor in the circuit produces the effect of three diodes. A temperature sensor using the band-gap principle can also be incorporated; the type used in Fig. 26.41c is the STP 35 (see Fig. 26.18). It operates as shown in Fig. 26.18 and delivers a voltage of 10 mV/K, i.e. about 3 V at room temperature. The interesting feature of this solution is that the temperature compensation circuit can be simultaneously used for temperature measurement.

One method of temperature compensation which dispenses with an additional temperature detector involves using the temperature dependence of the bridge resistors themselves for temperature compensation. If the bridge is operated with a constant current I_{ref} instead of a constant voltage U_{ref}, the voltage across the bridge increases with temperature by the same amount as its resistance. Unfortunately, the voltage increase of $TC_R = 1350\,ppm/K$ is not enough to compensate for the reduction in sensitivity of $TC_S = -2350\,ppm/K$.

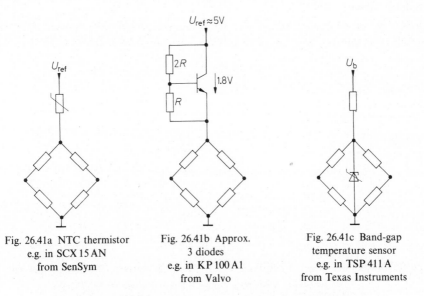

Fig. 26.41a NTC thermistor
e.g. in SCX 15 AN
from SenSym

Fig. 26.41b Approx.
3 diodes
e.g. in KP 100 A1
from Valvo

Fig. 26.41c Band-gap
temperature sensor
e.g. in TSP 411 A
from Texas Instruments

Fig. 26.41. Temperature compensation methods for pressure sensors

If, however, the current source in Fig. 26.42 is given a negative internal resistance, current I_B will rise as the voltage increases. The requirement that bridge voltage U_B shall rise by a factor of $|TC_S/TC_R|$ more quickly than with a constant current, produces the following condition

$$U_B = |TC_S/TC_R|R_B I_k = (R_i \| R_B)I_k \ .$$

This results in the following equation for determining the value of R_i

$$R_i = \frac{|TC_S|}{TC_R - |TC_S|} R_B = -2.35 R_B \ .$$

The circuit shown in Fig. 13.9 is again ideally suited for use as a current source. Figure 26.43 shows how it can be used for temperature compensation in a pressure sensor with a bridge resistance of $R_B = 3 \text{ k}\Omega$ (e.g. TSP 410 A from Texas Instr.). We select a short-circuit current of $I_k = 1 \text{ mA}$. This gives $R_1 = U_{ref}/I_k = 2.5 \text{ k}\Omega$. The rated operating voltage of the bridge is therefore

$$U_B = |TC_S/TC_R|R_B I_k = (2350/1350)\cdot 3 \text{ k}\Omega \cdot 1 \text{ mA} = 5.22 \text{ V} \ .$$

In order to obtain the component values for the circuit, the required internal resistance must first be determined:

$$R_i = \frac{|TC_S|}{TC_R - |TC_S|} R_B = -2.35 \cdot 3 \text{ k}\Omega = -7.05 \text{ k}\Omega$$

If $R_2 = 10 \text{ k}\Omega$ is then specified, we obtain

$$R_3 = \frac{R_2}{2R_i}\left[R_1 \overset{(+)}{-} \sqrt{R_1^2 + 4R_i(R_i + R_1)} \right] = 6.45 \text{ k}\Omega \ .$$

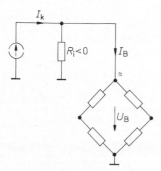

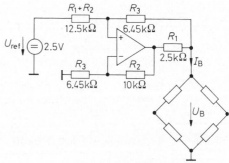

Fig. 26.42 Operation of a pressure sensor from a current source having a negative internal resistance

Fig. 26.43 Practical implementation of the current source

$$I_k = 1 \text{ mA} \qquad R_i = -7.05 \text{ k}\Omega$$

26.2.4   Commercially-available pressure sensors

Figure 26.44 gives some idea of the wide range of pressure sensors available. There are not only a large number of other manufacturers, but most of the types listed are merely representative of a whole family of sensors. It can be seen from Fig. 26.44 that in addition to the pressure sensors with a range of 1 to 2 bar, which are primarily designed for barometers, there are also types with very much smaller and greater measurement ranges. There are two designs of differential pressure sensor: one type measures pressure against atmospheric pressure, the other measures the difference in pressure between two connections.

The sensitivity of the sensors appears to vary considerably. The reason for this is the great diversity of measurement ranges. At full pressure and nominal supply voltage, they all deliver a difference signal of 50 . . . 250 mV. The only exception to this rule are the types incorporating amplifiers. These provide an amplified, temperature-compensated and calibrated output signal. The zero error with many types is of the order of the entire measurement range. The types with thermistor compensation (Fig. 26.41a) perform much better in this respect, since not only the sensitivity but also the zero point is calibrated by the manufacturer.

Type	Manufac- turer	Pressure range	Sensitivity	Zero error	Bridge resistance	TC compens. Fig. 26.41
TSP 410 A	TI	0 . . . 2 bar	20 mV/V bar	± 8 mV/V	3 kΩ	–
TSP 411 A	TI	0 . . . 2 bar	20 mV/V bar	± 8 mV/V	3 kΩ	c
KP 100 A1	Valvo	0 . . . 2 bar	13 mV/V bar	± 5 mV/V	1.8 kΩ	b
KPY 10	Siemens	0 . . . 2 bar	10 mV/V bar		6 kΩ	–
KPY 12	Siemens	± 2 bar	10 mV/V bar		6 kΩ	–
KPY 31R	Siemens	± 0.02 bar	250 mV/V bar		6 kΩ	–
MPX 2100 GVP	Motorola	0 . . . 1 bar	4 m V/V bar	± 0.1 mV/V	1.8 kΩ	a
MPX 3100*	Motorola	0 . . . 1 bar	2.5 V/bar	± 50 mV		a
136 PC 15	Honeywell	0 . . . 1 bar	10 mV/V bar	± 0.1 mV/V	6.8 kΩ	a
142 PC 15A*	Honeywell	0 . . . 1 bar	5 V/ bar	± 25 mV		a
242 PC 250G*	Honeywell	0 . . . 17 bar	0.3 V/bar	± 50 mV		a
126 PC 05	Honeywell	± 0.35 bar	50 mV/V bar	± 0.1 mV/V	6.8 kΩ	a
SCX 15 AN	SenSym	0 . . . 1 bar	7.5 mV/V bar	± 25 μV/V	4 kΩ	a
LX 0570 A	SenSym	0 . . . 350 bar	0.1 mV/V bar	± 10 mV/V	1.8 kΩ	b
SX 15	SenSym	0 . . . 1 bar	22 mV/V bar	± 3 mV/V	4.7 kΩ	–
BP 01	SenSym	± 0.4 bar	7.5 mV/V bar	± 60 μV/V	4 kΩ	a

*integrated amplifier;
measurement range 0 . . . = absolute pressure sensor;
measurement range ± = differential pressure sensor

Fig. 26.44 Examples of pressure sensors

26.3   Humidity measurement

Humidity specifies water content. Of particular interest is the water content of air. *Absolute humidity* H_{abs} is defined as the amount of water contained in unit volume of air:

$$H_{abs} = \frac{\text{Mass of water}}{\text{Volume of air}} \quad ; \quad [H_{abs}] = \frac{\text{g}}{\text{m}^3} \;.$$

The maximum amount of water that can be dissolved in air is given by the *saturation humidity* H_{sat}:

$$H_{sat} = H_{abs\,max} = f(\vartheta) \;.$$

Its magnitude is heavily dependent on temperature, as shown in Fig. 26.45. When saturation humidity is reached or exceeded, water condenses: the *dew point* is reached. Determining the dew point thus allows Fig. 26.45 to be directly employed to specify the absolute humidity.

Most of the reactions due to atmospheric humidity, which include such things as physical wellbeing, are dependent on the *relative humidity* H_{rel}:

$$H_{rel} = \frac{H_{abs}}{H_{sat}} \;,$$

it indicates the percentage of saturation humidity attained. The amount of the

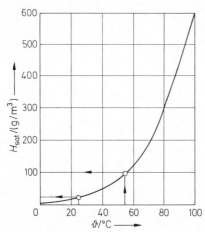

Fig. 26.45 Saturation humidity as a function of temperature

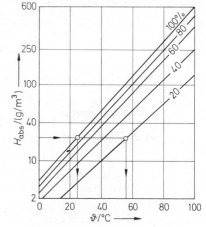

Fig. 26.46 Humidity as a function of temperature
Parameter: Relative humidity H_{rel}

For $H_{rel} = 100\%$, the plots in Figs. 26.45 and 26.46 coincide.

relative humidity can be determined with the aid of Fig. 26.45. If, for example, a dew point of 25°C is established by cooling the air, the absolute humidity $H_{abs} = 20$ g/m^3. However, at a temperature of e.g. 55°C, the air could take up $H_{sat} = 100$ g/m^3 of water. Therefore at 55°C the relative humidity is

$$H_{rel} = \frac{H_{abs}}{H_{sat}} = \frac{20 \text{ g/m}^3}{100 \text{ g/m}^3} = 20\% \quad .$$

The relationship between relative air humidity and temperature can be obtained directly from Fig. 26.45.

26.3.1 Humidity sensors

The example given above shows that the relative humidity can be determined by measuring the ambient temperature and the dew point. Although the dew point can be measured precisely and no further calibration is required, the cooling equipment required is complex [26.8]. The sensors commonly used for determining humidity simplify the measurement by providing an output that is a direct function of the relative humidity—the quantity generally of interest. They consist of a capacitor with a dielectric whose permittivity is humidity-dependent.

Figure 26.47 shows this type of device in schematic form [26.8]. The dielectric is made from aluminum oxide or a special plastic foil. One or both electrodes consist of a metal which is permeable to water vapor. The capacitance characteristic for a typical device is shown in Fig. 26.48. It can be seen that a specific basic capacitance C_0 occurs and that the increase in capacitance is non-linear. Within a restricted range, this non-linearity can be largely eliminated using a series capacitor.

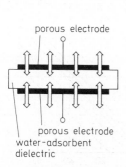

Fig. 26.47 Design principle of a capacitive humidity sensor

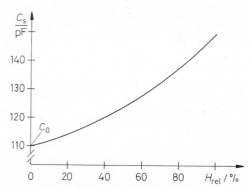

Fig. 26.48 Sensor capacitance versus relative humidity
Example: No. 2322691 90001 from Valvo

$$\frac{C_s}{C_0} = 1 + 0.4 \left(\frac{H_{rel}}{100\%} \right)^{1.4}$$

26.3.2 Interfacing circuits for capacitive humidity sensors

In order to determine humidity it is necessary to ascertain the capacitance of the humidity sensor. This means that any circuit for measuring capacitance could be employed here. For example, an AC voltage can be applied to the sensor and the flow of current measured, as shown schematically in Fig. 26.49. Although this method appears simple, it is actually quite complex, as it requires not only a calibrated AC meter, but also an AC voltage source with constant amplitude and frequency.

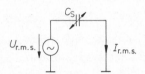

Fig. 26.49 Capacitance measurement by measuring the impedance

$$I_{\mathrm{r.m.s.}} = 2\pi U_{\mathrm{r.m.s.}} \cdot f \cdot C_{\mathrm{S}}$$

A simpler solution is to incorporate the sensor in an astable circuit, with the sensor determining its operating frequency or duty factor. Figure 26.50 shows a circuit of this type [26.9]. It consists of two multivibrators of the type shown in Fig. 8.29. Multivibrator M1 oscillates at a constant frequency of about 10 kHz if CMOS gates are used. It synchronizes multivibrator M2 whose ON time is determined by humidity sensor C_{S}. The ON times of both multivibrators are of equal duration at zero humidity; as the humidity increases, the ON time of M2

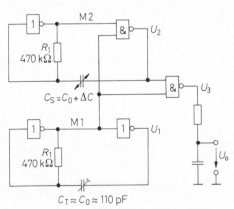

Fig. 26.50 Determining the increase in capacitance by measuring the increase in oscillation period
Gates: CMOS, e.g. CD 4001

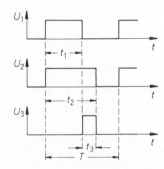

Fig. 26.51 Output signal resulting from the difference in switching times

becomes longer, as shown in Fig. 26.51. From the difference in the ON times, a signal U_3 is obtained which is proportional to ΔC and thus approximately proportional to the humidity. The lowpass filter at the output averages the signal.

A circuit providing a considerably higher degree of accuracy is shown in Fig. 26.52. Here the capacitance of the humidity sensor is determined in accordance with the definition of capacitance $C_S = Q/U$. Capacitor C_S is initially charged to U_{ref} and then discharged via the summing point. The average current flowing is

$$\bar{I}_S = U_{ref} \cdot f \cdot C_S \; ,$$

where f is the frequency at which the switch is operated. A DC voltage proportional to C_S is then produced at the output due to averaging by C_1.

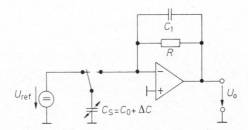

Fig. 26.52 Humidity measurement realized in switched capacitor technology

$$U_o = - U_{ref} \cdot R \cdot f \cdot C_S$$

In order to implement a humidity measuring circuit based on the principle illustrated in Fig. 26.52, additional devices are required for adjusting the zero point and the full-scale span. The complete circuit is shown in Fig. 26.53. Capacitor C_T is used for nulling. It is likewise charged to voltage U_{ref}, but is then applied to the summing point with reverse polarity. This produces a current given by

$$\bar{I}_T = - U_{ref} \cdot f \cdot C_T \; .$$

Feedback resistor R has also been replaced by a switched capacitor. Its average current is

$$\bar{I}_G = U_o \cdot f \cdot C_G \; .$$

Applying Kirchhoff's law to the summing point, i.e. $I_S + I_T + I_G = 0$ yields the output voltage

$$U_o = - U_{ref} \frac{C_S - C_T}{C_G} = - U_{ref} \frac{\Delta C}{C_G} \; .$$

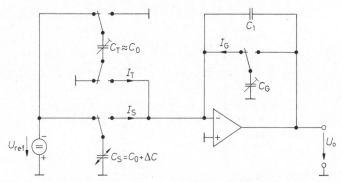

Fig. 26.53 Humidity measurement with nulling and sensitivity adjustment

$$U_o = - U_{ref}\, \Delta C / C_G$$

It can be seen that by using switched capacitor technology for nulling and gain adjustment, all the currents are proportional to f, thereby cancelling the switching frequency out of the result. This benefit is lost if resistors are used, as in normal SC techniques; this is also evident from the circuit in Fig. 26.52. The LTC 1043 from Linear Technology is particularly suitable for implementing the switches, since it not only contains four change-over switches but also a clock generator which drives the switches.

It is desirable to adjust the zero point and full-scale span with potentiometers rather than trimming capacitors. A method which can be employed without losing the benefits of pure SC technology is shown in Fig. 26.54. Here the current flowing through C_T or C_G is varied by the voltage tapped off via the potentiometers. In order to ensure that this does not increase the charging time, capacitors C_2 and C_3 are additionally employed and are selected large in relation to C_T or C_G [26.10].

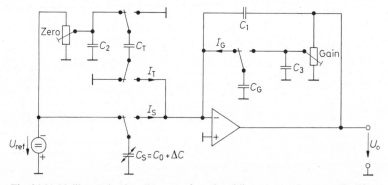

Fig. 26.54 Nulling and gain adjustment for a humidity sensor using potentiometers

26.4 Transmission of sensor signals

There is often a considerable distance or an environment with high levels of interference between the sensor and the point at which the signal is to be evaluated. For this reason, special action must be taken in such cases to ensure that the measured values are not impaired by external effects. Depending on the field of application and the protection class required, a distinction is drawn between electrical signal transmission and a more complex method employing electrically isolated transmission.

26.4.1 Electrical (direct-coupled) signal transmission

For long distance transmission the line resistance R_L cannot be ignored. Even small currents necessary for the operation of the sensor result in such large voltage drops that the measured value is invalidated. This problem can be solved by transmitting the measurement signal for evaluation via two additional lines in which no current flows. The measured quantity is then obtained by employing an instrumentation amplifier such as the one shown in Fig. 26.55. The voltage drop in the measurement circuit merely causes a common-mode signal $U_{CM} = I_0 R_L$ which disappears after subtraction.

One circuit can be dispensed with by specifying that the resistance in all the circuits shall be identical, giving the three-wire method shown in Fig. 26.56

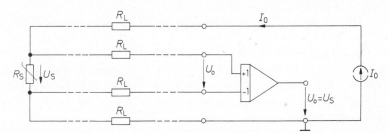

Fig. 26.55 Four-wire measurement, using a resistive temperature detector as an example

$$U_o = I_0 R_S = U_S \qquad U_{CM} = I_0 R_L$$

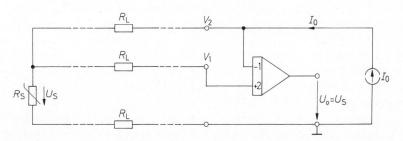

Fig. 26.56 Three-wire measurement, using a resistive temperature sensor as an example

$$V_1 = I_0(R_S + R_L) \qquad V_2 = I_0(R_S + 2R_L) \qquad U_o = 2V_1 - V_2 = I_0 R_S = U_S$$

[26.11]. The voltage drop across R_L can be eliminated in this case by formulating the expression

$$U_o = 2V_1 - V_2 = 2U_S + 2I_0 R_L - U_S - 2I_0 R_L = U_S .$$

If the sensor signals are small as, for example, in pressure sensors and thermocouples, they must be preamplified in the immediate vicinity of the sensor before the signal is transmitted over a long circuit. Figure 25.57 illustrates this principle. Although the output signal is affected by the voltage drop across R_L, if gain A is selected sufficiently large, this error becomes insignificant. It can be eliminated altogether if the four-wire method of Fig. 26.55 is additionally employed. However, one more instrumentation amplifier on the receiver side would then be required.

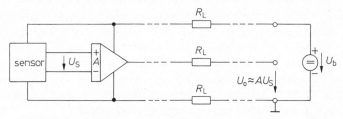

Fig. 26.57 Preamplifier for sensor reduces signal transmission errors

It is simpler in this case to convert the sensor signal into a current proportional to it. A current is unaffected by the line resistances. The principle is shown in Fig. 26.58. The voltage-controlled source converts sensor voltage U_S into a current $I_S = g_f U_S$. This produces a voltage drop of $U_o = g_f R_1 U_S$ across the load resistor. If $R_1 = 1/g_f$ is selected, the sensor signal is reproduced. However, the arrangement can be used at the same time to amplify the sensor voltage by making $A = g_f R_1 \gg 1$.

A further way of simplifying signal transmission is to ensure that the current consumption of the sensor and the voltage-controlled current source are constant. In this case, signal current I_S and supply current I_{sup} can be transmitted over the same line. Only two lines are then required, as shown in Fig. 26.59. They are used both to supply the sensor and interfacing circuit and to transmit the measurement signal. If current I_{sup} or the resulting voltage $R_1 I_{sup}$ are subtracted at the load resistor, the sensor signal will remain. As with current transmission in Fig. 26.58, the line resistances R_L have no effect on the measurement result. However, the supply voltage U_b must be large enough to prevent the current sources from being driven into saturation, in spite of all the voltage drops present in the circuit.

Currents $I_{sup} + I_S$ of a current loop are standardized. Their values are between 4 mA and 20 mA. Here 4 mA corresponds to the lower end of the range and 20 mA to the upper end. For unipolar signals the zero point is set to 4 mA. For bipolar signals it is set to 12 mA, giving a control range of ± 8 mA. If

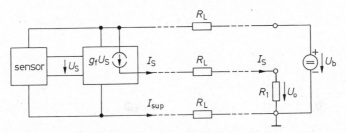

Fig. 26.58 Preamplifier with current output at the sensor eliminates errors in signal transmission. Example of a voltage-controlled IC current source: XTR 110 from Burr Brown

$$U_o = I_S R_1 = g_f U_S R_1 = A U_S$$

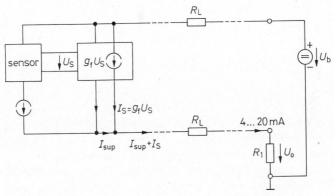

Fig. 26.59 Two-wire current loop for sensor signal transmission. IC types: XTR 101 from Burr Brown or AD 693 from Analog Devices

$$U_o = (I_{sup} + I_S) R_1 = R_1 I_{sup} + R_1 g_f U_S$$

$R_1 = 250\,\Omega$ is selected as is usual, both cases produce voltages of $U_o = 1 \ldots 5$ V at the receiver end.

Figure 26.60 shows the internal structure of a sensor interfacing circuit with current loop output. The core of the circuit is a precision current source consisting of transistor T, operational amplifier OA 1 and shunt resistor R_1. Current I_o assumes a value such that the input voltage difference of OA 1 becomes zero. If R_4 is omitted for simplicity's sake, this will occur when the voltage drop is $I_o R_1 = U_1$. Resistor R_4 is merely used to add the zero current of $I_Z = 4$ mA or 12 mA. The sensor signal is conditioned by the instrumentation amplifier and then controls the current source. The clever feature of the arrangement shown in Fig. 26.60 is that the load currents for the four operational amplifiers, the reference voltage source and any sensors connected to it also flow through shunt resistor R_1. Their sum is thus taken into account for current measurement. Transistor T then carries only the current lacking in the wanted output current. To ensure that the arrangement operates even with the smallest

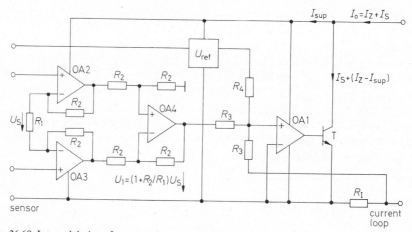

Fig. 26.60 Internal design of a current loop transmitter using the AD 693 from Analog Devices as an example

$$I_o = I_Z + I_S = \frac{R_3}{R_4}\frac{U_{ref}}{R_I} + \left(1 + \frac{R_2}{R_1}\right)\frac{U_S}{R_I}$$

loop current of $I_o = 4\,\text{mA}$, the sum of the load currents I_{sup} must be less than $4\,\text{mA}$. In commercially-available ICs, the internal current drain is less than $1\,\text{mA}$, so that up to $3\,\text{mA}$ is still available for operating the sensor.

A positive side-effect of the method described above is that faults can easily be detected: If the loop current is less than $4\,\text{mA}$, a fault has occurred, e.g. a shunt path or an open circuit.

26.4.2   Electrically-isolated signal transmission

For transmission over long distances and in environments with heavy electrical interference, noise signals of such magnitude can occur that the methods of signal transmission described above will not provide an adequate signal-to-noise ratio. In such cases there is only one viable solution: the use of fiber-optic transmission. This is affected neither by electrostatic nor electro-magnetic fields and can handle almost any potential difference. Figure 26.61 shows the principle involved in the optical transmission of sensor signals.

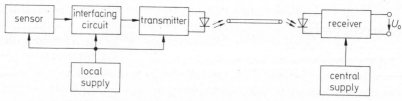

Fig. 26.61 Principle of optical transmission of sensor signals

However, analog signals are not usually transmitted over optical fibers, since the attenuation of the optical transmission paths is not well defined and is also subject to temperature variations and aging. The sensor signal is therefore converted into a serial digital signal in the transmitter. There are various ways of doing this. In the case of voltage-frequency conversion, the frequency is a linear function of the voltage; the duty factor of the output signal is a constant $1:1$. With voltage to duty factor conversion, the frequency is constant but the duty factor is a linear function of the voltage. Figure 26.62 shows the principle of the two methods. They are particularly useful in cases where an analog signal is to be recovered at the receiver end.

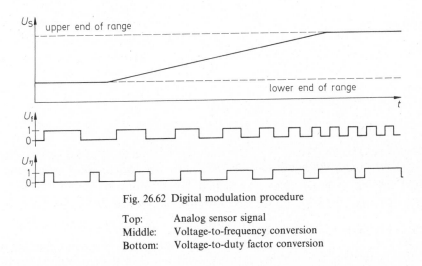

Fig. 26.62 Digital modulation procedure

Top: Analog sensor signal
Middle: Voltage-to-frequency conversion
Bottom: Voltage-to-duty factor conversion

Digital processing of the received signals is also possible by measuring the frequency or the duty factor digitally. However, if high accuracy is required, it is preferable to digitize the signal using a commercially available A/D converter at the sensor end and to transmit the result serially word by word.

26.5   Calibration of sensor signals

Some sensors are manufactured to such tight tolerances that no calibration is required, provided the interfacing circuit also employs components with sufficiently tight tolerances. In this case the sensor can be replaced without recalibration becoming necessary. However, this unfortunately applies only to a few temperature sensors. The general rule is that recalibration is always necessary when a sensor is replaced. Where a high degree of accuracy is required, regular recalibration may even be necessary.

26.5.1   Calibration of the analog signal

For an explanation of the calibration process without reference to the specific characteristics of the sensor, we shall consider the calibration circuit to be separated from the interfacing circuit of the sensor, as shown in Fig. 26.63. We shall assume that the sensor signal is a linear function of the physical quantity G or is linearized by the interfacing circuit. The input voltage of the calibration circuit can then be expressed in the form

$$U_i = a' + m'G \; . \tag{26.5}$$

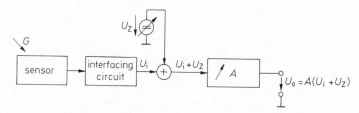

Fig. 26.63 Basic arrangement for calibration of sensor signals
by adjusting the zero point U_Z and gain A

The calibrated signal should generally be proportional to the measured quantity in accordance with

$$U_o = mG \; . \tag{26.6}$$

Figure 26.64 shows the voltage characteristic for a temperature measurement as an example. The calibration circuit must allow correction of the zero point and gain. An important constraint is that calibration should be possible *without iteration* i.e. there must be a procedure whereby one setting does not affect the other. This is possible with the arrangement shown in Fig. 26.63. Its output

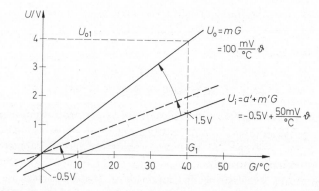

Fig. 26.64 Illustration of a calibration process; first nulling, then gain adjustment.
Example: clinical thermometer

voltage is

$$U_o = A(U_i + U_Z) \ . \tag{26.7}$$

Using equations (26.5/6), comparison of the coefficients produces the following calibration conditions:

Zero point: $\quad U_Z = -a' \ ,$

Gain: $\quad A = m/m' \ .$

For zero adjustment, the physical quantity $G = G_0$ associated with output value $U_o = 0$ is applied to the sensor. The output voltage is then adjusted to $U_o = 0$ by varying U_Z. This adjustment is independent of any setting of gain A: the only requirement is that $A \neq 0$. In Fig. 26.24 zeroing causes a parallel shift of the input characteristic through the origin.

For gain adjustment, we apply physical quantity G_1 and calibrate gain A so that the nominal value of the output voltage $U_{o1} = mG_1$ is produced. In Fig. 26.64 this corresponds to a rotation of the shifted input characteristic until it corresponds to the required function. Nulling is not affected by this, since gain adjustment merely involves varying factor A in Eq. (26.7).

It can be seen that the reverse sequence does not result in non-iterative adjustment. It is therefore absolutely essential for the zero adjuster to *precede* the gain adjuster in the signal path. The circuit arrangement in Fig. 26.63 is therefore invariable.

Calibration will now be further explained using the clinical thermometer example from Fig. 26.64. For zeroing, the sensor is set to temperature $\vartheta = 0°C$ and the output voltage adjusted to $U_o = 0$ by varying U_Z. This is the case for voltage

$$U_Z = -a' = +0.5 \text{ V} \ .$$

To calibrate the gain, the second calibration value is applied to the sensor, e.g. $G_1 = \vartheta_1 = 40°C$ and gain A is adjusted until the wanted value of the output voltage

$$U_{o1} = mG_1 = \frac{100 \text{ mV}}{°C} \cdot 40° = 4 \text{ V}$$

is obtained. The gain is therefore

$$A = \frac{m}{m'} = \frac{100 \text{ mV}/°C}{50 \text{ mV}/°C} = 2 \ .$$

The adjustment described requires that the zero point $U_o = 0$ be initially adjusted for $G = 0$. However, the situation may arise where physical quantity $G = 0$ cannot be implemented or cannot be implemented with the desired accuracy. We might also wish to set both calibration points close to the measurement range of interest, i.e. in the clinical thermometer example shown in Fig. 26.64 to $G_1 = 40°C$ and $G_2 = 30°C$, for example. This allows errors resulting from non-linearity to be minimized within this range. In order to obtain

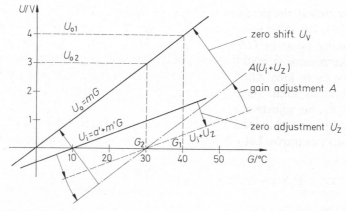

Fig. 26.65 Iteration-free adjustment procedure with two non-zero calibration points G_1, G_2

a non-iterative adjustment here, too, the zero point of the input characteristic curve can be shifted to one of these calibration values, as shown in Fig. 26.65, and an appropriate voltage added at the output. Additional voltage U_V in Fig. 26.66 is used for this purpose. It is preferable to dimension it for the smaller of the two calibration values:

$$U_V = U_{o2} = mG_2 \ .$$

For zeroing purposes, physical quantity G_2 is applied and voltage $U_i = U_Z$ or $A(U_i + U_Z)$ is zeroed by varying U_Z. To do this we do not need to measure into the circuit but follow the adjustment at the output. Calibration value $U_{o2} = U_V$ must then be obtained here. Since the output voltage of the amplifier after adjustment is precisely zero, it is independent of the value of A.

The second calibration value is then applied and gain A is adjusted as previously described. The shifted input characteristic in Fig. 26.65 will rotate until it possesses the correct slope. The calibrated output signal is then obtained by voltage addition to the output side.

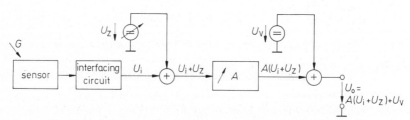

Fig. 26.66 Arrangement for non-iterative calibration of sensor signals
if none of the calibration points is zero

An example of the practical implementation of a calibration circuit is shown in Fig. 26.67. The input voltage and the voltage of the zero adjuster are added at the summing point of OA 1. The gain is set at the feedback resistor. The fixed-value resistor is used to limit the adjustment range; it also prevents the gain being set to zero. Amplifier OA 2 effects the output-side zero shift for the first calibration point. Since the amount of shift can be selected by a suitable choice of R_3, no adjustment is required here.

The adjustment procedure will now be further explained using the clinical thermometer example. Let the input and output characteristics be of the form

$$U_i = -0.5\,\text{V} + \frac{50\,\text{mV}}{°\text{C}}\,\vartheta \; ; \qquad U_o = \frac{100\,\text{mV}}{°\text{C}}\,\vartheta$$

and the calibration points

$$(\vartheta_2 = 30°\text{C}, U_{o2} = 3\,\text{V}) \; ; \qquad (\vartheta_1 = 40°\text{C}, U_{o1} = 4\,\text{V}) \; .$$

This gives an output-side zero shift of $U_v = U_{o2} = 3$ V. If $R_1 = 10\,\text{k}\Omega$ is specified, resistance $R_3 = 16.7\,\text{k}\Omega$ is obtained if the reference voltage is -5 V. For zeroing, we apply a temperature of $\vartheta_2 = 30°\text{C}$ to the sensor and adjust the output voltage to $U_{o2} = 3$ V. The voltage required for this purpose is

$$U_z = -U_{i1} = +0.5\,\text{V} - \frac{50\,\text{mV}}{°\text{C}}\cdot 30°\text{C} = -1\,\text{V} \; .$$

The output voltage of OA 1 is then zero and the value that happens to be set for A has no effect on the zero adjustment. To calibrate the gain, the other calibration point of $\vartheta_1 = 40°\text{C}$ is set and the output voltage adjusted to

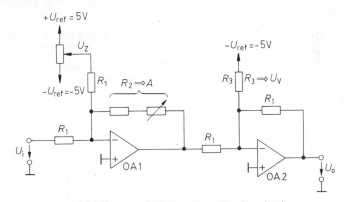

Fig. 26.67 Practical design of a calibration circuit

$$U_o = \underbrace{\frac{R_1}{R_3} U_{\text{ref}}}_{U_v} + \underbrace{\frac{R_2}{R_1}(U_i + U_z)}_{A}$$

$U_{o1} = 4$ V. This is obtained for a gain of

$$A = \frac{m}{m'} = \frac{100 \text{ mV/°C}}{50 \text{ mV/°C}} = 2 \; .$$

With $R_1 = 10$ kΩ, the calibrated condition produces a value of $R_2 = 20$ kΩ.

26.5.2 Computer-aided calibration

If we intend to undertake further processing of a sensor signal by a micro-computer, it is advantageous to calibrate the sensor with the microcomputer as well. As can be seen from Fig. 26.68, this not only obviates the need for an analog

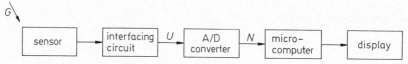

Fig. 26.68 Arrangement for computer-aided calibration of sensor signals

calibration circuit, but also allows calibration to be performed more easily and improves accuracy and stability. For calibration let us assume that the number N at the output of the A/D converter shown in Fig. 26.69 is a linear function of measured quantity G:

$$N = a + bG \; . \tag{26.8}$$

Calibration coefficients a and b are determined from two calibration points

$$(G_1, N_1) \quad \text{and} \quad (G_2, N_2) \; ,$$

by solving the conditional equations

$$N_1 = a + bG_1 \quad \text{and} \quad N_2 = a + bG_2$$

for a and b:

$$b = \frac{N_2 - N_1}{G_2 - G_1} \tag{26.9}$$

and

$$a = N_1 - bG_1 \; . \tag{26.10}$$

To compute the appropriate physical quantity from a measured value N, Eq. (26.8) must be solved for G:

$$G = (N - a)/b \; . \tag{26.11}$$

For practical calibration, the intended calibration values e.g. $G_1 = 30°$C and $G_2 = 40°$C are stored in a table. They are then applied in turn to the sensor and the microcomputer is instructed e.g. via push buttons to read in the appropriate measured values e.g. $N_1 = 1000$ and $N_2 = 3000$ and store them in the table.

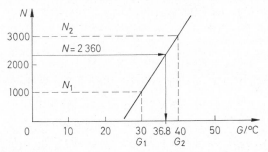

Fig. 26.69 Numerical calibration of a sensor with calibration points (G_1, N_1) and (G_2, N_2)

Using these entries, a program in the microcomputer can compute the calibration values in accordance with Eqs. (26.9/10) and store them in the table also:

$$b = 200/°C \quad \text{and} \quad a = -5000 .$$

Calibration is now complete. The analysis program can then compute values G_i in accordance with Eq. (26.11). For a measured value of $N = 2360$, the example gives a temperature of

$$G = \frac{N - a}{b} = \frac{2360 + 5000}{200/°C} = 36.8 \,°C .$$

For computer calibration, the hardware characteristic is therefore taken as given, its equation is formulated and is then used to map measured values N_i onto physical quantities G_i. It is therefore unnecessary to shift or rotate characteristic curves as in analog calibration. Any calibration point can be chosen: calibration is always non-iterative since the calibration points are determined by solving a system of equations.

A particularly difficult problem is posed by the calibration of sensors whose signals are not merely a function of the quantity sought, but on a second value as well. The most prevalent form of such unwanted dual dependence occurs in the temperature-dependence of sensor signals. Pressure sensors are an example of this, and they will be used here to illustrate the procedure involved. Measured value N comprises four components:

$$N = a + bp + c\vartheta + d\vartheta p , \tag{26.12}$$

where

p pressure,
ϑ temperature,
a zero error,
b pressure sensitivity,
c temperature coefficient of the zero point,
d temperature coefficient of the sensitivity.

To determine the four coefficients a, b, c and d, four calibration measurements are performed, each of which differs in one quantity.

$$N_{11} = a + bp_1 + c\vartheta_1 + dp_1\vartheta_1 , \qquad N_{21} = a + bp_2 + c\vartheta_1 + dp_2\vartheta_1 ,$$

$$N_{12} = a + bp_1 + c\vartheta_2 + dp_1\vartheta_2 , \qquad N_{22} = a + bp_2 + c\vartheta_2 + dp_2\vartheta_2 ,$$

and we obtain

$$d = \frac{N_{22} + N_{11} - N_{12} - N_{21}}{(p_2 - p_1)(\vartheta_2 - \vartheta_1)} , \qquad b = \frac{N_{22} - N_{12}}{p_2 - p_1} - d\vartheta_2 ,$$

$$\qquad\qquad\qquad\qquad\qquad\qquad\qquad\qquad\qquad\qquad (26.13)$$

$$c = \frac{N_{22} - N_{21}}{\vartheta_2 - \vartheta_1} - dp_2 , \qquad a = N_{22} - bp_2 - c\vartheta_2 - dp_2\vartheta_2 .$$

Calibration is now complete and the pressure can then be computed from Eq. (26.12):

$$p = \frac{N - a - c\vartheta}{b + d\vartheta} . \qquad\qquad\qquad (26.14)$$

To give an example of how calibration is performed, let us assume that the four calibration values required are to be obtained at pressures of $p_1 = 900$ mbar and $p_2 = 1035$ mbar and at temperatures of $\vartheta_1 = 25°C$ and $\vartheta_2 = 50°C$. This produces the measured values shown in Fig. 26.70. Using Eq. (26.13), we obtain from them the calibration coefficients

$$a = -1375 , \qquad\qquad b = 5.18\,\frac{1}{\text{mbar}} ,$$

$$c = 1.71\,\frac{1}{°C} , \qquad\qquad d = -0.0119\,\frac{1}{\text{mbar} \cdot °C} .$$

This calibration is very precise since it not only calibrates the zero point and gain but also takes account of the temperature coefficients of the sensitivity and zero point. This method allows low-cost, uncalibrated sensors to be used for performing precision measurements.

For pressure measurement we use Eq. (26.14). If, for example, a measured value $N = 3351$ is obtained for a temperature of $\vartheta = 15°C$, this gives a pressure of

$$p = \frac{N - a - c\vartheta}{b + d\vartheta} = \frac{3351 + 1375 - 1.71 \cdot 15}{5.18 - 0.0119 \cdot 15}\,\text{mbar} = 940\,\text{mbar} .$$

	$\vartheta_1 = 25°C$	$\vartheta_2 = 50°C$
$p_1 = 900$ mbar	$N_{11} = 3061$	$N_{12} = 2837$
$p_1 = 1035$ mbar	$N_{21} = 3720$	$N_{22} = 3456$

Fig. 26.70 Example of pressure calibration

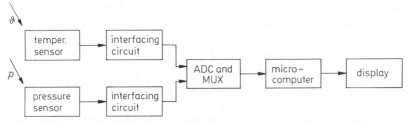

Fig. 26.71 Arrangement for computer-aided temperature and pressure calibration and measurement

Obviously, a calibrated temperature measurement is required to enable proper account to be taken of the influence of temperature. The temperature measurement will of course also be calibrated by computer in the same way as described above. The resulting block diagram is shown in Fig. 26.71. The pressure and temperature sensor signals are conditioned by the interfacing circuits and are fed to an analog-to-digital converter with built-in multiplexer. The microcomputer receives measured values N and computes from them the calibration coefficients during calibration and the measured quantities during normal operation. To enable sufficient accuracy to be attained, the A/D converter must have an accuracy of at least 12 bits. As A/D converters possessing this degree of accuracy are not available in single-chip microcomputers, separate A/D converters such as the AD 7582 from Analog Devices, which also contains an input multiplexer, have to be employed.

The sensor signal processor TSS 400 from Texas Instruments [26.12] is specially designed for evaluation of sensor signals. In addition to a 12-bit A/D converter with 4-channel analog multiplexer it contains an LCD interface. Figure 26.72 shows that only a few external components are required for the application of the TSS 400 as a digital barometer and thermometer. The output signal of the pressure sensor is amplified by a subtractor op-amp circuit and level shifted by a voltage divider. A PTC thermistor is connected to the second A/D converter channel. In order to reduce the current consumption the sensor supply voltage is switched on only when a new sample is to be taken. In this way the average current consumption can be reduced from several milliamps to a few microamps.

The LCD interface consists of 20 segment lines and 4 backplane connections. Up to 80 segments can therefore be driven if a display with 4 separate backplane connections is used. The chip contains 8 R-output lines, 4 K-lines with configurable direction which can be used to scan keys and a serial I/O data line.

The serial data line can be used to communicate with an external serial EEPROM. The outputs R 0 and R 7 act as control lines in this application. In the EEPROM the calibration values can be stored along with the user program. The on-chip standard ROM contains an interpreter for the sensor operating language. The user program can then be written in high level commands that are fetched from the EEPROM during execution and interpreted by the ROM routines. The RAM is entirely available for variables.

The user program can also be stored as a low level assembler program in the ROM by a user specific mask option. In this case the calibration values should be stored in the RAM. The EEPROM is then no longer needed and the circuit is simplified. Obviously, a mask version is only cost effective if a batch of 10 000 or more ICs is manufactured.

The chip contains a sophisticated power saving feature. The A/D converter is switched off when it is not in operation. The CPU can be switched off also, leaving only the timer and the LCD interface active. In this standby mode a supply current of only 4 µA is required. Therefore the entire circuit can be fed from a single lithium cell for up to 10 years.

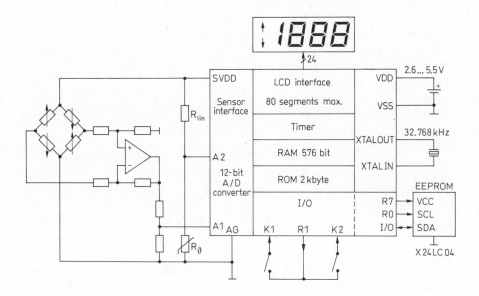

Fig. 26.72 Signal processor TSS 400 as a digital barometer and thermometer

27 Electronic controllers

27.1 Underlying principles

The purpose of a controller is to bring a physical quantity (the controlled variable X) to a predetermined value (the reference variable W) and to hold it at this value. To achieve this, the controller must counteract in a suitable way the effect of disturbances [27.1, 27.2].

The basic arrangement of a simple control circuit is shown in Fig. 27.1. The controller influences the controlled variable X by means of the correcting variable Y so that the error signal $W - X$ is as small as possible. The disturbances acting on the controlled system (plant) are represented formally by the disturbance variable Z which is superimposed on the correcting variable. Below, we shall assume that the controlled variable is a voltage and the system is electrically controlled. Electronic controllers can then be employed.

In the simplest case, such a controller is a circuit amplifying the error signal $W - X$. If the controlled variable X rises above the reference signal W, the difference $W - X$ becomes negative. The correcting variable Y is thereby reduced by a factor defined by the amplifier gain. This reduction counteracts the increase in the controlled variable, i.e. there is negative feedback. At steady state, the remaining error signal is smaller, the larger the gain A_C of the controller. It can be seen from Fig. 27.1 that for linear systems

$$Y = A_C(W - X) \quad \text{and} \quad X = A_S(Y + Z) , \tag{27.1}$$

where A_S is the gain of the controlled system. Hence, the controlled variable X

$$X = \frac{A_C A_S}{1 + A_C A_S} W + \frac{A_S}{1 + A_C A_S} Z . \tag{27.2}$$

It is now obvious that the response of the control system to a reference input, $\partial X / \partial W$, approaches unity more closely the greater the loop gain

$$g = A_C A_S = \frac{\partial X}{\partial (W - X)} \tag{27.3}$$

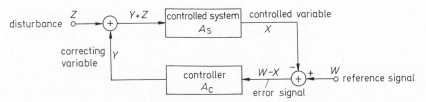

Fig. 27.1 Block diagram of a feedback control loop

The response to a disturbance, $\partial X/\partial Z$, approaches zero more closely the larger the gain A_C of the controller.

It must be pointed out, however, that there is a limit to the value of the loop gain g since, if the gain is too large, the unavoidable phase shifts within the control loop give rise to oscillations. This problem has already been discussed in connection with the frequency compensation of operational amplifiers. The objective of control engineering is to obtain, despite this restriction, the smallest possible error signal and good transient behavior. For this reason, an integrator and a differentiator are added to the proportional amplifier, and the P-controller is thus turned into one exhibiting PI or even PID action. The electronic realization of such circuits is dealt with below.

27.2   Controller types

27.2.1   P-controller

A P-controller (controller with proportional action) is a linear amplifier. Its phase shift must be negligibly small within the frequency range in which the loop gain g of the control system is larger than unity. For example, an operational amplifier with resistive feedback is a P-controller of this kind.

To determine the maximum possible proportional gain A_P, we consider the Bode plot of a typical controlled system, represented in Fig. 27.2. The phase lag is 180° at the frequency $f = 3.3$ kHz. The negative feedback then becomes a positive feedback. In other words, the phase condition of Eq. (15.3) for a self-sustaining oscillation is fulfilled. The value of the proportional gain A_P

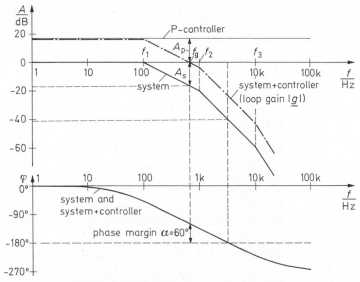

Fig. 27.2 Bode plot of a system and a P-controller

determines whether or not the amplitude condition of Eq. (15.2) is also fulfilled. For the example in Fig. 27.2, the gain $|A_S|$ of the system at 3.3 kHz is about $0.01 \cong -40$ dB. If we select $A_P = 100 \cong +40$ dB, the loop gain at this frequency would then be $|g| = |A_S| \cdot A_P = 1$, i.e. the amplitude condition of an oscillator would also be fulfilled and the system would oscillate permanently at $f = 3.3$ kHz. If $A_P > 100$ is chosen, an oscillation with exponentially rising amplitude is obtained; and for $A_P < 100$, a damped oscillation occurs.

There is now the question of how much A_P must be reduced for an optimum transient behavior. An indication of the damping of the transient response can be obtained directly from the Bode diagram: the *phase margin* is the phase angle required at the *gain crossover frequency* f_g to make a phase lag of 180°. The gain crossover frequency f_g is the critical frequency for which the loop gain is unity and is therefore often called the unity loop-gain frequency. Hence, the phase margin

$$\alpha = 180° - |\varphi_{\text{loop}}(f_g)| = 180° - |\varphi_S(f_g) + \varphi_C(f_g)| , \qquad (27.4)$$

where φ_S is the phase shift of the system and φ_C that of the controller. For the case of a P-controller, by definition $\varphi_C(f_g) = 0$, so that

$$\alpha = 180° - |\varphi_S(f_g)| . \qquad (27.5)$$

A phase margin of $\alpha = 0°$ results in an undamped oscillation, since the amplitude condition and the phase condition for an oscillator are simultaneously fulfilled; $\alpha = 90°$ represents the case of critical damping. For $\alpha \approx 60°$, the step response of the closed control loop shows an overshoot of about 4%. The settling time is then at a minimum. This phase margin is therefore optimum for most cases. The oscillogram in Fig. 27.3 provides a comparison of the step responses obtained for different phase margins.

To determine the optimum P-controller gain, we examine the Bode diagram to find the frequency at which the controlled system has a phase shift of 120°. In the example in Fig. 27.2, that frequency is 700 Hz. This can be made the critical frequency by selecting the P-controller gain, A_P, such that $|\underline{g}| = 1$. Thus, from

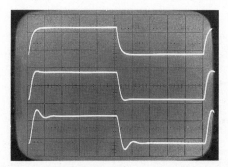

Fig. 27.3 Step response as a function of the phase margin, for constant gain crossover frequency f_g.
Upper trace: $\alpha = 90°$, middle trace: $\alpha = 60°$, and lower trace: $\alpha = 45°$

Eq. (27.3)

$$A_P = \frac{1}{A_S} = \frac{1}{0.14} = 7 \quad \text{or} \quad A_P^* = -A_S^* = -(-17\,\text{dB}) = 17\,\text{dB} .$$

This case is plotted in Fig. 27.2. The low-frequency limit value of the loop gain is therefore

$$g = A_S A_P = 1 \cdot 7 = 7 .$$

At steady state, this gives us, from Eq. (27.2), a relative deviation of

$$\frac{W - X}{W} = \frac{1}{1 + g} = \frac{1}{1 + 7} = 12.5\% .$$

If the controller gain is increased to obtain a smaller deviation, the transient response suffers. A proportional gain of any magnitude can only be set for systems which behave like a first-order lowpass filter, because the phase margin is then greater than 90° at any frequency.

27.2.2 PI-controller

The previous section has shown that for reasons of stability, the gain of a P-controller must not be too large. One way of improving the control accuracy is to increase the loop gain at low frequencies, as Fig. 27.4 illustrates. In the

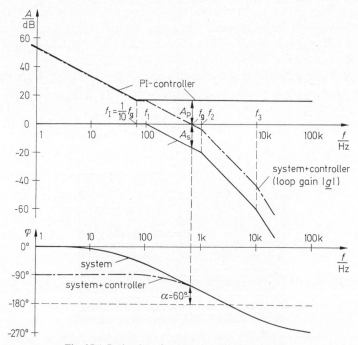

Fig. 27.4 Bode plot of a system and a PI-controller

vicinity of the critical frequency f_g, the frequency response of the loop gain thereby remains unchanged so that the transient behavior is not affected. However, the remaining error signal is now zero since

$$\lim_{f \to 0^-} |g| = \infty \ .$$

To implement a frequency response of this kind, an integrator is connected in parallel with the P-controller, as shown in Fig. 27.5. The Bode plot of the resulting *PI-controller* (controller with proportional-integral action) is presented in Fig. 27.6. It can be seen that for low frequencies, the PI-controller acts as an integrator and for high frequencies as a proportional amplifier. The change-over between the two regions is characterized by the cutoff frequency f_I of the PI-controller. At this frequency the phase shift is $-45°$, and the controller gain $|\underline{A}_C|$ is 3 dB above A_P.

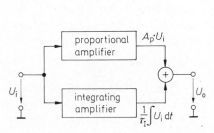

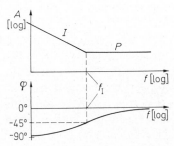

Fig. 27.5 Block diagram of the PI-controller   Fig. 27.6 Bode plot of the PI-controller

To determine the cutoff frequency f_I, we calculate from Fig. 27.5 the complex controller gain

$$\underline{A}_C = A_P + \frac{1}{j \omega \tau_I} = A_P \left(1 + \frac{1}{j \omega \tau_I A_P} \right) \ .$$

Hence,

$$\underline{A}_C = A_P \left(1 + \frac{\omega_I}{j \omega} \right) \quad \text{where } \omega_I = 2\pi f_I = \frac{1}{\tau_I A_P} \ . \tag{27.6}$$

A PI-controller can also be realized using a single operational amplifier, the appropriate circuit being shown in Fig. 27.7. Its complex gain is

$$\underline{A}_C = -\frac{R_2 + 1/j \omega C_1}{R_1} = -\frac{R_2}{R_1} \left(1 + \frac{1}{j \omega C_1 R_2} \right) \ . \tag{27.7}$$

By comparing coefficients with Eq. (27.6), we obtain the controller parameters as

$$A_P = -\frac{R_2}{R_1} \quad \text{and} \quad f_I = \frac{1}{2\pi C_1 R_2} \ . \tag{27.8}$$

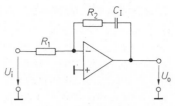

Fig. 27.7 PI-controller.

$$A_P = -\frac{R_2}{R_1}, \quad f_I = \frac{1}{2\pi C_1 R_2}$$

Designing a PI controller is quite simple if we make use of the fact that the I-component does not change the phase margin. The size of the P-component (gain) is therefore retained, i.e. in the example given $f_g = 700$ Hz, $A_P = 7$.

In order to ensure that the I-component does not reduce the phase margin, it is necessary to select $f_I \ll f_g$. However, it is not advisable to select it unnecessarily low, as it will then take longer for the integrator to bring the deviation to zero. The upper limit for f_I is approximately $0.1 f_g$. The I-component then reduces the phase margin by less than 6°. Figure 27.4 has been plotted using these parameters. The appropriate transient behavior of the error signal is shown by the oscillogram of Fig. 27.8. It is obvious from the lower trace that, with these optimum parameters, the PI-controller settles to zero error signal in the same time interval that a purely P-action controller requires to adjust to a relative error signal of $1/(1 + g) = 1/8 = 12.5\%$.

The effect of a less than optimum f_I is demonstrated by the oscillogram in Fig. 27.9. For the upper trace, f_I is too small: the settling time is increased. For the lower trace, f_I is too large: the phase margin is reduced.

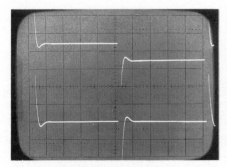

Fig. 27.8 Error signal.
Upper trace: P-controller.
Lower trace: PI-controller with optimum f_I

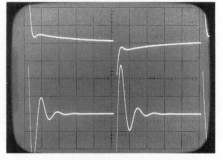

Fig. 27.9 Error signal of the PI-controller.
Upper trace: f_I too small.
Lower trace: f_I too large

27.2.3   PID-controller

By connecting a differentiator in parallel as in Fig. 27.10, a PI-controller can be extended to become a PID-controller (controller with proportional-integral-derivative action). Above the differentiation cutoff frequency f_D, the circuit behaves like a differentiator. The phase shift rises to $+90°$, as can be seen from the Bode plot in Fig. 27.11. This phase lead at high frequencies can be used to partially compensate for the phase lag of the controlled system in the vicinity of f_g, allowing a higher proportional gain, so that a higher gain crossover frequency f_g is obtained. The transient behavior is thereby speeded up.

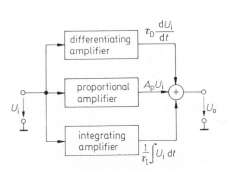

Fig. 27.10 Block diagram of the
PID-controller

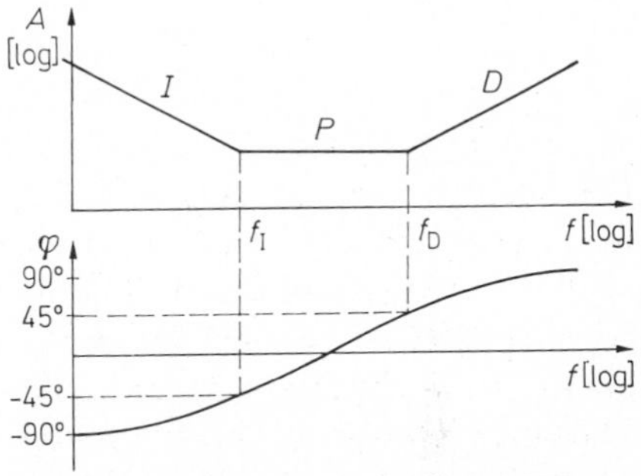

Fig. 27.11 Bode plot of the PID-controller

The selection of the controller parameters will again be illustrated for our example system. In the first step, we raise the proportional gain A_P until the phase margin is only about 15°. In this case, we can infer from Fig. 27.12 that $A_P = 50 \triangleq 34$ dB and $f_g \approx 2.2$ kHz, as against 700 Hz for the PI-controller. If the differentiation cutoff frequency is now chosen to be $f_D \approx f_g$, the phase lag of the controller at frequency f_g is approx. $+45°$, i.e. phase margin is increased from 15° to 60°, and we obtain the desired transient behavior.

To determine the integration cutoff frequency f_I, the same principles apply as for the PI-controller, i.e. $f_I \approx \frac{1}{10} f_g$. This results in the frequency response of the loop gain shown in Fig. 27.12.

The reduction in settling time is illustrated by a comparison of the oscillograms for a PI- and a PID-controller, shown in Fig. 27.13.

In order to implement a PID-controller we must first determine the complex gain from the block diagram in Fig. 27.10.

$$\underline{A}_C = A_P + j\omega\tau_D + \frac{1}{j\omega\tau_I} = A_P\left[1 + j\left(\frac{\omega}{\omega_D} - \frac{\omega_I}{\omega}\right)\right], \qquad (27.9)$$

where

$$f_D = \frac{A_P}{2\pi\tau_D} \quad \text{and} \quad f_I = \frac{1}{2\pi A_P\tau_I}. \qquad (27.10)$$

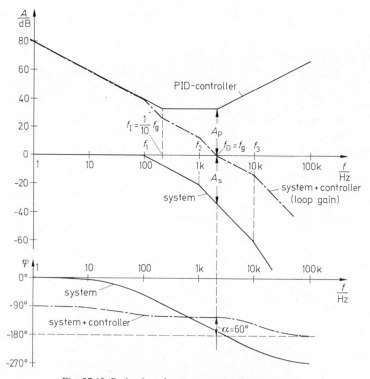

Fig. 27.12 Bode plot of a system and a PID-controller

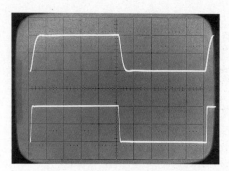

Fig. 27.13 Comparison of the transient behavior of a system with PI-controller (upper trace) and with PID-controller (lower trace)

A circuit having the frequency response of Eq. (27.9) can also be realized using a single operational amplifier; this is shown in Fig. 27.14. Its complex gain is given by

$$\underline{A}_C = -\left[\frac{R_2}{R_1} + \frac{C_D}{C_I} + j\omega C_D R_2 + \frac{1}{j\omega C_I R_1}\right].$$

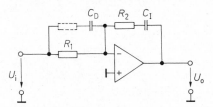

Fig. 27.14 PID-controller.

$$A_P = -\frac{R_2}{R_1}, \quad f_1 = \frac{1}{2\pi C_1 R_2}, \quad f_D = \frac{1}{2\pi C_D R_1}$$

Hence, with $\dfrac{C_D}{C_1} \ll \dfrac{R_2}{R_1}$,

$$\underline{A}_C = -\frac{R_2}{R_1}\left[1 + j\left(\omega C_D R_1 - \frac{1}{\omega C_1 R_2}\right)\right]. \qquad (27.11)$$

A comparison of the coefficients with those in Eq. (27.9) yields the controller parameters

$$A_P = -\frac{R_2}{R_1}, \quad f_D = \frac{1}{2\pi C_D R_1}, \quad f_1 = \frac{1}{2\pi C_1 R_2}. \qquad (27.12)$$

27.2.4 PID-controller with adjustable parameters

To determine the different controller parameters, we assumed that the parameters of the controlled system were known. However, these data are often difficult to measure, particularly for very slow systems. It is therefore usually better to establish the optimum controller parameters by experiment. A circuit is then required which allows *independent* adjustment of the controller parameters A_P, f_1 and f_D. It can be seen from Eqs. (27.12) and (27.10) that this condition can be fulfilled neither by the circuit in Fig. 27.14 nor by that in Fig. 27.10 since, for any variation in A_P, the cutoff frequencies f_1 and f_D will also change.

For the circuit in Fig. 27.15, however, the parameters are decoupled and can therefore be adjusted independently. The complex gain of the circuit is

$$\underline{A}_C = \frac{R_P}{R_1}\left[1 + j\left(\omega C_D R_D - \frac{1}{\omega C_1 R_1}\right)\right]. \qquad (27.13)$$

Comparing coefficients with Eq. (27.9) gives the controller parameters:

$$A_P = \frac{R_P}{R_1}, \quad f_D = \frac{1}{2\pi C_D R_D}, \quad f_1 = \frac{1}{2\pi C_1 R_1}. \qquad (27.14)$$

Controller optimization is again illustrated with reference to our example system. In the first step, switch S is closed to render the integrator inactive.

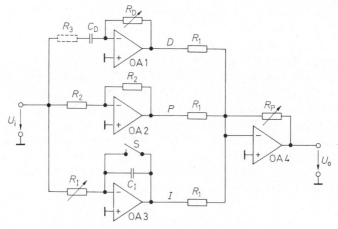

Fig. 27.15 PID-controller with decoupled parameters.

$$A_P = \frac{R_P}{R_1}, \quad f_I = \frac{1}{2\pi C_I R_I}, \quad f_D = \frac{1}{2\pi C_D R_D}$$

Resistor R_D is made zero, i.e. the differentiator does not contribute to the output signal. The circuit is therefore a purely P-action controller.

We now apply a square wave to the reference signal input and record the transient behavior of the controlled variable X. Starting from zero, A_P is increased until the step response is only slightly damped, as in the upper trace of Fig. 27.16. The step response is then that obtained for the system in Fig. 27.12, for a phase margin of 15° and without derivative or integral controller action.

In the second step, the differentiation cutoff frequency f_D is lowered from infinity by increasing R_D, and is adjusted to a value for which the desired damping is achieved (see Fig. 27.16, lower trace).

In the third step, we consider the transient behavior of the error signal $W - X$. After opening switch S, the integration cutoff frequency f_I is increased until the settling time is at a minimum. The appropriate oscillograms have already been shown in Figs. 27.8 and 27.9.

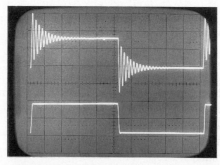

Fig. 27.16 Experimental determination of the proportional and derivative controller parameters

The great advantage of this optimization method is that the optimum controller parameters represented by Fig. 27.12 are obtained immediately and without iteration. Using the controller parameters found in this way, the simple PID-controller in Fig. 27.14 can be designed.

The *oscillation test*, i.e. the occurrence of an only slightly damped oscillation (Fig. 27.16), also allows calculation of all the data required for designing the PID controller: the oscillation frequency is the critical frequency $f_{\text{osc.}} = 1/T_{\text{osc.}} = f_{\text{g}}$. The gain for which oscillation occurs yields the P-gain $A_{\text{C osc.}} = A_{\text{P}}$. The differentiation cutoff frequency is selected equal to the oscillation frequency $f_{\text{D}} = f_{\text{osc.}}$ and the integration cutoff frequency equal to one tenth of the oscillation frequency $f_{\text{I}} = \frac{1}{10} f_{\text{osc.}}$. Taken together, these parameters produce the design parameters for a PID controller:

$$
\begin{array}{|l|}
\hline
A_{\text{P}} \approx A_{\text{C osc.}} \; , \\[2mm]
\tau_{\text{D}} \approx T_{\text{osc.}} \; , \\[2mm]
\tau_{\text{I}} \approx 10 \, T_{\text{osc.}} \; . \\
\hline
\end{array}
$$

27.3   Control of non-linear systems

27.3.1   Static nonlinearity

We have assumed so far that the equation for the controlled system is

$$X = A_{\text{S}} \cdot Y$$

i.e. that the controlled system is linear. For many systems, however, this condition is not fulfilled so that in general

$$X = f(Y) \; .$$

For small changes about a given operating point X_0, each system can be considered linear as long as its transfer characteristic is continuous and differentiable in the vicinity of this point. In such cases, the derivative

$$a_{\text{S}} = \frac{\text{d}X}{\text{d}Y}$$

is used so that for small-signal operation

$$x \approx a_{\text{S}} y \; ,$$

where $x = (X - X_0)$ and $y = (Y - Y_0)$. For a fixed point of operation, the controller can now be optimized as described above. However, a problem arises if larger changes in the reference variable are allowed: since the incremental system gain a_{S} is dependent on the actual point of operation, the transient behavior varies as a function of the magnitude of W.

This can be avoided by providing linearity, i.e. by connecting a function network of Section 12.7.5 in front of the controlled system. The corresponding

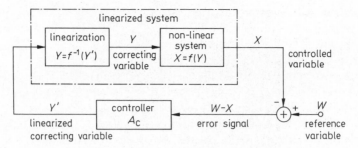

Fig. 27.17 Linearization of a system having static nonlinearity

block diagram is shown in Fig. 27.17. If the function network is used to implement the function $Y = f^{-1}(Y')$, we obtain the required linear system equation

$$X = f(Y) = f[f^{-1}(Y')] = Y' \; .$$

If, for instance, the system exhibits exponential behavior, i.e.

$$X = A e^{Y} \; ,$$

the function network must be a logarithmic one having the characteristic

$$Y = f^{-1}(Y') = \ln \frac{Y'}{A} \; .$$

27.3.2 Dynamic nonlinearity

A different kind of nonlinearity of a controlled system may be due to the rate of change of some quantity in the system being limited to a value which cannot be raised by increasing the correcting variable. We have encountered this effect in operational amplifiers as a limitation of the slew rate. For large input steps and controllers with integral action, the above effect leads to large overshoots which decay only slowly.

The reason for this is as follows. For optimized integral action of the controller and for a small voltage step, the integrator reaches its steady-state output voltage at the precise instant when the error signal becomes zero. For double the input step of a linear system, the rate of change in the system, as well as that of the integrator, would double. The increased reference value would therefore be reached within exactly the same settling time.

For a system having a limited slew rate, only the rate of change of the integrator is doubled, whereas that of the system remains unchanged. This results in the controlled system reaching the reference value very much later and the integrator overshooting. The controlled variable therefore greatly exceeds the reference value and the decay takes longer, the farther the integrator output voltage is from the steady-state value. The decay time constant for this non-linear operation therefore becomes larger for increasing input steps.

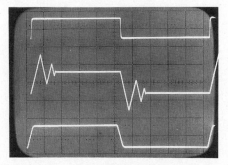

Fig. 27.18 Transient behavior of the controlled variable for a limited system slew rate.
Upper trace: small-signal characteristic.
Middle trace: large-scale characteristic.
Lower trace: large-signal characteristic for a slew-rate limited reference variable

The effect is avoided by increasing the integration time constant (i.e. reducing f_I) until no overshoot is incurred for the largest possible input step. However, this results in considerably prolonged settling times for small-signal operation (see Fig. 27.9 lower trace).

A much more effective measure is to limit the slew rate of the reference variable to the maximum slew rate of the controlled system. This ensures linear operation throughout, and the overshoot effect is thus avoided. This will not increase the settling time for large reference signals, since the controlled variable cannot change any faster anyway. This is illustrated by the oscillogram in Fig. 27.18.

In principle, a lowpass filter could be used to limit the slew rate, but this would also reduce the small-signal bandwidth. A better solution is shown in Fig. 27.19. If a voltage step is applied to the circuit input, amplifier OA 1 saturates at the output limit U_max. The output voltage of OA 2 therefore rises at

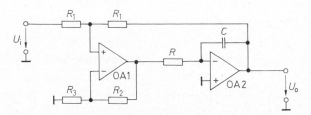

Fig. 27.19 Slew rate limiter for the reference variable. Resistors R_2, R_3 limit the gain of OA 1 and provide additional frequency compensation.

Steady-state output voltage: $\qquad U_\mathrm{o} = -U_\mathrm{i}$

Maximum slope of output voltage: $\qquad \dfrac{\mathrm{d}U_\mathrm{o}}{\mathrm{d}t} = \dfrac{U_\mathrm{max}}{RC}$

the rate

$$\frac{dU_o}{dt} = \frac{U_{max}}{RC}$$

until it reaches the values $- U_i$, determined by the overall feedback. A square-wave voltage would therefore be shaped into the required trapezoidal voltage. The signal remains unchanged if the rate of change of the input voltage is smaller than the predetermined maximum. The small-signal bandwidth is therefore not affected.

27.4   Phase-locked loop

A particularly important application of feedback control in communication systems is the phase-locked loop (PLL). Its purpose is to control the frequency f_2 of an oscillator in such a manner that it is the same as the frequency f_1 of a reference oscillator, and to do this so accurately that the phase shift between the two signals remains constant. The basic arrangement of such a circuit is illustrated in Fig. 27.20.

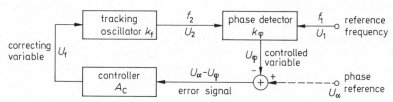

Fig. 27.20 Principle of the phase-locked loop (PLL)

The frequency of the tracking oscillator can be varied by means of the control voltage U_f, according to the relationship

$$f_2 = f_0 + k_f U_f \ . \tag{27.15}$$

Such voltage-controlled oscillators (VCOs) are described in Chapter 15. For low frequencies, the second-order differential equation circuit of Section 15.4 or the function generators of Section 15.5 can be employed. For higher frequencies, the emitter-coupled multivibrator of Fig. 8.21 is more suitable, or any LC oscillator if a varactor diode is connected in parallel with the capacitor of the oscillating circuit. However, the linear relationship of Eq. (27.15) then holds only for small variations around the point of operation, f_0, as the incremental control constant (VCO "gain") $k_f = df_2/dU_f$ is dependent on the operating point.

The phase detector produces an output voltage which is defined by the phase angle φ between the tracking oscillator voltage U_2 and the reference alternating voltage U_1;

$$U_\varphi = k_\varphi \cdot \varphi \ .$$

The integrating property of the controlled system is of particular interest. If frequency f_2 deviates from the reference frequency f_1, the phase shift φ will increase proportionally with time and without limit. The error signal in the closed loop therefore rises, even for a finite controller gain, until both frequencies are exactly the same. The remaining error signal of the *frequency* is thus zero.

The remaining error signal of the *phase shift*, however, does not usually become nil. From Fig. 27.20 we deduce that $U_\alpha - U_\varphi = U_f/A_C$; hence

$$\alpha - \varphi = \frac{f_1 - f_0}{A_C k_f k_\varphi} , \qquad (27.16)$$

where f_0 is the VCO frequency for $U_f = 0$. If it is important not only to keep the phase shift constant but also hold it precisely at a predetermined value

$$\alpha = U_\alpha/k_\varphi = -\varphi ,$$

a PI-controller must be used for which $A_C(f = 0) = \infty$. In many applications it is sufficient to control for identical frequencies ($f_1 = f_2$), i.e. for a *constant* phase shift (the angle α being unimportant) so that the control input U_α can be omitted. Voltage U_φ is then the error signal.

To determine the controller parameters, the frequency response of the system must be known. As mentioned before, the phase detector exhibits integral behavior so that the phase shift is given by

$$\varphi = \int_0^t \omega_2 \, d\tilde{t} - \int_0^t \omega_1 \, d\tilde{t} = \int_0^t \Delta\omega \, d\tilde{t} , \qquad (27.17)$$

where $\tilde{t}$ is a dummy time variable of integration. To determine the frequency response of the controlled system, we modulate frequency ω_2 sinusoidally with a modulating frequency ω_m around the centre frequency ω_1. Hence

$$\Delta\omega(t) = \widehat{\Delta\omega} \cos \omega_m t .$$

By inserting this in Eq. (27.17), we obtain

$$\varphi(t) = \frac{\widehat{\Delta\omega}}{\omega_m} \sin \omega_m t .$$

Taking into account the phase lag of 90°, we obtain in complex notation

$$\frac{\underline{\varphi}}{\underline{\Delta\omega}} = \frac{1}{j\omega_m} , \qquad (27.18)$$

which is the equation for an integrator. With the constants k_f and k_φ, the complex gain of the controlled system is then

$$\boxed{\underline{A}_s = \frac{\underline{U}_\varphi}{\underline{U}_f} = \frac{2\pi k_f k_\varphi}{j\omega_m} = \frac{k_f k_\varphi}{j f_m}} . \qquad (27.19)$$

As will be seen later, the measurement of the phase shift involves a certain delay and the factor k_φ is therefore complex, i.e. the order of the system is raised.

The behavior of a phase-locked loop generally depends on the type of phase detector used. The most important circuits will now be discussed.

27.4.1   Sample-and-hold circuit as phase detector

The phase angle φ between two voltages U_1 and U_2 can, for example, be measured by sampling with a sample-and-hold circuit the instantaneous value of U_1 when U_2 has a positive-going zero crossing. For this purpose, U_2 is used, as in Fig. 27.21, to activate an edge-triggered one-shot producing the sampling pulse for the sample-and-hold circuit. It can be seen in Fig. 27.22 that the output voltage of the circuit is given by

$$U_\varphi = \hat{U}_1 \sin \varphi \ . \tag{27.20}$$

Around the point of operation ($\varphi = 0$), the detector characteristic is approximately linear:

$$U_\varphi \approx \hat{U}_1 \varphi \ .$$

Hence, the factor of the phase detector

$$k_\varphi = \hat{U}_1 \ . \tag{27.21}$$

It is obvious from Fig. 27.23 that a further possible operating point where $U_\varphi = 0$, would be at $\varphi = \pi$. Then, $k_\varphi = -\hat{U}_1$. The sign of the controller gain defines which of the two operating points is assumed. Further stable points of

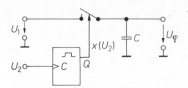

Fig. 27.21 Sample-and-hold circuit as a phase detector

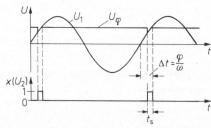

Fig. 27.22 Voltage waveform in the phase detector. The dips in U_φ disappear to a great extent if the sampling time t_s is not much larger than the time constant of the sample-and-hold circuit

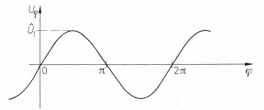

Fig. 27.23 Transfer characteristic of a sample-and-hold circuit as phase detector

operation occur at intervals of 2π. This indicates that the phase detector does not recognize a displacement by a whole number of periods.

If a triangular waveshape U_1 is employed rather than the sinusoidal one, a triangular detector characteristic is obtained. For rectangular input voltages U_1, the circuit is obviously unusable.

Dynamic behavior

The phase detector described determines a new value for the phase shift only once during a period of the input waveform and consequently has a dead time. The delay is between 0 and $T_2 = 1/f_2$, depending on the instant at which a change in phase occurs. The average delay is therefore $\frac{1}{2}T_2$. To allow for this, the "gain" k_φ of the phase detector for higher phase modulation frequencies f_m must be written in complex form so that

$$\underline{k}_\varphi = k_\varphi e^{-j\omega_m \cdot \frac{1}{2}T_2} = \hat{U}_1 e^{-j\pi f_m / f_2} . \tag{27.22}$$

With Eq. (27.19), we therefore obtain for the complex gain of the entire controlled system

$$\underline{A}_s = \frac{k_f \underline{k}_\varphi}{j f_m} = \frac{k_f \hat{U}_1}{j f_m e^{j\pi f_m / f_2}} ,$$

or

$$|\underline{A}_s| = \frac{|\underline{U}_\varphi|}{|\underline{U}_f|} = \frac{k_f \hat{U}_1}{f_m} \quad \text{and} \quad \varphi_m = -\frac{\pi}{2} - \frac{\pi f_m}{f_2} . \tag{27.23}$$

Controller parameters

For the controller it is best to choose a circuit without derivative action since the output voltage of the sample-and-hold element changes only in steps. According to Eq. (27.23), the phase shift φ_m between $\underline{U}_\varphi$ and $\underline{U}_f$ at frequency $f_m = \frac{1}{4}f_2$, is $-135°$. The phase margin is thus $45°$ if we adjust the proportional gain A_p in such a way that the gain crossover frequency $f_g = \frac{1}{4}f_2$. By definition, at $f_m = f_g$,

$$|\underline{g}| = |\underline{A}_s| \cdot |\underline{A}_c| = 1 .$$

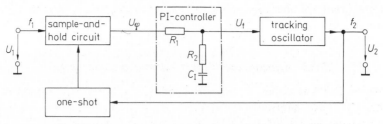

Fig. 27.24 PLL with sample-and-hold circuit as phase detector

With $\underline{A}_C = A_P$ and Eq. (27.23), this results in

$$A_P = \frac{f_g}{k_f k_\varphi} = \frac{f_2}{4 k_f \hat{U}_1} \; .$$

A typical example is $f_2 = 10\,\text{kHz}$, $k_f = 5\,\text{kHz/V}$ and $k_\varphi = \hat{U}_1 = 10\,\text{V}$. Hence, $A_P = 0.05$. The controller can in this case be a passive voltage divider.

To reduce the remaining phase error [see Eq. (27.16)], the gain at low frequencies can be raised by integral action ($f_1 \approx \frac{1}{10} f_g = \frac{1}{40} f_2$). It is advisable, however, to limit the low-frequency value of the gain to a finite value A_1, since otherwise the integrator would drift and saturate for as long as the loop is not in the locked condition. The VCO can thereby be detuned to such an extent that the loop will not acquire lock.

The passive voltage divider can be extended in a simple way to become a PI-controller with limited gain A_1, by connecting a capacitor in series with the resistor R_2, as illustrated in Fig. 27.24. The controller parameters are then

$$A_P = \frac{R_2}{R_1 + R_2} \; ; \quad f_1 = \frac{1}{2\pi R_2 C_1}; \quad A_1 = 1 \; .$$

Pull-in

After switch-on there is usually a frequency offset $\Delta f = f_1 - f_0$. The phase shift therefore rises proportionally with time. According to Fig. 27.23, this produces an alternating voltage at the output of the phase detector, having the frequency Δf and the amplitude $\hat{U}_\varphi = \hat{U}_1$, so that the tracking oscillator is thus frequency modulated by the voltage

$$U_f = A_P \hat{U}_1 \sin \Delta \omega t \; .$$

There will therefore be an instant at which the frequencies are identical, and the loop will pull in and acquire lock. The precondition for this is that the frequency offset $\Delta f = f_1 - f_0$ is smaller than the sweep width

$$\Delta f_{2\,\text{max}} = \pm k_f A_P \hat{U}_1 \; . \tag{27.24}$$

This maximum permissible offset is known as the *capture range* and represents the normal range of operation of the loop. For our example, it is $\pm 2.5\,\text{kHz}$, i.e. 25% of f_0.

27.4.2   Synchronous demodulator as phase detector

Section 25.3.4 describes the application of the multiplier as a phase-sensitive rectifier. If two sinusoidally alternating voltages, $U_1 = E\cos\omega_1 t$ and $U_2 = E\cos(\omega_2 t + \varphi)$, are applied to the inputs, the output voltage will be

$$U_0 = \frac{U_1 U_2}{E} = \tfrac{1}{2}E\cos[(\omega_1 + \omega_2)t + \varphi] + \tfrac{1}{2}E[\cos(\omega_1 - \omega_2)t - \varphi] \ . \quad (27.25)$$

For $\omega_1 = \omega_2$, there is an oscillation with double the frequency, superimposed on a DC voltage of the magnitude

$$U_\varphi = \bar{U}_0 = \frac{E}{2}\cos\varphi \ , \qquad (27.26)$$

in accordance with Eq. (25.22).

This function is represented in Fig. 27.25. It becomes immediately obvious that the voltage cannot be used as control variable in the vicinity of $\varphi = 0$, as the sign of the error signal cannot be detected. The two operating points $\varphi = \pm\pi$ are well suited, however, because voltage U_φ has a zero crossing. The sign of the gain determines at which of the two points lock-in occurs. Further stable points of operation occur at intervals of 2π. This implies that this kind of phase detector also cannot recognize a phase displacement by a whole number of periods, i.e. by a multiple of 2π.

Within a range of about $\pm\pi/4$ around the stable point of operation, φ_0, the characteristic of the phase detector is approximately linear, so that, with $\varphi = \varphi_0 + \vartheta$,

$$U_\varphi = \frac{E}{2}\cos(\varphi_0 + \vartheta) = \pm\frac{E}{2}\sin\vartheta \approx \pm\frac{E}{2}\vartheta \ . \qquad (27.27)$$

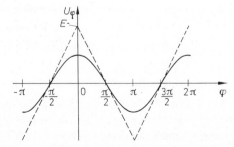

Fig. 27.25 Mean absolute value of the output voltage of a multiplier for sinusoidal input voltages of the amplitude E. Dashed line: multiplier mean output voltage for a square-wave input signal with the levels $\pm E$

The sensitivity (phase detector "gain") is therefore

$$k_\varphi = \frac{U_\varphi}{9} = \pm \frac{E}{2} \ . \tag{27.28}$$

If instead of the two sinusoidal voltages, two square-waves with the magnitude $\pm E$ are applied, the detector characteristic becomes triangular, as shown by the dashed lines in Fig. 27.25. The stable points of operation are again at $\varphi_0 = \pm (\pi/2) \pm n \cdot 2\pi$, the sensitivity in this case being

$$k_\varphi = \pm \frac{2E}{\pi} \ . \tag{27.29}$$

For square-wave input voltages, an analog multiplier is obviously no longer required. In this case, considerably higher frequencies are achieved with the transistor modulator in Fig. 22.21.

If the ripple of U_φ is to be kept small, a lowpass filter must be connected to the multiplier output, the cutoff frequency f_c of which is small against $2f_1$, in accordance with Eq. (27.25). This is a definite disadvantage since, unlike in the previous circuit, the proportional gain of the controller must now be chosen so low that the gain crossover frequency $f_g \approx f_c$. At this frequency, the phase shift of the controlled system together with that of the lowpass filter is already $- 135°$. If $f_g \approx f_c \ll f_1$, the control loop obtained would be impractical because of its very slow response. In principle, it could be speeded up by derivative action of the controller, but this would nullify the effect of the lowpass filter i.e. increase the ripple.

An increase of the control system bandwidth at the expense of the ripple of U_φ can be attained very simply by using a proportional action controller and omitting the lowpass filter. A phase margin of 90° is then available for any proportional gain chosen, i.e. the control loop is aperiodically damped.

Because of the feedback, the ripple of U_φ causes the tracking oscillator to be frequency modulated with twice the signal frequency. This results in a distortion of the output sine wave. For square-waves, the mark-space ratio is changed. The proportional gain must not be too high if the distortion is to be kept within tolerable limits. The condition $f_g \leq \frac{1}{3}f_1$ can be used as a rule of thumb.

The resulting arrangement is shown in Fig. 27.26 and is available as an integrated circuit PLL. Usually, the multiplier is simplified and reduced to a modulator, as in Fig. 22.21. The types NE 560 . . . 566 from Signetics and 74 HC 4046 from National, for instance, are based on this principle.

When operated without a lowpass filter, the circuit is usable only in those applications where it is important to have frequency f_2 identical to f_1 and where the shape and phase shift of the output signal are not significant; for example, as a discriminator for frequency demodulation. The reference oscillation is used as input signal. If the VCO frequency f_2 is linearly dependent on U_f, this voltage is proportional to the frequency deviation Δf_1. The superimposed ripple can be filtered out by a steep lowpass filter outside the control loop.

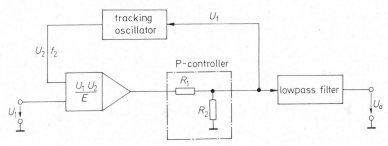

Fig. 27.26 PLL with a multiplier as phase detector for frequency demodulation

27.4.3 Frequency-sensitive phase detector

One drawback of the phase detectors described above is that they possess only a limited capture range, i.e. they cannot pull in if the initial frequency offset exceeds a certain limit. The reason for this is that the phase-equivalent signal U_φ for a frequency deviation is an alternating voltage symmetrical about zero. The voltage U_f therefore effects a periodic frequency modulation of the tracking oscillator, but never a systematic tuning in the right direction, i.e. towards the lock-in frequency.

The phase detector in Fig. 27.27, however, is different in this respect in that it produces a signal having the correct sign information for any given frequency offset. The circuit basically comprises two edge-triggered D flip-flops. For control purposes, the input voltages $U_1(t)$, $U_2(t)$ are converted into the rectangular signals x_1 and x_2 [27.3].

We now assume that both flip-flops are reset. If voltage U_2 leads voltage U_1, i.e. $\varphi > 0$, we first obtain a positive edge of x_2 which sets flip-flop F_2. It remains set until the following positive edge of x_1 sets flip-flop F_1. The state in which both flip-flops are set, exists only during the propagation delay time, since they are jointly reset subsequently by gate G. It can be seen from Fig. 27.28 that the output of the subtractor shows a sequence of positive rectangular pulses. Correspondingly, a sequence of negative pulses is obtained if the positive-going edge of x_2 occurs *after* the positive-going edge of x_1, i.e. if $\varphi < 0$. This behavior is summarized in the state diagram of Fig. 27.29.

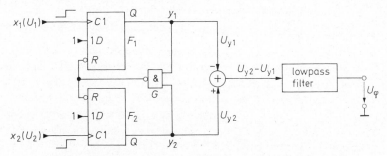

Fig. 27.27 Phase detector with memory for the sign of the phase shift

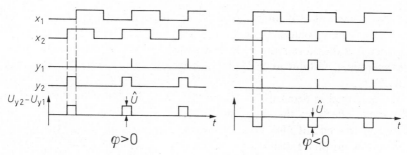

Fig. 27.28 Input and output signals of the phase detector

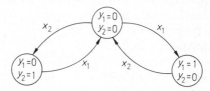

Fig. 27.29 State diagram of the phase detector

The duration of the output pulses is equal to the time interval between the positive-going zero crossings of $U_1(t)$ and those of $U_2(t)$. Hence, the mean value of the output voltage

$$U_\varphi = \hat{U}\frac{\Delta t}{T} = \hat{U}\frac{\varphi}{2\pi} . \tag{27.30}$$

As the value of the time interval increases proportionally with φ until the limits $\pm 360°$ are reached, a range of linear phase measurement of $\pm 360°$ is obtained. When this limit is exceeded, the output voltage jumps to zero and increases again, still having the same polarity. The result is the sawtooth characteristic in Fig. 27.30.

The basic difference between this characteristic and all previous ones is that, for $\varphi > 0$, U_φ is always positive and, for $\varphi < 0$, always negative. This is the reason for the frequency sensitivity of the detector. If frequency f_2 is, for instance, larger than f_1, the phase shift increases continuously and proportionally with time. As shown in Fig. 27.30, we then obtain for U_φ a sawtooth voltage having

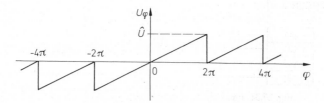

Fig. 27.30 Transfer characteristic of the phase detector

a positive mean value. If this detector is used in a phase-locked loop, it always indicates a leading phase. For a controller with integral action, the tracking frequency f_2 is therefore reduced until it coincides with f_1. The capture range is thus theoretically infinite and in practice limited only by the input voltage range of the VCO.

We described in Section 27.4.2 how the averaging lowpass filter has a very unfavorable effect on the transient behavior. For this reason, it is usually omitted in this circuit also. If one wishes to have $\varphi = 0$ (with the aid of an I-controller), no phase distortions are incurred, since in this case $U_\varphi = 0$ even without filtering. The flip-flops then produce no output pulses.

One drawback of the circuit is that very small deviations in phase are not detected, since the flip-flops would then have to produce extremely short output pulses which would be lost due to the limited rise times within the circuit. This is the reason why the phase jitter (phase noise) is somewhat larger than that with the sample-and-hold detector [26.4].

If a PLL with a large capture range and small phase jitter is required, this circuit can be combined with a sample-and-hold detector. After lock-in has been accomplished, the sample-and-hold detector is switched into the loop instead of the frequency-sensitive phase detector.

Integrated phase detectors employing this principle are listed in Fig. 27.34.

27.4.4 Phase detector with extensible measuring range

With the phase detectors described so far it is not possible to detect a phase shift of more than one oscillation period, as the phase measuring range is limited to values below 2π. There are applications, however, for which a phase delay of several oscillations must be recovered. The phase detector in Fig. 27.31 is suitable for this purpose. It is based on the up-down counter as illustrated in Fig. 10.35, which is insensitive to coinciding clock pulses.

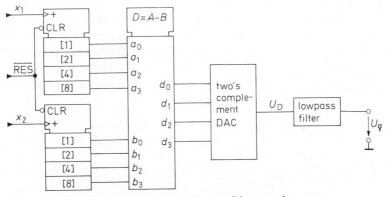

Fig. 27.31 Phase detector with extensible measuring range

Range in example: $+7$, -8 periods

Near zero phase shift, the detector behaves in the same way as the previous circuit; if x_2 leads x_1, positive pulses of the magnitude U_{LSB} arise, the duration of which is equal to the interval between the zero crossings of the input voltages. For a phase lag, negative pulses occur. The mean value of the pulses is

$$U_\varphi = \bar{U}_D = U_{LSB}\frac{\Delta t}{T} = U_{LSB}\frac{\varphi}{2\pi} \; .$$

If the phase displacement reaches the value 2π, the value for the interval Δt jumps from T to 0. In contrast to the previous circuit, however, the output does not assume zero voltage, but remains at U_{LSB}, as the difference D simultaneously increases by 1. Generalizing, the resultant output voltage is given by

$$U_\varphi = U_{LSB}\left(D + \frac{\Delta t}{T} \right) = U_{LSB}\cdot\frac{\varphi}{2\pi} \; .$$

The expression $D + \Delta t/T$ indicates the number of periods by which the two signals are displaced. The resulting detector characteristic is shown in Fig. 27.32 for 4 bits. The measuring range can be increased as required by extending the counting range.

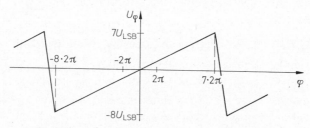

Fig. 27.32 Detection characteristic of the phase detector

27.4.5   PLL as a frequency multiplier

A particularly important application of the PLL is that of frequency multi-plication. A frequency divider is connected to each of the two inputs of the phase detector, as illustrated by Fig. 27.33. The frequency of the tracking oscillator

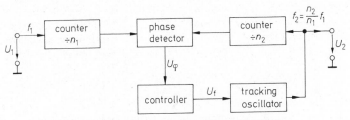

Fig. 27.33 Frequency multiplication with a PLL

assumes such a value that

$$\frac{f_1}{n_1} = \frac{f_2}{n_2} .$$

In this manner, the frequency of the tracking oscillator

$$f_2 = \frac{n_2}{n_1} f_1$$

can be adjusted to any rational multiple of the reference frequency f_1.

In this application the phase detector may operate at a frequency consider-ably lower than that of the tracking oscillator. It must therefore be ensured that the control voltage U_φ contains no ripple. An undesired frequency modulation would otherwise occur instead of simply the distortion of the output waveform, as described in Section 27.4.2.

The frequency multiplier circuit can be used to generate, with crystal accu-racy, frequencies above 50 MHz for which there are practically no crystals available. For this purpose we use a crystal oscillator operating at e.g. $f_1 = 10$ MHz and select $n_2 > n_1$. If it is merely a question of obtaining an integral multiple of the crystal frequency, we can select $n_1 = 1$, thereby dispens-ing with the input divider. However, if we would like, for instance, to step through the frequencies from 90 to 100 MHz in 100-kHz increments, the crystal frequency must first be divided down to 100 kHz with $n_1 = 100$. We can then generate all the desired frequencies using a divider factor $n_2 = 900$ to 1000. This is the principle on which the digital tuners widely used in today's radio and TV receivers are based [27.7].

A number of integrated PLL components are listed in Fig. 27.34.

Type	Manufacturer	Technology	Frequency range	Principle
Phase detectors				
MM74C932	National	CMOS	... 1 MHz	Freq./phase det.
MC4044	Motorola	TTL	... 20 MHz	Freq./phase det.
MC12040	Motorola	ECL	... 80 MHz	Freq./phase det.
AD9901	**Analog Dev.**	**TTL/ECL**	**...200 MHz**	**Freq./phase det.**
AD834	Analog Dev	Bipolar	... 500 MHz	Analog multiplier
AD539	Analog. Dev.	Bipolar	... 60 MHz	Analog multiplier
MPY634	Burr Brown	Bipolar	... 10 MHz	Analog multiplier
XR2228	Exar	Bipolar	... 50 MHz	Analog multiplier
LF398	National	Bifet	... 0.3 MHz	Sample & hold
HA5330	Harris	Bipolar	... 5 MHz	Sample & hold
Voltage-controlled oscillators (VCOs)				
74LS624	**Texas Instr.**	**TTL**	**... 20 MHz**	**Multivibrator**
MC4024	Motorola	TTL	... 20 MHz	Multivibrator
XR2209	Exar	Bipolar	... 1 MHz	Multivibrator
VFC110	Burr Brown	Bipolar	... 4 MHz	Charge compens.
VFC122	Burr Brown	Bipolar	... 0.5 MHz	Charge compens.
AD654	Analog Dev.	Bipolar	... 0.3 MHz	Charge compens.
MC1658	Motorola	ECL	...150 MHz	Multivibrator
MC1648	Motorola	ECL	...225 MHz	LC-oscillator
Phase-locked loops (PLLs)				
CD4046	RCA	CMOS	... 1 MHz	Phase det. + VCO
MM74HC4046	**National**	**CMOS**	**... 20 MHz**	**Phase det. + VCO**
PC74HCT7046	**Valvo**	**CMOS**	**... 20 MHz**	**Phase det. + VCO**
NE567	Signetics	TTL	... 0.5 MHz	Phase det. + VCO
XR2212	Exar	TTL	... 0.3 MHz	Phase det. + VCO
XR210	Exar	TTL	... 20 MHz	Phase det. + VCO
XRS200	Exar	TTL	... 30 MHz	Phase det. + VCO
DP8530	National	ECL/TTL	...125 MHz	Phase det. + VCO + divider
DP8512	**National**	**ECL**	**...225 MHz**	**Phase det. + VCO + divider**
74LS297	Texas Instr.	TTL	... 50 MHz	Digital PLL

Fig. 27.34. Integrated circuits for PLLs

28 Appendix

28.1 Addresses of some semiconductor manufacturers and distributors

International Headquarters	German Office or Distributor
Advanced Micro Devices 901 Thompson Place P.O. Box 3453 Sunnyvale, CA 94088 USA Phone: (408) 732–2400	Advanced Micro Devices (AMD) Rosenheimer Str. 143b D-8000 München 80 Phone: 089–4114–0 Fax: 089–406490
Altera Corporation 3525 Monroe Street P.O. Box 58163 Santa Clara, CA 95051 USA Phone: (408) 984–2800 Fax: (408) 248–6924	Electronic 2000 AG Stahlgruberring 12 D-8000 München 82 Phone: 089–42001–0 Fax: 089–42001–129
Analog Devices One Technology Way P.O. Box 9106 Norwood, MA 02062 USA Phone: (617) 329–4700 Fax: (617) 326–8703	Analog Devices GmbH Edelsbergstr. 8–10 D-8000 München 21 Phone: 089–57005–0 Fax: 089–57005–157
Apex Corporation 5980 N. Shannon Road Tucson, AZ 85741 USA Phone: (602) 742–8600 Fax: (602) 888–3329	Emtron GmbH Rudolf-Diesel-Str. 14 D-6085 Nauheim Phone: 06152–61081 Fax: 06152–69347
Atmel Corp. 2125 O'Nel Drive San Jose, CA 95131 USA Phone: (408) 441–0311 Fax: (408) 436–4200	Bacher GmbH Schleißheimer Str. 87 D-8046 Garching Phone: 089–3204026 Fax: 089–3207512
AT & T Microelectronics 555 Union Boulevard Allentown, PA 18103 USA Phone: (800) 372–2447	AT & T Microelectronic GmbH Bahnhofstr. 27A D-8043 Unterföhring Phone: 089–95086–0 Fax: 089–95086–333

International Headquarters	German Office or Distributor

Brooktree Corp.
9950 Barnes Canyon Road
San Diego, CA 92121
USA
Phone: (619) 452–7580
Fax: (619) 452–1249

Tekelec Airtronic GmbH
Kapuzinerstr. 9
D-8000 München 2
Phone: 089–5164–0
Fax: 089–5164–10

Burr Brown
International Airport
P.O. Box 11400
Tucson, AZ 85734
USA
Phone: (602) 746–1111
Fax: (602) 889–1510

Burr Brown GmbH
Kurze Str. 40
D-7024 Filderstadt
Phone: 0711–7704–0
Fax: 0711–7704–109

Comlinear Corp.
4800 Wheaton Drive
Fort Collins, CO 80525
USA
Phone: (303) 226–0500
Fax: (303) 226–0564

TransTech GmbH
Allee 18
D-7100 Heilbronn
Phone: 07131–68052
Fax: 07131–68059

Crystall Corp.
P.O. Box 17847
2024 E. St. Elmo Road
Austin, TX 78760
USA
Phone: (512) 445–7222
Fax: (512) 445–7581

Atlantik Elektronik GmbH
Fraunhoferstr. 11A
D-8033 Martinsried
Phone: 089–857000–0
Fax: 089–8573702

Cypress Semiconductor
3901 North First Street
San Jose, CA 95134
USA
Phone: (408) 943–2600
Fax: (408) 943–2741

Cypress GmbH
Münchener Str. 15a
D-8011 Zorneding
Phone: 08106–2855–59
Fax: 08106–20087

Dallas Semicond.
4350 Beltwood Pkway
Dallas, TX 75244
USA
Phone: (214) 450–0400
Fax: (214) 450–0470

Astek GmbH
Gottlieb Daimler Str. 7
D-2358 Kaltenkirchen
Phone: 04191–8007–0
Fax: 04191–8007–33

Datel
11 Cabot Boulevard
Mansfield, MA 02048
USA
Phone: (508) 339–3000
Fax: (508) 339–6356

Datel GmbH
Bavariaring 8
D-8000 München 15
Phone: 089–530741
Fax: 089–536337

International Headquarters	German Office or Distributor
Degussa AG Leipziger Str. 10 6450 Hanau Federal Republic of Germany Phone: (49) 6181–320–0 Fax: (49) 6181–320–236	Degussa AG Leipziger Str. 10 D-6450 Hanau Phone: 06181–320–0 Fax: 06181–320–236
Electronic Designs 42 South Street Hopkinton, MA 01748 USA Phone: (508) 435–2341 Fax: (508) 435–6302	Bacher GmbH Schleißheimer Str. 87 D-8046 Garching Phone: 089–3204026 Fax: 089–3207512
Elantec, Inc. 1996 Tarob Court Milpitas, CA 95035 USA Phone: (408) 945–1323 Fax: (408) 945–9305	Scantec GmbH Behringstr. 10 D-8033 Planegg Phone: 089–8598021 Fax: 089–8576574
Exar Corp. 2222 Qume Drive San Jose, CA 95161 USA Phone: (408) 434–6400 Fax: (408) 943–8245	Rohm Electronics GmbH Mühlenstr. 70 D-4052 Korschenbroich 1 Phone: 02161–6101–0 Fax: 02161–642102
Fairchild Semi. Div. of National Semicond.	
Fujitsu Limited 6-1 Marunouchi 2-chome Chiyoda-ku Tokyo 100 Japan Phone: 81–3–216–3211	Fujitsu GmbH Lyoner Str. 44–48 D-6000 Frankfurt 71 Phone: 069–6632–0 Fax: 069–6632–122
General Electric Semi. Div. of. Harris Semiconductor	
General Instrument Corp. 600 West John Street CS 620 Hicksville, NY 11802 USA Phone: (516) 933–3333 Fax: (516) 933–3236	General Instrument GmbH Freischützstr. 96 D-8000 München 81 Phone: 089–95997–0 Fax: 089–9570489
Harris Semicond. 1301 Woody Burke Road Melbourne, FL 32905 USA Phone: (407) 724–3739	Harris GmbH Putzbrunnerstr. 69 D-8000 München 83 Phone: 089–63813–0 Fax: 089–6377891

International Headquarters	German Office or Distributor
Heraeus Sensor GmbH Heraeusstr. 12–14 6450 Hanau 1 Federal Republic of Germany Phone: (49) 6181–35–5708 Fax: (49) 6181–35–735	Heraeus Sensor GmbH Heraeusstr. 12–14 D-6450 Hanau 1 Phone: 06181–35–5708 Fax: 06181–35–735
Hewlett-Packard Co. 370 West Trimble Road San Jose, CA 95131 USA Phone: (408) 435–7400 Fax: (408) 435–5865	Hewlett-Packard (HP) GmbH Hewlett-Packard-Straße D-6380 Bad Homburg Phone: 06172–16–0 Fax: 06172–16–1309
Hitachi, Ltd. New Marunouchi Bldg. 5–1 Marunouchi 1-chome Chiyoda-ku Tokyo 100 Japan Phone: 3–212–1111	Hitachi Components GmbH Hans-Pinsel-Str. 10A D-8013 Haar Phone: 089–4614–0 Fax: 089–463068
Honeywell SPT 1150 E. Cheyenne Mountain Blvd. Colorado Springs, CO 80906 USA Phone: (303) 577–1000 Fax: (303) 577–3716	Honeywell GmbH Kaiserleisstr. 39 D-6050 Offenbach Phone: 069–80641 Fax: 069–812620
Hybrid Memory Elm Road North Shields, NE 29 8 SE United Kingdom Phone: 091–258–0690	MSC GmbH Werner v. Siemens Str. 1 D-7513 Stutensee 3 Phone: 07249–758–170 Fax: 07249–8746
Hybrid Systems Div. of Sipex Corp.	
Integrated Device Technology 3236 Scott Boulevard Santa Clara, CA 95054 USA Phone: (408) 727–6116 Fax: (408) 492–8674	IDT GmbH Gottfried-von-Cramm-Str. 1 D-8056 Neufahrn Phone: 08165–5024 Fax: 08165–62896
Inmos Ltd Div. of SGS-Thomson 1000 Aztec West Almondsbury Bristol BS12 4SQ United Kingdom Phone: 0454–616616	SGS-Thomson (ST) GmbH Bretonischer Ring 4 D-8011 Grasbrunn Phone: 089–46006–130 Fax: 089–46006–140

International Headquarters	German Office or Distributor
Intel Corp. 3065 Bowers Avenue Santa Clara, CA 95051 USA Phone: (408) 765–8080	Intel GmbH Dornacher Str. 1 D-8016 Feldkirchen Phone: 089–90992–0 Fax: 089–9043948
ITT Semiconductors 55 Merrimack Street Lawrence, MA 01843 USA Phone: (508) 688–1881 Fax: (508) 975–7109	Intermetall (ITT) GmbH Hans-Bunte-Str. 19 D-7800 Freiburg Phone: 0761–517–0 Fax: 0761–517–788
International Rectifier 233 Kansas Street El Segundo, CA 90245 USA Phone: (213) 772–2000	International Rectifier GmbH Saalburgstr. 157 D-6380 Bad Homburg Phone: 06172–37066 Fax: 06172–37065
Intersil Div. of Harris Semiconductor	
Isdata Inc. 800 Airport Rd. Monterey, CA 93940 Phone: (408) 373–7359 Fax: (408) 373–3622	Isdata GmbH Haid-und-Neu Str. 7 D-7500 Karlsruhe Phone: 0721–693092 Fax: 0721–174263
Lattice Corp. 5555 N.E. Moore Ct. Hillsboro, OR 97124 USA Phone: (503) 681–0118 Fax: (503) 681–3037	Lattice GmbH Sendlinger-Str. 64 D-8000 München 2 Phone: 089–329099–0 Fax: 089–329099–99
Linear Technology Corp. 1630 McCarthy Blvd. Milpitas, CA 95035 USA Phone: (408) 432–1900 Fax: (408) 434–0507	Linear Technology GmbH Untere Hauptstr. 9 D-8057 Eching Phone: 089–3195023 Fax: 089–3194821
Logic Devices, Inc. 628 East Evelyn Avenue Sunnyvale, CA 94086 USA Phone: (408) 720–8630	Neumüller GmbH Eschenstr. 2 D-8028 Taufkirchen Phone: 089–61208–0 Fax: 089–61208–248
LSI Logic Corporation 1551 McCarthy Blvd. Milpitas, CA 95035 USA Phone: (408) 433–8000 Fax: (408) 434–6422	LSI Logic GmbH Arabellastr. 33 D-8000 München 81 Phone: 089–926903–0 Fax: 089–917096

International Headquarters	German Office or Distributor

Maxim Inc.
120 San Gabriel Drive
Sunnyvale, CA 94086
USA
Phone: (408) 737–7600
Fax: (408) 737–7194

Maxim GmbH
Sandstr. 21
D-8000 München 2
Phone: 089–5234083
Fax: 089–5236622

MHS Electronic
La Chantrerie
Route de Gachet CP 3008
44087 Nantes Cedex 03
France
Phone: (33) 40303030
Fax: (33) 40300216

Matra (MHS) GmbH
Erfurter Str. 29
D-8057 Eching
Phone: 089–310005–0
Fax: 089–310005–55

Micro Power Sys. Inc.
3151 Jay Street
Santa Clara, CA 95054
USA
Phone: (408) 727–5350
Fax: (408) 748–9045

Micro Power Sys. GmbH
Ernsbergerstr. 14
D-8000 München 60
Phone: 089–837091
Fax: 089–8340402

Mitsubishi Corp.
Mitsubishi Denki Bldg.
Marunouchi
Tokyo 100
Japan
Phone: 3–218–2860

Mitsubishi Electric GmbH
Gothaer Str. 8
D-4030 Ratingen 1
Phone: 02102–486–145
Fax: 02102–486–367

Monolithic Memories
Div. of Advanced Micro Dev.

Motorola Semicond. Inc.
3102 North 56 Street
P.O. Box 52073
Phoenix AZ 85018
USA
Phone: (602) 952–3000

Motorola GmbH
Schatzbogen 7
D-8000 München 82
Phone: 089–92103–0
Fax: 089–92103–101

Murata Ltd.
Nagaokakyo-Shi
Kyoto 617
Japan
Phone: 075–951–9111

Murata GmbH
Holbeinstr. 21–23
D-8500 Nürnberg 70
Phone: 0911–6687–0
Fax: 0911–6687–193

National Semicond. Corp.
2900 Semiconductor Drive
P.O. Box 58090
Santa Clara, CA 95052
USA
Phone (408) 721–5000

National Semiconductor GmbH
Industriestr. 10
D-8080 Fürstenfeldbruck
Phone: 08141–103–0
Fax: 08141–103–554

International Headquarters	German Office or Distributor
NEC Ltd. 33-1 Shiba 5 Chome Minato-co Tokyo 108 Japan Phone: 3–454–1111	NEC Electronics GmbH Oberratherstr. 4 D-4000 Düsseldorf 30 Phone: 0211–650302 Fax: 0211–6503327
Oki Ltd. 10-3 Shibaura 4-chome Minato-ku Tokyo 108 Japan Phone: 03–454–2111	Oki Electronic GmbH Hellersberg Str. 2 D-4040 Neuss 1 Phone: 02101–15960 Fax: 02101–103539
Optek Techn. Inc. 1215 W. Crosby Road Carrollton, TXX 75006 USA Phone: (214) 323–2200 Fax: (214) 323–2396	Optek Techn. Inc. Werner Friedmann Bogen 7 D-8000 München 50 Phone: 089–1413057 Fax: 089–1404476
Performance Semicond. 610 E. Weddell Drive Sunnyvale, CA 94089 USA Phone: (408) 734–9000	Alfatron GmbH Schleißheimer Str. 87 D-8046 Garching Phone: 089–329099–0 Fax: 089–329099–59
Philips Components P.O. Box 523 5600 MD Eindhoven The Netherlands Phone: (040) 757005	Valvo GmbH Buchardstr. 19 D-2000 Hamburg 1 Phone: 040–3296–0 Fax: 040–3296–213
Plessey Limited Cheney Manor, Swindon Wiltshire, SN2 2QW United Kingdom Phone: 0793–518000 Fax: 0793–616763	Plessey GmbH Ungererstr. 129 D-8000 München 40 Phone: 089–360906–0 Fax: 089–360906–55
Precision Monolithics Inc. 1500 Space Park Drive P.O. Box 58020 Santa Clara, CA 95052 USA Phone: (408) 727–9222 Fax: (408) 727–1550	Precision Monolithics (PMI) Breite Str. 2 D-7000 Stuttgart 1 Phone: 0711–2293–0 Fax: 0711–291568
Raytheon 350 Ellis Street Mountain View, CA 94039 USA Phone: (415) 968–9211 Fax: (415) 966–7620	Raytheon Halbleiter GmbH Thalkirchner Str. 74 D-8000 München 2 Phone: 089–539693 Fax: 089–531439

International Headquarters	German Office or Distributor

RCA
Div. of Harris Semi.

Reticon EGG	Reticon EGG GmbH
345 Potrero Avenue	Hohenlindener Str. 12
Sunnyvale, CA 94086	D-8000 München 80
USA	Phone: 089–918061
Phone: (408) 245–2060	Fax: 089–9101283
Fax: (408) 738–6979	

Rockwell	Rockwell International GmbH
4311 Jamboree Road	Fraunhoferstr. 11b
Newport Beach, CA 92658	D-8033 Martinsried
USA	Phone: 089–8576016
Phone: (714) 833–4700	Fax: 089–8575793

Seeq Inc.	Metronik GmbH
1849 Fortune Drive	Leonhardsweg 2
San Jose, CA 95131	D-8025 Unterhaching
USA	Phone: 089–61108–0
Phone: (408) 432–1550	Fax: 089–6116468

Sen Sym	Sensortechnics GmbH
1255 Reanwood Avenue	Aubinger Weg 27
Sunnyvale, CA 94089	D-8039 Puchheim
USA	Phone: 089–80083–0
Phone: (408) 744–1500	Fax: 089–80083–33

SGS-Thomson Microelectr.	SGS-Thomson (ST) GmbH
7 Avenue Gallieni	Bretonischer Ring 4
94253 Gentilly, Cedex	D-8011 Grasbrunn
France	Phone: 089–46006–130
Phone: 47407575	Fax: 089–46006–140
Fax: 47407910	

Siemens Semic. Inc.	Siemens AG
2191 Laurelwood Road	Balanstr. 73
Santa Clara, CA 95054	D-8000 München 80
USA	Phone: 089–4144–0
Phone: (408) 980–4500	Fax: 089–4144–2563
Fax: (408) 980–4596	

Siemens Opto. Inc.	Siemens AG
19000 Homestead Road	Balanstr. 73
Cupertina, CA 95014	D-8000 München 80
USA	Phone: 089–4144–0
Phone: (408) 257–7910	Fax: 089–4144–2563

Signetics Corp.	Valvo GmbH
Div. of. Philips	Buchardstr. 19
811E Argues Ave.	D-2000 Hamburg 1
Sunnyvale, CA 94088	Phone: 040–3296–0
Phone: (408) 991–2000	Fax: 040–3296–213

International Headquarters	German Office or Distributor
Silicon General 11861 Western Avenue Garden Grove, CA 92641 USA Phone: (714) 898–8121 Fax: (714) 893–2570	Astronic GmbH Grünwalder Weg 30 D-8024 Deisenhofen Phone: 089–6130303 Fax: 089–6131668
Siliconix Ltd. Morriston Swansea SA6 6NE United Kingdom Phone: (0792) 310100 Fax: (0792) 310401	Siliconix GmbH Johannesstr. 27 D-7024 Filderstadt 1 Phone: 0711–70002–0 Fax: 0711–70002–37
Sipex Corp. Hybrid Systems Division 22 Linnell Circle Suburban Industrial Park Billerica, MA 01821 USA Phone: (617) 667–8700 Fax: (617) 667–8310	Sipex GmbH Rheinstr. 32 D-6100 Darmstadt 11 Phone: 06151–291595 Fax: 06151–292762
Sony Corp. 6-7-35 Kitashinagawa Shinagawa-ku Tokyo 141 Japan Phone: 03–4482111	Sony GmbH Hugo-Eckner-Str. 20 D-5000 Köln 30 Phone: 0221–5966–0 Fax: 0221–5966–349
Sprague Comp. 115 Northeast Cutoff Worcester, MA 01615 USA Phone: (508) 853–5000	Sprague Halbleiter (SSG) GmbH Klaus Hofstetter Weg 3 D-7824 Hinterzarten Phone: 07652–1066 Fax: 07652–767
Standard Microsystems Corp. 35 Marcus Boulevard Hauppauge, NY 11788 USA Phone: (516) 273–3100	Standard Microsystems (SMC) GmbH Arabellastr. 5 D-8000 München 81 Phone: 089–919594 Fax: 089–918173
Teledyne Semicond. 1300 Terra Bella Avenue Mountain View, CA 94039 USA Phone: (415) 968–9241 Fax: (415) 967–1590	Teledyne GmbH Abraham-Lincoln-Str. 38-42 D-6200 Wiesbaden Phone: 06121–768–0 Fax: 06121–701239
Telefunken Electronic GmbH Theresienstr. 2 7100 Heilbronn Federal Republic of Germany Phone: (49) 7131–67–0 Fax: (49) 7131–67–2340	Telefunken Electronic GmbH Theresienstr. 2 D-7100 Heilbronn Phone: 07131–67–0 Fax: 07131–67–2340

International Headquarters	German Office or Distributor
Texas Instruments Inc. P.O. Box 8090 Dallas, TX 75380 USA Phone: (214) 995–2011	Texas Instruments GmbH Haggertystr. 1 D-8050 Freising Phone: 08161–804893 Fax: 08161–84516
Toshiba Corp. 1-1 Shibaura 1-chome Minato-ku Tokyo 105 Japan Phone: 457–3495	Toshiba Electronics GmbH Hansa Allee 181 D-4000 Düsseldorf 11 Phone: 0211–5296–0 Fax: 0211–5296–400
TRW Electronics P.O. Box 2472 La Jolla, CA 92038 USA Phone: (619) 457–1000 Fax: (619) 455–6314	TRW GmbH Konrad-Celtis-Str. 81 D-8000 München 70 Phone: 089–7103–0 Fax: 089–7103–180
Unitrode Corp. 580 Pleasant Street Watertown, MA 02172 USA Phone: (617) 926–0404 Fax: (617) 924–1235	Unitrode GmbH Hauptstr. 68 D-8025 Unterhaching Phone: 089–619004 Fax: 089–617984
VLSI-Technology Inc. 1109 McKay Drive San Jose, CA 94131 USA Phone: (408) 434–3100 Fax: (408) 263–2511	VLSI Technology (VTI) GmbH Rosenkavalierplatz 10 D-8000 München 81 Phone: 089–92795–0 Fax: 089–92795–145
Waferscale Inc. 47280 Kato Road Fremont, CA 94538 USA Phone: (415) 656–5400 Fax: (415) 657–5916	Bacher GmbH Schleißheimer Str. 87 D-8046 Garching Phone: 089–3204026 Fax: 089–3207512
Weitek Corp. 1060 E. Arques Avenue Sunnyvale, CA 94086 USA Phone: (408) 738–8400 Fax: (408) 738–1185	Tekelec Airtronic GmbH Kapuzinerstr. 9 D-8000 München 2 Phone: 089–5164–0 Fax: 089–5164–10
Western Digital Corp. 2445 McCabe Way Irvine, CA 92714 USA Phone: (714) 863–0102	Western Digital GmbH Zamdorferstr. 26 D-8000 München 80 Phone: 089–9220060 Fax: 089–914611

International Headquarters	German Office or Distributor
Xicor Inc. 851 Buckeye Court Milpitas, CA 95035 USA Phone: (408) 432–8888 Fax: (408) 432–0640	Xicor GmbH Bretonischer Ring 15 D-8011 Grasbrunn Phone: 089–461008–0 Fax: 089–4605472
Xilinx 2100 Logic Drive San Jose, CA 95124 USA Phone: (408) 559–7778 Fax: (408) 559–7114	Metronik GmbH Leonhardsweg 2 D-8025 Unterhaching Phone: 089–61108–0 Fax: 089–6116468
Yellow Springs Inc. Yellow Springs, Ohio 45387 USA Phone: (513) 767–7241 Fax: (513) 767–9353	Kipp & Zonen GmbH Obere Dammstr. 10 D-5650 Solingen 1 Phone: 0212–587575 Fax: 0212–587599
Zilog Inc. 210 Hacienda Ave. Campbell, CA 95008 USA Phone: (408) 370–8000	Zilog GmbH Peschelanger 11 D-8000 München 83 Phone: 089–672045 Fax: 089–6706188
Zoran Corp. 3450 Central Expressway Santa Clara, CA 95051 USA Phone: (408) 720–0444 Fax: (408) 749–8057	Scantec GmbH Behringstr 10 D-8033 Planegg Phone: 089–8598021 Fax: 089–8576574

28.2 Types of the 7400 logic families

28.2.1 Families of the various manufacturers

Manufacturer	TTL	CMOS
Texas Instruments	(SN 74) (SN 74 S) SN 74 LS SN 74 ALS SN 74 AS SN 74 F	SN 74 HC SN 74 HCT SN 74 AC SN 74 ACT SN 74 BCT
Valvo	(PC 74) PC 74 LS PC 74 F	PC 74 HC PC 74 HCT PC 74 AC PC 74 ACT

Hersteller	TTL	CMOS
National	DM 74 LS DM 74 ALS DM 74 AS 74 F	MM 74 HC MM 74 HCT 74 AC 74 ACT 74 FCT
Motorola	MC 74 LS MC 74 F	MC 74 HC MC 74 HCT
RCA		CD 74 HC CD 74 HCT CD 74 AC CD 74 ACT
SGS		M 74 HC M 74 HCT
IDT		IDT 74 HCT IDT 74 FCT

28.2.2   Arranged by function

Type	NAND gates	Output	Pins
00	Quad 2-input NAND	TP	14
01	Quad 2-input NAND	OC	14
03	Quad 2-input NAND	TP	14
10	Triple 3-input NAND	TP	14
12	Triple 3-input NAND	OC	14
13	Dual 4-input NAND Schmitt trigger	TP	14
18	Dual 4-input NAND Schmitt trigger	TP	14
20	Dual 4-input NAND	TP	14
22	Dual 4-input NAND	OC	14
24	Quad 2-input NAND Schmitt trigger	TP	14
26	Quad 2-input gate NAND 15 V O/P	OC	14
30	8-input NAND	TP	14
37	Quad 2-input NAND buffer	TP	14
38	Quad 2-input NAND buffer	OC	14
40	Dual 4-input NAND buffer	TP	16
132	Quad 2-input NAND Schmitt trigger	TP	14
133	13-input NAND	TP	16
(134	12-input 3-state NAND	TS	16)
1000	Buffer '00' gate	TP	14
1003	Buffer '03" gate	TP	14
1010	Buffer '10' gate	TP	14
1020	Buffer '20' gate	TP	14

TP = totem pole, OC = open collector, TS = tristate, O/P = overvoltage protection
( ) = only available in "Standard-" or "Schottky-" TTL, therefore not for new designs

Type	NAND gates	Output	Pins
4023	Triple 3-input NAND	TP	14
7003	Quad 2-input NAND Schmitt trigger	TP	14
7006	3/4-input NAND/NOR gates	TP	24
8003	Dual 2-input NAND	TP	8

Type	NOR gates	Output	Pins
02	Quad 2-input NOR	TP	14
23	Dual 4-input strobe expandable I/P NOR	TP	16
25	Dual 4-input strobe NOR	TP	14
27	Triple 3-input NOR	TP	14
28	Quad 2-input NOR buffer	TP	14
33	Quad 2-input NOR buffer	OC	14
36	Quad 2-input NOR	TP	14
(260	Dual 5-input NOR gate	TP	14)
1002	Buffer '02' gate	TP	14
1036	Quad 2-input NOR	TP	14
4002	Dual 4-input NOR	TP	14
4078	8-input NOR	TP	14
7002	Quad 2-input NOR Schmitt trigger	TP	14

Type	AND gates	Output	Pins
08	Quad 2-input AND	TP	14
09	Quad 2-input AND	OC	14
11	Triple 3-input AND	TP	14
15	Triple 3-input AND	OC	14
21	Dual 4-input AND	TP	14
1008	Buffer '08' gate	OC	14
1011	Buffer '11' gate	TP	14
7001	Quad 2-input AND Schmitt trigger	TP	14

Type	OR gates	Output	Pins
32	Quad 2-input OR	TP	14
802	Triple 4-input OR NOR	TP	
832	Hex 2-input buffer	TP	20
1032	Buffer '32' gate	TP	14
4075	Triple 3-input OR	TP	14
7032	Quad 2-input OR Schmitt Trigger	TP	14

Type	AND-OR gates	Output	Pins
(50	Dual 2 wide 2-input AND-OR-Invert	TP	14)
51	Dual 2 wide 2-input AND-OR-Invert	TP	14
54	4 wide 2 input AND-OR-Invert	TP	14
64	4-2-3-2 input AND-OR-Invert	TP	14
(65	4-2-3-2 input AND-OR-Invert	OC	14)

Type	EXOR gates	Output	Pins
86	Quad exclusive OR	TP	14
(135	Quad exclusive OR/NOR	TS	16)
136	Quad exclusive OR	OC	14
266	Quad 2-input exclusive NOR	OC	16
386	Quad exclusive OR	TP	14
810	'86' with inverting outputs	TP	14
811	'810' with open collector	OC	14
7266	'266' with totem pole output	TP	16

Type	Expander	Output	Pins
(53	4 wide 2-input AND-OR-Invert	TP	14)
55	2 wide 4-input AND-OR-Invert	TP	14

Type	Gate combinations	Output	Pins
7006	3-4 input NAND, 3-4 input NOR	TP	24
7008	Triple 2-input NAND, 2-input NOR, Dual INV	TP	24
7074	Dual D-FF, 2-input NAND/NOR, Dual INV	TP	24
7075	Dual D-FF, Dual 2-input NAND, Dual INV	TP	24
7076	Dual D-FF, Dual 2-input NOR, Dual INV	TP	24

Type	Inverters	Output	Pins
04	Hex inverter	TP	14
05	Hex inverter	OC	14
(06	Hex inverter/buffer 30 V O/P	OC	14)
14	Hex inverter Schmitt trigger	TP	14
(16	Hex inverter/buffer 15 V O/P	OC	14)
(17	Hex buffer 15 V O/P	OC	14)
19	Hex inverter Schmitt trigger	TP	14
1004	'04' gate buffer	TP	14
1005	'05' gate buffer	OC	14
4049	Hex inverting buffer	TP	16

Type	Non-inverting drivers	Output	Pins
(07	Hex buffer 30 V O/P	OC	14)
34	Hex buffer	TP	14
35	Hex buffer	OC	14
125	Quad 3-state buffer	TS	14
126	Quad 3-state buffer	TS	14
1034	Hex buffer	TP	14
1035	Hex buffer	OC	14
4050	Hex buffer	TP	16

O/P = overvoltage protection
( ) = only available in "Standard-" or "Schottky-" TTL, therefore not for new designs

Type	Line drivers	Output	Pins
(128	Quad 2-input NOR line driver	TP	14)
(140	Dual input NAND line driver	TP	16)
(425	Quad gates active low enable	TS	14)
804	Hex 2-input NAND line driver	TP	20
805	Hex 2-input NOR line driver	TP	20
808	Hex 2-input AND line driver	TP	20
832	Hex 2-input OR line driver	TP	20
1631	Quad differential line driver	TS	16
1804	'804' with Center Vcc, GND	TP	20
1805	'805' With Center Vcc, GND	TP	20
1808	'808' With Center Vcc, GND	TP	20
1832	'832' With Center Vcc, GND	TP	20

Type	Flip-flops, transparent	Output	Pins
75	Quad D-latch	TP	16
77	Quad D-latch	TP	16
(100	Dual 4-bit D-latch	TP	24)
(116	Dual 4-bit D-latch	TP	24)
(118	Hex SR flip-flop	TP	16)
(119	Hex SR flip-flop	TP	24)
279	Hex SR flip-flop	TP	16
375	Quad D-latch	TP	16
873	Dual 4-bit D-latch	TS	24
880	'873' inverting	TS	24

Type	Flip-flops, master-slave	Output	Pins
(70	JK flip-flop, preset, clear	TP	14)
(72	JK flip-flop, preset, clear	TP	14)
73	Dual JK flip-flop, clear	TP	14
74	Dual D flip-flop, preset, clear	TP	14
76	Dual JK flip-flop, preset, clear	TP	16
78	Dual JK flip-flop, preset, clear	TP	14
107	Dual JK flip-flop, clear	TP	14
109	Dual JK flip-flop, preset, clear	TP	16
(111	Dual JK flip-flop with data lock-out	TP	16)
112	Dual JK flip-flop, preset, clear	TP	16
113	Dual JK flip-flop, preset	TP	14
114	Dual JK flip-flop, preset, clear	TP	14
171	Quad D flip-flop, preset, clear	TP	16
173	Quad D flip-flop, clear, enable	TS	16
174	Hex D flip-flop, clear	TP	16
175	Quad D flip-flop, clear	TP	16
(276	Quad J$\overline{\text{K}}$ flip-flop, preset, clear	TP	20)
(376	Quad J$\overline{\text{K}}$ flip-flop, clear	TP	16)
378	Hex D flip-flop, enable	TP	16
379	Quad D flip-flop, enable	TP	16
3074	'74' metastable resistant	TP	14
7074	Dual D-FF + NAND, NOR, inverter	TP	24
7075	Dual D-FF + NAND, inverter	TP	24
7076	Dual D-FF + NOR, inverter	TP	24

Type	Shift registers		Output	Pins
91	8-bit shift register		TP	14
95	4-bit shift register	PIPO	TP	14
96	5-bit shift register	PI	TP	16
164	8-bit shift register	PO	TP	14
165	8-bit shift register	PI	TP	16
166	8-bit shift register	PI	TP	16
(178	4-bit shift register	PIPO	TP	14)
(179	4-bit shift register	PI	TP	16)
194	4-bit shift reg. right/left	PIPO	TP	16
195	4-bit shift register	PIPO	TP	14
(198	8-bit shift reg. right/left	PIPO	TP	24)
(199	8-bit shift register	PIPO	TP	24)
295	4-bit shift reg. right/left	PIPO	TS	14
299	8-bit shift reg. right/left	PIPO	TS	20
(322	8-bit shift reg. sign protection	PIPO	TS	20)
323	8-bit shift reg. right/left	PIPO	TS	20
395	4-bit shift register	PIPO	TS	16
396	Quad 2-bit shift register	PO	TP	16
673	16-bit shift register	PO	TP	24
674	16-bit shift register	PI	TP	24

Type	Shift registers with data register		Output	Pins
594	8-bit shift reg. w. output reg.	PO	TP	16
595	8-bit shift reg. w. output reg.	PO	TS	16
596	8-bit shift reg. w. output reg.	PO	OC	16
597	8-bit shift reg. w. input reg.	PI	TP	16
598	8-bit shift reg. w. input reg.	PIPO	TS	20
599	8-bit shift reg. w. output reg.	PO	OC	16
671	4-bit shift reg. w. output right/left	PO	TS	20
672	4-bit shift reg. w. output reg. right/left	PO	TS	20
962	8-bit shift reg. dual rank	PIPO	TS	18
963	8-bit shift reg. dual rank	PIPO	TS	20
964	8-bit shift reg. dual rank	PIPO	TS	20

Type	Asynchronous counters	Output	Pins
68	Dual decade counter	TP	16
69	Dual 4-bit binary counter	TP	16
90	Decade counter	TP	14
92	Divide-by-12 counter	TP	14
93	4-bit binary counter	TP	14

PI = parallel input, PO = parallel output
( ) = only available in "Standard-" or "Schottky-" TTL, therefore not for new designs

Type	Asynchronous counters	Output	Pins
(176	Decade counter (presettable)	TP	14)
(177	4-bit binary counter (presettable)	TP	14)
196	Decade counter	TP	14
197	4-bit binary counter	TP	14
290	Decade counter	TP	14
293	4-bit binary counter	TP	14
390	Dual decade counter	TP	16
393	Dual 4-bit binary counter	TP	14
490	Dual decade counters	TP	16
4017	Decade counter	TP	16

Type	Frequency divider (asynchronous)	Output	Pins
56	Frequency divider: 50	TP	8
57	Frequency divider: 60	TP	8
(97	6-bit binary rate multiplier	TP	16)
(167	4-bit decade rate multiplier	TP	16)
292	30-bit programmable freq. divider	TP	16
294	16-bit programmable freq. divider	TP	16
4020	14-bit binary counter	TP	16
4024	8-bit binary counter	TP	16
4040	12-bit binary counter	TP	16
4059	16-bit programmable freq. divider	TP	24
4060	14-bit binary counter, oscillator	TP	16
7060	14-bit binary counter, oscillator	TP	16

Type	Synchronous counters	Output	Pins
160	4-bit decade counter, sync. load	TP	16
161	4-bit binary counter, sync. load	TP	16
162	4-bit decade counter, sync. load	TP	16
163	4-bit binary counter, sync. load	TP	16
168	4-bit decade up/down counter, sync. load	TP	16
169	4-bit binary up/down counter, sync. load	TP	16
190	4-bit decade up/down counter, async. load	TP	16
191	4-bit binary up/down counter, async. load	TP	16
192	4-bit decade up/down counter, async. load	TP	16
193	4-bit binary up/down counter, async. load	TP	16
264	Look-ahead carry for counters	TP	16
269	8-bit binary up/down counter, sync. load	TP	24
560	4-bit decade counter, sync./async. load	TS	20
561	4-bit binary counter, sync./async. load	TS	20
568	4-bit decade up/down counter, sync. load	TS	20
569	4-bit binary up/down counter, sync. load	TS	20
579	8-bit binary up/down counter	TS	20

Type	Synchronous counters	Output	Pins
668	4-bit decade up/down counter, sync. load	TP	16
669	4-bit binary up/down counter, sync. load	TP	16
867	8-bit binary up/down counter, sync. load	TP	24
869	8-bit binary up/down counter, sync. load	TP	24
4017	Divide-by-10 counter, decoded outputs	TP	16
4022	Divide-by-8 counter, decoded outputs	TP	16
4510	Dual 4-bit decade up/down counter, async. load	TP	16
4516	4-bit binary up/down counter, async. load	TP	16
4518	Dual 4-bit decade counter	TP	16
4520	Dual 4-bit binary counter	TP	16
7022	Divide-by-8 counter, decoded outputs	TP	16

Type	Synchronous counters with data register	Output	Pins
590	8-bit binary counter, w. output reg.	TS	16
591	8-bit binary counter w. output reg.	OC	16
592	8-bit binary counter w. input reg.	TP	16
593	8-bit binary counter w. input reg.	TS	20
690	4-bit decade counter w. input reg.	TS	20
691	4-bit binary counter w. output reg.	TS	20
692	4-bit decade counter w. output reg.	TS	20
693	4-bit binary counter w. output reg.	TS	20
696	4-bit decade counter w. output reg.	TS	20
697	4-bit binary counter w. output reg.	TS	20
698	4-bit decade counter w. output reg.	TS	20
699	4-bit binary counter w. output reg.	TS	20

Type	Bus drivers (unidirectional)	Output	Pins
230	8-bit bus driver, 4-bit inverting	TS	20
231	8-bit bus driver, data inverting	TS	20
240	8-bit bus driver, data inverting	TS	20
241	8-bit bus driver	TS	20
244	8-bit bus driver	TS	20
365	6-bit bus driver	TS	16
366	6-bit bus driver, data inverting	TS	16
367	6-bit bus driver	TS	16
368	6-bit bus driver, data inverting	TS	16
465	8-bit bus driver	TS	20
466	8-bit bus driver, data inverting	TS	20
467	8-bit bus driver	TS	20
468	8-bit bus driver, data inverting	TS	20
540	8-bit bus driver, data inverting	TS	20
541	8-bit bus driver	TS	20
742	'540' with open collector	OC	20

Type	Bus drivers (unidirectional)	Output	Pins
743	'541' with open collector	OC	20
746	'540' with input pull-up resistor	TS	20
747	'541' with input pull-up resistor	TS	20
756	'240' with open collector	OC	20
757	'241' with open collector	OC	20
760	'244' with open collector	OC	20
762A	'230' with open collector	OC	20
763	'231' with open collector	OC	20
827	10-bit bus driver, non-data-inverting	TS	28
828	10-bit bus driver, data inverting	TS	28
1240	'240' reduced power	TS	20
1241	'241' reduced power	TS	20
1244	'244' reduced power	TS	20
2240	'240' with serial damping resistor	TS	20
2241	'241' with serial damping resistor	TS	20
2244	'244' with serial damping resistor	TS	20
2540	'540' with serial damping resistor	TS	20
2541	'541' with serial damping resistor	TS	20
2827	'827' with serial damping resistor	TS	24
2828	'828' with serial damping resistor	TS	24
29827	10-bit bus driver, non-data-inverting	TS	24
29828	10-bit bus driver, data inverting	TS	24

Type	Bus drivers with transp. latch	Output	Pins
373	8-bit latch	TS	20
533	8-bit latch, data inverting	TS	20
573	'373' bus pinout	TS	20
580	'533' bus pinout	TS	20
666	8-bit latch, readback	TS	24
667	8-bit latch, data inverting, readback	TS	24
841	10-bit latch	TS	28
842	10-bit latch, data inverting	TS	28
843	9-bit latch	TS	28
844	9-bit latch, data inverting	TS	28
845	8-bit latch	TS	28
846	8-bit latch, data inverting	TS	28
990	8-bit latch, readback	TP	20
991	8-bit latch, data inverting, readback	TP	20
992	9-bit latch, readback	TS	24
993	9-bit latch, data inverting, readback	TS	24
994	10-bit latch, data readback	TS	24
995	10-bit latch, data inverting, readback	TS	24
29841	10-bit latch	TS	24
29842	10-bit latch, data inverting	TS	24
29843	9-bit latch	TS	24
29844	9-bit latch, data inverting	TS	24
29845	8-bit latch	TS	24
29846	8-bit latch, data inverting	TS	24

Type	Bus driver with edge-triggered D flip-flops	Output	Pins
273	8-bit D flip-flop with clear	TP	20
374	8-bit D flip-flop	TS	20
377	8-bit D flip-flop with enable	TP	20
534	'374' data inverting	TS	20
563	8-bit D flip-flop, data inverting	TS	20
564	8-bit D flip-flop, data inverting	TS	20
574	'374' bus pinout	TS	20
575	'574' with synchronous clear	TS	24
576	8-bit D flip-flop, data inverting	TS	20
577	'576' with synchronous clear	TS	24
821	10-bit D flip-flop	TS	24
822	10-bit D flip-flop, data inverting	TS	24
823	9-bit D flip-flop	TS	24
824	9-bit D flip-flop, data inverting	TS	24
825	8-bit D flip-flop	TS	24
826	8-bit D flip-flop, data inverting	TS	24
874	8-bit D flip-flop	TS	24
876	8-bit D flip-flop, data inverting	TS	24
878	Dual 4-bit D flip-flop	TS	24
879	Dual 4-bit D flip-flop, data inverting	TS	24
996	8-bit D flip-flop, data readback	TS	24
1821	10-bit D flip-flop	TS	24
1823	10-bit D flip-flop, data inverting	TS	24
3374	8-bit metastable-resistant flip-flop	TS	20
3674	8-bit metastable-resistant flip-flop	TS	24
29821	10-bit D flip-flop	TS	24
29822	10-bit D flip-flop, data inverting	TS	24
29823	9-bit D flip-flop	TS	24
29824	9-bit D flip-flop, data inverting	TS	24
29825	8-bit D flip-flop	TS	24
29826	8-bit D flip-flop, data inverting	TS	24

Type	Transceiver (bidirectional)	Output	Pins
242	4-bit transceiver, data inverting	TS	14
243	4-bit transceiver	TS	14
245	8-bit transceiver, bus pinout	TS	20
446	4-bit transceiver, data inverting	TS	16
449	4-bit transceiver	TS	16
620	8-bit transceiver, data inverting	TS	20
621	8-bit transceiver	OC	20
622	8-bit transceiver, data inverting	OC	20
623	8-bit transceiver	TS	20
638	8-bit transceiver, data inverting	TS/OC	20
639	8-bit transceiver	TS/OC	20
640	8-bit transceiver, data inverting	TS	20
641	8-bit transceiver	OC	20
642	8-bit transceiver, data inverting	OC	20
643	8-bit transceiver, true/inverting	TS	20

Type	Transceiver (bidirectional)	Output	Pins
644	8-bit transceiver, true/inverting	OC	20
645	8-bit transceiver	TS	20
758	'242' with open collector	OC	20
759	'243' with open collector	OC	20
833	8-bit transceiver, parity gen.	TS	24
834	8-bit transceiver, inverting, parity	TS	24
853	8-bit transceiver, parity gen.	TS	24
854	8-bit transceiver, inverting, parity	TS	24
861	10-bit transceiver	TS	24
862	10-bit transceiver, data inverting	TS	24
863	9-bit transceiver	TS	24
864	9-bit transceiver, data inverting	TS	24
1242	'242' reduced power	TS	14
1243	'243' reduced power	TS	14
1245	'245' reduced power	TS	20
1640	'640' reduced power	TS	20
1645	'645' reduced power	TS	20
2242	'242' with serial damping resistor	TS	14
2620	'620' with serial damping resistor	TS	20
2623	'623' with serial damping resistor	TS	20
2640	'640' with serial damping resistor	TS	20
2645	'645' with serial damping resistor	TS	20
29833	8-bit transceiver, parity gen.	TS	24
29834	8-bit transceiver, inverting, parity	TS	24
29853	8-bit transceiver, parity gen.	TS	24
29854	8-bit transceiver, inverting, parity	TS	24
29861	10-bit transceiver	TS	24
29862	10-bit transceiver, data inverting	TS	24
29863	9-bit transceiver	TS	24
29864	9-bit transceiver, data inverting	TS	24

Type	Transceiver with edge-triggered register	Output	Pins
543	8-bit reg. transceiver	TS	24
544	8-bit reg. transceiver, data inverting	TS	24
614	8-bit reg. transceiver, data inverting	OC	24
615	8-bit reg. transceiver	OC	24
646	8-bit reg. transceiver	TS	24
647	8-bit reg. transceiver	OC	24
648	8-bit reg. transceiver, data inverting	TS	24
649	8-bit reg. transceiver, data inverting	OC	24
651	8-bit reg. transceiver, data inverting	TS	24
652	8-bit reg. transceiver	TS	24
653	8-bit reg. transceiver, data inverting	OC/TS	24
654	8-bit reg. transceiver	OC/TS	24
852	8-bit reg. transceiver	TS	24
856	8-bit reg. transceiver	TS	24
877	8-bit reg. transceiver	TS	24

Type	Tridirectional transceiver	Output	Pins
440	4-bit tridir. transc.	OC	20
441	4-bit tridir. transc., data inverting	OC	20
442	4-bit tridir. transc.	TS	20
443	4-bit tridir. transc., data inverting	TS	20
444	4-bit tridir. transc., true/inverting	TS	20

Type	Comparators	Output	Pins
85	4-bit magnitude comparator	TP	16
518	8-bit identity comparator	OC	20
519	8-bit identity comparator	OC	20
520	8-bit identity comparator	TP	20
521	8-bit identity comparator	TP	20
522	8-bit identity comparator	OC	20
526	16-bit identity comparator, fuse progr.	TP	20
527	12-bit identity comparator, fuse progr.	TP	20
528	12-bit identity comparator, fuse progr.	TP	16
677	16-bit address comparator	TP	24
678	16-bit address comparator w. output latch	TP	24
679	12-bit address comparator	TP	20
680	12-bit address comparator w. output latch	TP	20
682	8-bit magnitude comparator	TP	20
683	8-bit magnitude comparator	OC	20
684	8-bit magnitude comparator	TP	20
685	8-bit magnitude comparator	OC	20
686	8-bit magnitude comparator	TP	20
687	8-bit magnitude comparator	OC	20
688	8-bit identity comparator w. enable	TP	20
689	8-bit identity comparator w. enable	OC	20
812	12-bit ident. comp., fuse progr. + 1-of-4 dec.	TP	24
866	8-bit magnitude comparator w. inp./outp. latch	TP	28
885	8-bit magnitude comparator w. input latch	TP	24
29806	6-bit identity comparator + 1-of-4 decoder	TP	24
29809	9-bit identity comparator	TP	24

Type	Decoders, demultiplexers	Output	Pins
42	BCD to 10 line decoder	TP	16
(45	BCD to 10 line decoder	OC	16)
131	3 to 8 line decoder w. addr. register	TP	16
137	3 to 8 line decoder w. addr. latch	TP	16

( ) = only available in "Standard-" or "Schottky-" TTL, therefore not for new designs

Type	Decoders, demultiplexers	Output	Pins
138	3 to 8 line decoder	TP	16
139	Dual 2 to 4 line decoder	TP	16
(141	BCD to 10 line decoder	OC	16)
145	BCD to 10 line decoder	OC	16
154	4 to 16 line decoder	TP	24
155	Dual 2 to 4 line decoder	TP	16
156	Dual 2 to 4 line decoder	OC	16
(159	4 to 16 line decoder	OC	24)
237	3 to 8 line decoder w. addr. latch	TP	16
238	3 to 8 line decoder	TP	16
239	Dual 2 to 4 line decoder	TP	16
259	3 to 8 line decoder w. output latch	TP	16
445	BCD to 10 line decoder	OC	16
538	3 to 8 line decoder	TS	20
539	Dual 2 to 4 line decoder	TS	20
4514	4 to 16 line decoder w. addr. latch	TP	24
4515	4 to 16 line decoder w. addr. latch	TP	24

Type	Multiplexers, digital	Output	Pins
150	16-input multiplexer	TP	24
151	8-input multiplexer	TP	16
152	8-input multiplexer	TP	16
153	Dual 4-input multiplexer	TP	16
157	Dual 2-input multiplexer	TP	16
158	Quad 2-input multiplexer	TP	16
250	16-input multiplexer	TS	24
251	8-input multiplexer	TP/TS	16
253	Dual 4-input multiplexer	TS	16
257	Dual 2-input multiplexer	TS	16
258	Dual 2-input multiplexer	TS	16
298	Dual 2-input mux. w. output register	TP	16
352	Dual 4-input multiplexer	TP	16
353	Dual 4-input multiplexer	TS	16
354	8-input multiplexer w. input data latch	TS	20
355	8-input multiplexer w. data + address latch	OC	20
356	8-input multiplexer w. data reg. + addr. latch	TS	20
398	Quad 2-input multiplexer w. data reg.	TP	20
399	Quad 2-input multiplexer w. data register	TP	16
604	Octal 2-input multiplexer w. data register	TS	28
605	Octal 2-input multiplexer w. data register	OC	28
606	Octal 2-input multiplexer w. data register	TS	28
607	Octal 2-input multiplexer w. data register	OC	28
850	16-input multiplexer w. address register	TS	28
851	16-input multiplexer w. address latch	TS	28
857	Hex 2-input multiplexer, masking	TS	24

Type	Analog Multiplexers/Demultiplexers	Output	Pins
4016	Quad analog switch	R	14
4051	8 to 1 line mux./demux., level conv.	R	16
4052	Dual 4 to 1 line mux./demux., level conv.	R	16
4053	Triple 2 to 1 line mux./demux., level conv.	R	16
4066	Quad analog switch	R	14
4067	16 to 1 line mux./demux.	R	24
4316	Quad analog switch, level conv.	R	16
4351	8 to 1 line mux./demux., level conv.	R	18
4352	Dual 4 to 1 line mux./demux., level conv.	R	18
4353	Triple 2 to 1 line mux./demux., level conv.	R	18

Type	Code converters	Output	Pins
(184	5-bit BCD to binary converter	OC	16)
(185	5-bit binary to BCD converter	OC	16)
484	8-bit BCD to binary converter	TS	20
485	8-bit binary to BCD converter	TS	20

Type	Priority encoders	Output	Pins
147	10-line to binary priority encoder	TP	16
148	8-line to binary priority encoder	TP	16
278	4-bit priority encoder, input latch	TP	14
348	8-line to binary priority encoder	TS	16

Type	Display Decoder	Output	Pins
(46	BCD to seven segment for LEDs	OC	16)
47	BCD to seven segment for LEDs	OC	16
48	BCD to seven segment	TP	16
49	BCD to seven segment for LEDs	OC	16
(143	BCD counter, latch, 7-segment dec. for LEDs	OC	24)
(144	BCD counter, latch, 7-segment dec. for LEDs	OC	24)
247	BCD to seven segment for LEDs	OC	16
248	BCD to seven segment	TP	16
4511	BCD to seven segment w. latch for LEDs	TP	16
4543	BCD to seven segment w. latch for LCDs	TP	16

Output R: switch acts as a resistor between input and output

Type	Monostables	Output	Pins
(121	Monostable	TP	14)
122	Monostable, retriggerable	TP	14
123	Dual monostable, retriggerable	TP	16
221	Dual monostable	TP	16
422	Monostable, retriggerable	TP	14
423	Dual monostable, retriggerable	TP	16
4538	Dual monostable, retriggerable	TP	16

Type	Oscillators	Output	Pins
(124	Dual voltage-controlled oscillator	TP	16)
320	Crystal-controlled oscillator	TP	16
321	Crystal-controlled osc., freq. divider	TP	16
624	Voltage-controlled oscillator	TP	14
625	Dual voltage-controlled oscillator	TP	16
626	Dual voltage-controlled oscillator	TP	16
627	Dual voltage-controlled oscillator	TP	14
628	Voltage-controlled oscillator	TP	14
629	Dual voltage-controlled oscillator	TP	16

Type	Phase-locked loops	Output	Pins
297	Digital phase-locked loop	TP	16
4046	Phase-locked loop	TS	16
7046	PLL w. lock detector	TS	16

Type	Adders	Output	Pins
(82	2-bit binary full adder	TP	14)
83	4-bit binary full adder	TP	16
183	Dual carry-save full adder	TP	14
283	4-bit binary full adder	TP	16
385	Quad serial adder/subtractor	TP	20
583	4-bit BCD adder	TP	16

Type	Arithmetic logic units (ALU)	Output	Pins
181	4-bit arithmetic logic unit	TP	24
281	4-bit parallel binary accumulator	TP	24
381	4-bit arithmetic/function generator	TP	20
382	4-bit arithmetic/function generator	TP	20
681	4-bit binary accumulator	TP	20
881	4-bit arithmetic logic unit with status check	TP	24
1181	4-bit arithmetic logic unit	TP	20
1881	4-bit arithmetic logic unit with status check	TP	24

Type	Parallel carry logic	Output	Pins
182	Look-ahead-carry unit for 4 adders	TP	16
282	'182' cascadable	TP	20
882	Look-ahead-carry unit for 8 adders	TP	24

Type	Multipliers	Output	Pins
261	4 × 2 binary multiplier	TP	16
(274	4-bit × 4-bit binary multiplier	TS	20)
275	7-bit × 4-bit binary multiplier	TS	20
285	4 × 4 multiplier	TP	16
384	8-bit multiplier, serial	TP	16
1010	16 × 16 multiplier/accumulator	TS	64
1016	16 × 16 multiplier	TS	64
1017	16 × 16 multiplier	TS	64

Type	Pipeline registers	Output	Pins
818	8-bit pipeline/shadow register	TS	24
819	8-bit pipeline/shadow register	TS	24
29818	8-bit pipeline/shadow register	TS	24

Type	Register files	Output	Pins
170	4 × 4-bit register file	TP	16
(172	16 × 4-bit register file	TP	24)
670	4 × 4-bit register file	TS	16
870	Dual 16 × 4-bit register file	TS	24
871	Dual 16 × 4-bit register file	TS	28

Type	RAMs	Output	Pins
189	16 × 4-bit static RAM	TP	16

Type	FIFOs	Output	Pins
222	16 × 4-bit FIFO	TS	20
224	16 × 4-bit FIFO	TS	16
(225	16 × 5-bit FIFO	TS	20)
227	16 × 4-bit FIFO	OC	20
228	16 × 4-bit FIFO	OC	16
229	16 × 5-bit FIFO	TS	20
232	16 × 4-bit FIFO	TS	16
233	16 × 5-bit FIFO	TS	20
234	64 × 4-bit FIFO	TS	16
235	64 × 5-bit FIFO	TS	20
236	64 × 4-bit FIFO	TS	16
7030	64 × 9-bit FIFO	TS	28
7202	1024 × 9-bit FIFO	TS	28
7402	64 × 5-bit FIFO	TS	18

Type	Parity generators	Output	Pins
180	8-bit parity generator	TP	14
280	9-bit parity generator/checker	TP	14
286	'280' with bidirectional port	TP	20
656	8/9-bit par. gen./check, transceiver	TS	24
658	8/9-bit par. gen./check, transceiver	TS	24
659	8/9-bit par. gen./check, transceiver	TS	24
664	8/9-bit par. gen./check, transceiver	TS	24
665	8/9-bit par. gen./check, transceiver	TS	24
864	8/9-bit par. gen./check, transceiver	TS	24
865	8/9-bit par. gen./check, transceiver	TS	24

Type	Error correction	Output	Pins
616	16-bit error detection and correction	TS	40
617	16-bit error detection and correction	OC	40
630	16-bit parallel error correction circuits	TS	28
631	16-bit parallel error correction circuits	OC	28
632	32-bit error correction with byte write	TS	52
633	32-bit error correction with byte write	OC	52
634	32-bit error detection and correction	TS	48
635	32-bit error detector and correction	OC	48
636	8-bit error detection and correction	TS	20
637	8-bit error detection and correction	OC	20

Type	Dynamic RAM controllers	Output	Pins
600	Memory timer controller for 4 K/16 K	TS	20
601	Memory timer controller for 64 K	TS	20
602	Memory timer controller for 4 K/16 K	TS	20
603	Memory timer controller for 64 K	TS	20
608	Memory cycle controller	TS	16
764	256-K DRAM controller	TS	40
765	256-K DRAM controller	TS	40
2967	256-K DRAM controller	TS	48
2968	256-K DRAM controller	TS	48
6301	1-M DRAM controller		
6302	1-M DRAM controller		

Type	Memory mappers	Output	Pins
610	Memory mapper with latch	TS	40
611	Memory mapper with latch	OC	40
612	'610' without latch	TS	40
613	'611' without latch	OC	40

Type	8-bit building blocks	Output	Pins
887	Microprogrammable 8-bit ALU	TS	68
888	Microprogrammable 8-bit ALU, cascadable	TS	68
890	14-bit microsequencer with stack	TS	68
897	16-bit expandable barrel shifter	TS	68

Type	32-bit building blocks	Output	Pins
8818	16-bit microsequencer	TS	85
8832	32-bit registered integer ALU	TS	208
8833	64-bit to 32-bit barrel/funnel-shifter	TS	156
8834	64-word by 40-bit register file	TS	156
8835	16-bit microsequencer with stack	TS	156
8836	32-bit by 32-bit integer multiplier accumulator	TS	156
8837	64-bit floating point processor	TS	156
8838	32-bit barrel shifter	TS	84
8839	32-bit shuffle exchange network	TS	85
8841	Crossbar switch for 16 4-bit buses	TS	156
8847	64-bit floating point/integer processor	TS	208

Type	Miscellaneous Types	Output	Pins
31	Hex delay element	TP	16
(120	Dual pulse synchroniser	TP	16)
(265	Quad complem. output gate	TP	16)
350	4-bit shifter, combinatorial	TS	16

E 3 ±20%	E 6 ±20%	E 12 ±10%	E 24 ±5%	E 48 ±2%	E 96 ±1%	E 3 ±20%	E 6 ±20%	E 12 ±10%	E 24 ±5%	E 48 ±2%	E 96 ±1%
1.0	1.0	1.0	1.0	1.00	1.00		3.3	3.3	3.3	3.32	3.32
					1.02						3.40
				1.05	1.05					3.48	3.48
					1.07						3.57
			1.1	1.10	1.10				3.6	3.65	3.65
					1.13						3.74
				1.15	1.15					3.83	3.83
					1.18			3.9	3.9		3.92
	1.2	1.2	1.2	1.21	1.21					4.02	4.02
					1.24						4.12
				1.27	1.27					4.22	4.22
			1.3		1.30				4.3		4.32
				1.33	1.33					4.42	4.42
					1.37						4.53
				1.40	1.40					4.64	4.64
					1.43	4.7	4.7	4.7	4.7		4.75
				1.47	1.47					4.87	4.87
	1.5	1.5	1.5		1.50						4.99
				1.54	1.54				5.1	5.11	5.11
					1.58						5.23
			1.6	1.62	1.62					5.36	5.36
					1.65						5.49
				1.69	1.69			5.6	5.6	5.62	5.62
					1.74						5.76
				1.78	1.78					5.90	5.90
		1.8	1.8		1.82						6.04
				1.87	1.87				6.2	6.19	6.19
					1.91						6.34
				1.96	1.96					6.49	6.49
			2.0		2.00						6.65
				2.05	2.05		6.8	6.8	6.8	6.81	6.81
					2.10						6.98
				2.15	2.15					7.15	7.15
2.2	2.2	2.2	2.2		2.21						7.32
				2.26	2.26				7.5	7.50	7.50
					2.32						7.68
				2.37	2.37					7.87	7.87
			2.4		2.43						8.06
				2.49	2.49			8.2	8.2	8.25	8.25
					2.55						8.45
				2.61	2.61					8.66	8.66
					2.67						8.87
		2.7	2.7	2.74	2.74				9.1	9.09	9.09
					2.80						9.31
				2.87	2.87					9.53	9.53
					2.94						9.76
			3.0	3.01	3.01						
					3.09						
				3.16	3.16						
					3.24						

Fig. 28.1 Standard series of values per DIN 41426 or IEC 63

28.4 Color coding

Color	1st digit	2nd digit	Multiplier	Tolerance
none				± 20%
silver			× 0.01 Ω	± 10%
gold			× 0.1 Ω	± 5%
black		0	× 1.0 Ω	± 20%
brown	1	1	× 10 Ω	± 1%
red	2	2	×100 Ω	± 2%
orange	3	3	× 1 kΩ	
yellow	4	4	× 10 kΩ	
green	5	5	×100 kΩ	
blue	6	6	× 1 MΩ	
violet	7	7	× 10 MΩ	
grey	8	8	×100 MΩ	
white	9	9		

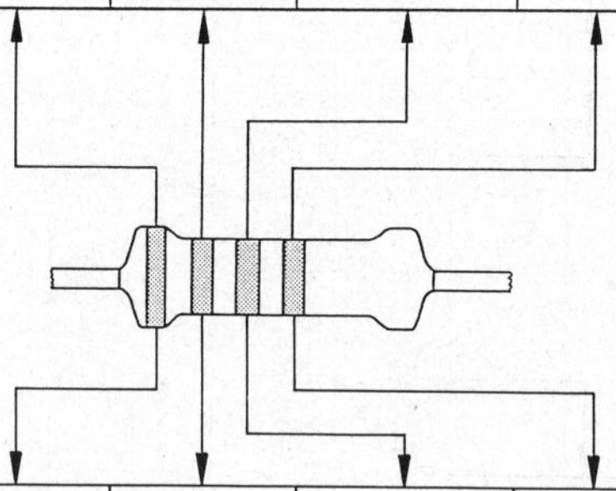

Example	yellow	violet	red	silver
4.7 kΩ	4	7	× 100 Ω	10%

Fig. 28.2 4-ring color code per DIN 41429

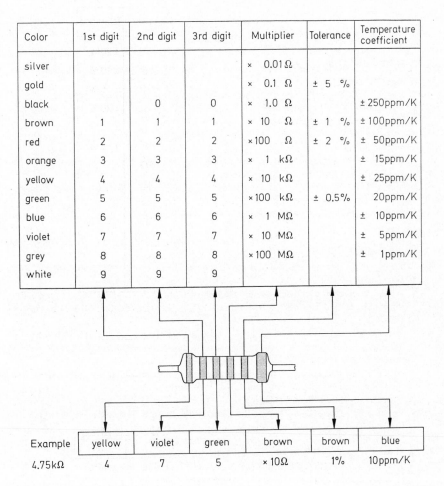

Color	1st digit	2nd digit	3rd digit	Multiplier	Tolerance	Temperature coefficient
silver				× 0.01 Ω		
gold				× 0.1 Ω	± 5 %	
black		0	0	× 1.0 Ω		± 250ppm/K
brown	1	1	1	× 10 Ω	± 1 %	± 100ppm/K
red	2	2	2	×100 Ω	± 2 %	± 50ppm/K
orange	3	3	3	× 1 kΩ		± 15ppm/K
yellow	4	4	4	× 10 kΩ		± 25ppm/K
green	5	5	5	×100 kΩ	± 0.5%	20ppm/K
blue	6	6	6	× 1 MΩ		± 10ppm/K
violet	7	7	7	× 10 MΩ		± 5ppm/K
grey	8	8	8	×100 MΩ		± 1ppm/K
white	9	9	9			

Example	yellow	violet	green	brown	brown	blue
4.75kΩ	4	7	5	× 10Ω	1%	10ppm/K

Fig. 28.3 5/6 ring color code per IEC 62. The temperature coefficient is usually only specified if it is less than 50 ppm/K

Literature

1.1 Weyh, U.; Benzinger, H.: Die Grundlagen der Wechselstromlehre. München, Wien: R. Oldenbourg 1967.

1.2 Brophy, J.J.: Basic Electronics for Scientists. New York: McGraw-Hill 1977.

2.1 Unbehauen, R.: Elektrische Netzwerke. Eine Einführung in die Analyse. Berlin, Heidelberg, New York: Springer 1981.

2.2 Schüßler, H.W.: Elektrische Netzwerke und Systeme I. Mannheim: Bibliographisches Institut 1981.

3.1 Müller, R.: Grundlagen der Halbleiter-Elektronik. Halbleiter-Elektronik, Bd. 1. Hrsg. v. W. Heywang u. R. Müller, Berlin, Heidelberg, New York: Springer 1979.

3.2 Unger, H.-G.; Schulz, W.: Elektronische Bauelemente und Netzwerke I. Braunschweig: Vieweg 1979.

4.1 Sheingold, D.H. (Editor): Nonlinear Circuits Handbook. Analog Devices, Inc., Norwood, Mass., 1974, p. 165.

4.2 Hart, B.L.; Barker, R.W.J.: Early-Intercept Voltage: A Parameter of Voltage-Driven B. J.T. s. Electronics Letters 12 (1976) No. 7, pp. 174–175.

4.3 Turner, C.R.: Interpretation of Voltage Ratings for Transistors. Publication SMA-2, RCA, Harrison.

4.4 Wanka, H.: Gefahr durch den zweiten Durchbruch. Markt & Technik (1981) No. 9, pp. 6–8.

4.5 Pippenger, D.: Current-mirror ICs Aid in Current Handling. EDN 26 (1981) No. 13, pp. 109–112.

4.6 Cooke, H.F.: Causes of Noise. Publication M-1, Texas Instruments, Dallas; München.

4.7 Mantena, N.R.: Sources of Noise in Transistors. Hewlett-Packard-Journal 21 (1969) No. 2, pp. 8–11.

4.8 Müller, R.: Bauelemente der Halbleiter-Elektronik. Halbleiter-Elektronik, Bd. 2. Hrsg. v. W. Heywang u. R. Müller. Berlin, Heidelberg, New York: Springer 1979.

5.1 Wüstehube, J.: Feldeffekt-Transistoren. Valvo, Hamburg, 1968.

5.2 Tiefert, K.H.; Tsang, D.W.; Myers, R.L.; Li, V.: The Vertical Power Mosfet for High-Speed Power Control. Hewlett-Packard-Journal 32 (1981) No. 8, pp. 18–23.

5.3 Beneking, H.: Feldeffekttransistoren. Halbleiter-Elektronik, Bd. 7. Hrsg. v. W. Heywang u. R. Müller. Berlin, Heidelberg, New York: Springer 1973.

5.4 Schaeffer, L.: VMOS, a Breakthrough in Power Mosfet Technology. Publication AN 76-3, Siliconix, Bernhausen

5.5 Graeme, J.D.; Gene, E.T.; Huelsman, L.P.: Operational Amplifiers. New York: McGraw-Hill 1973, p. 61.

6.1 Härtel, V.: Das Opto-Kochbuch. Freising: Texas Instruments 1975.

6.2 Optoelectronics Designer's Catalog. Hewlett-Packard, Palo Alto; Frankfurt.

6.3 Photoconductive Cell Application Design Handbook. Clairex, Mount Vernon, N.Y.

6.4 Camatini, E.: Progress in Electro-Optics. New York, London: Plenum Press 1975.

6.5 Walter, K.H.: Ein universeller Ansteuerbaustein für Flüssigkristallanzeigen. Siemens Components 19 (1981) No. 5, pp. 160–165.

7.1 Solomon, J.E.: The Monolithic Op Amp: A Tutorial Study. IEEE Journal of Solid-State Circuits 9 (1974) No. 6, pp. 314–332.

7.2 Hammerl, M.: CMOS-speziell für analoge ICs. Design & Elektronik, October 1985, pp. 131–134.

7.3 Blaesner, W.: Operationsverstärker mit weitem Gleichtakt- und Ausgangsspannungsbereich. Design & Elektronik, 28. 4. 1987, No. 9. pp. 112–114.

7.4   Sheehan, G.; Johnson, J.; Wilhelm, T.: Software-Configured Family Boards Speed Testing. Analog Dialogue 14 (1980) No. 3, pp. 8–13.

8.1   Shah, A.; Pellandini, F.; Birolini, A.: Grundschaltungen mit Transistoren. Zürich: Verlag des Akademischen Maschinen- und Elektro-Ingenieur-Vereins und der ETH 1972.

9.1   Whitesitt, J.E.: Boolesche Algebra und ihre Anwendungen. Braunschweig: Vieweg 1964.

9.2   Blood, W.R.: MECL-System Design Handbook. Motorola.

9.3   Schaltzeichen, Digitale Informationsverarbeitung, DIN 40900 Teil 12. Berlin: Beuth.

9.4   Bürgel, E.: Neue Normen und Schaltzeichen der digitalen Informationsverarbeitung, München: Franzis 1978.

9.5   Mann, F.A.: Explanation of New Logic Symbols. Dallas: Texas Instruments.

9.6   Twaddell, W.: The 80s Belong to CMOS. EDN 26 (1981) No. 13, pp. 89–100.

9.7   Karakotsios, K.; Wakeman, L.: CMOS Support Logic Helps Build Unified High-Speed Systems. Electronics 54 (1981) No. 25, pp. 137–140.

9.8   Giloi, W.; Liebig, H.: Logischer Entwurf digitaler Systeme. Berlin, Heidelberg, New York: Springer 1980.

10.1 Kraft, G.D.; Toy, W.N.: Mini/Microcomputer Hardware Design. Englewood Cliffs: Prentice-Hall 1979 pp. 87–91.

10.2 Schaltbeispiele. Handbuch der Firma Intermetall, Freiburg 1967, p. 40.

10.3 Wendt, S.: Entwurf komplexer Schaltwerke. Berlin, Heidelberg, New York: Springer 1974.

10.4 Clare, C.R.: Designing Logic Systems Using State Machines. New York: McGraw-Hill 1973.

11.1 Seitzer, D.: Arbeitsspeicher für Digitalrechner. Berlin, Heidelberg, New York: Springer 1975.

11.2 Huse, H.: Speicherentwurf mit DRAM-Controllern. Design & Elektronik, 19. 12. 1986, No. 26, pp. 94–104.

11.3 Voldam, Willibald: Die Speicheransteuerung mit RAM-Controllern. Design & Elektronik, 27. 5. 1986, No. 11, pp. 149–151.

11.4 Iversen, W.R.: Dual-Port RAM Transfers Data More Efficiently. Electronics 55 (1982) No. 20, pp. 47–48.

11.5 Wyland, D.C.: Dual-Port-RAMs Simplify Communications in Computer Systems. Application Note AN-02, IDT.

11.6 Hallau, D.: Die vielfältigen Anwendungsmöglichkeiten von FIFO-Speichern. Design & Elektronik, 9. 6. 1987, No. 12, pp. 109–114.

11.7 Evans, M.: Nelson-Matrix Can Pin Down 2 Errors per Word. Electronics 55 (1982) No. 11, pp. 158–162.

11.8 Peterson, W.W.: Weldon, E.J.: Error-Correction Codes. Cambridge, Mass.: The MIT-Press 1972.

11.9 Berlekamp, E.R.: Algebraic Coding Theory. New York: McGraw-Hill 1968.

11.10 Fleder, K.: Schaltkreis zur Erkennung und Korrektur von Fehlern in Speichersystemen. Application Note, Texas Instruments, 1984, EB 161.

11.11 Landers, G.: 5-Volt-Only EEPROM Mimics Static-RAM Timing. Electronics 55 (1982) No. 13, pp. 127–130.

11.12 Gupta, A.; Chiu, T.; Yound, S.: 5V-only EEPROM-Springboard for Autoprogrammable Systems. Electronics 55 (1982) No. 3, pp. 121–125.

11.13 Orlando, R.: NOVRAM oder EEPROM – welcher Speicher für welche Anwendung? Design & Elektronik, October 1985, pp. 62–68.

11.14 Voldan, W.: Alles über PALs, Markt & Technik, 7. 11. 1986, No. 45, pp. 324–332.

11.15 Agrawal, D.; Mubarak, F.: Elektrisch löschbare PLDs mit Eingangs-/Ausgangs-Makrozellen. Elektronik, 27. 11. 1987, No. 24, pp. 66–74.

11.16 Wichmann, B.: Doppel-Array mit programmierbaren AND- und OR-Feldern. Design & Elektronik, 7. 1. 1988, No. 1, pp. 116, 117.

11.17 Huber, R.: Logic-Cell-Arrays, die programmierbaren Gate-Arrays. Design & Elektronik, 7. 1. 1988, No. 1, pp. 109–114.

12.1 Henry, P.: JFET-Input Amps are unrivaled for speed and accuracy. EDN, 14. 5. 1987, No. 10, pp. 161–169.

906   Literature

12.2   Roberge, J.K.: Operational Amplifiers. New York, London, Sydney, Toronto: J. Wiley 1975.
12.3   Hentschel, C.; Leitner, A.; Traub, S.; Schweikardt, H.; Eberle, V.: Designing Bipolar
        Integrated Circuits for a Pulse/Function Generator Family. Hewlett-Packard-Journal 34
        (1983), No. 6, pp. 33–38.
12.4   Gilbert, B.: A Monolithic Microsystem for Analog Synthesis of Trigonometric Functions
        and Their Inverse. IEEE Journal of Solid-State Circuits, 17 (1982), No. 6, pp. 1179–1191.
12.5   Arnold, W.F.: Analog Multiplier Compensates Itself. Electronics 50 (1977) No. 25, p. 130.
12.6   Wagner, R.: Laser-Trimming on the Wafer. Analog Dialogue 9 (1975) No. 3, pp. 3–5.
12.7   Sheingold, D.H. (Editor): Nonlinear Circuits Handbook. Analog Devices. Inc., Norwood,
        Mass. 1974. pp. 289–294.
12.8   Tietze, U.: Analogmultiplizierer mit isolierenden Kopplern. Elektronik 17 (1968) No. 8, pp.
        233–238.
12.9   Graeme, J.G.: Applications of Operational Amplifiers. New York: McGraw-Hill 1973.
13.1   Schenk, Ch.: Ein neues Schaltungskonzept für eine bipolare, spannungsgesteuerte
        Präzisions-Stromquelle. Nachrichtentechn. Z. 27 (1974) pp. 102–104.
13.2   Tietze, U.; Schenk, Ch.: Bipolar steuerbare Leistungsstromquelle mit Power-MOSFETs.
        Elektronikpraxis 16 (1981) No. 10, pp. 142–144.
13.3   Antoniou, A.: 3-Terminal Gyrator Circuits Using Operational Amplifiers. Electronics
        Letters 4 (1968) 591.
13.4   Schenk, Ch.: Neue Schaltungen spannungsgesteuerter Stromquellen und ihre Anwendung in
        elektronischen Y-Gyratoren. Dissertation, University of Erlangen-Nürnberg, 1976.
13.5   Rollett, J.M.; Greenaway, P.E.: Direct Coupled Active Circulators. Electronics Letters
        4 (1968) 579.
14.1   Ghausi, M.S.: Principles and Design of Linear Active Circuits. New York: McGraw-Hill
        1965, p. 84.
14.2   Weinberg, L.: Network Analysis and Synthesis. New York: McGraw-Hill 1962, p. 494.
14.3   Steffen, P.: Die Pole auf der Ellipse. Elektronikpraxis 17 (1982) No. 4, pp. 16, 17.
14.4   Saal, R.: Handbuch zum Filterentwurf. Berlin: Elitera 1979.
14.5   Storch, L.: Synthesis of Constant-Delay Ladder-Networks Using Bessel Polynomials. Proc.
        IRE 42 (1954) 1666.
14.6   Schaumann, R.: A Low-Sensitivity, High-Frequency, Tunable Active Filter without External
        Capacitors. Proc. IEEE Int. Symp. on Circuits and Systems 1974, p. 438.
14.7   Unbehauen, R.: Synthese elektrischer Netzwerke. München, Wien: R. Oldenbourg 1972.
14.8   Heinlein, W.E.; Homes, W.H.: Active Filters for Integrated Circuits. München, Wien: R.
        Oldenbourg 1974.
14.9   Lacanette, K.: Universal Switched-Capacitor Filter Lowers Part Count. EDN, 3. 4. 1986,
        No. 7, pp. 139–147.
14.10   Cormier, D.: Programmable Switched-Capacitor Filter ICs Cut Component Count in Many
        Filter Types. EDN, 26. 6. 1986, No. 13, pp. 71–80.
14.11   Shear, D.: Comparison Reveals the Pros and Cons of Designing with Switched-Capacitor
        ICs. EDN, 25. 6. 1987, No. 13, pp. 83–90.
15.1   Boyd, H.: Destroy your Microwave Transistors. Electronic Design 15 (1967) No. 20, p. 98.
15.2   Luckau, H.; Sellar, D.; Weil, G.: Integrierter Quarzoszillator Q 052. Bauteile Report of
        Siemens: 14 (1976) No. 5, pp. 162–166.
15.3   Blood, W.R.: MECL-System Design Handbook. Motorola. 3rd Ed. 1980, pp. 216–224.
15.4   Riedel, R.; Vyduna, J.; Crume, B.: Funktion Generator Lets User Build Waveforms of
        Varying Shape. Electronics 55 (1982) No. 9, pp. 143–147.
15.5   Riedel, R.J.; Danielson, D.D.: The Dual Function Generator: A Source of a Wide Variety of
        Test Signals. Hewlett-Packard Journal 26 (1975) No. 7, pp. 18–24.
15.6   Clayton, G.B.: Voltage-Controlled Amplifier Phase-Adjusts Wave Generator. Electronics 52
        (1979) No. 3, p. 118.
15.7   Smith, J.I.: Modern Operational Circuit Design. New York: Wiley–Interscience 1971.
16.1   Müller, R..: Bauelemente der Halbleiter-Elektronik. Halbleiter-Elektronik, Bd. 2. Hrsg. v. W.
        Heywang u. R. Müller. Berlin, Heidelberg, New York: Springer 1973.

16.2 Cherry, E.M.; Hooper, D.E.: The Design of Wide-Band Transistor Feedback Amplifiers. Proc. I.E.E. 110 (1963) 375–389.

16.3 De Vilbiss, A.J.: A Wideband Oscilloscope Amplifier. Hewlett-Packard Journal 21 (1970) No. 5, pp. 11–14.

16.4 NN: A New Approach to Op Amp Design. Application Note 300-1 of Comlinear.

16.5 Biebel, H.: Höhere Bandbreite mit Strom-Rückkopplungs-Verstärken. Elektronik 36, 23. 12. 1987, No. 26, pp. 106–110.

16.6 Hansford, A.: Use of Transimpedance Amplifiers Minimizes Design Tradeoffs. EDN, 26. 11. 1987, No. 24, pp. 205–214.

16.7 Williams, J.: Composite Amplifiers Yield High Speed and Low Offset. EDN 22. 1. 1987, No. 2, pp. 137–150.

17.1 Chessman, M.; Sokal, N.: Prevent Emitter-Follower Oscillation. Electronic Design 24 (1976) No. 13, pp. 110–113.

18.1 Kühn, R.: Der Kleintransformator. Prien: C.F. Winter 1964.

18.2 Hanncke, W.: Kleintransformatoren und Eisenkerndrosseln. Würzburg: Vogel 1970.

18.3 Koellner, R.: Netzteilberechnung in Basic. Funkschau 53 (1981) No. 6, pp. 93–95.

18.4 Koch, E.: Integrierter Leistungs-Spannungsregler ist einstellbar und kurzschlußfest. Elektronik 26 (1977) No. 11, pp. 71–73.

18.5 Widlar, R.J.: New Developments in IC Voltage Regulators. IEEE Journal of Solid-State Circuits 6 (1971) No. 1, pp. 2–7.

18.6 Nelson, C.T.: Supermatched bipolar Transistors Improve DC and AC Designs. EDN 25 (1980) No. 1, pp. 115–120.

18.7 McDermott, J.: Ultraprecision IC Voltage References Serve Varied Circuit Needs. EDN 26 (1981) No. 8, pp. 61–74.

18.8 Knapp, R.: Selection Criteria Assist in Choice of Optimum Reference. EDN, 18. 2. 1988, No. 4, pp. 183–192.

18.9 Bingham, D.: CMOS Makes Voltage Converter a Paragon of Efficiency. Electronics 53 (1980) No. 20, pp. 141–146.

18.10 Kohlrausch, F.: Praktische Physik, Bd. 2. Stuttgart: Teubner 1968.

18.11 Schaltnetzteile mit Sipmos-Leistungstransistoren. Extract from "Schaltbeispielen 1982/83" of Siemens.

18.12 Power Mosfet Gate Drive Ideas. Application Bulletin 32 (1980) of Hewlett-Packard.

18.13 A 300 Watt, 100 kHz, Off-line Switch Mode Power Supply. Application Note 977 (1980) of Hewlett Packard.

18.14 Rischmüller, K.: Hochvolttransistoren als Chopper. Technical Information No. 40 of Thomson.

18.15 Shaughnessy, W.J.: LC-Snubber Networks Cut Switcher Power Losses. EDN 25 (1980) No. 23, pp. 175–180.

18.16 Wüstehube, J.: Schaltnetzteile. Grafenau: Expert 1982.

19.1 Ware, F.; McAllister, W.: CMOS Chip Set Streamlines Floating Point Processing. Electronics 55 (1982) No. 3, pp. 149–152.

19.2 Spaniol, O.: Arithmetik in Rechenanlagen. Stuttgart: Teubner 1976.

19.3 Bucklen, W.; Eldon, J.; Schirm, L.; Williams, F.: Single-Chip Digital Multipliers Form Basic DSP Building Blocks, EDN 26 (1981) No. 7, pp. 153–163.

19.4 Schmid, H.: Decimal Computation. New York, London, Sydney, Toronto: J. Wiley 1981.

19.5 Flores, I.: The Logic of Computer Arithmetic. Englewood Cliffs, N.J.: Prentice-Hall 1963.

19.6 Peatman, J.B.: The Design of Digital Systems. Tokyo: McGraw-Hill Kogakusha 1972.

19.7 Barna, A.; Porat, D.I.: Integrated Circuits in Digital Electronics. New York, London, Sydney, Toronto: J. Wiley 1973.

19.8 Hwang, K.: Computer Arithmetic. New York, London, Sydney, Toronto: J. Wiley 1979.

20.1 Klein, M.: Software-Entwurfstechniken. Elektronikpraxis 15 (1980) No. 1, pp. 8–11.

20.2 Dalton, W.F.: Design Microcomputer Software Like Other Systems-Systematically. Electronics 51 (1978) No. 2, pp. 97–101.

20.3 Zschocke, J.: Mikrocomputer-Aufbau und Anwendungen. Braunschweig, Wiesbaden: Vieweg 1982.

20.4 Bonzon, M.; Queyssac, D.; Schneider, K.: Mikroprozessoren: Aufbau und Arbeitsweise. Handook of Motorola.

20.5 M 6800-Mikroprozessor Programmierhandbuch. Handbook of Motorola.

20.6 M 6800-Microprocessor Applications Manual. Handbook of Motorola.

20.7 Leventhal, L.A.: 6800-Programmieren in Assembler. München: te-wi Verlag 1978.

21.1 Cushman, R.H.: Byte-Wide-Memory Standard Gains Adherents as Designers Discover its Advantages. EDN 27 (1982) No. 15, pp. 53–58.

21.2 Hutcheson, R.: Understanding PIA Operation Increases Your Design Options, EDN 25 (1980) No. 18, pp. 175–184.

21.3 Deutsche Normen- Informationsverarbeitung: 7-Bit-Code. DIN 66003. Berlin, Köln: Beuth.

21.4 Weissberger, A.J.: Upgrade Data Communications with an RS-449 Interface. EDN 27 (1982) No. 4, pp. 167–176.

21.5 Laws, D.A.; Levy, R.J.: Use of the Quad Driver/Receiver Family in EIA RS-422 and 423 Applications. Application Note of AMD.

21.6 Fenger, C.; Muhlemann, K.: High-Resolution LCD Panels Change Demands on Driver Electronics. EDN, 14. 4. 1988, No. 8, pp. 157–162.

21.7 Technisches Pflichtenheft: Richtlinien für die Messung der Pflichtenheftsbedingungen an Videogeräten. Nr. 8/1.1. München: Institut für Rundfunktechnik 1981.

21.8 Schönfelder, H.: Fernsehtechnik. Darmstadt: Justus von Liebig.

21.9 CRTC Design and Applications Manual. Application Note AN 8 of Synertek.

21.10 Bresenham, J.E.: Algorithm for Computer Control of a Digital Plotter. IBM Systems Journal 4 (1965) No. 1, pp. 25–30.

21.11 Lambinet, P.: Basic Routines for Graphic Display Processors. Application Note NA-028 A of Thomson-Efcis.

21.12 Amazeen, B.; Holloway, P.; Mercer, D.: Monolithic DA Converter Operates on a Single Supply. Electronics 53 (1980) No. 5, pp. 125–131.

21.13 M 6800-Microprocessor Applications Manual. Handook of Motorola.

22.1 Frenzel, D.: CMOS-Schalter und -Multiplexer ohne Latch up-Effekt. Elektronik 27 (1978) No. 1, pp. 57–60.

22.2 Muto, A.S.; Peetz, B.E.; Rehner, R.C.: Designing a Ten-Bit, Twenty-Megasamples-per-Second Analog-to-Digital Converter System. Hewlett-Packard-Journal 33 (1982) No. 11, pp. 9–20.

22.3 Gillooly, D. L.; Henneuse, P.: Multifunction Chip Plays Many Parts in Analog Design. Electronics 54 (1981) No. 7, pp. 121–129.

22.4 Pease, R.A.: Understand Capacitor Soakage to Optimize Analog Systems. EDN 27 (1982) No. 20, pp. 125–129.

23.1 McGuire, P.L.: Digital Pulses Synthesize Audio Sine Waves. Electronics 48 (1975) No. 20, pp. 104, 105.

23.2 Yuen, M.: DA Converter's Low-Glitch Design Lowers Parts Count in Graphic Displays. Electronics 52 (1979) No. 16, pp. 131–135.

23.3 Seitzer, D.; Pretzl, G.; Hamdy, N.: Electronic Analog-to-Digital Converters. Chichester, New York, Brisbane, Toronto, Singapore: J. Wiley 1983.

23.4 Lammert, M.; Olsen, R.: 1 μm Process Shrinks and Speeds up Flash Converter. Electronics 55 (1982) No. 9, pp. 135–137.

23.5 Bolm, E.D.: Dynamic Testing Describes Behavior of High-Frequency ADCs. EDN, 14. 4. 1988, No. 8, pp. 215–222.

23.6 Pratt, W.J.: High Linearity and Video Speed Come Together in AD Converters. Electronics 53 (1980) No. 22, pp. 167–170.

23.7 Little, A.; Burnett, B.: S/H Amp-ADC Matrimony Provides Accurate Sampling. EDN, 4. 2. 1988, No. 3, pp. 153–166.

23.8 Jones, L.T.; James, J.R.; Clark, C.A.: Precision DVM Has Wide Dynamic Range and High System Speed. Hewlett-Packard-Journal 32 (1981) No. 4, pp. 23–31.

23.9 Hnatek, E.R.: A User's Handbook of D/A and A/D Converters. New York. London, Sydney, Toronto: J. Wiley 1976.

23.10 Loriferne, B.: Analog-Digital and Digital-Analog Conversion. London, Philadelphia, Rheine: Heyden 1982.

23.11 Zander, H.: Analog-Digital-Wandler in der Praxis. Haar: Markt und Technik 1983.

24.1 Unbehauen, R.: Systemtheorie. München, Wien: R. Oldenbourg 1983.

24.2 Pohlmann, K.C.: Principles of Digital Audio. Howard W. Sams & Co., Indianapolis 1986.

24.3 Schönfelder, H.: Digitale Filter in der Video-Technik. Berlin: Drei-R-Verlag 1988.

24.4 Azizi, S.A.: Entwurf und Realisierung Digitaler Filter. München, Wien: R. Oldenbourg 1983.

24.5 Bucklen, W.; Eldon, J.; Schirm, L.; Williams, F.: Digital Processing Facilitates Signal Analysis. EDN 26 (1981) No. 8, pp. 133–146.

24.6 Windsor, B.; Toldalagi, P.: Simplify FIR-Filter Design with a Cookbook Approach. EDN, 3. 3. 1983, pp. 119–128.

24.7 Schüßler, W.: Eigenschaften und Entwurf digitaler Filter. NTZ, 24 (1971) No. 6, pp. 289–352.

24.8 Programs for Digital Signal Processing. Edited by the Digital Signal Processing Committee IEEE ASSP. New York: IEEE Press 1979.

24.9 Cushman, R.H.: DSP-Filter Software Offers Design Help to Novices. EDN, 10.7.1986, pp. 152–162.

24.10 Texas Instruments: Digital Filter Design Package. Filter Design Program for PC/DOS or VAX/VMS.

24.11 Jackson, L.B.: Digital Filters and Signal Processing. Boston, Dordrecht, Lancaster: Kluwer 1986.

24.12 Bose, N.K.: Digital Filters, Theory and Applications. New York, Amsterdam: North-Holland 1985.

24.13 Haight, J.D.: Simplify FIR-Filter Design with a CMOS Filter-Control Chip. EDN, 6 .8. 1987, pp. 157–164.

24.14 Friedlander, B.; Porat, B.: The Modified Yule-Walker Method of ARMA Spectral Estimation. IEEE Transactions on Aerospace Electronic Systems. AES-20 (1984) No. 2, pp. 158–173.

24.15 Yassaie, H.: Digital Filtering with the IMS A 100. Application Note 1 of Inmos, Bristol, 1986.

24.16 Jonuscheit, H.; Kapust, R.; Göring, H.D.: Aufwand bei Digitalfiltern gesenkt. Halbband-filter-Struktur reduziert Zahl der Rechenoperationen. Elektronik, 22. 7. 1988, No. 15, pp. 82–84.

25.1 Grandl, P.: Was ist ein Trennverstärker. Elektronikpraxis 17 (1982) No. 2, pp. 29–34.

25.2 Morong, B.: Isolator Stretches the Bandwidth of Two-Transformer Design. Electronics 53 (1980) No. 15, pp. 151–158.

25.3 Counts, L.; Kitchin, Ch.; Jung, W.: Low-Cost RMS/DC ICs Upgrade AC Measurements. EDN 27 (1982) No. 2, pp. 101–112.

25.4 Buchana, R.M.: Match True-RMS Detection to Accuracy, Cost Requirements. EDN 27 (1982) No. 1, pp. 139–142.

25.5 Ott, W.E.: A New Technique of Thermal RMS Measurement. IEEE Journal of Solid-State Circuits 9 (1974) No. 6, pp. 374–380.

25.6 Williams, J.: Thermal-Tracking IC Converts RMS to DC. EDN, 19. 2. 1987, No. 4, pp. 137–151.

25.7 Koeppe, W.; Peters, E.G.; Schröder, D.: Spitzenwertmessung mit Track & Hold-Verstärkern. Design & Elektronik, 8. 7. 1986, No. 14, pp. 75–79.

26.1 Hencke, H.: Lasergetrimmte Temperatursensoren für Messungen von − 40 bis + 150 °C. Design & Elektronik, 20. 1. 1987, No. 2, pp. 69–73.

26.2 Wetzel, K.: Der Heißleiter als Temperatursensor. Design & Elektronik, 15. 4. 1986, No. 8, pp. 83–85.

26.3 Timko, M.; Suttler, G.: Temperature-to-Current Transducer. Analog Dialogue 12 (1978) No. 1, pp. 3–5.

26.4 Williams, J.: Clever Techniques Improve Thermocouple Measurements. EDN, 26. 5. 1988, No. 11, pp. 145–160.

26.5 Ehrler, G.; Nagy, G.: Silizium-Drucksensoren. Elektronikpraxis 18 (1983) No. 9, pp. 30–33.

26.6   Werner, F.: Absolutdrucksensoren. Industrieelektrik und Elektronik (1986) No. 7, pp. 24, 25.

26.7   Werner, F.: Signalaufbereitung für moderne temperaturkompensierte Drucksensoren. Markt & Technik (1986) No. 37, pp. 74–78.

26.8   Sherman, L.H.: Sensors and Conditioning Circuits Simplify Humidity Measurement. EDN 30, 16. 5. 1985, No. 12, pp. 179–188.

26.9   N.N.: Sensor zur Messung der relativen Luftfeuchte. Valvo: Technical Information TI 790423.

26.10   Williams, J.: Monolithic CMOS-Switch IC Suits Diverse Applications. EDN 29 (1984) No. 21, pp. 183–194.

26.11   Schlitz, J.M.; Weiß, W.D.: Intelligenz im Meßwandler. Elektronik 18 (1985) No. 18, pp. 69–73.

26.12   Bierl, L.; Brenninger, H.; Diewald, H.: Sensor & Systems, TSS 400 Application Report of Texas Instruments, Freising.

27.1   Oppelt, W.: Kleines Handbuch technischer Regelvorgänge. Weinheim, Bergstraße: Verlag Chemie 1972.

27.2   Schlitt, H.: Regelungstechnik in Verfahrenstechnik und Chemie. Würzburg: Vogel 1978.

27.3   Warnkross, V.: Schneller Phasen- und Frequenzdetektor. Elektronik 28 (1979) No. 21, pp. 85, 86.

27.4   Breeze, E.G.: High Frequency Digital PLL Synthesizer. Application Note, Fairchild.

27.5   Best, R.: Theorie und Anwendung des Phase-locked Loops. Stuttgart: AT-Fachverlag 1982.

27.6   Gardner, F.M.: Phaselock Techniques. New York, London, Sydney: J. Wiley 1966.

27.7   Greenshields, D.: Einsatz eines Video-Taktgenerators. Design & Elektronik, 24. 5. 1988, No. 11, pp. 91–98.

List of tables of integrated circuits

A overview of all digital circuits of the 7400-family is to be found on pages 883 through 900.

Index

Boldface page numbers identify major chapter sections dealing with the particular topic, i.e. they indicate the principal reference to the topic.

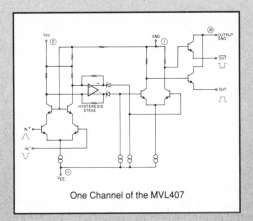

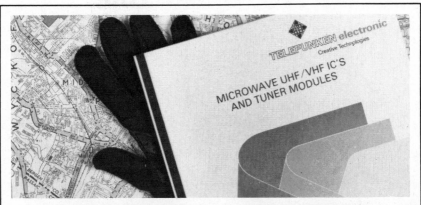